AIMING FOR GLOBAL ACCOUNTING STANDARDS

Aiming for Global Accounting Standards

The International Accounting Standards Board, 2001–2011

KEES CAMFFERMAN AND STEPHEN A. ZEFF

OXFORD

UNIVERSITY PRESS

OXFORD
UNIVERSITY PRESS

Great Clarendon Street, Oxford, OX2 6DP,
United Kingdom

Oxford University Press is a department of the University of Oxford.
It furthers the University's objective of excellence in research, scholarship,
and education by publishing worldwide. Oxford is a registered trade mark of
Oxford University Press in the UK and in certain other countries

Published in the United States of America by Oxford University Press
198 Madison Avenue, New York, NY 10016, United States of America

British Library Cataloguing in Publication Data
Data available

ISBN 978–0–19–964631–9

Foreword

I was no stranger to the politics of global financial reporting when I became chairman of the IASB in 2011. After all, I had served as co-chairman of the Financial Crisis Advisory Group to the IASB and the FASB, while from 2009 I served as chairman of the IFRS Foundation Monitoring Board, the supervisory body of the IFRS Foundation.

However, at the time of my appointment I had much to learn about the background of the organization and the rationale for the decisions that determined the structure and orientation of the IFRS Foundation. I subscribe to the often-quoted view that those who fail to learn from history are condemned to repeat it. Thankfully, on the day of my appointment I was handed a copy of *Financial Reporting and Global Capital Markets: A History of the IASC, 1973–2000* by Camfferman and Zeff. That book proved to be an indispensable companion during my first year as chairman of the IASB and it still provides a frequent source of reference about the history of the IFRS Foundation.

Camfferman and Zeff's book stopped where the IASB began, so a more up to date sequel was an obvious project to undertake. Thankfully, the history of the IASB during its first decade provides ample material for the authors to explore. It is a story of remarkable achievement and leadership, of some frustration, but above all a story of incredible global cooperation in something as fundamental as financial reporting. Progress rarely occurs in a linear fashion, and this book provides an excellent, authoritative account of the achievements but also the many challenges that have had to be overcome on the road towards global accounting standards.

However, those challenges should not dilute our focus on the mission of the organization. The quality and consistency of financial reporting around the world has been considerably enhanced by the work of the IASB and the many others who passionately believe in its mission of global accounting standards. In the decade covered by this book, more than 100 countries have moved from national accounting standards of varying quality to IFRS as the single set of high quality, global financial reporting standards. Our own research shows that the standards are mostly used in full and without modification. That is a remarkable achievement, even if we still have further work to do.

The fact that this story can be told owes much to the openness and transparency of the IFRS Foundation and the IASB, as well as the candour of those interviewed by the authors. I congratulate Camfferman and Zeff on an excellent account of this first decade of the IASB and I recommend this book to anyone with an interest in the remarkable history of IFRS.

Hans Hoogervorst
Chairman, International Accounting Standards Board

Preface

In 2008, IASB Chairman Sir David Tweedie invited us to undertake this project as a follow-on to our book on the history of the IASC, *Financial Reporting and Global Capital Markets: A History of the International Accounting Standards Committee, 1973–2000* (Oxford University Press, 2007). The IASC Foundation approved the project and agreed to reimburse our travel costs. Our plan was to conclude the research and writing by 2014, to enable us to complement our data-gathering during the period covered by our history, 2001–11, with acquisition of further historical perspective by tracing the evolution of earlier developments during the post-period from 2011 to 2014.

The IASB was the first international accounting standard setter whose pronouncements were imposed as requirements on thousands of listed companies around the world. The standards issued by the IASC, by contrast, were not mandated by any regulators but were adopted voluntarily by a number of listed companies, in whole or in part. Hence, the stakes for the IASB as a global standard setter have been much higher than for the IASC.

As set out in our Introduction, a great deal of the data-gathering occurred through interviews. We had also done much interviewing for the IASC study, but most of the interviewees for that study were retired, while almost all of the interviewees for the IASB study were still active professionals with busy schedules. We are grateful to our interviewees for their time spent preparing for and taking the interviews, and for the additional time that several of them devoted to commenting on draft chapters.

We are in debt to the IASB for making available hard-copy and digital files of correspondence and documents, and to their staff for responding so graciously to our many questions for information and other assistance. In particular, we thank Yael Almog, Ailie Burlinson, Jenny Cale, Katherine Maybin, Kathryn McCardle, Chris Samarakkody, Tom Seidenstein, and Janet Smy. For reasons explained in our Introduction, we express bountiful thanks to Yuji Nishino, of Japan's Financial Accounting Standards Foundation. By the same token, we thank Board members Tatsumi Yamada and Zhang Wei-Guo for greatly facilitating our interview trips to Japan and China, respectively.

We express appreciation to Peter Walton for giving us access to *IStaR* and to Steve Burkholder for providing us with access to BNA's newswire.

We thank the following assistants and students who have transcribed many of our interviews: Sarah Diez, Corey Haas, Thomas Heijnen, Kristen Hogan, Elise McCutchen, Jasdeep Rai, Deyanira Verdejo, Wilco de Vries. Annie Wong also gave valuable help on the index. We also thank Rie Ohno and Tatae Akiyama, who expertly translated our many interviews in Japan.

We wish to acknowledge the substantial assistance provided by our universities, the Vrije Universiteit Amsterdam and Rice University.

We, as authors, are solely responsible for this work.

Kees Camfferman
Stephen A. Zeff

June 2014

Contents

List of Figures   xvi
List of Tables   xvii
List of Abbreviations   xviii
The International Accounting Standards Board until 2011:
A Basic Chronology   xxiii

1. Introduction   1
   1.1. Origins of this Book   1
   1.2. General Considerations of Method   2
   1.3. Scope   4
   1.4. Sources   5
   1.5. Structure of the Book   7

2. Evolution of the IASC into the IASB   8
   2.1. The Origins of International Accounting Standards   8
   2.2. 1987: A Turning Point for the IASC   10
   2.3. The Restructuring of the IASC   15

3. Setting Up the IASB   17
   3.1. Portentous Changes as the IASC Becomes the IASB   17
   3.2. The Selection of the First Trustees   18
         3.2.1. The Trustees Begin Their Work   22
   3.3. The Selection of Sir David Tweedie as Chairman   23
   3.4. The Selection of the Other Board Members   25
         3.4.1. The Eleven Other Full-time Members   27
         3.4.2. The Two Part-time Members   30
         3.4.3. The Final Stage in the Selection Process   31
         3.4.4. Liaison Members   32
   3.5. The Board as a Group   34
   3.6. Residence in London   37
   3.7. Successor to Bob Herz in 2002   39
   3.8. The Standards Advisory Council   39
   3.9. The Interpretations Committee: From SIC to IFRIC   43
   3.10. Technical and Administrative Staff   46
   3.11. Fundraising   47
         3.11.1. Implications of Sarbanes-Oxley's Automatic Funding
                 for the FASB   52
         3.11.2. Copyright Policy   53
   3.12. Trustee Activity and Turnover in Trustee Membership   54

4. The First Wave of Jurisdictional Adoptions of IFRSs   56
   4.1. The EU's Adoption of International Accounting Standards   57
        4.1.1. The Financial Services Action Plan   57
        4.1.2. The IAS Regulation   59
        4.1.3. The Launch of the Endorsement Mechanism and the
               Creation of EFRAG   61
        4.1.4. Completing the Regulatory Arrangements   63

4.2. Early Adopters: Hong Kong and South Africa   65
4.3. Following the EU: Australia and New Zealand   66
4.4. Acceptance of the IASB's Standards in Jurisdictions Around
the World   69
4.5. The United States   71
     4.5.1. The SEC Weighs In   72
     4.5.2. The Norwalk Agreement   75
     4.5.3. The SEC Begins to Ponder the Lifting of the Reconciliation
       Requirement   77
4.6. Japan   79
     4.6.1. Launch of the ASBJ   80
     4.6.2. Initial Ambivalence over IFRSs   81
     4.6.3. A Japanese Listed Company Adopts IFRSs Beginning in 2002   84
     4.6.4. Equivalence Assessment by the EU   84
4.7. Outreach by the Board and Trustees   86
4.8. The IASB and the National Standard Setters   90

5. The IASB sets its Agenda: 'Improvement, Convergence, Leadership'   93
5.1. Setting the Initial Agenda   93
     5.1.1. The 'Stable Platform' of Standards   97
5.2. Basic Values   98
5.3. Working Procedures   99
5.4. Early Achievements   103
     5.4.1. Improvements   103
     5.4.2. IFRS 1: First-time Adoption of IFRSs   106
     5.4.3. IFRS 2: Share-based Payment   107
     5.4.4. IFRS 3: Business Combinations   112
5.5. Initial Difficulties   115
     5.5.1. Insurance Contracts   115
     5.5.2. Performance Reporting   120
5.6. An Interim Standard on Extractive Industries   125
5.7. Exploring Convergence   128
     5.7.1. Short-term Convergence with US GAAP   129
     5.7.2. IFRS 5 and the Difficulties of Short-term Convergence
       with US GAAP   131
     5.7.3. Good Intentions for Joint Projects with the FASB   132
     5.7.4. The IASB and the FASB: Learning to Work Together   133
     5.7.5. A Case of non-US Convergence: The Revision of IAS 19
       in Line with UK GAAP   135

6. Financial Instruments: The Confrontation with Europe   138
6.1. The Inherited Interim Standard   138
6.2. From Limited Improvements to a Politicized Debate   141
     6.2.1. Behind the Criticism: Fair Value and Hedge Accounting   142
     6.2.2. Behind the Criticism: France   144
     6.2.3. Political Intervention   144
     6.2.4. A Counterpoint: Brazil   145
6.3. 'The IASB Does Not Listen'   146
6.4. The IASB Attempts to Close the Books on IAS 39   152
6.5. The Fair Value Option and the European Central Bank   155
6.6. The Carve-outs   157
6.7. IFRS 7: The IASB and the Banks Produce a Principles-based
Standard   160

7. The IASC Foundation's First Constitution Review: Debating
   Governance and Due Process 165
   7.1. Debate Over the IASB's Legitimacy, Accountability, and
        Due Process 165
   7.2. The IASB Modifies its Due Process 167
   7.3. The First Constitution Review 170

8. The United States Begins to Warm to the IASB 177
   8.1. Nicolaisen's Roadmap of April 2005 177
   8.2. The Roadmap Unblocks the IASB's Constitution Review 179
   8.3. Chairmanship of Cox and the Emergence of a More Formal
        Dialogue with European Regulators 182
   8.4. The SEC Lifts the 20-F Reconciliation Requirement 184
   8.5. The SEC's Initiative to Allow US Issuers to Adopt IFRSs 191
   8.6. The Proposing Release on the Mandatory Adoption of IFRS
        by US Issuers 194

9. The IASB's Vexed Relation with Europe 200
   9.1. A New Start? 200
   9.2. Removal of One of the Carve-outs: The Fair Value Option 202
   9.3. Enhancement of EFRAG 204
   9.4. IFRIC 3: The IASB Stumbles over Emission Rights 206
   9.5. The EU Promotes IFRSs to the World: The Equivalence
        Assessments 210
   9.6. New Pressures on the IASB from the EU 214
        9.6.1. Institutional Changes in Europe 215
        9.6.2. EU Pressure for IASB Reform 217
        9.6.3. IFRS 8 Provides the Spark 219
        9.6.4. The IASB's Response 223
        9.6.5. Defusing the Conflict 225

10. Adopt or Adapt: Diversity in Acceptance of IFRSs 229
    10.1. Canada Chooses IFRSs over US GAAP 229
    10.2. China 233
    10.3. South Korea 238
    10.4. Japan Seeks its Place in the Convergence Process 240
         10.4.1. The Tokyo Agreement 244
    10.5. Protection of the IASB's Brand: Compliance with IFRSs 247
         10.5.1. Société Générale Controversially Claims IAS 1's
                 'Fair Presentation' Override 249
    10.6. Protection of the IASB's Brand: Jurisdictional Variations from IFRSs 252
         10.6.1. The IASB and the IAASB Respond to Jurisdictional Variations 255
         10.6.2. IOSCO Issues a Statement on the Financial
                 Reporting Framework 258

11. The IASB's Organization Matures 261
    11.1. The Trustees 262
         11.1.1. Trustee Appointments Process 262
         11.1.2. Changes in Trustee Chairmanship 262
         11.1.3. Appointments of the Other Trustees 263
         11.1.4. The Trustees as a Group 267
    11.2. Continuity and Change in the Composition of the Board 269
         11.2.1. The Board as a Group 281
    11.3. Evolution of the Standards Advisory Council 284
    11.4. IFRIC 287

11.5. Enhanced Oversight and Elaboration of Due Process
Requirements   289
   11.5.1. Due Process, a Continuing Discussion   292
11.6. Responsiveness, Communications, and Transparency   293
11.7. Specialized Advisory Groups   296
11.8. Relations with National Standard Setters   298
11.9. Changes in the Technical Staff   301
   11.9.1. Staff Numbers and Staff Policies   301
   11.9.2. Staff Comings and Goings   302
   11.9.3. Director-level Technical Staff   306
   11.9.4. Tom Seidenstein   307
11.10. Fundraising from 2002 to 2011   307
   11.10.1. Casting Around for Funding Alternatives   308
   11.10.2. 2006: A Turning Point   314
   11.10.3. What was the Foundation Saying Publicly From
        2002 to 2006?   319
   11.10.4. The Big Fundraising Drive Continues   320
   11.10.5. New Funding and New Challenges   323
   11.10.6. The EU, the United States, and the Rest of the World   326
   11.10.7. Analysis of Contributions by Country and Regions   329
   11.10.8. Fundraising: Small Sums, Large Efforts   331

12. **Concepts and Convergence: An Ever Closer Relation with the FASB**   333
12.1. The IASB's Standard-setting Activities in the Middle of
the Decade   333
12.2. Planning the Convergence of IFRSs and US GAAP   334
   12.2.1. The SEC Roadmap and the Origins of the 2006 MoU   334
   12.2.2. The February 2006 MoU   338
   12.2.3. The 2008 MoU and the Emergence of the 2011 Deadline   341
12.3. The IASB and the FASB: Still Learning to Work Together   345
12.4. Business Combinations Phase II   347
12.5. A Tangle of Issues in the Revision of IAS 37   351
12.6. Revenue Recognition   355
12.7. Revision of the Conceptual Framework   358
   12.7.1. Reliability   361
   12.7.2. Stewardship   363
   12.7.3. Elements, Recognition, and Measurement   366
   12.7.4. The Reporting Entity   367
   12.7.5. Limited Results of the Conceptual Framework Project   368
   12.7.6. Status of the Revised Conceptual Framework in Some
        Adopting Jurisdictions   369
12.8. Financial Statement Presentation   370
   12.8.1. Phase A: No Single Performance Statement   371
   12.8.2. Phase B: The IASB Again Shrinks Back from Calling
        Net Income into Question   375
12.9. Financial Instruments: Long-term Convergence and
Short-term Maintenance   378
   12.9.1. Full Fair Value as a Long-term Objective   378
   12.9.2. Maintenance and Improvement of IAS 39: Removing
        the Carve-outs   381
   12.9.3. Maintenance and Improvement of IAS 32: Puttable
        Financial Instruments   382

12.10. IFRS for Small and Medium-sized Entities — 385
12.11. Management Commentary — 391
12.12. Interpretations: IFRIC's Activities — 392
    12.12.1. Negative Agenda Decisions — 393
    12.12.2. IFRIC 12: Service Concession Arrangements — 395
    12.12.3. IFRIC 15: Agreements for the Construction of Real Estate — 399

13. The IASB Survives the Financial Crisis — 401
13.1. A Slow Build-up of Pressure — 401
13.2. Emergence of the Reclassification Issue — 404
13.3. The IASB's Crisis of 13 October 2008 — 407
13.4. Problems in Adopting the Amendment in Selected Other Jurisdictions — 413
13.5. Application of the Reclassification Option — 414
13.6. Devising a Response to Financial and Political Turmoil — 415
13.7. G20 Summit in Washington in November 2008 — 417
13.8. Loan Impairment, Dynamic Provisioning, and the Role of the Prudential Regulators — 420
13.9. The FASB also Feels the Sting of Political Pressure — 421
13.10. Pressure on the IASB to Level the Playing Field — 424
13.11. The FCAG Speaks Out Against Political Pressure — 428
13.12. IFRS 9 and the Parting of the Ways of the IASB and the FASB — 431
13.13. Intermezzo: Pressure of a Different Kind — 435
13.14. The European Commission Fails to Endorse IFRS 9 — 436

14. Preparing the IASB for the Second Decade — 439
14.1. A Strategic Review by the Trustees — 440
14.2. Narrowing the Issues and Moving Forward — 442
14.3. 'Independence with Accountability' — 442
14.4. Joint Statement from Four Public Bodies on a Monitoring Group — 444
14.5. Run-up to the Constitution Review — 447
14.6. The First Phase of the Constitution Review — 449
    14.6.1. Size and Composition of the IASB Board — 453
    14.6.2. The January 2009 Trustees' Meeting — 455
14.7. Other Issues Considered During the Strategy Review — 457
14.8. Part Two of the Constitution Review — 460
    14.8.1. Objectives: Principles-based Standards — 461
    14.8.2. Objectives: Range of Entities and Economic Settings — 462
    14.8.3. Objectives: Globally Accepted Standards — 463
    14.8.4. Collaboration with Other Organizations — 463
    14.8.5. Board Due Process: Agenda and Oversight — 464
    14.8.6. Board Due Process: Fast-track Procedure — 466
    14.8.7. Composition and Organization of the Trustees — 467
    14.8.8. Organization of the Board — 467
    14.8.9. Name Change — 468
    14.8.10. Issues Left for Future Consideration — 469
    14.8.11. From Constitution Review to the Next Strategy Review — 470
14.9. Organization of the Monitoring Board at its First Meeting — 470
14.10. The Monitoring Board Establishes its Presence — 473
14.11. Tommaso Padoa-Schioppa Becomes the Successor to Gerrit Zalm — 475

14.12.	Choosing the Successor to David Tweedie	478
	14.12.1. David Tweedie—in Retrospect	483
14.13.	The Trustees and the Monitoring Board Begin Parallel Reviews	485
	14.13.1. Outcomes of the Strategy and Governance Reviews	488

15. **The Uncertain Path Towards a Single Global Standard** — 494

15.1.	Many Latin American and Caribbean Countries adopt IFRSs	494
	15.1.1. Chile	496
	15.1.2. Argentina	496
	15.1.3. Brazil	497
	15.1.4. Mexico	499
	15.1.5. Colombia	500
	15.1.6. Group of Latin American Accounting Standard Setters (GLASS)	501
	15.1.7. Compliance and Languages	501
15.2.	Africa	502
15.3.	Russia Goes for IFRSs	503
15.4.	The United States: The SEC Does Not Decide on IFRSs	505
	15.4.1. Change in SEC Chairman from Christopher Cox to Mary Schapiro in January 2009	505
	15.4.2. Comments on the Proposing Release	508
	15.4.3. The Series of Instalments in the SEC Staff's Work Plan, from 2010 Onwards	512
15.5.	Japan Pulls Back from Adopting IFRSs	517
	15.5.1. Building Momentum Towards IFRS Adoption	517
	15.5.2. Hesitation Sets In	522
	15.5.3. The Prospect of IFRS Adoption Fades	526
15.6.	China's Substantial Convergence	527
	15.6.1. Application and Development of the Converged Accounting Standards	527
	15.6.2. China Seeks Recognition of Equivalence	530
15.7.	Attempts in India to Adopt IFRSs	533
15.8.	The Asian-Oceanian Standard-Setters Group (AOSSG)	537
15.9.	Other Forms of Regional Cooperation in Asia	538
15.10.	The EU Holds on to IFRSs	539
	15.10.1. Another Enhancement of EFRAG	541
	15.10.2. UK GAAP Moves Closer to IFRSs	542
	15.10.3. The French Standard Setter Strikes Out on its Own	543
	15.10.4. Standard-Setter Crisis in Germany	544

16. **The IASB and the FASB Rush to Complete the Convergence Programme** — 546

16.1.	Tension Rises as 2011 Approaches	547
	16.1.1. A Tight Schedule	547
	16.1.2. Renewed Commitment	548
	16.1.3. An FAF Threat Leads to a Modification of the Work Plan	550
	16.1.4. The Target is Missed	553
16.2.	Review of Technical Projects	557
16.3.	Consolidation and Joint Arrangements	557
	16.3.1. Consolidation and Special Purpose Entities	558
	16.3.2. From Joint Ventures to Joint Arrangements	561
	16.3.3. A Difficult European Endorsement	563
16.4.	Fair Value Measurement: Leapfrogging to Convergence	564

16.5.   Employee Benefits: An MoU Project Without the FASB   569
16.6.   Revenue Recognition   573
16.7.   Leases   576
16.8.   Financial Instruments   583
         16.8.1. Mixed Measurement or Fair Value   584
         16.8.2. Impairment   587
         16.8.3. Derecognition   589
         16.8.4. Hedge Accounting   591
         16.8.5. Offsetting   592
16.9.   Insurance Contracts   593
16.10.   Liabilities and Equity   597
16.11.   Financial Statement Presentation: No Single Performance
         Statement (Again)   599
16.12.   Income Tax: The Last Failure of Short-term Convergence   603

17. Epilogue   607
17.1.   A Changing Board in a Changing World   607
17.2.   The SEC's Reluctance to Move Towards IFRSs   608
17.3.   Mixed Signals from Other Jurisdictions   609
17.4.   Recalibrating the Organization   611
17.5.   Winding Down the Convergence Effort with the FASB   612
17.6.   Expansion of Trustee and Board Roles   614
17.7.   A World of National Standard Setters   614
17.8.   European Parliament Politicizes Funding of the IFRS
        Foundation   616
17.9.   US Financial Accounting Foundation Controversially
        Contributes up to $3 Million to the IFRS Foundation   616

Appendix 1 Trustees, Members of the Board, the Advisory Council,
and the Interpretations Committee   619
Appendix 2 Standards and Interpretations   629
Appendix 3 IASC–IFRS Foundation Summary Financial Data 2001–11   634
Appendix 4 List of Interviewees   636
Appendix 5 Sources and Referencing   641

Index   643

List of Figures

3.1	Sir David Tweedie	24
3.2	The initial members of the IASB Board, 2001	28
11.1	John Smith	269
11.2	Jan Engström	271
11.3	Philippe Danjou	273
11.4	Zhang Wei-Guo	274
11.5	Stephen Cooper	276
11.6	Prabhakar Kalavacherla	277
11.7	Patrick Finnegan	278
11.8	Patricia McConnell	278
11.9	Amaro Gomes	279
11.10	Elke König	280
11.11	Paul Pacter	280
11.12	Darrel Scott	280
11.13	The IASB Board in 2007	282
14.1	Advertisement for IASB chairman, January 2010	480

List of Tables

3.1 Founding IASB Board members by region and designated professional
background 34

3.2 Initial members of the Standards Advisory Council 42

3.3 Initial voting members of IFRIC 45

3.4 Contribution commitments by country and region, 2001 49

11.1 Contributions by country and region, 2007–11 330

12.1 Major projects of the IASB–FASB Memorandum of Understanding, 2006–11 339

12.2 The IASB's projects for short-term convergence with US GAAP, 2006–11 340

13.1 Members of the Financial Crisis Advisory Group (FCAG) 430

List of Abbreviations

AARF	Australian Accounting Research Foundation
AASB	Australian Accounting Standards Board
AcSB	Accounting Standards Board (Canada)
ACTEO	Association pour la Participation des Entreprises Françaises à l'Harmonisation Comptable Internationale
AFM	Autoriteit Financiële Markten (Authority for the Financial Markets, the Netherlands)
AICPA	American Institute of Certified Public Accountants
AIMR	Association for Investment Management and Research (United States), subsequently CFA Institute
AMF	Autorité des Marchés Financiers (France)
ANC	Autorité des Normes Comptables (Accounting Principles Authority, France)
AOSSG	Asian-Oceanian Standard-Setters Group
ARC	Accounting Regulatory Committee (European Union)
ASAF	Accounting Standards Advisory Forum
ASB	Accounting Standards Board (United Kingdom)
ASBJ	Accounting Standards Board of Japan
ASEAN	Association of Southeast Asian Nations
ASRB	Accounting Standards Review Board (New Zealand)
BAC	Business Accounting Council (Japan)
BADC	Business Accounting Deliberation Council (Japan)
CAS	Chinese Accounting Standard
CBI	Confederation of British Industry (UK)
CCCTB	common consolidated corporate tax base (EU)
CEA	Comité Européen des Assurances
CEBS	Committee of European Banking Supervisors
CESR	Committee of European Securities Regulators
CFA	Chartered Financial Analyst
CFC	Conselho Federal de Contabilidade (Federal Council of Accounting, Brazil)
CGA-Canada	Certified General Accountants Association of Canada
CICA	Canadian Institute of Chartered Accountants
CINIF	Consejo Mexicano para la Investigación y Desarrollo de Normas de Información Financiera (Council for Research and Development of Financial Information Standards, Mexico)
CNBV	Comisión Nacional Bancaria y de Valores (National Banking and Securities Commission, Mexico)

CNC	Conseil National de la Comptabilité (National Accounting Council, France)
CNV	Comisión Nacional de Valores (National Securities Commission, Argentina)
COB	Commission des Opérations de Bourse (France)
COFRI	Corporation Finance Research Institute (Japan)
CONSOB	Commissione Nazionale per le Società e la Borsa (Italian securities regulator)
Corp Fin	Division of Corporation Finance, Securities and Exchange Commission (United States)
CPA	Certified Public Accountant
CPC	Comitê de Pronunciamentos Contábeis (Accounting Pronouncements Committee, Brazil)
CRUF	Corporate Reporting Users Forum
CSA	Canadian Securities Administrators
CSRC	China Securities Regulatory Commission
CTCP	Consejo Técnico de la Contaduría Pública (Technical Council of Public Accountancy, Colombia)
DPR	Deutsche Prüfstellung für Rechnungslegung (Financial Reporting Enforcement Panel in Germany)
DRSC	Deutsches Rechnungslegungs Standards Committee (Germany), also known in English as the German Accounting Standards Board
DSOP	Draft Statement of Principles (IASC)
DTI	Department of Trade and Industry (United Kingdom)
EBF	European Banking Federation, also FBE
ECB	European Central Bank
ECOFIN	Council of the European Union, Economic and Financial Affairs
ED	Exposure draft (IASB)
EEC	European Economic Community
EITF	Emerging Issues Task Force (FASB)
EFRAG	European Financial Reporting Advisory Group
ERT	European Round Table of Industrialists
ESMA	European Securities and Markets Authority
EU	European Union
FACPCE	Federación Argentina de Consejos Profesionales en Ciencias Económicas (Argentine Federation of Professional Councils in Economic Sciences)
FAF	Financial Accounting Foundation (overseeing the FASB)
FAS	(Statement of) Financial Accounting Standards (United States)
FASAC	Financial Accounting Standards Advisory Council (advisory body to the FASB)
FASB	Financial Accounting Standards Board (United States)
FASF	Financial Accounting Standards Foundation (Japan)
FBE	Fédération Bancaire Européenne, also EBF

FCAG	Financial Crisis Advisory Group
FEE	Fédération des Experts Comptables Européens
FEI	Financial Executives International (until 2000, Financial Executives Institute) (United States)
FER	Fachkommission für Empfehlungen zur Rechnungslegung (Swiss accounting standard setter)
FIFO	first-in, first-out (inventory cost flow)
FRC	Financial Reporting Council (Australia, United Kingdom)
FRS	Financial Reporting Standard (UK ASB)
FRSB	Financial Reporting Standards Board (New Zealand)
FRSSE	Financial Reporting Standard for Smaller Entities (UK)
FSA	(1) Financial Services Agency (Japan)
	(2) Financial Services Authority (United Kingdom)
FSB	Financial Stability Board
FSC	Financial Supervisory Commission (South Korea)
FSF	Financial Stability Forum
GAAP	generally accepted accounting principles (originally United States, subsequently also used to indicate other national reporting frameworks, but with the meaning of generally accepted accounting practice in the United Kingdom and several other countries)
GDP	gross domestic product
GLASS	Group of Latin American Accounting Standard Setters
HKFRS	Hong Kong Financial Reporting Standard
HKICPA	Hong Kong Institute of Certified Public Accountants
IAASB	International Auditing and Assurance Standards Board (IFAC)
IAFEI	International Association of Financial Executives Institutes
IAIS	International Association of Insurance Supervisors
IAS	International Accounting Standard
IASB	International Accounting Standards Board
IASC	International Accounting Standards Committee
IASCF	International Accounting Standards Committee Foundation
ICAEW	Institute of Chartered Accountants in England and Wales
ICAI	Institute of Chartered Accountants of India
IETA	International Emissions Trading Association
IFAC	International Federation of Accountants
IFASS	International Forum of Accounting Standard-Setters (formerly NSS)
IFRIC	International Financial Reporting Interpretations Committee
IFRS	International Financial Reporting Standard
IGC	Implementation Guidance Committee (on IAS 39)
IMA	Investment Management Association (United Kingdom)
IMCP	Instituto Mexicano de Contadores Públicos (Mexican Institute of Public Accountants)

IMF	International Monetary Fund
IOSCO	International Organization of Securities Commissions
IPSASB	International Public Sector Accounting Standards Board
ISA	International Standard on Auditing (IAASB)
IVSC	International Valuation Standards Committee
JICPA	Japanese Institute of Certified Public Accountants
JIG	Joint International Group (an IASB–FASB joint working group)
JWG	Joint Working Group (of standard setters on financial instruments, 1997–2000)
KASB	Korea Accounting Standards Board
LIFO	last-in, first-out (inventory cost flow)
MD&A	Management's Discussion and Analysis (also known as Management Commentary)
MEDEF	Mouvement des Entreprises de France (French business confederation)
METI	Ministry of Economy, Trade and Industry (Japan)
MIF	Multilateral Investment Fund (Inter-American Development Bank)
MoF	Ministry of Finance (China)
MoU	Memorandum of Understanding
NACAS	National Advisory Committee on Accounting Standards (India)
NASB	National Accounting Standards Board (Russia)
NDK	Nihon Dempa Kogyo Co. Ltd (Japan)
NOFA	National Organization for Financial Accounting and Reporting Standards Foundation (Russia)
NSS	National Standard-Setters
OCA	Office of the Chief Accountant (SEC)
OCI	other comprehensive income
OECD	Organisation for Economic Co-operation and Development
OIC	Organismo Italiano di Contabilità
PAFA	Pan African Federation of Accountants
PIOB	Public Interest Oversight Board (IFAC)
PwC	PricewaterhouseCoopers
R&D	research and development
ROSC A&A	Report on the Observance of Standards and Codes, Accounting and Auditing (of the World Bank)
SAB	SEC's Staff Accounting Bulletin
SAC	Standards Advisory Council (IASB)
SAICA	South African Institute of Chartered Accountants
SARG	Standards Advice Review Group (European Union)
SC1	Standing Committee 1 (IOSCO)
SEBI	Securities and Exchange Board of India
SEC	Securities and Exchange Commission (United States)

SIC	Standing Interpretations Committee (IASC)
SMEs	small and medium-sized entities
SPE	special purpose entity
STRGL	statement of total recognized gains and losses (UK)
SVS	Superintendencia de Valores y Seguros (Securities and Insurance Supervisor, Chile)
SWP	Strategy Working Party (IASC, 1997–9)
TEG	Technical Expert Group (EFRAG)
TFOSS	Task Force on Standard Setting (Canada)
UN	United Nations
UNCTAD	United Nations Conference on Trade and Development
UNICE	Union of Industrial and Employers' Confederations of Europe, subsequently BUSINESSEUROPE
WTO	World Trade Organization
XBRL	eXtensible Business Reporting Language (XML-based computer software language developed specifically for the automation of business information requirements)

Abbreviations used in references to source materials (see also Appendix 5):

AP	Agenda paper (of the IASB Board)
CL	Comment letter (to the IASB)

The International Accounting Standards Board until 2011: A Basic Chronology

1973   National accountancy bodies found the International Accounting Standards Committee (IASC)

1997   IASC's Strategy Working Party begins to consider restructuring of IASC

1999   IASC Board agrees to restructuring as independent standard setter overseen by an IASC Foundation

2000   Nominating committee appoints IASC Foundation trustees, with Paul Volcker as chairman

Trustees appoint Sir David Tweedie as first chairman of restructured IASC

International Organization of Securities Commissions (IOSCO) endorses IASC's core standards, and recommends improvements

European Commission unveils plan for mandatory adoption of IASC standards in the European Union (EU) by 2005

2001   IASC Foundation trustees announce membership of restructured Board

IASC Foundation changes name of IASC to IASB and name of standards to IFRSs, Board holds first meeting

Enron accounting scandal, accompanied by others, occur in United States

2002   EU enacts IAS Regulation requiring listed company use of IFRSs by 2005

Australia and New Zealand announce plans for mandatory IFRS use by 2005 and 2007

Robert Herz resigns from IASB Board to become chairman of Financial Accounting Standards Board (FASB)

IASB and FASB announce Norwalk Agreement

2003   IASC Foundation trustees begin first periodic review of Constitution

2004   IASB completes 'stable platform of standards' as first phase of its technical work

EU endorses IASB's financial instruments standards with two carve-outs

2005   EU and Australia complete successful large-scale transition to IFRSs

Tommaso Padoa-Schioppa briefly succeeds Volcker as chairman of IASC Foundation trustees, Phil Laskawy becomes acting chairman following Padoa-Schioppa

Chief Accountant Donald Nicolaisen of the US Securities and Exchange Commission (SEC) publishes roadmap for lifting 20-F reconciliation

IASC Foundation trustees complete revision of Constitution

2006   IASB and FASB publish Memorandum of Understanding (MoU) outlining convergence work plan

Canada announces plan for transition to IFRSs in 2011

China publishes revised set of accounting standards, 'substantially converged' with IFRSs, effective 1 January 2007

2007   South Korea announces transition to IFRSs in 2011

IASB and Accounting Standards Board of Japan sign Tokyo Agreement on convergence of standards

IASC Foundation trustees begin strategic review in preparation of second periodic review of Constitution

Brazil announces transition to IFRSs in 2010

US SEC lifts 20-F reconciliation requirement for foreign registrants using IFRSs.

European Commission, US SEC, and Japan's Financial Services Agency (FSA) propose Monitoring Board to oversee the IASC Foundation

2008   IASC Foundation selects Gerrit Zalm as trustee chairman

IASB and FASB publish updated MoU, aiming for completion of convergence work plan by June 2011

US SEC issues roadmap proposal on required use of IFRSs by domestic registrants, decision expected in 2011

Financial crisis breaks; EU forces IASB to amend financial instruments standards without due process; G20 summit issues call for 'single set of global accounting standards'

2009   IASC Foundation creates Monitoring Board, which elects Hans Hoogervorst as chairman

US SEC rethinks plan for use of IFRSs by domestic companies

IASB and FASB drift apart in attempt to develop a converged financial instruments standard

IASB and FASB agree to redouble efforts to complete MoU work plan by June 2011

Japan's FSA permits voluntary use of IFRSs, envisages decision on mandatory use in 2012

2010   IASC Foundation renames itself IFRS Foundation

IFRS Foundation again appoints Tommaso Padoa-Schioppa as trustee chairman, but he dies in December of that year

Robert Herz retires suddenly from the FASB chairmanship, and is succeeded by Leslie Seidman

IFRS Foundation appoints Hans Hoogervorst to succeed David Tweedie in July 2011

2011   IFRS Foundation appoints Tsuguoki Fujinuma and Robert Glauber as acting co-chairmen of the trustees following the death of Padoa-Schioppa

IASB and FASB fail to complete MoU work plan by June

Last of initial IASB members, including David Tweedie, retire

SEC takes no decision on adoption of IFRSs in the United States

1

Introduction

To say that the International Accounting Standards Board (IASB) and its International Financial Reporting Standards (IFRSs) currently occupy a central place in financial reporting is to state the obvious. Nevertheless, it bears repeating just how remarkable and unprecedented the IASB's rise to prominence has been in the history of accounting. It has meant not only that today it is hardly possible to conduct a technical accounting discussion without some reference to IFRSs, but it has also meant that many people—in governments, in legislative bodies, in regulatory functions, in business, or in academia—who do not at all think of themselves as accountants, have been forced to develop a position vis-à-vis the IASB. Since 2001, the IASB and its standards have entered the working lives of countless individuals around the world, all of whom have had to respond to it, with varying degrees of urgency and intensity, in the context of their own background and responsibilities. As a result, the IASB is hardly an obscure body. Knowledge about it is widespread and most of what it does, or fails to do, is hotly debated. There has been an outpouring of publications about it in many languages in the professional and academic literature, as well as in the general media. Many people have developed a deep expertise on specific technical topics, or on the impact of IFRSs on financial reporting in their own country. But while many people know bits of the IASB's story, and know them well, it may still be useful to write a more general account of how the IASB came to occupy its present pivotal position, and how the various jurisdictions that have adopted its standards or have considered doing so have responded to the IASB—as well as of the interactions between the IASB's technical work and its political environment. This book aims to give such a general evolutionary account, in the hope that many people who need to take note of, or deal with, the IASB will find it a useful complement to their own experience or a useful companion in their own research.

1.1 ORIGINS OF THIS BOOK

This book has been written at the invitation of the IASB itself. In 2007, we published *Financial Reporting and Global Capital Markets: A History of the International Accounting Standards Committee, 1973–2000*, which aimed to give a similar general history of the International Accounting Standards Committee (IASC), the IASB's predecessor body. As we explained in that previous book, it was the IASB, and in particular its chairman, Sir David Tweedie, who asked us in

2002 to write a history of the IASC. By that time, the IASC had ceased to exist and, although the IASB had adopted the IASC's standards, it was for our purposes little more than the custodian of the IASC's archives. For the IASB, it was presumably not too difficult to allow us to have complete editorial freedom to write about the IASC as we thought proper.

Towards the end of 2007, Tweedie approached us again with the suggestion that we write a similar book about the first decade of the IASB. We realized that, despite the general similarity of the objective, there would be significant differences between the two projects. The IASB was, and is, a living organization with considerable responsibilities on the world stage. Moreover, it has been at the centre of some intense controversies, and continues to provoke mixed reactions. A practical point in terms of historical writing was that, at the time we were invited to undertake the study, several years of the IASB's first decade were still in the future and, as it turned out, these were certainly not the least eventful. With this in mind, we submitted a proposal to the IASC Foundation trustees, which was accepted in July 2008. As a result, we were provided with a lump-sum budget to cover travel expenses, which have consisted mainly of the costs of conducting interviews around the world. We did not ask for, and were not offered, an honorarium or fee. This meant that our time spent on this project was funded by our universities, where we continued to fulfil our normal teaching obligations in alternation with work on this book.

The trustees did not impose restrictions on our research or our writing. We have not been asked to submit our drafts for approval, but we did express from the start our intention to circulate our drafts for comment, both inside and outside the IASB organization. We were given to understand that the IASB would assist us with access to documentation, although the precise limits of that access were not specified in advance. In our view, the IASC Foundation trustees reposed considerable confidence in us by commissioning a research project under such conditions, and we wish to express our sincere appreciation for that.

1.2 GENERAL CONSIDERATIONS OF METHOD

Our ideal in writing this book has been to be objective, but we are aware that we can never be judged to have been fully successful in this regard, not even by ourselves. The IASB's work has sparked intense debate and controversy, and it is illusory to expect that anyone could portray the IASB in a way that will not be contradicted. Apart from that, during our work on this book and on our earlier book on the IASC, we have, for more than a decade, regularly breathed the atmosphere of the IASB's offices in London. If there is such a thing as the IASB's view of the world, it is inevitable that we have to some extent imbibed it.

Even if we did not say so here, most readers would have no great difficulty in discerning from this book that we are broadly sympathetic to the idea of a global set of accounting standards and to the way the IASC and the IASB have tried to achieve it. That leaves open many important questions as to the exact content of global standards and the way they should be set. Major questions remain with respect to the degree of desirable or inevitable variation of practice around a global norm, and therefore with respect to the way IFRSs should be allowed, required, or adapted for use in different countries. Nonetheless, we feel no compunction in stating our belief that financial reporting, considered at a global level, is currently in much better shape than it would have been if the multiplicity of national generally accepted accounting principles (GAAPs) had not been affected by the strong harmonizing impulses provided by the IASC and the IASB.

That said, we have consciously attempted to become aware of and understand differences of view on the IASB and IFRSs, not least through our extensive interviewing (see Section 1.4). As indicated above, we have adopted the policy of circulating sections of our drafts for comment, both inside and outside the IASB, to ensure that we have captured important alternative points of view and have provided a reasonably balanced treatment. In our writing, we have attempted to explain why controversies have arisen and what consequences they had, rather than to take a position on who was right. We had no commission to be apologists for the IASB, and we have attempted not to write as if we did.

We have not approached our research on the basis of a specific theoretical framework. Apart from a general disposition to welcome the emergence of international accounting standards, as mentioned above, the most important assumption underlying our writing is that the events with respect to the IASB over the last decade are best described as a process of collective discovery. We congratulate Nicolas Véron on his happy choice of a title for his 2007 analysis of the IASB, *The Global Accounting Experiment*.[1] Although this has forced us to think of a different title, the word 'experiment' does evoke the trial and error with which both the IASB and all its constituents have approached the task of building a global standard-setting structure for financial reporting. One can debate whether the biblical characterization of Abraham who 'went out, not knowing whither he went' is more applicable to the IASB in 2001 or to the leaders of the European Union (EU) when they announced, in 2000, the mandatory use of IFRSs, but it is clear that both the IASB and those who dealt with it have climbed a steep learning curve. Both the IASB and its constituents had to have frequent recourse to improvisation in response to each other's actions and to unexpected events. More fundamentally, the events of the last decade have demonstrated that the world may find it easy to agree in the abstract that a single set of high-quality global accounting standards is a desirable objective, but that it is still far away from consensus about the specific content of such standards, or even the proced-ures through which such standards should be developed. The IASB itself is not monolithic, and its decisions are taken in a process of collective and incremental decision-making that no one, not even the chairman, controls. In our writing, we have attempted to do justice to this 'emergent' nature of the IASB and its standards by portraying the actions of the IASB, of other organizations, of countries, or of key individuals in each, as much as possible in terms of their own logic or rationales.

A final aspect of our approach is that we have not aspired to write the definitive book about the IASB. This is *a* book, which we believe will make a useful

---

[1] Nicolas Véron, *The Global Accounting Experiment*, Bruegel Blueprint Series No. 2 (Brussels: Bruegel, 2007).

contribution to the literature at the current stage. It benefits from the fact that all participants were still around, that memories are still fairly fresh, and that we could even witness some events at first hand. On the other hand, closeness to the events brings inevitable limitations. Not everyone is yet able or willing to talk freely, our short time perspective means that we lack much of the benefit of hindsight, and we have thought it only natural to exercise a degree of discretion with respect to details about individuals who are still active in this area and who have given us their confidence. In view of the opportunities and constraints of the present moment, we have attempted to write the story of the IASB to the best of our abilities, but we look forward to future publications which will further enrich our insight and perhaps take issue with our interpretations.

1.3 SCOPE

The period covered in this book is approximately the first decade of the IASB. While the start of the IASB is clearly marked, finding a cut-off point at the end was less straightforward. We did decide that we wanted such a cut-off point at least a few years before submission of the manuscript to the publisher. We believe that this space has given us at least a minimum of historical perspective from which to assess even the more recent events covered in the book. We decided to draw the line in the middle of 2011, when the last of the first generation of Board members, including David Tweedie, retired from the Board. While this end point obviously does not provide an absolute caesura, it does seem to mark a change of pace and a point at which both the IASB and the world at large began to pause for reflection on the future role of international accounting standards. In an 'epilogue' chapter, we do attempt to review events between the middle of 2011 and the completion of the manuscript, but we do so in outline only, in a different style from the 'historical' chapters which make up the bulk of the book.

Another important aspect of scope is that we do not merely want to give the history of the IASB by itself, as an organization. A central theme that we wish to bring out in the book is how jurisdictions around the world have developed their response to what might be called the challenge posed by the very existence of the IASB. Moreover, many aspects of the evolution of the IASB itself are understandable only in the light of its interactions with the outside world. The obvious problem with this ambition is that, as the IASB likes to point out, 'more than a hundred' countries and other jurisdictions allow or require the use of IFRSs in one way or another, and we could not begin to discuss in any detail the great variety of experiences with the IASB and IFRSs of all of these places. In the light of events, we believe it is reasonable that the main focus of this book, when it comes to the worldwide reception of IFRSs, is on the EU and the United States. In addition, we have devoted special attention to events in China and Japan, not only because of the political and economic significance of these countries, but also because the story of the engagement of each country with the IASB and IFRSs is different again in important respects from the already strongly different stories of the EU and the United States. Many other countries, including Australia, Brazil, Canada, India, and Russia, reflect yet again other facets of the story of the IASB, and we have tried to make appropriate references throughout the book, but without any pretention to comprehensiveness. We are aware that, in doing so, we, like the IASB, can be criticized for a lack of balance, in particular with respect to developing countries and to countries with emerging economies.

A third question of scope is the extent to which the book should deal with the IASB's technical work. Both the IASB's publicly available documentation and the professional literature provide for more information about the content and progress of the IASB's technical projects than we could ever present in this book. Nevertheless, we do devote a considerable portion of this book to discuss technical projects, for two reasons. One is that a general grasp of how the IASB's agenda has developed may provide useful contextual information for studying any of the standards or projects in depth. The other reason is that it is simply impossible to understand the IASB itself, or the reactions it provoked, without some understanding of the nature of the questions it was dealing with and the answers it was trying to give. We have, however, been selective by focusing on those aspects of projects that, in our view, throw a light on the IASB's way of operating, the challenges it faced, its priorities, its outlook, and its relations with various constituents. This may mean that relatively minor aspects of some standards are highlighted while other aspects go unreported, but we are confident that interested readers will have no difficulties finding more comprehensive discussions in the professional literature.

1.4 SOURCES

There is a wealth of information in the public domain about the IASB, more than we could possibly do justice to. In terms of primary documentation, the IASB itself has, especially since around 2005, published a large part of its agenda papers on its website. Meetings of the IASB Board and the trustees are, with only limited exceptions, open to the public. Apart from the IASB's own webcasts, third parties provide reports on these meetings, in particular the extensive reports in *IFRS Monitor* (formerly known as *IStaR*). Other major sources reporting in detail on events as they happen are *World Accounting Report*, BNA's *Daily Tax Report*, and Deloitte's IAS Plus website. Primary documentation with respect to organizations other than the IASB is available in such forms as rule proposals, parliamentary records, or comment letters and other correspondence published on the originating organizations' websites. Some potentially relevant materials from other organizations were not available to us. The International Organization of Securities Commissions (IOSCO) declined to give us access to the minutes of meetings of its Standing Committee 1 on multinational disclosure and accounting.

As indicated above, the IASB has allowed us some access to documents that are not on the public record. We have accepted it as self-evident that a going concern like the IASB, if only because of its responsibilities as an employer and a public entity, could not give us automatic access to all information concerning the activities of Board members and staff. In practice, this has meant that we were given access to minutes and agenda papers, as well as to much of the correspondence at the chairman level. (See Appendix 5 for more information about archival sources and the way they are cited in the text.) Apart from that, we have made requests for information on specific questions as they arose. We have attempted to exercise our judgement with respect to what could reasonably be asked in such cases, and we have not encountered a situation in which a request for a specific piece of documentation was refused.

Another important source of information has been the interviews which we have conducted with people who are, or have been, involved with the IASB in a wide range of capacities: twenty-two members of the Board and a number of staff, fourteen trustees of the IASC/IFRS Foundation, members of the Standards Advisory Council (SAC) and the International Financial Reporting Interpretations Committee (IFRIC), other national standard setters and their staff, securities and prudential regulators, government agencies, users, auditors, preparers and industry associations, academics, and others. In all, we conducted more than 170 interviews between 2008 and 2013, some with two or more interviewees, and in a few cases more than once with the same person. Our interviews were conducted mainly in Europe and the United States. In addition, we conducted separate interview trips to Australia and New Zealand, China, and Japan (see Appendix 4 for a list of interviewees). Apart from rare exceptions where a telephone interview had to be conducted, all of the interviews were face to face. We have been gratified by the fact that only a few of the individuals we approached have declined to be interviewed. We have been much impressed by the generosity of many people who have given us their time and have shared their insights and recollections with us. Without in any way detracting from our appreciation of other interviewees, we believe that separate mention should be made of the incomparable support we received from the Financial Accounting Standards Foundation (FASF) and the Accounting Standards Board of Japan (ASBJ), which it oversees. We still marvel at how Mr Yuji Nishino of the FASF managed to organize an immensely valuable series of twenty-nine interviews in Tokyo, all scheduled during office hours during a two-week period, and with expert consecutive translation which was necessary for most of the interviewees. No one on the schedule he prepared for us missed the interview appointment.

In selecting our interviewees, we have aimed to cover a broad range of 'takes' on the IASB, both sympathetic and critical, a range of functional and geographical backgrounds, as well as a reasonable spread across the various episodes that we sought to discuss in the book. Although we did attempt to conduct our interviews in a planned fashion, starting with a list of around a hundred prospective interviewees in 2008, we substantially modified our plans as we went along, not unlike the IASB's style of working. Not only did the financial crisis, as it erupted in full severity in the autumn of 2008, bring new characters into the story, the interviews that we did, or the materials that we studied, inevitably pointed towards people we had not been aware of, or whose significance we had failed to appreciate. When we decided to draw our research to a close, we still had a list of more than several score people we would have liked to have seen.

The interviews were based on questions sent in advance, and they typically lasted between one and two hours. All but a few were recorded and transcribed, and all were conducted on a confidential basis. This means that we have undertaken to obtain our interviewees' approval when citing from or referring to interviews in our writing other than when the matters cited were innocuous, such as statements of fact. The main purpose of the interviews was to help us develop our awareness and understanding of issues, to gain insight into the causes and consequences of events and developments, and to understand different points of view. In that respect, the interviews have been an invaluable guide through the mass of written sources which we could never have hoped to master without this assistance. While we do quote from the interviews, or refer to them as sources of specific information, their main influence on our writing has been more subtle, and is reflected in matters of emphasis and even choice of words. Given the confidentiality of the interviews, this aspect of our work is not easily verifiable. However, we have attempted throughout to relate insights gained from interviews to referenced documentary sources in order to allow readers to form their own views of the way in which we have presented situations and events.

We have also attempted to do justice to the voluminous academic and professional literature on the IASB, as well as to commentary in the traditional news media and on the web, but we do not lay any claim to completeness. Although we draw on reportage in several other languages, it will be clear from the notes that the vast majority of what we cite has appeared in English.

1.5 STRUCTURE OF THE BOOK

After this introduction follows a brief chapter which reviews the history of the IASC and the circumstances leading to its replacement by the IASB, thus forming a bridge between our previous book on the IASC and the present volume. The body of the book is composed of fourteen thematic chapters in a roughly chronological order. This means that chapters dealing with the development of the IASB as an organization alternate with chapters on its technical work and on the reception of IFRSs around the world. The book ends with an epilogue, Chapter 17, reviewing events between the middle of 2011 and early 2014.

The relatively short span of time, ten years, covered in this book might have justified a purely thematic structure in which the three main themes—the IASB's organization, its relations with and impact on the world at large, and its standard-setting activity—would form the main elements. Cutting up each of these three elements in chronologically ordered sections, as we do, makes for a slightly more complicated book, because many story lines in which the IASB was involved do cut across our chapter divisions. Yet we believe our approach is more suitable to convey the sense of discovery that we think characterized the IASB during this period, and for highlighting the interaction between simultaneous events at the IASB and in various jurisdictions. We have used our chronological chapter divisions flexibly, with considerable overlap of the periods covered in the consecutive chapters. We have attempted to place specific episodes in the chapter where they seemed to reach their climax or an important turning point, even though part of the episode might, strictly chronologically, belong in an earlier or later chapter.

As several 'boards' make their appearance in this book, we have adopted the convention of using 'Board' for the IASC and IASB Board and 'board' for all others in shorthand references, following the use of the full name.

2

Evolution of the IASC into the IASB

2.1 THE ORIGINS OF INTERNATIONAL ACCOUNTING STANDARDS

When the IASB was formed in 2001, it could draw on almost three decades of international standard-setting history, dating back to 1973. It was then when Sir Henry Benson, a former president of the Institute of Chartered Accountants in England and Wales (ICAEW) and a forceful figure, persuaded the professional accountancy bodies in ten countries, including five others in the United Kingdom and Ireland, to send delegations to a newly established International Accounting Standards Committee (IASC), to be based in London.

This was breaking new ground. By no means all countries had established national bodies issuing guidance on best accounting practice—the appellation of 'standards' was not yet universally in vogue—and in several countries where such a body was in existence, it had only recently been created. To be sure, the accountancy bodies in the United Kingdom and Ireland, the United States, and Canada had, since 1967, been collaborating in the publication of a series of booklets that presented and explained the recommended practices in their countries. This latter programme was also launched by Benson, and it served to acquaint the accountancy bodies in each of the cooperating countries, as well as in others around the world, with some of the latest thinking and recommendations from abroad. As such, it provided a platform of experience and international awareness for moving to the next stage, which was setting accounting standards at the international level.

The founding countries in the IASC were, in alphabetical order, Australia, Canada, France, Germany, Japan, Mexico, the Netherlands, the United Kingdom (in a joint delegation with Ireland), and the United States. Benson became the first IASC chairman. Under the Agreement and Constitution signed by all of the countries, they were to use their 'best endeavours' to ensure that published accounts comply with the IASC's standards and that auditors satisfy themselves that the accounts comply with them.

At that time, there were major differences between the national accounting laws and standards across all of the founding countries. In some countries, such as the United States, the United Kingdom, and Australia, there were vibrant securities markets, and it was the aim of their standard-setting bodies, to greater or lesser degree, to recommend accounting and disclosure practices for use by investors in the market and shareholders. In the European Economic Community (EEC), the

Fourth Company Law Directive on annual accounts was still in the drafting stage, and there was much diversity of accounting practice among the member states. In countries such as France and Germany, the dictates of income tax law, not the needs of investors in the securities market, were the major influence on accounting requirements. Thus, transparency of financial information in the securities market was the most important desideratum in only some of the founding countries. Because of these differences, the delegations from the nine countries agreed at a high level of principle to set accounting standards, not with a specified purpose or a specific subset of companies in view, but in the 'public interest' (as stated in the IASC's Agreement).

Each delegation was to have a maximum of three members: two voting members and a staff observer. When voting on exposure drafts and final standards, each delegation would have a single vote. All of the members of the nine delegations were serving part-time, as they were partners in audit firms, sole practitioners, university academics, financial executives in companies, or employees of the accountancy bodies—all in their respective home countries. The IASC's full-time technical staff consisted of a secretary and two assistants, a complement which did not increase significantly in number until the early 1990s. The IASC's finances came from contributions from the signatory accountancy bodies and, before long, also from associate members, namely, accountancy bodies in other countries that agreed to use their 'best endeavours' to gain support for the IASC's standards. During the early years, the Board met three to four times a year, mostly in London, but beginning in the middle 1980s mostly at sites around the world. The delegations paid most of their own travel costs.

The IASC's first standard made its debut in January 1975, but it carried no legal force in any jurisdiction. They were recommendations pronounced by a body in the private sector. Yet, it was hoped, perhaps naïvely, that the sponsoring national accountancy bodies would earnestly use their 'best endeavours' to gain acceptance of the standards in their respective countries. In fact, during the early years of the IASC, the view prevailed that it was mostly in developing countries, not in the countries represented on the Board, that its standards seemed to gain a modicum of acceptance, although solid evidence to support this view was scarce. What was clear was that the World Bank became a major supporter of the IASC's standards early on, and it played a pivotal role in persuading developing countries, the Bank's principal clientele, to adopt them in their financial reports to the Bank. In the Board-member countries it soon became clear that, with the exception of Canada, the member bodies had no powers to enforce the standards. Some member bodies (as in the United States, the United Kingdom, Canada, and Australia) comforted themselves with the view that compliance with their superior national accounting standards implied compliance with the IASC's standards. Others (as in France, Germany, and Japan) quietly accepted that companies would be loathe to adopt the IASC's standards to the extent that they were out of harmony with their national accounting tradition.

Other international organizations, such as the United Nations (UN), the Organisation for Economic Co-operation and Development (OECD), and the European Commission disbelieved that, as a private-sector body, the IASC was capable of developing and issuing accounting standards that served the public interest. Public-sector organizations were apt to suspect private-sector bodies of possessing only a narrow, business-centred self-interest, while a private-sector body like the IASC tended to view these public-sector organizations as being hopelessly bureaucratic and easily susceptible to political influence. The European Commission continued its programme of accounting directives without paying much heed to the IASC. Around 1980, the UN and the OECD made stabs at becoming active in the field of accounting or disclosure standards for multinational companies, but neither succeeded in becoming a viable alternative to the IASC.

The IASC's earliest standards dealt with such familiar subjects as the disclosure of accounting policies, accounting for merchandise inventories, the preparation of consolidated accounts and use of the equity method, and accounting for depreciation. They were not entirely devoid of controversy, because what was an accepted practice in one or several countries was unknown—or even regarded as anathema—in others, because of the considerable diversity in accounting and financial cultures alluded to above.

From its founding in 1973 to 1987, the IASC issued some two dozen standards, covering such additional subjects as accounting for changing prices, research and development, income taxes, tangible fixed assets, leases, revenue recognition, government grants, foreign exchange, business combinations, and borrowing costs. Many of the standards allowed 'free choices' (such as LIFO, FIFO, and weighted average for inventories, any 'systematic' method of depreciation, capitalization or expensing of R&D, historical cost or revaluation for tangible fixed assets, and purchase or pooling of interests, with loosely defined restrictions on pooling). While, compared with US standards, they specified few norms of application and little required disclosure, they nonetheless included many requirements that were in advance of most other leading countries' standards. The IASC's Constitution required that a final standard be approved by a three-quarters majority, and, given the wide diversity of practice among the countries represented on the Board, it was verily impossible to secure this super majority for a standard without options. Moreover, members from a number of countries believed that a good standard was not necessarily one without options, but rather one which provided flexibility to capture differences in circumstances.

In the same period between 1973 and 1987, the number of delegations gradually increased to include South Africa (1978–2000), Nigeria (1979–87), Italy (1983–93), Taiwan (1984–7), and an international committee of financial analysts (1986–2000). In addition, several score other countries' accountancy bodies signed on as associate members. Representatives of the Board's member bodies as well as of associate members composed the small steering committees which did the initial drafting of the standards. With the creation of a consultative group, the IASC took a limited step of bringing a wider range of parties from outside the accountancy profession into its organization. Word was therefore beginning to spread about the IASC's work.

2.2 1987: A TURNING POINT FOR THE IASC

In 1987, two major, intertwined developments occurred to alter the direction and influence of the IASC. Leaders of the Board came to the belief that it was essential that the Board review and improve the standards so that they contained fewer options and were founded on an explicit conceptual framework. In this way, they hoped that the standards would be taken more seriously in developed countries, in particular those with active equity capital markets. The standard setters and securities market regulators in those countries—principally, the United States, the United Kingdom, Canada, and Australia—had dismissed the IASC's standards as being below the quality of their national standards, and thus not worthy models for improvement. They did not regard the IASC as a serious standard setter.

But in 1987, a confederation of more than forty regulatory bodies known as the International Organization of Securities Commissions (IOSCO) began to be a force on the world stage, especially as the US Securities and Exchange Commission (SEC) was starting to take it seriously as an agent of change to improve the way in which the world's securities markets were operated and governed. The increase during the 1980s in the cross-border trading of securities had captured the SEC's attention, thus motivating its interest in becoming active in IOSCO. Once the SEC had joined up, its chairman promptly became a member of IOSCO's executive committee. Since then, the SEC has always had a commanding voice in IOSCO's affairs.

One of IOSCO's announced concerns was the highly variable quality of accounting standards from one country to the next, and it viewed the IASC as having the potential to contribute to enhancing this quality around the world. IOSCO therefore approached the IASC with a proposition: if the IASC would review and revise its existing standards with a view towards removing 'free choices', providing more disclosure and detailed guidance on application, and expand its coverage of subjects, IOSCO would one day consider endorsing these improved standards for acceptance by its regulator members as a basis for reporting in cross-border listings. The IASC knew that the SEC was a key player in IOSCO, and the IASC's driving ambition from the late 1980s onward was that, once IOSCO were to endorse its standards, the SEC would lift its requirement imposed on foreign registrants using other than US generally accepted accounting principles (US GAAP) to reconcile their profit and shareholders' equity to their US GAAP equivalents. The IASC therefore had to adopt the SEC's emphasis on providing information for use by investors. Thus, the emergent thinking within the IASC about the next step in its evolution dove-tailed nicely with what IOSCO wanted it to achieve.

A special steering committee of the IASC then proceeded to review its standards and propose the elimination of as many alternatives as practicable. This was called the comparability project. In its deliberations, the committee was in constant conversation with an IOSCO working party composed of the chief accountants of the SEC, France's Commission des Opérations de Bourse, and the Ontario Securities Commission. The committee's work led to the IASC Board's *Statement of Intent* in 1990 to move forward with effectuating numerous eliminations, standard by standard, in order to respond to IOSCO's challenge. The *Statement of Intent* signalled the IASC's readiness to produce standards of higher quality, and it was noticed with heightened interest in some countries, such as Japan, which until then had paid little attention to the IASC.

While the comparability project was in train, the IASC completed its *Framework for the Preparation and Presentation of Financial Statements*, its conceptual framework, in 1989. The IASC's *Framework* was much influenced by the recently completed conceptual framework issued by the US Financial Accounting Standards Board (FASB).

To IOSCO, a move to eliminate many accounting alternatives in the IASC's standards was not enough. At its 1988 annual conference, IOSCO reminded the IASC that it also wanted the IASC 'to ensure that its standards are sufficiently detailed and complete, contain adequate disclosure requirements, and are prepared with a visible commitment to the needs of users of financial statements'.[1] This was surely an expression of the SEC's views as well. In 1990, following on from its *Statement of Intent*, the IASC empanelled an improvements steering committee to meet IOSCO's broader expectation. In November 1993, the IASC completed the revision of ten of its standards, eliminating most options, and providing for fuller disclosure and more implementation guidance. But in 1994, IOSCO, while accepting most of these standards, found deficiencies in the others, and it raised a number of issues requiring attention. It also looked for completion of the development or revision of yet other standards, especially the one on financial instruments. This reaction was a keen disappointment to the IASC.

The IASC and IOSCO agreed to a revised work programme, and the IASC redoubled its efforts to complete an entire 'core' set of standards to IOSCO's satisfaction by December 1998. The IASC was able to increase the size of its technical staff, and it began to hold more frequent and longer Board meetings in order to complete the 'core' set as expeditiously as possible. The biggest obstacle was the standard on financial instruments. After years of effort, the Board realized that it did not have the time to fashion its own standard on this immensely complex subject before its self-imposed deadline of December 1998. At a late stage, it opted to compose its standard by drawing on the extensive literature on the subject already issued, or in preparation, by the FASB. In December 1998, IAS 39, on financial instruments, was the final standard to be approved in the 'core' set, and it, like many others, was controversial within the Board. The IASC then transmitted the standards, both revised and new, to IOSCO for its assessment.

All the while, developments were occurring within the Board and among the leading national standard setters. Originally, the IASC was funded and controlled by its founding member bodies. In 1982, this changed to a form of collective ownership by the accountancy profession, as appointments to Board positions were from that moment on made by the council of the International Federation of Accountants (IFAC), and IFAC provided a part of the IASC's funding. In practice, however, IFAC followed the IASC Board's recommendations on appointments, and the IASC operated with complete autonomy. By 1996 the IASC had expanded the size of its Board membership to sixteen delegations. The Nordic Federation of Public Accountants joined from 1990 to 2000. The IASC made an effort to secure more representation from developing countries, to wit Korea (1988–92), Jordan (1989–95), India jointly with Sri Lanka (1993–2000), and Malaysia (1995–2000). From 1995 to 2000, South Africa shared its delegation with Zimbabwe. Another objective in expanding the size of the Board was to assure representation from preparers, in addition to the users (financial analysts) who had joined in 1986.

---

[1] International Organization of Securities Commissions, *Annual Report 1988*, 8.

Delegations from the Federation of Swiss Industrial Holding Companies (1995–2000) and the International Association of Financial Executives Institutes (1996–2000) also joined the Board. Increasingly, too, a number of accountancy bodies began to appoint key members of their national standard setters to their Board delegations, thus signalling the greater gravitas they associated with the Board and the standards it was issuing. Despite all of this broadening, two things remained true: (a) most of the members of the delegations were professional accountants, and (b) the professional bodies, through their delegations, controlled the Board.

Yet this increase in the number of Board delegations presented significant challenges. When one adds the usual dozen or more observers and staff to the sixteen delegations, each composed of three members, the number of persons sitting around a very large table exceeded sixty, and at some meetings even seventy. And many of those in attendance had to cope with the highly technical and fast-moving deliberations in their second language. The meetings were not easy for all.

Fundraising was always a challenge to the IASC. In the 1990s, it was especially important because of the need to increase the size of the IASC's technical staff during the final push to provide IOSCO with the completed 'core' standards. An increasing proportion of finance came from the sale of publications, but this was not sufficient. In 1995, the IASC established an advisory council composed of leading figures from key countries, and they aided significantly in the fundraising effort.

Although by the 1990s no national jurisdiction yet required the use of international accounting standards (IASs), some large European companies adopted them voluntarily. Swiss multinationals, led by Nestlé and Roche, were among the first. Even before them, several US companies had begun affirming in the 1980s that the accounting principles used in their annual financial statements were 'consistent in most important respects' or 'in alignment' with IASs. Prominent among them were General Electric and Exxon. But this expression of compliance was more a gesture because it did not require them to change their accounting. The adoption by the Swiss multinationals truly signalled the acceptance of the IASC as a credible standard setter.

The national standard setters in the United States, the United Kingdom, Canada, and Australia were taking notice. In the early 1990s, a body known as the G4+1, composed of representatives of the standard setters in these four countries plus the Secretary-General of the IASC began meeting regularly to discuss issues that should, in their view, be taken up by the IASC. Even though New Zealand was added in 1996, the group continued to be referred to as the G4. This initiative was viewed apprehensively by members of the Continental European delegations on the IASC Board, as being a challenge from the Anglo-American bloc to the IASC's aspiration to become the accepted world standard setter. As a counter-ploy to the G4, the European delegations to the Board made a stab at forming their own bloc, but their endeavour failed. The participating delegations preferred to use their resources to strengthen their respective national programmes. Agreement was not made easier by the fact that the UK delegation was already committed to the G4.

In the 1990s, important developments in Europe furthered the cause of the IASC. The European Commission, for many years dismissive towards the IASC, finally agreed to attend Board meetings as an observer. Equity capital markets were becoming more important in some Continental European countries, and the European Commission came to realize that its programme of directives, which focused on the harmonization of company law in the member states of the European Union (EU), was being overtaken by an increasing tendency in Europe to view financial reporting, at least for the subset of listed companies, in terms of providing useful information to equity investors. In 1993, Daimler Benz, the largest German multinational, shocked German industry by being the first German company to list in New York, thus requiring it to reconcile its profit and shareholders' equity according to German accounting rules to their equivalents under US GAAP. Daimler's decision made it clear that German GAAP was not sufficient for the new reality of equity capital markets, and it had two telling implications.

First, it caused German and other Continental European companies to be more disposed to consider IASs as an alternative to national GAAP in their financial reporting. In 1995, the European Commission proposed a policy of 'putting the Union's weight behind' the IASC.[2] It called upon member states to remove obstacles to the application of IASs. This led to an increase in the number of German companies in particular moving from their national GAAP to IASs, or at least claiming compliance with both simultaneously. Prominent examples included Bayer and Deutsche Bank.

The second implication of Daimler's decision was that it opened an avenue, not only for the adoption of IASs, but also for the adoption of US GAAP by European companies. More German companies followed Daimler to New York and thus had to reconcile to US GAAP. The most prominent instance was Deutsche Telekom in 1996. This created a demand for the use of US GAAP as the primary basis of reporting. In early 1997, when the German stock exchange established the Neuer Markt for small, high tech companies, it insisted that this new market's quoted companies adopt either US GAAP or IASs, not German GAAP, in their financial statements. In 1998, most German listed companies were given the option to apply US GAAP or IASs in their consolidated financial statements to satisfy the reporting requirements under company law.

For European companies seeking a listing in the United States, the main question was still whether the SEC would lift its reconciliation requirement for financial statements prepared on the basis of IASs. This was also a concern of the New York Stock Exchange, which believed that many world-class multinationals were not coming to New York to list because they wished to avoid the SEC's 'odious' reconciliation requirement. Yet the SEC gave no signs of acting precipitously. In 1996, it had announced that it expected to see '3 key elements' in the IASC's 'core' standards. They were, first, that the standards constitute 'a comprehensive, generally accepted basis of accounting'; second, they 'must be of high quality—they must result in comparability and transparency, and they must provide for full disclosure'; and third, they 'must be rigorously interpreted and

---

[2] *Accounting Harmonisation: A New Strategy vis-à-vis International Harmonisation*, COM 95 (508), paragraph 1.4.

applied'.[3] This set the bar for acceptance of IASs at a high level, and thus excited a concern in Europe over an invasion of US GAAP once that would become the standard of choice for the largest European companies.

2.3 THE RESTRUCTURING OF THE IASC

By 1997, when the IASC could see that it was making good progress in completing the 'core' standards to be forwarded to IOSCO for its possible endorsement, its leaders' thoughts began to turn to the future of the IASC as a standard setter. The SEC had made it known that its possible future acceptance of IASs hinged not only on IOSCO's endorsement of the standards (the SEC being the dominant IOSCO member when making that decision) but also the future structure, composition, and process of the IASC as a standard setter. The SEC would not have confidence in a part-time body composed of members who were selected by accountancy bodies and other organizations with a vested interest in the standards. Instead, the SEC wanted to see a small, independent, full-time body composed of technical experts, without regard to geographical representation and assisted by a large and competent technical staff. The SEC thus said, in effect, that the FASB model should be suitable as well for the IASC.

The SEC was not alone in looking for a restructuring of the IASC. In the wake of the Asian financial crisis of 1997, the G7 finance ministers acknowledged the significance of the IASC as part of the new global financial architecture that they believed should be put in place. Detaching the IASC from the accountancy profession would make sense in such a vision, but this could be done in more than one way. The European Commission wanted to see a large, representative, part-time body to be sure that European interests were adequately represented. The views of the SEC and the European Commission on the restructuring of the IASC were thus diametrically opposed. The IASC appointed a Strategy Working Party in 1997 to consider various concepts of a restructured standard setter, and there were continuing struggles within the working party and among the various interested private- and public-sector organizations over the configurations reflected in the working party's successive internal draft recommendations. The national accountancy bodies, for their part, were reluctant to give up their collective influence over the IASC. Yet national standard setters were not prepared to be part of a new IASC if their technical accounting decisions could be vetoed by such as professional accountancy bodies. Regulators and numerous organizations representing the interests of users, auditors, and preparers intoned with their discordant views on the working party's eventual recommendations issued for exposure, and there seemed to be little scope for a coherent consensus that would satisfy any of the major players.

The debates and controversy over the IASC's new structure carried over into 1998 and 1999. Finally, towards the end of 1999, the SEC made known its final

---

[3] 'SEC Statement Regarding International Accounting Standards', SEC news release 96–61, 11 April 1996.

demand, which was a restatement of its well-known position: a small, independent, full-time standard setter whose members would be chosen for their technical expertise alone. Geographical origin was not to be considered when selecting members. The SEC warned that, if the IASC were to depart from that model, it would not accept the outcome. The implication of not agreeing to the SEC's terms meant that the IASC would 'lose' the United States. US GAAP and not IASs would become the de facto global standard for use by companies accessing international capital markets. Another fear, if the IASC Board were to reject the SEC's solution, was that the G4 would overtake the IASC as the global standard setter. The pressure was intense, but at the decisive meeting in November 1999 all of the Board's delegations, although not uniformly happy with their predicament, voted for a structure, composition, and process that would align with the SEC's terms as expressed by SEC Chief Accountant Lynn Turner.

The IASC's Strategy Working Party issued a report elaborating the restructuring decision,[4] and on this basis the Board confirmed its decision at its December meeting. Sir Bryan Carsberg, the IASC's secretary-general then drafted a Constitution for the new organization, closely following the language of the Strategy Working Party's final report. The new IASC Board was to be overseen by nineteen independent trustees who would represent different regions of the world and a loosely prescribed mix of backgrounds. The trustees would select the Board members based on a number of factors under the over-arching criterion of technical expertise, and without regard to their geographical origin. The trustees would also raise the finance, establish the norms of due process for the Board, and monitor the Board's performance. The Board would have twelve full-time and two part-time members, with a prescribed mix of auditors, preparers, users, and academics. The Board would be served by an adequate technical and research staff. The Board was to assign half of its members to liaise regularly with designated national standard setters. As a continuation of the IASC's consultative group, an advisory council was established to enable interested parties from around the world to meet and counsel the Board. The Board would be complemented by an interpretations committee, a continuation of the interpretations committee which the IASC had set up in 1997. The trustees would select the members of this council and committee. The Board would require a simple majority to approve final standards, and it was expected to follow proper due process.

The decision to restructure the IASC implied the end of the formal link with IFAC established in 1982. Under the terms of the existing Constitution, this decision, including the new Constitution, still had to be ratified by a meeting of the national accountancy bodies constituting IFAC's membership. This ratification occurred in May 2000, following which the changes could be put into effect. The sequence of events that led from the decision to restructure the IASC late in 1999 to the installation of the new Board early in 2001 is discussed in Chapter 3.

---

[4] *Recommendations on Shaping IASC for the Future: A Report of the International Accounting Standards Committee's Strategy Working Party* (IASC, 30 November 1999).

3

Setting Up the IASB

3.1 PORTENTOUS CHANGES AS THE IASC
BECOMES THE IASB

The series of decisions in 2000 and early 2001 to give effect to the restructuring of the IASC were of necessity taken in a period of promise tinged with uncertainty both for the trustees and for the new Board members they appointed. There was no question that the restructured IASC—for which the name IASB was agreed in December 2000—would continue the mission of issuing standards at the highest achievable level of quality, consistent with the conceptual framework it had set for itself in 1989. But what standing would these standards attain? Although no jurisdiction had mandated company compliance with the IASC's standards, three important developments occurred in 2000 that offered hopeful, but still uncertain, prospects.

In February 2000, the US Securities and Exchange Commission (SEC) issued a lengthy concept release which, while approving of the IASC's new design, said that the IASC needed to be supported by an 'infrastructure that assures that the standards are rigorously interpreted and applied'.[1] Elements of the infrastructure included 'high quality auditing standards' and an independent and high quality auditing standard setter, 'audit firms with effective quality controls worldwide', 'profession-wide quality assurance', and 'active regulatory oversight'. This laundry list of further reform measures allowed the inference that, even with the endorsement of the IASC's 'core' standards by the International Organization of Securities Commissions (IOSCO), which was shortly expected, the SEC would demand progress in other areas before it was prepared to lift its reconciliation requirement for foreign registrants not using US generally accepted accounting principles (US GAAP).

In May 2000, IOSCO announced its endorsement of the IASC's 'core' standards for use by its regulator members around the world, albeit with strings attached.[2] It raised more than one hundred unresolved substantive issues. Moreover, as the SEC would have insisted, IOSCO recommended 'that its members allow multinational issuers to use [the] 30 IASC standards as supplemented by reconciliation, disclosure and interpretation where necessary to address outstanding substantive

[1] 'International Accounting Standards', Release Nos. 33-7801, 34-42430, International Series No. 1215, File No. S7-04-00, 16 February 2000 <http://www.sec.gov>.
[2] 'IASC Standards', IOSCO press release, 17 May 2000; 'IASC Standards—Assessment Report: Report of the Technical Committee of the International Organization of Securities Commissions', May 2000, both at <http://www.iosco.org>.

issues at a national or regional level'. This recommendation was consistent with the SEC's well-established practice with respect to the use of non-US GAAP by foreign registrants, and this provision may have served to reinforce outsiders' view that the SEC was not prepared at this stage to consider lifting its reconciliation requirement.

But the major development in 2000 was the announcement in June by the European Commission that it was proposing legislation to require that all companies domiciled and listed in the European Union (EU) be required to use the IASC's standards in their consolidated financial statements by 2005, subject to an endorsement process (see Section 4.1). This momentous declaration surprised many and seemed to assure the restructured IASC of a 'clientele' of some 6,700 companies for its standards. Yet it could not be taken for granted that the European Parliament and Council would implement this proposal.

What about the rest of the world? Would any securities market authorities in major countries beyond the United States and the EU—Japan, Canada, and Australia—adopt the new Board's standards for required use by listed companies? Or would the new Board, like its predecessor, be dependent on national standard setters adapting or converging their national GAAPs with international standards, one by one? It was not accidental that the newly restructured Board was, like the IASC before it, to have close ties with national standard setters.

The restructuring of the IASC meant that it would no longer enjoy the security of its organizational and financial link with the worldwide accountancy profession. Instead, it became an independent body under the oversight of a board of trustees who were charged with raising funds that, for a long enough period, had to be sufficient to persuade highly talented candidates for the dozen full-time Board positions to leave their present employment and sign on to this uncertain enterprise. These were the circumstances in which the first trustees—in just under six months—had to launch the new organization. We now turn to a discussion of the steps in this launch process.

3.2 THE SELECTION OF THE FIRST TRUSTEES

The dawning of the IASB occurred when, in December 1999, the IASC Board completed its approval of the restructuring by appointing a nominating committee of distinguished leaders from around the world. The IASC would continue to function for another year, holding its last meeting in December 2000, but its replacement was now just a matter of time. The sole function of the nominating committee was to select the first set of nineteen trustees to oversee the establishment and operation of the restructured IASC Board, including the selection of its members. Future trustee appointments would be made by the trustees themselves, in a process of cooptation. The nominating committee's members were as follows:[3]

---

[3] 'Shaping IASC for the Future: Board Takes First Step in Implementing Proposed Structure— Nominating Committee Approved', IASC press release, 17 December 1999, <http://www.iasc.org.uk> accessed through web.archive.

- Karl H. Baumann, chairman of the supervisory board of Siemens and deputy chairman of the Deutsches Rechnungslegungs Standards Committee (Germany)
- James E. Copeland, Jr, chief executive officer, Deloitte Touche Tohmatsu (United States)
- Howard Davies, chairman, Financial Services Authority (United Kingdom)
- Arthur Levitt, chairman, Securities and Exchange Commission (United States)
- Michel Prada, chairman, Commission des Opérations de Bourse (France)
- Andrew Sheng, chairman, Hong Kong Securities and Futures Commission
- James Wolfensohn, president, the World Bank.

One cannot overstate the influence of Arthur Levitt in this entire process. The leaders of the IASC regarded the support of the SEC for the restructured Board as indispensable to its future success, given that acceptance of the IASC's standards by the SEC would remain a central strategic objective of the new organization. Effectively, Levitt composed the membership of the nominating committee, and it was hardly a surprise that he was tapped to be its chairman. What might have caused surprise, given the impending announcement by the European Commission to require the use of the IASC's standards in the EU, was the absence of an EU official on the committee. The Commission had in fact been approached to name a member, but had declined to do so.[4] The absence of a Japanese member was keenly noted in Japan (see Section 4.6.1). The committee held three meetings between December 1999 and April 2000: in Levitt's conference room at the SEC in Washington, at the Commission des Opérations de Bourse in Paris, and in the Deloitte offices in New York City. On 13 January, the committee issued a news release in which it solicited names of possible candidates for the board of trustees.[5]

The Constitution mandated that six trustees come from North America, six from Europe, four from the Asia–Pacific region, and three from any area, subject to achieving an overall geographic balance. It also specified that five trustees were to be nominated by the International Federation of Accountants (IFAC), a last vestige of the IASC's origins in the accountancy profession. Three trustees should be selected after consultation with international organizations of preparers, users, and academics towards the aim of obtaining one trustee from each of those backgrounds. The remaining eleven trustees would be chosen at-large.

The nominating committee, and especially Levitt, believed that the trustee group had to be composed of figures of the highest international standing, and that its chairman had to be instantly recognized as a world leader, one whose power and dignity would make it difficult to turn down if invited to serve on the Board. They settled on the candidacy of Paul A. Volcker, the highly respected former chairman of the US Federal Reserve Board, and Levitt personally recruited Volcker for the position.

---

[4] See Kees Camfferman and Stephen A. Zeff, *Financial Reporting and Global Capital Markets: A History of the International Accounting Standards Committee, 1973–2000* (Oxford: Oxford University Press, 2007), 494.

[5] 'IASC Nominating Committee Begins Trustee Selection Process; SEC Chairman Arthur Levitt Named Committee Chair', nominating committee press release, 13 January 2000, reproduced in *SEC News Digest*, 2000–9 (13 January 2000), 1–3 <http://www.sec.gov>.

After Volcker accepted, the nominating committee proceeded quickly to secure acceptances of the remaining eighteen trustees. On 22 May 2000, it announced the board of trustees. This announcement did not come a moment too soon, as will shortly be seen.

At its meeting in March 2000, the IASC Board had unanimously approved the new Constitution,[6] and on 24 May 2000 in Edinburgh, where IFAC was holding its assembly of members (held only every two and a half years), the 104 member bodies in attendance unanimously approved the restructuring and, by implication, the nominating committee's choice of trustees. This approval effectively severed the link between the IASC and the worldwide accountancy profession. IFAC's remaining right to make a limited number of trustee recommendations was abolished in 2005.

The initial nineteen trustees were distributed geographically as follows: five from the United States, two each from Japan and the United Kingdom, and one each from Australia, Brazil, Canada, Denmark, France, Germany, Hong Kong, Italy, the Netherlands, and South Africa. The trustee appointments were the following:[7]

- Paul A. Volcker (chairman), former chairman, Federal Reserve Board (United States)
- Roy Andersen, deputy chairman and chief executive officer, The Liberty Life Group (South Africa—IFAC nominee)
- John H. Biggs, chairman, TIAA-CREF (United States—user representative)
- Andrew Crockett, general manager, Bank for International Settlements; chairman, Financial Stability Forum
- Roberto Teixeira da Costa, former chairman, Comissão de Valores Mobiliários (Brazil)
- Guido A. Ferrarini, professor of law, Università degli Studi di Genova (Italy—academic representative)
- L. Yves Fortier, chairman, Ogilvy Renault, barristers and solicitors, former ambassador of Canada to the United Nations (Canada)
- Toshikatsu Fukuma, chief financial officer, Mitsui & Co. Ltd (Japan)
- Cornelius A.J. Herkströter, former chief executive, Royal Dutch/Shell Group (the Netherlands—preparer representative)
- Hilmar Kopper, chairman of the supervisory board and former chief executive, Deutsche Bank (Germany)
- Philip A. Laskawy, chairman, Ernst & Young International (United States—IFAC nominee)
- Charles Yeh Kwong Lee, chairman, Hong Kong Exchanges and Clearing Ltd (Hong Kong)

---

[6] IASC meeting of 13–17 March 2000, minute 1.

[7] 'IASC Nominating Committee Announces Initial Trustees', nominating committee press release, 22 May 2000 <http://www.iasc.org.uk> accessed through web.archive. For the identification of the five IFAC nominees and the three trustees appointed after specific consultation with user, preparer, and academic organizations, see IASCF trustees meeting of 13 March 2003, agenda paper 6A. See Appendix 5 for a discussion of archival sources.

- Sir Sydney Lipworth QC, chairman, Financial Reporting Council and chairman or deputy chairman of the boards of directors of several major companies (United Kingdom)

- Didier Pineau-Valencienne, chairman, Association Française des Entreprises Privées and former chief executive of Schneider Electric (France)

- Jens Røder, senior partner, PricewaterhouseCoopers (Denmark—IFAC nominee)

- David S. Ruder, former chairman, Securities and Exchange Commission (United States)

- Kenneth H. (Ken) Spencer, former chairman, Australian Accounting Standards Board and retired partner in KPMG (Australia—IFAC nominee)

- William C. Steere, Jr, chairman and chief executive officer, Pfizer Inc. (United States)

- Koji Tajika, co-chairman, Deloitte Touche Tohmatsu (Japan—IFAC nominee).

Four of the trustees were current or former regulators or overseers of capital markets: Volcker, da Costa, Lee, and Ruder, while Lipworth chaired a body that oversaw an accounting standard setter. The others were from audit firms, the companies sector, the financial community, academe, and the legal profession.

John Biggs and David Ruder were, at the time, also trustees of the Financial Accounting Foundation (FAF), the body which was responsible for the oversight, administration, and financing of the US Financial Accounting Standards Board (FASB). In 1996, when Arthur Levitt was critical of the lack of representatives of the public interest on the FAF, he used his authority as SEC chairman to force the FAF to appoint four additional trustees, of whom two were Biggs and Ruder.[8] Moreover, during the lengthy deliberations of the IASC's Strategy Working Party, which paved the way for the restructuring of the IASC in 1997–99, on which Ruder served, Levitt and Ruder kept in close touch on the developments.[9] Hence, it would be no surprise that Levitt tapped both Biggs and Ruder for this new assignment.

As a former chairman of the Australian Accounting Standards Board, Ken Spencer brought expert knowledge of accounting standard setting to the trustees. Moreover, he knew the international landscape of accounting standard setting very well, having been an active participant in, and sometime chairman of, the meetings of the G4+1 during the 1990s. As indicated in Chapter 2, the G4+1 was a discussion group composed of representatives from the accounting standard setters in Australia, Canada, the United States, and the United Kingdom, with the addition of New Zealand in 1996. The group met quarterly to develop their views on contentious issues they believed would merit the attention of the IASC. Spencer therefore had a clear view of what was expected of the new Board, and knew many of the people who might be considered for appointment to it.

Ruder, Spencer, Sydney Lipworth, and Jens Røder were among the early leaders of the trustees. As chairmen of the various trustee committees, they, together with

---

[8] See Paul B.W. Miller, Rodney J. Redding, and Paul R. Bahnson, *The FASB: The People, the Process, and the Politics* (Burr Ridge, IL: Irwin/McGraw-Hill, 1998), 186–92.

[9] Camfferman and Zeff, *Financial Reporting and Global Capital Markets*, Chapter 13.

Paul Volcker, were grouped into an executive committee dealing with matters arising in between trustee meetings. Lipworth in particular, who was resident in London, tackled the myriad financial, legal, and tax issues in the early functioning of the IASB, including such matters as securing financial support for basing the IASB in London, finding office space for the organization, and resolving the tax status of the IASB's revenue from sales of publications. Røder had been president in 1995–6 of the Fédération des Experts Comptables Européens (FEE), the grouping of Europe's national accountancy bodies, and therefore was knowledgeable about the workings of the EU.

The predominance of the United States, Europe, and Japan, with fourteen of the nineteen trustees, was an evident reflection of where the world's major capital markets were located. Also, the United States, Japan, and Germany became the three largest sources of finance for the Board and thus were always well represented on the trustees, one of whose critical functions was the raising of funds.

3.2.1 The Trustees Begin Their Work

The trustees held their inaugural meeting on 28 June 2000 in New York City, chaired by Paul Volcker, with seventeen of the nineteen trustees participating. The three major issues facing the trustees at this meeting and the next two, held in October and December 2000, were the selection of the fourteen members of the newly restructured IASC Board, raising the funds to support the Board, and the incorporation of the new IASC entity. Because it was hoped that the new Board could begin operations on 1 January 2001, the trustees wanted to move with dispatch on all three matters. The selection of the Board members and the trustees' fundraising efforts are discussed in Sections 3.3, 3.4, and 3.11. With respect to the legal form of the entity, the trustees resolved in December 2000 that the organization be established as the IASC Foundation (IASCF), a not-for-profit corporation registered in the State of Delaware, in the United States, although its operations were to continue in London. The alternative of incorporation in the United Kingdom had been considered, but rejected when it was found the organization would probably not be accorded charitable status in the United Kingdom. This seemed possible in the United States by adopting the same legal form as the FAF, which was also a Delaware corporation. An important consideration was that it was expected that more than half the contributions to finance the organization would come from the United States. The Foundation qualified for Section 501(c)(3) status as a charitable organization under the US Internal Revenue Code, thus making it eligible to receive tax-deductible contributions. In addition, it was believed that Delaware's corporation law offered well-developed and appropriate indemnification for an internationally diverse group of trustees, at a level that would be more complex to arrange under UK law.[10]

---

[10] IASCF trustees meeting of 11 December 2000, minute 4; interview with Thomas Seidenstein, 14 October 2009; 'IASC Restructuring Completed', *IASB Insight*, March 2001, 4.

3.3 THE SELECTION OF SIR DAVID TWEEDIE
AS CHAIRMAN

At the trustees' first meeting in June 2000, the selection of the Board chairman became an urgent issue. It was known that Sir David Tweedie had an interest in the chairmanship. He was lauded as unquestionably the ablest candidate. But he had been approached to head one of the premier universities in Scotland, his native land. Even though he had dedicated his recent professional life to standard setting—he had been the full-time chairman of the UK national standard setter since 1990 and also had been serving part-time on the IASC Board since 1995—he was tempted by the university offer. The trustees had to decide at their June meeting whether to name Tweedie as the chairman without following the expected due process of inviting applications and conducting interviews with the candidates, else, it was believed, he would certainly accept the university appointment. Trustees' Chairman Volcker did not know Tweedie personally, but he heard undiluted praise of him from the likes of Arthur Levitt, SEC Chief Accountant Lynn E. Turner, and FASB Chairman Edmund L. Jenkins. Among the trustees, David Ruder had come to know and respect Tweedie from their service on the IASC's Strategy Working Party. Ken Spencer was a close friend of Tweedie's, and the meetings of the G4+1, which both had chaired, had helped to cement the bond. The die was cast. Even before the trustees' meeting, Levitt, Turner, Jenkins, and Ruder had telephoned Tweedie to urge him to accept an offer they were sure would be extended.[11] Ken Spencer also telephoned Tweedie to urge him to take the chairmanship.[12] Volcker had asked Tweedie to come to New York at the time of the meeting, in case the trustees wanted an opportunity to meet with him, but this proved to be unnecessary.[13] At the meeting, no one spoke against Tweedie. The trustees thereupon decided to waive the normal process of inviting nominations and applications, followed by interviews, and voted unanimously to offer Tweedie the Board chairmanship. He promptly accepted. Tweedie would recall in a letter to Levitt, 'It was the fact that you and Lynn [Turner] were supporting and encouraging me to join the campaign for one set of high quality global standards that ultimately persuaded me that I should do it'.[14] On 29 June, the day after the trustees' meeting, the IASC issued a press release announcing the appointment.[15] As chairman, he would also serve as the organization's chief executive.

David Tweedie (see Figure 3.1) obtained a Ph.D. from the University of Edinburgh in 1969 and qualified as a Scottish chartered accountant in 1972. From 1973 to 1978, he was an accounting lecturer at the University of Edinburgh. From 1978 to 1981, he served as the technical director of the Institute of Chartered Accountants of Scotland, and in 1982 he joined the major Scots audit firm of Thomson, McLintock & Co. as its national research partner. When, as part of the

---

[11] Interview with Lynn Turner, 19 November 2004.

[12] This was reported in Tweedie's eulogy given at Spencer's funeral in Melbourne on 6 April 2004. (The text of the eulogy is available from the authors.)

[13] Communication from David Tweedie to the authors, 25 February 2013.

[14] Letter from David Tweedie to Arthur Levitt, 24 January 2001, IASB archive, file 'US convergence'.

[15] 'Shaping IASC for the Future: First Meeting of IASC Trustees and Appointment of New IASC Board Chair', IASC press release, 29 June 2000 <http://www.iasc.org.uk> accessed through web.archive.

Figure 3.1 Sir David Tweedie

formation of the worldwide KPMG, his firm merged in 1987 with Peat, Marwick, Mitchell & Co. to become Peat Marwick McLintock, Tweedie moved to London as national technical partner with the merged firm. In 1989, following three years as vice chairman of the UK Auditing Practices Committee, he became its chairman. During his ten years (1990–2000) as chairman of the newly formed UK Accounting Standards Board (ASB), he was widely known for his leadership and resourcefulness in tackling and resolving difficult issues. His record at the ASB made it clear that he was willing to be controversial when advancing his views on improved financial reporting. On the IASC Board, he played an influential role in the deliberations, and he was the originator of the G4+1 and one of its most active members. He was knighted by the Queen in 1994.

Tweedie, whose residence was in North Berwick, Scotland, a seaside town some twenty-five miles east of Edinburgh, had been commuting to London so as to be in the ASB offices most of each week. Although the trustees, at their June meeting, discussed options other than London for the location of the Board, the selection of Tweedie as chairman probably laid to rest any serious consideration of sites outside the United Kingdom. Furthermore, the existence of the IASC's operating structure in London made maintaining the status quo the easier decision. Lest there be any doubt, on 2 October 2000 the Lord Mayor of London wrote to Paul Volcker to offer a package of support services and funds, including £350,000 per year for three years towards the cost of offices, so that the IASC's head office would remain in London.[16]

---

[16] Letter from the Right Hon. The Lord Mayor Clive Martin to Paul Volcker, 2 October 2000, IASB archive, file 'Lipworth'.

3.4. THE SELECTION OF THE OTHER BOARD MEMBERS

Paul Volcker, to whom the trustees had delegated the authority to compose a nominating committee, chose an eight-member committee, with Ken Spencer in the chair. The other members were Roberto da Costa (Brazil), Guido Ferrarini (Italy), Philip Laskawy (United States), Charles Lee (Hong Kong), Jens Røder (Denmark), David Ruder (United States), and Koji Tajika (Japan). As indicated above, Spencer was a natural choice given his knowledge of the field. He was held in high regard as a member of the accountancy profession, and Volcker had been urged by those in the profession to name him as the committee chairman. While he had great respect for David Tweedie, Spencer was a strong chairman and would hold to his own views.[17]

The nominating committee then proceeded to invite applications for the remaining thirteen Board positions—eleven full-time and two part-time. They retained Clive & Stokes International, an executive search firm based in London, to assist in administering the process of securing nominations but not to conduct a full search, 'because this would be expensive and not add sufficient value to what we can do for ourselves'.[18] The committee planned to recommend its nominees to the trustees by November or early December. This meant that the new Board could not, as originally hoped, commence operations as early as 1 January 2001.

The committee sought the names of candidates from national standard setters, professional accountancy bodies, regulatory agencies, and other groups around the world, and twelve of the thirteen members eventually selected to accompany Tweedie on the Board were named by one or more of these sources.[19] Display advertisements were placed in the *Financial Times* and *The Wall Street Journal* and posted on the IASC's website. The advertisements characterized the new organization, and set out the desirable attributes which the trustees were seeking in candidates:

> The IASC is an independent private body, currently based in London, formulating, publishing and promoting in the public interest, global accounting standards and gaining their universal acceptance. A new Constitution has been agreed with the governance of the IASC residing with nineteen trustees, under the Chairmanship of Mr Paul Volcker, who will provide a balanced international perspective.
>
> Eleven full-time and two part-time Board members will be appointed to join the incoming Chairman, Sir David Tweedie. The Constitution requires Members to include practicing auditors, preparers, users of financial statements and academics.
>
> Members must possess a high degree of relevant technical expertise. Other important qualifications include a substantial knowledge of the associated global environment, a high level of analytical and judicial decision making ability, first class administrative and communication skills.

---

[17] Tweedie later said that Spencer 'had a significant hand in selecting the IASB'. See Tweedie's Ken Spencer Memorial Lecture in March 2007 <http://www.frc.gov.au>.

[18] Letter dated 18 July 2000 from Spencer to the nominating committee (supplied by David Ruder).

[19] Only Anthony Cope was not nominated by one of these bodies. Of the total of sixty-eight nominees from these sources, the FASB submitted the most, twenty, which included seven of those eventually selected as Board members (undated memorandum for use by nominating committee, supplied by David Ruder).

> Important personal qualities will be self motivation; a high level of integrity, objectivity and discipline, a desire and the ability to work in a collegial atmosphere, a commitment to IASC's mission and the public interest, and the drive and dedication to handle a diverse and demanding workload.[20]

The emphasis on 'technical expertise' reflected the Constitution's specification that such expertise was the 'foremost qualification for membership of the Board' (paragraph 24), in turn a reflection of the victory of the proponents of an 'independent expert model' over those advocating a 'representative model' in the restructuring of the IASC.[21]

In the end, more than 200 applications and nominations were received and evaluated. Spencer, in consultation with Sir Bryan Carsberg (the IASC's secretary-general) and Tweedie, with advice from the search firm, winnowed the number down to a 'long short-list' of forty-four candidates. Interviews were conducted in Tokyo, New York, and London by five-member panels composed of Spencer, Ruder, Tweedie (as an observer), and the two other members of the nominating committee from Asia, the Americas, and Europe, respectively.

In line with the 'independent expert model', the Constitution stated that 'the selection of members of the Board shall not be based on geographic representation' (paragraph 25). Yet the trustees realized that all of the Board members could not come from just two or three countries with strong traditions in accounting standard setting. They certainly attended to geography at least as a constraining factor, but their task was more difficult because the nominations and applications received were seriously unbalanced in this respect. Almost 60 per cent of the candidates originated from the United States and the United Kingdom combined, with the United States making up the largest proportion by far (42 per cent). At the other extreme, only two names were put forward from Japan, only two from all of Africa (both from South Africa), and none from Latin America.[22] To complicate the trustees' work further, the Constitution stated that the Board was to be composed of a minimum of five practising auditors, three preparers, and three users, and should have at least one academic. The greatest challenge to the trustees was in finding appointable users. A further constraint imposed by the Constitution was that seven of the Board members were to liaise with national standard setters, so that 'the selection process will therefore necessarily involve consultation between the Trustees and the national standard setters concerned' (paragraph 27).

The nominating committee's selection process did not escape criticism. The Financial Executives Institute (FEI) took note of the fact that Carsberg and Tweedie were taking part in the process. In a letter to Paul Volcker sent in August 2000, the FEI wrote, 'We understand that the Trustees have invited the IASC Secretariat and the newly appointed Chairman to play an integral role in the steps taken to establish the new Board. We strongly believe that the responsibility for identifying and selecting Board members should reside exclusively with the

---

[20] Advertisement text appearing in *The Wall Street Journal*, 29 August 2000.

[21] See Camfferman and Zeff, *Financial Reporting and Global Capital Markets*, Chapter 13.

[22] 'IASC Board Selection', memorandum from Thomas Seidenstein to IASC trustees, 6 October 2000, IASB archive, file 'Lipworth'.

Trustees.' The FEI added that 'There is a significant risk of the appearance of "cronyism" in this selection process that you must take all necessary pains to avoid'.[23] The involvement of Tweedie in every step of the selection process for the other Board members is worthy of comment. Had the chairman been selected only after following the same due process as was used for the other members of the Board, which would have been the trustees' plan before it became known that Tweedie might accept a competing position, he would not have had an opportunity to influence the thinking of the nominating committee on the choice of the other members. From Tweedie's standpoint on the other hand, he believed it was important to have a board that was technically sound and was one with which he could work effectively, whether he agreed with their views or not. While it is clear that the nominating committee paid close attention to Tweedie's views, and that his advice tipped the scales in some cases, it seems likely that the committee by itself would not have selected a vastly different board from among the available candidates.

3.4.1 The Eleven Other Full-time Members

The nominating committee agreed on a recommendation of eleven full-time members and two part-time members (see Figure 3.2). Recollections differ about the number of candidates for the Board whom David Tweedie supported with his advice to the nominating committee.[24] For example, he seems to have conveyed his favourable views of James J. (Jim) Leisenring and Patricia L. (Tricia) O'Malley, an American and Canadian, respectively. Both had served on the G4+1, Leisenring being the group's chairman at the time he agreed to join the IASB. Leisenring had been the FASB's director of research and technical activities from 1982 to 1987 and a member of the FASB from October 1987 to June 2000 (and vice chairman from January 1988 onwards). Prior to his service at the FASB, he was a partner in a small audit firm in Michigan. From 1992 to 1996, he was the FASB's observer at meetings of the IASC Board. Leisenring was known not only for his keen analytical mind but also for his unsparing style of debate when he detected disingenuousness or a sacrifice of principle in the arguments of others around the table. While his technical ability made him a candidate supported by strong recommendations, he was, among a slate of candidates that the trustees in the end approved unanimously, the one whom

---

[23] Letter to Paul Volcker, dated 24 August 2000, signed by Bryan R. Roub, FEI chairman; Philip D. Ameen, chair, FEI Committee on Corporate Reporting; and Philip B. Livingston, FEI president and CEO <http://www.financialexecutives.org> accessed through web.archive.

[24] Biographies of the original and subsequent Board members may be found at <http://www.iasplus.com>. For the original Board members, see also *IASB Insight*, March 2001, 5–8. Interpretations in this section are based to a large extent on written communications which the authors have received from, as well as on interviews with, Mary Barth, 17 March 2009 and 2 August 2010; Hans-Georg Bruns, 30 June 2009; Anthony Cope, 14 January 2011; Colin Fleming, 14 October 2008; Robert Herz, 17 February 2009; Thomas Jones, 16 February 2009; Philip Laskawy, 18 February 2009; Arthur Levitt, 20 April 2005; Patricia O'Malley, 26 May 2009; David Ruder, 17 June 2009; John Smith, 16 March 2009; Kenneth Spencer, 26 May 2003; Lynn Turner, 19 November 2004; David Tweedie, 29 July 2008; Paul Volcker, 31 July 2009; Peter Walton, 13 October 2008; and Geoffrey Whittington, 19 March 2009.

Figure 3.2 The initial members of the IASB Board, 2001. *Standing, left to right*: Jim Leisenring, Geoffrey Whittington, Bob Herz, Tatsumi Yamada, Gilbert Gélard, Hans-Georg Bruns, Tony Cope, Harry Schmid, Bob Garnett, Warren McGregor. *Seated, left to right*: Patricia O'Malley, David Tweedie, Tom Jones, Mary Barth.

they most deliberately considered. The IASC Constitution specified that seven of the full-time Board members were to liaise with the national standard setter in their home country, and it was known that the FASB favoured Leisenring as the liaison to its board. O'Malley, formerly a technical partner in KPMG Canada, had been appointed the first full-time chairman of Canada's Accounting Standards Board (AcSB) in 1999. From 1988 to 1997, she served on Canada's Emerging Issues Committee, and in 1997 she became the part-time vice chairman of AcSB and began attending meetings of the G4+1. O'Malley was appointed in the auditor category. Leisenring, because he did not fit into any of the categories, was listed as 'other'.

Tweedie wanted British-born Thomas E. (Tom) Jones on the Board, especially for his ability to manage relations with 'political' parties outside the Board. Since 1980, he had been the chief financial officer and eventually executive vice president of Citicorp/Citigroup, and from 1991 to 1998 was a trustee and eventually vice president of the FAF, the trustee group which oversees the FASB. Jones had worked in Italy and Belgium for previous employers, and he speaks Italian. Early in his career he worked for Peat, Marwick, Mitchell & Co. (now part of KPMG) in the United Kingdom and became an English chartered accountant in 1963. Since 1996, he had headed the delegation on the IASC Board representing the International Association of Financial Executives Institutes, and in July 2000 he became the Board's chairman (the first chairman who had not been a partner in an audit firm). Jones was appointed to the new Board as a preparer and was named its vice chairman.

Tweedie did not know that Geoffrey Whittington had applied for the Board, but, once the application was received, Tweedie made it clear that he wanted him to be a member. Whittington, an accounting professor at Cambridge University, had served on Tweedie's ASB throughout the 1990s, initially as the academic advisor and then as a part-time member. He and Tweedie had co-authored two books and several articles, and they had served for four years together on the research committee of the Institute of Chartered Accountants of Scotland. He became an English chartered accountant in 1963 and received a Ph.D. from Cambridge in 1971. When Whittington was named to the Board, he was designated as a user because of his ten years' service on the UK Monopolies and Mergers Commission.[25]

Another candidate favoured by Tweedie was Warren McGregor, the executive director of the Australian Accounting Research Foundation from 1989 to 1999 (and previously its technical director), the staff observer for the Australian delegation to the IASC Board from 1986 to 1999, and another active member in the G4+1. In 1999, he and Kevin Stevenson formed a boutique accounting practice in Melbourne. McGregor was known as a staunch advocate of the use of fair values. Like Leisenring, McGregor was placed in the 'other' category.

British-born Anthony T. (Tony) Cope had worked as a financial analyst in the United States for thirty years, eventually becoming senior vice president of an investment advisory and asset management firm in Boston. In 1993, he was appointed to the FASB, and from 1996 onwards he was the FASB's observer at meetings of the IASC Board. Like Tweedie, he had been a member of the IASC's Strategy Working Party. Spencer and Tweedie urged Cope to apply for Board membership because of his long record as a user. He was duly classified as one of the user representatives although he had been a standard setter for the past seven years.

An application was received from Robert P. (Bob) Garnett, a South African chartered accountant who was executive vice president-finance of Anglo American plc, one of the world's largest mining companies, which had adopted IASs in 1997. He was a member of an IASC steering committee which produced a report on extractive industries accounting in November 2000. He therefore would have been known at least to Ken Spencer, who served as the steering committee's chairman. In a highly diverse career, Garnett had previously been technical director of the South African Institute of Chartered Accountants, a consulting partner in Arthur Andersen & Co., an investment analyst for four years, and for three years the general manager of a merchant bank. He joined Anglo American in 1994. For the past four years, he was a part-time member of South Africa's Accounting Practices Board. Garnett was appointed to the Board as a user even though his recent experience was as a preparer.

Gilbert Gélard had been serving on the French delegation to the IASC Board since 1988, first as the staff observer and then as a full member of the delegation. Like Garnett, his experiences covered a broad range. He served as a financial

---

[25] When challenged in a letter from Professor John Flower to name the third user appointed to the Board, Paul Volcker replied that it was Whittington because of his service on the Monopolies and Mergers Commission. See 'Puzzling and Disappointing', *Accountancy*, 127/1294 (June 2001), 26. For Flower's letter, see 'The Third Man', *Accountancy*, 127/1292 (April 2001), 28–9.

executive for two large French industrial groups and then, from 1987 to 1995, was in charge of technical and international affairs for the Ordre des Experts Comptables, in Paris. He then became a professional practice partner of KPMG, and since 1997 he had been a part-time member of the Conseil National de la Comptabilité, France's accounting standard setter. Gélard was appointed to the Board as an auditor. He speaks eight languages.

Harry K. Schmid, a retired financial executive after a long career in the Nestlé Group and a member since 1995 of the delegation on the IASC Board representing the Federation of Swiss Industrial Holding Companies, was appointed to the Board as a preparer. He had chaired the accounting expert group of the Federation and of the European Round Table. Nestlé was one of the early adopters of IASs. Schmid lived in Latin America for seventeen years, where he was responsible for finance and control of a Nestlé subsidiary. He had served for many years on the Fachkommission für Empfehlungen zur Rechnungslegung (FER), the Swiss accounting standard setter. He speaks four languages. When serving on the IASC Board, as well as on the IASB Board, he was known for his unyielding opposition to the many proposed disclosure requirements which he regarded as unnecessary. Like Garnett, he had experience in the application of IASs.

It was regarded as essential that a Board member come from Asia, and Japan was, for many, the logical choice. The appointment was given to Tatsumi Yamada, who was a member of the Japanese delegation to the IASC Board since 1996. He was a partner in ChuoAoyama Audit Corporation, the Japanese affiliate firm of PricewaterhouseCoopers, and he was also a member of Japan's Business Accounting Deliberation Council, the body which advised the Ministry of Finance on accounting principles. While at Chuo, he was seconded for three years as manager in charge of research and development of accounting standards for the Corporation Finance Research Institute (COFRI), a think-tank established in 1990 and financed by corporations to conduct policy-oriented research on the improvement of Japanese financial reporting. He was appointed to the Board as an auditor.

One of the least widely known of the new Board members, at least in international accounting circles, was Hans-Georg Bruns, the chief accounting officer of DaimlerChrysler AG. In 1993, he was in charge of adapting the accounting system at Daimler-Benz AG to US GAAP, when Daimler became the first German company to list on the New York Stock Exchange, and he became a convert to investor-oriented financial reporting. In 1998, he was responsible for the accounting and disclosure activities attendant to the merger between Daimler and Chrysler Corporation. In joining the Board, he had a personal objective of getting rid of the SEC's reconciliation requirement for foreign companies adopting IASs. Bruns holds a doctorate from the Universität Mannheim. He was the chairman of the Schmalenbach-Gesellschaft für Betriebswirtschaft, an important German think-tank on business economics. Unlike Schmid, Bruns was not yet familiar with IASs when he joined the Board as a preparer.

3.4.2 The Two Part-time Members

Originally, it was expected, or at least hoped, that company executives might be persuaded to accept the two part-time positions. But it soon became evident that it was impracticable for chief financial officers or executives at a comparable level of importance in their companies to divide their time with another demanding responsibility. The only preparers who could be recruited, it was believed, were those who were nearing, or at, retirement, and therefore would serve as full-time members.

The two part-time members who were selected were qualified accountants and came from the United States: Robert H. (Bob) Herz and Mary E. Barth. At the time, Herz was head of the US national office of PricewaterhouseCoopers. He had been an audit partner in Coopers & Lybrand, where he became the senior technical partner in 1996. He had served on the FASB's Emerging Issues Task Force and Financial Instruments Task Force. He had lived in Argentina, where he acquired knowledge of Spanish, before taking his undergraduate studies at the University of Manchester, in Britain. He recalls that, at a conference they were both attending, Jim Leisenring suggested that he apply for one of the part-time openings on the Board, and once Herz had obtained the permission of his partners in the firm, he did so.[26] Mary Barth was unusual in that, after becoming an audit partner of Arthur Andersen & Co., she obtained a Ph.D. from Stanford University in 1989 and, following a stint at Harvard University, became a professor of accounting at Stanford. She has been a leading author of research articles. Barth was a member of the AICPA's Accounting Standards Executive Committee and the FASB's Financial Accounting Standards Advisory Council. She established herself as one of the most active speakers at Board meetings.

Both Herz and Barth made arrangements with their firm and university, respectively, to enable them to serve as part-time Board members. Yet, as they both soon came to appreciate, a part-time Board member is expected to do the same homework and attend the same meetings as the full-time members.

3.4.3 The Final Stage in the Selection Process

At the trustees' third meeting, on 11 December 2000 in London, with sixteen of the nineteen members participating, they unanimously approved the committee's slate of nominees for the thirteen open Board positions.[27] It was noted that, in October, the nominating committee had said that it intended to provide some options to the trustees, but in the end the committee decided against doing so. It was then necessary to secure the formal agreement of the national standard setters to the liaison assignments, although the nominating committee had already satisfied itself, on an informal basis, of the necessary support of the candidates in their home countries. Once the formal agreements were in hand, Spencer, Ruder, and Røder telephoned the successful candidates during the week of 18 December. All accepted their appointments. Each full-time member, excluding the chairman, was to be paid a gross annual remuneration of £325,000, before any UK or home country taxation, and the two part-time members were to receive £162,500 each. The chairman's

---

[26] Robert H. Herz, *Accounting Changes: Chronicles of Convergence, Crisis, and Complexity in Financial Reporting* (AICPA, 2013), 25.

[27] IASCF trustees meeting of 11 December 2000, minute 9.

remuneration was set at £400,000 per annum.[28] Tweedie anticipated that the new Board could meet in February and March 2001 to develop its agenda and priorities, and that it would be ready to begin full-time in April.

It was infeasible, because of the approaching holidays, to announce the Board membership until January. On a more formal note, the trustees' power to appoint Board members was conditional on securing sufficient funds for the new organization (see Section 3.11). Although this had not stopped the trustees from announcing the appointment of Tweedie, it was now considered desirable to make more progress with fundraising and the incorporation of the Foundation as a legal entity. Finally, the trustees announced the full membership of the Board on 25 January 2001, and also that its new name would be the International Accounting Standards Board.[29] At the trustees' December 2000 meeting, it was David Tweedie who proposed this new name, and it was agreed to by the trustees.

The Constitution stipulated that the Board members' terms should be staggered, and that the initial appointments should therefore be for a mixture of three-, four-, and five-year terms. The trustees settled this point in March 2001; that is, after the names of the Board members had already been announced. The decision was based on a proposal by David Tweedie, who had surveyed the members for their preferences.[30] The terms were set, in the main, so that the terms of one user and one preparer should expire in each year and that the terms of all North Americans and all Europeans should not expire at once. The following was the proposal: Barth, Bruns, Cope, and O'Malley should have three-year terms; Garnett, Gélard, Herz, Leisenring, and Schmid should have four-year terms; and Jones, McGregor, Tweedie, Whittington, and Yamada should have five-year terms. But Bruns and Jones agreed to swap terms: Bruns would serve a five-year term, and Jones would serve a three-year term. All members were eligible for reappointment, and they were given reason to believe that, with satisfactory performance, they would be reappointed to a second term. At their October 2001 meeting, the trustees decided to allow Board members with initial terms of three years to serve up to ten years on the Board.[31] This decision, which was not publicly known, and may not have been known to the Board members either, was never put to effect. As Board reappointments became a matter of some controversy in subsequent years (see Section 11.2), the trustees did not refer back to this possibility.

3.4.4 Liaison Members

As mentioned above, the Constitution required that seven of the fourteen Board members liaise with national standard setters, which meant that these members would be expected to spend a considerable fraction of their time elsewhere than in

[28] Memorandum dated 15 December 2000 from Thomas Seidenstein to Jens Røder, David Ruder, and Kenneth Spencer (supplied by David Ruder); IASCF trustees meeting of 28 June 2000, minute 4(iii).

[29] 'IASC Trustees Announce New Standard-setting Board to Reach Goal of Global Accounting Standards', IASC press release, 25 January 2001 <http://www.iasplus.com>. See also 'SEC Chairman Arthur Levitt Congratulates IASC on Selection of New Board Members', SEC press release 2001–17, 25 January 2001 <http://www.sec.gov>.

[30] IASCF trustees meeting of 8 March 2001, agenda paper 3.

[31] IASCF trustees meeting of 15 October 2001, minute 6.

London. It was important to the new Board that it coordinate its agenda and projects with national standard setters so as 'to promote the convergence of national accounting standards and International Accounting Standards'.[32] The Constitution did not specify the countries with which liaisons should be established, nor the exact number of such relations, and it was accepted that one Board member could maintain more than one liaison relationship. So, while it was probably self-evident that standard setters like the FASB in the United States or the ASB in the United Kingdom would be included, there was some room for debate about the others. For instance, in their initial deliberations the trustees suggested that the Netherlands might be included, or that the EU, rather than individual countries, should be considered as a candidate.[33] It was left to the nominating committee to formulate a proposal, as part of the search process. By October 2000, the nominating committee proposed the standard setters of Australia, Canada, France, Germany, Japan, the United Kingdom, and the United States. The choice was 'based on the need to work with the standard setters that are particularly strong currently in order to draw upon their resources and harmonize agendas'.[34] This was an interesting way of putting it, given that the Accounting Standards Board of Japan was not even established until July 2001. Nor had the German standard setter, created in 1998, yet had the opportunity to establish a strong track record in international convergence work. The proposed set of standard setters could perhaps also be seen as the G4 with the addition of three standard setters with less experience but from major economies. The G4 parallel became even clearer when New Zealand's Financial Reporting Standards Board was subsequently added as the eighth liaison standard setter. At its meeting of 30 January–1 February 2001, the G4+1 agreed to disband, as 'successful restructuring of IASC to create an IASB designed to include an active partnership with national standard-setters would obviate the need for the G4+1'.[35] As finally agreed, the liaison assignments were the following:

- Bruns—Deutsches Rechnungslegungs Standards Committee
- Gélard—Conseil National de la Comptabilité
- Leisenring—Financial Accounting Standards Board
- McGregor—Australian Accounting Standards Board and New Zealand's Financial Reporting Standards Board
- O'Malley—Accounting Standards Board (Canada)
- Whittington—Accounting Standards Board (United Kingdom)
- Yamada—Accounting Standards Board of Japan.

It was also expected that the non-liaison members would play an informal liaison role in their home country or other countries, especially in emerging economies.[36]

---

[32] Quoted from paragraph 27 of the IASC Constitution.
[33] IASCF trustees meeting of 28 June 2000, minute 4(i).
[34] IASCF trustees meeting of 30 October 2000, minute 4(i).
[35] 'Meeting of the G4+1 in London', undated [9 February 2001] G4+1 communiqué <http://www.asb.org.uk> accessed through web.archive; 'G4+1 Disbands', news item posted 12 February 2001 <http://www.iasplus.com>; 'Farewell to G4', *World Accounting Report*, March 2001, 2.
[36] IASCF trustees meeting of 30 October 2000, minute 4(ii).

The stipulation that seven Board members serve their national standard setter in a liaison capacity seems, at the margin, to have influenced the nominating committee when making the selections. Before putting the finishing touches on their list of thirteen nominees, the committee had to ascertain that the seven were acceptable by their respective national standard setters. Yamada's liaison assignment had to be dealt with differently, because, as indicated, the Accounting Standards Board of Japan was not established until July 2001: the nominating committee observed that Yamada had the support of the Japanese Institute of Certified Public Accountants and of Nippon Keidanren.[37]

As noted earlier, in the discussion of the selection of the trustees, there was some liaison at the trustee level as well. Two of the trustees, John Biggs and David Ruder, were also trustees of the FAF in the United States. Another trustee, Sydney Lipworth, was chairman of the UK's Financial Reporting Council, which oversaw the ASB.

3.5 THE BOARD AS A GROUP

On various points in the preceding sections, several factors have been mentioned that put their mark on the initial IASB. They can be drawn together to give an impression of how the newly constituted Board, as a group, approached its standard-setting task, and it can be seen that the Board's strengths and weaknesses were closely related. Table 3.1 provides a summary of the new Board members by region and designated background.

It was never called into question that the Board was highly qualified in a technical sense. This was a conscious decision by the nominating committee, as well as by the other trustees, who realized that the new Board's chances to succeed as a global standard setter depended heavily on its ability to meet the FASB on equal terms. Eleven of the fourteen members were qualified accountants (other than Bruns, Cope, and Schmid), and Bruns and Schmid had held important accounting positions in their companies. Cope had served for seven years on

Table 3.1. Founding IASB Board members by region and designated professional background

	North America	Europe	Asia/Pacific	Other
Auditors	Herz	Gélard	Yamada	
	O'Malley	Tweedie		
Preparers	Jones	Bruns		
		Schmid		
Users	Cope	Whittington		Garnett
Academic	Barth			
Other	Leisenring		McGregor	

[37] 'Board Recommendations and Nominations Process', unnumbered agenda paper for IASCF trustees meeting of 11 December 2000, 19.

the FASB. More particularly, the members shared a wealth of standard-setting experience. Nine members—Cope, Garnett, Gélard, Leisenring, O'Malley, Schmid, Tweedie, Whittington, and Yamada—had served on their national standard setter, and McGregor had headed the research foundation that supported the Australian standard setter. Six members also served on the IASC Board (Gélard, Jones, McGregor, Schmid, Tweedie, and Yamada) or attended Board meetings, and spoke, as observers (Cope and Leisenring). Four members—Leisenring, McGregor, O'Malley, and Tweedie—had been members of the G4+1, which made it easy for them to continue their collaboration in the Board and provide a strong sense of direction. Herz, because of his position in his firm, was significantly involved with standard setting in the United States and therefore knew Leisenring and Cope. Because of these overlapping experiences, most of the Board members had known each other before the first meeting, thus facilitating the socialization of the new Board. It was further facilitated by holding a Board dinner every month, with spouses invited. As Tricia O'Malley recalled, 'It helped to have others to talk to who were in the same boat—having uprooted ourselves to move to London. So it did turn into family, because the spouses got to know each other, and that was part of making it work.'[38]

With all this shared experience, it was easy for the initial Board to reach quick agreement on the main issues that needed to be addressed, as well as on the general shape of the answers. But the Board's confidence in its own expertise was also a source of problems. One close observer whom we interviewed, after acknowledging that 'the Board were brilliant', also noted that 'One of the biggest failings of the first five-year period was trying to get to the ultimate answer too quickly'.

As soon became evident, previous national standard-setting experience was not a sufficient qualification to be a member of an *international* standard setter. One Board member whom we interviewed said that, beyond technical expertise, 'there is *far* more importance, which has taken us too long to fully appreciate, of the need to communicate—"communicate" means two ways: not just telling people what we're doing, not pretending to listen and then making up our own minds, but actually looking at the needs of the different constituency groups, geographical and professional, that are going to be using our standards'.

The initial Board's idealistic intention to set 'best of breed' standards or the 'gold standard' (as David Tweedie said on many occasions) was reinforced by the fact that, at the very beginning, there were as yet few companies in the world directly applying the IASB's standards. Certainly with hindsight, and perhaps also at the time, Board members described the IASB in its initial years as a 'think-tank'.[39] The implication was that the Board could afford to dispense with compromise in the pursuit of high quality standards.

There were recent memories of the restructuring of the IASC, and in particular of the arduous debate over the 'independent expert model' that was finally embedded in the revised Constitution. This would have underscored the need to

---

[38] Interview with Patricia O'Malley, 28 May 2009.

[39] Interview with David Tweedie, 29 July 2008; memorandum by David Tweedie, dated 3 October 2006, IASCF trustees meeting of October 2006, agenda paper 6.

defend the Board's independence, but it also created an image of the Board as defensive, aloof, and even arrogant. Such an outcome might have been even more likely because the massing of standard-setting experience was complemented by a thin presence of recent user and preparer experience. As indicated above, it was difficult to recruit practising users for the Board. Therefore, for the first several years the members classed as users were users more in name than because of recent experience as security analysts or portfolio managers.

The country influence, at least arguably, shifted rather markedly from the former IASC Board to the new IASB Board. In the old IASC Board, each country delegation possessed one vote. But the five US members of the new IASB Board would, if they were in agreement on an exposure draft or standard, account for five of the fourteen votes, and the two UK members could cast a further two if they were also to agree. It was not lost on interested parties on the European Continent, especially in France, that the seven US and UK members plus the single members from Canada, Australia, and South Africa—collectively constituting an Anglo-American bloc of accounting ideology—could command more than the simple majority of eight members needed to approve exposure drafts and standards. Yet it was made clear by the trustees that the members were to vote their own views and were not on the Board to represent their countries. On the day the new Board was announced, 25 January 2001, BNA reported that 'Some voiced worries about an adverse reaction to an IASB seen as too heavily weighted toward "Anglo-Americans" or members of the informal group of standard-setters known as the G4+1'. BNA quoted Volcker as saying, 'I don't think this is an American imperialistic effort'.[40]

Even so, the Board members from North America formed almost a board within the Board. They would bring to the table their memories of US GAAP and the standard-setting process developed by the FASB, which really had no match in the world in terms of depth of experience, rigour, and professionalism. They would also bring memories of the strong tradition of independent standard setting embedded in the FASB, and also of the frequent and bitter contests to maintain that independence from insistent lobbyists.

It was apparent from the beginning that some of the North American Board members—in particular Barth, Leisenring, and O'Malley—dominated the debates around the Board table, at least in terms of speaking time.[41] Yet their contributions were by no means interchangeable. O'Malley often used her widely acknowledged expertise to play a moderating role, trying to clarify the different positions that were articulated around the table and to seek common ground. Jim Leisenring was another formidable debater, but his style was blunt and readily dismissive of weakly thought-out arguments or inconsistent thinking. Yet, both were indispensable in developing the technical solutions that the Board needed. Leisenring recalls how, during the early years, after comments by other members on the prominent role of the North Americans in the debates, the North Americans had

---

[40] Steve Burkholder, 'Leisenring, Cope, Jones, and 10 Others Formally Named to New International Board', *BNA Daily Tax Report*, 26 January 2001.

[41] For a quantitative analysis of Board member interventions in the debates during the IASB's early years, see Peter Walton, 'Les délibérations de l'IASB en 2002 et 2003: une analyse statistique', *Comptabilité—Contrôle—Audit*, 15/1 (June 2009), 35–54.

agreed among themselves not to speak during the next day of the meeting: 'It was awfully quiet. Not much happened for a long time until David said, "what the hell is going on?" So he started calling on us. He didn't have much choice.'[42] While this was part of the good-natured give and take within the Board, Leisenring did not pull his punches in discussions with other Board members, or with the staff. Nor did he do so in discussions with the IASB's constituents, sometimes leading to amazement or outrage if they were used to more deferential treatment.

Bruns, Gélard, Schmid, and Yamada all had a good command of English, yet it was not their first language. This never caused any significant communication problems, but it could add considerably to the fatigue often felt by Board members after multiple-day meetings of sometimes fast-paced technical discussion. When Yamada had difficulty following the fast-paced discussion, he would motion with his hands to slow down. Non-English speakers sometimes had difficulty understanding the Scots and Australian accented English of Tweedie and McGregor, respectively.

As with all the other Board members, Chairman Tweedie brought his background with him to the IASB. He had participated actively in the G4+1's work, and he had been a successful chairman of the UK ASB for ten years. His achievements in reforming financial reporting in the United Kingdom, sometimes in the face of strong opposition, probably gave him confidence that the IASB would be able to pull off some quick victories on the basis of the preparatory work already undertaken by the ASB.

Within the Board membership there was a smaller group upon which Tweedie relied for collegial support to carry forward his strategy for the Board's work on projects. Foremost among those were Tom Jones, the vice chairman, who some characterized as the Board member who could assure Tweedie of the number of votes on which he could count. Another was Warren McGregor, who was Tweedie's informal lieutenant. A third was Jim Leisenring on whom Tweedie frequently relied to sort out technical impasses. These three plus a few others—in practice apparently depending on who was available at the moment—composed a strategy committee which Tweedie used as a sounding board for issues he was trying to resolve.[43]

3.6 RESIDENCE IN LONDON

An issue that came up for consideration by the trustees, raised by Ken Spencer, was the residence of the full-time Board members in London. The Constitution was silent on the issue of residence, and the Strategy Working Party had taken a relaxed position on the issue in its final report in November 1999:

> The importance of building mutual trust and teamwork amongst Board Members is recognised. However, it is also recognised that only the Chairman would be required

[42] Interview with James Leisenring, 2 August 2010.
[43] One listing shows the membership as Tweedie, Jones, Bruns, Leisenring, McGregor, and O'Malley. 'Agenda paper for Weybridge meeting', 9 September 2003, 50. IASB archive, 'Awayday' files.

to be located in the central office of IASC. Perhaps some of the other full-time Board Members not having formal liaison roles would also choose to be located in the central location. Other full-time Members with liaison responsibilities and part-time Members would be likely to remain in their home countries to carry out their other responsibilities.[44]

The trustees believed that a 50–50 split in time would be a reasonable assumption.[45] Plans were made to ensure a permanent presence of Board members by asking them to spend two weeks each month in London. Members coming in from other continents would add a week before or after each Board meeting, while the European members would schedule their presence in the remaining weeks. In practice, the distribution turned out to be skewed towards absence from London. The two part-time members would, of course, not be moving to London. The seven liaison members spent much of the time between Board meetings in their home countries, where their national standard setters typically provided them with office space. Of the remaining five members, only David Tweedie and Geoffrey Whittington were regularly in the IASB office between meetings. Whittington, a resident of Cambridge, managed to be in the IASB office on most days. No one moved their residence to London. One member chose not to move to London in order to avoid being subject to the high UK income tax rate. For another member, being allowed to reside at home, outside the United Kingdom, was a condition for accepting membership. Some Board members bought or rented apartments in London from the start, and others did so subsequently. But initially there was not an assured minimum presence of Board members, and the IASB's offices could be very quiet at times. This limited the occasions for Board members to exchange views or to confer with staff between Board meetings, other than by email or telephone. Two Board members recalled the exasperation of a trustee who wandered around the office on an unannounced visit, saying words to the effect of: 'Where the hell are all these people we are paying—what are they doing?' This absence of most members from London other than during Board meeting weeks was viewed soon as a problem that needed addressing.

In subsequent years, the trustees began strongly encouraging newly appointed Board members to take up residence in London, and most did so. Outsiders remarked on the absence of Board members from the office. In February 2004, at the initial stage of the trustees' quinquennial Constitution review, IOSCO's Technical Committee, together with its Standing Committee 1 (SC1) on multinational disclosure and accounting, raised the issue in a comment letter to Paul Volcker. They wrote: 'We believe that the Trustees should consider whether the proper balance of time spent in the office versus at offsite meetings or working from remote locations has been achieved.'[46] SC1 had noticed instances in which the IASB's staff and the Board were not on the same page, because the staff could not go down the hall and consult with one or more Board members.[47]

---

[44] 'Recommendations on Shaping IASC for the Future: A Report of the International Accounting Standards Committee's Strategy Working Party', November 1999, paragraph 50.

[45] IASCF trustees meeting of 30 October 2000, minute 4(ii).

[46] Letter dated 9 February 2005 from Andrew Sheng, chairman of the Technical Committee, to Paul Volcker <http://www.iosco.org>.

[47] Interview with Scott Taub, 17 June 2009.

3.7 SUCCESSOR TO BOB HERZ IN 2002

On 24 April 2002, the FAF announced the appointment of Bob Herz as FASB chairman in succession to Edmund L. Jenkins, who was to retire on 30 June.[48] Herz resigned from the IASB in June, and his five-year term at the FASB was to commence on 1 July. While Herz's departure, after only one year of service, was a loss to the IASB, his appointment as FASB chairman offered the opportunity, as will be seen, of even closer cooperation between the boards on a mutual convergence of their standards. The Norwalk Agreement between the two boards, attesting to this cooperation, which is discussed in Chapter 4, was issued on 30 October 2002.

The IASB Foundation placed an advertisement for a new part-time member with a background in auditing in the *Financial Times* and *The Economist*, which was posted on the IASB website during the week of 24 June, and the deadline for the receipt of applications was set as 17 July.[49] Half of the twenty-two applicants came from the United States and the United Kingdom, roughly equal between them. The nominating committee interviewed five candidates on 13 August.[50] Paul Volcker announced on 18 September that John T. Smith, a partner in Deloitte & Touche, in New York City, was appointed to complete Herz's four-year term as a part-time Board member, beginning his service on 1 October. Smith was the firm's director of accounting policies and he was already known at the IASB. He was a member of the IASB's International Financial Reporting Interpretations Committee (IFRIC, to be discussed in Section 3.9), from which he would resign. He had also been serving as chairman of the IAS 39 (Financial Instruments) Implementation Guidance Committee for the IASB.[51] By the time that Smith joined the Board, David Tweedie was beginning to express concern that so few Board members were in the office between Board meetings. Smith, therefore, although a part-timer, began to be a frequent presence in the office.

3.8 THE STANDARDS ADVISORY COUNCIL

In addition to the Board, the trustees were to appoint the members of an interpretations committee and a Standards Advisory Council (SAC).[52] As stated in the Constitution, SAC:

---

[48] 'Robert H. Herz Named Chairman of the Financial Accounting Standards Board', FAF press release, 24 April 2002 <http://www.fasb.org>.

[49] 'IASC Foundation update', *IASB Insight*, July 2002, 2.

[50] 'Board Candidates', memo by Kenneth Spencer, dated 18 July 2002; and email from Thomas Seidenstein to the nominating committee, dated 18 July 2002 (supplied by David Ruder).

[51] 'IASC Foundation update', *IASB Insight*, October 2002, 2.

[52] Interpretations in this section are based to a large extent on written communications which the authors have received from, as well as on interviews with, Jeannot Blanchet, 14 January 2011; Colin Fleming, 14 October 2008; Trevor Harris, 18 February 2009; Philip Laskawy, 18 February 2009; David Ruder, 17 June 2009; David Sidwell, 19 February 2009; and David Tweedie, 29 July 2008.

provides a forum for participation by organisations and individuals, with an interest in international financial reporting, having diverse geographic and functional backgrounds, with the objective of (a) giving advice to the Board on agenda decisions and priorities in the Board's work, (b) informing the Board of the views of the organisations and individuals on the Council on major standard setting projects and (c) giving other advice to the Board or the Trustees (paragraph 42).

SAC was to provide the Board and the trustees with a broad base of informed opinion on both substantive and procedural issues, including the specific directions the Board was taking in its standard-setting process. The Constitution provided that SAC 'shall comprise about thirty members' and will 'be appointed for renewable terms of three years' (paragraph 43). SAC members were not to be paid and, in general, were to cover their own travel costs. SAC was to meet at least three times a year, and its meetings were to be open to the public.

At their meeting on 11 December 2000, in which they approved the membership of the Board, the trustees took up the matter of how to select the members of SAC. This issue had to be addressed right at the beginning, because paragraph 36(d) of the Constitution required that the Board 'consult the Standards Advisory Council on major projects, agenda decisions and work priorities'. Therefore, the Board could not properly begin its work until it had carried out this consultation, although, as will be seen in Chapter 5, this did not prevent the Board from quickly making up its mind about its initial agenda.

The trustees decided that David Tweedie, assisted by the secretariat the trustees had begun to set up for themselves, should draw up a preliminary list of possible members, publish an advertisement, and send letters to constituency bodies seeking nominations.[53] Early in January, the nominating committee ran an advertisement in *The Wall Street Journal* and the *Financial Times*, and posted it on the IASC's website. Interested parties were asked to submit their curriculum vitae by 7 February. In the end, the committee received 175 applications and nominations.[54]

After conferring with Volcker and Tweedie, Ken Spencer, the chairman of the trustees' nominating committee, presented a paper to the trustees at their 8 March 2001 meeting on how to compose SAC. He reviewed the trustees' preliminary discussion at their previous meeting that was useful in guiding the selection: the need for strong representation from Europe and Asia, for the inclusion of members from developing countries, for financial institutions and financial regulators to be represented, and for observer status for the US SEC and the European Commission. He proposed the following potential composition of a SAC membership of thirty: EU, six; North America, six; Asia, excluding Japan, five; other Europe, three; Latin America, three; Africa/Middle East, three; Japan, two; and Australia/New Zealand, two. He wanted at least one member from each of the Big Five audit firms as well as representatives of regulators, national standard setters, academics, users, international organizations, and preparers. In his report, Spencer thereupon proposed to apportion the eligible applicants and nominees into

---

[53] IASCF trustees meeting of 11 December 2000, minute 9(ii).
[54] 'IASC Restructuring Completed', *IASB Insight*, March 2001, 4.

'A' and 'B' categories. Those in the 'A' category were regarded as 'essential' members of SAC from their respective geographical regions. They numbered twenty-three. Those in the 'B' category, which numbered forty-two, were considered to be well-qualified for membership of SAC but 'were not necessarily seen as clear-cut choices among the candidates in a person's country'.[55]

At their meeting, the trustees discussed the committee's report, and they agreed to send their recommendations of 'B' candidates to Spencer by 22 March. After receiving their suggestions, he was to prepare a report of his committee and send it to the trustees for final action.[56] In a conference call on 15 May of the trustees' executive committee (Volcker, Lipworth, Røder, Ruder, and Spencer), the nominating committee's report, which recommended forty-six members for SAC, was discussed. Spencer pointed out that the committee was concerned to have broad representation of all of the interests, and he expressed the view that the actual attendance at SAC meetings 'will likely be well below full membership'. In order to counter the perceived large representation of audit firm partners, the trustees added three names to reflect other backgrounds.[57] They then approved a SAC membership of forty-nine, with three observers. This was about two-thirds larger than had been envisaged by the framers of the Constitution. Ken Spencer was reported to have said, 'it's better to have people in the tent than outside the tent'.[58]

On 25 June, the IASB announced the composition of SAC (see Table 3.2).[59] Thirteen of the forty-nine SAC members were partners in audit firms, eleven were preparers, ten were national standard setters, six represented international organizations, four were users, three were academics, two were national regulators, and a few others were in assorted categories. Several of the members fell into more than one category, such as an audit firm partner or an academic who was also a standard setter. It was rather surprising that France, Germany, and the United Kingdom together accounted for only five members, yet ten came from the United States and three from Canada. It is noteworthy that three of the members (Philippe Danjou, Tricia McConnell, and Ian Mackintosh[60]) subsequently became Board members and that another three members (Marvin Cheung, David Shedlarz, and David Sidwell) subsequently became trustees. Jeannot Blanchet was recruited from SAC for IFRIC. Some members of the trustees looked upon SAC as a proving ground for future Board, trustee, and IFRIC positions. Also, at least ten of the SAC members had been interviewed as candidates for membership on the Board the previous year, and in some cases SAC may well have been seen as a way of offering viable but unsuccessful candidates for Board membership an alternative way of remaining involved with the Board's work. It is also of interest that ten of SAC's members had served in delegations to the IASC Board, and several others had attended IASC Board meetings as observers or guests. In the IASC

---

[55] 'Standards Advisory Council Recommendations', IASCF trustees meeting of 8 March 2001, unnumbered agenda paper.

[56] IASCF trustees meeting of 8 March 2001, minute 8.

[57] IASCF trustees meeting of 15 October 2001, agenda paper 1A.

[58] Interview with Thomas Seidenstein, 7 July 2011.

[59] 'IASC Foundation Trustees Name Standards Advisory Council to Provide Advice to IASB', IASC Foundation press release, 25 June 2001. See also *IASB Insight*, July 2001, 4.

[60] Mackintosh was different in that he served as chairman of the UK ASB from 2004 to 2011, when he became vice chairman of the IASB.

Table 3.2. Initial members of the Standards Advisory Council

Africa		Japan	
Peter Wilmot	South Africa	Eiko Tsujiyama	Japan
Ndung'u Gathinji	Kenya	Yoshiki Yagi	Japan
Asia, excluding Japan		**Latin America**	
Raja Arshad-Uda	Malaysia	Nelson Carvalho	Brazil
Marvin Cheung	Hong Kong	Héctor Estruga	Argentina
Feng Shuping	China	Rafael Gómez Eng	Mexico
Il-Sup Kim	South Korea		
Yezdi Malegam	India	**Middle East**	
Reyaz Mihular	Sri Lanka	Adir Inbar	Israel
		Rifaat Ahmed Abdel Karim	Bahrain
Australia, New Zealand			
Ian Ball	New Zealand	**United States and Canada**	
Peter Day	Australia	Jeannot Blanchet	Canada
		Michael Conway	United States
Central and Eastern Europe		Jerry Edwards	United States
Larissa Gorbatova	Russia	Trevor Harris	United States
Rita Ilisson	Estonia	Philip Livingston	United States
		Patricia McConnell	United States
European Union		Paul McCrossan	Canada
David Damant	UK	Gabrielle Napolitano	United States
Philippe Danjou	France	David Shedlarz	United States
Stig Enevoldsen	Denmark	Keith Sherin	United States
Douglas Flint	UK	David Sidwell	United States
Alberto Giussani	Italy	Norman Strauss	United States
Sigvard Heurlin	Sweden		
Benoit Jaspar	Belgium	**International organizations**	
Jean Keller	France	Fayezul Choudhury	World Bank
Carmelo de las Morenas	Spain	Arne Petersen	IMF
Jochen Pape	Germany	Ian Mackintosh	IFAC Public Sector Committee
Maija Torrko	Finland	Rafael Sánchez de la Peña	IOSCO
Willem van der Loos	Netherlands	John Carchrae	IOSCO
		Arnold Schilder	Basel Committee

Official observers
European Commission
United States SEC
Financial Services Agency of Japan

Foundation's 2001 *Annual Report*, David Tweedie made clear that he had a comparatively technical role in mind for SAC: 'The formation of the Standards Advisory Council (SAC) has made it possible for other standard-setters to become involved in the IASB's work.'[61]

Peter Wilmot, a standard setter and former audit firm partner who was a member of the South African delegation to the IASC for eight years in the 1980s and 1990s, was chosen as vice chairman of SAC, with David Tweedie being the ex-officio chairman. The vice chairman was to liaise with Tweedie and

---

[61] IASC Foundation, *Annual Report 2001*, 5.

the technical staff when setting SAC's agenda, to review all documents to be sent to the SAC members, to chair all sessions on technical accounting issues and SAC administration, to select and chair SAC's agenda committee, and to keep Tweedie aware of the views of the SAC members.[62] The trustees granted Wilmot an honorarium for this service.

SAC's inaugural meeting with the IASB Board was held on 23–4 July 2001, in London. The two major items on which the Board sought the SAC members' views were the IASB's proposed, initial technical agenda (see Section 5.1) and the proposed changes to the structure, procedures, and name of the Standing Interpretations Committee inherited from the IASC (see Section 3.9).

SAC's next four meetings with the IASB were on 16–17 October 2001 in Washington, 18–19 February 2002 in London, 20–21 June 2002 in Berlin, and 15–16 November 2002 in Hong Kong.[63] It regularly met three times a year.

SAC had teething problems. Its meetings did serve to expand the organization's reach, but absences were a problem. During a number of the early meetings, 20 or more per cent of the SAC members did not attend. Yet, even with these absences, the addition of most of the Board members and several of the staff made for very large and almost unmanageable meetings. One Board member recalled that, in large meetings like those of SAC, 'You have to raise your hand in order to get in the queue to speak, and sometimes somebody would say something outrageous, and it would be fifteen minutes before a Board member could challenge it, by which time the meeting would turn on to something else'. Some SAC members believed that the Board did not really listen, and some criticized the arrogance of some of the Board members when SAC members were critical of agenda decisions, drafts, or due process. To the Board and staff, the feedback was discordant and difficult to synthesize. One staff member lamented, 'It is very difficult to listen when a group over there says, "don't do it", and another group says, "do it", and a further group says, "do it, but do it this way"'. Reflecting on four years' experience with SAC, a trustee committee wrote in February 2005, 'In this forum interests are widely divergent, which has sometimes made discussions disjointed. For example, some members are interested in the technical details of standard setting, while others prefer to discuss broader strategy and priorities.'[64] By 2005, the trustees were contemplating actions to make the meetings more useful to both the Board and the SAC members.

3.9 THE INTERPRETATIONS COMMITTEE: FROM SIC TO IFRIC

The IASB had inherited the IASC's Standing Interpretations Committee (SIC), which was created in 1996 and began work the following year. Its membership and its formal arrangements were largely unaffected by the restructuring of the

---

[62] IASCF trustees meeting of 15 October 2001, agenda paper 9.

[63] For reports on the October 2001 and February 2002 meetings, see 'SAC Meets in Washington', *IASB Insight*, January 2002, 5–6, 11, and 'SAC Meets in London', *IASB Insight*, April 2002, 4–6.

[64] IASCF trustees meeting, London, March 2005, agenda paper 5A.

IASC into the IASB. When it was set up, SIC had twelve part-time members, ten of whom came from audit firms, including all of the Big Six firms. It was chaired throughout by Paul G. Cherry, a partner in an audit firm and a former chief accountant of the Ontario Securities Commission. Cherry succeeded Tricia O'Malley as chairman of Canada's AcSB when she was appointed to the Board of the IASB. SIC's interpretations had to be approved by a three-fourths majority of the IASC Board to become effective. During its four years of service to the IASC Board, SIC proposed twenty-five interpretations that secured this approval.

The IASB's Constitution, in paragraphs 38–41, provided for a continuation of SIC very much as it had been set up by the IASC. But instead of a three-fourths majority of the IASC Board, the new Board was to approve the interpretations by a simple majority. Within SIC itself, it was provided that the approval of a draft or final interpretation required that no more than three members vote against.

As the IASB Board began its operations, SIC continued to work on its stack of projects, and it submitted a proposed interpretation to the new Board at its first meeting in April 2001. Perhaps inevitably, a discussion arose in the Board about SIC's role now that there was a new, full-time, and independent IASB.[65] A review of SIC was agreed, focusing on two issues. The first was whether it should henceforth submit not only final interpretations to the Board for approval, but also obtain clearance by the Board before publishing an exposure draft. The other issue, emanating mainly from SIC itself, was whether its role should be expanded beyond the interpretation of existing standards to include producing guidance on issues where no standards were yet available.[66] The latter change, it was noted, would make SIC a bit more like the interpretations body of the FASB, the Emerging Issues Task Force (EITF). Both questions were answered in the affirmative by the Board and were combined in a package of changes, including a change of name from SIC to IFRIC and the creation of a non-voting chairman. It was expected that the chairman would be either a Board member or a senior member of the IASB's staff. IFRIC would remain a body of volunteers, and IASCF would cover their travel expenses only. After being exposed for comment, the required changes to the Constitution were approved by the trustees in March 2002.[67]

Well before that, in October 2001, the trustees had agreed on a thorough revision of the committee's membership (see Table 3.3). Of IFRIC's initial twelve voting members, five continued on from SIC, and seven were new appointments. The twelve included representatives of each of the Big Five (as they then were) audit firms, one partner in a local audit firm, three company executives, two users, and an academic. While auditors remained the largest contingent, their preponderance was considerably reduced compared to SIC. Preparer representation was deliberately expanded from one (the position formerly held by Harry Schmid, who had since become a Board member of the IASB) to three. As before, the European Commission and IOSCO were designated as official observers. The IOSCO observer was regularly a member of the SEC's accounting staff. The trustees also decided to appoint Kevin M. Stevenson as the non-voting chairman.

---

[65] IASB meeting of 18–20 April 2001, minute 10.

[66] AP 5/2001 paper 11; see also IASCF trustees meeting of 15 October 2001, agenda paper 3C.

[67] IASCF trustees meeting of 5 March 2002, minute 4.

Table 3.3. Initial voting members of IFRIC

Junichi Akiyama	Professor, Tama University, Japan
Phil Ameen	Vice president and comptroller, General Electric Company, United States
Christian Chiarasini	Partner, Arthur Andersen, France
Claudio de Conto	General manager, administration and control, Pirelli S.p.A., Italy
Clement K. M. Kwok	Managing director and chief executive, Hong Kong and Shanghai Hotels Limited, Hong Kong, China
Wayne Lonergan	Managing director, Lonergan Edwards & Associates, Australia
Domingo Mario Marchese	Partner, Marchese, Grandi, Mesón & Asociados, Argentina
John T. Smith	Partner, Deloitte & Touche, United States
Mary Tokar	Partner, IAS Advisory Services, KPMG International, United States
Leo van der Tas	Partner, Ernst & Young, the Netherlands
Patricia Walters	Senior vice president, Association for Investment Management and Research, United States
Ian Wright	Partner, PricewaterhouseCoopers, United Kingdom

Stevenson had been a member of SIC, and had just taken up his new staff position as the IASB's director of technical activities. The Constitution provided little guidance on the membership of the interpretations committee, but, in consultation with the Board, the trustees' nominating committee established a set of criteria among which, naturally, technical expertise figured prominently. The nominating committee also proposed that 'an appropriate geographic balance' should be sought, and the new IFRIC was rather more balanced than the Board in the sense that it had a greater proportion of members from outside the English-speaking world.[68]

Responding to the announcement of these decisions, France's Conseil National de la Comptabilité sourly observed in its comment letter on the proposed changes that it was not sure of the usefulness of its participation in the IASCF's due process, because the January 2002 issue of *IASB Insight* had already announced the reconstituted interpretations committee.[69] Generally, though, the changes to the interpretations structure attracted little, and largely positive, comment.

The change from SIC to IFRIC, which included the broadening of its mandate, gave rise to the expectation that the volume of interpretations would begin to increase significantly. This, however, did not happen. In December 2001 and March 2002, the Board approved the issue of seven out of the eight interpretations proposed by the SIC in 2001, and cancelled the remaining project. With this final effort, SIC had completed its own work programme, and the new IFRIC found itself with a blank agenda. It was not until May 2004 that its first interpretation, IFRIC 1, was published. This was a slow start, particularly for those whose point of reference was FASB's EITF, which had issued forty-four abstracts in its first year alone (1984). In September 2002, Stevenson reported to the Board that, whereas

[68] For the criteria, see IASCF trustees meeting of 15 October 2001, agenda paper 4. The exact proportion depends on whether one includes the IFRIC chairman and how one classifies Hong Kong, but it can be observed that the smaller IFRIC included the same number of nationalities as the Board.

[69] Letter from Antoine Bracchi to IASCF trustees, dated 15 February 2002, included in agenda paper 2, IASC trustees meeting of 5 March 2002. See 'Re-inventing Interpretations', *IASB Insight*, January 2002, 1–2.

IFRIC had expected to be 'deluged' with requests for interpretations, very few such requests had actually been received. He attributed this in part to the fact that so many standards were then under consideration by the Board, but also to a certain reluctance on the part of the large audit firms to submit issues.[70] Developing appropriate expectations concerning IFRIC's role and level of activity would remain an important issue throughout the IASB's first decade.

3.10 TECHNICAL AND ADMINISTRATIVE STAFF

As the old IASC Board wound down, some of the staff were preparing to depart, while others stayed on. And new staff arrived to serve both the IASB and the IASCF.

Sir Bryan Carsberg, the IASC's secretary-general, departed in May 2001 to become chairman of Council and senior pro-chancellor of the University of Loughborough. James S. Saloman, the technical director, was on a two-year secondment from PricewaterhouseCoopers in Toronto, and he returned to the firm in 2001.

Peter Clark, who had joined the IASC's staff in 1994, was promoted in 2008 to director of research and continues in that position to this day, the lone technical staff member who has served continuously from the old Board up to the present. Colin Fleming, a Bermudian, who had joined the IASC in 1999 as a project manager, and was serving as editor of *IASC Insight* and then *IASB Insight*, became the IASC's webmaster after Paul Pacter left the staff in 2000. Fleming departed in January 2005 to join Deloitte in London. Frank Palmer, Rieko Yanou, and Magnus Orrell joined in 2000, also on secondments. In 2002, Palmer and Yanou returned to practice in Australia and Japan, respectively. Orrell, a Swede who had come from the European Commission, left in 2003 to enter practice in the United States.

Board members, including David Tweedie, naturally drew on their networks in recruiting staff, and as these networks overlapped it is not necessarily evident who recruited whom. But the heavy Anglo composition of the Board's initial staff, including some who were known to one or more Board members, becomes evident. Among those whom Tweedie knew well were Kimberley Crook, a New Zealander, who came directly from the UK ASB, and Anne McGeachin from KPMG London, who had recently completed a secondment at the ASB. Tweedie had known Jim Paul and Annette Kimmitt from the Australian Accounting Standards Board, as they had presented papers at G4+1 meetings.

In 2001, there were several other staff arrivals: Sandra Thompson and Richard Barker, United Kingdom; Marie-Christine Batt (PwC, France), Kristin Hazzis (Governmental Accounting Standards Board, United States), Christine Lee (Deloitte, United States), and Galina Ryltsova (Arthur Andersen, Russia). Thompson, who came from Arthur Andersen in London, had previously been on the ASB's staff. In 2005, she left to join an international audit firm. Barker, a senior lecturer at Cambridge's Judge Institute of Management Studies, had completed his Ph.D. at Cambridge under Geoff Whittington. A part-time academic fellow, Barker

---

[70] *IStaR*, September 2002, 14.

concluded his IASB service in 2007. Batt and Lee were on secondment, which they completed in 2003. Hazzis, the IASB's first technical associate, left in 2003 to enter practice. Ryltsova left in 2005 to join a large UK audit firm.

In July 2001, Wayne S. Upton came as director of research after extensive service with the FASB. Tweedie knew him from G4+1 meetings, and actively encouraged him to express an interest in the position. In February 2002, Kevin Stevenson arrived from Australia, where he had been Warren McGregor's partner in their small accounting firm, to become director of technical activities. Stevenson was formerly executive director of the Australian Accounting Research Foundation and a partner in PwC in Melbourne. As the two senior technical staff members, Stevenson and Upton shared the responsibility for directing the work on the Board's technical agenda. Stevenson returned to Australia in 2005, while Upton remained beyond the period covered in this book.

Upon his appointment as chairman of the trustees, Paul Volcker brought with him Thomas R. (Tom) Seidenstein, an American who had come to know him during his undergraduate years at Princeton University. In 2000, Seidenstein was working at CCS, the fundraising consultancy that had been retained by the IASCF, and Volcker recruited him to join the IASCF on 1 September 2000 as executive officer to the chairman and secretary of the corporation. In February 2001, with Volcker's blessing, David Tweedie and Tom Jones asked Seidenstein to move to London as director of operations. That appointment took effect in April, and he made the move to London in May. In 2008, his title was changed to chief operating officer to reflect his broader responsibilities and to enable Tweedie to differentiate him from the other directors in the organization. Seidenstein's formal titles, coupled with his limited public appearances, might easily give an insufficient impression of his central role in assisting Tweedie, as chief executive, and the trustees in developing the strategies of the organization and in conducting the increasingly complex political negotiations in which it was involved. Both Tweedie and Seidenstein were the linchpins between the Board and the trustees. Seidenstein remained with the Foundation until December 2011, when he joined Fannie Mae (Federal National Mortgage Association) in Washington. He retained his title as secretary of the corporation throughout his long tenure at the Foundation.

Also at the Foundation level, Kurt Ramin, a German who had been with Coopers & Lybrand in New York City, continued from the IASC as commercial director until 2005, when he left the organization. Michael Butcher, who had been secretary to the ASB for eight years, arrived as editorial director in 2001, and the following year he succeeded Colin Fleming as editor of *IASB Insight*. He remained with the Foundation until 2008.

3.11 FUNDRAISING

The restructured IASC succeeded a body that was financed almost entirely from private-sector sources. In its 1999 *Annual Review*, the IASC said that its revenues came from three main sources: fees paid by the sponsors of Board delegations and from the IFAC on behalf of associate members of the IASC, sales of publications, and voluntary contributions from audit firms, companies, and financial institutions around the world, as well as from international development banks and the US Agency for International Development.[71] In comparison with the level of costs incurred by the old IASC, the Board members of the restructured IASC would not be serving as volunteers, and the technical staff would be much larger.

At their first meeting on 28 June 2000, the trustees took note of the estimate of £10 million (US$15 million)[72] made by the Strategy Working Party (SWP) of the annual budget required for the restructured IASC.[73] The SWP said that this figure 'includes the remuneration of Trustees, Board Members, technical and administrative staff, the costs of meetings and accommodation and other costs. The Working Party notes that this sum is in the same general order of magnitude as the budget of the Financial Accounting Standards Board in the United States' (paragraph 90). Following the meeting, Chairman Paul Volcker chose himself as chairman of the finance committee. The other members were Biggs, Fukuma, Herkströter, Lipworth, Kopper, and Steere.

In testimony to the US Senate Committee on Banking, Housing, and Urban Affairs on 14 February 2002, Volcker described the fundraising program in the first two years as follows:

> The international arrangements [i.e. the financing of the IASB] were set up pretty much on the model of FASB. There are two sources of income, including, selling the standards themselves, and an explanation in our case [is that] such sales are limited at this stage. In FASB, it accounts for more than half of [its] revenues. Since many, many accountants and auditors need to have these, it is a source of revenue. The rest of it is financed by contributions from industry.
>
> We started fresh with contributions from industry. Just to give you a picture of what we have done, we started at the end of 2000, the beginning of 2001. We solicited approximately 300 of the largest companies around the world. I wrote to them, or my associate trustees wrote to them in other countries. We are in the process of soliciting actually another 150 now, another tier. We have had a pretty good response.
>
> Our expenses we estimated at about $15 million a year. We have that covered in the early years from these initial solicitations. About 150 almost, corporations have contributed. The major accounting firms are picking up about a third of the tab.
>
> I might point out in connection with the interest in this effort, we have contributions from over 30 central banks and international institutions that are interested in this effort and wanted to indicate their support with relatively small contributions.
>
> But together, that comes to over a million dollars [from the central banks] . . . .
>
> As it turns out, about a third of our funding comes from the United States, about a third from Europe, about a third from Japan, Latin America, and others.[74]

[71] International Accounting Standards Committee, *Annual Review 1999*, 9. The full-page list of contributing organizations was shown on page 13. For more about the IASC's fundraising, see Camfferman and Zeff, *Financial Reporting and Global Capital Markets*, 240–9.

[72] The exchange rate between the US dollar and the UK pound fluctuated between $1.40/£1 and $1.45/£1 from September 2000 to June 2002.

[73] IASCF trustees meeting of 28 June 2000, minute 5(ii); the SWP's final report, *Recommendations on Shaping IASC for the Future* (30 November 1999), paragraph 90. By contrast, the IASC's total revenues for 1999 were £2,637,000 for a wholly part-time board. See Camfferman and Zeff, *Financial Reporting and Global Capital Markets*, 241.

[74] *Accounting Reform and Investor Protection*, Hearings before the Committee on Banking, Housing, and Urban Affairs, United States Senate, 107th Congress, 2nd Session, 14 February 2002, Volume I, 114–15.

Volcker's rendering of the geographical distribution of funding sources placed more emphasis on Latin America than was actually borne out in the first several years. To be sure, some significant funding was raised from Brazil, and contacts were made with potential contributors in Argentina and Mexico. But Japan largely shouldered the funding burden in the world beyond the United States and Europe (see Table 3.4). Volcker's statement correctly emphasized the central role of the trustees themselves in contacting potential contributors, even though the trustees retained CCS, a fundraising consultancy, to assist with the administration of the funding programme.

The trustees' funding strategy was to draw up a list of organizations with target amounts for each and to assign these to individual trustees, taking into account their country of origin and perceived or self-assessed fundraising ability. The objective was to seek annual commitments for up to five years, and not to raise too much money from any single donor because of independence concerns. The largest individual amounts, $1 million each, were pencilled in for the Big Five audit firms. At the 30 October 2000 meeting, Volcker reported that he had already received $1 million commitments from the first two of the Big Five audit firms he had approached. The other three would follow shortly after. Volcker was minuted as saying that 'He was hopeful that, after the accounting firms, the stock exchanges and large financial firms should underwrite a large portion of the IASC's needs, as

Table 3.4. Contribution commitments by country and region, 2001

Country and region	Annual contribution (US$)	Percentage of total
Japan	2,550,000	0.14
Hong Kong	100,000	0.01
Other Asia–Pacific	85,000	0.00
Total Asia–Pacific	**2,735,000**	**0.16**
United States	3,507,000	0.20
Brazil	320,000	0.02
Canada	265,000	0.02
Other Americas	60,000	0.00
Total Americas	**4,152,000**	**0.24**
South Africa	115,000	0.01
Total Africa	**115,000**	**0.01**
Germany	1,875,000	0.11
Switzerland	775,000	0.04
Netherlands	739,900	0.04
United Kingdom	718,030	0.04
France	650,000	0.04
Belgium	200,000	0.01
Italy	200,000	0.01
Other Europe	240,000	0.01
Total Europe	**5,397,930**	**0.31**
International audit firms	5,000,000	0.28
International organizations	200,000	0.01
Total international	**5,200,000**	**0.30**
Total	**17,599,930**	**1.00**

Note: Table shows commitments, mainly for five years but in some cases for three years, received by October 2001. Countries grouped as 'other' committed to contribute less than $100,000 each.

Source: IASCF trustees meeting of 15 October 2001, appendix to agenda paper 5.

they would be one of the primary beneficiaries of high quality, harmonized standards'.[75] He said he would work with Biggs and Ruder, both of whom were also serving on the FAF, to ensure that the IASC avoided fundraising conflicts with the FASB. At the meeting on 11 December 2000, Pineau-Valencienne and Herkströter reported on funding commitments they had already received, and various trustees offered to make contacts with additional sources, focusing on their countries or regions. Crockett volunteered to approach central banks, and Volcker opened important doors. It was reported that, in the United States, the Business Roundtable, the Chambers of Commerce, and Financial Executives International had offered assistance.[76] Chairman Volcker spoke at a meeting of the Business Roundtable (an association of chief executives of leading US companies) in February 2001 about the Foundation's funding strategy, and said he would write a personal letter to ask each company to consider making an annual commitment of $10,000 to $25,000, based on its annual revenue.[77] He led a major push for funds in the United States.

By 26 February 2001, the trustees reported having received $14.8 million in pledges. They were aiming for the original budgeted amount for the first year's operations of $15 million, which they had subsequently revised upward to $16.5 million.[78] In a table which summarized the commitments received by 29 July 2001, the total dollar amount of commitments from 137 donors exceeded $17 million. The implication of these figures was that, early in 2001, the point was passed where sufficient funding was secured to assume the viability of the new organization.

This was important in formal terms, as the Constitution approved in May 2000 consisted of two parts: one (part B) described the new organization, and one (part C) described the old IASC which continued to function until the trustees activated part B. This would then authorize the trustees to assume all of the assets and liabilities of the existing IASC, appoint members of the Board, the interpretations committee, and the advisory council, and to establish their operating procedures, among other things. The Constitution allowed the trustees to assume these powers 'as soon as they are reasonably satisfied that sufficient funding can be secured' (paragraph 16). At their December 2000 meeting, the trustees unanimously approved a proposal by Ruder that the trustees authorize Volcker to activate part B of the Constitution as soon as they are confident that the IASC can raise the required funds.[79] In October, Volcker had indicated that this would be the case when commitments for $12 million, annually, had been obtained.[80] Finally, on 19 January 2001, the finance committee reported having received sufficient funding commitments to put part B of the Constitution in force, and therefore the formal appointment of all of the Board members could proceed.[81]

---

[75] IASCF trustees meeting of 30 October 2000, minute 3.

[76] IASCF trustees meeting of 8 March 2001, agenda paper Va.

[77] IASCF trustees meeting of 15 October 2001, agenda paper 5A.

[78] IASCF trustees meeting of 8 March 2001, agenda paper Va.

[79] IASCF trustees meeting of 11 December 2000, minute 6.

[80] IASCF trustees meeting of 30 October 2000, minute 3.

[81] 'International Accounting Standards Committee, Resolution of the Trustees: Enforcement of Part B of the Constitution, 19 January 2001' (memorandum supplied by David Ruder).

Volcker himself was clearly the biggest fundraiser, even when it is allowed that the Big Five audit firms in his portfolio may not have been the hardest targets. The trustees accounting for the largest commitments, in descending order, were Volcker ($1 million from each of the Big Five audit firms, $200,000 each from Nasdaq and the New York Stock Exchange, $50,000 from the Federal Reserve Board, and $2.6 million mainly from US companies and financial institutions), Fukuma ($2.5 million from Japanese companies, mostly via Keidanren), Kopper ($2 million mainly from German companies and banks), Crockett ($900,000 from central banks, development banks, and the Bank for International Settlements), Pineau-Valencienne ($800,000 from mainly French companies), Herkströter ($700,000 from Dutch and Belgian companies and the Amsterdam Stock Exchange), and Lipworth ($700,000 from UK companies and the London Stock Exchange). Other trustees had the following fundraising responsibilities: Biggs (TIAA-CREF and help with the New York Stock Exchange), Da Costa (Brazilian enterprises), Steere (US pharmaceutical companies), Fortier (Canadian banks and the Toronto Stock Exchange), Ferrarini (Italian companies), Andersen (South African companies), and Lee (Hong Kong Stock Exchange).[82] Volcker, Kopper, and Pineau-Valencienne secured commitments from Swiss companies and banks. But both Volcker and Biggs found, to their chagrin, that most US investment institutions—the users—refused to contribute.[83] In Japan, the Tokyo Stock Exchange asked its listed companies to donate, and, in the end, the vast majority of them did.[84]

In the IASCF's 2001 *Annual Report*, the Statement of Activities displayed total contributions during the calendar years 2000 and 2001 as being £929,000 (US $1.3 million) and £12.8 million (US$18.3 million), respectively, and the list of 188 contributors consumed an entire page of the report.[85] Although the amount pledged by each contributor was not shown, the contributors were grouped by generic pledge levels. The fact that the Big Five audit firms had made commitments to give $1 million each per year was disclosed. Thirty-five contributors, composed of US, European, and Brazilian companies and financial institutions, were named as 'underwriters', which, it said, meant that they had pledged between $100,000 and $200,000 per year for five years. The 102 contributors classed as 'supporters', mostly companies and banks (one-third from Japan), gave less than $100,000 per year. The twenty-eight central banks listed on the page typically pledged no more than $10,000 to $50,000 each, but the magnitude of their contributions was not revealed in the report. In addition, there were international development banks and various associations among the listed contributors. Compared to 2001, the amount of contributions received declined somewhat over the next few years, to a low of £9.3 million in 2004, the most important single reason being the demise of Arthur Andersen. It was not until 2006 that annual contributions once again exceeded £10 million (see Appendix 3 for a eleven-year summary of income and expenses).

---

[82] IASCF trustees meeting of 15 October 2001, agenda papers 5 and 5-attachment.
[83] Interviews with Paul Volcker, 31 July 2009, and with John Biggs, 16 February 2009.
[84] Interview with Tsuguoki Fujinuma, 26 January 2011.
[85] IASCF, *Annual Report 2001*, 13, 20.

Revenues from publications were the Foundation's other major source of funding, although these were offset by the substantial cost of sales. During the Foundation's first four years, from 2001 to 2004, the revenues from the sales of publications and related revenue, after subtracting the direct cost of sales, ranged between 10 and 16 per cent of the amount received in contributions.

The remuneration of Board members and staff was by far the most important item of expense. But as the build-up of staff occurred gradually over the first few years, the Foundation was able to report significant surpluses during 2001–3, also because of favourable exchange rate movements. Hence, the decrease in contributions in 2002–4 did not amount to a significant constraint on the Board's activities.

3.11.1 Implications of Sarbanes-Oxley's Automatic Funding for the FASB

The US Senate Banking Committee hearing on 14 February 2002, from which a portion of Volcker's testimony was quoted above, was held in the aftermath of Enron's collapse on the heels of an accounting scandal. Senator Paul S. Sarbanes, the Committee chairman, pointedly raised the issue of whether the financing of both the IASB and the FASB should have 'an automatic nature'. He added, 'Some levy that may be placed on one or another of the economic transactions or economic activities that take place which would automatically engender a revenue stream, rather than rely on contributions?'[86] Sarbanes' interest in how the IASB was being financed may have been piqued by an article, 'Volcker Sought Enron Funds for Accounting Board: Memo', published that morning on the Reuters newswire. Volcker had been called earlier that day by a *Financial Times* journalist who was writing a similar story. The article reported on an email written by the Enron engagement partner at Arthur Andersen, which was released by Senator Carl Levin, saying that Volcker had called Kenneth Lay, the chairman of Enron, to solicit a $500,000 contribution. The email went on to ascribe a view to Lay that he hoped the contribution would buy influence at the IASB.[87] In the Washington climate at that time, anything relating to Enron captured the attention of Congress.

In the Sarbanes-Oxley Act of 2002, which was enacted in July, it was prescribed in Section 109 that the standard setter to be designated by the SEC under Section 108 was to be financed by an Annual Accounting Support Fee assessed against issuers. This provision was inserted in the Act by Sarbanes himself.[88] The

[86] *Accounting Reform and Investor Protection*, Hearings before the Committee on Banking, Housing, and Urban Affairs, United States Senate, 107th Congress, 2nd Session, 14 February 2002, Volume I, 115.

[87] For the Reuters article, see *The Financial Express*, 14 February 2002 <http://www.financialexpress.com/news/volcker-sought-enron-funds-for-accounting-board-memo/37689/>. Also see Michael Peel and Peter Spiegel, 'Enron Looked to Buy Influence over Accounting', *Financial Times*, 14 February 2002, and Floyd Norris, 'A Fund Plea from Volcker Aroused Hopes at Enron', *The New York Times*, 14 February 2002. Paul Volcker wrote a letter to the *FT* on its reportage: 'IASB, Funding and Enron', *Financial Times*, 25 February 2002.

[88] Communication to the authors, 30 September 2011, from Steven B. Harris, who was then a senior staff member of the Senate Banking Committee and was one of the principal draftsmen of the Act.

FASB came to be designated as the standard setter. In the light of Congress' decision to finance the FASB by an automatic fee, without the need to raise funds through contributions, the burden fell on the IASCF trustees to begin thinking about a comparable approach to raising its own funds, so as not to lose credibility in the United States. Suddenly, the model on which the trustees had originally built their fundraising strategy was no longer acceptable in the United States. The trustees recognized this, and the possibility of listing fees or similar funding mechanisms was raised with the European Commission, with the SEC, and with relevant organizations in some other countries. Securing forthcoming responses, however, proved to be difficult, and legal obstacles abounded.[89] By the time of the review of the Foundation's Constitution in 2005 the trustees could report little progress and had to reiterate their intention to deal with the matter of long-term funding (see Section 11.10). Perhaps the trustees could have tried harder, but the criticism which eventually emanated from the United States about the Foundation's dependence on voluntary contributions did not always note the lack of response with which the trustees' overtures on this point had met in the United States and elsewhere.

3.11.2 Copyright Policy

As revenues from publications were expected to become a significant source of income, the protection of the copyright on IASB publications required the trustees' vigilance, and the Foundation was occasionally involved in litigation over rights to the translations of standards. Copyright became an even more vexing issue once jurisdictions began to adopt the IASB's standards for mandatory application. The European Commission argued that, once it has endorsed a standard or interpretation, the Commission and the European Parliament would not be able to subject this legislation to the IASB's copyright protection, as they believed the standards were part of the primary and secondary legislation which should be accessible, free of charge, through publication in the *Official Journal* and, digitally, in the EU's EUR-Lex database. The Commission therefore insisted on a waiver of copyright, but only for the bare standards, omitting the basis for conclusions, any dissenting opinions, illustrative or guidance notes, and the like. The IASB was assured that publication in the *Official Journal* would not occur earlier than six months following endorsement of a standard or interpretation. At their meeting on 5 March 2002, the trustees had little choice but to accede to this arrangement.[90]

At the same meeting, the trustees adopted a policy which authorized national standard setters to publish, without copyright protection, (1) IASB consultative documents (such as discussion papers) for distribution within their jurisdictions, and (2) final IASB documents once they become part of their national standards or other official pronouncements. The IASB's logo, however, was reserved for the

---

[89] IASCF trustees meeting of 3–4 November 2003, minute 8; agenda paper 6B for this meeting.

[90] IASCF trustees meeting of 5 March 2002, minute 7; agenda paper 5F for this meeting.

IASB's own publications.[91] The IASB would be entitled to sell its own final standards and interpretations in publication packages to generate revenue as a supplement to contributions.

3.12 TRUSTEE ACTIVITY AND TURNOVER IN TRUSTEE MEMBERSHIP

The Constitution envisaged a trustee oversight model that was based on that of the FAF overseeing the FASB.[92] As with the FAF, the trustees were not to become involved in technical matters. It would seem that, as a group, the trustees understood and accepted the importance of this boundary from the beginning. In the early years in particular, with the debates on the restructuring of the IASC still fresh in many people's minds, the trustees scrupulously respected the independence of the Board, to the point of sometimes seeming remote from the perspective of the Board members. As will be seen in subsequent chapters, the growing impact of the IASB and its standards around the world led the trustees, on various occasions, to debate the exact location of the boundary that they should not overstep, and to reconsider the relationship between the trustees' oversight responsibility and the Board's responsibility for technical matters. In general, though, the trustees saw the composition of the Board through the appointment of its members and the securing of adequate funding, described above, as the core of their responsibilities. Over the years, the trustees have operated mainly on the basis of consensus, with very few issues requiring a formal vote.

The participation at the trustees' first sixteen meetings, through to June 2005, was generally quite good. Paul Volcker, Sydney Lipworth, Jens Røder, and David Ruder attended every meeting. But William Steere did not attend any of his eight meetings, and he was the first trustee to be rotated off the board. John Biggs missed seven of his fourteen meetings. At a number of the meetings, one or two of the trustees participated by telephone.

Ken Spencer missed only the two meetings held before his death at age 66 on 31 March 2004, following a short illness. Of the trustees, he had the deepest knowledge of the travails of the old IASC, and he was dedicated to the mission of the IASB. His death was a great loss to the Foundation. David Tweedie flew to Melbourne to speak at his funeral. Philip Laskawy succeeded Spencer as chairman of the nominating committee as part of his long period of leadership service on the trustees.

The initial terms of the trustees were staggered so that they served for one and a half, two and a half, or three and a half year terms, all beginning in May 2000 and ending on 31 December 2002, 2003, or 2004 (see Appendix 1 for a full list of the trustees and their terms). The trustees agreed to the procedure for appointing successor trustees which was set out in a memo from Paul Volcker in June 2002, as follows: The outgoing trustee would nominate one or more potential replacement candidates. The trustees would then consult the appropriate organizations and

---

[91] IASCF trustees meeting of 5 March 2002, agenda paper 3, paragraphs 9–12; minute 5 of that meeting.
[92] IASCF trustees meeting of 28 June 2000, minute 1.

associations in the home country or region of the outgoing trustee and would seek support for nominations. Once the trustees as a whole received the list of candidates, they were at liberty to comment on the proposed names and consult with interested parties prior to agreeing the appointment. In addition, the trustees advertised the position in *The Economist* and on the IASB website, and informed SAC and liaison national standard setters of the opening.[93] Normally, trustees would be limited to two terms. The trustee nominating committee coordinated the selection process.

Ten of the trustees, including all four who were current or former regulators or overseers of securities markets, renewed their terms for a further three years. Eight stepped down at or before the end of one term: John Biggs, Andrew Crockett, Guido Ferrarini, Toshikatsu Fukuma, Hilmar Kopper, Didier Pineau-Valencienne, William Steere, and Koji Tajika. As mentioned above, Ken Spencer died in March 2004.

The two retiring Japanese trustees, Fukuma and Tajika, were succeeded by Toro Hashimoto, former chairman of Fuji Bank, and Tsuguoki (Aki) Fujinuma, the chairman and president of the Japanese Institute of Certified Public Accountants. Fujinuma went on to serve three terms, concluding his long service in December 2013. Biggs, from the United States, was succeeded by Antonio Vegezzi, the president and director of Capital International SA, the Swiss subsidiary of the Capital Group, one of the largest global asset managers. During his service as a trustee, Vegezzi took the lead in strengthening the trustees' oversight of the Board's due process. Crockett was succeeded by Malcolm D. Knight, who had succeeded Crockett as general manager of the Bank for International Settlements. Knight, who had formerly been senior deputy governor of the Bank of Canada, was to serve two terms, until December 2007. Ferrarini, the Italian law academic, was succeeded by Oscar Fanjul, of Spain, vice chairman of Omega Capital and the former founder chairman and chief executive of Repsol. Kopper, from Germany, was succeeded by Max Dietrich Kley, deputy chairman of the management board of BASF. Pineau-Valencienne, from France, was succeeded by Bertrand Collomb, the chairman of Lafarge as well as chairman of the Association Française des Entreprises Privées (French Association of Private Enterprise). Collomb went on to become vice chairman in January 2006 and a very influential chairman of the trustees' nominating committee. Steere, from the United States, was succeeded by Sir Dennis Weatherstone, the British-born former chairman of J.P. Morgan & Co., in New York City. Spencer, from Australia, was succeeded by Richard G. Humphry, the chief executive of the Australian Stock Exchange who had been one of the drivers for the adoption of IASs in Australia since the middle of the 1990s.

One activity which the trustees sanctioned was taking responsibility for developing an XBRL taxonomy for IFRSs. This was done at the initiative of Kurt Ramin, the Foundation's commercial director. The trustees believed that, if they did not oversee its development, no one would do it properly. Over the years, the Foundation employed a small staff to deal with XBRL, but we will not cover this development in our book, because it was not integrated with the work of the Board.[94]

---

[93] IASCF trustees meeting of 19 November 2002, agenda papers 4 and 4B.
[94] See 'Building an IAS/IFRS Taxonomy Using XBRL', *IASB Insight*, October 2002, 17–22.

4

The First Wave of Jurisdictional Adoptions of IFRSs

When the IASC was restructured, eventually to become the IASB, the new body was conceived as a standard setter among national standard setters. It was hoped that the IASB would become the first among equals, the centre of a circle of national standard setters, but it would have to establish such a position by means of coordination, collaboration, and the quality of its ideas. It possessed no legal authority to compel companies in any country to adopt its standards. As David Tweedie put it in March 2001:

> As IASB cannot insist on the same standard being promulgated throughout the world, the objective of a single set of high-quality global standards will be achieved only if all standard-setters accept that goal and are willing to make every effort to achieve it. IASB's role, in co-operation with the national standard setters, is to lead the process by facilitating a world-wide partnership. Ideally, IASB should be the crucible in which ideas from different parts of the world are put to the test and the best idea selected.[1]

It soon transpired, however, that the 'world-wide partnership' was a complex patchwork of countries, or rather jurisdictions in the more precise language usually employed by the IASB, and they reacted very differently and at different speeds to the prospect of a global set of accounting standards held out by the IASB. Some countries enthusiastically embraced IFRSs and made the IASB their de facto or de jure standard setter. Others embarked on various forms of convergence, often without committing to full adoption. And some took an attitude of wait and see.

This chapter reviews the responses evoked around the world by the IASB during its first years, until about 2004. The chapter starts with the European Union (EU), whose decision to require the use of IFRSs by listed companies starting in 2005 instantly ensured the IASB a clientele and thus a degree of impact on accounting practice far beyond anything ever achieved by the IASC. The chapter continues with a review of moves towards IFRSs in other countries, for several of which the EU's decision was an important stimulus. Two major economies, however, the United States and Japan, were not about to adopt IFRSs anytime soon, and their initial relations with the IASB are discussed next. The chapter concludes with a review of the IASB's early outreach activities, before returning to the IASB's relations with national standard setters.

---

[1] David Tweedie, 'Convergence Is the Aim', *IASB Insight*, March 2001, 1.

4.1 THE EU'S ADOPTION OF INTERNATIONAL ACCOUNTING STANDARDS

The idea of placing the IASC's standards at the centre of the EU's policy for financial reporting regulation was already articulated in the 1990s.[2] A consensus gradually developed that the EU's approach to accounting regulation needed to be revised. The EU had traditionally approached accounting regulation from the angle of company law harmonization, and it had issued directives addressed at member states, requiring that they be incorporated in national law and made applicable to all companies. By 1995, it was widely felt that this procedure was inadequate to deal with the more sophisticated reporting practices of listed companies. These required more highly developed accounting standards which could be modified with greater flexibility. Alternative policies were explored under the guidance of Karel Van Hulle, the head of the Accounting Unit in the Internal Market Directorate, and for many years the interface between the European Commission and the IASC. One option, the creation of a European accounting standard setter, lacked political support among the member states. For some years it looked as if another option, the use of US generally accepted accounting principles (US GAAP) by the most internationally oriented enterprises, might be adopted by default. An increasing number of European companies took listings in the United States and began to report under, or reconcile to, US GAAP. This option, and the implied cession of authority over accounting standards to the United States, was not politically acceptable either. This left the IASC's standards as the only viable alternative. Moreover, the IASC's standards were often seen to have an advantage over US GAAP in that they were not as voluminous and were less based on detailed rules and implementation guidance.[3] Opinions might differ whether this was by design or because the IASC simply had not had the time and resources to develop standards that were as rigorous as US GAAP, but the difference was notable and before long would be expressed more sharply in terms of a contrast between 'principles-based' and 'rules-based' standards.

4.1.1 The Financial Services Action Plan

In the late 1990s, the tentative view that the EU should move towards the IASC's standards was swept up in a much broader regulatory initiative to create a European capital market, an initiative that, in turn, became caught up in fundamental debates about the governance of the EU. In order to understand the IASB's subsequent, and sometimes tempestuous, relationship with the various EU institutions, it is necessary to briefly review this wider background.[4]

---

[2] As discussed in Chapter 2. See also Kees Camfferman and Stephen A. Zeff, *Financial Reporting and Global Capital Markets: A History of the International Accounting Standards Committee, 1973–2000* (Oxford: Oxford University Press, 2007), 418–31.

[3] 'EU Financial Reporting Strategy: The Way Forward', COM(2000) 359, 13 June 2000, paragraph 15.

[4] On these developments, see John F. Mogg, 'Regulating Financial Services in Europe: A New Approach', *Fordham International Law Journal*, 26/1 (2002), 58–82, and Karel Van Hulle, 'From Accounting Directives to International Accounting Standards', in Christian Leuz, Dieter Pfaff, and

In 1998, the European Commission outlined its views on the creation of a single European market for financial services, and in 1999 it followed up with a document that became known as the Financial Services Action Plan.[5] The Action Plan listed more than forty regulatory actions in areas ranging from takeover bids to the prudential supervision of pension funds. One of the actions to be taken was to develop a financial reporting strategy for the EU to allow companies that wished to raise capital on international markets, both within and outside the EU, to prepare financial statements on the basis of a single set of internationally accepted reporting standards.

At their Lisbon summit of March 2000, the EU leaders decided to push this agenda forward. They adopted the ambitious objective of making Europe 'the most competitive and dynamic knowledge-based economy in the world', and called for implementation of the entire Action Plan by 2005. Dealing with such a massive legislative agenda in such a short period of time posed a huge challenge to the EU's decision-making procedures.

In principle, legislation on issues relating to the EU's internal market had to be passed jointly by the European Council and the European Parliament, at the initiative of the European Commission. As long ago as the 1960s, it had been recognized that this cumbersome procedure was not appropriate to deal with relatively minor and technical issues, and procedures were developed to delegate implementing authority to the European Commission. As these procedures typically involved that the Commission would exercise its authority with the advice of expert committees of member state representatives, they were known by the collective name of 'comitology'.[6] In 1987, standardized comitology procedures were established, which were revised in 1999. The European Parliament, whose powers and status continued to increase during the 1990s, followed the spreading use of comitology with some misgivings. The Financial Services Action Plan brought these concerns to the fore, because it would require a substantial further transfer of implementing authority to the Commission.

In July 2000, the European Council charged a 'committee of wise men', chaired by Alexandre Lamfalussy, with the task of developing a regulatory strategy to implement the Action Plan. In February 2001, the committee produced its report which outlined a way of using the existing comitology procedures in the area of securities markets, a priority area in the Action Plan.[7] The so-called 'Lamfalussy process' was subsequently used in banking and insurance as well. To take the case of securities regulation as an example, the Lamfalussy process envisaged a comitology procedure in which the Commission would adopt implementing measures

---

Anthony Hopwood (editors), *The Economics and Politics of Accounting: International Perspectives on Research Trends, Policy, and Practice* (Oxford: Oxford University Press, 2005), 349–75.

[5] Communications of the European Commission, 'Financial Services: Building a Framework for Action', 28 October 1998, and 'Financial Services: Implementing the Framework for Financial Markets: Action Plan', COM (1999) 232, 11 May 1999.

[6] On comitology, see Gregor Schusterschitz and Sabine Kotz, 'The Comitology Reform of 2006: Increasing the Powers of the European Parliament Without Changing the Treaties', *European Constitutional Law Review*, 3 (2007), 68–90.

[7] *Final Report of the Committee of Wise Men on the Regulation of European Securities Markets*, Brussels, 15 February 2001.

in cooperation with two other specialized bodies. The first was a 'comitology' committee in the strict sense of the word, consisting of member state representatives. The committee, the European Securities Commission, would in effect exercise the powers of the Council and the Parliament. The second committee was a technical committee, formed by the national securities regulators, which became known as the Committee of European Securities Regulators (CESR), and which would provide most of the input for the regulatory process.

These proposals could be implemented only after a year of negotiations between the Commission and the Parliament, necessary to allay the Parliament's concern to maintain a degree of control over financial services legislation. It took a solemn declaration by Commission President Romano Prodi on 5 February 2002 that the Commission would respect the Parliament's current rights and seek to enhance these rights in future treaty revisions, before the implementation of the Financial Services Action Plan could proceed.

4.1.2 The IAS Regulation

The debates over the Financial Services Action Plan formed the institutional background against which the proposal to make the IASB's standards mandatory for European companies was implemented in EU legislation.

It was obvious to all concerned that it was formally necessary to incorporate International Accounting Standards into EU law. The way to do this was already outlined in the Commission's June 2000 proposal, and elaborated in a draft regulation submitted to the Parliament in February 2001.[8] This was shortly before the IASB's first meeting at which it decided to use the name International Financial Reporting Standards (IFRSs) for new standards, as opposed to the International Accounting Standards (IASs) issued by the IASC (see Section 5.1). Soon, the entire body of standards became known as IFRSs, yet the regulation has always been known as the IAS Regulation. From this point onward we refer to the standards to which the IAS Regulation applies as IFRSs. The essence of the IAS Regulation was that IFRSs, if and when endorsed for use in the EU on a standard-by-standard basis, would apply directly to the consolidated financial statements of listed companies, that is, without incorporation in national company law or accounting standards. Parent company financial statements remained within the domain of company law and the accounting directives, but member states could elect to allow or require the use of IFRSs in this context as well, as well as in the financial statements of unlisted companies.

A 'comitology' approach was proposed by which each standard issued by the IASB would be formally adopted by the European Commission, supported by two committees. The Commission would propose the endorsement to an Accounting Regulatory Committee (ARC) of member state representatives, supported by expert advice from a private-sector technical committee. The European

---

[8] For the draft Regulation, see COM(2001) 80, 13 February 2001. For a more extensive discussion of the contents of the enacted Regulation EC 1606/2002 of 19 July 2002, see Alexander Schaub, 'The Use of International Accounting Standards in the European Union', *Northwestern Journal of International Law & Business*, 25 (Spring 2005), 609–29.

Parliament would have a limited right to object to a proposed standard, but only on the ground that the Commission was acting ultra vires, and the Council of Ministers would have the power to ignore such an objection. So far, the process was not unlike many other uses of the comitology approach. What was altogether new was that the accounting standards to be adopted would be developed entirely outside the sphere of influence of the EU institutions, at the initiative of an independent private-sector body in London. In this way, an existing legislative procedure was transformed into an endorsement process.

This required a delicate balancing act. On the one hand, users of the accounting standards concerned with global harmonization of financial reporting would have to be assured that, for all practical purposes, all standards issued by the IASB would be endorsed without delay, and that there would be no 'European' version of the standards. On the other hand, given the background of institutional tension over the implementation of financial services legislation, any suggestion of mere rubber stamping had to be avoided.

The Lamfalussy committee did not concern itself with financial reporting, and Karel Van Hulle, the principal draftsman of the IAS Regulation, was always careful to emphasize that it was *sui generis*, and not a part of the Lamfalussy proposals. Yet it was easy to associate the IAS Regulation with the entire package of financial services legislation, and to note some similarities in the proposed use of comitology.[9] Hence, the IAS Regulation was not adopted until after the more general procedural agreement on financial services reform had been reached between the Commission and the Parliament. The Parliament was also careful to ensure that the recitals to the IAS Regulation included a reference to Prodi's February 2002 declaration to the European Parliament (recital 8), thus marking out this topic for inclusion in the future extension of the Parliament's legislative powers. The Parliament also successfully argued for the inclusion of more explicit criteria by which the applicability of IFRSs should be decided, such as that they be 'conducive to the European public good' (article 3.2). As a clarification of what this might mean, the Parliament introduced a clause in the preamble of the Regulation, instructing the European Commission to 'take into account the importance of avoiding competitive disadvantages for European companies operating in the global market place' (recital 15).[10] These words seemed to echo the argument made around the same time by certain European companies that the IASB's work on the expensing of share-based payment or the treatment of goodwill should not disadvantage them with respect to their American competitors (see Sections 5.4.3 and 5.4.4). The endorsement criteria were presented as a 'real safeguard against the arbitrary endorsing' of IFRSs.[11]

Apart from the institutional tensions, there were practical problems to be resolved. Contrary to the Commission's proposal, the European Parliament

[9] Interview with Karel Van Hulle, 20 January 2009. For the view that the IAS Regulation was seen as a 'parallel' to the Lamfalussy process, see Schaub, 'The Use of International Accounting Standards', 621.

[10] European Parliament, Committee on Legal Affairs and the Internal Market, 'Report on the Proposal for a European Parliament and Council Regulation on the Implementation of International Accounting Standards', A5-0070/2002, 28 February 2002.

[11] Schaub, 'The Use of International Accounting Standards', 617–18, where Schaub also interprets the 'public good' clause in terms of the avoidance of competitive disadvantage.

insisted that, as formal legislation, the whole body of IFRSs had to be translated into all of the EU's official languages, of which there were twelve at the time, but the number of which was soon to grow to twenty with the accession of ten new member states in Eastern and Southern Europe. This required a massive translation effort. Translations of IFRSs were already available in some languages but not necessarily based on the most recent versions of the standards. The European Commission set up a complex organization in which the translation work was shared among the IASB, the Commission's translation services, and the member states. At the same time, the Commission negotiated an agreement with the IASB over the copyright of the standards and the translations, all of which had to be published in the EU's *Official Journal*.

Another complication was the legacy of a sizeable number of large European companies, particularly from Germany, that had adopted US GAAP as their primary reporting standard during the 1990s, and which were reluctant to switch to IFRSs as long as the US Securities and Exchange Commission (SEC) retained its requirement to reconcile to US GAAP. For these companies, the mandatory transition date to IFRSs was delayed from 2005 to 2007. Although at the time there could not have been more than a hope that the reconciliation requirement would be lifted as early as 2007, it was in fact lifted in November 2007, as discussed more fully in Chapter 8.

4.1.3 The Launch of the Endorsement Mechanism and the Creation of EFRAG

Despite the various institutional and technical difficulties, the mood at the time was mainly optimistic. Following the Enron scandal of 2001, it became a commonplace that US GAAP was deficient because of its rules-based approach, while IFRSs had the virtue of being principles-based. Consequently, there was a feeling that the EU was moving out from under the shadow of the United States with respect to the quality of its accounting standards. On the eve of the adoption of the IAS Regulation in June 2002, the responsible Commissioner holding the Internal Market portfolio, Frits Bolkestein, observed: 'IAS are the best standards that exist. . . . they are part of making sure Enron cannot happen here'.[12]

The extent to which the Commission, and the European Parliament, were able to judge the quality of IFRSs is an interesting question. David Tweedie remarked on several occasions that Europe took the step to adopt IFRSs 'with great courage and in total ignorance'.[13] There is no doubt that the Commission staff, and in particular Karel Van Hulle, had a clear knowledge of the contents and history of the IASC's standards, having attended IASC meetings as an observer throughout the 1990s. As a member of the IASB's Standards Advisory Council, he also was informed about the IASB's plans for the further development of the standards, and he was actively supported with technical expertise by Allister Wilson, of Ernst

---

[12] Speech by Frits Bolkestein, 'The Financial Services Action Plan', 3 June 2002, SPEECH/02/49 <http://europa.eu/rapid>.

[13] See, e.g. 'Fair Cop; Accounting: Fair-value Accounting Becomes a Political Issue', *The Economist*, US edition, 4 October 2008.

& Young, who acted as Van Hulle's advisor. But how far this knowledge was spread, and to what extent participants in the decision over the IAS Regulation relied on Van Hulle's knowledge and unquestioned authority, is another matter. There was awareness that the banking and insurance industry had concerns over fair value accounting, but this issue was essentially deferred for future resolution.[14]

The main emphasis in designing the European endorsement mechanism was certainly not on the possibility that IFRSs might not be endorsed, but on a pro-active involvement in the IASB's standard-setting process that would ensure that IFRSs would remain appropriate for Europe.[15] This was made clear when the 'technical level' of the endorsement mechanism was set up in the form of the European Financial Reporting Advisory Group, EFRAG. At the invitation of the European Commission, the Fédération des Experts Comptables Européens (FEE) took the lead, together with the employers' federation UNICE, in bringing to-gether a group of European-wide industry associations to sponsor the creation of a private-sector advisory committee. In a March 2001 agreement (also known as 'joint proposals') among these 'founding fathers', most attention was given to EFRAG's expected pro-active role in providing early advice to the IASB on views in Europe relating to ongoing technical projects.[16] For FEE, the creation of EFRAG was a natural outgrowth of its earlier attempts, during the 1990s, to create a platform for the 'European voice' in the deliberations of the IASC.[17]

The formal role of EFRAG in the endorsement procedure was designed to minimize the chances of negative endorsement advice. This was desirable from the point of view of EFRAG's sponsors from the business community which were strongly in favour of a European adoption of the IASB's standards and did not wish to see the policy diluted by selective endorsements. Negative advice by EFRAG would be tantamount to non-endorsement, because the Commission was unlikely to proceed with the proposal in such a case. As with all EU legislation, the Commission had the sole right of initiative, and the IAS Regulation allowed but did not require it to propose new IFRSs for endorsement. The Commission would put the endorsement on hold rather than making itself vulnerable to a challenge from member states or the Parliament that it ignored the view of its main technical advisor.

The March 2001 'joint proposals' stated that 'Rejection of IAS should be exceptional and should be contemplated only as a last resort' (paragraph 11), and stopped just short of stating that the endorsement of the existing body of

---

[14] See the report of the EU's Social and Economic Committee (an advisory body to the Council), 11 July 2001, 2001/C 260/15, O.J. 17.9.2001, paragraph 3.15. The combined report of the European Parliament's Economic and Monetary Affairs and Legal Affairs Committees did not attempt an evaluation of the quality of the standards. See European Parliament, Session Document A5-0070/2002, 28 February 2002.

[15] Report of the European Parliament's Economic and Monetary Affairs Committee, Session Document A5-0070/2002, 28 February 2002, 24.

[16] 'Expert Level of the Endorsement Mechanism—The Establishment of the "European Financial Reporting Advisory Group" (EFRAG)', March 2001 <http://www.iasplus.com>.

[17] Interview with Saskia Slomp, 19 January 2009. See also the discussion of a 'European mechanism' in FEE's 'Discussion Paper on a Financial Reporting Strategy within Europe', 8 October 1999, and Camfferman and Zeff, *Financial Reporting and Global Capital Markets*, 445–6.

standards should be a foregone conclusion (paragraph 18). When EFRAG was set up in June 2001, its voting arrangements were deliberately skewed by requiring a qualified majority to give a *negative* opinion. The actual advice was to be given by an eleven-member part-time Technical Expert Group, initially chaired by Johan van Helleman, a former member of the Dutch IASC delegation. EFRAG began working with a small staff from a Brussels office in the second half of 2001. In June 2002, just before the formal enactment of the IAS Regulation, it set the endorsement mechanism in motion by issuing its positive endorsement advice on the complete body of extant standards. Yet, as discussed more fully in Chapter 6, the process began to falter almost immediately afterwards when the political level, represented by the European Commission and the ARC, failed to complete the endorsement procedure with respect to the financial instruments standards. The IASB's extant standards were endorsed in time for application in the EU starting on 1 January 2005, but with two so-called carve-outs from IAS 39 *Financial Instruments: Recognition and Measurement.*

4.1.4 Completing the Regulatory Arrangements

As the pioneer of large-scale IFRS adoption, the EU also had to discover what supporting or consequential regulatory measures were required for the proper functioning of the IAS Regulation.

In November 2003, shortly after completing the endorsement of the original IASC standards (except for IAS 32 and IAS 39), the European Commission issued a document of 'comments' on the IAS Regulation, intended as 'authoritative clarification' on selected topics that apparently had given rise to questions.[18] Many of these concerned the complex relationships between the IAS Regulation, the EU's accounting directives, and national accounting legislation. For instance, there was a chicken-and-egg problem that the IAS Regulation required application of IFRSs to consolidated financial statements, but that IFRSs itself contained requirements on whether a company should prepare consolidated financial statements at all. The comments clarified that the determination of whether a company should prepare consolidated financial statements continued to be a matter of company law, but that the scope of consolidation would then be determined by IFRSs.

Another topic addressed in the Commission's November 2003 document was the status, under EU law, of the IASB's conceptual framework, non-mandatory implementation guidance, bases for conclusions, and other appendices which are not part of the standards. None of these fell within the scope of the IAS Regulation and would therefore not be formally endorsed. Nonetheless, companies applying the standards would on occasion be referred to the framework, particularly when choosing accounting policies for issues not covered in IFRSs. Also, each endorsed

---

[18] 'Comments Concerning Certain Articles of the Regulation (EC) No 1606/2002 of the European Parliament and of the Council of 19 July 2002 on the Application of International Accounting Standards and the Fourth Council Directive 78/660/EEC of 25 July 1978 and the Seventh Council Directive 83/349/EEC of 13 June 1983 on accounting', European Commission, November 2003 <http://ec.europa.eu/internal_market/accounting>.

standard included the usual introductory paragraph that it 'should be read in the context of the background material and implementation guidance'. By a simple reminder of these facts, the Commission document attempted to signal that these texts, while not part of the law, could nonetheless not be ignored. In an appendix, the document included the full text of the conceptual framework, so that this at least (but not all the appendices and implementation guidance) would have some recognition in the EU legal literature and would be translated into all the official languages.

The Commission's document also touched upon on the question of how the financial statements should describe the accounting policies applied. Subsequently, this would become a somewhat controversial issue with respect to the wording of the auditor's report when the EU carve-outs created differences between IFRSs, as issued by the IASB, and IFRSs, as endorsed in the EU. As discussed in Chapter 10, the emergence of jurisdictional variations of IFRSs posed a threat to the IASB's mission of establishing global standards. However, in November 2003 these developments were still in the future, and while the Commission suggested a description of accounting policies in terms of IFRSs 'as adopted for use in the European Union', it believed a simple reference to IFRSs was in order when the accounting standards applied were not different from those issued by the IASB.

Parallel to the introduction of IFRSs, the member states of the EU engaged in a major operation to set up national enforcement mechanisms, to be in place by 1 January 2005, so as to ensure the consistent application of IFRSs across the EU.[19] In most member states, prior to 2000, the auditor was looked to as the main, if not the only, source of assurance of compliance with accounting law or standards. However, during the 1990s a trend was discernible to set up more robust securities regulators, some of which also began to take up responsibilities related to financial reporting. This movement gained focus with the Financial Services Action Plan and the 'Lamfalussy' process described above, when CESR was created in 2001. Apart from all other responsibilities entrusted to CESR and its heterogeneous member bodies under the Action Plan, the IAS Regulation (recital 16) called for 'a proper and rigorous enforcement regime', and looked to CESR for developing a common approach to enforcement. Before being transformed into the European Securities and Markets Authority (ESMA) in 2011, in the wake of the financial crisis, CESR played a major coordinating role in developing the common principles of IFRS enforcement and in the exchange of information among regulators on the application and interpretation of IFRSs in Europe. While the details of that story are beyond the scope of this book, it is important to note that, for Europe at least, the transition to IFRSs, which for many was a culture shock and an intense learning process, coincided with an equally demanding process of learning to exercise active regulatory oversight of financial reporting, and of learning to live with such oversight.

A final consequence of the IAS Regulation that may be noted here is that it brought up the question of the accounting standards to be applied by non-EU

---

[19] See Philip Brown and Ann Tarca, 'A Commentary on Issues Relating to the Enforcement of International Financial Reporting Standards in the EU', *European Accounting Review*, 14/1 (2005), 181–212.

companies listing securities in EU markets. Previously, this matter had been left to the member states, but the creation of a single European capital market would seem to require a common answer. The Financial Services Action Plan had recognized this point, and in June 2004 the European Commission embarked on a process of assessing the equivalence of third-country accounting standards with IFRSs, in order to determine whether these standards would continue to be accepted as a basis for reporting in the EU. This equivalence assessment process is discussed more fully in Chapter 9. Its significance was that the EU, a major jurisdiction, assumed the authority to pronounce on what was, or was not, equivalent to IFRSs. The question of what constituted a global accounting standard was not therefore to be answered by the IASB alone. As seen in Sections 4.6.4 and 10.4, the equivalence assessment was followed with particular interest in Japan.

4.2 EARLY ADOPTERS: HONG KONG AND SOUTH AFRICA

While the EU's decision to adopt IFRSs was of signal importance, some other jurisdictions were already engaged in a serious process of harmonization with IASs before 2000. The most notable of these were Hong Kong and South Africa.

Jardine Matheson Holdings, a landmark of the Hong Kong economy, adopted IASs as the basis for its financial reporting in 1990, setting off a debate on the future of Hong Kong Statements of Standard Accounting Practice.[20] Until then, the Hong Kong standards had been based on UK standards, but it was gradually recognized that this orientation should be changed. One reason was the impending handover of sovereignty over Hong Kong in 1997. Another was the growing international recognition of the IASC's standards. In 1994, the Hong Kong Society of Accountants adopted a strategy of harmonization with IASs. In July 2001, the Society (which became the Hong Kong Institute of Certified Public Accountants in September 2004 in another step to de-emphasize the former UK orientation) took a further step by adopting a strategy of convergence with IASs. By that time, Hong Kong Statements of Standard Accounting Practice were said to be 'similar, but not identical' to IASs, but for the standing of Hong Kong as an international financial centre it was believed to be essential to adopt international standards, both in accounting and in auditing.[21] The aim was to issue Hong Kong Accounting Standards and Hong Kong Financial Reporting Standards that were word-for-word identical to the corresponding IASs and IFRSs.[22] The most important problem that was foreseen was the treatment of leased property under IASs. Virtually all property in Hong Kong was held under leases, including investment properties, but the implication of adopting IFRSs as they were at the time would be that much of this could not be capitalized as assets on the balance sheet. But before Hong Kong saw itself obliged to adopt a divergent standard, the IASB

---

[20] Winnie C.W. Cheung, 'A Positive Look at Hong Kong Accounting Standards', *The Hong Kong Accountant*, May/June 1991, 25.

[21] 'HKSA Standard Setting Strategy', *The Hong Kong Accountant*, May 2002, 4.

[22] Interview with Winnie Cheung, 28 March 2011.

adjusted its standards in 2003 (see Section 5.4.1), so that by 2005 Hong Kong Financial Reporting Standards had become virtually 100 per cent identical to IFRSs.

South Africa had been aggressively harmonizing its standards with IASs since 1993. Its Accounting Practices Board aligned existing standards with IASs and adopted new IASs as they were issued. In principle, it had the ability to make adjustments as IASs were converted into local standards, but by 2001 differences between the two sets of standards had all but disappeared.[23] As a result, South African companies were among the first in the world to grapple with the South African equivalent of the financial instruments standard IAS 39. Initially, it had been planned to copy the effective date of IAS 39, which had been set by the IASC at 1 January 2001. This proved too much for the South African banking industry and other affected companies, and IAS 39 was adopted with a delay of eighteen months. Even so, it gave South African companies a head start in coping with the more complex aspects of IFRSs. Only a limited number of European companies applied IFRSs, and thus IAS 39, on a voluntary basis before 2005, and the effective date of the Hong Kong equivalent, HKAS 39, had been set at 1 January 2005.

In May 2003, the JSE Securities Exchange amended its listing rules to require, rather than allow, the use of IFRSs as of 1 January 2005. Because of the preceding convergence of South African standards with IFRSs, the transition to IFRSs in 2005 was 'pretty much a non-event'.[24]

4.3 FOLLOWING THE EU: AUSTRALIA AND NEW ZEALAND

Neither South Africa nor Hong Kong had a strong national accounting tradition or a set of accounting standards that was clearly indigenous. Australia and New Zealand had strong reputations in accounting standard setting which, coupled with their status as developed economies, made their adoption of IFRSs highly significant. From the perspective of all four, the designation of the IASB as 'Europe's standard setter' or IFRSs as 'European accounting standards', which could sometimes be heard during the IASB's years, was clearly inappropriate.

In 2002, Australia, a country whose accounting profession and standard setter had long been playing a major world role, committed to the adoption of IFRSs in a 'big bang'. Its Financial Reporting Council (FRC), a statutory body within the federal government which oversees the Australian Accounting Standards Board (AASB), a government agency, announced, with striking suddenness, a strategic directive on 3 July 2002 to require companies to convert from Australian GAAP to

---

[23] Following the adoption of the IASC's last standard, IAS 41.The April 2003 'Report on Observance of Standards and Codes (ROSC): South Africa' published by the World Bank refers (paragraph 33) to 'minor inconsistencies' between South African GAAP and IFRSs.

[24] Interview with Darrel Scott, 12 March 2013. See also Iain Edwards, Peter Schelluch, Adel Du Plessis, Jean Struweg, and Andrew West, 'Globalisation and Accounting Reforms in an Emerging Market Economy: A Case Study of South Africa', in Jayne M. Godfrey and Keryn Chalmers (editors), *Globalisation of Accounting Standards* (Cheltenham, UK: Edward Elgar, 2007), 277.

full adoption of IFRSs by 1 January 2005.[25] The FRC's decision met with some controversy, and the FRC did not even inform the AASB of its decision prior to making the announcement.[26] The AASB had been, for several years, pursuing a programme of harmonizing with IASs/IFRSs.[27] Ruth Picker, who was an AASB member from 2000 to 2005, has written, 'The reaction of AASB members to the FRC's strategic directive was one of shock'.[28] The decision was precipitated by the EU's adoption in June 2002 of its IAS Regulation. The FRC chairman, Jeffrey Lucy, said in a media release: 'Australia certainly cannot afford to lag Europe in this regard.'[29] The new directive would apply to all reporting entities, including the not-for-profit sector, not just listed companies. This reflected Australia's traditional policy of having a single body setting 'sector-neutral' accounting standards applicable to all entities, unlike many other countries where not-for-profit standards are set in a separate process. During the decade, responses from Australia to technical projects undertaken by the IASB would often be coloured by concerns over the implications for the not-for-profit sector.

The adoption of IFRSs in Australia took the form of approval, by the AASB, of 'Australian equivalents to IFRSs'. When, in July 2004, the AASB approved the IASB's extant standards, it deleted a number of options that had not been available under Australian accounting standards, it added some disclosures that had been required under Australian accounting standards, and it provided some Australian guidance. The AASB believed that these modifications would 'provide a sound basis' for the transition from the previous Australian standards the following year. For example, it deleted the 'indirect method' option in IAS 7 *Cash Flow Statements* because the previous Australian standard required the 'direct method'. It also deleted the option to use proportionate consolidation when accounting for joint ventures. It added a requirement to disclose auditor remuneration in the Australian equivalent of IAS 1 *Presentation of Financial Statements* because the disclosure had been required in the previous Australian standard. After the Big Four audit firms pressed the view that Australia should require companies to use 'pure' IFRSs, these deletions, most of the disclosures, and the guidance were removed from the equivalents in 2007. Warren McGregor, the IASB Board member who served as the liaison to Australia and New Zealand, and others also urged the AASB to adopt IFRSs as issued by the IASB. One of the arguments made for restoring the deleted options was that the overseas parents or subsidiaries of

[25] For a news report, see Tom Ravlic, 'Australia to Use International Accounting Standards in 2005', *The Age*, 4 July 2002, Business 3.

[26] See Stephen Haswell and Jill McKinnon, 'IASB Standards for Australia by 2005: Catapult or Trojan Horse?' *Australian Accounting Review*, 13/1 (March 2003), 8–16; and Bryan Howieson and Ian Langfield-Smith, 'The FRC and Accounting Standard-setting: Should I Still Call Australia Home?', *Australian Accounting Review*, 13/1 (March 2003), 17–26.

[27] See Keith Alfredson, 'Pathway to 2005 IASB Standards', *Australian Accounting Review*, 13/1 (March 2003), 3–7.

[28] Ruth Picker, 'Too Special to Go Global? Too Small to Be Special? An Insight into Australia's Decision to Adopt IFRS and the Consequences for Its Own Standard Setting and Application', in Jayne M. Godfrey and Keryn Chalmers (editors), *Globalisation of Accounting Standards* (Cheltenham, UK: Edward Elgar, 2007), 100.

[29] See 'Adoption of International Accounting Standards by 2005', Bulletin of the Financial Reporting Council 2002/4, 3 July 2002 <http://www.frc.gov.au>.

Australian companies might use these very options in their own financial statements.[30]

New Zealand, because of the closeness of its economy to that of Australia, had little option but to follow the Australian example. In December 2002, New Zealand's Accounting Standards Review Board, a Crown entity, following extensive consultations, announced that all reporting entities, again including the not-for-profit sector, would be required to adopt IFRSs by 1 January 2007, with an option to adopt IFRSs as early as 1 January 2005.[31] As in Australia, the formal approach was to issue 'New Zealand equivalents to IFRSs'. In November 2004, New Zealand's standard setter, again with an eye to Australia, proposed to delete the 'indirect method' from its equivalent of IAS 7, because its previous standard, FRS-10, did not allow it. The standard setter also proposed to add disclosures that were previously required by New Zealand accounting standards. These proposals came to the attention of the IASB. Tony van Zijl, the chairman of New Zealand's Financial Reporting Standards Board, had enquired of David Tweedie in May 2003 whether, if his board were to delete the 'indirect method' option from IAS 7 and perhaps add some disclosures, entities would still be able to claim compliance with IFRSs. Tweedie replied that the IASB's strategy committee had discussed this matter and had agreed that, 'If a jurisdiction chose to add to the disclosure requirements of IFRSs, or to remove options in IFRSs, then, provided no other changes were made, companies complying with locally modified standards could hold out their financial statements as being in conformity with IFRSs'.[32] This was an interesting adaptation by the IASB to accommodate New Zealand. And it enabled the IASB's leadership to affirm publicly that Australia and New Zealand were en route to fully adopting IFRSs. New Zealand thereupon adopted these deviations.[33] But after Australia had restored its deleted options and removed most of its additional disclosures and guidance, New Zealand moved, in April 2011, to harmonize with Australia by conforming its standards with pure IFRSs.[34]

The matter of the wording of the auditor's opinion also surfaced in Australia and New Zealand, as it did in the EU. In 2005, when Australian companies began complying with the Australian equivalents to IFRSs, and when some New Zealand companies early-adopted New Zealand equivalents to IFRSs, the auditors gave a single opinion, as required by law: the financial statements complied with Australian (or New Zealand) Accounting Standards. But this affirmation did not

---

[30] Interviews with Warren McGregor, 18 and 19 May 2011, and with Angus Thomson, 22 March 2012. See ED 151'Australian Additions to, and Deletions from, IFRSs' (AASB, November 2006). Also the letter from Jan McCahey of PricewaterhouseCoopers to David Boymal, chairman of the AASB, dated 19 August 2005 (supplied by Jan McCahey).

[31] Joseph Bebbington and Esther Song, *The Adoption of IFRS in the EU and New Zealand: A Preliminary Report* (Christchurch, NZ: National Center for Research on Europe, University of Canterbury, 2004), 28–31. For New Zealand in particular, see Liz Hickey, John Spencer, Tony van Zijl, and Joanna Perry, 'Adoption of IFRS—Background and Process', *Chartered Accountants Journal*, July 2003, 4–7.

[32] Letter from David Tweedie to Tony van Zijl, dated 7 July 2003, and letter from Tony van Zijl to David Tweedie, dated 21 May 2003, IASB archive, file 'Australia/New Zealand'.

[33] NZ IAS 7 *Statement of Cash Flows* (FRSB, November 2007).

[34] *Amendments to New Zealand Equivalents to International Financial Reporting Standards to Harmonise with International Financial Reporting Standards and Australian Accounting Standards (Harmonisation Amendments)* (FRSB, April 2011).

signal to the world that their national accounting standards were, with only minor deviations, the same as IFRSs. David Tweedie and Warren McGregor were concerned that questions were being raised outside of Australia, especially in Europe, where the European Commission had approved two carve-outs from IFRSs in November 2004, whether Australia had actually adopted IFRSs or not. Critics of the European Commission's action cited Australia as having adopted IFRSs without carve-outs, but doubts arose over the lack of an affirmation by Australian auditors of companies' compliance with IFRSs. Both Tweedie and McGregor, together with Richard G. Humphry, the Australian member on the IASC Foundation board of trustees, recommended that an effort be made to embed IFRSs in Australian law, much as was happening in the EU, rather than incorporating IFRSs into Australian accounting standards.[35] But, in the end, the Australian auditing standard setter acted in 2007 to issue Auditing Standard ASA 2007-1, which obliged auditors to give a second opinion, on compliance with IFRSs.[36] In New Zealand, auditors began giving both opinions in the light of a guidance statement on how best to reflect the new accounting standards framework.[37]

In both Australia and New Zealand, their Parliaments retain the right of veto over accounting standards. In Australia, once a standard has been issued it becomes law. Thereafter, the Parliament has fifteen sitting days in which to disallow it. Because there are sometimes long periods when the Parliament is not in session, fifteen sitting days could extend to four or five months.[38] In New Zealand, once an accounting standard has been issued and then is entered in the *New Zealand Gazette*, the Parliament has twenty-eight calendar days in which to disallow it. But in New Zealand, unlike Australia, the standard does not become law until the expiry of the twenty-eight days.[39]

4.4 ACCEPTANCE OF THE IASB'S STANDARDS IN JURISDICTIONS AROUND THE WORLD

Mostly beginning in the 1990s, a number of developing countries and emerging economies, more tentatively than Hong Kong and South Africa, began efforts to point towards a possible future adoption of IFRSs, usually transitioning from harmonization to partial convergence and then towards full convergence. In some of these countries, the EU's decision probably helped to sustain or increase the momentum of such projects. For many, the World Bank was a catalyst. Following

---

[35] Interview with Warren McGregor, 18 and19 May 2011, and communication to the authors from David Tweedie, 4 March 2012.

[36] Auditing Standard ASA 2007-1 *Amendments to Australian Auditing Standards* (Australian Government: Auditing and Assurance Standards Board, June 2007).

[37] See Craig Fisher and Joanna Perry, 'Complying with IFRS: Guidance Amended', *Chartered Accountants Journal*, July 2007, 28–9. The guidance statement was an amendment of AGS-1012, *Audit Implications of the Transition to NZ Equivalents to IFRS*.

[38] Interview with Angus Thomson, 22 March 2012.

[39] Communication from Kevin Simpkins to the authors, dated 2 April 2013.

several financial crises in the late 1990s, particularly the Asian financial crisis of 1997, the Bank began a major programme to produce Reports on the Observance of Standards and Codes (ROSC), Accounting and Auditing (A&A), which was part of a Standards and Codes initiative jointly begun in 1999 by the Bank and the International Monetary Fund to strengthen the international financial architecture. A World Bank team would conduct extensive research in each country and then draft a lengthy report summarizing its findings on A&A. It would then conclude by recommending, with respect to accounting, that countries consider accelerating their acceptance of IFRSs or beginning a process of convergence and eventual adoption of IFRSs. The Bank's focus was mostly on developing countries and those with emerging economies. As the Bank makes substantial loans and grants to these countries, it would possess considerable leverage in countries' decisions on such matters. By the end of 2004, the Bank had published A&A reports on the following thirty-one countries: Bangladesh, Bosnia and Herzegovina, Chile, the Czech Republic, Ecuador, Egypt, Estonia, Ghana, Hungary, India, Jamaica, Jordan, Kenya, Korea, Lebanon, Lithuania, Macedonia, Mauritius, Mexico, Moldova, Morocco, Nigeria, Peru, Poland, Romania, Slovakia, Slovenia, South Africa, Sri Lanka, Tunisia, and Ukraine.[40] The Bank found the use of highly diverse accounting standards and practices across the countries. A number of countries had adopted some of the IASC's standards in the 1990s but had not kept up with subsequent changes. Others had been following an elongated process of aligning their standards with the IASC's, later the IASB's standards, for quite some years, while others had taken only a few initial steps in that direction. Still others had not begun any process towards alignment or convergence.

In May 2001, Singapore's Disclosure and Accounting Standards Committee recommended that all companies adopt the IASB's standards by 2003.[41] Yet the convergence of Singaporean Statements of Accounting Standards with IFRSs has continued to be an ongoing process. In 2001 and 2002, such countries as Kyrgyzstan, Tajikistan, Tanzania, and Ukraine announced steps towards the adoption of IFRSs by 2003 or 2004.[42] Some further countries announced in 2003 or 2004 that they had gone over to IFRSs, but again these affirmations were instances of self-reporting: Guatemala, Kazakhstan (banks only), Nicaragua, and Philippines. In addition, Malaysia and Vietnam were well along in a convergence process with IFRSs.[43] China had embarked on a programme of setting accounting standards, partly inspired by those of the IASC, in the 1990s, and the acceleration of its efforts in 2004 and 2005 are discussed in Chapter 10. Russia had embarked on a programme of convergence with the IASCs standards in 1998, and use of IFRSs became mandatory for Russian banks in 2004, but,

---

[40] The Bank can publish a country study only if the country's government accedes to its publication, and in a few cases it has taken a couple of years to obtain the permission.

[41] 'Adoption of IAS Proposed in Singapore', news item posted 29 May 2001 <http://www.iasplus.com>.

[42] See the entries for these four countries, respectively, at 15 May 2002, 6 August 2002, 20 November 2002, and 21 November 2002 <http://www.iasplus.com>.

[43] See the entries for these five countries, respectively, at 5 April 2003, 28 October 2004, 12 October 2003, and 19 December 2004 at <http://www.iasplus.com>.

beyond that, the country's moves towards IFRS adoption remained hesitant until 2011 (see Section 15.3).[44]

The IASB itself did not systematically gather intelligence on how many jurisdictions required or permitted the use of IFRSs. It was not until 2013 that the organization announced an initiative to document country-by-country progress towards adoption of IFRSs, which eventually led to the posting of more than one hundred jurisdictional profiles on the IASB's website.[45] But estimates of the policies and practices of jurisdictions on the use of IFRSs were posted on IAS Plus, the website maintained by Deloitte Touche Tohmatsu, based on information gathered from its offices around the world, and this was an important source of information for the IASB as well. Yet much of this information was highly subjective and tinged by politically sensitive exceptions and exemptions, and thus was difficult to use as a basis for counting. Nonetheless, beginning in the IASC Foundation's 2003 *Annual Report*, David Tweedie would confidently assert that 'From 1 January 2005 more than ninety countries will either require or permit the use of International Financial Reporting Standards'.[46]

4.5 THE UNITED STATES

No country's imprimatur was sought more avidly by the IASB than that of the United States. Throughout the 1990s, the IASC had single-mindedly pursued the objective of acceptance of its standards for use by foreign companies listing in the United States, and it seems fair to assume that to the newborn IASB, a signal by the US SEC that it would consider lifting the 20-F reconciliation requirement for foreign registrants that were using IFRSs would be prized as much as the EU's requirement that all listed companies must use IFRSs. From the beginning, the IASB was assiduous in nurturing its relations with the SEC and with the Financial Accounting Standards Board (FASB). While at the outset, the FASB was in principle just one of the IASB's original liaison standard setters, the IASB paid close attention to the FASB's activities when setting its initial agenda (see Chapter 5), and a 'special relationship' between the two boards began to emerge during 2002.

Both the IASC Foundation trustees and the Board decided to hold their meetings in Washington, DC, on 15 October and on 18–20 October 2001, respectively. On 15 October, the trustees, together with the Board, hosted an informal dinner. Trustees Chairman Paul Volcker had written letters inviting a number of distinguished figures from the legislative and regulatory community to attend. Among those at the dinner, apart from all Board members and most trustees, were James D. Wolfensohn, the president of the World Bank; SEC

---

[44] 'Russian Banks Begin Adopting IFRS in 2004', news item posted 3 November 2003 <http://www.iasplus.com>; see also 'White Paper on Corporate Governance in Russia', Russian Corporate Governance Roundtable, undated paper [2002] <http://www.oecd.org>.

[45] 'IFRS Foundation Charts Progress towards Global Adoption of IFRS', IFRS Foundation press release dated 5 June 2013.

[46] IASC Foundation, *Annual Report 2003*, 10.

Chairman Harvey L. Pitt, his chief accountant, Robert K. Herdman, and Deputy Chief Accountant John M. Morrissey; immediate past SEC Chairman Arthur Levitt (who had chaired the nominating committee in early 2000 which selected the IASC Foundation trustees); eight Senators and Representatives from Congress; a Treasury official; and a representative of the Basel Committee who was attached to the Federal Reserve Board, as well as FASB Chairman Edmund Jenkins. The dinner signified the importance which the trustees attached to developing contacts with 'official Washington'.

At the same time, the two standard setters made a tentative start to improve their contacts. In August 2001, FASB Chairman Jenkins had proposed to David Tweedie that, in connection with the IASB's scheduled meeting on 18–20 October 2001 in Washington, DC, 'it would be a good idea if your Board and our Board could meet together briefly. The principal objective of such a meeting would be for all of us to become better acquainted in the interest of our ongoing standard setting partnership.'[47] Jenkins had a discussion of non-technical issues in mind, so that the meeting could be either open or closed. Thus, the FASB and its senior staff, in a rare meeting outside of Stamford or Norwalk other than for public hearings, travelled to the capital to meet with the IASB on 17 October for an hour, followed by a reception in the IASB's hotel. While both Tweedie and Jenkins spoke in favour of convergence, Jenkins made it clear that, 'while it is committed to convergence, the FASB would continue to respond to the needs of its constituents when deciding its agenda priorities'.[48] This view would have presented an obstacle to full-bodied convergence. Although this first joint meeting of the boards was historic, it was not mentioned in either of the boards' newsletters or reported in the press.

4.5.1 The SEC Weighs In

An important stimulus for the two boards to increase their cooperation came from the SEC, where convergence between US accounting standards and IFRSs was an important agenda issue. As early as December 2001, Robert Herdman, a scant two months after becoming the SEC's chief accountant, advocated 'near-term convergence' of the US and global accounting standards 'as critical to a continued, efficient expansion of our global capital markets'. He said that international accounting 'will be a major focus for the Chief Accountant's office'.[49] Up to a point, this view could be seen as a continuation of the Commission's earlier policy as described in its concept release of 16 February 2000 entitled 'International Accounting Standards'. In the release, the Commission said that it had 'pursued a dual objective of upholding the quality of financial reporting

---

[47] Letter from Jenkins to Tweedie dated 28 August 2001, IASB archive, 'FASB' file.

[48] AP 11/2001 paper 10A ('Minutes of a Joint Meeting of the International Accounting Standards Board and the U.S. Financial Accounting Standards Board held in Washington DC, USA, on 17 October 2001'). Also in attendance were the chairman and another member of the American Institute of Certified Public Accountants' Accounting Standards Executive Committee.

[49] Speech by Robert K. Herdman, 'Advancing Investors' Interests', 6 December 2001 <http://www.sec.gov>.

domestically, while encouraging convergence towards a high quality global financial reporting framework internationally'.[50] Hence, such convergence had previously been viewed by the SEC as an important desideratum. Yet there was a new note of urgency to Herdman's statement.

Until well into 2001, few people in the United States would have thought of IFRSs, and of convergence between US GAAP and IFRSs, in any terms other than of facilitating listings by foreign companies. The idea that IFRSs might supplant US GAAP would have seemed utterly unrealistic given the long-standing perception, both in the United States and elsewhere, that US GAAP was the most sophisticated body of accounting standards in existence. To be sure, the notion of allowing US companies to choose between US GAAP and IFRSs in order to introduce regulatory competition was advanced in the academic literature, in particular by Shyam Sunder of Yale University, but for practical purposes US GAAP continued to reign supreme.[51]

However, the Enron scandal that broke in late 2001, quickly followed by several other notorious cases of accounting manipulation, shook confidence in the US financial reporting system and gave rise to the idea, not least at the SEC, that there might actually be something that the United States could learn from IFRSs. As already indicated above, the rules-laden corpus of FASB standards became a source of concern. David Tweedie was certainly willing to put forward the advantages of IFRSs in this regard. On 14 February 2002, he and Paul Volcker gave testimony in a hearing before the US Senate Banking Committee. Tweedie said, 'We hope that a clear statement of the underlying principles will allow companies and auditors to deal with these situations without becoming entangled in the web of detailed rules, rules which can allow the unscrupulous to game the standards'.[52] The distinction of 'principles-based' versus 'rules-based' accounting standards was coined by SEC Chairman Harvey Pitt and Chief Accountant Herdman in four speeches given in February and April, 2002.[53] While this terminology for characterizing the FASB's emphasis on rules-based standards was new, the general complaint about detailed accounting standards in the United States was not: in the late 1960s, critics had already assailed the Accounting Principles Board for putting out 'cookbooks'.[54] In an interview, Herdman has said that a strong motivation behind his push in 2002 for convergence between US and international accounting standards was his concern, following Enron, that US GAAP was too rules-based and that it would benefit from convergence with the

---

[50] 'International Accounting Standards', release Nos. 33-7801, 34-42430; International Series No. 1215 <http://www.sec.gov>.

[51] Ronald A. Dye and Shyam Sunder, 'Why Not Allow FASB and IASB Standards to Compete in the U.S.?', *Accounting Horizons*, 15/3 (September 2001), 257–71.

[52] *Accounting Reform and Investor Protection*, Hearings before the Committee on Banking, Housing, and Urban Affairs, United States Senate, 107th Congress, 2nd Session, Volume I, 110.

[53] Harvey L. Pitt, 'Remarks at the Winter Bench and Bar Conference of the Federal Bar Council', 19 February 2002; and 'Remarks at the SEC Speaks Conference', 22 February 2002. Robert K. Herdman, 'Improving Standard Setting to Advance the Interests of Investors', 11 April 2002; and 'Moving Toward the Globalization of Accounting Standards', 18 April 2002 <http://www.sec.gov>.

[54] See Stephen A. Zeff, 'How the U.S. Accounting Profession Got Where It Is Today: Part I', *Accounting Horizons*, 17/3 (September 2003), 197.

more principles-based international standards.[55] In a speech on 11 April 2002, Herdman said that the FASB 'must accelerate its efforts to achieve short-term convergence with the International Accounting Standards Board'.[56]

Against the same background of accounting scandals, a provision in the Sarbanes-Oxley Act, enacted on 30 July 2002, charged the SEC to designate a national accounting standard-setting body which, among other things, 'considers, in adopting principles, . . . the extent to which international convergence on high-quality accounting standards is necessary or appropriate in the public interest and for the protection of investors' (Sec. 108(a)(2)).[57] This provision, which was not included in the Oxley bill, H.R. 3763, passed by the House of Representatives in April 2002, was probably inserted at the suggestion of the Senate Banking Committee chairman, Paul S. Sarbanes. Following the testimony before the Senate Committee by Volcker and Tweedie on 14 February 2002, Sarbanes expressed the view that the development of US accounting standards that were 'conducive' to international harmonization would move the US towards better standards and thus 'correct deficiencies in [US] standards that Enron has reflected'.[58]

As the SEC gave thought to encouraging the FASB to work more closely with the IASB, the two boards agreed, in April 2002, to undertake a joint project on business combinations (see Sections 5.4.4 and 12.4). Shortly afterwards, on 24 April, the Financial Accounting Foundation's (FAF) trustees announced the appointment of Bob Herz, then a part-time member of the IASB, as chairman of the FASB, effective on 1 July 2002 (see Section 3.7). This gave the FASB a chairman with a distinctly international outlook who had acquired an intimate knowledge of the IASB and its activities.

One of the FASB's decisions made in the first month after Herz became chairman was to place the topic of accounting for employee stock options on its agenda. As discussed more fully in Chapter 5, this was one of the IASB's initial projects, and the FASB, in its news release announcing this decision, referred at some length to the IASB's recently concluded deliberations (in which Herz had participated) on accounting for share-based payment, including stock options, and to the IASB's intention to issue a proposal for public comment during the fourth quarter of 2002.[59] Herz knew that the IASB had decided tentatively in favour of requiring companies to expense the fair value of employee stock options, which the FASB had tried to do in 1993–5 but was defeated by persistent lobbying by the high tech sector. In an interview, Herz remarked that, following

---

[55] Interview with Robert Herdman, 18 February 2009.

[56] Herdman, 'Improving Standard Setting to Advance the Interests of Investors'.

[57] Public Law 107–204, 30 July 2002, 116 Stat. 745. In April 2003, the SEC designated the FASB as that standard-setting body, 'Securities and Exchange Commission Reaffirms Status of Pronouncements of the Financial Accounting Standards Board', SEC press release 2003–53, 25 April 2003 <http://www.sec.gov>.

[58] *Accounting Reform and Investor Protection*, Hearings before the Committee on Banking, Housing, and Urban Affairs, United States Senate, 107th Congress, 2nd Session, 14 February 2002, Volume I, 139.

[59] 'FASB's Plans Regarding the Accounting for Employee Stock Options', FASB press release, 31 July 2002 <http://www.fasb.org>.

Enron, there was a new attitude in the United States, and it made sense to take up the stock option issue again.[60]

4.5.2 The Norwalk Agreement

The FASB's interest in working with the IASB went further than individual projects such as accounting for business combinations and employee stock options. In October 2002, the two boards issued a joint programmatic statement known as the Norwalk Agreement, which signalled to the world that they intended to work more closely together than they had before.

Paul Pacter has suggested that the provision, cited above, in Sarbanes-Oxley 'provided some impetus and support for the Norwalk agreement'.[61] Herz himself discounts the importance of the provision in the Sarbanes-Oxley Act as a precipitating factor, and instead says that, upon becoming FASB chairman, he believed that a formal programme of convergence between the two boards was the next logical step after the long period of cooperation between them since the early 1990s.[62] Prior to accepting the FASB appointment, he had consulted with SEC officials, Paul Volcker, as well as David Tweedie and others at the IASB, in order to obtain a broad reading of the range of views. During the summer of 2002, he held a series of strategic planning meetings with the other FASB board members, and one of the topics taken up was the development of an agreement in principle with the IASB.[63]

In its early years, the IASB made a practice of holding some of its meetings outside London (see Section 4.7), and in March 2002 its updated meeting schedule showed that it planned to hold one of its regular meetings in Norwalk in September. Although nothing was said at the time about a joint meeting with the FASB, the choice of this venue for a Board meeting in the United States suggested that such a meeting was considered. The announcement of the Board's meeting in Norwalk occurred four weeks prior to the news that Herz would become FASB chairman on 1 July, but the Norwalk meeting had already been planned well before that time.[64] With Herz' move to the FASB, and his interest in developing the FASB's ties with the IASB, the meeting acquired greater significance, and even more so because the SEC took a strong interest in the preparations.

On 1 August 2002, Herdman hosted a gathering in the SEC's offices in Washington with Tweedie, Herz, IASB Vice Chairman Tom Jones, and FASB

---

[60] Interview with Robert Herz, 17 February 2009.

[61] Paul Pacter, 'What Exactly is Convergence?', *International Journal of Accounting, Auditing and Performance Evaluation*, 2/1–2 (2005), 73.

[62] Communication from Robert Herz to the authors, dated 5 March 2010.

[63] Interview with Robert Herz, 17 February 2009. For Herz's view of the convergence process, see his book, *Accounting Changes: Chronicles of Convergence, Crisis, and Complexity in Financial Reporting* (AICPA, 2013), Chapter 4.

[64] The schedule of meetings for 2002 attached to the minutes of the IASB Board meeting of 18–20 December 2001 (administrative session) includes the Norwalk meeting in September, but does not indicate a meeting with the FASB. Nor is a meeting with the FASB indicated in the first published meeting schedule showing the Norwalk meeting, in *IASB Update*, March 2002, 4.

board member Michael J. Crooch (a former member of the IASC's US delegation) to discuss the differences between US GAAP and IFRSs. During the meeting, they discussed numerous possible short-term and long-term projects as well as a number of other standards issues.[65] At the conclusion of the meeting, Herdman recalls that he said he would like to see both boards place on their agenda a project for convergence with the other.[66]

Given these extensive preparations, the boards' joint meeting on 18 September did not quite give the impression of a momentous event. It was held at the FASB's offices, and it lasted a full day, sandwiched between three days of a regular IASB meeting. The IASB's newsletter presented it as an 'educational joint board meeting', and the discussion consisted of a polite exchange of views on the few projects on which the boards were already cooperating to some extent. They also explored the possibility of a short-term convergence project.[67] David Tweedie 'said that it had been decided that a sub-committee of members of both boards should deal with convergence issues and liaise with the staff. They would try to identify upcoming reconciliation issues.'[68] He then asked for a vote on the principle of convergence, and it passed unanimously. This vote evidently laid the ground for the Norwalk Agreement which was not announced at the meeting, but at the end of October.

At a news conference following the joint meeting, Tweedie was quoted as confirming that the SEC's accounting staff 'had been working with IASB and FASB to plan for the possible joint effort to eliminate—or at least reduce, said Herz—the existing differences in the two panels' rules'.[69] Tweedie was also reported as saying: 'For the first time we have agreed to address the differences between our standards.'[70]

On 29 October, the two boards released a Memorandum of Understanding (MoU) that they would begin a systematic process of bringing their respective standards into compatibility with each other.[71] The MoU was labelled 'The Norwalk Agreement', in which it was stated that the boards 'pledged to use their best efforts to (a) make their existing financial reporting standards fully compatible as soon as is practicable and (b) to coordinate their future work programs to ensure that once achieved, compatibility is maintained'. The MoU was specific with respect to the intention to conduct a short-term project to remove a variety of individual differences between US GAAP and IFRSs, and an exposure draft was expected in 2003. Beyond that, the MoU contained more generally worded intentions to remove other differences through joint projects and coordination of the boards' agendas. The accompanying press release by the two boards characterized the MoU as 'marking a significant step toward

---

[65] Agenda papers for the meeting, IASB archive, 'US convergence' file.

[66] Interview with Robert Herdman, 18 February 2009.

[67] See *IASB Update*, September 2002, 1; Peter Walton, 'Norwalking on Egg Shells', *Accounting & Business*, 5/9 (October 2002), 13.

[68] 'IASB–FASB Meeting', *World Accounting Report*, October 2002, 2.

[69] Steve Burkholder, 'IASB and FASB Signal Commitment to Cut Differences in Accounting Rules', BNA's *Daily Tax Report*, 182 DTR G-7, 19 September 2002.

[70] 'Q&A Viewpoints on Convergence', *The FASB Report*, no. 236, 30 September 2002, 2.

[71] 'Memorandum of Understanding: 'The Norwalk Agreement' <http://www.fasb.org/news/memorandum.pdf>.

formalizing their commitment to the convergence of U.S. and international accounting standards' even though the terms 'converge' and 'convergence' nowhere appeared in the Agreement itself.[72]

In its press release issued on the day when the Norwalk Agreement became public, the European Commission lost no time in entreating the SEC to lift its reconciliation requirement. The release stated: 'The announcement is a major step towards a global system of accounting standards and will in particular help the US Securities and Exchange Commission (SEC) to accept financial statements prepared by EU companies in accordance with IAS, without reconciliation to US GAAP, for the purposes of listing on US markets.'[73] The SEC's press release, issued on the same date, in which Chairman Pitt 'applauded' the two boards' decisions, was less specific and characterized the significance of the Norwalk Agreement in terms of better information for investors in the United States and around the world.[74] It addressed neither the question of whether US GAAP might be in need of improvement, post-Enron, nor did it mention the reconciliation requirement.

That Herdman saw convergence in terms of improving US GAAP was indicated above. That he also thought of it in terms of lifting the reconciliation requirement had already been made clear in a speech on 18 April 2002 in Cologne, Germany: 'If by 2005 there has been sufficient progress in the development of the financial reporting infrastructure and short-term convergence of accounting standards, then I believe the SEC should consider the question of whether foreign private issuers from EU member countries should be required to continue to reconcile from IAS to U.S. GAAP.'[75] But Herdman's work was interrupted in November 2002 when he resigned as chief accountant, at the same time as Harvey Pitt resigned as SEC chairman.[76] In February 2003, William H. Donaldson took office as SEC chairman. He was a former chairman of the New York Stock Exchange and, like Arthur Levitt before him, was one of the comparatively few SEC chairmen who were not lawyers. It was not until September that a new chief accountant was appointed: Donald T. (Don) Nicolaisen, a former partner in Price Waterhouse and then PricewaterhouseCoopers. Deputy Chief Accountants Jackson M. Day and Scott A. Taub served successively as acting chief accountants during the interim.

4.5.3 The SEC Begins to Ponder the Lifting of the Reconciliation Requirement

One task completed by the SEC staff during the interregnum was in response to Section 108(d) of the Sarbanes-Oxley Act of 2002 which instructed the SEC 'to

---

[72] 'FASB and IASB Agree to Work Together toward Convergence of Global Accounting Standards', IASB–FASB press release, 29 October 2002.

[73] 'Financial Reporting: Commission Welcomes IASB/FASB Convergence Agreement', IP/02/1576, 29 October 2002 <http://europa/eu/rapid>.

[74] 'Actions by FASB, IASB Praised', SEC press release 2002–154, 29 October 2002 <http://www.sec.gov>.

[75] Herdman, 'Moving Toward the Globalization of Accounting Standards'.

[76] See 'Agency Faults SEC on Handling of Audit Panel', *The Washington Post*, 20 December 2002, E01.

conduct a study on the adoption by the United States financial reporting system of a principles-based accounting system'.[77] The SEC published its staff study in July 2003, concluding that there was indeed reason to modify the approach to standard setting in the US, in the sense that 'the adoption of objectives-oriented principles-based accounting standards in the U.S. would be consistent with the vision of reform that was the basis for the Sarbanes-Oxley Act'.[78] As a staff study, it did not purport to express the Commission's view. The study warned against overly idealistic perceptions of IFRSs, and in section I(F) it contained a rather sour characterization of the IASB's standards in relation to those of the FASB (footnotes omitted):

> Many have pointed to International Financial Reporting Standards ('IFRSs'), issued by the International Accounting Standards Board ('IASB') and selected for adoption in Europe by the European Commission ('EC'), as an example of a principles-based regime. We do not believe the line of demarcation to be quite so simple. As they currently stand, the IFRSs do not embody the objectives-oriented approach to principles-based accounting standard setting. Indeed, a careful examination of the IFRSs shows that many of those standards are more properly described as rules-based. Other IFRSs could fairly be characterized as principles-only because they are overly general. Accordingly, we reject the notion that IFRSs constitute a model for principles-based accounting standards.

In terms of means and ends, the study portrayed the adoption of an objectives-oriented approach to standard setting primarily as beneficial for the United States, with the added benefit that it would facilitate convergence. Convergence, in term, would bring many benefits both in the United States and worldwide, one being the possible elimination of reconciliation requirements in the United States and elsewhere (Section V(E)). In section IV(B), the study referred favourably to the two boards' continuing efforts on convergence, although, as discussed in Section 5.7, there was not yet much progress to report in July 2003.

When Don Nicolaisen took office as chief accountant, the lifting of the reconciliation requirement moved to the foreground as the principal motivation for convergence. From almost his first day in office, there was 'immense pressure' from Europe to accept IFRSs in foreign company filings without the reconciliation requirement, thus eliminating the companies' cost of having to maintain two GAAPs. Chairman Donaldson instructed Nicolaisen to 'deal with it'. So Nicolaisen thought the time was right for him to put on paper his views on what it would take to do away with the reconciliations for foreign issuers using IFRSs.[79] In a speech in December 2003, he said that one of the challenges he took on as chief accountant was 'to develop a roadmap, if you will, of the steps necessary for financial statements prepared using International Accounting Standards (IAS) to be accepted by the Commission'.[80] As will be seen in Chapter 8, in April 2005

---

[77] *Public Law 107–204* (30 July 2002), Sec. 108(d)(1)(A), 116 Stat. 769.

[78] *Study Pursuant to Section 108(d) of the Sarbanes-Oxley Act of 2002 on the Adoption by the United States Financial Reporting System of a Principles-Based Accounting System* (SEC, 25 July 2003), VI <http://www.sec.gov>.

[79] Interview with Donald Nicolaisen, 1 August 2009.

[80] Donald T. Nicolaisen, 'Remarks before the 2003 Thirty-First AICPA National Conference on Current SEC Developments', 11 December 2003 <http://www.sec.gov>.

Nicolaisen published a momentous 'roadmap' towards lifting the SEC's Form 20-F reconciliation requirement for foreign private issuers using IFRSs in US capital markets.

Meanwhile, the prospect of a lifting of the reconciliation requirement and the conditions under which this might happen were frequently touched upon in public statements. In May 2004, Deputy Chief Accountant Scott Taub made a point of saying in a speech, 'we are preparing for a time when IFRS financial statements can be accepted without reconciliation to US GAAP'.[81] One of the ways in which the Office of the Chief Accountant was preparing for a lifting of the reconciliation requirement was, as Taub said, its decision to monitor IASB projects in a very similar way to its monitoring of FASB projects.

In a speech in June 2004, Nicolaisen said he was 'eager to embrace IFRS because I believe our investors in the US will benefit', a view he echoed in a speech in December 2004, when he added, 'Anticipating that investors will embrace IFRS, OCA [Office of the Chief Accountant] is considering the steps that need to be taken to allow us to eliminate the reconciliation from IFRS to U.S. GAAP'.[82] Nicolaisen repeated three themes during the year: that the IASB must continue to operate as a truly independent standard setter, that the IASB and the FASB should collaborate to eliminate differences between their standards, and that the SEC was looking forward to reviewing the quality and consistency of IFRSs in perhaps as many as five hundred financial statements for 2005 which were expected to be filed by foreign private issuers once the IAS Regulation took effect.

In a release issued on 11 March 2004, the SEC echoed Nicolaisen's views by affirming that the two boards' convergence towards a high-quality set of accounting standards, coupled with 'developments promoting uniform interpretation and effective enforcement' of IFRSs around the world, 'would provide an opportunity for us to consider' lifting the reconciliation requirement.[83]

4.6 JAPAN

Japan presented a unique challenge to the fledgling IASB. It was obvious that Japan had to be included in any effort to develop a global set of accounting standards. Yet Japan was not ready to embrace IFRSs, as the EU had done. Compared to the United States, which was in many respects familiar territory to the IASB, much more groundwork needed to be laid to become acquainted with the principal actors in Japan and establish working relationships. Around the time when the IASB was formed, there were significant changes in the Japanese institutions involved in accounting standard setting.

[81] Scott A. Taub, 'International Convergence and Public Oversight of Accounting and Auditing Standards', 20 May 2004, Amman, Jordan <http://www.sec.gov>.

[82] Donald T. Nicolaisen, 'Remarks before the Public Hearing on the IASC Constitution Review', 3 June 2004; 'Remarks before the 2004 AICPA National Conference on Current SEC and PCAOB Developments', 6 December 2004 <http://www.sec.gov>.

[83] 'First-time Application of International Financial Reporting Standards', Release Nos. 33-8397; 34-49403; International Series No. 1274, Part B.

4.6.1 Launch of the ASBJ

Until 2000, Japanese company financial reporting was regulated by the Ministry of Finance under both companies and fiscal legislation.[84] From 1953 to 2000, accounting standards had been set by the Business Accounting Deliberation Council (BADC), an advisor to the Securities Bureau of the Ministry of Finance.[85] By tradition, a considerable fraction of the members of the BADC, all of whom served part-time, were distinguished accounting professors, and all of its chairmen were likewise accounting professors. In July 2000, the government created the Financial Services Agency (FSA) as the financial markets regulator, which in turn oversaw a reform of accounting standard setting. The BADC was relieved of the task of setting accounting standards—although it continued to set auditing standards—and became an advisory body to the FSA. For unknown reasons, it was renamed (in English) the Business Accounting Council (BAC). The role of the BAC has been specified as being 'to study and deliberate standard-setting on business accounting and auditing, the unification of cost accounting and the establishment and improvement of business accounting systems, and to report the findings to or submit the recommendations to the Prime Minister, the Commissioner of the Financial Services Agency and the related government offices'.[86]

In July 2001, accounting standard setting was entrusted to the private sector, in a deliberate attempt to move accounting standard setting away from the Ministry of Finance, discredited by a number of financial scandals in the 1990s. With support from the business community, the Accounting Standards Board of Japan (ASBJ) was established, together with its governing body, the Financial Accounting Standards Foundation (FASF). The arrangements were based on the FASB model. The FASF raised the necessary funds and appointed the members and staff of the ASBJ. The full-time chairman from 2001 to 2007 was Professor Shizuki Saito, of the highly respected Tokyo University and a former long-time member of the BADC. The first full-time vice chairman was Ikuo Nishikawa, the former executive director of the Japanese Institute of Certified Public Accountants. The appointment of Saito carried forward the long tradition of involving accounting professors in the setting of accounting standards. Presumably, no founding chairman of a national standard setter would have wished simply to preside over the adoption of IFRSs. But as will be seen, Saito had particularly strong

---

[84] Some of the content of this subsection is based on a script entitled 'Recent Ten-Year History of Accounting in Japan', which the ASBJ prepared in 2010 for use by the authors. See also the discussion of Japan in George J. Benston, Michael Bromwich, Robert E. Litan, and Alfred Wagenhofer, *Worldwide Financial Reporting: The Development and Future of Accounting Standards* (Oxford: Oxford University Press, 2006), Chapter 8.

[85] The translation 'Business Accounting Deliberation Council' was used by all of the commentators from Japan writing in English (interview with Shizuki Saito, 25 January 2011). For the work of a leading authority, see Kiyomitsu Arai, *Accounting in Japan* (Tokyo: Waseda University, 1994), 18. Some argue that a more apt English translation of the name should be Business Accounting Standards Council, but, according to Arai, that was the name of the body that preceded the BADC.

[86] Cabinet Order for the Organization of the Financial Services Agency, Article 24, paragraph 2.

ideas about the proper development of Japanese GAAP. In an interview published in 2013, David Tweedie ventured the view that Saito was opposed to IFRSs.[87]

Apart from domestic reasons favouring the creation of a private-sector standard setter, some believed that this was a condition for the IASC Foundation trustees to accord Japan a seat on the IASB. This belief originated during the debates on the restructuring of the IASC, when it looked for some time as if the IASC might become a body in which qualifying (private-sector) standard setters would be represented. It was noted in Japan that, in the same context, a German private-sector accounting standard setter had been created in 1998.[88] Yet it is not evident that the existence, or non-existence, of private-sector standard setters played a role in the IASC Foundation trustees' deliberations when selecting the initial Board members. Indeed, the French standard setter was, and still is, part of the Ministry of Finance, and in 2000 the AASB was reconstituted as a federal government agency.

It had already come as a shock to the Japanese government that, because it was not represented on the IASC's nominating committee which was to select the IASC Foundation trustees, it might also not be represented on the trustees, or the Board. Japan's Ministry of Finance approached SEC Chairman Arthur Levitt, the chairman of the nominating committee, to urge that Japan be given two seats on the trustees and one on the Board.[89] In the end, two of the nineteen trustees chosen by the nominating committee were from Japan, and they were instrumental in assuring that Japan was, together with the United States, one of the top two contributors of funds to the IASC Foundation. In their turn, the IASC Foundation trustees appointed a Japanese Board member, Tatsumi Yamada, and the ASBJ was recognized as the IASB's liaison standard setter in Japan.

4.6.2 Initial Ambivalence over IFRSs

While an anxiety over the appointment of Japanese members to the IASC Foundation trustees and to the Board showed that there was a strong interest in Japan to be involved in the activities of the IASB, this did not mean that there was a corresponding keenness to allow or require the use of IFRSs in place of Japanese GAAP. If Saito was sceptical of IFRSs, he was by no means alone. By tradition, Japan had looked to the United States for guidance on accounting principles and standards, and US GAAP, with its extensive application guidance, was generally seen as superior to IFRSs. The perception that IFRSs were principles-based did not serve as a recommendation in Japan.

Since the 1970s, the Ministry of Finance allowed a limited group of large Japanese companies listed in the United States to file consolidated statements based on US GAAP rather than Japanese GAAP to satisfy the Ministry's reporting requirements. In April 2002, this option was extended to all of the thirty-five or so

---

[87] Steve Burkholder, *Financial Reporting in Japan: Uncertainty in a Shift to IFRS*, Accounting Policy & Practice Special Report (Bloomberg BNA/Tax Management Inc., 15 March 2013), 24.

[88] Interview with Kazuo Hiramatsu, 3 February 2011; Camfferman and Zeff, *Financial Reporting and Global Capital Markets*, 413.

[89] Interview with Tsuguoki Fujinuma, 26 January 2011.

Japanese companies reporting on Form 20-F with the US SEC. No such move was contemplated at that time regarding IFRSs.

Apart from familiarity with, and a general preference for, US GAAP, there was considerable scepticism in Japan regarding some of the IASB's early technical work. As indicated in Chapter 5, the projects on insurance and performance reporting were especially controversial. Within the IASB, there certainly was awareness that there was no great receptiveness to IFRSs in Japan. In 2002, Board member Tony Cope described the prospects of IFRS adoption in Japan as 'pretty slim'.[90] To be sure, this was not unique to Japan, because the IASB was confronted in many countries with an unwillingness to change, or with a disagreement over aspects of IFRSs. But in Japan, rejection of IFRSs sometimes seemed to touch on deeper sentiments of national identity. David Tweedie often recalled how, during one of his early visits to Japan, a Japanese interlocutor referred to the IASB, and not in a complimentary tone, as 'the black ship', a reference to the squadron of US naval vessels which, in 1854, compelled Japan to end its policy of isolation.[91]

In terms of overall policy, the view at the FSA and the ASBJ, but also at Nippon Keidanren, the highly influential business federation, was that international convergence of accounting standards should be pursued as a three-way process among IFRSs, Japanese GAAP, and US GAAP, with mutual recognition as a first step.[92]

In order to establish the credentials of Japanese GAAP as the third pillar of global accounting convergence, and to enhance understanding of Japanese views abroad, one of the ASBJ's initial projects was to develop a conceptual framework. This task was assigned to a working group, although it is understood that the resulting draft framework, completed in July 2004, was strongly coloured by Saito's views. The distinctive feature in the draft framework was its assertion of the importance of net income, relative to comprehensive income. It defined net income to include, in effect, all realized gains and losses attributable to the parent company's shareholders. While possibly compatible with the IASB's framework, it was certainly at variance with the direction in which the IASB would subsequently attempt to revise its framework together with the FASB (see Section 12.7). It was also in conflict with the IASB's ongoing work on performance measurement (see Section 5.5.2). In the following years, the ASBJ's draft framework therefore became a focal point in sometimes heated debate between the IASB and the ASBJ about the nature and objectives of convergence.

To the world outside Japan, it was not always easy to detect what balance Japan was seeking to strike between participating in the work of the IASB and maintaining a distinct body of Japanese accounting standards. It could easily appear as if Japan preferred to remain aloof from IFRSs, perhaps motivated by the pride and confidence the Japanese had in the quality of their own accounting standards. This was illustrated when, in 2002, a research study sponsored by the large international audit networks identified Japan as one of only three countries (together with

[90] Tony Cope, cited in BNA's *Daily Tax Report*, 5 November 2002, 214 DTR G-4.

[91] Interviews with David Tweedie, 29 July 2008 and 15 October 2009.

[92] 'Seeking International Collaboration on Accounting Standards', Nippon Keidanren policy statement, 21 October 2003 <http://www.keidanren.or.jp>.

Iceland and Saudi Arabia) out of fifty-nine countries surveyed 'that do not currently intend to converge with IFRS'.[93] This prompted the ASBJ to issue a passionate assertion of its commitment to convergence with international standards.[94]

Regional cooperation was also on the Japanese agenda. On 8 February 2002, at the suggestion of Tatsumi Yamada, the Japanese Board member, the ASBJ began to hold annual meetings with the Chinese Accounting Standards Committee (within the Ministry of Finance) and the Korea Accounting Standards Board on mutual problems and issues. Like Japan, China and Korea were interested in engaging with the IASB but were not ready to throw in their lot unreservedly with IFRSs. The inaugural three-country meeting was held in Tokyo. The aim of the meetings was to provide updates on domestic developments, coordinate the three countries' perspectives, and promote a regional voice on accounting standards issues.[95]

During these early years, the position of Tatsumi Yamada was not easy. He found himself charged with a liaison responsibility between two environments where very different views of financial reporting prevailed. The ASBJ established the International Issues Standing Committee in order to deliver its views to the IASB and assist Yamada as the liaison. In one respect, this was helpful, as it was noted by other Board members that Yamada, with a dedicated team behind him, came very well prepared to Board meetings, often with his own set of briefing papers. Yet it could easily give rise to misunderstanding over the nature of the liaison relationship: the ASBJ expected Yamada to represent the Japanese view to the IASB in a way which the IASB, and no doubt Yamada himself, found to be incompatible with his status as an independent Board member.[96] Yamada said he believed that his decisions on standards should be 'for the world', not 'for Japan'. He saw his role as representing the IASB to Japan, even if it meant being critical of some Japanese accounting practices.[97] Yamada's name had been advanced as a candidate for the Board in 2000 with the support of the Japanese Institute of Certified Public Accountants but before the ASBJ had been created. Therefore, the ASBJ, once in operation, inherited a liaison from the IASB who may not have been its choice for the Japanese member of the IASB despite his international credentials: Yamada had served for four years in the Japanese delegation to the IASC, and from 1997 to 2000 had been a member of the important Financial Instruments Joint Working Group of Standard Setters. Yet, despite this experience, there was a strong perception in Japan that he was too young—in a society where seniority is a paramount consideration.

---

[93] *GAAP Convergence 2002: A Survey of National Efforts to Promote and Achieve Convergence with International Financial Reporting Standards*, International Forum for Accountancy Development (IFAD), 2002, 16.

[94] 'Our Stance on Convergence', ASBJ statement dated 24 April 2003 <http://www.asb.or.jp> accessed through web.archive.

[95] Responses by Wang Jun, Vice Minister of Finance, to interview questions, dated 29 August 2011.

[96] See also the characterization of Yamada's position in Warren McGregor, 'Personal Reflections on Ten Years of the IASB', *Australian Accounting Review*, 22/3 (2012), 230.

[97] Interview with Tatsumi Yamada, 19 May 2011.

4.6.3 A Japanese Listed Company Adopts IFRSs Beginning in 2002

The unique case of a company which adopted IFRSs on a voluntary basis was the exception to the rule that there was limited interest in IFRSs in Japan. Many Japanese companies that have been focused on generating a market for their shares overseas have, for years, prepared a 'voluntary English language annual report', because their filings with the FSA (and previously with the Ministry of Finance) were written in Japanese. Typically, it was assumed as a matter of course that the English language annual report was a straight translation from the official filing in Japanese GAAP. Yet it was possible, without requiring the permission of any government agency, to use a different GAAP in the English report, because the English version is an unregulated document. The one company to avail itself of this possibility to use IFRSs in its English report was a middle-sized listed company, Nihon Dempa Kogyo (NDK), which filed its annual financial statements with the FSA in Japanese GAAP, but, beginning in 2002, used IFRSs in its voluntary English language annual report. The company apparently believed that financial statements prepared in accordance with IFRSs would be more understandable to foreign investors. The company used IFRSs in its voluntary annual report in every year from 2002 to 2010, when, in the latter year, the FSA for the first time allowed listed companies to file their financial statements by the use of IFRSs (see Chapter 15). NDK was the only Japanese listed company to use IFRSs in its voluntary English language annual report prior to 2010, and in each year it received a clean opinion from its external auditor, KPMG AZSA LLC.

4.6.4 Equivalence Assessment by the EU

Interest in Japan in the convergence activities of the IASB and FASB was buoyed when the two bodies announced their Norwalk Agreement in October 2002.[98] Yet the main reason why Japan began to take more interest in IFRSs was found in Europe. As indicated earlier, and discussed more fully in Chapter 9, the EU began a process in 2004 of benchmarking the GAAPs of Japan, Canada, and the United States against IFRSs in order to decide whether those countries' companies could continue to use their respective national GAAPs in EU capital markets without the need to make supplemental statements or disclosures. This assessment of equivalence with IFRSs proved to be an important catalyst to change views in Japan towards the relationship between Japanese GAAP and IFRSs.

In June 2004, a broad-based study group of the Ministry of Economy, Trade, and Industry (METI) issued a 'Report on the Internationalization of Business Accounting in Japan'. The study group was chaired by Kazuo Hiramatsu, an accounting professor and president of Kwansei Gakuin University, who had served on the IASC's Strategy Working Party in 1997–9, which had paved the way to the restructuring of the IASC into the IASB. Although Hiramatsu was supportive of the IASB's mission, he found that the large Keidanren presence on

---

[98] Interview with Yoshiki Yagi and Shigeo Sakase, 25 January 2011.

the committee was not keen on convergence.[99] Keidanren was certainly attuned to the interests of the large number of Japanese companies raising debt or equity capital in EU markets, yet it held on to mutual recognition rather than convergence as the preferred strategy. The report therefore noted the impending equivalence assessment by the EU with concern, but the main conclusion it drew was that it was necessary to 'energetically and effectively conduct PR activities overseas to disseminate information about Japanese accounting standards and the fundamental concepts behind them, as well as Japan's philosophy and stance towards international convergence', in other words, to persuade the world that Japanese GAAP merited recognition as equivalent to IFRSs.[100] Hiramatsu recalled that, as a matter of compromise, a reference to convergence in the long term was included as well, as he believed that acceptance of Japanese GAAP in the EU required that Japan show an 'attitude of convergence'. The report also called for more active involvement by Japan with the IASB.[101]

Against this background, the ASBJ published a statement on its Medium-Term Operating Policy in July 2003, which presented a basic strategy towards international convergence in two phases.[102] Professor Saito, in looking back, characterized the two phases as follows, drawing on the notion of competition in accounting standard setting as developed in the writings of Professor Shyam Sunder, of Yale University:

> The first [phase] was to reduce the differences between standards as swiftly as possible in order to provide an environment for markets to support the existence of two (or more) sets of accounting standards at the same time. For this to be realized, it is necessary for both IFRSs and Japanese GAAP to be accepted by markets of both the EU and Japan, so that the companies can choose standards for disclosing their financial reports. This scheme allows a competition of both standards within a sound market procedure, and leads us to the second phase where investors assess the quality of the standards and select those of high quality and low costs. This selection process would result in a further convergence. The role of the national standards setters at this point would be to improve the existing standards based on the evaluation of markets.[103]

Within the framework of this policy, the ASBJ could make short-term adjustments in order to obtain the equivalence recognition by the EU, a pragmatic step that would have been welcomed by Keidanren. Yet the ASBJ also asserted that it

---

[99] Interview with Kazuo Hiramatsu, 3 February 2011.

[100] 'Report on the Internationalization of Business Accounting in Japan', Study Group on the Internationalization of Business Accounting, Ministry of Economy, Trade and Industry, June 2004, 19 <http://www.meti.go.jp/english/report/downloadfiles/IBAreporte.pdf>.

[101] Interview with Kazuo Hiramatsu, 3 February 2011.

[102] 'Medium-Term Operating Policy of the Accounting Standards Board of Japan', 15 July 2004 <http://www.asb.or.jp> accessed through web.archive.

[103] Shizuki Saito, 'Significance of Convergence and the Role of IFRS in Japan', in Hans-Georg Bruns, Robert H. Herz, Heinz-Joachim Neubürger, and David Tweedie (editors), *Globale Finanzberichterstattung/Global Financial Reporting: Festschrift für Liesel Knorr* (Stuttgart: Schäffer-Poeschel Verlag, 2008), 61. Saito cited Sunder's article, 'Regulatory Competition among Accounting Standards within and across International Boundaries', *Journal of Accounting and Public Policy*, 21/3 (Autumn 2002), 219–34. As will be brought out in Chapter 8, SEC Chairman Christopher Cox espoused the view that IFRSs and US GAAP should be similarly subjected to a market test.

had a long-term role in maintaining Japanese GAAP as distinct from IFRSs, to allow accounting standards to be subjected to market testing. In the July 2004 policy statement, the ASBJ presented cooperation with the IASB as a central element of its activities, but mainly with a view to improving IFRSs, and not, as implied by the idea of market testing, identity of Japanese GAAP with IFRSs as an end in itself.

There is no evidence that the IASB accepted that market testing was an integral part of its mission to develop a global accounting standard, but it duly noted the ASBJ's plan to reduce differences and took the initiative to approach the ASBJ with the suggestion to do so jointly.[104] The two boards thereupon announced in October 2004 that they had 'started talks about a joint project to minimise differences' between IFRSs and Japanese accounting standards 'towards a final goal of convergence of their standards'.[105] Minimizing differences meant that, for each topic, they would retain the superior of the two standards, a process reminiscent of the IASB's short-term convergence project with the FASB. ASBJ Chairman Saito recalls how, in discussion with David Tweedie, he raised the question of what criterion would be used to determine superiority, drawing attention to the fact that the ASBJ's draft conceptual framework and the IASB's framework were not identical. Whereas Tweedie agreed at the outset that the criteria for making the choice would be by reference to both conceptual frameworks, he then began to argue that unification of the frameworks should be given priority.[106] In a joint statement by the two boards in January 2005, it appeared that the question of the conceptual frameworks was put on the back burner and that a phased approach would be followed. The first phase would concentrate on removing selected differences between the standards, excepting those which were currently being reconsidered jointly by the IASB and the FASB, and excepting 'standards that are divergent owing to differences in the respective conceptual frameworks or basic philosophies'.[107] Differences between the frameworks would be addressed at a yet to be determined moment. With these relatively modest ambitions began a series of semi-annual meetings between the two boards to 'reduce differences' in their standards.

Further discussion of accounting standards developments in Japan appear in Chapters 10 and 15.

4.7 OUTREACH BY THE BOARD AND TRUSTEES

Most, if not all, of the countries discussed above took their steps towards IFRSs, if any, in response to their own varying circumstances, in several cases following the

---

[104] That the initiative was taken by the IASB was indicated by Shizuki Saito, interview, 25 January 2011.

[105] 'IASB and Accounting Standards Board of Japan Start Talks about a Joint Project for Convergence', IASB press release dated 12 October 2004.

[106] Interview with Shizuki Saito, 25 January 2011.

[107] 'ASBJ and IASB Agree to Next Steps in Launching Joint Project for Convergence', ASBJ press release dated 21 January 2005 <http://www.asb.or.jp> accessed through web.archive.

example of the EU, rather than because of active prompting by the IASB. During the early years of the Board, apart from public speeches by David Tweedie and other Board members, the Board's main outreach effort was to hold several of its meetings outside of London, in a pattern reminiscent of that of the IASC. Thus, from 2001 to 2004, the IASB held eight of its monthly meetings in Washington, Paris, Tokyo, Berlin, Hong Kong, Rome, Toronto, and Oslo, apart from its joint meetings with the FASB, one of which each year was held in Norwalk, Connecticut, from 2002 onwards. The aim was to 'fly the flag' and establish contacts with regulators and other local constituencies, and to secure wider support for the IASB and its goals. In Japan, as seen above, there was as yet little enthusiasm for IFRSs, and to hold a Board meeting in Tokyo was probably an important signal for the IASB to make. But the meetings in France, Germany, Italy, Norway, and Hong Kong would not have been necessary to make new converts, as these jurisdictions were already on a path towards adoption of IFRSs.

Gradually, it was realized that these overseas Board meetings were not a good use of the Foundation's resources. They were costly to organize, and were less effective than meetings in London because, for cost reasons, the number of staff attending was limited. In addition, the benefits in terms of outreach were limited, as the Board sometimes found itself meeting in front of empty public galleries. In May 2004, Jim Leisenring proposed, during one of the Board's strategy retreats, to stop meeting outside London, and the other Board members unanimously agreed.[108] After the June 2004 meeting in Oslo, which had already been planned, the Board never again met outside of London or Norwalk, so it could no longer use these meetings to network with national standard setters and the local business and financial communities.

The trustees did not typically seem to plan most of their meetings with a view to spreading the message on IFRSs widely around the world. Six of their fourteen meetings between 2001 and 2005 were held in London. Four of the others were held in the United States (three in Washington and one in New York City) and were used to forge contacts, as discussed above. During their June 2004 visit to New York City, they held a joint meeting and a reception followed by dinner with the FAF trustees to compare notes on fundraising strategies and tactics. During their November 2003 meeting in Brussels—one of their two meetings held in Brussels between 2001 and 2005—the trustees met informally with Commissioner Frits Bolkestein and staff of the European Commission. At their June 2005 meeting in Paris, the trustees hosted a discussion and dinner with French business executives. A special case was the meeting of both the trustees and Board in Hong Kong in November 2002, coincident with the 16th World Congress of Accountants, during which both Tweedie and Paul Volcker spoke at the opening session. In addition, the trustees held a small dinner with Hong Kong officials and business representatives. But there was no trustee outreach beyond the cities where they met, and they rarely gave talks that were publicly reported. In subsequent years, as will be seen, the trustees began meeting more broadly around the world.

The IASB's main ambassador, therefore, was David Tweedie, who tirelessly circled the globe to spread the message. Often accompanied by Tom Jones and

---

[108] 'Draft Note of Meeting at Ware', 20 and 21 May 2004, minute 129, IASB archive, 'Awayday' files.

one or more other Board members, he conferred with standard setters to discuss national differences from IFRSs and the Board's work programme, and he gave seminars to the local business community. At some stops, he and Jones would also meet with government ministers or regulators.[109]

A facet of outreach that was promoted by the trustees, beginning in 2002, was to launch an educational programme that would contribute to worldwide consistency in the implementation of the IASB's standards. David Tweedie, in his report to the trustees in June 2002, had recommended establishment of an education department. In line with the surge of interest in IFRSs as principles-based standards in the first half of 2002, he related this to the Board's intention to keep its standards principles-based. He wrote as follows under the heading 'Principles versus rules':

> The Board is aware that producing more and more rules is liable to be counterproductive. The IFRIC has already been warned that many of us on the Board do not expect a stream of interpretations which, in essence, become rules. The Board at present is looking closely at drafts of its first two proposed International Financial Reporting Standards and is seeking to reduce their length and decide with which issues it is not essential to deal in an accounting standard. At the same time it is trying to ensure that the few underlying principles in each standard are made clear by presenting them in **bold**[original emphasis] as opposed to plain type. The Board's view is that much of the detail of the standards could be removed if we were, as discussed elsewhere, to establish an education department that could produce non-binding guidance for those who need it. Such guidance would make clear that it had not been subject to due process nor vetted by the Board, but would be of use in dealing with the unusual transaction that would not fit easily into an IFRS without greatly extending its length. Such guidance too, would be helpful for emerging economies and those smaller accounting firms that do not have the resource of a technical department.[110]

The idea of an educational role for the IASB took a different turn in November 2002. Kurt Ramin, the Foundation's commercial director, and Guido Ferrarini, chairman of the trustees' recently created education committee, proposed to develop a proficiency-testing programme that would lead to the awarding of a certificate or diploma to those who would give advice on the application and implementation of IFRSs. The trustees exposed the proposal for public comment in December 2002.[111] There was a wide range of views among the thirty-seven commentators, but most of them, especially professional accountancy bodies, audit firms, and preparers, registered their opposition. Quite a number believed that running a proficiency-testing programme was not compatible with the role of the IASB and that testing and certification was generally the responsibility of national accountancy bodies and not standard setters. At their meeting in March 2003, the trustees charged the education committee to study the matter further with a view towards finding a way to address some of the concerns voiced by

---

[109] See, for example, IASCF trustees meeting of 29 July 2003, agenda paper 4A, paragraphs 48–51, and IASCF trustees meeting of 24–5 October 2004, agenda paper 3A, paragraph 54.

[110] IASCF trustees meeting of 12 June, agenda paper 2, paragraph 29.

[111] IASCF trustees meeting of 19 November 2002, minute 3; 'Proposal for a Testing and Certification Programme' (IASC Foundation, December 2002).

commentators. They also decided to create the position of Director of Education.[112]

In May 2003, Elizabeth (Liz) Hickey, who was an immediate past member, formerly chairman of New Zealand's Financial Reporting Standards Board (FRSB) and a part-time member of the Securities Commission there, was appointed to the new position of Director of Education, with effect from 1 August 2003. As chairman of the FRSB from 1996 to 2002, she participated in the meetings of the G4+1. Hickey was to assist the trustees in the 'preparation of explanatory and educational materials' related to IFRSs and in 'assuring the quality of the educational products carrying the IASC Foundation logo'.[113]

At the trustees' first meeting which Hickey attended, in November 2003, she recommended against moving ahead with a proficiency-testing programme 'because the IASC Foundation simply did not have the resources to give testing priority'. She recommended that the Foundation should focus in the near term on creating educational materials to support existing and newly created IFRSs. The trustees, though believing that 'training was critical in many of the emerging economies', accepted her recommendation, and the testing and certification programme came to an end.[114]

At their June 2004 meeting, the trustees approved the membership of eight members from around the world, plus Hickey as chairman, of an Education Advisory Group, a body which was first mooted in 2002 and which was to give advice on the educational needs to support IFRSs and on the priorities and markets for the Foundation's educational products and services.[115] The Education Advisory Group held its first meeting by conference call in October 2004.

While the IASC Constitution, which was approved in 2000, did not refer explicitly to a trustee role in regard to producing educational materials to support IFRSs, its broad provisions were construed as authorizing that class of activity. Nonetheless, the trustees proposed to include an explicit reference to developing educational materials in the enumeration of their duties, as part of the first review of the Foundation's Constitution. At the trustees' meeting in June 2004, Chairman Volcker informed the trustees of his surprise that, during the Constitution review hearing in New York City, there was a largely negative reaction to this proposal.[116] One reason was further discussed at the October 2004 meeting when Volcker asked for an explanation of the difference between education and interpretation. Hickey replied, according to the minutes, that 'there is a balance to be maintained between providing education material that is useful, and not straying into interpretation'.[117] At the same October meeting the trustees voted to insert section 16(j) in the Constitution to add the following to their duties: 'foster and review the development of educational programmes and materials that are consistent with the organisation's objectives'.

---

[112] IASCF trustees meeting of 13 March 2003, minute 4.

[113] 'IASC Foundation Appoints Elizabeth Hickey as Director of Education', IASC Foundation press release, 19 May 2003.

[114] IASCF trustees meeting of 3–4 November 2003, minute 6.

[115] IASCF trustees meeting of 2–3 June 2004, agenda paper 4B.

[116] IASCF trustees meeting of 4 June 2004, minute 5.

[117] IASCF trustees meeting 24–5 October 2004, minutes 2(c) and 4.

4.8 THE IASB AND THE NATIONAL STANDARD SETTERS

This chapter began with the observation that the IASB was created as a standard setter among standard setters. This section reviews the IASB's relations with national standard setters in the light of the very different reception accorded to IFRSs around the world, as discussed in the preceding sections.

During the IASB's early years, national standard setters were the only bodies with which the Board maintained a form of regular dialogue at the technical, standard-setting level. Preparers and users of financial statements, as well as their representative organizations, did seek the Board's ear from the beginning, but typically on an ad hoc basis, without a framework of regular meetings.

From the vantage point of the IASB, there were two circles of national standard setters: an inner circle consisting of the eight liaison standard setters (see Section 3.4.4) and an ill-defined outer circle of organizations from several dozen jurisdictions where private- or public-sector organizations with at least some responsibility for accounting standards were known to exist. The latter group included established organizations that had worked for many years with the IASC, for instance from Malaysia, the Netherlands, and the Nordic countries, but also many recently created bodies about which little or nothing was known at the IASB.

The liaison standard setters were actively involved in the IASB's work, in the first place by means of regular meetings of their chairmen with the IASB Board. The first such meeting took place in May 2001, to discuss the IASB's initial agenda, followed by similar meetings after four- to six-month intervals. In addition, the liaison standard setters had privileged access to the Board's agenda papers (which were not then made available to the public) and were therefore in a position to comment on the Board's activities on an ongoing basis. A more intensive form of cooperation was the undertaking of joint projects on a bilateral basis, in which staff from the IASB and a liaison standard setter would work together to develop agenda papers to be discussed by both boards. As discussed more fully in Chapter 5, the initial agenda included projects with the standard setters from France and the United Kingdom. A joint project with the US FASB was adopted in April 2002. The standard-setting bodies in both Australia and New Zealand, as they were no longer producing standards for listed companies, sought to have a strong presence with the IASB, both in terms of providing staff and in doing project work.[118] The AASB provided staff for the IASB's work on pensions, and it took the lead in a project on behalf of the IASB on extractive industries.

Of the other national standard setters, some had a regular point of contact with the IASB. The Dutch and Nordic standard setters, for example, had a kind of 'secondary' liaison relationship with the IASB, in that Board member Geoffrey Whittington occasionally attended their meetings to provide briefings. Other Board members also gradually assumed, or were assigned, liaison responsibilities of varying intensity for certain countries or regions, including their national standard setters, if any. The Secretary-General of the Chinese Accounting Standards Committee, Madame Feng Shuping, was a member of the initial Standards

---

[118] Interview with Warren McGregor, 18 and 19 May 2011.

Advisory Council, as were chairmen of the South Korean, Malaysian, Russian, and Sri Lankan accounting standard setters. For all the others, it was left to their own initiative to make themselves known to the IASB and to signal an interest in its work, for instance through comment letters on exposure drafts.

The IASB made its first attempt to address the heterogeneous group of non-liaison standard setters in its entirety in November 2002, on the occasion of the International Federation of Accountants' (IFAC) World Congress of Accountants in Hong Kong. In conjunction with IASB Board and trustee meetings there, the Board organized the first 'World Standard Setters Conference' in what was intended to become a regular annual series. Perhaps inevitably, the first conference was mainly a means for the IASB to brief the national standard setters, rather than to engage in a technical interchange of views. The IASB also used the occasion to present the recently concluded Norwalk Agreement to the chairmen of the standard setters in attendance. In subsequent years, the IASB sought to give the conference more of the character of a two-way dialogue.

The category of liaison standard setters soon came to be reconsidered. As the adoption of IFRSs by companies in the EU moved closer, it became ever clearer that the European national standard setters would soon lose their mandate to develop their own standards for listed companies. In 2002, Australia, followed by New Zealand, announced plans to adopt IFRSs. Among the liaison standard setters, this left only the standard setters from Canada, Japan, and the United States with an independent role. The Norwalk Agreement announced in October 2002 signalled that the 'world-wide partnership' of standard setters could well be replaced by a bilateral relationship of the IASB and the FASB, with all other standard setters relegated to, at best, the second plane. In the second half of 2002, the IASB was already giving thought to discontinue the periodic plenary meetings where all eight liaison standard setters were represented.[119] The status of liaison members lapsed in 2005 as a result of the Constitution review (see Chapter 7).

The weakening position of the European national standard setters raised the question of the status of EFRAG, the advisory body on accounting standards created by FEE and others in the private sector at the behest of the European Commission. EFRAG was emphatically not a standard setter, but it evidently set out to acquire the kind of expertise normally associated with a standard-setting body. In 2001, even before EFRAG was formally set up, FEE President Göran Tidström, who was about to become chairman of EFRAG's Supervisory Board, wrote to David Tweedie to request a liaison relationship on a par with the liaison standard setters. A similar request was repeated later that year, but the IASB tried to steer clear of a formal commitment. In November, Tweedie wrote to Tidström that the IASB Board was 'extremely keen' to work with EFRAG but was not prepared to grant it access to agenda papers or a guaranteed place on advisory committees. The main reason he gave was that this would make it difficult for the IASB to refuse similar requests from other organizations such as the SEC and IOSCO.[120] While this is certainly plausible, it may be surmised that the IASB's

---

[119] IASCF trustees meeting of 19 November 2002, agenda paper 10, paragraphs 20–3.

[120] Letter from Tidström to Tweedie, dated 5 February 2001; letter from Tweedie to Tidström, dated 22 November 2001, both in IASB archive, file 'EFRAG'.

caution was at least partly inspired by the fact that EFRAG at this stage was still an unknown quantity, with as yet very little staff capacity to contribute to the IASB's technical work. In substance, however, the IASB did devote considerable attention to EFRAG. As a matter of policy, the IASB regularly sent a Board member (often Tom Jones) to attend meetings of EFRAG's Technical Expert Group. In September 2002 Tidström wrote again, this time to the trustees, for an invitation to participate in the meetings of the liaison standard setters. EFRAG's significance in dealing with the EU was noted, and this time the trustees decided to grant EFRAG the right to send an observer to the meetings with the liaison standard setters.[121]

---

[121] IASCF trustees meeting of 19 November 2002, minute 7; agenda paper 10 for that meeting; letter from Göran Tidström to Paul Volcker, dated 16 September 2002, appended to agenda paper 10.

5

The IASB Sets its Agenda

'Improvement, Convergence, Leadership'

This chapter reviews how the newly formed IASB approached its task of setting accounting standards. The IASB had to determine its agenda, i.e. the list of technical projects it would take up (see Section 5.1), and it had to settle on a style of working (see Sections 5.2 and 5.3). The discussion of initial technical projects in this chapter (see Sections 5.4–5.6) covers some early successes, projects completed in a short period of time. But there were also projects that turned out to be more intractable, both conceptually and in terms of strong constituent opposition, and which would remain on the Board's agenda for many years to come. The theme of international convergence of accounting standards was of particular importance in the IASB's first decade. Section 5.7 describes the IASB's initial approach to convergence, and how, within a few years, convergence acquired the specific meaning of 'convergence with US Generally Accepted Accounting Principles (US GAAP)'.

5.1 SETTING THE INITIAL AGENDA

In April 2001 the IASB held its first formal meeting in the provisional setting of a London hotel. As a newly conceived body, there was a clear expectation that it would strike out on a course of its own. Yet, at the same time, there was a legacy that it could not ignore.

One of the first acts of the Board was to pass a resolution that 'All Standards and Interpretations issued under previous constitutions continue to be applicable unless and until they are amended or withdrawn'.[1] With the reference to 'previous constitutions', the Board signalled that it thought of itself as a continuation of the IASC rather than as an entirely new creation. Indeed, in its supporting memorandum, the staff remarked that such a resolution was not strictly necessary, as there was an 'unbroken line' from one organization to the other.[2] But in the debate preceding the passing of the resolution, Board members made it clear that they viewed it as a practical measure, to avoid any uncertainty on the part of users of

---

[1] IASB Board meeting of 18–20 April 2001, minute 2(a).
[2] AP 4/2001 paper 1.

the standards, but not as an unqualified expression of approval of the handiwork of the IASC. The Board wanted to make a new beginning, as was also suggested by changing the name of the standards. In March, the trustees adopted the suggestion from the Board to use 'International Financial Reporting Standards' (IFRSs) for new standards, to set them apart from the earlier International Accounting Standards (IASs). The standards issued by the UK Accounting Standards Board (ASB) were known as Financial Reporting Standards, and it might be surmised that this proposal came from David Tweedie. However, in December Tweedie had suggested the name of 'International Financial Accounting Standards' to the trustees, who had deferred making a decision at that time. The Board's subsequent preference for IFRSs was explained by pointing out pressures on the Board to move into areas such as management's narrative discussions (known as Management's Discussion & Analysis in the United States and Canada, and as Operating and Financial Review in the United Kingdom).[3]

To aid the Board in developing its initial agenda, the technical staff—all of whom at that point had continued from the IASC—briefed the Board on the stages of development of about half a dozen technical projects that the IASC had been working on. In some cases, notably the projects on insurance contracts and extractive industries, substantial discussion papers had already been published, but on other projects the work had only just begun. As one of its last acts, the IASC Board had approved a lengthy document addressed to its successor, in which it recommended that the IASB continue work on these projects, together with suggestions for new projects.[4]

Another legacy from the IASC was the quest for endorsement of IASs by securities regulators around the world. The International Organization of Securities Commissions (IOSCO), at its annual conference in Sydney in May 2000, had passed a resolution recommending that its regulator members allow the use of thirty 'core standards', comprising most of the IASC's standards, by multinational issuers. Yet the endorsement was less than complete. It allowed IOSCO members to impose additional requirements, including reconciliation, disclosure, and interpretation. The IASC's ultimate prize, acceptance of its standards by the US Securities and Exchange Commission (SEC) without reconciliation, was still not within reach. In February 2000, the SEC issued a concept release in which it connected the acceptability of IASs in the United States not merely with the quality of the standards themselves, but also with the sufficiency, around the world, of the supporting infrastructure of auditing standards and enforcement of compliance.[5] These conditions were obviously outside the control of the IASB, but, even regarding the standards themselves, IOSCO expected it to do more work. IOSCO's May 2000 endorsement resolution came with an appendix of some 200 'outstanding issues' that had to be addressed before the endorsement could

---

[3] IASCF trustees meeting of 11 December 2000, minute 3(ii); IASCF trustees meeting of 8 March 2001, agenda paper 2.

[4] 'Statement by the Board of the International Accounting Standards Committee, December 2000', *IASC Insight*, December 2000, 9–16.

[5] 'International Accounting Standards', release Nos. 33-7801, 34-42430, International Series No. 1215, 16 February 2000 <http://www.sec.gov>.

become unconditional.[6] This huge undifferentiated list reflected IOSCO's inability to articulate a clear consensus on its priorities. In the early days of his chairmanship, David Tweedie sought a meeting with IOSCO's Technical Committee to convey the view that, drafted in this way, IOSCO's report was useless to the IASB. As a result, he obtained the assurance that IOSCO was willing to take a more holistic view of the IASB's standards. An effort was made, led by the SEC's Mary Tokar, to provide the IASB with a more focused statement of IOSCO's most pressing concerns.[7]

A third element where some continuity was in evidence was that the IASC, during the latter half of the 1990s, had worked closely with a number of national standard setters from the English-speaking world in the so-called G4+1 (see Chapter 2). The G4+1 had aimed to promote international convergence of accounting standards by producing a series of discussion papers on financial reporting issues. As one of the standard setters participating in the G4+1, the IASC had invited comments on the papers, and early in 2001 some of these were still being processed by the IASC staff. Given the IASC's involvement in the G4+1 and the fact that four IASB Board members had been active participants in the G4 +1 meetings, it is not surprising that the G4+1 papers were seen as important directions in identifying new projects that the IASB might take up, preferably in cooperation with other national standard setters.

There was, however, one circumstance that the IASC so far had not faced. In June 2000, the European Commission had announced its plan to require the use of IASs by all listed companies in the European Union (EU), beginning in 2005. While it was true that a number of large European companies had already adopted the IASC's standards on a voluntary basis during the 1990s, the IASB now had to consider whether the standards were ready to be used on a required basis by large numbers of companies that might not be sympathetic to all of their contents.

Against this background, the Board and staff, in consultation with the liaison standard setters, developed a list of suitable projects. Some twenty-five projects were identified, out of which ten were seen as first priorities. The others were classified as second priorities or research projects requiring more preparatory research.[8] The Board was bound by the Constitution not to make its agenda decisions without consulting the Standards Advisory Council (SAC), which held its first meeting in July. By that time the Board's thinking was well advanced. As discussed in Chapter 3, many members of the initial Board had extensive experience in standard setting, and might perhaps be forgiven if they believed that they knew very well what the most urgent issues were. Although the SAC members provided many comments and suggestions, on balance their expressed views made little impact on the Board's choices. One of the strongest messages coming out of SAC was that many members believed that standards for small and medium-sized enterprises should be a priority. However, as discussed in Chapter 12, the Board was as yet unwilling to address this issue.

---

[6] 'IASC Standards—Assessment Report', Report of the Technical Committee of the International Organization of Securities Commissions, May 2000, 46–105 <http://www.iosco.org>.

[7] IASB Board meeting of 18–20 April 2001, minute 14; interview with David Tweedie, 29 July 2008.

[8] Compare, for instance, the listing in agenda paper 3 for SAC meeting of 23–4 July 2001 with the final list in IASB meeting of 25–7 July 2001, minute II.

When making the final choice, the Board tried to strike a balance among 'improvements' to existing standards, 'convergence' of existing international and national standards, and 'leadership' in areas where none of the existing standards was considered suitable as a basis for convergence. Although these three categories and their boundaries were fluid, they do provide a framework for considering the Board's initial choice of nine projects, made immediately after its first meeting with SAC.[9]

Among these nine projects, the Board's decision to address accounting for share-based payment was widely regarded as its most daring choice, and it left no doubt about its ambition to show leadership.[10] It was also a choice that ran counter to strongly expressed views within SAC, coming in particular from some of its US members. This was a highly controversial topic on which the US Financial Accounting Standards Board (FASB) had spectacularly failed to make progress during the 1990s in the face of strong political lobbying. Ironically, it was on share-based payment that the IASB was to score its first major success, whereas it was mired for the next ten years in two other 'leadership' projects that, at least initially, were not regarded as nearly as controversial as share-based payment. The first of these projects, accounting for insurance contracts, was an area of great international diversity in practice, where the IASB hoped to build on the work of an IASC steering committee. The second was performance reporting, a topic which the G4+1, as well as the IASC itself, had wrestled with during the later 1990s.

The fourth project on the IASB's agenda was business combinations and goodwill. For the time being, this was more about convergence than leadership, as the FASB was about to complete a major revision of its standards in this area, which the IASB believed it needed to consider.[11]

The remaining five agenda projects were improvements of various kinds. One project was explicitly labelled 'improvements to existing standards' and it was expected to include amendments to a range of standards, primarily in order to meet IOSCO's expectations. Amendments to IAS 32 and IAS 39, on financial instruments, were considered as a separate project (see Chapter 6). This reflected partly the specialist nature of the subject matter, and partly that the work to develop further guidance on this topic was already in progress since the closing days of the IASC. Similarly, a fundamental review of IAS 30 *Disclosures in the Financial Statements of Banks and Similar Financial Institutions* was another IASC project that the IASB decided to continue. This project would in due course result in IFRS 7 (see Section 6.7). A fourth improvements project was to develop guidance on the first-time application of the standards. Of all the initial agenda projects, this was the one most clearly inspired by the impending mass transition to IFRSs in the EU. The last improvements project was a small one, to make sure that the *Preface to Statements of International Accounting Standards* reflected the transition from the IASC to the IASB.

---

[9] Compare, for instance, the different classifications in the IASB meeting of 22–5 May 2001, minute 15, and in the Foundation's *Annual Report 2001*, 6–7.

[10] See e.g. 'Accountancy—Going for the Jugular', *Financial Times* (UK edition), 9 August 2001.

[11] See AP 7/2001 paper 5.

5.1.1 The 'Stable Platform' of Standards

After setting the initial agenda, the next time for the Board to discuss its future activities was in April 2002. This was followed by rounds of consultations with SAC, national standard setters, and other parties, and during the second half of the year the revised outlines of its work programme were becoming clear.[12]

The enactment of the IAS Regulation in the EU in June 2002 firmly established 1 January 2005 as the date of large-scale implementation of IFRSs in the EU. Of course, this date had been known ever since the European Commission announced its plan in June 2000, and it had definitely played a part in determining the IASB's initial work programme.[13] Yet it seems that the imminence of the transition announced by the European Commission in 2000 for some 7,000 companies to adopt their standards did not penetrate the consciousness of all Board members—especially those from outside of Europe—until the IAS Regulation became a reality in June 2002.[14] The enactment of the Regulation concentrated the minds at the IASB, in particular because it was followed the next month by the formal announcement that Australia would also adopt IFRSs by 2005. In response to these events, the idea of a 'stable platform' of standards emerged: the timely completion of standards required for implementation in 2005, followed by a period of calm, during which no new standards applicable in 2005 would be issued.[15] As it turned out, the stable platform was itself somewhat of a moving target. The target date, initially said to be the end of 2003, was subsequently fixed at March 2004, and, as discussed more fully in Chapter 6, by that time the Board still had difficulties in wrapping up its project to improve the financial instruments standards.[16] At some point, the Board may have believed that it would be able to complete its entire initial agenda by early 2004. Yet some initial projects were soon excluded from the stable platform, the composition of which remained subject to minor variations until March 2004.[17]

---

[12] IASCF trustees meeting, 19 November 2002, agenda paper 2.

[13] IASCF trustees meeting, 15 October 2001, agenda paper 2.

[14] Interviews with Mary Barth, 17 March 2009; Thomas Jones, 16 February 2009; and Patricia O'Malley, 28 May 2009.

[15] See AP 10/2002 paper 7A for a first attempt to plan comprehensively for transition to IFRSs in 2005. The staff proposal in this document contains the essence of the subsequent 'stable platform', although that wording is not used.

[16] See IASCF trustees meeting of 19 November 2002, agenda paper 2, for the December 2003 date. A period of stability beginning on 1 January 2004 was also suggested to the IASB by CESR's standing committee on accounting (CESRfin), letter from H. Bjerre-Nielsen to David Tweedie, dated 27 November 2002. In response (letter to Bjerre-Nielsen, dated 4 December 2002), Tweedie wrote that the Board was likely to need 'one or two months in 2004 to complete the set', IASB archive, file 'CNC'.

[17] For an initial listing of projects, see IASB meeting of 23–5 October 2002, minute 5. Subsequent modifications included the removal of the second phase of the business combinations project and changes in response to the shifting planning of short-term convergence with the FASB.

5.2 BASIC VALUES

Something which the Board perhaps might have done, but did not, was to issue a statement outlining its general standard-setting philosophy. That did not mean that such a vision was absent, and it had at least two elements: the IASB's conceptual framework, and the notion of principles-based standards.

The conceptual framework, adopted by the IASC in 1989 as the *Framework for the Preparation and Presentation of Financial Statements*, occupied a central position in the IASB's work. This was true in the formal sense of the requirement in the IASB's original Constitution that members of the Board 'shall agree contractually to act in the public interest and to have regard to the IASC framework (as amended from time to time) in deciding on and revising standards' (paragraph 28). The status already accorded to the conceptual framework by the Constitution could have been a reason why the framework was not mentioned in the resolution passed by the Board in April 2001, by which it adopted all of the IASC's extant standards and interpretations. Alternatively, the omission could have been an oversight, given that it was subsequently asserted that the framework had, in fact, been adopted by the Board in April 2001.[18] Whatever the formalities, frequent proof was given throughout the decade that the framework, and in particular its asset and liability approach, did indeed play an important role in the Board's deliberations.

But the Board was well aware that the existing framework was not a sufficient basis for its work, and that it was urgently in need of improvement. An important lacuna was that it hardly addressed measurement at all, and thus did not, for instance, discuss the concept of fair value and its application. The IASB's constituents soon perceived that fair value was an important element of the Board's intellectual outlook. It could be seen and criticized as an implicit addendum to the conceptual framework, resting on important but unspecified assumptions about the nature of enterprises, the role of financial reporting, and the functioning of markets.[19]

Despite the acknowledged shortcomings of the framework, the Board did not add a framework project to its initial agenda. The Board contemplated a number of distinct projects of a conceptual nature that it might subsequently undertake. High priority topics included measurement, generally, and the recognition of revenue and liabilities. For the moment, the Board looked to some of its liaison standard setters that were already working on these topics or might be asked to conduct research on behalf of the IASB. As will be seen, the IASB and the FASB agreed in 2004 on a joint project to revise their frameworks.

A second element of the IASB's outlook on standard setting was the ideal of principles-based standards. As discussed in Chapter 4, this notion gained

---

[18] The framework is not mentioned in the resolution as reproduced in *IASB Update* for April 2001 nor in the minutes of the April 2001 Board meeting. However, starting with the 2002 bound volume of IFRSs, the framework was preceded by a note that it was 'adopted by the IASB in April 2001'.

[19] See e.g. 'Michel Pébereau: Il est grave qu'un bilan donne une idée excessive de l'entreprise', *Le Monde*, 7 August 2002. For the views of a former Board member, see Geoffrey Whittington, 'Fair Value and the IASB/FASB Conceptual Framework Project: An Alternative View', *Abacus*, 44/2 (2008), 139–68.

currency after Enron and other accounting scandals in the United States. For some time, it was common to compare IFRSs favourably with US GAAP as archetypes of principles-based and rules-based standards, respectively. Even though on closer inspection the distinction was not so clear-cut, it was not without ground. The IASC had already drawn attention to it in the 'legacy' document by which it gave advice to its successor:

> Some [standard setters] produce detailed rules, leaving little to individual judgment. Others concentrate more on the general principles and leave more to judgment in applying the principles. IASC has followed the latter course. . . . While recognising the need for standards to be detailed enough to avoid unintentionally giving choices, the Board encourages the new Board to continue IASC's present practice in this regard.[20]

It is not apparent that the IASB immediately established principles-based standard setting, in the sense of not including detailed rules, as an important objective. At the start, dealing with IOSCO's many recommendations for improvement was still a priority, and from that perspective many of the IASC's standards needed to be improved by adding, rather than removing, implementation guidance. But at least by early 2002, David Tweedie was willing to use the epithet of 'principles-based' himself to explain the merits of the Board's standards (see Section 4.5). By that time, references to 'the Board's objective of developing principles-based standards' began to appear in the agenda papers when discussing the distribution of guidance between the body of standards and appendices.[21]

5.3 WORKING PROCEDURES

In addition to deciding upon its agenda, the IASB had to formulate the procedures it would follow in developing and issuing its standards. Its May 2000 Constitution was clear about some of the minimum requirements of due process, in particular the need to publish an exposure draft on all projects and to consider the comments received, to hold a mandatory consultation with SAC on major projects and agenda decisions, and to secure a majority of eight out of fourteen votes necessary to approve a standard, exposure draft, or interpretation by the Board. On other aspects, though, the Constitution gave suggestions rather than prescriptions, and put much emphasis on the Board's independence in determining its agenda and handling of all technical matters.

The Board elaborated on the steps of due process in a revised *Preface to International Financial Reporting Standards*, which was exposed for comment in November 2001 and approved in April 2002. In addition to the minimum steps required by the Constitution, the *Preface* listed additional steps that the Board would 'normally, but not necessarily' take, such as forming an advisory group, publishing a discussion document preceding an exposure draft, and considering

---

[20] 'Statement by the Board of the International Accounting Standards Committee—December 2000', *IASC Insight*, December 2000, 10.

[21] See e.g. AP 4/2002 paper 7A, paragraph 110.

the desirability of holding public hearings and conducting field tests (*Preface*, paragraph 18).

The revision of the *Preface* sparked a debate in the Board over the fact that IASs contained paragraphs in bold-faced ('black') lettering, and paragraphs in normal type ('grey'). This could be traced back to the earliest standards of the IASC, where a distinction was made between the actual standard in bold type and the explanatory material in normal type. In practice, the distinction had served as a safety valve for the IASC, because it allowed the compromise of moving contentious material to the grey-lettered sections, creating ambiguity about the degree of expected compliance. For that reason, those who advocated more rigorous standards, as well as a more disciplined standard-setting process, opposed the use of this two-tier lettering. Under pressure from IOSCO, the IASC had done much to eliminate ambiguous guidance from the grey-letter paragraphs, but it had retained the distinction and the Board itself stopped short of asserting clearly that the two kinds of paragraphs had equal authority.[22] Such an assertion was put forward as the staff's view in an article written by Paul Pacter for *IASC Insight* in June 2000.[23] The IASB was initially inclined to discontinue the use of two different types, but reconsidered its position when it appeared that many comment letters supported the practice. In April 2002, a majority of the Board was persuaded that a limited use of bold-facing to highlight the main principles of a standard would be helpful to users, particularly those from non-English-speaking countries. It might also be useful to the Board itself, as it would provide some discipline in the quest for principles-based standards which it had by that time espoused. The black-lettering was therefore retained, although it was now made unambiguously clear that all paragraphs were equally authoritative. Nonetheless, Tony Cope, Jim Leisenring, and Warren McGregor voted against the *Preface* because of their belief that using different types would encourage flexibility in the application of the standards.[24]

While the issue of black and grey lettering was the most substantive style issue discussed at this stage, some other seemingly minor decisions were taken that also reflected something of how the Board members were seeking to define the nature of their standards. The decision to use 'shall' instead of 'should' in all standards, including the ones inherited from the IASC, was inspired by a proposal from Warren McGregor who wished to clarify that the standards were imperative rather than permissive. Yet the Board did not adopt McGregor's proposal to use 'must' rather than 'shall', and asserted in public that the change from 'should' to 'shall' was not intended to change the requirements of the standard.[25] Another change in wording proposed by McGregor was that the standards would be addressed to reporting 'entities' rather than to 'enterprises'. In his view, 'entity' was a neutral term that would open the way to application of the standards by not-for-profit entities as well. The notion of 'sector neutrality', according to which

[22] Kees Camfferman and Stephen A. Zeff, *Financial Reporting and Global Capital Markets: A History of the International Accounting Standards Committee, 1973–2000* (Oxford: Oxford University Press, 2007), 285–6.

[23] See Paul Pacter, 'It's All Black and White', *IASC Insight*, June 2000, 14.

[24] IASB meeting of 16–19 April 2002, minute 5.6; *IStaR*, April 2002, 5–6.

[25] AP 5/2001 paper 5, paragraph 16–19; IASB meeting of 22–5 May 2001, minute 3; exposure draft 'Proposed Improvements to International Accounting Standards' (IASB, May 2002), 11.

standards were addressed to both for-profit and not-for-profit entities, was well established in the setting of Australian accounting standards. Yet, while the Board accepted the change in wording, the rationale it gave revealed no desire to move into the area of not-for-profit accounting. According to the Board, 'entity' was a more neutral term, reflective 'of its objective that Standards are used by all profit-oriented entities preparing general purpose statements'.[26]

The procedures for developing a standard and for voting were established at an early stage and remained largely unchanged during the period covered in this book.[27] Board debates were based on agenda papers produced by the staff. Over a series of meetings, these papers set out the various issues to be treated in the standard, and offered alternative solutions with arguments in favour and against. Meeting by meeting, the Board voted on issues raised by the staff or on ways forward suggested by the chairman following the debate in the Board. Once the staff believed that the Board had reached decisions on all issues, they asked the Board's permission to begin drafting the text of a discussion paper, exposure draft, or standard. With more complex projects, the drafting normally resulted in previously overlooked questions to be discussed in open Board meetings. The final vote on a document was not taken in a Board meeting. From the outset, it was expected that a pattern of monthly meetings, between which many Board members would be out of the office, would make it difficult to arrange such final votes in public without running into long delays caused by last-minute changes. Instead, it was agreed to conduct final votes in the form of written ballots, cast by email. To this end, the staff circulated one or more pre-ballot drafts of the document, to collect minor editorial changes as well as any substantial points requiring further discussion in Board meetings. By this stage, the chairman would have asked in an open meeting whether any Board members intended to vote against the standard. Although all Board members remained free to change their mind until the final ballot, this procedure evidently minimized the probability of last-minute surprises. Board members cast their votes on a ballot draft presented as such by the staff, following which the text was handed over to the production department.

The Constitution specified that exposure drafts and standards should be published with dissenting opinions, if any (paragraph 36). Within the Board, it soon was accepted as a rule that dissenting opinions (known as alternative views in exposure drafts) should not be used gratuitously. A no-vote should be cast as if it was decisive, and only when the Board member believed that the standard as a whole would not improve financial reporting.[28]

Apart from the disclosure of dissenting opinions, the Constitution provided no other guidance on what the components or accompanying documents of a standard should be. Continuing the IASC's practice, the IASB published its standards, or amendments of standards, as separate booklets, typically consisting

---

[26] AP 5/2001 paper 5, paragraph 20–3; IASB meeting of 22–5 May 2001, minute 3; exposure draft 'Proposed Improvements to International Accounting Standards' (IASB), May 2002, 11.

[27] See AP 9/2001 paper 8 for the procedures as proposed by Wayne Upton.

[28] Interview with David Tweedie, 29 July 2008; and with Patricia O'Malley, 28 May 2009. See 'New Board Member Orientation: Supplement to the Rules of Procedure', administrative meeting of 21–2 May 2007, agenda paper 5 (IASB archive, 'Awayday' file), for a subsequent statement of the policy.

of an introduction, the text of the new standard or amendments, implementation guidance and/or illustrative examples, the final vote and any dissenting opinions, and a basis for conclusions. The latter would give a brief history of the project leading up to the standard, the issues faced by the Board in developing the standard, and the arguments it had considered.

The IASC had held open meetings since 1999, knowing that this was what the SEC expected of a credible world-class standard setter. It was therefore a matter of course that the IASB would operate 'in the sunshine' as well. In contrast to the part-time IASC, the IASB's members were expected to be together much more frequently in their London office, and care had to be taken to ensure that the sunshine policy would not be undermined by a majority of Board members getting together for technical discussions outside of public meetings. For instance, the Board experimented with closed educational sessions in which groups of Board members were briefed by the staff. The meetings were held twice, once for each half of the Board membership. However, they were discontinued once a suspicion was aroused among some of the IASB's constituents that these meetings were used for stitching up answers in private. Subsequently, whenever occasional educational sessions were held, they were open to the public.

The Board retained the IASC practice of closing parts of its meetings to the public, when it went into administrative session. Although here it also did not escape the suspicion that technical matters were sometimes brought up in these sessions, the practice was continued throughout the decade.

While Board meetings were open to the public, the meetings were not always easy to follow, because the Board was reluctant during its early years to publish its agenda papers. Observer notes were made available, but these were initially very succinct. Access to the full agenda papers was reserved for the liaison standard setters, who considered it a valuable privilege.[29]

An important procedural issue, that was not explicitly addressed in the *Preface*, was the role of steering committees in relation to the staff. In the IASC tradition, steering committees composed of volunteers who were not, in the majority, members of Board delegations, had been very important. In the early years of the IASC, the steering committees shouldered most of the work of developing drafts for the Board, with the IASC's limited staff playing a supporting role. There had been occasional difficulties, though, when steering committees acted too much on their own. During the 1990s, as the IASC's staff grew in size and experience, suggestions were made to give the leading role in developing Board papers to the staff. However, as many IASC member bodies strongly favoured the steering committee system, no fundamental changes were made.

The IASB no longer had any sponsoring member bodies to consider, and it looked forward to building up its staff to levels never contemplated by the IASC. It is therefore not surprising that the IASB took a critical look at the ten steering committees it inherited from the IASC. Staff recommended that, henceforth, such committees would be used in advisory roles only, and that, based on a review of their membership, only three of the existing committees be continued. The others should be disbanded, although some of their members might be retained as

---

[29] Interview with Andrew Lennard, 13 October 2008.

consultants.[30] Consequently, only three of the IASB's first nine projects were initially undertaken with a committee in place (insurance, financial instruments, and the revision of IAS 30). To underline the changed approach, the name 'steering committee' was abandoned in favour of 'advisory group'.[31] Until 2004 the IASB created few new advisory groups.

Hence, the IASB placed most of the responsibility for maintaining progress on technical projects on its staff. Because the IASB was still ramping up its staff, this sometimes meant that projects were carried forward by quite small teams. Some of the major early projects which the resource-rich FASB would have assigned to an entire team, such as share-based payment or business combinations, were handled at the IASB by hardly more than a single project manager.[32] The staff were supervised by the director of research, Wayne Upton, who arrived from the FASB in July 2001, and the director of technical activities, Kevin Stevenson, who took up his position in February 2002. The FASB, after which the IASB had been modelled, saw its standard setting as a 'staff-driven' process, with a strong emphasis on the independence of the staff vis-à-vis the board. The expectation, or suggestion, could be heard that the IASB would follow the FASB's example in this case as well.[33] Chairman Tweedie was of the view that, in the normal course of things, the staff should lead the way in setting up and pursuing a project, guided by responses from the Board to staff proposals. However, he insisted from the beginning on his prerogative of intervening in projects which he believed were taking a wrong turn.[34] While this prerogative may not have been asserted prominently or used frequently, it was invoked decisively on selected occasions, as will be seen in later chapters.

5.4 EARLY ACHIEVEMENTS

5.4.1 Improvements

A large share of the IASB's energy during its first years was expended on a project to make 'general improvements' to the IASC's standards. Even though the IASC had worked very hard throughout the 1990s to improve the quality of its standards, the new Board required little persuasion to accept that more improvements were needed. As indicated above, initially the most frequently cited reason for this was that IOSCO's endorsement of the standards had come accompanied by a long list of items requiring further attention.[35] And while IOSCO would not insist that the IASB go slavishly down its list of concerns, it was quite clear that more work

[30] 'Future Role and Responsibility of Steering Committees and Other Committees', IASB meeting of 18–20 April 2001, unnumbered agenda paper.

[31] Interview with Geoffrey Whittington, 19 March 2009.

[32] Interviews with Colin Fleming, 14 October 2008, and with Patricia O'Malley, 28 May 2009.

[33] Donald E. Tidrick, 'A Conversation with James J. Leisenring, IASB member', *The CPA Journal*, 72/3 (March 2002), 48–51.

[34] Interview with David Tweedie, 18 May 2011, and with Wayne Upton, 7 July 2011.

[35] For the relationship between the improvements project and IOSCO's endorsement, see also 'The IOSCO Endorsement', *IASB Insight*, March 2001, 15–16.

needed to be done. In the 1990s, eliminating alternatives and strengthening application guidance were seen as the main desiderata by the 'securities regulators', a general label behind which one always felt the dominating presence of the US SEC. Apart from IOSCO, the improvements project offered an opportunity for maintenance work. The IASC itself would have admitted that some of its work during the 1990s had been hastily done. And then there were the accumulated interpretations of the Standing Interpretations Committee (SIC) which could be incorporated into the standards themselves. While all these reasons for undertaking an improvements project were valid enough, there was also the less explicit but still palpable sense that the new, professional, and independent Board was keen to make its mark and to show that it could take things further than the part-time IASC. Whereas the IASC, for instance, had agonized over the abolition of LIFO and ultimately failed to do so, the new IASB expected to be able to reach agreement quickly that LIFO should go, as it did in October 2001.[36]

Removing LIFO was an example of the relatively easy modifications or 'quick fixes' that the Board believed it could make to the existing standards, and which might make the project 'a source of short-term success'.[37] But the improvements project became more complex and burdensome than originally expected, even though Board and staff were aware from the beginning of the danger of scope-creep. In the course of the project, the Board had to consider a great diversity of issues. At a high level of principle, for instance, the Board discussed whether IAS 1 *Presentation of Financial Statements* should continue to include a 'fair presentation override', which required companies to depart from the standards if compliance would result in misleading information. This issue had already been controversial when the IASC revised IAS 1 in the 1990s. This time it was again the smallest majority which voted to retain the override, albeit with the introduction of additional restrictions.[38] On this issue, the Board knew it had to take account of diametrically opposed legal systems in countries adopting IFRSs: whereas in the EU, a 'true and fair view' override was embedded in the Fourth Directive, the cornerstone of EU accounting law, a similar override had deliberately been removed from the Australian Corporations Act in 1991. A clause (paragraph 23) therefore had to be added to IAS 1 by which the override was replaced by a requirement for additional disclosure in jurisdictions where the regulations prohibit a departure from accounting standards.

At a very practical level, the Board considered a problem raised by Hong Kong, where virtually all land was held under leases of very long duration. This made the leases, as it was argued, economically equivalent to an ownership interest, yet IAS 17 *Leases* required them to be classified as operating leases which could not be capitalized by the lessee. This was not just a theoretical issue, as property investment was a major element of the Hong Kong economy. Moreover, since 1994 Hong Kong had been in the vanguard of jurisdictions adopting the IASC's standards (see Section 4.2). Hence, the Board introduced an amendment to IAS 40 *Investment Property*, which allowed certain operating leases to be capitalized.

---

[36] See Camfferman and Zeff, *Financial Reporting and Global Capital Markets*, 278–9; IASB meeting of 18–20 October 2001, minute 7.

[37] IASB meeting of 18–20 April 2001, minute 11; SAC meeting of 23–4 July 2001, agenda paper 3.

[38] 'Improvements Project Nears Completion', *World Accounting Report*, March 2002, 2.

When completed in December 2003, about a year beyond the initial target date, the improved standards were presented in almost 600 pages of amended text, newly developed supporting material, and bases for conclusions.[39] Thirteen standards were revised, with consequential amendments made to almost all of the other extant standards. Several SIC Interpretations were withdrawn and one standard was eliminated. This was IAS 15 *Information Reflecting the Effects of Changing Prices*, which had been optional in its entirety since 1989 and was virtually ignored in practice. The complex improvements project put a heavy strain on the Board and its still modest staff, and when it was completed there was a sense of relief and a hope that the Board might henceforth be able to devote more time to true leadership projects.[40]

In 2005, IOSCO issued a general statement of support for the IASB, in which it noted that 'the IASB has engaged in standards setting efforts that have addressed many of the issues noted in the 2000 Assessment Report'.[41] But at this stage IOSCO, which had absolutely dominated the IASC's activities during the 1990s, was no longer the central point of reference in the IASB's work. IOSCO had taken on a monitoring role, being represented in SAC, and having an observer on the interpretations committee, IFRIC.

While originating with IOSCO, the improvements project took on a new significance when the implications of the EU's planned adoption of IFRSs began to sink in.[42] Looking back in 2008, David Tweedie even suggested that the EU had somehow derailed the IASB's planning:

> The Board's initial proposals to revise its 34 inherited standards over a period of some eight years had to be abandoned because of an announcement by the European Commission, which . . . would require the consolidated accounts of listed companies in the EU to comply with international standards . . . from 2005.
>
> The initial work of the Board in its first years of existence was therefore to repair the 34 standards that it inherited by cutting and pasting, by removing particularly bad sections of those standards that had been heavily criticised by national regulators and by patching in better solutions. The Board was never allowed to pursue its original vision of producing a set of interlocking standards that would be adopted by standard-setters throughout the world looking for appropriate solutions to particular problems.[43]

However, as seen above, the European Commission had announced its plans in 2000, before the Board was formed. The improvements were not a requirement by the EU nor a condition for the adoption of the standards. In fact, in one respect the European Commission felt that the IASB's improvements project was hindering its own preparations for the introduction of IFRSs in the EU. In September 2003 all of the original IASs with the exception of IAS 32 and IAS 39 were

---

[39] Target date: IASCF trustees meeting, 15 October 2001, agenda paper 2.

[40] 'IAS 2005—Tweedie Speaks Out', *Accountancy*, 31 January 2004; interview with Patricia O'Malley, 28 May 2009.

[41] 'Statement on the Development and Use of International Financial Reporting Standards in 2005', IOSCO Technical Committee, February 2005 <http://www.iosco.org>.

[42] IASCF trustees meeting, 15 October 2001, agenda paper 2.

[43] David Tweedie, 'Beancounters or Market Drivers? The Role of the Reporting Accountant', speech delivered at the ICAS Conference, 4 September 2009 <http://www.ifrs.org> accessed through web. archive.

endorsed for use in the EU, and were translated in all of the EU's official languages. After undertaking this massive and costly effort, staff at the European Commission were not pleased that they had to redo some of their work in order to incorporate the host of greater and lesser changes introduced by the improvements project.[44]

5.4.2 IFRS 1: First-time Adoption of IFRSs

The first International Financial Reporting Standard was published by the IASB in June 2003, based on an exposure draft of July 2002. The standard was developed in cooperation with the Conseil National de la Comptabilité (CNC), the French liaison standard setter. As it turned out, IFRS 1 would remain the only successfully completed project conducted jointly with one of the liaison standard setters, other than the FASB. Cooperation with a European standard setter was natural, given the massive transition to IFRSs expected in the EU in 2005. Even though the Board intended to write a general purpose standard, not just one intended for Europe, interest outside of Europe was limited, at least as measured by the number of comment letters received on the exposure draft.[45]

This was not a highly conceptual project. Its essence was to determine, on largely pragmatic grounds, what relief should be granted from the basic principle—already established in a 1998 SIC Interpretation—that an entity's first IFRS-based financial statements should be prepared as if IFRSs had always been applied.[46] The core of the standard consisted of a list of options and exemptions, for instance concerning the restatement of business combinations accounted for under previous GAAP. The IASB did not form a fully-fledged advisory group to help it in identifying the relevant issues, but it did consult a group of experts from the Big Five accountancy firms.[47] The CNC, however, did form a broad-based advisory group in France.[48] The resulting standard, while not perhaps as eye-catching as some of the IASB's other work, was generally welcomed as a necessary and useful addition to the corpus of international standards, even though within the Board occasional misgivings remained about whether the standard and its subsequent amendments did not provide too much relief.

Because IFRS 1 amounted to a formal rite of passage, it could occasionally create inconvenience for companies that moved more gradually to IFRSs by means of national standards converged with IFRSs. This was the case in Hong Kong, where national standards since the early 2000s were already virtually identical to IFRSs, but where the national standard setter never required companies to apply IFRS 1. This meant that, in later years, companies that thought they already applied IFRSs discovered that they could not assert in their financial statements that they did so without going through the formalities of IFRS 1.

---

[44] Interview with Karel Van Hulle, 20 January 2009.

[45] AP 12/2002 agenda paper 8D. Of the 79 comments letters, 56 came from Europe. Of the 23 non-European responses, 16 came from the IASC's traditional constituency of accountancy bodies, standard setters, and accounting firms.

[46] SIC-8 *First-time Application of IASs as the Primary Basis of Accounting* (IASC, January 1998).

[47] AP 11/2001 paper 2B.   [48] AP 11/2001 paper 2A.

In South Africa, which had followed a similar convergence policy as Hong Kong, listed companies were required to apply IFRS 1 upon transition to IFRSs in 2005. This was frequently welcomed as an opportunity to make selective use of the options and exemptions offered in IFRS 1 to clean up companies' balance sheets.[49]

5.4.3 IFRS 2: Share-based Payment

As indicated above, the project on share-based payment was easily the most courageous project on the IASB's initial agenda. The explosive growth of employee stock options in the late 1980s and early 1990s had drawn attention to the fact that the value of these options was traditionally not reflected in a company's income statement, on the basis of the argument that the issue of options was a transaction among current and future shareholders, which had to be accounted for as a direct movement in equity. In the eyes of many, this led to an overstatement of profits, because a significant component of employee remuneration was never recognized as an expense. In the United States, APB Opinion 25 *Accounting for Stock Issued to Employees* (dating from 1972) did require expensing of stock options as a matter of principle, but it was easy to design share-based compensation arrangements resulting in a charge of zero to the income statement. When the FASB considered this issue in the early 1990s, and indicated its intent to require the recognition of the fair value of all stock options as an expense, an unprecedented storm of protest arose. Congress, mobilized by heavy corporate lobbying, threatened to intervene, and the FASB was forced to retreat.[50] FAS 123 *Accounting for Stock-based Compensation*, issued in 1995, gave companies the option to expense the fair value of share-based payment, or to continue to apply APB Opinion 25, with disclosure in the notes of the effect of the fair value-based expense. The latter option was chosen by virtually all publicly traded companies, with only Winn-Dixie and Boeing choosing to expense.

Although FAS 123 was compromised, as the FASB itself admitted, it was the only national standard providing any serious guidance on the issue.[51] Internationally, share-based payment remained a significant gap in accounting regulation while the value of options granted to executives and other employees soared to new records, both in the United States and elsewhere. In July 2000 the standard setters working together in the G4+1 had issued a discussion paper which signalled that they had not given up on the issue, and still preferred to move towards expensing.[52] Outside the English-speaking world, the Deutsches Rechnungslegung Standards Committee (DRSC) was developing an exposure draft. The IASB's liaison standard setters showed themselves supportive when told, early in 2001, that there was a strong consensus in the new IASB that share-based

---

[49] Interview with Darrel Scott, 12 March 2013.

[50] Stephen A. Zeff, 'The U.S. Senate Votes on Accounting for Employee Stock Options', in Stephen A. Zeff and Bala G. Dharan (editors), *Readings & Notes on Financial Accounting*, 5th edition (New York: McGraw-Hill, 1997), 507–17; Lawrence Revsine, Daniel W. Collins, and W. Bruce Johnson, *Financial Reporting & Analysis* (Upper Saddle River, NJ: Prentice Hall, 2002), 806–10.

[51] FAS 123, Basis for Conclusions, paragraph 62.

[52] *G4+1 Position Paper: Accounting for Share-Based Payment* (IASC, July 2000).

payment should be a priority project.[53] However, it was equally natural that those who had strongly opposed the FASB in the United States prepared themselves to oppose the IASB just as tenaciously. During the first SAC meeting, in July 2001, Philip B. Livingston, president and CEO of Financial Executives International (FEI), threateningly reminded the Board that the FEI had spent more than $50 million to defeat the FASB on the issue, and that it was prepared to do so again.[54] Tom Jones, who had himself taken part in some of the FEI's lobbying of the FASB when he was still with Citigroup, was well-placed to help the Board evaluate such a threat.

In the second half of 2001, a head-on collision appeared to be in the making. At the Board's September meeting, the first after setting the agenda, the IASB tentatively agreed that share-based payment should give rise to an expense in the income statement.[55] It further underlined this intention by extending the comment period on the G4+1 discussion paper, thus making it, in effect, its first due-process document for this project. The main author of the G4+1 paper, Kimberley Crook, had joined the IASB's staff from the UK ASB, and she was now put in charge of this project for the IASB. It was clear from which direction the wind was blowing, because the FEI swiftly responded with a press release in which it denounced the IASB's 'foregone conclusion'. It blamed some members of the IASB for restarting 'this acrimonious fight'.[56] Both sides began mobilizing their allies. The FEI took the lead in forming an 'International Employee Stock Option Coalition', bringing together many veterans of the earlier battle with the FASB.[57] Congress was alerted and in October 2001 Representative Michael Oxley wrote to the SEC that the IASB's course was 'unnecessary and unwise'.[58] On the other hand, the IASB made sure to stay in touch with sympathizers in the United States, where financial analysts and investors were mounting a campaign to improve accounting for stock options. For this group, among whom Warren Buffett was prominent, the IASB's moves were a welcome support.[59] Paul Volcker, the chairman of the IASC Foundation trustees, took his considerable presence to

---

[53] 'Stock Options, Combinations Top Agenda for International Accounting Standards Board', BNA's *Daily Tax Report*, 23 April 2001, 78 DTR G-1; 'National Rulemakers Endorse IASB's Tentative Plan for Stock Options Project', *Daily Tax Report*, 25 May 2001, 102 DTR G-7; interview with Wayne Upton, 7 July 2011.

[54] 'Inaugural Meeting of the SAC', *World Accounting Report*, September 2001, 12; Stephen A. Zeff, '"Political" Lobbying on Proposed Standards: A Challenge to the IASB', *Accounting Horizons*, 16/1 (March 2002), 44–5.

[55] IASB meeting of 10–13 September 2001, minute IX.

[56] 'Stock Option Accounting Project Could Undermine March Toward Global Accounting Standards', FEI news release, 21 September 2001. In April 2001, Livingston and Leisenring had already exchanged warning shots on including share-based payment on the IASB agenda, 'IASB's Rulemaking Plans Not Yet Clear; Panel to Pursue Standard Convergence', BNA's *Daily Tax Report*, 10 April 2001, 69 DTR J-1.

[57] 'New Business Coalition Boosts Work Against IASB Stock Options Accounting Rulemaking', BNA's *Daily Tax Report*, 17 December 2001, 240 DTR G-5.

[58] 'US Lawmaker Blasts Stock Options Proposal', Reuters newswire, 17 October 2001; 'Lawmakers Protest IASB's Pursuit of New Standard for Stock Options', BNA's *Daily Tax Report*, 18 October 2001, 200 DTR G-6.

[59] Email correspondence between David Tweedie and Jane B. Adams (Credit Suisse First Boston), 4 October 2001, and copy of letter from Buffett to Adams, dated 2 October 2001, IASB archive, 'Share options' file.

the stage and addressed an FEI conference in November, not in order to comment directly on the issue itself, but to defend the IASB's right to deal with stock option accounting in the interest of developing high quality global standards.[60]

SEC Chief Accountant Robert Herdman, just taking office in October 2001, was not enthusiastic about the immediate prospect of a renewed fight over share-based payment. He would have preferred the IASB to adopt the FASB's standard, based on the argument that the IASB should seek short-term convergence rather than divergence with US GAAP. He accepted, however, Tweedie's argument that a simple copying of US GAAP would not create a level playing field, because many European companies could, for legal or other reasons, not design their option packages in the way that US companies did under APB Opinion 25 and FAS 123 to avoid a charge to profit or loss.[61]

European enterprises joined in. Letters from companies and from the European Round Table of Industrialists began to arrive at the IASB. Fifteen major multi-nationals (Bayer, DaimlerChrysler, Ericsson, Hoffmann-La Roche, Jefferson Smurfit, ING, Lafarge, Nestlé, Nokia, Océ, Philips, Pirelli, Repsol YPF, Saint-Gobain, and UBS) wrote similar letters making the case that European enterprises should not be placed in a position of competitive disadvantage vis-à-vis their American competitors by having to expense share-based payment.[62] What tended to be overlooked in such letters was that the status quo favoured European companies. These were typically not required to expense at all, while the US companies were to some degree constrained in the design of their arrangements to achieve a charge of zero. Nevertheless, European business had the ear of its politicians. The European Commission urged caution. It advised the IASB to begin with a disclosure-only standard, and to move forward on the basis of international consensus only, which meant, of course, that the IASB should not move too far ahead of the FASB.[63]

However, despite all these signs of a gathering storm, the IASB was able to publish a standard requiring the expensing of share-based payment in February 2004 with perhaps surprising ease. Of course, before IFRS 2 *Share-based Payment* could be published, there were lengthy debates in the course of 2002 and 2003. In response to the IASB's November 2002 exposure draft, individual businesses and preparer organizations wrote to repeat their objections.[64] An ephemeral European Employee Stock Options Coalition made its appearance in 2003,

---

[60] Julia Irvine, 'A Good Guy to Have on Your Side', *Accountancy*, 27 December 2001; Paul Volcker, 'Notes for Remarks at Financial Executives International Conference on November 12, 2001', typescript, copy in IASB archive, 'Share options' file; 'Volcker Defends IASB Stock Options Effort; Board Vice Chairman Cautions Opponents', BNA's *Daily Tax Report*, 218 DTR G-3, 14 November 2001.

[61] Interview with Robert K. Herdman, 18 February 2009; 'In Harsh Words, Battle Signaled over IASB Moves toward Expensing Stock Options', BNA's *Daily Tax Report*, 18 October 2001, 200 DTR G-5.

[62] Stephen A. Zeff, 'Political Lobbying on Accounting Standards: US, UK and International Experience', in Christopher Nobes and Robert Parker, *Comparative International Accounting*, 12th edition (Harlow, England: Pearson, 2012), 252.

[63] Letter from Alain Joly to David Tweedie, dated 28 November 2001; letter from John Mogg to David Tweedie, dated 28 January 2002, both in IASC archive, 'Share options' file.

[64] For a quantitative analysis of the comment letters on the exposure draft, see Begoña Giner and Miguel Arce, 'Lobbying on Accounting Standards: Evidence from IFRS 2 on Share-based Payments', *European Accounting Review*, 21/4 (2012), 655–91.

following the US model of corporate lobbying.[65] But none of this had a noticeable impact on the progress of the IASB's project, because the political conditions had changed fundamentally. The accounting scandals involving Enron and other US companies broke in late 2001 and the first half of 2002, and, as a result, political support evaporated for anything that could be construed as corporate pleading against improved transparency. In the United States, many major companies, including Coca-Cola and General Electric, announced their intention to adopt expensing on a voluntary basis.[66] The FASB was now emboldened, or encouraged, to take up the issue of stock options again.[67] A month after Robert Herz assumed the chairmanship in July 2002, the FASB announced its intention to issue an invitation to comment on the IASB's forthcoming exposure draft, as a first step in considering any changes to US standards.[68] The topic was formally placed on the FASB's agenda in March 2003, and a revised version of FAS 123, which required expensing, was published in December 2004, although not without attempts at political intervention from Congress. Even allowing for the change in circumstances, the IASB could claim to have blazed a trail where the FASB had failed to go. Several members of the Board looked back on IFRS 2 as the IASB's greatest success during its first decade.

At a conceptual level, though, the IASB's achievement was more modest, as it found that it had to rely to a greater extent on the FASB's work than originally intended. While it was easy for the Board to agree that share-based payment should be expensed, it found it more difficult to decide on the appropriate measurement of the expense item. The G4+1 paper favoured vesting-date measurement, but the Board decided at an early stage to move towards the grant-date approach of FAS 123. However, there was a view within the Board that FAS 123 did not handle the grant-date approach properly, in particular with respect to the treatment of vesting conditions. Under FAS 123, the number of options or other equity instruments charged to profit or loss was adjusted ('trued up') during the vesting period as the probability that vesting conditions would be met was revised. The result was that, cumulatively over the vesting period, an expense was recognized only for options that actually vested. A reason for the Board's discomfort with this approach was that it was inconsistent with the main principle it had adopted, namely, that the expense recognized for share-based payment represented the value of the employee services received. Under FAS 123 no expense would be recorded for non-vested options, even though the employee in question might have rendered valuable services.

Apart from its wish to write a conceptually sound standard, the Board in this case may also have seen a practical reason for adhering to principle. The argument

---

[65] 'Options Rule Poses Profit Threat', *Financial Times* (London edition), 6 June 2003; letter from Rory Knight to David Tweedie, dated 6 June 2003, IASB archive, 'Share options' file.

[66] 'Standard Setters are Targeting Stock Options Again: After Enron Reform Will be Harder to Resist', *Financial Times* (London edition), 11 November 2002. It was Warren Buffett who, in early 2002, persuaded some major companies to begin expensing the fair value of stock options. See Floyd Norris, 'G.E. is Latest to Reconfigure Stock Options', posted 1 August 2002 <http://www.nytimes.com>.

[67] 'Investment Company Institute Urges FASB to Require Companies to Expense Options', BNA's *Daily Tax Report*, 22 August 2002, 163 DTR G-6.

[68] 'FASB's Plans Regarding the Accounting for Employee Stock Options', FASB press release dated 31 July 2002 <http://www.fasb.org>.

that the expense for share-based payment did not represent the value of the equity instruments themselves, but the value of employee services consumed, was the Board's main weapon against the traditional line of reasoning that share-based payment was a transaction among shareholders that should have no impact on profit or loss.[69] Compromising on this principle might expose the Board to the charge that it was simply an activist standard setter, bent on expensing stock options by any means. The FEI, at least, was ready to make this charge, as Philip Livingston wrote to Volcker: 'Charging a fictitiously calculated stock option expense to the income statement has never been about good accounting. . . . It has been about shareholder activist displeasure and their lack of control over the granting of stock options to executives.'[70]

In its November 2002 exposure draft, the IASB tried what it believed to be a conceptually superior approach, based on units of services received. This did not appeal to many respondents, not least because of practical difficulties in application.[71] After considering the arguments again, the staff recommended in May 2003 that the Board adopt the FAS 123 approach, not because it was conceptually superior, but for practical reasons.[72] One of these reasons was that it was understood that the FASB, which, as indicated above, had taken up stock options again, was not likely to change on this point. Although share-based payment was not a part of the short-term convergence agenda agreed between the two boards at the time of the Norwalk Agreement (see Section 5.7)[73] both the IASB and the FASB were taking note of each other's decisions to avoid, if possible, further divergence between the two sets of standards.[74] The proposal to adopt the FASB solution caused some soul-searching in the IASB about balancing principle and pragmatism. Geoffrey Whittington, who had consistently argued that the Board should seriously consider vesting-date measurement, maintained that the FASB approach was a hybrid of the vesting-date and grant-date approaches, and that, if the Board just had to do what the FASB did, 'it may as well stop its debate there'.[75]

At this stage, there were perhaps good reasons for a pragmatic approach. The comments received on the exposure draft showed that, while many companies continued to oppose the expensing of share-based payment, the battle on this point had been won. It was now time to move forward and to settle a host of remaining specific issues so that the standard could be published before the March 2004 target date for the 'stable platform'.

---

[69] See IASB meeting of 19–22 February 2002, minute 12, where it was agreed that this point needed to be publicly explained, in response to criticism that recognition of expenses with respect to share-based payment was inconsistent with the IASB's conceptual framework. The explanation occurred in 'Share-Based Payment', *IASB Insight*, April 2002, 7–8.

[70] Letter from Philip B. Livingston to Paul Volcker, dated 11 February 2002, IASB archive, 'Share options' file.

[71] AP 5/2003 paper 14A.   [72] AP 5/2003 paper 14B; see also *IStaR*, May 2003, 34.

[73] See IASB Board meeting of 17 and 19–20 September 2002, minute 2, for the IASB's understanding of the convergence agenda.

[74] 'FASB Actions on Options Measurement Signal Potential Divergence from IASB', BNA's *Daily Tax Report*, 8 May 2003, 89 DTR G-8.

[75] *IStaR*, May 2003, 34–5.

5.4.4 IFRS 3: Business Combinations

Like share-based payment, accounting for business combinations was an area where accounting standard setters had been at work during the 1990s to rectify what they perceived as a long-standing deficiency in financial accounting. The deficiency in this case was the approach of accounting for some business combinations by means of the pooling of interests method (known as 'merger accounting' in the United Kingdom). This approach, designed originally for mergers of equals, had long been controversial because of widespread 'dirty pooling': the application of the pooling method to what were, in effect, acquisitions.[76] The attractions of pooling were that it did not give rise to the recognition of goodwill, which in some countries had to be amortized through profit or loss, and that the assets and liabilities of neither partner in the business combination had to be remeasured to their fair values.

The use of pooling was curtailed in Canada as early as 1974. Australia had eliminated the pooling method altogether in 1985 with AAS21, and the UK ASB had intended to restrict its use significantly with its FRS 6, issued in 1994. The FASB had for many years not touched the issue, perhaps mindful that the demise of its predecessor, the Accounting Principles Board, had been hastened by its struggle with accounting for business combinations in the late 1960s. In 1996, at the urging of the SEC, the FASB added a wide-ranging project on business combinations to its agenda, and in December 1998, the G4+1 issued a position paper, prepared by FASB staff, arguing that the pooling method should be eliminated and all business combinations should be accounted for as purchases.[77] This paper, as well as a concurrent project of Canada's Accounting Standards Board, may have served to give the FASB some international cover when, in September 1999, it issued an exposure draft, 'Business Combinations and Intangible Assets', in which it proposed the abolition of pooling, as well as the reduction of the amortization period for goodwill from forty to twenty years. The latter step would have brought about a degree of convergence with the IASC's standards, because IAS 22 *Business Combinations* (revised 1998) included a rebuttable presumption that the proper amortization period for goodwill should not exceed twenty years. IAS 22 had a requirement for pooling, but only in 'exceptional circumstances', when it was not possible to identify one of the partners in a business combination as the acquirer. In its final years, the IASC had considered business combinations again in the light of the G4+1 paper, but had made little progress. One of its steering committees was preparing a discussion paper, a draft of which was submitted to the IASB in May 2001.[78]

However, in December 2000, a week before the IASC Board's final meeting, the FASB decided to make a major change to its proposals. It did so in response to strong political lobbying against the mandatory amortization of goodwill, which promised to upset many income statements as a result of the FASB's decision to

---

[76] For the origin of the phrase, see A.J. Briloff, 'Dirty Pooling', *The Accounting Review*, 42/3 (July 1976), 489–96.

[77] *G4+1 Position Paper: Recommendations for Achieving Convergence on the Methods of Accounting for Business Combinations* (IASC, December 1998).

[78] AP 5/2001 paper 9.

drop pooling altogether.[79] While maintaining its decision to abolish pooling, the FASB now decided that it could accept, as a matter of principle, the replacement of the amortization of goodwill by regular tests for impairment, with the effect that goodwill would remain on balance sheets for an indefinite period of time. The FASB's modified proposal was exposed for comment in February 2001, just as the IASB was holding its first informal agenda discussions. In June 2001, the FASB issued its new standards, FAS 141 *Business Combinations* and FAS 142 *Goodwill and Other Intangible Assets.*

Given the history of earlier activity in the G4+1, it was natural for the IASB to see business combinations as a priority convergence project with the abolition of pooling as an important objective. However, now that the FASB had changed tack, there was also another reason why the Board could hardly avoid adding the project to its agenda: European companies were anxious to make sure that they too would no longer be required to amortize goodwill.

In July 2001, Tweedie received a letter from Novartis. The Swiss company was an early adopter of IASs. Its chief accounting officer, Malcolm Cheetham, had participated in several IASC steering committees, and served as a member of the delegation of the Federation of Swiss Industrial Holding Companies to the IASC Board in 1999–2000. This degree of involvement arguably gave Novartis some claim to the IASB's attention. The letter did not comment on the abolition of pooling as such, but on the consequent need to amortize goodwill. The letter was written in strong language: the company argued that it was 'not prepared to be strategically disadvantaged by using IAS', and effectively threatened to switch to US GAAP unless the IASB would speedily—the date of 1 January 2002 was suggested—remove the requirement to amortize goodwill.[80] As seen above in the discussion of share-based payment, this was not the only time that the argument of competitive disadvantage was raised. And although Novartis was not itself in an EU member state, its concerns were widely shared across Europe. By the summer of 2001, presumably because of lobbying by EU companies, the goodwill amortization issue had made its appearance in the political debate over the proposed IAS Regulation.[81] The need to avoid competitive disadvantage was included in recital 15 to the IAS Regulation enacted in 2002 (see Section 4.1.2).

It was therefore for more than one reason that the Board added a project on business combinations to its agenda, split into two phases. Phase I was to deal mainly with the high-level issue of pooling of interests accounting and the treatment of goodwill, while phase II would consider more specific aspects of accounting for business combinations which were also still on the FASB's agenda. The Board members accepted, with varying degrees of enthusiasm, that phase I was effectively about 'catching up with the United States'.[82]

Immediately after obtaining SAC's views about its initial agenda, in July 2001, the Board formally began the substantive discussions on phase I, and without

---

[79] See Dennis R. Beresford, 'Congress Looks at Accounting for Business Combinations', *Accounting Horizons*, 15/1 (March 2001), 73–86; Zeff, ' "Political" Lobbying on Proposed Standards', 50–1.

[80] Letter from R. Breu, chief financial officer, and M.B. Cheetham, head of group financial reporting and accounting, to David Tweedie, dated 13 July 2001, IASB archive, file 'SAC'.

[81] Email from Gilbert Gélard to David Tweedie, dated 31 July 2001, IASB archive, file 'EFRAG'.

[82] *ISAS Report* (subsequently *IStaR*), July 2001, 2.

delay it voted tentatively that all business combinations should be accounted for by using the purchase method.[83]

Within the Board, the strongest reservations were expressed by Geoffrey Whittington, who believed that the Board was rushing to a predetermined conclusion, and by Tatsumi Yamada, who maintained that, at least in Japan, there were instances of mergers of equals for which pooling was the appropriate treatment.[84] Yamada's concerns were reiterated by the IASB's Japanese liaison standard setter, the Accounting Standards Board of Japan (ASBJ).[85] The elimination of pooling was still a sore point when, in subsequent years, Japan began to consider the adoption of IFRSs.

In September 2001, the Board took the next step when it voted in principle to adopt an impairment-only approach to goodwill. Most of the staff work on this project fell to Annette Kimmitt, recently recruited from the Australian Accounting Standards Board (AASB). Based on the key decisions taken in 2001, she prepared the way for the Board towards an exposure draft of a new standard on business combinations to replace IAS 22, together with consequential amendments to IAS 36 *Impairment of Assets* and IAS 38 *Intangible Assets*. The exposure drafts were published in December 2002.

In developing these drafts, the Board continually had to strike a balance between making amendments with a view to convergence with the United States, and deferring issues for more fundamental subsequent consideration. The most obvious issue in this regard was the approach to testing goodwill for impairment, and for determining the new carrying amount of impaired goodwill, points on which significant differences between US GAAP and IFRSs existed. The Board agreed with the staff that a fundamental reconsideration of IAS 36 was not in order at this time. These differences could be accepted for the time being as long as the main convergence prizes, the prohibition of pooling and the replacement of amortization by an impairment test, were being won.[86] The Board therefore limited itself to clarifications and additional guidance with respect to the impairment method.

On the basis of the comment letters, the Board concluded that there was considerable support for the two main changes, which were duly reflected in the final standard. Phase I of the business combinations project was concluded with the publication of IFRS 3 *Business Combinations* in March 2004, together with amended versions of IAS 36 and IAS 38. As part of the preparation of the final standard, IASB Board members and staff conducted field visits at companies in Australia, France, Germany, Japan, South Africa, Switzerland, and the United Kingdom in order to discuss the practical implications of the impairment-only approach to goodwill. They also held round-table discussions in the United States and Canada to learn about early experience with the application of the new US standards.[87]

---

[83] IASC Board meeting of 25–7 July 2001, minute 5.
[84] *ISAS Report*, July 2001, 7.
[85] IASB Board meeting with national standard setters, 10–11 September 2001, minute 4.
[86] AP 12/2001 paper 1A, paragraph 24; Board debate as reported in *IStaR*, December 2001, 2–3.
[87] AP 7/2003 paper 13H.

Meanwhile, the FASB and the IASB had agreed in 2001 run a phase II business combinations project on a joint basis. This project, formally added to the IASB's active agenda in April 2002, was to deal with issues arising from the application of the purchase method, as well as with the 'new basis' or 'fresh start' method, expected to apply to business combinations under common control. Although this was a joint project, it was recognized that the FASB staff would take the lead in the joint project team. Both boards planned to consider the same agenda papers, but they would typically not do so in joint meetings, and the IASB was expected to discuss the papers after the FASB had done so. It was recognized from the start that each Board scoped the project somewhat differently, and that each would in the end write its own exposure draft and standard to replace or amend FAS 141 and IAS 22, respectively.[88] As can be seen, this first joint project with the FASB preceded the Norwalk Agreement by about half a year, but as it became caught up in the wider IASB–FASB convergence programme, it will be further discussed in Chapter 12.

5.5 INITIAL DIFFICULTIES

During its first years, the IASB scored some successes, but it also ran into serious difficulties with other projects. Its most eye-catching problems were in the area of financial instruments, where the IASB became embroiled in major political complications with the EU. These developments are discussed in Chapter 6. But, while financial instruments dominated the headlines, two 'leadership' projects from the Board's initial agenda were quietly running into the ground.

5.5.1 Insurance Contracts

After a long hesitation, the IASC Board had decided to take up a project on insurance accounting in 1997, and installed a steering committee to produce an initial document. The steering committee, chaired by Warren McGregor, made rapid progress and produced a 450-page issues paper in 1999, which was exposed for comment.[89] By the time the IASC was wound up, the steering committee was still digesting the comment letters, and the IASC Board did not really have an opportunity to take the project any further.

The IASB adopted the project for the reasons given in the issues paper: the economic significance of the insurance industry, coupled with the great variety in accounting practices around the world.[90] Accounting rules for the insurance sector were typically set by regulators rather than standard setters, and exemptions from general accounting rules or standards for insurance companies were common. Recently, the insurance supervisors, united in the International Association of

---

[88] For project arrangements see AP 11/2001 papers 11 and 11A, AP 4/2002 paper 4.

[89] 'Insurance: An Issues Paper Issued for Comment by the Steering Committee on Insurance', two volumes (IASC, November 1999).

[90] IASCF trustees meeting of 15 October 2001, agenda paper 2.

Insurance Supervisors (IAIS), had taken an interest in the international harmonization of accounting standards for the insurance industry. Like its counterpart in securities regulation, IOSCO, before it, the IAIS had set up a working group to follow and participate in the IASC's work. Following the 1997 Asian financial crisis, accounting standards became part of the agenda for strengthening the international financial system. The IAIS, as well as IOSCO and the Basel Committee, were instructed by the G7 Finance Ministers, in October 1998, to review the extant IASs.[91] As it was not too difficult to note that there was a large hole in these standards with respect to insurance accounting, the IAIS had, by 2000, identified accounting standards as one of its priority issues.[92] The heightened interest from regulators probably made it impossible for the IASB to sidestep this issue even if it had been inclined to do so.

In line with the IASC discussion paper, the IASB Board defined the project in terms of accounting for insurance contracts, not in terms of accounting by insurers. For most of its life, the IASC had been reluctant to issue industry-specific standards, and the IASB has continued this attitude. Although the IASB Board never formally affirmed this reluctance in a resolution or a policy statement, it was well understood from the beginning that it preferred to develop generally applicable standards for specific transactions and events, so as to avoid the difficulties of defining the nature of a 'bank' or an 'insurer'.[93] The extent to which the Board succeeded is open to question, because there is a thin line between an industry standard and a standard on a topic, such as insurance contracts, that virtually coincides with an industry. Just as the distinction between principles-based and rules-based standards is fuzzy, so too the IASB's stance on industry standards was not one of black and white. Even so, it may fairly be said that the IASB consciously avoided the path taken in the United States where the tangle of industry-specific guidance was increasingly seen as a major contributor to the vexed complexity of US GAAP.[94]

The steering committee which had produced the 1999 issues paper was still active as the IASB took office, and it was working to develop a 'draft statement of principles' or DSOP, the IASC's customary due-process step preceding an exposure draft. The first half of this DSOP became available after the Board's summer recess, but the Board did not get round to a substantive discussion until November 2001. Many Board members had no particular expertise in this area, in which, as Technical Director Upton put it, there was a prevailing 'tendency to view insurance accounting as a sort of black-box, the workings of which are known only to members of a secret society'. In its briefing documents, and in educational sessions held for the benefit of the Board, the staff attempted to present the issues in terms of basic and generally applicable accounting concepts—assets, liabilities, and equity; measurement; revenue recognition—and to dispel the view that 'insurance

---

[91] 'Declaration of G7 Finance Ministers and Central Bank Governors', 30 October 1998 <http://www.imf.org>.

[92] IAIS, *2000 Annual Report*, 15.

[93] Communications to the authors from Peter Clark, Warren McGregor, and James Leisenring, all dated 31 May 2011. See also IASB Board meeting of 18–20 April 2001, minute 13, for Leisenring's concerns over industry standards.

[94] As in 'Final Report of the Advisory Committee on Improvements to Financial Reporting to the United States Securities and Exchange Commission' (Pozen Committee report), 1 August 2008.

is different'.[95] This appealed to the Board, which, as indicated above, was wary of introducing industry-specific exceptions. However, it also opened up a Pandora's box of what came to be known as 'cross-cutting issues'. For many years to come, the Board would struggle with the problem that, to make progress on insurance, it first needed to make progress on issues such as revenue recognition, liabilities, and performance reporting, or to risk pre-judging these other issues by pressing ahead on insurance.

Some of these linkages among projects already became visible as the Board discussed the DSOP in late 2001 and early 2002. The steering committee presented the essential choice to the Board as one between a 'deferral and matching' approach, which had traditionally prevailed in insurance accounting, and an 'asset and liability' approach. It recommended the latter, as consistent with the IASB's conceptual framework. Like the FASB's conceptual framework, to which it was much indebted, the IASB's conceptual framework saw assets and liabilities as the fundamental elements of financial statements, from which revenues and expenses, defined as changes in assets and liabilities, were derived. Although by no means all the IASC's standards had been made consistent with this approach, it certainly had had a significant influence as the IASC revised its standards during the 1990s.

In a formal sense, an asset and liability approach could be combined with any measurement basis for assets and liabilities, and the conceptual framework did little more than enumerate the different measurement bases used in practice. Even so, in the minds of many, fair value accounting became easily associated with a primary focus on the measurement of assets and liabilities. Towards the end of the 1990s, there was a growing momentum in favour of fair value accounting and standards like IAS 40 *Investment Property* and IAS 41 *Agriculture* were clear manifestations of this tendency. Similar ideas were taking shape with respect to financial instruments. A joint working group (JWG) of standard setters, including the IASC, had been instructed in 1997 to develop the general principle of measuring all financial instruments at fair value in the form of a draft standard (see Section 6.1). The JWG published its draft in 2000.

Caught up in the flow towards fair value accounting, the insurance steering committee adopted this perspective in its 1999 discussion paper. It argued that insurance contracts had the essential features of financial instruments, so that, if a full fair value standard on financial instruments were to be issued, insurance contracts should follow this approach.[96] However, as 2001 progressed, it became ever clearer that the momentum towards fair value was weakening, and that a full fair value approach to financial instruments was receding into the future. In its DSOP, the steering committee maintained its recommendation of an asset and liability approach, but in terms of measurement it argued more generally for a so-called prospective approach. This still might mean measurement at fair value if and when a fair value standard on financial instruments were issued, but in the meantime would mean measurement on the basis of entity-specific estimates of future cash flows.[97] In whatever guise, a prospective approach raised significant

[95] AP 9/2001 paper 5C.   [96] 'Insurance: An Issues Paper', paragraphs 537, 556.
[97] DSOP Chapter 3, AP 11/2001 paper 5D.

conceptual issues on which the Board was by no means united. One implication was that so-called day-one profits might have to be recognized at the inception of an insurance contract. Whereas Board members such as Warren McGregor and Tricia O'Malley might see the recognition of such profits as a consequence of trying to measure the economic reality of insurance contracts, others were more uncomfortable with this possibility.[98] Another major problem arising from the perceived commonality between insurance contracts and financial instruments related to renewal options in insurance contracts. It was noted that long-term insurance contracts were typically renewable annually at the option of the policy holder. Although it could be expected that a large proportion of contracts would be renewed, an insurance company could not compel renewal. Hence, while the expectation of renewals was valuable, the question was whether it met the definition of an asset. Some Board members argued that, in the case of financial instruments, written options could never give rise to an asset. If the renewal option was viewed as an intangible asset representing the value of customer relationships, the question was why other similar intangible assets could not be recognized as well.[99] A parallel of particular significance for the Board were bank deposits that could be withdrawn on demand. As discussed in Section 6.2, this latter point sparked the Board's first major confrontation with the European banking industry and the European Commission.

But before all these issues could be discussed in detail, the fair value proposals in the 1999 issues paper had caused considerable alarm in parts of the insurance industry, especially outside the United Kingdom, Canada, and Australia, where fair value had already obtained a degree of general acceptance.[100] As the chapters of the DSOP were gradually made available on the IASB's website during the second half of 2001, it appeared that a shift from fair value to a prospective approach did little to assuage the industry's concerns. It was notable, for instance, that in Japan, where the prospect of direct application of IFRSs was still remote, the insurance industry took a lively and critical interest in the IASB's work. When the Board met outside London, as it still regularly did in its early years, its public meetings sometimes attracted few spectators. However, it was observed that, when the Board met in Tokyo in March 2002, the public gallery was filled with observers from the Japanese insurance industry.[101] At the same time, insurance industry associations from Japan, Germany, and the United States joined forces to lobby the IASB directly and through the press, and to call for a reconsideration of the IASB's planning, which still aimed for the publication of an exposure draft by the end of the year.[102]

---

[98] See the Board debate as reported in *IStaR*, December 2001, 12–15.

[99] For an early discussion of this point, see the Board debate as reported in *IStaR*, December 2001, 12–15.

[100] See AP 12/2001 paper 12A, for a review of responses on selected topics from the 1999 issues paper.

[101] *IStaR*, March 2002, 19.

[102] IASB Board meeting of 28 March 2002, administrative items minute 6. See also 'Versicherer wehren sich gegen geplante Bilanzregel: Verbände aus Japan, US und Deutschland einig', *Financial Times Deutschland*, 29 April 2002, 30; 'Life Insurers to International Accounting Standards Board: Don't Put Insurers, Stockholders, Consumers at Risk', PR Newswire Europe, 27 March 2002. For the project planning, see AP 3/2002 paper 5A.

Two months later, however, in May 2002, the Board reconsidered its timetable. Citing the transition to IFRSs in the EU in 2005, it noted that it was not realistic to develop a complete standard in time.[103] However, the Board knew that it had to do something: as part of the improvements project, it was about to propose the introduction of a 'GAAP hierarchy' into IAS 8 *Accounting Policies, Changes in Accounting Estimates and Errors* to apply in cases where IFRSs lacked a standard on a specific accounting issue. The proposed rule would require companies to consider 'pronouncements of other standard-setting bodies that use a similar conceptual framework [as the IASB]'. The implication was that, without an IFRS on insurance contracts, companies switching to IFRSs in 2005 would for all practical purposes be required to adopt the relevant portions of US GAAP. That this was feasible had been shown by Allianz, a major German insurer, which had followed this approach since it adopted IASs on a voluntary basis in 1998. To the Board, though, this was highly unattractive. If the Board would eventually succeed in developing its own standard, it would not win goodwill among companies that would have to change twice. More importantly, there was a fear that, once in place, US GAAP would be difficult to remove and would block the Board's efforts to develop a new standard.[104] Although the revised IAS 8 was softened to say that companies 'may' consider pronouncement of other standard setters, US GAAP was likely to remain an important point of reference for insurance companies.

Over the following months of 2002, the Board agreed on a way to split the project into two phases. In a limited phase I, it sought to issue a standard that exempted insurance contracts from the requirements of IAS 8. This would allow them to continue using their previous accounting policies while claiming compliance with IFRSs. At the same time, it sought to impose a degree of discipline on the process by requiring a loss-recognition test, and by ruling out certain practices that were deemed to be incompatible with the conceptual framework, such as the recognition of catastrophe provisions that do not meet the definition of a liability. While seemingly simple, it still took the Board until July 2003 before it could publish a phase I exposure draft, as it had to consider carefully which elements from its discussions thus far it should introduce in the interim standard, and what consequences the introduction of blocks of alien GAAP in IFRS-based financial statements might have for the application of other standards. Phase I was concluded with the issue of IFRS 4 *Insurance Contracts*, in March 2004.

The original idea was that phase II would continue in parallel with phase I, so that a final standard might be issued in 2004 or 2005. The Board did indeed continue its discussions during the second half of 2002. In January 2003 it came back to the fundamental measurement issue and resolved that insurance liabilities should be measured at fair value. Expecting to develop a standard on that basis, it also introduced a requirement in the phase I exposure draft that the fair value of insurance liabilities should be disclosed in the notes from 31 December 2006 onwards. However, after January 2003, phase II came to a standstill. The project was not resuscitated until the middle of 2004, only to run into further protracted

---

[103] IASB Board meeting of 22–4 May 2002, minute 4.
[104] See the Board's discussion as reported in *IStaR*, May 2002, 17–20.

delays. As discussed more fully in Chapter 16, no insurance standard had been published by the end of the period covered in this book. These delays robbed the proposed fair value disclosure of its basis, as the Board was not in a position to give guidance on its measurement, and it was therefore dropped from IFRS 4.[105]

5.5.2 Performance Reporting

The project on performance reporting built on a long history of initiatives by standard setters in the English-speaking countries to reconsider some of the fundamental features of financial statements. In the early 1980s, the FASB's conceptual framework project brought about the ascendancy of an asset and liability approach to financial reporting. As a natural part of that approach, the FASB's Concepts Statement No. 3 *Elements of Financial Statements of Business Enterprises* (1980) introduced the notion of 'comprehensive income' into the literature, defined as all changes in net assets from non-owner sources. This called into question the role of net income, the traditional bottom-line earnings based on the realization principle, as the primary indicator of enterprise performance.[106]

Before the FASB was able to make significant progress in incorporating comprehensive income into its standards, the UK ASB issued FRS 3 *Reporting Financial Performance* in 1992. FRS 3 introduced the 'statement of total recognized gains and losses' (STRGL) as one of the primary financial statements, thus moving those gains and losses that had traditionally been recognized directly in equity from the relative obscurity of the notes or supplementary schedules to a comparable degree of prominence as the gains and losses recognized in the income statement. Spurred on by, among others, the Association for Investment Management and Research (AIMR, since 2004 the CFA Institute), one of the main organizations of financial statement users, the FASB published FAS 130 *Reporting Comprehensive Income* in 1997. FAS 130 required a presentation of other comprehensive income (OCI) either in a single performance statement, in a separate statement, or as part of a statement of changes in equity. The last, and least prominent, option was introduced under pressure from industry. The ASB and FASB standards were limited to issues of presentation, in the sense that they by and large accepted the distinction in existing standards between items recognized in profit or loss (i.e. in the income statement), and items of OCI. However, more was at stake, because at the same time a tendency was discernible to use OCI (to give it its American name) to resolve some ongoing controversies. An increasing use of fair value to measure financial instruments, for instance, or the immediate recognition of actuarial gains and losses on defined benefit plans, might be made more acceptable by recognizing the resulting gains and losses in OCI rather than in profit or loss.

In the debates on these issues, it became clear that both the ASB and FASB were quite inclined to reconsider performance measurement in a more fundamental

---

[105] AP 11/2003 paper 9G.

[106] See L. Todd Johnson, Cheri L. Reither, and Robert J. Swieringa, 'Toward Reporting Comprehensive Income', *Accounting Horizons*, 9/4 (December 1995), 128–37.

way. One of the essential issues to be resolved was the acceptability of what came to be known as 'recycling': reporting value changes in the income statement upon realization after they had previously been reported as unrealized changes in OCI. Traditionally, this question had been settled on an ad hoc basis, and in different ways by different standard setters. For instance, gains on re-measuring property, plant, and equipment to fair value were not recycled under IFRSs, in contrast to exchange gains and losses on foreign subsidiaries. During the 1990s the question was posed, but not resolved, whether recycling was acceptable in principle. With recycling, a move to a single performance statement could be seen as a largely presentational issue: net income would remain, albeit as a subtotal rather than a bottom-line number. Without recycling for any item, the performance statement would no longer include a traditional net income number based on the realization principle. The ASB and the FASB were at variance on this point. The ASB was inclined to reject recycling, whereas under US GAAP all items of OCI were sooner or later recycled.

Meanwhile, other G4 standard setters had made, or were making similar moves. The IASC had modified IAS 1 *Presentation of Financial Statements* in 1997 to the effect that non-owner movements in equity had to be shown in one of the primary financial statements. Faced with similar protests as the FASB, the IASC had allowed companies a choice between reporting such items either in a second performance statement or in a statement of changes in equity. The way towards further reform was pointed to in a 1999 G4+1 discussion paper, which laid the basis for one of the IASC's final steering committees, set up in March 2000.[107] The ASB continued in the lead, though, and issued an exposure draft, FRED 22, in December 2000, in which it proposed to move towards a single performance statement which included all recognized gains and losses.

All of these previous events provided sufficient momentum for the IASB to consider performance reporting as one of its first priorities. To undertake the project jointly with the ASB was natural given the ASB's recent work. An alternative was offered by the FASB, which had issued its own agenda proposal for a project on performance reporting in August 2001, and had signalled its willingness to do so jointly with the IASB.[108] This did not happen, at least not for the time being: the IASB teamed up with the ASB, and the FASB went off on its own.

One reason for the IASB's choice of partner may have been that Tweedie was aware that the ASB was strongly motivated because it saw a revised presentation of performance as an essential facilitator of its simultaneous revision of accounting for pensions.[109] The fact that the ASB already had an exposure draft out may well have led Tweedie and other Board members to believe that the IASB could issue a standard before long. This belief may have been reinforced by the Board's

---

[107] *Reporting Financial Performance: A Discussion Paper Issued for Comment by the Staff of the International Accounting Standards Committee* (IASC: August 1999). The steering committee appointed in March 2000 included two persons who would become initial members of the IASB: Anthony Cope and Patricia O'Malley, as well as a future IASB Board member, Patricia McConnell, who was then a Board member of the IASC. Two steering committee members were appointed to the initial SAC: Jean Keller and Adir Inbar. The other members were Egbert Eeftink (Netherlands), Kwon-Jung Kim (Korea), and John Spencer (New Zealand). AP 10/2001 paper 3A, appendix.

[108] BNA's *Daily Tax Report*, 9 September 2001, 172-DTR G-1.

[109] Interview with Allan Cook, 18 March 2009; see also Section 5.7.5.

stated intention to exclude recognition and measurement issues from the scope of the project, so that it would largely be limited to a different presentation of accounting numbers determined in accordance with other standards.[110] In the light of subsequent events, that was perhaps not a realistic intention, and Board members who had been working on this issue in the 1990s might have been aware of that.

The Board did not take long to make up its mind that it was looking towards a single statement of performance. Like the expensing of share-based payment and the abolition of the amortization of goodwill, this was one of the fundamental decisions taken within months of establishing the initial agenda. The Board's preference for a single statement of performance was expressed in October 2001, in line with FRED 22 and a DSOP prepared by staff member Colin Fleming (retained from the IASC) and the IASC steering committee.

In October 2001, the Board also tentatively accepted the steering committee's view that there should be no recycling.[111] How the Board thought it could reconcile this with a 'presentation only' approach to this project is not so easy to see. Around the same time, the IASB recruited Richard Barker from Cambridge University as its first 'research fellow' to take over the role of project manager from Fleming for this project. David Tweedie approached Barker at the suggestion of Geoffrey Whittington, who, also at Cambridge, had supervised Barker's Ph.D. thesis.

The steering committee was disbanded, the IASC's DSOP was shelved, and early in 2002 Barker proposed, on behalf of the staff of both the ASB and the IASB, the outlines of a 'matrix' approach to performance reporting. The performance statement would be ordered vertically by presenting financing items separately from all other items, which would be grouped under the label of 'business'. In addition, there would be a horizontal split by presenting two different columns: 'income' and 'valuation adjustments' (as well as a third, 'totals', column). The 'valuation adjustments' column was to include both realized and unrealized holding gains.[112] The DSOP, as well as earlier proposals mentioned above, had focused on the vertical classification of income and expense items. The idea of using multiple columns had occasionally been considered before, but not pursued.[113]

For the vertical ordering of the performance statement, Barker fell back on mainstream equity valuation theory. The proposed breakdown into a financing and a business section was justified by the notion that the value of operational activities must be considered independently from the capital structure of the firm. With this vertical ordering, the concepts of net income and OCI would disappear, as well as the need for recycling, as the components of OCI would be apportioned to the financing and business sections (or to a third category for tax items, added later during the project). All in all, Barker's proposals pointed the Board towards a radical break with accepted practice, rather than towards a swift conclusion of the project.

---

[110] Colin Fleming, 'Reporting Performance', *IASB Insight*, January 2002, 12.

[111] IASB meeting of 18–20 October 2001, minute 11.

[112] AP 1/2002 paper 3. See also Richard Barker, 'Reporting Financial Performance', *Accounting Horizons*, 18/2 (June 2004), 157–72, for a more extensive discussion of the matrix approach reflecting the IASB's discussions up to that point.

[113] For example, in the G4+1 discussion paper *Reporting Financial Performance*, 49–50.

The Board accepted the proposal as the basis for further work and continued to debate its implications during each meeting up to December 2002, in tandem with the ASB. By the end of the year, a first version of an exposure draft was readied. Earlier, in July, the Board had briefly considered whether it should issue a discussion paper first, as suggested by the ASB, but it had decided that the G4 paper had essentially fulfilled that role. Gilbert Gélard noted that some speed was in order with a view to the 2005 implementation of IFRSs in Europe.[114]

The ASB's suggestion to proceed cautiously, and the Board's decision to press ahead, came at a time when the discussion had moved from general principles to the practical implications of the matrix approach, with the result that it must have become ever clearer to the Board just how controversial the project was becoming.

One of these implications concerned cash flow hedges. Under IAS 39, fair value changes of derivatives used in such hedges were reported in OCI, to be recycled to profit or loss at a later stage to offset the effect of recognizing the hedged item. The logical implication of the matrix principle was that the fair value changes of the derivative would be shown in the revaluation column, whereas the hedged item might be recognized in the income column in a different period. This, of course, would be the end of this form of hedge accounting. The Board had no great liking for hedge accounting, but it recognized that it would not do to end cash flow hedge accounting as part of the performance reporting project, while it was simultaneously preparing an exposure draft of an improved IAS 39 which left cash flow hedging intact (see Chapter 6). Staff and most Board members therefore tended towards an exception or practical expedient to allow at least some form of cash flow hedge accounting. Reacting to this turn of events, ASB Chairman Mary Keegan wrote to the IASB that a fix for cash flow hedge accounting would be 'an incongruous conflict with the principled approach of the project'. According to the ASB, the project's proposals would 'require a major change in thinking by the business community and the case for this change is unlikely to be convincing unless the proposals clearly follow coherent principles'.[115]

At this stage, if not before, it should have been clear that it was no longer possible to maintain that this project was just about a modified ordering and presentation of the accounting numbers produced by existing standards. The Board had got itself into deep water, and what was more problematic, it had done so with relatively little due process. Before the end of 2002, the IASB had not consulted widely about this project. The steering committee had not been replaced by a new working group, and consultations had been limited mainly to SAC and the liaison standard setters. Even so, in the course of 2002 the Board had had several occasions to learn that the ASBJ, as well as many of their Japanese constituents, were very uneasy about the direction the project was taking.[116] At the Board's October 2002 meeting with national standard setters, the ASBJ

---

[114] IASB meeting of 16–19 July 2002, minute 7.6 and administrative items minute 4.2; see also *IStaR*, July 2002, 41.

[115] Letter from Mary Keegan to David Tweedie, dated 4 July 2002, AP 7/2002 paper 8A (supplement).

[116] During the March 2002 Board meeting in Tokyo, Barker found it necessary to reassure the ASBJ observers about the future direction of the project. See *IStaR*, March 2002, 12. See also letter from Eiko Tsujiyama to David Tweedie, dated 12 July 2002, agenda paper 2D for meeting with national standard setters, 28 October 2002.

presented an elaborate criticism of the IASB's work so far.[117] ASBJ Chairman Shizuki Saito, an accounting academic, was deeply versed in the literature on income concepts, and was quite determined to make sure that the IASB was careful about its first principles. But this was no mere academic issue: in Japan, all the complexities of the project had already been subsumed in a simple rallying cry that could easily be understood by non-technicians as well: the alarm was sounded that the IASB was 'abolishing net income'.[118] Yoshiki Yagi, executive vice president of Hitachi Ltd and a member of SAC, recalled that he used to put forward his critical views on this issue with such persistence that Tweedie gave him the nick-name of 'Mr Net Income'.[119]

Apart from Japan, awareness of what the IASB was doing increased during the first months of 2003, when the Board conducted a series of field visits on the basis of Barker's draft standard. These were consultations organized by the liaison standard setters in their respective countries, with considerable leeway for the liaison standard setters to choose the format, the invited preparer and user representatives, and the degree of involvement of the IASB. Through the field visits, but also through unsolicited comments coming in, it became apparent that the 'abolition of net income' was the single most important concern, both for users and preparers, in other countries as well as Japan.[120] A closely related criticism was that the IASB was attempting to make important changes to recognition and measurement in other standards 'by stealth', or 'through the back door'.[121] In June and July 2003, when the results of the field visits were discussed, the Board still appeared inclined to push ahead, and Barker understood he had approval to draw up a formal exposure draft.[122] Shortly afterwards, however, the project foundered. An abrupt 'sunset review' was undertaken in October by a group of IASB Board and staff members, in consultation with Mary Keegan and Allan Cook from the ASB. It was concluded that the project suffered not merely from political difficulties, but that the boards faced unresolved technical difficulties as well. There was broad consensus in the two boards in favour of a single performance statement, but beyond that elementary point opinions diverged considerably, without much prospect of speedy resolution.[123] The conceptual problems posed by the matrix approach were exemplified by the apparently simple but unresolved question of inventory write-downs: should these go into the income column, assuming that obsolescence or sale below cost were part of regular operations, or into the re-measurement column?[124] The IASB Board adopted the conclusion of the review that the project should proceed, but with the more cautious objective of another discussion paper as the next step.[125]

---

[117] See agenda papers 2-2D for the 28 October 2002 meeting with national standard setters.

[118] 'IASB Eyes Shift to Comprehensive Income as Early as 2005', *Nikkei Report*, 24 September 2002; 'Japan Accounting Board to Lobby Against Comprehensive Income', *Nikkei Report*, 26 October 2002.

[119] Interview with Yoshiki Yagi and Shigeo Sakase, 25 January 2011.

[120] AP 6/2003 paper 6; interview with Richard Barker, 19 March 2009.

[121] AP 11/2003 paper 7; Gilbert Gélard, cited in *IStaR*, June 2003, 22.

[122] Interview with Richard Barker, 19 March 2009. In the second half of 2003, an article by Barker ('The Revolution ahead in Financial Reporting: Reporting Financial Performance', *Balance Sheet*, 11/4 (2003), 19–23) suggested that a new single-statement standard might be in place for voluntary adoption by 2005, and become mandatory in 2006.

[123] AP 11/2003 paper 7.   [124] Interview with Andrew Lennard, 13 October 2008.

[125] IASB meeting of 18–19 November 2003, minute 9.1.

This paper never appeared. Although the precise sequence of decisions is not clear, the net effect was that the IASB ended its cooperation with the ASB, and embarked upon a new project together with the FASB. In the second half of 2003, the IASB and the FASB took up the idea of collaboration on performance measurement. Both boards had tried to keep track of each other's progress during the preceding two years, which on occasion had considerably complicated at least the IASB's discussions. At the joint IASB–FASB Board meeting of October 2003, it was agreed to form a joint working group on performance reporting to consider convergence, and it was subsequently clarified that this was to be a tripartite group, involving the ASB as well.[126] Discussion papers prepared by a working party from the three boards were put forward for discussion in March and April 2004. Although these envisaged further tripartite cooperation, a decision to undertake the project just between the IASB and the FASB was either taken or confirmed at the joint IASB–FASB meeting of April 2004.[127] No public comment was made by the IASB on the ASB's disappearance from the scene. The last word from the ASB, as late as July 2004, was that it was 'working with the IASB and the US FASB in partnership on this priority project'.[128] One may surmise that the prospect of undertaking a complex and controversial project with three standard setters was not attractive to any of the participants. As the IASB and the FASB were preparing themselves for more intensive cooperation, and as time was running out for UK GAAP as the standard for listed companies in the United Kingdom, it is not too difficult to see why the ASB was the one to leave.[129] The new project with the FASB did not effectively start until 2005, and is discussed in Chapter 12.

5.6 AN INTERIM STANDARD ON EXTRACTIVE INDUSTRIES

In November 2000, the IASC had published a major 'issues paper' on accounting in the extractive industries (i.e. mining and petroleum).[130] IASB Board member Bob Garnett had been a member of the steering committee that produced the issues paper, and was apparently supportive of an active pursuit of this topic by

---

[126] Compare *IASB Update* November 2003, 7 and *IASB Update* March 2004, 7.

[127] IASB–FASB meeting of 22–3 April 2004, minute J3 (essentially reproduced in *IASB Update*, April 2004) appears to present the joint project as having already started. AP 4/2005 paper 2 notes that the decision to undertake a joint project was taken at the 22 April 2004 meeting. The IASCF *Annual Report 2003* (page 9) still describes the project as 'a joint project . . . with the UK Accounting Standards Board and the FASB'. However, the *Annual Report 2004* (page 9) does not mention the ASB in connection with this project, but simply states that the IASB and the FASB 'suspended [their projects] in late 2003 while they decided on the most effective way forward'.

[128] *Inside Track* (ASB), issue 40, July 2004, 7.

[129] In March 2004, FASB Chairman Herz was reported to have said that he 'supported continuing to work jointly with the IASB and ASB on the project, but he expressed concern regarding the composition of the Group. He stated that the uncertain future of U.K. GAAP, given the 2005 effective date for International Financial Reporting Standards, could lead to complications in the convergence process.' Extract from 31 March 2004 FASB meeting minutes, attached to AP 4/2004 paper 10.

[130] 'Extractive Industries: An Issues Paper Issued for Comment by the IASC Steering Committee on Extractive Industries' (IASC, November 2000).

the IASB.[131] Yet, although the topic was recognized as a potential leadership project, the Board did not adopt it as part of its initial agenda. To prepare the way for a subsequent agenda decision, the analysis of comment letters on the issues paper, expected to come in by June 2001, was to be subcontracted to the South African standard setter.[132] It is not evident that the Board ever discussed the responses to the issues paper, but the idea that this might be a good project in which to involve one or more national standard setters from countries with important extractive industries did not go away. After considering various combinations, the Board finally decided to ask the AASB, the Australian standard setter, to lead a project team in which the Canadian, Norwegian, and South African standard setters would participate.[133] The idea to ask Australia to take the lead seems to have emerged in mid-2002, when the IASB learned that Australia would adopt IFRSs starting in 2005, and it may have been something that David Tweedie wanted to be able to bring up when he was to visit Australia in August of that year.[134] At any rate, the impending Australian transition brought the need for transitional requirements with respect to extractive industries into focus, just as the enactment of the European IAS Regulation had done earlier in 2002 for insurance contracts. Before undertaking a fundamental research project, the Australian-led project team was therefore asked to make recommendations on implementation of IFRSs in 2005 by companies active in extractive industries.

In April 2003, AASB Chairman Keith Alfredson, accompanied by two staff members, came to London to discuss an elaborate proposal outlining both the short-term options available to the Board with respect to IFRS transition in 2005, as well as possible routes to be taken in a long-term project to develop a completely new standard. As might be expected, the analysis by the AASB-led team showed that any plans the Board might want to make turned on the perennial question in extractive industry accounting of the capitalization of exploration and evaluation costs, also known as pre-development costs. As it stood, IFRSs provided no explicit guidance on this issue. Possibly relevant standards such as IAS 16 and IAS 38 had scope exceptions for extractive industries, which meant that companies had to choose their policies on the basis of the 'GAAP hierarchy' of IAS 8. In theory, this made it an attractive option for the Board to do nothing, because the implication was that companies were restricted to choosing practices that were consistent with the IASB's conceptual framework. However, after considerable discussion, the Board concluded that this was not a feasible route. Given the critical stance of many Board members with respect to current practice, it would mean that the Board expected many companies to reduce their capitalization significantly upon transition to IFRSs, but without the Board itself being able to indicate by how much: both within the Board and

---

[131] A presentation by Garnett, scheduled for the May 2001 Board Meeting, included a suggested June 2003 date for an exposure draft. See AP 5/2001 paper 3 and attached presentation slides.

[132] AP 6/2001 paper 8.

[133] In April 2002, thought was given to asking the Australian, Canadian, and South African standard setters to 'explore the responses' to the 2000 issues paper. IASB meeting of 16–19 April 2002, administrative items, minute 3. In May 2002, the Board agreed on a 'research project' to be led by South Africa, and in which Australia, Canada, and Norway would participate. IASB meeting of 22–4 May 2002, administrative items, minute 11.

[134] IASB meeting of 16–19 July 2002, administrative items, minute 10.

the project team there were different views on the extent of capitalization allowed by the criteria of the conceptual framework. On the other hand, any interim measures aimed at articulating basic criteria for capitalization would be controversial, and risked pre-judging the expected long-term project.[135] Given the time pressure to issue a standard for application by 2005, the Board decided at the same April 2003 meeting on the approach it would take: to do no more than remove uncertainty about application of the GAAP hierarchy by specifying that companies could continue to apply their previous policies with respect to the capitalization of pre-development costs.[136]

This 'grandfathering' of existing practices was the same approach that the Board had decided to take a little earlier to conclude phase I of its insurance contracts project. Consequently, it led to an almost verbatim repetition of the alternative views of Board members voting against both standards. The dissenters asserted that companies should not be allowed to claim conformity with IFRSs when they have not been required to justify their choice of accounting policies by reference to the conceptual framework.[137] However, only Garnett, Leisenring, and Smith voted against both standards, citing this reason, whereas Mary Barth, Gilbert Gélard, and Warren McGregor used this argument to support their dissent to one standard only, and apparently found sufficient other reasons to vote in favour of the other.

A grandfathering approach still left some difficulties to resolve, in particular in specifying how companies should assess capitalized pre-development costs for impairment. Nonetheless, the project proceeded quite rapidly to an exposure draft in January 2004 and a final standard in December 2004, entitled IFRS 6 *Exploration for and Evaluation of Mineral Resources*. The original idea was to cast the project in terms of amendments to an existing standard, in particular IAS 38, but it was decided at a late stage, in November 2003, to make it a separate standard in order to highlight the similarity of treatment with IFRS 4 on insurance contracts.[138] IFRS 6 and IFRS 4 were not identical twins, however. IFRS 4 was a much more complicated standard, if only in its scope definition, including extensive application guidance. Moreover, there was an important and deliberate difference in the way companies were exempted from applying the GAAP hierarchy under both standards. Unlike IFRS 6, IFRS 4 did not explicitly require companies to select their accounting policies to result in information that is both relevant and reliable. The difference underlined just how critical the Board was of some the insurance accounting practices sanctioned or required by insurance regulators.[139]

---

[135] This paragraph is a summary of the analysis of issues in AP 4/2003 paper 7A and the corresponding Board discussion as reported in *IStaR*, April 2003, 2–7.

[136] A different interpretation of IFRS 6, in terms of regulatory capture of the IASB by industry interests, is offered by Corinne L. Cortese, Helen J. Irvine, and Mary A. Kaidonis, 'Powerful Players: How Constituents Captured the Setting of IFRS 6, An Accounting Standard for the Extractive Industries', *Accounting Forum*, 34 (2010), 76–88.

[137] Compare IFRS 4 *Insurance Contracts*, March 2004, DO3 and DO4 with *IFRS 6 Exploration for and Evaluation of Mineral Resources*, December 2004, DO2 and DO4.

[138] AP 12/2003 paper 12, footnote 1.

[139] IFRS 4 exempted reporting entities from IAS 8.10–12, IFRS 6 merely from IAS 8.11–12. Compare IFRS 4 BC80 and IFRS 6 BC18 for the Board's justification of the difference.

5.7 EXPLORING CONVERGENCE

During 2003 and 2004, 'convergence' was one of the main themes on the IASB's agenda and, following the Norwalk Agreement, this meant in particular convergence with US GAAP. But prior to the Norwalk Agreement the IASB had thought about convergence in broader terms. In the spring of 2002, the IASB had again reflected comprehensively on its agenda, for the first time since it had drawn up an initial list of projects in July of the previous year. 'Convergence' was one of the key topics to emerge. Directors Wayne Upton and Kevin Stevenson clarified that 'the staff uses convergence to describe topics in which several standard setters have standards that are broadly similar and that differ in a limited number of provisions'.[140] In this light, the Board agreed to consider a project, somewhat similar in nature to the improvements project, in which a raft of relatively minor changes would be combined in a package. As made clear in the staff's definition, convergence was thought of in a multilateral sense, aimed at reducing differences with several sets of national standards simultaneously. In the IASB's early years, 'convergence' was also used in a different but still multilateral sense of selecting the high quality or 'best-of-breed' solutions from national standards in order to make these the global 'gold standard'.[141]

Some of the IASB's earliest thinking on convergence seems to have been prodded by issues with UK standards, in particular in the areas of pensions and income taxes. As is discussed below, the IASB undertook its convergence project on retirement benefits specifically with reference to the United Kingdom. A tinge of Anglo-centrism was perhaps also visible in the staff's first systematic attempt to identify potential convergence projects, which was based on a comparison of the IASB's standards with Australian, Canadian, UK, and US GAAP.[142] On the basis of information provided by the liaison standard setters from other countries, a more comprehensive analysis of potential convergence topics was completed and presented to the Board in September 2002.[143]

By that stage, events were taking a different turn. The IASB's initial considerations on convergence as a possible topic apparently prompted SEC Chief Accountant Robert Herdman to write to David Tweedie in April 2002 to make inquiries about the IASB's plans.[144] As discussed in Section 4.5, this led to a meeting between Tweedie, Herdman, and FASB Chairman Bob Herz in early August. At this meeting, plans for a short-term convergence process were explored that would remove those differences between IFRSs and US GAAP which, in the experience of the SEC, most often appeared in the Form 20-F reconciliation schedules produced by foreign registrants (referred to in shorthand as reconciling differences).[145] On this basis, the FASB and the IASB boards, meeting jointly in

---

[140] AP 4/2002 paper 6.

[141] Examples of this point of view can be found in David Tweedie's Chairman's report in the IASCF *Annual Report* for 2002 (page 9) and 2003 (page 5).

[142] AP 6/2002 papers 6A and 6B.   [143] AP 9/2002 paper 5B.

[144] As apparent from Tweedie's letter to Herdman, dated 12 April 2002, IASB archive, 'US Convergence' file.

[145] See the various documents attached to 'Itinerary for David Tweedie's Visit to Washington and New York, 1 & 2 August 2002', IASB archive, 'US Convergence' file.

Norwalk in September, adopted a strategy for convergence of IFRSs and US GAAP.[146] The strategy, summarized in the Norwalk Agreement issued at the end of October, included both a short-term convergence project and the intention that the boards would work together to develop entirely new standards.

5.7.1 Short-term Convergence with US GAAP

In line with the IASB's earlier thinking on convergence, the short-term convergence project was initially thought of as a package of relatively small changes, in which differences would be quickly eliminated by selecting the best alternative out of existing US GAAP and IFRSs. Generally, the boards expected that the best alternative would be found in the standards of the board that had most recently addressed the issue. Informally, this was expressed as the belief that there was 'low-hanging fruit' which could be picked to yield swift yet substantial progress towards the reduction of the reconciling differences in the IFRS-based financial statements of foreign registrants with the SEC. In the Norwalk Agreement, the boards announced their intention to issue exposure drafts on most or all of these issues in the course of 2003, but without indicating the number of issues they had in mind. The underlying project planning available to the two boards in September 2002 identified some twenty topics, and suggested that it might be possible to have revisions of all the relevant standards—US GAAP or IFRSs, as the case might be—in place by the third quarter of 2004.[147] In adopting this plan, the IASB Board showed itself aware that this might be somewhat optimistic, and it was noted that, if convergence in the short term on any topic proved to be too difficult, a separate project might have to be set up.[148] Even so, the neat phalanx of exposure drafts and standards envisaged in the September 2002 project plan probably fell apart sooner and more comprehensively than even the more sceptical minds at the IASB had expected. During 2003 and 2004, the IASB made stabs at a number of possible short-term convergence topics, including earnings per share and accounting under conditions of hyperinflation. Until October 2003 the Board's newsletter, *IASB Update*, presented all of these activities under a separate heading, 'Convergence', but this practice was discontinued after October 2003. By that time, the 'short-term convergence project' had been broken up into in a small number of surviving but separate projects, including:

- A project to revise, or perhaps simply withdraw, IAS 20 *Accounting for Government Grants and Disclosure of Government Assistance*. This idea was discussed a few times during 2003 and 2004, and again picked up briefly in 2006. After that, it languished for many years as a footnote in the IASB's work programme, as a 'deferred' or 'suspended' project. With respect to convergence, it is interesting to note that the IASB considered withdrawing IAS 20 as a possible means of furthering convergence, because companies reporting under IFRSs would then, following the 'GAAP hierarchy' in IAS 8,

---

[146] AP 9/2009 papers 2A, 2B, 2C.
[147] AP 9/2002 paper 2B; see *IASB Update*, September 2002, 2–4 for a list of topics.
[148] IASB meeting of 17 and 19–20 September 2002, minute 2.2.

have to consider other sources of guidance.[149] While US GAAP could not be dismissed, the IASB Board and staff were not convinced that the relevant US GAAP, although more recent than the venerable IAS 20 (issued in 1982), was much of an improvement on IAS 20. In line with the IASB's original 'multilateral' view of convergence, a serious look was taken at the relevant Australian guidance, which seemed to offer a much more attractive approach.[150]

- A revision of IAS 12 *Income Taxes*. This project never disappeared from the active agenda, but an exposure draft for a new standard was not issued until 2009. Later that year, the IASB decided to abandon its proposal and to limit itself to making minor amendments to IAS 12, which were effected in 2010 (see Section 16.12).

- A revision of IAS 37 *Provisions, Contingent Liabilities and Contingent Assets*. This was a mixture of short-term convergence (with FAS 146) and an attempt to deal with some of the consequences of the IASB–FASB joint project on business combinations. An exposure draft was issued in June 2005, but, as discussed more fully in Chapter 12, the project foundered in a tangle of cross-cutting issues with other projects, including insurance contracts and revenue recognition.

Only a handful of projects from the initial short-term convergence programme agreed at Norwalk eventually resulted in new or changed standards within something like the original time-frame. It turned out that it was more difficult than expected to make minor changes in isolation, without touching on other aspects of the standards concerned. In addition, headwind was generated because both boards had constituents who disliked small changes that did not address a recognized problem with the existing standard.

The FASB issued three statements between November 2004 and May 2005 that were a direct result of short-term convergence. FAS 151 *Inventory Costs* brought some of the language on inventory cost in line with IAS 2, and FAS 153 *Exchanges of Nonmonetary Assets* reflected changes made to IAS 16 in the course of the IASB's initial improvements project. Probably the most substantive change was FAS 154 *Accounting Changes and Error Corrections*, which introduced, among other things, the retrospective application of accounting changes into US GAAP, in line with IAS 8. An exposure draft of a fourth change, on earnings per share, was issued in 2003 but was followed by revised exposure drafts in 2005 and 2008.[151] The project was removed from the FASB's agenda in January 2014, having been paused since 2009.

As noted above, the FASB also made a significant convergence move by modifying FAS 123 on stock-based compensation. In March 2003, as the IASB was still receiving comment letters on its proposal to require the expensing of stock options, the FASB added a similar project to its agenda, completed in

---

[149] As proposed by the IASB's staff in AP 1/2003 paper 4B.

[150] AP 1/2003 paper 4B. FAS 116 *Accounting for Contributions Received and Contributions Made* was issued in 1993. The Australian UIG Abstract 11 *Accounting for Contributions of, or Contributions for the Acquisition of, Non-Current Assets* had been issued in 1996.

[151] FASB exposure drafts 1200-200 (15 December 2003), 1240-001 (30 September 2005), 1240-100 (7 August 2008).

December 2004. Although clearly inspired by a general conviction on the part of the FASB of the importance of convergence—'it is embedded in everything we do', as FASB Chairman Herz asserted at the time[152]—the revision of FAS 123 was not seen as a part of the short-term convergence project. As discussed more fully in Section 5.4.3, the FASB was largely adopting its own earlier thinking on the subject, which had played such an important role in shaping IFRS 2.

5.7.2 IFRS 5 and the Difficulties of Short-term Convergence with US GAAP

One of the standards produced by the IASB under the initial short-term US GAAP convergence programme was IFRS 5 *Non-current Assets Held for Sale and Discontinued Operations*, published in March 2004, in the nick of time to complete the 'stable platform' of standards that the IASB had promised to be in place before large-scale implementation of IFRSs in the EU and Australia would begin in 2005. IFRS 5 replaced the six-year-old IAS 35 *Discontinuing Operations*, and it reflected many of the relevant features of FAS 144 *Accounting for the Impairment or Disposal of Long-lived Assets* (2001). Whereas IAS 35 was limited to presentation issues only, IFRS 5 also dealt with measurement issues, including its somewhat controversial suspension of depreciation of non-current assets held for sale.

The Board's deliberations over IFRS 5 illustrated why short-term convergence proved so hard to achieve. First of all, as with other convergence projects, it was difficult to keep a tight rein on the scope of the project. It touched on other issues—restructuring costs, the treatment of subsidiaries and associates, and the recycling of gains and losses—that were being dealt with in other projects of the IASB—the revision of IAS 37, business combinations phase II, and performance reporting. Another problem was that FAS 144, even though it was the more recent standard and therefore was assumed to reflect the most up-to-date thinking on the subject, was found to have difficulties of its own. With FAS 144, the FASB had tried to tighten the definition of discontinued operations so that reporting companies would be required to apply the standard to smaller units, but it appeared in practice that it had not succeeded in providing a satisfactory demarcation of the type of asset dispositions included in its scope. After the IASB learned that the FASB's Emerging Issues Task Force was still struggling with the wording of FAS 144, doubts emerged as to whether the IASB should knowingly adopt a problematic definition for the sake of convergence. Would it not be better for the IASB to retain the essentials of the definition in IAS 35 until both boards could agree on a better one? The IASB Board discussed this problem as late as February 2004, and Hans-Georg Bruns, whose primary motivation for joining the Board had been convergence with US GAAP, argued that the IASB 'had started the project as part of convergence. They had done a lot and now at five minutes to midnight they were saying they should draw back. Their primary aim should be to converge. They should issue this standard and continue the dialogue with the FASB.'[153] But

---

[152] 'Financial Accounting Standards Board', BNA's *Daily Tax Report*, 6 January 2003, 03 DTR S-35.
[153] *IStaR*, February 2004, 10.

a majority of the Board did want to draw back, with the result that IFRS 5 carried forward most of the definition of IAS 35, an admitted limitation to the degree of convergence achieved.

The exposure draft ED 4 (July 2003) was the first opportunity for the IASB's constituents to express their views on the practice as opposed to the general principle of convergence between IFRSs and US GAAP. At a high level of generality, most respondents expressed support for the convergence efforts of the IASB and the FASB, and none were opposed. Apart from that, the draft was poorly received. Many respondents criticized the draft for being prescriptive and rules-based, and attributed that to its close dependence on FAS 144. The IASB staff acknowledged that they had stayed as close to the wording of FAS 144 as possible, in order to achieve convergence, but 'that the resulting ED has a very different style to other IASB publications'.[154] Particularly from Europe, the IASB was criticized for rushing out a poorly drafted standard on a topic where the existing standard was not obviously faulty and might even be superior to ED4, at a time when companies were already struggling with the coming transition to an unstable set of standards. At this time, only Ernst & Young used a phrase that would subsequently come to summarize this type of criticism when they wrote that 'we do not believe in convergence purely for the sake of convergence', but many others expressed the same thought in different words.[155] However, Europe did not speak with one voice. Some European companies whose shares were traded in the United States, including BP, Nokia, Swiss Re, and UBS, thought that the IASB had correctly emphasized short-term convergence, and some of them exhorted the IASB to go even further in aligning its standard with FAS 144.[156]

IFRS 5 did not differ fundamentally from ED4. For Harry Schmid, who left the Board shortly afterwards, it provided the occasion for his single dissent to a final standard, essentially because he believed it was a clear example of the kind of artificial, rules-based standards which he believed the Board should not be issuing.[157] IFRS 5 appears never to have been a popular standard, and it probably helped to feed an incipient critical attitude in Europe towards the IASB's convergence with US GAAP.[158]

5.7.3 Good Intentions for Joint Projects with the FASB

The Norwalk Agreement referred optimistically to continuation of the joint projects that the two boards were currently undertaking, but only one such project

---

[154] AP 12/2003 paper 7, paragraph 10; see also IASB meeting of 17–19 December 2002, minute 3.2.

[155] CL77 (Ernst & Young). See also, for instance, CL12 (CAR, the Netherlands), CL13 (IDW, Germany), CL29 (PWC), CL35 (FAR, Sweden), CL46 (DRSC, Germany), CL47 (ICAEW, UK), CL48 (CNC, France), CL56 (EFRAG), CL62 (Grant Thornton), CL85 (FEE). IASB archive, comment letters ED 4.

[156] CL21 (Nokia), CL32 (UBS), CL51 (Swiss Re), CL53 (BP).

[157] Interview with Harry Schmid, 22 April 2010.

[158] For criticism of IFRS 5, see Mike Bonham et al., *International GAAP 2010: Generally Accepted Accounting Practice under International Financial Reporting Standards* (Ernst & Young/Wiley, 2010), 275, and the brochure *IFRS 5, Non-current Assets Held for Sale and Discontinued Operations: Practical Guide to Application and Expected Changes* issued by Mazars in 2009 <http://www.mazars.com>.

could be said to be under way in September 2002, the so-called phase II project on business combinations. This had been agreed upon only as recently as April 2002, and was therefore still in a very early stage. It was not to be completed until 2008, and is discussed more fully in Chapter 12. At the September 2002 meeting, the boards also agreed to conduct their separate embryonic projects on revenue recognition on a joint basis.[159] This again turned out to be a project of very long duration, and no member of either board would serve to see the project completed. Following the Norwalk Agreement, the two boards took good note of each other's work on certain topics, particularly performance reporting and share-based payment, but these could not be said to be joint projects. When the two boards met again, in October 2003 in Norwalk, their staffs observed that the coordination of the future work programmes of the two boards really still had to begin.[160]

At the April 2004 joint meeting, IASB–FASB convergence was put on a more systematic footing. For this meeting, a working party of senior staff members (Sue Bielstein and Todd Johnson for the FASB, Wayne Upton and Kevin Stevenson for the IASB) developed a proposal for a joint agenda as well as for working procedures. There was no shortage of candidates for joint projects, including heavyweight topics such as leasing, insurance, employee benefits, intangible assets, and financial instruments. These and some others were included in a list of potential projects from which the boards agreed to select projects when resources permitted.[161] In 2004 only one new joint project was adopted, again following recommendations made in April, but certainly not the least ambitious. Following the consultation processes required for the setting of each board's agenda, it was agreed in October 2004 to undertake a joint project to develop a common conceptual framework (see Section 12.7).

5.7.4 The IASB and the FASB: Learning to Work Together

The convergence process between the two boards was a learning experience for both sides.[162] In a sense, standard setting always involves learning, as it takes time for the standard setter to become aware of and understand the technical issues of a project. But in working together, the boards also had to learn how to arrive at a shared understanding of the problem at hand, as well as shared solutions. In doing so, they faced organizational, procedural, and cultural challenges. Even though the IASB had been set up on the basis of the FASB model, the organizations differed in

---

[159] The FASB had adopted its project in May 2002, the IASB in July, AP 9/2009 paper 3A.

[160] AP 10/2003 paper 15, paragraph 1.

[161] See AP 4/2004 (joint meeting) paper 11B for the staff's proposed priorities. See AP 10/2004 (joint administrative meeting) paper 1 for a summary of the boards' decisions.

[162] This section is based on interviews with Peter Clark, 29 July 2008; Robert Herz, 17 February 2009; Kim Petrone, 17 February 2009; Suzanne Bielstein, 3 August 2009; Harry Schmid, 22 April 2010; Warren McGregor, 18 and 19 May 2011; Wayne Upton, 7 July 2011; Alan Teixeira, 13 February 2012; Paul Pacter, 15 February 2012; Darrel Scott, 12 March 2013; and Thomas Linsmeier, 11 June 2013; communication from Suzanne Bielstein to the authors, dated 20 March 2014; 'Notes on Staff Discussion of Working with FASB', memo from Wayne Upton dated 29 August 2004, IASB archive, file 'FASB'.

several greater and lesser respects. Some of these differences were already apparent when the boards first began to work together, while others came to the fore when the convergence process was intensified, as discussed in subsequent chapters.

From October 2003 onwards, the two boards met twice a year, with selected staff in attendance. Until 2009, a rhythm was maintained of an April meeting in London and an October meeting in Norwalk. These joint meetings were essential for the members of the boards to get to know each other and to understand each other's positions, as well as for developing a common agenda. In the initial stages, they were not decisive for making progress on convergence. As long as the emphasis was on short-term convergence, each board could, to some extent, work on its own to converge its standard with that of the other, as long as a good mutual understanding of the issues was assured. For this purpose, apart from the joint meetings, video conferencing was regularly used from late 2003 onwards to allow the staff of one board to participate in sessions of the other board. There were also periodic trips by staff across the Atlantic.

When the boards did meet, the difference in size was manifest. The FASB had seven members (which dropped to five between 2008 and 2010), while the IASB had fourteen, increased to a maximum of sixteen in 2009. Twenty-one board members sitting around a table would have difficulty discussing technical issues in depth, but the adjustment in debating style required for large meetings was greater for the FASB than for the IASB.

Differences in debating style also arose for reasons unrelated to board size. Especially in the early years, when many Board members were not in the London office outside meeting weeks, debate at IASB Board meetings was important for arriving at a common understanding of issues and for an exchange of views. In contrast, FASB board members were more likely to come to a meeting with a shared analysis and a good knowledge of each other's thinking. One reason for this was that the FASB members were all in residence in Norwalk so that staff could easily confer with the board members prior to a meeting, and board members themselves could likewise confer informally. In addition, in 2002 the FASB had adopted a practice of holding open education sessions a week before a decision-making session. The IASB could not copy this because of the residence of many Board members outside the United Kingdom. For these reasons, the FASB tended to coalesce a little earlier round certain views than the IASB. As a result, IASB meetings could look inefficient from an FASB point of view, whereas FASB meetings could appear as overly scripted when looked at from the IASB.

Initially, differences in resources were an important constraint in planning truly joint projects. In the early years of the IASB, the size of its technical staff was a small fraction of that at the FASB, although that disparity was gradually addressed. For the April 2004 meeting, the staffs had prepared a tentative staff allocation for convergence projects, based on the assumption of nineteen full-time equivalent technical staff at the IASB compared to fifty-six at the FASB. Allowing for the needs of non-convergence projects and interpretations, this implied that IASB staff would be outnumbered by more than three to one on the major joint projects (including the conceptual framework) and by two to one on short-term convergence projects. As the staff observed: '[t]his could have implications for the respective constituencies of the two Boards, or at least inferences might be taken. These could have political and financial ramifications. For example, some may see combining resources as a takeover.'[163] The FASB was conscious that, particularly in Europe, convergence was watched with suspicion for signs of US dominance, and it deliberately tried not to make its initial superiority in staff resources appear all too evident.

The IASB staff included several seasoned members, but also had junior staff with little or no standard-setting experience. To the latter, especially if their first language was not English, it could feel as if they had to punch above their weight when working together in teams with a larger number of veteran FASB staff. Staff at the FASB could consult the two reference librarians at the FAF's library when they were looking for resource material, yet the IASB did not, and has not, had a proper library, let alone reference librarians.

In 1973, when the FASB began operations, the development of a fully-fledged research library was a high priority. Of course, that was in the pre-digital age, when journals were accessible only in hard copy. Over the years, the FASB has built a large library, staffed with research librarians who can assist technical staff and board members in finding literature that bears on current projects. The IASB had a small library, which it disposed of in 2004. It was not until recently that it began building a collection of digital research resources.

In terms of working procedures, the boards agreed in April 2004 to reserve the label 'joint project' for new major projects that would be conducted with a single project team preparing papers to be discussed by each board, and with the intention to produce the same final pronouncements. For a few projects that were already on the agenda of one of the boards, a 'modified joint approach' was envisaged, according to which that board would take the lead until a suitable point was reached where the other board could join, such as the publication of a discussion paper. There were two candidates for this approach: accounting for insurance contracts, on which the IASB was already working, as discussed above; and the FASB's project on the distinction between equity and liabilities (both discussed further in Chapter 16). On other ongoing projects, such as consolidation and performance reporting, the boards would work 'concurrently' rather than 'jointly'. That is, they affirmed their intention to reach converged outcomes, even though they would continue to work on the issues separately.

5.7.5 A Case of Non-US Convergence: The Revision of IAS 19 in Line with UK GAAP

As convergence with the FASB gradually came to absorb most of the IASB's energies, it is noteworthy that in 2004 the Board completed a convergence project based on a national set of standards other than US GAAP. This was a revision of IAS 19 *Employee Benefits*, issued in December 2004. This project was agreed in June 2002, that is, before the Norwalk Agreement, and the aim was to consider whether the existing option in IAS 19 to defer the recognition of actuarial gains and losses should be replaced by a requirement to recognize such gains and losses

---

[163] AP 4/2004 (joint administrative meeting) paper 12, paragraph 13 and Appendix A.

immediately.[164] Although this project was undertaken with support from Australia's AASB, it was obvious that the main focus was on UK accounting standards. FRS 17 *Retirement Benefits* had been issued late in 2000, with mandatory application beginning in 2003. One of its key features was that actuarial gains and losses had to be recognized immediately, although outside of profit or loss, in what was known in the United Kingdom as 'total recognized gains and losses' and what would become known under IFRSs as 'other comprehensive income'. The UK ASB was anxious that this hard-fought change would not be undone in 2005, when UK-listed companies were to make the transition to IFRSs in their consolidated financial statements.[165]

The deferral of actuarial gains and losses in IAS 19 had its roots in the comparable provisions in FAS 87 *Employers' Accounting for Pensions* issued in 1985. Already, in the 1980s, it was recognized that this was a pragmatic solution which sat uncomfortably with the FASB's conceptual framework. Hence, when the staffs of the IASB and the AASB took up the issue, they had no difficulty in concluding that 'the conceptual arguments for immediate recognition are overwhelming', and in July 2002 the IASB Board tentatively adopted the view that actuarial gains and losses should be recognized immediately.[166] Nevertheless, concern was expressed both in the Board and in SAC that this would not only create a divergence with US GAAP, but also with just about any set of national standards other than UK GAAP.[167]

It may be noted that the Board took its decision on immediate recognition as a matter of principle, apart from the important practical question of where in the financial statements these recognized gains and losses should appear. Whereas most practitioners would put this presentational question in terms of a choice between recognition in profit or loss or in equity, the Board at this stage was thinking along very different lines. As seen in Section 5.5.2, the Board was exploring a radically new 'matrix' approach to the presentation of gains and losses in its concurrent project on performance reporting. Under this approach, income and expense items relating to retirement benefits would be scattered across the rows and columns of the performance statement. As there would be no net income number under this approach, the question of whether net income should include actuarial gains and losses did not arise. This link between the revision of IAS 19 and the performance reporting project was deliberately emphasized by the IASB in its public presentations.[168]

During the rest of 2002, and most of 2003, the Board continued its work on IAS 19, elaborating the details of the immediate recognition of actuarial gains and losses with reference to the matrix-model of the performance reporting project. At the same time, it considered some other issues with IAS 19, including the possibility of borrowing elements from the guidance in US GAAP. Early in 2003, the project had already expanded to such an extent that the Board discussed whether it should attempt to write a completely new standard on retirement

[164] AP 6/2002 paper 6, paragraph 15.
[165] ASB chairman's report, included in *2003 Annual Review: Financial Reporting Council*, 31; interview with Allan Cook, 18 March 2009.
[166] AP 7/2002 paper 4D, paragraph 15; IASB meeting of 16–19 July 2002, minute 4.8.
[167] IASB meeting of 16–19 July 2002, minute 4.4; *IStaR*, July 2002, 32.
[168] AP 11/2003 paper 6.

benefits. Warren McGregor was strongly in favour, believing that the Board had an opportunity to settle a range of tough issues quickly, which otherwise would continue to plague the Board for a long time. Others were sceptical, and believed that a widening of the scope would provoke so much debate and opposition that it would be impossible to finish the project quickly. Geoffrey Whittington, for instance, observed that he would not want to risk the Board's impending achievement in eliminating deferred recognition of actuarial gains and losses by such a move. The Board, including McGregor, thereupon agreed not to pursue this path, but to mark the fundamental revision of IAS 19 as a priority for its future agenda.[169]

In August 2003, a pre-ballot draft was completed, with publication of an exposure draft planned for December of that year. However, late in 2003 the Board abruptly decided to put its performance reporting project on hold, thus pulling the rug out from under its project to revise IAS 19. The consequences were considered during the November and December 2003 Board meetings. The Board members were unwilling to postpone the immediate recognition of actuarial gains and losses in order to wait for the uncertain outcome of a restarted performance reporting project. Apart from its preference in principle, the Board was sensitive to the significance of preserving immediate recognition in the United Kingdom. The Board also noted that the AASB wished to see the UK solution included in IFRSs in time for their adoption in Australia. However, the Board probably did not need the staff's reminder that to require immediate recognition in profit or loss on the basis of the current version of IAS 1 would lead to 'total rejection of the proposal'.[170] It was, of course, possible to follow the staff's recommendation to make minor amendments to IAS 1 with a view to 'providing a home for actuarial gains and losses', yet the Board pondered the risk of being seen to pre-judge the performance reporting issue by the back door of an amendment to IAS 19.[171] In a carefully constructed compromise (reflected both in the April 2004 exposure draft and the resulting amendments to IAS 19 and IAS 1 issued in December 2004), the Board decided to allow but not to require immediate recognition of actuarial gains and losses. It introduced an additional option in IAS 19 to recognize such gains and losses immediately outside of profit or loss. To use the option, however, companies were simultaneously required to use the existing option in IAS 1 to present all changes in equity apart from transactions with owners in a separate statement. And while the existing IAS 1 did not give this particular type of statement of changes in equity a distinctive name, the Board now decided that it should be titled 'statement of recognized income and expense'.

Hence, the Board did take its performance reporting project one step further as part of its convergence project on retirement benefits. Something very much like the UK STRGL had now become part of IFRSs. As might perhaps be expected, many UK companies availed themselves of this option under IAS 19 upon their transition to IFRSs in 2005.[172] The traditionally exclusive role of the income statement as the representation of a company's performance began to be challenged not just in theory, but also in the practice of IFRS application.

---

[169] IASB meeting of 19–21 February 2003, minute 2.6; *IStaR*, February 2003, 16–18.
[170] AP 11/2003 paper 6, paragraph 11.
[171] AP 11/2003 paper 6, paragraph 13; *IStaR*, November 2003, 11–13.
[172] KPMG/Isabel von Keitz, *The Application of IFRS: Choices in Practice* (KPMG, 2006), 33–4.

6

Financial Instruments

The Confrontation with Europe

Among the IASB's initial technical projects, the topic of accounting for financial instruments acquired a special significance. During the 1990s, it had already been well-established that accounting for financial instruments was complex, and that it could be controversial. Even so, it took many of the IASB's new constituents, as well as the IASB itself, by surprise that opposition from the European banking sector to the IASB's work on this topic escalated to a high-level political conflict that jeopardized the European Union (EU)'s adoption of IFRSs before it had even taken effect.

6.1 THE INHERITED INTERIM STANDARD

IAS 39 *Financial Instruments: Recognition and Measurement* had been approved by the Board of the IASC in December 1998. By then, the IASC had laboured for almost a decade to produce a financial instruments standard, but its work was unfinished.[1] IAS 39 (together with its companion standard IAS 32 on presentation and disclosure) was presented as an interim solution, necessary for the timely completion of the set of 'core standards' which the IASC had undertaken to submit to the International Organization of Securities Commissions (IOSCO) by 1998. Towards that end, IAS 39 had been put together under high pressure, building on the relevant sections of US generally accepted accounting principles (US GAAP) when, in the course of 1997, it appeared that it would take too long to complete the more fundamental approach that the IASC had wanted to take. After the IASC had failed to make progress on the basis of two earlier exposure drafts, issued in 1991 and 1994, the IASC steering committee on financial instruments had, in March 1997, published a discussion paper that suggested a radical break with established practice.[2] The discussion paper advocated measuring all financial

---

[1] See Kees Camfferman and Stephen A. Zeff, *Financial Reporting and Global Capital Markets: A History of the International Accounting Standards Committee, 1973–2000* (Oxford University Press, 2007), 361–77, for a discussion of the IASC's financial instruments project.

[2] 'Accounting for Financial Assets and Financial Liabilities: A Discussion Paper Issued for Comment by the Steering Committee on Financial Instruments' (IASC, 1997).

instruments at fair value, with changes in fair value recognized in profit or loss. The proposal was so radical that it served as a wake-up call for the banking industry, alerting it to the growing significance of the IASC, and causing alarm about the IASC's apparent eagerness to extend the use of fair value. The 1997 discussion paper was a catalyst to bring the international banking industry together: shortly after its publication, the American, Australian, Canadian, European, and Japanese banking associations formed an accounting working group, a degree of cooperation they had not hitherto attempted. This working group, in turn, proved to be an important step towards the creation of the International Banking Federation in 2004.[3]

In contrast to the 1997 discussion paper, IAS 39 was certainly not a full fair value standard. It embodied a mixed-measurement approach in which important categories of financial instruments were measured along traditional lines at amortized cost. To the extent that fair value had to be applied, fair value changes were directly reported in profit or loss for some instruments, while unrealized fair value changes of instruments classified as available for sale were recognized in equity (that is, in other comprehensive income, to use the language subsequently adopted by the IASB). IAS 39 took a firm position on derivatives which always had to be measured at fair value. Apart from certain forms of hedge accounting, fair value changes on derivatives had to be recognized in profit or loss.

Because of this mixture of traditional practices and innovation, IAS 39 would never be a popular standard. It was already controversial in the IASC itself, where it mustered just enough votes to pass. Proponents of a full fair value model saw it as a harmful and conceptually unsound compromise, which, once in place, could only hinder progress towards the final resolution of the financial instruments issue. For others, it already went too far in extending the use of fair value measurement. And just about everyone disliked IAS 39 for its inevitable complexity, which was necessary to resolve the numerous tensions arising out of a mixed-measurement approach. Even though IAS 39 was already a very lengthy document compared to previous IASC standards, it was soon agreed that it still left many questions unanswered. Following the publication of IAS 39, extensive implementation guidance in the form of questions and answers was published on the IASC's website. This was produced by the IASC staff together with a volunteer implementation guidance committee (IGC) chaired by John Smith, at the time a US partner of Deloitte & Touche and subsequently appointed to the IASB Board. While the guidance was generally seen as helpful, the fact that it was so much needed only reinforced the impression that the standard itself was flawed.[4]

Even if IAS 39 by itself was contentious enough, it was made more controversial by the continuing work on a full fair value standard by the so-called Joint Working Group of Standard Setters (JWG). This was a broad-based group in which national standard setters from Australia, Canada, France, Germany, Japan, New Zealand, the Nordic countries, the United Kingdom, and the United States were represented, as well as the IASC. Among its members were the future IASB Board

[3] Interviews with Donna Fisher and Michael Gullette, 29 June 2010; Russell Picot, 26 May 2009; and Wilfried Wilms, 2 July 2009.

[4] See e.g. 'FBE Observations on the IAS 39 Improvements Programme', European Banking Federation, 15 February 2002 <http://www.fbe.be> accessed through web.archive.

members Jim Leisenring, Tricia O'Malley, and Tatsumi Yamada. The JWG was formed with the brief of translating the ideas in the IASC's 1997 discussion paper into a draft standard, in order to explore the practical implications of a full fair value approach. The banking federations, through their own newly-established working group, sought contact with the JWG, but actual cooperation was limited. The banks were unwilling to discuss application problems before it was settled that fair value was in fact relevant to all of a bank's financial instruments, something the banks were not prepared to concede.[5] The JWG published its draft standard in December 2000, and it was left to the IASB, as the IASC's successor, to consider the comments on the draft and to decide on further action.[6]

That IAS 39 was the most controversial element of the IASC's legacy of standards was apparent from the moment the IASB commenced operations in April 2001. At its first meeting, the IASB adopted all of the IASC's extant standards but some Board members, including Geoffrey Whittington, only reluctantly agreed that this should include IAS 39.[7] Just a few weeks before, the Fédération Bancaire Française had raised an alarm over this standard in a circular letter to the authorities of the EU and European banks.[8] From Germany, a country where a significant minority of listed companies was already applying the IASC's standards on a voluntary basis, came a rumble of discontent as some of the banks prepared their first quarterly reports on the basis of IAS 39, which had become effective on 1 January 2001.[9]

As in 1998, criticisms of IAS 39 came from diametrically opposed positions. Whereas the banks opposed fair value measurement of financial instruments not held for trading, the Board tended to view the mixed measurements of IAS 39 as a major problem, and identified further consideration of a full fair value model as an 'area of some urgency'.[10] A majority of the Board was inclined to expend its resources on pursuing the work of the JWG rather than on maintaining a flawed interim standard. Nonetheless, the Board included a project to make limited improvements to IAS 32 and IAS 39 in its initial agenda. These improvements were seen as necessary in the short term, not least in order to provide a more clearly defined status within the body of standards for the IGC's series of questions and answers. A decision whether to continue the JWG's work was deferred. Canada's Accounting Standards Board (AcSB), which earlier had provided much of the motive power behind the IASC's work on financial instruments as well as behind the JWG, volunteered to take the lead in analysing the comment letters received on the JWG draft. The IASB was happy to accept the offer, and listed a 'comprehensive project' on financial instruments among its potential future agenda topics.[11]

---

[5] Interview with Gérard Gil, 19 February 2010.

[6] Joint Working Group of Standard Setters, 'Draft Standard and Basis for Conclusions: Financial Instruments and Similar Items' (IASC, 2000).

[7] IASB meeting of 18–20 April 2001, minute 2(a). See also 'IASB Meets for the First Time', *World Accounting Report*, May 2001, 2.

[8] 'La Fédération bancaire française monte au créneau contre la "juste valeur"', *Les Echos*, 9 April 2001, 32.

[9] 'Deutsche Banken wehren sich gegen neue Bilanzierungsvorschriften', *Die Welt*, 8 May 2001, Wirtschaft, 11; 'Neues aus dem Elfenbein-Turm', *Börsen-Zeitung*, 8 May 2001, 8.

[10] AP 6/2001 paper 9. See also SAC meeting of 23–4 July 2001, agenda paper 3.

[11] IASB meeting of 25–7 July 2001, minute II.

6.2 FROM LIMITED IMPROVEMENTS
TO A POLITICIZED DEBATE

In January 2002, the Board discussed the responses to the JWG draft with its eight liaison standard setters. But the Board did not really need the comment letters to know that a move to a full fair value model was strongly opposed by many preparers, even by those who were generally supportive of the IASB and its mission. Banking supervisors, notably the European Central Bank (ECB), had also weighed in with their concerns.[12] Notwithstanding an assertion by the IASB and its liaison standard setters that the momentum should not be lost, there was un-certainty over the next steps to be taken. By April the IASB's staff recommended not to pursue the objective of a standard based on the JWG proposals. The main reasons given were a lack of staff resources and that 'the JWG paper showed that constituents struggled to respond to so many complex and fundamental issues in one go'.[13] But perhaps equally to the point were the staff's observations that 'there is a lot of hostility to the basic model proposed' and that 'the IASB already has one controversial project on its agenda in share-based payment. It may well be wise to progress the financial instruments project in a way that minimizes controversy in the short term.'[14] Fears that the IASB would move directly to a full fair value model receded, although those who opposed such a move were not reassured about the IASB's longer-term objectives.[15] Nevertheless, as Alex Milburn, the Canadian chairman of the JWG, had feared, the interim solution began to take root.[16] Some standard setters that had postponed developing their own standards on financial instruments, notably the Accounting Standards Board (ASB) in the United Kingdom and its Australian and Canadian counterparts, now began to put standards in place that were in line with IAS 39.[17]

Meanwhile, the short-term improvements to the existing financial instruments standards quickly turned into the IASB's most controversial project, mainly because critics of IAS 39 used the occasion to push for more changes than the Board initially wished to contemplate. With hindsight, David Tweedie wondered whether it might not have been better to leave IAS 39 alone, in order to make it clearer that the IASB was not to be blamed for its shortcomings.[18]

The looming trouble was not, it seems, fully anticipated in the Board, which over the turn of the year 2001–2 agreed quite rapidly to a slate of modifications to IAS 39 and IAS 32. An exposure draft was published in June 2002. Although the 336-page exposure draft looked imposing, it did not propose any changes to the basic principles of recognition and measurement. Most of its bulk was made up of

---

[12] On the ECB's views, see 'Fair Value Accounting in the Banking Sector', undated [November 2001] note stating the ECB Governing Council's position on the JWG draft <http://www.ecb.eu>.

[13] 'The Long-term Financial Instruments Project—Next Steps', staff memo dated April 2002, paragraph 12, IASB archive, file 'Financial Instruments—JWG'.

[14] 'The Long-term Financial Instruments Project—Next Steps', paragraphs 3 and 8.

[15] See the various comments in 'IASB Admits Full Fair Value is a Pipe Dream', *Accountancy*, 22 January 2002, 7.

[16] Email from Alex Milburn to David Tweedie, dated 19 January 2001, IASB archive, file 'Financial Instruments—JWG'.

[17] See also Ian Hague, 'Filling in the GAAP', *CA Magazine*, June–July 2003, 43.

[18] Interview with David Tweedie, 29 July 2008.

numerous smaller changes intended to provide clarification, and remove inconsistencies. Much of the IGC's guidance was incorporated into the standard as well, even though the Board had made up its mind that it did not want any more interpretations, and had disbanded the IGC.

One of the more notable changes was the introduction of a fair value option, according to which an entity might designate any financial instrument, at the time of initial recognition, for subsequent measurement at fair value through profit or loss. The option would apply to both assets and liabilities. According to the staff, such a change would reduce the complexity of IAS 39 by giving enterprises more flexibility to deal with mismatches arising out of the mixed-measurement model, and it would be consistent with the JWG's conclusion that fair value is the most relevant measurement attribute for financial instruments.[19] In the light of subsequent events, it is interesting to note that the European Commission had been one of the parties suggesting such a fair value option to the IASB, in particular regarding liabilities.[20] Although this was not pointed out by the staff, the idea of a fair value option was not new. It had been considered by the IASC during the 1990s, and, as late as November 1998, the UK delegation (then including David Tweedie) had unsuccessfully tabled a proposal to allow fair value measurement for all financial assets and liabilities.[21]

While the Board may have thought of the proposed amendments as a relatively modest attempt to make the standards more useful in practice, the exposure draft provoked a storm of protest. By December 2002, when the staff had managed to digest the comment letters, it had become evident that many respondents objected not so much to the changes that the Board was proposing, but to IAS 39 as such. At this stage, the EU had yet to take the decision to endorse all extant IASs. This gave European critics of IAS 39 the opportunity to broaden the debate beyond the changes proposed by the Board. From the point of view of the critics, such a broader debate was justified by the perception that, in its final stages, IAS 39 had been pushed through at high speed with inadequate due process.[22] The IASB, on its part, believed that it could not reasonably be asked to reopen all prior discussions on IAS 39, and that the EU had adopted its IAS Regulation in full knowledge of IAS 39 and its problems.

6.2.1 Behind the Criticism: Fair Value and Hedge Accounting

While there was no shortage of criticism of IAS 39 by preparers generally, the banking sector took the lead. It was not the case that banks were opposed to fair value measurement as such.[23] Most banks readily accepted the merits of fair value

---

[19] AP 11/2001 paper 3A, 1–6.   [20] AP 11/2001 paper 3B, 17.

[21] IASC Board meeting of 9–13 November 1998, minute 9. See also Camfferman and Zeff, *Financial Reporting and Global Capital Markets*, 375.

[22] This criticism was voiced, among others, by the Basel Committee, in its 'Report to G7 Finance Ministers and Central Bank Governors on International Accounting Standards', Basel Committee on Banking Supervision, April 2000, paragraphs 52 and 53 <http://www.bis.org>.

[23] This paragraph draws on interviews with Gerald Edwards, 6 June 2012; Gérard Gil, 19 February 2010; Geoffrey Mitchell, 15 October 2009; Russell Picot, 26 May 2009; and Arnold Schilder, 4 June 2012. For a critique of IAS 39 by HSBC's Douglas Flint, see 'A Passion for Clarity', *Financial Times*, 6

measurement for assets and liabilities that were part of their trading portfolios, and for which market prices were available on a continuing basis. For assets and liabilities held for longer periods or until maturity (often referred to collectively as the 'banking book'), it was a different matter. Here, the notion of fair value could conflict with deep-seated views on the nature of banking and of the financial system. While some banks saw themselves primarily as traders in financial markets, others thought of their activities in terms of making long-term investments in the real economy. From their point of view, continually updated fair value numbers could easily be unreliable as well as misleading. Such numbers would introduce a degree of volatility in the accounting numbers that did not capture the long-term commitments of the banks, and might actually deter them from making such commitments. By the same token, bank regulators were often sceptical of the volatility introduced by fair value, believing this might pose risks to the stability of the financial system.

Some of these concerns remained at the abstract level of general views on the role of financial markets in the economy. But some problems with fair value were very specific. After IAS 39 was published in 1998, banks argued that it interfered with their risk management practices for the banking book. The requirement that all derivatives be measured at fair value would result in accounting volatility in the banking book, where most of the hedged assets and liabilities were measured at amortized cost. IAS 39 suggested hedge accounting as a way of dealing with this problem, but it allowed hedge accounting under tightly constrained circumstances only. As many banks saw it, this made hedge accounting a remedy of limited practical use.

The banks suggested that, to avoid the appearance of volatility introduced into their financial statements by IAS 39, they would have to limit the use of derivatives to manage their risks. They argued that it was unacceptable for accounting standards to force such changes in the way companies were managed. The banks objected in particular to IAS 39's prohibition of applying hedge accounting to hedges at portfolio level (known as macro-hedges) and to hedges based on internal transactions within a group.

Most of these concerns had already been made known to the IASC, and were reiterated to the IASB on various occasions in 2001 and 2002. The IGC had attempted to show, in discussions with the banks, how some of their problems could be solved within the rules of IAS 39.[24] Nonetheless, the banking sector asserted that the IASB had failed to respond adequately.[25] Some of these early discussions were quite acrimonious, leading to mutual recriminations between the IASB and the banking industry. Banking regulators noted the strained

February 2003, 2. For the point of view of the two main German banking associations, see '"Starre Haltung des IASB ist inakzeptabel"', *Börsen-Zeitung*, 17 October 2002, 19.

[24] Notably Questions 121–1 and 121–2 on portfolio hedge accounting.

[25] Among other communications, early in 2002, the IASB received a memo from the European Banking Federation, 'FBE Observations on the IAS 39 Improvements Programme', dated 15 February 2002 (<http://www.fbe.be> accessed through web.archive), as well as a letter from the French Conseil National de la Comptabilité, dated 5 February 2002, representing the views of its financial instruments working group (IASB archive, file 'CNC'). On the IASB's lack of response, see EBF letter to EFRAG, dated 17 June 2002 <http://www.fbe.be> accessed through web.archive.

communications between the IASB and the banks with concern. The Accounting Task Force of the Basel Committee on Banking Supervision made various attempts to improve the dialogue between the IASB and its banking constituents.

6.2.2 Behind the Criticism: France

It was soon observed that the French banks were particularly active and vocal in their opposition to IAS 39, probably for a number of reasons. For all of the European banks, it was an exasperating experience to run into an accounting standard setter that could seem excessively independent-minded. Yet one assumes that, to the French banks in particular, it amounted to a culture shock. They were used to operating in an environment of close cooperation between the leading financial firms and state-sponsored regulators like the accounting standard setter, the Conseil National de la Comptabilité (CNC). A small number of key individuals in the French financial sector took a strong interest in the matter. Michel Pébereau and Daniel Bouton, the presidents of BNP Paribas and Société Générale, respectively, and Claude Bébéar, the president of the insurance company AXA, formed an active and influential nucleus of opposition to the IASB in France. Pébereau espoused opposition to the IASB as a personal cause. Upon his retirement in 2011, he cited his failure to make himself heard when, in the early 2000s, 'the IASB had committed itself on the road towards a systematic application of full fair market value' as his single regret, looking back on eighteen years of service with the bank.[26]

But it seems likely that opposition by the French banks and insurers to a set of accounting requirements hardly understood outside a circle of experts would not have been as effective if it had not chimed with widely prevailing views in France, including a wariness of financial capitalism and a strong desire to maintain national sovereignty. The IASB was an easy target, as it constituted an Anglo-American challenge. As will be seen in other places in this book, the IASB soon learned that France was a unique and difficult case among the many countries adopting IFRSs. Yet the large French non-financial companies tended to welcome the move to IFRSs as an important simplification of accounting practices in their international operations, even if they had their doubts over some aspects of IFRSs.[27]

6.2.3 Political Intervention

In September 2002, the chairmen of eight French banks raised the issue to the political level by sending another circular letter to their counterparts in the EU member states and to the European Commission to call for a 'political initiative' to delay the endorsement of IAS 39, and perhaps all IASs, by the EU.[28] In their letter,

---

[26] BNP Paribas, 'Procès-verbal de l'Assemblée générale mixte des actionnaires du 11 mai 2011', <http://www.bnpparibas.com>.

[27] Interviews with Françoise Flores, 4 May 2013; and Patrice Marteau, 18 February 2010.

[28] Circular letter by Michel Pébereau and others, dated 18 September 2002 <http://www.fbf.fr>.

the bank chairmen placed their specific technical objections in the widest possible context by including a reference to the Enron scandal that had erupted a year earlier: 'The IAS/IFRS in their present state are largely inspired from the same theory that guides the United States Generally Accepted Accounting Principles (US GAAP), a theory that lies at the heart of the current accounting crisis and loss of confidence in financial reporting and markets.' Although, in response, the Bundesverband deutscher Banken (German Banking Federation) reiterated its view that all IASs should be endorsed, it shared the concerns of the French banks. Moreover, the German bankers observed that 'in view of the inflexible attitude displayed by many Board members, however, we see a danger that the IASB may take an en-bloc endorsement as carte blanche to refuse to make any meaningful changes to the standard. This must be prevented at all costs. We therefore urge the European Commission to bring all its influence to bear on the IASB to carry out the necessary overhaul of IAS 39.'[29]

By November 2002, concerns over the impact of IFRSs on financial stability had resonated within the European Parliament. It adopted a resolution on prudential supervision including a call for suspension of the endorsement of IAS 39.[30] Also in November, the Accounting Regulatory Committee (ARC), in its first session, agreed that the European Commission should urgently invite the IASB to 'a thorough, open due process debate with all interested parties, to address all the problems they have with IAS 39 including those related to the improvements proposed to IAS 32 and 39'.[31] The IASB had already been aware of 'some lobbying' in France against IFRSs in general, and IAS 39 in particular, but a telephone call following the November ARC meeting from David Wright of the European Commission's Internal Market Directorate made it clear to the IASB that the issue had developed to the point where 'the "EU-2005" transition could be at stake'. Reflecting the ARC's conclusions, Wright called into question the sufficiency of due process on IAS 39, and urged the IASB to hold public hearings.[32]

6.2.4 A Counterpoint: Brazil

The preceding discussion and the remainder of this chapter concentrate on reactions to IAS 39 emanating from Europe, because the European constituents did claim a large share of the IASB's attention. Far less conspicuously, and perhaps hardly noticed at the IASB, was the fact that Brazil's central bank had decided in 1999 to follow IAS 39, as well as IAS 32, in developing accounting guidance for Brazilian banks. The relevant regulations were issued in 2001 and 2002, both

---

[29] Letter from Manfred Weber and Wolfgang Arnold (BdB) to Frits Bolkestein, dated 18 November 2002, copy in IASB archive, file 'IAS 39'; see also 'BdB fordert Brüssel zum Handeln auf', *Börsen-Zeitung*, 22 November 2002, 18.

[30] Resolution 2002/2061(INI), OJ 29.1.2004, C25E/397.

[31] Summary record, ARC meeting of 6 November 2002 <http//ec.europa.eu/internal_market/accounting>.

[32] AP 10/2002 paper 10A; AP 11/2002, paper 10B, 'Administrative Items—November 2002 Board Meeting'.

effective in the course of 2002. The introduction of fair value measurement for derivatives and the introduction of the concept of hedge accounting were seen as important improvements by the central bank.[33]

The decision was part of a general policy of improving the accounting framework for banks to the level of international best practice, and thought had been given to adopt US GAAP. The choice for the IASC's standards was not purely based on their quality. It was also based on the perception that US GAAP, as national standards set in another country, might be less appropriate, and that it would be easier for Brazil to become involved in the IASC's decisions than in the development of US GAAP. IOSCO's endorsement also favoured the IASC's standards.[34] The Brazilian guidance was said to be 'similar to' IAS 39 and 'based on' IAS 32, making it less than an unqualified adoption. There was no immediate follow-up in the form of adoption of other standards, nor an attempt to follow the subsequent improvements to IAS 39. Yet it was an important precursor of the general adoption of IFRSs by Brazil announced in 2007 (see Chapter 15).

6.3 'THE IASB DOES NOT LISTEN'

In its meetings of November and December 2002, the IASB was aware that it needed to signal its willingness to engage in dialogue with its critics, but it was less certain precisely what it should talk about. In its analysis of comment letters, the staff noted that there was 'overwhelming opposition' to some aspects of hedge accounting, yet the exposure draft had left the essential provisions of the original IAS 39 on this point unchanged.[35] Moreover, the staff had not identified any new arguments. Its recommendation was therefore that the Board 'devote some time' to studying the issue of hedge accounting before finalizing the amendment, even though further study was not likely to lead to any fundamental changes. In response to the European Commission's urgings, the Board agreed to hold public roundtables. The IASB's Constitution mentioned the possibility of holding a public hearing (paragraph 36(e)), but the Board had so far not yet considered holding one. It therefore had to decide how such an open consultation would be conducted. The format of a roundtable was chosen, because it was thought to be less prone to becoming adversarial than a formal public hearing.[36] The Board decided to invite the writers of the comment letters to a series of meetings, to be held the following March in Brussels and London. Director of Research Wayne Upton drew on his experience at the Financial Accounting Standards Board (FASB) to inform the Board that the purpose of such a meeting should be 'mutual education'. An important secondary objective was to demonstrate the Board's willingness to listen and its earnestness in seeking to understand fully constituents' views.[37] The Board members agreed, but some feared that the meetings might raise false expectations: whereas the Board would like to confine the

---

[33] No title, Banco do Brazil, *Focus* newsletter, 12 April 2002 <http://www4.bcb.gov.br>.
[34] Interview with Amaro Gomes, 15 February 2012.
[35] AP 12/2002 paper 3A, 37–9.   [36] AP 11/2002 paper 10B; AP 12/2002 paper 3.
[37] AP 12/2002 paper 3, 1.

meetings to the scope of the exposure draft, it was only to be expected that participants would raise other issues as well.[38] In the end, an open format was chosen, in which all of the main issues raised in the comment letters were included in the questions sent out beforehand.[39]

More than a hundred participants, the vast majority from EU member states, attended the roundtables in March 2003, divided into more than nine sessions.[40] If the point of the roundtables was to show that the IASB was willing to listen, they certainly were held none too soon. There was a rising tide of anger in Europe over the IASB's perceived aloofness. The chief financial officer of Crédit Agricole, going into the meeting, was reported to have characterized the IASB's attitude so far as 'close to autistic'.[41] In an interview, Chairman Paul Volcker of the IASC Foundation trustees emphasized the trustees' awareness of their responsibility to prevent the Board from retreating into an ivory tower, but pointed to the roundtables as evidence that the Board was not doing that.[42] While the roundtables did not resolve the conflict, they did engender hope that a negotiated solution might be found. The IASB signalled its willingness to reconsider some of the issues in the exposure draft, as well as some new issues, in particular through consultation with the European Banking Federation (EBF, in source material also referred to by the French acronym FBE).[43]

As the Board contemplated its options in the wake of the roundtables, the impending date of 1 January 2005 for the mandatory adoption of IFRSs in the EU loomed large. The Board had included the revised IAS 39 and 32 in its 'stable platform' of standards that should be in place by March 2004 in order to provide reporting companies with sufficient time to prepare for the transition. But now it was evident that neither the original IAS 39 nor a version based on the June 2002 exposure draft stood a chance of being endorsed by the European Commission, because neither dealt with the main grievances of the banks in the area of hedge accounting. The Board concluded that it would have to address these issues and perhaps go through another exposure cycle. Given the tight time constraint, this meant that the contents of the new exposure draft had to be decided at the July 2003 meeting, at the latest.

By June 2003, the Board was ready to decide that most of the changes it would make to the June 2002 exposure draft would not require re-exposure, not least because its position on several important issues had moved closer to the original IAS 39, compared to the exposure draft. Hence, the most crucial issue as far as timing was concerned was hedge accounting, where it was accepted that some form of exposure would be necessary. From April to June, Board members Bob Garnett, Gilbert Gélard, Jim Leisenring, and John Smith, supported by staff members Wayne Upton and Sandra Thompson, held a series of meetings with representatives of the EBF, headed by Thomas Naumann of Commerzbank, in order to work out a solution to the most controversial questions: the application of hedge accounting to portfolio hedges of interest rate risk, and, more particularly,

[38] *IStaR*, December 2002, 2.   [39] AP 1/2003 paper 2A.

[40] 'Acceptances—Final', IASB Board meeting files March 2003.

[41] 'Financial Instruments', *Financial Times*, 10 March 2003, 19.

[42] 'Ex-Fed Chief Defends IASB', *Financial Times*, 17 March 2003, 26.

[43] 'Round Tables a Qualified Success?', *World Accounting Report*, April 2003, 3.

whether such hedge accounting might also be applied to demand deposits.[44] The controversy arose from a fundamental difference of perspective. Like the IASC when it developed IAS 39, the IASB approached financial instruments from a balance-sheet perspective, focusing on the recognition and measurement of individual items that conformed to the definitions of assets and liabilities in its conceptual framework. In line with the conclusions of the JWG, the Board began with the assumption that fair value was, in principle, the most relevant measurement attribute for all financial instruments. From this point of view, it was natural to consider as axiomatic the rule that all derivatives be measured at fair value.[45] Banks, on the other hand, were from a risk management perspective not necessarily interested in fair values of derivatives used for hedging purposes. They used derivatives, principally interest rate swaps, to reduce the interest rate exposure on income flows from large, heterogeneous portfolios of imperfectly matched assets and liabilities, or, put differently, to protect the interest margin on such positions.[46] Based on this perspective, banks had traditionally measured hedging derivatives at cost, and, as was clear from the comment letters on the June 2002 exposure draft, they fully intended to continue doing so.

Both sides acknowledged the magnitude of the differences, but seemed willing to find a solution, and they recognized the necessity of making certain accommodations.[47] The banks accepted, at least as a working assumption, that all derivatives should be measured at fair value. This, of course, immediately brought the issue of hedge accounting to the fore, because the hedged items would typically be measured at amortized cost. On this point, the IASB made a concession. In application guidance issued in 2000, the IGC had explained how, under the original IAS 39, hedge accounting might be applied to macro-hedges of interest rate risk, but the IASB now acknowledged that this was of limited use to the banks. In particular, it noted that, whereas the existing rules might allow cash flow hedge accounting for such positions, it was 'virtually impossible' to obtain fair value hedge accounting.[48] This difference mattered because, even though both types of hedge accounting would reduce volatility in income, under cash flow hedge accounting effectively hedged positions would still produce volatility in equity.

The fair value hedge accounting provisions had been drafted with individual assets and liabilities in mind. To apply them to large pools of items changing on a daily basis was a challenge from a systems point of view that not all banks were yet

[44] The other banks represented in the working party were said to be Barclays, BNP Paribas, and HSBC. See 'European Banks near Deal on Derivative Reporting Rules', *Financial Times*, 20 June 2003, 20. For a review of this episode, including a summary of the issues, see also Geoffrey Whittington, 'The Adoption of International Accounting Standards in the European Union', *European Accounting Review*, 14/1 (2005), 127–53.

[45] 'The Round Table Discussions on IAS 32 and IAS 39', introductory note sent to participants at roundtable meetings, agenda paper 2A, SAC meeting February 2003.

[46] For expositions of this point of view see, for instance, 'FBE Observations on the IAS 39 Improvements Programme'; and letter from Philippe Bordenave to David Tweedie, dated 14 November 2003 (comment letters on August 2003 exposure draft of IAS 39 amendments, CL 57).

[47] AP 5/2003 paper 1A 'Administrative Items—April 2003 Board Meeting'. See also 'Normes comptables: l'IASB face à la Fédération bancaire européenne', *Les Echos*, 28 April 2003, 26.

[48] AP 5/2003 paper 7C, 6.

ready to meet.[49] The concession made by the IASB was therefore to allow that a notional amount of either assets or liabilities, derived from the net amount at risk from interest rate changes within a portfolio of assets and liabilities, be designated as the hedged item in a fair value hedge. In the income statement, fair value changes in the derivative used as a hedging instrument would be offset against those fair value changes in the notional amount that were due to the hedged risk. On the balance sheet, these latter fair value changes would not be allocated to individual assets or liabilities, but would be shown as separate line items. Until June 2003, hopes were expressed that an agreement along these lines could be reached.[50] Yet two questions, both rather arcane to non-accountants, and perhaps to many accountants as well, continued to keep the two sides apart. Given that these issues came to be emblematic of the difficulties between the IASB and the EU, they merit some further attention.

One of these two issues was a basic problem of the proposed approach to portfolio-hedge accounting. The notional amount (the hedged item) was an abstract representation of just a portion of a larger underlying group of specific assets or liabilities. The question then was how, if at all, the notional amount would be affected by unexpectedly early or late repayments of, say, assets in the underlying portfolio. If an individual loan was repaid early by the debtor, should it be assumed that it was always, sometimes, hardly ever, or only for a certain percentage a part of the notional amount? The answer to the question determined how likely it was that such prepayments, or a revision of the expectation of prepayments, would cause the hedge to become ineffective, so that gains and losses would have to be recognized. The banks were divided over the significance of these prepayment options. German banks tended to view them as less import-ant in practice than did French banks, because of differences in prevailing loan conditions.[51] But in general, all banks favoured solutions that cushioned them to some extent against the recognition of ineffectiveness. When, at its June 2003 meeting in Rome, the Board, with the exception of Gilbert Gélard (against) and Tom Jones (abstention), opted for a solution implying a low threshold for recognition of hedge ineffectiveness, something snapped.[52]

As the question presented itself to the Board, it was more complicated than described here, and it took some time for the Board and the staff to understand it fully.[53] Yet at heart it was just an example of an allocation problem. And as had been recognized in the accounting literature for decades, this was a type of problem which, on a fundamental level, could be resolved by arbitrary solutions only.[54] The Board's justification for its choice was therefore to a large extent based

---

[49] Interview with Geoffrey Mitchell, 16 October 2009.

[50] 'European Banks Near Deal on Derivative Reporting Rules', *Financial Times*, 20 June 2003, 20.

[51] 'Rückslag bei Gespräche über IAS 39', *Börsen-Zeitung*, 27 June 2003, 18. The reason given for the difference is that German banks tended to be protected against prepayment by penalty clauses, whereas banks from France, Spain, and Italy were not.

[52] AP 7/2003 paper 6, 2; 'Les négociations sur les normes comptables dans la banque sont dans l'impasse', *Les Echos*, 26 June 2003, 25. For the vote, see *IStaR*, June 2003, 40.

[53] See for the evolution of views: AP 5/2003 paper 7C, AP 6/2003 paper 9C, and AP 7/2003 paper 6B.

[54] See Arthur L. Thomas, *The Allocation Problem in Financial Accounting Theory* (Evanston, Ill: American Accounting Association, 1969), and the subsequent literature based on this study.

on arguments of internal consistency with other aspects of IAS 39.[55] It was motivated as well by a general keenness to make sure that any hedge ineffectiveness would be forced into the open, and there was considerable scepticism in the Board whether, in practice, financial instruments could be found or devised that would effectively mirror the idiosyncratic interest-sensitivity of prepayments. Clearly, such arguments would not necessarily have been persuasive to the banks, particularly if they held different views on whether particular risks were effectively hedged or not.

Related to the general question of determining hedge effectiveness was a more specific stumbling block in the form of the so-called 'core deposits'. This referred to the relatively stable total amounts of demand deposits appearing on bank balance sheets, but consisting, of course, of many continuously changing individual account balances. The French banks in particular wished to include these deposits in portfolios to which fair value hedge accounting for interest rate risks was applied, because, for practical purposes, these were predictable long-term liabilities that hedged the interest rate risk on assets of similar duration.[56] Up to that point, the Board did not disagree, at least not as long as the notional amount used as a hedged item, as mentioned above, was an asset. But in the case where a bank wished to hedge a notional liability representing core deposits, the Board decided in July 2003 that it could not allow fair value hedge accounting. This, again, was a clash between two different mindsets. For the Board, it was a matter of principle that the fair value of a liability with a demand feature could not be lower than the amount payable on demand. To assume otherwise would create problems with another general principle in IAS 39, namely, that all financial instruments are initially recognized at fair value. If that fair value could be assumed to be lower than the nominal amount, 'day one profits' would have to be recognized on new deposits, a conclusion the Board was unwilling to draw. Moreover, it was anomalous to the Board to apply fair value hedge accounting to liabilities whose fair values could not, in its view, change at all in response to interest rate changes. In fact, the Board went so far as to suggest that interest rate hedges of core deposits were fully ineffective.[57] While this was logical from the Board's point of view, it implied that the banks had a defective view of risk management. To the banks, therefore, the Board's arguments were offensive as well as unpersuasive.[58] The banks had no desire to measure core deposits in the balance sheet at anything other than nominal value, and were not really interested in the question of whether that was equal to fair value or not. From their perspective, there was a real interest rate risk associated with core deposits that they wished to hedge with derivatives. They had not asked for the measurement of these derivatives at fair value but had accepted this because they recognized that it was an important principle to the IASB. From their point of view, it would have been reasonable for the IASB to adopt a pragmatic attitude to dealing with the

[55] See IAS 39, BC201.

[56] AP 5/2003 paper 1A 'Administrative Items—April 2003 Board Meeting'.

[57] Exposure draft 'Fair Value Hedge Accounting for a Portfolio Hedge of Interest Rate Risk' (IASB, August 2003), BC14(d).

[58] See AP 7/2003 paper 6C, 'Core Deposits in a Portfolio Hedge of Interest Rate Risk' (a paper by the EBF).

resulting volatility in income. One bank representative involved in the negoti-ations concluded in July: 'We are facing ideologues. The IASB understands our concerns, but nevertheless doesn't change its approach.'[59]

The IASB's strict adherence to principle must be seen in the light of the politicization of the issue which had reached new heights of intensity after a spell of relative calm produced by the roundtables in March. Early in June 2003, the chairmen of the main French banks paid a visit to the European Commission to discuss their concerns over bank regulation, among which IAS 39 figured prominently.[60] Around the same time, it became clear that the European Com-mission planned not to include IAS 32 and IAS 39 in the package of IASs that was scheduled for endorsement in the upcoming ARC meeting on 16 July. This move was welcomed not just by the banks: the European Round Table of Industrialists wrote a scathing letter to Commissioner Frits Bolkestein, in which it condemned IAS 39 as an expression of the IASB's 'obsession' with valuation at the expense of meaningful performance measures.[61] On 4 July, President Jacques Chirac of France wrote to Chairman Romano Prodi of the European Commission to express his approval of this split endorsement by referring to the 'dire consequences for financial stability' that the accounting standards on financial instruments would have.[62] As an intervention by a head of state on accounting standards, the letter was without precedent, but the opinion it expressed was commonplace. As a matter of historical perspective, it may be noted that a little over ten years earlier, the US Secretary of the Treasury Nicholas F. Brady had written in very similar language to the FASB to argue that its proposal to apply market value accounting to marketable securities 'could have serious, unintended effects on the availability of credit as well as on the stability of the financial system'.[63]

In line with the Commission's proposal, all extant standards, but not IAS 32 and IAS 39, were accepted for endorsement by the ARC on 16 July. While Chirac's letter did not alter the decisions made by the EU, the highly publicized interven-tion clearly revealed the power and intensity of the French banks' lobbying effort in opposition to the IASB.

It was under these circumstances that the Board met later in July 2003 to put the finishing touches on the exposure draft on the portfolio hedging of interest rate risk, which was published in August. The Board confirmed that it would not follow the well-understood preferences of the banks on recognition of ineffect-iveness and the inclusion of core deposits on the basis of expected maturities. Annoyance with the banks' political campaign may have stiffened the Board's resolve to reject pragmatic modifications in favour of a principled approach.[64]

---

[59] 'Le débat sur les nouvelles normes comptables prend un tour politique', *La Tribune*, 15 July 2003, 18.

[60] 'IAS: les banquiers français plaident à Bruxelles', *Les Echos*, 11 June 2003, 23.

[61] Letter from Alain Joly to Frits Bolkestein, dated 5 June 2003 <http://www.ert.be>. The ERT, at that date, was aware of the proposed 'split endorsement'.

[62] The letter is reproduced as Appendix A in David Alexander, 'Legal Certainty, European-ness and Realpolitik', *Accounting in Europe*, 3 (2006), 79–80.

[63] Letter from Treasury Secretary Nicholas F. Brady to Dennis R. Beresford, FASB chairman, dated 24 March 1992 (available from the authors).

[64] *IStaR*, July 2003, 20.

6.4 THE IASB ATTEMPTS TO CLOSE
THE BOOKS ON IAS 39

In July 2003, before the Board began a holiday recess, it had determined its policy on IAS 39. It confirmed its earlier decision that there would not be a re-exposure of the improved IAS 39, with the exception of the macro-hedging issue. Although some members, including Tatsumi Yamada and Tricia O'Malley, were in favour of partial re-exposure of other modifications as well, other members, including John Smith, believed that this would merely give opponents of the standard a 'second shot', and that, following the roundtables and subsequent discussions, it was not likely that re-exposure would produce new insights.[65] While there was frustration on the part of the banks over the perceived lack of responsiveness of the IASB, there was comparable frustration at the IASB about the perceived tendency of the banks to revisit issues on which the Board believed it had reached agreement with the banks.

From this point onwards, it would still take several months to deal with a variety of 'sweep issues' before the improved versions of IAS 32 and IAS 39 were finally published in December 2003. At that time, David Tweedie declared in a meeting with German journalists that these standards 'were no longer subject to political influence, or negotiable, and would have to be accepted as a whole by the EU'.[66] The only point that clearly remained to be settled was macro-hedging, on which an exposure draft of a further amendment to IAS 39 had been issued in August. However, as Tweedie was aware, another issue was coming to a boil just as he was speaking. This was the so-called fair value option, to be discussed further below.

After completing the improved version of IAS 39, the Board turned its attention, from December 2003 to February 2004, to the comment letters received on the macro-hedging exposure draft which had been published in August 2003. While most commentators commended the Board for responding to the concerns of the financial industry, a common refrain was that the Board had not gone far enough.[67] This was clear in particular on the issue of core deposits, where a large majority of respondents argued for a wider possibility to apply hedge accounting. The Board's staff, which continued to meet with representatives of the EBF, was receptive to this point of view.[68] The staff argued for a relaxation of IAS 39's strict position that the fair value of a liability with a demand feature cannot be less than the amount payable on demand, and hence for a somewhat wider scope for hedge accounting.[69] There was some sympathy for this within the Board as well, but in the end the Board decided that it was not yet ready to consider all of the conceptual ramifications. It was recognized that the so-called 'deposit intangible' (i.e. the positive value of the probability that not all demand deposits would be withdrawn at once) was a significant issue, but the Board did not wish to address

---

[65] *IStaR*, July 2003, 49.

[66] 'IASB legt Derivate-Standards vor; IAS 32 und IAS 39 nicht mehr verhandelbar: Makro-Hedging läuft aber separat', *Börsen-Zeitung*, 17 December 2003, 17.

[67] See AP 12/2003 paper 6 for a general characterization of the comment letters.

[68] As indicated in AP 1/2004 papers 4B and 4C.

[69] AP 1/2004 paper 4B, paragraphs 30–44.

this issue in isolation because parallel 'unit of account' issues were then being discussed in the context of insurance accounting and revenue recognition. Hence, there was great reluctance in the Board to make ad hoc decisions. Bob Garnett may have captured the majority feeling in the Board when he observed that this was a major measurement issue 'that could not be swept through in fifteen minutes' and that the Board had already made a substantial concession by allowing fair value hedge accounting for macro-hedges.[70] Therefore, apart from a number of clarifications, the final amendment to IAS 39 published in March 2004 was similar to the exposure draft, and so ran counter on several points to the clear wishes of the financial industry. In its comment letter, the EBF had anticipated the nature of the Board's sensitivities when it wrote: 'the right thing to do from a risk management point of view may become the wrong thing from an accounting point of view. It is essential for such clashes between accounting theory and risk management policies to be avoided.'[71] Unfortunately for the EBF, the IASB was not about to avoid conflict by making concessions on accounting theory.

When the Board took these decisions, the political pressure had not abated. The evening before the start of the January 2004 Board meeting, when the Board decided not to do anything more about the core deposits, there had been a very tense moment when European Commissioner Frits Bolkestein took the floor to give a welcoming address at a working dinner in Brussels. The dinner meeting had been organized by the Commission in its own Breydel building to discuss ways forward on financial instruments, and the diners included Board members, trustees, Commission staff, chief executives from the banking industry, and banking regulators. Some of Bolkestein's remarks came as a complete surprise to the Board members and trustees present. They heard him say that a joint committee or working group was to be formed in which the banking industry would in effect have an equal say with the IASB in further work on financial instruments. To those attending from the IASB, this was unacceptable. Moreover, they had come to the dinner in the belief that any ideas the Commission might have about a decision-making group of this kind had been shelved when the agenda for the meeting was coordinated in advance.[72] When the incompatibility of views became apparent, Bolkestein warned that failure to reach agreement would put at risk the adoption of IAS 39 by the EU. This prompted Paul Volcker, the chairman of the trustees, to defend the Board's mandate to take its decisions independently, and that, once a standard was completed, it was 'take it or leave it' for the EU.[73] An appearance of agreement was achieved only because both sides

---

[70] *IStaR*, January 2004, 32. See also IASB meeting of 20–3 January 2004, minute 3.1–8.

[71] 'FBE Comments on the Proposed Amendments to IAS 39', dated 18 November 2003 (comment letters on August 2003 exposure draft of IAS 39 amendments, CL 105).

[72] Communication from Thomas Seidenstein to the authors, dated 23 October 2012.

[73] For reports on the dinner, see 'IASB Set to Rebuff Brussels on Rules', *Financial Times*, 21 January 2004, 29; 'Take It or Leave It: New Rules Offer Harmony for Europe's Accounting Standards, But Who Will Play by Them?', *Financial Times*, 31 March 2004, 17. In Volcker's own report on the dinner, he contrasts the Commission's proposal for a high-level group to seek 'consensus' with the IASB with the need to achieve closure well before 2005, following which 'it will be up to the European Union to decide whether to accept or to reject the IASB's standards'. Memorandum from Paul Volcker to IASCF trustees, dated 27 January 2004, IASB archive.

accepted that a purely consultative committee would be convened.[74] The day after the acrimonious dinner, as a Board meeting was in progress, the EU finance ministers announced their support for Bolkestein's efforts in the 'difficult discussions' on IAS 32 and IAS 39.[75]

With the issuance of the hedge accounting amendment in March 2004, the IASB formally met its deadline of a 'stable platform' of standards by that date. However, that stability was called into question by a flurry of continued negotiations over further hedge accounting amendments during the next few months. The EBF hoped to resolve the dispute by tabling a proposal for a new type of hedge accounting, which it called 'interest rate margin hedge accounting'. A paper, drafted by Andreas Bezold (then between positions at Dresdner Bank and Deutsche Postbank, and a member of the Technical Expert Group of the European Financial Reporting Advisory Group, EFRAG) was submitted to the IASB in March. The IASB Board members and staff who engaged in discussions with the EBF were sceptical about the compatibility of these proposals with IAS 39 and the IASB's conceptual framework. Nevertheless, they embarked on a series of meetings with the EBF in order to discuss the proposal in more detail. Meanwhile, other ideas were explored at a higher level, as David Tweedie met with the chief executives of several banks from Britain and Continental Europe. As a compromise result of the unfortunate dinner meeting in January, a high-level European consultative group on accounting issues affecting financial institutions was set up. To be sure, this was to be a purely advisory group, but some saw its first meeting, scheduled for early June, as offering the hope of last-minute compromise.[76]

While dealing with Europe, the IASB still had to be mindful of other constituencies. In fact, the announcement in February 2004 of the high-level consultative group prompted a small wave of applications for membership from outside Europe, requiring the IASB to explain as well as it could why this group would be purely European.[77] Among these other countries was Australia which had also committed to a transition to IFRSs in 2005. The possibility of further modifications to IAS 39, together with speculations about delayed endorsement, raised the question of which financial instruments standard, if any, Australian companies should adopt by 1 January 2005. In March 2004 Jeffrey Lucy, chairman of the Australian Securities and Investments Commission, spoke of Australia's 'predicament'. David Tweedie, visiting Australia around the same time, met with finance directors of major companies to discuss their concerns.[78]

---

[74] 'IASB Creates Advisory Group at EU's Request', *Financial Times*, 3 February 2004, 29. Tweedie recalls that he suggested setting up such a group in order to offer Bolkestein a way out, rather than in response to a request from the Commission. Interview with David Tweedie, 29 July 2008.

[75] 'Council Meeting: Economic and Financial Affairs, Brussels, 20 January 2004', 5082/2/04 REV 2, 8.

[76] 'Norme IAS 39: vers un possible compromis', *Les Echos*, 10 June 2004, 17.

[77] Interview with David Tweedie, 29 July 2008.

[78] 'EU Digs in on International Accounting Standard', *Australian Financial Review*, 31 March 2004, 8.

6.5 THE FAIR VALUE OPTION AND THE EUROPEAN CENTRAL BANK

Meanwhile, in the early months of 2004, the fair value option became a major complication in the IASB's efforts to reach closure on IAS 39. Compared to the intricacies of hedge accounting, this issue was not difficult to understand and was easily politicized. In this case, the IASB did respond, and, some would say, bend, to the pressure.

As indicated above, the June 2002 exposure draft proposed to introduce a 'fair value option'. The IASB's staff had concluded that a majority of respondents supported the proposal, or at least did not object, but that there were also a significant number of disagreements.[79] Companies were generally supportive, given that the option was intended as a fix of acknowledged problems with the mixed-measurement model. In that sense, a fair value option was a second-best solution for banks such as BNP Paribas and Société Générale which preferred to see these problems solved by allowing that some instruments would *not* be measured at fair value, rather than the other way round.[80] Behind such suggestions may have been suspicions that, by means of the fair value option, the Board was preparing the way for a mandatory full fair value approach envisaged in the earlier proposals by the JWG.[81]

The comments from most of the regulators reflected scepticism, and they called for further thinking.[82] The securities regulators in IOSCO's Standing Committee 1 on multinational disclosure and accounting were uneasy with an option that might lead to earnings manipulation and different treatment of identical financial instruments.[83] The Basel Committee had expressed misgivings about the option even though it recognized its merits as an attempt to allow enterprises to avoid some of the complexities of hedge accounting. It mentioned the inclusion of an entity's own credit risk in the fair value measurement of liabilities as a significant problem.[84] Many other respondents also mentioned the counterintuitive result that an entity would report a gain on liabilities measured at fair value when its own credit risk deteriorates. When the Board discussed the fair value option in April 2003, it agreed to leave it in place. Some Board members were uncomfortable with the 'own credit risk' problem, but it was agreed that it followed from a consistent application of the definition of fair value. John Smith noted that they had 'had a red flag from the regulators', but this was something to be resolved by calling for more disclosure.[85] This was not the way the regulators saw it, as shown by

---

[79] AP 4/2003 paper 5A.

[80] Identical letters from Daniel Bouton and Philippe Bordenave to David Tweedie, dated 14 October 2002 (comment letters on June 2002 ED of amendments to IAS 32 and IAS 39, CL 45 and 45A).

[81] The existence of these concerns was acknowledged by David Tweedie in a letter to Michel Pébereau (BNP Paribas), dated 13 January 2004, IASB archive, file 'IAS 32 IAS 39 2004'. However, Tweedie wrote 'I can assure you that is not the case'.

[82] See table in AP 12/2002 paper 3C, 4.

[83] Letter from Jackson M. Day to David Tweedie, dated 6 November 2002 (comment letters on June 2002 ED of amendments to IAS 32 and IAS 39, CL 135).

[84] Letter from William McDonough to David Tweedie, dated 18 October 2002 (comment letters on June 2002 ED of amendments to IAS 32 and IAS 39, CL 97).

[85] *IStaR*, April 2003, 18.

a June 2003 letter from IOSCO's Standing Committee 1, which repeated earlier concerns and asked the Board to reconsider this issue.[86] The Board, however, again concluded that disclosure should be the main answer to the regulators' concerns.[87]

But in November 2003, the IASB received signals that became too strong to ignore. ECB President Jean-Claude Trichet, who had just assumed office on 1 November, wrote to the IASB to convey his concerns over the implications for financial stability if the fair value option were to be widely applied.[88] This should not have come as a complete surprise to the IASB. As seen above, in its reaction to the JWG report, the ECB had already rejected an expansion of the use of fair value in the financial statements of banks beyond the trading book. Trichet's critical view of full fair value accounting for financial instruments was on record.[89] The timing of the ECB's current intervention, at a late stage of the IASB's due process, was due to a request from the European Commission for advice on the issue.[90] It was not unusual for the Commission to look to the ECB for advice, and the fair value option was a technical topic that was known to be controversial for reasons of financial stability, an issue of great concern to the ECB. But the Commission would have known that the ECB disliked the option, so that a request for advice could only lead to a derailing of the endorsement of IAS 39. By this time, it was already more than evident that the European endorsement of IAS 39 was going to be a very difficult process, and it would have been impossible for the European Commission to propose the standard for endorsement in the face of negative advice from the ECB. That the ECB had concerns became more widely known in February 2004, when strong criticism of fair value accounting was expressed in an article in the ECB's *Monthly Bulletin*.[91] In the article, the reliability of fair value measures was questioned, and the worrying prospect was raised of pro-cyclical effects on banks' lending behaviour. Whether or not fair value accounting had implications for financial stability would become a matter for vehement public debate in later years, following the financial crisis of 2008 (see Chapter 13). At this stage, the issue did attract far less attention and was overshadowed by the hedge accounting controversy, but the ECB's objections were sufficient for the IASB to take heed.

On 4 February, a meeting was held between representatives of the ECB and the IASB, during which it was agreed that certain modifications to the standard would be proposed to the Board.[92] These modifications would restrict the scope of the fair value option to a few specific situations where they would offer practical relief from the complexities of IAS 39 without fundamentally altering its mixed-

---

[86] Letter from Scott A. Taub to David Tweedie, dated 12 June 2003, IASB archive, file 'IOSCO'.

[87] IASB meeting of 22–4 July 2003, minute 5.8.

[88] Letter from Jean-Claude Trichet to David Tweedie, dated 21 November 2003, IASB archive, file 'IAS 32 IAS 39 2003'.

[89] 'Normes comptables: Jean-Claude Trichet n'est "pas convaincu" par les propositions de l'IASC', *Les Echos*, 28 June 2001, 26.

[90] Interview with David Wright, 19 January 2009; and with Mauro Grande, 30 June 2009.

[91] 'The Impact of Fair Value Accounting on the European Banking Sector: A Financial Stability Perspective', *ECB Monthly Bulletin*, February 2004, 69–81. But see also the concerns expressed by Bank of England Deputy Governor Sir Andrew Large, reported in 'Controversy over IAS 39 Raises Fundamental Questions', *Credit Control*, 25/8 (1 January 2004), 9.

[92] AP 2/2004 paper 11.

measurement character. The fair value option would still allow, for instance, measuring a host contract together with an embedded derivative at fair value, rather than require the two to be separated.

When this proposal was formally put to the Board in February 2004, the members unsurprisingly expressed concern that such a last-minute change was proposed after the completion of a lengthy due process on the improvements to IAS 39. Tatsumi Yamada made a statement conveying the opinion of the Accounting Standards Board of Japan (ASBJ) that it was unacceptable that the IASB had ignored the ASBJ's earlier concerns over the fair value option, but was now reacting in response to the ECB. Tom Jones tried to argue that there was a difference between the EU, which had committed to use the standards in full, and Japan, which had not, but Geoffrey Whittington emphasized that it was not correct to withhold an option, which the Board had believed was proper and useful, from all companies in all countries because of objections from a regional banking regulator.[93] In the end, a majority of Board members agreed to proceed with the proposals, persuaded by the argument that the modified option would still allow most of the intended applications.[94] An exposure draft was published in April 2004.

What is perhaps surprising is that the Board at this stage did not recall that in 2003 it had informed Australia and New Zealand that the removal of an option in IFRSs from local accounting standards that were otherwise identical to IFRSs would still allow companies that complied with the local standard to claim compliance with IFRSs (see Section 4.3). Following this logic, the IASB might have pointed out to the European Commission that it should remove the option itself. This is, of course, what subsequently happened with the so-called carve-outs. But at this stage, with the endorsement of IAS 32 and 39 still undecided, the IASB may have believed that it was the wiser course to pay heed to the publicly expressed misgivings of a major EU institution, without whose support the European Commission was unlikely to proceed with the endorsement process at all.

6.6 THE CARVE-OUTS

By June 2004 a decision about the endorsement of IAS 32 and 39 for use in the EU could no longer be postponed if, given the requirements of the cumbersome EU endorsement process, there was to be a complete set of standards available for use on 1 January 2005. On 2 June, Commissioner Bolkestein informed the EU's finance ministers that it was 'high noon' in the negotiations between the EU and the IASB.[95]

To recapitulate, at that stage the improved versions of both standards had been published by the IASB in December 2003. A further amendment had been made in March 2004 to allow a degree of macro-hedge accounting. An exposure draft to limit the fair value option had been issued in April. However, intense negotiations

---

[93] *IStaR*, February 2004, 33–5. See also 'Compromises at the IASB', *World Accounting Report*, March 2004, 2.

[94] IASB meeting of 18–20 February 2004, minute 7.2.

[95] 'Dispute Over Bank Hedging of Core Deposits Seen as Last Hurdle for EU to Commit to IAS', BNA's *Daily Tax Report*, 106 DTR G-4, 3 June 2004.

were still in progress over further changes to hedge accounting, and it was not a foregone conclusion that the fair value option amendment would be widely acceptable.

The European endorsement mechanism got off to a difficult start when it became known that EFRAG's Technical Expert Group (TEG) was deeply divided over IAS 39. After fierce debate, a 4 June draft ballot on the endorsement of IAS 39 resulted in five votes in favour and six against. When it was formed, TEG's voting rules had deliberately been written to require a qualified majority for rejecting a standard and a simple majority for recommending a standard for endorsement, in order to make rejection an unlikely event. The vote on IAS 39 fell into the no-man's-land in between, and drew attention to the fact that no fewer than three TEG members came from France, all of whom voted against a positive endorsement advice.[96] When, a month later, the final vote had not changed, EFRAG had to draw the lame conclusion that it could not express an opinion on IAS 39. EFRAG did recommend endorsement of IAS 32.[97]

Meanwhile, a final attempt at compromise failed on 9 June, during the first meeting of the EU's high-level consultative group with the IASB. The banking representatives rejected an IASB proposal that IAS 39 should be endorsed in exchange for a firm commitment by the IASB to consider the EBF's interest rate margin hedge proposals.[98] A few days later, the European Commission sounded out the ARC about an endorsement under this condition, but four member states, said to be France, Belgium, Italy, and Spain, announced that they were not prepared to vote in favour of endorsement. Under the EU's complicated voting rules, they formed a blocking minority.[99] The unsuccessful high-level consultative group was allowed to die a quiet death after meeting two or three times.

In order to move forward, the Commission's staff, on 9 July, unveiled a plan to propose for approval to the ARC a version of IAS 39 from which a small amount of text had been eliminated, both from the standard and from the associated application guidance. These 'carve-outs', as the Commission called them, consisted of two parts.

One carve-out was a simple removal of the fair value option for liabilities, leaving the option for assets intact. The ostensible reason for limiting this carve-out to liabilities was that the EU's Fourth Company Law Directive had recently been changed to allow the measurement of assets, but not liabilities, at fair value. The concerns of the ECB went beyond liabilities, however, and it was clear that a more comprehensive revision of the fair value option was required before this carve-out could be removed. Such a comprehensive reconsideration was already envisaged in the IASB's April 2004 exposure draft, so that the carve-out was really just a reminder to make sure that the IASB would deliver.

---

[96] 'Endorsement Thrown into Confusion', *World Accounting Report*, July/August 2004, 2.

[97] Letter from Stig Enevoldsen to Alexander Schaub, dated 8 July 2004 <http://www.efrag.org>.

[98] 'Normes comptables: le refus des banques', *Le Figaro Économie*, 10 June 2004, 1; 'IASB Offers to Try Compromise on IAS 39 But EU Bankers still Unsatisfied with Plan', *Daily Tax Report*, 111 DTR G-8, 10 June 2004.

[99] Summary record, ARC meeting of 14 June 2004 <http://ec.europa.eu/internal_market/account ing>. For the identity of the four countries, see 'Bruxelles ne se prononcera pas sur l'IAS 39 avant juillet', *Les Echos*, 15 June 2004, 31.

The other carve-out was a quite complex collection of eliminated sentences and paragraphs intended to allow the designation of core deposits as hedged items and to relax the effectiveness criteria for portfolio hedges of interest rate risk, mainly with a view to allow hedges of 'core deposits'. Despite the appearance of delicate surgery, the carve-out created a gap of uncertain dimensions in the standard. As was pointed out both at the IASB and by EFRAG, the relaxation of effectiveness testing could well have unintended consequences beyond the area of application envisaged by the Commission and open the way to abuses. Moreover, some paragraphs that stood in the way of the intended purpose of the carve-out could not be eliminated because of their function beyond hedge accounting, and the Commission had to rely on the questionable expedient of giving directions on their interpretation in the recitals to the endorsement regulation.[100]

It is possible that some members of the Commission's staff had already quietly envisaged such carve-outs as a potential emergency measure at the time when the EU's IAS Regulation was drafted.[101] Yet for most people, the idea that it was possible to endorse a standard with small deletions was new. The ARC tentatively expressed its support for this approach, although the United Kingdom, Sweden, and Denmark, and perhaps other member states that favoured integral adoption of IAS 39, questioned the legality of the carve-outs.[102] Nevertheless, the proposal opened the way for the carved-out IAS 39 to be formally placed on the EU's statute books on 19 November 2004, only some six weeks before IFRSs became mandatory for EU listed companies.

The EU carve-outs would acquire a symbolic value that went far beyond their practical significance. By their very existence, they raised the spectre of more such carve-outs, both by the EU and by other jurisdictions adopting IFRSs, leading to a dilution of the ideal of comparable financial reporting. Such carve-outs did happen, for instance when the Philippines adopted IFRSs as of 1 January 2005, with certain modifications to IAS 39 and other standards.[103] To the chagrin of officials at the European Commission, carve-outs in other jurisdictions attracted

---

[100] 'Analysis of EC Proposal, with Amendments', memorandum from Wayne Upton to David Tweedie, dated 16 July 2004, IASB archive, file 'EU'; communication from James Leisenring to the authors, December 2012; letter from Stig Enevoldsen to Alexander Schaub, dated 26 September 2004 <http://ec.europe.eu/internal_market/accounting>. An important paragraph that could not be carved-out was IAS 39.49, indicating that the fair value of a liability with a demand feature cannot be lower than the amount payable on demand. Recital (8) to Commission Regulation No. 2086/2004 of 19 November 2004 includes an assertion about the compatibility of this paragraph with portfolio hedge accounting of core deposits.

[101] As asserted by Karel Van Hulle, interview, 20 January 2009.

[102] Summary record, ARC meeting of 9 July 2004 <http://ec.europa.eu/internal_market/account ing>. In the final vote in the ARC, on 1 October 2004, four member states voted against the adoption of IAS 39 with carve-outs, and three member states abstained. The United Kingdom, Denmark, and Sweden were said to oppose the carve-outs in 'EU vor Einigung über Buchhaltungsnorm IAS 39— Mehrheit für "Carve-out"-Lösung', *Neue Zürcher Zeitung*, 9 September 2004. See also BNA's *Daily Tax Report*, 9 November 2004, 174 DTR G-4, 9 September 2004.

[103] 'Conversion to IFRS: The Philippine Experience', remarks by Fe B. Barin, chairperson, Philippine Securities and Exchange Commission at the IASCF Conference on International Financial Reporting Standards, 29–30 August 2007 <http://demo.sec.gov.ph>. It was this speech which caused the Deloitte website IAS Plus to modify its earlier statement, posted on 4 November 2005, that 'the Philippines has adopted all IFRSs for 2005 without modification'.

little world attention, while the EU carve-outs were notorious. They could be cited to illustrate the threat to the IASB's independence posed by political pressure from the EU, although, of course, it was also possible for David Tweedie to see them as a 'badge of honour' for resisting such pressure.[104]

Obviously, no EU company could apply the fair value option because of the carve-out, but, as it was only an option, their financial statements would still be in accordance with IFRSs. As discussed in Chapter 9, the fair value carve-out was removed with relative ease in 2005, following an amendment to IAS 39.

The hedge accounting carve-out created more difficulties and, as discussed more fully in Chapter 12, it remained in place beyond the period covered in this book. Hedge accounting was not mandatory under IAS 39, so the carve-out did not prevent companies from complying with full IFRSs. In November 2004, the Commission even wrote that member states could *require* their companies to comply with full IFRSs on this point, although few member states, if any, seem to have done so.[105] Yet the carve-out was clearly meant to be used, and it created the possibility to depart from IFRSs. Given that European banks were not even required to disclose whether they applied the carve-out, let alone what its effect on the reported numbers was, it is not easy to estimate how frequently it was used, and to what effect. A study on the implementation of IFRSs carried out on behalf of the European Commission concluded that, out of forty-three large banking groups, eleven banks from six countries used the carve-out in 2005 and/or 2006. In the case of twenty-nine others it was clear that they did not, while in three cases no definite conclusion could be drawn on the basis of public data.[106] In subsequent years, the carve-out gained an occasional new convert, while other banks abandoned its use.[107]

6.7 IFRS 7: THE IASB AND THE BANKS PRODUCE A PRINCIPLES-BASED STANDARD

The sometimes acrimonious debate between the IASB and the banking industry over IAS 39 could easily obscure that, at the same time, the parties were working together quite constructively on a different topic. This was the project to revise

---

[104] Interview with David Tweedie, 29 July 2008.

[105] 'IAS 39 Financial Instruments: Recognition and Measurement—Frequently Asked Questions (FAQ)', European Commission MEMO/04/265, 19 November 2004 <http://europa.eu/rapid>.

[106] The eleven banks said to be using the carve-out were Dexia, Fortis, KBC (all three from Belgium), BNP Paribas, Crédit Agricole, Société Générale (all three from France), Commerzbank (Germany), Unicredit (Italy), ING, Rabobank (the Netherlands), and Nordea (Sweden). See *Evaluation of the Application of IFRS in the 2006 Financial Statements of EU Companies: Report to the European Commission* (Ineum Consulting, December 2008) <http://ec.europa.eu/internal_market/accounting>. ING had not used the carve-out in 2005 (see Section 8.1). According to *The Impact of IFRS on European Banks: 2005 Reporting* (Ernst & Young, 2006), 48, Sanpaolo IMI (Italy) used the carve-out in 2005.

[107] For example, Commerzbank reportedly used the carve-out in 2005 and/or 2006, but began affirming that it did not use the carve-out in its 2009 financial statements. Aegon (the Netherlands), on the other hand, began using the carve-out in its 2012 financial statements.

IAS 30 *Disclosures in the Financial Statements of Banks and Similar Financial Institutions*, which finally resulted in IFRS 7 *Financial Instruments: Disclosures*, issued in August 2005. IAS 30 (1990), while not a very old standard, had had a difficult birth, from which it showed some scars. Moreover, it had never been aligned with IAS 32 and IAS 39, the subsequent standards on financial instruments. The IASC had already seen the need for its revision, and started a project in 2000 which the IASB decided to retain as part of its initial agenda. This was a project that the Board simply could not abandon. At the time, banking supervisors were hammering out the Basel II framework (completed in June 2004), which included as its 'third pillar' a set of disclosure requirements, particularly with respect to risk. The IASB staff reminded the Board that it would be incompatible with its aspirations to leadership to leave this important field to others. More positively, it was noted that both banks and bank regulators desired the active involvement of the IASB. This offered the opportunity to build bridges with the banking sector, clearly on edge over IAS 39 and the work of the JWG.[108] As the staff summarized it: 'The bank disclosure project would seem to have a lot of upside potential, but little downside risk. Indications are that banks and banking supervisors generally are very much supportive of the project to revise IAS 30. Therefore, the bank disclosure project could serve as a valuable means of promoting a constructive dialogue with banks.'[109]

With the project, the IASB inherited a steering committee. As discussed in Section 5.3, the Board was inclined to break with the IASC's reliance on steering committees, but in this case it retained the committee, added some members, and changed its name to the Financial Activities Advisory Committee.[110] Although the name change might suggest otherwise, the Board let it play a very active role in the development of a new standard, rather than using it as a passive sounding board.

The committee was initially chaired by Geoffrey Mitchell (a former IASC secretary-general, then with Barclays), soon succeeded by Russell Picot, group chief accountant of HSBC. Picot's active participation in the IASB's work was in line with the fact that, among preparers of financial statements, HSBC was one of the most significant supporters of the IASB. HSBC's finance director (since 2010, the chief executive) Douglas Flint, a Scottish chartered accountant, was a long-standing acquaintance of David Tweedie's and had served with him on the UK ASB. From 2001 to 2004, Flint was a member of SAC. Although on occasion Flint was critical of the IASB's work on financial instruments, when the endorsement of IAS 39 by the EU hung in the balance, he came out with a strong public message of support, stating that HSBC would adopt IAS 39 even if the EU rejected it.[111]

---

[108] AP 5/2001 paper 15.

[109] AP 4/2001 paper 2, paragraph 11.

[110] As of November 2001, the membership of the committee consisted of (AP 11/2001 paper 4) Russell Picot (HSBC, chairman), Chris Begy (Bank of Montreal), Judith Downes (ANZ Banking Group), Wolfgang Kolb (Dresdner Bank), Peter Jepson (Ford Financial Europe), Michael J. Castelli (American International Group), Anik Sen (UBS Warburg), Steve Ball (PricewaterhouseCoopers), Tadayuki Matsushige (Ernst & Young), and Hans Schoen (KPMG). Karl-Heinz Hillen (Bundesbank) and Robert F. Storch (Federal Deposit Insurance Corporation) attended as observers for the Basel Committee, Richard Thorpe (Financial Services Authority, United Kingdom) for IOSCO, and Vittorio Pinelli for the European Commission.

[111] 'HSBC Signals Controversial Accounting Move', *Financial Times*, 31 March 2004, 15.

Both the committee and the Board had some difficulty in finding the right approach for this project. One problem was how to define its scope. It was noted that the line dividing banks from non-banks had become blurred, so that it was questionable whether a separate standard for banks was still in order. Moreover, demarcation lines had to be drawn with IAS 1 *Presentation of Financial Statements* and IAS 32 *Financial Instruments: Disclosure and Presentation*. After trying to avoid the word 'bank' by defining the project in the cumbersome terms of 'deposit-taking, lending, and securities activities', it was finally agreed that the project would be defined in terms of disclosures relating to financial instruments. The possibility of aiming for an amendment to IAS 32 was considered but rejected in favour of developing a new standard, to which the disclosure requirements of IAS 32 would be transferred.

Another, more fundamental, question was in what sense the new standard should be principles-based. The idea of developing a standard based on articulated disclosure principles had been put forward by the committee and the staff in the early stages of the project.[112] Yet a lengthy draft standard put on the table in July 2002 did not strike the Board as a particularly good instance of principles-based standard setting.[113] Nonetheless, while it called for principles, the Board also continued to worry about the risk of companies using boilerplate language to comply with the standard, and about the necessity of minimum requirements and application guidance. So, when a revised proposal was produced, based on a single principle and a small number of high-level requirements, Jim Leisenring's critical comment was that the Board 'risked becoming enamoured of disclosures which sounded good but produced nothing meaningful'.[114]

Over time, however, the staff, the committee, and the Board were able to strike a balance, and in July 2004 an exposure draft, ED 7, was published which was generally well-received. The resulting IFRS 7 mainly followed the exposure draft and could, with some justification, be presented as an example of principles-based standard setting. IFRS 7 contained just two bold-faced paragraphs, stating as basic principles that an entity should disclose information that enables the users of financial statements to evaluate the significance of financial instruments for its financial position and performance, and to evaluate the nature and extent of risks arising from financial instruments to which the entity is exposed (IFRS 7.7; IFRS 7.31).

In the light of criticism, already mounting at the time, that the Board's agenda was too much dominated by convergence with US GAAP, it is of some interest to note that it was as an afterthought that the Board decided to add a reference in its July 2004 exposure draft to the FASB's contemporaneous project on fair value measurement. The FASB's project was to lead to an exposure draft in June 2004, which contained some disclosure requirements that had counterparts in the IASB's ED 7. Jim Leisenring observed in May 2004 that 'he was concerned that it would look like the two boards had not spoken to each other'.[115] While this was

---

[112] AP 11/2001 paper 4, paragraphs 43–5.

[113] See the discussion as reported in *IStaR*, July 2002, 23–9, and December 2002, 6–10.

[114] *IStaR*, December 2002, 7; for the Board's reaction to earlier proposals see IASB meeting of 27–30 November 2001, minute II.

[115] *IStaR*, May 2004, 16.

apparently not far from the truth with respect to this issue, the Board agreed to include a question in the exposure draft on the respective merits of the two boards' proposals. It also intended to ask the FASB to make a similar cross-reference, but the FASB's exposure draft did not mention the IASB's project.[116]

A question that took up considerably more of the Board's time was how to deal with banking supervision in this project. When the Board decided that the project would be about financial instruments in general, and not specifically about banks, it did no more than push the banks a little below the surface. The Board still had to ensure that the general-purpose language of the standard was appropriate both for non-financial companies and for the specific regulatory regimes under which banks, but also insurance companies, had to operate. By means of an observer in the IASB's Financial Activities Advisory Committee, the Basel Committee maintained a direct link with the IASB, and the degree of coordination achieved was one of the reasons for the favourable reception of the IASB's exposure draft.

In the initial stages of the project, when it was still focused on banks, the question had been raised of requiring the disclosure of entity-specific capital requirements (such as minimum solvency ratios) imposed by banking supervisors. The committee's view, accepted by the Board, was that information about such requirements is relevant to users of financial statements because of their potentially constraining effect on banks' operating and financial policies. Hence, just as IAS 32 called for disclosures regarding loan covenants, the disclosure of regulatory capital requirements would be in order.[117] It is possible that the bank representatives on the committee did not just have the information needs of investors in mind, but may also have been interested in the potential of this disclosure to signal their own strength. But when proposals along this line were developed, during the first months of 2003, the IASB was informed both by the Basel Committee and the European Commission that some bank regulators were strongly opposed to such disclosures, particularly of entity-specific requirements imposed on individual banks.[118] While the Basel Committee acknowledged that it might be of interest to the market to be informed of the regulator's assessment of a bank, it expressed the concern that such disclosures could not be made without upsetting the delicate process of bank supervision. Even if disclosure were desirable, it would be difficult to convey information about the often complex mix of formal and informal regulatory interventions to the market in a way that would not be misleading.

While the Board and its advisory committee were willing to accept this point, they were not immediately willing to abandon a potentially useful disclosure altogether. The result was a carefully worded requirement in ED 7, applicable to all entities, to disclose information about 'capital' and its management by the

---

[116] See Question 9 in ED 7 'Financial Instruments: Disclosures' (IASB, July 2004). FASB's exposure draft 'Fair Value Measurements' (Financial Accounting Series No. 1201-100) was issued on 23 June 2004.

[117] AP 11/2001 paper 4, paragraph 38.

[118] Letter from Jan Brockmeijer (chairman of Basel Committee Transparency Group) to Thomas Jones, dated 19 March 2003, AP 5/2003 paper 8A; letter from Jean-Claude Thebault (European Commission, DG Internal Market–Financial Institutions) to Thomas Jones, dated 21 March 2003, AP 5/2003 paper 8B.

entity. Although the requirement merely called for qualitative disclosures about any externally imposed requirements, it did call for quantitative disclosures about capital targets set by management (paragraph 47(b)). As it was assumed that, for regulated entities, these targets would at least be equal to regulatory requirements, the proposed disclosure was seen as an indirect way of eliciting at least some quantitative information about regulatory requirements.[119]

The IASB staff reported that respondents to ED 7 'overwhelmingly' disagreed with the proposed requirements on capital disclosure, making this easily the most controversial part of the exposure draft.[120] When the Board again considered the issue, early in 2005, the requirement did in fact look a little awkward. It had originated in the banking background of the project, but it now looked out of place in a standard on financial instruments. While there was some support from both users and preparers for the view that information about capital was relevant for all entities, there was also something strained about a general-purpose requirement, as it was hard to forget that the potential relevance of the disclosure was far greater for regulated than for non-regulated entities. Moreover, for non-regulated entities it was difficult to see how information on capital targets set by management could avoid problems with subjectivity and manipulation, or why IFRSs should call for disclosure of these particular targets rather than any other targets set by management. Finally, the Board noted that the concept of 'capital' played at best a minor role in its own conceptual framework, and was used there in a different sense than in the exposure draft.[121] As a result, the capital disclosures were removed from IFRS 7 and included in an amendment to IAS 1, published together with IFRS 7 in August 2005. The controversial requirement to disclose quantitative targets was deleted. What remained of the capital disclosure requirement was probably not very effective, and could serve as an illustration of the difficulties the Board had experienced in drafting principles-based disclosure standards. On the basis of a survey, the UK ASB reported in 2010 that a majority of UK companies surveyed either failed to disclose information on management of financial capital at all, or 'provided largely boilerplate information'.[122]

---

[119] See comments by Russell Picot reported in *IStaR*, January 2005, 31–2.

[120] AP 12/2004 paper 8, paragraph 15.

[121] See the report in the Board's discussion in *IStaR*, January 2005, as well as AP 1/2005 paper 2A; and the basis for conclusions in *Capital Disclosures: Amendments to International Accounting Standard IAS 1 Presentation of Financial Statements* (IASB, August 2005).

[122] *Financial Capital Management Disclosures* (London: Accounting Standards Board, December 2010).

7

The IASC Foundation's First Constitution Review

Debating Governance and Due Process

7.1 DEBATE OVER THE IASB'S LEGITIMACY, ACCOUNTABILITY, AND DUE PROCESS

As the high-profile conflict over financial instruments unfolded during 2003 and 2004, it naturally led to a debate about the status and organization of the IASB, both within the organization itself and among its constituents. As the countries of the European Union (EU) still made up the lion's share of jurisdictions committed to adopt IFRSs, it was natural that this debate focused on redefining the relationship between the IASB and the EU. However, accounting for financial instruments was only one issue, although a very important one, among several causes of growing dissatisfaction with the IASB. As discussed in Chapter 5, the project on performance reporting raised strong criticisms in both Europe and Japan over the IASB's perceived radicalism in 'abolishing' net income. The increasing emphasis in the IASB's agenda on convergence with US generally accepted accounting principles (US GAAP) following the Norwalk Agreement of 2002 began to give rise to questions about whether this was really in the interest of European companies. All of these issues pointed towards the fundamental question of what mandate this self-assured private-sector organization based in London actually had to set standards for the world and to what extent those affected by its standards should have the right and the means to influence its decisions.

Similar questions had already been raised in the debates over the restructuring of the IASC into the IASB in the late 1990s. At that time, the insistence by the US Securities and Exchange Commission (SEC) on adopting the organizational model of the Financial Accounting Standards Board (FASB) had prevailed, so that the IASB had been set up as an organization with independence and technical expertise as its core values, rather than representation and accountability. Officials of the European Commission had been deeply involved in the debate over the restructuring of the IASC, and would have been well aware of the issue when the Commission proposed, in 2000, the adoption of IFRSs for use in the EU. The creation of the EU's endorsement procedure (see Section 4.1) can be seen as an acknowledgement that the IASB's standards had to be anchored in a system of political accountability before they could be imposed as legal requirements on reporting companies. But even so, many in Europe who were dealing with the IASB or were affected by its standards discovered only at a late stage that they had to work with a standard setter that took its independence very seriously. For example, Alexander Schaub, who became director-general of the European Commission's Internal Market Directorate in 2003, found that his extensive international regulatory experience in the area of competition policy had not prepared him at all to work with a board like this.[1]

The question of Europe's influence over the IASB was already raised in 2002, when the IAS Regulation was enacted. In July of that year Pervenche Berès, a French member of the European Parliament and subsequently one of the Parliament's leading critics of the IASB, posed the question: 'How does the Commission . . . intend to strengthen its influence within this body so that it is able to defend the European common interest effectively?' To which the Commission confidently replied: 'As the main client of the IASB, the Union has a great influence over the decisions of the IASB. . . . The Commission is confident of the Union's capacity to make its views heard within the IASB.'[2] Less than a year later, awareness that there might be a problem with the EU's influence had reached the highest political levels, as indicated by the July 2003 letter on IAS 39 from the French President to the President of the Commission (see Section 6.3). Early in 2004 Berès could taunt the Commission in the European Parliament by referring to the 'wayward effects of the so-called autonomy of the IASB'.[3]

The trustees' response to criticism of the Board's substantive decisions was typically to point to the Board's complete responsibility for its technical agenda. Paul Volcker, the initial chairman of the trustees, made no secret of his own misgivings with respect to fair value and other aspects of IAS 39, yet he unswervingly maintained the line that the trustees' responsibility was limited to ensuring that the IASB followed its established due process.[4] In their meetings of November 2002 and March 2003, the trustees considered the Board's handling of the financial instruments project, and took note that concerns over the Board's procedures were not confined to the EU, but had been expressed in Japan as well. In general, though, the trustees appeared to be satisfied with the Board's adherence to due process.[5]

However, by July 2003 the political temperature had risen to such a degree that the minutes of the trustee meetings begin to show some doubt whether enough had been done. While some trustees emphasized that 'it was important to safeguard the IASB's ability to make difficult and unpopular decisions', others pointed to the need to 'improve communications with relevant parties', even if only to 'counteract perceptions that the IASB's processes were not sufficiently transparent'. The latter conclusion was adopted, specifically with regard to Europe, and it

---

[1] Interview with Alexander Schaub, 20 January 2009.

[2] Oral question by Pervenche Berès, 19 July 2002, and Commission response, 5 September 2002, Question 41, H-0602/02 <http://www.europarl.europa.eu>.

[3] Record of plenary session, 9 February 2004, 1-054 <http://www.europarl.europa.eu>.

[4] See, for instance, letter from Paul Volcker to Jean-Claude Trichet, dated 13 September 2001, IASB archive, file 'FI-JWG'; see for comparable views letter from Paul Volcker to Frits Bolkestein, dated 17 July 2003, IASB archive, file 'Bolkestein—meetings with'.

[5] IASCF trustees meetings of 19 November 2002, minute 4, and of 13 March 2003, minute 3.

was agreed that the trustees should take a more active role in these communications.[6] Volcker became increasingly active in consulting with the European Commission and the European Central Bank (ECB) about ways to resolve the financial instruments controversy, while maintaining his stance on the ultimate responsibility of the IASB to take its own decisions.[7]

At the same July meeting, the trustees began to consider a review of the IASC Foundation Constitution. Such a periodic review was called for in the Constitution itself, the first to start no later than February 2004, and to come into effect no later than February 2006. This review was never intended to be a formality, but 'a review of the entire structure of IASC [i.e. the IASB] and its effectiveness' (article 22(b)). While the review was not prompted by the financial instruments controversy, the circumstances made the upcoming review more momentous than may have been anticipated when the Constitution was drafted. This was not lost upon the European Commission, which, two weeks before the trustees' July meeting, had already briefed the European finance ministers. The latter had taken note in their formal Council conclusions that 'the Commission, as part of that [Constitution] review, intends to urge the International Accounting Standards Board (IASB) to ensure that all parties concerned are given a full opportunity to participate in the elaboration of the standards, including their economic impact, and to discuss with the IASB its present institutional structure to ensure that it is conducive to the achievement of the aforementioned objective'.[8] With this political loading, the first Constitution review was a major project, only completed in June 2005. Before considering this process in more detail, attention will be paid to a more immediate response by the Board to its critics.

7.2 THE IASB MODIFIES ITS DUE PROCESS

There was undoubtedly something in the attitude of the early Board that could make it seem arrogant and not inclined to consult widely. David Tweedie fondly remembered the days of the G4+1, when a small group of bright people had thought freely and widely on accounting issues. He liked to quote a remark made by Jim Leisenring on one of these occasions: ' "If we just locked the door and we all stayed in here for a fortnight it would solve most of the major accounting problems." ' Looking back in 2013, Tweedie added: 'I have always believed that if three or four of the right sort of people get together you can have a good chance of hammering out solutions to problems in a relatively short period.'[9] Regardless of the merits of Tweedie's point of view, it was bound to create a conflict with constituents who believed that the IASB owed it to them to adopt a much more consultative style of standard setting.

---

[6] IASCF trustees meeting of 29 July 2003, minute 3.

[7] See e.g. letters from Paul Volcker to Jean-Claude Trichet and Frits Bolkestein, both dated 18 December 2003, IASB archive.

[8] 2520th Council Meeting—Economic and Financial Affairs, Brussels, 15 July 2003, 11180/03, 14.

[9] 'Response by Sir David Tweedie', in *The Accounting Hall of Fame: Sir David Philip Tweedie: Remarks, Citation, and Response* (The Ohio State University/Fisher College of Business, 2013), 22–3.

Moving ahead of the Constitution review process, the Board itself reconsidered and modified its operating procedures. Some might think that it was the leverage provided by the EU endorsement process which made a Board that 'was not listening' more amenable to outside views. In June 2004, Tommaso Padoa-Schioppa, then a member of the executive board of the ECB, but later to become Volcker's successor as chairman of the IASC Foundation trustees, wrote to Volcker:

> The ECB has shown interest from an early stage to participate in the debate on the new accounting standards, and particularly on FVA [fair value accounting]. However for some time it proved rather difficult to have our contributions properly taken into consideration. It would seem that other parties interested in the process also shared this concern. Then, once the procedure approached the endorsement phase within the EU regulatory framework, the debate became more open and we are pleased with the way in which exchange of views and common understanding have developed until now.[10]

Whatever the precise impetus might have been, the IASB began consultations with the staff of the European Commission, to discuss the latter's suggestions for improved due process.[11] In January 2004 David Tweedie announced several steps taken with the aim of 'improving communication with [the Board's] constituents and the transparency of the Board's deliberative processes'.[12] These included more extensive observer notes posted on the website ahead of meetings, more timely publication of comment letters on exposure drafts, and experimentation with webcasts.

In another development, the IASB began to make more use of working and advisory groups, a raft of which came into being in 2004. While the creation of each group was a separate decision with its own specific background, taken together they did indicate a change of approach by the Board, which initially had been reluctant to establish such groups.[13]

An Analyst Representative Group grew out of a meeting with financial analysts in November 2003, organized by Standards Advisory Council (SAC) member and former IASC Board member David Damant. It may be noted in passing that Damant's involvement with the IASC went all the way back to November 1973.[14] During many years, he had actively encouraged and cultivated contacts between the IASC and financial analysts. The creation of the Analyst Representative Group showed how he continued to play this role during the first years of the IASB.

---

[10] Letter from Tommaso Padoa-Schioppa to Paul Volcker, dated 28 June 2004 <http://www.iasc.org.uk> accessed through web.archive.

[11] 'Notes of the Meeting between European Commission staff and the IASB', 7 January 2004, appendix to memo from Paul Volcker to IASC Foundation trustees, dated 14 January 2004, IASB archive; Communication from Thomas Seidenstein to the authors, dated 23 October 2012.

[12] 'The Chairman's Page—A Personal View by Sir David Tweedie', *IASB Insight*, January 2004, 4.

[13] Volcker characterized some of the groups created in 2004 as 'a reflection of the organization's new emphasis on early consultation'. Paul Volcker, 'Maintaining Progress toward International Accounting Standards', remarks before the ARC, 25 February 2005 <http://ec.europa.eu/internal_market/accounting>.

[14] Kees Camfferman and Stephen A. Zeff, *Financial Reporting and Global Capital Markets: A History of the International Accounting Standards Committee, 1973–2000* (Oxford: Oxford University Press, 2007), 205–6.

To help reinvigorate the difficult projects on insurance and performance measurement, new working groups were set up in September and November 2004, respectively. Also in September, a financial instruments working group was established to deal with the next steps in that contentious area. Starting in January 2004, regular meetings to discuss the IASB's ongoing projects took place with a group of European finance directors representing a task force on IFRSs from the European Round Table of Industrialists (ERT). Like the Analyst Representative Group, this was not a group set up and composed by the IASB itself. Rather, the initiative was taken by the finance directors, and it illustrated how both the Board and its constituents were feeling their way towards more effective forms of consultation than just the formal comment letter process.

The Board summarized these changes, as well some others it was considering, in a discussion paper, 'Strengthening the IASB's Deliberative Processes' issued in March 2004.[15] In this paper, the Board asserted that it had hitherto looked to the best practices of national standard setters. However, in response to public concerns, it said it now aimed to set 'a new global standard for transparency and consultation'. Yet the proposals contained in the paper were incremental improvements rather than radical innovations. Apart from the initiatives mentioned above, and a stated intention to develop a due process manual, the main innovations proposed were the publication of a summary of the Board's responses to major points raised in exposure drafts, the publication of near-final versions of exposure drafts and standards, and a commitment to provide an explanation in case any non-mandatory due process steps were omitted in the course of a project. The Board explained that it had so far not issued discussion papers because it had relied mainly on work by the G4+1. It stated its intention to make more use of such papers, as well as of advisory groups, public hearings, field visits, and field testing in the future. Somewhat defensively, the Board emphasized how its work so far had been dominated by the need to finish the improvements project in time, for which these due process elaborations had been neither possible nor strictly necessary.

Based on the comments received, the IASB's staff concluded that there was strong support for these measures, but it was also apparent that many respondents, particularly in Europe, were looking for more constraints on the Board's autonomy.[16] Many respondents volunteered comments that were more at home in the parallel review of the Constitution by the trustees, such as comments on the voting threshold for the publication of standards and exposure drafts and approval of the IASB's agenda by the trustees. This was not unnatural, given that, within the IASB itself, the due process reforms and the review of the Constitution were seen as a combined effort to deal with the tensions that had arisen with the EU. Still, there was a limit to what the Board, as opposed to the trustees, could do. So, in September 2004, the Board decided to continue with the approach described in its March discussion paper.[17] Consequently, the Board set out to prepare a handbook of policies and procedures to supplement the information on due

---

[15] 'Strengthening the IASB's Deliberative Processes', posted on the IASB website 24 March 2004 <http://www.iasplus.com>.
[16] AP 9/2004 paper 12.   [17] IASB meeting of 21–4 September 2004, minute 7.

process in the *Preface* to IFRSs. Because the production of such a manual was subject to due process itself, the IASB's *Due Process Handbook* was not approved by the trustees until March 2006.

7.3 THE FIRST CONSTITUTION REVIEW

In July 2003, the trustees appointed a Constitution Review Committee, chaired by Paul Volcker, the other members being John Biggs, Roberto Da Costa, Toru Hashimoto, Cornelius Herkströter, Philip Laskawy, and Sir Sydney Lipworth. The committee made sure to consult widely at every step, beginning with a public invitation to suggest issues for the review in November 2003. This led to a progress report in March 2004, listing ten main issues, and tentative trustee positions on each.[18] Comments were invited and roundtables were held from June to October 2004 in New York, London, Tokyo, and Mexico City. In June 2004, the committee also met with a delegation of SAC. In November 2004, the trustees issued a full set of proposals, again inviting comments. The range of issues dealt with during the review included the effectiveness of SAC and whether or not the Constitution should specify a role for the IASB regarding financial reporting by small and medium-sized entities. However, it was evident throughout that the question at the heart of the review was the independence of the Board in developing standards. In tandem with the Constitution review, the controversy over IAS 39 continued to intensify, culminating in the EU's carve-outs in November 2004. This inevitably raised the stakes in the debate over the Constitution, which ultimately became a question of who should control the IASB.

It may be recalled that the notion of independence had been deeply ingrained in the IASB's initial organization. At the insistence of the US SEC, a structure had been chosen for the IASB that strongly resembled that of the FASB. In 2003, the trustees still had direct access to this recent history in the person of trustee David Ruder. A former SEC chairman, Ruder had been an active member of the Strategy Working Party which prepared the way for the restructuring of the IASC. With Volcker's support, he consistently and persuasively reminded the trustees of the need to guard the Board's independence.[19]

The questions in the Constitution review touching on the independence of the Board might be grouped under three broad headings. The first was the composition of the Board, in particular whether it should be representative, either geographically or by interest group. The second was whether, and to what extent, the oversight role of the trustees regarding the Board's technical work should be strengthened. The third was whether the trustees should continue to be

---

[18] 'Next Steps for the Constitution Review Following Initial Consultation' (IASC Foundation, 22 March 2004), and 'An Update on the Constitution Review and Information Regarding Public Hearings' (IASC Foundation, 7 May 2004) <http://www.iasplus.com>.

[19] For Ruder's position, as well as for an extensive discussion of the first review of the IASC Foundation Constitution, see David S. Ruder, Charles T. Canfield, and Hudson T. Hollister, 'Creation of World Wide Accounting Standards: Convergence and Independence', *Northwestern Journal of International Law & Business*, 25/3 (Spring 2005), 513–88.

autonomous in appointing their own successors, or whether trustee appointments should be subject to a form of outside monitoring or control. With some simplification, it may be said that the emphasis of the discussion gradually shifted from the first to the second and then to the third question.

In November 2003, the trustees apparently expected that the main battle would be fought over the composition of the Board. In an initial inventory of possible issues, it was noted that the question of ultimate oversight had been much discussed during the IASC's restructuring, but 'since that debate, there has not been a challenge to the Trustees' role as the oversight body'. On the other hand, 'there is likely to be a push by some to move toward a more representative board that reflects geographic or professional backgrounds'.[20] It was noted that this might imply a larger Board. However, the trustees', or at least Volcker's, initial thinking was that, if the trustees supported an independent Board, they should rather consider *reducing* the size of the Board and discontinuing the part-time members.[21]

The trustees' initial analysis of the issues was mirrored in the discussion, in February 2004, between the European Commission and EU member states in the Accounting Regulatory Committee (ARC). As the first of four key objectives, the Commission listed 'the need for a more balanced European representation on the IAS Board and relaxation of the job specifications to fulfil to become a Board member'. The other three key objectives mentioned by the Committee were reform of SAC, impact assessments, and due process improvements 'to bring about transparency and remedy the general perception of a lack of good governance and communication between the IASB and interested parties'. After discussion, it was concluded that 'the Board should also include people with more practical experience and that the recourse to some more part-time Board members may help in this respect'. Neither the trustee oversight nor the appointment of the trustees themselves seem to have been thought of at this stage as matters requiring particular attention.[22]

During the first half of 2004, the trustees carefully developed their position, responding to some of the demands for change, but drawing clear lines on other points. In the Foundation's *Annual Report* for 2003, Volcker set the tone by recalling that the trustees 'have emphasized that they are willing to examine any aspect of the Constitution'. At the same time, he asserted that the basic structure established in 2000—including the independence of the Board—'has been critical in gaining the confidence of the rising number of countries that are committed to International Financial Reporting Standards or the convergence process'.[23] In their listing of issues and tentative positions published in May, the trustees had discarded all thought of reducing the size of the Board, and were willing to

---

[20] IASCF trustees meeting 4 November 2003, agenda paper 3, appendix 1; see also minutes of IASCF trustees constitution committee meeting, 3 November 2003.

[21] IASCF trustees meeting 4 November 2003, agenda paper 3, appendix 1; see also IASCF trustees meeting 29 July 2003, agenda paper 5.

[22] Summary record, ARC meeting of 3 February 2004 <http://ec.europa.eu/internal_market/accounting>.

[23] 'Report of the Chairman of the Trustees', IASC Foundation, *Annual Report 2003*, 2.

consider a possible increase in part-time members to four.[24] They also indicated their receptiveness to claims that the Board had a too narrow, technical focus by proposing to replace 'technical expertise' as the foremost qualification for membership of the Board by 'professional competence and practical experience'. A few years earlier, at the time of the restructuring of the IASC, the SEC had insisted on the primacy of 'technical expertise'. It would therefore have been of interest to the trustees to learn that the SEC's staff was now comfortable with the proposed change. As the SEC staff saw it, there was no objection to the suggestion that those who had experience with applying IFRSs might make better Board members than those who had no such experience.[25] The proposed wording eventually found its way into the revised Constitution. However, the trustees did not want to introduce criteria amounting to geographical representation, as this would be inconsistent with the independence of the standard-setting process.

By the middle of 2004, at the latest, the trustees' oversight function had become a prominent issue. In June, the IASC Foundation trustees met with the trustees of the Financial Accounting Foundation (FAF), which oversees the FASB. The two groups of trustees compared notes on how to balance trustee oversight with the need to maintain the independence of the standard-setting board. One assumes that on this point Ruder would again have been able to brief his IASC Foundation colleagues, as his term as IASC Foundation trustee (2000–5) partly overlapped an earlier term as FAF trustee (1996–2002).

The IASC Foundation trustees were willing to acknowledge that there might be a problem with their oversight. In their May progress report, they had proposed to 'strengthen the language of the Constitution' by clarifying that the trustees' duty to review annually the strategy and effectiveness of the organization included 'careful consideration of the IASB's agenda', and to make more explicit the trustees' responsibility to approve and oversee consultative arrangements and due process. Commenting on these issues in 2005, Volcker acknowledged that the 'review [of the agenda] in the past has been perfunctory, in large part out of concern of impinging on the Board's independence'.[26]

An issue that also made its appearance in 2004 was the appointment of the trustees themselves. In their May 2004 progress report, the trustees noted that the process of selection had been called into question. Here the trustees drew the line, and asserted their belief that they themselves should remain responsible for the selection of new trustees in case of vacancies.

The trustees' final proposals for the review of the Constitution, approved for publication in October 2004, were not significantly different on the points discussed above. If anything, they veered slightly back towards a stronger assertion of the Board's independence, for instance by clarifying that the 'careful consideration of the IASB's agenda' did not include determination of that agenda, and by maintaining the number of part-time members at two.

The trustees had in fact received important support for maintaining the independence of the Board. During the public hearings, SEC Chief Accountant

---

[24] 'An Update on the Constitution Review and Information regarding Public Hearings' (IASC Foundation, 7 May 2004) <http://www.iasplus.com>.

[25] Interview with Scott Taub, 17 June 2009.

[26] Volcker, 'Maintaining Progress toward International Accounting Standards', 6.

Don Nicolaisen strongly emphasized his belief that it was 'critically important' to have an independent accounting standard setter, and he linked the continued operation of the IASB as a 'strong, independent standard setter' with the prospect of the elimination of the Form 20-F reconciliation.[27] Similarly, the Basel Committee on Banking Supervision at more than one point during the Constitution review put the maintenance of the independence of the standard-setting process at the core of its written submissions.[28]

On the other hand, pressure was building in Europe during the second half of 2004 for some form of political accountability of the IASB organization. The European Parliament had signalled its interest in September, and in December Pervenche Berès, by that time chairing the Parliament's Economic and Monetary Affairs Committee, drew attention with a speech in which she discussed the IASB as an example of 'potential democratic accountability loopholes' in EU financial regulation.[29] The speech was noted in the ARC, and echoed in the Commission's response to the trustees' October 2004 proposals.[30] In his letter to the trustees, Director-General Alexander Schaub placed the need for 'serious improvements' to the IASB's 'overall accountability' at the centre of his reaction, and at the top of his list of concerns was 'that an appropriate procedure for the selection and appointment of the Board of Trustees should be established. The trustees should not select and appoint their own successors.'[31]

This comment letter was written after Volcker had met with the EU's ARC in February 2005. To what extent the appointment of trustees was discussed in that meeting is not apparent from the record.[32] What is clear is that Volcker expressed the trustees' acceptance of the need for improved consultation, for more active trustee oversight, and for limited changes with respect to Board membership criteria and the voting threshold. He also held out the prospect of a European trustee chairman, to succeed himself at the end of his term in 2005. However, all of these changes were placed in the context of the overriding imperative 'to foster the independence of judgment of a highly professional, decision-making Board'.[33]

By March 2005, the trustees felt ready to take their final decisions on most of the elements of the Constitution review, except for the appointment of the trustees, which was deferred to the trustees' next meeting in June. In March, this issue had become the focal point of EU concerns. The demand by the new EU

---

[27] 'Prepared Statement of Donald T. Nicolaisen, Chief Accountant, US Securities and Exchange Commission, at the Public Hearing on the IASC Constitution Review, June 3, 2004' <http://www.sec.gov>.

[28] Basel Committee on Banking Supervision, 'Submission to the Public Hearing Held by the IASC Foundation Constitution Committee', dated 29 June 2004 <http://www.iascfoundation.org> accessed through web.archive.

[29] Pervenche Berès, 'The Integration of European Financial Markets: What Challenges Ahead?', speech given at CESR annual conference, 6 December 2004 <http://www.esma.org>.

[30] Summary report, ARC meeting of 20 December 2004 <http://ec.europa.eu/internal_market/accounting>.

[31] Letter from Alexander Schaub to Thomas Seidenstein, dated 7 March 2005 <http://ec.europa.eu/internal_market/accounting>.

[32] Trustee appointment is not addressed in the written version of Volcker's statement (Volcker, 'Maintaining Progress toward International Accounting Standards'), nor is it mentioned in the summary report of the ARC meeting of 25 February 2005 <http://ec.europa.eu/internal_market/accounting>.

[33] Volcker, 'Maintaining Progress toward International Accounting Standards', 4.

Internal Market Commissioner, Charlie McCreevy, who had succeeded Frits Bolkestein in November 2004, for further consultation on this point was apparently too strong to be ignored.[34] But, as discussed more fully in Chapter 8, Paul Volcker at this point sensed, or knew, that McCreevy would be willing to drop most of his reservations if the latter could claim definite progress towards the elimination of the SEC's 20-F reconciliation requirement for European companies listing in the United States on the basis of IFRSs. As the SEC staff was just about to publish a 'roadmap' to that effect, it was not too difficult for the SEC to allow McCreevy, following a visit to Washington in April 2005, to present the roadmap as the result of an agreement between the SEC and the European Commission. At the same time, and in frequent consultations between the SEC, the European Commission, and the IASB, it was ascertained that this degree of public commitment by the SEC towards ending the reconciliation was sufficient for the European Commission to drop most demands with respect to trustee appointment. The Commission was willing to accept that change would be limited to the creation by the trustees of a high-level Trustee Appointments Advisory Group, which would review proposed trustee appointments. At the same time, it was made clear that the SEC would be willing to accept this minor limitation on the hitherto unconstrained authority of the trustees to appoint their own successors.[35]

This agreement was reflected in the trustees' final report on the Constitution review, issued in July 2005, where it was proposed that 'the Trustees undertake to establish a high level advisory group, comprising five to eight leaders of official international and regional organisations. This body will be consulted on the nominations before the Trustees' ultimate decision on Trustee appointments.'[36] The Advisory Group, which was not actually mentioned in the revised Constitution, was assembled by the trustees themselves, who also drafted terms of reference for the group. These included the provision that the chairman of the trustees would also chair the meetings of the Advisory Group.[37] In fact, Paul Volcker continued as chairman of the Advisory Group after his term as trustee ended in December 2005, and until the Advisory Group was effectively replaced by the Monitoring Board established in 2009 (see Chapter 14). When its initial membership was announced in November 2005, the trustees described it as a 'broadly representative advisory group', without spelling out which constituencies the Group was supposed to represent. Both from the accompanying text and from the appointments themselves, however, it could easily be inferred that the trustees were looking to involve international organizations that had an official status as well as an interest in accounting standards, in order to provide the IASB with links to public authorities and hence with a degree of public legitimacy that its original Constitution failed to provide. The Trustee Appointments Advisory Group brought together, ex officio, Roger Ferguson, chairman of the Financial Stability Forum (succeeded by Mario Draghi), Rodrigo de Rato y Figaredo, managing

---

[34] IASCF trustees meeting of 18 March 2005, minute 6.

[35] Interview with Thomas Seidenstein, 14 October 2009.

[36] *Changes in the IASCF Constitution: Report of the IASC Foundation Trustees* (IASC Foundation, July 2005), paragraph C17.

[37] The terms of reference are attached to 'Leaders of International Organisations Appointed to Advise Trustees', IASC Foundation press release, 22 November 2005 <http://www.iasplus.com>.

director of the International Monetary Fund (succeeded by Dominique Strauss-Kahn), Paul Wolfowitz, president of the World Bank (succeeded by Robert B. Zoelick), Jean-Claude Trichet, president of the ECB, Donald Kaberuka, president of the African Development Bank, Haruhiko Kuroda, president of the Asian Development Bank, Luis Alberto Moreno, president of the Inter-American Development Bank, and Jane Diplock, chairman of the executive committee of the International Organization of Securities Commissions (IOSCO). Although several of these institutions had long recognized the significance of accounting standards to their work, one assumes that Volcker's role was still indispensable in bringing together such a high-level group.

The Trustee Appointments Advisory Group was a first and very tentative step to anchor the hitherto free-floating IASB organization in a form of international public governance. It may be noted that the step could hardly be other than tentative, given that there was as yet no well-developed international regulatory architecture in which the IASB could easily find a place. In a sense, the Financial Stability Forum and IOSCO themselves were informal networks lacking official status.

As indicated above, the trustees agreed the other substantive changes to the Constitution in March 2005. These included the insertion of the needs of small and medium-sized entities and emerging economies in the statement of the Foundation's objectives (see also Section 12.10); strengthened language concerning the trustees' oversight role (see Section 11.5); the introduction of 'professional competence and practical experience' as the main qualifications for Board membership; and an increase of the voting threshold to approve standards and interpretations from eight to nine votes out of fourteen. This last change was made particularly in response to demands from Europe. Some of the American trustees were reluctant to make the change, knowing that experimentation with supermajorities at the FASB had been inspired by the desire of some constituents to slow down the pace of standard setting. The suggestion by insurance industry associations from Europe, Japan, and the United States to increase the threshold to eleven votes out of fourteen was probably indicative of such a desire, born out of alarm over the IASB's project on insurance contracts.[38] However, compared to the overriding objective of preserving the IASB's independence, the increase of the threshold by just one vote was seen as a relatively minor point by the trustees.

The trustees also agreed not to change the size of the Board or the number of part-time members, and not to introduce geographical criteria for Board membership.[39] Nonetheless, as with the composition of the initial Board, maintaining a degree of geographical balance remained an important factor in practice when the trustees decided on the appointment of new Board members (see Section 11.2). In addition to these implicit geographical criteria, the trustees had to adhere to the explicit quota which the original Constitution prescribed for the number of members with a background as auditors, preparers, users, and academics. It was soon discovered that this combination imposed almost impossible restrictions

---

[38] Letter from the American Council of Life Insurers and others to Thomas Seidenstein, dated 23 February 2005, CL15 <http://www.iasb.org.uk> accessed through web.archive.

[39] See the trustees' final report: *Changes in the IASCF Constitution: Report of the IASC Foundation Trustees* (IASC Foundation, July 2005).

when vacancies on the Board had to be filled. Moreover, finding the required minimum of three users was always a problem, regardless of geographical background. It was therefore agreed to adopt a more flexible wording, requiring that the IASB 'as a group provides an appropriate mix of recent practical experience among auditors, preparers, users and academics' (paragraph 21).

Another change made at this time was the elimination of the requirement that seven Board members should maintain formal liaison relationship responsibilities with designated national standard setters. This change seems to have been made at the suggestion of the Board rather than its constituents. As discussed more fully in Section 11.8, the Board felt that, on the whole, these special liaison relationships had not worked satisfactorily. Therefore, the revised Constitution simply referred in general terms to 'liaison with national standard setters and other official bodies concerned with standard-setting' (paragraph 22).

Compared to the views expressed by some of the IASB's constituents during the consultations, the total package of changes made in the first review of the Constitution was quite limited and showed that the trustees were committed to maintaining the basic features of the organization. In the Foundation's *Annual Report* for 2005, the result of the Constitution Review was summarized by the observation that 'the Trustees confirmed the conclusions reached by regulators and experts involved with the Strategy Working Party that developed the original 2000 Constitution'.[40] Yet it is likely that the limited nature of the changes made in 2005 did not fully reflect the significance of this Constitution review for the trustees' own understanding of the nature of the IASB and their role in it.[41] The review, conducted while the IAS 39 saga continued to unfold, increased awareness among the trustees of the strength and complexity of the political forces which confronted the IASB. The view gained currency among the trustees that the FASB model might have been a good starting point to launch the IASB, but that the model now needed further reconfiguration in order to function in an international setting where mandatory application of IFRSs was spreading rapidly. At the time of the first Constitution review, the trustees did not yet seek to develop the IASB's organizational model by making significant modifications to the hard-wiring of the Constitution. Rather, the various minor changes signalled the trustees' recognition that, in addition to fostering technical expertise, the organization needed to improve its abilities to work effectively with an increasingly complex body of constituents who had invested considerable trust in the IASB and expected much in return. In addition, the Constitution review marked a turning point in the trustees' view of their own role, leading them to the conclusion that they should be more active in their oversight of the Board, and to be seen by the outside world to be active.

---

[40] 'Report of the Chairman of the IASC Foundation Trustees', IASC Foundation *Annual Report 2005*, 3.

[41] This assessment draws on interviews with John Biggs, 16 February 2009; Bertrand Collomb, 16 February 2010; Jens Røder, 23 March 2010; and David Ruder, 17 June 2009, without suggesting that all interviewees would assess the Constitution Review in the terms offered here.

8

The United States Begins to Warm to the IASB

8.1 NICOLAISEN'S ROADMAP OF APRIL 2005

An important step towards the acceptance of IFRSs by the US Securities and Exchange Commission (SEC) was taken in the first half of 2005. SEC Chief Accountant Don Nicolaisen's article setting out a possible roadmap for eliminating the Form 20-F reconciliation requirement, entitled 'A Securities Regulator Looks at Convergence', was published in the Spring 2005 issue of the *Northwestern Journal of International Law & Business*.[1] During 2004, David Ruder, a professor of law at Northwestern University, and an influential member of the IASC Foundation trustees, invited Nicolaisen, David Tweedie, and Bob Herz, among others, to write articles for a symposium issue of the journal devoted to the convergence of accounting standards. As can be seen from Nicolaisen's speeches in December 2003 and June 2004 (see Section 4.5), the development of the ideas for the article had been in gestation for some time. Ruder's invitation was motivated by the contents of these speeches and what Ruder learned of the views of Nicolaisen through his own and Tweedie's contacts at the SEC.[2] The invitation from Ruder focused Nicolaisen's mind on getting the article written by the deadline for the issue, and in October 2004 he hired Julie A. Erhardt, formerly a partner in Arthur Andersen who had subsequently served as a fellow at the Financial Accounting Standards Board (FASB) and then at the IASB, as deputy chief accountant with a full-time commitment to international issues, a new position. Upon her arrival, she became the principal draftsman of the article. It is uncommon for the SEC to float a policy proposal in the form of a journal article, and Nicolaisen exposed successive drafts to the chairman, the commissioners, the Division of Corporation Finance (Corp Fin), the Office of International Affairs, and the Office of the General Counsel, as well as within the Office of the Chief Accountant, for comments.[3] On the whole, the commissioners believed that it was a useful initiative, but, of course, the article was written in Nicolaisen's name with

---

[1] Donald T. Nicolaisen, 'A Securities Regulator Looks at Convergence', *Northwestern Journal of International Law & Business*, 25/3 (Spring 2005), 661–86. The article was posted on <http://www.sec.gov> under the date of April 2005.

[2] Interview with David Ruder, 17 June 2009.

[3] Interviews with Donald Nicolaisen, 1 August 2009; Ethiopis Tafara, 29 June 2010; and Scott Taub, 17 June 2009.

the usual disclaimer that the views expressed were his own and not necessarily those of the Commission. His draft article was published as-is: it was not edited by the journal's editorial staff.[4]

Few chief accountants other than Nicolaisen could, or would, have developed and published a roadmap towards lifting the reconciliation requirement, which since 1982 had been a pillar of SEC policy for foreign private issuers that did not use US GAAP (generally accepted accounting principles). He was an internationalist whose judgement was highly respected within the Commission, he admired the achievements thus far of the IASB, and he believed that the reconciliation requirement was an obstacle to progress.

Nicolaisen believed it was essential that the United States not adopt an isolationist position: it risked being excluded from the growing worldwide debate about global financial reporting standards unless it engaged constructively with the new order. So he 'placed a bet' on the IASB to become the world's leading standard setter.[5] In the article, he referred to the European Union's (EU's) adoption of IFRSs for its listed companies as 'a bold and critically important decision' (page 662), and he extolled 'the widespread use of a single set of high quality accounting standards, applied globally and consistently' (page 663).[6] He used 'convergence' to embrace both adoption by a jurisdiction and the process of reducing differences between a jurisdiction's standards and IFRSs (pages 666–7). He expected 'the number of foreign private issuers who use IFRSs to increase [from the approximately forty now] to approximately 300 for 2005 and to nearer 400 by 2007—the end of the phase-in period for certain companies' transition to reporting under IFRSs. Thus, a critical mass of SEC filings soon will contain financial statements prepared under IFRSs' (page 667, footnote omitted). In speeches given in 2004, Nicolaisen had given estimates of some five hundred registrants filing on the basis of IFRSs in 2005 (see Section 4.5), and the reduction of the estimate to three hundred was made without comment. Nonetheless, Nicolaisen wrote that the 'critical mass' of financial statements for 2005 would enable the staff 'to see convergence in action' (page 662). This would be the trial period.

As to the possible roadmap itself, Nicolaisen wrote, 'it is my personal belief that if developments surrounding IFRSs—the standards, their application, and convergence—continue in the right way, then within this decade the SEC staff should be in a position to recommend that the Commission eliminate the requirement for foreign private issuers to reconcile financial statements prepared under IFRSs to U.S. GAAP' (page 673). Appendix I to the article contained the actual roadmap, including a timeline affirming that by 2009 'or possibly sooner' the staff may well be in a position to make this recommendation (page 686). The staff would review (a) the 'faithfulness and consistency' of the application and interpretation of IFRSs in the financial statements, (b) their reconciliations to US GAAP, and (c) the progress on convergence between IFRSs and US GAAP (page 686).

Nicolaisen's timeline within the roadmap was the most difficult element in his article on which to secure agreement among the commissioners and other senior

---

[4] Interviews with William Donaldson, 19 February 2009; and with Donald Nicolaisen, 1 August 2009.

[5] Interview with Donald Nicolaisen, 1 August 2009.

[6] Page references to Nicolaisen, 'A Securities Regulator Looks at Convergence'.

staff in the Commission, because it defined a commitment. He said: 'Really the toughest [points] throughout were the question of the timetable itself, and then what would be acceptable milestones along the way. Most of the dialogue tended to be around that.'[7] The IASB, which hoped that the SEC would lift its reconciliation requirement as soon as possible, was content with Nicolaisen's choice of 2009 as the ultimate year in which the staff would make its recommendation to the Commission.

Coincident with the publication of Nicolaisen's roadmap, the SEC published a rule, dated 12 April 2005, which permitted foreign private issuers that were switching from their home country GAAP to IFRSs to provide only two years of comparative financial statements instead of the normal three. The rule was clearly intended as a gesture of practical support for the adoption of IFRSs in the EU, which Nicolaisen had lauded in his roadmap article. Yet the SEC did not follow events in Europe uncritically. It took cognizance of the EU's two carve-outs of IAS 39, and it required any EU companies seeking to take advantage of this accommodation to reconcile 'IFRS as adopted by the EU' to 'IFRS as published by the IASB', in addition to the usual reconciliation of either of the two to US GAAP.[8] This was the SEC's first expression of concern over jurisdictional variations from IFRSs, and it seems likely that this additional reconciliation was not welcomed in Europe.

Yet, if the SEC intended to ensure that companies disclosed the impact of the carve-outs, it was less than successful. The Dutch financial conglomerate ING gamed the SEC by postponing for one year its application of the portfolio hedge accounting provisions of IAS 39. As a result, its 2005 financial statements were in conformity with IFRSs as issued by the IASB, and it could avail itself of the SEC's accommodation with respect to comparative figures. In the financial statements included in its Form 20-F filing for 2006, ING declared that it did apply the provisions for portfolio hedge accounting under the EU carve-out. But, as it elected to reconcile to US GAAP with a limited application of hedge accounting, the line item in its reconciliation relating to hedge accounting was a mixture of regular hedge accounting effects and the effects of the carve-out. Its reported US GAAP numbers differed from what it would have reported if US GAAP had been its primary basis of reporting, thus calling the effectiveness of the reconciliation requirement into question.[9]

8.2 THE ROADMAP UNBLOCKS THE IASB'S CONSTITUTION REVIEW

Apart from the coincidental timing occasioned by the invitation to contribute a paper to the *Northwestern Journal of International Law & Business*, the

---

[7] Interview with Donald Nicolaisen, 1 August 2009.

[8] 'First-time Application of International Financial Reporting Standards', Release Nos. 33-8567; 34-51535; International Series Release No. 1285 (SEC, 12 April 2005), 28 and 29. Unless otherwise indicated, all documents originating with the SEC and referred to in this chapter, including press releases and speeches by Commissioners and staff, were retrieved from <http://www.sec.gov>.

[9] See ING Groep NV Form 20-F, 2005, note 2.4.3, and Form 20-F 2006, pages F-63 and F-148–9 <http://www.sec.gov>.

publication of Nicolaisen's roadmap reflected above all the gradual evolution of thought within the SEC about the acceptability of IFRSs in US markets. It seems highly unlikely that the moment of publishing the roadmap was deliberately chosen with reference to simultaneous events involving the IASB and the EU. But, as it happened, the roadmap appeared just in time to allow a break-through in the ongoing discussions about the review of the IASB's Constitution. As discussed in Chapter 7, by March 2005 the IASC Foundation trustees had made up their minds about all of the issues they had raised in the course of the Constitution review, except for the question of whether any limitations should be imposed on the unlimited authority of the trustees to make appointments to fill vacancies in their own ranks. EU Commissioner Charlie McCreevy, who had taken up office in November 2004 in succession to Frits Bolkestein, had made it clear that simply maintaining the status quo on this point would not be accepted in the EU. On the other hand, and also mentioned in Chapter 7, Nicolaisen had, in the course of public hearings organized by the IASC Foundation trustees during the Constitution review, expressed the view that maintenance of the IASB as an independent organization was a key issue for the SEC when considering the acceptability of IFRSs in the United States. Clearly, the trustees had to find their way forward carefully.

Yet Paul Volcker, the chairman of the trustees, did see room for agreement. On 31 March 2005, following consultations with McCreevy, he wrote to SEC Chair-man William Donaldson, informing him of the state of the discussions on the Constitution review. According to Volcker, 'the strong reaction of Charlie McCreevy at this point is that the linchpin of his effort to deal with the European criticism must be a strong and open commitment by the SEC to support rapid progress toward minimal reconciliation, and not long after, full recognition of IFRS for U.S. listings'.[10] Volcker suggested that such a commitment by the SEC might allow the European Commission to accept that trustee appointments would continue as before, except perhaps for relatively modest concessions that might in their turn be acceptable to the SEC. These included an advisory or consultative group to 'review' proposed trustee appointments, and offering the prospect of appointing a European to chair the trustees after Volcker's impending retirement, 'provided he is dedicated to "convergence"'.

Volcker's letter does not show whether he was aware that Nicolaisen's roadmap would, in a matter of days, be posted on the SEC website, as well as be published in the *Northwestern Journal of International Law & Business*. But the fact that it was, evidently made it only a small step for the SEC to make the kind of gesture that Volcker was asking for. Volcker knew that McCreevy was scheduled to make his first visit to Washington later in April as part of the ongoing transat-lantic Financial Markets Regulatory Dialogue, which the European Commission had maintained since 2002 with the US Treasury, the Federal Reserve, and the SEC.[11] That McCreevy wanted to use the occasion to discuss the reconciliation

---

[10] Letter from Paul Volcker to William Donaldson, dated 31 March 2005; letter from Charlie McCreevy to Paul Volcker, dated 3 March 2005, IASB archive, file 'EC–EU'.

[11] See Charlie McCreevy, 'One Big, Less-regulated Family', *The Wall Street Journal Europe*, 19 April 2005, A12.

requirement with the SEC, and even to look for a 'roadmap', was not a secret either.[12] In 2004, the EU had initiated an assessment of the equivalence with IFRSs of accounting standards in several countries, including the United States, in order to determine whether they could continue to be used for purposes of listing in the EU after the EU's own transition to IFRSs in 2005 (see Chapter 9). In speeches, McCreevy had been threatening that, unless the SEC were to take steps towards lifting the reconciliation requirement for foreign private issuers using IFRSs, the EU would consider requiring US companies listed in Europe to reconcile their US GAAP financial statements to IFRSs. Strictly speaking, this threat was not relevant to the SEC, because it was not part of the SEC's remit to be concerned with facilitating the overseas listings of US companies. Yet it was politically significant to McCreevy and, by implication, for US politicians who were concerned about the US–EU relationship. Against this background, in his 31 March letter to Donaldson referred to above, Volcker concluded his linking of the IASB's Constitution review with the lifting of the reconciliation requirement: 'Thus, the possibility of an "April Concord". But you and the SEC are the key!'

And indeed, having met Donaldson on 21 April, McCreevy claimed that 'agreement' on a roadmap towards lifting the reconciliation requirement had been reached with the SEC, a claim that was echoed in the press.[13] In his press release, McCreevy said: 'I very much welcome the constructive approach the SEC is taking to moving these critical issues forward.' He added that 'the bandwagon [towards high-quality global accounting standards] has now started', while acknowledging that European companies, auditors, and regulators all had their part to play in delivering the consistent application and enforcement of IFRSs that were known to be important to the SEC.

The SEC presumably would not wish to deny McCreevy his achievement, knowing its significance for completing the IASC Foundation's Constitution review. Yet its own press release was rather more restrained, simply stating that both sides had 'discussed . . . a "roadmap" developed by SEC staff'.[14] In the release, Donaldson reaffirmed his support for the IASB–FASB convergence programme but stopped short of endorsing the roadmap.

A few months later, SEC Commissioner Roel C. Campos did testify to support within the Commission for the roadmap. In his reconfirmation hearing before the Senate Banking Committee on 26 July 2005, he said, 'At some point in the near future, we at the Agency and through our chief accountant are interested in reaching the point where it will no longer be necessary for those companies that use IFRS to reconcile to U.S. GAAP. That will promote transatlantic commerce

---

[12] Charlie McCreevy, 'Competiveness and Growth in the EU through the Development of an Integrated Capital Market and Banking System', speech given on 1 April 2005 for the Institute of International Finance, SPEECH/05/194 <http://europa.eu/rapid>.

[13] 'Accounting Standards: EU Commissioner McCreevy Sees Agreement with S.E.C. as Progress toward Equivalence', European Commission press release IP/05/469, 22 April 2005 <http://europa.eu/rapid>. See also the report on McCreevy's visit in the summary record of the ARC meeting of 20 May 2005 <http://ec.europa.eu/internal_market/accounting>. For press comment, see e.g. 'U.S. Moves to Give European Companies Special Accounting Status', *The New York Times*, 22 April 2005, 6; 'Roadmap Laid for Atlantic Harmony', *Accountancy Age*, 28 April 2005, 2.

[14] 'Chairman Donaldson Meets with EU Internal Market Commissioner McCreevy', SEC press release 2005-62, 21 April 2005.

and industry.'[15] Among the commissioners, Campos, who was a member of IOSCO's Technical Committee, had been a strong supporter of the roadmap.

In April 2005, IOSCO's Technical Committee had itself said that it 'encourages members to continually evaluate such supplemental treatments [e.g. reconciliation] as the implementation of IFRS continues and as the global financial reporting infrastructure is enhanced to encourage the consistent application and enforcement of IFRS. By this approach it is hoped that issuers would be allowed in the foreseeable future to make use of IFRS without reconciliation.'[16] This statement would not have been issued without the behind-the-scenes support of the SEC.

8.3 CHAIRMANSHIP OF COX AND THE EMERGENCE OF A MORE FORMAL DIALOGUE WITH EUROPEAN REGULATORS

Christopher Cox, a lawyer and a Republican Congressman from California, succeeded Donaldson as SEC chairman in August 2005. Nicolaisen departed as chief accountant in October 2005 and was succeeded in August 2006 by Conrad W. Hewitt, of Ernst & Young. Scott Taub again served as acting chief accountant during the interval. As will be seen below, Chairman Cox played a pivotal role in advancing the cause of IFRSs in the United States. More generally, his chairmanship was marked by important developments in the SEC's international policy.

The SEC took a major step towards transatlantic collaboration in August 2006 when it signed a joint work plan with the Committee of European Securities Regulators (CESR), by which its staff 'will share information about areas of IFRS and US GAAP' with CESR-Fin (the group of financial reporting experts in CESR) 'that raise questions in terms of high-quality and consistent application'. In addition: 'The staff of the SEC and the staff of CESR Members will consult on issuer-specific matters regarding the application of US GAAP and IFRS in order to facilitate a solution that contributes to the consistent application of US GAAP or IFRS by companies that are both listed in the EU and registered with the SEC.'[17] This protocol may have been more important to regulators in Europe, who were not all that familiar with the SEC's rigorous comment process on financial statements, than it was to the SEC, but it was helpful to both. To be sure, the SEC's staff had for years been holding bilateral conversations with foreign

---

[15] Testimony of Roel C. Campos, in *Nominations of Christopher Cox, Roel C. Campos, Annette L. Nazareth, Martin J. Gruenberg, John C. Dugan and John M. Reich*, Hearing before the Committee on Banking, Housing, and Urban Affairs, United States Senate, 109th Congress, First Session, 26 July 2005 (Washington, DC: U.S. Government Printing Office, 2006), 23 <http://www.gpo.gov>.

[16] 'Statement on the Development and Use of International Financial Reporting Standards in 2005', IOSCO Technical Committee, February 2005, 4 <http://www.iosco.org>.

[17] 'SEC and CESR Launch Work Plan Focused on Financial Reporting', SEC press release 2006-130, 2 August 2006. This consultative procedure was discussed by Corp Fin Director John W. White in 'IFRS and U.S. Companies: A Look Ahead', speech at FEI's Global Financial Reporting Convergence Conference, 5 June 2008.

regulators. They had also been engaging in active dialogue since the early 1990s with other major securities market regulators in IOSCO's Technical Committee. The SEC's accounting staff made a practice of consulting other regulators on issues of concern during meetings of IOSCO's Standing Committee 1, which an SEC staff member always chaired.[18] These discussions had culminated in IOSCO's 'Multilateral Memorandum of Understanding Concerning Consultation and Cooperation and the Exchange of Information' in May 2002.[19] The SEC and CESR had been engaged in a dialogue on matters of mutual interest since 2003.[20]

Following the launch of the joint work plan with CESR in 2006, the SEC negotiated protocols, or bilateral agreements, with the UK's Financial Services Authority, the UK's Financial Reporting Council (a private-sector body that was not part of CESR), and other EU regulators.[21] The work plan and the protocols were concluded by Ethiopis Tafara, the director of the SEC's Office of International Affairs.

By 2007, the SEC was seriously contemplating selective areas, not limited to accounting, in which mutual recognition with overseas regulators might be pursued.[22] As we detailed in our book on the history of the IASC, the SEC in the early 1990s categorically eschewed mutual recognition arrangements with foreign regulators (other than with the Ontario Securities Commission).[23] This strong view persisted within the SEC until the middle 2000s. The SEC was never comfortable with mutual recognition, because it would mean giving a regulator in another jurisdiction the power to decide what was acceptable to the SEC.[24] Yet during an SEC roundtable held on 12 June 2007, at which the Commission explored the possibility of various forms of mutual recognition with overseas regulators, former SEC Chairman David Ruder, who had served on the IASC Foundation trustees from 2000 to 2005, held up the SEC's encouragement of convergence of IFRSs with US GAAP with a view towards lifting the reconciliation requirement as an example of a policy area where the pursuit of mutual recognition had proven to be beneficial. Ruder used the case of accounting standards to illustrate how the United States could achieve much more success on the world stage by being collaborative than by acting unilaterally. He said:

---

[18] Interview with Scott Taub, 17 June 2009.

[19] 'Multilateral Memorandum of Understanding Concerning Consultation and Cooperation and the Exchange of Information', IOSCO, May 2002 <http://www.iosco.org>.

[20] See 'SEC–CESR Set out the Shape of Future Collaboration', SEC press release 2004-75, 4 June 2004.

[21] By 2012, the SEC concluded such agreements with the United Kingdom, Belgium, Bulgaria, Portugal, Norway, Germany, and Spain. See the section 'Issuers and Financial Reporting' at <http://www.sec.gov/about/offices/oia/oia_cooparrangements.shtml>.

[22] 'Unofficial Transcript of Roundtable Discussion on Mutual Recognition, Tuesday, June 12, 2007' <http://www.sec.gov/news/openmeetings>; and John W. White, 'Corporation Finance in 2008—International Initiatives', speech given on 14 January 2008, which dealt at length with mutual recognition.

[23] Kees Camfferman and Stephen A. Zeff, *Financial Reporting and Global Capital Markets: A History of the International Accounting Standards Committee, 1973–2000* (Oxford: Oxford University Press, 2007), 312–13, 314–15.

[24] Interview with Scott Taub, 17 June 2009.

The experience that I had at the IASB when we were trying to create accounting standards was that to the extent that the U.S. seemed to be trying to impose U.S. GAAP on the world there wasn't much cooperation. But once it became apparent that the approach was to be cooperative and to engage the rest of the world in the process, there was a great opportunity for progress.[25]

8.4 THE SEC LIFTS THE 20-F RECONCILIATION REQUIREMENT

It is understood that in a meeting on 14 December 2005 with CESR Chairman Arthur Docters van Leeuwen, Cox avowed that he was committed to implementing the roadmap, and he said this with the knowledge and consent of the other commissioners.[26] Cox therefore elevated Nicolaisen's roadmap to 'a Chairman's roadmap', thus endowing it with enhanced authority.[27] On 8 February 2006, even before the SEC's staff could begin assessing the application and interpretation of IFRSs by foreign private issuers, McCreevy met with Cox in Washington, and in an SEC press release it was stated that 'Chairman Cox reaffirms his commitment to the "roadmap" to eliminate, by 2009 at the latest, the SEC requirement for foreign private issuers to reconcile IFRS-based financial statements to US GAAP'.[28] Even though the term 'reaffirms' was employed, this was the first public expression of support for Nicolaisen's roadmap by an SEC chairman.

On 20 November 2006, Henry M. Paulson, Jr, the Secretary of the Treasury, made known his support for lifting the reconciliation requirement.[29] Hence, there was some pressure on the SEC emanating from the Treasury. Further, in January 2007, New York City Mayor Michael Bloomberg and US Senator Charles Schumer released the report they had commissioned from McKinsey & Company, *Sustaining New York's and the US' Global Financial Services Leadership*, which recommended, inter alia, that the SEC should consider recognizing IFRSs used by foreign companies without a reconciliation to US GAAP.[30]

According to the roadmap, the SEC staff would prepare for the lifting of the reconciliation requirement by monitoring the convergence of US GAAP and IFRSs as well as the filings of foreign registrants. On the first point, the SEC

---

[25] 'Unofficial Transcript', 12 June 2007, 173.

[26] Communication from Christopher Cox to the authors, dated 16 June 2012. The roadmap is not mentioned in 'Meeting between Chairman Christopher Cox and CESR Chairman Arthur Docters van Leeuwen', SEC press release 2005-177, 15 December 2005.

[27] Interview with Christopher Cox, 22 June 2010.

[28] 'Accounting Standards: SEC Chairman Cox and EU Commissioner McCreevy Affirm Commitment to Elimination of the Need for Reconciliation Requirements', SEC press release 2006–17, 8 February 2006.

[29] 'Remarks by Treasury Secretary Henry M. Paulson, Jr, on the Competitiveness of U.S. Capital Markets', at the Economic Club of New York, 20 November 2006, reproduced as Appendix C in the *Final Report* of the Advisory Committee on the Auditing Profession, dated 6 October 2008, C:4 <http://www.treasury.gov>.

[30] *Sustaining New York's and the US' Global Financial Services Leadership*, 23 <http://www.nyc.gov/html/om/pdf/ny_report_final.pdf>. Also see Kevin LaCroix, 'The Bloomberg/Schumer Report on U.S. Capital Market Competitiveness', blog posted 23 January 2007 <http://www.dandodiary.com>.

actively involved itself in the planning of convergence, resulting in the publication of a memorandum of understanding (MoU) by the IASB and the FASB in February 2006. As discussed more fully in Chapter 12, the MoU included a work plan with targets for 2008, ostensibly intended to provide the SEC with a basis for assessing progress towards convergence by that time.

With respect to monitoring the application of IFRSs, it was noted above that Nicolaisen estimated in his roadmap that some three hundred foreign private issuers would file their 2005 financial statements prepared using IFRSs, so that the SEC's accounting staff could assess their faithfulness and consistency in adhering to IFRSs. But even though this was already a downward revision of an earlier estimate, the number of these filings received was significantly less. In a speech on 11 December 2006, Deputy Chief Accountant Julie Erhardt reported that only forty such filings, reflecting the use of IFRSs, had so far been received, namely, where both the company and auditor affirmed compliance with IFRSs as promulgated by the IASB. She speculated on the reasons for the shortfall. One was the adoption by companies of a 'home jurisdictional adaptation of IFRS'.[31] Evidently, the staff of the Office of the Chief Accountant did not regard financial statements that were said to comply with 'IFRS as adopted by the EU' as being in compliance with pure IFRSs. Yet, except for perhaps two dozen European banks that were using the remaining EU carve-out (see Section 6.6), only one of which was a foreign private issuer registered with the SEC, that wording effectively signified compliance with IFRSs as issued by the IASB. In April 2007, Commissioner Campos referred to Erhardt's report and said that forty was 'hardly a critical mass'. He added that 'we need to get to the bottom of this issue, and see more companies filing audited financial statements in the manner contemplated by the roadmap'.[32]

On 6 March 2007, the SEC held a roundtable on Nicolaisen's roadmap. This was almost two years after the roadmap had been published, and a year after Cox first publicly affirmed his commitment to the roadmap. The lapse of time may reflect Cox's priorities as incoming SEC chairman, but now it would seem that the issue of IFRSs had reached the top of his list, and the pace of events quickened perceptibly.

The roundtable consisted of three panel sessions, to which the SEC invited a wide range of twenty-one key participants in the capital-raising process: issuers, accountants, investors, credit rating agencies, investment bankers, and lawyers. This was the first in a series of roundtables held on IFRS issues under Cox's chairmanship. They were intended to educate the commissioners, all of whom were lawyers and not accountants, and the chairman as well as the other commissioners were regularly in attendance.[33] At the outset of the roundtable, Cox said: 'Once unveiled, the Roadmap took on a life of its own. Governments, regulators, and standard setters around the world have been relying on it to determine their actions. And so it is important that I repeat today what I have said before: We are committed to this process, and we aren't looking back.' In his

---

[31] Julie A. Erhardt, 'Remarks before the 2006 AICPA National Conference on Current SEC and PCAOB Developments', dated 11 December 2006.

[32] Roel C. Campos, 'Remarks before the IOSCO Annual Conference', dated 12 April 2007.

[33] Interview with Christopher Cox, 22 June 2010.

opening remarks, Cox already looked beyond the lifting of the reconciliation requirement. He described the purpose of the roundtable as 'to consider the possibility that International Financial Reporting Standards and U.S. GAAP might co-exist in U.S. capital markets'. He explained that the SEC's commitment to the roadmap meant that the 'SEC was seriously contemplating a system in which, not only foreign issuers, but also domestic issuers, will have that choice [between US GAAP and IFRSs]'.[34]

Former Chief Accountant Don Nicolaisen was also present at the roundtable. Reflecting on Cox's remarks, he ventured his view that the next step after lifting the reconciliation requirement should be to make IFRSs mandatory rather than optional for US companies. One close observer of the SEC said that this was the first time that 'anybody like Don had publicly stated that this possibility was even on the radar screen or an option'.[35]

While the roundtable opened these wider vistas, for the moment the main focus remained on the lifting of the reconciliation requirement. EU Commissioner McCreevy, also in attendance, came out strongly in favour of removing the reconciliation, citing both accounting and auditing standards as 'outriders', or precursors of deeper EU–United States cooperation in other policy areas. He reminded the SEC that the acceptance of US GAAP in EU capital markets had been extended to 2009 (see also Section 9.5), so that the EU timetable and the SEC roadmap for lifting the reconciliation requirement were aligned.

In a speech given on 23 March, less than three weeks after the roundtable, John W. White, the SEC's Corp Fin director, summarized the panellists' views and said that he was encouraged by the 'striking consensus among various speakers at the Roundtable that the Commission should end its reconciliation requirement with regard to IFRSs as soon as possible'. He added:

> I was struck by how consistently the investor panelists told us they were not really using the reconciliation and in some sense preferred IFRS to U.S. GAAP. They pointed out that for many industries and peer groups, IFRS is the most common accounting standard and so in order to understand that industry or sector, analysts must know IFRS and in fact, institutional investors sometimes 'reconcile' U.S. GAAP financial statements to IFRS in order to make their comparisons and investment decisions.[36]

Chairman Cox believed that the United States was already a two-GAAP country because there was so much activity of a global nature in the US capital market and because US investors were exposed in their portfolios to companies using IFRSs in their home countries. Also, he concluded that there was abundant evidence and documentation that the reconciliation was of minimal use.[37] He believed that the roundtable participants' responses were 'resoundingly positive' that the benefits of

---

[34] Christopher Cox, 'Chairman's Address to the SEC Roundtable on International Financial Reporting Standards', speech dated 6 March 2007. For remarks by Cox and others at the roundtable, see 'International Financial Reporting Standards Roadmap Roundtable', 6 March 2007, unedited transcript (not paginated) <http://www.sec.gov/spotlight/ifrsroadmap.htm>. On Cox's remarks, see also 'Reconciliation Roundtable', *World Accounting Report*, April 2007, 7.

[35] Interview with Danita Ostling, 28 June 2010.

[36] John W. White, 'Seeing down the Road: IFRS and the U.S. Capital Markets', speech dated 23 March 2007.

[37] Interview with Christopher Cox, 22 June 2010.

eliminating the reconciliation requirement were achievable in practice.[38] Other arguments in favour of lifting the reconciliation requirement considered at the SEC included that the SEC allowed foreign issuers to submit the reconciliation as late as six months after the end of the financial year, which meant that it was untimely information.[39] Further, the reconciliation might not even be displayed in the companies' annual report to shareholders, because a fair number of them would release their annual report in their home jurisdiction within ninety days, and some sixty days later they would file their Form 20-F reconciliation with the SEC.[40]

During the first months of 2007, it was not just Cox who came out in favour of the roadmap. On 9 February 2007, even before the roundtable was held, SEC Commissioner Kathleen L. Casey affirmed that 'the Commission is committed to the roadmap announced in 2005'.[41] In a speech on 20 March, Commissioner Annette L. Nazareth also endorsed the roadmap.[42] Commissioner Roel Campos affirmed on 12 April that 'the SEC is *absolutely* committed to doing what we can to facilitate meeting the goals of roadmap'.[43] Clearly, the Commission was of a mind to carry forward the terms of the roadmap.

Then, on 24 April, the SEC issued a momentous press release, announcing 'a series of actions' in the wake of its roundtable. First, the Commission 'anticipates issuing a Proposing Release this summer' to lift the reconciliation requirement for foreign private issuers using IFRSs. 'In addition', it added, reflecting the statements by Chairman Cox at the roundtable, 'the Commission plans a Concept Release relating to issues surrounding the possibility of treating U.S. and foreign issuers similarly in this respect by also providing U.S. issuers the alternative to use IFRS'. Both John White and Conrad Hewitt said that the Division of Corporation Finance and the Office of the Chief Accountant, respectively, were working expeditiously to develop their recommendations in sufficient time for the Commission's consideration.[44]

In March 2007, an independent, bipartisan Commission on the Regulation of U.S. Capital Markets in the 21st Century, established by the U.S. Chamber of Commerce, recommended that the process of convergence between the FASB and IASB be completed within five years and that the SEC establish a process for eliminating its reconciliation requirement on a case-by-case basis with countries whose accounting standards are sufficiently equivalent to US GAAP.[45]

On 30 April 2007, in an initiative stimulated by German Chancellor Angela Merkel, the United States and the EU agreed to establish a Transatlantic Economic Council, with the objective of reducing non-tariff barriers to trade and investment.

---

[38] Christopher Cox, 'Opening Remarks at the SEC Open Meeting', speech dated 25 July 2007.

[39] Interview with Conrad Hewitt, 1 August 2010.

[40] Interview with Scott Taub, 17 June 2009.

[41] Kathleen L. Casey, 'Remarks before SEC Speaks', speech dated 9 February 2007.

[42] Annette L. Nazareth, 'Remarks for the Council of Institutional Investors', speech dated 20 March 2007.

[43] Roel C. Campos, 'Remarks before the IOSCO Annual Conference', speech dated 12 April 2007, original emphasis.

[44] 'SEC Announces Next Steps Relating to International Financial Reporting Standards', SEC press release 2007-72, 24 April 2007.

[45] Commission on the Regulation of U.S. Capital Markets in the 21st Century, *Report and Recommendations*, 47–8 <http://www.uschamber.com>.

The underlying accord, known as the 'Framework for Advancing Transatlantic Economic Integration between the United States of America and the European Union', resolved, among other things, to 'Promote and seek to ensure conditions for the U.S. Generally Accepted Accounting Principles and International Financial Reporting Standards to be recognized in both jurisdictions without the need for reconciliation by 2009 or possibly sooner'.[46] While it might seem that this agreement signed by President George W. Bush ratcheted up the pressure on the SEC, all signs indicate that, by the time this agreement had been negotiated and signed, the SEC was well on its way towards making a decision to lift the reconciliation requirement sooner rather than later. The accord did no more than affirm the SEC's avowed intention, and seemed to have little impact on the SEC's pace and direction.[47] On 17 May, if it were actually needed, the US Treasury Department made known its support of lifting the reconciliation requirement by 2009, but by then the die was cast.[48]

Then, on 20 June 2007, with full staff support, a unanimous Commission proposed for public comment a rule that would eliminate the reconciliation requirement for foreign private issuers using 'the English language version of IFRS as published by the IASB'.[49] The SEC believed it was essential that, to avoid the reconciliation, foreign issuers must not be using 'jurisdictional variations' from pure IFRSs and that the translation of the English version of IFRSs into other languages must not become the source of such variations.

On 2 July, the date on which the proposing release was issued, the SEC's staff published their 'Staff Observations in the Review of IFRS Financial Statements', which included the annual reports of one hundred foreign private issuers preparing their financial statements on the basis of IFRSs for the first time. In line with a policy established in 2004, the staff placed on the public record all of its comment letters and the filer responses.[50] The staff reported that they had not yet reached 'comprehensive conclusions' about compliance with IFRSs or consistent application. In line with previous expressions of concern over jurisdictional variations, the staff made the following general observation:

> We found that the vast majority of companies asserted compliance with a jurisdictional version of IFRS and that most also asserted compliance with IFRS as published by the International Accounting Standards Board, commonly referred to as the IASB. In the vast majority of the companies we reviewed, the company's auditor

[46] 'Framework for Advancing Transatlantic Economic Integration Between the United States of America and the European Union', press release dated 30 April 2007 <http://georgewbush-whitehouse.archives.gov>.

[47] Interview with Conrad Hewitt, 1 August 2010.

[48] 'Paulson Announces First Stage of Capital Markets Action Plan', dated 17 May 2007, reproduced as Appendix E, *Final Report* of the Advisory Committee on the Auditing Profession, dated 6 October 2008, E:2 (see also Appendix F, F:2) <http://www.treasury.gov>.

[49] 'Acceptance from Foreign Private Issuers of Financial Statements Prepared in Accordance with International Financial Reporting Standards without Reconciliation to U.S. GAAP', 2 July 2007, Release Nos. 33-8818; 34-55998; International Series Release No. 1302. For the webcast of the meeting at which the decision was taken, see <http://www.sec.gov/news/press/pressarchive/2007press.shtml>.

[50] 'SEC Staff to Publicly Release Comment Letters and Responses', SEC press release 2004-89, 24 June 2004. Previously, the letters could be obtained via Freedom of Information Act requests lodged with the SEC. For the letters, see <http://www.sec.gov/divisions/corpfin/ifrs_reviews.htm>.

opined on the company's compliance with the jurisdictional version of IFRS that the company used, but did not opine on the company's compliance with IFRS as published by the IASB.[51]

But the tenor of the staff report was not censorious. Most of the observations dealt with financial statement format and the insufficiency of disclosure. That the first round of IFRS financial statements raised issues mostly of format and disclosure, and not measurement, led the staff to believe that they did not need to look at second-year and third-filings. They concluded that the letters sent to the IFRS users were no greater in number and no more serious in nature than those which the staff had in the past been sending to US registrants.[52]

The rule proposal attracted more than 120 letters of comment, more than half coming from outside the United States.[53] Almost unanimously, the non-US letter-writers supported, and even lauded, the SEC's proposal. Yet some European letter-writers argued that the SEC should accept 'IFRS as adopted by the EU'.[54] US letter-writers varied from opposing the lifting of the reconciliation requirement, counselling caution, to favouring it. An underlying concern among those who were sceptical was that the move would lessen the incentive to continue the FASB–IASB convergence process. The CFA Institute and Standard & Poor's opposed the proposal, arguing that the reconciliation contained useful information and that lifting the requirement might impede FASB–IASB convergence. Fitch Ratings, on the other hand, supported the proposal. The Big Four audit firms, plus Grant Thornton and BDO, supported the proposal. Neither the American Institute of Certified Public Accountants (AICPA) nor the FASB responded, but the Center for Audit Quality, which is affiliated with the AICPA, favoured it. Two key US Senators, Christopher C. Dodd and Jack Reed, wrote to express 'serious concerns' about the move. Reed's securities subcommittee of the Banking Committee, which oversees the SEC, held a hearing on IFRSs on 24 October, at which former SEC Chief Accountant Lynn E. Turner was roundly critical of the proposal, and analyst Jack T. Ciesielski and Professor Teri Yohn both argued that that the move was premature.[55] Issues were raised about the robustness of IFRSs and the lack of stable funding for the IASB. A committee of the American Accounting Association, after reviewing the research literature, also concluded that a decision to lift the reconciliation requirement was, at best, premature.[56] To be sure, a number of commentators were critical of lifting the

---

[51] 'Staff Observations in the Review of IFRS Financial Statements', item posted 2 July 2007 <http://www.sec.gov/divisions/corpfin/ifrs_staffobservations.htm>.

[52] Interviews with Julie Erhardt, 20 February 2009, and Conrad Hewitt, 1 August 2010.

[53] For the comment letters, see <http://www.sec.gov/comments/s7-13-07/s71307.shtml>.

[54] See also Floyd Norris, 'A Plan to Let S.E.C. Accept Foreign Rules is Opposed', *The New York Times*, 25 September 2007, C4 (US edition).

[55] *International Accounting Standards: Opportunities, Challenges, and Global Convergence Results*, Hearing before the Subcommittee on Securities and Insurance and Investment of the Committee on Banking, Housing, and Urban Affairs, United States Senate, 110th Congress, First Session, 23 October 2007 (Washington, DC: U.S. Government Printing Office, 2010).

[56] See Patrick E. Hopkins et al., 'Response to the SEC Release: Acceptance from Foreign Private Issuers of Financial Statements Prepared in Accordance with International Financial Reporting Standards without Reconciliation to U.S. GAAP File No. S7-13-07', *Accounting Horizons*, 22/2 (June 2008), 223–40.

reconciliation requirement, yet Cox and his senior staff had been buoyed by the 'striking consensus' in the roundtable of 6 March 2007 in favour of ending the requirement.

Acting swiftly, and with full staff support, the Commission voted 4–0 on Thursday 15 November 2007, a scant seven weeks after the close of the comment period on the proposal, to lift the reconciliation requirement for foreign private issuers using IFRSs as issued by the IASB, effective immediately.[57]

At the IASB in London on that Thursday, five time zones ahead of Washington, the Board was holding a regular meeting, and everyone was eyeing the clock, anticipating the SEC's big decision. When the Commission took up the second item on its agenda, on lifting the reconciliation requirement, David Tweedie suspended the Board's meeting so that the members and staff could watch, in stunned silence, the live video feed of the Commission's historic decision.[58]

Charlie McCreevy immediately issued a press release to welcome 'this historic step by the SEC on the road towards global accounting standards'.[59] The IASB also welcomed the decision, and Chairman Stig Enevoldsen of the European Financial Reporting Advisory Group (EFRAG) said that the Commission's decision 'makes this a grand day for global accounting'.[60]

In view of the stipulation in IOSCO's endorsement of the IASC's core standards in May 2000 that regulators may continue to impose a reconciliation requirement, and the SEC's daunting concept release issued in February 2000 which had called for creation of a financial reporting infrastructure, it had seemed to many in the international community that the SEC would never give up its reconciliation requirement for foreign private issuers using IFRSs.[61] Yet it finally happened in November 2007.

In view of jurisdictional variations in the adoption of IFRSs around the world, including the remaining carve-out in the EU, the SEC insisted that the foreign private issuers (in note 1 to their financial statements) as well as their auditor explicitly affirm compliance with IFRSs as issued by the IASB. Chairman Cox later said: 'This was meant to send a strong signal that the dilution of a truly global

---

[57] The release was actually issued on 21 December, as 'Acceptance from Foreign Private Issuers of Financial Statements Prepared in Accordance with International Financial Reporting Standards without Reconciliation to U.S. GAAP', Release Nos. 33-8879; 34-57026; International Series Release No. 1306. See also 'SEC Takes Action to Improve Consistency of Disclosure to U.S. Investors in Foreign Companies', SEC press release 2007-235, 15 November 2007. For the webcast of the SEC's open meeting, see <http://www.sec.gov/news/openmeetings.shtml>. For news reports, see 'SEC ends GAAP Reconciliation Requirement for Foreign Firms Using IASB-issued IFRSs', BNA's *Daily Tax Report*, 16 November 2007; 'Historic Day for International Accounting', *World Accounting Report*, December/January 2008, 2; Jeremy Grant and Jennifer Hughes, 'US Watchdog Scraps Need for Two Sets of Accounts', *Financial Times*, 16 November 2007; and David Reilly and Kara Scannell, 'Global Accounting Effort Gains a Step', *The Wall Street Journal*, 16 November 2007.

[58] As related in the interview with Mary Barth, 17 March 2009.

[59] 'Accounting Standards: Commissioner Charlie McCreevy Welcomes the US Securities and Exchange Commission's Move to End Reconciliation to US GAAP', European Commission press release IP/07/1705, 15 November 2007 <http:europa.eu/rapid>.

[60] 'The IASB Welcomes SEC Vote to Remove Reconciliation Requirement', IASB press release, 15 November 2007; 'Removal of the SEC Reconciliation Requirement for Foreign Companies listed at US Exchanges', EFRAG press release, 16 November 2007 <http://www.efrag.org>.

[61] 'New Attempt at Consolidation', *World Accounting Report*, December/January 2008, 3.

standard through an accretion of national variations is inconsistent with the very purpose of IFRS.'[62] As a concession to the EU, the SEC gave the one foreign private issuer from the EU which was using the carve-out, the banking and insurance group ING, a two-year reprieve. During these two years, it could continue to use the carve-out without providing a reconciliation to US GAAP, under the condition that it would provide a reconciliation to IFRSs as issued by the IASB.[63] ING did so, but in line with its previous practice described above, it reconciled to a version of IFRSs with limited application of hedge accounting, simply by rolling back the total effect of all hedge accounting affected by the carve-out. ING continued this practice when, two years later, the SEC did not extend the reprieve. The group continued to use the carve-out in its published annual accounts. Solely for purposes of SEC filings it prepared a set of financial statements that were acknowledged to be different from what they would be if 'full IFRSs' were ING's primary basis of reporting. ING's staff had the impression that, over time, financial analysts made little use of the group's reconciliations, whether to US GAAP or to full IFRSs. To them, it seemed that analysts compared European banks' financial statements without considering whether the banks applied the carve-out or not.[64]

8.5 THE SEC'S INITIATIVE TO ALLOW US ISSUERS TO ADOPT IFRSs

On 25 July 2007, a bit more than a month after approving its rule proposal to lift the reconciliation requirement, the Commission unanimously approved a concept release on the possible future voluntary use of IFRSs by US issuers.[65] The issue of the release had been recommended by both the Office of the Chief Accountant and the Division of Corporation Finance. Commissioner Campos said that the release was an example of the Commission thinking ahead and anticipating issues.[66] In a speech at the SEC's open meeting at which the concept release was to be approved, Chairman Cox elaborated on the views he had expressed at the March roundtable. He regarded (1) the SEC's support for convergence between the FASB and the IASB, (2) Nicolaisen's roadmap, (3) the proposal approved on 20 June to lift the reconciliation requirement, and (4) the concept release as steps that, collectively, comport with the Commission's backing for 'IFRS and U.S. GAAP co-existing and even freely competing in U.S. capital markets'. He said he viewed the concept release as 'the mirror image of allowing foreign private issuers to file IFRS financial statements without reconciling their financial

---

[62] Christopher Cox, 'Remarks before the U.S. Chamber of Commerce', speech dated 18 April 2008.

[63] The EU had not requested this concession. Interview with Conrad Hewitt, 1 August 2010.

[64] Interview with Hans Buurmans and Harm van de Meerendonk, 24 March 2010.

[65] 'Concept Release on Allowing U.S. Issuers to Prepare Financial Statements in Accordance with International Financial Reporting Standards', Release Nos. 33-8831; 34-56217; IC-27924 (SEC, 7 August 2007).

[66] Roel C. Campos, 'Remarks at the Open Meeting: Concept Release on Allowing U.S. Issuers to Use IFRS', 25 July 2007.

statements to U.S. GAAP, in that it would give U.S. issuers the same choice that foreign private issuers would have'.[67] This is an ideology that quite a number of accounting academics have supported.[68]

Among the some eighty comment letters received on the concept release (excluding a dozen letters from students on a university course), all of the Big Four audit firms, plus Grant Thornton, approved of the suggestion to allow the use of IFRSs, but they pointed to the need for a careful plan for the transition or conversion towards an eventual *requirement* to adopt IFRSs. They did not favour an indefinite period of competition between the two sets of standards, a view that was shared by a considerable number of the other letter-writers, especially those from the United States. As seen above, former SEC Chief Accountant Don Nicolaisen had asserted at the March roundtable his belief that eventually US issuers should be required to report on the basis of IFRSs. Corp Fin Director White had, following the roundtable, characterized Nicolaisen's comment as 'very intriguing', but in the concept release the SEC had espoused the notion of competition.[69]

One of the most notable views expressed against the idea of competition, and in favour of a planned transition to IFRSs, occurred in the joint letter from the chairmen of the FASB and the Financial Accounting Foundation (which oversees the FASB):

> Investors would be better served if all U.S. public companies used accounting standards promulgated by a single global standard setter as the basis for preparing their financial reports. This would be best accomplished by moving U.S. public companies to an improved version of International Financial Reporting Standards (IFRS). We believe permitting extended periods of choice between U.S. Generally Accepted Accounting Principles (GAAP) and IFRS results in a two-GAAP system that creates unnecessary complexity for investors and other users of financial information. Permitting choice would add to the overall complexity of our reporting system.[70]

A number of letter-writers said that, in their view, it was premature to allow US issuers to use IFRSs in the US capital markets, even though many foreign private issuers, perhaps over the writers' objection, would now be able to do so. The writers raised such matters as the lack of stable funding for the IASB and the lack of robustness of its standards that had earlier been cited in opposition to the lifting of the reconciliation requirement.

---

[67] Christopher Cox, 'Opening Remarks at the SEC Open Meeting', 25 July 2007.

[68] See the AAA Financial Accounting Standards Committee 'A Perspective on the SEC's Proposal to Accept Financial Statements Prepared in Accordance with International Financial Reporting Standards (IFRS) without Reconciliation to U.S. GAAP', *Accounting Horizons*, 22/2 (June 2008), 241–8; Shyam Sunder, 'Regulatory Competition among Accounting Standards within and across International Boundaries', *Journal of Accounting and Public Policy*, 21/3 (Autumn 2002), 219–34; and George J. Benston, Michael Bromwich, Robert E. Litan, and Alfred Wagenhofer, *Worldwide Financial Reporting: The Development and Future of Accounting Standards* (New York: Oxford University Press, 2006), 236–40.

[69] John W. White, 'Seeing down the Road: IFRS and the U.S. Capital Markets', speech dated 23 March 2007.

[70] Letter from Robert E. Denham, FAF chairman, and Robert H. Herz, FASB chairman, to Nancy M. Morris, SEC, dated 7 November 2007 <http://www.sec.gov/comments/s7-20-07/s72007-20.pdf>.

On 13 and 17 December 2007, the SEC held two roundtables to obtain a broad range of feedback on the concept release, perhaps because of the relatively low number of comment letters received.[71] Most or all of the commissioners, as well as the senior staff, attended both roundtables. At the outset of the first roundtable, Chairman Cox positioned the issue before the Commission: 'Now that the Commission has addressed the consistency of application of IFRSs, to help U.S. investors gain better comparability among foreign issuers [i.e. lifting the reconciliation requirement], the question becomes what does this mean for U.S. companies?' (page 6).[72] During the roundtable on 17 December, Cox made it clear that, to him, the question was not whether US companies would transit to IFRSs, but when and how they should be allowed to do so: 'we are actually already in the middle of a transition to IFRS in the U.S. market' (page 5). Cox acknowledged that there were pitfalls along the road to a global standard, and during the 13 December roundtable he warned about a possible 'cacophony of standards [around the world], the result if IFRS is Balkanized into so many different national flavors'.[73] Yet he explained that the SEC's insistence on the use of 'IFRSs as issued by the IASB' by foreign registrants was meant 'to encourage the development of IFRS as a uniform global standard' (page 4).

In the same vein, Bob Herz, the FASB chairman, one of the panellists on 17 December, raised the spectre that the possibility of jurisdictional variations in IFRSs could end up as 'a Tower of Babel under a common label'. He did so not in order to disown the 'dream' of global standards shared by himself and the IASB's other founding members at the outset of their mission, but to indicate the work required to make the dream a reality (page 91–3). This work included dealing with those elements of US GAAP that had no counterpart in IFRSs, in order to prevent a 'U.S. flavor of IFRS, which I don't think is actually what is desired' (page 136).[74]

Several of the US panellists on both days expressed concerns about the cost of imposing IFRSs on small publicly traded companies, but Paul G. Cherry, chairman of Canada's Accounting Standards Board, which had already begun a transition towards mandatory adoption of IFRSs, said on 17 December, 'We have a lot of small cap public companies. Initially, there was some sentiment in that sector that this might be too onerous for them. That evaporated very early on. They did not want a stigma put on their market as being inferior or second class to the others' (page 120). A few panellists said that allowing US issuers to use IFRSs might, together with lifting the reconciliation requirement, dampen the incentive for the FASB and the IASB to continue their convergence apace.

During the two roundtables, the panellists from the audit firms and companies did not support a proposal for competition between US GAAP and IFRSs over an indefinite period. They argued for a well-designed transition plan to a single accounting standard, that is, IFRSs, else companies would not take IFRSs seriously. Gerald I. White, a long-time securities analyst and chairman of the Corporate Disclosure Policy Council of the CFA Institute, said on 13 December,

---

[71] For the webcasts and transcripts of the roundtables, see <http://www.sec.gov/spotlight/ifrsroadmap.htm>. John White summarized the comments raised in 'Corporation Finance in 2008—International Initiatives', speech dated 14 January 2008.

[72] The page numbers refer to the transcripts, which were separately produced for each roundtable.

[73] 'vulcanized' emended to 'Balkanized'.   [74] 'Babble' emended to 'Babel'.

'my experience tells me that when managements have reporting options, they generally don't exercise those options in ways that favor investors' (page 39). Some months later, John White said, 'One observation that I came away with from the roundtables we had in December was panelists' lack of enthusiasm for a period of optional use without a date certain as to mandatory use of IFRS'.[75] Conrad Hewitt's recollection was that 'a date certain for mandatory use [of IFRSs] was emphasized by panelists'.[76]

The panellists from the user community were the most sceptical of the direction in the SEC's concept release. To illustrate that 'there are some very, very significant differences between these two standards', Jeff Mahoney of the Council of Institutional Investors on 13 December cited the findings from a study reported in Jack Ciesielski's analyst newsletter: in a sample of 130 reconciliations from foreign filers using IFRSs in 2006, eighty-four of the companies showed higher earnings under IFRSs than US GAAP, with a median difference of 12.9 per cent, and forty-four of the companies showed lower earnings under IFRSs, with a median difference of 9.1 per cent.[77] The study found that the greatest excess of IFRS earnings over US GAAP earnings for a company was 826.4 per cent, while the highest excess of US GAAP earnings over IFRS earnings was 268.3 per cent. Mahoney regarded these results as evidence of the sometimes startling differences between the two GAAPs (pages 110–11). However, a point that was rarely if ever made when the magnitude of reconciliations was discussed was that foreign registrants did not necessarily reconcile to a form of US GAAP that they would have adopted as their primary basis for reporting. As seen above, some non-US banks reconciled from IFRS numbers based on the application of hedge accounting to US GAAP numbers calculated without hedge accounting.[78]

8.6 THE PROPOSING RELEASE ON THE MANDATORY ADOPTION OF IFRSs BY US ISSUERS

In a speech on 10 January 2008, Chairman Christopher Cox began the year by alerting his audience at an AICPA conference that 'IFRS is coming'.[79] On 23 January, Corp Fin Director John White rather more cautiously stated that the Commission's concept release issued the previous July, which would allow US issuers to use IFRSs, 'is a project that appears to have some momentum'.[80] The latter observation appears somewhat understated, as the SEC was already busily at work to ensure that the IASB and IFRSs would be up to standard for widespread

[75] John W. White, 'IFRS and U.S. Companies: A Look Ahead', speech dated 5 June 2008.

[76] Conrad Hewitt, 'IFRS and U.S. Companies', speech dated 29 May 2008.

[77] 'It's Not a Small World, After All: The SEC Goes International', *The Analyst's Accounting Observer*, 16/11, 24 September 2007.

[78] Apart from ING, this could be seen in the Forms 20-F for 2005 of National Westminster Bank and Lloyds TSB Group.

[79] Christopher Cox, 'International Business: An SEC Perspective', speech dated 10 January 2008.

[80] John W. White, 'Corporation Finance in 2008—A Focus on Financial Reporting', speech dated 23 January 2008.

use in the United States. The three main areas of interest of the SEC were the IASB's governance, its funding, and the progress of convergence of IFRSs with US GAAP. On governance, the SEC was, since the second half of 2007, deeply involved in efforts to set up a body overseeing the IASC Foundation, efforts which would bear fruit in early 2009 with the creation of a Monitoring Board (see Chapter 14). Securing a more stable funding basis for the IASB was a perennial question (see Chapter 11). It was also one on which, outside the United States, there was only so much that the SEC could do. On convergence, however, the SEC could make its views count.

In January 2008, Chief Accountant Hewitt took an important initiative by raising the question with the chairmen of the FASB and the IASB, Bob Herz and David Tweedie, whether the convergence programme as embodied in the February 2006 MoU between the two boards could not be accelerated. This matter was first raised in a consultation involving Hewitt, Herz, and Tweedie only, followed by a meeting at the SEC's offices involving other members and senior staff of both boards.[81] Recollections are in agreement that in these meetings Hewitt expressed his view that the two boards were not moving forward very fast with their convergence work. Hewitt believed the boards could move faster, and offered suggestions about priorities and project organization. His apparent reason for doing so was his, or Cox's, belief that the SEC should before long set a target date for the start of transition to IFRSs by US companies, and that this starting date would have to be chosen sometime after the expected completion of the MoU projects, in order to give companies an opportunity to prepare. In the course of these consultations, two related target dates emerged: 2013 for the US transition to IFRSs, and therefore 2011 for the completion of the MoU.

What is not easily established on the basis of the parties' recollections is whether these dates originated with Hewitt, or whether they were suggested to Hewitt by Tweedie. Given the frequency of contacts between the IASB and the SEC, the source of the dates will probably remain unclear. What is clear, however, is that Hewitt's views chimed with those of Tweedie. In a communication to the trustees discussing Hewitt's remarks, Tweedie volunteered as his own observation that the rate of progress on convergence was 'leisurely'.[82] It was generally known that Tweedie's term would end in 2011, and it was therefore easy to surmise that it would be a matter of personal satisfaction for Tweedie to see the major convergence projects successfully completed before leaving office. If so, this was obviously not an argument Tweedie could employ himself, but he did connect the completion of the MoU with his own departure by pointing out on more than one occasion that a 2011 deadline would have to mean June 2011, because it would not do to leave the completion of such major projects in a matter of months to a new chairman and to a Board without some of its most experienced members.

---

[81] Unless otherwise indicated, the reconstruction of events in this section is based on interviews with Suzanne Bielstein, 3 August 2009; Robert Herz, 17 February 2009; Conrad Hewitt, 1 August 2010; James Leisenring, 2 August 2010; David Tweedie, 15 October 2009; and Wayne Upton, 7 July 2011. The initial meeting of Hewitt, Herz, and Tweedie may have been a conference call (as reported in agenda paper 5E for the January 2008 IASCF trustees' meeting), or there may have been both a meeting of the three and a conference call.

[82] IASCF trustees meeting of 28–30 January 2008, agenda paper 5E.

Moreover, June 2011 had already acquired a certain significance for the IASB, as it was the target date for convergence of Japanese GAAP with IFRSs according to the August 2007 Tokyo Agreement (see Section 10.4). While it is therefore possible that the 2013 date for transition to IFRSs in the United States suggested itself to Hewitt and his staff as desirable on the basis of the SEC's own plans and priorities, it seems more likely that he did not put forward this date without some idea that it would match with Tweedie's view of what was both possible and desirable in terms of completion of the convergence work plan.

How the two boards heeded Hewitt's suggestions and modified their work plan, and thus published an updated MoU in September 2008, is discussed more fully in Chapter 12. One aspect, however, was that the world first glimpsed something of the SEC's planning when the FASB and the IASB discussed the acceleration of the convergence programme in their April 2008 joint meeting. An agenda paper containing a proposal for such an accelerated programme was posted, then withdrawn, and then posted again with some revisions. This maladroitness drew some attention to the paper, which, apart from being rather outspoken about some of the difficulties in the convergence process, also contained the quite explicit expectation that the remaining major capital markets, 'including the US', would adopt IFRSs 'no later than 2013' or, alternatively, 'within the next five years or so'.[83] This was a more specific forecast than was available so far in the SEC's public utterances. In a speech on 18 April, Chairman Cox showed himself committed to produce a timetable, but did not yet comment on its specific contents:

> Later this year, as a result of a joint effort in the Division of Corporation Finance and the Office of the Chief Accountant led by Wayne Carnall and Julie Erhardt, the staff will formally propose to the Commission an updated 'roadmap' that lays out a schedule, and appropriate milestones on which the schedule will be conditioned, for continuing the progress that the United States is making in moving to accept IFRS in this country.
>
> The rapidly increasing interest in IFRS in the United States, and the rapidly increasing acceptance of IFRS in the rest of the world, also reflect a growing consensus that these standards will in fact be able to deliver the high quality, consistency, and global comparability that so many have advocated for so long.[84]

On 29 May, SEC Chief Accountant Hewitt reported that the staff had begun working on the roadmap, which he regarded as the next step following the concept release and the two panel meetings in December.[85] And on 5 June, Corp Fin Director White, after treating his audience to a lengthy discussion of the policy issues facing the SEC on IFRSs, concluded, 'I truly believe that the endpoint [of this process] will be U.S. issuers using IFRS and that it is time to move in

---

[83] AP 4/2008 paper 3, version revised 15 April 2008, paragraphs 4 and 65. For comments on the withdrawal of the agenda paper, see 'IASB Technical Director Hickey Resigns; Project Woes in Withdrawn FASB–IASB Paper', BNA's *Daily Tax Report*, 16 April 2008, 73 DTR I-2, and 'The Internet: Lesson 1', *World Accounting Report*, May 2008, 11.

[84] Christopher Cox, 'Remarks before the U.S. Chamber of Commerce', speech dated 18 April 2008. Carnall was chief accountant in the Division of Corporation Finance.

[85] Conrad Hewitt, 'IFRS and U.S. Companies', speech dated 29 May 2008; interview with Conrad Hewitt, 1 August 2010.

that direction'.[86] In a speech on 23 June, Chairman Cox pointed towards the roadmap as a Commission rule that would enable audit firms, issuers, and university educators to prepare before 'a do-or-die switch [to IFRSs] is required of everyone'.[87] Clearly, Cox had retreated from his view, reported above, that a viable option would be to allow US issuers to choose between US GAAP and IFRSs for an indefinite period.

While the SEC was contemplating the use of IFRSs by listed companies, the AICPA paved the way for its application by private companies. In May 2008, the AICPA's governing council amended its Code of Professional Conduct to designate the IASB as a body authorized to establish professional standards.[88] As a result, companies not required to report on the basis of US GAAP could now choose to report on the basis of IFRSs with an unqualified opinion from a US auditor that the financial statements were in accordance with generally accepted accounting principles.

The SEC's Advisory Committee on Improvements to Financial Reporting, which had been set up in June 2007 to 'examine the U.S. financial reporting system, with a view to providing specific recommendations as to how unnecessary complexity in that system could be reduced and how that system could be made more useful to investors', issued its final report on 1 August 2008, in which it confirmed the direction in which the SEC was evidently heading: 'we encourage the development of a roadmap to identify issues and milestones to transition to this end state in the U.S., with sufficient time to minimize disruptions, resource constraints, and the complexity arising from such a significant change.'[89]

On 4 August, the SEC held a roundtable on how IFRSs and US GAAP had performed during the subprime crisis. IASB member John Smith and FASB member Leslie F. Seidman participated as observers with a right to the floor. This was still very early in the impact of the global economic and financial crisis, i.e. prior to the collapse of Lehman Brothers. Some of the discussion touched upon the question whether US issuers should adopt IFRSs. Once again, Jeff Mahoney, general counsel of the Council of Institutional Investors, expressed himself critically. He contended that 'many U.S. investors, including many on [the FASB's Investors Technical Advisory Committee]' believed that four deficiencies in IFRSs must be repaired before any move was made towards a greater use of IFRSs in the United States: revenue recognition, fair value, consolidation policy, and derecognition related to securitization accounting.[90] He also argued that the SEC must

---

[86] John W. White, 'IFRS and U.S. Companies: A Look Ahead', speech dated 5 June 2008.

[87] Christopher Cox, 'Making Disclosure More Useful for Public Company Directors', speech dated 23 June 2008.

[88] 'AICPA Council Votes to Recognize the International Accounting Standards Board as a Designated Standard Setter', AICPA press release dated 18 May 2008 <http://www.ifrs.com>. The ifrs.com website was launched the next day by the AICPA. See also 'AICPA Formally Recognizes IASB as Authorized IFRS Standard Setter', BNA's *Daily Tax Report*, 97 DTR G-3, 20 May 2008.

[89] *Final Report of the Advisory Committee on Improvements to Financial Reporting to the United States Securities and Exchange Commission*, dated 1 August 2008, 2 <http://www.sec.gov>. See Appendix C for the statement of the committee's objectives.

[90] 'Roundtable Discussion on International Financial Reporting Standards', 4 August 2008, unpaginated transcript <http://www.sec.gov/spotlight/ifrsroadmap.htm>.

address the competence and independence of the IASB before deciding on whether US issuers should use IFRSs.

Then, on 27 August in an open meeting, the Commission voted unanimously for a proposing release which contained a roadmap that allowed a limited number of US issuers to adopt IFRSs in 2009 and targeted mandatory adoption by all US issuers by 2014–16. In making that decision, the Commission was enthusiastically supported by the Office of the Chief Accountant, the Division of Corporation Finance, the Office of the General Counsel, the Office of Economic Analysis, and the Office of International Affairs.[91] The release, which ran to 165 pages, was finally issued on 14 November.[92] It was titled, 'Roadmap for the Potential Use of Financial Statements Prepared in Accordance with International Financial Reporting Standards by U.S. Issuers'. Because of requests from many companies having financial years ending on 31 December for additional time in which to respond, the Commission extended the usual comment period from 90 days to 150 days.[93]

Under the proposed rule, the SEC would limit the option for US issuers to use IFRSs as early as 2009 'to a group of larger U.S. companies in industries in which IFRS is the most-used set of standards globally' (page 32).[94] The SEC assumed, conservatively in its view, that '110 U.S. issuers, representing the approximate minimum number of those presently eligible to use IFRS accounting under the proposals, would elect to switch from U.S. GAAP to IFRS' (page 118). If, with respect to all other companies, the SEC had earlier in the year been thinking of a transition to IFRS in 2013, this had now become 2014, at the earliest. The year 2011, which had by now become the focal point of the joint work plan of the IASB and the FASB, was identified as the year in which the SEC would decide whether to proceed with rule-making to require that US issuers begin adopting IFRSs over a phased period 'if it is in the public interest and for the protection of investors to do so' (page 10). The release set out seven milestones along the path towards mandatory use of IFRSs, four of which related to conditions to be achieved in order to proceed with the last three steps, involving rule-making. The four initial milestones, expressed in the words of the SEC, were as follows (page 10):

- improvements in accounting standards;
- the accountability and funding of the IASC Foundation;
- the improvement in the ability to use interactive data for IFRS reporting;
- education and training relating to IFRS.

Further: 'In addition to the milestones, the Commission also expects to consider, among other things, whether IFRS as issued by the IASB is a globally accepted set of accounting standards and whether it is consistently applied' (page 20). Clearly,

---

[91] For the webcast of the open meeting, see <http://www.sec.gov/news/openmeetings.shtml>.

[92] 'Roadmap for the Potential Use of Financial Statements Prepared in Accordance with International Financial Reporting Standards by U.S. Issuers', Release nos. 33-8982, 34-58960, File no. S7-27-08 (SEC, 14 November 2008). Normally, the SEC promulgates releases within two weeks of a Commission's decision, but at times the press of other rule-making business, as well as the complicated nature of the release, has delayed their publication.

[93] The extension was announced on 3 February 2009. See <http://www.sec.gov/rules/proposed/2009/33-9005.pdf>.

[94] This series of page numbers refers to pages in the proposing release.

the SEC contemplated a profound and wide-ranging enquiry before taking any step towards mandating the use of IFRSs. Depending on the class and size of the filer, IFRSs would become mandatory during a staged transition period from the end of 2014 to the end of 2016. The SEC estimated 'the costs for issuers of transitioning to IFRS to sum to approximately $32 million per company and relate to the first three years of filings on Form 10-K under IFRS' (page 130). In the release, the SEC acknowledged that US filers using the LIFO inventory method would have to change to another inventory method and 'may experience a change in taxable income' (page 39).

The comments received on the proposing release, together with related discussion, are taken up in Chapter 15.

9

The IASB's Vexed Relation with Europe

9.1 A NEW START?

With the endorsement of a carved-out version of IAS 39 in November 2004, the European Union (EU) completed the formal preparations for the transition of listed companies to IFRSs as of 1 January 2005. Clearly, these preparations had taken much longer, and had created much more friction and mutual resentment between the IASB and various official and private-sector parties in the EU than was anticipated in the upbeat, but perhaps naïve, mood at the 2000 Lisbon summit where the adoption of IFRSs was first announced. By the end of 2004, the two sides had come to know each other much better, and had not always liked what they learned. Nonetheless, the first-time adoption of IFRSs by thousands of EU companies remained a momentous event, and both the IASB and the EU appeared inclined to celebrate the occasion by turning over a new leaf and by attempting to cultivate a more constructive relationship.

At staff level, the Commission and the IASC Foundation had already developed good contacts during the intense negotiations over IAS 39 and the review of the Foundation's Constitution. Some personal changes also seemed to bode well. The new EU Internal Market Commissioner Charlie McCreevy, in office since November 2004, was not only a former finance minister but he had also become an Irish chartered accountant in his early days. Given the range of backgrounds from which the Internal Market Commissioner might have been recruited, this seemed to provide a good basis for developing a working relationship with the IASB, headed by the Scottish chartered accountant David Tweedie. Well within his first year in office, McCreevy could already claim the roadmap of the chief accountant of the US Securities and Exchange Commission (SEC) towards the lifting of the 20-F reconciliation for companies using IFRSs as a significant outcome of the EU–US dialogue on financial regulation (see Section 8.2). In the favourable atmosphere created by the roadmap, the first review of the IASC Foundation Constitution could be concluded on a comparatively harmonious note in June 2005, instead of becoming a source of conflict between the IASB and the European Commission.

The IASC Foundation trustees were looking for a European to succeed Chairman Paul Volcker, whose term ended in 2005. By the end of that year, it was announced that Volcker's successor would be the Italian Tommaso Padoa-Schioppa, who had served from 1998 to May 2005 on the executive board of the European Central Bank (ECB). In that capacity, and in the course of discussions over IAS 39, the IASB had come to know and respect him, and there was every reason to expect that he would play a central role in building bridges between the IASB and its European constituents. Unfortunately for the IASB, Padoa-Schioppa's term was cut short in May 2006 when he was called to serve as finance minister in the Prodi government in Italy. Yet, brief as it was, Padoa-Schioppa's term was already seen to have made a distinctly positive contribution.

Meanwhile, the transition to IFRSs in Europe—and, as was sometimes acknowledged but more often forgotten in Europe, also in Australia, Hong Kong, and South Africa—proceeded with an immense effort, innumerable practical difficulties, but without major incidents, and on the whole more smoothly than many had expected.[1] As a major study undertaken by the Institute of Chartered Accountants in England and Wales (ICAEW) on behalf of the European Commission concluded: IFRS implementation in the EU had been 'challenging but successful'.[2] For Europe in particular, it was indeed a challenge. Whereas accounting standards in Australia, Hong Kong, and South Africa had already, well before 2005, reflected the investor-oriented philosophy underlying IFRSs, as well as much of the look and feel of the specific requirements of IFRSs, this was not necessarily true in all EU member states. National accounting frameworks in the EU differed greatly in their degree of prior convergence with IFRSs, as well as in the strength of the influence of company and tax law over financial reporting. Apart from adopting a new set of accounting standards, EU member states were simultaneously engaged in a movement to strengthen and harmonize their enforcement of accounting standards. During the 1990s, the European members of the International Organization of Securities Commissions (IOSCO) had been a motley group of organizations with very different competencies and resources. Some had hardly any powers at all to enforce compliance with accounting standards, which in several member states was left largely to the auditor. In the context of the Financial Services Action Plan, it was recognized that improved market confidence required oversight of the enforcement of financial information by independent administrative authorities. Some of these were new creations, like the Autoriteit Financiële Markten (AFM, Netherlands Authority for the Financial Markets) or the Deutsche Prüfstellung für Rechnungslegung (DPR, Financial Reporting Enforcement Panel) in Germany, which had to find their roles as enforcing agencies at the same time as companies were learning how to apply IFRSs.[3] All had to learn how to work together

---

[1] See, for a series of interviews with auditors, preparers, users, and regulators reflecting on the transition: *International Financial Reporting Standards: Views on a Financial Reporting Revolution* (KPMG International, 2006). See also Martin Hoogendoorn, 'International Accounting Regulation and IFRS Implementation in Europe and beyond: Experiences with First-time Adoption in Europe', *European Accounting Review*, 15/3 (supplement), (2006), 23–6; Eva K. Jermakowicz and Sylvia Gornik-Tomaszevski, 'Implementing IFRS from the Perspective of EU Publicly Traded Companies', *Journal of International Accounting, Auditing and Taxation*, 15/2 (2006), 170–96; *Investor Perspectives on IFRS Implementation: Collection of Essays* (Fédération Française des Sociétés d'Assurances/Association Française de la Gestion Financière, December 2007).

[2] *EU Implementation of IFRS and the Fair Value Directive: A Report for the European Commission* (Institute of Chartered Accountants in England and Wales, 2007), 25.

[3] The Dutch AFM was created as a general securities market regulator in 2002. It formally assumed its task with respect to enforcement of accounting standards on 31 December 2006, but it had done preliminary work on an informal basis during the preceding years. The German DPR was set up in 2004 specifically for the task of monitoring compliance with accounting standards, and began its work on 1 July 2005.

in the Committee of European Securities Regulators (CESR) in order to ensure a reasonable degree of uniformity across the EU in the application and interpretation of IFRSs.[4]

The large audit firms had worked hard to make companies aware of the impending transition and to prod them into making timely preparations, and many of their clients had paid heed. Inevitably the quality of compliance varied, with many companies relying initially on workarounds and ad hoc fixes to obtain some of the required accounting numbers and disclosures. It took time before the requirements of IFRSs fully permeated companies' accounting systems so that subsidiaries could send IFRS-compliant financial statements up for consolidation.[5]

The estimated costs of transition varied considerably. The finding of the ICAEW study that transition costs ranged from 0.05 per cent of turnover for the large companies to 0.3 per cent of turnover for smaller companies has been much cited. As the study itself noted, these typical figures hide considerable variation and difficulties in distinguishing the incremental costs of IFRS adoption from other costs of maintenance and improvements. As in the case of Sarbanes-Oxley, many companies used the occasion of the shift to IFRSs to take a fresh look at their accounting systems. Apart from costs, there remained enough cause for disgruntlement. Closer acquaintance with IFRSs certainly did not mean the end of criticism of the IASB's standards by both users and preparers of financial statements. One could also emphasize the extent to which IFRSs had not succeeded in improving comparability of financial statements in the EU by pointing towards differences in implementation among companies and countries.[6] Yet, despite all that, the feeling seemed to prevail that, with the adoption of IFRSs, European financial reporting had taken a major step forward.

9.2 REMOVAL OF ONE OF THE CARVE-OUTS: THE FAIR VALUE OPTION

The year 2005 also saw a détente of sorts between the EU and the IASB in the field of accounting for financial instruments. As seen in Chapter 6, the IASB had published an exposure draft in April 2004, proposing to restrict the option in IAS 39 to designate any financial asset or financial liability as accounted for at 'fair value through profit or loss'. With the exposure draft, the IASB attempted to address the concerns of banking regulators over the possible consequences for

---

[4] See for instance CESR standard No. 1 'Enforcement of Standards on Financial Information in Europe', March 2003, and CESR standard No. 2 'Coordination of Enforcement Activities', April 2004, and the supporting documentation at <http://www.esma.europa.eu>.

[5] Interviews with Jeannot Blanchet, 14 January 2011; and with Hans de Munnik, 22 March 2010.

[6] Apart from the ICAEW study cited before, see for instance the comment by Ernst & Young that, while the firm considered the implementation of IFRSs 'a resounding success overall', IFRS financial statements 'retain a strong national identity', *IFRS: Observations on the Implementation of IFRS* (Ernst & Young, 2005), 6–7. See also Christopher Nobes, 'The Survival of International Differences under IFRS: Towards a Research Agenda', *Accounting and Business Research*, 36/3 (2006), 233–45.

financial stability of an inappropriate use of this fair value option by banks. Although these concerns were not limited to Europe, and had been voiced by the international community of banking regulators through the Basel Committee, the ECB was particularly anxious to see a restriction of the option. The fair value option had prompted one of the two carve-outs applied by the European Commission when IAS 39 was endorsed for use in the EU in November 2004.

The fair value carve-out applied to liabilities only, but the IASB's April 2004 exposure draft proposed a comprehensive restriction of the fair value option, including both assets and liabilities. The Board had issued this draft somewhat hastily and without great enthusiasm. Three members (Bob Garnett, Geoffrey Whittington, and Tatsumi Yamada) had voted against the exposure draft, not least because of the conspicuous role of the ECB in bringing about the amendment. Gilbert Gélard, who voted in favour, remarked that 'it was fortunate that they [the assenting Board members] did not have to explain why they did not dissent'.[7]

When the Board discussed the comment letters on this draft in the autumn of 2004, it was clear that, apart from regulators, there was little support for restricting the option.[8] Many preparer organizations from around the world argued that an unrestricted fair value option was necessary to redress mismatch problems arising from the mixed-attribute model of IAS 39. The insurance industry in particular strongly advocated the retention of the full fair value option.[9]

Part of the criticism was directed at the way the exposure draft was worded, and it was conceded by the Board that the draft was technically flawed.[10] More fundamentally, the very fact that the exposure draft was issued at all raised the question of the role of prudential supervisors, such as bank regulators, in setting accounting standards. Should their concerns over financial stability carry weight in the Board's deliberations, or should the Board design its standard purely on the basis of the information needs of investors? That the exposure draft was inspired by the ECB was public knowledge, and the Board was warned, among others, by the Bundesverband Öffentlicher Banken (Germany), that accepting an apparently political compromise would damage its credibility. More specifically, respondents criticized a proposed insertion in paragraph 9 of IAS 39 which acknowledged that prudential supervisors might have the power to oversee the application of fair value measurement requirements. As the staff noted when the exposure draft was prepared, this sentence had been inserted at the insistence of 'regulators', who believed it was 'of paramount importance'.[11] Misgivings had been expressed in the Board, particularly by Geoffrey Whittington, but the view had prevailed that the sentence simply stated the obvious, and was therefore harmless.

In November 2004, Tom Jones claimed that the matter might be settled within weeks.[12] Yet it still took several months of negotiation between the ECB, the Basel

---

[7] *IStaR*, March 2004, 9.   [8] AP 9/2004 paper 4A.

[9] 'International Financial Reporting Standards—"The Unlimited Fair Value Option Should be Maintained in IAS 39" Says CEA President Gérard de La Martinière', Comité Européen des Assurances (CEA) press release dated 17 January 2005. See also 'ABI Urges Retention of Fair Value Option', *Financial Times*, London edition, 28 December 2004, 13.

[10] *IStaR*, December 2004, 21.   [11] AP 2/2004 paper 11, 7.

[12] 'IASB Official Hopes IAS 39 Fair-value Option Can Be Resolved in Matter of Weeks', *European Report*, 10 November 2004.

Committee, the banking and insurance industries, and the IASB to arrive at a form of words for the amendment to IAS 39 that sufficiently restricted the fair value option for the regulators but that left enough of the benefits of the option intact for the reporting companies.

In addition, further consultation with the regulators was required to finesse the sensitive statement in the standard about their supervision of the application fair value option. In the end, this was transformed into an acknowledgement by the IASB in the basis for conclusions appended to IAS 39 that prudential supervisors 'may wish to understand the circumstances in which a regulated financial institution has chosen to apply the fair value option' (BC79A). The Board also explained how it had attempted to make some of its disclosures useful to prudential supervisors as well as to investors. The Basel Committee issued a corresponding statement in which it explained how prudential supervision of the application of the fair value option should neither add accounting requirements to those issued by the IASB, nor contravene the IASB's guidance.[13] By the time a widely-attended roundtable meeting took place in London on 16 March 2005, most parties were ready to voice their agreement.[14] An amendment to IAS 39 was issued by the IASB on 16 June, albeit with dissents from Barth, Garnett, and Whittington. The Accounting Regulatory Committee (ARC) approved the amendment unanimously on 8 July, so that one carve-out was formally removed later that year.[15] As discussed more fully in Section 12.9, the removal of the remaining hedge accounting carve-out proved to be a much more intractable problem.

While the Board itself may not have been very happy with the way in which the fair value option was restricted, the episode was of considerable help in fostering the IASB's contacts with the banking regulators, both in Europe and in North America.[16] It was at this stage that Tommaso Padoa-Schioppa became closely involved on behalf of the ECB, leading David Tweedie to form a very favourable impression of him.[17]

9.3 ENHANCEMENT OF EFRAG

As the relationship between the IASB and its European constituents became more tempestuous than had been envisaged in 2000, the effects were felt by the European Financial Reporting Advisory Group (EFRAG), the technical expert body created to represent the European view to the IASB. In July 2003, the EU Council of finance ministers (ECOFIN) noted with approval that 'the [European]

---

[13] *Supervisory Guidance on the Use of the Fair Value Option for Financial Instruments by Banks* (Basel Committee on Banking Supervision, June 2006) <http://www.bis.org>. The Basel Committee had issued an earlier version as a consultative document in July 2005.

[14] 'Industry Agrees New Fair-value Accounting Standard', Reuters News newswire, 16 March 2005.

[15] Commission Regulation (EC) No 1864/2005 of 15 November 2005.

[16] See letters from David Tweedie to Donna M. Bovolaneas (Office of the Superintendent of Financial Institutions Canada), to Jaime Caruana (Bank for International Settlements), and to Roger Ferguson (US Federal Reserve), all dated 22 April 2005, IASB archive, file 'EC–EU September 2004–'.

[17] Letter from David Tweedie to Tommaso Padoa-Schioppa, dated 22 April 2005, IASB archive, file 'EC-EU September 2004–'.

Commission intends promptly to consider ways to enhance the role and the working process of the European Financial Reporting Advisory Group (EFRAG) in order to ensure that European concerns are taken into proper consideration in the international accounting standard setting process'. EFRAG's 'founding fathers', a coalition of the Fédération des Experts Comptables Européens (FEE) and several European business associations which had created EFRAG in 2001 at the suggestion of the Commission (see Section 4.1), paid heed and initiated a rapid 'enhancement'. At that time, EFRAG was still a small operation, running largely on the time contributed by the unremunerated members of its Technical Expert Group (TEG). By November 2003, it could be said that there was general support in Europe for a strengthening of EFRAG's financial and technical resources.[18] The next month, EFRAG's Supervisory Board issued a public consultation document, which explicitly linked the proposed enhancement to the financial instruments controversy, and the enhancements were effected early in 2004.[19] These included the appointment of a full-time chairman of TEG and a full-time technical director, as well as the hiring of several project managers. The chairmen of the French, German, and UK national standard setters became ex-officio members of TEG. With an elaborate and open due process, TEG assumed more of the trappings of an accounting standard setter. Through various working groups and consultation procedures it aimed to position itself at the centre of the European response to the IASB.

While there was general support for giving EFRAG more muscle, there was disagreement in Europe over what it should be used for. Within some member states, and one assumes mainly those in which the strongest objections to IAS 39 were being voiced, there was support for a more overtly political role for EFRAG. Others, however, wanted EFRAG to remain an independent technical committee.[20] Within the December 2003 consultation document, this disagreement found expression in a somewhat confused proposal that EFRAG's Supervisory Board, or TEG, should consider 'the strategic political and/or economic impact IFRS might have'.[21] While some of this language was retained in the final conclusions, it had virtually disappeared from the presentation of the enhancement in EFRAG's 2004 *Annual Review*.

Perhaps contrary to some expectations, EFRAG did not seek to play an adversarial role vis-à-vis the IASB. Such expectations might have been raised by the appointment of Stig Enevoldsen, a Danish partner of Deloitte, as the first full-time chairman of TEG, in April 2004. Enevoldsen had been a TEG member since 2001, and was well known at the IASB. As IASC chairman from 1998 to 2000, he had been heavily involved in the debate over the restructuring of the IASC, when he had argued tenaciously, but in the end unsuccessfully, against the imposition of

---

[18] Summary record of ARC meeting of 21 November 2003, item 2 <http://ec.europa.eu/internal_market/accounting>. In other references to ARC meeting records in this chapter, this website reference is assumed.

[19] 'Proposals for the Enhancement of the Role and Working Process of EFRAG' (EFRAG, 5 December 2003) <http://www.efrag.org>.

[20] Summary record of ARC meeting of 21 November 2003, item 2.

[21] For a comment see Stephen Zeff, 'What Does EFRAG Want?' *World Accounting Report*, March 2004, 4.

the 'independent expert' model and in favour of a more representative model for the IASB. Since 2001 he had been an outspoken member of the IASB's Standards Advisory Council. His appointment as TEG chairman in the context of moves to seek more European influence over the IASB could easily give rise to the expectation of confrontation.[22]

Yet Enevoldsen, although sensitive to the political context in which EFRAG operated, consistently emphasized the technical and apolitical nature of its work.[23] Both he and Paul Ebling, his technical director who had joined EFRAG from the UK Accounting Standards Board, were determined to develop EFRAG's technical capacity to the point where it could not be ignored by the IASB. As discussed more fully in Section 9.4, they embarrassed the IASB in 2005 by rejecting IFRIC 3 on emission rights in 2005. But, in general, EFRAG sought to play the role of a critical ally of the IASB, rather than that of an opponent.

As indicated in Section 4.8, EFRAG's TEG was allowed to participate as an observer in the meetings of the IASB with its liaison standard setters since April 2003. When the liaison standard setters disappeared as a separate category in 2005, the Board agreed to hold periodic meetings on its convergence work programme with the chairman of TEG, accompanied by the chairmen of the French, German, and UK standard setters. In a formal sense, this put EFRAG on an equal footing with the US Financial Accounting Standards Board (FASB) and the Accounting Standards Board of Japan (ASBJ), which also held regular convergence meetings with the IASB Board.

9.4 IFRIC 3: THE IASB STUMBLES OVER EMISSION RIGHTS

As discussed in Chapter 3, the IASB's interpretations body, the International Financial Reporting Interpretations Committee (IFRIC), was slower to get off the mark than some had expected. After being reconstituted in 2002, it issued its first interpretation in May 2004. By February 2005, IFRIC had published eleven exposure drafts, which by then had led to five new interpretations and one amendment to an existing interpretation. IFRIC required Board clearance before issuing exposure drafts, and the Board's approval before the publication of an interpretation.

Among IFRIC's early output, IFRIC 3 *Emission Rights* undoubtedly attracted most attention. In some respects, it was a miniature version of the IASB's troubles with financial instruments. As in the project to improve IAS 39, IFRIC and the Board struggled to base a conceptually correct solution on a foundation of inherited IASC standards which the Board believed to be deficient. And as in the case of the improved version of IAS 39, IFRIC 3 ran into difficulties with the EU.

---

[22] See e.g. 'EFRAG', *World Accounting Report*, February 2004, 5.

[23] Stig Enevoldsen and Thomas Oversberg, 'Importance of a European Voice in International Standard Setting—The Role of EFRAG', in Hans-Georg Bruns et al. (editors), *Globale Finanzberichterstattung/Global Financial Reporting: Entwicklung, Anwendung und Durchsetzung von IFRS* (Stuttgart: Schäfer Poeschel, 2008), 99.

The main reason for IFRIC to take up the issue of emission rights as one of its first projects was that the transition of European companies to IFRSs on 1 January 2005 would coincide with the coming into effect of an EU emission rights trading scheme, one of the first major schemes of its kind to be implemented in line with the Kyoto Protocol.[24] Without any guidance in the existing body of IFRSs, this was believed to be an urgent issue.

IFRIC and the Board came to the conclusion that an interpretation had to be based on a discordant mix of standards inherited from the IASC and based on different conceptions of accounting: IAS 38 on intangible assets (for emission rights received or bought), IAS 20 on government grants (for the required credit to offset any recognized emission rights received for free, as would be the case in the initial stages of the EU's scheme), and IAS 37 on provisions (for the liability incurred by actually emitting greenhouse gases). IAS 37 required periodic remeasurement of provisions to settlement value, with changes recorded in profit or loss. IAS 38, while it allowed fair value measurement, called for fair value changes in intangible assets to be reported in other comprehensive income, not in profit or loss. IAS 20, dating back to 1982, must have looked simply antediluvian to many Board members, as it was based on a deferral and matching approach, with no possibility of remeasurement at all. As indicated in Section 5.7, the Board was toying, since early 2003, with the idea of replacing or withdrawing IAS 20.

IFRIC reluctantly drew what it believed to be the only possible conclusion from this combination of standards: the emission rights, the liability, and the government grant all had to be accounted for separately under their respective standards, giving rise to various mismatches and to income statement volatility.[25] A government grant would be recognized as deferred income at an amount equal to the fair value of the emission rights at their grant date. This amount would be released over time into profit or loss. However, the cost of recognizing a liability as emissions took place would be based on the market value of emission rights at subsequent dates. While some of this mismatch might in theory be corrected by measuring the emission right assets at fair value, IAS 38 did not allow these fair value changes to be reported in profit or loss. IFRIC recognized these problems, but observed to the Board that its mandate tied it to the existing text of IFRSs, and that it could not anticipate any changes to IAS 20 or other standards that the IASB might want to make.[26]

IFRIC's first exposure draft, D1, issued in May 2003, was based on IFRIC's conclusion as described above. The comment letters received confirmed IFRIC's views of why its interpretation was problematic, yet, having reconsidered its position, it still believed that D1 was the most appropriate interpretation of the existing standards.[27] As a way out, IFRIC proposed that the Board should defer issuing the interpretation until it had amended IAS 38 to allow fair value changes of emission rights to be recognized in profit or loss. The Board accepted this idea

---

[24] For the background to IFRIC3, as well as an extensive discussion of its technical issues, see Allan Cook, 'Emission Rights: From Costless Activity to Market Operation', *Accounting, Organizations and Society*, 34 (2009), 456–68. A short review of the history of IFRIC 3 by the IASB staff can be found in AP 9/2005 paper 8.

[25] On IFRIC's reluctance, see *IStaR*, April 2003.   [26] AP 4/2003 paper 13.

[27] *IFRIC Update*, October 2003, 1.

in December 2003, but decided that it would aim for a package in which it would expose both the change to IAS 38 and its yet-to-be-drafted proposal to withdraw IAS 20.[28] Nothing came of this, however, apparently because of agenda and staff constraints.[29] In October 2004, IFRIC decided that the impending start of the EU emissions trading scheme made it urgent to have some guidance in place in order to avoid divergent and possibly unacceptable accounting practices.[30] Having agreed on IFRIC 3, which was substantially identical to D1, it asked the Board for approval. In its October 2004 meeting, the Board voted 11–2, with one abstention, to approve the interpretation.[31]

IFRIC had certainly not hidden from the Board that D1 'did not receive wide acceptance', and that it was still receiving 'unsolicited letters expressing concern'.[32] Yet absent from IFRIC's advice to the Board and, as far as can be seen, from the Board's October 2004 discussion, is any explicit reference to a possible problem with the endorsement of IFRIC 3 for use in the EU.[33] Stig Enevoldsen, the chairman of EFRAG's TEG, recalled that he had repeatedly given warning to the IASB that EFRAG would not support the endorsement of an interpretation based on D1.[34] If so, his warnings apparently did not register with the Board.

In February 2005 it became known that EFRAG in a draft endorsement letter was poised to advise against the endorsement of IFRIC 3, a position which it reiterated in its final advice of May 2005. In EFRAG's view, the various mismatches in IFRIC 3 meant that it would not always result in information that faithfully represents economic reality, so that 'it is not in the European interest to adopt IFRIC 3 in its present form'.[35] There had apparently been some lobbying by affected companies in Brussels against the proposed interpretation, yet it is not evident that, prior to EFRAG's negative advice, there would have been sufficient political support in Europe to block the endorsement of IFRIC 3.[36] However, once expressed, EFRAG's reservations found easy support across the EU, and it was clear that there was no basis for the European Commission to proceed with endorsement.[37] If EFRAG had been looking for an opportunity to demonstrate that it was not merely a rubber stamp, it could hardly have wished for an easier target: an unpopular proposal, of which the IASB itself had explained the weaknesses at some length.[38]

---

[28] IASB meeting of 17–19 December 2003, minute 6.4 and 6.10.

[29] According to the IASB staff, in AP 9/2005 paper 8.　　　[30] AP 10/2004 paper 4B.

[31] *IStaR*, October 2004. Smith and Garnett voted against, Leisenring abstained.

[32] AP 10/2004 paper 4B, paragraph 3.

[33] Potential problems with EU endorsement are not mentioned in AP 10/2004 paper 4B, nor in the record of the Board's discussion in *IStaR*.

[34] Interview with Stig Enevoldsen, 3 July 2009.

[35] Letter from Stig Enevoldsen to Alexander Schaub, dated 6 May 2005 <http://www.efrag.org>.

[36] IAS-Vorschriften droht in EU neuer Rückschlag—Emissionsrechte-Standard findet keine Akzeptanz', *Börsen-Zeitung*, 23 February 2005, 6.

[37] Summary record of ARC meeting of 25 March 2005.

[38] See e.g. the European Banking Federation's allegation that a positive endorsement advice on IAS 39 would make EFRAG seem 'toothless', letter from Maurizo Sella (EBF) to Paul Rutteman (EFRAG), dated 17 June 2002 <http://www.fbe.be>, accessed through web.archive.

For a few months, both IFRIC and EFRAG endeavoured to develop a way forward. IFRIC worked on a proposal for an amendment to IAS 38, and EFRAG came up with an alternative approach based on a form of hedge accounting in line with IAS 39. IFRIC brought both proposals before the Board in June 2005.[39] However, the Board concluded that the effectiveness of either route was uncertain as long as IAS 20 had not been dealt with. After some debate, Chairman Tweedie summed up the discussion by observing that 'the mistake they had made was to rush [IFRIC 3] out'. Abruptly, he proposed to withdraw IFRIC 3, and the Board agreed.[40] Although the Constitution did not with so many words refer to withdrawals of standards or interpretations, the absence of even minimal due process steps was striking.

The way out had already been suggested to the IASB by the European Commission. Following EFRAG's negative advice, it had asked the IASB to defer the effective date of IFRIC 3, and also provided the IASB with some justification for doing so: the Commission pointed out that the European emission allowance scheme was not yet fully operational, and that markets in emission rights were developing more slowly than expected. Both circumstances figured prominently in the IASB's public explanation of its decision.[41]

Because of EFRAG's role, the IFRIC 3 episode invited comparisons with the clash between the EU and the IASB over IAS 39.[42] Yet, whereas the conflict over IAS 39 raised important questions about the EU's willingness to accept the IASB's independence, and the IASB's ability to withstand political pressure, IFRIC 3 mainly reflected on the Board's own judgement. Leaving the matter with IFRIC because the Board did not have time to deal with the issue itself may have been justified initially.[43] However, once it had become clear that the limitations of IFRIC's mandate did not allow it to arrive at a satisfactory conclusion, the Board could have taken matters into its own hands, either by not approving the final interpretation, or by giving a higher priority to amending the relevant standards, or by dealing with the entire problem itself.

The withdrawal of IFRIC 3 raised the interesting question of whether an interpretation was really needed, or whether reporting companies would, following IFRIC's apparently inexorable logic, arrive by themselves at what IFRIC had believed to be 'the most appropriate interpretation' of the existing standards.[44] During the June 2005 Board meeting, this question was raised in an exchange

---

[39] AP 6/2005 paper 12A. See also *IFRIC Update*, June 2005.

[40] *IStaR*, June 2005, 33. Barth and Leisenring voted against. The agenda papers for the June Board meeting are based on the proposals by IFRIC and EFRAG to amend IAS 38 or IAS 39, and do not suggest a withdrawal. Similarly, Tweedie's written report to the IASCF trustees meeting, held one day prior to the Board meeting, mentions the possibilities of amendment or deferral, not withdrawal. IASCF trustees meeting of 21 June 2005, agenda papers 2A and 2B. The report in *IStaR*, June 2005, 32, suggests the proposal was first raised in a paper distributed during the Board meeting.

[41] Letter from Alexander Schaub to David Tweedie, dated 13 May 2005, IASB archive, file 'EU'; *IASB Update*, June 2005, 1; 'IASB Withdraws IFRIC Interpretation on Emission Rights', *IASB Insight*, July 2005, 6.

[42] See e.g. Robert K. Larson, 'Constituent Participation and the IASB's International Financial Reporting Interpretations Committee', *Accounting in Europe*, 4/2 (2007), 207–54.

[43] This was the initial rationale for leaving the project with IFRIC, according to Wayne Upton cited in *IStaR*, June 2005, 32.

[44] *IFRIC Update*, September 2004, 1.

between Wayne Upton, who suggested that 'it was difficult to think people would forget that IFRIC 3 existed', and John Smith who countered that 'he was sure some people could manage to forget'.[45] To make sure that people would, in effect, be allowed to forget IFRIC 3, the report on the meeting in *IASB Update* was careful to note that the 'Board affirmed its view that IFRIC 3 is *an* [emphasis added] appropriate interpretation of existing IFRSs', a phrase that was frequently cited in the professional literature on accounting for emission rights.[46] A survey of European companies by the audit firm PricewaterhouseCoopers and the International Emissions Trading Association (IETA), published in 2007, revealed a considerable variety of approaches used in practice, with only a small minority of companies following the approach of IFRIC 3. The audit firm described the main approaches which it considered acceptable, some of which differed markedly from IFRIC 3.[47]

9.5 THE EU PROMOTES IFRSs TO THE WORLD: THE EQUIVALENCE ASSESSMENTS

The European Commission liked to cast itself as the IASB's 'first customer', but it also assumed a role as the IASB's salesman. The immediate cause of this development were some relatively obscure implementing measures from the EU's Prospectus Directive (2003) and Transparency Directive (2004), two major pieces of legislation which, like the IAS Regulation, followed from the Financial Services Action Plan adopted by the EU in 2000.[48] In support of the general objective of creating a single European capital market, the two directives were aimed at harmonizing and upgrading requirements in the EU on information to be provided by listed companies, both when issuing securities to the market and on an ongoing basis. Both directives called for financial statements to be included among the information to be provided by companies on various occasions, and obviously referred to the IAS Regulation for the specific requirements. But whereas the IAS Regulation was directed exclusively at companies governed by the laws of EU member states, the Transparency and Prospectus Directives encompassed non-EU, or third-country, companies seeking listings in the EU as well. The default requirement under both directives was that these non-EU companies would have to provide financial statements prepared on the basis of IFRSs as adopted by the EU. Without further measures, this would have been a

---

[45] *IStaR*, June 2005, 32.

[46] *IASB Update*, June 2005, 1. That the choice of language was deliberate may be inferred from an email from David Tweedie to David Boymal, dated 30 June 2005 (IASB archive, file 'IFRIC'), in which Tweedie wrote: 'I stress that IFRIC came up with *an* [original emphasis] interpretation for existing standards—if there are others that meet requirements of our standards then companies are clearly free to judge them when using professional judgement.'

[47] *Trouble-entry Accounting—Revisited* (PricewaterhouseCoopers, 2007).

[48] Directive 2003/71/EC of 4 November 2003 (Prospectus Directive) and Directive 2004/109/EC of 15 December 2004 (Transparency Directive). See also Committee of European Securities Regulators (CESR), 'Technical Advice on Equivalence of Certain Third Country GAAP and on Description of Certain Third Countries Mechanisms of Enforcement of Financial Information', June 2005, CESR/05-230b <http://www.esma.eu>.

major policy change: before the move towards a single European capital market, the individual member states had typically allowed listings from outside the EU on the basis of other than just domestic accounting standards, even though not all foreign standards might be accepted, and restrictions might apply depending on the type of security and the type of listing. Exact numbers were not easy to come by, but early in 2007 it was reported that there might have been up to 600 companies listing in the EU using generally accepted accounting principles (GAAP) from at least thirty-three non-EU countries.[49] Among these, the more than 200 users of US GAAP formed by far the largest contingent, also including non-US companies. Evidently, the most sensitive potential consequence of the Transparency and Prospectus Directives was that US companies might have to reconcile their financial statements to IFRSs, just as the US SEC had for many years required EU companies to reconcile to US GAAP.

Both directives, however, included provisions that allowed the Commission to designate third-country accounting standards and enforcement mechanisms as equivalent to IFRSs as adopted by and enforced in the EU, and therefore as a suitable basis for a European listing and for raising capital in the EU. The Prospectus Directive established a deadline for making this designation: in the absence of a recognition of equivalence, third-country issuers seeking admission to regulated markets in the EU after 1 January 2007 would have to restate to the European version of IFRSs.[50] In June 2004, the Commission set the equivalence assessment process in motion by asking CESR for technical advice on the equivalence of Canadian, Japanese, and US GAAP with IFRSs. After companies using US GAAP, companies using Japanese GAAP (presumably all from Japan) formed the second largest group of listed companies not applying IFRSs. In 2004, Canada probably came in third place, before it was overtaken by India.[51]

It is not apparent that interested parties in Canada and the United States were greatly disturbed by the equivalence assessment, perhaps out of a perception that the risk of not being granted equivalence was slight.[52] With respect to Canada, the equivalence assessment soon lost its significance anyway. On 31 March 2005, Canada's Accounting Standards Board issued a draft of a strategic plan in which

[49] 'First Report to the European Securities Committee and to the European Parliament on Convergence between International Financial Reporting Standards (IFRS) and Third Country National Generally Accepted Accounting Principles (GAAPs)', European Commission, COM(2007) 405 final, 6 July 2007, table on pages 4–5 <http://ec.europa.eu/internal_market/accounting>. CESR is cited as the source of the table, and a similar table is included in 'CESR's Advice to the European Commission on the Work Programmes of the Canadian, Japanese and US Standard Setters, the Definition of Equivalence and the List of Third Country GAAPs Currently Used on the EU Capital Markets', 6 March 2007, CESR/07-138, pages 20–1 <http://www.esma.eu>. The Commission's table lists a total of 594 issuers, apparently a summation of the data in CESR's table, which separately lists 298 share issuers and 296 debt issuers, which may mean that the Commission's number is an overestimation to the extent that it includes companies with both listed debt and shares. CESR notes that its numbers may not be complete and may include double counting of companies listed in more than one member state.

[50] Article 35, Commission Regulation (EC) No. 809/2004 of 29 April 2004 implementing Directive 2003/71/EC.

[51] No data over 2004 are available, but CESR's March 2007 report shows eighty-four companies from Japan, seventy from India, and forty-five from Canada.

[52] See e.g. 'Treasury Official Sobel Urges Progress on Trans-Atlantic Accounting Standards', BNA's *Daily Tax Report*, 16 November 2004, 220 DTR G-5.

IFRSs were envisaged as the basis for financial reporting by all Canadian public companies (see Section 10.1).

In contrast, the position of US GAAP was still unchallenged in the United States, and by 2005 there were no serious plans yet to require or allow US companies to use IFRSs. If suggested at all, the idea that US GAAP might not be good enough for Europe would probably have been greeted with derision. The European Commission did frequently refer to the equivalence assessment in its appeals to the SEC to lift its Form 20-F reconciliation requirement for European companies using IFRSs, suggesting that the SEC's failure to do so might result in the imposition of a similar requirement for US companies listing in Europe.[53] Yet the Prospectus and Transparency Directives indicated that equivalence should be assessed purely on technical grounds, and did not mention reciprocity as a condition. At the technical level, the SEC had already encouraged the 2002 Norwalk Agreement that declared the FASB's commitment to seek convergence with the IASB. As discussed in Chapter 8, the SEC was steadily moving of its own accord towards lifting the reconciliation requirement, and the EU's equivalence assessment had at most a marginal, if any, impact on the evolution of the SEC's views.[54]

However, the EU's equivalence assessment did have a great impact in Japan, as discussed more fully in Sections 4.6 and 10.4. The news from Europe did much to shift Japanese opinion away from the belief that Japanese GAAP merited equal standing next to US GAAP and IFRSs, to a view that convergence with IFRSs should become the dominant focus of the ASBJ. The ASBJ and the IASB began a convergence project in January 2005 to remove differences between their standards, which in practical terms amounted to unilateral convergence of Japanese GAAP towards IFRSs.

Perhaps inspired by the SEC Chief Accountant's roadmap, published in 2005, towards lifting the reconciliation requirement, and by the moves in Japan and Canada to converge with or even adopt IFRSs, the European Commission began to represent its equivalence assessment more explicitly as an instrument to encourage a worldwide movement towards the use of IFRSs as a single global standard. In December 2006, just before the original deadline of 1 January 2007, the Commission extended the transition periods envisaged in the Prospectus and Transparency Directives, but for most countries it added conditions with respect to convergence. Canada, Japan, and the United States were granted an unconditional extension of the transition period to 1 January 2009, matching the SEC's increasingly prominent use of the year 2009 in its utterances on lifting the 20-F reconciliation. According to McCreevy, an extension of the deadline 'gives us leverage in our efforts to obtain the removal of reconciliation requirements for EU issuers abroad', which could hardly be a reference to any country other than the

---

[53] See e.g. 'From Quantity to Quality: The Future of Internal Market Regulation', speech by Charlie McCreevy, European Policy Centre policy breakfast briefing, Brussels, 7 April 2005, SPEECH 05/203 <http://europa.eu/rapid>.

[54] See e.g. Alan L. Beller (Director, Division of Corporation Finance, SEC) 'Remarks Before the Practicing Law Institute Fifth Annual Institute on Securities Regulation in Europe' speech dated 5 December 2005 <http://www.sec.gov> for remarks dissuading the European Commission from taking steps against the use of US GAAP in Europe while the SEC was preparing for a lifting of the 20-F reconciliation requirement.

United States. However, there was also a broader purpose: McCreevy characterized the prolongation of the transition period as 'the most efficient way to promote the use of IFRS'.[55] Financial statements based on GAAP from countries other than Canada, Japan, and the US would also continue to be accepted without reconciliation until 2009, provided that:

(i) the third country authority responsible for the national accounting standards in question has made a public commitment, before the start of the financial year in which the prospectus is filed, to converge those standards with International Financial Reporting Standards;

(ii) that authority has established a work programme which demonstrates the intention to progress towards convergence before 31 December 2008.[56]

What this meant in practice was not entirely clear, as it was left to the securities market regulators of the members states to satisfy themselves that these conditions had been met in, say, Tunisia, Venezuela, and Zambia (each with one company listed in the EU in 2007). The European Commission did not require itself to keep track of the rapidly changing details of progress towards IFRSs around the world, a task which even the IASB itself found to be daunting. Given that countries such as Australia, Israel, and South Africa had already adopted IFRSs for use by their listed companies, determining whether a country had committed to convergence was a substantive issue with respect to a small number of major countries only, in particular China, India, and South Korea. The European Commission, assisted by CESR, provided periodic reports on convergence in these and selected other countries to the European Parliament.[57]

When the European Commission announced the extension of its transition period, in December 2006, China had already declared earlier that year that it considered its standards to be substantially converged with IFRSs, a claim which the IASB had countenanced (see Section 10.2). In March 2007, South Korea made a formal declaration with respect to convergence (see Section 10.3), followed by more tentative steps by India in July (see Section 15.7). Although Japanese GAAP continued for the moment to be accepted without conditions, the ASBJ's commitment to convergence expressed in the Tokyo Agreement of August 2007 fell neatly into this series (see Section10.4).

The significance of the European Commission's activities was recognized at the IASB. In July 2007, David Tweedie reported to the IASC Foundation trustees:

[55] 'The Use of Non-EU Accounting Standards on EU Stock Markets Is Extended for Two More Years', European Commission press release IP/06/1691, 6 December 2006 <http://europa.eu/rapid>.

[56] For the Prospectus Directive, see Commission Regulation 1787/2006/EC of 4 December 2006, article 2; identical language regarding the Transparency Directive was used in Commission Decision 2006/891/EC of 4 December 2006, except that 'in which the prospectus is filed' was replaced with 'to which the financial statements relate'.

[57] 'First Report to the European Securities Committee and to the European Parliament on Convergence between International Financial Reporting Standards (IFRS) and Third Country National Generally Accepted Accounting Principles (GAAPs)', European Commission, COM(2007) 405 final, 6 July 2007; 'Report on Convergence between International Financial Reporting Standards (IFRS) and Third Country National Generally Accepted Accounting Principles (GAAPs) and on the Progress towards the Elimination of Reconciliation Requirements that Apply to Community Issuers under the Rules of these Third Countries', 22 April 2008 <http://ec.europa.eu/internal_market/accounting>.

One of the major factors driving the convergence initiatives in Japan, India, China, Korea, and other major economies is the equivalence exercise being undertaken by the European Commission and the Committee of European Securities Regulators. The EU must decide by 2009 whether to require reconciliations for accounting systems not deemed as equivalent. This has focussed energy on the need to reach conclusion on the convergence programmes described in a timely manner.[58]

As it happened, the EU did not make all of its final decisions by 2009. In December 2008, US GAAP and Japanese GAAP were recognized as equivalent with IFRSs as adopted in the EU, without any time limit. Financial statements on the basis of Canadian, Chinese, Indian, and South Korean accounting standards continued to be accepted on a temporary basis, until 31 December 2011.[59] By default, accounting standards from all other countries were no longer acceptable from 1 January 2009 onwards. For good measure, and in a clause that was intelligible only within the logic of the EU's endorsement process, 'IFRSs as issued by the IASB' were also recognized as equivalent to 'IFRSs as adopted by the EU'.[60]

While important, the EU's equivalence assessments were not the only factor behind the significant moves towards IFRSs made by several countries in 2007 and subsequently. In April 2007, when addressing the European Parliament, Tweedie did not mention the equivalence assessments. Instead he observed:

> In my travels throughout the world, I am struck by the fact that the appropriate regulatory authorities have been willing to adopt IFRSs only with reasonable confidence that IFRSs will be accepted in US markets eventually. This certainly is the case in China, India, Korea, the rest of the Asia-Oceania region, Canada, and Latin America, all of which have close ties with both Europe and the United States.[61]

It may well have been true that, worldwide, the United States was still seen as the ultimate arbiter of the fate of IFRSs as the global accounting standard. In that case, the persuasive powers of the EU in promoting third-country convergence with IFRSs derived much of their strength from calculations by these third countries about what the US would or would not eventually do. Nevertheless, between 2004 and 2007, before the SEC opened a fundamentally new perspective on the future of IFRSs by starting a debate about domestic use of IFRSs in the United States, the EU's equivalence assessment provided an important short-term focal point for countries considering moving towards IFRSs.

9.6 NEW PRESSURES ON THE IASB FROM THE EU

Notwithstanding the European Commission's efforts to promote the use of IFRSs, relations between the IASB and the EU again went through a difficult period

---

[58] IASCF meeting of 2–3 July 2007, agenda paper 2, paragraph 10.

[59] Commission Decision 2008/961/EC of 12 December 2008 (Transparency Directive) and Commission Regulation (EC) 1289/2008 of 12 December 2008 (Prospectus Directive).

[60] Commission Decision 2008/961/EC, paragraph 1(a).

[61] 'Statement by IASB Chairman Sir David Tweedie before the Economic and Monetary Affairs Committee of the European Parliament', 10 April 2007, 6.

between 2006 and 2008. As indicated above, there certainly were indications from 2005 onwards that the IASB might look forward to more stable relations with Europe, compared to the tensions over financial instruments of 2003 and 2004. A good working relationship and a degree of mutual understanding had come into being between the European Commission, EFRAG, and the IASB, holding out the promise that standards developed by the IASB would be endorsed for use in Europe without undue friction. However, such hopes were upset by the emergence of the European Parliament as a significant actor, at a time when some of the IASB's work, particularly on segment reporting, service concessions, and small and medium-sized entities, met with opposition in Europe. This produced a complex tangle of issues, from which both Europe and the IASB could extricate themselves only by reconsidering and modifying the processes by which IFRSs were produced by the IASB and endorsed for use in Europe.

9.6.1 Institutional Changes in Europe

As described in Chapter 4, the EU's IAS Regulation of 2002 was enacted against a background of inter-institutional tension. The European Parliament had agreed to a delegation of authority to the European Commission in the form of the endorsement process of IFRSs under the condition that the endorsement of IFRSs would be one of the policy areas to be included in a future expansion of the Parliament's powers. The time to redeem this promise came in July 2006, when a new type of legislative procedure was added to the EU's legal framework.[62] The original 'regulatory procedure' used in the IAS Regulation of 2002, it may be recalled, allowed the Commission to endorse IFRSs for use in the EU upon the advice of the ARC, a committee of member state representatives. Under this procedure, the European Parliament's powers of intervention were limited to expressing any concerns to the Council of Ministers, which could elect to ignore such a representation made by the Parliament. Under the new 'regulatory procedure with scrutiny', however, the Parliament itself obtained the right to block a standard within three months after the ARC had approved its endorsement. In a joint statement published in October 2006, the Parliament, the Council, and the Commission included the IAS Regulation in a list of twenty-five existing directives and regulations, ranging from money laundering to pesticides, into which the new procedure had to be incorporated 'as a matter of urgency'.[63] Even so, the IAS Regulation was not amended until March 2008.[64] From early 2007 onwards, the Parliament acted as if it already had obtained its new powers with respect to endorsement of IFRSs.

The Parliament's hitherto limited formal powers over endorsement of IFRSs had not prevented it from exercising a certain influence in this area, particularly through the activities of a small number of parliamentarians who took a critical view of the IASB. Among these were Pervenche Berès (France, Socialist), the

---

[62] Council Decision 2006/512/EC of 17 July 2006.   [63] O.J.21 October 2006, C255.
[64] Regulation (EC) 297/2008 of 11 March 2008, amending Regulation (EC) 1606/2002.

chairman of the Parliament's Economic and Monetary Affairs Committee, and three German members, Alexander Radwan and Klaus-Heiner Lehne (both Christian-Democrat) and Wolf Klinz (Liberal-Democrat). Critical views expressed by these and some other members had already helped to make the EU's endorsement process of IFRSs a little more complex even before the extension of the Parliament's formal powers.

Because some of the criticisms expressed in the Parliament with respect to the IASB reflected disapproval of the central role of a private-sector body in the development of legislation, it is not surprising that the question was raised whether EFRAG's advice was not also coloured by private interests.[65] EFRAG exposed itself to such criticisms because its earliest endorsement recommendations contained no more than succinct arguments in support of its position. What also raised eyebrows was that EFRAG could comment very critically on IASB exposure drafts, yet recommend a substantially unchanged standard for endorsement.

The European Commission responded in two ways. In March 2006, it signed a 'Working Arrangement' with EFRAG, which represented the first official recognition of EFRAG as the European Commission's advisory body on IFRSs, apart from an oblique reference in the recitals of the IAS Regulation. Among other duties listed in the 'Working Arrangement', EFRAG was to consult widely before issuing its advice, and to justify how it reached its conclusions.[66] The Commission also announced in 2006 that it was creating an additional group to oversee the work of EFRAG.[67] This group, which came to be known as the Standards Advice Review Group (SARG), was charged with advising the Commission whether EFRAG's endorsement advice was 'well-balanced and objective'.[68] Although the Commission was itself satisfied with the quality of EFRAG's work, it wanted to deflect the Parliament's criticisms of the body. SARG's role was therefore to make sure that EFRAG's due process was properly reported in its endorsement advice.

SARG began operating in March 2007 under the chairmanship of Geoffrey Mitchell. Mitchell's involvement with international accounting standards went back to his service as secretary-general of the IASC from 1982 to 1985. More recently, in several positions with Barclays until 2006, he had been closely involved in the IASB's work on financial instruments. Another member of SARG who knew the IASB well was Liesel Knorr. She had served as the IASC's technical director from 1994 to 1999. In 1999, she became secretary-general of the recently created Deutsches Rechnungslegungs Standards Committee (DRSC) which was shortly afterwards recognized as one of the IASB's liaison standard setters. In a curious development, illustrative of how the EU was still discovering how to organize its dealings with IFRSs, she served for a brief period both on SARG and on EFRAG, whose work SARG was charged to review.[69]

---

[65] See e.g. written question P-3697/01 by Jean-Maurice Dehousse (PSE) to the Commission, 8 January 2001.

[66] 'Working Arrangement between European Commission and EFRAG', 23 March 2006 <http://ec.europa.eu/internal_market/accounting>.

[67] Summary record of ARC meeting of 24 April 2006, 6.

[68] Commission Decision 2006/505/EC of 14 July 2006.

[69] Knorr was appointed to SARG in February 2007. In July 2007, she became chairman of the Deutsche Standardisierungsrat, the standard-setting board operating under the aegis of the DRSC. This

Although SARG's critical questioning did cause some annoyance at EFRAG, the latter did accept the need to improve its reports.[70] For example, EFRAG attempted to clarify the relationship between sometimes highly critical comments it might make on an IASB exposure draft and its subsequent positive endorsement advice even when the IASB had not addressed all of EFRAG's concerns.

Whatever the origins of SARG, its creation illustrated the challenge of building up a proper institutional framework for IFRSs in the EU. Whatever may have been believed at the time of the original announcement of IFRS adoption in 2000, it had since become clear that the EU was not going to be a passive recipient of the IASB's standards. Political realities in the EU, as well as actual experience with a strong-willed IASB, led to highly elaborate procedures for embedding IFRSs in the European legal framework, and to continued active involvement in the IASB's affairs.

9.6.2 EU Pressure for IASB Reform

EU interest in the IASB was not limited to the endorsement of IFRSs, but extended to the governance and functioning of the IASB itself. This interest was expressed with at least two voices, one striking a moderate tone, coming from the European Commission, and the other more strident, emanating from the European Parliament.

In July 2006, the EU finance ministers, meeting as the ECOFIN Council configuration, discussed the IASB. The thrust of the 'Council conclusions', the published summary of the discussion, was to encourage the IASB in its efforts to put in place a stable funding system (see Section 11.10). In addition, the IASB was exhorted to continue to:

(1) strengthen its governance structure, with a view to adequately take into account the public interest, including financial stability aspects;
(2) strengthen its due process with stakeholders—including work planning and setting of standards as well as their interpretations—in particular relating to consultation, so that views of all IFRS users and investors are fully taken into account. In this context, impact assessments, field testing and reasoning behind any actions should be developed; and cooperation with other standard setting bodies should involve stakeholders using IFRS; as well as
(3) ensure that stakeholders are adequately represented in the IASC Foundation, IASB and International Financial Reporting Interpretations Committee (IFRIC) governing bodies, bringing additional technical expertise.[71]

It was not too difficult to discern, behind the views of the Council, several of the grievances expressed by various parties in Europe during the preceding years, including the complaint that the IASB 'is not listening', the perceived prominence

made her an ex-officio member of EFRAG, although, like the chairmen of the French and UK standard setters, without voting rights.

[70] Interviews with Stig Enevoldsen, 3 July 2009; Jan Klaassen, 24 July 2008; and Geoffrey Mitchell, 15 October 2009.

[71] '2741st Council Meeting, Economic and Financial Affairs, Brussels, 11 July 2006', C/06/209, press release 11370/06 (Presse 209), 12 <http://europa.eu/rapid>.

of Americans in the IASB, the overriding influence of US GAAP convergence on the IASB's technical work and the concomitant lack of consultation over the IASB's agenda, and the ECB's concerns over the full fair value option. From the Council's conclusions it was clear that, at government level, the EU's member states did not believe that the IASC Foundation's recent Constitution review had settled all these matters satisfactorily. The Council instructed the European Commission to monitor developments and to report on a regular basis whether 'effective progress has taken place'.

The Commission delivered its first progress report in January 2007, not omitting to send a copy to the IASC Foundation trustees.[72] To the trustees, the Commission staff expressed its satisfaction that 'significant improvements' had already been made to the governance of the IASB and the Foundation, but that further action was needed. In the report, the Commission was careful to list changes made during and since the review of the IASC Foundation's Constitution in 2005, but otherwise it mainly elaborated on the three points already indicated by the Council, calling in particular for more extensive consultation, assessment of impact and the costs of standards, and feedback to constituents on what the IASB had done with their input. In addition, the Commission reiterated the need for the IASB and the Foundation to give more weight to jurisdictions applying IFRSs, both in its due process and when making appointments.

Meanwhile, in October 2006, the Economic and Monetary Affairs Committee of the European Parliament had initiated a procedure of its own to draft a report on IFRSs and the governance of the IASB. The rapporteur, Alexander Radwan, delivered a first version in March 2007 under the provocative title of 'IFRS tested, IASB failed'.[73] In the report, Radwan expressed his conviction that:

> the IASCF/IASB is far from being transparent and balanced. The rapporteur is also convinced that democratic control with the organisation must be improved. Moreover, the European Parliament is only involved at the very latest stages of the decision making process when the final standard has to be turned into EU law. . . . Therefore it must be ensured that the European Parliament is involved when [the] work program for the IASB is drawn up and when the accounting standard project is being considered.

After reviewing a range of potentially controversial topics on the IASB's agenda, Radwan concluded that '2007 could be [a] decisive year in the cooperation between the London based standard setter, the Commission, the Council and the European Parliament'.

---

[72] 'Commission Services Working Paper on Governance Developments in the IASB (International Accounting Standards Board) and IASCF (International Accounting Standards Committee Foundation)', with cover letter from Jörgen Holmquist to Philip Laskawy, dated 18 January 2007, IASCF trustees meeting of 2–3 April 2007, attachment to agenda paper 3B.

[73] European Parliament, 'Working Document on International Financial Reporting Standards (IFRS) and the Governance of the IASB', 30 March 2007, ECON_DT(2007)386323. The quotations are taken from page 3–4, and 5, respectively <http://www.europarl.europa.eu>.

9.6.3 IFRS 8 Provides the Spark

As indicated in Radwan's preliminary report, there was no shortage of IASB projects with sufficiently inflammatory content to strain the developing triangular relation between the Parliament, the Commission, and the IASB. Among those mentioned by Radwan were the IASB's project to develop a standard for small and medium-sized entities, service concessions, performance reporting, and the always contentious financial instruments. As discussed more extensively in Chapter 12, all of these projects caused mounting resentment across Europe. All were frequently mentioned whenever the IASB or IFRSs were discussed in the European Parliament during 2007 and 2008. But, as it happened, the tinder was lit by a standard that Radwan had not mentioned, IFRS 8 on operating segments.[74]

IFRS 8 *Operating Segments* was the result of one of the few projects undertaken by the IASB under the banner of short-term convergence with US GAAP that was successfully completed. IFRS 8 replaced IAS 14 *Segment Reporting*, a standard last revised by the IASC in 1997. During the 1990s, the revision of IAS 14 was one of the rare IASC projects undertaken in cooperation with the FASB, and the intention had been for the two organizations to issue similar standards. In the end, they had not been wholly successful in this, and IAS 14 differed in important respects from its counterpart, FAS 131 *Disclosure About Segments of an Enterprise and Related Information*, issued by the FASB in 1997.[75] Compared to IAS 14, FAS 131 was a more radical expression of the so-called management approach. It required the publication of segment information in line with information regularly provided to senior management, both with respect to the identification of segments and with respect to the accounting policies used in determining segment results. While IAS 14 acknowledged the importance of internal reporting structures, it imposed certain minimum requirements on the number and size of reportable segments, as well as a minimum of information on a geographical basis if segments were identified according to lines of business, and vice versa. IAS 14 also stipulated that segment results should be measured using the same basis of accounting as used in the consolidated financial statements.

At the time of the Norwalk Agreement, segment reporting was identified as a potential convergence project even though it was noted that segment reporting was a matter of disclosure, not of measurement of the amounts in the financial statements, so that lack of agreement between IFRSs and US GAAP on this point did not give rise to reconciling differences.[76] A project on this topic was added to the agenda, but until 2005 it led a marginal existence. On the rare occasions when it was discussed, it was thought of, at least by the IASB, as a joint project in which the two boards would determine which of their two standards offered the better

---

[74] For an overview of the IFRS 8 episode, see Louise Crawford, Christine Helliar, and David Power, *Politics or Accounting Principles: Why Was IFRS 8 so Controversial?* (London: ICAEW Centre for Business Performance, 2010).

[75] See Kees Camfferman and Stephen A. Zeff, *Financial Reporting and Global Capital Markets: A History of the International Accounting Standards Committee, 1973–2000* (Oxford: Oxford University Press, 2007), 393–5.

[76] AP 9/2002 (joint meeting) paper 2B, paragraph 12.

solution.[77] But in January 2005, the IASB staff was ready to recommend, on an apparently unilateral basis, that the IASB Board should adopt the management approach of FAS 131 in order to achieve convergence. This recommendation was based on a review of academic research and discussions with Board members, as well as on the views expressed by the IASB's Analyst Representative Group. In addition, it was noted that 'it was thought unlikely that the FASB would consider moving away from the current management approach'.[78] From this point on-wards, the project took shape and proceeded rapidly to the publication of an exposure draft issued in January 2006, followed, after Board discussions in July and September, by a final standard in November of that year.

The IASB made no secret of the fact that it had not just adopted the general principles of FAS 131, but had literally copied most of its wording into IFRS 8. In that light, it was only to be expected that Jim Leisenring's dissenting view on IFRS 8 was almost identical to his dissent to FAS 131 in 1997, when he was a member of the FASB. This time, Gilbert Gélard signed on to Leisenring's dissent, whereas, at the FASB, Leisenring had been the only one to vote against the standard. The fact that Leisenring, the man who was widely regarded as the personification of American influence on the Board, voted against a standard that became emblem-atic of this perceived American influence is just one of the reasons why the subsequent controversy over IFRS 8 needs more than a simple explanation.

That it did become controversial was largely a surprise to the IASB.[79] Of course, the Board was well aware of the main issue, which also formed the core of the dissenting opinion expressed by Leisenring and Gélard: should the management approach to segment reporting be conditioned by requirements to prevent op-portunistic reporting by management? In particular, should the freedom of management to define segment results be restricted by more detailed reconcili-ations to the consolidated numbers, or even by a requirement to use the same accounting policies in the segment numbers as in the consolidated accounts? The Board itself had debated this issue, and it had taken note of the fact that the users in its Analyst Representative Group and respondents to the exposure draft held divergent views on this point. Yet, on balance, it believed that the reasoning underlying FAS 131—FASB's original basis for conclusions was reproduced in its entirety in the basis for conclusions to IFRS 8—was still valid. And if the US standard was the better one, the logic of short-term convergence dictated that it should be adopted without modifications.

Following the exposure draft, another arabesque began to wind its way through the story. But perhaps because it seemed unrelated to anything the Board was preoccupied with at the moment, the Board may have misjudged its potential as a source of controversy. When the comment letters came in, it appeared that eighty out of 182 letters originated in a letter-writing campaign organized by Publish What You Pay, a global network of civic-society organizations originating in the

---

[77] AP 10/2003 (joint meeting) paper 11, paragraph 6.

[78] AP 1/2005 paper 6. The quotation is taken from paragraph 55.

[79] Interviews with Mary Barth, 17 March 2009, and with Patricia O'Malley, 28 May 2009. According to a news item in *Accountancy Age*, 'IASB sources have admitted they are baffled by the fierce opposition to IFRS 8, which was consulted on last year', Nicholas Neveling, 'MPs Join European Parliament in Segment Standards Row', 3 May 2007 <http://www.accountancyage.com>.

United Kingdom. The aim of the network was to increase corporate disclosure with respect to activities in the extractive industries, in order that more of the benefits of these activities may accrue to the inhabitants of resource-rich countries. As part of the campaign many charities and other non-governmental organizations that, until then, had been beyond the IASB's purview wrote in to argue that the scope of the IASB's proposed standard should be extended to deal with this issue, and that the standard should call for detailed country-by-country disclosure on transactions between governments and enterprises in the oil, gas, and mining industries. The IASB had until recently also been beyond the purview of the Publish What You Pay campaign: this type of country-by-country disclosures had not been mentioned in comment letters when the IASB prepared IFRS 6, its standard on extractive industries accounting, in 2003 and 2004 (see Section 5.6).[80] The IASB's exposure draft did call for disclosures on the geographical breakdown of revenues and non-current assets, but not nearly at the level of detail that the campaigners for country-by-country disclosures had in mind.

When the Board discussed country-by-country disclosures on the basis of the comment letters in September 2006, it seemed a little unsure about how it should deal with this point. While several members expressed their sympathy with the concerns raised by Publish What You Pay, questions were raised about the Board's mandate with respect to more overtly political questions, whether the trustees should be involved, or whether this issue would better be addressed by the World Bank, the International Public Sector Accounting Standards Board, or other international organizations. The only thing the Board seemed sure of was that it did not want this short-term convergence project to be delayed by taking up this issue as part of the segment reporting standard, as this would certainly require re-exposure. The issue was therefore noted for future consideration.[81]

Initially it looked as if the Board had made the right judgement, given that IFRS 8 seemed headed for rapid endorsement by the EU. EFRAG re-debated the question of stricter requirements for the measurement of segment results and registered the concerns of some of its members on this point, but it nevertheless issued a positive and unanimous endorsement advice in January 2007.[82] A month later, in February, IFRS 8 was accepted unanimously by the ARC. Neither EFRAG nor the ARC mentioned the issue of country-by-country disclosures. As the original comitology procedure still applied, no further decisions were required to bring IFRS 8 on the EU's statute book.

But, from March 2007 onwards, a vociferous opposition to IFRS 8 flared up in the United Kingdom, contributing to a serious complication in the European endorsement process. The Investment Management Association (IMA), the

---

[80] AP 4/2003 paper 7C, paragraph 59, prepared by the AASB staff, does mention Publish What You Pay and its concerns, but gives no indication that Publish What You Pay had sought contact with the IASB. This agenda paper mentions that the IASB had received a letter from George Soros 'expressing the desire for disclosure requirements regarding payments made by multinational extractive industries companies to host governments'. No comment letters were received from non-governmental organizations on the 2004 exposure draft, and the issue of country-by-country disclosure appears not to have been raised (see analysis of comment letters in AP 6/2004 paper 9E).

[81] Based on Board discussion as reported in *IStaR*, September 2006, 31–3.

[82] Letter from Stig Enevoldsen to Jörgen Holmquist, dated 16 January 2007 <http://ec.europa/eu/internal_market/accounting>. For unanimity, see summary record of ARC meeting of 2 February 2007, 2.

National Association of Pension Funds, and the Association of British Insurers all approached the European Commission to request that the application of IFRS 8 in the EU be postponed.[83] Other investors and investor groups in the United Kingdom were said to be supportive of the initiative to approach the Commission, or at least to be critical of IFRS 8. Neither the National Association of Pension Funds nor the Association of British Insurers had sent comment letters to the IASB on the exposure draft. The IMA had written, but while its comment letter did contain critical remarks, its restrained language had apparently led the IASB staff to classify it among those which supported the management approach of the exposure draft.[84] One can empathize with the IASB that it read a different message in the IMA's May 2006 comment letter, which said 'in principle we welcome the IASB replacing IAS 14, Segment Reporting, with the US SFAS 131', from what the IMA was said to have written to the European Commission in March 2007: 'In adopting IFRS 8, the Commission would be rushing ahead with an unnecessary and imperfect standard.'[85]

What might have been more predictable is that the country-by-country disclosure issue came back to haunt the IASB. Richard Murphy, an English chartered accountant who had become an activist on economic and taxation issues, and who had stimulated the interest of Publish What You Pay in the IASB's work on segment reporting, was not about to accept the IASB's dismissal of the issue. In a vigorous campaign, he criticized the IASB for refusing to give a hearing to Publish What You Pay and argued the more general point that the publication of IFRS 8 was illustrative of fundamental problems with the mandate, accountability, and procedures of the IASB.[86]

All of these concerns resonated with critical views of the IASB that had already been developing among some members of the European Parliament, as indicated above. On 18 April, the Economic and Monetary Affairs Committee, chaired by Pervenche Berès, tabled a motion in which the view was expressed that IFRS 8 should include a defined measure of segment profit or loss, and in which the concern was stated 'that the Commission is proposing, contrary to the principles of better regulation, to import into EU law an alien standard without having conducted any impact assessment'. The motion called on the Commission to carry out an impact assessment urgently, failing which the Parliament would do so itself.[87] A few days later, the Parliament agreed to postpone a vote on the

---

[83] 'War of Words Sparked over New Standard', and 'UK Investors in Plea to Brussels over IFRS 8', *Financial Times*, 21 March 2007, 30.

[84] AP 7/2006 paper 5B, classification of CL162.

[85] Letter from Liz Murrall and Uner Nabi (IMA) to Kil-woo Lee (IASB), dated 26 May 2006, IFRS 8 comment letters, CL 162; 'IMA Urges the European Commission to Defer the Introduction of IFRS 8—Operating Segments', IMA press release dated 15 March 2007 <http://www.investmentuk.org>. For the IASB's view that IMA's views were not expressed consistently, see letter from David Tweedie to Liz Murrall, dated 23 March 2007, IASB archive, file 'covered correspondence'; and 'Statement by IASB Chairman Sir David Tweedie before the Economic and Monetary Affairs Committee of the European Parliament', 10 April 2007.

[86] Murphy's activities and comments during 2007 with respect to IFRS 8 are recorded in detail on his blog at <http://www.taxresearch.org.uk/Blog/category/ifrs-8>. Penny Sukhraj, 'International Investors Wade into Segments Row', news item posted 24 May 2007 <http://www.accountancyage.com>.

[87] Motion for a Resolution, 18 April 2007, B6-0157/2007 <http://www.europarl.europa.eu>.

resolution until September, having learned that the Commission had consented to conduct an impact study.[88]

While the Commission staff carried out this unexpected task, the controversy rumbled on, mainly in the United Kingdom. A motion tabled in the House of Commons did attract some support for the statement 'That this House finds [IFRS 8] . . . totally unacceptable because it gives company directors carte blanche to decide what they disclose and how they disclose it'. Apart from calling for an in-depth impact assessment, the motion also stressed the importance of country-by-country disclosure.[89] While the motion had no practical effect, it helped to keep the question in the news. The UK Accounting Standards Board, when it wrote to the European Commission in favour of endorsement of IFRS 8, came under similar criticism as the IASB, namely, that its letter did not properly reflect the views of those opposing the standard.[90]

While mainly confined to the United Kingdom, opposition to IFRS 8 obtained a more international flavour with the publication, in April 2007, of an influential report on the IASB by Nicolas Véron, of the Brussels-based think-tank Bruegel. The report backed the need for an impact assessment on IFRS 8.[91] In May, the International Corporate Governance Network wrote to the European Commission to express its doubts about the compatibility of the management approach of IFRS 8 with the principles of sound corporate governance.[92]

9.6.4 The IASB's Response

The IASB, or at least the Board leadership and the IASC Foundation trustees, took note of the shifting institutional situation in Europe. In January 2007, former trustee Jens Røder alerted the trustees to the impending expansion of the Parliament's powers over the endorsement process. Røder was a partner in PricewaterhouseCoopers in Copenhagen and a former president of FEE, and at that point in time he served as 'senior advisor' to the trustees. He advised a programme of active communication with key members of the Parliament in order to remove the recurring perception that 'the IASCF is a closed, self-perpetuating organisation'.[93] By the time the trustees were able to discuss this, at their meeting in April of that year, events had overtaken them. Both the European Commission's report on the governance of the IASB and Radwan's far more critical draft report had come out. The controversy over IFRS 8 had erupted in March, and, although the European Parliament had not yet tabled its motion, it was obvious that the IASB was heading for another entanglement with the EU institutions.

---

[88] Intervention by Pervenche Berès in plenary session of 25 April 2007, CRE 25/04/2007, 11.8.

[89] Early day motion 1369, tabled 27 April 2007, by Austin Mitchell MP <http://www.parliament.uk>.

[90] ASB *Inside Track* 52, July 2007, 6; Penny Sukhraj, 'Not a Standard Row', 31 May 2007, <http://www.accountancyage.com>.

[91] Nicolas Véron, *The Global Accounting Experiment*, Bruegel Blueprint 2 (Brussels: Bruegel, 2007).

[92] Letter from Christiana Wood to Pierre Delsaux, dated 9 May 2007 <http://www.icgn.org/policy-committees>.

[93] Email from Jens Røder to selected trustees, dated 19 January 2007, reproduced as appendix to agenda paper 9B, IASCF trustees meeting of 2–3 April 2007.

Even if their role had allowed it, there was not much that the trustees could do directly about IFRS 8. It had been issued by the Board, and it was up to the EU to decide on its endorsement. Nevertheless, the trustees were inclined to respond to events, not least because this fitted in with some initiatives that they themselves were already taking with respect to communications and governance. With the aid of their recently appointed director of corporate communications, Mark Byatt, a programme was developed for establishing regular contacts with the European Parliament at the staff, Board, and trustees levels.[94] A 'procedures committee' of trustees (subsequently known as Due Process Oversight Committee) had been working since 2006 to develop recommendations for more effective trustee oversight (see Section 11.5). In April 2007, the trustees agreed to a set of proposals by the committee which were explicitly designed to address some of the concerns raised by the European Commission in January. They also noted the need for the trustees to engage with the European Parliament and to publicize their action on oversight issues. The trustees accepted, among other things, that the IASB should publish feedback statements when issuing standards to explain how it had dealt with issues raised in the comment letters, and that it should develop a framework for cost-benefit analysis.[95] In general, the trustees aimed to impose a greater degree of accountability on the Board while continuing to emphasize the need to preserve the Board's independence.

David Tweedie was scheduled to meet with the European Parliament's Economic and Monetary Affairs Committee on 10 April, a week after the trustees' meeting. Tweedie's statement summarized much of the discussions and conclusions of the trustees' meeting, and one of its two main messages was that the IASB was trying hard to listen and respond to concerns expressed in Europe with respect to the IASB's governance and work programme.[96] Although this was not Tweedie's first appearance before the European Parliament, he acknowledged the need to 'rectify' the previous lack of regular contact with the Parliament. The other key message of Tweedie's speech was that the US SEC was close to lifting its 20-F reconciliation requirement. This message was delivered less explicitly, and Tweedie was careful to deny that he was making any prediction, but the range of facts and circumstances which he cited all pointed towards a high probability that use of IFRSs would be allowed in the United States by foreign and, in due course, perhaps even US companies. Both Tweedie and the trustees must have been well aware that demonstrable progress towards acceptance of IFRSs in the United States would be more effective in removing objections to the IASB or IFRSs in Europe than anything they could do or say themselves. They would also have known, conversely, that a conspicuous political conflict over one of the IASB's standards in Europe at this point in time would not be helpful in encouraging the SEC to make its decision.[97]

---

[94] IASCF trustees meeting of 2–3 April 2007, agenda paper 9B.

[95] IASCF trustees meeting of 2–3 April 2007, minutes D and G; see also agenda paper 3B.

[96] 'Statement by IASB Chairman Sir David Tweedie before the Economic and Monetary Affairs Committee of the European Parliament', 10 April 2007. Expressed more compactly, the trustees' press release 'Summary of the IASC Foundation Trustee Meeting April 2007', dated 23 April 2007, includes the same points as Tweedie's 10 April statement.

[97] In a further letter to the European Commission, dated 29 June 2007, the IMA wrote that 'we do not believe that [our reservations on IFRS 8] should stand in the way of the broad aims of convergence and in particular, the proposed consultation announced by the SEC on 24 April 2007 on changes to its

9.6.5 Defusing the Conflict

In the European Parliament's calendar, both IFRS 8 and Radwan's report on the IASB were scheduled for discussion in the latter part of 2007. It would seem that, during the Parliament's summer break, the relations between the EU and the IASB had improved, not least because of the SEC's actions. As discussed in Chapter 8, the SEC had approved a rule proposal in June to lift the reconciliation requirement, and in July it approved a concept release contemplating the voluntary use of IFRSs by US companies.

In July, the ECOFIN Council had received and accepted a second report by the European Commission on the governance and funding of the IASB. The significance of the trustees' decisions at their April meeting now became clear, as the various measures announced by the trustees formed the basis for a generally positive assessment by the Commission and the Council. Even though the Council was somewhat more guarded in its wording, both EU institutions acknowledged that steps had been taken in the right direction. It remained to be seen how the IASB would implement its plans with respect to, for instance, impact assessments, and issues such as 'geographically balanced representation' were again marked for continued attention.[98] Nonetheless, two of the three main EU institutions were indicating that the IASB, though by no means perfect, was certainly acceptable enough to remain in good standing with the EU.

The IASB continued its plans to build better relations with the third main institution, the European Parliament. On 10 July, the same day as the ECOFIN meeting, Bertrand Collomb, the French vice chairman of the IASC Foundation, accompanied by the German trustee, Max Dietrich Kley, appeared before the Parliament's Economic and Monetary Affairs Committee. In his statement, Collomb reminded the committee of the ongoing developments at the SEC, which he characterized as a 'breakthrough', vindicating the IASB's convergence strategy. In an apparent attempt to allay some of the concerns expressed over IFRS 8, he observed:

> To my mind, this is a sign that the momentum is behind IFRSs and a more principle-based approach to accounting, and not—as some fear—a movement towards exporting US GAAP to the international system.[99]

In addition, Collomb could announce a further modification of the IASB's due process. In their July meeting, the trustees had accepted a proposal from the Board that, henceforth, new standards and major interpretations would include a clause calling for a post-implementation review after two full years of implementation.

rules to allow the use of IFRS in financial reports filed by foreign private issuers registered with the Commission' <http://www.investmentfunds.org.uk> accessed through web.archive.

[98] 'Commission Services Working Paper on Governance and Funding Developments in the IASB (International Accounting Standards Board) and IASCF (International Accounting Standards Committee Foundation), 2nd Report', no date [July 2007] <http://ec.europa.eu/internal_market/accounting>; '2813st Council Meeting, Economic and Financial Affairs, Brussels, 10 July 2007', press release 11464/06 (Presse 160), 13–14 <http://europa.eu/rapid>.

[99] 'Prepared Statement of Bertrand Collomb, Vice Chairman of the International Accounting Standards Committee Foundation, before the Open Coordinators Meeting of the Economic and Monetary Affairs Committee of the European Parliament, 10 July 2007' <http://www.iasplus.com>.

Collomb emphasized that this would apply to IFRS 8, even though it had already been published, as well as to IFRIC 12 on service concessions and to modifications following from the business combinations project.

In preparation of the European Parliament's debate on IFRS 8, the Commission's staff produced its 'analysis of potential effects' in September 2007.[100] The staff had struggled to find a proper approach to this task. This was not surprising given that the IASB at this stage had done little more than express its intention to conduct impact assessments in the future, and was still in the earliest stages of articulating the objectives and methods of such studies. It was clear that EFRAG was better equipped than the Commission to conduct impact assessments, however defined, and that EFRAG would in the future be asked to play a role in this respect. But in this particular case it would have been awkward to ask EFRAG to review its own advice that endorsement of IFRS 8 was in the European interest. Apart from reviewing the IASB's and EFRAG's due processes, as well some of the same academic literature that the IASB had already reviewed, the Commission relied heavily on public consultations through a hasty questionnaire survey of users, auditors, preparers, and academics. It was perhaps not a strong report, but it did provide the basis for the Commission's recommendation that IFRS 8 be endorsed.

Attempts were made in the United Kingdom to keep the controversy over IFRS 8 alive. Richard Murphy continued to make the case for country-by-country disclosures. Tim Bush, of Hermes Pensions Management, pursued the line of criticism opened up by the IMA and other UK investor and financial statement user groups. Prem Sikka, an academic at the University of Essex known for airing his distrust of the corporate sector in public commentary, cited the alleged unresponsiveness of the IASB to the concerns of both investors and non-governmental organizations to point out 'the folly of allowing private organizations to make public policies'.[101] At the same time, these broader policy issues continued to be explored in the European Parliament by Alexander Radwan, who circulated a revised draft of his report in September 2007.[102] Repeating the criticism that the IASB is 'undemocratic and outside of democratic control', his report called, among other things, for a forum of stakeholders, including legislators, to appoint the IASC Foundation trustees. The Parliament's Legal Affairs Committee, in its advice on the Radwan report, suggested wording for a draft Parliamentary resolution, including the statement that IASB 'lacks democratic control and pluralistic input', and criticizing the 'increasingly theoretical dimension of the IASB's projects'.[103]

---

[100] 'Endorsement of IFRS 8 *Operating Segments*: Analysis of Potential Effects—Report', MARKT F3 D(2007), 3 September 2007 <http://ec.europa.eu/internal_market/accounting>.

[101] Prem Sikka, 'Unaccountable', comment posted 4 September 2007 <http://www.guardian.co. uk>. On Murphy, see the posts from September–November 2007 at <http://www.taxresearch.org. uk>. Tim Bush, 'IFRS 8: What Is it Good For?', *Accountancy Age*, 20 September 2007, 9. See also Prem Sikka, 'There's No Accounting for Accountants', comment posted 29 August 2007 <http:// www.guardian.co.uk>.

[102] 'Draft report on International Financial Reporting Standards (IFRS) and the Governance of the IASB', 24 September 2007, ECON_PR(2007)392258 <http://www.europarl.europa.eu>.

[103] 'Opinion of the Committee on Legal Affairs for the Committee on Economic and Monetary Affairs on International Financial Reporting Standards (IFRS) and the Governance of the IASB (2006/ 2248(INI))', 5 October 2007, PE 388.441v02-00 <http://www.europarl.europa.eu>.

The IASB, for its part, continued to devote a considerable share of its corporate communications activities to develop its relations with members of the European Parliament.[104] However, some oil was also poured on the fire when Gerrit Zalm, who had recently assumed the chairmanship of the IASC Foundation trustees, was quoted in the press in October saying that: 'One of my first priorities will be no new carve-outs in Europe and trying to get rid of the existing carve-out, because if Europe is doing this, other countries could get the same inspiration and then all the advantages of the one programme fade away.'[105] This was not likely to go down well with parliamentarians who were about to demonstrate by a vote on one of the IASB's standards that they had a full right to an independent view on which accounting standards were suitable for Europe.

Nonetheless, it seemed that at least the Parliament was satisfied that its main point had been sufficiently made. This point was not so much that IFRS 8 was deficient, or that the Parliament wished to be involved in detailed discussions of individual standards, but rather that IFRSs should be developed and endorsed with appropriate procedures and under democratic control.[106] When the Parliament accepted the proposed endorsement of IFRS 8 on 14 November 2007, it did so with a motion in which it stressed that 'Parliament will actively use its right of scrutiny' and underlined 'that the IASB/International Accounting Standards Committee Foundation and the Commission in particular must therefore engage more closely with the Parliament and EU stakeholders than they have done to date'. In the motion, the Commission was taken to task for the deficiencies of its impact assessment, and instructed to do better with respect to future standards. The IASB was reminded 'that the convergence of accounting rules is not a one-sided process where one party simply copies the financial reporting standards of the other party'.[107] The Commission had tried to keep the issue of country-by-country disclosure separate from the endorsement of IFRS 8, a point that the Parliament was now willing to accept. Yet in its motion it expected future action by the Commission and the IASB, and it would keep the issue alive.[108]

To the extent that the Parliament did exercise its right of 'scrutiny' during the next few years with respect to the endorsement of the IASB's standards, it did so in a more low-key fashion than over IFRS 8. EFRAG regularly published 'endorsement updates' on its website, a table in which the endorsement status of each

---

[104] IASCF trustees meeting of 31 October–1 November 2007, agenda paper 11A, paragraphs 4–9.

[105] 'Europe Told Not to Disrupt Move to Global Accounting Standards', *Financial Times*, 18 October 2007, 19. See also 'IASB Chair Sparks Fresh Tensions with European Regulators', *Accountancy Age*, 25 October 2008, 4; 'Europe Called Threat to Accounting Convergence', news item posted 18 October 2007 <http://www.cfo.com>.

[106] See remarks by Berès and Radwan cited in 'Convergence is More than "Cut and Paste"', *Accountancy Age*, 27 September 2007, 2; remarks by Radwan cited in '"Die Aufgabe der Politik bei IFRS wird nicht verstanden"', *Börsen-Zeitung*, 17 November 2007, 11; interview with Alexander Radwan, 19 April 2010.

[107] European Parliament resolution of 14 November 2007, P6_TA(2007)0526, paragraphs 7, 2, 9, and 3 <http://www.europarl.europa.eu>.

[108] See for instance the letter from Jörgen Holmquist to Richard Murphy, dated 12 June 2007, accessible through Murphy's post of 3 July 2007 <http://www.taxresearch.org.uk>. See also European Parliament resolution of 23 September 2008 on the follow-up to the Monterrey Conference of 2002 on financing for Development 2008/2050(INI), P6_TA(2008)0420, paragraph 24 <http://www.europarl.europa.eu>.

individual standard, amendment, or interpretation was monitored and in which separate columns provided space to tick off the votes by EFRAG and the ARC as they occurred. For a while, during 2008, it added a column providing for opinions by the European Parliament and the Council. As this column was completely blank, it gave the ominous impression that both bodies might interfere, unpredictably, at any moment. The column disappeared early in 2009, and no further resolutions comparable to the one on IFRS 8 were passed, or even taken up, by the European Parliament. This did not mean that it lost interest in the IASB, but henceforth this interest was largely confined to the high-level issues of the IASB's governance. From late 2007 onwards, these issues concentrated on the formation of a Monitoring Board, which therefore figured prominently in the motion finally adopted by the Parliament, in April 2008, on the basis of the Radwan report.[109]

The EU endorsement process settled down into a new, but more complicated, routine. As discussed above, the creation of SARG had already introduced an extra step, and now the debate over IFRS 8 had added impact assessments to the endorsement process. As indicated above, the IASB had accepted that such assessments were ultimately its responsibility, but for the time being it fell to the European Commission to make sure that an adequate assessment was made of the effects of new standards that were already in the endorsement pipeline. Doing the impact study on IFRS 8 had shown just how much of a burden this would be on the Commission's slender accounting staff, so that it was keen to entrust this work to EFRAG.[110]

---

[109] 'European Parliament Resolution of 24 April 2008 on International Financial Reporting Standards (IFRS) and the Governance of the International Accounting Standards Board (IASB)', P6_TA (2008)0183 <http://www.europarl.europa.eu>.

[110] Summary record of ARC meeting of 1 October 2007, minute II.

10

Adopt or Adapt

Diversity in Acceptance of IFRSs

The year 2005 saw the transition to IFRSs by listed companies in a number of jurisdictions, in particular the member states of the European Union (EU), Australia, Hong Kong, and South Africa. Although each of these jurisdictions had followed its own road towards IFRSs, as discussed in Chapter 4, the shared significance of the 2005 date made it easy to see them together as a 'first wave' of IFRS adopters. This designation implied that there was also a subsequent 'second wave', and, indeed, momentum in favour of IFRSs continued after 2005. Preparations by the US Securities and Exchange Commission (SEC) for lifting the Form 20-F reconciliation requirement for IFRS users (see Chapter 8) were vital in sustaining this momentum. But it also found expression in decisions in a number of major economies to adopt IFRSs or at least to commit to convergence with IFRSs. The first part of this chapter consists of a discussion of four of these countries: Canada, China, South Korea, and Japan. Other countries also considered their policies with respect to IFRSs, and some of these, including India and Brazil, are discussed in Chapter 15. The four countries discussed in this chapter took important, but different, policy decisions with respect to IFRSs in the period 2005–7; whereas Canada and South Korea committed unreservedly to a mandatory use of IFRSs by their listed companies, China and Japan were not ready to do so. They adopted policies to make significant changes to national standards, adapting them to IFRSs, but stopping short of full adoption.

By the second half of the decade there was a growing realization that the IASB's oft-proclaimed success of 'more than a hundred countries' allowing or requiring the use of IFRSs covered a complex reality of straightforward IFRS adoption, local adaptations known as jurisdictional variations, and uneven compliance. The second part of the chapter describes how the IASB and other organizations attempted to respond to such threats to the 'IFRS brand'.

10.1 CANADA CHOOSES IFRSs OVER US GAAP

During the era of the IASC, from 1973 to 2000, the Canadian delegation, including especially its members from the Canadian Institute of Chartered Accountants (CICA)—the original and subsequently the lead sponsor of the Canadian delegation—was the most enthusiastic of all of the delegations in supporting the IASC's mission to develop a single, global set of accounting standards.[1]

Canada's securities market was very small compared with those in New York, Tokyo, and London—about 3 per cent of the global capital market. Foreign multinationals listed in these other markets which were seeking to list also on the Toronto Stock Exchange were usually not willing to endure the cost of conforming to Canadian generally accepted accounting principles (GAAP), which, while largely similar to US GAAP, nonetheless reflected many differences. Foreign flows of capital in and out were important to the Canadian market.[2] In this respect, until 2004, Canada had much in common with South Africa and Australia, when they too moved towards adoption of IFRSs. Beginning in 2004, the Canadian Securities Administrators (CSA) allowed Canadian companies registered with the SEC to file their financial statements in Canada using US GAAP.[3] Prior to this important change, the hundreds of Canadian companies that were SEC registrants had to reconcile their shareholders' equity and earnings to US GAAP, which was a costly process. Hence, beginning in 2004, Canadian companies registered with the SEC were like companies in Japan (since 1978) and Germany (since 1998) that were registered with the SEC in that they were authorized to use US GAAP in filings in their home countries.

In the late 1990s, the CICA leadership was looking for a way towards supplanting its GAAP by a set of standards recognized and accepted internationally. In 1998, the CICA published the final report of its Task Force on Standard Setting (known as TFOSS).[4] The task force proposed two linked options: harmonizing more closely with US GAAP, thus eliminating the differences, while at the same time continuing to work actively with the IASC to establish a single set of global standards (pages 23–4). TFOSS thus tried to ride two horses at the same time. The following year, the Certified General Accountants Association of Canada (CGA-Canada), another sponsor of the Canadian delegation to the IASC and a rival body to the CICA, announced a policy position in favour of the adoption in Canada of IASs to replace Canadian GAAP.[5] Probably reacting to the TFOSS report, it argued that the adoption of the Financial Accounting Standards Board's (FASB)

---

[1] Kees Camfferman and Stephen A. Zeff, *Financial Reporting and Global Capital Markets: A History of the International Accounting Standards Committee, 1973–2000* (Oxford: Oxford University Press, 2007), 7, 165–6. Much of the discussion in this section is based on 'IFRS: Canada's Decision', a case prepared in 2011 for the Richard Ivey School of Business, The University of Western Ontario, which consists of an extensive recorded interview with Paul G. Cherry. Citations to the Cherry interview are keyed to 'Cherry interview'. He was the full-time chairman of Canada's Accounting Standards Board from May 2001 to June 2009. The authors are grateful to Patricia O'Malley, Marion Kirsh, and Paul Cherry for advice received on this section. For another analysis of the IFRS developments in Canada, see Karthik Ramanna, 'The International Politics of IFRS Harmonization', *Accounting, Economics, and Law—A Convivium*, 3/2 (April 2013), 12–16.

[2] Cherry interview, 5.

[3] National Instrument 52–107 *Acceptable Accounting Principles, Auditing Standards and Reporting Currency* (CSA, January 2004), accessible at <http://www.osc.gov.on.ca>. See also 'Canadian Regulators Okay Use of US GAAP', news item posted 14 May 2003 <http://www.accountingweb.com>.

[4] CICA Task Force on Standard Setting, *Final Report* (Toronto: CICA, 1998).

[5] *The Case for International Accounting Standards in Canada* (Vancouver, BC: Certified General Accountants Association of Canada, 1999).

standards was a 'flawed choice'. That Canadian GAAP was being set by a board of the CICA, in which CGA-Canada had declined to cooperate as an invited participant, could have been one reason why CGA-Canada would have liked to see Canadian GAAP supplanted by IASs.

In 2001, Tricia O'Malley, a former KPMG partner who, in 2000, had become the full-time chairman of Canada's Accounting Standards Board (AcSB), became one of the founding members of the IASB. Paul Cherry, a former chief accountant of the Ontario Securities Commission and a former partner in Pricewaterhouse-Coopers, succeeded her as the AcSB chairman until June 2009. Cherry had also served in the Canadian delegation to the IASC from 1989 to 1995 and 1999 to 2000.

Under Cherry's leadership, the AcSB then began an extended consultation over two years with the AcSB's constituents about the best path for Canada to follow in accounting standards.[6] In May 2004, the AcSB issued an invitation to comment and an accompanying discussion paper, seeking advice on its five-year strategic plan for 2006–11.[7] The board said that its current strategy, following TFOSS, was to set its own GAAP while working to support the international convergence of accounting standards and harmonizing with US GAAP. It asked for comments on whether the board should instead adopt either US GAAP or IFRSs for all entities in place of its own GAAP. After studying the sixty-eight comments received, hearing the views of 106 individuals who attended roundtable meetings, and conferring with key stakeholder groups, the board issued another invitation to comment in March 2005 in which it proposed its strategic plan to begin a transitional period, expected to be five years, towards the eventual adoption of IFRSs for public companies.[8]

Paul Cherry found that the following consensus emerged: 'continuing to have a unique Canadian set of standards did not make sense for our public companies, that U.S. GAAP was absolutely high quality but too expensive, not affordable, and that we do not have the [compliance] infrastructure in place on a consistent basis across the country to deliver against U.S. GAAP.... On that basis, the view was that international standards are the way to go.... If we committed to adopting IFRS, we could have greater influence in its future evolution and keep it on the path that we think is most appropriate.'[9] Canadian thinking was also influenced by the EU's decision in 2002 to require the some 6,700 listed companies in their fifteen member states to adopt IFRSs in their consolidated statements by 2005, as well as by the Australian decision in 2002 to do the same. Another development that may have spurred on the AcSB was the publication in April 2005 by SEC Chief Accountant Don Nicolaisen of his roadmap for the eventual lifting of the Form 20-F reconciliation requirement by 2009 for foreign issuers using IFRSs.

---

[6] For a news report on the evolution of Canadian thinking on IFRSs, see Lawrence Richter Quinn, 'Closing the Gap', *CAmagazine*, 136/6 (August 2003), 16–22.

[7] 'Accounting Standards in Canada: Future Directions', discussion paper and accompanying invitation to comment (Accounting Standards Board, May 2004) <http://www.frascanada.ca>.

[8] 'Invitation to Comment: Accounting Standards in Canada: Future Directions, Draft Strategic Plan' (Accounting Standards Board, 31 March 2005) <http://frascanada.ca>. See also Robert Colapinto, 'The Future Direction of Accounting Standards', *CAmagazine*, 138/4 (May 2005), 20–2.

[9] Cherry interview, 10.

It was clear that IFRSs were gaining significant momentum, and US GAAP had been perceived as losing much of its lustre following the accounting scandals of Enron, WorldCom, and other companies. In addition, since 2004 the European Commission was engaged in assessing Canadian GAAP for equivalence with IFRSs (see Section 9.5). Even if the imposition of an EU reconciliation requirement for Canadian companies seemed just a remote possibility, simply eliminating the question altogether would be a positive side-effect of a Canadian move to IFRSs.

After consulting again with constituents, including the academic community, about how quickly it could develop IFRS educational materials for use in the universities, the AcSB concluded that Canada required a transition period of five years prior to the date for changing over to IFRSs. Cherry knew that the IASB had a number of major projects under way, as part of the programme of convergence with the US FASB (see Chapter 12). Having these projects completed prior to the changeover would make the transition easier.[10]

In January 2006, the AcSB ratified its strategic plan and announced its decision to begin the process of transition towards full adoption of IFRSs.[11] It announced an 'expected' changeover date of 1 January 2011, but it did not commit to the date until February 2008, following a review of the progress until then.[12] It would be the task of the AcSB to incorporate into Canadian GAAP all of the IFRSs in time for the changeover. In the end, the AcSB, companies, audit firms, and users, as well as the academic community, collaborated to complete the transition in time, and IFRSs replaced the *CICA Handbook* on the appointed date, 1 January 2011.[13] At the same time, the CICA disbanded its Emerging Issues Committee, because the interpretations of IFRSs were to be made only by the IASB's interpretations committee in London (known since 2010 as the IFRS Interpretations Committee).

A number of rate-regulated utilities were allowed to defer their transition to IFRSs in the expectation that the IASB would issue a standard on rate-regulated activities. In December 2008, the Board had indeed added such a project to its agenda. But work on the project was suspended in September 2010, because the Board believed that it could not resolve the conceptual and technical issues expeditiously in the light of its effort to complete the major convergence projects by 2011. The subject again made it on the Board's agenda in December 2012 after the IFRS Interpretations Committee, responding to enquiries from Canada and Brazil, decided not to add it to its own agenda. Finally, in January 2014 the Board issued IFRS 14 *Regulatory Deferral Accounts*, 'a limited-scope Standard to provide a short-term, interim solution for rate-regulated entities that had not yet adopted

---

[10] Cherry interview, 10.

[11] See 'Canada's Accounting Standards Board Ratifies its Strategic Plan, Approves Convergence with International Reporting Standards', CICA media release dated 10 January 2006. <http://www.iasplus.com>; 'Canadian Accounting Standards—Global Positioning: The New Direction', *Bulletin #1* of the Accounting Standards Board of Canada (May 2006); and *The CICA's Guide to IFRS in Canada* (Toronto: CICA (2006)) <http://ocaq.qc.ca/pdf/ang/6_presse/infoca/2007/InfoCA1185_Guide_EN. pdf>.

[12] 'Canada's CAs Call Firm IFRS Commencement Date Good News', CICA press release dated 13 February 2008 <http://www.cica.ca>.

[13] See Jeff Buckstein, 'Finishing Touches', *CAmagazine*, 144/1 (January/February 2011), 40–2; and Robert Colapinto, 'IFRS: The First Quarter', *CAmagazine*, 144/6 (August 2011), 28–34.

IFRS' (paragraph IN7). IFRS 14 allowed entities to continue their pre-IFRS recognition and measurement practices for rate-regulated activities, even if these were not in all respects in conformity with the IASB's conceptual framework. Hence, the Canadian utilities were able to complete their adoption of IFRSs. This was the third instance, following insurance contracts (IFRS 4) and extractive industries (IFRS 6), where the IASB used an interim standard to 'grandfather' existing practices. The three dissents on IFRS 14 rehearsed the objections against this approach expressed on the two earlier occasions.

As to the affirmations to be made by both the company and the auditor, in 2010 the CSA, which supported the move to IFRSs, amended National Instrument 52–107 *Acceptable Accounting Principles and Auditing Standards*. In it, the CSA requires the preparation of financial statements in accordance with Canadian GAAP as well as a statement of compliance (by both the company and the auditor) with IFRSs. In the notes to the financial statements as well as in the auditor's report, reference may be made to both Canadian GAAP and IFRSs, or instead only IFRSs.[14] It was appreciated that some years would be required for provincial legislation and contracts which referred to Canadian GAAP to be modified.

In a companion policy to its national instruments on IFRSs, the CSA made crystal clear that companies and auditors must use IFRSs as issued by the IASB and not something altered by their national standard setter. It is interesting that the introduction to Part I of the *CICA Handbook* states, 'International Financial Reporting Standards are incorporated into the Handbook without modification'.

10.2 CHINA

The rise of China was one of the major developments of the decade, and the IASB, among many other organizations, had to come to come to terms with it. Whereas in 2001 China might still have been thought of as being at the margins of the movement towards international accounting harmonization, a few years later it had become much more active in closing the gap. Moreover, because of its firm policy of pursuing convergence but not committing to full adoption of IFRSs, it set an important precedent.

From China's perspective, accounting standards were an integral component of the institutions to be developed in support of the programme of fundamental economic reform and opening to the outside world which it had pursued since the late 1970s and which, particularly from 1992 onwards, ushered in a period of sustained, strong economic growth. While opening to the outside world always was an important element of this programme, the domestic need for strong, stable, and high-quality institutions to manage and support the rapid growth was paramount. Hence, while the development of Chinese accounting standards has been characterized by a willingness to adapt and adjust to international developments, this has consistently been combined with a determination to

---

[14] For National Instrument 52–107, as amended on 1 October 2010, see <http://www.osc.gov.on.ca>.

ensure that the resulting standards are suitable for whatever specific conditions are believed to prevail in China.

From the 1980s onwards, accounting institutions were gradually built up under the guiding hand of the Ministry of Finance, in which a 1985 Accounting Law (revised in 1993) had vested the central authority in all accounting matters. With financial support from the World Bank and technical support from Deloitte, a programme of issuing accounting standards began with the publication of a 'basic standard' in 1993. In a flurry of activity, drafts for a further thirty specific standards were developed over the next three years, but final standards were issued only gradually, from 1997 onwards, as it was realized that the Chinese environment was not yet ready to support such a fully fledged system of accounting standards.[15] By the end of 2001, the last standards in this programme were issued, bringing the total to sixteen.

Meanwhile, companies issuing so-called B-shares (initially for foreign investors only) were required from 1992 onwards to prepare financial statements both according to local regulations and according to IASs.[16] As the IASC's standards rapidly gained in complexity during the 1990s, one assumes that factors inhibiting the development of local standards must have caused practical difficulties in the application of IASs as well. China's interest in the IASC was confirmed in 1997, when the IASC Board met, for the first and only time, in Beijing. From that point onwards, Chinese observers, mainly from the Ministry of Finance, attended most Board meetings. When the IASC was replaced by the IASB in 2001, no mainland Chinese candidates applied, or were nominated, for Board or trustee positions. The Chinese observer position at the IASC was replaced by membership of the IASB's Standards Advisory Council (SAC). This position was initially held by Madame Feng Shuping, who, as director-general of the accounting division in the Ministry of Finance, had welcomed the IASC to Beijing in 1997. China also developed its own international contacts. In February 2002, the Chinese standard setter began a series of meetings with its counterparts in Japan and South Korea to discuss common issues and problems.

Between 2001 and 2004, China did not figure prominently on the IASB's horizon, although Board member Tatsumi Yamada, in addition to his liaison role with the Japanese standard setter, attempted to liaise with China as well. An official of the Ministry of Finance was attached to the IASB staff in 2002–03, but the IASB was mainly preoccupied with Europe and the United States. In China itself, there appeared to be a degree of hesitation about what the next step in the development of its accounting standards should be. However, that China was preparing itself for a next step was fairly clear. In 2001, China had joined the World Trade Organization (WTO) and, although the accession protocol did not contain specific commitments with respect to accounting standards, the Ministry of Finance cited WTO accession as an important motivation for advancing

---

[15] Chen Yugui, *Zhongguo Kuaijizhunze Guoji Xiediao* [International Harmonization of Chinese Accounting Standards] (Beijing: Zhongguo Caizheng Jingji Chubanshe, 2008), 90.

[16] See Chen Shimin, Sun Zheng, and Wang Yuetang, 'Evidence from China on Whether Harmonized Accounting Standards Harmonize Accounting Practices', *Accounting Horizons*, 16/3 (September 2002), 183–97, for background information and descriptive statistics on application of IASs by B-share companies.

accounting reform. In 2002, a target date of 2005 began to circulate.[17] The impression was given that, in 2003 or 2004, some twenty further standards would be added to the suite of sixteen standards already issued up to 2001.[18] This, however, did not happen.

Around the turn of the year from 2004 to 2005, it became clear at the IASB that developments were beginning to move apace in China, although there was some uncertainty about what exactly was happening. In December 2004, the IASB learned with some surprise that Madame Feng, whom David Tweedie had only just met on a visit to Beijing, had been replaced. It took some time before contact with her successor, Wang Jun, was established. Wang had just resumed his already long career at the Ministry of Finance after a four-year break to pursue Ph.D. studies. His appointment marked a turning point in the Chinese accounting standards programme. The significance attached to accounting was further underlined by Wang's rapid promotion to vice minister in 2005. His position as director-general of the accounting division was assumed by Liu Yuting. Liu remained in this position until the end of 2010 and directed the effort to implement the policies set by Wang. Around the time of Wang's appointment, a decision was taken to accelerate the Chinese accounting standards programme.[19]

In April 2005, IASB Board member Tatsumi Yamada was sent to Beijing to learn more about developments there. He was informed about plans of the Ministry of Finance to issue a great number of exposure drafts for new and revised standards during 2005, and was asked whether the IASB could send a team to China to assist in convergence. In addition, the ministry made it known that it wished to continue to be represented on SAC, and that it would like to see a Chinese trustee appointed when the impending revision of the IASB's Constitution would increase the number of trustees from nineteen to twenty-two.[20] The latter issue was not altogether new, and had already been explored in contacts between Tweedie and the Ministry of Finance late in 2004.[21] Although there may have been some hesitation among the trustees about the appointment of government officials as trustees, the significance of China was indisputable. In November 2005, the trustees agreed the appointment of Liu Zhongli, the current president of the Chinese Institute of Certified Public Accountants (within the Ministry of Finance) and former finance minister.

Meanwhile, at the technical level, events were proceeding at a very rapid pace. Responding to the ministry's call, a small IASB team consisting of Yamada and staff members Wayne Upton and Paul Pacter was sent to Beijing in October to

---

[17] Chen Yugui, *Zhongguo Kuaijizhunze*, 55–88; Feng Shuping, 'Strengthen Co-operation to Promote International Convergence of Accounting Standards', speech at the IASB's National Standard Setters' Meeting, 18 November 2002 <http://www.iasplus.com>.

[18] Liu Yuting, *Zhongguo Qiye Kuaijizhunze: Gaige yu Fazhan* [Chinese Business Accounting Standards: Reform and Development] (Beijing: Renmin Chubanshe, 2010), 31; See also Liu Yuting, cited in 'China to Release New Accounting Rules Next Year', *Business Daily Update*, 10 December 2003, accessed through LexisNexis.

[19] Liu Yuting, *Zhongguo Qiye Kuaijizhunze*, 50, refers to a decision 'in 2005' by the Party Committee of the Ministry of Finance.

[20] Undated memo by Tatsumi Yamada, attached to email from Yamada to Tweedie, dated 6 April 2005, IASB archive, 'China' file.

[21] Letter from Tweedie to Feng, dated 18 November 2004, IASB archive, 'China' file.

prepare the way for a visit by a Board delegation, including Tweedie, in November. Pacter's formal position at the IASB, as part-time director for the small and medium-sized entities project, did not perhaps fully reflect how well qualified he was for the China assignment: while with Deloitte in Hong Kong in the early 2000s, he had been deeply involved in that firm's role as consultant to the Ministry of Finance on accounting standards.

Upton and his colleagues soon realized that the IASB was faced with an urgent question of great strategic significance. By October 2005, the ministry had issued some twenty exposure drafts for new standards, and had begun work on revising the previously issued sixteen. The completion date for the entire project was February 2006. This was a project of massive proportions, pushed through at a speed that was incomparably faster than the IASB's due process. The ministry's stated aim was 'convergence in substance', which, as confirmed many times since, meant that the ministry rejected in principle any literal incorporation of IFRSs in Chinese standards, or direct applicability of IFRSs in China. Chinese standards would have their own structure, which could differ significantly from IFRSs, but would be written in order to achieve the same outcomes in terms of accounting numbers in the financial statements. The structure envisaged by the Ministry of Finance, and subsequently realized, was of a basic standard, roughly comparable to the IASB's conceptual framework, and thirty-eight specific standards, ordered by topic, and mostly containing the key, bold-faced paragraphs of the corresponding IASs and IFRSs. These standards would be accompanied by an 'Implementation Guidance' (*yingyong zhinan*) supplement for most standards, which would still be relatively brief compared to the IASB's texts. The bulk of the detailed requirements of IFRSs, and perhaps more, would be included in so-called 'Explanatory Guidance' (*jiangjie*), issued by the Ministry of Finance, ostensibly as educational material.[22] Such a three-layered approach was not new: already by 2000, similar 'implementation guidance' and 'explanatory guidance' had been developed for the standards extant at that point. But when the IASB team visited in October 2005, little if any of the supplementary documents for the new or revised standards were as yet available, let alone in English translation. As none of the IASB team could read Chinese, they had to base their views on the degree of convergence likely to be reached on English translations of the rather skeletal specific standards, as well as on advice from two Big Four representatives from Hong Kong who provided assistance in the discussions. As Upton wrote to Tweedie from Beijing: 'we are taking a lot on faith here.'[23] Yet there was little time to ponder these issues because, as indicated above, the ministry was planning the launch of the new set of standards for next February. Moreover, the Ministry of Finance made known that it would be pleased to have a public statement by the IASB in which it welcomed the new standards and acknowledged a high degree of convergence, or equivalence, with IFRSs.[24]

---

[22] For these plans see Liu Yuting's December 2005 statements reproduced in Liu Yuting, *Zhongguo Qiye Kuaijizhunze*, 47.

[23] 'Progress Report on MoF Meetings', memo by Wayne Upton to David Tweedie, dated 4 October 2005, IASB archive, 'China' file.

[24] Email from Tatsumi Yamada to David Tweedie, dated 4 October 2005, IASB archive, 'China' file.

The reaction of the IASB's team, after detailed discussions with the Ministry of Finance, was one of cautious optimism. They were clearly impressed by the determination of the ministry to pursue convergence, and by its willingness to make very significant changes to the draft standards on the basis of advice from the IASB representatives. Yet concerns remained over the possibility that the yet-to-be-developed implementation guidance might undermine the principles in the standards. In addition, there were evident gaps in the standards, such as a complete omission of any discussion of defined benefit pension plans, which were said not to exist in China. Finally, there remained a small number of acknowledged differences between the Chinese standards and IFRSs. These included a prohibition on the reversal of impairment losses, the treatment of government grants as an addition to capital, and a requirement to use 'pooling of interests' for business combinations under common control.[25]

Based on these findings, Tweedie wrote to Wang Jun in October to express the IASB's appreciation of the ministry's commitment to move towards IFRSs, and its understanding of the reasons why China was choosing a particular approach to convergence. He reiterated that the IASB encourages countries to adopt IFRSs in full, and that convergence should be seen as a 'process towards full adoption'. He added that, 'As a matter of policy, the IASB does not express a view about whether a jurisdiction or a standard is "converged with" or "equivalent to" IFRS'.[26] Evidently, these points required further discussion between the ministry and the IASB.

In November 2005, Tweedie visited Beijing with a delegation of Board members. At the conclusion of the visit, Tweedie and Wang issued a joint statement, sometimes referred to as the 'Beijing Agreement'. In the statement, the Chinese side reiterated the view that convergence, not adoption, was the objective: 'China stated that convergence is one of the fundamental goals of their standard-setting programme, with the intention that an enterprise applying CASs [Chinese Accounting Standards] should produce financial statements that are the same as those of an enterprise that applies IFRSs. How to converge with IFRSs is a matter for China to determine.'[27]

The IASB's position that full adoption should be the end point was not repeated. Instead, the joint statement said: 'The IASB notes that, in converging their national standards with IFRSs, some countries add provisions and implementation guidance not included in IFRSs to reflect the circumstances of those countries. This is a pragmatic and advisable approach with which China agrees.' Allowing for the differences in circumstances, this was at least a different tone than in the 'take it or leave it' view expressed by the IASB to the European Commission two years earlier, during the acrimonious debates preceding the EU carve-outs.

The IASB's willingness to reach out to China was further underlined on 15 February 2006, when David Tweedie attended, as expected, the ceremony in Beijing at which the new set of standards was presented. In his speech, Tweedie

---

[25] Memo from Wayne Upton to Board members, dated 9 October 2005, IASB archive, 'China' file.
[26] Letter from David Tweedie to Wang Jun, dated 18 October 2005, IASB archive, 'China' file.
[27] 'Joint Statement of the Secretary-General of the China Accounting Standards Committee and the Chairman of the International Accounting Standards Board', 8 November 2005 <http://www.ifrs.org>.

observed, 'The adoption of the new Chinese accounting standards system brings about substantial convergence between Chinese standards and International Financial Reporting Standards (IFRSs), as set by the International Accounting Standards Board (IASB)'.[28]

The Ministry of Finance also suggested a modification of IFRSs. Applying IAS 24 *Related Party Disclosures* without an exception for state-owned entities would be very onerous for a country like China, although not only there. This issue had already been raised earlier in the International Financial Reporting Interpretations Committee (IFRIC), but this time the Board agreed to add an item to its agenda.[29] An exposure draft was issued in 2007, and a revised standard in 2009.

10.3 SOUTH KOREA

From 1988 to 1992, South Korea sent a delegation to the Board of the IASC, but this did not, apparently, produce a strong interest in IASs within the country. The East Asian financial crisis of 1997 was a precipitating factor in creating such an interest among South Korean leaders. With encouragement from the International Bank for Reconstruction and Development and the International Monetary Fund, a newly created standard setter, the Korea Accounting Standards Board (KASB), began reforming Korean GAAP to become closer to IASs/IFRSs, such that about 90 per cent convergence was achieved by 2006. A further expression of South Korean interest in IFRSs was in the KASB's series of joint meetings with the standard setters in China and Japan beginning in February 2002, which continue today, to discuss common problems and issues. Yet the domestic and international capital markets did not credit the country's improvement in financial reporting transparency, and a 'Korean discount' persisted. Leaders also took note of the many countries or regions moving to adopt IFRSs, especially the EU, Australia, and Canada. Another factor was the move by the EU to review the equivalence of foreign countries' GAAPs with IFRSs.[30] Without such equivalence, those countries' companies trading in European securities markets would have to reconcile their GAAP to IFRSs. This prospect may have been considered more seriously in South Korea than in Canada.

In February 2006, the government appointed a broad-based task force to look into the appropriateness of adopting IFRSs and to prepare a roadmap. Finally, on 15 March 2007, the country's Financial Supervisory Commission (FSC) and the KASB held a ceremony in Seoul to announce a roadmap which called for a transition from South Korean accounting standards to mandatory adoption of IFRSs by listed companies. As in China a year before, the Korean side attached great importance to the fact that David Tweedie, accompanied by Tatsumi Yamada, was present on the occasion. According to the roadmap, the transition to IFRSs would take place on 1 January 2011, with voluntary adoption beginning

---

[28] 'China Affirms Commitment to Converge with IFRSs', IASB press release dated 15 February 2006.

[29] For the Chinese suggestion, see AP 5/2006 paper 6, paragraph 2 and 29–34.

[30] Communication to the authors from Chungwoo Suh, dated 1 April 2014.

in 2009 for all but financial service companies. The decision had come as a surprise both to the IASB and to Japan.

The press release that was issued on the day following the announcement ceremony said, 'it has been generally assumed that the level of confidence of foreign investors and others in Korea's corporate accounting has not matched the efforts undertaken thus far, in part because of accounting standards that differ from IFRS and other globally prevailing standards'.[31]

When word had reached the IASB of the decision prior to the announcement ceremony, there had been some uncertainty about the nature and scope of the KASB's commitment—for example, would it be a staged convergence or actually an adoption? South Korea's planned adoption of IFRSs involved two carve-outs: proportionate consolidation from IAS 31 and the immediate expensing of borrowing costs from IAS 23.[32] Both were options under IFRSs in 2007, but South Korea correctly anticipated their eventual elimination by the IASB. It is understood that the KASB had planned to modify certain other standards, but the IASB dissuaded it from doing so. In the end, South Korea adopted IFRSs fully.

In March 2013, the KASB, together with the Financial Supervisory Service, the regulator which operates under the oversight of the FSC, published a 110-page book, *IFRS Adoption and Implementation in Korea, and the Lessons Learned*, which treats the adoption and implementation process at length.[33] It was revealed that fourteen entities early-adopted IFRSs in 2009, and a further fifty-nine entities early-adopted IFRSs in 2010. A total of 3,126 entities, including 1,783 listed entities, began applying IFRSs in 2011. Under South Korean GAAP, companies and their auditors were much more accustomed to having specific and detailed guidance than was available under IFRSs. The KASB wrote candidly about the 'hardship' involved in the transition to IFRSs:

> The IFRS adoption process in Korea was rather a bumpy ride: there were troubles relating to unexpected additional costs, lack of accounting professionals, unwelcoming public sentiment, etc. While trying to overcome the stumbling blocks, however, Korea realised that the followings are essential in promoting successful implementation of IFRS in any country: invigorating discussions about IFRS among constituents at home and abroad; preventing the psychological stress of stakeholders from getting exaggerated by providing sufficient education and promotion of IFRS; and receiving more robust support from the IFRS Foundation.[34]

In regard to support from the IFRS Foundation, from the first half of 2009, Wayne Upton, the IASB's director of international activities, travelled to Seoul every six or eight months to provide a kind of implementation support for companies and auditors who were still used to a more detailed accounting regimen—a Korean IFRIC, as he has called it. Companies and audit firms prepared detailed papers, and he participated in a publicly aired conversation, without drawing

[31] 'Road Map for the Adoption of International Financial Reporting Standards', FSC press release dated 16 March 2007 <http://www.fsc.go.kr>.

[32] 'Korea: Convergence with IFRS', *World Accounting Report*, April 2007, 15.

[33] *IFRS Adoption and Implementation in Korea, and the Lessons Learned: IFRS Country Report*, Korea Accounting Standards Board/Financial Supervisory Service [March 2013] <http://eng.kasb.or.kr>. Much of the history in this section is drawn from this report.

[34] *IFRS Adoption and Implementation in Korea*, 9.

conclusions but nonetheless providing insight into how to think through problems of application.[35] While this form of support was much appreciated by the KASB, it ventured the suggestion that a single director of international activities might be hard-pressed to handle all of the communications between the IASB and the growing number of countries requiring support in their adoption of IFRSs. Another note of criticism was that 'the IFRS Foundation and IASB may have been more active in resolving the issues raised by European nations or accounting firms who are major financial contributors to the IFRS Foundation, rather than the issues raised by new adopters of IFRS'.[36] In 2011, South Korea contributed £437,000, organized through the KASB, to the IFRS Foundation, exceeded in Asia/Oceania only by Japan, China, and Australia.

The first South Korean to serve as an IFRS Foundation trustee was Duck-Koo Chung, whose appointment began on 1 January 2011, coincident, as it happens, with the effective date of his country's adoption of IFRSs. He was formerly a minister of commerce, industry, and energy. The first South Korean Board member, Chungwoo Suh, was appointed on 1 July 2012. He was an accounting professor at Kookmin University, Seoul, and was the KASB chairman from 2008 to 2011, when he led the preparations to adopt IFRSs. He holds a Ph.D. in Accountancy from the University of Illinois at Champaign-Urbana.

10.4 JAPAN SEEKS ITS PLACE IN THE CONVERGENCE PROCESS

As seen in Section 4.6, there was a widely shared view in Japan during the first years of the decade that the international accounting landscape should be organized on the basis of the mutual recognition of equivalence of three sets of high-quality standards: IFRS, US GAAP, and Japanese GAAP. Some thought that the quality of Japanese GAAP, as it was, provided a sufficient basis for such a recognition. Others recognized that the acceptance of this vision outside Japan also required an ongoing, active Japanese participation in the movement of accounting standards convergence that was building up around the IASB and IFRSs. The importance of convergence was brought home in 2004 by the start of the EU's programme of assessing the equivalence of Japanese GAAP and IFRSs. The implication that the continued use of Japanese GAAP in European capital markets was not a foregone conclusion was taken very seriously in Japan, perhaps more so than in all other countries subject to the EU's assessment. The result had been that the Accounting Standards Board of Japan (ASBJ) and the IASB announced, in January 2005, a joint project to reduce differences between their standards.

Beginning in the first quarter of 2005, representatives of the two boards began holding semi-annual meetings, alternately in Tokyo and London. The first meeting was held on 9–10 March in Tokyo, with the IASB sending five members plus

---

[35] Interview with Wayne Upton, 7 July 2011; see also *IFRS Adoption and Implementation in Korea*, 95.
[36] *IFRS Adoption and Implementation in Korea*, 97.

senior staff to confer with four members of the ASBJ. IASB Chairman David Tweedie and the ASBJ's full-time Chairman Shizuki Saito headed their respective delegations.[37]

Despite the initiative to hold these meetings, the relationship between the IASB and the ASBJ during the next few years was not easy. The ASBJ continued to pursue the idea of mutual recognition in which Japanese GAAP would maintain its place next to IFRSs and US GAAP, with a continuous exchange of ideas among the three standard setters on an equal footing. This idea was not shared by the IASB, nor was it in line with events outside Japan.

The stated aim of the joint IASB–ASBJ project was to revise IFRSs when Japanese GAAP was found to be superior to IFRSs, and vice versa.[38] It turned out that, of the various possible modifications of IFRSs put forward by the ASBJ, the IASB accepted only one minor point. When the IASB undertook to solve the problem of Chinese state-owned enterprises by amending IAS 24 *Related Party Disclosures*, it included in the project a clarification of the definition of a related party at the suggestion of the ASBJ.[39] Apart from this point, narrowing the differences between IFRSs and Japanese GAAP became a one-sided exercise of aligning Japanese GAAP with IFRSs. The ASBJ started several projects on topics where differences had been identified.

Meanwhile, in June 2005, the Committee of European Securities Regulators (CESR) provided the European Commission with its technical advice as part of the EU's assessment of the equivalence of the GAAPs of Japan, Canada, and the United States with IFRSs.[40] As regards Japan, CESR's advice was that Japanese GAAP 'as a whole, [is] equivalent to IFRS' (paragraph 2). But its recommendation that Japanese GAAP be accepted as equivalent to IFRSs was qualified by the proposal that Japanese GAAP be amended with 'remedies' (mainly additional disclosures) for twenty-six specific differences (pages 44–62). CESR's advice was perceived by many in Japan as a verdict that Japanese GAAP was not up to standard. This was painful, although some would say that CESR's analysis had its shortcomings, too. The prevailing view was that the ASBJ had to show greater determination to converge Japanese GAAP with IFRSs, to safeguard the interests of Japanese companies raising capital in Europe.

The accelerating pace of convergence between IFRSs and US GAAP was quickly becoming another source of concern in Japan. The 2005 roadmap of the SEC chief accountant, followed by the February 2006 Memorandum of Understanding (MoU) between the IASB and the FASB (see Chapters 8 and 12) showed the increasing possibility that the SEC would eliminate the Form 20-F reconciliation requirement for IFRS users by 2009, without any prospect of a similar move with respect to Japanese GAAP. This naturally raised fears that Japanese GAAP would be relegated to second-tier status, and again resulted in calls on the ASBJ to act.

---

[37] 'The ASBJ and the IASB Hold Initial Meeting on Joint Project for Convergence', ASBJ press release dated 11 March 2005 <https://www.asb.or.jp>.

[38] Interview with Tatsumi Yamada, 19 May 2011.

[39] AP 5/2006 paper 6, paragraphs 19–27.

[40] 'Technical Advice on Equivalence of Certain Third Country GAAP and on Description of Certain Third Countries Mechanisms of Enforcement of Financial Information' (CESR, June 2005) <http://www.esma.europa.eu>.

One policy option open to the ASBJ was simply to converge unilaterally with IFRSs in order to eliminate the differences identified by CESR. However, IFRSs were a moving target because of the major overhaul of standards envisaged in the 2006 IASB–FASB MoU. Rather than waiting passively for the outcome of this process, another policy option for the ASBJ was to pursue a tripartite solution, by seeking a place at the table with the IASB and the FASB. The ASBJ's actions are perhaps best interpreted as an attempt to pursue both options simultaneously.

In January 2006, the ASBJ issued a report, 'Statement on Japan's Progress toward Convergence between Japanese GAAP and IFRSs', in which it reviewed its convergence project with the IASB, and set out its plans for addressing CESR's list of differences.[41] A large part of the report could be read as a statement of a unilateral convergence policy. The report showed that by then the ASBJ was planning work on a wide range of topics, partly identified in the convergence project with the IASB, and partly resulting from CESR's assessment. The ASBJ's timetable was still somewhat indeterminate, because for many issues it listed the prospects for 2008 as 'at least a tentative discussion'. In defence of what might look like a cautious approach, the ASBJ pointed to the ongoing convergence efforts of the IASB and the FASB, which were likely to change many of the existing differences between IFRSs and Japanese GAAP.

In the course of 2006, signs of impatience appeared with the ASBJ's open-ended planning. In June 2006, Nippon Keidanren issued a position paper in which it expressed its concern over the possible 'isolation of Japanese GAAP' and called for an acceleration of the convergence of accounting standards.[42] In July 2006, as if to echo this sentiment, the Planning and Coordination Committee of the Financial Services Agency's Business Accounting Council, citing the timetable for the EU's equivalency assessment, called upon the ASBJ to shift to a more proactive approach to convergence. The committee urged the ASBJ to develop a 'time-framed convergence programme' so that acceptable progress could be achieved by early 2008, in time for the EU's assessment report which would lead to its final decision on equivalency.[43]

At the same time, the idea of building a three-legged world based on US GAAP, IFRSs, and Japanese GAAP continued to be supported in Japan. At a high level came the announcement in January 2006 by Japan's Financial Services Agency (FSA) and the US SEC of terms for establishing a structure and agenda for a dialogue between the two bodies.[44] This was to involve regular meetings between high-level representatives, with an ad hoc information exchange at the staff level. Among the topics to be taken up were accounting and auditing standards. The dialogue was patterned closely on a similar dialogue announced in 2004 by the

---

[41] 'Statement on Japan's Progress toward Convergence between Japanese GAAP and IFRSs: In Reference to Technical Advice on Equivalence by CESR' (ASBJ, 31 January 2006) <https://www.asb.or.jp>.

[42] 'Nippon Keidanren Supports to Accelerate the Convergence of Accounting Standards and to Seek Mutual Recognition of Standards in Japan, the United States, and Europe', Nippon Keidanren press release dated 20 June 2006 <http://www.keidanren.or.jp>.

[43] 'Towards the International Convergence of Accounting Standards' (Planning and Coordination Committee, Business Accounting Council, 31 July 2006) <http://www.fsa.go.jp>.

[44] 'SEC and Japan Financial Services Agency Announce Terms for Increased Cooperation and Collaboration', SEC press release 2006–14 dated 30 January 2006 <http://www.sec.gov>.

SEC and CESR.[45] With respect to the substance of the dialogue, the Keidanren position paper of June 2006, mentioned above, advocated the mutual recognition of accounting standards among Japan, the United States, and the EU by 2009.

In May 2006, with the explicit support of Minister of State for Financial Services Tatsuya Ito and SEC Chairman William Donaldson, the ASBJ held the first of what was planned as a series of periodic meetings with the FASB, mirroring the periodic meetings between the ASBJ and the IASB.[46] In the press release issued on the occasion of this first meeting, held in Tokyo, ASBJ Chairman Saito expressed his view of tripartite convergence as follows:

> I am confident that periodic meetings-to-be between representatives of the ASBJ and the FASB, two national standard setters for the world's largest capital markets, will be of great significance in the history of international convergence of accounting standards. In collaboration with the IASB, the ASBJ and the FASB will work together with all their might to support the sound and proper order of capital markets in the world.[47]

There was some surprise at the IASB when it first learned of the planned ASBJ–FASB meeting, sometime before the IASB's own convergence meeting with the ASBJ in March 2006. However, this had no discernible effect on the relations among the three standard setters. Following the March 2006 IASB–ASBJ meeting, Saito wrote to Tweedie with further proposals about the ASBJ's role in the work programme announced by the IASB and FASB in their February 2006 MoU.[48] Although, according to Saito, the ASBJ would prefer to participate in all MoU projects, it was hampered by limited staff resources. Therefore, Saito proposed a new type of arrangement in which the ASBJ would gain access to all project papers and correspondence, would provide input 'from the ASBJ and its constituents', but would not as a rule have its staff assume the authorship of agenda papers. Not surprisingly, the IASB steered clear of this suggestion, given that it often found it difficult enough to achieve progress on joint projects while working with the FASB alone. In response to Saito's letter, Tweedie reiterated the IASB's usual policies on cooperation with national standard setters: they could either make staff available to work as regular members of a project team under the IASB's supervision, or they could choose to monitor projects and provide comments, based on agenda papers as provided to the Board members.[49] Discussion of this issue continued for some time, with the practical result that the ASBJ decided, for the first time, to second a staff member to work in London, at the expense of the ASBJ. Previously,

---

[45] 'SEC–CESR Set out the Shape of Future Collaboration', SEC press release 2004–75 dated 4 June 2004 <http://www.sec.gov>.

[46] 'Chairman Donaldson Meets with Japan Minister of State for Financial Services Ito', SEC press release 2005–71 dated 3 May 2005 <http://www.sec.gov>. Interview with Ikuo Nishikawa, 24 January 2011.

[47] 'Representatives of the Financial Accounting Standards Board and the Accounting Standards Board of Japan Meet In Pursuit of Global Convergence', FASB/ASBJ press release dated 22 May 2006 <http://www.fasb.org>.

[48] Letter from Shizuki Saito to David Tweedie, dated 12 May 2006, IASB archive, 'Japan' file.

[49] Letter from David Tweedie to Shizuki Saito, dated 8 June 2006, IASB archive, 'Japan' file. The letter refers to 'project papers as they are posted on the IASB intranet' which would, for practical purposes, amount to agenda papers as provided to the Board. At this stage, the IASB had not yet adopted a policy of making its agenda papers fully available to the public, so that access to the Board papers was a privilege enjoyed by standard setters such as the ASBJ.

the ASBJ had limited itself to assigning staff located in Tokyo to work as members of IASB project teams. The ASBJ was not, however, given a special role in the IASB–FASB convergence process. The ASBJ–FASB meetings continued on a separate track, with the ASBJ in charge of developing most of the agenda and preparing most of the papers. The FASB was impressed with the quality of the ASBJ's work and found the meetings useful because of the high level of the technical discussions and for exchanging views between two standard setters which were both looking to their respective regulatory agencies to develop policies on the use of IFRSs.[50]

The Financial Accounting Standards Foundation (FASF), overseeing the ASBJ very much as the Financial Accounting Foundation has overseen the FASB, also sought to establish an international presence. Hiroshi Endo, the secretary-general of the FASF from 2004 to 2010, proactively sought cooperation with foundations and standard setters in other countries. Several times a year he would travel overseas to visit the United States, Europe, and countries in Asia/Oceania, accompanied by a board member or technical staff, to compare notes with counterpart bodies.[51]

10.4.1 The Tokyo Agreement

By late 2006, the tension between the ASBJ's two policy lines began to build up. An intensified effort to converge Japanese GAAP with IFRSs sat uneasily with the unwillingness of the ASBJ, and of Chairman Saito in particular, to give up on the mission to forge a distinct approach to setting accounting standards for the country—by which Japanese GAAP would be accepted at home and abroad as a fully fledged, equal alternative to IFRSs and US GAAP. Saito argued that the size and importance of Japan and its capital market warranted that Japan should retain ownership of its standard-setting process.[52] Towards that end, the ASBJ discussed over the course of 2006 whether it should complete its project to develop a conceptual framework.[53] Specifically, it considered issuing an exposure draft based on its 2004 discussion paper.

As discussed in Chapter 4, the ASBJ's discussion paper differed in a number of fundamental respects from the IASB's conceptual framework. It is understood that the proposed move towards an exposure draft was not well received by the FSA, Keidanren, and the Japanese Institute of Certified Public Accountants (JICPA). An important reason for caution was the belief that the European Commission saw convergence of the conceptual frameworks as essential to the equivalence assessment.[54]

---

[50] Interviews with Thomas Linsmeier, 11 June 2013, and with Leslie Seidman, 11 June 2013.

[51] Interview with Hiroshi Endo, 31 January 2011.

[52] Interview with Shizuki Saito, 25 January 2011.

[53] For the ASBJ's plan to finalize its framework, see 'The ASBJ and the IASB Hold Fourth Meeting on Joint Project towards Convergence', ASBJ press release dated 29 September 2006 <http://www.asb. or.jp>.

[54] For the significance attributed to the European Commission's views, see Ikuo Nishikawa, 'A Decade at the ASBJ: From the Past and to the Future', English translation of an article originally published in *Accounting Standards and Disclosure Quarterly*, 34/9 (September 2011) <http:/www.asb.or.jp>.

The draft framework had also been a source of friction between the ASBJ and the IASB in their joint meetings, as the two parties continued to differ on the role of the ASBJ's conceptual framework in arbitrating differences between their two standards.[55] Apart from differences over the framework, the IASB was impatient to convert the discussions with the ASBJ into what the IASB considered as 'real' convergence—that is, with a deadline for completion. The ASBJ, for its part, thought that indefinite convergence was the necessary corollary of maintaining Japanese GAAP on an equal plane with, but not necessarily identical to, IFRSs.[56]

In April 2007, Saito was succeeded, after completing two three-year terms as ASBJ chairman, by Ikuo Nishikawa, the ASBJ's full-time vice chairman. Nishikawa resolved one problem by not taking up the conceptual framework. Although the ASBJ did issue a revised discussion paper on the framework in 2007, the conceptual framework project was then relegated to the backburner indefinitely. Nishikawa also agreed to a deadline for the conclusion of the ASBJ's convergence programme. This took the form of a 'Tokyo Agreement' between the IASB and the ASBJ, announced in August 2007.[57]

The idea of a 'Tokyo Agreement' was attractive both to the IASB and the ASBJ. For the IASB, a public announcement including a convergence timetable meant that it could claim that one of the world's leading economies had joined the movement towards IFRSs. To the ASBJ, an apparent parallel with the 2002 'Norwalk Agreement' would confirm its special relationship with the IASB. Indeed, the IASB was not averse to putting pressure on the ASBJ by intimating that the semi-annual convergence meetings, another marker of the ASBJ's preferential status, would not be continued in the absence of a clear convergence timetable.[58] But, as seen above, other parties in Japan were also concerned about the pace of convergence and its implications for the European equivalence assessment.

The Agreement was negotiated not only by the ASBJ and the IASB, the two signatories, but also behind the scenes by the FSA, Keidanren, and the JICPA—the three heavyweights in regulation, corporate society, and the accounting profession, respectively.[59] Without doubt the Agreement represented a concession by Japan to the IASB, in terms of Japan's 'ownership' of its standard-setting process. The negotiation of the Agreement was therefore mainly about the size of the concession and any benefits accruing to the ASBJ. The IASB could point out that Canada and, very recently, South Korea had committed to adopting IFRSs and suggested that India was not far behind. For Japan not to engage in a convergence-cum-deadline towards eventual agreement with IFRSs would be to isolate the country from fast-moving developments around the world. In line with Canada and South Korea, David Tweedie would have liked to see a reference to 'adoption' of IFRSs in Japan included in the statement. The FSA, however, was not yet ready

---

[55] Interview with Atsushi Kogasaka, 26 January 2011.

[56] Interview with Ikuo Nishikawa, 24 January 2011.

[57] 'The ASBJ and IASB Announce Tokyo Agreement on Achieving Convergence of Accounting Standards by 2011', ASBJ press release dated 8 August 2007 <https://www.asb.or.jp>. The text of the agreement is attached to the press release.

[58] Interview with Tatsumi Yamada, 19 May 2011; interview with David Tweedie, 29 July 2008.

[59] On the parties involved in the negotiations, see email from Ikuo Nishikawa to David Tweedie and email from Tatsumi Yamada to David Tweedie, both dated 19 July 2007, IASB archive, file 'Japan'.

to take this step, as it believed that adoption implied a restriction on its authority to control the standard-setting process and issue interpretations.[60]

The Agreement therefore did not refer to 'adoption', but spoke of 'the final goal of accomplishing convergence' and 'the ultimate objective of convergence' between Japanese GAAP and IFRSs. According to the Agreement, the ASBJ's main obligation was to eliminate, by 30 June 2011, the differences between Japanese GAAP and IFRSs that would remain after the conclusion of the short-term projects to address the EU's concerns for equivalence.

The Tokyo Agreement gave no explanation of the choice of 30 June 2011 as a target date for convergence. As seen above, Canada and Korea were by then known to aim for transition to IFRSs in 2011, but not specifically on 30 June. A few months after the Tokyo Agreement, early in 2008, the June 2011 date would emerge in the context of an acceleration of the work programme for the IASB–FASB MoU. In that context, the target date was justified as the date on which the terms of the last original IASB Board members, including that of Chairman Tweedie, would end (see Section 12.2). It would seem that, at the time of the Tokyo Agreement, this date already figured prominently in Tweedie's planning.

As mentioned before, the contours of IFRSs by 2011 could still only be partially discerned because of the ongoing work on the IASB–FASB MoU. In 2007, several convergence projects were already causing anxiety, in Japan and elsewhere. It was feared, for instance, that the two boards might move towards full fair value for financial instruments. Japanese constituents also strongly disapproved of the way the IASB and the FASB toyed with the idea of abolishing net income, or at least its prominent presentation as the bottom line of the income statement (see Sections 12.8 and 12.9). More than in any other country, net income was then considered in Japan as a fundamental accounting concept, and any attempt to downplay its significance, let alone remove it from the income statement, was strongly resisted. Hence, the main point of the negotiations preceding the Tokyo Agreement was to find wording to express the degree of Japan's commitment to what might be the eventual outcome of the MoU projects.[61] The conclusion reached—in wording which avoided mentioning the FASB and the MoU—was that the ASBJ's commitment to converge did not apply to major IASB projects with an effective date later than 30 June 2011. At the time the Tokyo Agreement was signed, the IASB–FASB MoU did not yet contain any firm deadlines for most projects, and the ASBJ might well have hoped that this would allow it to make up its own mind about net income, fair value, and other problematic topics. Yet in 2007 it would have been very difficult for anyone to predict the outcome of the IASB–FASB cooperation with confidence. As seen above, Canada's transition to IFRSs in 2011 was based on the assumption that by then the major projects would have been completed.

The IASB on its part committed to work closely with the ASBJ 'to ensure the acceptance of the international approach in Japan'. It was agreed to set up staff working parties at the director level to discuss 'major issues emerging in the development of accounting standards'. While this wording did not amount to 'a place at the table' next to the IASB and the FASB, as the ASBJ had demanded more

---

[60] Email from Tatsumi Yamada to David Tweedie, dated 27 July 2007, IASB archive, file 'Japan'.
[61] Email from Tatsumi Yamada to David Tweedie, dated 27 July 2007, IASB archive, file 'Japan'.

than once, it was more than the IASB promised to many of 'over a hundred countries' that had adopted IFRSs and that were equally concerned about what the IASB–FASB convergence process might have in store for them.

The announcement of the Tokyo Agreement apparently resonated in the Japanese corporate world. A major manufacturing company executive whom we interviewed grouped it with the SEC's 2008 roadmap as factors that changed preparers' mentality towards IFRSs. He said: 'After the Tokyo Agreement and the issuance of the roadmap in 2008 by the SEC of the United States, we came to view convergence with IFRSs and moving towards requiring IFRSs in Japan to be a natural course for Japan to take, given the globalization of the economy.'

In order to carry out the terms of the Tokyo Agreement, the ASBJ released a project plan in December 2007. It classified the some two dozen project topics into the categories of short-term, medium-term, and medium to long-term, and set out the timetable for the publication of drafts and final standards.[62] One important consequence of the Tokyo Agreement has been an intensification of staff-level communication and travel between the ASBJ and the IASB.[63]

10.5 PROTECTION OF THE IASB'S BRAND: COMPLIANCE WITH IFRSs

As the IASB became more successful in terms of persuading countries or companies to adopt its standards, it was increasingly recognized that the IASB, and its standards, represented a valuable brand that needed to be protected. Challenges to the claim that IFRSs were a global reporting standard came from two sources: jurisdictional variations and variations in compliance. The former refers to the decisions by national or regional adopting agencies (e.g. the national standard setters and government ministries) to modify or exclude one or more provisions in IFRSs from mandated practice in their jurisdiction. The latter deals with a failure of reporting companies to apply IFRSs fully or correctly, made possible by a failure of auditors or regulatory agencies to compel such compliance. A mixed record on compliance was the oldest challenge and is discussed first, before the issue of jurisdictional variations is taken up in Section 10.6.

In the 1990s, the IASC was increasingly bedevilled by the practice of 'IAS-lite', the selective adoption of IASs by companies.[64] In 1997, the IASC attempted to provide redress by including a requirement in IAS 1 *Presentation of Financial Statements* that enterprises should disclose whether their financial statements comply with IASs and that financial statements should not be described as complying with IASs 'unless they comply with all the requirements of each applicable Standard and each applicable Interpretation' (paragraph 11). This was the IASC's first utterance on protecting the integrity of its brand name. It suffered from the inherent limitation that companies willing to depart from

---

[62] 'ASBJ Project Plan', *ASBJ Newsletter*, 25 December 2007, 1–2.
[63] Interview with Ikuo Nishikawa, 24 January 2011.
[64] Camfferman and Zeff, *Financial Reporting and Global Capital Markets*, 409.

one requirement in IASs would not necessarily be deterred from doing so by another such requirement. Just as the IASC before it, the IASB had no enforcement powers, even though the IASC Foundation's original Constitution stated that 'to promote . . . the rigorous application of [the] standards' was one of the organization's objectives (paragraph 2(b)).

From the perspective of the IASB it was therefore fortunate that the truly large-scale use of IFRSs commencing in the 2000s coincided with a movement in which jurisdictions around the world ratcheted up their financial reporting compliance function.[65] The US SEC was the 'mother of all securities regulators'. It was founded in 1934 and has used a very heavy hand to secure compliance by publicly traded companies with US GAAP.[66] The SEC had also made it abundantly clear from the 1990s onwards that it expected similar vigilance by regulators in other countries as a condition for accepting the IAS-based financial statements of foreign registrants without reconciliation to US GAAP.[67] Yet in most other countries external monitoring of compliance with financial reporting standards was, until recently, weak or nonexistent. As jurisdictions began to recognize the importance of compliance, they set up new bodies or invigorated existing bodies in accordance with their own governmental structures and regulatory cultures. Some were attached to a ministry, while others were free-standing entities. The authority given to them, as well as the size of their budget and the competence of their staff, varied profoundly from one jurisdiction to another. Notwithstanding these developments, it is still true today that no other jurisdiction's regulator can begin to compare with the SEC in terms of the size of its staff and the rigour which it uses in enforcing compliance with national GAAP.

In the EU some member states had already, prior to 2000, set up public-sector or private-sector bodies to monitor compliance with accounting standards, but others had not. The European Commission's proposal to require the use of IASs by listed companies included a recognition that the expected benefits from IASs were conditional on rigorous and consistent enforcement throughout the EU.[68] The Financial Services Action Plan, of which the IAS proposal was a small part, envisaged an enhanced role of national securities regulators. While ensuring compliance with IASs remained a national rather than a European responsibility, there was a stated expectation in the IAS Regulation (recital 16) that CESR, formed in response to the Financial Services Action Plan, would undertake to coordinate EU regulators' performance with respect to compliance with accounting standards. CESR took up the challenge, among others, by agreeing on common principles of enforcement, reporting on the implementation and compliance of IFRSs in the EU, and establishing a European database of IFRS enforcement decisions taken by its members. On 1 January 2011, the EU launched

---

[65] For an empirical investigation of this point, see Hans B. Christensen, Luzi Hail, and Christian Leuz, 'Mandatory IFRS Reporting and Changes in Enforcement', *Journal of Accounting and Economics*, 56/2–3, Supplement 1 (December 2013), 147–77.

[66] Stephen A. Zeff, 'A Perspective on the U.S. Public/Private Sector Approach to the Regulation of Financial Reporting' *Accounting Horizons*, 9/1 (March 1995), 52–70.

[67] Camfferman and Zeff, *Financial Reporting and Global Capital Markets*, 331–4 and 344–5.

[68] 'EU Financial Reporting Strategy: The Way Forward', communication from the European Commission to the Council and the European Parliament, COM(2000) 359 final, Brussels, 13 June 2000, paragraphs 26 and 28 <http://ec.europa.eu/internal_market/accounting>.

the European Securities and Markets Authority, an agency set up as a more powerful successor to CESR. Although its enhanced oversight powers did not include a direct responsibility for financial reporting, it has cajoled national securities market regulators to improve the standard of their performance in enforcing compliance with IFRSs.

Outside the EU, similar movements to create regulatory agencies or to expand their powers could be observed in jurisdictions including Canada, China, and Japan. It might be thought that, at the global level, the International Organization of Securities Commissions (IOSCO) might have played a coordinating and stimulating role comparable to that of CESR. However, IOSCO lacked a clear mandate such as CESR had, and it would seem that compliance with IFRSs was for some time relegated to a lower priority within IOSCO by pressing issues such as reforming auditing in the wake of Enron.[69]

Traditionally, ensuring compliance with financial reporting standards had in many countries been left exclusively to the external auditor. The first-line responsibility of the auditor did not change with the spread of active enforcement by regulators, but the increasing risk of being corrected by a regulator may well have spurred on the audit firms to be less tolerant of practices that could be labelled as 'IAS-lite' or 'IFRS-lite'. Apart from the influence of the regulators, it is likely that the vast increase in the number of clients using IFRSs helped to foster a much deeper understanding on the part of the audit firms of what IFRSs required or prohibited, leading to a stricter application. One sign of this was noted by a non-US company listed in the United States and that had applied IFRSs on a voluntary basis prior to 2005. A senior accounting officer interviewed for this book recalled that around 2005 the number of items requiring a reconciliation between IFRSs and US GAAP began to mushroom, not only because of changes made to IFRSs, but also because the company's auditor concluded that previous interpretations of IFRSs in line with US GAAP were no longer tenable.

Given their international reach, the Big Four audit firms have played a significant role in securing compliance with IFRSs around the world, and making compliance more consistent. Each of the firms has centralized its decision-making on the application of IFRSs in an international office or centre of expertise. They issue their own IFRS manuals which their partners and staff are expected to follow in conducting audits. The firms also regularly confer among each other to address issues of diverse practice within and among jurisdictions. While some may construe this as standard setting behind closed doors, the firms regard it as a sharing of views and exchanging of information in areas of IFRSs where they find that practice diverges.

10.5.1 Société Générale Controversially Claims IAS 1's 'Fair Presentation' Override

The inevitable question posed by the trend towards more active compliance monitoring by regulators in many countries, and the efforts of the audit firms,

---

[69] Interview with Philippe Richard, 17 February 2010.

is whether they resulted in a high level of compliance with IFRSs around the world, but the question defies easy answers. Regulators have published reports on compliance, such as CESR's 2007 report on the initial implementation of IFRSs in the EU.[70] Numerous academic studies have investigated compliance with specific standards or in specific countries.[71] It is not easy to draw general conclusions from this heterogeneous body of evidence, other than that compliance has not been of uniform quality and tends to vary with certain company characteristics and country-level factors also found to be associated with financial reporting quality. Moreover, many investigations focus of necessity on compliance with disclosure requirements, which is easily observed compared to compliance with recognition and measurement provisions, but provides at best a partial view of compliance.

It is perhaps not surprising that the subject of compliance with and enforcement of IFRSs has tended to be discussed more vividly in response to anecdotal evidence than on the basis of the less easily digested body of available empirical evidence.

A case that was very well suited to attract attention and to illustrate the sometimes fine line between the legitimate exercise of judgement and non-compliance with IFRSs was reported in March 2008. Floyd Norris, the chief financial correspondent of *The New York Times*, wrote that Société Générale (SocGen), France's third largest bank, 'created a furor in accounting circles' when it invoked IAS 1's 'fair presentation' override to report the €6.4 billion loss sustained in January 2008 by rogue trader Jérôme Kerviel, in its 2007 annual results rather than in those for 2008.[72] This was very likely the first use of the override in IAS 1, *Presentation of Financial Statements*, by a European listed company, or perhaps by a listed company anywhere, since the override was established by the IASC in 1997.

Kerviel had begun his 'unauthorized and concealed trading activities' at the bank as early as 2005, and by the end of 2007 he had accumulated trading profits of €1.5 billion.[73] But the tide turned abruptly against him in January 2008, when

---

[70] 'CESR's Review of the Implementation and Enforcement of IFRS in the EU', CESR, 07–352, November 2007 <http://www.esma.europa.eu>.

[71] To name but a few: Christopher Hodgdon, Rasoul H. Tondkar, David W. Harless, and Ajay Adhikari, 'Compliance with IFRS Disclosure Requirements and Individual Analysts' Forecast Errors', *Journal of International Accounting, Auditing and Taxation*, 17 (2008), 1–13; Martin Glaum, Peter Schmidt, Donna Street, and Silvia Vogel, 'Compliance with IFRS 3- and IAS 36-required Disclosures across 17 European Countries: Company- and Country-level Determinants', *Accounting and Business Research*, 43/3 (2013), 163–204; Ismail Ufuk Misirlioglu, Jon Tucker, and Osman Yükseltürk, 'Does Mandatory Adoption of IFRS Guarantee Compliance?', *The International Journal of Accounting*, 48/3 (September 2013), 327–63.

[72] Floyd Norris, 'Société Générale Invokes Special Accounting Rule to Absorb Kerviel Losses', *The New York Times*, 6 March 2008, B1 <http://www.nytimes.com>. The article also appeared in the *International Herald Tribune* on the same date. Also see 'Secondary Shock at Soc Gen', *World Accounting Report*, April 2008, 8.

[73] For the characterization, see Note 40, page 247, in the *2008 Registration Document* (i.e. the 2007 annual report) of Société Générale. See also page 52 of the *2008 Registration Document* <http://www.societegenerale.com>. Floyd Norris, 'Defending SocGen', *The New York Times*, 10 March 2008 <http://economix.blogs.nytimes.com/2008/03/10/defending-socgen/>.

his tally suffered a reversal of €7.9 billion, at which point the bank announced the fraudulent trading and the trader's huge losses for the month.

Under the IASB's applicable accounting standards, IAS 10 *Events after the Balance Sheet Date*, and IAS 37 *Provisions, Contingent Liabilities and Contingent Assets*, the losses of €6.4 billion should have been reflected in the 2008 consolidated financial statements. But the bank, in all likelihood, wished to get the losses behind it, so they would not be a topic of discussion as late as March 2009, when its 2008 accounts were to be published. SocGen said in Note 40 to its 2007 financial statements that 'the Group considered that this presentation was inconsistent with the objective of the financial statements described in the framework of IFRS standards and that for the purpose of a fair presentation of its financial situation at December 31, 2007, it was more appropriate to record all the financial consequences of the unwinding of these unauthorized activities under a separate caption in consolidated income for the 2007 financial year'. The bank's joint auditors, Ernst & Young Audit and Deloitte & Associés, made a point of saying that, in their opinion, the treatment of the losses discussed in Note 40 did not justify a qualification on the consolidated financial statements.[74] There was no sign that the Autorité des Marchés Financiers (AMF), France's stock market regulator, objected to the treatment. A senior staff member at one of the securities regulators on the Continent confided to the authors that some of the other regulators in Europe were livid that the AMF went along with the claimed override.[75] SocGen could argue that it provided an informative disclosure in its Note 40.

The controversial accounting treatment was also the subject of an article in the *Financial Times*, which reported that 'Regulators and accountants are questioning Société Générale's use of a "get out" clause' so as to accelerate the accounting recognition of the losses.[76]

The IASB, for its part, did not comment on the application of IAS 1's 'fair presentation' override to such a case, but Floyd Norris quoted two Board members, both from the United States, who were critical of its use in this context.[77]

In a way, the SocGen case played a similar role to the EU's carve-outs of IAS 39 in 2004. Just as the carve-outs were used by only a handful of banks, there was no reason to believe that the unique circumstances of the SocGen case made it representative of the application of IFRSs by European companies generally. Nevertheless, it became emblematic of the potential risk posed to the idea of a global set of accounting standards by the actions of jurisdictional authorities.

---

[74] The auditors' opinion appears on pages 266 and 267 of the bank's *2008 Registration Document*.

[75] Not included in list of interviewees in Appendix 4.

[76] Jennifer Hughes, 'SocGen Accounting Prompts Queries', *Financial Times*, 11 March 2008, 27. For a critical news report by a leading forensic accountant in Canada, see Al Rosen, 'SocGen "Rogues" Show Flaws in Accounting Rules', *Financial Post*, 9 April 2008 <http://investorvoice.ca/PI/3470.htm>. Rosen asserted that the bank's accountants 'buried the credibility of IFRS'.

[77] The Board members so quoted were Anthony Cope and John Smith. See Norris, 'Société Générale Invokes Special Accounting Rule to Absorb Kerviel Losses'.

10.6 PROTECTION OF THE IASB's BRAND: JURISDICTIONAL VARIATIONS FROM IFRSs

As mentioned above, the IASC had amended IAS 1 *Presentation of Financial Statements* in 1997 to require reporting entities to make a statement of compliance. In December 2003, the IASB, without exposing the changed wording for comment, unanimously voted to strengthen this requirement even further, as follows:

> An entity whose financial statements comply with IFRSs shall make *an explicit and unreserved statement* of such compliance in the notes. Financial statements shall not be described as complying with IFRSs unless they comply with all the requirements of IFRSs. (IAS 1.14, emphasis added)

As soon became clear, the problem was not so much that the language of the requirement needed to be strengthened, but to determine what it meant when a company did not apply IFRSs directly, but complied with IFRSs as adopted or adapted by its home jurisdiction.

This question first rose to prominence in connection with the adoption of IFRSs in the EU. In November 2003, the European Commission issued a release clarifying some aspects of the IAS Regulation of June 2002. In a section of the release dealing with the note on the statement of accounting policies in companies' financial statements, the Commission said that, while it would be consistent with the IASB's position, in IAS 1, on companies' affirmation of compliance with IFRSs to say 'in accordance with all International Financial Reporting Standards as adopted for use in the EU', it believed that, where 'no standards have been rejected and all standards issued by the IASB have been endorsed', companies could simply affirm compliance with IFRSs.[78] A year later, just after the Commission endorsed IAS 39, on financial instruments, with two carve-outs, it gave advice that companies (or banks) using the carve-outs must affirm compliance with IFRSs as adopted by the EU.[79] But all companies not affected by the carve-outs could continue to affirm compliance with IFRSs.

The branding issue raised by the EU carve-outs resonated in the United States in April 2005, when the SEC issued a release which allowed first-time adopters of IFRSs, switching from their home country GAAP to IFRSs, to provide only two years of comparative financial statements rather than the normal three.[80] To be eligible to avail themselves of this accommodation, foreign private issuers from the EU had to provide a one-time reconciliation of any differences between 'IFRSs as adopted by the EU' and 'IFRSs as published by the IASB'. Up to that time, the

---

[78] European Commission, 'Comments Concerning Certain Articles of the Regulation (EC) No 1606/2002 of the European Parliament and of the Council of 19 July 2002 on the Application of International Accounting Standards and the Fourth Council Directive 78/660/EEC of 25 July 1978 and the Seventh Council Directive 83/349/EEC of 13 June 1983 on Accounting', Brussels, November 2003, section 2.1.4 <http://ec.europa.eu/internal_market/accounting>.

[79] 'IAS 39 Financial Instruments: Recognition and Measurement—Frequently Asked Questions (FAQ)', European Commission Memo/04/265, Brussels, November 19, 2004 <http://ec.europa.eu/internal_market/accounting>.

[80] 'First-time Application of International Financial Reporting Standards', Securities and Exchange Commission, release nos. 33-8567; 34-51535 <http://www.sec.gov>.

addition of 'as published by the IASB' to IFRSs would probably have been regarded as redundant by most people, and it had so far rarely been used in the literature. Following the SEC's release, 'IFRSs as issued by the IASB', or its colloquial equivalent 'full IFRSs', began to be much more widely used.

In December 2005, the European Commission announced a new position on companies' affirmations with IFRSs, taken in consultation with the Accounting Regulatory Committee, that *all* EU listed companies were expected to affirm compliance with 'IFRSs as adopted by the EU'.[81] This position was at variance with the view it expressed in November 2003, above. This choice of wording for the affirmation of compliance was understandable in the light of the legal position in the EU, where Commission needs to endorse every new standard and interpretation before it becomes binding on EU listed companies. To be sure, the Commission has never suggested that companies could not also assert compliance with full IFRSs, and for the vast majority of European companies that did not use the carve-outs it would presumably not have been costly to make such a double affirmation and to obtain a double auditor's opinion. Yet they were not required to do so, causing a potential problem for readers in other parts of the world, who would not know whether, and to what extent, an EU company's financial statements deviated from full IFRSs. In subsequent years, it appeared that this problem could also appear when the EU was slow to endorse a standard, creating temporary differences between full IFRSs and 'IFRSs as adopted by the EU'.

It might be argued that in a formal sense the Commission's guidance did not contravene the IASB's policy as stated in IAS 1. As adopted by the EU, IAS 1 included paragraph 14 requiring 'an explicit and unreserved statement of compliance' with IFRSs, but the Commission could maintain that any reference to 'IFRSs' in a text adopted by the EU could have no other meaning but 'IFRSs as adopted by the EU'. Even so, it was clear that the EU's reservation of the option not to endorse IFRSs in full, and its requirement of a statement of compliance with a jurisdictional adoption of IFRSs, ran counter to the IASB's intentions and posed a threat to the IASB's brand.

In communicating the Commission's decision to its members, the Fédération des Experts Comptables Européens (FEE) was anxious to mitigate this threat, as it 'strongly encouraged' companies to disclose in the notes to their financial statements any differences between their accounting policies and full IFRSs. FEE also recommended that companies should affirm whether they are in full compliance with IFRSs as published by the IASB. FEE said that the affirmation that auditors give in their reports on the financial statements should be consistent with that made by the company in its note to the accounts. Some EU companies sought and obtained a second opinion from their auditors, namely, that their financial statements complied with 'IFRS as published (or issued) by the IASB' so that readers of its financial statements outside the EU would know that they comply

---

[81] 'Reference to the Financial Reporting Framework in the EU in Accounting Policies and in the Audit Report and Applicability of Endorsed Standards', communication dated December 2005 to its member bodies by the Fédération des Experts Comptables Européens (FEE) <http://www.fee.be>. See also summary record of ARC meeting of 30 November 2005, minute VII(1) <http://ec.europa.eu/internal_market/accounting>.

with full IFRSs.[82] The second opinion was particularly important for EU companies that were listed or traded in the United States, because the SEC has since 2007 required such an auditor affirmation if a company is to avoid the reconciliation requirement.

As the IASB became more concerned over differences between IFRSs as adopted by the EU and IFRSs as issued by the IASB, a seemingly innocuous concession made by the IASB in 2004 to Australia and New Zealand returned to haunt the Board. The standard setters in Australia and New Zealand had wanted to delete several options in IFRSs—options that had not been available previously under their national GAAPs—and add some disclosures in their two countries' adopted versions of IFRSs. At the time, in order to induce them to be among the first adopters of IFRSs, the Board's strategy committee assured the New Zealand standard setter, and implicitly also its Australian counterpart, that these amendments would not bar companies from claiming that they complied with IFRSs (see Section 4.3). At around the same time, the auditing standard setters in the two countries stipulated that auditors would be required, once companies began adopting IFRSs as amended (in 2005 in Australia, and in 2007 in New Zealand), to affirm in their reports that the financial statements comply with Australian or New Zealand accounting standards (not with IFRSs), as required by company law. The auditor could give a second opinion, at the company's request, stating compliance with IFRSs. The IASB's leadership, once confronted with the European Commission's carve-outs, realized that its concession to Australia and New Zealand might be seized upon by other jurisdictions, and it was probably relieved to learn that the standard setters in both countries decided in 2007 to reverse their positions and therefore restore the deleted options (see the fuller discussion in Chapter 4.) However, the removal of options continued on a small scale in other jurisdictions, for instance in South Korea (see Section 10.3) and Brazil (see Section 15.1.3).

Apart from modifications of the text of IFRSs upon adoption in a jurisdiction, another potential source of jurisdictional variations consisted of local interpretations or implementation guidance provided by a national standard setter or securities regulator. The IASB consistently attempted to dissuade jurisdictions from issuing local guidance, and to emphasize that requests for interpretations should be sent to IFRIC. As discussed more fully in Chapter 12, however, IFRIC's reticence in acting upon interpretation requests meant that local interpretations continued to appear. The IASB found it hard to keep track of IFRS adoption in general, and even more so to gain an understanding of the existence and significance of local interpretations. Typically, such interpretations were truly limited, either because they were of a temporary nature or were related to strictly local circumstances. For instance, France, Germany, Hong Kong, and Italy all occasionally issued guidance of such a limited nature.[83] In other jurisdictions,

---

[82] Christopher W. Nobes and Stephen A. Zeff, 'Auditors' Affirmations of Compliance with IFRS around the World: An Exploratory Study', *Accounting Perspectives*, 7/4 (2008), 279–92.

[83] In France, the AMF issued a statement 'Classement des OPCVM de trésorerie en équivalent de trésorerie au regard de la norme IAS 7 « Tableau des flux de trésorerie » : l'AMF se réfère à l'analyse de l'AFG et de l'AFTE', *Revue Mensuelle de l'Autorité des Marchés Financiers*, no. 23, March 2006, 15–23. The German DRSC and its interpretations committee have since 2006 issued a small number of

however, guidance was sometimes issued that modified the results of applying a standard in ways that were not intended by the IASB. IFRIC 15, which was not well received in many jurisdictions, was a case in point (see Section 12.12.3).

A problem relating to jurisdictional variations was that, in a number of jurisdictions, companies and their auditors referred to reporting requirements in addition to IFRSs. In many cases, this would have no bearing on the application of IFRSs, for instance when company law imposed requirements on the directors' report or other information not covered by IFRSs. However, for a foreign investor it might be difficult to distinguish between cases where additional requirements would, or would not, have an impact on the application of IFRSs. For example, the management of the Spanish banking Group BBVA explained in the notes to its 2006 financial statements that they had been prepared 'in accordance with EU-IFRSs, taking into account best practices of Bank of Spain Circular 4/2004'.[84] Another example: the audit report in Embraer's 2011 annual report refers both to IFRSs and to 'accounting practices adopted in Brazil', whatever that means.

10.6.1 The IASB and the IAASB Respond to Jurisdictional Variations

At the February 2006 meeting of SAC, it was reported that 'SAC members expressed concern about the risk that local variations of IFRSs could undermine the brand. The Board agreed that there is a risk and noted it will raise the issue with the Trustees.'[85] At the trustees' next meeting, in March, Chairman David Tweedie brought the matter forward from SAC. The minutes stated: 'It was noted that some countries have chosen not to adopt IFRSs in full. This results in the description in the financial statements and auditor's report of the basis of accounting referring to "compliance with International Financial Reporting Standards as adopted in [name of country/region]".' The trustees 'agreed that the use of the IFRS brand was an important issue and tasked the IASB with developing an approach on this matter [and] to bring it to the Trustees at their next meeting'.[86]

The IASB staff thereupon developed a proposal to amend IAS 1 *Presentation of Financial Statements*, as part of a set of minor amendments known as 'annual improvements to IFRSs'. In the background paper which the staff prepared for the Board's November 2006 meeting, it professed a concern about 'the potential for misunderstanding by the users of the financial reports described as being based on IFRSs that are not in compliance with IFRSs; and harm to the IFRS brand'.[87] The staff explained that, just as the IASB could not require jurisdictions to adopt IFRSs in their entirety, neither could it prevent them from using the word 'IFRSs' to designate a nationally applicable accounting framework as 'IFRSs as adopted in X'. This was true even though 'IFRSs' and 'International

---

'Anwendungshinweise'. Italy's OIC has issued a small number of 'Applicazione' and 'Guida Operativa' related to IFRSs since 2009. On Hong Kong, see 'Policy on Providing Interpretations or Rulings on Financial Reporting Issues', HKICPA, 17 April 2007 <http://www.hkicpa.org.hk>.

[84] BBVA *Annual Report 2006* (English version), 187.
[85] SAC meeting of 27–9 February 2006, minute 3.5.
[86] IASCF trustees meeting of 23–4 March 2006, minute 5.
[87] AP 11/2006 paper 2A, paragraphs 5 and 7.

Financial Reporting Standards' were trademarks of the IASC Foundation. This was an issue the IASB could not solve alone. Both at Board and at trustee level, contact was sought with the International Auditing and Assurance Standards Board (IAASB) and with IOSCO.[88] Staff reported that the IAASB was already considering issuing a requirement that an auditor's unqualified opinion was possible only when:

(a) the notes to the financial statements include an appropriate explanation of the differences between the applicable financial reporting framework and IFRSs, including an indication of the significance in the case of an reporting entity; and

(b) the auditor's report draws attention to this note and the fact that the applicable financial reporting framework differs from IFRSs.

The staff asserted that the IASB could support the IAASB by requiring the explanation that the IAASB was looking for. The following addition was proposed to IAS 1, following paragraph 14, cited above, which called for a statement of compliance in the notes to the financial statements if, and only if, the financial statements comply with IFRSs:

14A Where the entity's financial statements are described as being based on IFRSs but are not fully compliant with IFRSs, the entity shall disclose:

(a) all instances where IFRSs are not complied with; and
(b) indicate the significance of those differences in its financial statements.

The proposal was actively discussed at the Board's November and December meetings. Some Board members were concerned about officially condoning non-compliance with standards, or the awkwardness, as Jan Engström put it, of the Board itself 'regulating how not to use their standards'. There was some sentiment for a more forceful requirement, but one that did not mandate a quantitative reconciliation as the proposal seemed to do.[89] The Board finally agreed 14–0 to expose the following amendment to IAS 1:

14A When an entity refers to IFRSs in describing the basis on which its financial statements are prepared but is not able to make an explicit or unreserved statement of compliance with IFRSs, the entity shall:

(a) describe each difference between the basis on which its financial statements are prepared and IFRSs that are applicable to its financial statements; and
(b) describe how its reported financial position and performance of the entity would have differed if it had complied with IFRSs.[90]

This proposed amendment came close to calling for a quantitative reconciliation between IFRSs and the basis on which the financial statements were prepared, but instead it called for a descriptive reconciliation, leaving open the possibility of supplying actual figures.

---

[88] AP 12/2006 paper 10A, paragraph 15–16.
[89] *IStaR*, November 2006, 7–8 and December 2006, 20–1.
[90] Exposure draft 'Improvements to International Financial Reporting Standards' (IASB, October 2007), 57. For the staff proposal, see AP 12/2006 paper 10A, paragraph 18.

The publication of the proposal had to wait until the Board had assembled the entire package of assorted amendments to IFRSs which was published in October 2007 as an omnibus exposure draft of 'Improvements to International Financial Reporting Standards'. The delay meant that the IAASB preceded the IASB: in July 2007 it published an exposure draft of a comprehensive rewording of International Standard on Auditing (ISA) 700 *The Independent Auditor's Report on General Purpose Financial Statements*. In its own proposal, the IAASB referred to the forthcoming IASB proposal to amend IAS 1 and drew attention to the possibility that the absence of the required disclosure could mean that the description of the applicable financial reporting framework was misleading, even if the relevant framework (i.e. 'IFRSs as adopted in X') did not include the proposed amendment to IAS 1.[91]

Even before the IASB's exposure draft was published, it was clear that at least Chairman Tweedie was not convinced that it represented the right solution. He thought that IAS 1, as it stood, was clear enough. It just needed to be better enforced to make companies that complied with full IFRSs say so explicitly, even if in a formal sense they complied with a national requirement. The proposed amendment was a plan B in case ongoing discussions with auditors and regulators were to fail.[92]

Early in June 2007, Tweedie had written the following in a letter to Paul Koster, chief executive of CESR and chairman of the Netherlands' Autoriteit Financiële Markten (Financial Markets Authority):

> A description such as IFRSs 'as adopted by country X' is disguising the fact that some countries are 'carving out' sections of standards (in some cases entire standards) with which certain interests in the country disagree. This is undermining the IFRS brand, indeed, we rather wish such countries would not refer to IFRS and simply make reference to their own national accounting standards.[93]

In the letter, Tweedie reacted negatively to the proposal by 'auditors'—presumably a reference to the IAASB—that the IASB insert a provision in IAS 1 that companies affirming compliance with 'IFRS as adopted by . . . ' should be required to disclose the omitted sections or standards, because this would imply that the IASB sanctioned the deletion of parts of IFRSs. He suggested to Koster that 'perhaps the most appropriate way to resolve the problem would be for regulators through CESR and IOSCO to seek clarification for the market by demanding that if companies use the term IFRS in describing the basis for their financial reports, they should state whether this is full IFRS—or, if not, what departures from full IFRS have been made'. IOSCO's Standing Committee 1 could see how the IASB was reacting to pressure to say something about companies not complying fully with IFRSs that might nonetheless assert compliance, and it agreed to take on the issue, which led to the Technical Committee's statement which we discuss next.[94]

---

[91] Exposure draft 'ISA 700, The Independent Auditor's Report on General Purpose Financial Statements' (IAASB, July 2007), paragraphs A9–A11.

[92] *IStaR*, July 2007, 20–1.

[93] Letter from David Tweedie to Paul Koster, undated but evidently written in early June 2007, IASCF trustees meeting of 2–3 July 2007, agenda paper 2(iii).

[94] Interview with Richard Thorpe, 16 October 2008.

10.6.2 IOSCO Issues a Statement on the Financial
Reporting Framework

In February 2008, IOSCO published a statement by its Technical Committee in which it commented on the risk of misunderstanding by investors and other users of financial statements in circumstances 'where national standards assert that [the financial statements] are based on but do not fully implement International Financial Reporting Standards (IFRS), i.e. when IFRS have been modified or adapted to the particular circumstances of a national market'. The committee said that 'investors run the risk of making investment decisions without a full understanding of financial statement data if they are not fully aware of the basis on which financial statements are prepared, and of the accounting standards that underpin the company's policies'.[95] To address this possible source of misunderstanding, the committee recommended that 'all annual and interim financial statements that are prepared on the basis of national standards that are modified or adapted from IFRS and published by publicly traded companies should include at a minimum the following statements':

1. A clear and unambiguous statement of the reporting framework on which the accounting policies are based;
2. A clear statement of the company's accounting policies on all material accounting areas;
3. An explanation of where the accounting standards that underpin the policies can be found;
4. A statement that explains that the financial statements are in compliance with IFRS as issued by the IASB, if this is the case; and
5. A statement that explains in what regard the standards and the reporting framework used differs from IFRS as issued by the IASB, if this is the case.

Although IOSCO's statement could appear as a direct answer to Tweedie's letter to Koster, it is more likely that this letter was only a part of a wider discussion among IOSCO member bodies and the IASB. In all likelihood, IOSCO's statement was drafted in the first instance by its Standing Committee 1, which was chaired, as always, by a senior member of the SEC's accounting staff (Julie Erhardt). Tweedie would certainly have raised the matter with the SEC as well as with CESR. It had been known for some time that the SEC was critical of jurisdictional variations from IFRSs, a point which it made forcefully in November 2007, when it decided to lift its Form 20-F reconciliation requirement for foreign private issuers using IFRSs. The SEC was probably among the members of Standing Committee 1 who expressed their doubts about the proposed amendment to IAS 1 on the ground that it 'could legitimize the practice of amending IFRSs for national use'.[96]

---

[95] 'Statement on Providing Investors with Appropriate and Complete Information on Accounting Frameworks Used to Prepare Financial Statements' (IOSCO Technical Committee, 6 February 2008) <http://www.iosco.org>.

[96] IASCF trustee meeting of 2–3 July 2007, minute E.

While the EU carve-out had helped to place the issue of jurisdictional variations on the agenda, it was not the main reason behind IOSCO's statement, given that the carve-out was used by only a small number of banks. Rather, the statement was inspired by a more general concern in IOSCO over countries that claimed to have adopted IFRSs, but had not adopted certain standards, or were using older versions of IFRSs.[97]

IOSCO's statement provided the justification to the IASB and the IAASB not to proceed with their proposals. This was probably welcome to both organizations, as their exposure drafts had been coolly received. The IASB staff's analysis of the comments received on the proposed amendment to IAS 1 showed that the commentators generally opposed it, and the following four bullet points in the staff's analysis conveyed the principal arguments against the proposal:

- Although many respondents understand the Board's reasoning behind this proposal, nearly two-thirds disagree that this amendment will achieve its aim and about a third object to including this as an annual improvement

- Most point out that this is an issue for regulators or auditors rather than standard-setters, and inappropriate for individual entities to address through disclosures comparing IFRSs and other non-IFRSs frameworks

- The proposal creates an onerous burden and ignores the time lapse between the Board's adoption of changes and jurisdictional endorsement process for new requirements; and if this 'gap' spans a year-end reporting period, the disclosure requirement applies only in years with such a delay for all historical periods reported, and arises on an irregular basis for irregular accounting items

- Many also perceive this as an endorsement by the Board of non-compliance with IFRSs that will dilute the IFRS brand and handicap the convergence effort.[98]

In February 2008 the Board put the matter on hold by excluding it from re-deliberations on the improvements package of which it had been part.[99] During the same year, the IAASB considered the responses to its proposal, which in various ways expressed doubt that auditors, or the IAASB, were best placed to deal with the problem. Pointing both to IOSCO's statement and the probability that the IASB would not proceed to amend IAS 1, the IAASB concluded that it would continue to monitor developments but not otherwise pursue the matter.[100] As amended in 2009, ISA 700, by now titled *Forming an Opinion and Reporting on Financial Statements*, included some additional guidance on the auditor's evaluation of whether the financial statements adequately refer to or describe the applicable financial reporting framework, developed in conjunction with the IASB. Some of the more obviously inappropriate statements a company might make about compliance with a reporting framework were ruled out, including the use of imprecise language such as 'the financial statements are in substantial compliance with International Financial Reporting Standards'.[101] The truly

---

[97] Interview with Sophie Baranger, 17 February 2010.

[98] AP 2/2008 paper 4B, appendix 2.

[99] 'Annual Improvements', *IASB Update*, February 2008, 1.

[100] ISA 700 (Redrafted) *Forming an Opinion and Reporting on Financial Statements* (IAASB, March 2009), Basis for Conclusions, paragraphs 50–65.

[101] ISA 700, paragraphs A6 and A7. See also 'IAASB CAG Paper', IAASB CAG Agenda (March 2008), agenda item C.3.3.1 (Clarity—Proposed ISA 700 (Redrafted)), paragraph 4 <https://www.ifac.org>.

sensitive question, whether the auditor should call into question the judgement of a competent national authority to require or allow something other than full IFRSs, had been dropped. The IAASB decision, in turn, provided the final argument for the IASB to remove the issue permanently from its agenda.[102]

It is curious that the IASB said nothing publicly about the IOSCO statement, which was, after all, issued to facilitate financial statement users' understanding of company deviations from IFRSs. Only France's AMF issued a press release on IOSCO's statement. Michel Prada, the long-time chairman of the AMF, was also chairman of IOSCO's Technical Committee, which issued the statement. In the release, the AMF acknowledged that, of course, companies must affirm compliance with 'IFRS as adopted by the EU'. Yet it encouraged companies, as part of the need to be transparent about their accounting framework, to include in a note the Internet address of the European Commission where the complete text of the endorsed standards could be found. Further, where companies complied with full IFRSs, they were also encouraged to make a positive statement to this effect. Companies that were using the remaining carve-out should disclose that fact and provide a narrative explanation of the differences between the accounting policies used and IFRSs.[103] There is anecdotal evidence that, following the AMF's release, more French companies began to assert, or to assert more explicitly, compliance with IFRSs as issued by the IASB. This was true, for instance, of Lafarge, the company where IASC Foundation trustee Bertrand Collomb had been a top executive.[104]

---

[102] AP 3/2009 paper 10, paragraph 7; *IStaR*, March 2009, 3.

[103] 'L'Autorité des marchés financiers invite les émetteurs à suivre la recommandation de l'Organisation internationale des commissions de valeurs sur la transparence en matière de référentiel comptable utilisé', AMF press release dated 12 February 2008 <http://www.amf-france.org>.

[104] Another example would be BNP Paribas, which, starting in its 2007 annual report, began to make its use of the carve-out more explicit.

11

The IASB's Organization Matures

This chapter reviews the evolution of the IASB, following its set-up and initial years as described in Chapter 3, until the middle of 2011. According to the original Constitution, power in the IASC Foundation rested with a board of trustees. The changing composition of the body of trustees is discussed in Section 11.1. One of the most elementary and critical roles of the trustees was the appointment of the IASB Board. Section 11.2 describes how the trustees approached this task, and what this meant for the make-up of the Board. The trustees also appointed the members of the Standards Advisory Council (SAC) and of the International Financial Reporting Interpretations Committee (IFRIC), as discussed in Sections 11.3 and 11.4.

Apart from personnel changes in the trustees, the Boards, and other groups, the organization also changed in the way it approached the task of developing IFRSs. To a large extent, these changes reflected a growing awareness that the Board, while remaining independent in its technical work, should be more responsive to constituents' views, or at least make its responsiveness more visible and demonstrable. Three aspects are discussed in particular. Section 11.5 considers the continuous enhancement of due process, reflecting a consciousness on the part of the trustees that they should be much more active in their exercise of oversight of the Board. Other changes followed from efforts to improve communications and transparency (Section 11.6) and the elaboration of the Board's consultative arrangements, both in its use of specialized advisory groups and in its evolving relations with national standard setters (Sections 11.7 and 11.8).

The Board could not have functioned without a growing technical staff, the evolution of which is the subject of Section 11.9.

Finally, another elementary task of the trustees was to ensure sufficient funding of the Foundation's activities (Section 11.10). Here, the challenge was to reduce or remove the threat to the Board's independence arising out of the original system of voluntary contributions.

All of the issues mentioned above and discussed in this chapter were addressed within the basic framework of the original Constitution, which had not been fundamentally altered by the first Constitution review concluded in 2005. The Constitution established the IASC Foundation as an independent, private-sector entity, with no formally established public accountability. This was increasingly recognized as a problem and was finally resolved by the creation of a Monitoring Board in 2009, which meant a limitation in principle of the previous autonomy of the trustees. This development is covered in Chapter 14, apart from occasional references to the Monitoring Board in this chapter.

11.1 THE TRUSTEES

11.1.1 Trustee Appointments Process

Changes in the composition of the trustees until the end of 2005 were discussed in Chapter 3. According to the Constitution, the trustees themselves were responsible for making new appointments in case of any vacancies, and this did not change with the first Constitution review. However, as discussed in Chapter 7, the trustees responded to criticism that they were a self-perpetuating body by installing, in 2005, a Trustee Appointments Advisory Group, which would advise on the selection of trustees, including reappointments. The final decision on such appointments remained with the trustees themselves. The Group seems to have been a kind of reincarnation of the nominating committee, composed of distinguished public servants, which appointed the original trustees in 1999 (see Section 2.3). The members of the Group were personages at the highest international level, including the managing director of the International Monetary Fund and the president of the World Bank (see Section 7.3 for further discussion). It seems likely that it required personal invitations from no less than Paul Volcker to persuade such eminent figures to join the Group, albeit that its workload was light and infrequent. Meetings of the Group were rarely, if ever, convened, but the views of its members on proposed trustee appointments were regularly solicited.

11.1.2 Changes in Trustee Chairmanship

In a speech in February 2005 to the EU's Accounting Regulatory Committee (ARC), at a time when there was every reason to mind the strained relations between the IASB and some of its European constituents, Paul Volcker seemed predisposed towards a European chairman to succeed him:

> When the new effort to work toward international standards was agreed five years ago, I think there was an understanding among many that the Trustees' chair would usefully be from the United States, given the past skepticism—even antipathy—by some Americans toward the effort. Substantial American support and close collaboration with U.S. standard setters is now more firmly in place. My term expires this year. To my mind at least, a chairman equally dedicated to the principle of common international standards but drawn from another part of the world—certainly including a continental European—would now be appropriate.[1]

The trustees apparently agreed that his successor should be a European. Volcker's second and final term ended on 31 December 2005, and early in 2005 the trustee selection committee began the search in earnest. The trustees advertised for the position in *The Economist* and on the IASB website. Following the search, Volcker consulted informally with EU Commissioner Charlie McCreevy about the suitability of several candidates to succeed him: Mario Monti, a former EU competition commissioner; Hans Tietmeyer, a former president of the Deutsche Bundesbank;

---

[1] Paul A. Volcker, 'Maintaining Progress toward International Accounting Standards', remarks before the ARC, 25 February 2005 <http://ec.europa.eu/internal_market/accounting>.

and Tommaso Padoa-Schioppa, an Italian central banker who was president of the Basel Committee on Banking Supervision and then became a founding member of the executive board of the European Central Bank. Then Volcker himself talked with the candidates. Monti and Tietmeyer declined interest in the position, but Padoa-Schioppa appeared willing to pursue the conversation.[2] Padoa-Schioppa had recently been actively engaged with the IASB in discussions over modifications to the fair value option in IAS 39, so that the corresponding EU carve-out might be removed. It seems that a mutual appreciation grew up in the course of these contacts.

In December 2005, the trustees appointed Tommaso Padoa-Schioppa as chairman, effective in January 2006. But a few months later, in May, he had to resign abruptly when Italian Prime Minister Romano Prodi appointed him to be minister of economy and finance. Philip Laskawy, one of the founding trustees, succeeded him as chairman with the understanding that he would step down as soon as a successor to Padoa-Schioppa was appointed, which did not occur until the end of 2007. For the time being, the trustees once again had an American chairman. The trustees searched for another European candidate, who proved difficult to find. Meanwhile, in December 2006, Laskawy reached the end of his second term. As a rule, a trustee's term was renewable only once, but the Constitution as amended after the first review in 2005 allowed a separate appointment as chairman, regardless of prior service as a trustee. The trustees availed themselves of this clause to appoint Laskawy to a third term of three years, to enable them to complete the search for a new chairman, again with the understanding that he would serve until a replacement was found.[3] In December 2007 Gerrit Zalm, who had served three Dutch governments as minister of finance, became chairman. The trustees named Laskawy to serve as vice chairman under Zalm, having sought legal advice as to whether he could continue serving as a trustee if he were appointed vice chairman.[4] Laskawy continued as a trustee until December 2009, by far the longest term of service of any of the trustees during the IASB's first decade. But Zalm's term also had to be attenuated. In late 2008 the Dutch government persuaded him to take charge of the administration of the troubled bank ABN AMRO, leading him to resign after only two and a half years of service. As discussed more fully in Chapter 14, the trustees found Tommaso Padoa-Schioppa willing to assume the chairmanship once again. Unfortunately, he died in December 2010, having taken office in July. Tsuguoki Fujinuma and Robert Glauber, who had been appointed vice chairmen in July 2010, assumed the position of acting co-chairmen. They held this position beyond the period covered in this book, until the appointment of Michel Prada, a former chairman of the Autorité des Marchés Financiers (France), whose term began in January 2012.

11.1.3 Appointments of the Other Trustees

One of the changes to the Constitution in 2005 was to increase the number of trustees from nineteen to twenty-two. The geographical distribution was to be at

[2] IASCF trustees meeting of 14–15 November 2005, agenda paper 3.
[3] IASCF trustees meeting of 26–7 October 2006, minute J.
[4] IASCF trustees meeting of 31 October–1 November 2007, agenda paper 9A.

least six trustees from North America, at least six from Europe, and at least six from Asia-Pacific (compared with at least four of the nineteen in the initial Constitution), plus four trustees from any region to achieve an overall geographical balance. As successor appointments and reappointments were made, members from an expanded set of countries were named to the board of trustees: Spain and Switzerland in 2005, and China, India, and Poland in 2006. By 2008, North America and Europe each had seven trustees, while Asia-Oceania (renamed from Asia-Pacific) had six of the twenty-two. In addition, South Africa and Brazil had one each. The last new country to be represented was South Korea, added in 2011.

In advertisements placed to solicit applicants for trustee positions, the required qualities were, with minor variations, stated as follows:

> A suitable candidate must demonstrate a firm commitment to the IASC Foundation and the IASB as a high quality global and independent standard-setter, be financially knowledgeable, and have an ability to meet the time commitment. Applicants should have an understanding of, and be sensitive to the challenges associated with the adoption and application of high quality global accounting standards developed for use in the world's capital markets and by other users.[5]

While advertisements were duly placed when there were vacancies, it would seem that the consultations with significant constituent organizations in the relevant geographical areas were by far the most important source of trustee candidates. Apart from consulting the Trustee Appointments Advisory Group, the trustees typically made sure that appointments enjoyed support in their home countries. While the European Commission had no formal role in the trustee appointment process, the trustees took care to ascertain the support of the Commission for European candidates, or its acquiescence in decisions such as the change of Laskawy's role from chairman to vice chairman upon the appointment of Zalm.[6]

Between 2005 and 2008, Max Dietrich Kley (Germany), Bertrand Collomb (France), Oscar Fanjul (Spain), Tsuguoki Fujinuma (Japan), and Antonio Vegezzi (Switzerland) all were reappointed to second terms.

In January 2005, Richard G. Humphry (Australia), formerly managing director and chief executive of the Australian Stock Exchange, succeeded Ken Spencer whose term had been shortened by his death.

January 2006 saw by far the greatest single change in the composition of the trustees so far, as no fewer than eight new trustees were appointed, more than a third of what was by then a board of twenty-two members. Junichi Ujiie, of Japan, chairman of Nomura Holdings Inc., succeeded Toru Hashimoto, who retired after his three-year term. Sir Sydney Lipworth, of the United Kingdom, was succeeded by Sir Bryan Nicholson, who had succeeded Lipworth as chairman of the UK Financial Reporting Council. Nicholson became one of the leaders of the trustees and eventually chaired the trustees' nominating committee. Charles Lee, of Hong Kong, was succeeded by Marvin Cheung, retired chairman and chief executive of KPMG Hong Kong as well as a member of SAC from 2001 to 2005. Sir Dennis Weatherstone and David Ruder, both from the United States, were succeeded by

---

[5] IASCF trustees meeting of 21 June 2005, agenda paper 5.
[6] For support of a European trustee, see IASCF meeting of 23–4 March 2006, agenda paper 9; on Laskawy, see IASCF trustees meeting of 31 October–1 November 2007, agenda paper 9A.

William J. McDonough, the retired founding chairman of the Public Company Accounting Oversight Board and former president of the Federal Reserve Bank of New York, and by Samuel A. DiPiazza, Jr, the chief executive of Pricewater-houseCoopers United States. In addition, David L. Shedlarz, vice chairman of Pfizer Inc. and who had served on SAC from 2001 to 2005, was appointed as a US trustee. With Paul Volcker's retirement, Shedlarz's appointment restored the North American contingent to six. Shedlarz was hardly a model trustee: he missed ten of the eleven meetings during his three-year term.

Two appointments in January 2006 that signalled a shift towards Asia were Liu Zhongli, president of the Chinese Institute of Certified Public Accountants and China's former minister of finance, and T. V. Mohandas Pai, board member and chief financial officer of Infosys Technologies Limited and board chairman of Progeon Limited, India. These were the initial appointments from China and India.

The cumulative effect of the previous appointments was what might be called a generational shift among the trustees. Whereas up to the end of 2004 only six new trustees had been appointed, leaving the founding members in a solid majority, about a year later, early in 2006, the position was reversed, and the founding trustees had been reduced to a minority of six in a group expanded to twenty-two members. Compared to the Board (see Section 11.2), the renewal of the trustees occurred rather earlier, and less gradually.

In March 2006, Jens Røder, of Denmark, retired from the trustees less than half way through his second term, but he was named a senior adviser to the trustees with the right to attend meetings during the remainder of his term, until December 2007.[7] Succeeding Røder from March onwards was Dr Alicja Kornasiewicz, from Poland. She was chairman and chief executive of CA IB Group and chairman of the supervisory board of Bank BPH, the third largest bank in Poland. She served as secretary of state and first deputy minister of the Ministry of the State Treasury from 1997 to 2000.

In January 2007, Roy Andersen, of South Africa, was succeeded by Jeff van Rooyen, chief executive of Uranus Investment Holdings, a broad-based black empowerment company. Van Rooyen was also vice chairman of the executive committee of the International Organization of Securities Commissions (IOSCO) and was former chief executive of South Africa's Financial Services Board. L. Yves Fortier, of Canada, was succeeded by Paul Tellier, former president and chief executive of both Bombardier and Canadian National Railway, a Crown corporation. Cornelius Herkströter, of the Netherlands, was succeeded by Kees Storm, former chairman of the management board of Aegon, a major Dutch insurance group, and chairman of the supervisory board of KLM. He served on SAC from 2005 to 2007. In the event, Storm served only one year of this three-year term. A third appointment in January 2007 brought the number of trustees back to twenty-two. This was David Sidwell, the chief financial officer of Morgan Stanley, New York City, who had served on SAC from 2001 to 2005.

In January 2008, Richard Humphry of Australia (having missed four of ten meetings), was succeeded by Jeffrey Lucy, chairman of the Financial Reporting

---

[7] IASCF trustees meeting of 14–15 November 2005, minute 7.

Council and member (and former chairman) of the Australian Securities and Investments Commission. William McDonough, of the United States, who had to resign at the end of the second year of his three-year term (having attended only three of seven meetings), was succeeded by Dr Robert R. Glauber, former chief executive of the National Association of Securities Dealers and former under-secretary of the Treasury for finance. Glauber played a leadership role on the trustees. As indicated above, he was appointed vice chairman in July 2010, together with Fujinuma, and with him he became acting co-chairman in December 2010. Roberto Teixeira da Costa, of Brazil, was succeeded by Pedro Malan, former Brazilian minister of finance and former president of the Banco Central do Brasil. Luigi Spaventa, of Italy, completed Storm's term. He was formerly chairman of the Commissione Nazionale per le Società e la Borsa (CONSOB), the Italian securities regulator. Malcolm Knight, who was classified as coming from an international organization, was succeeded in January 2008 by Gerrit Zalm.

In January 2009, Marvin Cheung, Samuel DiPiazza, Bryan Nicholson, Mohandas Pai, Liu Zhongli, and Robert Glauber all were appointed to second terms. Clemens Börsig, of Germany, chairman of the supervisory board of Deutsche Bank, succeeded Max Dietrich Kley. Junichi Ujiie, of Japan, was succeeded by Noriaki Shimazaki, board member and executive vice president of Sumitomo Corporation. David Shedlarz, of the United States, was succeeded by Scott Evans, executive vice president-asset management of TIAA-CREF and chief executive of TIAA-CREF Investment Management LLC.

In December 2009, Alicja Kornasiewicz, of Poland, retired a year before the end of her second term. She had missed seven of thirteen meetings, including all of her last six, because of ill health.

In January 2010, Jeff van Rooyen, David Sidwell, Paul Tellier, and Luigi Spaventa were appointed to second terms. However, Spaventa retired as a trustee in June 2010 shortly before Padoa-Schioppa, also an Italian, began a three-year term. Bertrand Collomb, of France, was succeeded by Yves-Thibault de Silguy, vice chairman and lead director of Vinci and a former EU commissioner for economic, monetary, and financial affairs. Philip Laskawy, of the United States, was succeeded by Harvey Goldschmid, a law professor at Columbia University and a former commissioner of the Securities and Exchange Commission (SEC). He was also co-chairman of the IASB–FASB Financial Crisis Advisory Group.

In January 2011, Tsuguoki Fujinuma, Jeffrey Lucy, and Pedro Malan began new terms after being reappointed. In Fujinuma's case it was to be a third term, agreed when he was appointed vice chairman in July 2010. As indicated above, by the time his third term began he was serving as acting co-chairman. Oscar Fanjul, of Spain, was succeeded by Antonio Zoido, board chairman and chief executive of Bolsas y Mercados Españoles, the operator of all stock markets and financial systems in Spain. Zoido had served on the IASC's Advisory Council in 1998–99, when he was president of the Madrid Stock Exchange. The trustees succeeded in making two appointments to fill the open chairs of Zalm, Vegezzi, and Kornasiewicz. One was Duck-Koo Chung, who became the first South Korean trustee. He was formerly minister of commerce, industry, and energy. The second was Dick Sluimers, of the Netherlands, who was chairman of the management board of the APG Group, a financial services provider.

Since 2010, encouraged by Chairman Bryan Nicholson of the nominating committee, the trustees have been seeking women candidates for the trustees.[8] So far, the only woman trustee has been Alicja Kornasiewicz, who took a shortened term.

11.1.4 The Trustees as a Group

Despite considerable turnover, as recited above, the composition of the trustees in terms of their credentials and background was quite stable during the ten years under study, except for a gradual geographic expansion. New trustees continued to be recruited from among senior executives of large corporations, audit firms, and stock exchanges, with more than a sprinkling of people from governmental and regulatory backgrounds. As new trustees were chosen, their previous experience in regulating or overseeing capital markets, or in other public service, was evidently an important primary criterion. The following trustees who were appointed between 2005 and 2008 possessed such experience: Nicholson, McDonough, Liu, Kornasiewicz, van Rooyen, Tellier, Lucy, Glauber, Malan, and Spaventa, as well as Chairmen Padoa-Schioppa and Zalm.

The essential roles of the trustees, as defined by the Constitution, were to appoint members of the Board and successor trustees, to ensure sufficient funding, and to exercise oversight over the Board's activities. A strict reading of the independence of the Board would have meant that the trustees should not discuss the substance of the Board's agenda. On the other hand, it would have been difficult to recruit eminent and highly qualified individuals as trustees if they were to confine their discussions solely to matters of process and procedure. But there was an opportunity for the trustees to convey their wisdom on the substance of the Board's work, to be sure informally and unofficially. From the beginning, the custom was adopted for David Tweedie to report on the Board's agenda at every trustees' meeting. The trustees would give their views, knowing that a well-advised Board would weigh them with others.

Inevitably, some trustees found that they could not devote enough time to their role, or that it was not, after all, something which captured their interest. Yet those who were actively engaged still formed a sizeable group of estimable ability and experience, to the point that occasionally the question was raised whether the organization really drew all of the potential benefits which such a group might have to offer. One trustee confided, 'if you are going to bring people of this calibre half way around the world, and the meeting lasts only a day and a quarter, people are going to wonder why they're doing it'. Both to members of the Board and to the IASB's constituents, the trustees other than the chairman were not very visible, except during the two Constitution reviews. Their activity, such as fundraising, occurred mostly behind the scenes. Some assumed a role in furthering the cause of IFRSs in their home countries, but to the extent that they gave speeches or wrote articles at all, these were not collected on the IASB's website, again with the exception of the chairmen. Nor did the trustees evince an interest in enhancing

---

[8] IFRS Foundation trustees meeting of 5–7 July 2010, agenda paper 3, Appendix A.

the role played by regulators in assuring that the IFRSs were faithfully followed by listed companies. One early member of the trustees said that the trustees were not in 'the compliance business'. That was something, he said, for governments to worry about.

The trustees continued to schedule their quarterly meetings (but only three in 2006) at venues around the world, which gave them the opportunity to 'rub shoulders' with local standard setters, regulators, company executives, and members of the financial community. From 2006 to 2010, their yearly pattern was to meet once in London, once in the United States (in Washington or New York City), once in Asia, and once somewhere else. The Asian venues were Tokyo, Beijing, Seoul, and New Delhi. The other locations were Berlin, Madrid, Rome, Amsterdam, and Rio de Janeiro.

During the first five years, two trustees stood out: Paul Volcker and David Ruder. Volcker was a dominating figure both in personality and stature—he was six feet, seven inches (2.01 meters) tall. He was world-renowned for his service in the United States as a central banker. As the first chairman of the Foundation trustees, he gave the organization instant credibility. Among the trustees, Volcker was such a strong figure that, at least a few suggested, the other trustees were not as outspoken or as active as they might have been, and let Volcker take the lead. He played a particularly strong role in fundraising in the United States.

David Ruder, a former chairman of the US SEC and until 2002 a trustee in the Financial Accounting Foundation (FAF), which oversees the Financial Accounting Standards Board (FASB), continually preached the importance of the IASB being independent and of leaving the Board alone. He was also a valuable link between the Foundation and the SEC. He was a proponent of the Foundation operating just like the FAF. While the FAF was certainly an important point of reference, there was a difference from the beginning. While the FAF trustees' meetings lasted for only three hours or so, the Foundation trustees would meet for a day or more. Even if this may have reflected no more than the complexities of setting up an international organization, it does suggest a somewhat more intensive involvement on the part of the Foundation trustees.

During the second five years, a leading figure among the trustees was Bryan Nicholson. A proactive trustee, he chaired the nominating committee and played a key role in the delicate process of selecting the successor to David Tweedie as Board chairman as well as in the selection of Tommaso Padoa-Schioppa to succeed Gerrit Zalm as trustees' chairman. With his impeccable contacts at the highest levels in the United Kingdom, he paved the way for his country to become the 'lead nation' in establishing a levy on listed companies to support the Foundation and the Board, to be emulated by other countries. Finally, when Chairman Gerrit Zalm took over the helm of the nationalized ABN AMRO in 2008, and thus had much less time to devote to the IASC Foundation, Nicholson deftly stepped into the void to manage the day-to-day affairs for which Zalm did not have the time. The most important among these duties was frequent conversations with David Tweedie.

Another trustee who stood out during the second half of the decade was Antonio Vegezzi, who took the lead, following the first review of the Foundation's Constitution, to elaborate the due process requirements governing the work of the Board and of IFRIC.

Even though Tommaso Padoa-Schioppa served as chairman for two periods of only four and six months, he made a considerable mark. He argued that it was important for the trustees to conduct a strategy review in 2010 (which they did), and he acted decisively in persuading Hans Hoogervorst, who was then chairman of the Monitoring Board, to become a candidate to succeed David Tweedie as Board chairman.

11.2 CONTINUITY AND CHANGE IN THE COMPOSITION OF THE BOARD

In considering the changes in the Board, the most notable fact is that the number of such changes was limited, because eleven out of the fourteen founding Board members were reappointed to second terms.

The first new appointment to the Board was discussed in Chapter 3, where it was shown how John Smith (see Figure 11.1) succeeded Bob Herz in September 2002, after Herz was named chairman of the FASB. Smith's appointment was part-time. In June 2007, he retired from Deloitte in New York City and was reappointed as a full-time member of the Board for a five-year term.

Apart from Herz, the other two initial Board members who were not reappointed were Harry Schmid, from Switzerland, who retired at the end of March 2004 before the end of his term, and Geoffrey Whittington, of the United Kingdom, who did not seek a second term when his first term concluded on 30 June 2006. Because all of the other original Board members were reappointed, mostly for five-year terms, it was not until the second half of 2009 that a majority of the Board consisted of second-generation members.

Figure 11.1 John Smith

The reappointment of the founding Board members was a matter of recurring debate among the trustees. Because of the members' staggered initial terms, this question first came up in connection with the scheduled end of the terms of four Board members in June 2004. When this was first discussed in July 2003, the assumption was apparently that all would be reappointed, if willing. Plans to search for candidates were made with respect to the vacancy to be left by Schmid only, as he had already apprised the trustees of his wish to retire.[9] The assumption of reappointment went back to an understanding believed to have been given to the Board members when their applications were invited or discussed in 2000, that they could reasonably expect a second term, assuming adequate performance. This was justified by the perception that the founding Board members—the full-time members—had taken something of a risk by giving up their positions to embark on a venture with an uncertain outcome.[10] However, as discussed in Section 7.3, once the review of the IASB's Constitution gathered speed in the second half of 2003, the trustees understood that reappointment was a sensitive issue. In November 2003, for instance, the trustees met with EU Commissioner Frits Bolkestein, who emphasized the importance of a stronger European contingent on the IASB.[11] From this perspective it was a little awkward that all of the four members slated for reappointment in 2004—Mary Barth (a part-timer), Tony Cope, Tom Jones, and Tricia O'Malley—were North Americans, even though Cope and Jones also held British passports.

Geography was not the only issue. The preponderance of former standard setters and technically proficient members on the initial Board had provoked reaction from outside observers on how the Board functioned. One trustee whom we interviewed said that the general external view which he heard was 'that the first Board was too academic, not closely enough related to the real world, too inclined to want to take a purist view of the standard-setting process, rather than recognition that you've got to make it fly [that is, to make its standards acceptable]'. As the trustees began to consider modifications to the Constitution's criteria for Board membership, to provide for a Board with a broader range of backgrounds and experience, the question was discussed whether the trustees should 'lock in' nearly one-third of the membership before the Constitution review was completed, or whether they should aim for more turnover.[12] Yet in March 2004 the trustees decided to proceed with the reappointments. To accelerate the turnover of the Board, they limited the second terms of Cope and O'Malley. In doing so, they honoured the wish for a shorter term that these two Board members had expressed earlier.

The only fresh appointment made in 2004, therefore, following a public announcement and interviews by the trustees' nominating committee, was of Jan Engström (see Figure 11.2), from Sweden, who, in May 2004, was appointed to succeed Harry Schmid. Engström was put forward by the European Round

---

[9] IASCF trustees meeting of 29 July 2003, minute 6.
[10] IASCF trustees meeting of 25 October 2004, agenda paper 8B, paragraph 3; IASCF trustees meeting of 21 June 2005, minute 4; interview with Thomas Seidenstein, 14 October 2009; interview with Jens Røder, 23 March 2010.
[11] IASCF trustees meeting of 3–4 November 2003, minute 1.
[12] IASCF trustees meeting of 9 March 2004, minute 7.

Figure 11.2 Jan Engström

Table of Industrialists (ERT), a network of directors of multinational companies. The ERT had completed an arduous search for a suitable and willing preparer from the Continent, preferably one with a wider perspective—whose company background was not in technical accounting. Engström had served for thirty years in various senior positions for Volvo in Sweden and Latin America, including as chief financial officer successively of the Volvo Group and of Volvo Bus Corporation.[13] Of all the Board members appointed thus far, he was the furthest removed from accounting. Upon his appointment, Engström was encouraged by the trustees to bring some common business sense into setting standards. In May 2009 he was reappointed to a second five-year term, which expired on 30 June 2014.

If it was true that David Tweedie had a considerable sway over the naming of the initial Board members—so that the Board was composed predominantly of those with whom he had worked before and was comfortable—the appointment of Jan Engström marked a departure in the sense that Engström, and most subsequent appointees, were people who were new to Tweedie's experience.

The trustees again had to deal with reappointments in October 2004, as the terms of three Board members—Bob Garnett, Gilbert Gélard, and Jim Leisenring—were to expire in June 2005. In a memo to the trustees, David Tweedie recommended all three for reappointment. Although the trustees emphasized that they had no objections to reappointing these three members, there was now an even stronger view among the trustees that turnover was important, and that two terms of five years was too long for Board membership.[14] But after debating the

---

[13] More extensive biographies of Engström and all Board members may be found at <http://www.iasplus.com/en/resources/ifrsf/iasb-ifrs-ic/iasb-history>.

[14] IASCF trustees meeting of 25 October 2004, minute 8; IASCF trustees meeting of 18 March 2005, minute 7.

matter at some length, the trustees decided in March 2005 to reappoint the three, all for full five-year terms. The press release announcing the reappointments gave some further information about the trustees' reasons for the reappointments, compared to the succinct statement issued a year earlier to announce the previous set of reappointments.[15] This time, the trustees did mention, and apparently for the first time in public, the understanding given to the initial Board members concerning their reappointment.

This second reappointment decision provoked critical reactions, particularly in Europe, and especially in France. In a joint letter, the presidents of the two main accountancy bodies and of the banking, insurance, and general employers' associations in France sharply criticized the trustees for not issuing a call for nominations and for a general lack of transparency in the reappointment process. They asserted that similar views were held by their counterparts at the European level, including the Fédération des Experts Comptables Européens (FEE), UNICE, and the European Banking Federation.[16] Trustees Chairman Paul Volcker strongly rejected the allegation that the trustees had not followed due process and hit back by expressing his 'doubts about the commitment of French business to the basic concept of international accounting standards, a concept embedded in EU law'.[17] Nonetheless, the trustees were struggling to square a strong desire held by many of them to speed up turnover within the Board with an equally strong sense that the commitment to the founding Board members had to be honoured.

The issue of reappointment presented itself one last time in June 2005, in connection with the ending of the terms of the remaining five founding Board members, including the chairman, in June 2006. The trustees treated Tweedie separately from the other four, and they agreed to reappoint him for a second five-year term, subject to his acceptance. The decision was reaffirmed later that year and was publicly announced in December 2005.

Of the other four members whose terms would end in June 2006, only Geoffrey Whittington indicated that he would not seek a second term. This meant that the reappointment of Hans-Georg Bruns, Warren McGregor, and Tatsumi Yamada had to be considered. The nominating committee conceded that the original Board members were given to believe that they would be reappointed if their performance had been satisfactory, but the committee believed that 'the conditions under which the IASB was operating had changed'. The majority of the committee was in favour of advertising for the positions, and that the advertisement should note 'the three IASB members were seeking reappointment and that would be taken into account'. David Tweedie, while he did not have responsibility in the matter of selection, took issue with the nominating committee. The minutes of the trustees' meeting said, 'He [Tweedie] pointed out that he believed that a commitment had been made, he had done some persuading to convince

[15] 'IASC Foundation Reappoints Four IASB Members' and 'IASC Foundation Reappoints Three IASB Members', IASCF press releases dated 26 May 2004 and 7 April 2005, respectively.

[16] Letter from Vincent Baillot (CNCC), Jean-Pierre Alix (CSOEC), Daniel Bouton (FBF), Gérard de la Martinière (FFSA), and Ernest-Antoine Seillière (MEDEF) to Paul Volcker, dated 20 April 2005, attached to agenda paper 4A, IASCF trustees meeting of 21 June 2005.

[17] Letter from Paul Volcker to Baillot, Alix, Bouton, de la Martinière, and Seillière, dated 29 April 2005, attached to agenda paper 4A, IASCF trustees meeting of 21 June 2005.

individuals to join the IASB and sacrifice their positions at the time, and feels honor-bound by his commitment'. In a compromise solution, the trustees agreed to advertise for all four positions, but to indicate that the three current Board members would be given 'particular consideration'.[18]

Perhaps because of the discouragement implicit in the advertisement, the trustees received only around twenty-five nominations for the four positions, following which interviews were held with the three current members as well as with selected applicants. The nominating committee reported that it had drawn up its short list of interviewees, with particular emphasis on finding candidates from a preparer or user background, to reflect the trustees' thinking on the 'diversity of practical experience' in the Board during the recent review of the Constitution.[19] The result of the procedure was that the three Board members were reappointed for five-year terms. In the vacancy created by Whittington, the trustees appointed Philippe Danjou (see Figure 11.3), of France, who had served on SAC since 2001 and who joined the Board in November 2006. While Danjou was neither a preparer nor a user, as a former regulator he did bring a different kind of background to the Board. He had been a partner in Arthur Andersen & Co. in Paris prior to becoming chef, then directeur des affaires comptables (chief accountant) in 1997 of France's Commission des Opérations de Bourse (the stock exchange regulator), which merged into the Autorité des Marchés Financiers in 2003. His first term expired on 30 June 2011, and he was subsequently reappointed to an additional five-year term. Danjou was the first of several ex-regulators who were to join the Board.

Figure 11.3 Philippe Danjou

---

[18] IASCF trustees meeting of 21 June 2005, minute 4, and meeting of 14–15 November 2005, minute 8.
[19] IASCF trustees meeting of 23–4 March 2006, agenda paper 8.

From the second half of 2006 onwards, the challenges facing the trustees with respect to Board appointments took on a different character. They now had to face the obvious consequence of their earlier decisions to reappoint all of the founding Board members who sought second terms, which was the prospect of having to compose an almost entirely new Board over the next five years. In doing so, they had to take note of the growing number of countries adopting IFRSs, even though the Constitution did not prescribe a geographical balance within the Board. Moreover, as the nominating committee observed in October 2006, with a subtle reference to the recent tendency to seek a greater variety of backgrounds, there still was a need to 'retain individuals with strong technical skills'.[20] The trustees took their first steps in this direction in October 2006 when they reappointed John Smith to a second term of five years, starting in July 2007. At the same time, they changed his membership status from part-time to full-time. Smith was generally regarded as one of the Board's leading technicians, in particular with respect to financial instruments.

By July 2007, two full-time positions would be available, as the second terms of Tony Cope and Tricia O'Malley were ending. In addition to reappointing Smith, the trustees decided in October 2006 to fill the first of these two positions by appointing Zhang Wei-Guo (see Figure 11.4) to a five-year term on the Board. Zhang had been chief accountant and director-general of the department of international affairs of the China Securities Regulatory Commission (CSRC), having joined the Commission in 1997. Prior to then, he had been an accounting professor at the Shanghai University of Finance and Economics, from which he had received a Ph.D. in economics. As discussed in Section 10.2, China had made very rapid moves towards convergence with IFRSs from late 2005 onwards.

Figure 11.4 Zhang Wei-Guo

---

[20] IASCF trustees meeting of 26–7 October 2006, agenda paper 7C.

Following the decision to appoint a Chinese trustee in November 2005, the appointment of a Board member from China was a logical next step. Zhang's appointment to the Board expanded the number of members from Asia-Oceania from two to three.

The appointment of Zhang and the reappointment of Smith were not preceded by a call for nominations. The trustees had already discussed Zhang's candidacy together with that of Danjou during the earlier round of appointments in June 2006. They appointed Danjou and proceeded to obtain assurances from the Ministry of Finance and the CSRC that they supported Zhang's candidacy, with a view towards appointing Zhang to fill one of the vacancies in July 2007. After receiving assurances from both bodies, the trustees appointed Zhang to the Board.[21] Apparently the trustees felt that the results of that search process in early 2006 also provided a sufficient basis for the reappointment of John Smith.

This left the part-time position vacated by Smith. The trustees decided to leave this position open for the time being, as they wished to consider the possibility of reducing the size of the Board and of eliminating the part-time positions.[22] In January 2007, however, Hans-Georg Bruns, of Germany, one of the founding members, unexpectedly announced that he would retire on 30 June, for personal reasons, one year after he had been reappointed to a second five-year term. The trustees thereupon decided to advertise for both a part-time and a full-time position, with the understanding that they were looking for a user and a preparer, possibly from Germany and Canada, to replace Bruns and O'Malley.[23]

The user was found first, although from the United Kingdom rather than Canada. In August 2007 Stephen Cooper (see Figure 11.5) began serving on the Board in a part-time capacity. Users had always been hard to find, and, as indicated in Chapter 3, the three users on the initial Board—Cope, Garnett, and Whittington—were somewhat dubiously designated as such. But there was no doubt that, with Cooper, the Board gained its first 'genuine' user, coming directly from practice. A chartered accountant, Cooper was a managing director in the equities division of UBS Investment Bank. An analyst specializing in equity valuation and accounting, he had been voted the Number 1 analyst in Europe for several years. Cooper was a familiar face for the Board, as he had been an active member of the Analyst Representative Group, which had been meeting regularly with the IASB since 2004 (see Section 11.7). In January 2009, Cooper resigned from UBS and ascended to a full-time position on the Board, where he had already established himself as a leader in the discussions.

Cooper was the last part-time member to be appointed. The Constitution as revised in 2009 allowed for a maximum of three part-time members, but this has so far remained a dead letter and is likely to remain so. Part-time membership, initially thought of as a means of attracting preparer candidates, came to be regarded as an unreasonably demanding assignment. The part-time member had to attend all of the meetings and read all of the papers in the same way as

---

[21] IASCF trustees meeting of 26–7 October 2006, agenda paper 7C.

[22] IASCF trustees meeting of 26–7 October 2006, minute 3. However, the 6 November 2006 press release announcing the decisions with respect to Smith and Zhang stated that 'The trustees are in the process of completing their search for the remaining IASB position to be vacated in June 2007'.

[23] IASCF trustees meeting of 2–3 April 2007, paper 8B.

Figure 11.5 Stephen Cooper

did the full-time members, in addition to holding down a job in a company, audit firm, or university. David Tweedie, in reflection, believed that part-time member-ship is not really feasible.[24]

Although the appointment of Cooper brought the number of Europeans on the Board back to the original five, the trustees continued an active search for a German preparer into the first half of 2008. Not being successful, they decided in March to open the search to candidates from all countries.[25] This resulted in the appointment of Prabhakar Kalavacherla (see Figure 11.6), of India, who began a term of four and a half years beginning on 1 January 2009. Kalavacherla (known as PK) had been a partner in the San Francisco office of KPMG with responsibility for reviewing IFRS financial statements and filings with the SEC. Previously, he had worked in India, where he was born, and in Europe. He holds an Indian passport.

In the course of 2008, the pressure on the trustees' nominating committee increased. Not only was the Bruns vacancy difficult to fill, the next regular vacancies were already coming up, with the end of the second terms of Barth and Jones in 2009. Moreover, it became likely that the size of the Board would soon be increased from fourteen to sixteen as a result of the ongoing second review of the Constitution (see Section 14.6). Nominating committee chairman Bertrand Collomb was also looking further ahead to the changes in 2010 and 2011, and began reminding his colleagues that the search for a new Board chairman had to begin well in advance of Tweedie's retirement on 30 June 2011. Tweedie himself had urged the trustees to be careful when making new appointments and to avoid disrupting the Board's work by the appointment, in rapid succession, of many new

---

[24] Interview with David Tweedie, 5 June 2013.
[25] IASCF trustees meeting of 8–9 July 2008, minute 13.

Figure 11.6 Prabhakar Kalavacherla

members who needed to familiarize themselves with what was happening in the Board.[26]

After Mary Barth left the Board, Tweedie recruited her under the title of 'academic adviser' to return periodically to London to conduct orientation sessions for newly arriving Board members. Previously, Liz Hickey, when she was director of technical activities, also had oriented new Board members. As vice chairman, Tom Jones had been a valued help to Tweedie as his counsellor. When the Board was about to take a critical vote, Tweedie would rely on Jones to take a sounding of Board members and then advise him of what changes needed to be made to get the matter through. A plan was made that, after Jones's retirement from the Board, he should continue to work out of the New York office of the Board. But the New York office, which was envisaged as a twin for the Board's planned office in Asia, never was established. The trustees agreed with Tweedie that Jones should be retained in the organization. The organization needed outreach, especially to the SEC and to Congress, and Jones, a resident of the United States, could be helpful. Listed as an adviser, he attended the trustees' meetings for the next year.

Tweedie would have liked to appoint another vice chairman, either John Smith or Warren McGregor, but the trustees declined to do so. They thought that a new vice chairman would be perceived as Tweedie's successor.[27]

In January 2009, the trustees announced their decision to change the Constitution to expand the size of the fourteen-member Board by two. On that occasion, they also introduced the following geographical quotas for the sixteen-member Board: normally, four from North America, four from Europe, four from Asia-Oceania, one

---

[26] IASCF trustees meeting of 8–9 July 2008, minute 13.
[27] Interview with David Tweedie, 5 June 2013.

each from Africa and South America, and two to achieve overall geographical balance. With the appointment of Kalavacherla, the number of members from Asia-Oceania increased from three to four and reached its regular size. The fact that Europe already had five members meant that the appointment of a German preparer was not on the cards for the time being. Three additional appointments made to the Board in 2009, therefore, came from other geographical areas: Patrick Finnegan (see Figure 11.7) and Patricia (Pat) McConnell (see Figure 11.8), both from the United States, and Amaro Luiz de Oliveira Gomes (see Figure 11.9), from Brazil. All began five-year terms on 1 July.

Finnegan and McConnell succeeded Mary Barth and Tom Jones, both from the United States, whose second five-year terms ended on 30 June. Following Barth's retirement, and as Cooper had changed to a full-time position in January 2009, all of the Board members were serving on a full-time basis. Finnegan was previously director of the financial reporting policy group of the CFA Institute's Center for Financial Market Integrity. McConnell, a CPA, had previously been senior managing director, equity research, for Bear, Stearns & Co., and had managed the firm's periodic research report sent to clients, *Accounting Issues*, for many years. From 1990 to 2000, she had served in the financial analysts' delegation to the IASC Board, and from 2001 to 2006 she was a member of SAC. McConnell therefore became the only member of a delegation to the IASC Board who was appointed to the IASB Board since 2001. With the appointments of Finnegan and McConnell, together with Stephen Cooper, the user component of the Board acquired a larger prominence. Gomes had been head of the financial system regulation department of the Banco Central do Brasil. In that capacity, he had been playing a lead role in the adoption of IFRSs in Brazil, which was achieved in 2010. Gomes' appointment

Figure 11.7 Patrick Finnegan   **Figure 11.8** Patricia McConnell

Figure 11.9 Amaro Gomes

was the first from South America. There was a desire among the trustees to bring in regulators, in addition to users and preparers, and that was a factor in tapping Gomes as a Board member.

After the retirements of Geoff Whittington in 2006 and Mary Barth in 2009, there was no further appointment of someone whose background was primarily as an academic. Zhang Wei-Guo came closest, having been a full-time accounting academic in Shanghai for twelve years before becoming a regulator in 1997. Possibly, an academic background was not the first that came to mind when the trustees looked for candidates in terms of 'professional competence and practical experience' following the first Constitution review. Yet the FASB has always counted an immediate past academic among its members. Academics have also played important roles in the national standard-setting bodies of several jurisdictions, including Japan, South Korea, Taiwan, and Norway.

Three members were appointed in 2010: Elke König (see Figure 11.10), from Germany; Paul Pacter (see Figure 11.11), from the United States; and Darrel Scott (see Figure 11.12), from South Africa. König and Pacter began their terms on 1 July, while Scott began his service in October. König's and Scott's terms were for five years, while Pacter agreed to a two-year term. They succeeded Gilbert Gélard, from France, Jim Leisenring, from the United States, and Bob Garnett, from South Africa, all of whose second five-year terms ended on 30 June.

With König, the Board finally obtained its German preparer. She holds a doctorate in political science and had been a senior financial executive in the insurance industry: for the past eight years with the Hannover Re Group and previously with Munich Re. König was the fourth woman to serve on the Board, following Barth, O'Malley, and McConnell.

The Board gained another preparer with Scott, who was previously chief financial officer of the FirstRand Banking Group, one of the largest financial

Figure 11.10 Elke König

Figure 11.11 Paul Pacter

Figure 11.12 Darrel Scott

institutions in South Africa. He had served on SAC from 2005 to 2007 and on IFRIC from 2007 to 2010.

By 2010, the Board was, if anything, less technically deep than the trustees might have liked. In particular with the departure of Leisenring, the Board had lost one of its technical mainstays. There were few former national standard setters still on the Board. The appointment of Paul Pacter could be seen as an attempt to redress the balance. Pacter had been, for many years, a member of the senior technical staff of the FASB and subsequently of the IASC and the IASB, and he directed the IASB's major project on IFRS for small and medium-sized entities (SMEs). Since December 2000, as a director in Deloitte Hong Kong, he founded and maintained the firm's IAS Plus website. He is a CPA and holds a Ph.D., having been an accounting professor early in his career.

On 30 June 2011, the three remaining members who had joined the Board in 2001 retired: David Tweedie, the chairman, from the United Kingdom; Warren McGregor, from Australia; and Tatsumi Yamada, from Japan. They were succeeded by Hans Hoogervorst, the chairman, from the Netherlands; Ian Mackintosh, the vice chairman, from Australia/United Kingdom; and Takatsugu (Tak) Ochi, from Japan. The circumstances of the appointments of Hoogervorst and Mackintosh are discussed more extensively in Chapter 14. Hoogervorst had been successively minister of finance and minister of health in Dutch governments and was most recently chairman, since 2007, of the Autoriteit Financiële Markten, the Dutch securities market regulator, as well as chairman of IOSCO's Technical Committee. He was the founding chairman of the Monitoring Board, which the trustees created in early 2009. Mackintosh, who was born in New Zealand, had been chairman of the UK Accounting Standards Board (ASB) since 2004, and he had been chairing the National Standard-Setters group, which was founded in 2005. Previously, he was a member, and later deputy chairman, of the Australian Accounting Standards Board, and was chief accountant of the Australian Securities and Investments Commission from 2000 to 2002. He then worked for the World Bank for two years. From 2001 to 2003, he served on SAC. Ochi had previously been assistant general manager of the financial resources management group of Sumitomo Corporation, in Tokyo. Sumitomo, a big supporter of the IASB, had just issued its first annual report using IFRSs. He was secretary-general of Nippon Keidanren's task force on early adoption of IFRSs and was an adviser to the Accounting Standards Board of Japan (ASBJ). Since 2006, he had been serving on IFRIC.

11.2.1 The Board as a Group

Mirroring the discussion in Section 3.5, this section reviews how the make-up of the Board evolved as a result of the cumulative effect of the individual appointments as related above. These changes were slow to take effect because of the trustees' decisions to appoint most of the initial Board members for a second term. Moreover, in David Tweedie's view, it could take new Board members up to two years of learning before they could fully make their presence felt in the Board's discussions.[28] For a long time, therefore, the Board retained its original character of a group of people able to build on long-standing previous acquaintance—some of the Board's critics would say: a group of buddies—with deep roots in standard setting and a strong attachment to the conceptual purity of its standards. But this character began to change as the original members gradually left the Board. In

---

[28] Interview with David Tweedie, 15 October 2009.

2007, Cope and O'Malley left the Board, followed in 2009 by Barth and Jones and in 2010 by Garnett, Gélard, and Leisenring. Certainly, by the latter date, there was a sense among the remaining members that a tipping point had been reached and that the Board had entered a new stage of life. One aspect of this new stage was a loss of some of the camaraderie that was so evident in the glow of idealism and newness that typified the Board's early years. Another, probably more important, aspect was, as a former Board member lamented, the gradual departure of members with previous experience in setting standards, which, the Board member said, called upon a different skill set than reading and interpreting them. Another Board member observed that the gradual retirement of Board members with strong technical expertise was occurring at a time when the issues facing the Board were more technically complex. For better or worse, the Board was becoming more diverse and more pragmatic (see Figure 11.13).

It is fruitless to attempt to characterize the change in the Board's overall attitude with any degree of precision, and, if anything, one should be careful not to overemphasize the difference between the old and the new Board. It is, for example, true that with Leisenring the Board lost a well-known character, the most frequent speaker (and typically the first to speak) at meetings, a unique combination of analytical power, deep knowledge of the standard-setting literature, and a gritty determination to set standards of the highest quality. Yet Pacter's knowledge of accounting standards was encyclopaedic, Cooper's analytical mind was widely esteemed, and, for instance, Zhang Wei-Guo justified his vote against the exposure draft on rate-regulated activities by an appeal to the IASB's conceptual framework. Nonetheless, there was a view that the Board had changed and that there was a greater openness to views expressed by constituents. Elke König, upon her appointment to the Board, assured the IASB's German

Figure 11.13 The IASB Board in 2007. *Standing, left to right*: Gilbert Gélard, Warren McGregor, David Tweedie, Tatsumi Yamada, Mary Barth, Zhang Wei-Guo, Jim Leisenring, Tom Jones, Philippe Danjou. *Seated, left to right*: John Smith, Jan Engström, Bob Garnett, Stephen Cooper.

constituents that she would not conform to a common perception, right or wrong, of Board members, as she was 'certainly not an accounting ayatollah'.[29] But it was also felt that discussions began to lack a certain depth and rigour, that the Board had to rely somewhat more on the staff for technical expertise, and that there was more readiness to accept ad hoc solutions for the sake of bringing a project to a close, rather than persevere in seeking consistent answers across standards. Philippe Danjou, who has served on the Board since November 2006, said, 'I think there is much more regard [than before] to the feasibility of the solutions, more regard to the possible impact, and probably more consideration of the acceptability of the solutions by the world at large'.[30]

Perhaps as important as the recruitment of new Board members from a different set of backgrounds was the fact that, over time, some of the remaining initial Board members began to adjust their view on the nature of their work, acknowledging that the acceptance of IFRSs was as important as their technical soundness. As Bob Garnett, one of the initial Board members, recalled in an interview:

> Over the years, [the Board has] come to a realization that actually the best way of improving financial reporting is not always to leap the closest to the concept, but to understand the concept, understand where we are, and understand just what direction we can move in. If we can get people to move from where they are now to somewhere that is better, then that is a bigger improvement of financial reporting than trying to take them all the way and getting a much lower level of acceptance, or at a much higher cost.[31]

Warren McGregor had always been known as the Board's most consistent advocate of fair value, and he remained faithful to his convictions throughout his two terms. Yet he observed:

> I've come to accept that, at an international level, one must be even more patient than one has to be at a national level. Change management is more acute at the international level. Jurisdictions have different levels of experience, in capital market reporting, different cultures, different stages of market development and so on. So, education and patience are necessary ingredients to successful financial reporting reform.[32]

'Change management' also entered David Tweedie's vocabulary. While he was, of course, a constant presence on the Board during its first ten years, his handling of the Board's technical agenda did, over time, become infused with a greater awareness of what it took to have new standards accepted in jurisdictions around the world. Moreover, it would seem that a streak of pragmatism which had always been part of his work as a standard setter became more noticeable as his impending retirement from the Board in 2011 made it desirable for him to bring as many projects as possible to a close.

Over the ten years, the Board has had members, with their number given, from the following countries: Australia (1), Brazil (1), Canada (1), China (1), France (2), Germany (2), India (1), Japan (1), South Africa (2), Sweden (1), Switzerland (1), the United Kingdom (3), and the United States (9). Numbers such as these, while

[29] 'Elke König setzt Bilanzstandards in London', *Frankfurter Allgemeine*, 21 April 2010, 19.
[30] Interview with Philippe Danjou, 14 February 2012.
[31] Interview with Bob Garnett, 22 June 2010.
[32] Interview with Warren McGregor, 18 and 19 May 2011.

meaningful, fail to convey the nuances of the geographical balance of the Board. Strictly speaking, geography should not have mattered, as Board members were appointed in a personal capacity, and were, neither before nor after 2009, supposed to be referred to as 'representing' a particular country or region. Few thought of Stephen Cooper as representing the United Kingdom. And few would think of Jan Engström as representing Sweden, and if one thought of him as representing European preparers, the emphasis would be on 'preparers' rather than 'European'. Yet it was clear that the Board continued to look to Tatsumi Yamada to learn about Japanese views, and that Zhang Wei-Guo was an indispensable link to China and its highly centralized system of accounting regulation emanating from the Ministry of Finance.

The United States was by far the largest supplier of Board members, and the only country with as many as five members serving at one time, from 2001 to 2007, with four serving concurrently after then. Following the United States, only the United Kingdom (for nine years) and France (for four years) had two members serving on the Board at the same time. The numerical dominance on the Board of members from the United States, in comparison with those from any other country, is evident. It was also often a point of complaint, especially in Europe, that a country which had not adopted IFRSs was so strongly represented on the Board.

Yet here again the numbers do not tell the full story. The frequent perception of the Board as being dominated by Americans can to a large extent be ascribed to the very active roles played by Mary Barth and Jim Leisenring in public Board meetings. Towards the end of the period, when the American contingent consisted of Patrick Finnegan, Pat McConnell, Paul Pacter, and John Smith, the perception that Board debates were geographically unbalanced had disappeared. Moreover, by that stage any collective influence attributed to the American contingent in the IASB would have paled in comparison to the direct influence of the FASB with which the Board was meeting on a virtually continual basis during the final push to complete the agenda of convergence projects by 2011.

The practice of dissenting to final Board pronouncements (i.e. disregarding alternative views on exposure drafts) is worth noting. When Jim Leisenring retired from the Board in 2010, he held the record for the number of dissents: sixteen. Tony Cope, his former colleague on the FASB, called him the 'king of dissenters'. During the period from 2001 to 2011, the other leading dissenters were Garnett, nine; Yamada, seven; and Barth, Smith, and Cope, six each. Save for Yamada, all of the frequent dissenters were Anglo-Americans. But not all Anglo-Americans were disposed to cast dissents. O'Malley, whom we characterized in Chapter 3 as a Board member whose temperament was one of building coalitions, registered only one dissent in her six years of service.

11.3 EVOLUTION OF THE STANDARDS ADVISORY COUNCIL

In 2001, when SAC was organized, it had forty-nine members from thirty jurisdictions, plus three observers, and it proceeded to meet with the Board three or four times annually. It soon became evident that SAC was attending too much to technical issues in Board drafts, when the Board already had channels open to national standard setters to address such matters, to say nothing of the comment letters received by the Board on its drafts. The initial composition of SAC had been more skewed towards members with technical backgrounds, and forty-nine was regarded as an excessive size for effective meetings.

In 2005, the trustees decided to restructure SAC. They provided 'clear guidance' that 'the restructured SAC's foremost role will be to provide broad *strategic* advice on the IASB's agenda priorities and insight into the possible benefits and costs of particular proposals' (emphasis added).[33] Rather than have David Tweedie serve as the chairman of a body advising his Board, even though the SAC meetings were always chaired by Peter Wilmot, the vice chairman, the trustees decided to amend the Constitution to provide for an independent chairman who had a standing invitation to attend trustees' meetings, in order to strengthen the link between SAC and the trustees. The chairman would be expected to devote one week per month to SAC's work, would have an initial term of three years, and would receive an annual stipend of £75,000. The first chairman was Nelson Carvalho, of Brazil, a professor at the Universidade de São Paulo and a member of SAC since 2001. The trustees advertised in *The Economist* and on the IASB website for applications to serve on the restructured SAC. Interest was strongest in Europe, Australia, and South Africa, where IFRSs had just been implemented, and it was somewhat less so in North America. In the end, SAC's membership was trimmed to forty, and the most notable change in composition was a reduction in the North American contingent from twelve to four (see Appendix 1 for a listing of SAC members). The number of Europeans rose from twelve to fourteen. Whereas the initial SAC membership included ten former members of delegations to the old IASC Board, the new SAC had only three. Eight SAC members were appointed to represent international organizations, such as the World Bank and the Basel Committee on Banking Supervision, up from six in the original SAC.[34] The trustees said that 'the SAC in future should comprise senior financial officers of corporations, investment analysts with knowledge of accounting issues, partners of audit firms with experience in auditing companies applying IFRSs, executives of international financial and development organizations, and other senior representatives of public interest bodies'.[35]

While not mentioned in the context of the Constitution review, a view was held within the IASB organization that SAC should act not merely as an advisory body, but that its members should also support the IASB in other ways, by serving as the IASB's 'ambassadors', or, as discussed in Section 11.10, to assist with fundraising.[36] Another informal function of SAC, appreciated by the trustees, was that it allowed them to identify several qualified candidates for the trustees, the Board, and IFRIC from SAC's ranks. Examples over the years were Marvin K.T. Cheung, David Sidwell, and Kees Storm (appointed to the trustees), Philippe Danjou and

---

[33] 'Restructured Standards Advisory Council Appointed', *IASB Insight*, October/November 2005, 12, and IASCF trustees meeting of 21 June 2005, agenda paper 3, paragraph C51.

[34] 'Restructured Standards Advisory Council Appointed', *IASB Insight*, October/November 2005, 12.

[35] IASCF trustees meeting of 21 June 2005, agenda paper 4B, 1.

[36] IASCF trustees meeting of 28–9 June 2006, agenda paper 7A.

Pat McConnell (appointed to the Board), Jeannot Blanchet (appointed to IFRIC), and Darrel Scott (appointed first to IFRIC and then to the Board).

A few years after the first Constitution review, the trustees again reconsidered the role and effectiveness of SAC. The matter arose as part of the trustees' strategy review undertaken in 2007 (see Section 14.1). An internal strategy document proposed that the members of SAC should be chosen from key stakeholder groups, including preparer, investor, and accountancy groups, thus transforming SAC into a representative body rather than one composed mostly of individuals serving on their own.[37] This was in line with David Tweedie's views; he was minuted as saying in a subsequent trustees' meeting 'that the problem with the SAC is that the membership is very large and each member is there in their personal capacity, and does not represent an organization or stakeholder body. Consequently, the views expressed are disparate and not particularly relevant to the IASB's work. The SAC would be far more helpful if it was composed of representatives of stakeholders and organisations.'[38]

Another aspect was that the trustees recognized that SAC's original set-up took insufficient account of the fact that members of SAC, although mainly serving in an individual capacity, might sometimes represent a vested interest. It was thought better to bring such interests out in the open.[39]

The restructuring of SAC was developed in a January 2008 staff paper. It was proposed that SAC should be composed of 'relevant groups' and organizations that could provide candidates to attend SAC meetings. The paper said, 'While there would not be a guarantee that particular organizations be represented, it seems that using well-recognized stakeholder organizations could be one way in ensuring balanced representation and the necessary liaison among SAC and their constituencies'. The paper suggested the names of more than thirty possible organizations around the world that might be contacted to name persons to attend future SAC meetings.[40]

The trustees thereupon decided to restructure SAC once again. Among other changes, they dropped the 'giving of strategic advice' as one of its roles. Some had questioned whether the Board had been asking the right questions that would enable SAC to provide such advice.[41] In July 2008, the trustees assented to a proposal developed by a subcommittee of trustees that the SAC members would serve primarily as representatives of organizations, while still providing scope for individual appointments. The chairman was to be rotated every three years. It was concluded that these changes required no changes to the IASC Foundation's Constitution.[42]

As part of the restructuring, the trustees provided for two vice chairmen from different regions than the chairman, chiefly to reduce the work load and travel requirements for the chairman. Paul Cherry, the former chairman of the IASC's Standing Interpretations Committee and immediate past chairman of Canada's

---

[37] IASCF trustees meeting of 31 October–1 November 2007, agenda paper 10B, 7.
[38] IASCF trustees meeting of 17–18 March 2008, minute 14.
[39] Interview with Jens Røder, 23 March 2010.
[40] IASCF trustees meeting of 28–30 January 2008, agenda paper 5B, 3–4.
[41] IASCF trustees meeting of 28–30 January 2008, agenda paper 5B, 3.
[42] IASCF trustees meeting of 8–9 July 2008, minute 4.

Accounting Standards Board, became SAC chairman in succession to Nelson Carvalho. Patrice Marteau, of France, and Charles Macek, of Australia, were appointed vice chairmen. The trustees anticipated that there might in the future be regional arrangements in addition to SAC's plenary meetings, although no such regional meetings ever occurred. In addition to the three officers, the new SAC membership on 1 January 2009 was composed of forty-three organizations, including five standard-setting bodies, the European Financial Reporting Advisory Group (EFRAG), and the six largest audit firms, as well as strong representation from the banking and insurance industries. Thus, the technical depth of the membership rose considerably. Membership from the United States vaulted from four to eleven.[43]

Within the Board, some members bridled at having to attend SAC meetings, believing they contributed little fresh insight. Other Board members regarded the meetings as fruitful and useful. Jan Engström said, 'I think it's interesting to hear people who are intelligent, dedicated, and experienced talk about what they are doing. So I think it has always been a good forum.'[44]

Within SAC, opinions about its effectiveness were also divided. Some members concluded that it was not worth their time. One member of SAC said that he found it to be a frustrating experience: it had too many members and seemed more like a forum for making political statements with little or no debate, and then moving on to the next topic. Others recognized the inevitable problems of running such a large advisory group. Most kept coming even though they had to pay their own travel costs.

World Accounting Report said in 2009: 'The new SAC is the third version of an organisation whose precise place within the governance structure has never been well articulated. . . . some observers have seen the SAC as a forum for the disgruntled. In its second iteration it was given an independent chairman and reduced in size but this, too, brought complaints from the excluded.'[45] As noted above, the third iteration focused on organizations, not individuals, and once again became strongly attuned to the technical in the roles and experience of its members.

11.4 IFRIC

The origins of IFRIC, were discussed in Section 3.9, and some of its technical activities are covered in Section 12.12. IFRIC's membership remained at twelve until 2007, when it was raised to fourteen. The trustees decided to make this change to the Constitution, outside of the normal five-year cycle of Constitutional reviews, as a further response to comments received on the draft of IFRIC's *Due Process Handbook*, put out for consultation in 2006. The main reason given for the proposal to expand the membership was to ensure sufficient preparer expertise at

---

[43] 'Trustees Announce Membership of Reconstituted Standards Advisory Council', IASCF press release, 19 February 2009.

[44] Interview with Jan Engström, 14 February 2012.

[45] 'New Standards Advisory Council', *World Accounting Report*, March 2009, 3.

IFRIC meetings.[46] Until then, the Constitution did not provide principles guiding the composition of IFRIC, but with this revision the notion that IFRIC should, like the Board, have a sufficiently diverse membership came to the fore. As modified in November 2007, the Constitution now required that the IFRIC members represent 'the best available combination of technical expertise and diversity of international business and market experience in the practical application of [IFRSs] and analysis of financial statements prepared in accordance with IFRSs' (paragraph 39). As IFRIC was initially constituted in early 2002, seven of its twelve members were auditors, and mutterings could occasionally be heard that IFRIC was too much dominated by the audit profession. The membership of IFRIC turned over faster than that of the Board, with the result that already by the middle of 2006 more than half of its members had been newly appointed since 2002 (see Appendix 1 for an overview of IFRIC membership). By the middle of 2006, preparers and auditors were evenly balanced, with users making up a minority of two. However, as noted by the staff, the preparer members tended to have more difficulty in attending all meetings. Increasing the absolute rather than the relative number of preparers was therefore cited as a justification for expanding the membership of IFRIC.[47]

Geographically, IFRIC did not change much, as a considerable majority of its members continued to be drawn from Europe, the United States, and Canada. The number of members from the Asia-Pacific region did not reach four until the appointment of a Chinese member, Li Feilong, in 2010. Latin America and Africa provided one member between them, first Domingo Mario Marchese (Argentina), followed by Darrel Scott (South Africa). Following the latter's appointment to the Board in 2010, the southern hemisphere was represented on IFRIC by Australia and New Zealand only.

Kevin Stevenson, the IASB's director of technical activities since 2002, had doubled as the first chairman of IFRIC. Upon his return to Australia early in 2005, the trustees appointed Bob Garnett, a member of the Board, rather than another senior staff member, as his successor. At around the same time, the new staff position of IFRIC coordinator was created. The first to hold the position was Allan Cook, a former technical director of the UK ASB. Until his appointment to the IASB staff, Cook had been a member of EFRAG's Technical Expert Group. Plans to expand the staff supporting IFRIC to six full-time equivalents would have given the interpretations body a resource base exceeding that of most national standard setters not many years before.[48] When Cook retired from the position in 2007, he was succeeded as IFRIC coordinator by Tricia O'Malley, whose second term as a Board member ended in June of that year. O'Malley remained with the IASB as director of implementation activities until July 2009, when she again assumed the chairmanship of Canada's Accounting Standards Board.

---

[46] IASCF trustees meeting of 17–18 January 2007, agenda paper 4D.

[47] IASCF trustees meeting of 17–18 January 2007, agenda paper 4D.

[48] The increase in staff assigned to IFRIC is mentioned in the IASC Foundation's *Annual Report 2005*, 15.

11.5 ENHANCED OVERSIGHT AND ELABORATION
OF DUE PROCESS REQUIREMENTS

Due process refers to those features of the decision-making processes of organizations such as the IASB that allow persons and organizations to convey their views on agenda decisions and the drafts of proposed pronouncements before they become final, and that ensure that such views are properly taken into account. The Foundation's first Constitution, approved in 2000, called for an elemental due process regarding the work of the Board, including the issue of exposure drafts and consultation with SAC over the setting of the agenda (paragraphs 31–3). Early in the work of the trustees, and out of respect for the Board's independence, there had been the view that trustees' oversight of the Board's performance, including its due process, should be carried out with a light touch. Around the time of the first Constitution review, both the Board and the trustees had modified their views in response to criticism that the Board's due process was inadequate (see Chapter 7). The Constitution, as revised in 2005, imposed on the trustees an explicit responsibility to establish consultative arrangements and due process for the Board, as well as for IFRIC and SAC, and to review compliance (paragraph 15(f)–(g)). A conspicuous consequence of this change was the publication of a *Due Process Handbook* for the Board, approved by the trustees in March 2006. A similar handbook for IFRIC followed in January 2007.

A little less visibly, the trustees began to ponder how to give effect to their extended oversight responsibility. The lead was taken by a five-member 'procedures committee' established by the trustees in 2004 to review the proposed composition of advisory groups and to consult with the Board about proposed due process arrangements for new projects.[49] This group, initially chaired by Max Dietrich Kley, laid the groundwork for a more systematic approach to oversight by extracting a list of trustees' responsibilities from the Constitution and developing 'effectiveness measures' or 'deliverables' for each of them. The intention was not merely to be more active in oversight, but also to find a means of demonstrating this to the outside world.[50] In due course, a series of tables and checklists were developed which guided the trustees through an annual cycle of decisions and activities, and which formed the basis for a much-expanded section on oversight in the Foundation's *Annual Report*, starting with the report for 2007.[51]

In January 2007, the chairmanship of the 'procedures committee' was taken over by Antonio Vegezzi, under whose leadership the committee increased significantly in importance. The committee, renamed the Due Process Oversight Committee in 2007, was expanded to seven, its mandate was revised more than once, and it was provided with support staff. Vegezzi continued to chair the committee until his retirement from the trustees in December 2010. If David Ruder had embodied the earlier hands-off policy justified by the Board's

---

[49] IASCF trustees meeting of 25 October 2004, agenda paper 4.

[50] IASCF trustees meeting 23–4 March 2006, minute 9; IASCF trustees meeting of 28–9 June 2006, agenda paper 2A.

[51] See IASCF trustees meeting of 2–3 April 2007, agenda paper 3C, for a first version of the list of effectiveness measures. See meeting of 29–30 January 2008, agenda paper 2, for a proposal to expand the oversight section in the annual report.

independence, Vegezzi became the personification of the trustees' enhanced oversight role.

On behalf of the trustees, the Due Process Oversight Committee monitored the Board's technical projects in considerable detail, in order to verify that all required steps had been properly taken and to stay abreast of its ever-changing work plan in order to identify potential risks to the quality of due process at an early stage. The committee took the lead in responding to complaints about specific infractions of the Board's due process.

The committee also established itself as the trustees' 'interface' with the Board. Chairman Tweedie had from the beginning attended all trustees' meetings, but around the time of the first review of the Constitution it was felt that the trustees and the Board should meet more directly. The full Board attended parts of two trustees' meetings in 2005, following which this was scaled down to a practice by which Tweedie came accompanied by three to five Board members, with geographical backgrounds to match the location where the trustees were meeting. While this practice probably helped to give the Board members a better understanding of the role of the trustees, the trustees were not satisfied that effective interaction had been established. It was therefore agreed that the Due Process Oversight Committee should meet twice a year with the full Board in closed administrative session for a more thorough but non-technical discussion of important issues facing the Board.[52]

The *Due Process Handbook* for the Board was revised in October 2008 to codify several innovations that had been introduced since the 2006 edition. As discussed in Chapter 9, these changes were mainly in response to pressures from the European Union where dissatisfaction over the IASB's governance and procedures still rankled and which erupted in politicized protest from time to time. In April and July 2007, the trustees announced several modifications, or plans for modifications, to the IASB's due process.[53]

A change with immediate effect was the introduction of feedback statements accompanying final standards, in which the Board would explain how it had responded to the significant issues raised during the comment phase. The first feedback statement was to be issued with the revised version of IFRS 3 *Business Combinations*, in January 2008 (see Section 12.4). A change with delayed effect was the introduction of post-implementation reviews, undertaken two years after the effective date of a new standard or a major change in a standard. The first standard to which this applied was IFRS 8 *Operating Segments*. When IFRS 8 was issued in November 2006, no mention was made of a post-implementation review, but by the middle of 2007 the endorsement of the standard for use in the EU was becoming a serious political problem which the announcement of a review policy might help to defuse (see Section 9.6). The Board began preparations for this first post-implementation review in July 2011.[54]

---

[52] IASCF trustees meeting of 2–3 April 2007, agenda paper 3A.

[53] 'Summary of the IASC Foundation Trustees Meeting April 2007', IASCF press release dated 23 April 2007; 'Summary of the IASC Foundation Trustees Meeting 2 and 3 July 2007 Madrid', IASCF press release dated 18 July 2007.

[54] AP 7/2011 paper 2B.

One of the more challenging due process problems facing the Board was how it should properly consider the consequences, effects, or impact of its standards, a point which also figured conspicuously in criticisms of the Board emanating from Europe. The 2006 *Due Process Handbook* already included a requirement for the Board to include cost-benefit considerations in its deliberations and to report on these in the basis for conclusions (paragraph 107), but this was hedged about with reminders that this would inevitably be subjective and qualitative, in the absence of well-established techniques for cost-benefit analysis in public policy fields.

Awareness soon developed that such a general exhortation might not be sufficient, and that the Board had to be more pro-active in defining what it could or could not do to answer demands that it should do 'impact assessments'.[55] It was again IFRS 8 which made this issue acute in April 2007, when the European Parliament insisted on an impact assessment before endorsing the standard, an expectation subsequently expanded to all standards submitted for endorsement (see Section 9.6). Also in April 2007, the trustees publicly expressed the view that it was desirable to develop a more explicit framework for cost-benefit analysis, to be incorporated into the IASB's due process. A tentative step was taken when, in the 2008 edition of the *Due Process Handbook*, some of the more defensive language was removed from the paragraphs on cost-benefit analysis, a term which was replaced by 'impact analysis'.

Meanwhile, the European Commission, assisted by EFRAG, had stepped in to provide the Parliament with an ad hoc 'effects study' on IFRS 8, and EFRAG has since continued to conduct such studies as a regular part of its process to develop endorsement advice. EFRAG has continued to argue that the IASB itself should take more responsibility for effects studies.[56] To encourage, or prod, the IASB in this direction, EFRAG and the UK ASB embarked on a research project to consider possible approaches to effects studies in accounting standard setting, resulting in a 2011 discussion paper with proposals addressed explicitly to the IASB.[57] The subject remained on the agenda, and in their April 2011 strategy review report the trustees recommended that an international study group, chaired by the IASB, be convened to develop an agreed methodology for field testing and effect analysis.[58]

The Board did not, within the period studied, adopt a consistent practice of issuing separate effects studies with each new standard or amendment. Apart from questions of methodology, one can see that pressures on the Board's agenda and the increasingly hectic pace of work, beginning with the financial crisis (see Chapter 13) and ending with the rush to complete, by 2011, as many as possible of the planned convergence projects with the FASB (see Chapter 16), were not conducive to the emergence of a stable approach to effect analysis. The first project to be concluded with a separately published effect analysis was business

---

[55] IASCF trustees meeting of 2–3 July 2007, agenda paper 3A(ii).

[56] See e.g. EFRAG *Annual Review 2010*, 16; *Annual Review 2011*, 13.

[57] 'Considering the Effects of Accounting Standards' (FRC/EFRAG, January 2011) <http://www.efrag.org>.

[58] Report of the Trustees' Strategy Review, *IFRSs as the Global Standard: Setting a Strategy for the Foundation's Second Decade* (IFRS Foundation, April 2011), 17.

combinations, completed in 2008,[59] but it was not until 2011 that similarly extensive documentation accompanied the publication of the suite of standards on consolidation and joint ventures, IFRS 10, 11, and 12.[60] IFRS 13, on fair value measurement, was also published in 2011, but its feedback statement contained just a short discussion of cost-benefit considerations, presumably because it was not expected to lead to great changes in practice.[61]

11.5.1 Due Process, a Continuing Discussion

Within the Board there was a certain wariness that calls for enhanced due process, and in particular for effects studies, while in themselves legitimate, could also be delaying tactics to hold back the Board from completing difficult projects. Nonetheless, Board members came to accept that the increased use of its standards around the world, and thus the expanding range of constituents with which it had to deal, necessitated more robust and transparent processes. In the end, the Board took pride in the quality of its due process. As David Tweedie commented in his final chairman's report:

> The way we set standards is also very different from when we began our work in 2001. Back then, we would publish proposals and wait for the comment letters to come in. Today's standard-setting involves developing our proposals using real-time feedback from expert advisory panels, while seeking feedback before, during, and after the formal comment period. We use a variety of methods to encourage the broadest possible participation in the standard-setting process.... At the end of this process, we publish feedback statements that explain what we heard, how we responded and the rationale for the choices that we made. I am not aware of any comparable organisation that can lay claim to consult so widely or communicate so effectively with its stakeholders.[62]

The implementation of the various due process reforms led the trustees to believe that criticisms of the IASB's due process as being fundamentally deficient, a view that could often be heard during the first part of the decade, had by 2011 largely disappeared.

By 2011, it would seem that the importance of adhering to sound due process in accounting standard setting was acknowledged around the world. Perhaps the most telling indicator was the common view that the trustees' decision in October 2008 to suspend the Board's due process—ironically at the same meeting where they approved the revised *Due Process Handbook*—was something that was not to be repeated (see Section 13.3).

---

[59] *Business Combinations Phase II: Project Summary, Feedback and Effect Analysis* (IASB, January 2008).

[60] *Effect Analysis: IFRS 10 Consolidated Financial Statements and IFRS 12 Disclosure of Interests in Other Entities* (IASB, September 2011) and *Effect Analysis: IFRS 11 Joint Arrangements and Disclosures for Joint Arrangements included in IFRS 12 Disclosure of Interests in Other Entities* (IASB, July 2011).

[61] *Project Summary and Feedback Statement: IFRS 13 Fair Value Measurement* (IASB, May 2011), 28–9.

[62] IFRS Foundation, *Annual Report 2010*, 22.

Nonetheless, there could still be disagreement over what due process meant in substance. The number of formal due process complaints reaching the trustees in the second half of the decade amounted to hardly more than a handful, but they could be significant. In April 2010, BUSINESSEUROPE, Nippon Keidanren, and Financial Executives International, claiming to represent 80 per cent of the world's capital markets, wrote to the trustees to complain about the Board's handling of its project to revise the standard on provisions, IAS 37.[63] The substance of their complaint is discussed more fully in Chapter 12, but in essence the associations objected fundamentally to parts of the proposed standard, and therefore with the Board's decision not to re-expose these parts. When the matter came before the Due Process Oversight Committee, a staff paper summarized the Board's position: it had considered the objections when the responses to the previous exposure draft were discussed, but the Board had maintained its views. It was willing to consider the objections once again when finalizing the standard, but this would not necessarily lead to a change of view. It also noted that the relevant due process steps had been observed, including consideration of the criteria for re-exposure in the *Due Process Handbook*, and that the Board had voted eight to seven not to re-expose.[64] In the end, the issue disappeared from sight when the Board decided, late in 2010, to defer completion of the project until after the middle of 2011. Meanwhile, it had served to illustrate a basic question regarding the trustees' due process oversight: is it possible to evaluate the quality of due process by a formal consideration of the steps taken in reaching a decision? Or is the fact that a decision, taken by close vote of the Board, is not accepted by a significant group of constituents in itself an indication of a shortcoming in due process? As discussed more fully in the context of the second Constitution review (see Chapter 14), the consensus view that the IASB's due process had greatly improved over time did not remove the underlying tension between the need to guarantee the independence of the Board and the need to obtain acceptance of its standards.

Finally, it may be observed that demands by constituents for enhancing the IASB's due process also imposed a price on these constituents themselves. Every exposure draft, discussion paper, roundtable, or working group was a call on constituents to invest more of their time in the standard-setting process. Similarly, while the call for more field tests was in itself understandable, the question of who would bear the costs of them was hardly ever raised.

11.6 RESPONSIVENESS, COMMUNICATIONS, AND TRANSPARENCY

As discussed in Chapter 7, a major theme in the first review of the IASC Foundation's Constitution was to ensure that the IASB would be a more responsive and

---

[63] Letter from Philippe de Buck, Yasuhisa Abe, and Arnold C. Hanish to Gerrit Zalm, dated 20 April 2010 <http://www.businesseurope.eu>.

[64] IFRS Foundation trustees meeting of 5–7 July 2010, agenda paper 7B.

accountable organization. The Board itself had consciously tried to improve its working procedures in order to enhance its transparency and its engagement with constituents. These efforts were partly defensive, in response to mounting criticism and opposition, such as over IAS 39. However, they also reflected a more positive sense of obligation to the growing number of parties affected by the IASB's standards, as more and more countries signalled an interest in requiring, allowing, or converging their standards with IFRSs.

During 2005, small groups of Board members and staff visited eighteen European countries in a series of what were called 'roadshows': one-day events organized in conjunction with national standard setters, intended as an occasion for dialogue with relatively small groups of users and preparers. The Board believed that these meetings were helpful in building bridges with Europe, even though their immediate tangible result was a laundry list of complaints and expressed concerns.[65] Despite the roadshows, such criticisms persisted and even grew in intensity, in particular as more and more of the Board's work became governed by the logic of convergence with US generally accepted accounting principles (US GAAP). In May 2006, during one of its strategy retreats, the Board members discussed a letter sent by Tommaso Padoa-Schioppa upon his resignation as chairman of the trustees. As paraphrased in the minutes of the meeting, the letter described his 'perception of the threats surrounding the IASB, which was facing rising hostility from those who wished to rein in its independence, or even replace it with bodies that were politically answerable. This was a risk not only in Europe, but also in Japan and possibly China. The letter warned that the IASB was in an exceptionally fragile position, and advised that the IASB should seek ways to defuse the looming threats.'[66] The meeting went on to discuss a miscellany of possible responses, major and minor. These included giving more attention to Europe, making greater use of field visits and field testing, and a greater willingness on the part of the Board to modify its stance on technical positions, excepting those which 'the IASB was prepared to defend to the last'. In addition, it was thought advisable to cultivate more tactful ways by which the Board could reject views with which it disagreed. This change should be reflected in a different style of debate in Board meetings and in a more nuanced reporting of these debates in *IASB Update*. In all, the Board concluded that: 'It was important that any gesture that the IASB made to appease its critics should not be viewed as empty gestures. They should be, and be seen as, a sincere attempt to respond sympathetically to legitimate concern.'[67]

Prior to the Board's May 2006 retreat, there was already an awareness that the Board needed to do a better job in getting its message across, and that this would require a more coordinated approach. Communications until then had been overseen by a committee of the Board, chaired by Tony Cope, and supported by members of staff who combined this with their other duties. In January 2006, it had been decided to recruit a full-time communications manager.

[65] 'IASB European Roadshows 2005', *IASB Insight*, July 2005, 6. A summary of views expressed during the first nine roadshows held in June 2005 is included in AP 7/2005 paper 1A.

[66] 'IASB Awaydays at Greywalls Hotel on 18 and 19 May 2006', revised draft dated 24 May, paragraph 1, IASB archive, 'awaydays' file.

[67] 'IASB Awaydays at Greywalls Hotel on 18 and 19 May 2006', paragraphs 3–4.

But the Board did not wait for its new communications manager to arrive. At the May 2006 strategy retreat referred to above, the members discussed their communications strategy on the basis of a critical review by Jan Engström.[68] Engström, who had joined the Board in 2004, was the second non-founding member to be appointed and the first without any previous involvement in the IASC or the IASB. Combined with his business experience at Volvo, he was well placed to see the weaknesses in the IASB's public relations efforts. As Engström saw it, these weaknesses included that the Board had an unclear image outside of its core audience of accounting professionals, and that the critical views which dominated the public debate about the IASB were perceived to be unanswered. In his report, he said that between 20 and 25 per cent of Board members' time had been spent on communications and outreach activities, but that this effort should be more focused, with clear objectives and deliverables for the use of that time. Based on his report, which was presented to the Board in May and to the trustees in June, the Board members and the trustees promptly agreed that communications should henceforth be an integral part of a project manager's responsibilities, to enable Board members and staff to give out clear and consistent messages on each project's rationale and expected benefits.

Towards the end of the year, Mark Byatt joined the organization as the IASC Foundation's director of corporate communications, coming from the audit firm of BDO Stoy Hayward, where he held a similar position, after spending seven years as group marketing director for Morse plc.

After he arrived, Byatt could help bring more focus and structure to the organization's attempts at outreach, which were continually refined during subsequent years. One of the outward signs of this was the introduction of a new house style for publications, introduced in the course of 2008. The 'hexagon' logo, which had been created for the IASC in the 1970s, was retained but was incorporated in a new logo prominently including the letters 'IFRS'. The nomenclature of the organization was also changed under Byatt's watch to give uniform prominence to 'IFRS': the IASC Foundation, SAC, and IFRIC became the IFRS Foundation, the IFRS Advisory Council, and the IFRS Interpretations Committee in 2010, respectively. At his suggestion, some thought was given to recasting the IASB as the IFRS Board, but it was felt that the name 'IASB' had already become too deeply rooted in use around the world to make such a change helpful. Another outward change he initiated, reflecting the demise of print media generally rather than the evolution of the IASB, was the discontinuation of the newsletter *IASB Insight*, which began as a quarterly newsletter, *IASC Insight*, in 1991, and whose last issue appeared in 2008. *IASB Update*, previously *IASC Update*, became exclusively electronic in 2009. Meanwhile, he made less visible but equally important improvements in the organization's monitoring of the press and in its cultivation of press contacts around the world. A constant theme was to make sure that important constituent views were heard earlier rather than later in the process. An example of this were roundtables on measurement, organized in January and February 2007 in London, Norwalk, and Hong Kong, just after the IASB and the FASB had embarked on this phase of their joint project to develop a

---

[68] IASCF trustees meeting of 28–9 June 2006, agenda paper 7A.

revised conceptual framework.[69] Byatt believed that it would take a lot of heat off the standard-setting process if constituents could make their views known at an earlier stage rather than when the Board had already made up its mind in the form of discussion papers or even exposure drafts. He also initiated an email alert system keyed to individual projects, which kept interested constituents abreast of every step in the Board's deliberation process. Another outreach vehicle consisted of conferences sponsored around the world by commercial conference organizers which brought the Board members and staff before sizable audiences of preparers, audit firm partners, and users. Sessions were held on the technical facets of emerging and completed standards.

In December 2007, the IASB was proud to announce that it ranked highly among thirty global organizations assessed by the One World Trust in its *Global Accountability Report*, scoring high on dimensions such as transparency and stakeholder engagement.[70] Although the report noted that this could be ascribed partly to the nature of the IASB's activities, which, compared with those of other non-governmental organizations, inherently required a greater amount of stakeholder participation, it was unqualified in holding the IASB out as an example of good practice. Yet some of the IASB's critics remained unconvinced.[71] One World Trust's 2008 report, the last one in the series, was based on a different sample of organizations, so that it provided no basis for judging the IASB's subsequent performance.

11.7 SPECIALIZED ADVISORY GROUPS

As shown in Chapter 7, the IASB began to make a greater use of advisory groups in 2004, sometimes relating to a specific project, sometimes representing a specific constituency. This development was a response to demands for more dialogue with constituents, and, as this demand persisted throughout the first decade, so did the IASB continue to cultivate a growing collection of advisory groups. Some of these were created at the initiative of the Board, and the members were appointed by the Foundation trustees. Other groups were self-organized and were recognized by the IASB as standing interlocutors.

In the Board's continuous quest to seek input from users, the self-organized Analyst Representative Group (ARG) was seen by the Board as a valuable resource. As discussed in Chapter 7, it grew out of a meeting between Board members and a group of financial analysts in 2003, including the future Board members Stephen Cooper and Pat McConnell. From 2004 onwards, the ARG,

---

[69] 'Discussing Measurement—Round Tables Provide the Platform', *IASB Insight*, Q3, 2007, 6–7. For a more detailed report on the roundtables, see AP 3/2007 paper 10A.

[70] Robert Loyd, Jeffrey Oatham, and Michael Hammer, *2007 Global Accountability Report*, The One World Trust, <http://www.oneworldtrust.org>. See also 'IASB Tops Global Rankings for Stakeholder Participation—Identified as "High Performer" for Transparency and Evaluation', IASCF press release dated 2 December 2007.

[71] 'Global Accounting Board Cheered, Jeered on Transparency', news item posted 11 December 2007 <http://www.cfo.com>.

with a membership of about a dozen, drawn from Europe, the United States, and Japan, met some three times a year with the Board for a day, to discuss the Board's work programme and issues arising out of major technical projects. In 2011, the group changed its name to Capital Markets Advisory Committee and endowed itself with a more formal structure, including a chairman and a vice chairman. It remained independent of the IFRS Foundation.

While it might seem natural to match a user group with a preparer group, this next step took some more time. In January of 2004, a series of periodic meetings began with a group of European finance directors representing the ERT. This 'CFO Task Force' was organized and initially chaired by Wolfgang Reichenberger, of Nestlé, with new members appointed on the basis of co-optation. The intention was to engage with a group of senior executives, dealing with high-level issues. Meetings with David Tweedie and a delegation of Board members continued through 2005, and were initially helpful in establishing communication and a degree of mutual confidence between the IASB and these European constituents. However, tensions arose over some of the IASB's technical work, in particular the Board's apparent drive to abolish net income in the course of its project on financial statement presentation (see Section 12.8). The series of meetings was allowed to lapse in 2006. In 2008, a new start was made with the creation of a Global Preparers Forum, a geographically broad-based group of some fifteen members, again self-organized. In July 2008, it began a series of regular one-day meetings with a delegation from the Board, in the same manner as the ARG. Typically, one of the two or three annual meetings of each group with the Board has been held jointly with the other.

At the tail-end of the period covered in this book, the Foundation trustees created an IFRS Emerging Economies Group (EEG) to enhance the participation of emerging economies in the standard-setting process. The group met for the first time in Beijing in July 2011. Although the group was created by the Foundation and initially chaired by Wayne Upton, the Foundation's director of international activities, its secretariat was established in China's Ministry of Finance. The Ministry of Finance was willing to play a leadership role in this area. Already in 2007, it had organized an international conference at which it launched a 'Beijing initiative', calling among other things for a regular mechanism for an exchange of views on accounting convergence among emerging economies and with the IASB.[72] In 2009, the idea had been picked up by Tweedie in a meeting with Wang Jun, the vice minister of finance, as a way of responding to recurrent criticism that the IASB was listening to the United States and Europe only.[73] The initial membership consisted of representatives from the emerging economies in the G20 plus Malaysia.

The preceding groups provided advice across projects by specific constituent groups. In addition, the Board worked with a number of broad-based working or advisory groups focusing on individual technical projects. These groups were created by the Board itself, following a call for applications, with membership

---

[72] 'Beijing Initiative for Promoting International Convergence of Accounting in Emerging and Transition Economies', Ministry of Finance (China) press release dated 12 July 2007 <http://www.ifrs. org>. See also IFRS Foundation trustees meeting of 13–14 July 2011, agenda paper 2J.

[73] IASF trustees meeting of 26–7 January 2010, agenda paper 3C.

approved by the trustees. Typically, such groups were formed for projects requiring specialized knowledge, as in the case of the working groups on insurance, leases, employee benefits, and financial instruments. Advisory groups were not formed for more general topics such as revenue recognition and the conceptual framework revision. An exception was the so-called joint international group on financial statement presentation, but this may have reflected the controversy provoked by the project rather than its specialized nature. A group supporting the development of the IFRS for SMEs was replaced, in 2010, by an SME implementation group, chaired by Paul Pacter (see also Section 12.10). Finally, as discussed in Chapter 13, the financial crisis prompted the creation of a temporary Financial Crisis Advisory Group and an expert advisory panel on valuation of financial instruments in illiquid markets.

11.8 RELATIONS WITH NATIONAL STANDARD SETTERS

From the beginning, a continuing challenge to the IASB has been to cultivate rewarding relations with national standard setters. As pointed out in Chapter 3, shortly after its establishment, the Board was conscious that, as it did not possess authority to require that companies around the world follow its standards, it needed the active support of the national standard setters to achieve its ambitious aims. Towards that end, the initial Constitution stipulated that seven of the fourteen Board members were to liaise with major national standard setters—in the United States, the United Kingdom, Japan, Germany, France, Canada, and jointly with Australia and New Zealand—and the Board decided to liaise informally with standard setters in a number of other countries as well. The liaison standard setters had the privilege of receiving confidential Board papers, and they had the opportunity to influence Board members' thinking at an early stage in the development of standards. The Board invited several of the liaison standard setters to undertake research projects, but there was some frustration that the Board sometimes altered the terms of the research project after it was well along, or dispensed altogether with the need for the project after the standard setter had virtually completed work (see also Sections 5.6 and 16.3.2).

The Board's thrice-yearly meetings with the liaison standard setters were held from May 2001 until April 2005. They were fairly fractious meetings, if only because of some of the strong personalities present. To be sure, the chairmen of some of the standard setters found it difficult to reconcile themselves to the prospect of no longer setting standards for listed companies in their own countries. They had lost this sovereignty over national standard setting and found themselves serving as 'junior partners' to the IASB.[74]

Well before 2005, it had become evident that a policy of favouring only the liaison standard setters with an early view of the Board's papers was no longer tenable. The policy was not effective in that, in practice, the agenda papers leaked widely, but the restriction still fuelled a sense of exclusion on the part of some

---

[74] Interview with David Tweedie, 6 January 2013.

non-liaison standard setters. South Africa, for instance, had for many years been a steadfast participant in the former IASC and was one of the earliest adopters of the IASB's standards. It would have had a claim to being a member of the inner circle. By 2005, with some 7,000 European listed companies, as well as companies in South Africa and Australia, already using IFRSs in their annual financial statements, the Board began to make its documents more generally available and to supply observers to its meetings with more informative notes and papers.

Another reason for reconfiguring the Board's relations with national standard setters was that the landscape of standard setting around the world had changed. Two of the liaison standard setters, the FASB and the ASBJ, had developed their own bilateral contacts with the IASB. In October 2002, the IASB and the FASB announced their Norwalk Agreement, in which the two bodies, with the support of the US SEC, resolved to engage in active collaboration, including joint meetings twice a year, towards the end of converging their standards. In March 2005, the Board began to hold semi-annual meetings with the ASBJ in order to bring their standards closer together as well.

Some of the other liaison standard setters had lost the ability to set standards themselves, at least for listed companies, once their countries adopted IFRSs. This was true for the Australian and European standard setters. In Europe, the question arose of the respective roles of the national standard-setters and EFRAG, whose Technical Expert Group (TEG) began commenting on the IASB's draft standards and which also sought to be counted among the liaison standard setters. In 2004 the chairmen of the three national standard setters in the United Kingdom, France, and Germany were accorded ex officio membership on the TEG, and the TEG chairman, accompanied by the three national chairmen, began holding periodic meetings with the Board (see also Section 9.3).

Meanwhile, as more countries were moving towards adopting IFRSs, the need for standard setters in these countries to develop relations with the IASB, and vice versa, gained in importance. Beginning in October 2002, at the World Congress of Accountants in Hong Kong, the Board organized regular meetings of World Standard Setters in order to cast a wide net. Thirty-nine representatives from some nineteen countries attended the first meeting; by 2012, the attendance at these annual gatherings had doubled.[75] But these meetings could not satisfy the standard setters that wished to participate on a plane with the liaison standard setters. Accordingly, in the Constitution review of 2005, the requirement for the Board to meet with liaison standard setters was deleted. In May 2005, the Board, during one of its strategy retreats, agreed that the meetings with the eight liaison standard setters should be widened to include all standard setters, and, as noted in Chapter 7, the Constitution was changed accordingly.[76]

With the encouragement of David Tweedie, Ian Mackintosh, the chairman of the UK ASB, convened a meeting of standard setters in September 2005 under the name, 'National Standard-Setters' (NSS), which included a much broader array of

---

[75] Jessica Lion, 'How the IASB Interacts with Domestic Standard Setters—A Network of Standard Setters', *Australian Accounting Review*, 22/3 (September 2012), 244.

[76] 'Note of Board Awaydays 19 and 20 May 2005', paragraph 5.2. IASB archive, 'awayday' files.

country participants than the eight liaison standard setters. This grouping could be thought of as occupying the middle ground between the previous, exclusive liaison arrangement and the unwieldy World Standards Setters meetings.[77] The number of national standard setters represented in the new NSS was in excess of twenty, and was restricted to bodies that were willing and able to make an active contribution to its deliberations. The NSS has since met half yearly, always with IASB representatives in attendance. Consciously falling back on the example of the G4+1 of the 1990s, the NSS has conducted basic research on major topics ahead of their consideration by the IASB. In addition, it has submitted comments on Board drafts.[78] From 2001 to 2005, therefore, an activity of the IASB to reach out to a select group of standard setters had been displaced by the world organizing itself to make its views known to the Board.

In 2011, Tricia O'Malley, a former IASB Board member from Canada, succeeded Mackintosh as chairman of the NSS, following the latter's appointment as vice chairman of the IASB. In 2012, the NSS was renamed the International Forum of Accounting Standard-Setters.

In a draft Memorandum of Understanding issued in February 2005, the Board attempted to give a comprehensive definition of the relationships it sought to maintain with national standard setters. The Memorandum of Understanding outlined mutual responsibilities in areas such as communication, participation in technical work, and implementation of standards. As regards its own responsibilities, the Board said that its standard-setting environment should 'encourage critical analysis of its proposals, and provide an open, transparent and credible process for arriving at its conclusions'. Conversely, it said that the 'Accounting standard-setters should be a key channel for information flowing to the IASB from government agencies, politicians and others who are engaged in non-technical debate'.[79] The national standard setters were also expected to encourage their constituents to participate in the IASB's due process, for instance by organizing their own roundtables or by encouraging membership applications for IASB working groups. In a more controversial vein, the Board attempted to address what would become known as the 'brand name issue' (see Section 10.6), because the Memorandum of Understanding also cautioned standard setters that, when adopting IFRSs in their jurisdictions, they 'should avoid amending the IFRSs in a manner that creates a non-compliance with the IFRSs' (paragraph 6.7). The Board strongly discouraged standard setters from issuing interpretations of IFRSs and to respect decisions by the IASB or IFRIC not to address an issue (paragraph 7.8).

Illustrating how the draft Memorandum of Understanding was received by some national standard setters, Board member Tatsumi Yamada was said to have reported that 'the ASBJ was troubled by the draft Memorandum of

---

[77] Interview with Andrew Lennard, 13 October 2008.

[78] 'In Focus: An Interview with Ian Mackintosh', *The CPA Journal*, 80/6 (June 2010), 24.

[79] 'Draft Memorandum of Understanding on the Role of Accounting Standard-Setters and Their Relationships with the IASB', paragraphs 3.18 and 3.20 <http://www.drsc.de/docs/press_releases/MoU_draft_0205.pdf>. Carrie Bloomer, a senior staff person at the FASB, did the original drafting of this Memorandum of Understanding, because it grew out of discussions among the liaison standard setters at their meetings in 2004.

Understanding, viewing it as a demand for a loyalty test, and implying a master/servant relationship'.[80]

The final version of the Memorandum of Understanding appeared under the softer title, 'Statement of Best Practice: Working Relationships between the IASB and other Accounting Standard-Setters', issued in February 2006. The 'should' recommendations in the draft tended to be expressed somewhat more circumspectly in the 'Statement of Best Practice'.

11.9 CHANGES IN THE TECHNICAL STAFF

11.9.1 Staff Numbers and Staff Policies

The technical staff was an indispensable part of the IASB's standard-setting activities. Board members held the staff in high regard, as competent and hard-working. They considered themselves generally well-served by the staff, even if this could sometimes seem different from the point of view of a staff member who saw an agenda paper torn to pieces by a critical Board.

By the end of the Board's initial year, 2001, the technical staff—which we define as the staff who participate in the standard-setting function—increased to a total of seventeen individuals, a few of whom had come from the IASC. Some of these worked part-time, or divided their time between standard setting and other work, such as supporting the trustees (see Section 3.10). Over the ensuing years, the technical staff steadily increased, reaching a total of twenty-six individuals by the end of 2005, and forty-one by the end of 2008. By May 2011, the tally had reached fifty-six.[81] Behind these numbers was a considerable degree of staff turnover. The total number of people who at one time or another served the IASB during its first decade in a technical capacity, including some brought in for just a few months to help with peak loads, is not exactly known, but can perhaps be estimated at around 150.

The high degree of staff turnover reflected a mixture of unplanned occurrences and deliberate policy.[82] The initial Board, made up mostly of experienced standard setters, was ready to go from the start, but a shortage of equally experienced staff was felt as a major bottleneck. The staff that could be recruited or borrowed on short notice from national standard setters or audit firms was generally capable enough, but in numbers it fell short of the Board's ambitions, so that the staff's workload in the first years was very heavy. The result was that, around 2004, the organization was faced with a significant amount of turnover, mainly because of

---

[80] 'Note of Board Awaydays 19 and 20 May 2005', paragraph 12.2, IASB archive, 'awayday' files.

[81] Staff numbers up to 2008 as reconstructed from IASC/IFRS Foundation annual reports and *IASB Insight*. For the May 2011 number, see Stephen A. Zeff, 'The Evolution of the IASC into the IASB, and the Challenges it Faces', *The Accounting Review*, 87/3 (May 2012), 828.

[82] The remaining paragraphs of this section are based on interviews with Elizabeth Hickey, 5 March 2012; Thomas Jones, 16 February 2009; Patricia O'Malley, 28 May 2009; and Alan Teixeira, 13 February 2012.

the termination of short-term contracts but in some cases also because of sheer exhaustion.

In subsequent years, when the size of the staff was no longer a serious constraint, the organization was able to build up its staff in a more balanced way. A high degree of turnover was still a matter of policy, as a significant proportion of the recruitments were relatively young people contracted to serve for a few years, following which they would go back to pursuing their professional careers. As staff members, they would have obtained a good understanding of the functioning of the IASB and be able to serve as its 'ambassadors' once leaving the IASB. Gradually, staff development policies were put in place to support staff members who, to an increasing degree, had no previous experience of standard setting.

Throughout the decade, the organization relied on a mixture of its own staff and staff seconded from other organizations. Over time, a policy emerged of relying for roughly 70 per cent on its own directly contracted staff and for 30 per cent on secondees. With the latter category, the IASB not only gained access to valuable technical expertise but also acquired the flexibility to adjust its capacity quickly. As the pace of standard setting became ever more frantic following the financial crisis, and with the rush to complete the Memorandum of Understanding with the FASB (see Chapters 13 and 16), this flexibility was of great value to the organization.

The use of secondees can give rise to possible conflicts of interest, even when the standard setter pays their salaries. Secondees from an industry, or an audit firm with clients in that industry, where strong views were held about the outcome of a particular technical project might find themselves under pressure to give undue weight to these views in the Board's papers. This possible threat to independence is a risk that must be balanced against the benefit of the relevant experience that a secondment can bring to a technical project. That this risk was not purely hypothetical was understood at the IASB, and the senior staff took care to avoid the problem when determining the size and composition of project teams.

11.9.2 Staff Comings and Goings

The aim of this section is to give credit to the technical staff by bringing a large proportion of them out as individuals. Equally importantly, the following review of staff movements provides vivid evidence of the many and diverse professional backgrounds and national origins from which they have been recruited and of the many and diverse firms, companies, and other institutions to which they went upon leaving the staff.

The information about the comings and goings of technical staff between 2002 and 2008 in this section was culled from *IASB Insight*, the Board's periodic magazine, which was discontinued in 2008, as well as from the IASC Foundation's annual reports, which provided information about the changes in staff until 2008. We have supplemented this published information with further particulars provided by the Foundation. The discussion below continues from Section 3.10 on technical staff during 2001–2. The two elements in parentheses following each name are the individual's employment prior to joining the staff followed by the individual's nationality.

During 2002, Annette Kimmitt was promoted to senior project manager, alongside Peter Clark and Sandra Thompson. In early 2005, she joined E&Y in Australia and eventually became the firm's Melbourne managing partner. Among those arriving during 2002 were Andrea Pryde (Arthur Andersen, United Kingdom) and Sue Lloyd (Deutsche Bank Sydney, New Zealand). Pryde continues on the staff as technical principal. Lloyd left the IASB and spent 2004–9 in merchant banking, before returning to serve as senior director, technical activities. In January 2014, she became a member of the Board. Other arrivals in 2002 were Kathie Bugg (Deloitte, United States), Lu Jianqiao (China Accounting Standards Committee, China), Claus Nielsen (KPMG, Denmark), Henry Rees (KPMG, United Kingdom), Brigitte Schuster (Austria), Julie Erhardt (Arthur Andersen, United States), and Yuichi Torikai (PwC, Japan)—attesting to the widening geographical background of the technical staff. The following year, Lu returned to the China Accounting Standards Committee. Also in 2003, Schuster left to resume her studies in Austria, and Erhardt, following her planned seven-month stint, returned to the United States for post-graduate studies. In 2004, she was appointed a deputy chief accountant at the SEC, and among her duties there was liaison with the IASB. Bugg, Nielsen, and Torikai were all on secondment, and returned to practice in 2004.

In 2003, Liz Hickey, formerly a director at E&Y in Auckland and a member of New Zealand's Securities Commission, came as director of education, and Paul Pacter (Deloitte Hong Kong, United States) rejoined the Board's staff as part-time director of standards for SMEs. Both were new positions. Pacter directed the project that led to the *IFRS for SMEs*, published in 2009, and then went on to become a member of the Board. Kevin Singleton joined as a project manager, on leave from KPMG UK. He left in 2004 to join a leading bank. Kathryn DeKauwe, who was in charge of the small library, departed, and in early 2004 the IASB disposed of the library's sparse holdings. Kimberley Crook was promoted to senior project manager and headed the share-based payment project. She left in 2005 to become technical director-accounting standards for the Financial Reporting Standards Board of the New Zealand Institute of Chartered Accountants. Arrivals during the year were Christoph Bonin (Deloitte, Germany), Kumar Dasgupta (E&Y, India), and Farhad Zaman (PwC United States, Bangladesh). Bonin and Zaman, who were practice fellows, returned to their firms in 2005. Dasgupta left in 2005 to join a leading UK bank.

In early 2004, Angus Murray (Australia) came from the Australian Accounting Standards Board but returned to Australia the following year. In November, Kevin Stevenson made it known that he wished to return to Australia during the first half of 2005. Liz Hickey succeeded him as director of technical activities, and in 2008 she returned to New Zealand. Arrivals were Joan Brown (Deloitte and staff of UK ASB, United Kingdom), Kil-woo Lee (Korea Accounting Standards Board (KASB), South Korea), and Noreen Whelan (General Electric, Ireland). In 2006, Lee, a visiting fellow, returned to the KASB. Whelan, the IASB's first industry fellow, returned to GE in 2006. Patrina Buchanan (Ireland) joined the education staff and then the following year shifted to the technical staff, where she became a project manager and in particular has headed the leases project.

In early 2005, Gavin Francis (UK merchant bank) and Jenny Lee (UK actuarial consultant) joined the technical staff. Lee, a project manager, departed in 2008 to pursue further studies. In 2008, Francis became the newly created director of capital markets; he left in 2011 for Barclays. The appointment in 2005 of Allan Cook to the newly created position of IFRIC coordinator was discussed in Section 11.4, as well as his succession by Tricia O'Malley in 2007. The number of other arrivals in 2005 signified the growing size of the technical staff: Sarah Broad (PwC, United Kingdom), Eduardo Manso Ponte (Comisión Nacional de Mercados y Valores, Spain), Luis Medina (from studies at the London School of Economics, Nicaragua), Amanda Quiring (staff of FASB, United States), Jeff Singleton (Australia Post, Australia), and Michael Thomas (E&Y, South Africa). The following year, Manso Ponte left to join IOSCO in Madrid. Broad and Singleton, both project managers, departed in 2007. Also in 2007, Medina went to the CFA Institute. Thomas, another project manager, left in 2008 to take up a position in Singapore, and Quiring stayed on to become a project manager and then departed in 2008 to pursue post-graduate studies. Three further arrivals, Jon Nelson (PwC, United States), Simon Peerless (staff of ASB, United Kingdom), and Lara Pope (E&Y London, New Zealand) all completed their secondments in 2007. A further arrival was Alan Teixeira (staff of the New Zealand Institute of Chartered Accountants, New Zealand), who went on to become a senior project manager and, in 2008, the director of technical activities, following which he has carried the title of senior director, technical activities.

Also in 2005, Michael Wells (University of KwaZulu-Natal, South Africa) joined the IASB in the new position of manager, educational projects, which became re-titled as director-IFRS education initiative. Wells succeeded Liz Hickey, who moved from education to technical activities in that year.

In early 2006, the following technical staff arrived: Michael Buschhueter (RSM, Germany), Candy Fong (Deloitte, Hong Kong), Rachel Knubley (PwC, United Kingdom), Li Li Lian (staff of International Public Sector Accounting Standards Board, Malaysia), and Zhang Xiangzhi (Ministry of Finance, China). Of these, Fong and Zhang were on secondments, which they completed in two years and one year, respectively. In 2008, Buschhueter rose to the position of project manager and was in charge of the projects on earnings per share and business combinations/consolidations. Lian has remained on the staff to become a technical manager and headed up the project on Chapters 1 and 3 of the conceptual framework. Other arrivals in 2006 were Hilary Eastman (Duff & Phelps London, United States), Denise Gómez Soto (staff of Consejo Mexicano de Normas de Información Financiera (CINIF), Mexico), Caron Hughes (Goldman Sachs, United Kingdom), Ewa Kwiatkowska (following her studies, Poland), and April Pitman (Fujitsu Services UK, Canada). Eastman and Gómez Soto both came as project managers. Hughes went to KPMG in Hong Kong a year later, and Kwiatkowska left within the year. Pitman, a project manager, continued on the staff. Two-year secondees who arrived were Colin Edwards (KPMG, United Kingdom), Sebastien Landry (Mazars, France), and Eiko Osawa (staff of ASBJ, Japan). Landry returned to his base in 2007, and Edwards and Osawa returned in 2008.

Technical staff arrivals in 2007 were Liz Figgie (UBS, United States), Sandra Hack (Germany), Mariela Isern (KPMG, Spain), Jane Jordan (consultant in Australia, United Kingdom), Christian Kusi-Yeboah (Swiss Re, Ghana/United Kingdom), Amy Schmidt (staff of Governmental Accounting Standards Board, (GASB)

United States), Michael Stewart (PwC, United Kingdom), Hans van der Veen (E&Y, Netherlands), Henri Venter (South Africa), and Carol Wong (PwC, Hong Kong). Stewart, van der Veen, and Wong all departed within the year, but Stewart returned as director of implementation activities in 2009, when Patricia O'Malley departed. Figgie remained on the staff until 2010 and then entered consulting. Isern eventually became a technical manager and took charge of the project on joint arrangements. Jordan was assigned to the fair value measurement project and left in 2010. Kusi-Yeboah joined the financial instruments team and then went to KPMG in 2011. Two-year-secondee arrivals were Dora Cheung (PwC, Hong Kong), Michelle Fisher (Deloitte HK, United Kingdom), and Yung Wook Kim (staff of KASB, South Korea). All three returned home the following year. Cheung joined the IFRIC team and took over the annual improvements project, and Fisher worked on the IFRS for SMEs project. She came back to the IASB as a senior technical manager in 2010.

In 2008, Liz Figgie and Rachel Knubley were promoted to senior project manager. Knubley managed the leases project and eventually the conceptual framework project. Arrivals as project managers were Jón Arnar Baldurs (Eimskip, Iceland), Mark Bunting (Rhodes University, South Africa), Martin Friedhoff (E&Y, Germany), Ryan Richards (KPMG, United States), Aida Vatrenjak (Corporate Solutions Consulting, Bosnia and Herzegovina), and Luci Wright (PwC, South Africa). Baldurs was in charge of the projects on other comprehensive income and employee benefits. He left in 2013. Bunting was assigned to the conceptual framework project. He left in 2009. Friedhoff became a senior project manager and eventually associate director, and managed the hedge accounting projects; he left in 2012 for E&Y but later worked on secondment remotely from New Zealand. Richards covered financial instruments and left in 2009; Vatrenjak was a manager on leases. Wright eventually became the investor liaison manager before departing in 2011 for E&Y. Three arrivals as technical associates were Manuel Kapsis (Hacker Young, Australia), Sunhee Kim (from studies, South Korea), and Barbara Ruane (GASB, United States). Kapsis was heavily involved with the project on employee benefits, and Kim was involved with the project on leases. Kim joined Financial Executives International in 2011. Five practice fellows arrived mostly from audit firms in 2008: Fabienne Colignon (Mazars, France), Michael Kraehnke (KPMG, United States), Michael Mueller (Deloitte, Germany), Masashi Oki (KPMG, Japan), Shelley So (PwC, Hong Kong), and Nikolaus Starbatty (Siemens, Germany). Of them, Mueller and Starbatty left within the year. Oki took over the project on hedges of investments in foreign operations.

Jeff Wilks (Brigham Young University, United States), who had served as project manager from 2006 to 2008 at the FASB on the revenue recognition project, arrived in 2008 for one year as academic adviser/technical consultant on the same project. In 2008, Leng Bing (Ministry of Finance, China) came for a year as a visiting fellow, leaving in 2009. The following special secondments relating to the conceptual framework project were completed in 2008: Kimberley Crook (from New Zealand's Financial Reporting Standards Board), Ian Hague and Rebecca Villmann (both from Canada's Accounting Standards Board), and Simon Peerless (from the UK ASB).

What is the benefit to national standard setters to second staff to the IASB? The benefit may vary as between high-budget and low-budget standard setters. The high-budgets, already with full-time, experienced technical staff, lose a staff member for a year or two with perhaps little received in return other than a better insight into the working of the IASB. The low-budgets, perhaps only with part-time technical staff, benefit from receiving back a staff member who is highly knowledgeable about standard setting at the international level.

11.9.3 Director-level Technical Staff

In 2001, the IASB started with two technical staff members at the director level, Wayne Upton and Kevin Stevenson. In 2004, Stevenson was succeeded by Liz Hickey, but the number of directors remained at two. In 2006 Paul Pacter became the third with the title of director of standards for SMEs. Pacter was appointed on a part-time basis to lead a specific project and his appointment therefore did not fundamentally alter the organizational structure.

A major change happened in April 2008 when the number of directors jumped to six in an overhaul of what the IASB then called its 'technical leadership team'.[83] Wayne Upton was given a new role as director of international activities, which made him the IASB's principal liaison officer with countries adopting IFRSs. In practice, his attention was initially directed mainly at Asia. Peter Clark succeeded Upton as director of research. The position of director of technical activities, vacant because of the recent departure of Liz Hickey, was filled by Alan Teixeira. This made Clark and Teixeira the two directors with a general responsibility for most of the IASB's technical agenda. In addition, there were three directors with a more specialized responsibility. Paul Pacter remained in position as director of standards for SMEs. A role of director of capital markets was created for Gavin Francis, which gave him the leadership role in the development of standards for financial instruments and related areas. Finally, Tricia O'Malley's role as IFRIC coordinator was upgraded to that of director of implementation activities.

The changes made in 2008 could reasonably be interpreted as part of the IASB's changing agenda and responsibilities. Yet developments in the subsequent years suggested that, to some extent, they were also tailored to the individuals at hand. When Paul Pacter was appointed to the IASB Board in 2010, he was not succeeded by another director of standards for SMEs. It was not difficult to surmise that the position had been created specifically for him. When Gavin Francis left in 2010, Sue Lloyd succeeded him as director of capital markets. The next year, however, she was given the more general title of senior director, technical activities. This title was given to Alan Teixeira as well. Apparently, it was felt that a dedicated director in the area of financial instruments was no longer needed, and the organization reverted to the original situation of two senior technical staff members sharing the responsibility for the overall agenda.

---

[83] 'Changes to Technical Leadership Team', IASB press release dated 14 April 2008.

In 2009, Michael Stewart replaced Tricia O'Malley as director of implementation activities. In 2011, Wayne Upton assumed the chairmanship of the IFRS Interpretations Committee, and the following year he dropped the title of director of international activities. Again, no successor was named.

One conclusion with respect to the technical staff at director level is inescapable: throughout the decade, they were exclusively from English-speaking countries, and therefore did not reflect the increasing diversity of the staff at other levels.

11.9.4 Tom Seidenstein

The Foundation's senior staff member, who was little known to the outside world, was Tom Seidenstein, an American who was briefly profiled in Chapter 3. A long-serving trustee has said, 'People will always talk about David Tweedie, but for those on the inside, we would say that it was David Tweedie and Tom Seidenstein who created this organization'. He attended all of the trustee meetings, and he drafted most of the speeches of the successive chairmen of the trustees. As director of operations, he oversaw the running of the IASB's office, including the legal and tax complications arising out of working with a multinational group of Board members, staff, and trustees. He was in charge of developing the Foundation's budget. Between trustee meetings, Seidenstein carried forward the trustees' initiatives and drafted agenda papers for their next meeting. He developed and nurtured relations with government and industry figures outside the Board, and he usually accompanied David Tweedie or the chairman of the trustees to important negotiations and consultations with other bodies. He and Tweedie were a tightly functioning team. He came at the same time as Tweedie, and he left five months after Tweedie's term ended in June 2011.

11.10 FUNDRAISING FROM 2002 TO 2011

Fundraising to support the operations of the IASB has been a constant preoccupation of the trustees and Foundation staff. As depicted in the summary of the Foundation's income and expenses in Appendix 3, the total contributions received gradually declined from £12.8 million in 2001 to a low of £9.3 million in 2004, and then began a steady rise until it ascended to £17.0 million (restated) in 2010 and £20.6 million in 2011. Contributions were made in different currencies, so that the trend in contributions expressed in sterling has to be interpreted with some caution because of exchange rate fluctuations. Nonetheless, as will be seen, the doubling of the contributions from 2004 to 2011, when one allows for the cumulative effect of inflation, can largely be explained by the eventually successful efforts of the trustees to persuade national governments and regulators, and eventually the EU, to assure the Foundation of a stable annual contribution from a central source within countries or regions. The initial funding system, as discussed in Chapter 3, was that the trustees had to go 'hat-in-hand' to audit firms, large companies, and financial institutions in their respective countries to solicit contributions, initially involving a five-year commitment from 2001 to 2005. The desirability of moving to a more permanent funding arrangement was seen at an early stage, but the realization of this ideal was an uphill struggle.

11.10.1 Casting Around for Funding Alternatives

As early as February 2001, shortly after the initial funding commitments had been received, the finance committee, chaired by Paul Volcker, posed the following question to the trustees: what are the next steps in broadening the fundraising programme beyond the world's largest international banks and industrial corporations?[84] The issue was considered by the trustees, but no immediate action was taken.[85] Yet, in 2002, most of the trustees signed up to contact more than 150 audit firms, financial institutions, industrial companies, business associations, and central and development banks around the world to continue the fundraising effort.

The need for continued activity was underlined in a report submitted in June 2002 by the trustees' finance committee. The report, 'Future of IASC Foundation's Financing', reviewed recent experience and began planning for the longer term.[86] The disappearance of Arthur Andersen from the roll of the big audit firms in 2002 meant the sudden loss of an annual contribution of US$1 million from 2003 onwards. It was believed that there would be increased difficulty in raising funds in Japan, and the companies in the Business Roundtable, in the United States, to which Volcker had written personal letters, yielded a disappointing result, as only six of 118 of its member companies had pledged or given funds. It was hoped that an increase in publication revenues would compensate for some of these setbacks. Because the initial donors' five-year commitments would expire in 2005, the trustees' finance committee began to examine alternatives for the future, 'in particular the establishment of user fees transmitted through the securities exchanges or official organizations'.

It was not coincidental that the idea of a levy system made its first appearance in the trustees' discussions at this point in time. The finance committee was aware of a levy system of fundraising to support the FAF, the FASB's oversight body, being discussed in the United States in the wake of the Enron accounting scandal. The Sarbanes-Oxley Act of 2002, passed by Congress in July, contained a provision, Section 109(e)(1), for the assessment of an 'annual accounting support fee . . . to be assessed and collected against each issuer . . . to provide for an independent, stable source of funding [for the designated standard-setting body which sets US GAAP]'. The fee was to be administered by the SEC. In the event, the SEC designated the FASB as the standard-setting body. When the Act was being drafted, Volcker tried to get the language broad enough to include funding for

---

[84] IASCF trustees meeting of 8 March 2001, agenda paper Va.

[85] IASCF trustees meeting of 15 October 2001, minute 5.

[86] IASCF trustees meeting of 12 June 2002, agenda paper 4.

the IASB and convergence, both in the Act and in the Senate Banking Committee's report. But in the end such language did not appear in either.[87]

When the finance committee's report was discussed in June 2002 by the trustees, including the idea of a user fee, Volcker drew attention to the levy being discussed in US Congressional circles. He speculated that such a levy, if it were to be legislated, could adversely affect the Foundation's fundraising in the United States. Nonetheless, the trustees recognized it as an example worth considering. They set up a seven-member working group, later called the Long-Term Funding (or Finance) Committee, to study long-term financing issues with a view towards considering 'the feasibility of a funding program that would ensure a source of funding independent of the conclusions of interested parties'. With an implicit recognition that there was more to this question than copying the proposed US system, it was minuted that the proposal 'should be robust enough to operate in multiple jurisdictions'.[88]

The Long-Term Funding Committee, chaired by Sir Sydney Lipworth, met in July 2002 and concluded that a levy on listed companies was the best alternative to the Foundation's current approach to funding, but it recognized that different countries would prefer different approaches for collecting a levy. As a first step, it was noted that the levy scheme authorized by the bill leading up to the Sarbanes-Oxley Act might not just be a threat to the Foundation's fundraising in the United States, but could also present an opportunity. The hope was expressed that the FAF might allocate a portion of the funds received to the IASB, called a 'pass-through'. It was reported that Volcker had met with SEC Chairman Harvey Pitt about funding sources for the IASB. Setting up a funding system would probably require a degree of coordination between the United States, the EU, and other countries using IFRSs, and Pitt, during an October visit to Brussels, had urged the European Commission 'to work to securing an independent source of funding for the IASB'.[89]

However, all of this was still very tentative and exploratory. Meanwhile, the trustees faced the immediate problem that some contributors failed to fulfil their pledges, or made signs of not renewing their commitments. The funding gap caused by the demise of Arthur Andersen still remained to be filled and there were other signs of donor attrition.[90] With an eye on the immediate future, the trustees continued with soliciting contributions where they could be found.

The Foundation's fundraising manager, Stefan de Greling, suggested 'target' companies to the trustees in their respective countries, especially ones where the trustees knew a high-level executive who could influence a decision. In particular, Charles Lee, the trustee from Hong Kong, agreed to draft letters in Chinese to companies in China he wished to solicit, and he was to pay personal calls on a number of the companies. An effort was to be made to recruit contributors in the Nordic countries and in Eastern Europe and Russia. In France, however,

---

[87] Communication to the authors from Thomas Seidenstein, dated 27 January 2014.
[88] IASCF trustees meeting of 12 June 2002, minute 5.
[89] IASCF trustees meeting of 19 November 2002, agenda paper 7.
[90] IASCF trustees meeting of 13 March 2003, minute 6.

fundraising efforts had slowed owing to opposition to IAS 32 and IAS 39. Several French business confederations, including MEDEF (Mouvement des Entreprises de France), were to sign a joint appeal letter together with the IASC Foundation to solicit a broad range of French companies. But the letter had not been sent because not all of the sponsoring parties were willing to sign it.[91] This experience with French reaction to the two standards was doubtless a reason why the trustees were seeking an independent, stable funding mechanism. In its first several years, the Foundation sought to deal with any such threats to its independence by building up a reserve fund of approximately one year's budget.

In October 2002, Tom Seidenstein reported the first sign of what might become a long-term national funding scheme. The Financial Reporting Council, the body which oversees the Australian Accounting Standards Board, made known that it would contribute AU\$1 million (£335,000) annually to the IASC Foundation for at least the next two years.[92] Assuming renewal beyond the first two years, this meant that the first national standard setter to agree to a multi-year funding commitment was in Australia.

The Long-Term Funding Committee met again in April 2003 to continue its consideration of the feasibility of various long-term funding options. A lengthy report to the trustees at their July meeting began by rehearsing the problems of the current system.[93] Having the trustees 'target' potential funding sources in their respective countries, the committee said, had 'major drawbacks'. For one, the report said that 'some business sectors are currently showing hostility towards the IASB and are likely to be reluctant to offer financial support'. The committee also worried over the perception that business interests could have undue influence over the Board's deliberative process. As discussed in Chapter 3, a news report appearing in February 2002 indicated that Enron, after being approached for a contribution, said that it would consider doing so 'on condition that it could help shape the board's policies'. Although Volcker had publicly rebutted the allegation that influence on the board was up for sale, the fact that the suggestion had been made still rankled with the trustees.[94]

The committee considered four options for post-2005, but the main result was a better understanding of the difficulties of each. The four options as seen by the committee were: funding from national business and accounting associations, listing fees, direct governmental funding, and self-financing through publications and related activities. As to self-financing, it observed that the FASB had, for years, raised about two-thirds of its funds via publications. But the IASB was still a very young body, and its net publication revenues accounted for less than 10 per cent of the Foundation's budget. Self-financing was clearly not a viable option. On funding from national and accounting associations, Keidanren in Japan was performing well, but Japan is unique in being a cohesive society. As noted

---

[91] All of this was reported in IASCF trustees meeting of 13 March 2003, agenda paper 5D.

[92] IASCF trustees meeting of 19 November 2002, agenda paper 5.

[93] IASCF trustees meeting of 29 July 2003, agenda paper 8C, undated and unsigned but apparently drafted by Lipworth.

[94] The article cited in the report was by Michael Peel, 'Accounting Board Feels Enron Effect', *Financial Times*, 15 February 2002. See Section 3.11 for further references, including Volcker's reply.

above, the initial results from working through the Business Roundtable in the United States were disappointing. In addition, the committee realized that 'Concentrating funding in the hands of business associations may encourage business to threaten withholding funds if a business group disapproves of the IASB's decisions'. The listing fees option was attractive but it required agreement among the world's regulators and stock exchanges, which would be difficult if not impossible to achieve. Direct governmental funding had been ruled out by the IASC's Strategy Working Party in 1999 when it drew up the blueprint for its successor body. The committee outlined the pros and cons of the options and left it to the trustees to propose a strategy.

This is more or less where matters remained for the next three years, as discussed in the following paragraphs: the specific problems of establishing funding mechanisms in the main countries and regions were explored further, and thought was given to establishing criteria for an equitable distribution of contributions from countries and regions. Meanwhile, the raising of voluntary contributions on an ad hoc basis continued.

The European trustees took steps to confer with the European Commission and the Committee of European Securities Regulators (CESR) on the idea of a listing fee.[95] In November 2003, Max Dietrich Kley said that he was discussing a listing fee with the Deutsche Börse but that there were legal impediments.[96] The legal challenges provided the real hurdle, not the amounts involved. The European trustees worked out that, if shared across all the listed companies on the fifteen main exchanges in the EU, a voluntary or compulsory fee of well below $1,000 per company would be sufficient, including a wide margin of error.[97] In October 2004, Jens Røder, Sydney Lipworth, and Cornelius Herkströter met with the outgoing EU Commissioner Frits Bolkestein to explore the Commission's views on possible funding options. Although Bolkestein agreed that something had to be done to assure funding for the Foundation and offered to look into ways the Commission could assist, the committee wrote that he:

> stressed the difficulty, if not the impossibility, of providing any legislative backing for a Europe-wide system, but thought that the Commission would be able to give its backing and endorsement to a voluntary system or to one adopted country by country domestically. He did, however, rule out any form of direct financial support from the Commission. He also informed the delegation that it would be difficult to gain full support for any Europe-wide initiative if the Constitution Review did not address some of the concerns voiced in the EU.[98]

As seen in Chapter 7, these European concerns included calls for significant changes to the IASB's governance, at a time when the relationships between the Board and many of its European constituents had become strained if not openly hostile.

---

[95] IASCF trustees meeting of 29 July 2003, minute 8.
[96] IASCF trustees meeting of 3–4 November 2003, minute 8.
[97] IASCF trustees meeting of 25 October 2004, agenda paper 6B, 3.
[98] IASCF trustees meeting of 25 October 2004, agenda paper 6B, 4.

Discussions were continued with Bolkestein's successor, Charlie McCreevy. It was reported that, in January 2005, the six trustees from EU countries had met with McCreevy to discuss the possibility of establishing a voluntary or mandatory levy system in Europe. Both McCreevy and his staff responded positively to the concept of a broadly spread, fee-based system. But, as with his predecessor, he said that no progress could be made on such a proposal without satisfying some of the European concerns as part of the Constitution review. At this point in time, the Constitution review was almost completed, but it was held up by McCreevy's insistence on further consultations.

Not much progress was made in the United States, either. In July 2003, it was agreed that Chairman Volcker was to pursue the idea of a 'pass-through' with the FAF and the SEC.[99] The result was awareness of a new difficulty: if a 'pass-through' were authorized, the SEC might wish to examine the IASC Foundation's budget—because the SEC already vetted the FAF's budget before approving the amount of the annual fee. 'Then', a November 2003 staff memo stated, 'other participating jurisdictions would probably demand similar access to the IASC Foundation's budget'.[100] At the November 2003 trustees' meeting, Volcker reported that it would be 'difficult' for the IASC Foundation to obtain funds via the mechanism established for the FAF by the Sarbanes-Oxley Act, and it seemed that that specific option was laid to rest.[101] The US trustees, in particular Chairman Volcker and David Ruder, continued to raise the question of funding with the SEC and members of Congress with an interest in standard setting. While those to whom they talked expressed sympathy for the cause, they did not suggest any solution. Moreover, it was reported early in 2005 that decision-makers in the United States were watching developments in Europe. As seen above, that meant that real progress could not be made until a satisfactory completion of the first Constitution review.[102]

That the trustees had been meeting, between 2001 and 2005, every other year in Washington—in October 2001, July 2003, and November 2005—and only once during that span in New York City suggested that they were keen to solidify their relations with the SEC and members of Congress. In October 2006, the trustees again met in Washington. As part of the effort to persuade the SEC to make the move towards IFRSs as well as on fundraising, David Tweedie, Tom Jones, Tom Seidenstein, and the US trustees 'worked' the SEC to be sure that the Commission and senior staff knew and understood what the IASB was doing and why. While they believed that the SEC gave them a good reception, this did not immediately translate into progress on establishing a funding system in the United States.

With respect to Japan, another major source of contributions, Toru Hashimoto, one of the Japanese trustees, remarked in November 2003 that Keidanren was unlikely to sustain its financial support for the Foundation after the initial five-

---

[99] IASCF trustees meeting of 29 July 2003, minute 8.

[100] IASCF trustees meeting of 3–4 November 2003, agenda paper 6B.

[101] IASCF trustees meeting of 3–4 November 2003, minute 8; for the relationship between progress on funding in Europe and in the United States and the Constitution review, see IASCF trustees meeting of 23–4 March 2006, agenda paper 11, paragraph 4.

[102] See e.g. IASCF trustees meeting of 18 March 2005, agenda paper 11, paragraph 18.

year period. He said that the preferred Japanese solution was to have 20 per cent of the Foundation budget supported by publication revenues and 80 per cent from a combination of listing fees, governments, and audit firms.[103] In March 2005, Hiroshi Endo, of Japan's Financial Accounting Standards Foundation (FASF), met with Tom Seidenstein. Endo said that, while it would be difficult to raise funds from major Japanese business enterprise as was done in the past, the FASF was exploring whether it could provide $2 million annually from its budget to support the IASC Foundation.[104]

The good news came as before from Australia. In 2005 the Financial Reporting Council continued its annual contribution, and this provided the example to New Zealand to consider a similar scheme.[105]

While the trustees explored how national funding systems could be set up, they also gave thought to the amounts to be raised with such schemes. In an October 2004 report, the trustees' Long-Term Funding Committee estimated that the Foundation would in the future need a budget of some $23 million, which would be financed by publication sales of about $2 million, interest on investments of $1 million, contributions from the Big Four audit firms of $4 to $5 million, and $15 million from other sources.[106] (The figures were given in US dollars because the funds were largely raised in US dollars.) By comparison, the Foundation's total expenses in 2004 were £12.0 million ($21.6 million), net publication sales were £1.2 million ($2.2 million), and contributions were £9.3 million ($16.7 million).[107]

In the same report, the Long-Term Funding Committee revealed the first attempt by the Foundation to develop criteria for the funding burden that should be shouldered by each country, according to either the market capitalization of domestic companies or gross domestic product (GDP). The report contained tables with dollar figures for the eleven largest countries with an interest in the IASB. It was thought that GDP was the more practicable alternative if only because, under the market capitalization approach, the United States would be charged with raising $8.1 million of the $15.0 million, or 54 per cent, of the total funding requirement—some 71 per cent above the EU's share, which was the next in line. Using the comparative GDP approach, the United States would be tasked with raising only $5.2 million, or 35 per cent of the total, just behind the EU share of $5.6 million. The report observed that the funding allocation according to the GDP approach 'is fairly close to the current situation'. The trustees signified their general support for a system to allocate the financial burden on listed companies and on countries in proportion to company size and country GDP, respectively. The idea was further explored in a March 2005 memo by the Foundation's staff, which proposed three different weighting schemes for EU member states and

---

[103] IASCF trustees meeting of 3–4 November 2003, minute 8.
[104] IASCF trustees meeting of 18 March 2005, agenda paper 11, paragraph 13.
[105] IASCF trustees meeting of 18 March 2005, agenda paper 11, paragraphs 20–2.
[106] IASCF trustees meeting of 25 October 2004, agenda paper 6B.
[107] IASC Foundation, *Annual Report 2004*, 16. The exchange rate generally prevalent in 2004 of $1.80 per British pound was used for the conversion.

associate states (Norway and Iceland), depending on their size and political significance.[108]

By 2005, it was evident that any alternative fundraising scheme could not be in place until 2007, if then. At the trustees' June 2005 meeting, Chairman Volcker said that the trustees' current concern should be persuading contributors to renew their current five-year commitments, about to run out, for a further two years and obtaining new contributors. Several trustees reported on possible renewals in their countries, but it was stated that the central banks, which had regarded their five-year commitments as 'seed money', might be more difficult to persuade to renew.[109] It was reported that the Big Four audit firms had confirmed an increase in their annual commitment from $1 million to $1.5 million for each, beginning in 2006–7.[110] The year before, Jens Røder, the trustee from Denmark, had already begun discussions with the Big Four audit firms to increase their contribution from $1 million to $1.25 million to compensate for the loss of funding occasioned by the collapse of Arthur Andersen. It was hoped that funding might be obtained also from the second-tier audit firms: Grant Thornton and BDO had already been contributing $50,000 annually.[111] Hence, progress was being made to provide for post-2005 funding, but it was still on an ad hoc basis. Coming back to the same donors and asking for two more years was 'a very painful effort', as Chairman Tommaso Padoa-Schioppa observed early in 2006.[112] The goal of a listing fee or other stable funding source in the major countries was as elusive as before.

11.10.2 2006: a Turning Point

In 2006, the quest for a stable funding system took a decisive turn. One reason was that the review of the Constitution had been completed in the previous year. As indicated above, this had held up progress on fundraising because the European Commission, for one, preferred to await the outcome of that process before proceeding with a consideration of funding alternatives. In addition, the Constitution review required a considerable proportion of the trustees' attention in 2004 and into 2005. Another factor was that, in January 2006, Paul Volcker had been succeeded by Padoa-Schioppa. While it was generally acknowledged that Volcker's fundraising abilities had been of great importance to the Foundation in its early years, there was also a perception that, as long as Volcker was around with his legendary ability to raise large contributions by picking

---

[108] IASCF trustees meeting of 18 March 2005, agenda paper 11. As the trustees were precluded by the time needed to move ahead with the Constitution review from considering this report at their March meeting, the staff re-sent the memorandum with minor updating as agenda paper 6A, IASCF trustees meeting of 21 June 2005.

[109] IASCF trustees meeting of 21 June 2005, minute 6.

[110] IASCF trustees meeting of 14–15 November 2005, agenda paper 5B.

[111] IASCF trustees meeting of 25 October 2004, agenda paper 6B.

[112] Tommaso Padoa-Schioppa, 'Current Structure of Funding and Reform Proposal: The Position of the IASCF', in *Future of IASB Funding*, conference transcript, 30 and 31 March 2006 (Frankfurt am Main: Deutsches Aktieninstitut, 2006), 21.

up the telephone, the search for a sustainable funding mechanism lacked a certain urgency. Padoa-Schioppa was determined that things should be put on a different footing.

In March and June 2006, the trustees discussed successive versions of a memo on the principles that should govern sustainable, long-term funding. The memo was written by Tom Seidenstein on behalf of the Long-Term Financing Committee (as it now came to be known).[113] The committee was now chaired by Cornelius Herkströter, as Lipworth, the previous chairman, had retired from the trustees at the end of 2005. Presumably partly for the benefit of the many new trustees who had recently been appointed, the memo reviewed *in extenso* the earlier conclusions about the unsustainable character of the current funding, and the difficulties of alternative approaches.

As finally agreed, the four principles were that the funding system should be (a) broad-based, in contrast to the current situation where the funds were contributed by fewer than 200 companies and organizations, (b) compelling, that is, not necessarily mandatory but with sufficient pressure to make free-riding difficult, (c) open-ended, in contrast to the current situation in which funding commitments expired at a fixed point in time, and (d) country-specific, with each country selecting an appropriate approach to raise their share of the funding required, calculated with GDP as the key determining factor.[114]

The fourth principle was detailed in a calculation of weights by country and region, with a discount applied to countries with a GDP per capita of less than US $10,000. The distribution of country weights by this formula was as follows: EU member states 34.7 per cent, United States 32.8 per cent, and Japan 12.4 per cent. Collectively, these three economies were to supply 79.9 per cent of the national contributions. Among EU countries, Germany had the highest country weight, followed by the United Kingdom, France, and Italy. It was estimated that, of a total target for 2008 of £16.0 million, £12.0 million would have to be raised by national or regional collective schemes, the remainder consisting of contributions by the large audit firms. Compared to actual contributions received in 2005, this implied the following targeted contributions for 2008: EU countries £4.2 million (2005: £2.7 million), United States £3.9 million (£2.0 million), and Japan £1.5 million (£1.1 million).

It may be noted that publication revenues were not considered in establishing the financing requirement. On this point, the trustees followed the recommendation of the Long-Term Financing Committee, which argued that when the new funding scheme took effect, 'the Trustees may wish to make the official IASB pronouncements available on the IASC Foundation's Website free of charge'. This change took effect in 2009. As disclosed in the summary of income and expenses in Appendix 3, the revenue from subscription and publication sales gradually

---

[113] IASCF trustees meeting of 23–4 March 2006, agenda paper 11; IASCF trustees meeting of 28–9 June 2006, agenda paper 8A; IASCF trustees meeting of 23–4 March 2006, minute 6; IASCF trustees meeting of 28–9 June 2006, minute L.

[114] IASCF trustees meeting of 28–9 June 2006, agenda paper 8A. For discussions of the four principles, see also IASC Foundation, *Annual Report 2006*, 6 and Padoa-Schioppa, 'Current Structure of Funding', 21–2.

rose until 2009, when it dropped by 13 per cent from 2008, and then remained approximately level for the next two years.

The trustees did not await the completion of their deliberations to begin work on bringing about the realization of funding schemes in specific countries or regions, and the immediate focus was on Europe. In March 2006, a week after the meeting at which the trustees agreed their statement of funding principles, a two-day conference on the funding of the IASB was held in Frankfurt am Main, in the offices of the Deutsche Bundesbank.[115] The conference was organized by the Deutsches Aktieninstitut, the leading think-tank on capital market issues in Germany. Max Dietrich Kley, the German trustee, as well as Padoa-Schioppa, had been instrumental in setting up the conference and ensuring the participation of key players from the European corporate and financial sectors, and senior officials from the European Commission, including Alexander Schaub, director-general of the internal market directorate. The participants engaged in a thorough discussion of all aspects of funding, including the parallel question of funding for EFRAG. While there was some harsh criticism of the IASB's activities, the tenor of the discussion was that decisions on funding should be kept separate from other grievances, such as IASB's emphasis on convergence with US GAAP or its perceived mishandling of the project to develop a standard for SMEs. Rather, the mood was that, now that Europe had adopted IFRSs, it was in its benefit that the IASB should be properly run, including a stable funding system. A practicable way had to be found to allow Europe to make its financial contribution.

A key question at the conference was what role the European Commission could play. Opinions on this point were divided. After Padoa-Schioppa had outlined the funding principles recently adopted by the trustees, he noted that the trustees would certainly not object if, in Europe, this would take the form of a mandatory fee scheme established across the EU. As a committed European, he would even be happy for the EU to have the power of taxation, but this was not the case under the current treaties, and therefore he did not think a compulsory contribution was legally possible. However, a law professor present at the meeting concluded, after a thorough discussion of the legal issues, that there was indeed a possibility for a compulsory contribution. This prompted Schaub to observe that he had already been convinced of that for some time, and that sooner or later the idea of stable EU funding would be more widely accepted. However, at present there was simply not the necessary political support, neither for a levy nor for a direct contribution from the Commission's budget. One reason was fear of setting a precedent with possible effects far beyond accounting. Another reason was that 'the drama around the IAS 39 endorsement has created a lot of unhelpful emotions'. In addition, Schaub said: 'One of the immediate necessities is to improve the public perception of the IASB procedures and to avoid that industry representatives too often turn up complaining about the absence of dialogue: in an

---

[115] Full transcripts of all presentations and discussions are included in *Future of IASB Funding*, conference transcript, 30 and 31 March 2006 (Frankfurt am Main: Deutsches Aktieninstitut, 2006).

excessive, but—I have to admit—not in a completely unfounded way.'[116] Later during the conference, Max Kley came back to this point by saying that 'In the past under Paul Volcker's leadership one of his main concerns was the independence of the IASB Board in comparison to FASB. Looking back, the Board of Trustees might have gone too far in this respect.'[117] As indicated elsewhere in this chapter, the IASB and the trustees certainly made efforts to improve their responsiveness to constituents' views. But all of this would take time, and the IASB's funding needs were imminent, given that the latest two-year commitments would expire in 2007. Pierre Delsaux, serving directly under Schaub in the Commission's staff, concluded that the main contribution that Europe could make at the moment was to express its political commitment in support of the trustees' plans.[118] While apparently limited, it was what the EU delivered. In July 2006, the EU finance ministers meeting as the ECOFIN Council welcomed 'the current private sector efforts to create a broad-based voluntary financing system for the IASB'.[119] The statement did not bind the EU member states to any particular course of action, but it could certainly be read as an encouragement to the member states to put in place some form of national funding scheme.

Meanwhile, a group of European trustees, headed by Bertrand Collomb, had assumed responsibility for seeking support for implementation of the trustees' funding principles in Europe.[120] At their October 2007 meeting, the trustees decided to enlist ex-trustee Sydney Lipworth to assist in coordinating the long-term fundraising efforts, particularly in Europe.[121] Whether prompted by ECO-FIN's statement or because of initiatives taken by the European trustees, plans to set up national schemes were hatched across the EU.

One of the first signs that plans for national levy systems might finally leave the drawing-board and become a reality was the announcement by UK trustee Bryan Nicholson in October 2006 that he had obtained 'agreements in principle' on a fee-based levy on listed companies in meetings with the Financial Reporting Council (FRC, which he previously chaired), the Financial Services Authority (FSA), HM Treasury, the Department of Trade and Industry, The Hundred Group, and other bodies. The FSA signified that it wanted the UK to be the 'lead nation' in adopting a fee-based levy.[122] In March 2007, the FRC proposed its annual business levy and pension and insurance levies for 2007/8, which for the first time included a small average contribution of £550 per listed company as the UK contribution to the IASB. The total amount expected to be raised by this increased levy was £700,000.[123] Lipworth hoped that the FRC levy, if successful,

---

[116] *Future of IASB Funding*, 79–80.   [117] *Future of IASB Funding*, 102.

[118] Pierre Delsaux, 'Listing Fees, Budgetary Option or Funding by National Governments', in *Future of IASB Funding*, 29. See for a similar view expressed by the Commission the summary record of ARC meetings of 17 February 2006, 7, and of 24 April 2004, 6–7 <http://ec.europa.eu/internal_market/accounting>.

[119] '2741st Council Meeting: Economic and Financial Affairs, Brussels, 11 July 2006', press release 11370/06 dated 11 July 2006 <http://europa.eu/rapid>.

[120] IASCF trustees meeting of 23–4 March 2006, minute 6.

[121] IASCF trustees meeting of 26–7 October 2006, minute K.

[122] IASCF trustees meeting of 26–7 October 2006, agenda paper 8C(i).

[123] IASCF trustees meeting of 2–3 2007, agenda paper 6, attachment ii.

could serve as a model for the rest of Europe.[124] In June 2007, after receiving comments, the FRC announced the new levy, thus making it final.[125]

The Netherlands was also quick off the mark. In November 2006 the finance minister, Gerrit Zalm, informed the national Parliament of a plan to institute a fee-based levy on listed companies to fulfil the country's funding quota. The proposal was said to be a response to ECOFIN's 'call on the member states' to set up national funding systems, and had been developed in consultation with Cornelius Herkströter, the Dutch trustee.[126] In the end, no levy was imposed. Beginning in 2008, when Zalm had already become the chairman of the IASC Foundation trustees, the Ministry of Finance made an annual contribution of €380,000 directly from its own budget, which, apart from a smaller contribution by the central bank, accounted for all of the money received from the Netherlands.[127]

At the March conference in Frankfurt it had been reported that a broad-based scheme to support both the IASB and EFRAG was in preparation in France, but this amounted to channelling voluntary contributions through ACTEO (Association pour la Participation des Entreprises Françaises à l'Harmonisation Comptable Internationale, an existing private-sector organization to represent the views of French businesses to the IASB). As a voluntary scheme, it still required active solicitation of French companies by Bertrand Collomb. The same situation prevailed in Germany, where voluntary contributions were already routed through the DRSC (the German standard setter), and where Max Kley tried to persuade companies to commit for longer periods. In Italy, Tommaso Padoa-Schioppa could himself take action when he exchanged his position as IASC Foundation chairman for that of finance minister in the Italian government, later in 2006. He supported legislation to require all companies to contribute to the Foundation through a central source, which in 2008 became the Organismo Italiano di Contabilità (OIC). The approval of this legislation made Italy the third EU member state, with the United Kingdom and the Netherlands, to provide a stable source of funding. The OIC, the Italian national accounting standard setter, had been founded in 2001.

Outside Europe, the trustees sought secure funding where they could, and continued to raise voluntary contributions otherwise, also for 2008 and beyond. The hat-in-hand system would not be displaced in one go.

US trustees Samuel DiPiazza and William McDonough were to chair a group to deal with the United States. In August 2006, the Foundation engaged the New York City-based fundraising consultancy CCS to work with the US trustees in promoting its fundraising effort in the United States. This was the same firm that had been engaged to help with the funding of the IASC in 2000–1. The trustees grandly set a 2008 funding target of $8.0 million for the United States, an enormous increase over its 2006–7 funding commitment of $3.1 million. A

[124] IASCF trustees meeting of 2–3 April 2007, minute G.

[125] IASCF trustees meeting of 2–3 July 2007, agenda paper 4(i).

[126] Tweede Kamer der Staten-Generaal, vergaderjaar 2006–2007, 21501-07, no. 541.

[127] See, for instance, 'Vaststelling van de Begrotingsstaten van het Ministerie van Financiën (IXB) en de Begrotingsstaat van Nationale Schuld (IXA) voor het Jaar 2014', Tweede Kamer der Staten-Generaal, vergaderjaar 2013–2014, 33750-IX, no. 2.

recommended campaign for the United States proposed a 'working goal of 100 companies contributing an average of $80,000 per annum' from among financial institutions, money managers/insurance, and non-financial multinationals'—this for a country whose securities regulator had not even devised a plan for going over to IFRSs for domestic companies.[128] One or more of the four US trustees were assigned to get in touch with the chief executives of about forty major US target enterprises.[129]

The two Japanese trustees—Tsuguoki Fujinuma and Junichi Ujiie—were to accelerate efforts in Japan. With hindsight, Japan's collective contributions through Keidanren had always been quite in conformity with the trustees' funding principles established in 2006, except that the commitment was not open-ended. A meeting of the principal parties involved with IFRSs in Japan in July 2006, and attended by the two Japanese trustees, agreed that funding from Japan would continue on largely the same footing in 2008 and beyond, with the FASF assuming responsibility for collecting and transmitting an agreed sum, contributed by preparers, users, and auditors. At the same, the intention was expressed to broaden the base of contributing companies from some thirty to five hundred.[130]

New Zealand, like Australia, agreed to continue funding at current levels through its Accounting Standards Review Board. Australian trustee Richard Humphry, formerly chief executive of ASX Limited (Australian Stock Exchange), was instrumental in securing the continuing support from Australia and New Zealand. Polish trustee Alicja Kornasiewicz was tasked with generating funding interest in the eight former Warsaw Pact countries that joined the EU in May 2004 and in Russia.

Apart from reliance on their own efforts, the trustees also identified the members of SAC in each of the countries, who, one supposes, might be asked to intercede with the executives of major companies whom they knew.[131] The use of SAC members for purposes of fundraising seems open to question. SAC was to function at arm's length from the IASB and was mandated to be consulted on the IASB's agenda and to give advice to the Board. It was also to give advice to the Foundation trustees, but this advice was probably intended to be given by SAC during its meetings and not individually, by suggesting fundraising contacts in companies.

11.10.3 What was the Foundation Saying Publicly from 2002 to 2006?

Apart from the 2006 Frankfurt conference, the deliberations reported above about the search for a stable funding scheme were internal to the Foundation, coupled with meetings that the trustees were continually having with prospective

---

[128] IASCF trustees meeting of 26–7 October 2006, agenda paper 8B(ii).
[129] IASCF trustees meeting of 26–7 October 2006, agenda paper 8B(iii).
[130] IASCF trustees meeting of 2–3 July 2007, agenda paper 4(i), 3–4.
[131] IASCF trustees meeting of 26–7 October 2006, agenda paper 8C(i).

contributors. But while all this was going on, what was the IASC Foundation saying to the public? The first public notice of the Foundation's quest for such a scheme appeared in its 2002 *Annual Report*. Chairman Paul Volcker said that the trustees had begun studying longer-term funding options, and the 'goal must be to maintain an assured source of funding free from concern that financial pressure could compromise the independence of the IASB's decision-making' (page 3). After referring to the levy on issuers prescribed by the Sarbanes-Oxley Act in the United States, he said that, as one option, the 'practicality of such an approach on an international scale will need to be assessed' (page 3). In the 2003 *Annual Report*, little more was said other than that 'the possibility of achieving agreement internationally [on an approach such as in the United States] is far from clear' (page 3).

In the Foundation's 2004 *Annual Report*, Volcker ventured further: 'the Trustees are investigating other funding mechanisms, such as listing fees or country-specific funding requirements spread by an agreed formula over a broad number of businesses' (page 2). For the first time, in the 2005 *Annual Report*, a full section of Chairman Tommaso Padoa-Schioppa's letter was given over to 'Establishing a broad-based funding system'. The tenor of the discussion was decisive, no longer one of just looking into options. It made clear the trustees' determination to have such a funding system in place by the end of 2006 for implementation in 2008. Padoa-Schioppa confidently said, 'We are now meeting public and private sector officials in the world's three largest economies—the European Union, Japan, and the United States—from where the great portion of the funding is expected' (page 2). Finally, in the 2006 *Annual Report*—at forty pages, the longest of the Foundation's first six annual reports—the characteristics of the new long-term funding scheme (broad-based, compelling, open-ended, and country-specific) were presented and discussed, and Chairman Philip Laskawy reported that: 'For the 2006 financial year, broad-based regimes were in place in Australia, France, Germany, Italy, Japan and New Zealand. This is reflected in the rise in the number of contributing organisations from 182 in 2005 to 286 in 2006' (page 7).

11.10.4 The Big Fundraising Drive Continues

The effects of the trustees' intensified fundraising efforts were modestly visible in the IASC Foundation's *Annual Report* for 2007. This disclosed the total contributions for the year of £11.277 million, up by about £0.9 million. The revenues from publications and other activities were £4.992 million. Thus, with interest and other income, the total revenues for the year were £16.925 million. This was in excess of the £16 million target, originally planned for 2008 but since applied also to 2007. Yet revenues fell £211,000 short of total expenses, in contrast to staff's earlier expectations of a comfortable surplus. For the first time, the *Annual Report* disclosed the contributions by countries and other major sources. The EU member states, the United States, and Japan, as well as the international audit firms, registered the following contributions (with the target amounts indicated in parentheses):

EU member states	£3.340 million (£4.200 million)
United States	£2.062 million (£4.200 million)
Japan	£1.027 million (£1.750 million)
Audit firms[132]	£3.239 million (£3.420 million)

The considerable shortfall for the United States was an issue, although some would point out that the audit firms were mostly based in the United States. Also in the *Annual Report* for 2007, the trustees remarked that Australia, Hong Kong, India, and New Zealand 'are providing direct contributions through the relevant regulatory authorities in an amount greater than, or equal to, their prorated portion' (page 10).

In the course of 2007 and 2008, the trustees continued their search for stable sources of funding, and chalked up some successes. At the trustees' January 2007 meeting, Max Dietrich Kley, the German trustee, once again voiced the view that the current fundraising scheme would not be sustainable beyond 2010 and that the trustees should approach the European Commission about authorizing a listing fee to cover Europe's share of the Foundation's budget. Bryan Nicholson, from the United Kingdom, agreed.[133] But no action was as yet forthcoming at the European level. Progress was reported in Denmark, Germany, France, and elsewhere in Scandinavia in funnelling voluntary company contributions through either a standard setter or a business association. Outside the EU, a voluntary funding scheme through a central body was established in Switzerland in 2007, even though Swiss listed companies could choose to report on the basis of US GAAP as well as IFRSs.[134] In the 2008 *Annual Report*, ten listed European countries either had a central funding scheme to collect voluntary contributions, a levy, or made payments out of the budget of a national organization—or were well towards doing so (page 16). No funding was received during 2008 from France, because the establishment of a central funding regime, supported by the Ministry of Finance, had taken longer than planned to establish.[135]

In 2007, when South Korea announced its decision to adopt IFRSs, Tom Seidenstein led an effort to secure annual direct funding via the KASB. In the South Pacific, Australia's Financial Reporting Council forwarded the contribution from both Australia (Au$800,000) and New Zealand (NZ$250,000) from grants received, respectively, from Australia's Treasury and the New Zealand government via the Accounting Standards Review Board. Because of the position of the Australian government, a mandatory levy was not in prospect.[136] In 2007, the fundraising agency CCS, already retained with an eye on the United States, began assisting the fundraising effort in Brazil.

A levy system had so far not been in view in the United States, but at their January 2008 meeting, the trustees worried that the suggestion that the SEC might consider a levy system to support the IASB would adversely affect fundraising in

---

[132] Includes BDO, Grant Thornton, and Mazars.

[133] IASCF trustees meeting of 17–18 January 2007, minute H.

[134] IASCF trustees meeting of 2–3 April 2007, agenda paper 6, attachment iii; IASCF trustees meeting of 29–30 January 2008, minute 12.

[135] IASCF trustees meeting of 15–16 January 2009, agenda paper 3.

[136] IASCF trustees meeting of 2–3 July 2007, agenda paper 4(i).

the United States. The trustees thought that US companies should be advised that they would not have to pay twice if such a system were implemented.[137] Funding from the United States was at risk from another source as well. In September 2008, Seidenstein reported that 'We are, however, facing attrition among some of our donors in the United States due to the turmoil in the markets'.[138] Fundraising was discussed at the trustees' October 2008 meeting in Beijing, which was dominated by unrelenting pressure on the IASB Board to amend a standard without due process in order to relieve banks of the need to recognize losses on their portfolio holdings. The onset of the financial crisis, Seidenstein said, had cost the Foundation about £500,000 because of voluntary donors being unable to make a payment.[139]

As money did not yet begin to flow abundantly from national schemes, it was decided in the course of 2007 to approach the Big Four audit firms once more, which were already giving $1.5 million each, to raise their commitment to $2 million. The firms agreed to do so, beginning in 2008.[140]

The Foundation's *Annual Report* for 2008 revealed that the total contributions for the year were £12.747 million, which was 13 per cent above the previous year but still well short of the target of £16 million. Yet, when the revenue from publications and related activities of £6.481 million and from interest and other income were included, the total revenue of £19.822 million exceeded the total expenses by £528,000. However, the Foundation had to report a nearly £3 million hedging loss on foreign exchange. A large fraction of the Foundation's revenues was received in US dollars and euros, while the expenses were incurred mainly in sterling. It was hoped to recoup the losses in 2009 and 2010 by a more stable foreign exchange hedging policy.[141]

The breakdown of the four largest sources of funding was as follows:

EU member states	£3.137 million (down by £203,000 from 2007)
United States	£1.891 million (down by £171,000 from 2007)
Japan	£1.592 million (up by £565,000 from 2007)
Audit firms	£4.230 million (up by £991,000 from 2007)

Some developments boded well for 2009 and beyond. In Asia-Oceania, in addition to the notable 55 per cent increase in the Japanese contributions, Hong Kong and India grew in their contributions as well.[142] A funding system had been established in China, so that all of Asia-Oceania, Australia, China (mainland), Hong Kong, India, Japan, New Zealand, and South Korea now either had a centralized system for gathering voluntary contributions or made a country contribution from an authoritative body (*Annual Report 2008*, pages 16–18).

---

[137] IASCF trustees meeting of 29–30 January 2008, minute 12.

[138] IASCF trustees meeting of 9–10 October 2008, agenda paper 7.

[139] IASCF trustees meeting of 9–10 October 2008, minute 8.

[140] IASCF trustees meeting of 2–3 July 2007, agenda paper 4(i); IASCF trustees meeting of 31 October–1 November 2007, agenda paper 7.

[141] IASCF trustees meeting of 15–16 January 2009, minute 6.

[142] IASCF trustees meeting of 15–16 January 2009, agenda paper 3.

11.10.5 New Funding and New Challenges

In 2009, Canada began transmitting contributions through the Canadian Institute of Chartered Accountants (which housed its standard setter), a decision reported to the trustees in September 2008. Yet, in the Americas, only Canada could so far count on a central funding agency. The United States, among major countries, was the conspicuous exception still to rely on voluntary contributions solicited by the trustees, because the SEC was powerless under the Sarbanes-Oxley Act of 2002 to exact a levy on issuers to support the IASB. Nor did the FAF, the American Institute of Certified Public Accountants, or any other body step forward to coordinate or centralize the IASC Foundation's fundraising.

A tantalizing disclosure in the *Annual Report* for 2008, which would relieve the European trustees of much of the ardour of begging for funds, was squirreled away in a footnote: 'The European Commission has proposed a €4 million per year contribution for 2011–2013', yet to be confirmed (page 16). This disclosure reflected an announcement by the European Commission on 26 January 2009 that it was proposing to contribute €5 million (not €4 million) annually for three years to the IASC Foundation, subject to approvals from the European Parliament and the Council.[143] As seen above, the European Commission was already pondering the possibility of EU funding for the IASB in 2006, if not before, but apparently it judged that the time was now ripe. The proposal was part of a wider package of measures to strengthen the regulatory framework following the financial crisis, and in terms of funding would benefit not only the IASC Foundation, but also EFRAG and the Public Interest Oversight Board of the International Federation of Accountants (IFAC). For all three, the Commission noted that reliance on non-diversified and voluntary funding from interested parties gave rise to continuous concerns about the independence of these bodies. This was not a new insight, and the Commission did not offer any suggestion that the IASB had in fact been influenced by means of funding, let alone in ways that would have contributed to the financial crisis. As in many other areas, it would seem that the financial crisis provided a good justification for actions that were already considered for other reasons.

On 1–2 April 2009, the trustees met jointly with the Monitoring Board (discussed more fully in Chapter 14) at the latter's inaugural meeting. Charlie McCreevy, the EU commissioner for the internal market representing the Commission on the Monitoring Board, confirmed the European Commission's proposal to earmark a maximum of €5 million as 'operating grants' to the Foundation for the years 2011 to 2013. He said that he hoped that the Parliament would approve the proposal by the end of April and added that, because the funding would come directly from the EU's budget, it would be paid in a way that

---

[143] 'Financial Markets: Commission Adopts Measures to Strengthen Supervisory Committees and Standard-setting Bodies for Accounting and Auditing', European Commission press release IP/09/125, 26 January 2009 <http://europa.eu/rapid>. For details of the proposal, see 'Proposal for a Decision of the European Parliament and of the Council Establishing a Community Programme to Support Specific Activities in the Field of Financial Services, Financial Reporting and Auditing', COM(2009) 14 final, 23 January 2009 <http://ec.europa.eu/internal_market/finances>.

preserved independence.[144] In the event, the European Parliament and the Council jointly approved the legal framework in September 2009, which would allow funding for the IASC Foundation and the other bodies. The maximum amount allocated to the Foundation was set at a little over €12 million in three years, or some €4.2 million per year.[145]

At their October 2009 meeting, the trustees asked themselves whether the EU funding might be a mixed blessing. It was queried whether the EU's promise of its annual contribution beginning in 2011 would replace voluntary funding from individual member states. Seidenstein observed that the €4 million was a concern because it was less than what was currently being received from the individual EU member states. He estimated that the amount of the shortfall would be in the neighbourhood of £500,000 less than the amount contributed by the EU member states in 2008. Although the European Commission justified its proposal in terms of bolstering the IASB's independence, Bryan Nicholson raised the spectre that the reverse might result. He said that 'the EU levy based funding announcement is of great concern since the IASC Foundation has no control over how much EU funding will be provided and the EU funding will be conditional, requiring the organisation to provide annual reports and be generally accountable which may limit its independence and ultimately politicize the standard-setting process. This level of intrusion will be a negative impact.'[146]

However, EU funding beginning in 2011 was a comparatively distant issue compared to some of the Foundation's current problems. Tom Seidenstein realized that it was one thing to establish national contribution schemes, but that their upkeep was another issue. He noted, in October 2009, that many countries did not provide any 'inflationary uplift' in their annual contributions.[147] Also, new developments in funding during 2009 were matched by new developments in expenditures. The increased number of Board meetings because of the acceleration of the convergence programme with the FASB, and in response to the financial crisis, as well as continuing attempts to enhance due process and outreach all came at a price. At the trustees' January 2009 meeting, David Sidwell, chairman of the audit committee, who had just completed a review of the five-year funding plan, argued that the organization needed to achieve further outreach. He said that the Foundation required more Board members and staff to set up satellite offices in Asia and the United States. He feared that, by 2010, the Foundation might incur a net operating deficit of between £1 million and £1.5 million, and the low level of funding (in relation to its share of GDP) in the United States was a continuing problem.[148] Although the minutes do not say that the trustees acted on the proposal to set up the two satellite offices, a remark by Chairman Gerrit Zalm

---

[144] Transcript of IASCF trustees and Monitoring Board meeting, 1 April 2009, 15–16 <http://www.iosco.org>.

[145] Decision No. 716/2009/EC of the European Parliament and of the Council of 16 September 2009, *Official Journal of the European Union*, 25 September 2009.

[146] IASCF trustees meeting of 7–8 October 2009, minute 15.

[147] IASCF trustees meeting of 7–8 October 2009, minute 15.

[148] IASCF trustees meeting of 15–16 January 2009, minute 4.

at the trustees' joint meeting with the Monitoring Board in April indicates that they did.[149]

In the light of the pressure on both revenues and expenses, the question was raised once again in the course of 2009 whether the Big Four audit firms could be prevailed upon to provide still more funding. When this point was raised at the October trustees' meeting, Samuel DiPiazza, who had just stepped down as chairman of the global firm of PricewaterhouseCoopers (PwC), said that it was a perception in the United States that the IASB organization was a tool of the big audit firms 'and as a consequence many believe that the big accounting firms should not finance the IASB or the FASB. Furthermore, the accounting firms will not be willing to provide any more funding.'[150] In fact, in 2011 the Big Four firms lifted their contributions to $2.25 million. The trustees and Foundation staff did try to limit the amount that the audit firms contributed as a percentage of the total in order to avoid the perception of a possible conflict.

To the outside world, the results for 2009 provided a new opportunity to review the Foundation's fundraising efforts. In the 2008 *Annual Report*, the trustees had for the first time displayed the 'expected financing contribution' for the coming year from each major country or other type of contributor, which aggregated in excess of £17 million (pages 15–18). The United States was charged with raising only £2.394 million, well below the optimistic figure advanced in 2006 for the following year, based on its share of world GDP. Japan's target was £1.915 million, and for the EU member states it was £4.092 million. The international audit firms were to contribute £5.745 million. This framework of target contributions had been discussed in April 2009 with the Monitoring Board, in keeping with the agreement between the trustees and the Monitoring Board that they would regularly discuss the adequacy and appropriateness of the sources of funding and any other revenue arrangements of the IASC Foundation.[151]

The IASC Foundation's *Annual Report* for 2009 showed that the total contributions for the year were £16.584 million, which was a small amount below the target for the year but was nonetheless an increase of 30 per cent over the previous year. Not all of this was due to fundraising: the appreciation of the euro and the dollar versus sterling were large factors as well.[152] Nonetheless, the total revenues of £22.649 million fell short of the total expenses of £22.956 million, which also had risen significantly from the previous year. The three largest contributing regions or countries, plus the international audit firms, gave the following amounts:

EU member states	£4.503 million (up by £1.366 million from 2008)
United States	£1.847 million (down by £44,000 from 2008)
Japan	£1.737 million (up by £145,000 from 2008)
Audit firms	£5.690 million (up by £1.460 million from 2008)

---

[149] Transcript of IASCF trustees and Monitoring Board meeting, 1 April 2009, 19.
[150] IASCF trustees meeting of 7–8 October 2009, minute 15.
[151] IASCF trustees meeting of 15–16 January 2009, minute 4.
[152] IASCF trustees meeting of 29 March–1 April 2010, agenda paper 6A.

The total contributions from only thirteen of the twenty-seven EU member states, almost entirely from Western Europe, increased by 44 per cent, and exceeded the target set in the 2008 *Annual Report*. In particular, Spain mounted its stable funding platform via the Bolsas y Mercados Españoles, led by trustee Oscar Fanjul, and the French funding scheme, through the Ministry of Finance, was now in operation. Germany, which contributed £1.235 million in voluntary contributions channelled through the German standard setter, was the third largest contributing country, behind the United States and Japan. Yet the good news from Europe only served to exacerbate the concern over the insufficiency of the EU's annual contribution of €4 million beginning in 2011, if this were to replace existing national contributions.

Although, of all countries, the United States continued to provide the largest amount, the flatness of the trend in US contributions and its evident shortfall compared to the target continued to be a great worry to the trustees.[153] The trustees' gloomy forecast for US contributions in 2010 was £1.812 million (*Annual Report 2009*, page 52). At the trustees' March/April 2010 meeting in London, Jeffrey Lucy, the Australian trustee, tweaked the noses of some of his colleagues by saying, 'Asia-Oceania are paying a considerable amount and it is now for the EU, North America, South America and other areas to start contributing equally'.[154] Although this was perhaps a little unfair on the EU, the US 'funding gap' and the question whether the EU member states would continue to provide support at present levels once the European Commission began to make its contributions were the two most pressing questions facing the trustees in 2010 and 2011.

11.10.6 The EU, the United States, and the Rest of the World

Tom Seidenstein prepared a major report, 'Update on Financial Efforts', for the trustees' January 2010 meeting. He proposed that the European trustees discuss the potential impact of the reduced European funding with the incoming internal market commissioner (not yet identified), the incoming internal market director-general, Jonathan Faull, and Sharon Bowles, the new chairman of the Parliament's Economic and Monetary Affairs Committee. When the European Commission had announced its plans for EU funding early in 2009, it had been clear from the start that this would be contingent on the EU's satisfaction with improvements in the IASB's governance, both through the establishment of the Monitoring Board and as part of the ongoing review of the IASC Foundation's Constitution. Seidenstein wrote, 'The Finance Committee took the strong view that it would be preferable to maintain the existing national schemes, rather than an EU-wide scheme, if there were strings attached or it led to a greater shortfall'. At the trustees' January 2010 meeting, the trustees echoed these concerns about any conditions that might attach to the EU's funding, especially if they were to impinge on the IASB's independence. The European trustees agreed with the

---

[153] IFRS Foundation trustees meeting of 11–13 October 2010, agenda paper 4.
[154] IASCF trustees meeting of 29 March–1 April 2010, minute 15.

importance of approaching the parties suggested by Seidenstein in his report about the need to increase the amount of funding.[155]

A few months later, at the Monitoring Board meeting of April 2010, Michel Barnier, the EU's new internal market commissioner, set out the terms for continued EU-wide funding: 'The first priority must be to ensure stable and sufficient funding from all jurisdictions. It is true that in September 2009 the EU adopted a legal basis to fund the IASB from 2011, but I must say that from the beginning that's not automatic and must be approved every year, both by the Council and by the Parliament and I counsel that it is not a formality.'[156] Yet the European Commission had just signed up as a formal member of the Monitoring Board, and the Foundation had concluded its second Constitution review in February 2010, suggesting that there were no insurmountable formal impediments left. Barnier may have wished to signal both to the IASB and the European Parliament that he was vigilant in keeping the IASB on the right course. The Foundation prepared itself to go through the detailed grant application procedure to secure the EU funds.[157]

With respect to the United States, Seidenstein recommended in January 2010 that the US trustees and the Foundation's staff meet with the SEC commissioners and senior staff to see if there might be the prospect of a US funding mechanism, through the SEC or otherwise, to address the problem that the US annual contribution had been regularly well below the country's GDP share.[158] As in the case of the EU, the Monitoring Board again brought the trustees directly into contact with the principal.

At the Monitoring Board's meeting with the trustees on 1 April, SEC Chairman Mary Schapiro gave some hope for a solution to the US funding problem: 'On behalf of the US gap I think the Trustees and the Monitoring Board all know that we're very committed to finding a solution to the US funding issue and we're working very hard on both a short-term and a long-term, stable, lasting approach to this.' She encouraged the trustees to work with the SEC's staff to see how some of this gap could be filled. Schapiro cautioned that 'a condition for the Commission to go forward in 2011 [with a decision on use of IFRSs by domestic listed companies is] that the IASB has sufficient, stable, long-term funding to help ensure its independence going forward'.[159] Perhaps the trustees would have preferred to be told how the SEC could help them to achieve that goal.

In the Foundation's 2010 *Annual Report*, it was stated that the total contributions were £16.641 million, which was less than one-half of a per cent above the figure for the previous year, and in line with expectations. Total revenues were £22.773 million compared with total expenses of £24.143 million, producing a deficit of £1.370 million. The acting co-chairmen described 2010 as 'a particularly challenging period from a financial perspective' (page 9). The EU member states,

---

[155] IASCF trustees meeting of 26–7 January 2010, minute 11.
[156] Transcript of IASCF trustees and Monitoring Board meeting, 1 April 2010, 10; 'department' emended to 'Parliament' <http://www.iosco.org>.
[157] IFRS Foundation trustees meeting of 11–13 October 2010, agenda paper 4B.
[158] IASCF trustees meeting of 25–7 January 2010, agenda paper 7.
[159] Transcript of IASCF trustees and Monitoring Board meeting, 1 April 2010, 10.

the United States, Japan, and the international audit firms accounted for the following contributions:

EU member states	£4.213 million (down by £292,000 from 2009)
United States	£1.898 million (up by £51,000 from 2009)
Japan	£1.850 million (up by £113,000 from 2009)
Audit firms	£5.437 million (down by £253,000 from 2009)

In February 2011, because of the sizable operating deficit in 2010 and expected further growth, the trustees' finance committee estimated the 2011 funding requirements to be 'circa £3.5 million' more than the Foundation received in 2010. The committee said that the trustees and staff were in the process of seeking increases from a number of countries. It was reported that China had confirmed additional funding of $200,000 (£124,000) beyond its £726,000 contributed in 2010 via a system being administered by the Ministry of Finance. China's GDP share was about £950,000.[160]

At the trustees' February meeting, the trustees' worry that EU funding might reduce but not make up for contributions from EU member states was somewhat relieved when it was reported that several EU countries were prepared to continue funding the Foundation during the transitional year of 2011.[161] This intelligence arrived in time to be incorporated in the 2010 *Annual Report*, where it was stated that a sum of £2.334 million was expected from six EU member states to supplement the EU-wide contribution. The EU countries named were Spain, France, Germany, the Netherlands, Italy, and the United Kingdom (page 61).

The Foundation's *Annual Report* for 2011 finally revealed whether EU member states would continue to make contributions during the first year in which the EU gave its €4.25 million (£3.653 million) grant. In fact, they did, as will shortly be seen. The total contributions for the year were £20.561 million, representing a 24 per cent advance on the figure for 2010 and some £400,000 above the expected increase of 'circa £3.5 million'. Total revenues were £26.121 million, and total expenses were £25.716 million, yielding the first operating surplus since 2008. The major contributors were as follows:

EU member states	£4.056 million (down by £156,000 from 2010)
United States	£1.737 million (down by £161,000 from 2010)
Japan	£1.713 million (down by £137,000 from 2010)
Audit firms	£5.825 million (up by £388,000 from 2010)

In the year in which the EU made the first of its three annual 'operating grants' to the Foundation, ten EU member states—all from Western Europe plus Bulgaria—remained loyal and carried forward with their contributions, with only a minor drop from their 2010 level. The total of £4.056 million for the EU member states was almost 75 per cent above the expected amount of £2.334 million which the

---

[160] IFRS Foundation trustees meeting of 9–11 February 2011, agenda paper 6.
[161] IFRS Foundation trustees meeting of 10–11 February 2011, 6.

trustees gave in their 2010 *Annual Report*. As it turned out, the Foundation trustees need not have worried about the size of the EU's contribution, because it turned out to be over and above what the EU member states were continuing to give.

But not all of the EU countries continued making contributions during the 2007–11 period. Hungary and Sweden dropped out as contributors in 2009, and Slovakia and Greece dropped out in 2010 and 2011, respectively. All but Sweden were small donors, all under £20,000. Sweden gave £221,000 in 2007 and £190,000 in 2008 through a private-sector foundation, and then stopped.

The total US contribution, although buoyed by a first-time grant from the FAF, was once again the biggest disappointment among major donor countries. Contributions received were down compared to 2010, and more than 20 per cent below the rosy estimate for the year of £2.210 million, reported in the 2010 *Annual Report*. The actual amount of the FAF's contribution was subsequently put at $500,000.[162] The FAF's contribution of its funds to the IFRS Foundation in 2011 was subjected to some criticism several years later in the United States (see Section 17.9).

11.10.7 Analysis of Contributions by Country and Regions

In Table 11.1, we present a comparative analysis of the contributions by country and region. Countries are named if they contributed at least £100,000 in one of the five years from 2007 to 2011. Otherwise, they are included in the 'Other' totals. Only the years 2007–11 are shown, because the IASC/IFRS annual reports began disclosing the geographical sources of contributions in 2007. As we have already discussed above, the trends in the contributions from the United States, Japan, and the international audit firms, they will not be treated here as well. Some of the countries' contributions will be compared to their relative share of their 2007 GDP.[163] We recognize that the relative share of GDP was not the only factor used by the Foundation trustees when setting their funding expectations.

Asia–Pacific. Omitting Japan, the two largest contributors from 2008 to 2011 were China and Australia. Australia's annual contributions were significantly ahead of its GDP share, while China's were well below its share. South Korea's contribution more than doubled in 2011, coinciding with the country's mandatory adoption of IFRSs. From 2008 to 2011, the Asia-Pacific area shouldered between one-fifth and one-quarter of the total contributions to the Foundation.

Americas. Brazil and Mexico were the only contributor countries in Latin America during the five-year period. Brazil's contributions in 2010 and 2011 were well under its GDP share, following a year, 2009, when it did not contribute at all. Mexico contributed a total of £55,000 in 2007 and 2008 and then did not contribute anything again. Canada's contributions from 2009 to 2011 were above

---

[162] 'Financial Accounting Foundation to Provide up to $3 Million to IFRS Foundation to Aid Completion of Joint IASB Projects', FAF news release dated 28 January 2014 <http://www.accountingfoundation.org>.
[163] For the GDP figures for 2007, see IASCF trustees meeting of 26–7 January 2010, agenda paper 7, appendix I.

Table 11.1. Contributions by country and region, 2007–11

Country and region	Annual contribution (£1,000)				
	2007	2008	2009	2010	2011
Australia	339	473	463	617	632
China	90	533	750	726	807
Hong Kong	–	–	132	123	120
India	174	218	247	251	257
Japan	1,027	1,592	1,737	1,850	1,713
South Korea	151	197	182	193	437
Other Asia–Pacific	86	91	117	164	204
Asia–Pacific	**1,867**	**3,104**	**3,628**	**3,925**	**4,170**
Asia–Pacific (% of total)	**0.17**	**0.24**	**0.22**	**0.24**	**0.20**
Brazil	139	8	–	198	229
Canada	63	15	453	512	507
United States	2,062	1,891	1,847	1,898	1,737
Other Americas (Mexico)	30	25	–	–	–
Americas	**2,294**	**1,939**	**2,300**	**2,607**	**2,472**
Americas (% of total)	**0.20**	**0.15**	**0.14**	**0.16**	**0.12**
Africa	**50**	**10**	**7**	**45**	**62**
Africa (% of total)	**0.00**	**0.00**	**0.00**	**0.00**	**0.00**
France	426		888	861	854
Germany	966	1,011	1,235	1,049	952
Italy	366	632	684	628	661
Netherlands	412	313	355	339	350
Spain	137	171	440	430	348
Sweden	221	190	–	–	–
Switzerland	240	211	169	188	195
United Kingdom	787	730	800	855	861
Other European countries	30	92	175	95	31
EU Institutions	25	25	34	31	3,686
Europe	**3,610**	**3,376**	**4,780**	**4,476**	**7,937**
Europe (%)	**0.32**	**0.26**	**0.29**	**0.27**	**0.39**
International audit firms	3,239	4,230	5,690	5,437	5,825
International organizations	185	50	68	62	62
Trustees (waived reimbursements)	34	37	110	89	32
International	**3,457**	**4,317**	**5,869**	**5,588**	**5,919**
International (% of total)	**0.31**	**0.34**	**0.35**	**0.34**	**0.29**
Total	11,277	12,747	16,584	16,641	20,561

Source: IASC/IFRS Foundation annual reports.

its GDP share. The absence of contributions from other countries in the Americas is a curiosity. The Americas accounted for between 12 and 15 per cent of the total contributions between 2008 and 2011.

Africa. South Africa, which was one of the first and most dedicated adopters of IFRSs, gave £50,000 in 2007 and £45,000 in 2010 but nothing at all in the other three years. A contribution through its Financial Reporting Council had been expected in 2009.[164] The contribution in 2010—much below South Africa's GDP share—was organized through the South African Institute of Chartered Accountants. Nigeria gave £62,000 in 2011 but nothing in the earlier years. Also during the

---

[164] IASCF trustees meeting of 9–10 October 2008, agenda paper 7.

five-year period, Uganda and Botswana contributed an aggregate of £12,000 and £5,000, respectively. Africa's share of the total contributions has been less than 1 per cent in each year.

Europe. From 2007 to 2010, Europe gave between 26 and 32 per cent of the total contributions. In 2011, buoyed by the EU's first major 'operating grant' to the Foundation, Europe's share of the total increased to 39 per cent. In all five years, the aggregate contribution from EU countries and the EU itself exceeded its GDP share. Switzerland's contributions were regularly above its GDP share. Russia contributed only £5,000 in 2007 and £18,000 in 2009.

11.10.8 Fundraising: Small Sums, Large Efforts

The trustees, in the April 2011 draft of their strategy review, properly drew attention to the fact that the total funding that had been sought by the Foundation was not all that much in the light of the important global mission of the IASB. The trustees wrote as follows:

> The 2011 budget for the IFRS Foundation (for all activities) is £26 million. This budget is relatively small compared with those of other international organisations with global reach and influence. Furthermore, the budgetary increases since the advent of the IASB in 2001 have failed to keep pace with the growing demands placed on the organisation.
>
> To 'adjust' to the global spread and to implement the strategy contained in this report, the Trustees believe that the budget may need to grow to approximately £40–45 million (at current sterling amounts, i.e. excluding future inflation) annually over a period of time. This would still be a relatively small amount when compared with other international financial institutions. Furthermore, it would mark significant savings when compared with the sum of resource requirements for all national accounting standard-setting before global adoption of IFRSs.[165]

It is not so easy to determine the proper benchmarks with which to compare the IASB in terms of funding. On the one hand, the IASB looks well-endowed compared with, say, the London-based International Coffee Organization (2011/ 12 budget of £3.2 million, with twenty-six staff). But on the other hand, if the IASB's budget were to grow to £45 million, it would be the same order of magnitude as that of the Universal Postal Union. Yet it seems reasonable to say that the costs of running the IASB were not large in terms of the means available to some of its larger constituents. When trustee Bryan Nicholson approached the chairman of the One Hundred Group of Finance Directors about financial support for the IASB, he said the chairman asked, 'how much is involved?' When he was told of the amount being sought, he replied that 'it's loose change. Are you sure you don't want more?'[166] Similarly, the contributions from the international audit firms which formed the stable basis of the IASB's budget

---

[165] *IFRSs as the Global Standard: Setting a Strategy for the Foundation's Second Decade*, Report of the Trustees' Strategy Review (IFRS Foundation, April 2011), 20.

[166] Interview with Bryan Nicholson, 19 May 2011. See a similar comment by trustee Yves-Thibault de Silguy, transcript of IASCF trustees and Monitoring Board meeting, 1 April 2010, 11.

must be seen in the light of the very substantial revenue generated for these firms as companies around the world have adopted IFRSs.

If the absolute sums involved were not very large, the trustees' laborious efforts throughout the decade to raise funds from a multiplicity of sources around the world appear all the more striking. It would seem that these efforts must be appreciated primarily in view of the imperative of being seen as truly broad-based. Just as it would have been easy for the IASB to recruit most of its staff from the United Kingdom and other English-speaking countries, so one assumes that, if truly necessary, the audit firms and the core group of regularly contributing companies could well have funded an even larger part of the IASB's budget. Yet in both cases the effort to draw on a broader range of sources was justified to establish the IASB's credentials as a truly international organization.

12

Concepts and Convergence

An Ever Closer Relation with the FASB

12.1 THE IASB'S STANDARD-SETTING ACTIVITIES IN THE MIDDLE OF THE DECADE

With the completion of the 'stable platform of standards' in 2004 (see Chapter 5), the IASB could well believe that an important mission had been accomplished on schedule. The package of standards had been readied for large-scale adoption, starting in 2005, in the European Union (EU), Australia, South Africa, and a number of other jurisdictions. The Board entered into a new phase of its life, roughly lasting from late 2004 to the middle of 2008.

This phase had two related features. The first was that convergence work with the US Financial Accounting Standards Board (FASB) now truly began to dominate the IASB's agenda. Working with the FASB had always been important to the IASB, certainly since the 2002 Norwalk Agreement, but the publication of the 'roadmap' towards lifting the 20-F reconciliation requirement by the chief accountant of the US Securities and Exchange Commission (SEC) in April 2005 gave a much stronger sense of purpose (see Section 8.1). In 2006, the IASB and the FASB published a Memorandum of Understanding (MoU) outlining a work programme for converging their standards. This MoU, updated in 2008, became the central point of reference in planning the IASB's technical work.

The second feature of this period was that, in the joint projects of the two boards, the emphasis shifted from modifying existing standards to writing completely new standards, including a rethink of basic accounting concepts. The members of the IASB Board experienced this as an interesting, perhaps even an exhilarating, phase when contrasted with the earlier grinding work of improving the IASC's standards. Yet, to many reporting companies that had recently moved to IFRSs, the prospect of a fundamental overhaul of the standards could be quite alarming, especially if done by a Board believed to be remote from the concerns of practice. The phrase 'accounting ayatollahs'—generally credited to Claude Bébéar, chairman of the French insurer AXA—gained currency.[1] The Board had

---

[1] Possibly the earliest use was in Bébéar's speech at the AXA annual general meeting of May 2003; see 'Bébéar en guerre contre les normes IAS', La Tribune, 2 Mai 2003, 17. For an international echo see Floyd Norris, 'Does Business Need a New Bottom Line?' posted 24 June 2005 <http://www.nytimes.com>. Bébéar was still quoted with approbation by Michel Pébereau in 2011, see 'Quand Pébereau

to navigate carefully between the SEC's expectation that convergence would lead to significant improvements in the standards and the craving by many companies for stability.

In the end, this phase did not result in as much change as the IASB might have hoped for, or as some of its constituents had feared. By the middle of 2008, most of the major projects the two boards were working on had not progressed beyond the stage of discussion papers or exposure drafts. The boards had to discover as they went along how much time they needed to come to grips with the issues they were addressing, and what it would take to bring their constituents along with them. By the middle of 2008, another phase was beginning, for two reasons. First, because of an accelerating trend towards adoption of IFRSs in countries around the world, and because of the possibility opening up that even the United States might move to IFRSs in the near future, the year 2011 came to occupy a central place in the IASB's planning, as the year 2005 had before. The need to have, once again, a relatively stable set of standards in place by 2011 concentrated minds that, until then, might have been too much inclined to continue exploring possibilities of fundamental accounting reform. As 2011 drew closer, the Board repeatedly trimmed its agenda, and several MoU projects were curtailed or deferred. Second, the financial crisis breaking in the second half of 2008 overturned much of the IASB's planning. The next phase in the IASB's technical work, from 2008 to 2011, is the subject of Chapter 16.

This chapter considers, first, the overall development of IASB–FASB cooperation as embodied in the MoU of February 2006, and then continues with a review of the main joint projects of the two boards. The final part of the chapter considers some of the remaining projects which the IASB did on its own, including the project to develop a standard for small and medium-sized entities (SMEs).

12.2 PLANNING THE CONVERGENCE OF IFRSs AND US GAAP

12.2.1 The SEC Roadmap and the Origins of the 2006 MoU

On 21 April 2005, European Commissioner Charlie McCreevy met with SEC Chairman William Donaldson in Washington to discuss SEC Chief Accountant Don Nicolaisen's roadmap towards lifting the Form 20-F reconciliation requirement for foreign registrants using IFRSs. On the same day, the IASB and the FASB were meeting in London for one of their joint meetings. The two boards could by then point towards some convergence achievements, but their approach had so far been haphazard and had lacked a strong sense of urgency. Discussions of the planning and organization of the convergence work had taken place at the leisurely pace of two joint meetings a year, starting in October 2003. Some

parle métier', *L'Express*, 23 November 2011, 20. It may be noted that Bébéar also applied the trope outside of accounting, for instance with reference to environmental legislation. See 'Non aux ayatollahs de la prudence', news item posted 25 October 2007 <http://www.lemonde.fr>.

important decisions about the future of IASB–FASB convergence work had been taken at the April 2004 joint meeting, but these needed time to bear fruit (see also Section 5.7.3).

For the April 2005 joint meeting, an agenda paper written by the two staffs suggested that 'reducing the reconciliation burden' should be the IASB's major strategic target. There was no indication in the paper that a complete lifting of the reconciliation requirement was in sight. The paper suggested that the SEC could be asked to consider a 'discrete' reconciliation, that is, a reconciliation with respect to selected standards only, rather than a complete reconciliation.[2] But during the April meeting, in an apparent response to Nicolaisen's roadmap, the emphasis shifted from 'reducing the burden of the 20-F reconciliation' to a resolution by the two boards to seek to determine the '"minimally required" standard-setting effort that would enable the SEC to lift the 20-F reconciliation requirement by or around 2008'. This knowledge would then guide the two boards' convergence actions in the short term.[3]

To give effect to this resolution, a meeting was held on 10 May 2005 which brought together David Tweedie and Jim Leisenring from the IASB, Bob Herz and Michael Crooch from the FASB, and FASB senior staff member Suzanne (Sue) Bielstein and, from the SEC, Chief Accountant Don Nicolaisen, Deputy Chief Accountant Julie Erhardt, and the director of the Office of International Affairs, Ethiopis Tafara. The roadmap had already made it clear that important conditions for lifting the reconciliation requirement were outside the IASB's control. There was not much the IASB could do about establishing effective enforcement mechanisms in countries where IFRSs were used, or about the consistent application of IFRSs. But the roadmap indicated that convergence between IFRSs and US generally accepted accounting principles (US GAAP) would be an important 'enabler' in the SEC's ultimate decision.[4] This raised the question of how far convergence should have to proceed, and on this point the SEC staff at the meeting provided an important clarification of the roadmap:

> In response to specific questions raised by Mr. Leisenring and others, Mr. Nicolaisen said that in his view, the failure of the Boards to eliminate particular differences between IFRS and US GAAP through short-term convergence or other major projects by 2008–2009 *would not* [original emphasis] impede the removal of the reconciliation by the SEC.[5]

What was already proposed in the roadmap was now confirmed. The SEC's chief accountant wished to see the differences between IFRSs and US GAAP reduced as much as possible, but he was not thinking in terms of a target list of specific changes to existing standards that needed to be completed as a condition for lifting the reconciliation requirement. Rather, he was looking for a clearly demonstrated commitment by the two boards to convergence, and to significant

---

[2] 'Convergence Review', AP 4/2005 paper 5.

[3] Memorandum from Suzanne Bielstein to FASB board members, dated 23 May 2005, IASB archive, file 'FASB'.

[4] Donald T. Nicolaisen, 'A Securities Regulator Looks at Convergence', *Northwestern Journal of International Law & Business*, 25/3 (Spring 2005), 672.

[5] Memorandum from Suzanne Bielstein to FASB board members, dated 23 May 2005, IASB archive, file 'FASB'.

progress towards that end by means of joint projects to develop new standards. In the words of David Tweedie:

> From the standard-setting standpoint, the approach taken in the roadmap was a revelation. The IASB and the FASB would no longer need to concentrate on a possibly endless series of changes . . . to get the reconciliation removed.[6]

To appreciate Tweedie's enthusiasm, it should be recalled just how much of the effort of both the IASC and the IASB since the late 1980s had been devoted to improving existing standards with a view towards satisfying the SEC. The IASB much welcomed a shift of emphasis 'from short-term elimination of differences to longer-term work aimed at improving existing practices'.[7]

Yet the change in emphasis did not mean that the SEC was no longer a demanding constituent. Well before the end of the relatively short period to 2009 as envisaged in the roadmap, the IASB and the FASB were expected to complete at least some of their existing short-term convergence projects, and to make significant progress on major projects for new standards. With respect to the latter, the SEC had its own ideas about priorities. In June 2005, the SEC staff published a major report on off-balance sheet issues, one of the many after-effects of the accounting scandals leading up to the Sarbanes-Oxley Act of 2002.[8] It was noted at the IASB that, because of political pressure on the SEC, the FASB was beginning to think about projects on accounting for pensions and leases, and that the IASB might have to follow suit.[9]

During the remainder of 2005, intensive consultations took place among the IASB, the FASB, and the SEC to develop a work plan, including relevant 'milestones' to guide the SEC's decision on the reconciliation requirement. The main outlines of the plan as it would subsequently be adopted were already visible in May 2005.[10] Following its annual agenda review in 2005, the IASB began work on several new projects. By November 2005, if not before, the IASB's intention was to formalize this work plan in a memorandum of understanding between the two boards. This MoU was publicly announced on 27 February 2006, but by that time work on the MoU programme was already well under way.[11]

Before considering the contents of the 2006 MoU, it may be helpful to review briefly some of the constraints faced by the IASB in setting its convergence agenda. At a practical level, the IASB found itself, in the middle of 2005, very short of staff resources, even to the point where the staff fell short of what was necessary for the existing workload. Even though recruitment was under way, the

---

[6] 'Report of the Chairman of the IASB', IASC Foundation, *Annual Report 2005*, 6.

[7] IASCF trustees meeting of 21 June 2005, minute 2.

[8] 'Report and Recommendations Pursuant to Section 401(c) of the Sarbanes-Oxley Act of 2002 on Arrangements with Off-balance Sheet Implications, Special Purpose Entities, and Transparency of Filings by Issuers' (US SEC, 15 June 2005) <http://www.sec.gov>.

[9] AP 7/2005 paper 9, paragraph 9–12.

[10] 'Targets', memo from Wayne Upton to David Tweedie, dated 25 May 2005, IASB archive, file 'FASB'.

[11] IASCF trustees meeting of 14–15 November 2005, agenda paper 7, paragraph 6; 'US FASB and IASB Reaffirm Commitment to Enhance Consistency, Comparability and Efficiency in Global Capital Markets', IASB–FASB press release dated 27 February 2006.

staff was cautious in recommending new projects such as the SEC might have in mind.[12]

Another consideration was that the IASB had to deal not only with the United States but also with other jurisdictions, not least the EU and Japan. Board members and trustees knew that developments surrounding convergence were followed with scepticism in Europe. In part, this reflected an aversion to change of any kind in the standards, following the strenuous exertions by reporting companies and their auditors to prepare for transition to IFRSs in 2005. However, there was also a fear that convergence would be a one-way street and would lead to the importation of US GAAP into IFRSs.[13] While this might be acceptable for the over two hundred EU companies with US listings for which the lifting of the reconciliation requirement was important, it was a potential source of great annoyance for the thousands of European companies that were not listed in the United States.[14] In this situation, the IASB's best course was probably to emphasize the fact that the European Commission had embraced the SEC staff's roadmap and, by implication, the need for convergence, and to seek to involve the European Commission's staff in the development of the IASB–FASB work plan. Even so, the fact that the Commission itself had to tread carefully in this matter did not make it an easy partner for the IASB. In a speech delivered in October 2005, EU Commissioner McCreevy emphasized that the convergence effort envisaged in the roadmap:

> should not destabilise the IFRS platform in Europe. I would like to stress that convergence is not an invitation to standard-setters to try and advance the theoretical frontiers of accounting. I will not take on board any revolutionary new standards.... We will not be adding any new carriages to the IFRS train just as it has left the station.[15]

In a cautiously worded comment to the trustees, David Tweedie concluded that 'My colleagues and I believe that our work programme with the FASB is generally consistent with the views expressed by Mr McCreevy', but he noted that McCreevy's remarks could be construed by others in a way that was contrary to what the SEC expected.[16] In January 2006, when appearing before the European Parliament's Economic and Monetary Affairs Committee, Tweedie emphasized that the work plan about to be agreed with the FASB was a programme 'involving minimal change to our existing agenda'.[17]

---

[12] AP 7/2005 paper 9, paragraph 4–5.

[13] AP 6/2005 paper 2B, paragraph 11–12; IASCF trustees meeting of 21 June 2005, minute 2. See also 'Accounting: All for One, and One for All', *Financial Director*, 4 July 2005, 17.

[14] 'Foreign Companies Registered and Reporting with the U.S. Securities and Exchange Commission, December 31, 2005' <http://www.sec.gov>. This document lists 246 entities from EU countries but may include some double counting of entities belonging to the same group.

[15] Charlie McCreevy, 'Address to the Global Public Policy Symposium', London, 20 October 2005, SPEECH05/627 <http://europa.eu/rapid>.

[16] IASCF trustees meeting of 14–15 November 2005, agenda paper 7, paragraphs 10–12.

[17] 'Prepared Statement of Sir David Tweedie, Chairman of the International Accounting Standards Board before the Economic and Monetary Affairs Committee of the European Parliament, 31 January 2006' <http://www.iasplus.org>.

It was not just Europe which had to be handled with kid gloves. As discussed in Section 10.4, in the early months of 2005 the IASB and the Accounting Standards Board of Japan (ASBJ) were feeling their way towards closer cooperation, and the first of a regular series of 'convergence' meetings was held in Tokyo in March 2005. The IASB must have been aware of a desire, or expectation, in Japan that it should be treated on a comparable footing with the United States, and that the ASBJ should either participate in IASB–FASB projects or establish its own direct consultations with the FASB.[18] But while the IASB continued to describe its work with both the FASB and the ASBJ in terms of convergence, it was easily seen that the word carried a different meaning with respect to the United States and Japan.[19]

12.2.2 The February 2006 MoU

Whereas the 2002 Norwalk Agreement had been couched in the relatively modest terms of achieving and maintaining 'compatibility' between US GAAP and IFRSs, the February 2006 MoU, entitled 'A Roadmap for Convergence between IFRSs and US GAAP', stated more boldly that 'A common set of high quality global standards remains the long-term strategic priority of both the FASB and the IASB'.[20] More specifically, the removal of the 20-F reconciliation requirement was identified as the immediate objective for 2006–8. In line with the way the SEC's chief accountant had expressed his views in 2005, the two boards declared that their responsibility was to make 'continued and measurable progress' on convergence, rather than to complete given projects by a set date. So, while the MoU did contain a work programme listing a series of projects, the expected progress on each project was typically stated in flexible terms such as 'to have issued one or more due process documents' (i.e. a discussion paper or an exposure draft) by 2008.

The core of the 2006 MoU consisted of eleven major projects (see Table 12.1). Only one of these had a firm expected completion date. This was the project to provide guidance on the application of the acquisition method of accounting for business combinations (a project known at the IASB as 'business combinations phase II'), on which the two boards had been working jointly since 2002. This was

---

[18] See, for instance, 'Comments on Draft Memorandum of Understanding on the Role of Accounting Standard Setters and their Relationships with the International Accounting Standards Board', letter from Shizuki Saito (ASBJ chairman) to Warren McGregor, dated 29 June 2005 <http://www.asb.or.jp> accessed through web.archive; 'Interim Report by Study Group on Corporate Accounting' (Ministry of Economy, Trade and Industry, September 2005), 1 <http://www.meti.go.jp>; 'Statement on Japan's Progress toward Convergence between Japanese GAAP and IFRSs' (ASBJ, 31 January 2006) <http://www.asb.or.jp> accessed through web.archive; letter from Shizuki Saito to David Tweedie, dated 12 May 2006, IASB archive, 'Japan' file.

[19] Compare, for instance, Tommaso Padoa-Schioppa's 'Work on the Convergence of Accounting Standards Must Go On', *IASB Insight*, May 2006, 2, with the article, 'The ASBJ and the IASB Hold Third Meeting on Convergence', in the same issue (pages 7–8).

[20] 'A Roadmap for Convergence between IFRSs and US GAAP—2006–2008', Memorandum of Understanding between the FASB and the IASB, 27 February 2006 <http://www.ifrs.org>. Unless otherwise indicated, all citations in this section are from this document.

Table 12.1. Major projects of the IASB–FASB Memorandum of Understanding, 2006–11

Project	Status with IASB in February 2006 MoU	Status with IASB in September 2008 MoU update	Status with IASB in June 2011
Business combinations	Active project	Concluded with revised standards (January 2008)	–
Consolidations	Active project	Active project, exposure draft about to be published	IFRS 10 and 12 issued (May 2011), work in progress on limited modifications
Fair value measurement	Active project	Active project, discussion paper published (May 2006)	Concluded with IFRS 13 (May 2011)
Liability/equity distinction	Active project	Active project, discussion paper published (February 2008)	No exposure draft, discussion deferred (November 2010)
Performance reporting (financial statement presentation)	Active project	Phase A concluded with revised IAS 1 (September 2007), phase B active, discussion paper about to be published	Limited amendments to IAS 1 (June 2011), further discussion deferred (November 2010)
Postretirement benefits	Not yet on agenda (active FASB project)	Active project, discussion paper published (March 2008)	Concluded with limited revisions to IAS 19 (June 2011)
Revenue recognition	Active project	Active project, discussion paper about to be published	Exposure draft issued (June 2010), active project
Derecognition	Research phase	Active project, no publications yet	Reduced in scope and concluded with limited amendments to IFRS 7 (October 2010)
Financial instruments (replacement of existing standards)	Research phase	Active project, discussion paper published (March 2008)	Partial standard issued (IFRS 9, November 2009), active project
Intangible assets	Research phase	Negative agenda decision (December 2007)	–
Leases	Research phase	Active project, no publications yet	Exposure draft issued (August 2010), active project

the first truly joint project of the two boards to develop a new standard. Although a few other joint projects had been agreed since 2002, the business combinations project was the only one on which substantive progress had been made by early 2006. According to the MoU, converged business combination standards were to be issued in 2007.

The other ten major projects included three on which the boards had at least done some work together: performance reporting, revenue recognition, and a comprehensive revision of the financial instruments standards. Work on all others had yet to commence, or had so far been undertaken by one of the two boards only.

The MoU also showed that the boards wished to put a lid on short-term convergence work. As indicated in Chapter 5, much of the two boards' convergence effort in 2003 and 2004 had been spent on an open-ended and shifting series of projects to eliminate relatively minor differences between their existing standards. The 'quick wins' expected from this effort had largely failed to materialize. In the MoU, the two boards now expressed the view that 'trying to eliminate differences between two standards that are in need of significant improvement is not the best use of the FASB's and the IASB's resources—instead, a new common standard should be developed that improves the financial information reported to investors'. By mid-2005, the IASB's portfolio of short-term convergence work had already dwindled to four distinct projects. What was new was that the MoU now contained a definitive list of ten short-term convergence projects: four to be examined by the IASB, four by the FASB, and two jointly (see Table 12.2 for the six projects involving the IASB).[21] By 2008, the boards should either have substantially completed these projects, or have made up their minds that they should not be addressed as short-term convergence projects. As shown in Table 12.2, some of these projects never took off. Three completed short-term projects are discussed in other chapters: the project resulting in IFRS 8 *Operating*

Table 12.2. The IASB's projects for short-term convergence with US GAAP, 2006–11

Project	Status with IASB in February 2006 MoU	Status with IASB in September 2008 MoU update	Status with IASB in June 2011
Borrowing costs	Active project (IASB only)	Concluded with amendments to IAS 23 (March 2007)	–
Impairment	Possible joint project	Deferred (April 2008), no longer mentioned in work programmes following September 2008	–
Income tax	Active joint project	Active project (IASB), FASB's work suspended	Concluded with limited revision of IAS 12 (December 2010)
Government grants	Deferred (IASB only)	Deferred	Deferred
Joint ventures	Active project (IASB only)	Active project, exposure draft published (IASB only, September 2007)	Concluded with IFRS 11 (May 2011)
Segment reporting	Active project, exposure draft published (IASB only, January 2006)	Concluded with IFRS 8 (November 2006)	–

[21] The fluid nature of the short-term convergence agenda may be seen from a comparison of the 2006 MoU with the work plan of about half a year earlier ('IASB Project Timetable 2005–2006', *IASB Insight*, July 2005, 13). Three projects appear in both lists (revision or replacement of IAS 12 on income taxes, IAS 14 on segment information, and IAS 20 on government grants). The fourth short-term project listed in July 2005 (IAS 37, provisions) was no longer a convergence project by the time of the MoU. In July 2005, joint ventures were listed as part of the research agenda. Borrowing costs (revision of IAS 23) was not listed in the July 2005 work plan, and first discussed by the Board in October 2005, although at that point it was affirmed that the project had been agreed in April 2004 (AP 10/2005 paper 12A, paragraph 1).

Segments (Chapter 9), the project on joint ventures, resulting in IFRS 11 *Joint Arrangements*, and a project resulting in amendments to IAS 12 *Income Taxes* (both in Chapter 16).

The MoU did not mention that the boards had already set out on a joint project to develop a revised conceptual framework, as it had no direct significance for the lifting of the reconciliation requirement. For a similar reason, the MoU did not mention the FASB's intention to join, in due course, the IASB in developing a standard for insurance contracts. This was not a pressing reconciliation issue as it affected only a small number of the SEC's foreign registrants using IFRSs.

The 2006 MoU was very much a continuation of the two boards' previous planning rather than a plan developed on a clean sheet of paper. Even so, it was ambitious in contemplating a fundamental review of several major topics. The tension between these ambitions and the desire on the part of many of the IASB's constituents for stability following the massive first-time adoption of IFRSs in 2005 remained unresolved. During the first half of 2006, as the implications of the MoU began to sink in and it became more widely understood what kind of changes the IASB and the FASB were contemplating, complaints that the boards were going too far and too fast began to multiply. In July, Tweedie acknowledged that 'the memorandum of understanding frankly scared a few people'. He announced a 'quiet period' in the sense that any standards currently under development would not become mandatory before January 2009.[22] That was perhaps not a major concession given that the first few significant IFRSs under the MoU, other than business combinations, were not expected until 2008 anyway.[23] Nevertheless, the fact that such a gesture was considered necessary is suggestive of the signals that were reaching the IASB.

12.2.3 The 2008 MoU and the Emergence of the 2011 Deadline

The single most important factor that sustained constituents' support for the IASB's convergence agenda with the FASB, notwithstanding a continuous rumble of discontent over the pace and scope of change, was the prospect of acceptance of IFRSs by the SEC. As discussed in Chapter 8, the SEC moved with surprising speed and lifted its reconciliation requirement in November 2007 with immediate effect. By then the IASB and the FASB had not even completed their business combinations project—although they would do so within weeks—let alone any of the other major projects from the 2006 MoU. The SEC's decision was consistent with its stated policy of looking for sustained efforts at convergence rather than completion of a specific agenda, but the decision could raise the question why the IASB's constituents would continue to support further convergence now that the main prize of access to US capital markets without using US GAAP had been won. Why should the IASB not declare victory, stop giving priority to convergence with US GAAP, and concentrate on the needs of jurisdictions that had already adopted

---

[22] Tweedie quoted in 'Accounting Board to Freeze Changes in Rules Until 2009', *Financial Times*, 24 July 2006, 17; 'IASB Takes Steps to Assist Adoption of IFRSs and Reinforce Consultation: No New IFRSs Effective until 2009', IASB press release, 24 July 2006.

[23] IASCF trustees meeting of 28–9 June 2006, agenda paper 3C.

IFRSs or had announced plans to do so?[24] The question was asked, but not with as much insistence as might be expected, due to the fact that a new and even more ambitious ultimate objective immediately took the place of the lifting of the reconciliation requirement. In August 2007, the SEC issued its concept release on the possible voluntary use of IFRSs by domestic listed companies, so that the movement towards a single global standard appeared to be rapidly accelerating.[25]

These developments had a significant influence on the work plans of the two boards. As discussed more fully in Chapter 8, SEC Chief Accountant Conrad Hewitt took the initiative in January 2008 for a series of meetings and consultations with the IASB and the FASB on the possibility of accelerating the convergence work programme to a 2011 deadline, with a view to US adoption of IFRSs beginning in 2013.[26] For the IASB, taking into account its expected Board turnover in 2011, this translated into a June 2011 target date. David Tweedie was certainly keen to embrace a 2011 target, and he may well have provided Hewitt with inspiration. Both within the IASB and the FASB, there was scepticism about the feasibility of this target, but probably more so at the FASB. However, with Hewitt and Tweedie behind it, it is understandable that the FASB went along in exploring the idea.

The task of working out the details was entrusted to a working group consisting of a member and a senior staff member of both boards: Thomas (Tom) Linsmeier and Sue Bielstein from the FASB, and Jim Leisenring and Wayne Upton from the IASB. The result was a proposal submitted to the two boards for their joint meeting in April 2008.[27] Leisenring was a former FASB board member, and Upton was a former senior staff member of the FASB. Therefore, when the composition of the working group became publicly known, the fact that it was a 'strictly US affair' of 'four FASB luminaries' drew some adverse comment in the press.[28] The composition of what became known internally as 'the gang of four' was perhaps a little at odds with the way it described its own objectives in the April 2008 agenda paper: 'to outline the improvements to existing IFRS that are needed to facilitate mandatory adoption of IFRS in all major capital markets' (paragraph 3). At that stage, one might think of Brazil, Canada, India, and Japan as major capital markets committed to moving to IFRSs or considering so to do. In several of these countries, the year 2011 had already been identified as a date of adoption or as an important milestone. The proposals left little doubt, though, that what the group really had been instructed to do was to take a hard look at what it would take, at a minimum, to prepare IFRSs for adoption in the United States, and for that purpose a better qualified group could not have been formed.

The group carried out its mission but showed itself highly sceptical. Mainly by significantly reducing the scope of existing projects, the four succeeded in making

---

[24] See e.g. remarks by Paul Boyle, cited in 'Rethink is Urged over Accounting Proposals', *Financial Times*, 11 July 2007, 23.

[25] 'Fast Adoption Raises Hopes of Happy Families', *Financial Times*, 11 September 2007, 2.

[26] Apart from documentation referred to in the notes, the reconstruction of events relating to the revision of the MoU is based on interviews with Suzanne Bielstein, 3 August 2009; Robert Herz, 17 February 2009; Conrad Hewitt, 1 August 2010; James Leisenring, 2 August 2010; David Tweedie, 15 October 2009; and Wayne Upton, 7 July 2011.

[27] AP 4/2008 (joint) paper 3.

[28] 'The Internet: Lesson 1', *World Accounting Report*, May 2008, 11.

recommendations that added up to a timely completion of most of the major projects. Yet they commented that 'a mid-2011 completion date goal requires that the Boards work more efficiently than they ever have' (paragraph 6). When the proposal was discussed at the joint meeting in April, it seems that none of the members of either board, nor their staffs, were under any illusions regarding the feasibility of the plan. Yet all voted to proceed, except one: Jim Leisenring, one of the four members of the working group.[29] Leisenring considered it intellectually dishonest, and in the long run also damaging to the IASB's standing, to commit publicly to a plan that the members knew would be virtually unachievable. To him, the April 2008 meeting marked a turning point in the Board's work, where the need to bring projects to a close and gain acceptance for the standards began to override the need for thorough debate, conceptual consistency, and high quality.[30] Other members, including Chairman Tweedie, saw this differently. It was plain to Tweedie that, without the pressure of a clear deadline, projects would continue to drift:

> *Everybody* works to deadlines. If you're in business and the client wants something, you set a deadline on it. You try and do it. You throw everything at it until you do it. I remember I said to them [i.e. those who were sceptical of deadlines]: When I was a student, President Kennedy was saying in 1961 they'd put a man on the moon by the end of the decade. Writing a pension standard can't be as complicated as that. I just felt *everything* was taking too long. So we were quite keen to have a target.[31]

Similarly, Warren McGregor believed it was important 'to put a stake in the ground' to concentrate minds at the Board and give off a strong outward signal of determination: 'Historically, standard setters were as slow as wet wicks, and many would like just to sit there and just pontificate, rather than actually make decisions. This injected a pretty strong sense of urgency.'[32]

The result of the April meeting was the publication, in September 2008, of an updated version of the MoU, presented as a progress report.[33] Publication was held up for several months as the IASB first had to mend fences with the European Commission. The Commission felt surprised by the sudden appearance of the revised work plan among the April 2008 agenda papers, and protested against what it saw as a lack of consultation and transparency in the setting of the Board's agenda.[34]

As may be recalled, the 2006 MoU had listed eleven major projects. Of these, business combinations could be ticked off because it was completed in 2008. One

---

[29] *IStaR*, April 2008, joint meeting supplement, 33.

[30] Interview with James Leisenring, 2 August 2010.

[31] Interview with David Tweedie, 21 December 2010.

[32] Interview with Warren McGregor, 18 and 19 May 2011.

[33] 'Completing the February 2006 Memorandum of Understanding: A Progress Report and Timetable for Completion', appended to IASB–FASB press release 'IASB and FASB Publish Update to 2006 Memorandum of Understanding', dated 11 September 2008.

[34] Interview with Jeroen Hooijer and Alain Deckers, 19 January 2009. Bob Herz (interview, 17 February 2009), recalled that the FASB was ready to publish in June but that publication was held up by the IASB's need to consult with the European Commission. See also letter from Pierre Delsaux to David Tweedie, dated 17 July 2008, IASB archive, file 'EU', and the ECOFIN conclusions of 8 July 2008 (2882nd Council meeting, press release 11236/09), 13 <http://www.consilium.europa.eu>.

other project, on intangible assets, had been dropped from the list when both the IASB and the FASB decided not to make it an active agenda topic. There was a long-standing difference between IFRSs and US GAAP on this point. Since FAS 2 *Accounting for Research and Development Costs* (1974), capitalization of most internally developed intangible assets was prohibited under US GAAP. In contrast, IAS 9 *Accounting for Research and Development Activities* (1978) had allowed capitalization, provided certain conditions were met. In 1993, this had been changed in mandatory capitalization under similar conditions, a requirement carried forward into IAS 38 *Intangible Assets* in 1998. The SEC saw this as an important difference and had wished to see the topic included in the 2006 MoU. Yet neither the IASB nor the FASB was inclined to take it up, because they could not see their way forward towards a widely-supported solution.[35] This was a great disappointment for the Australian Accounting Standards Board (AASB), which had undertaken to do the preparatory work and had developed an agenda proposal.[36]

The remaining nine projects from the 2006 MoU had by now all moved to the status of active projects. For only one of these—the development of a new standard on financial instruments—did the revised MoU not set a specific completion date. The other eight—financial statement presentation, leases, the liability/equity distinction, revenue recognition, consolidations, derecognition, fair value measurement, and post-employment benefits—were expected to be completed at various dates between 2009 and 2011. In addition, just two projects were left for the IASB from the former category of short-term convergence: joint ventures and the revision of the standard on income taxes, with expected completion in 2009 and 2010, respectively (see Table 12.2).[37] As before, two important joint projects remained outside the scope of the MoU: the revision of the conceptual framework and the insurance contracts project.

Following some general observations on IASB–FASB cooperation (Section 12.3), the remaining sections of this chapter cover selected technical projects, beginning with those projects in which the IASB worked closely with the FASB. First, Section 12.4 considers business combinations. The next two sections discuss the projects to revise IAS 37 on provisions (Section 12.5) and to develop a new standard on revenue recognition (Section 12.6), two projects that raised important conceptual issues and anticipated the formal revision of the conceptual framework, which is discussed in Section 12.7. The project on financial statement presentation (Section 12.8) also led the IASB and the FASB to discuss the fundamentals of financial reporting, in particular with respect to the role of net income.

The chapter then turns to projects that were not, or only to a lesser extent, governed by convergence with US GAAP. With respect to financial instruments (Section 12.9), the IASB had to steer a course between the pragmatic maintenance of existing standards and a fundamental revision together with the FASB. The standard for SMEs (Section 12.10) was an IASB-only project, as was a project to

---

[35] Interview with David Tweedie, 5 June 2013.

[36] AP 4/2007 paper 12B, for the draft agenda proposal. Letter from David Tweedie to David Boymal, 9 January 2008, IASB archive, file 'Australia'.

[37] The 2008 MoU did not specify a completion date for the income tax project, but the 2010 date was given in the October 2008 version of the work plan published on the IASB's website.

develop guidance on management commentary (Section 12.11). Finally, the chapter turns to the work of the International Financial Reporting Interpretations Committee (IFRIC) (Section 12.12).

12.3 THE IASB AND THE FASB: STILL LEARNING TO WORK TOGETHER

In Section 5.7.4, we discussed some of the challenges faced by the IASB and the FASB in developing an effective working relationship between two organizations that might appear similar but that differed in many respects.[38] Over time, some differences between the two organizations were resolved. The IASB's staff, for instance, gradually came to match that of the FASB in size and experience, but this did not necessarily make it easier for the two boards to reach shared conclusions. Other differences became more pronounced as the emphasis shifted from short-term convergence to joint projects with the intention to issue identical or near-identical exposure drafts of entirely new standards. When the boards had to work together more closely, small differences in outlook and procedures could assume a greater weight.

At a very basic level, the staffs sometimes had to resolve differences between British and American English when writing papers and drafts. More substantial was the difference between the IASB's policy of making most of its agenda papers publicly available, and the FASB's long-standing policy not to do so. The FASB continued to believe in its own policy, which was inspired by the belief that the staff should be able to write critical and candid analyses of all views. Yet it accepted as inevitable that papers on joint projects would be available on the IASB website.

The logistics of producing joint board papers were complicated by the need to have them reviewed by senior staff on both sides, and to resolve any difference of view which might arise. Another complication was that the FASB met weekly for a day and the IASB only monthly for a week. This affected the pacing of projects and their approval. The FASB staff had to learn that to miss a deadline for producing a paper by one meeting was more consequential at the IASB side than was the case at the FASB.

Other procedural differences made themselves felt in the course of the joint projects. The FASB had for some time not been in the habit of issuing discussion papers (preliminary views documents in the FASB's parlance) prior to exposure drafts. Following the first review of the IASC Foundation's Constitution, and the publication of the IASB's *Due Process Handbook*, the expectation that the IASB would normally begin each major project by issuing a discussion paper had been firmly established. The FASB followed the practice in the sense that all of the discussion papers it published between 2005 and 2011 related to joint projects with the IASB.

---

[38] The references to the sources on which Section 5.7.4 is based also applies to this section.

More fundamentally, the joint projects brought home that the FASB and the IASB differed in their general approach to standard setting. There was a style difference in the sense that FASB members were accustomed to more detailed analysis and examples. One IASB Board member recalled:

> The discussion papers prepared by the staff of the [FASB], sometimes you read it, and you said: 'That's fantastic!' I mean, as work, as analytical work, it was almost a thesis to become a Ph.D., a doctorate. So I don't question the quality of the work. It was really amazing. But it was just too much! It was just not necessary to do it like that.

There was a view at the IASB that, beyond a difference in style, there was a difference in objectives. The FASB was seen as preferring to approach a project comprehensively, by breaking it down into all aspects and sub-problems that the staff could identify, discussing these thoroughly one by one, and then assembling the result into a proposal for a standard. In contrast, the IASB, and David Tweedie in particular, liked to think of its approach as first considering what the answer to the main question was likely to be, and then to work out only those details that were necessary for a proper implementation in most, but not necessarily all, circumstances. The contrast between US GAAP and IFRSs as rules-based versus principles-based may often have been overstated, but there was no doubt that the FASB was accustomed to responding to demands for more extensive application and implementation guidance in its standards, much more than the IASB was willing to do. The difference may well reflect that many IASB Board members came from national accounting and business environments where, at least until recently, financial reporting standards had been minimally specified and lightly enforced. The FASB's members and staff, on the other hand, were all steeped in a reporting culture marked by the strength of the SEC's enforcement practice, which had no equivalent in any other jurisdiction. The IASB Board members were cosmopolitan enough to understand these differences and to appreciate some of the merits of the US system, and the reverse was true for the FASB. But a residual difference in outlook remained, and this difference was greater among the boards' constituents. As the number of countries adopting or about to adopt IFRSs increased, the IASB had to pay heed to a much wider range of views on the desired properties of accounting standards than the FASB.

Another difference was that the FASB thought of its standard setting as staff-led, or staff-driven, and it placed great value on the independence of the staff vis-à-vis the board. This was seen as favourable to an objective analysis of alternatives, and to collegiality among board members who would be criticizing staff proposals rather than the ideas of their fellows. The IASB had a different emphasis and saw its standard setting as Board-dominated. While it encouraged staff to take the initiative on projects and to speak freely, it was always on the understanding that the Board could respond by pointing the staff in a different direction. At the IASB, there was also a stronger inclination to involve Board members in the development of alternatives. Initially, this may have been a pragmatic response of an experienced Board faced with a shortage of staff. In subsequent years it appeared from the FASB point of view more as an attempt to speed up projects. Another variable was that IASB Chairman David Tweedie had more influence over the work of the staff, and more generally over the pace and progress of the IASB than any chairman could have had at the FASB. At the FASB, the chairman was seen as a first among equals, but that would not have been an apt description of the IASB chairman's position.

Given the different positions of the staffs, and the different expectations of their work, it was perhaps not surprising that occasional frictions arose. It was observed both at the IASB and the FASB that the two boards got along very well, but that the staff assigned to some of the projects found it difficult to cooperate, to an extent that could not simply be attributed to the sometimes inevitable mixing of incompatible personalities.

12.4 BUSINESS COMBINATIONS PHASE II

Phase II of the IASB's business combinations project was completed with a revised version of IFRS 3 *Business Combinations*, issued in January 2008, almost simultaneously with the corresponding FAS 141(R) *Business Combinations* issued in December 2007. As discussed in Chapter 5, the IASB's phase I had been a matter of catching up with the FASB in the abolition of the pooling of interests method and the replacement of goodwill amortization by a periodic impairment test. A joint phase II on the application of purchase accounting was already envisaged in 2001. In April 2002, the boards agreed to add such a project to their agendas.[39] This was well before their first substantive joint meeting in September of that year, which would lead to the two boards' Norwalk Agreement.

It was by no means the easiest topic to take on as a first joint project, as it entailed consideration of the accounting treatment of all items on the balance sheet of an acquired company.[40] But one issue acquired particular prominence, not least because of the inability of the two boards to reach convergence. This was the 'full goodwill' issue; that is, the question of how to measure goodwill and non-controlling interests in situations where the acquiring company obtains an interest of less than 100 per cent in the acquired company.

The measurement of goodwill and non-controlling interests were two sides of the same coin, but the boards first approached the question from the perspective of goodwill. In many countries the traditionally prevailing view had been a 'parent company perspective' following which goodwill was recognized as purchased goodwill, that is, the goodwill corresponding to the percentage of interest actually acquired.[41] But in the United States there was a notable line of academic literature going back many decades, arguing from an 'entity theory' perspective in favour of recognition of the hypothetical full goodwill that would have been paid for the acquisition of a 100 per cent interest.[42] In November 2002, the staffs argued that

[39] AP 11/2001 paper 11A and AP 4/2002 paper 4.

[40] As recalled by Thomas Linsmeier, interview, 11 June 2013.

[41] According to AP 11/2002 paper 2A, 'this method appears to be the most prevalent in practice [in the United States] and it is the method prescribed by the Big 4 accounting firms in each of their business combinations guides'. In the EU, the Seventh Directive (1983)'s treatment of goodwill as a consolidation difference would seem to have ruled out the full goodwill method.

[42] See Stephen A. Zeff, 'The Entity Theory of Recording Goodwill in Business Combinations: Old Stuff', *The CPA Journal*, 75/10 (October 2005), 80.

this full-goodwill method was conceptually more appealing, being more in line with the boards' view that goodwill is an asset, and with the concept of control underlying the practice of consolidation. Although potential problems with reliable measurement of full goodwill and questions concerning the relevance of full-goodwill information were duly noted, the staffs recommended the full-goodwill approach for conceptual reasons.[43]

The arguments proved persuasive to majorities of both boards, but with considerably more reservations at the IASB than at the FASB. After some rounds of debate in both boards, the FASB confirmed its choice for the full-goodwill method by five votes to two. A little later, in June 2003, the IASB voted nine to four with one abstention in favour of full goodwill. Tatsumi Yamada, Gilbert Gélard, Harry Schmid, and Geoffrey Whittington voted against, while Hans-Georg Bruns abstained.[44] This was the end of the debate as far as this issue was concerned, although—indicating the scope and complexity of the project, as well as the added difficulty of working with two boards—it took two more years before an exposure draft could be issued in June 2005. By then, Schmid had left the IASB, but Bruns' abstention had hardened into a no-vote, and the dissenters had been joined by Bob Garnett. The full-goodwill method was the main reason for the five to vote against the exposure draft of the revised IFRS 3.[45] They cited conceptual reasons and issues of reliability, and questioned whether the full-goodwill information would be relevant.[46] At the FASB, one board member recorded an alternative view in the parallel exposure draft to revise FAS 141, also issued in June 2005, but this dissent did not relate to the full-goodwill issue.[47]

It was a notable feat for the two boards to issue, for the first time, exposure drafts on a major issue that were almost word-for-word identical. The achievement was marred by the fact that the exposure drafts referred to unconverged concepts of 'control' in other standards (see Section 16.3 for the IASB's project on consolidation). Hence, the boards still had different definitions of what constituted a business combination, because these definitions were couched in terms of acquiring control.

The IASB's exposure draft was a complex package with implications beyond business combinations. For instance, because of the requirement that all identifiable assets and liabilities of the acquired company should be recognized at their fair values when first included in the consolidated financial statements of the acquirer, the Board had included some guidance on fair value measurement. This was extracted from an FASB draft standard which the Board, as part of the MoU, expected to use as the basis for its own standard on fair value measurement (see Section 16.4). Also included in the package were significant changes to IAS 37, the standard on provisions, discussed in Section 12.5.

Feedback on the exposure drafts was received both through comment letters and at roundtables organized by the two boards in London and Norwalk. The tenor of the responses was that the boards, or at least the IASB, had gone too far,

[43] AP 11/2002 paper 2A, 2–16.   [44] Both votes were reported in *IStaR*, June 2003, 28–9.
[45] *IStaR*, July 2004, 22.
[46] Exposure draft 'Amendments to IFRS 3 Business Combinations' (IASB, June 2005), AV2–7.
[47] Exposure draft 'Business Combinations: A Replacement of FASB Statement N0. 141', 1204-001 (FASB, 30 June 2005), B204–12.

too fast. It is not surprising that many preparers were not pleased to see a package of significant changes appear during what, for many, was still the year of transition to IFRSs. The European employers' federation UNICE, for instance, argued that the boards should at least have gone through the stage of a discussion paper before proposing something as radical as recognizing full goodwill. It also disapproved of the proposed fair value guidance which seemed to pre-judge the outcome of the separate fair value measurement project.[48] But it was not just preparers who were sceptical. Some user organizations, for instance the UK's Society of Investment Professionals, thought that a discussion paper would have been appropriate in order to investigate more fully whether an 'entity perspective' as implied by the full-goodwill method was really the best way of accounting from the point of view of valuing a holding company's shares.[49] Perhaps the strongest support for the proposals came from the US-based CFA Institute, which did believe that the full-goodwill method would improve transparency and comparability.[50]

By early 2006, the staffs had concluded that the full-goodwill proposal received little support, confirming their view that this was one of the most controversial issues in the exposure draft.[51] But whereas, in March, the FASB still solidly supported the staff's recommendation to continue with the full-goodwill method, the IASB's approval had slipped to a bare majority of eight out of fourteen.[52] There was a risk that the boards might not be able to agree on a single solution. As discussed in Chapter 7, the IASB's Constitution had been amended in 2005 to raise the threshold of approval for a standard from eight to nine votes out of fourteen. This was the first project where this tightened voting rule came into view as a factor in the Board's decisions, although one might also argue that the grossing up of goodwill was so controversial that it would not have passed under the previous voting rules either.[53]

An attempt was made by the staffs to shift attention away from goodwill, and to avoid the full-goodwill terminology altogether. Instead, the staffs proposed to start with the measurement of the non-controlling interest, and to consider the amount of goodwill as a residual. Non-controlling interests would in principle be measured at fair value, and the staffs conceded that this might result in the same numerical outcome as the original proposal. Yet they disagreed that 'this was just a "backdoor way" of getting to the full-goodwill method'.[54] There might also, perhaps, be scope for an exception based on the undue cost or effort to determine the fair value of non-controlling interests. The change of emphasis and wording

[48] Letter from Jérôme P. Chauvin to FASB, dated 24 October 2005, CL13 at <http://www.fasb.org>. All comment letters received on this project were posted on the FASB website.

[49] Letter from Tony Good to Alan Teixeira, dated 27 October 2005, CL 244.

[50] Letter from Patricia A. McConnell and Rebecca T. McEnally to David Tweedie, dated 26 November 2005, CL 273.

[51] AP 1/2006 paper 6A, paragraph 31; AP 3/2006 paper 2B, paragraph 13.

[52] See AP 10/2006 paper 5B (joint meeting), paragraphs 1–3 for a summary of the voting in March. The FASB's vote was said to have been six to one in favour of continuing with full goodwill.

[53] While Patricia O'Malley (interview, 28 May 2009) recalled that the change in the voting rule played a role in the final decision on the revised IFRS 3, Mary Barth (interview, 17 March 2009) and Robert Garnett (interview, 22 June 2010) expressed the view that the change in voting rules did not change the Board's decisions, neither in general nor in the case of the goodwill issue.

[54] AP 12/2006 paper 2A, paragraph 27.

did not help to break the deadlock. The FASB was willing to go along with the change of perspective, starting with the measurement of the non-controlling interest, but wanted this done simply at fair value, without any exceptions or options. The IASB wanted exceptions to fair value measurement but had difficulty defining the appropriate conditions.[55] No decision was reached while a host of other issues arising from the exposure drafts were being resolved. By the time of the boards' joint meeting in April 2007, the staffs were ready to begin drafting the standard and asked the boards to take positions on the final remaining differences. As the IASB could not muster up the required majority for any proposed conditions to depart from fair value measurement, it ended up with accepting an option. IFRS 3 revised, issued in January 2008, allowed a free choice between measurement of the non-controlling interest at fair value and at a proportionate share of the fair value of the acquired company's identifiable net assets. This in turn provoked a different set of dissents: Mary Barth, Bob Garnett, and John Smith now voted against the standard because of the free option. Barth and Smith noted that it had been a process of give and take, primarily for the sake of convergence, but 'the [IASB] Board's compromise on this particular issue diminishes the importance of convergence, establishes a precedent for allowing a choice when the two boards cannot reach agreement and may suggest that full convergence in the long term cannot be achieved'.[56] Jim Leisenring was reported to have said that 'he would be willing to line up, but was chagrined that the FASB had stuck to the principle and the IASB had not'.[57] In its standard, the FASB maintained the single requirement to measure the non-controlling interest at fair value. Of its seven members, Leslie Seidman was the only one to dissent, among other reasons because she did not support the recognition of goodwill for the non-controlling interests.[58]

More quietly, the fair value guidance disappeared from the IASB's standard, with the result that the final business combinations standards issued by IASB and FASB were based on somewhat different conceptions of fair value. Although the practical effect of the difference might not be great, it was another illustration of just how difficult it was to achieve complete convergence on a specific topic, because of the inevitable cross-references to other standards.

Apart from being the first major joint convergence project to be completed, business combinations phase II also was the first to give effect to a number of due process enhancements. At the completion of the project, the IASB Board published a feedback statement, separate from the basis for conclusions, summarizing the project and reflecting on what the Board had done with input received from constituents during the process. The Board also published a separate booklet which combined the feedback statement with an 'effect analysis', a generally qualitative assessment of the costs and benefits of the standards to users and preparers of financial statements.[59] Finally, this was the first project on which the

---

[55] See AP 3/2007 paper 2A; see also AP 4/2007 paper 2I, paragraphs 2–4; *IStaR*, April 2007 Joint Boards Supplement, 21–2.

[56] IFRS 3 *Business Combinations* (IASB, 2008), DO6.

[57] *IStaR*, April 2007 Joint Boards Supplement, 22.

[58] FAS 141 *Business Combinations* (FASB, revised 2007), 27–8.

[59] 'Business Combinations Phase II: Project Summary and Feedback Statement' (IASB, January 2008); 'Business Combinations Phase II: Project Summary, Feedback and Effect Analysis' (IASB, January 2008).

IASB committed to a post-implementation review, two years after the effective date of the standard. All of these innovations had been agreed by the trustees in April and July 2007 in response to prodding from the European Commission and the European Parliament for a more open and responsive standard setting process (see Sections 9.6.4 and 11.5).

12.5 A TANGLE OF ISSUES IN THE REVISION OF IAS 37

One of the Board's long-running and, in the end, inconclusive projects was the revision of IAS 37 *Provisions, Contingent Liabilities and Contingent Assets*. This was a project that, over time, took on different faces: short-term convergence, consequential amendment, stand-alone project, and revision of fundamental concepts with implications for several other projects. If it was not easy for the Board to maintain a firm grip on the project, it was even less so for the Board's constituents. The Board invested a large amount of time and effort in the project, and saw it as making a real contribution to its understanding of a range of issues, but the unfortunate impression among the IASB's constituents seems to have been that the Board was trying to make important changes too quickly if not surreptitiously. Regardless of its substantive merits, the shifting shape of the project caused people to raise questions about the rigour of the IASB's agenda-setting process.[60]

The origin of the project in 2002 was as an element in the short-term convergence programme established at the time of the Norwalk Agreement. The idea was to bring the requirements on the timing of recognizing restructuring costs in IAS 37 in line with the recently issued FAS 146 *Accounting for Costs Associated with Exit or Disposal Activities*. As with other low-hanging fruit targeted in the short-term convergence programme, the staff soon discovered that this modest objective could not be reached without reconsidering more fundamental aspects of IAS 37.[61]

Around the same time, also in 2002, the project acquired an additional dimension. As part of its business combinations project (phase I) resulting in IFRS 3, the Board had decided that the contingent liabilities of an acquired company should be recognized by their acquirer at their fair value in the initial accounting for the business combination. As the Board well knew, this was inconsistent with IAS 37, according to which contingent assets and liabilities were never recognized. The Board therefore marked the issue for further consideration during phase II of the business combinations project. This reconsideration meant that the Board embarked on a discussion of some of the most fundamental aspects of its conceptual framework before it added a revision of the framework to its agenda in October 2004.

At the heart of the issue was that the existing framework distinguished the question of whether something meets the definition of an asset or liability from the question of whether that asset or liability should be recognized in the balance

---

[60] Interview with Françoise Flores, 4 May 2013.   [61] AP 12/2002 paper 9A, paragraph 2.

sheet. Assets (liabilities) were conceived in terms of future inflows (outflows) of economic benefits, and the framework stipulated that, to recognize an asset or a liability, these future inflows or outflows had to be probable. However, the framework was not as clear as it might have been in distinguishing possible uncertainty over the *existence* of a present resource or obligation giving rise to possibly uncertain future benefit flows from the *probability* of these benefit flows, given the existence of an asset or liability. In IAS 37, both forms of uncertainty had been swept together under the categories of contingent assets and contingent liabilities. Thrown into the mixture were liabilities that were known to exist, and with sufficiently probable outflows, but whose value could not be estimated reliably. The Board believed that it could introduce improved conceptual clarity by removing the probability threshold altogether from the recognition criteria, and separating the uncertainty surrounding an asset or liability in 'element uncertainty' (the question whether the asset or liability exists) and 'measurement uncertainty' (the uncertainty over future benefit flows of an existing asset or liability, to be reflected in its measurement). For IAS 37, the practical conclusion was that the categories of contingent assets and liabilities could be abolished. What had been considered as contingent assets could be brought within the scope of IAS 38 on intangible assets. Most of what had been contingent liabilities could be recognized and measured with other provisions in a new class of items described as 'non-financial liabilities' (all liabilities other than those within the scope of IAS 39 on financial instruments). An example of what this might mean in practice was that companies involved as defendants in a lawsuit would have to recognize a liability for their 'stand-ready obligation' to perform as the court directs, in contrast to the situation under the existing IAS 37 where a lawsuit was the classical example of a contingent liability, not recognized on the balance sheet.

An exposure draft for a substantial modification of IAS 37 along these lines was issued in June 2005, as part of the business combinations (phase II) package. In addition to changing the recognition of liabilities, the Board had also made some modifications to the measurement requirements, although it believed that these were clarifications rather than changes in substance.

The Board was aware that the proposed changes were substantial, even though they were in a formal sense consequential amendments arising out of the business combinations project. In November 2004, the Board discussed whether the proposed changes to IAS 37 were sufficient to justify labelling the revised standard as a new IFRS rather than as a revised IAS 37. It was decided not to move to an IFRS, mainly because most Board members believed that this required reconsideration of other unsatisfactory aspects of IAS 37 as well, which would hold up the business combinations project.[62]

The responses to the exposure draft brought home that, whatever the merits of the proposals by themselves, the Board had failed to carry its constituents along. Stephen Cooper, appointed a Board member in 2007 but who had already been in frequent contact with the Board as a member of its Analyst Representative Group, characterized retrospectively how the Board's approach to standard setting in

---

[62] *IStaR*, November 2004, 5–7. See also AP 11/2004 paper 4.

projects such as the revision of IAS 37 implicitly, but incorrectly, assumed that 'high quality' would ensure acceptance:

> The whole focus was on getting the right accounting, and only if we could get the definitions and measurements of assets and liabilities right, if only we got the correct form of accounting, the rest of the world would see how clever we are and how wonderful this accounting is and everything would be OK.[63]

The view was widely held that the proposed changes were far too important to be handled as consequential amendments, and that they went well beyond anything required for short-term convergence, given that the FASB was not about to undertake a similar comprehensive review of liabilities. The Board was again berated for not issuing a discussion paper first, and was urged to clarify the concept of a liability first at framework level, before pre-judging any issues in the context of a specific standard.[64] What probably did not help the reception of the IAS 37 exposure draft was that it was packaged with the business combinations project, by itself already controversial because of the full-goodwill proposal, and that both were published as many companies were still preparing for their first set of annual financial statements to be published under IFRSs. The idea that the IASB was planning significant changes to the structure of the balance sheet with a possible effective date of 1 January 2007 seemed to make a mockery of the notion of a stable platform of standards, and was said in the press to be 'stretching the goodwill of financial directors to its limits'.[65]

When the Board took up the project again in February 2006, it accepted that there were procedural lessons to be learned. However, the members believed they were breaking important new ground in their consideration of liabilities, and that they had already made significant progress in clarifying basic concepts. Following the staff's recommendation, it was decided to continue the project on a stand-alone basis, to defer the planned completion by about a year, and to ensure careful consultation, not least through a series of roundtables planned for later in 2006. The Board was not ready to accept that it should first complete the revision of the framework before continuing with this project. Rather, it believed that the two projects should move forward together.[66] Thus, in a formal sense the revision of IAS 37 was taken out of the scope of convergence with US GAAP—it was not part of the 2006 or 2008 version of the MoU workplan—but it remained intricately tied up with convergence through its conceptual links with other projects.

For several years, from 2006 through 2009, the Board devoted ample time to debate the revision of IAS 37. In part, this reflected the appointment of new Board members who had to be introduced to the Board's thinking as it had developed. A large fraction of the Board's discussions were taken up with further reflection at the level of basic accounting concepts. Indeed, for some time the agenda papers were being produced jointly by the staff teams working on IAS 37 and the conceptual framework. Just how elementary the accounting issues were could be

---

[63] Interview with Stephen Cooper, 13 February 2012.

[64] See AP 2/2006 paper 8, appendix, for the staff's analysis of responses.

[65] Peter Williams, 'Accounting: Proposal is a Contingent Liability', *Financial Director*, 13 December 2005, 18.

[66] See the discussion as reported in *IStaR*, February 2006, 30–3.

seen from a simple case which became a standing example in Board discussions: a vendor selling a hamburger to a customer in a jurisdiction where the law stipulates that a vendor must pay compensation of £100,000 to a customer that has bought a contaminated hamburger, past experience showing that one in a million of the vendor's hamburgers is contaminated. This simple setting allowed the Board to ponder the difference between uncertainty whether an obligation exists and a known obligation of uncertain amount. The case also prompted debate about the nature of events that give rise to obligations, the difference between liabilities and business risks, and the role of the law in creating obligations.[67] As will be seen in the next section, the concept of a liability proved to be central in the Board's parallel discussions on revenue recognition, not to mention the insurance project. The intricate relationship among these projects and the conceptual framework project were clearly not conducive to fast progress.

While the definition of the elements of the financial statements and their recognition formed an important part of the deliberations, the Board also devoted much time to the measurement of non-financial liabilities. Here, again, the Board was continually refining its thinking on measurement in parallel projects, not least the project to develop a standard on fair value measurement and the project on insurance contracts. In the 2005 exposure draft on IAS 37, the Board had reached the conclusion that non-financial liabilities should be measured at the amount that the reporting entity would rationally pay to settle or transfer the obligation. This was not intended as a fair value measurement, but when the Board, during redeliberation, tried to clarify what it meant, it moved quite close to fair value when it explained the concept in terms of consistency with observable market prices, if available, and in terms of using hypothetical market prices in some circumstances. In particular, in the case of an obligation to provide services, the reporting entity might have to measure its obligation on the basis of what it would charge to another party to provide the service, including a profit margin. A significant minority of Board members, including Jan Engström and Philip Danjou, objected strongly to the idea of including a profit margin, not representing any expected cash outflows, in the measurement of a liability.

Looking back, Jim Leisenring thought of IAS 37 as the Board's only original work other than insurance contracts.[68] It is a fair question whether, after many years of fundamental debate, the Board was still merely clarifying the original IAS 37 and refining the proposals of its 2005 exposure draft. In that case, the Board would be justified in proceeding directly to issue a standard. But at a minimum, it would seem that the Board itself had arrived at a much deeper understanding of the issues covered in IAS 37, possibly at variance with the way the standard was applied in practice. Some Board members believed that a standard could be issued, others thought a partial exposure of just the measurement provisions would be sufficient, while Danjou and Engström favoured a complete re-exposure.[69] The Board agreed on the middle ground of partial re-exposure, with a staff draft of the complete standard—now presented as an IFRS rather than an IAS—posted on

---

[67] See, for instance, AP 5/2007 paper 7.

[68] Interview with James Leisenring, 2 August 2010.

[69] See record of Board debate in *IStaR*, October 2009, 26–8.

the website.[70] Out of fifteen members, Stephen Cooper, Philippe Danjou, Jan Engström, Prabhakar Kalavacherla, John Smith, and Zhang Wei-Guo voted against the exposure draft, mainly on account of the profit margin proposal.[71]

The reactions showed that the dissenters had properly gauged the views of the Board's constituents. An 'overwhelming majority' of respondents 'of all types and from all regions, and including most investor and analyst groups' opposed the idea of including a profit margin in a non-financial liability, whether explicitly estimated or implicit in the price which a contractor would charge for rendering the service.[72] Moreover, constituents were not deterred by a partial re-exposure from raising once again other points to which they strongly objected. The removal of the probability threshold for recognizing a provision was one of these points, although the staff had attempted to explain in an additional paper on the website that the practical effect in cases of lawsuits—the most controversial example—was likely to be limited.[73]

After some deliberations, the Board decided in November 2010 that the project would be deferred indefinitely.

12.6 REVENUE RECOGNITION

As suggested above, the project to revise IAS 37 was conceptually linked to the revenue recognition project, which provided another instance of significant conceptual discussions preceding and continuing in parallel with the formal conceptual framework project.

Both the IASB and the FASB recognized that revenue recognition required their attention. The IASB's standard, IAS 18 *Revenue*, had been issued in 1982 and, despite a revision in 1993, was thought to sit uneasily with parts of the IASB's conceptual framework. Moreover, while it might be adequate for straightforward sales transactions, it did not address the problems of complex transactions with multiple elements.[74] The FASB had never issued a general standard on revenue recognition, although industry-specific guidance was scattered throughout US GAAP. The SEC's Staff Accounting Bulletin (SAB) 101, issued in 1999 and amended in 2003 by SAB 104, was considered as the first authoritative statement on revenue recognition in the United States.[75] In the absence of detailed guidance in IAS 18, SAB 101/104 also came to serve as an important point of reference for

---

[70] Working draft, 'International Financial Reporting Standard [X]: Liabilities' (IASB, 19 February 2010).

[71] ED/2010/1 'Measurement of Liabilities in IAS 37: Limited Re-exposure of Proposed Amendment to IAS 37' (IASB, January 2010).

[72] AP 9/2010 paper 7 (Appendix A, observer version), Section 3.4.

[73] 'Recognising Liabilities Arising from Lawsuits', IASB staff paper, dated 7 April 2010.

[74] AP 9/2002 paper 3A, 3.

[75] SEC Staff Accounting Bulletin No. 101 *Revenue Recognition in Financial Statements*, 3 December 1999 and Staff Accounting Bulletin No. 104 *Revenue Recognition*, 17 December 2003. Staff Accounting Bulletins represent the interpretations and policies followed by the Division of Corporation Finance and the Office of the Chief Accountant in administering the disclosure requirements of federal securities laws.

users of IFRSs. Both boards had added projects on revenue to their agendas during 2002, and, at the joint IASB–FASB meeting in Norwalk in September 2002, before either board could make a real start, it was agreed to continue in the form of a joint project that would comprehensively reconsider revenue recognition. Removing inconsistencies from the existing standards and putting the standards on a sound conceptual footing, where necessary developing the relevant aspects of the conceptual frameworks, were among the main objectives.[76] From the beginning, the asset and liability approach at the heart of both boards' conceptual frameworks was accepted as the starting point, and the attempt was made to draw out the consequences in the form of specific recognition rules. This proved to be quite difficult, as more than one revenue recognition model could be developed on the basis of the frameworks. The IASB Board by itself, as well as together with the FASB, found it difficult to make up its mind about these alternatives. The main contenders in the initial stages of the project were known as the 'liability extinguishment view', according to which revenues were conceived in terms of a decrease in the 'performance obligation' to customers, and the 'broad performance view', which considered both increases in assets and decreases in liabilities, but only those resulting from the reporting entity's own activities. The two approaches could yield different answers in common situations such as subcontracting and the production of an inventory of readily saleable assets.[77] Board members showed themselves reluctant to accept the full consequences of either model as they worked through example after example. Already in May 2003, Chairman Tweedie observed that his Board was going round in circles, and this had not really changed a year later.[78]

Progress was made, but mainly in gaining a deeper understanding of the conceptual problems the boards were up against. For instance, if one assumed—as the boards did, at least as a working assumption—that performance obligations were to be measured at fair value, did this mean that the probability of future cash flows should affect just the fair value measurement, or should this probability also serve as a recognition threshold, as implied by the IASB's conceptual framework? This was, of course, the same issue of 'element uncertainty' versus 'measurement uncertainty' that the Board had encountered in thinking about contingent liabilities in the context of IAS 37. Perhaps even more than in that project, the Board increasingly recognized that it was hard to make progress on revenue recognition without reference to the conceptual framework revision project which had begun in 2004 (as discussed in Section 12.7).[79] Consideration of fair value raised several issues not addressed at all in the IASB's conceptual framework, such as the question of the proper reference market for the determination of fair value in the absence of active markets. Some of these were being dealt with in the FASB's parallel project on fair value measurement, which so far had no counterpart on the IASB side.

But even if fair value could be reliably measured, some of its consequences caused misgivings. Fair value was understood as measurement from the point of

---

[76] AP 9/2002 paper 3; see also *IStaR*, October 2002, 2.
[77] See AP 12/2003 paper 5 for a review of the two models.
[78] *IStaR*, May 2003, 13; see comment by Jan Engström, cited in *IStaR*, October 2004, 38.
[79] AP 1/2004 paper 5A, 16–18; *IStaR*, January 2004, 11.

view of market participants, and was therefore not entity-specific. So, should a selling entity really exclude its own efficiency or inefficiency relative to competitors from the fair value of the performance obligation? Was it acceptable that fair value measurement could result in up-front profit recognition at the inception of a contract, well ahead of traditional recognition criteria ('day-one profits')? To Jan Engström, who had joined the Board in May 2004 directly from an executive position in Volvo, the debates on revenue recognition were a shock, as the Board appeared to be a group of free-thinking theorists without an evident business orientation. He recalled asking incredulously whether he correctly understood that, if he signed a five-year contract to deliver 1,000 buses, he should recognize a profit immediately? He was rather disconcerted by hearing a Board member affirm that this would indeed be a desirable implication of the approach.[80]

Engström was not the only sceptic, and by the end of 2004 the project had become deadlocked because both boards were split over the merits of fair value as the basic measurement approach. Each board took some time to reconsider its options. The FASB took the lead and decided in May 2005 that it wanted to proceed with the project, but no longer on a fair value basis. What it had in mind was akin to the liability extinguishment view as mentioned above, coupled with measurement based on the consideration received or receivable from the customer. A month later, the IASB Board agreed. Although eight of its members favoured the fair value approach, all but Warren McGregor—always the Board's most consistent fair value advocate—were willing to follow the FASB, if only as a compromise.[81] But when a closer examination revealed all of the problems of an allocated customer consideration approach, fair value began to look more attractive once again. The boards reverted to a pattern that had characterized the revenue project from the start: whenever a particular approach seemed to gain the upper hand, it would become unstuck again as its opponents raised difficulties during the elaboration of the operational details.[82]

Following the February 2006 MoU, doubts arose whether the boards would be able to come up with as much as a discussion paper on revenue recognition by the end of 2007 if they continued their already lengthy and inconclusive debates. Therefore, during their joint meeting of October 2006, the staffs, at the initiative of Sue Bielstein (FASB) and Wayne Upton (IASB), proposed a change in approach. Recognizing that both boards were hopelessly split, approximately along the lines of fair value versus allocated consideration, and that the debates were becoming acrimonious, it was proposed to discontinue board discussion of the topic for some time. Meanwhile, two teams of board members should be formed, each to develop their favoured model. It was hoped that bringing fully developed models to the table would provide a better basis for decisions than developing models gradually with objections raised at every step. The envisaged 'preliminary views' paper could present both models, or just one if the boards were to succeed in making a choice.[83] The suggestion was adopted, and the teams (four board members each, plus staff) were formed. Internally, the camps were referred to as

[80] Interview with Jan Engström, 14 February 2012.
[81] *IStaR*, June 2005. See also AP 6/2005 paper 7.
[82] Interview with John Smith, 16 March 2009.
[83] AP 10/2006 paper 7; interview with Suzanne Bielstein, 3 August 2009.

the 'space cadets' and the 'dinosaurs', advocating fair value and allocated consideration, respectively. Mary Barth and Warren McGregor represented the IASB on the 'space cadet' team, with Ed Trott and Tom Linsmeier for the FASB. John Smith was seen as the IASB's leading 'dinosaur' and joined that team together with Gilbert Gélard from the IASB, and with George Batavick and Leslie Seidman from the FASB. Jim Leisenring played his usual role of provider of technical solutions by sitting on both teams.[84]

It took a year, until October 2007, before IASB Board discussions were resumed on the basis of two proposals, one based on customer consideration and the other on what was now called current exit price rather than fair value.[85] The ensuing debates revealed that the boards were still divided. Yet, as they were about to issue a discussion paper containing the two models side by side, the staff came up with a last-minute hybrid model. This was based on the customer consideration model but with remeasurement in some cases, in particular when contracts become onerous.[86] The compromise generated just enough support in both boards for a discussion paper based on this single model, published in December 2008, in time to meet the target of the 2006 MoU.[87] Although the composition of the IASB Board had not changed much, small changes in membership may have helped tip the balance. Stephen Cooper, joining the Board in August 2007, recalls the intense interest at the time in knowing which camp he would choose—and he was not supportive of the fair value alternative.[88]

Reflecting the acceleration of the work programme, the staff proposed in July 2008, even before the publication of the discussion paper, to begin work on an exposure draft, and to set June 2011 'as the deadline (rather than a goal) for issuing the general revenue recognition standard'.[89] It will be seen in Chapter 16 that the boards almost made this deadline before allowing completion to be delayed by several years.

12.7 REVISION OF THE CONCEPTUAL FRAMEWORK

In the late 1980s, when the IASC was drafting its conceptual framework, the FASB's was the only completed framework thus far issued by a national standard-setting body.[90] It was logical for the IASC to pattern its own framework on that of the FASB, not only because the FASB had spent untold resources in its development, but also because the IASC had begun a series of initiatives to improve its standards to the satisfaction of the International Organization of Securities

---

[84] *IStaR*, November 2007, 12; interview with Suzanne Bielstein, 3 August 2009.

[85] For a discussion of the two models, see Katherine A. Schipper, Catherine M. Schrand, Terry Shevlin, and T. Jeffrey Wilks, 'Reconsidering Revenue Recognition', *Accounting Horizons*, 23/1 (March 2009), 55–68.

[86] AP 5/2008 paper 7B.

[87] Discussion paper, 'Preliminary Views on Revenue Recognition in Contracts with Customers' (IASB, December 2008).

[88] Interview with Stephen Cooper, 13 February 2012.

[89] AP 7/2008 paper 6A, paragraph 2.

[90] In the case of the FASB, we refer to Concepts Statements 1, 2, 3, and 5.

Commissions (IOSCO), in which the US SEC was the major player.[91] The
Financial Reporting Group of Ernst & Young has written: 'The IASB document
clearly derives from the original FASB work embodied in its concepts statements
and in truth the IASB's framework is little more than a synopsis of the FASB
conceptual statements.'[92]

The FASB's and IASC's frameworks included very similar statements on the
objectives of financial statements, although the former characterized them as objectives of financial reporting, while the latter confined them to financial statements.
They both accorded stewardship separate standing as an objective. The two frameworks were also similar with respect to the qualitative characteristics of useful
financial information, with relevance and reliability occupying central places in
both. The IASC's treatment of the elements of financial statements (definitions of
assets, liabilities, equity, income, and expense) incorporated the FASB's preference
for the 'asset and liability' view over the 'income and expense' view. The frameworks
differed somewhat in their discussion of recognition. With respect to measurement,
the IASC reached the same indeterminate conclusion as did the FASB: both frameworks described present measurement practice without providing a conceptual basis
for recommending sound practice.[93]

The idea of revising the framework and dealing with some of its acknowledged
deficiencies had come up from time to time during the IASB's first years.[94] As
discussed above, the Board in its initial discussions on contingent liabilities and
revenue recognition during 2003 and 2004 was already immersing itself in conceptual questions. But given the dependence of the IASC's framework on that of the
FASB and the importance that convergence with US GAAP soon obtained in the
Board's strategic thinking, it may be surmised that the Board would not have lightly
undertaken a formal revision of its framework independently of the FASB.

In April 2004, at the third joint meeting of the IASB and the FASB since the
signing of the Norwalk Agreement, the two boards discussed a fundamental staff
proposal for coordinating their long-term agendas (see Section 5.7). An important
part of the proposal, accepted by the boards, was to launch a joint project to
update, refine, and improve the boards' conceptual frameworks. At their next joint
meeting, in October 2004, they discussed a project plan and decided to add a
project for a single, common conceptual framework to their agendas.[95]

From the FASB's standpoint, L. Todd Johnson, a senior staff member, wrote:
'Because the framework has not kept up with the changing times and changing
business practices, it needs updating and refining.' He added that the FASB's need

---

[91] See Stephen A. Zeff, 'The Evolution of the Conceptual Framework for Business Enterprises in the United States', *The Accounting Historians Journal*, 26/2, December 1999, 104–5.

[92] The Financial Reporting Group of Ernst & Young, *International GAAP* 2005 (London: Lexis-Nexis, 2004), 99 (parenthetical aside omitted). Chapter 2 of this work contains an analytical review of the series of conceptual frameworks from the 1960s to the 1990s.

[93] For this judgement of the FASB's concepts statement on recognition and measurement, see Reed K. Storey and Sylvia Storey, *The Framework of Financial Accounting Concepts and Standards* (Norwalk, CT: FASB, 1998), 158. For a discussion of the IASC's framework, see Kees Camfferman and Stephen A. Zeff, *Financial Reporting and Global Capital Markets: A History of the International Accounting Standards Committee, 1973–2000* (Oxford: Oxford University Press, 2007), 259–64.

[94] See reports of Board discussions in *IStaR*, July 2001, 3–4 and April 2002, 13.

[95] AP 4/2004 paper 11A; *IASB Update*, October 2004, 4.

'to revisit the framework has become more pronounced with the Board's decision to move toward producing accounting standards that are "principles-based"'.[96] The latter reason might not have been as compelling to the IASB at a time when it was commonplace to compare IFRSs favourably with US GAAP on this point. What probably would have weighed more heavily with the IASB than with the FASB was that a common framework might facilitate the convergence of their standards.

The joint conceptual framework staff team consisted initially of Kimberley Crook from the IASB together with Halsey G. Bullen and Todd Johnson from the FASB. Johnson wrote that, in order to make efficient use of the boards' resources, they would pursue an approach that did not 'comprehensively reconsider' the framework 'but rather focuses on those issues that are more likely to yield standard-setting benefits in the near term', namely 'troublesome conceptual issues that reappear time and time again in different standard-setting projects and in a variety of different guises'.[97] As seen above, the concept of a liability was central to several projects, and therefore was one of these 'crosscutting issues'.[98] To be sure, the IASB, if not also the FASB, needed to husband its resources carefully. Yet, even without such constraints, it is likely that neither board would have been inclined to start with a blank sheet of paper. During their October 2004 joint meeting, the boards showed that they had no intention of abandoning the 'asset and liability' approach enshrined in their frameworks, even though they were aware that some of their constituents would wish to reopen this discussion. Highlighting the potential problem, David Tweedie recalled the IASB's recent experience with IAS 39, when the Board had been accused of wanting to change only certain things and closing its mind on other issues.[99] It was agreed that a carefully worded educational document would be published jointly by the two boards, to explain the rationale of the project and to manage expectations.[100]

The staff optimistically proposed that the initial three phases of the conceptual framework project could be completed by 2009. Phase A (objectives and qualitative characteristics) was projected for completion in 2007; phase B (elements, recognition, and definition of measurement attributes) in 2008; and phase C (initial and subsequent measurement concepts) in 2009.[101] Beyond these three were phases D through H on, for the most part, lesser issues, with the entire project to be finished in 2010. As with many of the IASB's projects, this planning was overturned both by the inherent complexity of the project and by exogenous events such as the economic and financial crisis. In addition, the IASB had difficulties in matching the FASB's contribution of staff. Kimberley Crook returned to New Zealand in 2005,

---

[96] L. Todd Johnson, 'The Project to Revisit the Conceptual Framework', *The FASB Report*, *Financial Accounting Series*, No. 263-D, 28 December 2004, 6.

[97] L. Todd Johnson, 'The Project to Revisit the Conceptual Framework', 7.

[98] AP 4/2009 (joint meeting) paper 11A, paragraphs 31–2.

[99] *IStaR*, October 2004, 37.

[100] This document was published as Halsey G. Bullen and Kimberley Crook, 'A New Conceptual Framework Project', *Revisiting the Concepts* (FASB/IASB, May 2005), a draft of which was presented to the IASB Board as 'A New Conceptual Framework Project?', AP 1/2005 paper 11A. The deletion of the question mark in the published document may be noted.

[101] AP 2/2005 paper 11; see also FASB meeting of 23 February 2005, FASB memorandum 1, paragraph 35.

and had to be borrowed for the project from that country's Financial Reporting Standards Board, where she served as technical director. Canada's Accounting Standards Board (AcSB) also made staff available to help the IASB shoulder its part. It was not until 2007 that the IASB could once more assign one of its own project managers, Li Li Lian, to the conceptual framework project. By June 2011, as it turned out, the boards had just managed to complete phase A and had issued a phase D exposure draft on the reporting entity.

Whereas in the 1980s the FASB's conceptual framework had been the obvious point of reference for the IASC, other standard setters had since then worked on conceptual frameworks as well. When the IASB discussed the conceptual framework in September 2004, before the formal agenda decision was taken, Geoffrey Whittington and Tatsumi Yamada raised this point. Although Whittington spoke in general terms, the *Statement of Principles for Financial Reporting* issued by the UK Accounting Standards Board (ASB) in 1999 (on which he had then served) would not have been far from his mind. Yamada mentioned the draft conceptual framework published, but not yet adopted, by the ASBJ earlier that year. While the two boards emphatically stated their intention to draw on these other frameworks, it remained to be seen what this would mean in practice.[102]

Phase A, on objectives and qualitative characteristics, was the first to be completed, but not until several years after the originally planned date. The main stages in the project were the publication of a discussion paper in July 2006, followed by an exposure draft in May 2008, and by an amended version of the framework issued in September 2010.[103] This amended version consisted of two newly drafted chapters (numbered as 1 and 3) on the objective of general purpose financial reporting and on qualitative characteristics of useful financial information, and of the unmodified remaining text of the 1989 framework for the remaining topics. The two troublesome issues in phase A were the place of reliability among the qualitative characteristics and the position of stewardship in the objectives.

12.7.1 Reliability

In February 2005, Todd Johnson wrote that some FASB constituents had questioned certain of the board's past trade-offs between relevance and reliability when setting standards. They apparently were interpreting reliability to mean precision, whereas the FASB's Concepts Statement 2, on qualitative characteristics, said that the two principal components of reliability were representational faithfulness and verifiability. Precision, he said, was not a component of reliability in Concepts Statement 2. The real motivation, it seemed, was that those who equated reliability

---

[102] *IStaR*, September 2004, 3; Bullen and Crook, 'A New Conceptual Framework Project', 3.

[103] Discussion paper 'Preliminary Views on an Improved Conceptual Framework for Financial Reporting: The Objective of Financial Reporting and Qualitative Characteristics of Decision-useful Financial Reporting Information' (IASB, July 2006); Exposure draft 'Improved Conceptual Framework for Financial Reporting: Chapter 1: The Objective of Financial Reporting, Chapter 2: Qualitative Characteristics and Constraints of Decision-useful Financial Reporting Information' (IASB, May 2008); *The Conceptual Framework for Financial Reporting 2010* (IASB, September 2010).

with precision stood in opposition to the board's increasing use of fair value in its standards. Johnson wrote:

> The Board [i.e. the FASB] has required greater use of fair value measurements in financial statements because it perceives that information as more relevant to investors and creditors than historical cost information. Such measures better reflect the present financial state of reporting entities and better facilitate assessing their past performance and future prospects. In that regard, the Board does not accept the view that reliability should outweigh relevance for financial statement measures.[104]

The two boards were certainly sensitive to the potential links between qualitative characteristics, in particular reliability, and measurement, and they tried to avoid wording in the qualitative characteristics that would set them on a path leading inevitably to fair value in the measurement phase of the conceptual framework project.[105] They were also willing to accept that many constituents were not mischievously equating reliability with precision in a deliberate attempt to block fair value, but that the frameworks were truly unsatisfactory in their explanations of the meaning of reliability. When, after considerable discussion, they decided to discard the notion of reliability altogether, they did so on the grounds that the concept, given its connotations in daily use, could easily give rise to different interpretations, and that there seemed to be little prospect of a definition that would reflect a consensus of views.[106] As the boards reshuffled the deck of remaining related concepts—such as substance over form, verifiability, and neutrality—they finally agreed to place faithful representation on top, on a plane with relevance, as the two fundamental qualitative characteristics. In their view, faithful representation was the most suitable term to express what the original frameworks had intended with reliability. In the words of Board member John Smith, it also had the advantage, as an obviously technical term, that 'people would have to think about what it meant', thus avoiding some of the spontaneous associations frequently evoked by reliability.[107]

None of the members of either board registered an alternative view to this change in any of the three successive documents issued in 2006, 2008, and 2010. Yet Whittington, who left the Board shortly after the approval of the 2006 discussion paper, subsequently expressed his dissatisfaction with the removal of reliability.[108]

A majority of those who commented on the 2006 discussion paper disagreed with the proposal to replace reliability with faithful representation at the apex of the qualitative characteristics.[109] Some found the boards' reasoning in terms of clarification and avoidance of ambiguity unpersuasive and suggested that the

---

[104] L. Todd Johnson, 'Relevance and Reliability', *The FASB Report, Financial Accounting Series*, No. 265, 28 February 2005, 8. For a further discussion of these issues, see AP 5/2005 paper 7, especially paragraphs 38–46.

[105] See e.g. *IStaR*, October 2004, 33, and May 2005, 25.

[106] See the basis for conclusions in the 2006 discussion paper (BC2.26), the 2008 exposure draft (BC2.13), and the final version of 2010 (BC3.23).

[107] *IStaR*, May 2005, 27.

[108] Geoffrey Whittington, 'Fair Value and the IASB/FASB Conceptual Framework Project: An Alternative View', *Abacus*, 44/2 (2008), 139–68.

[109] See the comment letter analysis in AP 2/2007 paper 3A.

boards should try harder to define reliability unambiguously. Others suspected that a significant change in meaning was intended. Among these was the European Financial Reporting Advisory Group (EFRAG), which also showed itself sensitive to signals that the boards, in deciding on qualitative characteristics, were pre-judging the debate on measurement, for instance by suggesting in one example that current-value based amounts are more faithfully representational than cost-based amounts.[110] The latter point was also made by others, including the ASBJ.[111] The Hundred Group of Finance Directors (United Kingdom) volunteered the view that, all in all, 'Phase A seems to be setting the scene for performance measurement to be based on the difference between two balance sheets measured at fair value'.[112] Clearly, the boards were up against quite formidable suspicions with respect to their underlying intentions in the conceptual framework programme. By the time of the May 2008 exposure draft these suspicions had abated somewhat, but many respondents were still not convinced that faithful representation would be an improvement over reliability in terms of clarity of meaning and avoiding a diversity of interpretations.[113] Nonetheless, the revised framework issued in 2010 confirmed the choice of relevance and faithful representation as the two fundamental quali-tative characteristics.

12.7.2. Stewardship

In the revised framework of 2010, the boards agreed on a decision-usefulness objective (singular) of financial reporting to provide investors and creditors with financial information 'to help them assess the prospects for future net cash flows to an entity' (OB3). The objective of supporting investment decisions was part of the earlier FASB and IASC objectives, but the IASC's framework had also referred to 'a wide range of users' who might look to the financial statements for support in their 'economic decisions'. The more outspoken focus on the information needs of investors could be seen as a narrowing of the objectives of financial reporting. One possible objective of financial reporting that seemed to fall by the wayside was that of supporting management's accountability to shareholders and other stake-holders, often referred to as the stewardship role of financial reporting. The place of stewardship in the objective, or objectives, of financial reporting became a contested issue. In a July 2005 agenda paper, the joint staff quoted with favour a passage from paragraph 53 of the FASB's Concepts Statement 1 on objectives:

> Actions of past managements affect current periods' earnings, and actions of current management affect future periods' earnings. Financial reporting provides information about an enterprise during a period when it was under the direction of a particular

---

[110] Letter from Stig Enevoldsen to Li Li Lian, dated 17 January 2007 <http://www.efrag.org> (also accessible as CL 179 on July 2006 discussion paper at <http://www.ifrs.org>).

[111] Letter dated 29 November 2006, CL 172 on July 2006 discussion paper.

[112] Letter from Ken Lever to Li Li Lian, dated 3 November 2006, CL 126 on July 2006 discussion paper.

[113] See AP 12/2008 paper 2A for an analysis of comment letters on the 2008 exposure draft. Compare, for instance, CL 137 (EFRAG), CL 112 (The Hundred Group), and CL 35 (ASBJ) with the corresponding comment letters on the 2006 discussion paper.

management but does not directly provide information about that management's performance. The information is therefore limited for purposes of assessing management performance apart from enterprise performance.[114]

Believing that the boards did not intend their framework to imply that financial reporting can provide 'all the information for assessing management's stewardship or show all of the results of management's stewardship', the staff recommended that 'the information needed to assess stewardship or accountability should not be included as an explicit objective of financial reporting by business entities'. The staff then recommended that the converged framework should acknowledge that financial information is useful for other purposes than investment decisions, including the assessment of management's stewardship.[115] In this respect, it would fold stewardship into the overall objective of financial reporting.

Evidently, this staff recommendation sparked disagreement at the IASB, because Tony Cope, Geoffrey Whittington, and David Tweedie voted against it. All three had become Chartered Accountants in the United Kingdom, although Cope had made his professional career in the United States, in the financial services industry and as a member of the FASB. Whittington and Tweedie had been a member and chairman, respectively, of the UK ASB. Whittington and Tweedie filed alternative views to the discussion paper issued by the boards in 2006, which incorporated the staff recommendation.[116] Cope declined to join in the formal dissent.[117] To some degree, this difference over the place of stewardship reporting in the objectives reflected the institutional and legal differences between the United States and the United Kingdom. In the United States, financial reporting for publicly traded companies has been promoted and enforced by a federal securities commission. At the state level, corporation laws have provided limited support, at best, for stewardship reporting to shareholders. In the United Kingdom, by contrast, stewardship reporting has been deeply ingrained in company law for more than a century.[118] In their dissent, Whittington and Tweedie argued that, while it is accepted that 'information relevant to predicting future cash flows . . . will not provide a complete set of information for stewardship purposes', yet 'financial reports are unlikely to provide complete information for any specific purpose, including the prediction of future cash flows'. Stewardship, they claimed,

---

[114] AP 7/2005 paper 7 (FASB meeting of 27 July 2005, FASB memorandum 7), paragraph 24.

[115] AP 7/2005 paper 7, paragraphs 25, 30, and 38.

[116] For a news report, see 'First Conceptual Framework Paper', *World Accounting Report*, August/September 2006, 8. Two papers critical of the omission of stewardship as an objective are Andrew Lennard, 'Stewardship and the Objectives of Financial Statements: A Comment on IASB's *Preliminary Views on an Improved Conceptual Framework for Financial Reporting: The Objective of Financial Reporting and Qualitative Characteristics of Decision-Useful Financial Reporting Information*', *Accounting in Europe*, 4/1 (2007), 51–66; and *Stewardship/Accountability as an Objective of Financial Reporting: A Comment on the IASB/FASB Conceptual Framework Project* (Brussels: EFRAG and others, 2007) <http://www.efrag.org>.

[117] The names of the two IASB members who dissented were not made public, but their identities soon became known. In a communication to the authors dated 19 September 2012, Cope affirmed that he voted against the draft.

[118] See Stephen A. Zeff, 'The Objectives of Financial Reporting: A Historical Survey and Analysis', *Accounting and Business Research*, 43/4 (2013), 262–327. For UK views on the framework project, see also Peter Williams, 'In the Frame', *Financial Director*, 21 August 2006, 21.

'is at the heart of the financial reporting process in many jurisdictions'. Steward-ship and decision-usefulness, they argued, are parallel objectives, and to subsume stewardship within a decision-usefulness objective would lead to a failure to report financial information that is essential to the exercise of effective steward-ship.[119] On the FASB side, board member G. Michael Crooch said that the FASB was of the belief that, while an accounting for stewardship is very important, assessing stewardship 'is a somewhat narrow aspect of the broad objective of financial reporting'.[120] In general, members and staff of the FASB found it difficult to see what practical differences in accounting a reference to stewardship would make and challenged advocates of stewardship to come up with concrete examples.[121]

Despite scepticism on the part of the FASB, the boards included stewardship as a distinct element of the overarching decision-usefulness objective in their exposure draft issued in 2008. Yet, in the final version of the 'objectives' chapter of the framework issued in 2010, stewardship was merely mentioned by name in the introduction and the basis for conclusions. In the body of the framework, the word was not used 'because there would be difficulties in translating it into other languages'. The basis for conclusions asserted correctly that the framework did refer to stewardship in substance, where it pointed out the usefulness of 'information about management's discharge of responsibilities'.[122] But the reality was that the Board as a whole was not convinced that mentioning stewardship, by name or otherwise, made much of a difference. The staff had argued that stewardship really played no role in the section on qualitative characteristics, nor, so far, in discussions of the other sections of the framework.[123] With little discussion, the explicit reference to stewardship was discarded. By then, Whittington had retired from the IASB. Among the new generation of Board members, Prabhakar Kalavacherla, who had practised in the United States, expressed the view that the concept of stewardship was not necessary.[124] Tweedie, apparently stewardship's last advocate on the Board, was satisfied that the notion, if not the name, of stewardship was included in the framework and opted not to repeat his dissent.[125]

The elimination of reliability and of stewardship, at least as an explicit term, continued to rankle with some of the IASB's constituents. In 2013, EFRAG, together with the national standard setters from France, Germany, Italy, and the United Kingdom, identified this as one of the issues that needed to be revisited when the IASB undertook to complete work on its conceptual framework.[126]

---

[119] 2006 discussion paper, AV1.1–1.7. For further discussion by Whittington, see his 'Harmonisation or Discord? The Critical Role of the IASB Conceptual Framework Review', *Journal of Accounting and Public Policy*, 27/6 (2008), 495–502, as well as his 'Fair Value and the IASB/FASB Conceptual Framework Project', 139–68.

[120] 'Michael Crooch Talks about the Conceptual Framework', *The FASB Report, Financial Accounting Series*, No. 283, 31 August 2006, 2.

[121] Interview with Kimberley Crook, 20 March 2012.

[122] 2010 Framework, BC1.27–1.28 and OB4.   [123] AP 9/2009 paper 10A, paragraphs 27–32.

[124] *IStaR*, September 2009, 6–7.   [125] Interview with David Tweedie, 5 June 2013.

[126] 'Getting a Better Framework: Our Strategy' (EFRAG, ANC, DRSC, OIC, FRC, January 2013), paragraphs 3, 10, 11 <http://www.efrag.org>.

12.7.3 Elements, Recognition, and Measurement

Late in 2005, when it still looked as if the boards might move swiftly to an exposure draft for phase A, work began on the elements of financial statements, and in April 2006 planning started for the measurement phase.[127] The history of the FASB's conceptual framework had already shown that these topics were indisputably the most sensitive of the entire project. From its own experience, the Board was aware that the asset and liability approach and fair value measurement were at the heart of much of the criticism to which the IASB was exposed. The staff work on these phases occurred largely outside the IASB, involving staff from the FASB (Halsey Bullen, Kevin McBeth, and Todd Johnson) and Canada's AcSB (Ian Hague). It is possible that the preparation of papers outside of the IASB did not help the IASB Board in coming to grips with a project that was already inherently difficult. But whatever the reason, the rate of progress was not viewed with satisfaction at the IASB.

During several years, papers on measurement and elements were regularly discussed, both by the IASB itself and in joint meetings with the FASB. But in the second half of 2008, work on elements effectively ceased, even though the project remained marked as 'active' in the Board's work plans. Work on measurement continued for some time longer but petered out in the course of 2010. From late 2010 onwards, the IASB's work plan indicated that work on phases B and C would not resume until after June 2011, after the boards had completed their major convergence projects. The FASB stopped updating the project information page on its website in October 2010.

As suggested above, one of the main problems with the elements phase was the IASB's simultaneous wrestling with projects on insurance, the revision of IAS 37 on provisions, revenue recognition, and financial instruments with the characteristics of equity. The concept of liabilities was vital to all of these, and it was difficult to discuss elements without compromising the boards' own resolve not to 'peek ahead' to the practical implications for these projects.[128] Even so, it was not conducive to an orderly evolution of the elements project that the Board continued to refine its thinking on liabilities in the course of these projects to write specific standards. Where to draw the line between liabilities and equity remained a thorny issue in individual projects as well as in the framework, to the point that boards and staff for a while explored the radical idea of replacing liabilities and equity by a single credit-side element tentatively called 'claims', as well as the less radical idea of creating an intermediate category between equity and liabilities.[129]

The original plan for the framework project had suggested that the boards did not intend a fundamental reconsideration of the framework, but there was little trace of short-cuts at the start of the measurement phase. In fact, the FASB staff recommended that, both because measurement was such a large conceptual gap in the framework and because 'measurement issues continued to be highly charged

---

[127] For planning of the measurement phase see AP 4/2006 (joint meeting) paper 5A.

[128] 'Resist the temptation to "peek ahead"' was listed as 'precept#8' in 'Precepts for Conducting the Conceptual Framework Project', joint IASB–FASB meeting, April 2005, agenda paper 7.

[129] AP 2/2007 paper 3.

ones for the Board's constituents', this phase of the project should be conducted in a 'more measured way than a less difficult topic might require', and that it should be evident 'that the Boards have been thorough and deliberate in both fact and appearance throughout the measurement phase of the project'.[130] Hence, round-tables on measurement were held at an early stage, in January and February 2007 in Hong Kong, London, and Norwalk. As the IASB's website announced: 'The discussion around this objective will be unstructured. Any views on measurement that constituents wish to express are welcome.'[131] This was followed later in the year by a series of elaborate papers delving deeply into measurement theory, which might have provided some justification for the fairly routine criticism of the IASB as an 'academic' body.[132] But after this exploratory stage, the project settled down to address the main problem which was, of course, what to do with fair value. As some critics had feared, the Board and staff working on the project recognized that the objectives of financial statements and the qualitative char-acteristics of information that were being defined in phase A of the project could easily lead to a line of argument ending in universal fair value measurement. At the same time, it was recognized that this would simply not be acceptable, neither to a majority in the Board nor to the world at large. Given then that financial statements would for the foreseeable future remain based on a mixture of measurement bases, including both cost and fair value, the challenge was to write a proper justification for such a mixed-measurement system, including principles for determining the appropriate measurement bases for specific assets and liabilities. Despite several attempts, this challenge was not satisfactorily met before this phase came to a stop during 2010 in the Board's rush to complete as many of the projects of the MoU with the FASB as possible before the June 2011 target date.[133] It was, in words ascribed to Bob Herz, another instance of 'the urgent overtaking the important', a recurring problem in accounting standard setting.[134]

12.7.4 The Reporting Entity

The only other phase where a degree of progress was made dealt with the reporting entity. Neither board's conceptual framework contained more than a summary discussion of this subject, but it was noted by the staff that the Austra-lian conceptual framework already contained a thorough treatment of the subject since 1990.[135] In May 2008, the boards issued a discussion paper on the reporting

---

[130] AP 4/2006 (joint meeting) paper 5A, paragraph 5.

[131] <http://www.iasb.org> as of 17 February 2007, accessed through web.archive. See also the information document 'Conceptual Framework—Measurement Roundtable Discussions: Background Materials' (no date), <http://www.iasb.org> accessed through web.archive.

[132] See e.g. AP 7/2007 paper 2B.

[133] See AP 5/2009 paper 4, AP 6/2009 paper 5A, and AP 12/2009 paper 2A for successive staff attempts to elicit the boards' views on the implications of the objectives and qualitative characteristics standards for measurement.

[134] Interview with Thomas Linsmeier, 11 June 2013.

[135] AP 12/2005 paper 2B. The reference is to SAC 1 *Definition of the Reporting Entity* (Australian Accounting Research Foundation, 1990).

entity, which evoked no alternative views.[136] One of the boards' preliminary views was that a reporting entity should not be limited to legal entities and should be 'broadly described as being a circumscribed area of business activity' of interest to capital providers (paragraphs 22, 35). Another preliminary view was that control of an entity 'is the ability to direct the financing and operating policies of an entity' (paragraph 49). The boards also reached the preliminary view that consolidated statements should be presented 'from the perspective of the group reporting entity, not from the perspective of the parent company's shareholders' (Question 8). In reaching this view, the boards drew on the literature dealing with the 'entity' and 'proprietary' perspectives (or theories), without perhaps appreciating that the entity perspective, as designed by its originator, would require that interest charges be shown as a distribution of net income, not as an expense.[137]

Commentators on the discussion paper reminded the boards that parts of the discussion paper, including the concept of 'control', were simultaneously being addressed in a convergence project to develop a new standard on consolidation (see Section 16.3). This raised the question which of the two projects was leading. The solution adopted was to keep the discussion in the framework at a general level.[138] In March 2010, the two boards issued a terse exposure draft on the reporting entity, containing only twelve paragraphs plus the basis for conclusions.[139] The first two preliminary views mentioned above were affirmed in general terms, yet the exposure draft was silent on the perspective that should be used when presenting consolidated statements.

It was reported in November 2010 that, 'because of the need to give priority' to the major convergence projects targeted for completion in June 2011, the boards would not complete the chapter on the reporting entity until after that date.[140] It was announced in 2012 that the boards would not follow up on the reporting entity exposure draft with further joint work.

12.7.5 Limited Results of the Conceptual Framework Project

In the light of the ambitions with which the two boards had approached their common conceptual framework project, the results could hardly be seen as other than disappointing.[141] Despite a considerable expenditure of staff and board time over many years, the boards were not able to move beyond a revision of the curtain-raising chapters on objectives and qualitative characteristics. While these chapters were not devoid of interest, it was clear to all concerned that the heart of the matter was in the chapters on elements, recognition, and measurement. And

---

[136] Discussion paper 'Preliminary Views on an Improved Conceptual Framework for Financial Reporting: The Reporting Entity' (IASB, May 2008).

[137] See William Andrew Paton, *Accounting Theory, with Special Reference to the Corporate Enterprise* (New York: The Ronald Press Company, 1922), chapter XI.

[138] AP 3/2009 paper 14A; *IStaR*, March 2009, 29–30.

[139] ED/2010/2 'Conceptual Framework for Financial Reporting: The Reporting Entity' (IASB, March 2010).

[140] *IASB Update*, November 2010, 2.

[141] For Herz's view, see Robert H. Herz, *Accounting Changes: Chronicles of Convergence, Crisis, and Complexity in Financial Reporting* (AICPA, 2013), 249.

even where the revised chapters had provoked debate, there was not necessarily an immediate impact on the standards. The most notable case was probably IAS 8 *Accounting Policies, Changes in Accounting Estimates and Errors*, which continued to require reporting entities to select accounting policies—in the absence of specific guidance in IFRSs—by applying the criteria of relevance and reliability as defined in the 1989 framework (IAS 8.10).

After the completion of the Chapters 1 and 3, the boards lost the will to pursue the revision of their frameworks together. In 2012, IASB resumed work on the remaining sections of the framework by itself (see Section 17.5).

12.7.6 Status of the Revised Conceptual Framework in Some Adopting Jurisdictions

The revision of Chapters 1 and 3 of the IASB's conceptual framework provided a reminder that jurisdictions adopting IFRSs differed in their policies regarding the conceptual framework.

Canada's AcSB incorporated the new chapters in the *CICA Handbook* in January 2011, in line with its policy of bringing IFRSs into Canadian GAAP. Similarly, the Hong Kong Institute of Certified Public Accountants (HKICPA) was quick to amend its framework, in October 2010, by incorporating the IASB's two new chapters. A little oddly, however, the HKICPA left its own original introduction to the framework unchanged. This introduction had been written in 1997 to replace the IASC's own introduction to its 1989 framework, at a time when the Hong Kong Society of Accountants (which became the HKICPA in 2004) first incorporated the IASC's framework into Hong Kong standards. As a result, the HKICPA's introduction in 2010 still discussed financial reporting in terms of a broad range of users making economic decisions, and did not reflect the shift in focus to investors in the revised chapter on the objective of general purpose financial reporting.[142]

The AASB had adopted the IASC's 1989 framework in July 2004 but with some additional paragraphs and minor editorial modifications, in particular to reflect the fact that Australia's accounting standards also apply to not-for-profit entities. In 2007, the IASC's original wording was restored, but some of the additional Australian paragraphs were retained. The new chapters of the IASB's framework were adopted by the AASB in December 2013, again with some additional Australian paragraphs.[143]

In Chile, the Colegio de Contadores de Chile approved the IASC's 1989 framework in 2006, but, even though it adopted the full text of the extant IFRSs in 2009 through a *Boletín Técnico* (No. 79) with subsequent modifications, it has not, so far, amended the adopted conceptual framework.

---

[142] 'Conceptual Framework for Financial Reporting 2010' (HKICPA, October 2010), 5–6.

[143] CF 2013-1 *Amendments to the Australian Conceptual Framework* (AASB, December 2013). On the reception of the IASB's framework in Australia, see also Stewart Jones and Peter R. Wolnizer, 'Harmonization and the Conceptual Framework: An International Perspective', *Abacus*, 39/3 (2003), 375–87.

In the EU, the framework was not a part of endorsed IFRSs, and therefore had the same status as, for instance, implementation guidance that is not part of the standards. Yet the European Commission recognized that companies applying IFRSs may be required to consult the framework, and therefore it included the full text of the framework in a November 2003 document that clarified aspects of the IAS Regulation.[144] So far, this document has not been updated to reflect the IASB's revised framework.

More examples could be added to illustrate how the IASB's conceptual framework provides a peculiar challenge in incorporating IFRSs in national accounting regulations.

12.8 FINANCIAL STATEMENT PRESENTATION

As discussed in Chapter 5, the IASB had chosen 'performance reporting' as one of the leadership projects in its initial agenda and had actively pursued the project in cooperation with the UK ASB. An exposure draft aiming for a fundamental restructuring of the income statement was in preparation, but because of a combination of outside opposition and doubts within the Board itself, it was decided abruptly, late in 2003, to put the project on hold. The year 2004 was used for regrouping, initially on a tripartite basis with participation of the FASB, the IASB, and the ASB. By the end of the year the ASB had quietly dropped out of the picture.

The new plan as developed during 2004—initially still under the heading of 'performance reporting', subsequently under that of 'financial statement presentation'—was to proceed in two phases. Phase A was seen as a matter of resolving narrow differences between US GAAP and IFRSs. The dominant issue in this phase was the number and nature of the statements in which movements in equity should be shown. Conceptually, four types of equity movements could be distinguished in IFRSs: (a) items of profit or loss, (b) items of other comprehensive income, (c) the effects of accounting changes, and (d) the effects of transactions with owners. As it then stood, IAS 1 *Presentation of Financial Statements* required items of class (a) to be reported in an income statement, ending in profit or loss (net income). IAS 1 also required a 'statement of changes in equity' opening with profit or loss and including all items in the categories (b), (c), and (d). Alternatively, items of category (d) might be reported in the notes, in which case the second statement should be called a 'statement of recognized income and expense'. The main question in phase A was whether to combine (a) and (b) into a single performance statement, with total comprehensive income as the bottom line, which was a rarely applied option in FAS 130 *Reporting Comprehensive Income*, issued in 1997. At the start of the project it was assumed that, in phase

[144] 'Comments Concerning Certain Articles of the Regulation (EC) No. 1606/2002 of the European Parliament and of the Council of 19 July 2002 on the Application of International Accounting Standards and the Fourth Council Directive 78/660/EEC of 25 July 1978 and the Seventh Council Directive 83/349/EEC of 13 June 1983 on Accounting' (European Commission, November 2003) <http://ec.europa.eu/internal_market/accounting>.

A, net income (total of items of profit or loss, or (a)) would remain as a subtotal within such a statement, although it was no secret that several IASB Board members were sceptical of the traditional emphasis on net income.[145] As discussed in Section 5.5.2, this scepticism could be traced to discussions during the 1990s in the G4+1, which had highlighted the lack of a conceptual basis for the distinction between items of profit or loss and items of other comprehensive income. Phase B would consider the overall ordering and classification of items in the financial statements as well as the merits of 'recycling' items that had been previously reported in other comprehensive income to profit or loss upon realization.

12.8.1 Phase A: No Single Performance Statement

Although the IASB and the FASB had believed in April 2004 that they might issue a phase A exposure draft within a year, by April 2005 little more than preparatory work had been done. As had already been discovered with the short-term convergence projects following the Norwalk Agreement, it was not easy to find the most effective way for the two boards to work together.[146] The FASB staff were to take the lead on this project, but this did not obviate the need to coordinate with the IASB's staff. A further complication was that Japan's ASBJ, through a staff member stationed at the FASB, had also been allowed to participate in the project, albeit to an unspecified degree.

The preparatory work had once again highlighted the sensitive nature of the topic. Part of the plan for pulling the project afloat again was to set up an IASB–FASB joint working group (generally referred to as JIG, Joint International Group), consisting of some twenty-five senior executives, auditors, and analysts.[147] As seen in Chapter 7, this fitted into a more general pattern of creating advisory groups at the time of the first review of the IASC Foundation's Constitution, in response to criticism that the IASB was insufficiently responsive to the views of its constituents. Perhaps because of a lack of experience in composing such groups, or because it was felt that the sensitivity of the issues required great care in selecting the members, including involvement of the trustees, it took a rather long time to get JIG up and running. This held up the project, and, from the FASB's point of view, it was seen as a largely unnecessary delay.[148]

When JIG first met in January 2005, it served to strengthen rather than to alleviate criticism of the IASB. The tenor of the JIG meeting was that the executives were opposed to a single-statement approach, in particular one without a subtotal for net income. Perhaps contrary to the Board's expectations, the users did not provide strong support for a single performance statement, thinking that it was not really a priority. Users also indicated their preference for something like profit or loss as a subtotal: although they acknowledged its conceptual weaknesses,

---

[145] For project planning, see 'Reporting Comprehensive Income', *IASB Update*, April 2004, 5.

[146] See remarks by project manager Farhad Zaman as reported in *IStaR*, April 2005, 12.

[147] 'Membership of IASB and FASB International Working Group on Performance Reporting Announced', IASB press release dated 22 November 2004.

[148] Interviews with Richard Barker, 19 March 2009; and Kim Petrone, 17 February 2009.

it did provide a practical starting point for analysis and discussions with companies.[149] Some of the executives came away from the meeting with the impression that this was not what the Board wanted to hear, but that the Board was nonetheless intent on pressing ahead towards a single performance statement without profit or loss. There were some difficulties over approving the minutes of the meeting.[150]

From its earlier attempt at dealing with performance presentation, the IASB was aware that the view that net income should be retained was held with particular strength in Japan. But the view was not confined to Japan. Wolfgang Reichenberger, finance director of Nestlé and a member of JIG, organized a letter-writing campaign in which major companies from Europe, North America, and Japan wrote to the IASB and the FASB ahead of their April 2005 joint meeting to 'voice a strong endorsement of net income as a prominent measure of performance'.[151] Nestlé was a company that, since the early 1990s, had shown a strong interest in the IASC's work, in which one of its senior staff, Harry Schmid, actively participated. Schmid served in the IASC's delegation representing the Federation of Swiss Industrial Holding Companies from 1996 to 2000 and as an IASB Board member from 2001 to 2004. In 2004, Reichenberger had helped to form a group of European finance directors which had met a number of times with IASB Board members to discuss issues on the IASB's agenda (see Section 11.7). His activity on performance presentation was therefore part of a sustained though critical interest in the IASB.

At the joint meeting of the IASB and FASB in April 2005, the single-statement issue was seen as pivotal.[152] There was talk of showing the IASB Board's backbone and having the courage of its convictions. Some of the IASB's members, in particular those from the former G4 such as Tweedie, McGregor, and Leisenring, had been discussing performance reporting for many years and were convinced that it was finally time to move towards a single statement. The same was true for Tony Cope, who, as an FASB member in the 1990s, had dissented to FAS 130 for the reason that it allowed a choice between a single-statement and a two-statement presentation. Others were more cautious and pointed out that many countries lagged behind the United Kingdom, the United States, and Australia in terms of the debate over these issues, and had had less chance to gain experience with reporting formats in which comprehensive income was given more prominence. The boards agreed by a large majority on a single statement, but with a required subtotal for profit or loss.

This did not allay preparers' concerns. They continued to worry, reasonably or unreasonably, that there was more to the project than a mundane rearrangement of numbers that were already being reported anyway. As one commentator

---

[149] In the absence of minutes from the January JIG meeting, user and preparer views are based on 'Key Performance Ratio Finds that its Number May Be Up', *Financial Times*, 1 February 2005; letter from Philippe de Buck (UNICE) to Philip Laskawy, dated 1 June 2006, IASB archive, file 'covered correspondence', and the Board discussion as reported in *IStaR*, April 2005, 15–17.

[150] Letter from Philippe de Buck (UNICE) to Philip Laskawy, dated 1 June 2006, IASB archive, file 'covered correspondence'.

[151] Cover note from Wolfgang Reichenberger to David Tweedie and Robert Herz, dated 13 April 2005 and nineteen accompanying letters, supplied to the authors by Richard Barker.

[152] The representation of the April 2005 meeting is based on the report in *IStaR*, April 2005, 15–17.

observed at the time: 'It may . . . be that preparers believe that the [single] statement is a Trojan horse, and that having introduced it, the IASB will suddenly do away with traditional measures. There is no rational foundation for this, but it reflects the profound suspicion and the highly inaccurate mythology that seems to have built up regarding IFRS.'[153]

A second JIG meeting in June again ended in wrangling over whether Board and staff had really paid attention to what was said. At their June meeting, some of the trustees raised concerns that the Board was moving ahead with a preconceived idea to a conclusion for which many companies were not ready. They suggested that this would be unproductive because of opposition in the United States as well as in Europe. French trustee Bertrand Collomb, sensing that many trustees questioned the wisdom of having the project in its current form on the Board's agenda, asked whether the trustees could take a formal stance on the project. This was ruled out by Chairman Paul Volcker as inconsistent with the Constitution, but the message was clearly given that the Board should carefully attend to the views expressed by the trustees.[154]

In October 2005, during a discussion of the 'sweep issues' to be dealt with before the completion of the exposure draft, the question of a single statement came up suddenly for reconsideration by the IASB. The request came from 'some Board members' who saw the IASB 'heading for an unproductive "fight" with constituents, with each side seeing the other as entrenched in its views'.[155] Among these was Tom Jones, the Board's vice chairman, who had repeatedly indicated his belief that the Board was fighting the wrong fight.[156] Undoubtedly, the point was raised with the consent, if not direct encouragement, of Chairman Tweedie. From the discussion, it appeared that allowing a choice between a one-statement and a two-statement presentation would probably be supported by a majority of the Board for the sake of what David Tweedie called 'change management'.[157] Even with the option, the change could still be viewed as a small step in the right direction, because it would at least clearly separate transactions with owners from other changes in equity. An important question, given that this was a joint project, was what the FASB's response would be. In November 2005, when the Board made its final decision to introduce a two-statement option in the exposure draft, the FASB had not yet taken a formal position, but it was known that the FASB saw little point in a separate phase A exposure draft if there was so little change compared to FAS 130, which already contained such an option.[158] When the IASB issued its exposure draft in March 2006, it had to report that the FASB had decided to consider phases A and B together, and not to issue a separate phase A exposure draft.[159]

---

[153] Peter Walton, 'Editorial', *World Accounting Report*, November 2005, 1.

[154] IASCF meeting of 21 June 2005, minute 2; interview with Bertrand Collomb, 16 February 2010; see also Floyd Norris, 'Does Business Need a New Bottom Line?', posted 24 June 2005 <http://www .nytimes.com>.

[155] AP 10/2005 paper 11C, paragraph 6. This paper apparently had no parallel in the observer notes, see *IStaR*, October 2005, 35, suggesting a relatively late addition to the agenda.

[156] See e.g. 'Comprehensive Income Dispute', *World Accounting Report*, November 2005, 2.

[157] *IStaR*, October 2005, 36.   [158] *IStaR*, November 2005, 14.

[159] Exposure draft of amendments to IAS 1, 'A Revised Presentation' (IASB, March 2006), IN4.

Not much Board time was devoted to moving from the exposure draft to the final standard, although it took the staff some time to complete further editorial work. In September 2007 a revised version of IAS 1 was published, substantially in line with the exposure draft. Barth, Cope, Garnett, and Leisenring voted against. Cope had consistently expressed his belief that the Board should move towards a single performance statement. The others joined in the dissent and expressed their regret that the Board had introduced a conceptually flawed option despite its general preference to reduce alternatives.[160] The Board as a whole decided to express a preference for the single-statement approach in the basis for conclusions, an approach reminiscent of how the IASC had many times moved statements on controversial topics from the actual standards to the explanatory text.[161]

Apart from modifying the presentation of other comprehensive income, IAS 1 as reissued in September 2007 included changes in some of the key terms used in IFRSs. It introduced the FASB's term 'other comprehensive income' as a compact and clearly delineated term for what had hitherto been more loosely indicated as items 'recognized in equity', 'recognized directly in equity', or 'deferred to equity'. In line with the exposure draft, the names of the main financial statements were changed, even though a large majority of respondents had disagreed with this proposal.[162] Thus, in keeping with the language of the conceptual framework, the balance sheet became the 'statement of financial position'. On reconsideration, the name 'income statement' was retained (the exposure draft had referred to a 'statement displaying components of profit or loss'), but only as part of the two-statement option. A single performance statement was called a 'statement of comprehensive income'. Evidently, these changes caused a very large number of consequential amendments to all of the other standards. The IASB did not, and had never intended to, make these changes in nomenclature mandatory, so that many companies using IFRSs continued to call their balance sheets 'balance sheets'.

The introduction of the 'statement of financial position' probably did not help to improve the IASB's image as being somewhat remote from practice, even though it did not invent the name.[163] The FASB had made increasing use of this term in its pronouncements since the 1980s, and Australia and New Zealand had introduced it in their national standards in the 1990s. But to many constituents speaking languages other than English, the change seemed sudden and uncalled for. In some translations, the change was simply ignored, apparently not without the IASB's knowledge. In the official European translations of the new IAS 1 into German and Dutch, 'statement of financial position' was simply translated with 'Bilanz' and 'balans', respectively.[164] Because of the coordination of the EU's translation efforts with the IASB's policy on publishing translations,

---

[160] IAS 1 (2007), DO4 and DO6.
[161] IAS 1 (2007), BC 51–4. See Camfferman and Zeff, *Financial Reporting and Global Capital Markets*, 112.
[162] AP 12/2006 paper 14, paragraph 6.
[163] See for an example of sarcastic comment from Europe, Dieter Fockenbrock, 'Bilanzen ohne balance', *Handelsblatt*, 21 January 2009, 11.
[164] Commission Regulation (EC) No. 1274/2008 of 17 December 2008, German and Dutch versions.

the same wording was used in the German and Dutch versions published on the Foundation's website. Curiously, this meant that the German-language basis for conclusions contained the discussion of why the IASB believed that the change in wording was a good idea, but with a footnote that the German wording remained unaltered. For other languages, attempts were made to coin new names for the balance sheet, drawing on the national translations of the conceptual framework.

12.8.2 Phase B: The IASB Again Shrinks Back from Calling Net Income into Question

Phase A produced very little change in financial reporting practice, as all of the truly contentious issues had been shifted to phase B. These included not just the role of the income statement and the nature of other comprehensive income. Other issues that had fallen by the wayside or were deferred to phase B included per-share calculations (should total comprehensive income per share be reported?) and the question whether the cash flow statement should be prepared using the direct method, thus eliminating the popular alternative of the indirect method from IAS 7 *Statement of Cash Flows*. It was not until early 2006, when the phase A exposure draft was about to be published, that the boards turned in earnest to phase B. At this point, on the recommendation of the staff, the name of the project was changed from 'performance reporting' to 'financial statement presentation', to underline that in this phase the boards would consider the financial statements as a whole.[165] The FASB, still organizationally in the lead, put forward its staff member Kim Petrone as senior project manager, which contributed to the sense that a new phase was beginning. It was understood that the first step would be the publication of a discussion paper, rather than an exposure draft.

From the start, the idea was to build the project around a number of fundamental principles underlying the display of information in the financial statements. One of these principles was the notion of 'cohesiveness' among the main financial statements, that is, the idea that an item should be presented consistently across the balance sheet, the income statement, and the statement of cash flows. This formal notion was complemented by a more substantive idea, that items in all three statements should be classified in operating and financing items. This idea had already been explored by the IASB, at the suggestion of its staff member Richard Barker, during its first attempt at performance reporting from 2001 to 2003 (see Section 5.5.2). As before, the justification was found in terms of facilitating the assessment of an entity's future cash flows by classifying statement items in economically homogeneous groups, and reflected the common practice in financial analysis of separately valuing a firm's operating and financing activities. These ideas were accepted by the boards as the basis for further discussion, such as of the merits of additional categories for taxation, discontinued activities, and investment activities.

This approach led inevitably to the question of what to do with other comprehensive income. The IASB had found out in its earlier attempt at performance

---

[165] AP 3/2006 paper 6, paragraph 12.

reporting that any principled approach to ordering and classifying elements of income and expense must come into conflict with the existing standards. What was recognized as other comprehensive income in these standards—not necessarily identical under US GAAP and IFRSs—was based on a series of ad hoc decisions taken independently by both boards at various points in time. There was no clear conception of what these items had in common. In October 2006, the staff put the issue squarely before a joint meeting of the two boards in Norwalk, by recommending as a logical consequence of the cohesiveness principle that the current items of other comprehensive income should be distributed to the appropriate functional categories (such as operating, by then known as 'business', and financing), and that recycling be eliminated.[166] Pursuing the same logic, the staff added the recommendation that 'the subtotal of what is called net income should not be presented in the statement of comprehensive income'. The staff acknowledged 'that its recommendation could be viewed as revolutionary by many constituents'. Anticipating the criticism that the boards would introduce major changes under cover of a project ostensibly limited to mere presentation, the staff drew a further logical conclusion by recommending that the boards should openly broaden the scope of the project and undertake to review the accounting treatment of each item currently recognized in other comprehensive income.

Most members of both boards were sympathetic to the staff's views, or at least were willing to acknowledge the lack of a conceptual basis for other comprehensive income as currently defined. Among the IASB members, Tatsumi Yamada appeared isolated with his emphasis on the need to respect constituents' strong demand that net income, as well as recycling, be retained. Mary Barth and Warren McGregor, on the other hand, strongly supported the staff, with Barth reported as saying: 'If they were not prepared to propose this even in a discussion paper, she remained unconvinced they would ever do it.'[167] However, the view prevailed that what was desirable in the long term might not be achievable in the short term. In a vote, both boards expressed themselves against retaining other comprehensive income as a separate category in the long term. Conversely, only one FASB member (Tom Linsmeier) and three IASB members (Barth, Leisenring, and McGregor) were against retaining other comprehensive income in the short term.[168]

The distinction between the long and the short term may have been intended as reassuring, but anxiety about the boards' plans for the future of financial reporting flared up again, not least among the IASB's constituents. As discussed in Section 12.7, the boards had published a discussion paper on the objectives of financial reporting in July 2006, which was widely interpreted as a shift of emphasis towards the information needs of investors and away from more traditional objectives couched in terms of stewardship. The way in which the notion of assessing future cash flows was simultaneously guiding the financial

---

[166] AP 10/2006 paper 6C, paragraphs 38–58. Quotations in this paragraph are taken from this document.

[167] *IStaR*, October 2006, Supplement, 25–8. See also the report on the discussion by the IASB, prior to the joint meeting, *IStaR*, October 2006, 14–16.

[168] According to *IStaR*, October 2006, Supplement, 28, the vote against OCI in the long term was unanimous. However, Jan Engström was not present at the meeting.

statement presentation project seemed to justify fears that changes to the framework were not ornamental but intended to prepare the way for revolutionary change. The IASC Foundation trustees, at their October 2006 meeting, took note of the stir caused by the two projects and asked for a report. When this was discussed at their next meeting in January, concerns were expressed about a lack of support 'even among investor groups', and many trustees 'questioned the FASB's and the IASB's tactics in focusing on raising the elimination of net income at the outset'.[169]

Throughout 2007 and into 2008, the project continued on the premise that other comprehensive income and net income might disappear in the long term but would be retained in the short term. The boards considered alternative formats of a single performance statement that would do justice to the idea of functional classification but also include the current items of other comprehensive income as recognizable line items, as well as a subtotal for net income. This was far from easy. While it might look appealing, for instance, to collect all tax items in a single functional category, it could hardly be done without touching net income, because, under existing standards, items of other comprehensive income were presented net of tax. Apart from these technical problems, there were differences of view on how close the short-term solution should be either to current practice or to the long-term objective. The FASB tended towards presentations that de-emphasized other comprehensive income as a separate category, whereas the IASB was more evenly divided between those who favoured radical change and those who wanted to stay closer to existing practice.[170] After trying various expedients, the more traditional view prevailed, perhaps in part because the acceleration of the MoU programme being planned from early 2008 onwards increased the importance of keeping the project within manageable bounds. In their joint meeting of April 2008, the boards concluded that the project would be reduced in scope and would not, after all, address the presentation of other comprehensive income. Instead of describing several long-term and short-term alternatives for dealing with other comprehensive income, it was decided to present just one approach in which a single statement of performance would include other comprehensive as currently defined in a separate section.[171]

In June 2008, when the discussion paper was in the final stages of preparation for publication, both boards meeting by themselves reviewed these recent decisions. They confirmed that the discussion paper should include a paragraph briefly indicating the boards' long-term view on the statement of other comprehensive income.[172] A staff proposal in a pre-ballot draft put this in terms of 'the boards' preference for eliminating' the separate presentation of other comprehensive income, and hence for the elimination of recycling.[173] This caused David Tweedie to raise the issue one last time, concerned as he was that such a statement would be enough to embroil the IASB in a fight over something the Board might

---

[169] IASCF trustees meeting of 17–18 January 2007, minute C.
[170] For the distribution of views, see *IStaR*, December 2006, 35–7.
[171] See AP 6/2008 paper 9A for a staff review of decisions in April.
[172] Minutes of FASB meeting of 18 June 2008, paragraph 14 <http://www.fasb.org>; AP 6/2008 paper 9A and *IStaR*, June 2008, 34.
[173] AP 7/2008 paper 16.

never actually do, but which would block progress on the project on hand.[174] He was concerned in particular about Asia, as he knew very well that in Japan, where adoption of IFRSs was now seriously considered, there was a strong attachment to the concept of net income.[175] The Board thereupon agreed to remove the reference to the long-term view, a step in which the FASB apparently acquiesced.[176] With the publication of this discussion paper, the boards had met their target, established in the 2006 MoU, of publishing a due process document by the end of 2008.[177] The IASB had by then spent seven years reflecting on the presentation of financial statements, and the end was not yet in sight. As discussed in Chapter 16, the project would remain unfinished in 2011 when all of the initial members had left the Board.

12.9 FINANCIAL INSTRUMENTS: LONG-TERM CONVERGENCE AND SHORT-TERM MAINTENANCE

12.9.1 Full Fair Value as a Long-term Objective

There was never a time when financial instruments were not on the agenda of the IASB. When it was issued in 1998, IAS 39 was intended as an interim standard. As discussed in Chapter 6, the IASB had, from the beginning, its eye simultaneously on the improvement and maintenance of IAS 39 and on the more distant prospect of replacing it with a definitive standard. Initially, the focus had been on improvements, which embroiled the IASB in a conflict with the European banking industry. Yet, while the IASB was engaged in discussions with Europe over IAS 39, the question of convergence with US GAAP already began to weave itself into the story of financial instruments, following the Norwalk Agreement.

The IASB and the FASB began by considering whether accounting for financial instruments could benefit from short-term convergence projects. IAS 39 was derived from US GAAP, but there were numerous differences, some causing significant reconciling items for non-US companies reporting on Form 20-F to the SEC. More than a year was spent identifying worthwhile short-term financial instruments projects before the conclusion was reached, early in 2005, that there really were no such projects that would pass a cost-benefit test.[178] The issues that mattered were too complex to treat in isolation. Attention shifted to a long-term project to develop an improved and simplified financial instruments standard that the two boards would maintain together.

---

[174] AP 7/2008 paper 16 refers to 'a Board member' raising this point. The identification with Tweedie is based on *IStaR*, July 2008, 38, and interview with David Tweedie, 29 July 2008.

[175] *IStaR*, July 2008, 39.

[176] The issue appears not to have been discussed again at a public FASB meeting between July and October.

[177] Discussion paper 'Preliminary Views on Financial Statement Presentation' (IASB, October 2008).

[178] See AP 10/2005 paper 6A, paragraph 2, for a review of conclusions reached in April 2005.

For those who had followed the history of financial instruments accounting it would have come as no surprise that the ideal of improving and simplifying IAS 39 was almost instantaneously associated with the idea of fair value measurement for all financial instruments (often referred to as 'full fair value'). After all, much of the complexity of the existing standards stemmed from the mixed-measurement approach, combining fair value and amortized cost measurement for different classes of financial instruments. Already in April 2005, the staffs, who knew their history, wrote of possible approaches to a long-term project:

> Any suggestion that the Boards should move to full fair value will raise a large controversy between the Boards and many of their constituents. The previous attempt to define a full fair value model, the JWG [Joint Working Group] report, was widely criticised. The staffs are not suggesting that the Boards walk away from controversy. Rather, we suggest that the Boards consider whether this approach could gain support from a sufficient proportion of our constituents. Many of the staff consider a full fair value approach to be the clear conceptual winner. We question whether the approach is achievable in today's climate.[179]

Pursuing this line of thought, the boards agreed at their October 2005 joint meeting that it would be useful to make an explicit public statement that they saw full fair value as their long-term objective, without, however, adding an active project to their agendas. Neither the IASB nor the IASC before it had ever formally adopted such a long-term objective, although the discussions over IAS 39 in Europe in 2003 and 2004 had shown that the Board was certainly suspected of harbouring plans for full fair value. The FASB's view was already on record, as it had referred several times to a long-term full fair value objective in the basis for conclusions of FAS 133 *Accounting for Derivative Instruments and Hedging Activities* (1998).[180] Yet those references were not particularly conspicuous, and the turnover of FASB membership made a reaffirmation seem worthwhile. Therefore, in January 2006, both boards included a statement in the project updates on their websites that:

> The long-term objectives for simplifying and improving the accounting for financial instruments, assuming that technical and practical hurdles can be overcome, are:
>
> 1. To require that all financial instruments be measured at fair value with realized and unrealized gains and losses recognized in the period in which they occur
> 2. To simplify or eliminate the need for special hedge accounting requirements
> 3. To develop a new standard for the derecognition of financial instruments.[181]

The statement does not seem to have attracted much immediate attention, perhaps because there was already enough ammunition available to put the IASB under fire for its real or assumed predilection for fair value. By late 2005, early 2006, the use of fair value in the business combinations project and suggestions that the

---

[179] AP 4/2005 (joint meeting) paper 1, paragraph 16.
[180] FAS 133, paragraphs 247, 329, 335, 347, and 366.
[181] <http://www.iasb.org> and <http://www.fasb.org> as of January 2006, accessed through web. archive. The statement is cited in AP 4/2006 (joint meeting) paper 1, paragraph 2. The essence of the statement was already reported in *IASB Update*, October 2005, 5.

measurement phase of the conceptual framework project would herald a more general move towards fair value had contributed to a rather rancorous tone in public commentary on the IASB.[182] In that light, a statement on the long-term objectives for financial instruments that would merely lead to a research project might not be the most pressing concern. In February 2006, the research project became part of the MoU with the generally-worded target of publishing one or two due process documents by 2008.

The boards delivered on their undertaking by publishing a discussion paper, entitled 'Reducing Complexity in Reporting Financial Instruments', in March 2008. As implied by the title, this document did not discuss fair value accounting as an end in itself, but as the most plausible long-term approach to simplifying and improving financial instruments accounting. The argument was organized into two steps: one, the statement of the boards' belief that a long-term solution for reducing complexity was to use a single measurement method for all financial instruments, and, two, the argument by default that fair value seemed to be the only measurement attribute appropriate for all types of financial instruments. Although similar in substance to the long-term objectives established early in 2006, the approach appeared to be more circumspect and soft-spoken. The earlier statement of objectives was referred to in passing only, in one of the appendices.[183] The discussion paper emphasized that 'There are issues and concerns that have to be addressed before the boards can require general fair value measurement. It might take a long time to resolve all these issues and concerns'.[184] Part of the discussion paper was therefore devoted to possible interim steps to reduce complexity, such as simplifying hedge accounting.

By the time the paper was issued, the world was already in the first phases of the global financial crisis, characterized by alarm over the risks of various structured products and the concomitant disappearance of liquidity in many markets. While the timing was wonderful for suggesting simplification in an area where excessive complexity was increasingly seen as the root of the problem, it was not obvious to everyone that this was the time to suggest a greater reliance on fair value and, by implication, current market prices.[185] Calls for a suspension of fair value accounting could be heard with increasing urgency.[186] As discussed in Chapter 13, the financial crisis would prompt the IASB to come up with a new financial instruments standard with unprecedented speed. The new standard embodied a mixed-measurement approach, and the long-term objective of full fair value accounting would disappear behind the horizon.

[182] 'Opposition Mounts to IFRS 3 Draft', *Financial Times*, 24 October 2005, 28; 'IFRS Could Drive Directors to Commit Crime, Says AXA Head', *Financial Times*, 31 October 2005, 2; 'Complexity Dogs the Benefits of Fair Value: Deborah Hargreaves on Why the Ferocity of Debate on the Use of Market Valuations in Reports and Accounts has Persisted', *Financial Times*, 12 January 2006, 14.

[183] 'Reducing Complexity in Reporting Financial Instruments' (IASB, March 2008), paragraph C7.

[184] 'Reducing Complexity in Reporting Financial Instruments', paragraphs IN5 and 2.1.

[185] For commentary, see Peter Williams, 'IASB Looks for the Simple Life', *Financial Director*, 24 April 2008, 42; Glenn Cheney, 'FASB, IASB Call for Comments on Financial Instruments', *Accounting Today*, 22/9 (19 May 2008), 14.

[186] 'Fair Weather Fans Can't Expect Sir David to Shift', *Accountancy Age*, 29 May 2008.

12.9.2 Maintenance and Improvement of IAS 39:
Removing the Carve-outs

A practical implication of the October 2005 decision to adopt full fair value as the long-term objective was that the IASB and the FASB gave up the idea of aiming for convergence of the boards' existing mixed-measurement standards. Each board would be free to maintain and improve these as it saw fit.[187] Generally, the IASB was reluctant to continue tinkering with IAS 39, and it believed that many of its preparer constituents also wanted stability.[188] Nevertheless, there were some issues that required the IASB's attention. The most obvious one was whether something could be done to remove the last of the two IAS 39 carve-outs imposed by the EU in 2004. As discussed in Section 9.2, the carve-out relating to the fair value option was removed in November of 2005 following an amendment of IAS 39.

The other carve-out, relating to macro-hedges of interest rate risk, could not be removed as easily. For several years, until the middle of 2008, discussions continued between representatives of the European Banking Federation (EBF) and a group of Board members and staff of the IASB. The IASC Foundation trustees were eager for the issue to be resolved, and they continued to remind the Board of this.[189] The origin of the carve-out was that the IASB did not accept that certain hedges of interest payments on existing or future liabilities were effective in the sense of offsetting variability in hedged cash flows, as required by IAS 39. The EBF looked at it from a different angle and asserted that such hedges might nevertheless contribute to stabilizing the interest margin on a portfolio of financial instruments. The ineffectiveness perceived by the IASB was therefore not necessarily relevant from the perspective of a bank's asset and liability management. This difference of view had already been explored at length in 2003 and 2004, and subsequent discussions did not bring consensus. Periods of impasse alternated with moments when the two sides seemed tantalizingly close to reaching agreement. It was suggested that many problems followed from too restrictive interpretations by local auditors, and that minor changes in the wording of IAS 39 and its application guidance might be sufficient to allow the banks to apply hedge accounting in most situations where they thought this was appropriate.[190] Yet, by August 2008, David Tweedie wrote to the EBF with palpable exasperation that the EBF's report on the most recent round of discussions, held in May, showed that

---

[187] AP 10/2005 (joint meeting) paper 6A, paragraph 10.

[188] See the Board's discussion as reported in *IStaR*, July 2005, 4–5; see also memo from David Tweedie to Financial Instruments Working Group, dated 20 July 2005, IASB archive, file 'FIWG'.

[189] Interview with Thomas Jones, 16 February 2009.

[190] For a sense of impasse, see letter from Robert Garnett to Jörg Hessenmüller and Wilfried Wilms (EBF), dated 25 July 2005 and letter from David Tweedie to Jörg Hessenmüller and Wilfried Wilms (EBF), dated 15 December 2005, both in IASB archive, file 'general technical correspondence 2001–'. For a sense of optimism, tempered by earlier experience, see *IASB Update*, December 2006, 1–2, and the corresponding report in *IStaR*, December 2006, 48–51. That the issue might be resolved by an adjustment of local auditors' interpretations is mentioned, with caution, in a memo 'Interest Margin Hedging' from Wayne Upton to David Tweedie, dated 17 July 2007, IASB archive, file 'Interest Margin Hedge' and, more confidently, in a letter from David Tweedie to Michel Pébereau, dated 9 October 2007, IASB archive, file 'covered correspondence'.

they were still facing 'the fundamental difference between us that has existed for the last five years'. According to Tweedie, the EBF was not pursuing the possibility of providing better guidance to apply the existing rules, as agreed at the most recent meeting. Instead, it was simply restating positions discussed many times before and known to be unacceptable to the IASB, because they violated the Board's fundamental principle that all hedge ineffectiveness should be recognized in profit or loss.[191] The EBF, undoubtedly, would have seen this differently, but, by then, as with other issues in financial instruments accounting, the financial crisis was about to overturn all priorities. When, some two years later, the Board began to reconsider macro-hedging, the world had changed, Board membership had turned over, and all hedge accounting was considered afresh in the context of a new financial instruments standard, IFRS 9 (see Section 16.8). Nevertheless, because IAS 39 continued to be applied during the long transition to IFRS 9, the carve-out endured as a difference between 'IFRSs as issued by the IASB' and 'IFRSs as adopted by the EU'.

12.9.3 Maintenance and Improvement of IAS 32: Puttable Financial Instruments

A second short-term financial instruments issue which required the IASB's attention arose for entities with capital structures different from the ordinary limited liability company. What some cooperatives and partnerships, for instance, saw as their equity capital consisted of financial instruments that could be sold back by their owners to the cooperative or the partnership, at the initiative of the holder. This point had been considered by the Board during the project to improve IAS 32 and IAS 39, and the conclusion had been that such financial instruments were liabilities of the entity because they represented an obligation to pay cash on demand.[192] The Board accepted the consequence that such entities' financial statements under IFRSs might show zero equity, and that distributions to owners would have to be recognized as expenses. It believed that the financial statements, while reflecting these principles, might still be presented in a meaningful way with a suitable ordering and labelling of line items. It offered some illustrative examples of how to do this.[193]

From the perspective of the Board, this may initially have looked like a minor issue, not relevant to any but a few of the thousands of entities about to adopt IFRSs in 2005. Yet New Zealand and several EU member states had a long tradition of agricultural or banking cooperatives, many of which would be required to use IFRSs. The issue was given a higher profile when Fonterra, a cooperative dairy multinational and New Zealand's largest company, pointed out

---

[191] Letter from David Tweedie to Guido Ravoet (EBF), dated 14 August 2008, IASB archive, file 'covered correspondence'.

[192] This conclusion had already been drawn by the Standing Interpretations Committee (SIC) in its draft interpretation D34 (September 2001), following which the issue was taken up by the Board as part of the IAS 32 and IAS 39 improvements project.

[193] IAS 32 *Financial Instruments: Disclosure and Presentation* (IASB, December 2003), BC7–BC8 and IE32–IE33.

to the IASB that it faced the prospect of having its equity wiped out. Under New Zealand's transition rules, it would not have to adopt IFRSs until its financial year beginning in May 2007, but it did not wait until then to refer the issue to IFRIC. European cooperatives, more pressed for time, made an attempt to raise the issue to the political level in 2003, prior to the European endorsement of IAS 32 and IAS 39.[194] That it did not become as publicly contentious as the hedge accounting issue perhaps reflected the smaller political clout of these entities, compared to the major banks. What also may have helped was David Tweedie's suggestion that an IFRIC interpretation might provide a way forward.[195]

Although IFRIC did produce further guidance on applying the definition of a liability in the case of cooperatives, it referred an important part of the question back to the Board in 2004.[196] As it was understood by then, the question was not merely a matter of some entities reporting zero equity. In situations where ownership rights could be sold back to the entity for their fair value or a similar amount, the consequence of recognizing that amount as a liability would be that the entity would have to deduct an amount from its equity equal to the unrecorded goodwill corresponding to these ownership rights. Accounting for fluctuations in this deduction would mean that the entity would show greater losses as it performed better. The IASB's staff was ready to acknowledge that this was anomalous and merited further consideration.[197] The Board agreed in June 2004, but even so it was not until February 2008 that an amendment to IAS 32 was issued.

One reason for the delay was that the Board concluded that the most practicable approach to the amendment would not be to tinker with the definition or measurement of liabilities: as discussed elsewhere in this chapter, the Board was during these years too deeply involved in fundamental reflections on the liability concept to venture into any quick solutions. Rather, the amendment took the form of an explicit exception, such that some items meeting the definition of a liability could nevertheless be accounted for as equity instruments. Agreeing on the appropriate conditions for such an exception was not a trivial matter, as was pointed out repeatedly by John Smith, one of the Board members most alert to the potential abuse of accounting standards by means of opportunistic 'structuring' of contractual arrangements.[198] A practical constraint was a shortage of staff. This was generally a problem for the IASB around 2005, but was particularly acute for financial instruments. In July of that year, Tweedie claimed to have just two members of staff with expertise in that area.[199]

---

[194] Letter from Ivano Barberini and Iain Macdonald (International Co-operative Alliance) to Romano Prodi (European Commission), dated 18 November 2003, IASB archive, file 'Co-op banks'.

[195] Letter from David Tweedie to Etienne Pflimlin (European Association of Co-operative Banks), dated 2 December 2003, IASB archive, file 'Co-op banks'.

[196] IFRIC Interpretation 2 *Members' Shares in Co-operative Entities and Similar Instruments* (November 2004).

[197] AP 4/2006 paper 8.

[198] See reports of Board discussions in *IStaR*, September 2005, March 2006, May 2007. See also 'IASB Finds Limited Progress on Efforts to Extend Scope of Planned IAS 32 Relief', BNA's *Daily Tax Report*, 138 DTRI-1, 19 July 2007.

[199] Memo from David Tweedie to Financial Instruments Working Group, dated 20 July 2005, IASB archive, file 'FIWG'.

But perhaps the most important complication was a general problem faced by the IASB in setting global standards: how should it respond to claims that its standards did not properly account for local circumstances? To what extent could it set standards by reasoning on the basis of general principles, and to what extent did it have to make an effort to understand, in this case, the implications of such principles for limited liability partnerships under German company law, which faced a similar problem with their equity as many cooperatives?[200] That many in Germany saw a significant problem here was repeatedly brought to the attention of the IASB, but, from the German perspective, the IASB seemed slow to acknowledge that there was a problem. In February 2006, Harald Wiedmann, the chairman of the German national standard setter, wrote to Tweedie that 'This is an issue causing great unrest in Germany', and warned that it jeopardized the acceptance of both full IFRSs and the proposed IFRS for SMEs in his country.[201] The problems in Germany were not limited to small companies. In Germany there were several very large family-owned groups whose legal structures led them into difficulties with IAS 32. Some already had to report using IFRSs because of listed debt securities. Others were not required to use IFRSs but did so voluntarily or planned to do so, because they did not see German GAAP as a viable long-term alternative.[202] It was reported that some of these groups preferred qualified audit opinions to compliance with IAS 32.[203]

Early in 2006, several major family-owned companies in Germany grouped themselves in an association which began to engage in discussions about national and international accounting standard setting.[204] This was one more example that the influence of the IASB around the world was not limited to its standards. By prompting its constituents to organize themselves, the presence of the IASB has contributed in many countries to a much more elaborate institutional infrastructure for reflection and debate on financial reporting issues.[205]

In the end, the IASB did pay close attention to the legal details of the German situation. As finally published in 2008, the amendment to IAS 32 was crafted in close consultation with the German accounting standard setter.[206] The amendment succeeded in laying the issue to rest. It came just in time for New Zealand, but not before it had engendered considerable resentment if not downright hostility in Germany towards the IASB.

---

[200] For the German case, this point is articulated in Thomas Gruhn, 'Deutsche Gesellschaften ohne Eigenkapital: Unternehmen müssen Konsequenzen aus IAS 32 ziehen', *Börsen-Zeitung*, 12 April 2006, 2.

[201] Letter from Harald Wiedmann to David Tweedie, dated 3 February 2006, IASB archive, file 'covered correspondence'.

[202] 'Rechnungslegung: Streit um die Bilanz', *Der Handel*, 8 March 2006; see also Liesel Knorr, 'Nochmalige Diskussion über Eigenkapital nach IFRS', *Börsen-Zeitung*, 29 September 2007, 13.

[203] Christian Buchholz, 'Aufstand der Familienunternehmer', posted on 21 December 2006 <http://www.manager-magazin.de>.

[204] Known as Vereinigung zur Mitwirkung an der Entwicklung des Bilanzrechts für Familiengesellschaften (VMEBF). The 'Wir über uns' page on <http://www.vmebf.de> (accessed December 2013) reported that the association traced its origins to concerns over IAS 32.

[205] Earlier examples included the formation of ACTEO in France, in the latter days of the IASC, and the formation of the International Banking Federation, mentioned in Chapter 6.

[206] See comments by Wayne Upton, cited in *IStaR*, September 2007; see also *DRSC Quartalsbericht* Q1/2008, 2 and 4.

12.10 IFRS FOR SMALL AND MEDIUM-SIZED ENTITIES

The *International Financial Reporting Standard for Small and Medium-sized entities* (*IFRS for SMEs*), issued in 2009, was arguably one of the IASB's successes: a major project, starting from scratch but completed within the relatively short span of six years, and accepted, if not positively welcomed, in a wide a range of jurisdictions.[207] Yet, initially, the Board was not sure whether it wished to embark on such a project.

The idea that something might be done for smaller entities, in particular in developing countries which lacked an extensive infrastructure in accounting, had been considered already by the IASC. With World Bank support, this idea had been transformed into IAS 41 *Agriculture*, issued in 2000, which was industry-specific and not confined to smaller entities.[208] Meanwhile, the question of what to do for companies in emerging markets, or for SMEs in general, remained a low-priority item on the IASC's agenda. It appeared that the newly constituted IASB Board had no great appetite for it either, as it did not figure in the Board's initial agenda. Evidently, many Board members were concerned about a possible dilution or devaluation of the IASB's standards, in particular when a standard for SMEs would include departures from the recognition and measurement requirements in the full set of IFRSs. Some members of the Standards Advisory Council (SAC) shared this reluctance, but others kept the issue alive.[209]

At an early stage, David Tweedie and Tom Jones became convinced that the Board should undertake an SME project, for more than one reason. The EU's proposed IAS Regulation included a member state option to allow or even require the use of IFRSs by non-listed companies, and the European Commission apparently approached the IASB with a request to consider the implications.[210] Another interested party was the Intergovernmental Working Group of Experts on International Standards of Accounting and Reporting (ISAR), operating under the aegis of the United Nations Conference on Trade and Development (UNCTAD). This group, created in 1982 with a broad remit to consider issues in financial reporting, was by 2001 known to be considering the development of a simplified international accounting standard. Faint echoes seemed to be raised of the early 1980s, when it briefly looked as if the United Nations might set itself up as an accounting standard setter in competition with the IASC.[211] Yet ISAR saw itself as taking up the issue by default, and urged Peter Wilmot, the chairman of SAC, to press the importance of further attention to the issue by the IASB.[212] So did other organizations, including the Fédération des Experts Comptables

---

[207] For an extensive review of the history of the SME project, see Ronita Ram, *Development of the International Financial Reporting Standard for Small and Medium-sized Entities*, Ph.D. thesis, The University of Sydney, March 2012.

[208] Camfferman and Zeff, *Financial Reporting and Global Capital Markets*, 401–4.

[209] SAC meeting of 23–4 July 2001, minute 4.44–4.47; *IStaR*, April 2002, 13; SAC meeting of 20–1 June 2002, agenda paper 2, paragraph 18.

[210] Interview with David Tweedie, 29 July 2008.

[211] Camfferman and Zeff, *Financial Reporting and Global Capital Markets*, 187–92.

[212] Letter from Lorraine Ruffing (UNCTAD) to Peter Wilmot, dated 6 March 2002, IASB archive, file 'SME's'.

Européens (FEE) and the Organisation for Economic Co-operation and Development (OECD).[213]

By the middle of 2002, Tweedie and Jones had persuaded the Board that preparatory work should be undertaken by the staff, assisted by a small advisory panel, towards a project proposal for the Board. A brief sentence expressing the trustees' support appeared in the Foundation's 2002 *Annual Report*.[214] Given this groundwork, Tweedie was not pleased when discovering, early in 2003, that staff intended to propose to the Board *not* to place an SME project on the Board's agenda. In one of the interventions by which he occasionally asserted his chairman's prerogative, Tweedie had the agenda paper retracted, and he gave a new twist to the project.[215] He called on Paul Pacter, a former IASC staff member, then with Deloitte in Hong Kong, to develop a proposal, which was accepted by the Board in July.

By all accounts, the recruitment of Pacter was decisive for the success of the project. Over the course of his career, he had served first the FASB and then the IASC as a staff member, from which he brought not just a deep knowledge of US GAAP and IFRSs, but also much experience in the craft of standard setting. He had once before provided a key service to the IASC in the 1990s, when it was becoming bogged down in its financial instruments project. To meet the IASC's target date for submitting a set of core standards to IOSCO, Pacter single-handedly and on very short notice prepared a draft of what would become IAS 39 by extracting the relevant parts of extant and proposed US GAAP. Since 2000, he had been running Deloitte's IAS Plus website, demonstrating his knack for keeping abreast of both the details of the IASB's technical work and of its reception in countries around the world. The SME project required just such a person: someone with an overview of the entire range of standards, who could identify the essential points that needed to be translated into a simplified standard, who could hold his own against other technical experts who were sceptical of any watering-down of IFRSs, and, finally, an internationalist willing to travel the world to sell his product.

Although the Board went along with the project, its initial inclination was to ensure that the SME standard would remain closely aligned with the full body of IFRSs. The preliminary view expressed in a June 2004 discussion paper was essentially that an SME standard would be little more than a practical guide to IFRSs, with some disclosure relief. The SME standard would follow the structure of topics as in IFRSs, show the main principles for recognition and measurement extracted from these standards that should normally be sufficient to deal with SMEs' accounting needs, but it would contain a mandatory fall-back on IFRSs for any issues not covered in the SME standard. It was stated as a presumption, rebuttable on a case-by-case basis when developing the SME standard, that no modifications would be made to the recognition and measurement requirements of IFRSs. As if to call the entire project into question, the Board began the document by stating its view that 'full IFRSs are suitable for all entities'.[216]

[213] Letter from Göran Tidström (FEE) to David Tweedie, dated 11 December 2001; email from John R. Rieger (OECD) to David Tweedie, dated 17 May 2002, both in IASB archive, 'SME's'.

[214] 'Report of the Chairman of the Trustees', IASCF *Annual Report 2002*, 2.

[215] Interview with David Tweedie, 15 October 2009.

[216] Discussion paper 'Preliminary Views on Accounting Standards for Small and Medium-sized Entities' (IASB, June 2004), paragraph 4.

During the next several years, the Board gradually came round to the idea that the SME standard should be a self-contained document with its own organization of topics and without a mandatory fall-back. It was accepted that the SME standard, while obviously akin to full IFRSs, could nevertheless lead to different accounting treatments, and would evolve at its own pace rather than mimicking each change in IFRSs. The only Board member who maintained his opposition to the project from beginning to end was Jim Leisenring, who, earlier in his career as a member of the FASB, had already opposed the development of an SME standard in the United States. In his final dissenting view, he declared the *IFRS for SMEs* to be 'neither necessary nor desirable'.[217] This did not prevent him from contributing actively to the debates on the multitude of technical issues addressed by the standard.

The step to decouple the SME standard from full IFRSs was not lightly taken. It led to some discussion of whether this was allowed by the Constitution, which stated that one of the Foundation's objectives was 'to develop, in the public interest, a *single set* of high quality, understandable and enforceable global accounting standards' (paragraph 2(a), emphasis added). Some trustees were for this reason unwilling to countenance a separate set of standards for SMEs.[218] In November 2004, when the trustees published proposals for modifications to the Constitution, one proposal was to include an express reference 'to taking account of, as appropriate, the special needs of small and medium-sized entities and emerging economies'. A subtle point was that this clause was not added to the objective of developing accounting standards, cited above, but to a second objective of the Foundation listed in the Constitution: 'to promote the use and rigorous application of those standards' (paragraph 2(b)). In a comment on the proposal, the trustees said they wished to 'emphasise that the proposed change should not be interpreted as implying a separate set of accounting standards for SMEs based on different criteria'.[219]

When the trustees discussed the final change to the Constitution in March 2005, they took a further step. As revised, the Constitution still used the language of 'taking account of' the needs of SMEs, but now this was explicitly linked both to the objective of developing a single set of standards and to the objective of promotion of use and rigorous application of the standards. The commentary explained that 'the change is worded to enable the IASB to exercise its judgement on how to deal with these issues, while maintaining the rigour and essential consistency of the standards'.

In this decision, the trustees followed a staff recommendation, behind which one can assume the hands of Tweedie and Jones. Both wanted to defuse the argument used by some Board members that the Constitution prohibited the development of a separate SME standard.[220] Although the language of the revised Constitution was not as straightforward as it might have been, the view became current that the trustees had endorsed a separate SME standard. Subsequently the Board, with the exception of Leisenring, accepted the view that the Board's

---

[217] *IFRS for SMEs*, DO1.   [218] Interview with Philip Laskawy, 18 February 2009.
[219] 'Review of the Constitution: Proposals for Change' (IASCF, November 2004), paragraph 26.
[220] Interview with Thomas Jones, 16 February 2009. For the staff recommendation, see IASCF trustees meeting of 18 March 2005, agenda paper 6B, 3–4.

mission of developing a single set of standards was consistent with a separate set of SME standards in addition to full IFRSs.[221] In doing so, the Board followed a line of reasoning based on the conceptual framework. The framework's assertion that financial reporting should be directed at user needs and subject to a cost-benefit trade-off did not, it was believed, preclude that the trade-off might result in different answers for SMEs. A different answer was likely because the information needs of users of SME financial statements were likely to be different compared to public entities. A separate set of standards might thus be justified, provided it was consistent with other aspects of the framework, in particular the definitions of elements of financial statements.[222]

In modifying their views, Board members and trustees could find confirmation in the strong support for an SME standard expressed by many of the Board's constituents. Respondents to the June 2004 SME discussion paper were said to be 'overwhelmingly' in favour. Those who were not tended to agree that the IASB should address the needs of SMEs, but believed that it should do so in its main standards.[223] Beyond this basic consensus, however, opinions differed widely on how an SME standard should be drafted, and to what kind of entities it should apply. In that respect, the discussions around the SME standard were just another manifestation of the debate that had accompanied the IASC and its standards since 1973: while the general notion of a global accounting standard had always been intuitively appealing to most people, the difficulties began as soon as an attempt was made to define what this would mean in practice. The Board's struggle with the basic purpose and nature of the SME standard was symbolized by its almost embarrassing inability to settle on a name for the standard. Should it be a standard for 'SMEs', for 'non-publically accountable entities' (soon colloquially referred to as 'nappies'), 'private entities', or 'smaller entities'? Or should it be known as 'simplified IFRS'? Over the course of the project, the Board changed its mind a number of times, but ended up with 'SMEs', where it began.

The choice of a name might appear trivial, but the question of what kind of companies the Board had in mind while drafting the standard was not, as these might include anything from the proverbial corner grocery store to large but unlisted multinational enterprises. In the end, the Board came to the conclusion that there was little it could do to control the use of its SME standard. As in the case of full IFRSs, it would be up to individual jurisdictions to decide which entities would be allowed or required to follow the standard. The Board therefore limited itself to defining SMEs as entities that do not have public accountability, which in turn primarily meant entities without exchange-traded securities. Small listed companies were expressly not allowed to claim compliance with the standard.[224] The SEC staff felt strongly that there should be such a prohibition, but once the IASB had made it clear that it felt the same way, the SEC saw no need

---

[221] See the record of the October 2006 Board meeting in *IStaR*, October 2006, 32–3.

[222] *IFRS for SMEs*, BC44–BC47; communication from Warren McGregor to the authors, dated 11 April 2014.

[223] AP 12/2004 paper 5. Paragraph 6 claimed that 'nearly 90%' of respondents were in favour of an SME standard. Yet the accompanying spreadsheet (AP 12/2004 paper 5B) showed that 93 out of 116 (80%) of answers to this particular question were positive.

[224] *IFRS for SMEs*, paragraph 1.5.

to involve itself further in the project.[225] But as the Board would have known from its discussions about compliance with IFRSs and the protection of the IASB's brand name (see Chapter 10), there was little it could do to hold back regulators that were differently inclined than the SEC from allowing an inappropriate use of the standard.

The process of determining the details of the SME standard involved several years of discussion in which Pacter patiently guided the Board again and again through all of the issues making up a complete set of accounting standards, yet condensed to around 200 pages. Part of the process was the publication of an exposure draft issued in February 2007, also used as the basis for field testing. In the course of the discussions, a number of significant differences between the SME standard and full IFRSs were introduced. Accounting for financial instruments was considerably simplified and, as discussed more fully in Chapter 13, the approach of the SME standard would provide inspiration when the Board discussed what would become IFRS 9. While IFRS 3 (2003) had done away with amortization of goodwill, it was reintroduced for SMEs on the basis of a maximum useful life of ten years.

Once the idea was accepted that the SME standard might depart from the full standards, the thought naturally arose that the Board could anticipate in the SME standard the solutions it was still considering for the full standards, or that choices made in the SME standard might be seen to bind the Board in other ongoing projects. This was debated in particular with respect to retirement benefits and deferred taxation, and on the latter issue the SME standard adopted an approach that, for full IFRSs, had just reached the stage of an exposure draft by March 2009. At one point, late in 2008, the staff suggested that the SME standard should require a single performance statement, something which the Board had long wanted to include in its full standards, without ever succeeding. Recognizing the potential risk to the SME project, the Board decided, somewhat against its inclination, to include the same two-statement option in the SME standard that it had recently included in the revised version of IAS 1.[226]

The clearest indication that the SME standard addressed an urgent need, at least in some countries, was given by South Africa which did not wait for the final standard. In October 2007, its Accounting Practices Board adopted the exposure draft of the SME standard as a statement of generally accepted accounting practice for SMEs.[227] In August 2009, a month after the issue of the final standard, South Africa claimed to be the first country in the world to adopt the *IFRS for SMEs*. Other jurisdictions followed, and in its 2011 annual report the IFRS Foundation claimed that over eighty jurisdictions had adopted the standard or had announced plans to do so.[228] The IASB did not content itself with launching the standard, but also helped to build a supporting infrastructure. Under Pacter's leadership, initially in his capacity of director of standards for SMEs and subsequently as a Board member, a range of educational materials was

---

[225] Interview with Scott Taub, 17 June 2009.

[226] See AP 12/2008 paper 5A and record of Board discussion in *IStaR*, December 2008, 4–6.

[227] 'SA First Country to Adopt Proposed International Financial Reporting Standard for SMEs', press release, The South African Institute of Chartered Accountants, 3 October 2007.

[228] IFRS Foundation, *Annual Report 2011*, 38.

prepared in several languages. He also organized and offered 'train the trainer' workshops in many countries in Latin America, Africa, Asia, and Eastern Europe. The workshops were partly financed by the World Bank, which thus continued its support for building up accounting expertise in countries which benefited from its funding.

Yet the *IFRS for SMEs* was not uniformly welcomed in all countries. In France and Germany there was notable opposition to suggestions that the EU might voluntarily allow its use for purposes of complying with company law requirements, let alone require it. As discussed in Section 12.9, the first stages of the SME project coincided with considerable unrest in Germany over IAS 32, and had alerted many to the possibility that non-listed companies might, de facto if not de jure, become obligated to adopt IFRSs or the SME standard once the latter would be published. Reflecting this view, a project to modernize the accounting requirements of German company law, which began in 2005 and was concluded in 2009, emphatically did not build on the *IFRS for SMEs*, even though this was initially contemplated.[229] The final outcome was presented by the government as 'an answer to IFRSs' which were considered as unsuitable for companies not accessing public capital markets, while the *IFRS for SMEs* was also rejected as a good alternative.[230] One of the objections was that the *IFRS for SMEs* was still too complex and costly to implement for smaller companies. Another reason was the desire to maintain the traditional link between financial reporting and tax accounting. Similar views could be heard in France (see also Section 15.10.3).

Following the publication of the *IFRS for SMEs*, the European Commission undertook a public consultation as to its possible use in the EU. This revealed large differences of view across the member states, but the strong opposition to the standard in Germany was conspicuous.[231] After considering the options, the Commission decided not to accord the *IFRS for SMEs* a formal place in the EU's regulatory framework. Its adoption, or not, therefore became a matter for the individual member states, within any constraints imposed by the EU's accounting directives.[232]

Full IFRSs sometimes underwent modifications upon adoption, and the same was true for the *IFRS for SMEs*. When the standard was adopted for voluntary use in Hong Kong in 2010, the section on accounting for income tax was replaced with the relevant requirements from IAS 12. In March 2013, the United Kingdom and Ireland replaced most of their national GAAP by a single standard based on the *IFRS for SMEs*, but with substantial modifications.[233] Not unnaturally,

---

[229] 'Germany: Not Happy with SME Standard', *World Accounting Report*, March 2006, 15.

[230] 'Neues Bilanzrecht in Kraft: Milliardenentlastung für den Deutschen Mittelstand', press release, Bundesministerium der Justiz, 29 May 2009 <http://www.bmj.de> accessed through web.archive.

[231] 'Summary Report of the Responses Received to the Commission's Consultation on the International Financial Reporting Standard for Small and Medium-sized Entities' (European Commission, Internal Market and Services DG, May 2010) <http://ec.europa.eu/internal_market/accounting>. Over one-third of the 210 responses came from Germany, and all but a few of these did not consider the *IFRS for SMEs* suitable for widespread use within Europe.

[232] 'Financial Reporting Obligations for Limited Liability Companies—Frequently Asked Questions', MEMO/11/732, 25 October 2011 <http://ec.europa.eu/internal_market/accounting>.

[233] See FRS 102 *The Financial Reporting Standard Applicable in the UK and Republic of Ireland* (UK FRC, March 2013), page 4 and Appendix II.

considering that international comparability was less important for most SMEs than it was for listed companies, these modifications did not seem to attract much international attention, let alone the kind of opprobrium sometimes reserved for carve-outs from full IFRSs.

12.11 MANAGEMENT COMMENTARY

One of the IASB's minor projects, at least in terms of the limited amount of Board time spent on it, was the project to develop guidance on 'management commentary'. In six years from 2005 to 2010, it was discussed in seven Board meetings before the IASB issued its first 'practice statement', not a standard, in December 2010.

The project originated in 2002, when the IASB was still partnering with its eight liaison standard setters. As seen in Section 11.8, determining the working relationship of the Board with these national standard setters was not always easy. One format that was tried was to ask a liaison standard setter to conduct a research project in preparation of a decision by the Board to put a project on its agenda. The idea that the IASB might move into the area of what was referred to by the American name of Management's Discussion and Analysis (MD&A) had been considered when the Board deliberated on its initial agenda, and had been cited as one of the justifications for adopting the name International Financial Reporting Standards as opposed to the earlier International Accounting Standards (see Section 5.1).

The MD&A in the United States had originated in 1968 with the SEC, not the standard setter, and the SEC has subsequently revised and enhanced its guidance several times.[234] The MD&A is not covered by the auditor's report, and today it is not unusual for the MD&A of large US publicly traded companies to extend to as many as thirty pages. The SEC's Division of Corporation Finance reviews registrants' MD&A to be satisfied that they are sufficiently forthcoming. There was a view at the SEC that the IASB should steer clear of this territory, given that it might interfere with one of the SEC's responsibilities.[235]

But the topic was not just relevant to the United States. Canada's Ontario and Québec Securities Commissions imposed an MD&A requirement on listed companies in 1989.[236] During the 1990s, the UK ASB began to recommend the content of an 'Operating and Financial Review', which had been required as a kind of directors' report by Article 46 of the EU Fourth Directive as incorporated in UK companies legislation. In 1998, the Australian Stock Exchange amended its listing rules to require all listed companies to prepare a review of operations and activities for the reporting period, based on recommended practice by the Group of 100 senior finance executives.[237] In 2004, the German standard setter issued an

---

[234] *Guides for Preparation and Filing of Registration Statements*, Securities Act Release No. 4936, issued on 9 December 1968.

[235] Interview with Scott Taub, 17 June 2009.

[236] Policy Statement No. 5.10, *Annual Information Form and Management's Discussion and Analysis of Financial Condition and Results of Operations—Policy*, 12 OSCB 4275 (10 November 1989).

[237] See *Guide to Review of Operations and Financial Condition*, Group of 100 (2003), 4–5 <http://www.group100.com.au>.

accounting standard which provided guidance for the implementation of Article 46, Fourth Directive, as incorporated in German law.[238]

In 2002, New Zealand's Financial Reporting Standards Board volunteered to do initial work on the topic, and the standard setters from Canada, Germany, and the United Kingdom also expressed an interest. The four formed a project team with New Zealand in the lead.[239] In February 2005, the group produced a draft discussion paper, presented to the Board by Alan Teixeira, the leading draftsman, who would join the IASB later that year from New Zealand as project manager, subsequently to become director of technical activities. The Board seemed to take to the paper on 'management commentary', as the subject was referred to by then, and it was published as a discussion paper by the IASB in October 2005.[240] Of the various research projects undertaken by liaison standard setters in the IASB's early days, it was the most successful. It went on to an exposure draft in June 2009, and a final statement, as indicated, in December 2010.

The significance of information accompanying the financial statements, providing interpretation and explanation of the reported figures, was rarely contested. It was also readily accepted that this type of information fell within the scope of 'financial reporting' as understood in the IASB's conceptual framework. The question was always whether it was something that the IASB should take up, or leave to others, such as securities regulators. And if the IASB were to issue any guidance, what status should it have relative to its body of standards? If it were to be a standard, how could it be reconciled to the widely different legal requirements across the world? And if it was not a standard, what would that mean for any statements of compliance with IFRSs or the auditor's report? The complex of questions makes it understandable why the IASB, with many other demands on its time, chose the light format of an explicitly non-binding practice statement. Not all Board members were convinced that the Board could find a meaningful way out of these questions. Bob Garnett, Prabhakar Kalavacherla, and Jim Leisenring voted against the publication of the exposure draft, in part because they did not believe that such a non-authoritative document would lead to an improvement in financial reporting. Paul Pacter, when he joined the Board, expressed similar concerns. The vote on the final practice statement was not disclosed.[241]

12.12 INTERPRETATIONS: IFRIC's ACTIVITIES

By the end of 2004, it might well have been believed that IFRIC was coming up to speed.[242] So far, it had issued eleven exposure drafts, nine in 2004. Five of these

---

[238] DRS 15 *Lageberichterstattung* (DRSC, December 2004) <http://www.drsc.de>.

[239] IASB meeting with national standard setters, 28 October 2002, agenda paper 12.

[240] 'Management Commentary: A Paper Prepared for the IASB by Staff of its Partner Standard-setters and Others' (IASB, October 2005).

[241] For Pacter's views and Kalavacherla's intention to dissent, see *IFRS Monitor*, September 2010, 7.

[242] For an extensive analysis of IFRIC's activities until March 2007, see Michael Bradbury (IFRIC member 2004–8), 'An Anatomy of an IFRIC Interpretation', *Accounting in Europe*, 4/1–2 (2007), 109–22.

exposure drafts had resulted in final interpretations, all issued in 2004. At one point it was suggested that its output in subsequent years might reach eight to twelve interpretations per year.[243] However, this level was never achieved. Five new exposure drafts were issued in 2005, slipping to three in 2006, and then to two each in 2007 and 2008, and even fewer afterwards. In terms of final interpretations, 2004 had set a record that would not be broken. Only the year 2006, with four new interpretations, came close (see Appendix 2 for a listing of all interpretations). The low level of output was not so much caused by a lack of requests for interpretations, as by IFRIC's restraint in responding to such requests, as discussed in the next section.

12.12.1 Negative Agenda Decisions

As in the case of the Board, IFRIC's work was coming under increasing scrutiny from constituents, leading to calls for a better justification of its decisions. This was true in particular of IFRIC's decisions *not* to act upon requests for an interpretation received from outside parties. Between 2002 and December 2004, requests for fifty-six interpretations were rejected, followed by twenty-two and thirty-one rejections in 2005 and 2006, respectively.[244] Even when taking into account that a number of rejections by IFRIC were recommendations to the Board to address the issue, it is evident that this number was relatively large compared to IFRIC's output of exposure drafts, let alone its small number of final interpretations. IFRIC was deliberately acting with restraint. As Director of Technical Activities, Liz Hickey put it to the trustees in October 2006: 'One issue that both constituents and the IASB have to face is the extent to which, in a world of principle-based standards, it is appropriate to respond to every request for interpretation by developing a new rule. The IFRIC itself tries to base its Interpretations on principles but is under constant pressure to descend to greater detail.'[245] It was understood that David Tweedie, for one, did not wish to see the ambition to make IFRSs principles-based thwarted by a high volume of detailed interpretations. Bob Garnett, who chaired IFRIC from 2005 to 2011, shared that view, and he believed that the preferred way to deal with a problem was to fix the standard, rather than to issue an interpretation. This preference was reflected in a so-called annual improvements process adopted by the Board in 2006 and in which IFRIC actively participated.

Outside the IASB organization, some believed that IFRIC's restraint showed the influence of the international audit firms which were always strongly represented on IFRIC and its agenda committee. The audit firms were in a delicate position. Their unquestionable technical expertise made it inevitable that they played a leading role on IFRIC, but they would also be conscious that a client might prefer not to have one of its accounting policies ruled out by an IFRIC interpretation.

---

[243] 'IFRIC Review of Operations', IASCF trustees meeting of 18 March 2005, agenda paper 4A, Appendix A, paragraph 11.

[244] See the regularly updated decision summaries, compiled from *IFRIC Update*, on the IFRS foundation website.

[245] 'IFRIC Report', IASCF trustees meeting of 26–7 October 2006, agenda paper 5, page 2.

Moreover, as mentioned in Section 10.5, the Big Four firms developed elaborate procedures for ensuring uniform application of IFRSs by their clients, and they shared their conclusions in virtually continual consultation among themselves. This inspired a perception that the audit firms were reluctant to reopen these issues for debate in IFRIC.

The high number of rejections caused some resentment, not only when mixed with suspicions about the role of the audit firms. The IASB had always discouraged national interpretations of its standards and urged that requests for interpretations should be sent to IFRIC. This call was generally heeded, although the demand for local interpretations could never be entirely suppressed.[246] Some jurisdictions—for instance, Germany and Hong Kong—did issue interpretations or guidance on the application of IFRSs, but this tended to be incidental and limited to purely local or ephemeral issues. But, typically, national standard setters met demands for interpretations by undertaking to collect and screen such requests before passing them on to IFRIC. Preventing a multiplicity of national interpretations was clearly of importance for the EU, but exercising restraint on this point was seen to depend on whether IFRIC could deliver.[247] During 2005, EFRAG played an important role in steering the EU away from local interpretations. In line with EFRAG's thinking, the European Commission set up a European Roundtable for the Consistent Application of IFRS, emphatically not to issue its own interpretations, but to consider issues for referral to IFRIC. Against this background, it may be assumed that many who sent their requests to IFRIC did so in the belief that they were not doing so frivolously. A rejection by IFRIC could then well be perceived as an adverse comment on the judgement of those making the request. This was understood at the IASB, and it was observed during one of the Board's strategy retreats that 'There were two ways of irritating constituents; the first was to impose an unwelcome change, and the second was then to reject requests for an interpretation'.[248]

Such criticisms of IFRIC echoed criticisms directed at the Board at around the time of the first Constitution review. And just as the Board's procedures were modified to redress grievances over a perceived lack of openness and responsiveness, so IFRIC's procedures were adjusted. Starting in 2005, IFRIC began publishing tentative agenda decisions, allowing for public comment, before making a final decision to reject a request for interpretation. In January 2007, the trustees approved a *Due Process Handbook* for IFRIC, in line with the *Handbook* for the Board approved in March 2006. As a consequence, meetings at which potential agenda items were discussed were henceforth to be open to the public. The *Handbook* also codified criteria for making agenda decisions. These criteria implied, generally speaking, that the mere fact that a standard was unclear on

---

[246] For demand for national interpretations efforts see e.g. 'IFRIC and the National Standard Setters', *Accountancy*, 135/1342 (21 June 2005), 67; 'Big Four in Australia Call for IASB to Outsource Interpretational Work', *International Accounting Bulletin*, 28 January 2005.

[247] See 'Achieving Consistent Application of IFRS in the EU: A Discussion Paper' (EFRAG Supervisory Board, 27 July 2005) <http://www.iasplus.com>; see also letter from Philippe Danjou (CESR) to Kevin Stevenson, dated 16 April 2004, attached to letter from Richard Thorpe (CESR) to Thomas Seidenstein, dated 25 June 2004, (first) IASCF Constitution review comment letters <http://www.iasb.org.uk> accessed through web.archive.

[248] 'IASB Awaydays at Greywalls Hotel on 18 and 19 May 2006', IASB archive, 'awayday' files.

a particular point was not by itself sufficient for putting the item on IFRIC's agenda. Indications were required that an issue was widespread, or that it led to significant diversity in practice.[249]

Changes such as these did not modify IFRIC's overall approach, which remained more restrained in undertaking projects and issuing interpretations than some constituents might have liked. When, for instance, the adoption of IFRSs began to be seriously considered in Japan, the absence of detailed guidance was seen as an important weakness of IFRSs, and the suggestion could be heard that IFRIC should be given more resources, for instance by adding some full-time members.[250]

Just as the Board had to grapple with widely different expectations and preferences around the world about the level of specificity and detail in its standards, so did IFRIC with respect to its interpretations. On the one hand, IFRIC's greater openness respecting its rejection decisions was welcomed. The rejection notices, or 'non-IFRICs' as they were sometimes called, functioned in practice as a form of guidance, providing comfort to those who welcomed any reduction of ambiguity in the standards. On the other hand, the introduction of this form of de facto guidance could also cause annoyance, in particular where IFRIC motivated its rejection of an interpretation request by the argument that the standard was 'clear' in requiring a certain practice. This could be troublesome for companies that had believed that the standard was not clear, and that had adopted a different practice. They might be required by securities regulators in some countries to restate their earnings. Fears were expressed that stock markets would not be able to distinguish clearly between the comparatively innocuous effects of companies learning to apply IFRSs and the more serious accounting misdemeanours sometimes associated with earnings restatements.[251] Striking a proper balance between providing interpretations and not providing interpretations remained a challenge for IFRIC.[252]

12.12.2 IFRIC 12: Service Concession Arrangements

By the nature of its mandate, IFRIC's work tended to attract little attention outside the circle of accounting experts. One exception, IFRIC 3 on emission rights, was discussed in Section 9.4. Another notable interpretation was IFRIC 12, on service concession arrangements. This interpretation stands out among IFRIC's work by its length and complexity. It amounted to a small standard, and for several years it

---

[249] *Due Process Handbook for the International Financial Reporting Interpretations Committee (IFRIC)* (IASCF, 2007), paragraph 24. An example of how such criteria might be applied prior to the publication of the *Handbook* is the rejection notice 'IAS 17 Leases—Recognition of Contingent Rentals', *IFRIC Update*, May 2006, 6.

[250] The existence of these views in Japan was indicated by Takatsugu Ochi (interview, 31 January 2011) and Atsushi Kogasaka (interview, 26 January 2011). See also the comment letter submitted in phase two of the IASC Foundation's second Constitution review by the JICPA (CL 13, 26 March 2009).

[251] See 'Hundreds Face Restatement in Wake of Standards Chaos', *Accountancy Age*, 23 November 2006.

[252] See Ken Wild (then a member of IFRIC), 'Rules of Interpretation', *Accountancy Age*, 7 December 2006.

helped to keep IFRIC busy. It also gave rise to another episode in the story of the EU's struggles to come to terms with the IFRSs it had embraced.

The IASC's Standing Interpretations Committee (SIC) had identified accounting for 'public-private sector transactions' as a relevant agenda topic in 1999, thinking of phenomena such as the construction and operation of motorways by private contractors on the basis of government concessions. Upon reflection and consultation with the Board, it decided to limit itself to an interpretation specifying relevant disclosures. This interpretation was issued as SIC-29 *Disclosure—Service Concession Arrangements* and was approved by the IASB Board in December 2001. The initiative for continuing with the accounting aspects of concession arrangements came from the UK ASB. The ASB was considering the issue both because of its practical relevance to the United Kingdom, where significant experiments in public-private partnerships and financing arrangements were underway, and because of its conceptual proximity to other issues it was working on, including leases. Following one of the periodic meetings with its liaison standard setters, the IASB asked the ASB to lead a working group including the standard setters from Australia, France, and Spain—countries where concession arrangements for developing transport infrastructure were of considerable significance—to develop a proposal for a possible IASB project. The report was duly delivered for discussion with the liaison standard setters in April 2003. While it outlined a major, long-term project for the Board on fundamental issues of non-financial assets and executory contracts as the way to a comprehensive resolution, its main message was that at least some further guidance was necessary before 2005. Recognizing the pressure on its agenda, the Board recommended that IFRIC take up the matter, with a view to issuing an interpretation in the first quarter of 2004.[253]

The recommendation was accepted, and IFRIC began considering the topic at its meeting of September/October 2003.[254] As with its interpretation on emission rights, IFRIC struggled to develop guidance on the basis of inconsistent existing standards. It took IFRIC some time to work out on which of the existing concepts and requirements of IFRSs—leases, tangible assets, revenue recognition—its interpretation should be built. As 2004 drew to a close with no interpretation in sight, impatience in Europe was growing. At meetings of the Accounting Regulatory Committee (ARC), the need to have an interpretation ready for application in 2005 was repeatedly stressed, and the lack of progress on service concessions was mentioned as an example of the kind of malfunctioning that needed to be addressed in the IASC Foundation's ongoing Constitution review.[255] In January 2005, Alexander Schaub, the director-general of the European Commission's internal market directorate, wrote to David Tweedie to underline the 'urgent need' for guidance, and to remind the IASB of an earlier suggestion by EFRAG that, as a transitory measure, the IASB should countenance the continuation of existing practices. In the language of standard setting, this meant that such practices

[253] 'IASB Research Project—Accounting for Service Concession Arrangements', joint meeting of standard setters, April 2003, agenda paper 5.

[254] For the ASB's summary of events, see 'Service Concession Arrangements', *Inside Track* (ASB) 37, October 2003, 5.

[255] Summary reports of ARC meetings of 14 June, 30 November, and 20 December 2004 <http://ec.europa.eu/internal_market/accounting>.

should be 'grandfathered' as had been done in IFRS 4 and IFRS 6 with respect to accounting for insurance contracts and extractive industries, respectively (see Chapter 5).[256]

The IASB rejected Schaub's suggestion, and IFRIC did finally unveil its plans in a triplet of exposure drafts issued in March 2005.[257] The draft interpretation was concerned with projects where a private-sector enterprise would both build and operate infrastructure (e.g. a toll road or a bridge), but where the state retains control over the asset or would regain control at some point. In IFRIC's view, the contractor would not recognize the infrastructure as an asset, but it would recognize revenue for the construction of the asset. The credit entry for recognizing the revenue would be matched by a debit in the balance sheet. This could either be a receivable, in case of a cast-iron guarantee by the state that the contractor will recover the full construction costs, or it could be an intangible asset, when the contractor had a right to operate the infrastructure and to levy user charges, but no guarantee that these would be sufficient to recover construction costs. While most people agreed that IFRIC had correctly drawn its inferences from the existing standards, there were at least two problems with this approach. The first was conceptual, and it had troubled some IFRIC members as well: because of the recognition of the intangible asset, the total revenue over the life of the concession would be greater than the total stream of cash receipts, the additional revenue being exactly offset in the income statement by future amortization or impairment of the intangible asset.[258] The second problem was of a more practical nature: because many concession arrangements did not have cast-iron guarantees, and because the fair value of the right to levy an uncertain amount of future user charges might not be high, the interpretation was likely to give rise to significant up-front losses, compared to established accounting practices. Although the latter problem was not one that IFRIC could consider under its mandate, it did figure prominently in comment letters such as those from ASETA, the Spanish Association of Toll Motorways and Tunnels: 'The recognition of heavy losses during the initial years of operation, as mentioned above, though unrelated with the underlying performance of the project, could affect the parties' behaviour and possibly have negative effects on the development of concession infrastructure projects throughout the EU in the near future.'[259]

Many respondents questioned whether this was really a proper topic for IFRIC, and suggested that it should be handed back to the Board. Some IFRIC members sympathized with this view, at least as a matter of hindsight, but in view of the progress already made it was decided to soldier on.[260] Yet IFRIC members continued to have misgivings, and the issues were debated and re-debated through

---

[256] Letter from Alexander Schaub to David Tweedie, dated 12 January 2005, IASB archive, file 'EC-EU'.

[257] See 'Service Concessions', *IFRIC Update*, February 2005, 1–2. IFRIC D12 'Service Concession Arrangements—Determining the Accounting Model', IFRIC D13 'Service Concession Arrangements—The Financial Asset Model', and IFRIC D14 'Service Concession Arrangements—The Intangible Asset Model' (IFRIC, March 2005).

[258] See IFRIC 12, BC34–5.

[259] Letter from José Luis Feito to Elizabeth Hickey, 27 May 2005, CL22 <http://www.iasb.org> accessed through web.archive.

[260] See *IFRIC Update*, August 2005, 1.

the remainder of 2005 and well into 2006, before agreement was reached on a thoroughly fine-tuned version which left the main features of the exposure drafts intact. This was IFRIC 12 *Service Concession Arrangements*, issued in November 2006 with mandatory application as of 1 January 2008.

At this point, IFRIC was probably relieved to be done with the project, which had absorbed a considerable fraction of its energy and resources during more than three years. It now became the turn of the EU to wrestle with IFRIC 12. While some parties in Europe had clamoured for an interpretation in 2004, it was now obvious that IFRIC 12 was strongly disliked in some quarters, particularly in Spain. Moreover, European companies had made the transition to IFRSs in 2005 without the benefit of an interpretation on service concessions, which made it less obvious that such an interpretation was urgently needed. The endorsement process stalled.

A first sign of problems came in January 2007, when EFRAG first withdrew a draft of a positive endorsement recommendation, and then held an extra meeting at which it agreed again, with five votes to four and three abstentions, to draft a positive recommendation.[261] EFRAG issued its final positive endorsement advice in March, despite many protests from southern European infrastructure operators. Then the ARC was unable to reach a decision. For the better part of two years, IFRIC 12 was debated inconclusively in many of the ARC's meetings held between February 2007 and October 2008. The ARC's anonymized minutes showed how 'one member state in particular'—a reference to Spain—strongly objected to endorsement, not least because of the up-front recognition of losses. The member state representatives suggested and debated several ways forward, including approaching the IASB to make further changes, perhaps with the help of EFRAG, not to endorse at all, or to endorse an amended version of the interpretation by a 'carve-in' which would introduce an alternative accounting treatment into IFRIC 12.[262] Both the Commission and EFRAG cautioned against amendments. Some member states were not enthusiastic supporters of IFRIC 12, but warned against the consequences of non-endorsement for the ongoing processes of convergence and acceptance of IFRSs.[263] The process was delayed even further when, in November 2007, the Commission announced that it first had to undertake an effects study, in line with a resolution recently passed by the European Parliament (see Section 9.6). If the Commission had hoped that this would persuade the ARC to endorse, it was to be disappointed, because, even following the effects study, some member states continued to argue that more consultation was needed. It was only in November 2008, perhaps because it reached the point of exhaustion, and perhaps because the financial crisis had brought about a different sense of priorities, that the ARC voted in favour of endorsement, with one vote against and one abstention. Before the vote, the EU changed the

---

[261] 'Interpretation Endorsed—By a Whisker', *World Accounting Report*, February 2007, 4.

[262] This suggestion was already mooted by the Instituto de Contabilidad y Auditoría de Cuentas (ICAC), the Spanish accounting and auditing regulatory body, and by several Spanish toll-road operators in their comment letters on EFRAG's draft endorsement advice, accessible at <http://www.efrag.org>.

[263] Summary records of ARC meetings of 27 February, 16 March, 6 June, and 1 October 2007, <http://ec.europa.eu/internal_market/accounting>.

proposed mandatory application of the endorsed version from financial years starting after 31 December 2008 to financial years starting after the publication of the endorsed version, which would not occur until several months into 2009. This implied that many companies would not be required to follow the interpretation until their 2010 financial statements, creating a two-year gap with the effective date of the interpretation as issued by IFRIC. The Commission expressed the view that, in the interim, all companies, whether complying voluntarily with the interpretation or not, could claim compliance with 'IFRS as endorsed by the EU'.[264] The delay of more than two years in endorsing IFRIC 12 set a new record for the EU's endorsement process and drew renewed attention to the risk that jurisdictional standard-by-standard adoption procedures for IFRSs posed to the ideal of a single global set of standards.

12.12.3 IFRIC 15: Agreements for the Construction of Real Estate

IFRIC 15, which became one of the more controversial interpretations, was approved in July 2008. In response to a stream of inquiries, in March 2006 the issue was placed before IFRIC of how real estate sales where the agreement to sell residential units is reached prior to construction (known as 'off plan') should be treated in the light of the apparently conflicting guidance in IAS 11 *Construction Contracts* and IAS 18 *Revenue*. Some real estate developers recorded revenue only once they delivered the completed unit to the buyer (IAS 18), while others recorded revenue according to the stage of completion of the construction of a multi-unit building (IAS 11).

IFRIC's initial view was that most such contracts probably fell within IAS 18, as buyers did not play a major role in the conception and design of the construction. On 5 July 2007, the Board approved an IFRIC exposure draft, D21 'Real Estate Sales'. According to the Board's press release, the exposure draft proposed 'that revenue should be recorded as construction progresses only if the developer is providing construction *services*, rather than selling *goods* (completed real estate units)'.[265] The exposure draft suggested that the features indicating that the seller is providing construction services are typically not present in the 'off plan' sales agreements in many countries.

After receiving fifty-one letters of comment, IFRIC redeliberated the issue. In the end, the Board unanimously approved IFRIC 15 *Agreements for the Construction of Real Estate* on 3 July 2008 for annual periods beginning on or after 1 January 2009.[266] The interpretation was to be applied retrospectively, which, David Tweedie observed, some developers would like because they could report the revenue twice.[267] The final interpretation stipulated that entities undertaking the construction of real estate where the buyers have a significant ability to

---

[264] Summary record of ARC meeting of 6 November 2008, <http://ec.europa.eu/internal_market/accounting>.

[265] 'IFRIC Publishes Proposed Guidance on Real Estate Sales', IASB press release dated 5 July 2007.

[266] 'IFRIC Issues Clarification on Agreements for the Construction of Real Estate', IASB press release dated 3 July 2008.

[267] *IStaR*, June 2008, 30.

influence the final design should be accounted for under IAS 11 by the percentage-of-completion method. Where, alternatively, buyers have only a limited ability, or no ability, to influence the final design, the entities must defer the recognition of revenue, under IAS 18, until the delivery of the units to the buyers. The practical effect of this interpretation was, for many entities that were using the percentage-of-completion method, to postpone revenue recognition until handing over the completed unit to the buyers.[268]

Especially in Asia and South America, real estate developers have protested against IFRIC 15. Standard setters in a number of countries in those regions have either refused to implement the standard or have adopted it with accompanying guidance making it easier to use the percentage-of-completion method.

---

[268] See, for instance, Lau Chee Kwong, 'Does IFRIC 15 Matter? The Decision Usefulness of Accelerated Revenue and Earnings Recognition', *Asian Academy of Management Journal of Accounting and Finance*, 9/2 (2013), 49–74.

13

The IASB Survives the Financial Crisis

13.1 A SLOW BUILD-UP OF PRESSURE

The collapse of Lehman Brothers in September 2008 turned what had, until then, been a serious but manageable 'credit crunch' or 'credit crisis' into a violent financial storm, bringing 'business as usual' to an end for enterprises and governments around the world. The IASB, too, was shaken to its foundations when the financial crisis hit in full force. Yet the storm had been building for a long time, and it must be considered whether the IASB had been sufficiently watchful to batten down the hatches.

Worries about a US housing bubble and related imbalances in the markets for mortgages and structured products based on mortgages were increasingly voiced from early 2007 onwards.[1] Starting in July 2007, it became evident that various financial markets were rapidly drying up, as a loss of confidence spread widely through the international financial system. At the meeting of the IASC Foundation trustees on 2–3 July 2007, trustee Mohandas Pai called on the Board to 'identify developments in financial markets to which the IASB may need to respond', but this may have come just too early for the Board to discern clearly what it was that it had to respond to.[2] The next few months provided more clarity. In October 2007, responding to calls from the G7 finance ministers and central bank governors, the Financial Stability Forum (FSF) set up a high-level working group to analyse the situation and report, by April 2008, on recommended actions. This was of direct relevance to the IASB, given that the FSF provided the IASB with its main point of contact with the world of senior financial policy makers. Trustees' Chairman Paul Volcker had clearly been well-placed to introduce the IASB into this world, but so was Sir Andrew Crockett, the FSF's first chairman, who served as one of the first trustees of the IASC Foundation. David Tweedie, in his capacity of IASB chairman, had been attending the FSF's biannual meetings since March 2002.[3] Hence, Tweedie could report to the trustees in

---

[1] For a review of events related to the origins of the financial crisis see, among others, Markus K. Brunnermeier, 'Deciphering the Liquidity and Credit Crunch 2007–2008', *Journal of Economic Perspectives*, 23/1 (Winter 2009), 77–100.

[2] IASCF meeting of 2–3 July 2007, minute B. Agenda paper 2 for that meeting, containing David Tweedie's report on the IASB's activities, does not indicate that the Board at that stage was already responding to developments in financial markets.

[3] On the FSF/FSB's involvement with the IASB before and during the financial crisis, see Gerald A. Edwards, 'FSB Transparency Initiatives', *Financial Stability Journal* (Banco de España), 22 (May 2012), 55–73 <http://www.bde.es>.

November 2007 that the IASB was already working, under the aegis of the FSF, with regulators and the audit firms to develop policies for valuing investments in illiquid markets. He also noted that the crisis, as it was called by then, gave increasing relevance to the Board's ongoing projects on derecognition, consolidation, and special-purpose entities, but that these projects were not otherwise affected by the crisis. Noting the appearance of articles in the press that questioned the role of fair value in the current market problems, Tweedie asserted that 'our standards have held up well in the crisis'.[4] Some of the Board's activities to which Tweedie referred resulted in a paper on applying the fair value provisions of IFRSs in illiquid markets, published in December 2007 by the Global Public Policy Committee of the six largest international audit firms.[5] The paper indicated that some IASB Board members and staff had provided comments, suggesting that the IASB's role had been rather passive. In their paper, the audit firms explained the IASB's standards as they were, without breaking new ground. While the paper acknowledged, in line with IFRSs, that fair value was not by definition identical to observed market prices, the tenor of the paper was clearly that market prices could not lightly be ignored when determining fair values.

Around the turn of the year from 2007 to 2008, it would not have been apparent to the outside world that there was any sense of urgency at the IASB with respect to the credit crisis. At this time, discussions of the IASB's agenda were dominated by attempts to accelerate the completion of the projects in the Memorandum of Understanding (MoU) with the US Financial Accounting Standards Board (FASB) (see Chapter 12).[6] A notable public utterance by the IASB on accounting for financial instruments was the discussion paper, 'Reducing Complexity in Reporting Financial Instruments', published in March 2008. In this paper, which had been some time in the making and which was clearly not intended to deal with the immediate problems of applying IAS 39 *Financial Instruments: Recognition and Measurement*, the IASB had its eyes on the distant prospect of developing a completely new standard (see Section 12.9). Given that purpose, it may be understandable that neither the discussion paper nor the accompanying press release mentioned current events, but one assumes that many constituents could not but think of the credit crisis and the problem of illiquid markets when they read how the paper explored the way towards fair value measurement as a general requirement for all types of financial instruments.[7]

---

[4] IASCF trustees meeting of 31 October–1 November 2007, agenda paper 6A, 4. The articles referred to may have included Shyam Sunder and Stella Fearnley, 'Pursuit of Convergence is Coming at too High a Cost', *Financial Times* (London edition), 23 August 2007, 19. See also 'Fair Comment or Unfair Criticism?', *Accountancy Age*, 30 August 2007.

[5] 'Determining Fair Value of Financial Instruments under IFRS in Current Market Conditions' (Global Public Policy Committee, 13 December 2007) <http://www.iasplus.com>.

[6] The credit crisis does not appear as a consideration in a major staff paper on the Board's agenda discussed in December 2007 (AP 12/2007 paper 5). The credit crisis was not, apparently, discussed at the trustees' meeting of 29–30 January 2008, nor was the subject mentioned in Tweedie's activity report to the trustees (agenda paper 3 for the January 2008 meeting).

[7] 'IASB Publishes a Discussion Paper as First Step towards Reducing Complexity in Reporting Financial Instruments', IASB press release dated 19 March 2008 <http://www.iasb.org> accessed through web.archive.

If there was an outward appearance of serenity, this was not quite the internal reality. The IASB was aware that pressure was building for it to act. Such awareness came not only through the participation of IASB Board member John Smith in the FSF working group mentioned above.[8] It came also, for instance, from US Senator Jack Reed (Democrat of Rhode Island), who had written to the IASB in February for information about the steps which the Board was taking towards improved standards, in particular with respect to off-balance sheet risks.[9] In early April, the FSF delivered its report. Among the wide-ranging recommendations were two action points for the IASB. In particular, the IASB was expected to accelerate its ongoing project on consolidation and special-purpose entities in the light of the notorious off-balance sheet treatment of many sub-prime mortgages. The IASB was also to enhance its guidance on valuing financial instruments in inactive markets with the aid of an expert advisory group. The report was quickly endorsed by the G7 finance ministers and central bank governors, who included the two action points for the IASB among the 'immediate priorities for implementation within the next 100 days'.[10] One hundred days implied sometime in July, which, taken literally, would have been a tough and perhaps unrealistic demand of the IASB. However, within the IASB this was understood to mean 'that the process should be underway within 100 days', rather than that it should be finished in that timeframe.[11] But whatever the G7's intended meaning was, the introduction of the 'hundred days' target clearly brought a risk that the Board would be perceived as moving too slowly. Although they did not refer to the hundred days again, in June the finance ministers, meeting then in the G8 configuration, called on the IASB to 'accelerate its reviews' of the two issues.[12]

The project on consolidation and special-purpose entities had figured in the IASB's agenda since 2002 and was included in the 2006 MoU. The Board had spent quite some time on it in 2005 and 2006, but not, it seems, during most of 2007. When it was again brought before the Board in November 2007, the plan was still to move to a discussion paper sometime in the spring of 2008.[13] The FSF report called on the IASB to skip the discussion paper and to move directly to an exposure draft, a suggestion which the Board duly accepted during its April meeting. From the IASB's point of view, this may have had less to do with the credit crunch than with planning the acceleration of the IASB–FASB convergence work programme. Tweedie recalled making it known to the FSF that a request to

---

[8] IASCF trustees meeting of 17–18 March 2008, minute 7.

[9] Letter from Jack Reed to David Tweedie, dated 12 February 2008, IASB archive, 'covered correspondence' file.

[10] 'Statement of G-7 Finance Ministers and Central Bank Governors', Washington DC, 11 April 2008 <http://www.fin.gc.ca>. Between them, the website of the Department of Finance, Canada, and the website of the US Treasury (<http://www.treasury.gov>) contain most of the statements and press releases originating with the G7/G8 and the G20 referred to in this chapter. Extensive collections of documents can also be found at the websites <http://g8.utoronto.ca> and <http://g20.utoronto.ca>.

[11] Email from David Tweedie to Gerrit Zalm and Philip Laskawy dated 5 August 2008, IASB archive, unmarked file.

[12] 'Statement of the G-8 Finance Ministers Meeting', Osaka, 14 June 2008 <http://www.fin.gc.ca>.

[13] At this meeting, the topic was discussed in an educational session. The staff paper (AP 11/2007 paper 8A) did refer to 'recent financial instability', but rather to advise the Board not to follow the press in jumping to the conclusion that more consolidation is always better.

drop the discussion paper would be welcome to him.[14] Even so, the IASB was not even close to delivering a standard on consolidation and special-purpose entities by July 2008, as contemplated by the G7 finance ministers' 100-day deadline. As it turned out, the Board managed to publish an exposure draft in December 2008, which was already something of an achievement in itself (for further discussion of this project, see Section 16.3).

On the second issue of applying fair value to assets traded in illiquid, or inactive, markets, the IASB announced plans for the formation of an Expert Advisory Panel in May, and the panel held its first of several meetings in June. The panel brought together some twenty representatives from the financial industry, prudential regulators, and the major audit firms. The FASB attended as an observer.[15] The IASB published the panel's final report on 31 October 2008.[16] In line with the paper on the same topic produced by the large audit firms almost a year earlier, the report provided guidance on the application of existing IFRSs. This time, the point was made more forcefully that market prices cannot always automatically be accepted as indicators of fair value, and may require significant adjustments in situations of inactive markets.

13.2 EMERGENCE OF THE RECLASSIFICATION ISSUE

In the first half of 2008 the emphasis in the debate over accounting standards in relation to the financial crisis began to shift, away from the question of how fair value should be determined in illiquid markets, to the question of whether the use of fair value should be suspended altogether. This was related to the question of whether accounting standards, in particular fair value measurement, could have a pro-cyclical effect. Could it be that fair value was a cause of the financial crisis, if it encouraged the formation of speculative bubbles in good times? Could it be that fair value was exacerbating the current crisis, if the widespread reporting of unrealized losses eroded market confidence, or if companies had to react to deteriorating balance sheet positions and breaches of ratio covenants by forced sales of assets?[17] Questions such as these had been raised earlier in the decade, in particular when the European Central Bank objected to the introduction of a fair value option in IAS 39 (see Chapter 6). However, in the rather benign economic climate of 2003 or 2004, these questions were of a somewhat academic nature. Now, in the middle of an increasingly severe credit crisis, they acquired immediate urgency. From around March 2008 onwards, following another quarter of reported losses, calls for some kind of suspension of the use of fair value could be heard with

---

[14] Interview with David Tweedie, 5 June 2013.

[15] 'IASB Forms an Expert Advisory Panel', announcement dated 3 June 2008 <http://www.ifrs.org>, accessed through web.archive.

[16] 'Measuring and Disclosing the Fair Value of Financial Instruments in Markets that Are no Longer Active' (IASB, October 2008).

[17] For a review of the issues, see Christian Laux and Christian Leuz. 'The Crisis of Fair-value Accounting: Making Sense of the Recent Debate', *Accounting, Organizations and Society*, 34/6–7 (2009), 826–34.

increasing insistence from the banking and insurance industry, in the United States as well as in Europe.[18] In response, defenders of fair value argued that this would amount to 'shooting the messenger'. According to this view, reporting fair value losses might be painful, but it would allow a more accurate diagnosis of the problems and a more speedy resolution of the crisis than papering over losses in the hope that they might prove to be temporary.[19]

Those who wished to limit or suspend fair value accounting considered various approaches. One proposal, floated by three members of the European Financial Reporting Advisory Group (EFRAG), was to base fair value on twelve-month moving averages of market prices rather than on current prices, in order to smooth out some of the wilder fluctuations.[20] This did not seem to attract widespread support. It prompted EFRAG Chairman Stig Enevoldsen to emphasize that this was not an EFRAG point of view, and that, in his opinion, 'attempts to find instant solutions could do more harm than good'.[21]

A possible instant solution that did attract support was to allow a reclassification of certain financial assets. Under IAS 39, the measurement of financial assets depended on their classification. In particular, assets 'held for trading' were assigned to the category known as 'fair value through profit or loss'. Debt securities classified as 'held to maturity' were measured at amortized cost. If debt securities could be reclassified from the 'fair value through profit or loss' category to the 'held to maturity' category, recognized losses would be limited to cases of impairment for which, so it could be argued, a temporary drop of prices in illiquid markets was not a sufficient indicator. However, paragraph 50 of IAS 39 contained a categorical prohibition of reclassifications into, or out of, the 'fair value through profit or loss' category.

The idea of allowing a degree of flexibility in reclassifying assets out of the fair value category was suggested to both the IASB and the FASB by the Institute of International Finance in April 2008, and the two boards considered the idea, among other suggestions on fair value in illiquid markets, in their joint meeting on 21–2 April 2008. However, there was no sign that the boards were at all inclined to move in that direction.[22] The idea did not go away, though, and the IASB continued to be reminded of it, for instance in meetings of the Expert Advisory Panel on fair value in illiquid markets, which began meeting in June.[23] Awareness

---

[18] See for instance the overview in 'An Unforgiving Eye: Bankers Cry Foul over Fair Value Rules', *Financial Times*, 14 March 2008, 15.

[19] See for instance Jeff Diermeier (CFA Institute), 'Fair Value Is Not to Blame for Turmoil', *Financial Times*, 20 March 2008, 10; 'Investors Smack Banks for Fair-value Attack', news item posted 30 May 2008 <http://www.cfo.com>.

[20] Carsten Zielke, Michael Starkie, and Thomas Seeberg, 'Reporting Move Could Break the Write-down Spiral', *Financial Times*, 3 April 2008, 27.

[21] Stig Enevoldsen and Göran Tidström, 'No View Formed on the Credit Crunch', *Financial Times*, 14 April 2008, 8.

[22] Letter from Charles Dallara (IIF) to Robert Herz and David Tweedie, dated 18 April 2008. Tweedie's reply to Dallara dated 21 May 2008 did not address the reclassification issue specifically, but merely reiterated the text on the April joint board meeting as published in *IASB Update* of April 2008. Both letters in IASB archive, 'covered correspondence' file. *World Accounting Report* (May 2008, 3) reported that 'Neither Board had been impressed by the arguments' for reclassification.

[23] Interview with Sophie Baranger, 17 February 2010. See also letter from Klaus-Peter Müller and Manfred Weber (Bundesverband deutscher Banken) to David Tweedie, dated 21 May 2008, essentially

began to spread that US generally accepted accounting principles (US GAAP), under paragraph 15 of FAS 115 *Accounting for Certain Investments in Debt and Equity Securities*, already allowed in principle for reclassifications in or out of the 'held for trading' category, even though this was qualified by the comment that 'Given the nature of a trading security, transfers into or from the trading category . . . should be rare'. The difference between IFRSs and US GAAP on this point was noted in a report on the crisis by the Committee of European Banking Supervisors (CEBS), published in June 2008.[24] The banking supervisors had been alerted to this by the banking industry, but were not inclined to press forcefully for change. Rather, they made the general comment that 'CEBS members generally have little concern regarding reclassification rules applicable in IAS 39' (page 12). Their concerns mainly regarded lack of guidance in certain complex situations, as well as inconsistent application. Although they asked the IASB to analyse and eliminate the reclassification difference and other noted differences with US GAAP in the interest of maintaining the quality of IFRSs, they equally reminded the banks to be 'mindful of the strict classification rules that exist in IAS 39' (page 13).

With hindsight, it is not difficult to see that the perception that something meaningful could be done to address the crisis by a simple change in an arcane accounting rule, combined with the idea that banks in the European Union (EU) might not have access to the same degree of accounting flexibility as their American competitors, could easily become irresistible to European politicians. After all, the notion that European companies should not be placed at a competitive disadvantage by the use of IFRSs was already mentioned in the original IAS Regulation of 2002 (Recital 15, see also Section 4.1). However, it took some time before the boiling point was reached. In July, EU Commissioner Charlie McCreevy, in a speech on the Commission's response to the financial turmoil, referred favourably to the CEBS report. He rejected calls to temporarily disregard fair value accounting, because 'intervention right now risks adding to the confusion and [creating] even greater distrust in companies' accounts'. Although he did mention the need for coordination with international partners to ensure a 'level playing field' in accounting, he did so as part of his main message that 'possible changes to the accounting standards should be assessed carefully and ought to be subject to proper consultation'.[25]

The idea of a 'level playing field' also emerged in July 2008 in a draft report on the financial crisis by former International Federation of Accountants (IFAC) President René Ricol, written at the request of French President Nicolas Sarkozy with a view to France's assumption of the rotating presidency of the EU on 1 July. However, David Tweedie was still not inclined to embrace the notion of a change in the reclassification rules. Commenting on Ricol's draft to the chairman of the trustees, he wrote: 'we have asked for an interpretation of the American Standards to see what *exactly* they do allow. At a time when market commentators are calling

---

repeating the points of Dallara's (IIF) letter of 18 April, cited above, IASB archive, 'covered correspondence' file.

[24] 'Report on Issues Regarding the Valuation of Complex and Illiquid Financial Instruments' (Committee of European Banking Supervisors, 18 June 2008) <http://www.eba.europa.eu>.

[25] Charlie McCreevy, 'The Financial Turmoil—The Role of the EU-Commission', speech dated 3 July 2008 <http://europa.eu/rapid>.

for more transparency I can imagine a retreat to a more historical basis would be met with howls of anguish from investors and would probably damage the banks who wished to implement such a policy.'[26] In general, in holding off requests to allow reclassification out of the 'held for trading' category, Board and staff felt supported by comments they received from users that such reclassifications should not be permitted.[27] Another reason for doing so was provided by the fact-finding about the precise meaning of US GAAP. As Tweedie wrote to the trustees: 'Based on discussions with US accounting firms, some US regulators and FASB staff, it is the [IASB] staff's understanding that "rare" [as used in FAS 115], in practice, means never.'[28] From that perspective, one can see why reclassification was not on the Board's agenda for its 15–19 September 2008 meeting. Instead, its activities with respect to fair value in response to the crisis remained focused on improving disclosure and providing better guidance in determining fair values in illiquid markets. To accelerate this, the Board added a short-term project to its agenda in September to improve the fair value disclosures under IFRS 7. It intended to draw on the Expert Advisory Panel, whose draft report was published on 16 September.

13.3 THE IASB's CRISIS OF 13 OCTOBER 2008

Lehman Brothers' declaration of Chapter 11 bankruptcy on 15 September changed all previous calculations and plans with respect to the financial crisis. It also quickly eroded any restraint there may have been in calling for immediate changes to accounting standards. Ricol had submitted his final report to President Sarkozy on 2 September.[29] Creating a level playing field vis-à-vis the United States with respect to reclassification figured prominently among the recommendations thus placed on the desk of an important European head of state—and, indeed, the holder of the rotating EU Presidency at the time—determined to act decisively in the face of the financial crisis. Moreover, it was not a secret that leading figures in the French financial sector did not look kindly on the IASB. Events began to unfold rapidly.

In the margins of a hurriedly conducted FSF meeting on Monday 29 September—following a weekend when the UK government nationalized Bradford & Bingley, a mortgage bank; the German government pumped billions of euros of emergency loans into Hypo Real Estate, another major mortgage bank; and the Dutch, Belgian, and Luxembourg governments came to the rescue of the collapsing bancassurance group Fortis—David Tweedie first learned that

---

[26] Untitled copy of final draft of Ricol report, English version, dated 23 July 2008, part C, page 6; email from David Tweedie to Gerrit Zalm and Philip Laskawy dated 5 August 2008, IASB archive, unmarked file.

[27] AP 10/2008 paper 12, paragraph 4.   [28] AP 10/2008 paper 12, paragraph 14.

[29] *Rapport sur la crise financière: Mission confiée par le Président de la République dans le contexte de la Présidence française de l'Union européenne 2008, September 2008* <http://www.ladocumentation francaise.fr>. See in particular pages 12, 18, and 61.

the European Commission was preparing to move on accounting standards.[30] A similar message was conveyed to the Accounting Regulatory Committee (ARC) meeting two days later, on Wednesday 1 October. Reclassification was among the issues being considered, but the Commission emphasized that there was as yet no specific proposal on how to take matters forward.[31] On the next day, the IASB held an extra one-day Board meeting, dominated by crisis-related activities. This was followed by a press release on 3 October, announcing, among other steps already taken or to be taken, that:

> The IASB will assess immediately any inconsistencies in how IAS 39 and US GAAP practice address the issue of reclassifications and whether to eliminate any differences. The IASB will discuss these matters and will decide its position as part of its public meeting during the week of 13–17 October. At that meeting the IASB will assess the suitability of adopting the US GAAP approach and whether adapting IFRSs will provide relevant information to users of financial statements.[32]

After several months of holding out on reclassification, the Board had accepted that it could no longer afford not to take up the issue. It would turn out, however, that by then it was too late to do something without significant damage to the Board's reputation.

More pressure was applied on the next day, Saturday 4 October, when President Sarkozy convened a summit meeting of the European G8 members. At the end of the meeting, he announced, as one of five decisions, that the heads of state and government demanded a change in accounting rules regarding reclassification. The European Commission and the accounting standard setters, according to the President, would have to work urgently in order to settle the matter before the end of the month, a deadline evidently intended to allow application in the interim reports for the third quarter.[33] This call was repeated by the EU's finance ministers, meeting as the ECOFIN Council on Tuesday 7 October. From ECOFIN's language, it was apparent that, while the IASB might still find a role to play if it acted quickly, the ministers were counting on the Commission to move alone, if necessary.[34]

During the week of 6 to 10 October, both the IASB and the European Commission worked hard to prepare themselves for the IASB's Board meeting on Monday 13 October, when the key decisions would have to be taken. The IASB's staff worked on an exposure draft of changes to IAS 39 and IFRS 7 that attempted to replicate US GAAP as much as possible. This meant not merely allowing

---

[30] Interview with David Tweedie, 15 October 2009.

[31] Summary record of ARC meeting of 1 October 2008, minute VI.2 <http://ec.europa.eu/internal_market/accounting>.

[32] 'IASB Announces Next Steps in Response to Credit Crisis', IASB press release 3 October 2008.

[33] 'Situation financière internationale: sommet des membres européens du G8, conference de presse conjointe, propos du Président de la République, M. Nicolas Sarkozy', Paris, 4 October 2008 <http://www.ambafrance-uk.org>.

[34] 'The Council urged the Commission to amend without delay certain accounting rules applicable to banks' (page 2), and 'We also consider that the issue of asset reclassification must be resolved quickly. To this end, we urge the IASB and the FASB to work together on this issue and welcome the readiness of the Commission to bring forward appropriate measures as soon as possible' (page 8). Council of the European Union press release, 2894th Council Meeting, Economic and Financial Affairs, Luxembourg, 7 October 2008 <http://www.consilium.europa.eu>.

reclassifications, but also imposing certain restrictions and required disclosures of the effects of reclassification, both in the period in which the reclassification was made and in subsequent periods.[35] In doing so, the staff again ran into an old problem of convergence: simply copying some sentences from another set of GAAP does not necessarily create a level playing field, because such sentences tend to interact with other provisions in the standard. Some time was spent, therefore, in considering whether the changes might not place US banks, rather than European banks, at a disadvantage because of differences in the impairment rules of US GAAP and IFRSs to be applied following reclassification.[36]

At the same time, the European Commission's staff was working on a plan B to be implemented if the IASB would fail to adopt its measure in time, and in a manner to muster the necessary political support for European endorsement. Compared to the niceties which the IASB's staff was considering, the Commission could only forge a very blunt instrument, even had it been willing to do otherwise. The Commission's staff prepared a draft Regulation that would, just as in 2004, carve out a few words from IAS 39, apparently because even the financial crisis would not provide the Commission with the authority for adding new wording to the IASB's standards when endorsing these for use in Europe.[37] If implemented, this would have allowed almost unrestricted reclassification out of the 'fair value through profit or loss' category, with limited disclosure. In its draft preamble, the Commission did insist that the relevant disclosure provisions of IFRS 7 would have to be applied. However, it could not fine-tune these provisions to match the proposed changes in IAS 39, and therefore no disclosure in subsequent periods could be called for.

As it happened, a regular meeting of the IASC Foundation trustees was scheduled in Beijing on Thursday and Friday 9–10 October, towards the end of a tense week in which share prices fell by 20 per cent or more in many markets. It would seem that David Tweedie, as he flew to Beijing, was aware at least in general terms of the Commission's preparations, but he assumed that the Commission preferred the Board to act, and would grant it some time to do so, as long as ECOFIN's target of measures in place by the end of the month was met. Tweedie's plan then was to have the Board approve an exposure draft the next Monday, based on the staff's preparatory work, and to issue it with a very short comment period of perhaps a week. The IASB's *Due Process Handbook* prescribed a normal 120-day exposure period which, for 'exceptionally urgent' matters, could be shortened to 'no less than 30 days' (paragraph 98). Tweedie therefore wished to obtain the trustees' agreement to breach even this lower limit.

However, during the Beijing meeting, one of the trustees, Samuel DiPiazza, received a message on his Blackberry about a speech given the previous day,

---

[35] AP 10/2008 paper 12A. As far as can be ascertained, this document was available by 8 October. Paragraph 7 suggests that an earlier version, or parts of it, were circulated for comment to 'US commentators' before that date.

[36] AP 10/2008 paper 12 A, paragraph 7.

[37] 'Draft Commission Regulation Amending Regulation (EC) No 1725/2003 Adopting Certain International Accounting Standards in Accordance with Regulation (EC) No 1606/2002 of the European Parliament and the Council as Regards International Accounting Standard (IAS)', COM-AC_DRC(2008)D002268-01 <http://www.europarl.europa.eu>.

Wednesday 8 October, by Commissioner McCreevy before the European Parliament in which he said he was ready to follow up on ECOFIN's demand with legislative measures on the reclassification of bank assets with immediate effect. McCreevy made no reference to any action still expected from the IASB on this point, and he solicited the Parliament's cooperation to obtain speedy approval of the measure about to be put forward by the Commission.[38] This news caused consternation in Beijing. Although a telephone call to the Commission appeared to bring out that the Board might still have a respite of some days, it was clear to all now that the Commission's actions were becoming unpredictable. Even if the Board were to issue an exposure draft next Monday—and Tweedie still needed to get his Board to go along—the Commission might still impose its carve-out in the middle of the exposure period, however short. The question before the trustees was whether they should step back and let the Commission carry out its threat, or to authorize the Board to suspend its due process altogether, in order to issue an amendment to IAS 39 on the spot. Even though several of the trustees were persuaded that a relaxation of the reclassification rules was an urgently needed measure, the manner of bringing it about was clearly one of choosing the lesser of two evils: letting the European Commission create an ugly hole in the standards, with all of the accompanying risks for the prospects of a single global standard, or having the Board breach its own rules with a gun pointed to its collective head. After initially giving thought to a seven-day due process, in the end the trustees decided unanimously on a motion from Bryan Nicholson to give the Board permission to suspend due process altogether, given the urgency of the matter.[39]

Following the trustees' meeting, when Tweedie was being driven on Friday evening to the Beijing Airport, he again telephoned the European Commission. He learned that there were twelve days to go to the next meeting of the ARC, which would endorse either a change made by the IASB or the Commission's carve-out. But by the next morning, the IASB learned that the ARC was to meet as soon as Wednesday 15 October. President Sarkozy was convening an unprecedented emergency summit of the Eurozone heads of state and government in Paris on Sunday 12 October. One of the conclusions being prepared for the meeting was that the reclassification rules would be relaxed within the week, rather than by the end of the month as demanded earlier. It was all or nothing: on Monday, the Board would have to decide either to use the discretion given by the trustees to the full, or not to use it at all.

The weekend—a dramatic weekend of crisis meetings both in Washington and Paris, resulting in promises of vast rescue funds in desperate attempts to stop the collapse of the banking system—was spent finessing the IASB's exposure draft, now to become a standard immediately, and drumming up support in advance for what would be a very awkward decision. Consultations with the US Securities and

---

[38] The trustee's reference was to McCreevy's speech to the European Parliament of 8 October, SPEECH/08/513 <http://europa.eu/rapid>. McCreevy said, 'we are urgently putting changes to our accounting rules to ensure Banks in the EU can avail [themselves] of the same flexibility that is offered to banks in the US. Namely this will provide the option for individual banks if they want to move assets from their trading books to their banking books. This is a comitology measure which I hope the Parliament will be able to give its agreement as a matter of urgency.'

[39] IASCF trustees meeting of 9–10 October 2008, minute 1.

Exchange Commission (SEC) were particularly intense. Tweedie learned that the SEC would view the carve-out envisaged by the Commission, with hardly any restrictions on reclassification and little disclosure, as the end of international standards, as the United States would not take IFRSs under such conditions.[40] A month later, Tweedie was quoted in the press as saying: 'If the EU had done another carve-out then the US would have said this is impossible. That would have crippled the whole global process.'[41] But Tweedie was aware that the plug would not just be pulled by the United States: if the IASB would fail to modify its standard in response to the clamouring from Europe, political pressure for changes to the European accounting regime would become irresistible, and the IASB would in all likelihood lose its franchise to set accounting standards for the EU. To do nothing could mean that the entire programme to set international accounting standards would come down in flames. During this weekend, Tweedie seriously considered resigning.[42] One reason why he did not was that he shared the SEC's point of view that an injudicious European carve-out without adequate disclosure requirements did not just pose a threat to international standards; it would also carry the risk that the consequent lack of transparency might cause even further losses of confidence in markets already in the grip of panic. As Tweedie was reported to have told the Board members during their meeting on Monday, 'it was better if the changes were made by accountants rather than politicians'.[43] But there was also his fighting determination not to give up on international standards, as he later said: 'We want to make sure we win this project.'[44]

Sunday evening saw a press conference in Paris in which President Sarkozy announced as a fact that by next Thursday a revised accounting rule would have removed the 'handicap' of European companies compared to their US counterparts. The IASB was not mentioned, as the European Commission's Plan B had apparently become Plan A. Sarkozy thanked Commission President José Manuel Barroso for his 'essential role' in preparing this measure, and Barroso reciprocated by saying that this was a subject to which he 'attributed the greatest importance'. Sarkozy made a point of mentioning the support of British Prime Minister Gordon Brown for the accounting measure.[45] It must have been bitter for Tweedie to learn that he received no support from that quarter.

---

[40] Interview with David Tweedie, 15 October 2009.

[41] David Jetuah, 'Tweedie Nearly Quit after Fair Value Change', *Accountancy Age*, 11 November 2008.

[42] See Tweedie's statement in testimony on 11 November 2008 to the UK House of Commons' Treasury Committee, 'Banking crisis' (London: The Stationery Office Limited, 1 April 2009), volume I, 33.

[43] Quoted in Jennifer Hughes, 'Fair Value Accounting Rules Eased', *Financial Times*, 14 October 2008, 18.

[44] Tweedie's testimony before the UK House of Commons' Treasury Committee, 'Banking Crisis', volume I, 33.

[45] 'Conférence de presse conjointe de MM. Nicolas Sarkozy, Président de la République, José Manuel Barroso, Président de la Commission européenne, Jean-Claude Juncker, Président de l'Eurogroupe, et Jean-Claude Trichet, Président de la Banque central européenne, sur la réaction concertée de l'Union européenne face à la crise financière internationale, à Paris le 12 octobre 2008' <http://www.vie-publique.fr/discours/>.

On Monday morning, 13 October, the Board met first in a closed administrative session where the politics of the issue were aired. Mary Barth, Warren McGregor, Tatsumi Yamada, and Zhang Wei-Guo had been present at the trustees' meeting in Beijing, but the other Board members needed to be brought up to date about the fast-moving events and the trustees' decision to suspend due process. It was apparently concluded that action by the IASB might yet forestall the Commission's carve-out. Tweedie's arguments about the impact of a carve-out on the prospects of IFRS adoption in the United States and the importance of ensuring sufficient disclosure were persuasive. Apart from these rational considerations, one interviewed Board member observed that the EU's original carve-outs had left the Board 'a bit traumatized', and thus more inclined to avoid another one.

In the Board's open meeting which followed, it briefly discussed the proposed amendments to IAS 39 and IFRS 7. Next to the complete suspension of due process, there was another bitter pill for the Board to swallow. For the banks to escape recognizing, in their figures for the third quarter, any of the significant reduction in the market value of their debt securities following the collapse of Lehman would require backdating the effective date of the amendments to 1 July 2008. Some banks even argued for a 1 January 2008 effective date, citing the argument that FAS 115 had already allowed US banks to avoid losses in the first quarter.[46] The IASB staff tried hard to obtain evidence from the US of any reclassifications during the first quarter, but did not find anything of significance. The Board therefore refused a backdating to 1 January but had to accept an effective date of 1 July. If it did not do so, it might as well have spared itself the trouble of making any changes at all: a standard allowing prospective application only would not have had the least chance of endorsement for use in the EU. The Board did, however, make sure that an entity's decision to reclassify back to 1 July had to be made prior to 1 November 2008, after which date reclassifications could no longer be made retroactively. Following some discussion and well before the morning was over, the Board approved the amendments by a vote of eleven to two, with Jim Leisenring and John Smith dissenting. The *Financial Times* reporter, who observed the meeting, wrote that 'IASB members made their distaste clear but accepted this was an extreme situation'.[47]

The European Commission had carefully oiled up its normally cumbersome endorsement machinery, so that the amendments could be accepted for use in the EU with lightning speed. On Tuesday, EFRAG, suspending its own due process, recommended the amendments for adoption by the European Commission. On Wednesday, the Standards Advice Review Group, charged with overseeing EFRAG's due process, reported that EFRAG's opinion was 'balanced and objective'. That same day, the ARC, composed of delegates from the twenty-seven EU member states, unanimously affirmed its support. Commission President Barroso then asked the President of the European Parliament whether the Parliament would be willing to express its opinion expeditiously, and then to consider its normal three-month objection period as having expired.[48] This allowed the Commission

---

[46] AP10/2008 paper 12 'follow up', paragraph 12.

[47] Hughes, 'Fair Value Accounting Rules Eased', 18.

[48] Letter from José Manuel Barroso to Hans-Gert Pöttering, dated 15 October 2008, EP-PE_LTA (2008)010601. The Parliament's response appears to have been given effectively by Pervenche Berès,

to publish the amendment in the EU's *Official Journal* on Thursday 16 October, effective immediately.

The preceding events had been watched with misgivings by securities regulators. On 21 October, the Technical Committee of the International Organization of Securities Commissions (IOSCO), chaired at the time by SEC Chairman Christopher Cox, issued a statement on accounting standards in the context of the crisis, saying: 'We strongly support accounting standards that afford investors transparency, maintain market integrity, facilitate capital formation and are consistent with financial stability.'[49] It was not difficult to see this as a counterweight to the many voices advocating at that time a different order of priorities, with financial stability coming first and transparency last.

13.4 PROBLEMS IN ADOPTING THE AMENDMENT IN SELECTED OTHER JURISDICTIONS

While the European Commission was obviously well prepared for a swift endorsement of the reclassification amendment, other jurisdictions that had committed themselves to adopt IFRSs were taken by surprise by the amendment, made by the Board without any due process, and had to cope with it as best as they could.

As in the EU, the laws in Australia and New Zealand stipulate that the Parliament shall be conceded a specified time period in which to consider whether to reject a new accounting standard, prior to its becoming effective, but only in New Zealand did this obstacle preclude entities from reclassifying their securities with a backdating to 1 July.

In Australia, the Australian Accounting Standards Board (AASB) makes law when it approves a new accounting standard, although either house of Parliament can later disallow it. The Parliament is given fifteen *sitting* days for considering the disallowance of a new standard, and, if it were in recess at the time, fifteen sitting days could consume weeks or months. If a motion is made during that period to disallow, the Parliament is then given a further fifteen sitting days in which to vote on the motion. The AASB moved with dispatch to approve the IASB's 13 October amendments by 22 October, but by that time the Senate had only twelve sitting days left for the remainder of the year. The AASB issued a media release informing people that, even though the amending standard was not yet out, it was coming out, and, if they wished to take advantage of its retroactive application, they had to make the reclassification decision now.[50]

---

chairman of the Parliament's Committee on Economic and Monetary Affairs, see letter from Pervenche Berès to Hans-Gert Pöttering, dated 15 October 2008, EP-PE_LTD(2008)317454. Both letters are at <http://www.europarl.europa.eu>.

[49] 'IOSCO Technical Committee Statement on Accounting Standards Development and Enforcement', IOSCO press release 017/2008, 21 October 2008 <http://www.iosco.org>.

[50] AASB 2008–10 *Amendments to Australian Accounting Standards—Reclassification of Financial Assets* (AASB, 22 October 2008). Interview with Angus Thomson, 22 March 2012, and communication from Angus Thomson, dated 2 April 2013. The Senate did raise some questions about the amendment,

In New Zealand, a new accounting standard does not become effective until after allowing the Parliament twenty-eight calendar days in which to object. Hence, it was not possible for the New Zealand standard setter to adopt the IASB's October amendments in sufficient time for them to become effective prior to 1 November 2008, much to the disappointment, one supposes, of the banks and the prudential regulator. Directly as a result of this inability to implement the IASB's October amendments with immediate effect, the Accounting Standards Review Board (ASRB) wrote to the Minister of Commerce to seek an amendment to the Financial Reporting Act 1993 to enable entities to adopt a new accounting standard as soon as the board had it recorded in the *New Zealand Gazette*. In May 2011, under newly passed legislation, the standard setter, now the External Reporting Board, could in its discretion authorize entities to begin using a new accounting standard 'legally' as soon as it was gazetted, even if the standard were subsequently to be disallowed by the Parliament.[51]

In Hong Kong, the Hong Kong Institute of Certified Public Accountants (HKICPA) followed a strategy of adopting all new or amended IFRSs word for word as Hong Kong Financial Reporting Standards. It also shadowed the IASB's due process, issuing both exposure drafts and final standards nearly simultaneously with the IASB. It was therefore confronted with the question whether it should also follow the IASB in suspending due process, and decided to do so. The amendment was published on 15 October, effective as of 1 July.[52]

13.5 APPLICATION OF THE RECLASSIFICATION OPTION

In the light of the high drama surrounding the reclassification amendment, its application in practice appeared a little mundane. The quarterly reporting season started off with a high-profile announcement by Deutsche Bank that its net earnings for the third quarter, generally expected to be negative, amounted to a profit of €414 million, not least because of avoiding an €845 million write-down of reclassified assets. The bank made no secret of its use of the new accounting rules, and it attracted widespread comment, some of it critical.[53] After an initial jump, the bank's share price continued on a volatile decline until well into November. Whether this was because of a stigma attaching to what might look like dubious accounting, or simply because of continuing bad news for the banking sector as a whole, is hard to say. What is clear is that the financial press was able to comment on the effect of reclassifications on banks' reported profits only because of the

and a motion to disallow was tabled to provide more time for the government to respond. See <http://www.openaustralia.org/senate/?id=2009-02-12.12.1>.

[51] Communication from Kevin Simpkins to the authors, dated 2 April 2013.

[52] 'Hong Kong Adopts International Accounting Amendments for Reclassification of Financial Instruments: "Breathing room" for Banks in Financial Crisis', HKICPA press release dated 15 October 2008 <http://www.hkicpa.org.hk>.

[53] 'Profit, Not Loss, Thanks to Fair Value Tweak', news item posted 30 October 2008 <http://www.cfo.com>; 'Deutsche Bank', comment posted 30 October 2008 <http://www.ft.com>; 'Deutsche Bank Kicks off Funny Accounting Season; Commentary: Watering Down Accounting Rules Will Hurt in the End', comment posted 30 October 2008 <http://www.marketwatch.com>.

disclosure requirements attached by the IASB to the reclassification amendment. What is also clear is that not all banks followed Deutsche Bank in applying the new rules. Several banks were surprised by the amendment, about which the European Commission apparently had not consulted widely. Some did not believe that this was the most pressing accounting issue arising out of the crisis, but nonetheless availed themselves of the unexpected opportunity to improve their financial position as presented in the financial statements. According to one survey, only 37 per cent of 158 EU banks had reclassified assets under the revised IAS 39 by December 2008.[54] More significantly, those that did reclassify did not all do so in their results for the third quarter. The three largest French banks, for instance, Société Générale, BNP Paribas, and Crédit Agricole, began to apply the amendment only in the fourth quarter, as of 1 October 2008. This might well raise doubts whether the suspension of the IASB's due process and the backdating of the effective date of the amendment to 1 July really had been necessary to ward off a financial meltdown. A reported average increase by half a percentage point of tier 1 capital across European banks that did apply the amendment in 2008 was not negligible, given generally low capital ratios, but it did not bear out fears, in the midst of the October panic, that banks' equity would have been wiped out across the board without the amendment.[55]

13.6 DEVISING A RESPONSE TO FINANCIAL AND POLITICAL TURMOIL

Making the reclassification amendments did not get the IASB into calmer waters. The financial crisis remained at the top of the world's political agenda, and the idea that accounting was somehow part of the problem had not gone away. The reclassification issue had briefly become the focal point, but there were other points where the IASB was pressed for action. Some of these, notably off-balance sheet vehicles and the practical problems of determining fair values in the absence of active markets, had already been recognized during the 'credit crunch' phase of the crisis, as discussed above. As the crisis worsened, impairment rules were receiving increasing scrutiny, and it began to be noted that, because of the so-called 'incurred loss model' on which both IFRSs and US GAAP were based, overstatement of financial assets carried at amortized cost might be a bigger problem than any understatement of assets measured at fair value referenced to prices in illiquid markets (see also Section 13.8). In addition, the fact that some banks were reporting gains on the falling fair value of some of their own liabilities was drawing adverse comment. The IASB had to find its way through a welter of issues, and it had to coordinate any actions closely with the FASB because everyone was by now fully aware of the problem of regulatory arbitrage, by which one board would be played off against the other in case of any differences.

---

[54] Peter Fiechter, 'Reclassification of Financial Assets under IAS 39: Impact on European Banks' Financial Statements', *Accounting in Europe*, 8/1 (2011), 49–76, Table 2. Out of Fiechter's broader sample of 219 EU and non-EU banks, 35 per cent made use of the new rules.

[55] Fiechter, 'Reclassification of Financial Assets under IAS 39', 63 and Table 4.

The two boards had to minimize the risk of political intervention based on the argument of a 'level playing field'. This risk was apparent on both sides of the Atlantic. Both the IASB and the FASB were under pressure to make short-term changes. Responding to increasing calls for a suspension of fair value accounting after the Lehman collapse, the SEC and the FASB had issued a joint press release providing additional guidance on fair value measurement, reiterated shortly afterwards in an FASB staff position on 10 October. In both cases, the IASB followed with press releases asserting that its standards, as well as the guidance just being completed by its Expert Advisory Panel, were consistent with the emergency guidance on fair value measurement issued by the SEC and the FASB.[56] But the FASB's steps did not satisfy the banking industry. On the fateful Monday 13 October, the American Bankers Association had written to SEC Chairman Christopher Cox calling on the SEC to override the FASB's recently issued guidance on fair value, citing among others the draft declaration of the Eurozone summit held the day before.[57]

The European Commission issued a statement on Wednesday 15 October in which it declared that it would at short notice convene a meeting of all 'stakeholders' to discuss other possible issues in accounting standards, and that it would 'propose further amendments to IAS 39 and IFRS 7, by all legal means if necessary, by the end of October'.[58] The meeting was held on 21 October and was followed by a letter from the Commission to the IASB, dated 27 October, and referred to colloquially at the IASB as the 'four demands' letter, because it listed four specific matters which the Commission expected to be addressed before the end of the year, if not earlier.[59] The letter was not well received at the IASB, partly because it again implied the use of shorter comment periods than the normal due process requirements, and partly because it was believed that the letter did not properly reflect views expressed during the Commission's stakeholder meeting that no hurried changes should be made.[60] In addition, one assumes that the Board simply had no stomach for some of the requested changes, such as allowing

---

[56] See 'SEC Office of the Chief Accountant and FASB Staff Clarifications on Fair Value Accounting', SEC press release 2008–234, dated 30 September 2008 <http://www.sec.gov>, followed by 'IASB Staff Position on SEC-FASB Clarification on Fair Value Accounting', IASB press release dated 2 October 2008; and FASB Staff Position FSP 157-3 'Determining the Fair Value of a Financial Asset when the Market for that Asset is Not Active', 10 October 2008, followed by 'IASB Provides Update on Applying Fair Value in Inactive Markets', IASB press release dated 14 October 2008.

[57] Letter from Edward L. Yingling to Christopher Cox, dated 13 October 2008 <http://www.aba.com>.

[58] 'Commission Declaration', dated 15 October 2005 <http://ec.europa.eu/internal_market/accounting>.

[59] Letter from Jörgen Holmquist to David Tweedie, dated 27 October 2008 <http://ec.europa.eu/internal_market/accounting>.

[60] IASCF trustees meeting of 15–16 January 2009, minute 3. The issues raised in the Commission's letter would have been aired by at least some of the participants in the stakeholder meeting. While, for example, the letter from the European Banking Federation (EBF) to the European Commission prior to the stakeholder meeting had listed approximately the same issues as the European Commission in its letter to the IASB, other participants such as the Corporate Reporting Users Forum (CRUF) and the Confederation of British Industry (CBI) had argued against hasty changes in the standards, and certainly against unilateral changes made by the Commission. The EBF had emphasized the importance of coordination with the FASB, an aspect absent from the Commission's letter to the IASB. See EBF, CRUF, and CBI letters to Jeroen Hooijer, all dated 17 October 2008, at <http://circabc.europa.eu> under public consultations, accounting, '2008-10-21 IAS39 Stakeholder's Meeting'.

reclassification of assets accounted for under the fair value option. The Board had deliberately excluded this from its October 2013 amendments because it had no counterpart in US GAAP.

By the time the Commission's letter came in, however, the political scene was already shifting, and not necessarily to the IASB's disadvantage. A week before, it had been announced that a special summit of the Leaders of the Group of Twenty (G20) would be held in Washington on 15 November, to review the global financial architecture. This meant that accounting standards would be discussed in a new political setting with which the IASB so far had no experience. While this made the outcome unpredictable, a G20 summit offered as good an opportunity as any to make a pitch for a global accounting solution, and to prevent the IASB and the FASB being played off against each other.

One of the first cards played by the IASB and the FASB therefore was the announcement, on 16 October, that they planned to form a joint global advisory group 'to ensure that reporting issues arising from the global economic crisis are considered in an internationally co-ordinated manner'.[61] The advisory group would become known as the Financial Crisis Advisory Group (FCAG), discussed in Section 13.11. A few days later, at their regular joint meeting of 20–21 October, in Norwalk, the two boards confirmed their commitment to a global approach, and announced plans for a series of three joint roundtables in November and December in London, Norwalk, and Tokyo, to solicit views on the proper response by accounting standard setters to the financial crisis.[62] These would provide input for co-ordinated projects, both at the FASB and at the IASB, to develop a 'long-term solution' to financial instruments. Indeed, each board duly decided in November or December to add such a project to its active agenda. While this could be presented in terms of the boards' response to the financial crisis, an agenda decision was due at any rate in order to follow up on the joint March 2008 discussion paper on 'Reducing Complexity in Reporting Financial Instruments'. For the moment, however, the timing of this general financial instruments project remained vague, and the immediate focus of the response to the financial crisis, at least at the IASB, remained on a series of ongoing separate projects on topics such as derecognition, consolidation, disclosures, and fair value measurement.[63]

13.7 G20 SUMMIT IN WASHINGTON IN NOVEMBER 2008

That the G20 would take up accounting was apparent when, following a summit of G20 finance ministers and central bank governors held in São Paulo on 8–9 November, the communiqué stated their agreement that 'financial institutions

---

[61] 'IASB and FASB Create Advisory Group to Review Reporting Issues Related to Credit Crisis', IASB–FASB press release dated 16 October 2008.

[62] 'IASB and FASB Commit to a Global Approach to Enhance Market Confidence', IASB–FASB press release dated 20 October 2008.

[63] See draft work plan as of 31 December 2008, AP 1/2009 paper 9A, showing 'financial instruments: replacement of existing standards' with timing 'to be determined' and the first half of 2009 planned for the work of the FCAG.

should have common accounting standards and clear internal incentives to promote stability'.[64] Also, in a press briefing on 12 November, an assistant to President George W. Bush and a high-level US Treasury official said that the movement towards global accounting standards might be discussed by the leaders.[65] In 2003, a letter by the French President Jacques Chirac on IAS 39 had been seen as an unprecedented instance of accounting standards attracting the attention of a head of state (see Chapter 6). Now, it seemed, it was taken for granted that heads of state and government would sit down to discuss the merits of fair value accounting and similar issues.

Fully expecting that the G20 would address accounting as an issue in the financial crisis, the International Accounting Standards Committee Foundation (IASCF) trustees, IOSCO, and the Financial Accounting Foundation (FAF, which oversees the FASB) all wrote letters to President Bush, the host of the summit, setting out their views. The letter from the IASC Foundation trustees, which was signed by Chairman Gerrit Zalm, said, 'The Trustees believe that any steps taken outside the well-established and supported standard-setting process to amend fair value accounting would further undermine already scarce confidence in financial markets'.[66] While Zalm's letter emphasized the significance of joint action planned with the FASB, it was careful to explain the desired global response to the crisis in terms of the 'more than 100 countries' in which IFRSs were already used. The letter emphasized the IASB as an actor independent of the FASB, for instance in its consultations with the FSF and the Basel Committee. The IOSCO letter was accompanied by four statements, one of which dealt with accounting standards and governance, in which it said that it 'strongly supports' IFRSs as developed by the IASB. As Zalm had done in his letter, the IOSCO letter drew attention to the emergent Monitoring Board.[67] Compared to the IASC Foundation trustees' letter, the FAF's letter, signed by Chairman Robert E. Denham, was more consistent in portraying the desired response to the crisis as a joint IASB–FASB effort. The letter referred to the European Commission's request to the IASB for further changes by the end of the year, and said, 'We are very concerned about recent efforts in the United States and abroad that contemplate political solutions to perceived flaws in certain accounting standards. . . . We encourage the G-20 to support independent standard setting via a robust due process free from political interference.'[68]

---

[64] 'Communiqué, Meeting of Ministers and Governors, São Paulo, Brazil, 8–9 November 2008' <http://www.u20.utoronto.ca>.

[65] 'Press Briefing by Daniel Price and David McCormick on the Summit on Financial Markets and the World Economy', 12 November 2008 <http://georgewbush-whitehouse.archives.gov>. On 13 November, President Bush, said in a speech, 'One vital principle of reform is that our nations must make our financial markets more transparent. For example, we should consider improving accounting rules for securities, so that investors around the world can understand the true value of the assets they purchase.' 'President Bush Discusses Financial Markets and World Economy', 13 November 2008 <http://georgewbush-whitehouse.archives.gov>.

[66] Letter from Gerrit Zalm to George W. Bush, dated 11 November 2008 <http://www.ifrs.org>.

[67] Letter from Jane Diplock, Christopher Cox, and Guillermo Larrain to Mario Draghi, Guido Mantega, and Henrique Meirelles, dated 12 November 2008 <http://www.iosco.org>.

[68] Letter from Robert E. Denham to George W. Bush, dated 13 November 2008 <http://www.accountingfoundation.org>.

Following the G20 summit on 14–15 November, the world leaders stated in their communiqué a number of 'common principles for the reform of financial markets'.[69] They tasked their finance ministers to implement these principles by formulating recommendations in a number of specific areas, which included 'reviewing and aligning global accounting standards, particularly for complex securities in times of stress'. The accompanying 'action plan' enumerated the following measures under the heading of 'Strengthening Transparency and Accountability':

Immediate actions by March 31, 2009

- The key global accounting standards bodies should work to enhance guidance for valuation of securities, also taking into account the valuation of complex, illiquid products, especially during times of stress.

- Accounting standard setters should significantly advance their work to address weaknesses in accounting and disclosure standards for off-balance sheet vehicles.

- Regulators and accounting standard setters should enhance the required disclosure of complex financial instruments by firms to market participants.

- With a view toward promoting financial stability, the governance of the international accounting standard setting body should be further enhanced, including by undertaking a review of its membership, in particular in order to ensure transparency, accountability, and an appropriate relationship between this independent body and the relevant authorities. . . .

Medium-term actions

- The key global accounting standards bodies should work intensively toward the objective of creating a single high-quality global standard.

- Regulators, supervisors, and accounting standard setters, as appropriate, should work with each other and the private sector on an ongoing basis to ensure consistent application and enforcement of high-quality accounting standards.

Under the heading of 'reinforcing international cooperation', they recommended as a 'medium term action' that: 'Authorities, drawing especially on the work of regulators, should collect information on areas where convergence in regulatory practices such as accounting standards, auditing, and deposit insurance is making progress, is in need of accelerated progress, or where there may be potential for progress.' This extensive treatment of accounting vividly demonstrated how the subject had vaulted to the attention of world heads of government during the crisis.

In substance, the outcome must have been quite satisfactory to the IASB. The stated objective of 'a single high-quality global standard', even if read as referring to financial instruments only, was a significant political endorsement of the fundamental purpose of, first, the IASC and then the IASB. Calls for action on valuation of securities and off-balance sheet vehicles were broadly in line with the Board's agenda, and the 31 March 2009 deadline for immediate action presumably could be used to put aside the European Commission's request for changes by

---

[69] 'Declaration: Summit on Financial Markets and the World Economy', 15 November 2008 <http://www.treasury.gov>.

the end of the year. Enhancement of the governance of the IASB was already in progress as part of the second review of the IASC Foundation's Constitution, and, as discussed in Chapter 14, the trustees would formally agree to the creation of a Monitoring Board in January 2009.

It was recognized at the IASB that the favourable outcome was due mainly to the long-standing support of the US Treasury for the IASB and for the independence of accounting standard setting generally. The Treasury's view was of great significance, given the pivotal role of the US government in organizing the summit and preparing the communiqués. The US Treasury, supported by the UK Treasury, had opposed the use of much more interventionist language which had been called for by the French government, and the IASC Foundation had done its part to provide the two governments with all of the briefing they required.[70]

13.8 LOAN IMPAIRMENT, DYNAMIC PROVISIONING, AND THE ROLE OF THE PRUDENTIAL REGULATORS

From the start of the credit crisis, the focus of attention as far as accounting was concerned had mainly been on assets measured at fair value, and the determination of fair value in illiquid markets. By early 2009 attention was also being drawn to assets, in particular loans, measured on the more traditional basis of amortized cost. Under IAS 39, the recognition of credit losses on such assets was based on a so-called 'incurred loss' approach, which meant that losses could be recognized only on the basis of evidence of events subsequent to initial recognition with an impact on expected cash flows from the asset. This meant later recognition of credit losses compared to alternative 'expected loss' approaches, under which, for instance, an allowance for likely future losses on a portfolio of loans might already be formed before evidence of specific 'loss events' would come to light. That IAS 39 was based on an incurred loss approach was no secret, and it had been a matter of some discussion in the IASB's project to improve IAS 39 in 2001–03.[71] Banking supervisors generally preferred more conservative approaches to loss recognition based on expected losses, but the IASB, as well as the FASB before it, prodded by the SEC, were anxious to reduce the opportunities for earnings management associated with expected loss models. At the time, this issue was overshadowed by the row over hedge accounting (see Chapter 6), and the matter was allowed to rest for the time being.

The financial crisis raised the question of whether the relatively low level of provisions allowed by the incurred loss model of IFRSs had contributed to the current distress of the banking system. The Banco de España in particular drew attention to its system of 'dynamic provisioning' which it had, since 2000, imposed on Spanish banks and which it had maintained after the introduction of IFRSs in 2005. At the time, in 2008 and early 2009, the Bank felt confident to

---

[70] Interviews with Bryan Nicholson, 7 July 2011; Thomas Seidenstein, 7 July 2011; and David Tweedie, 21 December 2010.

[71] Kees Camfferman, 'The Emergence of the Incurred Loss Model in IAS 39', working paper, Vrije Universiteit Amsterdam, 2013, available at SSRN.

argue that this was one of the reasons why Spanish banks had not suffered so much from the financial crisis.[72] Loan loss provisioning became a topic at the FSF, and in the first months of 2009 it became clear at the IASB that the G20 at its next summit was likely to add loan loss provisioning to the list of topics it wished to see addressed quickly.[73] Apart from the technicalities of incurred loss versus expected loss models, the more fundamental questions began to be discussed whether accounting standard setters should consider the impact of their standards on financial stability, and whether prudential supervisors should be accorded a greater role in accounting standard setting, next to securities regulators.[74] That idea was not welcomed at the IASB, but the IASB's senior staff—Wayne Upton and Peter Clark—could see the merits of an expected loss approach, and on their advice the IASB and FASB, at their March 2009 joint meeting, agreed that loan loss provisioning should be included in the joint financial instruments project.[75]

13.9 THE FASB ALSO FEELS THE STING OF POLITICAL PRESSURE

As indicated above, the year 2009 opened with both the IASB and the FASB committed to undertake a significant project on the classification and measurement of financial instruments, apart from a number of other crisis-related projects. Although the stated intention was to work together, the nature, scope, and timing of the projects—sometimes referred to as a single joint project—remained fluid, not least because each board individually was still trying to discover the most appropriate response to its own turbulent environment.[76] The boards' joint meeting of 23–4 March 2009 was supposed to bring more clarity, and the staffs had prepared an analysis of the various issues. The debate was to be about general principles, such as the status of fair value as the generally most appropriate measurement basis, about amortized cost and possible other alternatives to fair

---

[72] See for instance Miguel Fernández Ordóñez, 'Speech by the Governor: 2008 International Monetary Conference–Central Bankers Panel', Barcelona, 3 June 2008; speech by Miguel Fernández Ordóñez, 'Procyclicality in the Banking Activity', Conference on Pro-cyclicality and the Role of Financial Regulation, Banco de España and Financial Stability Institute, Barcelona, 4 May 2009, both at <http://www.bde.es>.

[73] AP 3/2009 paper 7, paragraph 2.

[74] See for instance 'Dynamic Provisioning for Financial Instruments', FEE Policy Statement, March 2009 <http://www.iasplus.com>.

[75] See AP 3/2009 paper 7 (joint meeting), paragraphs 11 and 18.

[76] Compare AP 3/2009 paper 6 (joint meeting), which claims that the boards decided in November and December 2008 to add a 'joint project' to their agendas, with AP 11/2008 paper 10 which casts the plan in terms of distinct although obviously co-ordinated projects of IASB and FASB. The FASB work plan as of 1 January 2009 (<http://www.fasb.org>) labels the plan as 'improvements to recognition and measurement'. The IASB work plan as of 25 January 2009 characterizes the project as 'financial instruments: replacement of existing standards'. In Herz's discussion of the FASB's response to the financial crisis in late 2008 and early 2009, the IASB does not appear to play a major role. See Robert Herz, *Accounting Changes: Chronicles of Convergence, Crisis, and Complexity in Financial Reporting* (AICPA, 2013), 159–74.

value, as well as about criteria for determining the applicability of each measurement basis. In addition, the paper marked out further issues for subsequent discussion, including different treatments of gains and losses, a possible fair value option, and reclassifications subsequent to initial classification.[77] However, plans for an orderly discussion of these issues were upset by another round of political intervention, in some ways reminiscent of the events of October 2008.

During the first months of 2009, pressure was again building in the United States for some kind of intervention in fair value accounting. On 30 December 2008, the SEC published a major study, undertaken by its staff, on mark-to-market accounting, that is, fair value accounting in the wording normally used at the IASB. The SEC had been instructed by Congress, concerned over the role of accounting in the crisis, to perform the study under an instruction in the Emergency Economic Stabilization Act of 2008.[78] While the SEC staff generally did not see evidence for a significant role of fair value in, for instance, bank failures, and while they advised against a suspension of fair value accounting, they did point out a number of aspects where the requirements should be improved or refined. Two weeks later, a report by the Group of Thirty, a private-sector group of high-level experts on international economic and monetary affairs, published a report proposing a framework for financial stability which empathically recognized the potential for pro-cyclical effects on accounting, and called, with respect to fair value accounting, for a better balance between the information needs of investors and the business model of regulated financial institutions, including a greater role for prudential regulators in reviewing and co-ordinating accounting standards.[79] The working group which had produced the report was composed of a high proportion of former central bankers. It was chaired by Paul Volcker, former chairman of the IASC Foundation, with Tommaso Padoa-Schioppa, his successor as IASC Foundation chairman, serving as one of the two vicechairmen. Andrew Crockett, former general manager of the Bank for International Settlements and also a former IASC Foundation trustee, was another member.

The two reports appearing in quick succession helped to put the spotlight again on the issue of fair value accounting and provided support for the view that 'something had to be done' about fair value. But the banking industry, which had pushed continually for some kind of relief from fair value accounting since the start of the credit crisis, did not need any encouragement. In February, it organized a 'fair value coalition' with the support of the US Chamber of Commerce. Under this umbrella, individual banks as well as the American Bankers Association assiduously lobbied members of Congress, and backed up their efforts with substantial contributions to selected politicians' campaign funds.[80] Briefed in this manner, a subcommittee of the US House of Representatives organized a hearing

---

[77] AP 3/2009 paper 6 (joint meeting).

[78] 'Report and Recommendations Pursuant to Section 133 of the Emergency Economic Stabilization Act of 2008: Study on Mark-to-market Accounting', US SEC, Office of the Chief Accountant, 30 December 2008 <http://www.sec.gov>.

[79] *Financial Reform: A Framework for Financial Stability* (Washington: Group of 30, 2009).

[80] Susan Pulliam and Tom McGinty, 'USA Inc.: Congress Helped Banks Defang Key Rule', *The Wall Street Journal* (Eastern edition), 3 June 2009. See also the joint letter from the American Bankers Association and other industry groups to Paul Kanjorski and Scott Garrett, dated 11 March 2009, cited in Herz, *Accounting Changes*, 169–71.

on fair value accounting, in which FASB chairman Bob Herz and the SEC's acting chief accountant, James L. (Jim) Kroeker, appeared on 12 March, that is, two weeks before the planned joint meeting of the IASB and the FASB.[81] While Herz explained at the hearing how the FASB, since February, was already busy addressing the issues identified by the SEC staff study, and also how it was working with the IASB in a joint project aimed at comprehensive improvement, simplification, and convergence, the subcommittee chairman, Paul E. Kanjorski (Democrat from Pennsylvania), and several members made it clear in no uncertain terms that what they wanted now was speed. Although some subcommittee members, notably Alan Grayson (Democrat, Florida) criticized the demands for adjusting the accounting rules as a 'shoot-the-messenger' response, Herz was faced with an explicit threat of legislative action, and he was forced to commit the FASB to issue the guidance it was already working on within three weeks. During the hearings, Kroeker made no strong attempt to shield the FASB from this political pressure, and even suggested that the SEC might act if the FASB did not deliver on time.[82]

Within a week, on 17 March, the FASB published exposure drafts of three so-called staff positions. Apart from enhancing disclosure requirements, the proposals were intended to nudge reporting companies, and their auditors, away from using market prices in distressed markets as the basis for fair value measurement and towards reliance on model-based ('level 3') valuations. Another proposal was to split, under certain conditions, declines in the values of financial assets into losses because of credit deterioration, to be reported in profit or loss, and into losses related to other market factors, to be reported in other comprehensive income. Whereas the fair value proposal might perhaps be interpreted as a correction of an overly rigid interpretation in practice of FAS 157 *Fair Value Measurement*, rather than a relaxation of these rules, the proposed modification of impairment losses was a manifest change. Taken together, the proposals were either widely hailed as providing much-needed relief, or deplored as ill-advised patchwork under pressure, threatening the integrity of the standard-setting process.[83] After two weeks of dealing with a massive volume of comment letters, the FASB approved final versions of the staff positions in line with the proposals on 2 April, and allowed their application in determining the results for the first quarter of 2009.[84]

---

[81] 'Mark-to-market Accounting: Practices and Implications: Hearing before the Subcommittee on Capital Markets, Insurance, and Government Sponsored Enterprises of the Committee on Financial Services, US House of Representatives, 111th Congress, First Session', 12 March 2009, Serial 111–12 (Washington DC: US Government Printing Office, 2009).

[82] US House of Representatives, 'Mark-to-market Accounting', 30. See for this point also Herz, *Accounting Changes*, 173.

[83] See, for instance, 'FASB Bows: Fair Value to Get Overhaul', *American Banker*, 174/51 (17 March 2009), 1; 'A Fair Value Antidote is Rushed by FASB', news item posted 16 March 2009 <http://www.cfo.com>; 'FASB to Allow Companies More Leeway under Mark-to-Market', Dow Jones News Service, 16 March 2009; 'Investors: Stem the Anti-Fair Value Tide', news item posted 1 April 2009 <http://www.cfo.com>; 'Messenger, Shot', *The Economist* (US edition), 11 April 2009, 18.

[84] FASB Staff Position No. FAS 115–2 and FAS 124–2, 'Recognition and Presentation of Other-than-temporary Impairments', 9 July 2009; FASB Staff Position No. FAS 157–4, 'Determining Fair Value when the Volume and Level of Activity for the Asset or Liability Have Significantly Decreased and Identifying Transactions that Are Not Orderly', 9 July 2009.

13.10 PRESSURE ON THE IASB TO LEVEL
THE PLAYING FIELD

The IASB had to respond to the fast-paced events in the United States as well as it could. The timing of the FASB's activities was challenging, from the IASB's point of view. As indicated above, a joint meeting of the two boards took place on 23–4 March, in the middle of the exposure period of the FASB's staff positions. The FASB's final decision, on 2 April, coincided with the second G20 summit on financial markets and the world economy, in London, on 2 April. This was followed on 3–4 April by meetings of EU finance ministers and central bankers in Prague. Meanwhile, the IASC Foundation trustees met on 1–2 April, including the inaugural meeting of the Monitoring Board on 1 April. The number of near-simultaneous discussions of the IASB's response to the financial crisis in these pivotal few days made it difficult to keep track of the IASB's evolving plans.

As indicated above, by the start of the year, the IASB and the FASB were already considering a comprehensive replacement of their financial instruments standards, but the timing was still fluid. In January 2009, the IASB's work plan showed the timing as 'to be determined'. Following the joint meeting of the two boards in March 2009, their public statement declared that they had agreed to issue proposals 'in a matter of months, not years' to replace their respective standards with a common standard. Although no date was given, the idea was apparently to issue an exposure draft on classification and measurement, including the topic of loan loss provisioning, in the fourth quarter of 2009.[85] This was confirmed at the meeting of the IASC Foundation trustees on 1 April, when Tweedie reported plans for a 'complete rewrite' of IAS 39, including impairment rules, 'in conjunction with FASB over the next six months'. However, in a different part of the same meeting, Tweedie also raised concerns about the general timetable of convergence with the FASB, including financial instruments, and that the IASB might have to move unilaterally on some topics. In an apparent reference to the draft FASB staff positions, Bryan Nicholson observed that the trustees had to be prepared for further pressure from the banking industry to amend IAS 39. The trustees agreed that a piecemeal approach to the revision of the financial instruments standards was not desirable.[86] The latter point was emphasized in a press release issued by the trustees on 2 April, which meant that the trustees publicly took position against a quick copying of the FASB staff positions on the very day that these were approved.[87] The press release also referred to the plan for an exposure draft to replace IAS 39 within six months.

Nonetheless, the meeting of Eurozone finance ministers and central bankers the next day provided participants, including French Finance Minister Christine Lagarde, with a platform to call for urgent changes in the IASB's standards in response to the FASB's actions, for the sake of a level playing field. This call for

---

[85] 'IASB and FASB Announce Further Steps in Response to the Global Financial Crisis', IASB–FASB press release, 24 March 2009.

[86] IASCF trustees meeting of 1–2 April 2009, minute 3, minute 5.

[87] 'Trustees Express Support for Fundamental and Urgent Review of Financial Instruments Accounting, Conclude Inaugural Meeting with Monitoring Board', IASCF press release, 2 April 2009. See also 'IASB Rejects US Rule Changes', *Financial Times* (US edition), 3 April 2009, 13.

short-term action took up much of the finance ministers' final statement.[88] It may be noted that, by this stage, it would have been hard for even the closest students of accounting standards to assess accurately and dispassionately what the state of the playing field was following issue of the FASB staff positions on 2 April. In particular with respect to impairment, the view of the American Bankers Association was that, prior to April 2009, companies reporting on the basis of IFRSs had had the better deal, so that the modification introduced by the FASB staff positions was merely a form of catching up.[89] On the other hand, at the French Autorité des Marchés Financiers, by no means the IASB's strongest critic in France, it was seen as simply unfair that American banks could shift hundreds of millions of dollars in losses to other comprehensive income in the first quarter of 2009.[90]

Meanwhile, the G20 summit meeting in London had taken place on 2 April. In their communiqué issued following the summit, the G20 did not directly address the FASB staff positions, but accounting standards did again figure prominently. The G20 resolved 'to call on the accounting standard setters to work urgently with supervisors and regulators to improve standards on valuation and provisioning and achieve a single set of high-quality global accounting standards'.[91] The topic of provisioning had by then taken central stage, in addition to earlier concerns over valuation. In an accompanying 'Declaration on Strengthening the Financial System', the G20 said that they 'have agreed to strengthen international frameworks for prudential regulation . . . [and that] the FSB [Financial Stability Board], BCBS [Basel Committee on Banking Supervision] and CGFS [Committee on the Global Financial System], working with accounting standard setters, should take forward, with a deadline of end 2009, implementation of the recommendations published today to mitigate procyclicality, including a requirement for banks to build buffers of resources in good times that they can draw down when conditions deteriorate'.[92] Later in the Declaration the G20 declared their agreement that accounting standard setters should take action 'by the end of 2009' to:

> reduce the complexity of accounting standards for financial instruments; strengthen accounting recognition of loan-loss provisions by incorporating a broader range of credit information; improve accounting standards for provisioning, off-balance sheet exposures and valuation uncertainty; achieve clarity and consistency in the application of valuation standards internationally, working with supervisors; make significant progress towards a single set of high quality global accounting standards; and, within the framework of the independent accounting standard setting process, improve involvement of stakeholders, including prudential regulators and emerging markets, through the IASB's constitutional review.

This was a tall order indeed.

---

[88] 'Statement by the Informal Ecofin: Prague, 4 April 2009' <http://www.mfcr.cz>. See also 'Update: ECOFIN: EU Accounting Rules Should Be Like US—Italy Min', Dow Jones International News, 3 April 2009; 'French Fin Min: EU Accounting Rules Must Be Changed Urgently', Dow Jones International News, 4 April 2009.

[89] Interview with Donna Fisher and Michael Gullette, 29 June 2010.

[90] Interview with Sophie Baranger, 17 February 2010.

[91] 'The Global Plan for Recovery and Reform', 2 April 2009 <http://www.treasury.gov>.

[92] 'Declaration on Strengthening the Financial System', London, 2 April 2009 <http://www.treasury .gov>.

Following the flurry of meetings in early April, the IASB had to decide on its next steps. The Board was not keen to make a short-term adjustment in response to the FASB staff positions. In this, it was supported by the trustees, as indicated above, but also, as it appeared, by many of the IASB's constituents. Through its website, the IASB had issued a request for views on the draft FASB staff positions. The tenor of the reaction was that, with respect to fair value in illiquid markets, the FASB guidance was by and large in line with IFRS, especially when combined with the report of the IASB's own Expert Advisory Panel on the same subject, issued the previous October. Further changes could be made when the IASB completed its standard on fair value measurement, based on FAS 157.

With respect to impairment, the FASB staff positions clearly introduced a difference, as IAS 39 did not have a corresponding provision to hive off parts of losses on specific assets through other comprehensive income. Here the view, particularly from users, was that the IASB should not attempt to make piecemeal changes. Because of the interaction with other parts of the impairment rules, it was argued, limited changes were unlikely to result in a truly level playing field. Similar views were expressed in the Standards Advisory Council.[93] During its April meeting, therefore, the Board agreed unanimously not to make limited amendments in response to the FASB staff positions, and it continued on its course of developing a comprehensive exposure draft, including impairment, for publication later in the year, thus confirming the position taken in the trustees' press release of 1 April.[94]

Even so, the IASB did modify its plans in the next weeks. During the Board meeting of 19–21 May, Chairman Tweedie came up with a proposal to split the project: an exposure draft dealing with basic classification and measurement issues would be brought forward to July, to be followed by a final standard towards the end of the year. A separate exposure draft on impairment would follow later in the year. With a separate exposure draft on hedging, already envisaged, the replacement of IAS 39 would become a three-phased project resulting in a complete standard sometime in 2010. What was the reason for this change in planning, which was not mentioned in the agenda papers for the meeting? One report on the Board meeting suggests that Tweedie used the positive argument that the basic classification and measurement model on which the Board had by then more or less reached agreement (see Section 13.12 for details) would already remove many impairment issues existing under IAS 39.[95] Another report shows Tweedie using the negative reason that banks and other interested parties were only just beginning to think through the operational implications of alternative, 'expected loss' approaches to impairment, so that the impairment part of the project was not yet ready for an exposure draft.[96]

Yet a third reason, not incompatible with the first two, weighed heavily as well. Tweedie continued to feel the pressure from Europe to do something about levelling the playing field, following the FASB staff position on the treatment of

---

[93] For an analysis of comments, see AP 4/2009 papers 16, 16A, and 16B.

[94] *IStaR*, April 2009, 28.

[95] 'Financial Instruments: Recognition and Measurement', report on IASB Board meeting of 20 May 2009 <http://www.iasplus.com> accessed 26 June 2013.

[96] *IStaR*, May 2009, 35.

impairment losses. Following the IASB's Board meeting in April where the IASB 'ignored pleas from EU officials to loosen the rules', Christian Noyer, the Governor of the Banque de France, commented: 'What we can do is that Europe can very well reclaim its freedom.... It's not the IASB that makes the law in Europe. If we decide to take back control and write the accounting rules in the European directives ourselves without following the IASB, the issue would be resolved. So it's very simple.'[97]

At an informal ECOFIN meeting on 4–5 May, the view was expressed that, to bring matters forward, the IASB should be invited to the next ECOFIN meeting on 9 June.[98] Tweedie was warned in advance that he might be heading for a dangerous confrontation. Some of those present at the informal meeting of finance ministers and central bank governors in April had told him that unprecedentedly strong language had been used there against the IASB.[99] From the point of view of the European finance ministers, the IASB had failed to respond by the end of 2008 to the European Commission's 'four demands' letter (see Section 13.6). Although the IASB might initially have justified this by pointing to the G20's target of 31 March 2009, it had let that date pass as well, while the FASB was seen to take action. One can see that Tweedie might not wish to appear before the finance ministers with the announcement that there really would be no significant change during 2009 to accounting for financial instruments under IFRSs.

So when Tweedie did make his appearance before ECOFIN—together with Gerrit Zalm, the chairman of the trustees and a long-serving former Dutch finance minister—he announced boldly: 'the IASB will issue a final standard, available for use this year, that addresses issues related to impairment and the fair value option. This means that financial institutions in Europe and elsewhere will be able to use the new IFRS in 2009 financial statements.' Tweedie explained that 'the recent US FASB Staff Positions (FSPs) regarding fair value measurement and impairment caused the IASB to accelerate the timing of the approach announced on 1 April'.[100] The latter statement may have been true primarily in a political sense. As seen above, the substance of the staff positions had been known since the middle of March and the IASB did not initially see them as sufficient reasons for changing its planning.

The announcement was intended as a game-changing tactic, to break the cycle of pressure on the IASB and the FASB to follow each other's incremental changes.[101] Tweedie recalled that the announcement of the revised planning took the ECOFIN meeting by surprise, which would mean that news of the change in plans mentioned at the May Board meeting had not yet reached some of the

---

[97] 'EU Could Take back IASB Power—ECB's Noyer', news item posted 25 April 2009 <http://uk.reuters.com>. Noyer was also a member of the governing council of the ECB.

[98] 'Verslag Eurogroep en Ecofin raad van 4 en 5 mei', Tweede Kamer der Staten-Generaal, Vergaderjaar 2008–2009, 21501-07, No. 660. According to this source, the suggestion to invite the IASB was made by the Dutch finance minister.

[99] Interview with David Tweedie, 15 October 2009.

[100] 'Prepared Statement of Sir David Tweedie, Chairman of the International Accounting Standards Board, to the 2948th meeting of the COUNCIL OF THE EUROPEAN UNION (Economic and Financial Affairs): Luxembourg 9 June 2009', pages 1 and 4. <http://www.ifrs.org>.

[101] Communication from Thomas Seidenstein to the authors, dated 17 September 2013.

finance ministers.[102] Yet some must have been aware before their meeting, at least in general terms, that the IASB was planning to make changes applicable during 2009.[103] At any rate, the meeting did not descend into outright confrontation, and Tweedie's explanation of the revised work programme was said to have been appreciated by the Council.[104] For the moment, the IASB was given the benefit of the doubt: following the ECOFIN meeting, the French and German finance ministers, Christine Lagarde and Peer Steinbrück, wrote a joint letter to EU Commissioner McCreevy that they had noted the IASB's plans for a general reform of IAS 39. However, this did nothing to silence their demand for a levelling of the playing field vis-à-vis US GAAP by the end of the year, and they grimly added that: 'If the respective implementation will not take place, the European Union would need to ensure that the result is achieved in some other manner.' As to the content of the new standard, they expressed definite expectations with respect to provisioning for expected losses, a counter-cyclical role for accounting standards, less focus on short-term market valuation, and reclassification out of fair value. In forwarding the letter to the IASB, McCreevy wrote that he had resisted pressure to work on a 'standby measure', but that: 'To avoid this pressure mounting further I am sure I don't have to underline how important it is that the IASB is able to show good progress in good time.'[105]

13.11 THE FCAG SPEAKS OUT AGAINST POLITICAL PRESSURE

As mentioned in Section 13.6, the IASB and the FASB decided to create a high-level FCAG in October 2008. On 14 November 2008, the first day of the G20 summit in Washington, the two boards announced that Hans Hoogervorst, chairman of the Netherlands' Autoriteit Financiële Markten (Authority for the Financial Markets), and Harvey J. Goldschmid, a law professor and a former SEC commissioner, had agreed to serve as co-chairmen of the FCAG.[106] Its mission was 'to consider financial reporting issues arising from the global economic crisis', yet it would seem that Tweedie and Herz were not looking merely for technical advice, but also for a degree of cover from political pressure that the installation of a credible high-profile group might bring. If so, the idea may have recommended

---

[102] Interview with David Tweedie, 21 December 2010.

[103] This was true for the Dutch Ministry of Finance, as can be seen from its notes on the upcoming ECOFIN agenda sent to the Parliament on 29 May 2009, Tweede Kamer der Staten-Generaal, Vergaderjaar 2008–2009, 21501–07, No. 659.

[104] 'Verslag Eurogroep en Ecofin Raad van 8 en 9 juni', Tweede Kamer der Staten-Generaal, Vergaderjaar 2008–2009, 21501–07, No. 661.

[105] Letter from Christine Lagarde and Peer Steinbrück to Charlie McCreevy, dated 6 July 2009, copy attached to letter from Charlie McCreevy to David Tweedie, dated 7 July 2009, IASB archive, file 'covered correspondence'. For subsequent critical comment by Lagarde, see also 'Compte rendu: Commission des affaires européennes, Mercredi 14 octobre 2009', 5 <http://www.assemblee-nationale.fr>.

[106] 'Hans Hoogervorst and Harvey Goldschmid to Co-chair Advisory Group Considering Financial Reporting Issues Arising from Global Financial Crisis', IASB–FASB press release dated 14 November 2008.

itself in particular to Tweedie, whose Board did not have the benefit that the oversight of the SEC normally brought to the FASB.

On 30 December 2008, the boards announced the other sixteen members of the FCAG (see Table 13.1). In composing the membership, care had evidently been taken to bring together a group that would command respect for its financial expertise and its independent views, while at the same time ensuring that many had a good understanding of, and perhaps even sympathy for, the boards' approach to standard setting. Among those who, in various capacities, had shown themselves supportive of the IASB were: Don Nicolaisen, the former SEC chief accountant who had prepared the way for the lifting of the 20-F reconciliation; Tommaso Padoa-Schioppa, former IASCF chairman; and Jane Diplock, chairman of New Zealand's Securities Commission and the current chairman of IOSCO's executive committee, who had come out strongly in favour of the independence of the IASB in October 2008.[107] The FCAG also proved to be a fertile recruiting ground in that Hans Hoogervorst subsequently succeeded David Tweedie as Board chairman. Harvey Goldschmid and Wiseman Nkuhlu, of South Africa, became trustees of the IFRS Foundation in 2010 and 2013, respectively, while Michel Prada, a former French securities regulator whose involvement with the IASB went back to the restructuring of the IASC in the late 1990s, succeeded to the chairmanship of the trustees in January 2012.

The FCAG first met on 20 January 2009, and held a total of six meetings until July 2009, when it issued its report. During the spring of 2009, the FCAG provided an important platform where many of the technical issues through which the boards were attempting to chart their way forward were discussed in considerable detail.[108] But perhaps equally important was that the FCAG came out strongly in support of independent standard setting and against the political pressures both boards were facing during the first half of 2009. In its final report, the FCAG referred to the political pressure on the IASB and the FASB in October 2008 and March 2009, respectively, and observed that 'during the last several months, we have become increasingly concerned about the excessive pressure placed on the two Boards to make rapid, piecemeal, uncoordinated and prescribed changes to standards, outside of their normal due process procedures'.[109] As one of its main conclusions, the group affirmed that accounting standard setters 'must enjoy a high degree of independence from undue commercial and political pressures'. As a counterbalance it was noted that the standard setters must have a high degree of accountability to constituents, derived from appropriate due process and oversight in the public interest.[110] The latter observation encapsulated the essence of the IASB's first and second Constitution reviews, in which due process

---

[107] 'Commission Supports the Work of the International Accounting Standards Board', Securities Commission press release dated 23 October 2008 <http://www.seccom.govt.nz> accessed through web. archive, 5 July 2013; see also letter from Jane Diplock to David Tweedie, dated 23 October 2008, IASB archive, file 'Australia/New Zealand'.

[108] See Herz, *Accounting Changes*, 178, for a very positive appreciation of the FCAG's substantive contribution to the board's work.

[109] *Report of the Financial Crisis Advisory Group*, 28 July 2009, 15.

[110] *Report of the Financial Crisis Advisory Group*, 28 July 2009, 14.

Table 13.1. Members of the Financial Crisis Advisory Group (FCAG)

Harvey J. Goldschmid (co-chair)	former commissioner, US Securities and Exchange Commission	Hans Hoogervorst (co-chair)	AFM (the Netherlands Authority for the Financial Markets)
John Bogle	founder, Vanguard (United States)	Eugene A. Ludwig	former Comptroller of the Currency (United States)
E. Gerald Corrigan	Goldman Sachs; former president, New York Federal Reserve Bank (United States)	Yezdi Malegam	board member, Reserve Bank of India (India)
Fermín del Valle	former president, International Federation of Accountants (Argentina)	Klaus-Peter Müller	chairman of supervisory board, Commerzbank (Germany)
Jane Diplock	chairman, executive committee of International Organization of Securities Commissions (New Zealand)	Donald Nicolaisen	former chief accountant, US Securities and Exchange Commission (United States)
Raudline Etienne	chief investment officer, New York State Common Retirement Fund (United States)	Wiseman Nkuhlu	chairman of audit committee, AngloGold Ashanti; former economic advisor to the President of the Republic of South Africa (South Africa)
Stephen Haddrill	director general, Association of British Insurers (United Kingdom)	Tommaso Padoa-Schioppa	former Finance Minister (Italy)
Toru Hashimoto	former chairman, Deutsche Securities Limited (Japan)	Lucas Papademos	vice president, European Central Bank (Europe)
Nobuo Inaba	former executive director, Bank of Japan (Japan)	Michel Prada	former chairman, Autorité des Marchés Financiers (France)

improvement and the creation of the Monitoring Board, respectively, had been central issues.

13.12 IFRS 9 AND THE PARTING OF THE WAYS OF THE IASB AND THE FASB

The previous sections outlined the main steps by which the IASB decided in June 2009 to split its financial instruments project into three phases, with an exposure draft on classification and measurement published in July. It is time now to review the substance of the IASB's technical discussions as it prepared the standard that would become known as IFRS 9, and to consider how the IASB and the FASB moved towards different solutions.

As indicated above, the formal starting point of the Board's work, together with the FASB, in the autumn of 2008 was the March 2008 discussion paper, 'Reducing Complexity in Reporting Financial Instruments', which was widely seen as pointing towards a greater use of fair values in accounting for financial instruments, and perhaps towards a full fair value model. As seen in Chapter 12, the IASB and the FASB had said in 2006 that they saw measurement of all for financial instruments at fair value as their long-term objective. Of course, by the time the boards began their deliberations on steps to follow up on the discussion paper, the onset of the financial crisis meant that the long-standing debate on accounting for financial instruments had moved on to a completely new chapter. In March 2009, when the staffs had prepared their first substantive papers on the project to develop a new financial instruments standard, they observed:

> Inherent in the current economic state and the questions swirling around fair value accounting in the marketplace, the staff acknowledges that the debate regarding whether fair value is the most appropriate measurement basis for all financial assets and liabilities is not only being engaged globally but more passionately and by a wider array of constituents and other interested parties than at any other time in recent history. While it is true that there is a belief among many users that recognizing all financial instruments at fair value is not only conceptually but practically the only acceptable answer, others do not agree. The staff believes that recognizing all financial instruments at fair value *may* [original emphasis] not be the most appropriate measurement model to achieve an improvement to the usefulness, in particular the understandability and comparability of information provided to users of financial statements.[111]

As an illustration of the climate in which these words by the staff were written, one can cite the following passage from the report published in February 2009 by a high-level EU working group on reform of financial supervision, chaired by Jacques de la Rosière. Following an assertion of the contribution of fair value accounting to the financial crisis, it said:

> To ensure convergence of accounting practices and a level playing-field at the global level, it should be the role of the International Accounting Standards Board (IASB) to

---

[111] AP 3/2009 paper 9, paragraph 9.

foster the emergence of a consensus as to where and how the mark-to-market principle should apply—and where it should not.... If such a consensus does not emerge, it should be the role of the international community to set limits to the application of the mark-to-market principle.[112]

When the Board discussed the project in March, Tweedie established by a vote that nine Board members agreed that fair value for all financial instruments was conceptually the right answer. However, a second vote showed that a majority of the Board did not think that a long-term objective of full fair value, desirable or not, could be achieved for the time being. At least one Board member, Philippe Danjou, remembered the vote as a turning point in the Board's thinking on financial instruments.[113]

The Board therefore turned its attention to developing a simplified mixed-measurement model. In the spirit of reducing complexity, it was envisaged that there probably should be just two categories, fair value and amortized cost with appropriate impairment provisions. Apart from the question of whether the impairment model should include some form of expected loss recognition, the main issue facing the Board was therefore how to make the cut between fair value measurement and amortized cost measurement.[114] At a joint meeting with the FASB, a week later, it was agreed to explore three possible measurement bases—fair value, amortized cost, and remeasurement based on discounted cash flows—but with the intention of using not more than two measurement bases in the final standard. Although Tweedie wished to emphasize that no decision in favour of fair value had been taken, the possibility of using just one measurement basis was not ruled out either.[115] Both the IASB's own discussions and the joint meeting in March revealed that there was still considerable diversity of opinion within and between the boards about the criteria to be used to classify instruments in a mixed-measurement approach: should the distinction be made on the basis of characteristics of the instrument, such as cash flow variability, on the general business model under which it was held, or on management intent with respect to the specific instrument? The boards agreed to explore these issues further between March and July.

However, by May the IASB was already able to make up its mind. As suggested above, this speed may have been inspired by the realization that a concrete change in standards had to be produced by the end of the year. In May, the notion surfaced rather suddenly that the IASB already had a model available for distinguishing amortized cost financial instruments from fair value instruments.[116] This was the model of the *International Financial Reporting Standard for Small and Medium-sized Entities (IFRS for SMEs)*, about to be published in July 2009. This standard made a distinction between 'basic financial instruments', at amortized cost, and all others, at fair value. The distinction was made on the basis of the characteristics of the instrument, with the general intention that straightforward

---

[112] The High-Level Group on Financial Supervision in the EU, *Report*, 25 February 2009, paragraph 77 <http://ec.europa.eu/internal_market>.

[113] Interview with Philippe Danjou, 14 February 2012.

[114] *IStaR*, March 2009 (final edition), 21–3.   [115] *IStaR*, March 2009 (final edition), 55.

[116] This notion first appeared in appendix C to AP 5/2009 paper 5E. This appendix was a late addition to the paper, see *IStaR*, May 2009, 14.

debt instruments should be classified as 'basic'. It is not apparent that, when the SME standard was developed, it was thought of as a possible blueprint for a general financial instruments standard. But in May 2009, the Board agreed that it wished to pursue this approach in the replacement of IAS 39. At meetings in June, including some extra meetings early in the month, this was fleshed out by adding a business model condition: to qualify for amortized cost measurement, an instrument should not just have 'basic loan features', but should also be managed on a contractual yield basis.

Furthermore, the Board completed its exposure draft of a basic classification and measurement standard by making a number of decisions. It agreed that it wanted a restricted fair value option, as in IAS 39. It decided not to allow reclassification between the two categories, thus undoing, in effect, the change forced upon it in October 2008. The Board also agreed that fair value changes should in principle go through profit or loss, but it wanted to allow an exception for shareholdings held for strategic purposes. This issue was viewed with particular concern in Japan, where strategic cross-holdings were common, without an appetite to see gains and losses taken to profit or loss. For such holdings, the Board wanted to allow recognition of all gains and losses (both relating to remeasurement and to dividends) in other comprehensive income, but without recycling to profit or loss. The Board struggled for a while to develop a principle to identify assets eligible for this treatment, but decided in the end to make it a free choice, assuming that the prohibition of any recycling and reclassification would impose sufficient discipline. The exposure draft was published on 14 July.

At the FASB, meanwhile, thinking developed in a different direction. Following the joint meeting of March 2009, the FASB had considered the same general issues as the IASB in a series of education sessions: like the IASB, the FASB had considered the merits of three possible measurement bases, including fair value and amortized cost. It had also discussed classification criteria to be used in a mixed-measurement model, as well as impairment. On 15 July, the FASB held a decision-making meeting during which, following the recommendation from its staff, it tentatively agreed on a different approach from that adopted by the IASB. The approach adopted by the FASB was to have all financial instruments measured at fair value (but with display of the amortized cost amount on the face of the balance sheet), with fair value changes as a rule recognized in profit or loss, but in other comprehensive income in some cases. The criteria adopted for distinguishing between the two treatments of gains and losses were similar but not identical to those adopted by the IASB to distinguish between fair value and amortized cost measurement.[117] In terms of process, the FASB did not follow the IASB's phased approach but continued to aim for a comprehensive exposure draft to be issued sometime in 2010.

When the two boards met for a joint meeting in London in July, it was noted that little was said in public about the reasons why they reached different conclusions.[118] It was still possible to maintain, as members and staff of the boards did, that the two boards might yet converge, or that at least a solution

[117] Minutes of FASB meeting of 15 July 2009 <http://www.fasb.org>.
[118] 'Editorial', *World Accounting Report*, August 2009, 1.

might be found that would result in approximately the same effect on profit or loss under either board's approach.[119] Plans were made for the FASB to participate in roundtables to be organized by the IASB in the autumn and to ensure that the FASB would consider reactions both to its own tentative plans and to the IASB's exposure draft.[120] As the boards resumed their work after the summer, they continued to affirm their commitment to convergence.

Yet it was increasingly obvious that the IASB was getting entangled in a web of expectations that became simply incompatible. It was hard to see how it could at once move quickly, achieve convergence with the FASB, and arrive at a solution that had at least a modicum of acceptability for itself and its constituents. In September 2009, prior to the third G20 summit in Pittsburgh, the European Commission had written a memorandum to unite the EU member states on a common position. It wrote as follows about the EU's firm expectations of the IASB:

> The EU should also seek a renewed commitment from the G20 to accelerating the pace of delivery on accounting standards. . . . It is vital that the IASB delivers on appropriate reform of the accounting rules to ensure that financial stability concerns are fully taken into account to reduce pro-cyclicality in the system. Convergence to high quality accounting standards remains a top priority of the EU, in particular as regards financial instruments. The EU therefore needs to secure a strong political commitment to balanced convergence towards high quality standards no later than 2010.[121]

While there was pressure for speed from Europe, the FASB reassured the financial industry, alarmed by the radical nature of the FASB's tentative decision to measure all financial instruments at fair value, that 'there is a long and robust due process ahead on this issue' and that 'the FASB is taking a very measured and comprehensive approach to this complex issue'.[122] IASB Board member Bob Garnett highlighted some of the contradictions facing the IASB when, at one of the roundtables on financial instruments, he berated a representative of one of the French banks who had questioned the coherence of some of the IASB's proposals:

> If it hadn't have been for some people, and I do hold you partly responsible, as a European banker, for insisting that we address some of these issues by the end of the year—you have forced on us the need to address this on a piecemeal basis. . . . So, I'm sorry, be careful what you ask for in future, because the result that you get is something that you found is not palatable. . . . If we had more time, we could address more of these issues jointly with FASB, [holding] joint deliberations with them. You have imposed this timetable on us, this is the consequence of coming back to us.[123]

---

[119] 'Boards Compare Financial Instruments Notes', *World Accounting Report*, August 2009, 3; 'Impact of Financial Instruments Plan Hinges Partly on Entity Holdings, IASB Member Says', BNA's *Daily Tax Report*, 17 July 2009, 135 DTR I-1.

[120] 'Minutes of the July 24, 2009 Joint Board Meeting Accounting for Financial Instruments' <http://www.fasb.org>.

[121] 'European Commission Calls for United EU Position for G20 Summit in Pittsburgh', European Commission press release dated 17 September 2009, MEMO/09/397 <http://eurpa.eu/rapid>.

[122] FASB Communications manager Christine Klimek, speaking on behalf of Robert Herz, quoted in 'Banking Group Says Standard Setters Moving Too Fast on Financial Instruments', BNA's *Daily Tax Report*, 14 August 2009, 155 DTR G-2.

[123] 'IASB Member Garnett Publicly Blames European Bankers for Instruments Upheaval', BNA's *Daily Tax Report*, 9 September 2011, 174-DTR I-5.

In the end, the IASB continued to make speed rather than to wait for the FASB to develop a position that could serve as a plausible basis for a converged and internationally acceptable standard, as opposed to the FASB's plans for a full fair value standard. The IASB issued IFRS 9 *Financial Instruments* on 12 November 2009 with a mandatory application date of 1 January 2013, but allowing earlier application. The final standard, replacing parts of IAS 39, broadly confirmed the proposals of the July exposure draft. It established fair value through profit or loss as the default treatment of financial assets, but allowed a substantial exception to measure assets at amortized cost, essentially for loans and similar assets held under a business model with the objective to collect contractual cash flows. However, the wording of the standard was modified so that structured credit-linked investments could also qualify for amortized cost treatment. As this included assets such as the repackaged mortgages that had caused such concern in the financial crisis, it was a significant modification.

IFRS 9 was as yet an incomplete standard, dealing just with the recognition and measurement of financial assets. As implied in the IASB's phased approach, other parts of IAS 39 were expected to be replaced bit by bit. In November 2009, the IASB also issued an exposure draft on the impairment of amortized cost assets, setting out the Board's proposals for a shift towards an expected loss model for loan loss recognition. Already in March 2009, an exposure draft on derecognition had been published. What remained unresolved was the treatment of financial liabilities, including the tricky issue of fair value gains and losses relating to changes in own credit risk, which had been dropped from IFRS 9 during the redeliberation. And then there was the even trickier topic of hedge accounting, which included the potentially explosive question of how to deal with the EU's remaining carve-out on macro-hedging of interest rate risks.

13.13 INTERMEZZO: PRESSURE OF A DIFFERENT KIND

In the midst of the rush to produce IFRS 9, the IASB found time to make an amendment to IAS 32 *Financial Instruments: Presentation*. The amendment addressed a problem faced by companies whose equity is denominated in a currency other than their functional currency, for instance, Hong Kong companies doing most of their business in China. When these companies raised new equity in the form of a rights issue or a similar arrangement, the rights to acquire new shares had to be classified as derivatives by the issuing company and measured at fair value. The company would have to report any gains or losses on the derivatives in profit or loss, but without a net effect on equity over the entire transaction because an offsetting entry would be made directly to the reserves once the shares were issued. As early as 2005, IFRIC had recommended that the Board should amend IAS 32, but the Board had then declined to do so.

The question resurfaced with some urgency in the first half of 2009, when the banking group HSBC—with its share capital denominated in sterling, yet with the US dollar as functional currency—announced a rights issue. For reasons as outlined earlier, HSBC gave warning of a loss of US$4.7 billion in its report for the first quarter. HSBC believed this was nonsensical accounting. It approached the IASB to do something about it, but it saw the IASB as slow to act.[124] The group increased the pressure when, in its mid-year interim report, it invoked the 'fair presentation' override and departed from the requirements of IAS 32. As HSBC spelled out, citing IAS 1, this meant that it believed that following IAS 32 'would be so misleading that it would conflict with the objectives of financial statements set out in the IASB's framework'.[125] While the interim financial statements were unaudited, the auditor, KPMG, raised no objection in its review report, which suggested that HSBC would also have no difficulty obtaining an unqualified opinion on its annual accounts. In response, the IASB rushed out an exposure draft in August, and a revised standard in October, which addressed the issue.[126]

The substance of what became known as the 'HSBC amendment' was welcomed, because many people outside HSBC also thought that IAS 32 could lead to meaningless accounting numbers. Yet the amendment caused some grumbling among constituents about the way the IASB determined its priorities and set its agenda.[127] Over the years, many companies and industry organizations had approached the IASB with practical problems in the application of IFRSs, but it often seemed to them that the Board was too preoccupied—by its convergence agenda, for instance—to take note. Apparently, the Board would pay attention only when one of the world's largest groups, and moreover one known for its generally supportive stance of the IASB, publicly put aside one of the IASB's standards.

13.14 THE EUROPEAN COMMISSION FAILS TO ENDORSE IFRS 9

Even though IFRS 9 was not a complete standard on financial instruments, producing it in about a year from the initial agenda decision was a remarkable achievement, certainly compared with the cumbersome progress on some of the IASB's other projects. It had taken a major effort, including several additional Board meetings between May and October in addition to the pattern of monthly meetings which the Board had hitherto observed. Following the July exposure draft, the Board had conducted roundtables in London, Tokyo, and Norwalk. It held many small-group discussions with reporting companies, auditors, regulators, and investors. Constituents were kept informed through webcasts to which 'thousands of participants' were said to have listened.[128]

The main question now was whether the EU, from which most of the pressure had come for a change in accounting for financial instruments, applicable to the 2009 financial statements, would endorse the standard. This was clearly not a foregone conclusion. The IASB had produced a standard, but was this really what Europe had in mind? As indicated above, the progress of the project had been

[124] Interview with Russell Picot, 26 May 2009.

[125] 'HSBC Holdings Plc—Interim Management Statement', 11 May 2009; *2009 HSBC Holdings Plc Interim Report*, note 19 to the financial statements <http://www.hsbc.com>.

[126] *Classification of Rights Issues: Amendment to IAS 32* (IASB, October 2009).

[127] Interview with Alan Teixeira, 13 February 2012.   [128] AP 9/2009 paper 7, paragraph 3.

followed sceptically, if not with downright hostility, by the French and German finance ministries. In the course of the redeliberations following the exposure draft, the IASB had become even more familiar with the laundry list of European concerns, on which it issued a separate feedback statement with IFRS 9.[129] Some of these had been dealt with, such as the expansion of the amortized cost category to include certain structured products. The IASB had also made a small move on reclassification of assets—a sensitive point since October 2008. Reclassification was no longer categorically ruled out, as in the exposure draft, but allowed in the rare circumstances of a change in business model. Other issues were simply deferred, such as the treatment of liabilities and the whole question of impairment. And then there were fundamental concerns in the insurance industry that the abolition of the available-for-sale category (fair value through other comprehensive income, with recycling) would play havoc with their financial statements, as gains and losses on the insurance liability would no longer be aligned with gains and losses on investments. This had been dealt with by moving the mandatory application back to 2013, with a promise to review that date if by then the IASB's insurance project was still not completed. The European accountancy profession as represented by the Fédération des Experts Comptables Européens (FEE) argued that the IASB had responded sufficiently to European concerns. However, from the point of view of the IASB's European critics, there were still many question marks hanging over the financial instruments project.[130]

To make IFRS 9 available for application in 2009 would require a fast-track endorsement procedure on the part of the European Commission. Preparations were made accordingly. Already on 2 November, before the official publication of IFRS 9, EFRAG published a draft endorsement advice and impact assessment, based on a pre-ballot draft of the standard provided by the IASB.[131] EFRAG concluded that IFRS 9 should be endorsed. However, on 11 November, a day before the publication of IFRS 9, a meeting of the ARC took place during which the European Commission had its view confirmed that there would be insufficient political support to proceed with the endorsement of IFRS 9.[132] Two days later, EFRAG made it known that it would not, for the time being, finalize its endorsement advice. The German government was among those that did not yet support the endorsement of IFRS 9, both because of remaining concerns over the existing

---

[129] 'How the IASB Has Responded to European Concerns' (IASB, [November 2009]).

[130] Letter from Hans van Damme (FEE President) to Jörgen Holmquist (European Commission), dated 10 November 2009 <http://www.iasplus.com>. See also Edouard Salustro, 'Normes comptables: l'heure de vérité approche', *La Tribune*, 30 November 2009.

[131] 'Draft Endorsement Advice and Effects Study Report on IFRS 9 Financial Instruments' (EFRAG, 2 November 2011) <http://www.efrag.org>.

[132] The tentative views of the European Commission were already suggested to the IASB in a letter dated 4 November 2009 from Jörgen Holmquist to David Tweedie in which the IASB was urged to 'reflect further and assess the extent to which input from stakeholders . . . has been effectively translated into the new text' <http://ec.europa.eu/internal_market/accounting>. See also 'Meeting of the Accounting Regulatory Committee and Contact Committee of 11 November 2009' <http://ec.europa.eu>. These summary minutes merely report 'different views' about whether there should be an accelerated endorsement process. That the ARC decided on 11 November to postpone its consideration of endorsement of IFRS 9 is reported in 'Update on IFRS Endorsements in Europe', 14 November 2009 <http://www.iasplus.com>, accessed 5 July 2013.

text, and because of questions about the subsequent phases of the project.[133] Apparently, the weight carried by the German concerns was sufficient for the European Commission to halt the endorsement process.

The trustees of the IASC Foundation wrote to Commissioner McCreevy to express their 'surprise and disappointment' at the decision to defer the endorsement. The trustees strongly supported the Board by asserting that they were satisfied that the IASB 'has conducted a thorough, balanced, and fair process. The IASB has responded in an appropriate and timely manner to the issues raised by the G20, the European Commission, and other international stakeholders. It is for this reason, even if we understand the context of the EU's political constraints related to the accelerated endorsement procedure, we find the deferral decision particularly disappointing.' In his response, McCreevy indicated that this would be a matter for the next European Commission, to take office in 2010.[134] He also pointed at the 'changed financial outlook and market improvements', apparently meaning that the worst of the financial crisis was over, thus removing the need for urgent measures. Somehow, the need to level the playing field in response to the FASB staff position on impairment, still considered 'a key issue' as recently as September, was no longer felt.[135]

Because of the European Commission's decision, as well as its far-off effective date, IFRS 9 was doomed to a shadowy existence. For European companies, IAS 39 continued to apply as before. In other jurisdictions, including Hong Kong and Australia, IFRS 9 could be applied on a voluntary basis, but very few companies, apart from a handful of investment companies, seemed to be interested to use it.

---

[133] The concerns of the German government, as well as its support for the Commission's decision not to pursue the endorsement of IFRS 9 were made known to the IASB in a letter from Wolfgang Schäuble (finance minister) and Sabine Leutheusser-Schnarrenberger (justice minister) to David Tweedie, dated 27 November 2009, IASB archive, file 'covered correspondence'.

[134] Letter from Gerrit Zalm to Charlie McCreevy, dated 18 November 2009; letter from Charlie McCreevy to Gerrit Zalm, dated 19 November 2009 <http://www.iasplus.com>.

[135] Letter from Jörgen Holmquist to David Tweedie, dated 15 September 2009 <http://ec.europa.eu/internal_market/accounting>.

14

Preparing the IASB for the Second Decade

As seen in Chapter 7, the first review of the IASC Foundation's Constitution, completed in 2005, had left the essential features of the organization intact. It remained an independent, private-sector body in which the trustees had the exclusive right to appoint members of the IASB Board, and in which the Board was free to set its agenda and carry out its technical work. This unrestricted independence remained a source of controversy in jurisdictions adopting IFRSs. At the conclusion of the first Constitution review, the trustees themselves were aware that they needed to consider further how the IASB could best evolve to shoulder its new-found responsibility as the de jure or de facto standard setter for an increasing number of jurisdictions. From late 2006 onwards, the trustees were involved in an almost permanent discussion of this question. It was not, however, a neat, linear discussion. It consisted of a cluster of related processes, some initiated by the trustees, some by parties outside the organization.

Sections 14.1–14.3 show how the trustees began with an internal strategy review. This soon became caught up with an initiative by regulatory bodies to set up a third layer in the organization, consisting of a Monitoring Board to oversee the Foundation (Section 14.4). The creation of the Monitoring Board, in turn, became one of the key questions in the Foundation's second periodic review of its Constitution (Sections 14.5–14.8). Once created, the Monitoring Board (Sections 14.9–14.10) became involved in the process of selecting a new chairman for the trustees, and of a successor to David Tweedie, selections which were of vital importance to the future development of the IASB organization (Sections 14.11–14.12). As it was found that neither the completion of the second Constitution review, nor the creation of the Monitoring Board, had put to rest critical questioning of the IASB's overall functioning, both the trustees and the Monitoring Board decided that they had to undertake further strategic and governance reviews (Section 14.13).

If this chapter at times seems repetitive, that is because it was apparently necessary for the worldwide acceptance of the IASB and its standards to debate and re-debate many times the basic questions of the IASB's structure and governance. However, it would seem that after the more than five years of discussions covered in this chapter—which were a continuation of discussions going back to the 1990s—the IASB, its governing bodies, and a large proportion of its constituents were satisfied that the main issues had been properly settled.

14.1 A STRATEGIC REVIEW BY THE TRUSTEES

In October 2006, David Tweedie wrote to the Foundation trustees to propose that a committee of trustees, Board members, and the management team be formed to assist him in developing a 'vision' of what changes should be made to the organization so that it could fulfil its potential for the coming years.[1] After 2007, he said, all of the original trustees will have retired. When the Foundation was organized in 2001, 'the organization effectively was a think tank to produce standards for those countries or standard setters which wished to adopt them', but the chain reaction following the decision by the European Union (EU) in 2002 to require some 7,000 listed companies to use IFRSs in their consolidated financial statements eventually 'has meant that at present 100 countries either require all or some of their companies to use IFRSs or permit them to do so. . . . For the first time, IFRSs are being used in major markets throughout the world, and issues related to that implementation will inevitably arise.' Convergence efforts with the United States, he added, 'are reaching a critical phase'. He believed that, at this juncture, it was necessary to rethink the long-term future of the organization.

As seen in Chapter 4, Tweedie's thumbnail sketch of the IASB's early history downplays the extent to which the IASB already was, or was seen as, a standard setter with real-world responsibilities right from its inception in 2001, but there was no denying that the organization's reach had increased spectacularly since then. Therefore, at their October 2006 meeting, the trustees strongly supported Tweedie's proposal, but they said it should be a trustee-led initiative, not one for the trustees and the Board jointly.[2] The acting chairman of the trustees, Phil Laskawy, took the lead and created a strategy committee composed of himself, Bertrand Collomb, Samuel DiPiazza, Tsuguoki Fujinuma, and Antonio Vegezzi. David Tweedie and Tom Seidenstein, the secretary to the trustees and director of operations, were also included in the project, and they participated in the committee's meetings. In his dual capacity as chief executive of the IASC Foundation and Board chairman, Tweedie worked hand-in-glove with Seidenstein on many Foundation matters over the years.

On 29 December, Tweedie and Seidenstein launched the discussion by drafting a lengthy memorandum to the trustees' strategy committee, containing a comprehensive list of stated and implied questions that should be addressed, including:[3]

- What should be the role of the trustees in providing strategic advice to the Board without impairing its independence?
- What is the ideal size of the Board, should it continue to have part-time members, and should all members be required to relocate to London?
- What are the strategic issues relating to the Board's ongoing convergence process with the Financial Accounting Standards Board (FASB), and what should be the Board's relationship to the FASB after convergence is achieved?

---

[1] IASCF trustees meeting of 26–7 October 2006, agenda paper 6.
[2] IASCF trustees meeting of 26–7 October 2006, minute F.
[3] IASCF trustees meeting of 17–18 January 2007, agenda paper 7A, ATT(i).

- Should the trustees raise questions relating to strategy and priority in its consideration of the Board's agenda, so as to be sensitive to issues of the public acceptability of its prospective standards?
- How best can the organization develop a structure that will attract and retain technical staff, coupled with the administrative and support resources necessary for them to perform efficiently?
- What should the Board do so as not to risk its principles-based approach by moving towards the complexity and detailed application guidance in US generally accepted accounting principles (US GAAP)?
- What changes should be made to the due process of the International Financial Reporting Interpretations Committee (IFRIC) so as to improve its operations and efficiency?
- What steps should be taken to protect the IASB/IFRS brand owing to the risk of different national 'IFRSs'?
- How should the Board strengthen its communications to key communities?
- What should the Board do to maintain its educational programme for producing useful and relevant materials?
- Should the Board make any changes in its involvement with eXtensible Business Reporting Language (XBRL)?
- What communications strategy should the Board undertake to counteract misunderstanding and misinformation about its project to develop a standard for small and medium-sized entities?
- Should the trustees extend the Board's mandate to include not-for-profits and/or public-sector entities?
- Are there are further alternatives to the trustees' long-term strategy for funding?
- As a result of the addition of a growing number of operations staff, what organizational changes should be made to the 'very flat reporting structure leading to the Director of Operations' (i.e. Seidenstein)?

This was indeed a full array of daunting questions, reflecting many of the challenges faced at the time by the Board and the trustees as discussed throughout Chapters 8–12.

The strategy committee met in Paris prior to the trustees' January 2007 meeting in Tokyo. During the Tokyo meeting, trustee chairman Phil Laskawy was minuted as reporting 'that the Committee focused on a few topics, including developing the concept of "independence with accountability", enhancing the role of the IASB Chairman, improving the IASB's deliberative process and operating procedures, and the composition and performance criteria of the IASB'.[4] Above all, the enhancement of the IASB's independence and accountability stood out as the issue of overriding importance in the strategy review.

---

[4] IASCF trustees meeting of 17–18 January 2007, minute J.

14.2 NARROWING THE ISSUES AND MOVING FORWARD

During the next twelve months, until January 2008, the trustees worked out how to establish priorities for their unstructured initial list of issues, including plans to move from analysis to implementation. The outline of events, to be explained in more detail below, is that the trustees formally completed their strategy review at their meeting of October/November 2007. At that meeting they approved the final version of an internal document called 'The Pathway to a Global Standard', earlier versions of which had been discussed at the trustees' meetings of April and July. The 'Pathway' paper included many of the issues mentioned in the Tweedie-Seidenstein memorandum of December 2006, but put them in the context of an overall strategic vision, introduced a sense of priorities, and indicated for many of them how they might be dealt with, or were already being dealt with.

While for some of the proposals in the 'Pathway' paper there were no formal impediments to immediate implementation, others required modifications to the Foundation's Constitution. For these issues it was natural to look towards the next five-yearly review of the Constitution, due to begin in 2008 and to be completed in 2010. However, by the time the finishing touches were put to the 'Pathway' paper, the central issue of 'independence with accountability', which inevitably had Constitutional implications, had already moved beyond the stage of strategic reflection. By then, the trustees were already deeply engaged in negotiations with parties external to the organization about the creation of a so-called monitoring group to oversee the Foundation. Therefore, it was decided to tackle this issue—together with one other point concerning the composition of the Board—in an accelerated part one of the Constitution review, followed by a part two in which they could deal with all of other issues.

The following sections begin by tracing the discussions of the two topics that the trustees considered during part one of the Constitution review, which ended when they approved a package of Constitutional amendments in January 2009. This is followed by a discussion of other strategic issues considered in the 'Pathway' paper, and by an overview of part two of the Constitution review. Part two began in December 2008 and was concluded with a second slate of amendments approved in January 2010.

14.3 'INDEPENDENCE WITH ACCOUNTABILITY'

In a working paper drafted following the January 2007 trustees meeting, it was reported that they agreed that the strategy review 'should be comprehensive in its approach, encompassing both structural and operational issues of the organization'.[5] Yet, among the themes emerging from the initial discussions, two stood out

---

[5] IASCF trustees meeting of 2–3 April 2007, agenda paper 7. Quotations and attributions in this paragraph are taken from this document. As the document was surely drafted by Seidenstein, it is not easy to determine, in some areas, whether the views expressed were those of the trustees or of the draftsman.

as 'fundamental structural principles'. The first was 'independence with account-ability', on which it was observed:

> The Trustees recognized that the independence of the standard-setting process is fundamental to the organization's success. However, the organization needs to main-tain the trust and respect of those affected by standard-setting activities. The Trustees recognize that the IASC Foundation's unique structure makes demonstrating account-ability more difficult than it would be for a national standard-setter, who may need to report to a national securities regulator or national parliaments.

The second principle was 'responsible independence'. It was noted that there were constraints on independence. The Board was unlike other international standard-setting activities, where the normal pattern was for committees composed of national officials, representing their countries' interests, to make decisions on the basis of compromise. The IASB needed to exercise its unique independence in a responsible manner, because of the 'continuing risk that in some countries, those with power and interests on a national level may be just waking up to the fact of the IASB's success and its unique structure and may seek to return accounting standard-setting back to the more regularly practiced model of international standard-setting'. This was an accurate observation of a problem that the IASB repeatedly encountered in the course of its first decade. However, it would presumably have been hard for the trustees to elaborate on the notion of exercis-ing independence in a responsible manner without conveying their verdict on the Board's technical conclusions. This train of thought was not pursued, and the trustees' deliberations concentrated on the notion of 'independence with accountability'.

Seidenstein drafted a first version of the paper entitled 'The Pathway to a Global Standard'.[6] Independence with accountability was a key theme in the nine-page, single-spaced paper which, after being adopted by the strategy committee, was submitted to the trustees for their July 2007 meeting. In the paper, the committee acknowledged that commentators on the organization 'have questioned the self-perpetuating nature of the Trustees' and considered two reforms. The first was to have a group of trustees who would be elected representatives of different con-stituent groups. The second was that the trustees' selection of their own replace-ments would be approved by an external body prior to making the appointments. The paper rejected the first option because of the difficulty of identifying all of the relevant stakeholder groups and also because this approach risked a decline in the quality of the trustees. As to the second option: 'For "political" accountability, such an external group should be comprised of public officials who have a role in ensuring the adoption and implementation of IFRS' (page 4). The proposed external body was seen as a possible replacement of the existing Trustee Appoint-ments Advisory Group, which the trustees had set up in 2005 during the first Constitution review to address the same concerns over the trustee appointment process (see Section 7.3). The trustees considered the following organizations as possible candidates to be represented on the external body: securities regulators such as the US Securities and Exchange Commission (SEC), the Committee of

---

[6] IASCF trustees meeting of 2–3 July 2007, agenda paper 10A. Quotations and attributions in the remainder of this section are taken from this document.

European Securities Regulators (CESR), Japan's Financial Services Agency (FSA), and two other securities commissions in countries that have adopted IFRSs; the Basel Committee on Banking Supervision; the International Association of Insurance Supervisors; the Public Interest Oversight Board of the International Auditing and Assurance Standards Board (IAASB); the World Bank; and the International Monetary Fund (IMF). With such a membership, the new body could be thought of as an evolved version of the Trustee Appointments Advisory Group, but with a shift of emphasis towards securities regulators. This was the germ of the Monitoring Board, which was established early in 2009 but with a much narrower membership than suggested in 2007.

It was proposed that the trustees should not merely enhance the trustee appointment process, but should go further and create their own 'democratic accountability', that is, to demonstrate their responsiveness to markets' demands and therefore to 'ensure confidence in the accountability of the organization', without jeopardizing the fundamental independence of the process. Two steps that might be taken would be for the trustees to report 'formally to the external appointments body on oversight duties and activities once annually' and to establish annual meetings at which the trustees 'would report to the public and enable the public to express concerns' (page 4). A third possible step was to establish regional bodies, 'as already exists in Asia-Oceania', as 'a mechanism to receive input in a more formalized fashion' (page 5). This was presumably a reference to the IFRS Regional Policy Forum in the Asia-Pacific region, a meeting of the IASB with standard setters and regulators, the first of which was held in Sydney in October 2005. At their July meeting, the trustees expressed general support for this report, and said that it 'would serve as a basis for discussion when the Constitution Review began in 2008'. At that point the proposals had not yet been shared with any external parties, but Seidenstein emphasized the strategy committee's desire to begin consultations with outside groups in order to invite comment.[7]

14.4 JOINT STATEMENT FROM FOUR PUBLIC BODIES ON A MONITORING GROUP

While it may have been true that the trustees' strategy proposals had not been widely circulated prior to their meeting on 31 October and 1 November, it became apparent that one central element of the proposals had already acquired a life of its own. Immediately after the trustees' July meeting, the SEC had issued its rule proposal on 3 July 2007 to lift its reconciliation requirement for foreign registrants reporting on the basis of IFRSs (see Section 8.4). Shortly afterwards, senior SEC staff members, including especially Ethiopis Tafara, the director of the Office of International Affairs, were engaged in discussion with senior staff of the European Commission, in particular Pierre Delsaux, a director in the Internal Market and

---

[7] IASCF trustees meeting of 2–3 July 2007, minute J; IASCF trustees meeting of 31 October–1 November 2007, agenda paper 10A.

Services Directorate General. The SEC's proposal that the reconciliation would be lifted only for financial statements prepared on the basis of 'IFRSs as issued by the IASB' caused concern at the European Commission. The Commission saw its standard-by-standard endorsement process, resulting in 'IFRSs as adopted for use in the EU', as a means of keeping the IASB accountable to Europe. As seen in Section 9.6, pressure on the Commission was building up during 2007, both from the European Parliament and from some of the member states, to safeguard or enhance this kind of accountability, so from the Commission's point of view a weakening of the endorsement instrument at this time was not opportune.

The SEC staff pointed out that the European Commission could also, and perhaps more effectively, make the IASB publicly accountable by participating in an 'external mechanism' that would oversee the functioning of the IASC Foundation trustees—essentially a grouping of public authorities that would constitute a monitoring body. In an attempt to form such a body, the SEC and the European Commission thereupon approached Japan's FSA—bringing on board the world's three largest capital markets—together with representatives of other developed countries via the International Organization of Securities Commissions (IOSCO), and secured their collective agreement.[8] They then brought their proposal to the trustees at their meeting on 31 October–1 November 2007.[9]

Given the simultaneous developments in the United States, in Europe, and at the Foundation, as well as the continuous consultations and contacts on all sides, it is not easy to establish the precise origins of the Monitoring Board. Staff at the European Commission had certainly been thinking about the IASB's governance for some time, and if the SEC first broached the idea of a monitoring body to the Commission, it would have found the ground well prepared. Also, it is not clear to what extent the initiative by the SEC and the European Commission was prompted by knowledge of the trustees' own discussion of a possible external body in July, or, conversely, whether the trustees' discussions drew on incipient ideas held at the SEC or the European Commission. Be that as it may, by late October the genie was out of the bottle, and it was clear that the regulatory bodies brought forward their own views and did not merely intend to endorse blueprints prepared by the trustees. For instance, while a role for the SEC and the FSA was clearly in line with the trustees' thinking of giving more weight to securities regulators, the idea that the European Commission—as opposed to CESR—might play a role did not occur in the earlier strategy review documents. During the October/November trustees' meeting, concern was expressed over potentially less desirable outcomes. Chairman Laskawy 'stressed his view that he would not support any proposals that would weaken the Trustees as a body', and the minutes reported: 'Several of the Trustees cautioned that the organization should not become subject only to bilateral discussions between the European Union and the United States and needed to recognize that the IASC Foundation served the global community.'[10] Looking back, Seidenstein recalled the red lines which the trustees did not want to cross. These included: (1) that the monitoring body should have

---

[8] Interview with Ethiopis Tafara, 29 June 2010.
[9] IASCF trustees meeting of 31 October–1 November 2007, minutes 1 and 11.
[10] IASCF trustees meeting of 31 October–1 November 2007, minutes 1 and 11.

no authority over the IASB Board's agenda setting; (2) that the monitoring body should have no authority to approve IASB members; and (3) that the trustees would need to be the conduit through which the monitoring body could discuss issues with the IASB.[11]

But while the specific arrangements would remain a matter of heavy negotiations, the public bodies and the trustees were in agreement that the installation of a monitoring body in the Foundation's structure was an idea whose time had come. At their October/November 2007 meeting, the trustees signified their 'commitment to the approach taken by the Strategy Committee regarding the accountability of Trustees and their general commitment to the IASB's independence', and they decided to issue a press release on the strategy review to enable public consultation. The 6 November 2007 press release recited and briefly discussed four planks in the platform of reform adopted by the trustees: establishing a 'formal reporting link' to official organizations; developing a 'multi-layered, multi-faceted' approach to accountability to key stakeholder groups; creating a mechanism to encourage public input to the trustees on the Foundation's and the Board's policies, processes, and procedures; and continuing the efforts towards building a sustained, broad-based funding regime.[12]

The wording of the press release was intended to highlight similarities between the trustees' conclusions and the proposals developed by the regulatory bodies which the trustees knew would be aired at the same time.[13] Nevertheless, the trustees wished to avoid the impression that their hand was being forced by the regulatory bodies. In fact, both sides issued coordinated press releases.[14]

On 7 November, one day after the trustees' press release, the European Commission, Japan's FSA, the SEC, as well as IOSCO issued a joint statement proposing the creation of a monitoring body.[15] This body would have final approval over the trustees' nominations of new or continuing trustees and would meet regularly with the trustees 'to discuss, review and comment on the IASB's work program' and 'would have the opportunity to review the Trustees' procedures for overseeing the standard-setting process and ensuring the IASB's proper funding'. The Trustee Appointments Advisory Group would, under their proposal, continue in existence.[16]

Immediately afterwards, at the meeting of the Standards Advisory Council (SAC) on 8–9 November, Laskawy discussed a number of major points in the

[11] Communications from Thomas Seidenstein to the authors, dated 22 February 2013 and 1 March 2013.

[12] 'Trustees Announce Strategy to Enhance Governance, Report on Conclusions at Trustees' Meeting', IASCF press release dated 6 November 2007 <http://www.iasb.org> accessed through web. archive.

[13] IASCF trustees meeting of 31 October–1 November 2007, minutes 11 and 12.

[14] Laskawy was quoted as saying, 'we did have discussions with the regulators on our press release, and they had discussions with us on their press release, and we came out pretty much the same place', 'SAC: Don't Mention the War', *World Accounting Report*, December/January 2008, 8.

[15] That IOSCO played a role in the preceding discussions is not apparent from the minutes of the trustees' meetings.

[16] 'Statement of the European Commission, the Financial Services Agency of Japan, the International Organization of Securities Commissions (IOSCO) and the US Securities and Exchange Commission on Work to Enhance the Governance of the IASC Foundation', MEMO/07/451, Brussels, 7 November 2007 <http://europa.eu/rapid>.

'Pathway' paper approved by the trustees. Several of SAC's members expressed anxiety over the possible threat posed by a monitoring body to the Board's independence.[17] Jochen Pape, from Germany, was reported to have said: 'Where you say "mainly selection of trustees", my question is "what else?"'[18]

14.5 RUN-UP TO THE CONSTITUTION REVIEW

The October/November 2007 trustees meeting marked the transition from strategy review to review of the Constitution. At that meeting, the trustees voiced their support for the findings in the strategy committee's report (the 'Pathway' paper) and 'agreed that the Trustees should embark on a series of consultations that would lead into or be part of the Constitution Review that is required to begin next year. The report, however, would remain an internal document.' The next Constitution review was to begin by July 2008 and had to be completed two years later.[19] According to a note prepared by staff for submission to the trustees prior to their January 2008 meeting, the trustees had discussed that they might accelerate the Constitution review process in particular areas, which included the issues of trustee selection and oversight, the structure of SAC, and the size and composition of the Board.[20] The note proposed that the trustees would initially focus on developing the concept of a 'monitoring group' and the two other issues which they agreed to advance to the front of the process. During the period January–April, the trustees would consult with a broad range of key stakeholder groups. The note suggested that, if one or more of these three issues could be resolved quickly, they could be exposed for public comment. 'It would be preferable', the note said, 'to resolve the first issue described above [i.e. the monitoring group] as soon as possible' (page 2).

Evidently, one reason for moving so quickly on the issue of the monitoring group was the initiative advanced by the regulatory bodies for an 'external mechanism' to oversee the trustees and thus provide public accountability. With the issue so prominently on the table, it might be awkward to defer its resolution until the end of the Constitution review in the middle of 2010.

More specifically, as seen in Chapters 8 and 12, in early 2008 the IASB was engaged in discussions with the SEC about an acceleration of the convergence work plan of the IASB and the FASB, with a view to a possible adoption of IFRSs in the United States. In that light, clarifying the SEC's relation with the IASB had become a matter of some urgency. At the trustees meeting of January 2008, the acceleration of this part of the Constitution review was agreed in the context of a discussion of recent events in the United States.[21]

---

[17] Minutes of SAC meeting of 8–9 November 2007, 4–5. SAC's agenda papers included two brief extracts from the approved 'Pathway' paper, excluding the proposal to restructure SAC.

[18] 'SAC: Don't Mention the War', *World Accounting Report*, December/January 2008, 8.

[19] IASCF trustees meeting of 28–30 January 2008, agenda paper 5, page 1.

[20] IASCF trustees meeting of 28–30 January 2008 agenda paper 5. Quotations and attributions in this section are taken from this document.

[21] IASCF trustees meeting of 29–30 January 2008, minute 10.

Another likely reason would have been the IASB's wish to respond to criticisms of its lack of public accountability from the European Parliament, stridently expressed in the so-called Radwan report of 2007 and accompanying draft resolutions (see Section 9.6). While the language of the resolution adopted by the Parliament in April 2008 on the basis of the report was considerably softened, the Parliament had taken the view that the IASB's governance and accountability had to be improved by setting up a 'public oversight body'. As envisaged by the Parliament, the oversight body would have more extensive powers and a much broader composition than the monitoring group so far envisaged by the trustees, as it would involve 'all IASCF/IASB public stakeholders including, in particular, legislators and supervisors'.[22] Suggestions as these undoubtedly underscored the importance to the IASC Foundation's leadership to move fast on the approval and installation of the monitoring group.

In a paper which accompanied the January 2008 note, the staff suggested 'possible parameters' for a monitoring group. The paper referred to the Monitoring Group of the International Federation of Accountants (IFAC), and said that it could serve as a good starting point for the Foundation's proposed monitoring group. One could question that judgement. IFAC, which represents the worldwide accountancy profession, sets auditing standards via its IAASB. Through audit firms, the accountancy profession also implements the auditing standards. IFAC would require a monitoring body so as to provide assurance against regulatory capture. Its Monitoring Group had been established as part of a package of general reform proposals accepted by IFAC in 2003 in response to accounting and auditing scandals in a number of countries, which had given rise to the perception that the accountancy profession was not setting its standards in the public interest.

But regulatory capture was not the central issue with the IASC Foundation. As seen by many, the problem that a monitoring group should solve was that the IASB was too independent by half. As the staff paper put it: 'The creation of such an oversight body will help clarify the IASB's ultimate responsibility to the public interest, thereby enhancing public confidence in IFRSs' (page 7). But even though the rationale for setting up a monitoring group might differ as between IFAC and the IASB, citing the IFAC parallel had the advantage, from the IASB's point of view, of suggesting an acceptable precedent of how the powers of such a monitoring group might be kept within reasonable bounds.[23]

The staff's proposal, instead of designating as members the four public bodies (the European Commission, Japan's FSA, IOSCO, and the SEC) which had proposed a monitoring body for the Foundation in their joint statement on 7 November, was that the Foundation's monitoring group should comprise leaders of the following six organizations: the Basel Committee on Banking Supervision, the Financial Stability Forum, the International Association of Insurance Supervisors, IOSCO, the World Bank, and the European Commission.[24] These were also the members of IFAC's Monitoring Group, except that the European

---

[22] European Parliament Resolution of 24 April 2008 on International Financial Reporting Standards (IFRS) and the Governance of the International Accounting Standards Board (IASB) (2006/2248 (INI)), P6_TA(2008)0183 <http://www.europarl.europa.eu>.

[23] Communication to the authors from Thomas Seidenstein, 22 February 2013.

[24] IASCF trustees meeting of 29–30 January 2008, agenda paper 5A.

Commission was only an observer on the IFAC group. Although the SEC and Japan's FSA were not mentioned by name, they could hardly be overlooked. It was noted with some understatement that 'It is possible that securities regulators could seek greater representation on such a group, but that could be accomplished by having two or more IOSCO members' (page 2).

The paper proposed that the monitoring group would be responsible for approving the selection of trustees and would review the trustees' procedures for the following: '1) appointing members to the IASB, 2) reviewing the strategy of the IASC Foundation and the IASB and its effectiveness, including consideration, but not determination, of the IASB's agenda, 3) reviewing the IASB's compliance with its operating procedures, consultative arrangements and due process, and 4) ensuring proper funding for the IASB' (page 7).

In the discussion on strategy at the trustees' January 2008 meeting, they approved the suggestion to create a monitoring group and noted that the key issues for consideration and decisions were its composition and mandate. They 'confirmed that it was essential to preserve their [i.e. the trustees'] independence whilst maintaining their public accountability, transparency and commitment to due process'. Also during the meeting, Conrad Hewitt, the SEC's chief accountant, and Julie Erhardt, a deputy chief accountant, gave reports to the trustees. The following was minuted: 'Hewitt affirmed the SEC's commitment to the adoption of IFRSs and assured the Trustees that the SEC was trying to advance the effort.'[25] The trustees were thus apprised of the swift progress being made in the United States. In executive session, the trustees agreed that Chairman Gerrit Zalm should establish a Constitution review committee and that the issues of the monitoring group and the Board's composition—but not the size and composition of SAC— should receive the committee's immediate attention. After Seidenstein said that the monitoring group should be made up of representatives of official organizations, including securities regulators, the trustees 'agreed that the group should comprise more than securities regulators. This proposed composition of the [monitoring group] should ensure that representation was based on an even geographic spread. It was recommended that appointments onto the [monitoring group] would be for principals, and no substitutes would be allowed.'[26]

14.6 THE FIRST PHASE OF THE CONSTITUTION REVIEW

Prior to the trustees' March 2008 meeting, Tom Seidenstein drafted a proposed Constitution document, 'Proposals and Issues for the Constitution Review', dealing with the monitoring group and Board size and composition. The 'Proposals' document was intended to be submitted to interested parties for comment, once approved by the trustees.[27] It was divided into two parts: A, on the monitoring group and Board size and composition; and B, on other issues (yet to be drafted).

---

[25] IASCF trustees meeting of 29–30 January 2008, minutes 10 and 11.
[26] IASCF trustees meeting of 29–30 January 2008, minute 1.
[27] IASCF trustees meeting of 17–18 March 2008, agenda paper 2A.

In Part A, it was evident that the thinking within the Foundation over the desired composition of the monitoring group had evolved. The aim of the monitoring group was 'to establish a formal link to public institutions that have accountability to national governments' (paragraph 9), or, otherwise stated, 'should include primarily those regulatory and other official bodies generally charged with the establishment and enforcement of financial standards' (paragraph 12). Specifically, the monitoring group was to be composed as follows (paragraph 13):

(a) four members of the International Organization of Securities Commissions (IOSCO), represented by the Chairman of the Japan Financial Services Agency, the Chairman of the US Securities and Exchange Commission, the chair or deputy chair of the IOSCO Emerging Markets Committee, and the chair or deputy chair of the IOSCO Technical Committee,

(b) the responsible member of the European Commission or another member of the European Commission,

(c) the managing director of the International Monetary Fund, and

(d) the president of the World Bank.

Gone were the Basel Committee, the Financial Stability Forum, and the International Association of Insurance Supervisors (IAIS), and the IOSCO delegation was expanded to four members. The new composition included all four signatories of the joint statement issued on 7 November 2007, discussed above. The removal of the Basel Committee and the IAIS, and perhaps also of the Financial Stability Forum, reflected the SEC's strong preference not to include prudential regulators among the members of the monitoring group. The trustees valued the IASB's contacts with these bodies, and had initially thought that their membership was appropriate in a monitoring group conceived as an evolved version of the Trustee Appointments Advisory Group.[28] But apparently the trustees found the SEC's views to be persuasive, and satisfied themselves that their relations with these organizations would not be impaired if they were excluded from the monitoring group.

At their March 2008 meeting, the trustees discussed the proposed document and recommended some changes in wording.[29] Based on advice from the trustees, staff modified the 'Proposals' document to provide that no member of the monitoring group could serve in more than one capacity—for example, if the SEC chairman were also chairman of IOSCO's Technical Committee, the vice chairman of the latter would serve. It was also stated that the terms of reference of the relationship between the monitoring group and the trustees would be contained in a memorandum of understanding, which would be made public.

The trustees also agreed to a Constitutional coordinating group made up of Laskawy, Collomb, DiPiazza, Fujinuma and Vegezzi (who had been the members of the earlier strategy committee), and Chairman Zalm. Pedro Malan was added subsequently.

---

[28] Communications from Thomas Seidenstein to the authors dated 22 February and 1 March 2013.

[29] IASCF trustees meeting of 17–18 March 2008, minute 5.

Public consultations on the monitoring group and the composition of the Board began with four sessions with a total of thirty participants representing a wide array of stakeholder organizations in an all-day roundtable in London on 19 June. The roundtable was held prior to the publication of a consultation document. Chairman Zalm, together with Laskawy and Vegezzi, represented the trustees at the sessions.[30] As analysed by the staff, the comments received at the four sessions showed nearly unanimous support for the creation of the monitoring group.[31] But the participants' views on the specific construction, mandate, and membership varied considerably. The staff noted: 'A regular theme of the round-table participants was a concern that the MG [monitoring group] could politicize the IASB's standard-setting process and that [the] organisation would suffer from the MG's "mission creep"' (page 3). While many panellists believed that the proposal would give too much power to the monitoring group to influence the IASB, there were some who believed that it should play a more active role in the oversight, and even in the Board's agenda setting. Some from the investment community recommended specific investor representation on the monitoring group, while others called for the inclusion of prudential regulators. Views were offered for and against the continuance of the Trustee Appointments Advisory Group.

The next step was the publication of a consultation document. Prior to the trustees' July meeting, staff made numerous drafting changes, mainly to clarify, reorganize, and amplify the materials from the previous 'Proposals' paper.[32] Seidenstein reported on the roundtable in executive session at the trustees' July 2008 meeting, which led to an extensive discussion.[33] Chairman Zalm recommended that the composition and membership of the monitoring group should be the subject of a specific question in the consultation document, as the inclusion of a representative from the 'banking sector' (i.e. banking supervisors) might well be appropriate, and the trustees assented to do so. This was at variance with the views of the four signatories of the November letter, who had described the monitoring group as a 'mechanism for interaction between securities authorities and the IASCF' in a press release welcoming the June roundtable.[34] The trustees agreed that there would be public consultation on the draft memorandum of understanding between the monitoring group and the trustees so that the process would be seen to be accountable and completely transparent.

On 21 July, the Foundation issued a press release to announce the period of consultation on the recommended changes in the Constitution, with a deadline of 20 September set for the receipt of comments.[35] The exposure document was a twenty-five-page booklet entitled 'Review of the Constitution: Public

---

[30] IASCF trustees meeting of 8–9 July 2008, agenda paper 2; see also 'Trustees to Hold Round-table Discussions ahead of Constitution Proposals', IASCF press release dated 12 May 2008.

[31] IASCF trustees meeting of 8–9 July 2008, agenda paper 2A.

[32] IASCF trustees meeting of 8–9 July 2008, agenda paper 2B.

[33] IASCF trustees meeting of 8–9 July 2008, minute 3.

[34] 'Authorities Responsible for Regulation of Public Companies Announce Next Steps Regarding the Creation of a Group to Interact with the International Accounting Standards Committee Foundation', European Commission press release IP/08/966, 18 June 2008 <http://europa.eu/rapid>.

[35] 'Trustees Publish Proposals on Enhancements to Public Accountability and to IASB Composition', IASCF press release dated 21 July 2008.

Accountability and the Composition of the IASB—Proposals for Change'. The proposal with respect to the monitoring group was that it would consist of seven members, in line with earlier drafts. The World Bank and the IMF would be included, and the question was asked whether other organizations 'accountable to public authorities and with an interest in the functioning of capital and other financial markets' should be considered for membership.

The financial crisis which broke in September 2008, during the consultation period, precipitated heavy political pressure on the IASB to adjust its standards on financial instruments (see Chapter 13) and thus underlined the urgency of setting up a monitoring group that could shield the IASB from such pressure. On 21 October, IOSCO's Technical Committee issued a statement asserting the critical importance of independent accounting standard setting. The Technical Committee said: 'We strongly support the efforts of the International Accounting Standards Committee Foundation Trustees to enhance their, and the IASB's, accountability, legitimacy and independence.' While the notion of a monitoring group was not mentioned in so many words, in the light of the trustees' published proposals the statement could well be read as the Technical Committee's first public utterance that it wished to see such a Monitoring Board, and to see it as a board of securities regulators.[36]

In October, staff provided an analysis of the more than sixty comment letters received to date, about half of which came from Europe.[37] The preponderance of views roughly paralleled those heard during the roundtable on 19 June. Most commentators supported the establishment of the monitoring group, but there was a lack of consensus on its composition. A number of respondents, particularly those from the private sector, worried about possible political interference in the standard-setting process (page 3). Some argued that the monitoring group should include banking and insurance supervisors or an investor representative (pages 4–5). Some wanted greater clarity on the relative roles of the trustees and the monitoring group.

While all of these reactions were of interest, some crucial reactions were still missing. At the trustees' October meeting in Beijing, Chairman Zalm said in executive session that it would not be possible to conclude the first part of the Constitution review until they had received a formal comment letter from the regulators that were candidates for membership on the monitoring group.[38] Apparently, there was not merely a general lack of consensus on the composition of the monitoring group, but also among the organizations considered for membership. The trustees accepted the recommendation of the Constitution review

---

[36] 'IOSCO Technical Committee Statement on Accounting Standards Development and Enforcement', IOSCO press release 017/2008, 21 October 2008 <http://www.iosco.org>.

[37] IASCF trustees meeting of 15–16 January 2009, agenda paper 2B. Apparently, this paper, dated 'October 2008' and said to reflect the comments received until 2 October, was not part of the agenda papers of the trustees' meeting of October 2008, although it presumably was seen by the Constitution review committee prior to the full trustees' meeting. The paper gives more than one count of the number of letters received to date, but the totals and geographical distribution do not differ markedly from the final tally reported in April 2009. Quotations and attributions in this paragraph are taken from this document.

[38] IASCF trustees meeting of 9–10 October 2008, minute 1.

committee that it was not yet appropriate to conclude the first part of the Constitution review.[39]

14.6.1 Size and Composition of the IASB Board

As indicated above, the second major issue in part one of the Constitution review was the size and composition of the IASB Board. This, too, was an issue that arose out of the strategy review. Following the trustees' first round of discussions in January 2007, the preliminary views were reported to be that, while technical competence remained a clear priority, 'those from a purely technical background should not solely dominate the IASB'. There was sympathy for reducing the size of the Board from fourteen to twelve, by removing the part-time positions. A geographical mix, while not determining, was important to promote.[40]

The first version of the 'Pathway' paper, discussed in July 2007, addressed the trustees' own geographical make-up as well as that of the Board.[41] The trustees, it said, 'may need to give further thought about allocation of Trustee positions to Africa and Latin America' (page 6). As to the Board, while the trustees affirmed that they already took account of geographical diversity, the paper added: 'As more countries adopt IFRS, the demand for geographical diversity will increase.' The strategy committee had been discussing the optimum size of the Board and began contemplating a prescribed regional representation on the fourteen-member Board, initially four from Europe, four from North America, four from Asia-Oceania, and two from Africa, the Middle East, or South America. (The difference with Latin America, as used for the trustees, may not have been intentional.) This was a new departure. When the IASB's original Constitution was drafted, geographical membership criteria had been consciously rejected when it was agreed that the Board should operate on the basis of an independent-expert model rather than on the basis of a representative model. The same logic had prevailed during the first review of the Constitution. Given the increasing adoption of IFRSs around the world, it was now seen as important to make explicit the implicit search for geographical balance which was already a major factor in the trustees' appointment decisions (see Section 11.2). Explicit geographical criteria were expected to have a calming influence in a situation where the IASB was easily criticized for being too much dominated by either Europe or the United States, or by both relative to the rest of the world.[42]

The paper recommended leaving the Board at its current size or even expanding it to fifteen or sixteen members with an eye on the proposed geographical quota, 'even if efficiency purposes would be better served through a smaller board' (page 6). The latter was still a concern of some Board members and trustees. David Tweedie, for one, suggested a Board of twelve. In the final 'Pathway' paper the trustees slightly modified their stance. Instead of suggesting that the Board's

---

[39] IASCF trustees meeting of 9–10 October 2008, minute 1 and 9.

[40] IASCF trustees meeting of 2–3 April 2007, agenda paper 7.

[41] IASCF trustees meeting of 2–3 July 2007, agenda paper 10A. Quotations and attributions in this and the next paragraph are taken from this document.

[42] Interview with Philip Laskawy, 18 February 2009.

size be increased to fifteen or sixteen, the trustees now cautioned against a reduction below fourteen 'in light of the desire to maintain broad contact and understanding with a global constituency'.[43]

In January 2008 the pendulum had swung again, as a staff paper made the case for keeping the Board size at fourteen or, preferably, as some trustees and Board members had suggested, to consider expanding it to sixteen. This number was apparently seen as a convenient basis for geographical quotas.[44] Three reasons were given for expanding the size of the Board: the growing burden of the Board's liaison and communications tasks following increased acceptance of IFRSs, the legitimacy provided 'in the eyes of many' by professional as well as geographical diversity in the Board, and the benefit of a diversity of perspectives to the quality of the Board's deliberations: 'The introduction of IASB members from different backgrounds has enabled the IASB to account for issues that may not have been raised in the past' (page 2). The diversity of perspectives was also the main reason to recommend the continuation of the part-time Board members, 're-examining that position only if it becomes difficult to identify qualified part-time candidates' (page 3).

When this was discussed during the trustees' meeting, Chairman Zalm said that he favoured an increase in Board size to sixteen, with the regional quotas as recommended by the staff (four each from Asia-Oceania, Europe, North America, and any area). The trustees 'confirmed that of paramount importance was the maintenance of the IASB's competence and diversity/balance of backgrounds. The regional representation of the IASB members would also be kept in mind but would not be the final determining factor.' The trustees did not reach a decision at the meeting about the recommended size and composition.[45]

As indicated above, Tom Seidenstein had drafted a proposed Constitution document for the trustees' March 2008 meeting, 'Proposals and Issues for the Constitution Review', dealing both with the monitoring group and Board size and composition.[46] In his covering memorandum, he said that the trustees had agreed to 'the expansion of the IASB to 16 members', yet no such agreement was actually reported in the minutes of the trustees' January meeting.[47] The 'Proposals' document therefore recommended sixteen members, with the geographical distribution already considered: four each from North America, Europe, and Asia-Oceania, and four from any area, 'subject to maintaining overall geographical balance' (paragraph 19). In place of the existing provision that two of the fourteen members were to be part-time, the proposal provided that up to three of the sixteen members may be part-time. The supermajority requirement in the Constitution would be retained.

During the roundtables on part one of the Constitution review held in June 2008, many expressed concern that a larger size would slow down the standard-

---

[43] IASCF trustees meeting of 31 October–1 November 2007, agenda paper 10B, page 9.

[44] IASCF trustees meeting of 28–30 January 2008, agenda paper 5C. Quotations and attributions in this paragraph are taken from this document.

[45] IASCF trustees meeting of 29–30 January 2008, minute 1.

[46] IASCF trustees meeting of 17–18 March 2008, agenda paper 2A.

[47] IASCF trustees meeting of 17–18 March 2008, agenda paper 2.

setting process.[48] Also: 'A common concern expressed was that if the IASB becomes too large then it would break down into sub-groupings and its workings would become less transparent' (page 6). Some critics of the proposed geographic delineation of the Board cited the possible risk that Board members would represent their regions instead of relying on their own decision criteria. Some expressed concern that there was no provision for membership from Latin America or Africa or other emerging economies, thinking that there was nothing stopping the trustees from appointing all four of the remaining members from the regions already represented on the Board. This point was accepted by the trustees who considered a provision that the trustees should 'normally' appoint at least one Board member from Africa and South America. At the suggestion of Chairman Zalm, this was changed to a simple requirement of at least one Board member from each area.[49]

When the comment letters resulting from the public consultation were analysed, it appeared that there were mixed views on the increase in the size of the Board.[50] While many commentators understood the reason for the increase in size, many expressed the view that the larger Board membership would make it more unwieldy and less effective (page 7). Some believed that consultation with stakeholders was not part of the Board's duties. On geographic representation, some were strongly opposed because fulfilling this criterion would detract from the trustees' ability to appoint competent and experienced members, and that there was a risk that some members would become geographic representatives (page 8). Some expressed concern over the continued dominance of members from North America. There was general support for part-time membership. Most respondents 'were of the view that it would assist in achieving an improved level of practitioner representation on the Board' (page 9).

14.6.2 The January 2009 Trustees' Meeting

The January 2009 meeting of the trustees in New Delhi was when they took the fateful decision to create the Monitoring Board (the name now adopted for the monitoring group). They also acted to change the size and composition of the IASB Board.

Before the trustees could act, they were awaiting a joint comment letter from the proposed members of the monitoring group in order to learn their views of the trustees' proposal. By early January, a comment letter was finally in hand.[51] It was signed by Commissioner Charlie McCreevy on behalf of the European Commission, Chairman Jane Diplock for IOSCO, Commissioner Takafumi Sato for Japan's FSA, and Chairman Christopher Cox for the SEC. Throughout their

---

[48] IASCF trustees meeting of 8–9 July 2008, agenda paper 2A. Quotations and attributions in this paragraph are taken from this document.

[49] IASCF trustees meeting of 8–9 July 2008, agenda paper 2B; IASCF trustees meeting of 8–9 July 2008, minute 3.

[50] IASCF trustees meeting of 15–16 January 2009, agenda paper 2B. Quotations and attributions in this paragraph are taken from this document.

[51] IASCF trustees meeting of 15–16 January 2009, agenda paper 2A.

letter, they used Monitoring Board in place of Monitoring Group, to distinguish the new body from IFAC's Monitoring Group. The four bodies wrote, 'We strongly support the creation of a Monitoring Board. Establishing a formal link between capital markets authorities responsible for setting financial reporting in their jurisdictions and the IASC Foundation will strengthen investor confidence in IFRS, to the benefit of capital markets around the world.' They maintained their position that the Monitoring Board's membership should be limited to the aforementioned capital markets authorities. Hence, the IMF and the World Bank were not to be included, in contrast to the trustees' proposal in their consultation document. Prudential regulators were not entirely left out, as the signatories recommended that the Basel Committee on Banking Supervision should participate as a non-voting observer. By early 2009, the onset of the financial crisis had placed the influence of accounting standards on financial stability high on the political agenda, but it did not necessarily follow that securities regulators were willing to share their oversight of financial reporting with prudential regulators. The recommendation regarding the observer position for the Basel Committee could therefore be seen as a somewhat minimalist implementation of the call by the G20 in November 2008 that 'With a view toward promoting financial stability, the governance of the international accounting standard setting body should be further enhanced'.[52]

So the final composition of the Monitoring Board would come down to the four bodies that wrote the joint statement to the Foundation trustees on 7 November 2007, in which they proposed the creation of such a body. The four signatories set out the following five principal responsibilities of the Monitoring Board, the last of which was perhaps the least expected by the trustees:

   i) Approve Trustee nominees;

  ii) Review the adequacy and appropriateness of Trustee arrangements for financing the IASB;

 iii) Review the Trustees' oversight of the IASB's standard setting process, in particular with respect to its due process arrangements;

  iv) Confer with the Trustees regarding their responsibilities, in particular in relation to the regulatory, legal and policy developments that are pertinent to the IASCF's oversight of the IASB; and

   v) Refer matters of broad public interest related to financial reporting for consideration by the IASB.

They concluded their three-page letter by saying, 'We applaud the IASC Foundation's efforts to address concerns about the accountability of the IASC Foundation'.

In a January 2009 memorandum to the trustees, staff revised the proposed Constitutional amendments to reflect the name and final membership of the Monitoring Board in line with the apparently decisive letter from the four

---

[52] 'Action Plan to Implement Principles for Financial Reform', page 1, appendix to 'Declaration: Summit on Financial Markets and the World Economy', 15 November 2008 <http://www.treasury. gov>.

signatories.[53] Staff also recommended that the Trustee Appointments Advisory Group be disbanded.

In conjunction with the staff of the proposed members of the Monitoring Board, the Foundation's staff had developed a proposed Memorandum of Understanding.[54] This added one responsibility of the Monitoring Board ('Participate in the Trustee nomination process') and modified the fifth responsibility as follows: 'Refer matters of broad public interest related to financial reporting for consideration by the IASB *through the IASCF*' (emphasis added). Notwithstanding the trustees' earlier intentions that there should be a public consultation on the draft Memorandum of Understanding, the staff proposed that this was not required because the Memorandum of Understanding 'reflects the conclusions of a document that has received public review' (page 3). The amendments, staff said, were to take effect on 1 February 2009.

At their January 2009 meeting, the trustees approved the amendments to the Constitution with respect to the Monitoring Board, as well as the Memorandum of Understanding. They noted that both the IMF and the World Bank would continue to hold positions on SAC. As to the Board's size and composition, staff recommended a membership of sixteen with the geographic distribution according to the consultation document, which was also approved.

On 29 January, the Foundation issued a press release to announce the approval of the amendments. Attached to the release were the conclusions from the trustees' meeting and the Memorandum of Understanding. In April, the Foundation published the trustees' report on part one of their Constitution review.[55]

14.7 OTHER ISSUES CONSIDERED DURING THE STRATEGY REVIEW

During the strategy review process, many other issues from the December 2006 Tweedie-Seidenstein memorandum were discussed. The heterogeneity of the issues, as well as the fact that some, such as the creation of a Monitoring Board, were already taken up while the strategy review was still in process might obscure the fact that the trustees did attempt to formulate an over-arching vision. The final 'Pathway' paper began by recalling: 'In little more than six years, the possibility that the world's capital markets will have a common, internationally accepted set of accounting standards is closer than ever.'[56] If this was an understatement of the wonderment felt by many about the IASB's astonishing rise to prominence, the trustees were realistic enough to recognize that the adoption of IFRSs had been favoured by the forces of economic integration and the development of capital

---

[53] IASCF trustees meeting of 15–16 January 2009, agenda paper 2. Quotations and attributions in this section are taken from this document.

[54] IASCF trustees meeting of 15–16 January 2009, agenda paper 2C.

[55] *Changes in the Constitution: Report of the IASC Foundation Trustees on Part 1 of their Review* (IASCF, April 2009).

[56] IASCF trustees meeting of 31 October–1 November 2007, agenda paper 10B, paragraph 1. Unless otherwise indicated, paragraph references in this section are to this document.

markets. Nonetheless, the trustees were determined to grasp Fortune by the forelock (paragraph 3, original emphasis):

> The organization's strategy is and should be aimed at making *IFRSs the unrivaled global standard for financial reporting*. To be successful, the IFRSs should be the only set of high-quality accounting standards that are used by investors to make decisions regarding the allocation [of] capital for companies operating in the world's capital markets.

The trustees identified four elements of the Foundation's structure that required reinforcement, not just in terms of resources and operational effectiveness, but also 'to endow its work with the necessary legitimacy in the long-term' (paragraph 8). As will be seen, the four elements grouped a variety of issues requiring a variety of responses. Some were already being dealt with at an operational level, and others would become part of either part one or part two of the Constitution review, while others were simply identified as important questions that needed constant attention or further reflection.

The first element was, unsurprisingly, 'independence with public accountability', taking up six of the paper's eleven pages. Under this heading, the paper discussed what would become the Monitoring Board, as described above. But independence also meant creating a sustainable funding mechanism, a perennial issue facing the trustees (see Section 11.10). This section of the paper also touched on broader aspects of accountability. Apart from creating a Monitoring Board, the 'organization should continue to demonstrate that it is responsive to a broader range of interests and parties in the development of IFRSs' (paragraph 20). This included a restructuring of SAC (discussed in Section 11.3), but also the need to review the representative groups of users and preparers with which the IASB held regular meetings. The paper discussed why it was important for the IASB to strengthen its engagement with national standard setters, not least because the success of IFRSs might lead to a weakening of national standard setters as a result of reduced home support and declining resources. Keeping the accounting standard setters in the loop was important, because reaching them was 'an efficient way for the IASB to receive input and to communicate with those affected by its standards' (paragraph 24). A special case, of course, was the IASB's relationship with the FASB. As described in an April 2007 trustees agenda paper for the strategy review, support for this ongoing relationship up to, say, 2012 would be sustainable only if the SEC were to lift the US GAAP reconciliation requirement. Some trustees questioned whether the international community would accept an equal partnership between the IASB and FASB in the long term, especially 'as the relative importance of US capital markets diminishes naturally as other economies develop and a larger number of countries adopt IFRSs'.[57] The final Pathway paper, written just before the SEC would lift the reconciliation requirement in November 2007, summed up the position as follows (paragraphs 26–7):[58]

> In the future if the IASB were successful in making IFRSs the unrivalled global standard, it is unlikely that the IASB will be able to sustain a 'special relationship',

---

[57] IASCF trustees meeting of 2–3 April 2007, agenda paper 7.
[58] 'two internally used sets' emended to 'two internationally used sets'.

where a uniquely US body has a place at the table, on an indefinite basis. Already European and Asian standard-setters have expressed disquiet with the perceived 'undue' influence that FASB has in the process. The current status is justified by the aims of the Memorandum of Understanding and is a pragmatic approach for bringing together two internationally used sets of standards and winning the confidence of US market participants.... Therefore, the Trustees should begin the consideration of the post-MoU relationship with the US FASB. These discussions should include the US SEC, the Financial Accounting Foundation, and other US parties.

The second main element of the trustees' strategy paper was 'building a truly global organization'. This dealt with the debate among the trustees, as it then stood, on the size and composition of the Board, in particular its geographical make-up. As noted above, this was addressed in part one of the Constitution review. The paper noted that the IASB's staff already came from nineteen countries, but that the organization 'should have a policy that seeks a diversity of experiences' (paragraph 42).

The third strategic element was 'protecting the IFRS brand'. As discussed more fully in Sections 10.5 and 10.6, the main concerns here related to companies claiming compliance with IFRSs, or jurisdictions claiming adoption of IFRSs, without full compliance or adoption. However, as the strategy review progressed it became clearer that this was a regulatory issue rather than something over which the IASB or the Foundation had direct control, and the final Pathway paper simply stated the intention to continue working with IOSCO and the IAASB to ensure that there is a statement of full compliance with IFRSs in either the auditor's report or the financial statements. IOSCO eventually issued a statement in this vein, dealing with the financial statements, in February 2008 (see Section 10.6). Thought was given to the question whether the names of countries that use the IFRS brand without fully complying with IFRSs should be divulged.[59] The final Pathway paper concluded that a public survey should be conducted on a regular basis to identify countries where the accounting standards do not comply fully with IFRSs. The trustees looked to the World Bank or the major audit firms to take this up, because they already had access to the relevant information (paragraph 45). While that was true, one surmises that the trustees may also have thought of the complications that might possibly arise out of confronting jurisdictions with 'improper' adoption of IFRSs.

Apart from this, the 'brand' heading assembled such points as ensuring the quality of IFRS translations, a high quality XBRL IFRS taxonomy, protection of copyright, and establishing 'IFRS' as the key brand of the Foundation. As will be seen, the last point was taken up in part two of the Constitution review.

The fourth and final element of the strategy paper was 'operating in a non-bureaucratic, professional environment'. The words 'non-bureaucratic' and 'professional' were not explained, but the brief discussion of the issues suggested that the trustees had more in mind than simple stock phrases from the management literature. What was at stake was the tension between the technical quality and the acceptability of the IASB's standards. This touched upon the debate in the late 1990s on the IASC's basic structure, which ended with the adoption of the FASB

---

[59] IASCF trustees meeting of 2–3 April 2007, agenda paper 7.

model and the identification of technical expertise as the primary requirement for Board membership. The paper observed that 'While [the] IASB's working procedures are aimed at technical quality, they are not well suited for considering the acceptability of proposals. This is not to dismiss the need for discussion papers, exposure drafts, and other field research, but is a call to examine whether the process that the IASB uses to develop its discussion papers and exposure drafts is suitable for the environment in which the IASB operates' (paragraph 48). The paper did not specify in detail why the IASB's procedures fell short in terms of ensuring acceptability, but it went on to draw attention to the influence of the FASB example: 'Upon formation, the IASB adopted the working procedures used at the US FASB. This made sense, because the FASB was a well-established body with significant experience. However, the IASB's experience showed that dissecting parts of a project to a single issue sometimes inhibited the IASB from taking a more holistic view of its approach and potential workability' (paragraph 49). Again, this was not explained, but it seems a reflection of the frustration that some of the IASB Board, including its chairman, sometimes felt in working with the FASB on convergence, because of what was seen as the FASB's overly detailed approach to analysing and discussing technical projects (see also Section 12.3). It is true that the IASB was sometimes criticized for allowing its standards to become too detailed as part of the convergence with US GAAP. But it was equally true that, when the IASB had worked independently of the FASB, acceptability of its work was not guaranteed either, as illustrated by the Board's initial attempts at performance reporting (see Section 5.5.2) and the European carve-outs on financial instruments. At any rate, it was noted that 'any changes in the working procedures would need to account for the ongoing relationship with the FASB and that significant change may not be possible in the near-term' (paragraph 50).

A different emphasis in the Board's work was also suggested by the brief remarks on how the trustees might encourage 'a balanced approach' by means of IASB performance evaluations. While it was acknowledged that the trustees should not participate in the standard-setting work, the selection of Board members and the definition of performance criteria were in their remit. It was noted that the selection criteria for Board members in the Constitution emphasized technical qualities, but that a 'balanced scorecard' had been developed for use in performance evaluations, which might be used to evaluate reappointments (paragraph 50).

14.8 PART TWO OF THE CONSTITUTION REVIEW

For the second part of the Constitution review, multiple rounds of consultation by the trustees took place within a relatively short period. The first step consisted of a consultation document which they issued in December 2008. The consultation document was a 25-page booklet on the remaining Constitutional issues (formerly Part B). Its title was 'Review of the Constitution: Identifying Issues for Part 2 of the Review'. This was an exploratory consultation, as the title implied, and the trustees invited comments on any matters related to the Constitution not raised in this document. Comments were to be received by 31 March 2009.

As the comments on the consultation document were digested by the staff, preparations were made for roundtables with key stakeholder groups in September and October in London, New York, and Tokyo. With an eye on the 2010 deadline for completing the review, the trustees did not wait for the roundtables to take their next step. Just before the first roundtable, on 9 September 2009, the Foundation issued a second consultation document, a pamphlet of fifty-two pages containing the trustees' specific proposals.[60] Comments were invited before 30 November, and this allowed the trustees to complete part two according to the plan in January 2010, when they approved a number of amendments to the Constitution, effective as of 1 March 2010.[61]

This second phase of the Constitution review attracted attention from around the world, but, just as in part one of the review, the interest displayed by European constituents was notable. The December 2008 consultation paper attracted sixty-seven comment letters, of which thirty-one came from Europe.[62] Of the sixty-nine comment letters on the September 2009 proposals, thirty-three came from Europe.[63] Conversely, interest in the United States appeared tepid, given that the SEC was still considering the use of IFRSs by US companies. Only one letter was received from the United States on the September 2009 proposals, from Conrad Hewitt, the former SEC Chief Accountant. Eight persons from the United States attended the roundtable held in New York, compared to twenty-seven from Japan attending the roundtable in Tokyo.[64]

The more salient issues brought up in the course of this phase, and the related changes made to the Constitution, are briefly discussed in Sections 14.8.1–14.8.11.

14.8.1 Objectives: Principles-based Standards

The December 2008 consultation paper (paragraph 2) noted the opinion of the trustees that 'the commitment to drafting standards based upon clear principles remains vitally important and should be enshrined in the Constitution'. As seen in Chapters 4 and 5, the idea of IFRSs as principles-based standards had become part of the IASB's self-image at least since the Enron affair made the contrast between principles-based and rules-based standards a common theme in accounting discourse. While all commentators favoured a principles-based approach, there was no consensus that it should be expressly stated in the Constitution.[65] The trustees therefore revised their earlier opinion and followed the staff's

---

[60] 'Part 2 of the Constitution Review: Proposals for Enhanced Public Accountability' (IASCF, September 2009).

[61] For the planning, see IASCF trustees meeting of 1–2 April 2009, minute 7. See also *Report of the IASC Foundation Trustees on Part 2 of their Constitution Review: Changes for Enhanced Public Accountability and Stakeholder Engagement* (IASCF, April 2010).

[62] See the comment letter analysis in IASCF trustees meeting of 6–8 July 2009, agenda paper 1A. Referred to in the remainder of this chapter as trustees agenda paper 1A, July 2009.

[63] IASCF trustees meeting of 26–7 January 2010, agenda paper 2A. Referred to in the remainder of this chapter as trustees agenda paper 2A, January 2010.

[64] *Report of the IASC Foundation Trustees on Part 2 of their Constitution Review*, Appendix II and III.

[65] IASCF trustees meeting of 1–2 April 2009, agenda paper 1A, 8.

recommendation that no references to principles-based standards be inserted in the Constitution, as this would be a level of detail inappropriate for a constitutional document.[66] This, in turn, did not please some of the IASB's constituents, and both at the roundtables and in responses to the September 2009 consultation document there was strong to 'overwhelming' support for including a reference to principles-based standards in the paragraph on the objectives of the organization.[67] As a result, paragraph 2(a) of the Constitution was amended by adding that the Foundation sought to develop financial reporting standards 'based upon clearly articulated principles'.

14.8.2 Objectives: Range of Entities and Economic Settings

Ever since the late 1980s it was evident that the IASC, and subsequently the IASB, was firmly focused on setting standards for listed companies active in global capital markets. Even so, the question always recurred whether the reporting needs of 'other' entities, or companies in 'other' settings, should be considered as well. As mentioned in Chapters 7 and 12, this had resulted, in the first Constitution review, in the insertion of a reference to 'emerging economies' and the 'special needs of small and medium-sized entities' in the objectives of the Foundation. In the second Constitution review, the trustees raised the question whether this wording was still appropriate, and whether the Foundation's mandate should be widened by a reference to financial reporting in the public sector and by not-for-profit entities. This latter point had already been considered during the preceding strategy review. The final (October 2007) 'Pathway' paper concluded that 'the current timing is not conducive to expanding the organization's mandate' because it would divert resources and focus, and it would raise questions about the IASB's legitimacy in those fields.[68] If the trustees had been looking for confirmation of their view, they could not have wished for a clearer response. Almost all commentators on the December 2008 consultation document gave the view that, in the light of the IASB's very full agenda, it would be inappropriate to extend its mandate to not-for-profit and public-sector entities at this time.[69] As before, Australia and New Zealand remained the main source of support for so-called sector-neutral standards. The trustees tried to clarify the wording of the reference to emerging economies and small and medium-sized entities in the Constitution, which seemed to attract wide support.[70] Nonetheless, in the Constitution as approved in January 2010, this explicit reference was replaced by the more general 'to take account of, as appropriate, the needs of a range of sizes and types of entities in diverse economic settings' (paragraph 2(c)).

---

[66] IASCF trustees meeting of 6–8 July 2009, agenda paper 1B. Referred to in the remainder of this section as trustees agenda paper 1B, July 2009.

[67] For comments made during the London roundtable, see IASCF trustees meeting of 7–8 October 2009, agenda paper 7, referred to in the remainder of this section as trustees agenda paper 7, October 2009. For comment letters, see trustees agenda paper 2A, January 2010, 15.

[68] IASCF trustees meeting of 31 October–1 November 2007, agenda paper 10B, 2.

[69] Trustees agenda paper 1A, July 2009, 9.

[70] Trustees agenda paper 2A, January 2010.

To some extent, this reflected a recognition that the world had changed in a way that defied easy classification of economies into categories such as 'developing', 'emerging', 'transitioning', or 'developed'.[71]

14.8.3 Objectives: Globally Accepted Standards

The September 2009 consultation document proposed a change in section 2(a) of the IASB's objectives: from developing 'a single set of high quality, understandable, and enforceable global accounting standards' to 'a single set of high quality, understandable, enforceable and *globally accepted* financial reporting standards' (emphasis added). The reason given was: 'This would reflect the fact that relevant public authorities must take the decision to adopt the standards if they are to be become universally accepted' (page 11). Experience had shown that there could sometimes be a tension between global acceptance and what the Board saw as pursuit of high quality standards, but it was curious that the trustees' insertion of 'globally accepted' seemed to come almost as an afterthought, without any wording to suggest to the Board how it should consider resolving possible conflicts between the two. It was said that 'All commentators supported the proposed change to reflect that financial reporting standards should be globally accepted and saw this as further emphasizing the need for the IASB to consult widely and find support amongst a wide variety of constituents. It was also felt that this implicitly reinforced the requirement for the standards to be of a high quality.'[72] As will be seen below, impressing the need for consultation on the IASB and thus, one might say, further constraining the almost unlimited independence of the Board under the original Constitution, seemed to be an important consideration underlying many respondents' views on more than one issue dealt with in this part of the Constitution review.

14.8.4 Collaboration with Other Organizations

The original Constitution included a clause on liaison with national standard setters. As discussed in Chapter 3, this was a reference to a very specific form of cooperation with a clearly defined and small set of accounting standard setters. In the first Constitution review, the exclusiveness of these liaison relationships had been abandoned, and the scope of the clause had been broadened to include the expectation of liaison with 'other official bodies concerned with standard setting in order to promote the convergence' of national accounting standards and IFRSs (paragraph 28). In the December 2008 consultation document (paragraph 4), the trustees observed that there were other organizations 'that establish standards that are either based upon or have a close relationship with IFRSs', and they raised the question whether the Constitution should allow for the possibility of closer collaboration with such organizations. No examples were mentioned, but in

---

[71] *Report of the IASC Foundation Trustees on Part 2 of their Constitution Review*, 22.
[72] Trustees agenda paper 2A, January 2010, 15.

October 2008 the trustees had considered a proposal from the International Valuation Standards Committee (IVSC) for just such a kind of cooperation.[73] The origins of the IVSC went back to 1981, when the IASC's work on accounting for property, plant, and equipment resulting in IAS 16 brought it into contact with the property valuation industry. The IVSC was set up in a deliberate imitation of the IASC's model, and it had maintained good relations with the IASC as well as the IASB.[74] So, while cooperation with the IVSC was not problematic for the IASB, establishing a formal relationship as suggested by the IVSC might prompt a number of other organizations to make similar requests. Because of this latter concern, the staff advised the trustees to include this point in part two of the Constitution review.

During the consultations it became clear that the IVSC was indeed seen as a plausible candidate for cooperation, as well as the International Public Sector Accounting Standards Board (IPSASB) and the IAASB. It may be surmised that the Foundation would have been a little more wary to enmesh itself too closely with organizations responsible for prudential supervision and financial stability, as suggested by some European respondents.[75] It was probably not too difficult for the trustees to avoid choosing, by concluding that a listing of organizations by name in the Constitution was neither practicable nor appropriate. Meanwhile, a significant change of emphasis had occurred, as many respondents interpreted the issue less in terms of liaison and cooperation, and more in terms of the need for the IASB to consult more widely when setting standards. The trustees cited as the main reason for the almost unanimous support for modifying the Constitution on this point 'that wide consultation is imperative to reinforce the legitimacy of accounting standards'.[76] As amended in January 2010, paragraph 28 of the Constitution did indeed include 'other standard setters' next to accounting standard setters as the bodies with which the Board should liaise. But now it also said that liaison with standard setters or other bodies, should be established not merely in order to promote convergence, but also in order 'to assist in the development of IFRSs'. Compared to the original Constitution, which envisaged the Board setting standards in relative isolation, and working with only a small group of similar standard setters, there had been a considerable evolution.

14.8.5 Board Due Process: Agenda and Oversight

Part two of the Constitution review provided an opportunity to rehearse many familiar criticisms of the IASB, reducible to the general complaint that the Board, in its choice of priorities and in its actual standards, did not pay proper attention to the views of constituents, and that the trustees should do more to ensure that the Board did so. The open invitation to comment in the December 2008

---

[73] IASCF trustees meeting of 9–10 October 2008, agenda paper 5E.

[74] Kees Camfferman and Stephen A. Zeff, *Financial Reporting and Global Capital Markets: A History of the International Accounting Standards Committee, 1973–2000* (Oxford: Oxford University Press, 2007), 132.

[75] *Report of the IASC Foundation Trustees on Part 2 of their Constitution Review*, 30.

[76] *Report of the IASC Foundation Trustees on Part 2 of their Constitution Review*, 29.

consultation paper prompted a litany of grievances. A large majority of letter-writers from the user sector expressed concern over the relevance of some of the IASB's work. A significant number of commentators questioned the emphasis placed on convergence. Many felt that the Board's independence would be enhanced and receive greater legitimacy if the agenda-setting process were to become more transparent and the IASB were to become more accountable, 'including providing explanations and justifications for their prioritisation of the agenda'.[77] Many commentators had taken note of the ongoing efforts by the Board and the trustees to enhance due process (see Section 11.5). They 'welcomed the enhancements of the IASB's due process procedures in the form of feedback statements, post-implementation reviews and effect analysis'. But some were disappointed with the IASB's consultations and 'urged' the trustees to demonstrate enhanced oversight over the IASB to ensure that it 'takes account of feedback, [and] cannot over-rule overwhelming opposition'.[78] On the trustees' oversight activities: 'There was a strong sense in the responses that the Trustees should play a greater role in assessing the IASB's effectiveness, should be more active in the agenda setting process, and should demonstrate their review of the IASB's due process.'[79] Many commentators said that, despite the robust procedures that were in place and followed, there was a sense that the IASB did not sufficiently take stakeholder views into account. In addition, there was increasing concern over the length and complexity of financial statements prepared using IFRSs, over the IASB making significant changes in drafts without re-exposing them, and over the cost and uncertainty of frequent changes to IFRSs.

In their September 2009 consultation paper, the trustees responded with restraint. While recognizing the 'valid and important' concerns over trustee oversight, they proposed not to make any Constitutional amendments on this point, but by continuing with the due process improvements initiated at the time of the first Constitution review. With respect to the Board's agenda, they proposed a modification of the Constitution to provide for mandatory consultation with the trustees and with SAC while maintaining the Board's 'full discretion in developing and pursuing the technical agenda' (paragraph 37(c) of the 2009 Constitution).

From the roundtables and the comment letters on the September 2009 discussion paper, it appeared that, while there was 'nearly universal support' for the IASB to have the ultimate authority to set its own agenda, there was also a strong desire for a public consultation on the Board's agenda priorities, and significant support for making explicit the need for formal public consultation on the IASB's agenda.[80] On the proposal that the Board should consult the trustees and SAC when developing its technical agenda, almost all commentators replied that such consultation was simply not sufficient: 'It was imperative for the IASB to hold formal broad based consultation with all interested constituents on a regular basis so as to ensure that it becomes more transparent and the IASB become more accountable.'[81] The commentators also wanted the IASB to provide explanations

---

[77] Trustees agenda paper 1A, July 2009, 14.   [78] Trustees agenda paper 1A, July 2009, 15.
[79] Trustees agenda paper 1A, July 2009, 12.
[80] Trustees agenda paper 2A, January 2010. See also IASCF trustees meeting of 7–8 October 2009, minute 9.
[81] Trustees agenda paper 2A, January 2010, 25.

and justifications for its agenda priorities. Most commentators took the view that the Board's agenda and how it was set was one of the most critical aspects of what the Board did, a view which was adopted by the trustees.[82]

In evident recognition of these views, the trustees amended the Constitution in January 2010 to the effect that the Board was not merely required to consult the trustees and SAC, but that it was required to carry out a public consultation on its agenda every three years, the first of which to begin no later than 30 June 2011 (paragraph 37(d)(ii) of the 2010 Constitution).

A more subtle but important change with relevance to the Board's agenda was a modification of the objectives of the organization (paragraph 2(d)), where jurisdictions' convergence was now portrayed as a strategy to promote and facilitate the adoption of IFRSs, rather than as an end in itself. This change not only reflected a general 'convergence fatigue' after almost a decade of high-intensity convergence efforts, it also reflected more fundamental developments. In 2000, when the original Constitution was drafted, convergence was probably the only feasible way forward in the direction of global accounting standards. Since then, however, the experience that many countries were prepared to adopt IFRSs in lieu of national standards made adoption, not convergence, the mark for which the Board should aim in its technical work.

Other due process issues, including calls for more field testing, better cost-benefit analysis, and enhanced feedback, did not result in Constitutional changes, but the trustees 'acknowledged the need for the IASB to be more responsive to stakeholders and interested parties and will bear this in mind when carrying out their oversight function in the future'.[83]

14.8.6 Board Due Process: Fast-track Procedure

A specific due process issue that clearly required attention had arisen in October 2008 when, during the financial crisis, the trustees had permitted the Board to modify IAS 39 and IFRS 7 without following the normal due process requirements (see Section 13.3). The December 2008 consultation document raised the question whether a fast-track procedure for use in emergency situations should be included in the Constitution. It appeared that many commentators were opposed to such a procedure because it might lead to abuse. Almost all commentators suggested two minimum criteria for any fast-track procedure. One was that it should be available only if 'triggered' by the trustees or the Monitoring Board in circumstances that constitute an emergency or urgent situation. The second was that there should always be an exposure draft with a comment period of no less than thirty to sixty days.[84] Thirty days was in fact the absolute minimum established in Board's 2006 *Due Process Handbook* (paragraph 98) for 'exceptionally urgent' matters.

---

[82] *Report of the IASC Foundation Trustees on Part 2 of their Constitution Review*, 35.
[83] *Report of the IASC Foundation Trustees on Part 2 of their Constitution Review*, 35.
[84] Trustees agenda paper 1A, July 2009.

In the September 2009 consultation document, an amendment to the Constitution was proposed that would allow the Board, in exceptional circumstances and with prior approval from the trustees, to reduce an exposure period below the minimum specified in the *Due Process Handbook*, but not to dispense entirely with a comment period. Again, most reactions were cautious if not critical. During the roundtables, many panellists emphasized the 'sheer impracticability' of anything less than a thirty-day comment period for a proposed standard.[85] Staff said that many comment letters had opposed a fast-track procedure in the Constitution 'because there was fear that it would be used capriciously and/or used to achieve a predetermined outcome'. Many also said that the thirty-day period stipulated in the *Due Process Handbook* was sufficient in itself for a fast track.[86]

One can see how most of the IASB's frequently divided constituents could find common ground in an abhorrence of fast-track procedures: those who were keen on the Board's independence remembered that the Board had departed from its due process only because of intense political pressure, while those who were anxious to ensure the widest possible consultation by the Board were loath to create what might look like an escape clause.

In the end, the trustees adopted the proposal of the September 2009 consultation document, but with the added safeguard that a due process suspension required approval by a supermajority of 75 per cent of the trustees.

14.8.7 Composition and Organization of the Trustees

It was not evident from the responses to the December 2008 consultation document that commentators saw the geographical distribution of trustees as problematic.[87] Nonetheless, the staff recommended that seats for Africa and South America be added to the geographic make-up of the trustees, to match the similar changes agreed for the Board in part one of the review.[88] This change, as proposed in September 2009, met with near-universal approval, and was enshrined in paragraph 6 of the 2010 Constitution. A change to paragraph 10, allowing the trustees to appoint up to two of their members as vice chairmen, while maintaining a geographical balance among them, was also non-controversial. As it happened, this change served the Foundation well when the two vice chairmen had to take over in December 2010, following the sudden death of trustees' chairman, Tommaso Padoa-Schioppa (see Section 14.11).

14.8.8 Organization of the Board

The composition of the Board in terms of membership criteria had been dealt with in part one of the review, but some issues remained to be addressed. A proposal to allow up to two full-time Board members to serve as vice chairmen passed without

---

[85] IASCF trustees meeting of 25–7 January 2010, minute 9.
[86] Trustees agenda paper 2A, January 2010, 24.
[87] Trustees agenda paper 1A, July 2009.   [88] Trustees agenda paper 1B, July 2009.

significant discussion. Somewhat more controversial was the question whether the roles of chairman of the Board and chief executive officer of the Foundation, hitherto combined in the person of David Tweedie, should be separated. There was support for this view among commentators as well as the staff, but it was not adopted by the trustees, neither in the September 2009 consultation paper nor in the Constitution as amended in January 2010.[89] One assumes that Tweedie's view weighed heavily. Tweedie opposed the split because he believed that having to go through a chief executive officer with requests for budget or staff, compared to going directly to the trustees, was an unnecessary complication: it could hamper the standard-setting process, while it would not change the trustees' ultimate oversight responsibility.[90]

The terms of Board members constituted another issue. As discussed in Chapter 11, the reappointment of Board members had earlier on become a matter of debate among the trustees, as some trustees began to see a higher rate of turnover in the Board as desirable. This was not initially put forward by the trustees as an issue in public consultation, but, reflecting comments received, they proposed to limit the second term of Board members to three years, following an initial five-year term. In this way, the trustees sought to balance the need for continuity in the Board with the need to ensure a sufficient number of members with recent practical experience. Reactions to this proposal were said to be 'mixed', but the change was made, applicable to Board members appointed after 2 July 2009. Hence, Patrick Finnegan, Pat McConnell, and Amaro Gomes, all three appointed as of 1 July 2009, would still be allowed a second five-year term. The first appointment under the new rules was that of Elke König, who joined the Board in July 2010. As amended, the Constitution allowed the chairman and a vice chairman of the Board to serve a second term of five years, but neither was allowed to serve on the Board for more than a total of ten years (paragraph 31 of the 2010 Constitution).

14.8.9 Name Change

As discussed in Chapter 11, the idea of using the word 'IFRS' in the name of the various units of the organization—the Foundation, the Board, IFRIC, and SAC— to give the IASB a more clearly delineated public image had already come up in the context of a review of the IASB's public relations strategy and when the IASB attracted its first full-time director of communications. A similar recommendation, without prompting by the trustees, arose out of the comments on the December 2008 consultation paper.[91] As a result, the September 2009 consultation document proposed that the International Accounting Standards Committee Foundation should become the IFRS Foundation, and the International Accounting Standards Board the IFRS Board. No changes were proposed to the names of SAC and IFRIC. From the roundtables, it emerged that the change in name of the Foundation was generally supported, but opinion was divided on

---

[89] Trustees agenda paper 1B, July 2009, 20.   [90] Interview with David Tweedie, 5 June 2013.
[91] Trustees agenda paper 1B, July 2009, 1.

changing the name of the IASB to the IFRS Board. It was reported that 'The strongest opposition at the round tables' to changing the name of the Board was from the participants in Tokyo, who felt that the change 'would dilute a well-recognised brand and also cause legal difficulties since the term "IASB" has been incorporated into legislation and legal contracts in many jurisdictions around the world'.[92] Consequently, in January 2010, the IASC Foundation did become the IFRS Foundation, while the Board remained known as the IASB. The trustees changed the names of IFRIC and SAC to IFRS Interpretations Committee and IFRS Advisory Council, respectively. Further, all references in the Constitution to 'accounting standards' were changed to 'financial reporting standards'.

14.8.10 Issues Left for Future Consideration

On funding, the responses to the December 2008 consultation document were almost unanimous in that the trustees must find 'long term, sustainable funding in the form of some government sponsored levy based systems or defined and compulsory country based contributions'.[93] The trustees had already recognized this long before (see Section 11.10), and the work of the trustees in establishing national funding schemes was commended.

As discussed in Section 11.3, the membership of SAC had been renewed early in 2009. Without a change in the Constitution, the trustees had at that point decided to appoint the new members as representatives of stakeholder bodies, rather than in an individual capacity. Many commentators on the December 2008 consultation document noted that it was too early to determine whether the new SAC was working effectively and said they would reserve their opinion until a later date. Many commentators commended the trustees for strengthening and improving SAC.[94] The trustees thereupon proposed to make no Constitutional changes with respect to SAC, which found general acceptance.

The idea that the IASB might set up regional offices was broached during the strategy review, in the July 2007 'Pathway' paper. North Asia, North and South America, and South or Southeast Asia were suggested as possible locations. One Board member could be based in each regional office, leaving nine to ten Board members in London full-time. These offices could promote the visible presence of the Foundation and the IASB throughout the world.[95] This proposal was not carried forward into the final 'Pathway' paper, although it still contained an isolated, and unexplained, reference to regional offices in the context of staff requirements.[96] The matter resurfaced during the initial round of consultations on part two, when it was suggested that it might be desirable to set up regional offices in North America and Asia, 'which would facilitate discussions on critical projects and initiatives'.[97] This point was not picked up by the trustees in their September 2009 paper, but the idea came back during the roundtables. In Tokyo

---

[92] Trustees agenda paper 7, October 2009, 9.   [93] Trustees agenda paper 1A, July 2009, 13.
[94] Trustees agenda paper 1A, July 2009, 17.
[95] IASCF trustees meeting of 2–3 July 2007, agenda paper 10A, 7.
[96] IASCF trustees meeting of 31 October–1 November 2007, agenda paper 10B, paragraph 44.
[97] Trustees agenda paper 1A, July 2009, 20.

in particular, there was a call for creating liaison offices around the world. Not coincidentally, Tokyo was proposed by most of the participants.[98] Again, the point was not mentioned by the trustees in their final report on the Constitution review, and thoughts of a North American office faded away. However, the trustees did pursue the idea of an Asian-Oceanian liaison office immediately following the completion of the Constitution review, which was established in Tokyo in 2012 (see Section 15.5.3).[99]

14.8.11 From Constitution Review to the Next Strategy Review

As discussed above, the second review of the Constitution followed seamlessly on the strategy review initiated by the trustees in 2006. Equally seamlessly, the trustees moved from this Constitution review to their next strategy review. At the January 2010 meeting, following the trustees' approval of the amendments, Tom Seidenstein said that there were a number of extra-Constitutional matters that required attention: (1) that the trustees should 'undertake a full strategic review of the organization beyond June 2011, including financing of the organization'; (2) the trustees should 'undertake a full review of the effectiveness of the IFRS Advisory Council, including its size and membership'; and, as proposed by the Constitution committee, the trustees' Due Process Oversight Committee should 'review its activities and how the Trustees carry out their oversight functions'. The trustees agreed to take up all of these matters.[100]

14.9 ORGANIZATION OF THE MONITORING BOARD AT ITS FIRST MEETING

On 1 April 2009, the Monitoring Board, which was intended to enhance the public accountability of the IASB, met for the first time with the IASC Foundation trustees and IASB Chairman David Tweedie in London, in a public meeting. Those attending on behalf of their organizations were as follows (in addition to their staff aides):

- Hans Hoogervorst, chairman of the Netherlands' Autoriteit Financiële Markten (AFM, Financial Markets Authority), attending as vice chairman of IOSCO's Technical Committee
- Guillermo Larraín, chairman of Chile's Superintendencia de Valores y Seguros (Securities and Insurance Supervisor), attending as chairman of IOSCO's Emerging Markets Committee

---

[98] Trustees agenda paper 7, October 2009, 10.

[99] IFRS Foundation trustees meeting of 5–7 July 2010, agenda paper 4D refers to a discussion of the issue at the trustees' March meeting. See also IFRS Foundation trustees meeting, 6–7 July 2010, minute 5.

[100] IASCF trustees meeting of 26–7 January 2010, minute 7.

- Junichi Maruyama, deputy commissioner for international affairs, attending on behalf of the commissioner of Japan's FSA, who was unable to attend
- Charlie McCreevy, commissioner for the internal market of the EU
- Mary Schapiro, chairman of the SEC
- Sylvie Matherat, director of financial stability of the Banque de France and attending as observer on behalf of the Basel Committee on Banking Supervision.

The members elected Hans Hoogervorst as their chairman. Hoogervorst represented IOSCO's Technical Committee because its chairman was an SEC commissioner, and the SEC was already represented on the Monitoring Board. Hoogervorst became chairman of the Technical Committee the following year. At the time, Hoogervorst was also the chairman of IFAC's Monitoring Group which had, as seen above, to some extent inspired the creation of the IASC Foundation's Monitoring Board.

The Monitoring Board had been a matter of intense discussion between all of the parties involved from late 2007 onwards, and it might have been expected that its members came to their first meeting with a clear understanding of their mandates. As a body independent of the Foundation, the Monitoring Board had its own Charter, signed in advance of the first meeting by Jane Diplock, chairman of IOSCO's executive committee; by Christopher Cox, who was then the SEC chairman; and Takafumi Sato, the commissioner of the FSA. At the meeting, they also signed, together with Chairman Gerrit Zalm of the IASC Foundation, the Memorandum of Understanding which established the relationship between the two bodies.[101]

Yet it appeared that Charlie McCreevy felt he was not yet in a position to sign either the Charter or the Memorandum of Understanding. By April 2009, the terms of the Commission's mandate to represent the EU on the Monitoring Board had not yet been agreed with the European Parliament, and McCreevy caused some consternation during the Monitoring Board's first meeting by indicating that he, or rather his successor who would come in following elections to the Parliament in June, might have to consult the Parliament each time before giving his assent to trustee appointments. Of the trustees, Philip Laskawy in particular spoke out strongly against this, saying that the trustees had been very careful to avoid a politicization of the Monitoring Board: 'I think we signed up for a Monitoring Board that would be independent individuals who would not [be] representing some other group, but representing themselves.'[102]

The underlying problem was that McCreevy was generally anxious to avoid friction with the European Parliament. In particular, he did not wish to pick a fight with Pervenche Berès, the strong-willed chairman of the Parliament's Economic and Monetary Affairs Committee. She was critical of the European Commission for joining the Monitoring Board without a degree of Parliamentary

---

[101] For the Charter and Memorandum of Understanding not yet signed by McCreevy, see <http://www.ifrs.org/News/Press-Releases/Documents/MGCharter060409.pdf> and <http://www.ifrs.org/News/Press-Releases/Documents/MGMou060409.pdf>.

[102] 'IASCF Trustees and Monitoring Board Meeting, 1 April 2009' <http://www.iosco.org>.

oversight that was only proper from her point of view, but that was unacceptable to the other members of the Monitoring Board. Her views on this and related matters were reflected in a resolution approved by the Parliament on 9 October 2008.[103] Yet this was a problem that time might solve because, as indicated above, the next European elections were only a few months away. The Monitoring Board accepted this political reality and left the matter for future consideration. McCreevy was allowed to attend the meetings.

As it happened, Berès did not continue as chairman of the Economic and Monetary Affairs Committee in the Parliament elected in June 2009. Shortly before his retirement as EU commissioner in February 2010, McCreevy finally signed the Charter and the Memorandum of Understanding. The signings were made known at the Monitoring Board's meeting in April 2010. McCreevy's successor as the EU commissioner for the internal market was Michel Barnier, who attended the Monitoring Board meetings from April 2010 onwards.

According to the Charter, the Monitoring Board chairman served a two-year term and would maintain the secretariat. The Monitoring Board was not a legal entity and had no budget. The members were to pay their own costs. An important provision in the Charter was that the Monitoring Board was to make its decisions by consensus. This was similar to the arrangements in, for instance, IOSCO, which also operated by consensus. Yet in this case it was apparently of particular significance to the SEC, because without the implied veto the SEC might not be able to meet its legal oversight responsibility if the IASB were ever to be recognized as a source of accounting principles 'generally accepted' in the United States. In the drafting of the Memorandum of Understanding, a close eye had been kept on the SEC's 'Policy Statement' outlining its relation with the FASB.[104] This was apparent in the sensitive matter of the Monitoring Board's ability to refer agenda items to the IASB for consideration, and the IASB's right to decide that consideration of the issue was not advisable. On this point, the Memorandum of Understanding deliberately used wording borrowed from the SEC's Policy Statement.[105]

The Memorandum of Understanding specified that the Monitoring Board would approve nominations of trustees, but not of members of the IASB. In addition, the Monitoring Board was expected to confer regularly with the trustees on their oversight of the IASB. The Monitoring Board was to meet at least annually on its own and at least annually with all or a quorum of the trustees, the chairman of the trustees, and/or the chairmen of the trustees and the IASB. Neither the Charter nor the Memorandum of Understanding indicated whether meetings should be held in public. In practice, the Monitoring Board and the trustees have conducted part of their meetings in the open, but have also held significant discussions behind closed doors.

---

[103] European Parliament Resolution of 9 October 2008 on the IASCF Review of the Constitution, Public Accountability, and Composition of the IASB: Proposals for Change, P6_TA(2008)0469 <http://www.europarl.europa.eu>.

[104] For the position of the SEC relative to the FASB, see the SEC's 'Policy Statement: Reaffirming the Status of the FASB as a Designated Private-sector Standard Setter', Release Nos. 33-8221; 34-47743; IC-26028; FR-70, 25 April 2003 <http://www.sec.gov>.

[105] Interview with Thomas Seidenstein, 7 July 2011.

14.10 THE MONITORING BOARD
ESTABLISHES ITS PRESENCE

In about half a dozen meetings between April 2009 and July 2011, the Monitoring Board exercised the functions assigned to it in the Memorandum of Understanding. It approved trustee nominations and received reports from the trustees and IASB Chairman Tweedie on such matters as the ongoing review of the Constitution, the funding of the IFRS Foundation, the activities of the trustees' Due Process Oversight Committee, and the progress made by the IASB Board on its technical work plan. In addition, the members of the Monitoring Board briefed each other on developments in their own jurisdictions, such as Japan's decision in 2009 to allow companies to report on the basis of IFRSs and the SEC's ongoing deliberations on the possible use of IFRSs in the United States (on both countries, see Chapter 15).

Yet it was only to be expected that the senior figures making up the Monitoring Board, who as a rule attended the meetings in person, would not be content to spend their time in a purely passive role. In several respects, the Monitoring Board sought to be actively involved in the IASB, and in doing so explored what its remit allowed or required it to do. In April 2010, a year after its first meeting, and after the European Commission had formally signed on, the Monitoring Board took the initiative for a review of the governance of the IFRS Foundation (see Section 14.13). Another important development in 2010 was that the Monitoring Board involved itself in the selection of the successor to David Tweedie (see Section 14.12).

Meanwhile, the Monitoring Board was also used as a forum where the members, as well as the participating trustees, could set out their sometimes divergent views on accounting standards. The financial crisis, which was still in its acute phase when the Monitoring Board first met, provided an immediate topic for such discussions.

More than a quarter of the Monitoring Board's first meeting with the trustees, which ran for four hours, consisted of an intense discussion of what trustees chairman Gerrit Zalm called the 'main dish', the response to the financial crisis, in particular the issue of loan loss provisioning. This was a natural topic for discussion, given the sense of urgency generally felt at the time over the need to improve accounting for financial instruments (see Chapter 13). Yet it was also a sensitive topic, as neither the Monitoring Board nor the trustees had a formal role with respect to the IASB's technical work. The discussion was therefore interlaced with reminders by several of the participants that their meeting should be concerned with the Board's processes, and not with the substance of its work. Nevertheless, it became clear enough that all were intensely interested in the substance of the Board's response to the financial crisis.[106]

The financial crisis had once more thrown into relief the different perspectives of prudential and securities regulators on financial reporting by banks and insurance companies. As indicated above, the question whether prudential regulators should be included in the Monitoring Board had been raised, but answered

---

[106] 'IASCF Trustees and Monitoring Board Meeting, 1 April 2009' <http://www.iosco.org>.

in the negative, with the exception of the observer from the Basel Committee. In the Monitoring Board's press release issued after its first meeting, Hoogervorst was quoted as saying: 'Through the Monitoring Board, world securities regulators will have a means for engaging with the IASCF Trustees to provide a rigorous external review of IASCF operations, policies, and procedures, while at the same time protecting the independence of the IASB in its standard-setting work. As such, the Monitoring Board serves as a forum for IASCF accountability and gives securities regulators a formal means for providing input to the IASCF and IASB regarding the implementation of IFRS.'[107]

Yet in the Monitoring Board's second meeting, in July 2009, according to observers' notes, Charlie McCreevy said that he was 'increasingly of the view that for financial institutions, accounting and financial reporting should be more biased towards the needs of prudential regulators than the investor'. Trustees chairman Gerrit Zalm retorted that the banking industry representative at the SAC meeting the previous month had expressed 'exactly the opposite view'. Monitoring Board Chairman Hans Hoogervorst, who co-chaired the IASB–FASB Financial Crisis Advisory Group, pointed out that, in its final report, the group had asserted that, while financial reporting provided important information to prudential regulators, 'reporting to investors should have primacy'.[108]

The securities regulators' perspective prevailed in the statement issued by the Monitoring Board on 22 September 2009, two days before the beginning of the G20 summit in Pittsburgh, Pennsylvania. The Monitoring Board underscored the need for principled and transparent financial information for investor protection, market integrity, and capital formation. On its newly designed stationery, the Monitoring Board wrote:

> While it is useful to consider the intersection of banking supervision and financial reporting in light of the recent banking crisis, accounting standards should not be allowed to become a surrogate for robust bank risk management or effective bank supervision.... As securities market regulators, we believe it would be a mistake to attempt to rectify today's banking crisis by placing a burden on the investors in our public capital markets. Accounting standards must be designed to provide investors with information to assist them in efficiently allocating their hard-earned investment money.[109]

The Monitoring Board referred to the standards of both the IASB and the FASB. Hence not only the IASC Foundation but also the Financial Accounting Foundation (FAF) issued press releases to welcome the Monitoring Board's statement.[110] The Monitoring Board's statement was ascribed to Hoogervorst,

---

[107] 'Monitoring Board Meets with IASCF Trustees; Announces First Chair', press release of the IASC Foundation Monitoring Board, dated 2 April 2009 <http://www.ifrs.org>.

[108] See observer notes by Deloitte, posted 7 July 2009 <http://www.iasplus.com>.

[109] 'Statement of the Monitoring Board for the International Accounting Standards Committee Foundation on Principles for Accounting Standards and Standard Setting' (Monitoring Board, 22 September 2009) <http://www.iosco.org>.

[110] 'Trustees Welcome Monitoring Board Statement on Accounting Standards', IASC Foundation press release dated 22 September 2009; 'Financial Accounting Foundation Endorses Statement of the International Accounting Standards Committee Foundation Monitoring Board', release dated 22 September 2009 <http://www.accountingfoundation.org>.

Larraín, Katsunori Mikuniya (Japan's FSA commissioner), and Schapiro, all of whose names appeared on the stationery, but not to McCreevy, who was yet to sign the Memorandum of Understanding and therefore was not formally a member.

In April 2010, Michel Barnier continued to make McCreevy's point of the importance of prudential considerations. In his opening remarks, Barnier referred to 'concerns in Europe about the IASB governance', including: 'the fact that the IASB is reluctant to fully consider the economic impact of its standards, in particular in financial stability. In this context it is important for me to say at the very beginning of this meeting that we need to have closer cooperation with the users and the prudential regulators.'[111]

During the same meeting, following David Tweedie's report on the Board's progress in working with the FASB on financial instruments, Barnier said that he supported the efforts being made on convergence. He also emphasized the importance of achieving 'greater coherence between accounting standards and prudential regulators' wherever possible, saying that this is not necessarily against investors' interests, a point that was seconded by Sylvie Matherat, the Basel Committee observer.[112]

Discussions such as these were a part of the role the Monitoring Board was expected to play. The relation between accounting standards and financial stability, or the possibly conflicting viewpoints of prudential and securities regulators, remained important issues with distinct political overtones. But now the Monitoring Board could shield the IASB Board to some extent from the kind of political pressure under which it almost succumbed in October 2008. It was now apparent that a group of publicly accountable officials were overseeing the IASB, who took note of public policy concerns surrounding accounting standards, debated them among themselves, and could report on them to the political sphere, as represented by the G20. One interviewed IASB Board member observed that the establishment of the Monitoring Board had no influence on his daily work on the Board, but, somewhat like an insurance policy, 'it makes you sleep well at night'.

14.11 TOMMASO PADOA-SCHIOPPA BECOMES THE SUCCESSOR TO GERRIT ZALM

As originally envisaged, the primary role of the Monitoring Board was to approve trustee nominations. An appointment of particular significance came up during 2010. On 1 January 2008, Gerrit Zalm, an economist who was the Dutch finance minister from 1994 to 2002, became chairman of the trustees for a three-year term. But, as in other ways, the eruption of the financial crisis with full severity in the second half of 2008 upset this planning. In October 2008, the earlier acquisition of the Dutch ABN AMRO bank by a consortium of three European banks

---

[111] As reported in the transcript of the meeting, 'Monitoring Board and IASCF Trustees Meeting' 1 April 2010, 2, with emendation of 'potential regulators' to 'prudential regulators' <http://www.iosco.org/monitoring_board>.

[112] Meeting transcript 'Monitoring Board and IASCF Trustees Meeting', 1 April 2010, 6–7.

turned sour, and the Dutch government stepped in to nationalize the Dutch banking activities involved in the complex transaction. In November, the Dutch government called upon Zalm to restructure and stabilize the acquired banking business under the name of ABN AMRO, and to prepare the new bank for privatization in due course. It would be a daunting assignment. As Zalm's work level at the bank was that of a full-time job, he was able to devote less and less of his time and attention to the IASC Foundation. The pressure on him was such that he was unable to attend the trustees' quarterly meeting in October 2009. This did not go unnoticed among the trustees, and the outgoing and incoming chairmen of the trustees' nominating committee, Bertrand Collomb and Sir Bryan Nicholson, quietly began to contemplate the possibility of an early vacancy in the trustee chairmanship. So it did not come as a surprise when, at the trustees' 29 March–1 April 2010 meeting, Zalm made it known that he would not seek a second term and that, if a successor could be found before the end of the year, he would step down earlier than planned.[113] Still, it presented the nominating committee with something of a problem, in that it was already well along in the search for a successor to IASB Board Chairman Sir David Tweedie, who was to retire in June 2011. The choice of Tweedie's successor was planned for the June 2010 meeting of the trustees, and it would be awkward if the trustee chairman were to be selected after the decision had been made on a new Board chairman.

The problem was avoided because the nominating committee acted with dispatch. Its members already had their eyes on a candidate: Tommaso Padoa-Schioppa, who had resigned as trustee chairman in May 2006, after serving less than five months, to become the Italian finance minister in the government of Romano Prodi. But in May 2008 his commission ended after the Prodi government was voted out of office, and it seemed that he was once again available. As soon as the nominating committee learned from Zalm that he was prepared to make way for a successor, the question was put to Padoa-Schioppa, whose mind had already been prepared by occasional informal conversations with Tom Seidenstein and others. Padoa-Schioppa had remained in touch with the IASB, among other things through his membership of the Financial Crisis Advisory Group established in 2008. Following some discussion of the arrangements, not least the expectation that he make at least 40 per cent of his time available for the IASB, Padoa-Schioppa signified his interest in the appointment. The implication was that the nominating committee was preparing the recommendation of Padoa-Schioppa without any form of public search or wider consultation. This was a delicate point, as the Monitoring Board was to oversee the trustees' own adherence to due process, not least with respect to the appointment of trustees. Yet the nominating committee felt justified in what it planned to do because of the qualities of Padoa-Schioppa, whose departure in 2006 had been uniformly regretted by the IASB Board members and the trustees, and because the lengthy and arduous process of finding a successor to Paul Volcker in 2005 had revealed that suitable and available candidates were scarce indeed. Considerations such as these presumably helped to sway the members of the Monitoring Board. On 29 April 2010, the trustees held a telephone conference call during which

---

[113] IASCF trustees meeting of 29 March–1 April 2010, minute 5.

Nicholson, as chairman of the nominating committee, proposed the appointment of Padoa-Schioppa and announced that all of the members of the Monitoring Board had shown themselves supportive when informally briefed about the nominating committee's plans. The trustees unanimously agreed that the appointment should be formally proposed to the Monitoring Board.[114] The Monitoring Board concurred.

Padoa-Schioppa began his three-year term on 8 July 2010, the day after Gerrit Zalm chaired his final trustees meeting, which Padoa-Schioppa attended as an observer.[115] Tsuguoki Fujinuma, of Japan, and Robert Glauber, of the United States, were appointed as vice chairmen to serve under Padoa-Schioppa.

Notwithstanding the great regard in which Padoa-Schioppa was held, his fast-track appointment may have caused some misgivings among the members of the Monitoring Board. Earlier in 2010, the trustees had agreed the procedures for the appointment of new trustees with the Monitoring Board, and these included public advertising and an opportunity for the Monitoring Board to put forward names for consideration.[116] Early in April, an updated version of these procedures clarified that this also applied to the vacancy of a trustee chairman, which by then had become manifest.[117] So, although the Monitoring Board supported the appointment of Padoa-Schioppa, it may not have been coincidental that the trustees learned in May with respect to the still pending appointment of a chairman of the Board, that a request for a slower pace and for more Monitoring Board involvement was being voiced, in particular by Michel Barnier.[118] As discussed more fully in Section 14.12, the resulting delay in the appointment of a successor to David Tweedie provided Padoa-Schioppa with the opportunity to play a significant role in that process.

Once again, the IASB was not to profit from Padoa-Schioppa's appointment for long. He died unexpectedly on 18 December 2010 at the age of seventy, inciting a keen sense of loss in the organization. The trustees then named Fujinuma and Glauber as acting co-chairmen, in addition to their titles as vice chairmen, until another chairman could be recruited. During the process of recruiting a successor, Barnier expressed his appreciation for the care with which the search was undertaken. He emphasized the need for adherence to due process and transparency, 'not only for me but also for the European Parliament and the member states', because 'There was a clear lack of transparency last time'.[119]

In January 2012 the Monitoring Board approved the appointment of Michel Prada, the former chairman of France's Commission des Opérations de Bourse (which was merged in 2003 into the newly created Autorité des Marchés

---

[114] IASCF trustees meeting (telephone conference call) of 29 April 2010, minute 2.

[115] 'Statement of the Monitoring Board for the International Accounting Standards Committee Foundation Regarding the Appointment of Tommaso Padoa-Schioppa as Chair of the IASCF Trustees', Monitoring Board press release dated 18 June 2010 <http://www.iosco.org>.

[116] IASCF trustees meeting of 26–7 January 2010, agenda paper 5D.

[117] Appendix A, dated 7 April 2010, to agenda paper 3, IFRS Foundation trustees meeting of 5–7 July 2010.

[118] Memo from Bryan Nicholson to nominating committee members dated 14 June 2010, attached as Appendix D to agenda paper 3, IFRS Foundation trustees meeting of 5–7 July 2010.

[119] 'Monitoring Board and IFRS Foundation Trustees Meeting (Transcript of Public Meeting)', 1 April 2011, 7 <http://www.iosco.org>.

Financiers), as chairman. All of the successive chairmen, Volcker, Padoa-Schioppa, Zalm, and Prada have been men with significant records of public service.

14.12 CHOOSING THE SUCCESSOR TO DAVID TWEEDIE

Another matter in which the Monitoring Board became involved during 2010 was the selection of a successor to David Tweedie, whose second five-year term both as a member and chairman of the Board was to end in June 2011.[120]

In the trustees' meeting held in July 2009, Bertrand Collomb, the chairman of the nominating committee, said that it was imperative to start preparing to find a suitable candidate to succeed Tweedie as a matter of some urgency.[121] The trustees wanted the decision to be made soon so as to assure an orderly transition in the chairmanship. As Collomb was to step down as trustee in December 2009, he asked his successor as chairman of the nominating committee, Bryan Nicholson, to take the lead in the search.

The search was complicated when it became probable during 2009 that a parallel process had to be set in motion to find a new chairman of the trustees. Nicholson was concerned that the trustees would select the Board chairman before Zalm's successor as trustee chairman could participate in the selection. Further, he did not feel it was a good practice to change the chairmen of the trustees and the Board within a span of just six months. By acting swiftly, as seen above, the trustees arranged for Tommaso Padoa-Schioppa to take over the chairmanship from Zalm in July 2010.

In September 2009, Nicholson met individually with about a dozen of the leading standard setters who were attending the annual meeting of the World Standard Setters in London. He sought their views on (a) the role and qualities required for the Board chairman going forward, and (b) the names of suitable candidates for the position. He also posed these questions in one-on-one confidential meetings with existing and recently retired Board members, the IASB's technical directors, and selected other persons. These brainstorming sessions represented a substantial investment of time and energy in the opening stage of his search. Before he began this series of meetings, Nicholson held a detailed conversation with Tweedie himself and recalled him saying, 'when I took up this job, it was 80 per cent technical and 20 per cent "small p" political. Now it's the other way around.' Nicholson knew he had to look for a technical standard setter who could handle the politics, and he wondered if anyone could meet such a job specification. Nicholson thought of the required political credentials in terms of the following question: if the person phoned up Jean-Claude Trichet, the head of the European Central Bank, would Trichet take the call? Yet the overwhelming majority of those to whom he spoke in his series of interviews believed that it would be highly unlikely to find a candidate who could be both a technical

---

[120] Much of this section is drawn from interviews with Bryan Nicholson, 19 May 2011 and 7 July 2011; with Thomas Seidenstein, 7 July 2011; and with David Tweedie, 6 January 2013.

[121] IASCF trustees meeting of 6–7 July 2009, minute 5.

standard setter and a political heavyweight. Tweedie had been one of a kind. Moreover, an American candidate was out of the question, given European reactions to the US influence on the IASB through the convergence process, while the United States had still not signed up to IFRSs.

Yet there was one name that was put forward consistently: at this stage it became clear that Ian Mackintosh would probably be the only viable candidate with a standard-setting background. Mackintosh, a New Zealander, had made his early professional career in Australia, where he was a partner in Coopers & Lybrand, and where he was a member, and later deputy chairman, of the Australian Accounting Standards Board. He spent two years as chief accountant of the Australian Securities and Investments Commission and then two years working for the World Bank in Washington, DC. In 2004, he moved to London to become chairman of the Accounting Standards Board (ASB), his current position. In 2005 he founded and chaired the group of National Standard-Setters, which has met semi-annually and provided feedback to the IASB on its drafts and other initiatives. Nicholson knew Mackintosh well. In fact, it was Nicholson who, as chairman of the Financial Reporting Council, had been responsible for Mackintosh's appointment as ASB chairman. But despite Mackintosh's undoubted credentials, Nicholson concluded from his enquiries that the search needed to be extended with a shift in emphasis. Candidates should be searched for as well among those who first of all had the required political standing and skills, and who, in addition, possessed a general background in the financial reporting area: that is, persons who understood the issues, had shown an interest in the area, and were clever enough to hold their own with the Board members and technical standard setters within six months of being on the job.

From the outset, both Nicholson and Tweedie had had such a person in their sights. This was Hans Hoogervorst, whose qualities and support for the IASB Tweedie had first come to appreciate during the tense meetings of the Financial Stability Forum following the collapse of Lehman Brothers. At that time, Hoogervorst chaired the Dutch securities market regulator. He attended the Financial Stability Forum meetings on behalf of IOSCO, being, since 2008, vice chairman of IOSCO's Technical Committee. Prior to his service as a securities regulator, Hoogervorst had for almost ten years served as junior minister, minister of finance, and minister of health in successive Dutch governments. During the financial crisis, Hoogervorst was brought into the IASB's orbit, first by his appointment, in December 2008, as co-chairman of the Financial Crisis Advisory Group (FCAG). Next, in April 2009, he was elected as the first chairman of the IASB's Monitoring Board, again as the representative of IOSCO's Technical Committee. In the margins of one of the FCAG meetings, Tweedie informally mentioned the IASB chairmanship to Hoogervorst, and believed that Hoogervorst was interested. However, when the chairman search started in earnest, Hoogervorst was rising to greater prominence in IOSCO, on course to become the next chairman of the Technical Committee. In addition, rumours started to appear in the press from the second half of 2009 onward that he was being considered as the possible next president of the central bank in the Netherlands.[122] Whether or not

---

[122] 'Volksgericht', *De Telegraaf*, 14 October 2009, 21.

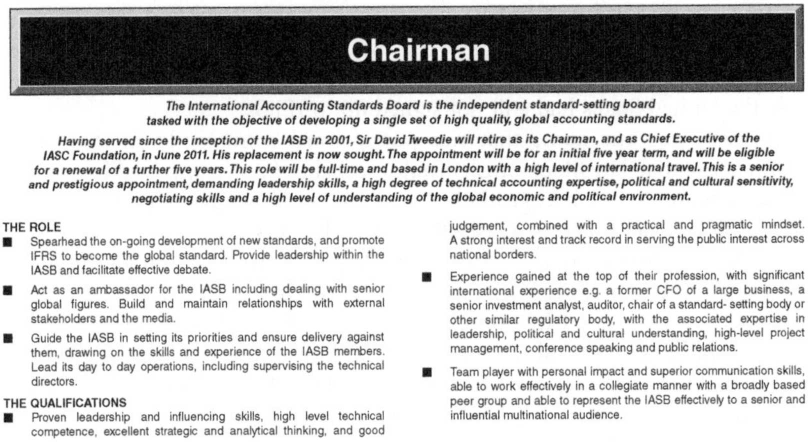

Chairman

The International Accounting Standards Board is the independent standard-setting board tasked with the objective of developing a single set of high quality, global accounting standards.

Having served since the inception of the IASB in 2001, Sir David Tweedie will retire as its Chairman, and as Chief Executive of the IASC Foundation, in June 2011. His replacement is now sought. The appointment will be for an initial five year term, and will be eligible for a renewal of a further five years. This role will be full-time and based in London with a high level of international travel. This is a senior and prestigious appointment, demanding leadership skills, a high degree of technical accounting expertise, political and cultural sensitivity, negotiating skills and a high level of understanding of the global economic and political environment.

THE ROLE

■ Spearhead the on-going development of new standards, and promote IFRS to become the global standard. Provide leadership within the IASB and facilitate effective debate.

■ Act as an ambassador for the IASB including dealing with senior global figures. Build and maintain relationships with external stakeholders and the media.

■ Guide the IASB in setting its priorities and ensure delivery against them, drawing on the skills and experience of the IASB members. Lead its day to day operations, including supervising the technical directors.

THE QUALIFICATIONS

■ Proven leadership and influencing skills, high level technical competence, excellent strategic and analytical thinking, and good judgement, combined with a practical and pragmatic mindset. A strong interest and track record in serving the public interest across national borders.

■ Experience gained at the top of their profession, with significant international experience e.g. a former CFO of a large business, a senior investment analyst, auditor, chair of a standard- setting body or other similar regulatory body, with the associated expertise in leadership, political and cultural understanding, high-level project management, conference speaking and public relations.

■ Team player with personal impact and superior communication skills, able to work effectively in a collegiate manner with a broadly based peer group and able to represent the IASB effectively to a senior and influential multinational audience.

Figure 14.1 Advertisement for IASB chairman, January 2010

Tweedie and Nicholson saw these other possibilities open to Hoogervorst as so many barriers to his candidacy as chairman of the IASB, no further action was taken, but, as chairman of the Monitoring Board, Hoogervorst remained well within sight.

On 3 December 2009, Nicholson wrote to Hoogervorst to inform the Monitoring Board of the trustees' plan to choose Tweedie's successor. He said that the plan was for the trustees to decide on the new chairman by their July 2010 meeting, with any external candidate joining the Board on 1 January 2011, six months before the end of Tweedie's term, thus allowing a seamless transition. He invited the Monitoring Board members to suggest names by 12 January. Nicholson was prophetic in writing, 'Of course, unpredictable things can happen, which is why we are starting early and thus giving ourselves some flexibility'.[123] Nicholson informed the trustees in December that the interviewing would take place sometime between the middle of May and the middle of June. He also said that the vice chairman, or two vice chairmen, as allowed by the Constitution, would most likely be chosen from among the existing members of the Board, in consultation with the incoming chairman.[124]

The advertisement for candidates, containing the attributes which were approved by the trustees, appeared in the 9 January 2010 issue of *The Economist* and on the IASB's website (see Figure 14.1). As can be seen in the reproduction, the qualities sought in candidates were daunting to a fault, as if the trustees had attempted to apply the dictum from *Parkinson's Law*: 'the perfect advertisement would attract only one reply, and that from the right man.'[125]

Shortly after Barnier joined the Monitoring Board as the new EU commissioner for the internal market, he began to express concerns over the search process, initially over its speed. Japan's FSA joined Barnier in wanting a more deliberative

---

[123] Letter from Bryan Nicholson to Hans Hoogervorst, dated 3 December 2006 <http://www.ifrs.org>.

[124] IASCF trustees meeting of 26–7 January 2010, minute 10.

[125] C. Northcote Parkinson, *Parkinson's Law* (London: John Murray, 1957), 25.

process, proceeding at a slower pace.[126] But it soon became clear that Barnier believed that the Monitoring Board should be more involved in the selection of the chairman of the IASB and not simply be presented with the trustees' choice at the end. While the trustees did inform the Monitoring Board of each step in the process, Barnier wanted more: effectively, he wanted a 'say'. As the EU was the major contributor of countries committed to adopting IFRSs, he needed to have full confidence in the person appointed as chairman of the IASB, whose standards he needed to get past the European Commission and through the European Parliament. Yet the decision to appoint the new Board chairman was to be made by the trustees alone. According to the Constitution, the Monitoring Board, composed of public authorities, was to have no formal role in the appointment process. A majority of the trustees were not immediately prepared to give the Monitoring Board a voice in the decision. After all, the powers to be granted to the Monitoring Board had been the subject of intense debate during the Constitution review concluded in January 2009, and it had been decided that the Monitoring Board would approve the appointment of trustees but would not be involved in the process of selecting the members of the Board.

During the months in which this dilemma became manifest to the trustees, the search process continued largely as planned. In February, the trustees' nominating committee began considering a long-list of nominations from organizations and applications by individuals coming from more than twenty-eight countries. By the end of March, the committee had reduced it to a shorter list. On 16 June, the nominating committee interviewed the candidates, and it was reported in the accountancy press that Ian Mackintosh and Fayezul Choudhury, vice president of corporate finance and risk management at the World Bank and formerly its controller, were among those on the shorter list.[127]

Choudhury, who began his career with Price Waterhouse in London, initially in public accounting and later in management consulting, had represented the World Bank on SAC from 2001 to 2005. The World Bank had been the staunchest supporter of the IASC from the beginning and has continued to give strong support to the IASB. Hence, a high-level representative from the World Bank would have been a serious candidate for the chairmanship.[128]

Yet Barnier continued to press his demand that the Monitoring Board should be involved in the selection of the chairman. As suggested in Section 14.11, the speed with which the trustees had moved to appoint Padoa-Schioppa in April may have stiffened Barnier's resolve. As before, Japan's FSA joined in Barnier's view, and there is no indication that the SEC took issue with him. The trustees were faced with a problem: some of them agreed with Barnier's procedural point, recognizing as inevitable that those who bear political responsibility for accounting standards must be allowed to assure themselves before the final decision that an acceptable candidate will be chosen. Other trustees, however, viewed Barnier's demand as a form of unacceptable political intervention. As a result, the process of

---

[126] IFRS Foundation trustees meeting of 5–7 July 2010, agenda paper 3, Appendix D (memorandum from Bryan Nicholson to the nominating committee, dated 14 June 2010).

[127] Mario Christodoulou, 'Candidates in Frame for Top IASB Role', *Accountancy Age*, 10 June 2010.

[128] In June 2012, Choudhury was named to succeed Ian Ball as chief executive of the International Federation of Accountants.

choosing a chairman began to slow. But by the time of the trustees' July 2010 meeting, the opposition of those trustees who wanted to follow the Constitution had been overcome, and it was agreed that the final candidate would meet with the Monitoring Board before the trustees would formally make their decision. Therefore, the trustees postponed their decision to select the chairman from July to October, and a meeting of the Monitoring Board was arranged with the final candidate selected by the nominating committee, who turned out to be Ian Mackintosh.[129]

After the Monitoring Board had met with Mackintosh, it became clear that, for all the concern over tension between the Monitoring Board and the trustees, there was no real difference of view. The Monitoring Board unanimously reached the identical conclusion as the nominating committee that, while Mackintosh was strong and more than acceptable on the technical side, he was not strong enough on the other elements required for representing the Board in the highest political councils. With very similar sentiments expressed by the Monitoring Board and the nominating committee, a different approach was necessary. Nicholson and Seidenstein went to Paris to consult with Padoa-Schioppa about revisiting the idea of approaching Hans Hoogervorst, the chairman of the Monitoring Board, to see if, by this time, he could be persuaded to become a candidate. They gave Hoogervorst a very short window in which to make a decision, as the trustees' October meeting was drawing near, and, in the end, he expressed his willingness to become a candidate and thus to resign his position on the Monitoring Board. By informal soundings, Nicholson and Padoa-Schioppa assured themselves that the other members of the Monitoring Board would support this move. At the same time, Nicholson approached Ian Mackintosh to see if he would agree to become the vice chairman. Hoogervorst was flown to Seoul for an interview with the nominating committee just prior to the October meeting of the trustees. He performed admirably in the interview, and, when the trustees met, Nicholson conveyed the nominating committee's unanimous recommendation that Hoogervorst be appointed chairman of the Board. Some of the trustees were restive about being presented with a fait accompli, different from the one they had expected. But the trustees as a whole recognized the logic of what was being proposed, as well as the qualities of the candidate, and in the end they unanimously approved the recommendation. The nominating committee separately, and unanimously, recommended Ian Mackintosh as vice chairman of the Board, in the knowledge that the Monitoring Board was supportive of this nomination as well.[130]

The course of events as outlined above differs in some respects from what has been suggested in public commentary. Nicolas Véron, an astute observer of developments at the IASB, was quoted in the press as saying, 'The sequence as it appeared to outside observers was that Mr. Mackintosh was the trustees'

---

[129] IFRS Foundation trustees meeting of 5–7 July 2010, agenda paper 3, Appendix D (memorandum from Nicholson to the nominating committee, dated 14 June 2010). See also Rachel Sanderson, 'Hunt for IASB Head Hits Hurdle', *Financial Times*, 16 August 2010, 1; Penny Sukhraj, 'Europe Opposes Process in Hunt for IASB Chair', *Accountancy Magazine*, 16 August 2010. That Ian Mackintosh was the final candidate was reported in the press, see Adam Jones and Nikki Tait, 'Former Dutch Minister to Be IASB Head', *Financial Times*, 12 October 2010.

[130] IFRS Foundation trustees meeting of 12–13 October 2010, minute 2.

preferred candidate for chair, but that Commissioner Michel Barnier vetoed him and that this led to the selection of Mr. Hoogervorst'.[131] Peter Walton wrote in *World Accounting Report*: 'People close to the situation say that the European Commission blocked the idea of an Anglo-Saxon accountant at the head of the IASB, especially yet another chairman of the UK standard-setter.'[132] To be sure, the trustees themselves had ruled out an American chairman, and one could well imagine that they would not have preferred a Briton as chairman to succeed Tweedie, but apart from that it would seem that nationalities played a minor role in the process and that Barnier's intervention was procedural, rather than directed at a particular candidate. Moreover, while Barnier may have been the most outspoken member of the Monitoring Board on this matter, and while his intervention may have touched nerves left raw from previous clashes between the IASB and the European Commission, his position was not fundamentally different from that taken by other Monitoring Board members, or from the prevailing view in the nominating committee.

14.12.1 David Tweedie—in Retrospect

By common consent, the choice of David Tweedie as the IASB's first chairman was at the heart of the organization's success, a view with which both those inside and outside the organization agreed. One Board member said, 'I don't think that anybody could have moved things as far and as fast as he managed to do'. As seen in the preceding section, there were no available candidates with the same exceptional combination of abilities. Tweedie was adept at leading the technical side of the IASB Board while at the same time able to cajole and charm ministers of finance, industry leaders, and chairs of securities regulators during his incessant travels around the globe. He devised strategies and plans for developing principled standards—that was his ideal—but was attuned to what was realistically feasible in the face of the cacophony of praise and criticism which the Board heard from a great many quarters. Chairing an international board was leagues more challenging than running a national board, which was difficult enough in itself. He himself found that out when he discovered that tactics and technical solutions that worked so well at the UK ASB, which he had chaired for ten years, did not work comparably well at the international level. A national standard setter knows the way that business is done in its own country, and it is eventually accountable to the country's stakeholders and its national government. At the international level, one could multiply that by many, eventually scores of, business cultures and national governments. Each country has its own way of doing business, its own national legislation, and its own stage of capital market development. As there had been no precedent for the international setting of accounting standards that were to be mandated for use by listed companies, both companies and their auditors had, with difficulty, to become accustomed to receiving financial reporting

---

[131] Jeff Buckstein, 'New IASB Head Seen as More Political', *The Bottom Line*, December 2010 <http://www.thebottomlinenews.ca>.

[132] Peter Walton, Editorial, *World Accounting Report*, November 2010, 1.

instructions from this recently established entity known as the IASB, based in London. Tweedie, therefore, had to sell the idea of standard setting that would promote the international comparability of financial reporting in global capital markets. And he was a formidable salesman.

Tweedie did much to shape the initial Board membership and brought with him some staff from the ASB. At the outset, with Ken Spencer as a sympathetic chairman of the trustees' nominating committee, Tweedie surrounded himself with, for the most part, familiar figures he respected from his service on the IASC board and from G4+1meetings—'friends of David', as one close observer dubbed them. He succeeded in persuading the trustees that the members of the initial Board should have their terms renewed in order to promote continuity in the development of standards. When Mary Barth and Tom Jones retired, he arranged to have them serve in special capacities at the Board, to continue to keep them involved.

No leader is without weaknesses, and without critics. Tweedie's ever-present sense of humour went over well in Britain but not always in other national cultures, where British humour, particularly in formal settings, is not necessarily appreciated, or where the idiom of his jokes was simply not understood. While he easily established a good rapport with a great variety of people in many different countries, his diplomatic skills often seemed to fall flat in Europe. Partly, this reflects that Europe was generally a hard-to-please constituency, and was home to some of the IASB's most determined critics. Yet some observers maintain that Tweedie never really understood, or tried to understand, Europe beyond the Channel. One person well versed in the workings of the EU observed in an interview, 'David Tweedie, like many British people, never quite understood the importance of the European Union'. Towards the end of the decade, it was tacitly agreed within the organization that his visits to the Continent should be limited as much as possible, because his presence there did more harm than good.

His drive to get standards out, especially in the rush to complete the major convergence standards near the end of his tenure (and that of the other two remaining initial Board members) was seen by some, including a few critics on the Board, as lowering the quality of the Board's work. When Tweedie represented the Board in meetings with company executives and government figures, critics have alleged that he was too accommodating a salesman by promising results that he could not—and he should have known that he could not—deliver. He could cast only one vote in Board meetings, and while he managed the Board's operation with a strong hand, sometimes directly intervening in the staff's work, he could not dictate the outcomes.

A consequence of Tweedie's fervent desire to move things along was that he might place items on the agenda, or take them off, without consulting even Board members. One Board member whom we interviewed said: 'One of the things that used to annoy the hell out of a lot of us was going to listen to his speeches, listening to him tell the audience about what was on the agenda. And we are sitting in the back and saying, "We never put that on the agenda!" . . . If you listened to his speeches, the agenda morphed depending on who he was talking to and what he thought they might want to have on the agenda.' The Board member added that 'we published the work plan on the website as a discipline so that David couldn't say anything in his speeches that wasn't on there'.[133]

14.13 THE TRUSTEES AND THE MONITORING BOARD BEGIN PARALLEL REVIEWS

As seen above, the trustees had concluded their second Constitution review in January 2010 with the resolution to undertake a full strategic review of the IFRS Foundation and its activities, looking ahead to the period beyond June 2011. This point in time was expected to be an important milestone, both because of the expected completion of the convergence agenda embodied in the Memorandum of Understanding between the IASB and the FASB, and because of the end of the term of the first chairman of the Board.[134] In contrast with the strategy review undertaken in 2007 and discussed earlier in this chapter, this new review was to be based on public consultation.

The trustees held a first discussion of the scope and method of the review at their meeting of 29 March–1 April 2010. At that meeting, it became clear that 'strategy' was interpreted in a wide sense, to include possible enhancements of the governance of the IFRS Foundation and the working of the IASB.[135] But before the trustees could begin to implement their plans, the Monitoring Board decided to undertake a review of its own, focusing on the governance of the IFRS Foundation, and thus overlapping to a considerable extent with the trustees' planned review.

The Monitoring Board's intention was formed during its 1 April 2010 meeting, that is, the one held in private on the same day as the trustees' own meeting, and briefly referred to during the public meeting of the Monitoring Board with the trustees on that same day in the context of the trustees' announcement of their plans for a review.[136] At that point in time, the scope of the Monitoring Board's review was not yet evident, and would not become clear to the trustees until a few months later.[137] As reported in April, it could easily appear as remaining restricted to the functioning and composition of the Monitoring Board itself, a natural step to take once the European Commission had at last formally taken its seat.[138] It was acknowledged in a jocular manner in the public meeting by Gerrit Zalm that the Monitoring Board's own arrangements were a matter beyond the competence of the trustees: 'we were involved when the Monitoring Board was

---

[133] Interview with Patricia O'Malley, 28 May 2009.

[134] IASCF trustees and Monitoring Board meeting of 1 April 2010, agenda paper 6.

[135] IASCF trustees meeting of 29 March–1 April 2010, minute 14.

[136] 'Monitoring Board and IASCF Trustees Meeting', 1 April 2010, 12–13 <http://www.iosco.org>.

[137] While it seems plausible that Padoa-Schioppa and the other members of the trustees' executive committee were more fully aware of the Monitoring Board's plans, the other trustees had to be informed at their meeting of 6–7 July on the basis of the Monitoring Board's 2 July press release. See IFRS Foundation trustees meeting of 6–7 July 2010, agenda paper 4C and IFRS Foundation trustees meeting of 6–7 July 2010, minute 4.

[138] This appears to be the interpretation in the Deloitte observer notes, 'Notes from Monitoring Board Meeting', posted 2 April 2010 <http://www.iasplus.com>.

created, but once it is created, we're lost. We're just a subject. We created our own god.'[139]

It was not until 2 July 2010 that the Monitoring Board made its intentions clearer in a public statement.[140] Its review was to encompass 'the overall governance model of the IFRS Foundation, including the composition of the Monitoring Board'. More specifically, the intention was to assess whether the current governance structure adequately:

- provides appropriate representation for relevant authorities such as capital market and other public authorities;
- creates sufficient transparency and accountability of the IASB to relevant authorities such as capital market and public authorities;
- ensures the appropriate involvement of all relevant stakeholders in the standards elaboration process;
- ensures that all relevant public policy objectives are taken into account in the standard setting process; and
- protects the IASB's independent standard setting process.

This amounted to more than a consideration of the Monitoring Board's own composition and functioning, and with respect to some of the points might well result in conclusions that could be implemented only with the agreement of the trustees. Because of this and because of the evident overlap with the trustees' planned review, the Monitoring Board's action could appear as an intervention in the trustees' responsibilities. Such an interpretation would be based in particular on signs from Europe that demands for reform of the IASB—which had never ceased since the IAS Regulation of 2002—were once again increasing in intensity. In his opening remarks at the 1 April 2010 meeting of the Monitoring Board with the trustees, Michel Barnier had not only emphasized the European Commission's support for IFRSs, but also 'the still weak accountability of the IASB towards public authorities'. It was also not too difficult to discern behind the elements of the Monitoring Board's planned review Barnier's expressed views on the necessity of involving prudential regulators in accounting standard setting and the importance of considering the implications for financial stability (see Section 14.10). In the press, comments by Barnier about a linkage between governance reforms at the IASB and the European Commission's proposed financial contribution to the IASCF Foundation (see Section 11.10) were described as 'a power grab by Brussels'.[141] In March 2010, the European Commission representative had informed the Accounting Regulatory Committee (ARC) that the Commission would continue to promote governance reforms to enhance the accountability of the IASB, and that its decision to formally join the Monitoring Board 'does not

---

[139] 'Monitoring Board and IASCF Trustees Meeting', 1 April 2010, 13 <http://www.iosco.org>.

[140] 'Statement of the Monitoring Board for the International Financial Reporting Standards Foundation Regarding the Governance Review of the IFRS Foundation', Monitoring Board press release dated 2 July 2010 <http://www.iosco.org>.

[141] 'Push for Accounting Convergence Threatened by EU Reform Drive', *Financial Times*, 5 April 2010, 1.

prejudge future questions about the role and composition of the Monitoring Board, nor indeed about broader governance reforms'.[142]

However, it should be noted that IASB governance was not an exclusively European preoccupation. The SEC staff's work plan for the consideration of the incorporation of IFRSs in the US financial reporting system, published in February 2010 (see Section 15.4) included an 'ongoing review of the functioning of the IASB's governance structure'.[143] Similarly, the FSA's June 2009 'roadmap' towards the adoption of IFRSs for use in Japan had emphasized the necessity of improvements in the IASC Foundation's governance and due process (see Section 15.5).

The heading of 'enhanced governance' could cover many different ideas, ranging from sustainable funding mechanisms to bolster the IASB's independence to suggestions that no Board members or trustees should be appointed from countries that had not adopted IFRSs, i.e. in particular not from the United States, or that the European Commission should be able to appoint directly a representative member of the Board. The latter view was said to be held within France's Ministry for the Economy and Finance.[144] The old notion that there should be a European accounting standard setter was circulating again, apparently reflecting a view that the IASB was beyond redemption by any amount of governance reform.[145] Against this background of unspecified, conflicting, or hostile calls for reform of the IASB's governance, it was seen as fitting within the IFRS Foundation that the Monitoring Board engaged itself actively in the public debate. This was one of the things expected of the Monitoring Board, and there was a fair degree of confidence that the Monitoring Board's views on the organization's future were not fundamentally at variance with the trustees' thinking. Even if Barnier could appear as the Monitoring Board's most critical member, it was recognized within the IASB that, in the end, the European Commission was interested in the worldwide success of IFRSs. In that sense, the Commission was the IASB's ally in Europe, even though it frequently had to act under pressure from member states with strong currents of opinion against the IASB, as in France.

Nonetheless, it was a little awkward that the broad scope of the Monitoring Board's review, which may have been decided on at some point following the April 2010 Monitoring Board meeting, did overlap with the strategy review to which the trustees had already committed themselves. Thought was given to conducting the two reviews together. However, the trustees accepted that it was necessary for the credibility of the Monitoring Board's review that it should be conducted in complete independence of the IFRS Foundation. Only in that way was there a prospect that the Monitoring Board's review could answer the

[142] Summary record of ARC meeting of 4 March 2010, minute IV <http://ec.europa.eu/internal_market/accounting>.

[143] Securities and Exchange Commission Release Nos. 33-9109; 34-61578, 'Commission Statement in Support of Convergence and Global Accounting Standards', 24 February 2010 <http://www.sec.gov>.

[144] 'La lutte d'influences entre Américains et Européens est loin d'être achevée', *Les Echos*, 14 October 2010, 32.

[145] 'Talk of a European standards board' was noted, and rejected, by IFAC President Robert Bunting in April 2010, see 'Europe Urged Not to Go it Alone on Accounting Rules', news item posted 14 April 2010, Reuters News. For the persistence of the idea of a European accounting standard setter during the 1990s, see Camfferman and Zeff, *Financial Reporting and Global Markets*, 420.

persistent complaints about a lack of public accountability, as well as defuse calls for a review that would even be independent of the Monitoring Board.[146] However, this did not rule out coordination of the two reviews, a point repeatedly made in the meeting of the Monitoring Board and the trustees in October 2010. Tommaso Padoa-Schioppa praised the 'extremely positive' relationship between the Monitoring Board and the trustees as both worked on their respective reviews. As if to remove all doubt about his position, Barnier stated that the point of developing processes of accountability and governance was 'not to undermine the IASB's independence—never'.[147]

The coordination agreed between the reviews was that the Monitoring Board would concentrate on the 'institutional' aspects of governance, that is, the composition of the IASB, the trustees, and the Monitoring Board itself as well as the allocation of responsibilities to each level. The trustees' review would consider the 'operational' aspects of fulfilling these responsibilities, which meant in particular issues of due process.[148] With such a division of labour, it was perhaps not likely from the outset that the Monitoring Board would propose a fundamental redistribution of responsibilities.

14.13.1 Outcomes of the Strategy and Governance Reviews

The initial thrust to the trustees' strategy review was given by Padoa-Schioppa, supported by Tom Seidenstein and in consultation with the trustees' executive committee, which at that time consisted, apart from Padoa-Schioppa, of Fujinuma and Glauber, the two vice chairmen, and the trustees Clemens Börsig, Samuel DiPiazza, Jeffrey Lucy, Bryan Nicholson, and David Sidwell. Padoa-Schioppa's contribution was cut short by his death in December 2010. The approach followed by the trustees was to publish a consultation paper in November 2010, followed by a report with proposed recommendations in April 2011.[149] The review was completed by a final report published in February 2012.[150]

Before the Monitoring Board's governance review was well underway, Hans Hoogervorst stepped down as chairman of the Monitoring Board in order to be eligible to succeed David Tweedie as chairman of the IASB Board. Masamichi Kono, the FSA's vice commissioner for international affairs, representing the FSA on the Monitoring Board, took over as acting chairman of the Monitoring Board. Kono also chaired the governance review working group. Other members of the

---

[146] IFRS Foundation trustees meeting of 6–7 July 2010, minute 4; interview with Thomas Seidenstein, 7 July 2011.

[147] 'Monitoring Board and IFRSF Trustees Meeting', 28 October 2010, 1–2 <http://www.iosco.org>.

[148] 'Consultative Report on the Review of the IFRS Foundation's Governance' (IFRS Foundation Monitoring Board, 7 February 2011), 9–10 <http://www.iosco.org>; 'Report of the Trustees' Strategy Review: IFRSs as the Global Standards: Setting a Strategy for the Foundation's Second Decade' (IFRS Foundation, April 2011), 3.

[149] 'Paper for Public Consultation: Status of Trustees' Strategy Review' (IFRS Foundation, 5 November 2010); 'Report of the Trustees' Strategy Review: IFRSs as the Global Standard: Setting a Strategy for the Foundation's Second Decade' (IFRS Foundation, April 2011).

[150] *IFRSs as the Global Standards: Setting a Strategy for the Foundation's Second Decade* (IFRS Foundation, February 2012).

working group were Zarinah Anwar, of the Securities Commission Malaysia, representing IOSCO's Emerging Markets Committee; Pierre Delsaux, representing the European Commission; Steven Maijoor, of the Dutch AFM, representing IOSCO's Technical Committee; and Ethiopis Tafara, representing the SEC.

The Monitoring Board published its consultation document in February 2011, in between the two preliminary publications by the trustees. The Monitoring Board's final report appeared in February 2012, on the same day and as a package with that of the trustees.[151] Evidently, the earlier view that it was important for the Monitoring Board to be seen as conducting its review independently of the trustees had changed to an emphasis on reaching an integrated and consistent package of conclusions, in line with views expressed by respondents to the trustees' April 2011 proposals.[152]

The conclusion of the reviews occurred beyond the period covered in this book, but the trustees' final report differed only in limited respects from its April 2011 proposals. The Monitoring Board's February 2011 consultation document was more open-ended, and probably caused some suspense among the trustees. Despite the evident coordination, the trustees by no means held the Monitoring Board on a leash. In its February 2011 consultation document, the Monitoring Board raised a number of questions, naturally including some relating to its own composition and functioning, but also on topics that hitherto had rested exclusively with the trustees. Even if some of these questions could hardly be avoided in any serious review, the mere fact that they were put on the table could appear threatening. The trustees may well have felt some anxiety whether the Monitoring Board would be able to resolve all of the following in a way that they themselves found fully acceptable:[153]

- 'Do you agree with the proposal to urge concrete efforts to deepen the pool of candidates for IASB membership from diverse geographical and professional backgrounds?'

- 'Do you agree with the proposal to separate the roles of IASB Chair and the CEO of the Foundation?' Here the Monitoring Board was directly second-guessing the trustees who, in the recently completed Constitution review, decided against separating the two functions (see Section 14.8.8).

- 'Do you agree with the proposal to provide increased transparency into the process for Trustee nominations?'

- 'Do you believe that the current arrangements for Monitoring Board involvement in the IASB's agenda-setting are appropriate, or should the Monitoring Board have an explicit ability to place an item on the agenda, or would you consider other alternatives that would enhance the Monitoring

---

[151] *Final Report on the Review of the IFRS Foundation's Governance* (IFRS Foundation Monitoring Board, 9 February 2012) <http://www.iosco.org>; 'Monitoring Board and the Trustees of the IFRS Foundation Announce Conclusions of their Governance and Strategy Reviews', IFRS Foundation and Monitoring Board press release dated 9 February 2012.

[152] See analysis of comments, IFRS Foundation trustees meeting of 11–13 October 2011, agenda paper 6A, 7.

[153] 'Consultative Report on the Review of the IFRS Foundation's Governance' (7 February 2011), 2–6.

Board involvement in the IASB agenda setting?' Even if carefully phrased in terms of the acceptability of the status quo, this question challenged the unquestioned tenet of the trustees and the IASB Board that the Board should be wholly independent in shaping its agenda.

- 'Do you believe that the Monitoring Board should have a more prominent role in the selection of the IASB Chair?'
- 'Do you agree that the Monitoring Board's responsibilities should explicitly include consultation with the Trustees as they further develop the framework to ensure proper balance in the composition of the IASB?'

Yet it was already clear in 2011 that the Monitoring Board had a firm view of the overall governance framework within which these questions should be considered, and that this view did not differ fundamentally from that of the trustees. In terms of process, the chairman of the Monitoring Board, Masamichi Kono, reassured the trustees in February 2011 that, in areas requiring changes to the IFRS Foundation Constitution, the Monitoring Board would not include in its final report anything that could not be agreed with the trustees.[154]

Considered as a package, one might say that the views of the trustees and the Monitoring Board expressed in the consultation papers of 2011 and the final reports of 2012 amounted to an affirmation of the existing structure, a call for relatively limited adjustments within that structure, and a sense that the effectiveness of the existing arrangements had to be better demonstrated to the outside world.

Viewed in a broader perspective, the trustees and the Monitoring Board reaffirmed the fundamental choice made in 1999 with respect to the restructuring of the IASC that the new organization, soon to become the IASB, was to be, above all, independent in setting standards. What had changed since then was the understanding of the necessary conditions for the viability of an independent international standard setter. In 1999, an alternative model of standard setting based on representation had been rejected, but at the time it was acknowledged that a standard setter needed more than independence to establish its legitimacy. The solution had been found in the combination of a Board of independent technical experts overseen by a board of trustees composed along representational lines.[155] As the experience of the previous decade had shown, this was insufficient to provide the IASB with the degree of legitimacy expected of a body setting standards that were mandatory in many countries. As seen above, the trustees had already taken the view early in their strategy review, in January 2007, that independence had to be paired with accountability. In 2011, the trustees wrote: 'The independence of the IASB in its standard-setting decision-making process, within a framework of public accountability, must be maintained. A primary role of the Trustees is to advocate for, and to preserve the independence of, the standard-setting process.'[156] The Monitoring Board made the same point in

---

[154] IFRS Foundation trustees meeting of 10–11 February 2011, minute 'Report of the Monitoring Board'.

[155] *Recommendations on Shaping IASC for the Future: A Report of the International Accounting Standards Committee's Strategy Working Party, Recommendations to the IASC Board* (IASC, November 1999), paragraphs 6–8.

[156] *IFRSs as the Global Standards* (February 2012), 15.

different words: 'Stakeholders share the Monitoring Board's view that the independence of the IASB is critical to the credibility of IFRSs. The governance structure should provide for a standard-setting environment that is independent of vested interests. At the same time, the long-term viability of IFRSs as global accounting standards depends on the IASB exercising its independence in a manner that serves the public interest by remaining accountable to investors, markets, and other market participants.'[157]

Both the trustees and the Monitoring Board stated their belief that the three-tier structure established in 2009, consisting of the Board, the trustees, and the Monitoring Board, provided an appropriate balance of independence and accountability.

The first two tiers, the Board and the trustees, were part of the original structure and had already been the subject of exhaustive discussion in the course of two Constitution reviews, and no major changes were proposed. The importance of diversity in the Board was affirmed, but this had already for many years been an important consideration in the trustees' appointment decisions. Ever since the first Constitution review, it had been acknowledged that a rigorous and transparent due process was indispensable to the Board's legitimacy, and many enhancements had been made over time. The trustees already had a very active Due Process Oversight Committee, but intentions were stated to provide it with more resources, to clarify its procedures, and to ensure that it would also report to the Monitoring Board. A point on which the Monitoring Board did second-guess the trustees was their proposal to split the roles of the chairman of the Board and the chief executive of the IFRS Foundation. David Tweedie had played both roles, and in the second Constitution review completed in 2010 the trustees had agreed to continue the practice. The Monitoring Board believed, and the trustees now accepted, that the independence of the Board was best served by avoiding any potential conflicts of interest between the two roles.

That the Board's independence would benefit from having a stable funding base was something that had been recognized long ago, and it was not for want of trying on the part of the trustees that some jurisdictions did not yet have stable funding systems in place (see Section 11.10). What was new was the trustees' ambition to see the annual budget grow from its current £26 million to approximately £40–45 million. This was in line with the trustees' ambitions for IFRSs, which were expressed with a forcefulness that was also in some respects new. In an apparent reflection on the chequered history of convergence, adoption, adaptation, and jurisdictional variants of IFRSs as documented in several chapters of this book, the trustees now stated that:

the IFRS Foundation must remain committed to the long-term goal of the global adoption of IFRSs as developed by the IASB, in their entirety and without modification. Convergence may be an appropriate short-term strategy for a particular jurisdiction and may facilitate adoption over a transitional period. Convergence, however, is not a substitute for adoption. Adoption mechanisms may differ among countries and may require an appropriate period of time to implement, but, whatever the

---

[157] *Final Report on the Review of the IFRS Foundation's Governance* (February 2012), 2.

mechanism, it should enable and require relevant entities to state that their financial statements are in full compliance with IFRSs as issued by the IASB.[158]

If, with some simplification, the trustees' original view had been that the IASB should produce the best possible standards but leave it to jurisdictions to decide whether and how to use them, they now took a more assertive stance on promoting and protecting the IFRS brand (see also Sections 10.5 and 10.6). The intention to be more actively involved in the implementation of IFRSs was also reflected in plans to establish more formal cooperation with securities regulators and other authorities to identify and redress situations of divergent implementation of IFRSs or inappropriate claims of compliance with IFRSs.

The third tier, the Monitoring Board, had only recently been added, and it was to be expected that at this level there would be more questions about its composition and functioning. Even so, the Monitoring Board members firmly held on to their original idea that the Monitoring Board should be composed exclusively of capital markets authorities. As seen above, they had rejected the membership of prudential regulators when the Monitoring Board was first set up, and they continued to do so now, although they committed to consider how interaction with prudential regulators could be improved beyond the existing observer status of the Basel Committee.

Yet the Monitoring Board intended to open itself to new members, in particular from emerging markets, and on the basis of criteria that were still to be developed. However, one important criterion was already stated: 'To become a member of the Monitoring Board will require domestic use of IFRSs in the relevant jurisdiction and financial contribution by the jurisdiction to the setting of IFRSs.'[159] This was a notable criterion, suggesting that the SEC was contemplating the prospect of either at least allowing the use of IFRSs by domestic listed companies, or of having to cede its place on the Monitoring Board to a more eligible body.

In view of the Monitoring Board's recent involvement in the selection of the successor to David Tweedie, despite the letter of the Memorandum of Understanding between the trustees and the Monitoring Board (see Section 14.12), it was a natural question whether the Monitoring Board should formally be given some powers on this point. The Monitoring Board found that most respondents to its consultation document expressed 'strong objections' to a more prominent role for the Monitoring Board, on the ground that it would undermine the Board's independence.[160] The existing situation of ultimate responsibility of the trustees to appoint the Board chairman was therefore maintained, but the Monitoring Board would be given the opportunity to express its views on a shortlist of candidates, assessed against a set of criteria previously agreed between the Monitoring Board and the trustees.

Perhaps the most contentious questions in the strategy and governance reviews related to the setting of the Board's agenda. A considerable portion of negative sentiment towards the IASB resulted from perceptions that the Board failed to

[158] *IFRSs as the Global Standards* (February 2012), 11.

[159] *Final Report on the Review of the IFRS Foundation's Governance* (February 2012), 13.

[160] *Final Report on the Review of the IFRS Foundation's Governance* (February 2012), 19.

address issues seen as problematical in practice, while spending much time on issues that were problematic in theory rather than practice. In addition, the overriding importance attached between 2005 and 2011 to convergence with US GAAP had given many constituents, as well as some members of the IFRS Advisory Council (previously SAC), the idea that the IASB had put itself in a position where it could not properly consider agenda suggestions. As seen in Section 14.8.5, this question had been discussed extensively during the second Constitution review, when the trustees had introduced the requirement for a three-yearly agenda consultation. As the first consultation was just underway when the strategy review was completed, the trustees proposed no new measures other than a commitment that the Board should provide full feedback.

At the level of the Monitoring Board, the question was framed in terms of whether the Monitoring Board should have an explicit ability to place matters on the IASB's agenda, as opposed to the existing arrangements under which the Monitoring Board could refer issues to the IASB but which also gave the IASB the possibility not to consider the issue. This may have been the issue which kept the trustees most in suspense whether a mutually acceptable position could be arrived at. The issue was not theoretical, given that tension over a perceived Monitoring Board intervention in the Board's work plan had arisen in the first half of 2011 (see Section 16.1.4). It turned out that, as on other issues, most respondents to the Monitoring Board's consultation documents emphasized the fundamental importance of the Board's independence. The existing arrangements were therefore left in place, except for a strengthening of the requirements on the IASB to justify a decision not to act on a Monitoring Board suggestion.

The Monitoring Board's conclusion that it would continue to operate on the basis of consensus, coupled with the decision to expand its membership, provided additional assurance that explicit agenda referrals to the Board would occur in 'extremely rare and urgent cases' only.[161]

---

[161] *Final Report on the Review of the IFRS Foundation's Governance* (February 2012), 17.

15

The Uncertain Path Towards a Single Global Standard

In 2007 and 2008, it might have seemed as if the world was heading for a simple endgame with respect to IFRSs. It seemed possible that the lifting of the 20-F reconciliation requirement by the US Securities and Exchange Commission (SEC) would be followed by a decision of the SEC, expected in 2011, that US domestic listed companies would move to IFRSs. Thus, the United States would set the ultimate seal of approval on the course set in 2000 by the European Union (EU). Other jurisdictions would have no choice but to follow sooner or later. IFRSs would become the single global accounting standard.

The reality of events from 2009 to 2011 was more complex. In parts of the world, the earlier momentum towards IFRS adoption continued. In particular, countries in Latin America for the first time joined the movement towards global accounting standards (see Section 15.1). Several countries in Africa (see Section 15.2) as well as Russia (see Section 15.3) also moved to IFRSs. But the crucial events occurred in the United States, where it became ever clearer that the SEC might not, after all, decide in favour of IFRSs (see Section 15.4). This had repercussions throughout the world, but especially in Asia. There, the three major economies of Japan (see Section 15.5), China (see Section 15.6), and India (see Section 15.7) were watching the United States for signs of a waxing or waning commitment to IFRSs. Meanwhile, the EU maintained a fractious loyalty to its original IFRS policy, with clear differences in the degree of support across member states (see Section 15.10).

15.1 MANY LATIN AMERICAN AND CARIBBEAN COUNTRIES ADOPT IFRSs

During most of the IASC period, from 1973 to 2000, the South and Central American republics evinced scant interest in the movement to develop a single, global set of accounting standards.[1] Mexico, of course, was one of the delegations

---

[1] Kees Camfferman and Stephen A. Zeff, *Financial Reporting and Global Capital Markets: A History of the International Accounting Standards Committee, 1973–2000* (Oxford: Oxford University Press, 2007), 180–1.

on the IASC Board, and there was a Brazilian included in the financial executives' delegation beginning in 1996, but in neither country did this produce a discernible tendency to move closer to the IASC's standards. As discussed in Chapter 4, the World Bank launched a programme in the late 1990s which involved an extensive review of developing countries' accounting and auditing, always at the invitation of countries, leading to its 'Reports on the Observance of Standards and Codes, Accounting and Auditing' (ROSC A&A).[2] In these lengthy reports, the World Bank invariably concluded the section on accounting by recommending that the country begin a programme towards the eventual adoption of IFRSs or that it fortify its existing programme aimed at adopting IFRSs. A recommendation by the World Bank to such countries would have carried considerable weight, as the Bank was viewed as a major source of infrastructure financing. This programme embraced not only developing countries but also countries with emerging economies. As a consequence, a larger world, including Latin America and the Caribbean, began to develop a heightened interest in adopting IFRSs or converging their national generally accepted accounting principles (GAAP) with IFRSs. In addition to the World Bank's impressive ROSC A&A initiative, the Inter-American Development Bank's Multilateral Investment Fund (MIF) provided financial assistance to nine Latin American countries to support training towards their IFRS adoption or convergence programmes.[3] Other development institutions, notably the Financial Sector Reform and Strengthening (FIRST) Initiative, a multi-donor grant facility based at the World Bank in Washington, DC, sponsored projects in Chile, El Salvador, Honduras, and Peru to build capacity for a transition to IFRSs.[4]

By the middle of the 2000s, five of the smaller Latin American and Caribbean countries had adopted IFRSs for listed companies: the Dominican Republic, El Salvador, Honduras, Jamaica, and Uruguay.[5] To be sure, especially in the smaller countries, 'adoption' may signify less than full compliance with the IASB's IFRSs. Fortin et al. wrote that, at the same time, 'the larger countries in the region continued to develop their own standards, which they felt were more amenable to their respective environments, and not as demanding as international ones'.[6] Yet by 2009, Fortin et al. wrote, most large countries in the region—Argentina, Brazil, Chile, and Mexico—had 'officially adopted' IFRSs for listed companies, with varying transition regimes. Only the large listed companies in Chile were complying with IFRSs by 2009, and compliance by all listed companies was not expected until 2011. Brazil adopted a 'progressive' or 'escalation' approach towards adoption from 2008 on, with completion of the cycle in 2010. Argentina and Mexico had both set 2012 as their deadline year for the required changeover.

---

[2] See 'Overview of the ROSC Accounting and Auditing Program' (Washington DC: The World Bank, January 2004) <http://www.worldbank.org/ifa/rosc_aa.html>. The same page links to the more than ninety country reports published under the programme.

[3] Henri Fortin, Ana Cristina Hirata Barros, and Kit Cutler, *Accounting for Growth in Latin America and the Caribbean: Improving Corporate Financial Reporting to Support Regional Economic Development* (Washington, DC: The World Bank, 2010), 87. The three authors of this work were the authors or co-authors of most of the ROSC A&A reviews of the countries in this region. As will be seen, this work provides indispensable information on the IFRS developments treated in this section.

[4] Fortin et al., *Accounting for Growth*, 87.   [5] Fortin et al., 78.   [6] Fortin et al., 78.

In addition, adoptions were signified by the Organization for Eastern Caribbean States (representing nine countries), as well as by Ecuador, Panama, Paraguay, and Peru.[7] Venezuela did not join the movement to IFRSs by 2012, and the fitful steps taken by Colombia will be discussed in Section 15.1.5.

15.1.1 Chile

In Chile, a regulatory body took the initiative to lead and manage the move towards IFRS adoption from beginning to end. In late 2006, the Superintendencia de Valores y Seguros (SVS, Securities and Insurance Supervisor) decided to require issuers in the stock market to issue IFRS financial statements by 2009. The SVS set up a dedicated website on the transition process, issued ten circulars on IFRS adoption, and 'conducted two surveys of securities issuers to assess their degree of preparedness for implementation and identify possible difficulties and bottlenecks in the adoption process'.[8] Despite some slippage at the end, the goal of bringing at least the big listed companies on board by 2009 was fulfilled. The transition by the remaining listed companies was successfully concluded in 2011. Fortin et al. wrote: 'Clearly, having a strong and active regulatory body to move the process forward must be seen as a prerequisite to successful IFRS implementation; and the regulator must be proactive throughout the adoption process [as the SVS was] to anticipate and manage the risk of delays that any such project is prone to face.'[9]

15.1.2 Argentina

Argentina provided another example of a securities regulator taking the initiative. In December 2009, the Comisión Nacional de Valores (CNV, National Securities Commission) announced that all companies that offered equity or debt securities would be required to prepare their financial statements using IFRSs, beginning with financial statements for the year ended 31 December 2012. Companies could voluntarily file their financial statements using IFRSs as early as January 2011. Companies already preparing IFRS financial statements on a supplemental basis might begin adopting IFRSs in 2010.[10] Neither banks nor insurance companies have so far been allowed to use IFRSs. As is the case in Canada (see Section 10.1), listed companies, in their notes to the financial statements, and auditors, in their report on the financial statements, are required to affirm compliance with IFRSs.

The Federación Argentina de Consejos Profesionales en Ciencias Económicas (FACPCE, Argentine Federation of Professional Councils in Economic Sciences), which brings together the professional councils of the twenty-three provinces and the federal capital, was charged with incorporating IFRSs into Argentine GAAP,

---

[7] Fortin et al., 78–9. Fortin et al. did not provide any adoption information about Guatemala and Nicaragua.

[8] Fortin et al., 86. [9] Fortin et al., 86.

[10] 'Argentina Will Require IFRSs in 2012', news item posted 31 December 2009 <http://www.iasplus.com>.

and the target year was achieved as planned. For required use by listed companies of newly issued IASB standards and interpretations, the FACPCE will continue to be the arbiter, but its role is limited to assessing whether they contradict any laws.

15.1.3 Brazil

Brazil's experience was quite different from that in Chile and Argentina. In Brazil, the lead role in the move towards IFRS adoption by listed companies was taken by the private sector. As in other countries, awareness that increasing country adoptions of IFRSs were beginning to make an indelible mark on global financial reporting led to an appreciation of the importance of IFRSs to the future financial competitiveness of Brazilian companies.

Apparently, much of the stimulus for the recognition in Brazil of the work of the IASC and then the IASB came from L. Nelson Carvalho, the only Brazilian to serve on the IASC Board. Carvalho participated in the financial executives' delegation to the IASC Board, beginning in 1996–7 as a technical adviser and then, from 1999 to 2000, as a full member of the delegation.[11] He had earlier been head of banking supervision at the central bank and then a commissioner of the securities commission, and he was also a member of the board of the futures and stock exchange and of the boards and audit committees of other companies. The IASC Board's quarterly meeting in March 2000 was held in São Paulo (for the first time in South America), probably owing to Carvalho's encouragement and initiative, thus offering the opportunity to bring important business, financial, government, and accounting figures in Brazil into touch with the IASC's leadership. Carvalho was a member of the IASB's Standards Advisory Council (SAC) from 2001 onwards, and its chairman from 2005 to 2008. He was appointed a member of the IASB–FASB Financial Crisis Advisory Group in 2008. Hence, he remained close to the IASB following his service on the IASC Board, and he was well placed in Brazil to convey his views at the highest levels about the importance to the business community of replacing its domestic accounting standards with high-quality international accounting standards.

Brazil was represented at an early stage—well before China and India, for example—at the level of the IASC Foundation trustees. The IASC nominating committee, headed by SEC Chairman Arthur Levitt, appointed Roberto Teixeira da Costa, formerly the founding chairman of the Brazilian securities commission, as one of the nineteen trustees to begin service in May 2000. He was the only South American chosen at that time for the original panel of trustees. When his second term ended in December 2007, he was replaced by Pedro Sampaio Malan, Brazil's former minister of finance and former governor of the Banco do Brasil.

---

[11] L. Nelson Carvalho and Álvaro A. Ricardino Filho, 'Brazil', in Gary J. Previts, Peter Walton, and Peter Wolnizer (editors), *A Global History of Accounting, Financial Reporting and Public Policy: Americas* (Bingley, UK: Emerald Group Publishing, 2011), 45. Much of this subsection on Brazil is drawn from this source. Also see L. Nelson Carvalho and Bruno M. Salotti, 'Adoption of IFRS in Brazil and the Consequences to Accounting Education', *Issues in Accounting Education*, 28/2 (May 2013), 235–42.

Since 1995, the Ministry of Finance had been considering a project of reform of the accounting section of company law. By the early 2000s, interest in this reform had shifted strongly towards possible future adoption of IFRSs, and new legislation pointing towards IFRSs was expected.

In October 2005, in anticipation of the new law, the Conselho Federal de Contabilidade (CFC, Federal Council of Accounting), with full support from the government, established an independent standard-setting committee, the Comitê de Pronunciamentos Contábeis (CPC, Accounting Pronouncements Committee). Its membership was broadly based, drawn from five organizations that had requested the CFC to set up such a body: Abrasca, the association of Brazilian listed companies; Apimec, the association of financial analysts; Fipecafi, a foundation associated with the Universidade de São Paulo; Ibracon, the Brazilian institute of auditors; and Bovespa, the stock exchange. Other regulatory bodies—the securities market and insurance supervisors, the central bank, and the tax authority—participated as observers without a vote.[12] To be enforceable, the CPC's pronouncements must be approved by the CFC and the relevant regulatory body. Fortin et al. characterized the CPC as 'an example of good practice' of independent, private-sector standard setting.[13] In January 2009, Carvalho became a member of the CPC.

The CPC became the centrepiece in a new arrangement for setting accounting standards in conformity with IFRSs, both for listed and unlisted companies. A revision of company law enacted on 28 December 2007 separated, for the first time, financial reporting from taxation. It confirmed the authority of the securities commission and the CFC to set accounting standards for listed and unlisted companies, respectively, but legally required them to ensure the conformity of Brazilian standards with IFRSs. Both could look to an independent entity—the CPC—for advice. The CPC thereupon began to produce a series of Brazilian standards that were translations of IFRSs, initially with some exceptions, but by 2010 virtually identical.[14]

The securities commission did not await the results. In July 2007, before the new law was passed, it issued a rule requiring listed companies to publish their consolidated financial statements using IFRSs as issued by the IASB, beginning with financial years ending in 2010. Between 2007 and 2009, listed companies could voluntarily adopt IFRSs instead of the Brazilian standards which the CPC was now steadily converging with IFRSs.[15]

By 2010, the transition was completed, in the form of either direct application of IFRSs (mandatory in the consolidated financial statements of listed companies, optional for non-listed companies) or in the form of converged Brazilian standards (in the parent company financial statements of listed companies or in the

---

[12] Fortin et al., 83; see also 'International Standards in Brazil', *World Accounting Report*, October 2007, 10–11.

[13] Fortin et al., 83.

[14] Jurisdiction page 'Brazil' <http://www.iasplus.com>, consulted 22 April 2014; 'Law No. 11,638: Changes to Accounting Practices in Brazil', undated Deloitte newsletter [2008] <http://www.iasplus.com>; 'IFRS and CPCs—The New Brazilian Accounting Environment', (PricewaterhouseCoopers, 2011) <www.pwc.com.br>.

[15] CVM Instruction 457, 13 July 2007, English translation <http://www/cvm.gov.br>.

financial statements of the larger non-listed companies). In 2006, the central bank had announced that all banks required to publish financial statements must begin complying fully with IFRSs in their consolidated statements, also starting with financial years ending in 2010.

All of the IFRSs were required to be used in consolidated financial statements except for one option. As Brazilian law does not allow companies to revalue their fixed and intangible assets, the revaluation options in IAS 16 and IAS 38 were not allowed.[16] This exception was similar to the several options that were not allowed in Australia and New Zealand in 2004 (see Chapter 4), because they were not permissible under their national GAAPs. In the Brazilian case, however, statute law prohibited use of the option. Yet Brazilian company law also requires reporting that goes beyond IFRSs, in that public companies must present a statement of value added—a financial statement that has never been discussed by the IASC or the IASB.

The IASC Foundation reciprocated Brazil's growing interest in adopting IFRSs, as well as the increasing economic importance of the country, by naming Amaro Luiz de Oliveira Gomes a member of the IASB on 1 July 2009. He was formerly head of the financial system regulation department of the central bank and had played a major role in the move by Brazil towards IFRSs.

In January 2010, Brazil was the fourth country in the world—following the United States, Japan, and China—whose accounting standard setter or equivalent body signed a Memorandum of Understanding with the IASB. Unlike these other agreements, which committed the signatories to convergence with IFRSs, Brazil asserted that 'it continues to be committed to progressively require the full adoption' of IFRSs.[17] The Memorandum was signed in the boardroom of the São Paulo futures and stock exchange by David Tweedie, representing the IASB, Juarez Domingues Carneiro, in his capacity of president of the CFC, and representatives of the standard-setting body, CPC, in the presence of Brazilian trustee Pedro Malan.

15.1.4 Mexico

In November 2008, the Comisión Nacional Bancaria y de Valores (CNBV, National Banking and Securities Commission) announced that all companies listed on the Mexican Stock Exchange would be required to use IFRSs starting in 2012. Early adoption was permitted beginning with 2008 financial statements.[18] Like South Africa and Israel, Mexico has not had an endorsement protocol. This means that IFRSs existing prior to 2012, and IFRSs issued subsequently, were immediately applicable to Mexican listed companies without the need for any

---

[16] Interview with Amaro Gomes, 15 February 2012. Also see 'Should IFRS Standards Be More "European"?', report by Philippe Maystadt, October 2013, annex 3 <http://ec.europa.eu/internal_market/accounting>.

[17] 'Memorandum of Understanding among the International Accounting Standards Board (IASB), the Brazilian Federal Council of Accounting (CFC), and the Brazilian Accounting Pronouncements Committee (CPC)', 28 January 2010 <http://www.iasplus.com>.

[18] Untitled CNBV press release 56/2008 dated 11 November 2008 <http://www.cnbv.gob.mx>.

action or decision by a Mexican entity, such as the CNBV, to approve them for use in Mexico. By 2012, all listed companies complied with IFRSs, according to plan. Banks and other financial institutions were still required to prepare their financial statements based on the rules of the bank regulator.

The process of using IFRSs to make improvements in Mexican GAAP for use by private companies was entrusted to the Consejo Mexicano para la Investigación y Desarrollo de Normas de Información Financiera (CINIF, Council for Research and Development of Financial Information Standards), which had been set up in 2004, succeeding the accounting principles committee of the Instituto Mexicano de Contadores Públicos (IMCP, Mexican Institute of Public Accountants).

15.1.5 Colombia

Colombia is perhaps the only country in the world whose Constitution explicitly authorizes the Congress to determine proper accounting practice to be used by companies in the private sector.[19] The Congress by law may delegate this authority to the executive branch or to other institutions. Colombia has been somewhat of an enigma. In July 2009, the Congress passed Law 1314, which required that Colombian GAAP be converged to IFRSs by 31 December 2013, for required use by public companies. The Congress entrusted the convergence process to a Consejo Técnico de la Contaduría Pública (CTCP, Technical Council of Public Accountancy), which had no staff, no budget, and only three politically appointed part-time members, none of whom possessed expertise in IFRSs. Clearly, this task was all but impossible for such a body. Furthermore, its recommendations had to be approved by two government ministries: Finance and Public Credit; and Commerce, Industry and Tourism. Little progress was expected from this initiative.

Some 237 public companies, eighty-seven public entities, and other companies with public debt are required by the Superintendencia de Finanzas (Finance Supervisor) to submit financial statements prepared in accordance with Colombian GAAP. It was understood that the Finance Supervisor was also working on convergence with IFRSs.

In October 2011, the CTCP published a paper, 'Proposed Standards of Accounting and Financial Reporting for Convergence with International Standards', seeking responses to a proposal that listed, and selected non-listed, companies should apply IFRSs as issued for use in Colombia, but in principle identical to the Spanish-language version of IFRSs, beginning in 2014.[20] The proposal suggested earlier voluntary application, which was confirmed on 30 December 2011, when the President of the Republic decreed that large and medium-sized companies may voluntarily adopt IFRSs.[21] It is understood that a delegation of executives

---

[19] *Report on the Observance of Standards and Codes, Accounting and Auditing: Colombia* (The World Bank, 25 July 2004), paragraph 24.

[20] 'Colombia Issues Proposal Paper on IFRS Convergence', news item posted 26 October 2011 <http://www.iasplus.com>.

[21] 'Voluntary Application of IFRSs in Colombia', news item posed 4 January 2012 <http://www.iasplus.com>.

from major Colombian companies went to Europe to discuss financing possibilities, and were informed by bankers and other capital market sources that they could not analyse and interpret financial statements using Colombian GAAP, and that, if the companies really wanted financing in Europe, they should adopt IFRSs. Upon their return to Bogotá, the company executives met with the president and persuaded him to issue the decree so as to enable companies to raise finance overseas.[22] Then, in September 2012, following receipt of submissions from the private sector concerning the unexpected difficulties of implementing IFRSs, the government deferred mandatory application of IFRSs from 2014 to 2015.[23] This is as far as Colombia has gone.

15.1.6 Group of Latin American Accounting Standard Setters (GLASS)

In June 2011, under the leadership of Brazil and with the strong encouragement from the IASB, thirteen national standard setters from Mexico in the north to Argentina and Chile in the south formed the Grupo Latinoamericano de Emisores de Normas de Información Financiera (GLASS, Group of Latin American Accounting Standard Setters). Its chairman and vice chairman were from Brazil and Argentina, respectively. Representatives from Uruguay, Chile, and Mexico were named to its board of directors.[24] Its aim, similar to that of the Asian-Oceanian Standard-Setters Group (AOSSG, see Section 15.8), is to convey comments from its region to the IASB on agenda matters and drafts.[25]

15.1.7 Compliance and Languages

Fortin et al. wrote that the ROSC A&A reviews 'have shown that noncompliance with A&A rules is an issue in nearly every country in the Latin American and Caribbean (LAC) region, particularly in nonfinancial sectors'.[26] They added, 'Of the regulated sectors, the banking sector tends to be subject to the most stringent enforcement, as banking supervisors consistently have more human and financial resources [e.g. in the central banks] than regulators of other sectors'.[27] As to listed companies, they wrote, 'The human and financial resources for enforcing stock markets track closely with the significance of the stock market: the regulators of the Brazilian, Chilean, and Panamanian stock markets are the best equipped to oversee those relatively larger exchanges'.[28] A noteworthy omission from this short list is the regulator of the Mexican stock market. It will be a challenge for the regulators in the smaller countries, as well as in Colombia, to acquire the necessary

---

[22] Interview with Amaro Gomes, 15 February 2012, and other sources.

[23] 'IFRS Adoption in Colombia Deferred to 2015', news item posted 28 September 2012 <http://www.iasplus.com>.

[24] Interview with Amaro Gomes, 15 February 2012.

[25] Resource page 'Group of Latin American Accounting Standard Setters (GLASS)' <http://www.iasplus.com> consulted on 22 April 2014.

[26] Fortin et al., 95.   [27] Fortin et al., 100.   [28] Fortin et al., 101–2.

human and financial resources, as well as legislative authority, to regulate effectively the listed companies' compliance with IFRSs.

All of the Spanish-speaking Latin American republics have agreed with Spain on a single translation for rendering the English version of IFRSs into Spanish. But the same is not true for Portuguese. Brazil and Portugal have not agreed on a single translation from English into Portuguese. Therefore, there are two official Portuguese translations of IFRSs.

15.2 AFRICA

Africa has evinced strong interest in the *IFRS for SMEs*, and several of the countries—mostly former British dependencies in the east and south—have adopted full IFRSs for required use by domestic companies traded in public markets. These include Botswana, Mauritius, Tanzania, Uganda, Zambia, and Zimbabwe, and, of course, South Africa, which was one of the first countries anywhere in the world to adopt IFRSs.[29] In 2010, the Nigerian federal government adopted a roadmap towards adoption of IFRSs and the *IFRS for SMEs*. In January 2011, it was confidently predicted that Nigeria, the continent's most populous country, 'is on course for IFRS implementation from January 2012'.[30] Listed and significant public interest entities in Nigeria issued their first financial statements using applicable IFRSs in 2012. Deloitte reported that one of the reasons given by the relevant government minister for adopting IFRSs was to attract foreign direct investment.[31]

In countries other than South Africa, whether there is an effective system for securing compliance with IFRSs by listed companies is an open question. In early 2011, an official of the World Bank was quoted as saying that 'there is no country resistance [in eastern and southern Africa] to IFRSs anymore', but, he added, 'It is the capacity, the professional accounting bodies, the regulators and auditors, that remain the problem'.[32] An official with the African Development Bank, remarking on the great variability from country to country in 'accounting capacity', was quoted as saying, 'the number of qualified accountants in Francophone countries is so limited. It will take years to get to the technical capabilities required. Even with a simplified version of IFRSs they will not be able to comply in the next ten years. By 2020 they would struggle to comply.'[33] Furthermore, Francophone thinking and practice have been profoundly influenced by the French accounting plan.

---

[29] Jurisdictional profiles on the IFRS Foundation website, consulted in June 2013. See also Robert Bruce, 'Africa Embraces IFRSs', 4 January 2011 <http://www.ifrs.org>.

[30] Bruce, 'Africa Embraces IFRSs'.

[31] Uwadiae Oduware, *IFRS Adoption in Nigeria & Optimizing the Gains of Global Investment Climate* (Akintola Williams Deloitte, December 2012) <https://www.wecadeloitte.com>.

[32] Bruce, 'Africa Embraces IFRSs'. For similar views based on survey results, see Akintola Owolabi and Francis O. Iyoha, 'Adopting International Financial Reporting Standards (IFRS) in Africa: Benefits, Prospects, and Challenges', *African Journal of Accounting, Auditing and Finance* 1/1 (2012), 77–86.

[33] Bruce, 'Africa Embraces IFRSs'.

In May 2011, the Pan African Federation of Accountants (PAFA) was formed, with support from the World Bank, in order to represent African professional accountants in international circles with a single, loud voice. It is composed of thirty-nine professional accountancy bodies in thirty-four countries. Although the officers of the body are based in Nigeria and Tanzania, its secretariat is being managed in Johannesburg by the South African Institute of Chartered Accountants (SAICA). At PAFA's annual meeting held in Tunis in May 2012, its general assembly voted to 'adopt' IFRSs.[34] Yet, being a federation, it cannot impose its will on its country members.

15.3 RUSSIA GOES FOR IFRSs

Of the five so-called BRICS countries (Brazil, Russia, India, China, and South Africa), the Russian Federation was least involved with the IASB. Apart from a representation on SAC, which was not renewed in 2009, it had no presence in the Board, the trustees, or in the International Financial Reporting Interpretations Committee (IFRIC). From the outside, its progress towards IFRSs appeared unsteady and seemed to gain momentum only when riding on the crest of a much bigger wave.

As mentioned in Chapter 4, plans to converge Russian standards with IFRSs could be traced back to the late 1990s. Between 2002 and 2004, several regulatory and legislative initiatives occurred, pointing towards mandatory use of IFRSs. Beginning in 2004, banks were required to submit their financial statements using IFRSs to the central bank.[35] It was recommended, but not required, that banks also publish these statements. Plans were floated and draft legislation prepared for mandatory adoption by a larger group of companies, with planned transition dates variously announced from 2004 to 2006.[36] But for several years no further word was heard, at least outside of Russia, about the fate of this legislation. Nonetheless, the number of companies using IFRSs did increase, apparently with the encouragement of several stock exchanges and the Federal Commission of Securities Markets.[37]

The Ministry of Finance, for its part, had been making efforts for almost two decades aimed at the introduction of IFRSs or at least a harmonization between national standards and IFRSs, mostly to little avail. But since June 2008, President Dmitry Medvedev had been publicly advocating the creation of an international

---

[34] 'PAFA General Assembly Resolves to Adopt International Standards', PAFA press release, [23 May 2012] <http://www.pafa.org.za>.

[35] 'Russia Will Adopt IAS Starting in 2004', news item posted 25 July 2002 <http://www.iasplus.com>.

[36] 'Russia Moves Toward Adopting IFRSs', news item posted 1 November 2004 <http://www.iasplus.com>; 'White Paper on Corporate Governance in Russia' (Russian Corporate Governance Roundtable, [2002]) <http://www.oecd.org>.

[37] Julia Kochetygova et al., 'Analytical Assessment of the Progress in Implementing the Recommendations of the White Paper on Corporate Governance' (Standard & Poor's, [2004]) <http://www.oecd.org>; Robert W. McGee and Gayle Mende, 'What Kind of Financial Reporting Standards do Russian Companies Use?', in Robert W. McGee (editor), *Corporate Governance in Transition Economies* (New York, NY: Springer, 2008), 217–20.

financial centre in Moscow. Just under two years later, he appointed the head of a task force to achieve that result.[38] On 27 July 2010, a legislative requirement on the mandatory adoption of IFRSs for public interest entities was introduced by Federal Law No. 208-FZ, 'On Consolidated Financial Statements'. This represented final approval of the draft law that had stalled in 2004. On 25 February 2011, the minister of finance announced a government decree that the ministry was to begin endorsing IFRSs in accordance with a specified procedure.[39] The aim of the decree was to set out the requirements of the Federal Law in greater detail. The decree stated that the ministry's endorsement decisions on particular standards were to be based on the recommendations from an independent, not-for-profit institution. Although deadlines were not specified in the decree, the minister informed the media that he expected that the currently existing IFRSs would be endorsed by the end of 2011. This led some observers to believe that no great haste was intended, and that listed companies would first be required to prepare their consolidated financial statements in full conformity with IFRSs for the 2013 calendar year (with 2012 comparative figures).[40]

In 2011, on the basis of a public tender, the ministry awarded the status of advisory body to the National Organization for Financial Accounting and Reporting Standards (or NOFA Foundation), formed in October 2003. Within the NOFA Foundation there is an expert body, the National Accounting Standards Board (NASB), which is composed of accounting experts. The endorsement procedure implies that, following receipt of the recommendation from the NASB, the Ministry of Finance issues the regulation on IFRS endorsement in cooperation with the Securities and Exchange Commission, the Central Bank, and the Ministry of Justice.[41]

By the middle of the year, signs began to appear that the movement to IFRSs might occur earlier rather than later. On 14 June 2011, the minister of finance made it known that, given timely completion of the endorsement procedure, application of IFRSs might begin in 2012 (with 2011 comparatives).[42] On 18 June 2011, it was reported that President Medvedev had met with the members of his advisory board on the creation and development of an international financial centre in Russia, at which he said, 'I have decided to transfer Russian issuers to international accounting standards'.[43]

---

[38] 'Russia to Draw up Plan for International Financial Center', news item posted 7 June 2008; 'Medvedev Formalizes Appointment of Moscow Financial Center Task Force Head', news item posted 18 May 2010 <http://en.rian.ru>.

[39] 'IFRSs to be Partially Adopted in Russia in 2012', news item posted 16 March 2011 <http://www.iasplus.com>.

[40] This inference was apparently drawn in 'IFRSs to be Partially Adopted in Russia in 2012', news item posted 16 March 2011 <http://www.iasplus.com>. See also Valery Bakhtin, 'IFRS in Russia—History and Horizons', commentary posted 31 October 2012 <http://www.integra-international.net> accessed April 2014.

[41] 'IFRS Application around the World: Jurisdictional Profile: Russia' <http://www.ifrs.org>, consulted June 2013.

[42] See David R. Borker, 'Stepped-up Progress on IFRS in Russia: History in the Making', *International Business & Economics Research Journal*, 11/2 (February 2012), 255–68.

[43] 'Dmitry Medvedev Met with Members of Advisory Board on Creation and Development of International Financial Centre in Russia', President of Russia website, 18 June 2011, <http://eng.kremlin.ru/news/2420>.

The next word received from the Russian government was that, by 25 November 2011, the Ministry of Finance had indeed endorsed all of the IASB's existing standards and interpretations, with mandatory application in 2012 for most listed companies. The Ministry of Finance reminded companies that had not already done so that they should immediately begin providing the necessary comparative figures for 2011.[44]

Initially, all extant standards and interpretations were endorsed, other than IFRSs 9 to 13 and IFRIC 20.[45] IFRS 9 had still not been endorsed by the EU, and the other pronouncements had only just been issued. Subsequently, IFRSs 9 to 13 were also endorsed for use in Russia.

15.4 THE UNITED STATES: THE SEC DOES NOT DECIDE ON IFRSs

15.4.1 Change in SEC Chairman from Christopher Cox to Mary Schapiro in January 2009

The policy of SEC Chairman Christopher Cox in favour of IFRSs had culminated in November 2008 with the issue of a 'roadmap' proposing release in which the SEC said it would allow as many as 110 large, internationally active domestic issuers to use IFRSs as early as 2009, and that it would decide in 2011 whether to require all domestic issuers to switch to IFRSs beginning in 2014 (see Section 8.6).[46] But the Cox era at the Commission was shortly to end, before he could carry the roadmap proposal forward. Prior to the Presidential election on 4 November 2008, Cox had announced that he would leave the Commission at the end of the Bush Administration.[47] This was well before the end of his five-year term, but Cox had been under great pressure during the Administration's handling of the meltdown of the US economy, as well as for the SEC's failure to act on the Bernard Madoff fraud.[48] It was not known whether his strong avowal of IFRSs would be similarly evinced by his successor, Mary L. Schapiro. She had served as a commissioner from 1988 to 1994, when international accounting standards were becoming important to the SEC, but they were mostly of interest at the level of the senior staff in the Office of the Chief Accountant and the Division of Corporation Finance. During her confirmation hearing on 15 January 2009 before the Senate Banking Committee,

---

[44] 'Russia to Make IFRS Mandatory', *Russian Survey*, December 2011, 4–5.

[45] 'Update on Russia's IFRS transition', news item posted 27 December 2011 <http://www.iasplus.com>.

[46] 'SEC Proposes Roadmap Toward Global Accounting Standards to Help Investors Compare Financial Information More Easily', SEC press release 2008-184, dated 27 August 2008; 'Roadmap for the Potential Use of Financial Statements Prepared in Accordance with International Financial Reporting Standards by U.S. Issuers', release Nos. 33-8982; 34-58960, 14 November 2008. Unless otherwise indicated, materials originating with the SEC referred to in this section are accessible at <http://www.sec.gov>.

[47] See Robert W. Rouse, 'New Broom Sweeps Clean', *The Journal of Corporate Accounting & Finance*, 20/3 (March/April 2009), 87.

[48] See e.g. the article in *Time* magazine, 'How Much Is the SEC's Cox to Blame?' dated 23 September 2008 <http://www.time.com>.

she had the following colloquy with Senator Jack Reed (who, as reported in Chapter 8, had expressed 'serious concerns' about lifting the 20-F reconciliation requirement for IFRS users):

Senator REED. Much of what you are going to do will have complications and consequences overseas as well as here in the United States, and one of the areas is the IFRS road map. We have repeatedly written to Chairman Cox to try to determine and develop a very deliberate road map. I think there was a rush to judgment on this issue. In fact, I met with the CEO of Honeywell Corporation who says similar concerns about disparate accounting treatment on the international rules that can be used to change income, can be used to treat R&D expenses differently. There is a host of potential, I hesitate to say—I won't. There is a potential arbitrage of the two systems which I think we have to avoid.

Can you give us a notion of how you would like to proceed with this international accounting movement, with the recognition I think we all have that in the global economy, eventually, standards hopefully will converge to high levels.

Ms. SCHAPIRO. Well, I would proceed with great caution so that we don't have a race to the bottom. I think we all can agree that a single set of accounting standards used around the world would be a very beneficial thing, allowing investors to compare companies around the world. That said, I have some concerns about the road map that has been published by the SEC and is out for comment now and I have some concerns about the IFRS standards generally. They are not as detailed as the U.S. standards. There is a lot left to interpretation. Even if adopted, there would still be a lack of consistency, I believe, around the world in how they are implemented and how they are enforced.

The cost to switch from U.S. GAAP to IFRS is going to be extraordinary, and I have seen some estimates that range as high as $30 million for each U.S. company in order to do that. This is a time when I think we have to think carefully about whether imposing those sorts of costs on U.S. industry really makes sense.

Perhaps, though, my greatest concern is the independence of the International Accounting Standards Board and the ability to have oversight of their process for setting accounting standards and the amount of rigor that exists in that process today.

I will tell you that I will take a big deep breath and look at this entire area again carefully and will not necessarily feel bound by the existing road map that is out for comment.[49]

During the same hearing, she directed some pointed criticism at the IASB in her responses to questions posed by Senator Carl Levin:

When it comes to international accounting standards, it's critical that these standards are converged in a way that does not kick off a race to the bottom. American investors deserve and expect high standards of financial reporting, transparency, and disclosure—along with a standard-setter that is free from political interference and that has the resources to be a strong watchdog. At this time, it is not apparent that the IASB meets those criteria, and I am not prepared to delegate standard-setting or oversight responsibility to the IASB.[50]

---

[49] Schapiro's testimony in *Nominations of: Mary Schapiro, Christina D. Romer, Austan D. Goolsbee, Cecilia E. Rouse and Daniel K. Tarullo*, Hearing before the Committee on Banking, Housing, and Urban Affairs, United States Senate, 111th Congress, First Session, 15 January 2009 (Washington, DC: US Government Printing Office, 2009), 21–2.

[50] *Nominations*, 90.

Schapiro's statements, and in particular her utterance that she 'will not necessarily feel bound by the existing road map' was widely quoted or cited in the press and in articles in the professional and academic literature.[51] Within the United States, it served effectively to quell discussion of the roadmap proposal. It soon became evident that the adoption of IFRSs, as reflected in the roadmap proposal, was no longer envisaged by the SEC. The confirmation hearing was closely watched abroad, and Schapiro's statements prompted doubts about the SEC's commitment to IFRSs.[52]

Under these circumstances, some key changes in SEC personnel also invited speculation about the course the SEC was likely to take. The end of 2008 saw the departure of John White, the Corp Fin director since March 2006. When announcing his decision to leave, the SEC said, 'In addition to spearheading the Commission's groundbreaking adoption of new rules to accept IFRS from foreign issuers, Mr. White led the Division in developing the recommendation of a multi-year roadmap for use of IFRS by U.S. issuers'.[53]

Chief Accountant Conrad Hewitt also departed in January 2009.[54] There was some restiveness early during the lengthy process of appointing a successor, which finally occurred in August, when Chairman Schapiro appointed Deputy Chief Accountant (DCA) James L. Kroeker—who was serving as acting chief accountant—to the post. Kroeker had been a national office partner in Deloitte before joining the Commission as DCA in February 2007.[55] The restiveness over the appointment of a chief accountant was sparked in February 2009, when Bloomberg reported that Schapiro was considering Charles D. Niemeier, a former chief accountant in the SEC's enforcement division, to succeed Hewitt.[56] Niemeier, a member shortly to retire from the Public Company Accounting Oversight Board, had been highly critical of IFRSs in a speech given in September 2008 to the New York State Society of Certified Public Accountants.[57] But it shortly became evident that Niemeier was not, in fact, a candidate.

---

[51] See e.g. Stephen Labaton, 'S.E.C. Nominee Offers Plan for Tighter Regulation', *The New York Times*, 15 January 2009, 3; Greg Millman, 'Execs Hail Mary Schapiro for Folding IFRS Roadmap', news item posted 26 January 2009 <http://www.ifrsreporter.com>; Sarah Johnson, 'SEC Pushes Back IFRS Roadmap', news item posted 4 February 2009 <http://www.cfo.com>; Peter Walton, *An Executive's Guide for Moving from U.S. GAAP to IFRS* (New York: Business Expert Press, LLC, 2009), 32; and Tom Tyson, 'The Convergence of IFRS and U.S. GAAP', *The CPA Journal*, June 2011, 27.

[52] Jennifer Hughes, 'IFRS Set to Turn Political as SEC Unfolds Its Roadmap', *Financial Times*, 22 January 2009, 18. The effect of Schapiro's statements in Europe was mentioned in interviews with David Wright, 19 January 2009; Jeremy Jennings, 20 January 2009; and with Nicolas Véron, 21 January 2009.

[53] 'John White, Director of Division of Corporation Finance, to Leave SEC after Leading Unprecedented Rulemaking to Enhance Disclosure to Investors', SEC press release 2008-265, dated 6 November 2008.

[54] 'SEC Chief Accountant Conrad Hewitt to Leave SEC', SEC press release 2008-281, dated 25 November 2008.

[55] 'James L. Kroeker Named Chief Accountant at SEC', SEC press release 2009-187, dated 25 August 2009.

[56] 'SEC May Pick Audit Board's Niemeier for Accounting (Update 2)', news item posted 11 February 2009 <http://www.bloomberg.com>.

[57] For reports of the speech, see 'PCAOB's Niemeier Slams IFRS at FAE Conference', news item posted 11 September 2009 <http://www.nysscpa.org> and 'Regulator Rips into Global Accounting Plan', news item posted 10 September 2010 <http://www.cfo.com>.

The departure of John White and the long delay in appointing a chief account-ant were factors explaining why the SEC did not return to a discussion of IFRSs during the remainder of 2009. Even more important, the Commission was preoccupied with the financial crisis, the fallout from the Madoff scandal, and other pressing regulatory issues.[58]

The appointment of Mary Schapiro coincided with the decision of the IASC Foundation trustees, in January 2009, to approve the creation of a Monitoring Board. As seen in Chapter 14, its membership was composed of the SEC chair-man, the chairman of Japan's Financial Services Agency, two high-level represen-tatives of the International Organization of Securities Commissions (IOSCO), and the EU commissioner for the internal market. The Monitoring Board held its first meeting on 1 April 2009, in London. Mary Schapiro made a point of regularly attending the meetings of the Monitoring Board, at which the trustees and the IASB chairman, David Tweedie, were also in attendance. The IASB leadership, somewhat disconcerted by Schapiro's confirmation hearing, believed that her attendance at Monitoring Board meetings were favourable to the cause of IFRSs in the United States, as these meetings enabled her to become much more knowledgeable about the structure and operation of the IASB, the issues and challenges facing the Board and the trustees, and the views of other securities market regulators.

15.4.2 Comments on the Proposing Release

The SEC received some 280 comment letters on the proposing release, which included many in which companies did no more than request an extension of the comment period.[59] Although PricewaterhouseCoopers (PwC) reported that 84 per cent of the writers of 204 of the comment letters said they supported a single set of global accounting standards, which the SEC had stated as an avowed goal in its release, many writers followed this up by arguing that the SEC needed to make modifications in the roadmap and that, at the least, it needed to undertake further study before proceeding to the next step.[60] Or they favoured convergence over adoption.

As might be expected, all of the Big Four audit firms, plus Grant Thornton, BDO Seidman, and McGladrey & Pullen, welcomed the roadmap. The firms were

---

[58] See e.g. the speech by Commissioner Kathleen L. Casey, 'Lessons from the Financial Crisis for Financial Reporting, Standard Setting and Rule Making', 17 November 2009.

[59] All of the comment letters are posted at <http://www.sec.gov/comments/s7-27-08/s72708.shtml>.

[60] PwC analysis as reported in Cheryl de Mesa Graziano, 'IFRS in the U.S. Raises Questions: "Convergence" or "Conversion"?' *Financial Executive*, 25/5 (June 2009), 14. For a broad-ranging discussion and analysis of the economic and policy factors relating to the possible adoption of IFRSs in the United States, see Luzi Hail, Christian Leuz, and Peter Wysocki, 'Global Accounting Conver-gence and the Potential Adoption of IFRS by the U.S. (Part I): Conceptual Underpinnings and Economic Analysis', and '(Part II): Political Factors and Future Scenarios for U.S. Accounting Stand-ards', *Accounting Horizons*, 24/3 (September 2010), 355–94 and 24/4 (December 2010), 567–88. For an empirical study covering 2007–09 on the benefits and costs of IFRS adoption by US companies from the investor point of view, see Philip P. M. Joos and Edith Leung, 'Investor Perceptions of Potential IFRS Adoption in the United States', *The Accounting Review*, 88/2 (March 2013), 577–609.

already urging their clients in no uncertain terms to prepare for transition to IFRSs. For example, booklets published for their US clients by Pricewaterhouse-Coopers and Deloitte in September and October 2008, respectively, urged their clients to prepare for the inevitable adoption of IFRSs. Under the title *Buckle Up (On the Road to IFRS)*, Deloitte said: 'Every company will eventually be going on this ride.'[61] In their support for IFRSs, the firms believed that the SEC's final rule should set a date certain. In its comment letter, KPMG wrote: 'The lack of a firm date for mandatory transition to IFRS is a source of uncertainty among financial reporting constituencies and is a disincentive for preparers, educators, and users to expend resources in support of a successful transition to IFRS.' In brief, the uncertainty induced by the 'milestones' test might itself make it more difficult to achieve one or more of the milestones. Deloitte made a point of saying that convergence was no substitute for adoption. Several of the firms expressed concern over the compressed timetable.

The American Institute of Certified Public Accountants (AICPA) also showed itself supportive, although it struck a more cautious note. It said that 'Creating an environment where our members and the U.S. financial reporting system can make an orderly transition to IFRS is a strategic initiative of the AICPA'. Thus, the AICPA supported the principle of mandatory adoption of IFRS for domestic companies, but it disagreed over particulars in the roadmap. It believed that the criteria that companies must satisfy to be eligible for early adoption were too restrictive and might not yield a sufficiently large and diverse sample of adopters, including small companies, as a basis for judging how well the transition was proceeding. The AICPA also believed that a decision made by the SEC in 2011 to move towards a mandatory phased adoption by 2014–16 would not provide companies with a reasonable period of time in which to complete their transition to IFRS. It also believed that the move to IFRS 'cannot be viewed in a vacuum—the auditing, regulatory, and litigation environment in the U.S. must adapt to allow for adoption of IFRS'. The AICPA, as well as the Big Four firms and others, called upon the IASC Foundation trustees to develop a stable and secure funding system, which was one of seven milestones enumerated by the SEC as preconditions to adoption.

The FASB's Investors Technical Advisory Committee, in a letter signed by Jack Ciesielski, opposed the roadmap proposal, saying that the committee continued to support the 'best of breed' convergence between the FASB and the IASB. It said: '[T]he proposal does not establish that the current U.S. GAAP reporting system is inherently ineffective, uninformative, or otherwise flawed. Nor does it establish that IFRS is inherently superior to U.S. GAAP.... We wish to reiterate our considerable doubts regarding the highly aggressive and seemingly unrealistic timetable outlined in the proposal, and strongly urge the Commission to reconsider the proposed milestones.' Yet the CFA Institute welcomed the roadmap proposal, saying, 'We believe this is the only investor-friendly approach to converting financial reporting in the U.S. to IFRS'. It did not, however, support

---

[61] *Buckle Up (On the Road to IFRS)*, Straight Talk Book No. 11 (Deloitte Development LLC, 2008), 9; *IFRS and US GAAP: Similarities and Differences*, IFRS Readiness Series (PricewaterhouseCoopers LLP, 2008), 3.

the limited early adoption proposal, because permitting free choice would 'create a two-GAAP system for U.S. filers, introducing complexity for investors and allowing for accounting arbitrage among preparers'.

Standard & Poor's, a major user, argued that the two boards should work together to develop a 'comprehensive disclosure framework and related principles', and that the SEC should require that this framework be implemented before the US converts to IFRS.

A number of US-based multinationals wrote to support the SEC's proposed roadmap, albeit with reservations, yet quite a few companies, such as Raytheon and Wal-Mart Stores, argued that the benefits of the conversion to IFRS did not outweigh the costs. Boeing argued that continued convergence between the IASB and the FASB was superior to adoption. One analyst tallied the disparate views expressed in the seventy-five letters from large US issuers: ten mildly favoured the proposal, while twelve mildly opposed it; eighteen strongly favoured the proposal, while thirty-five strongly opposed it. The primary focus of forty-eight of the commenters was the cost of transition.[62] The Business Roundtable, an association of chief executive officers of leading US companies with $4.5 trillion in total annual revenues, did not pronounce its view on the overall roadmap proposal, apart from favouring continued convergence between the two boards. It counselled that companies eligible for early adoption were likely to decline the option because of the risk that the SEC, in the end, would not mandate IFRSs. It also contended that, in view of the fact that more than one-third of US companies used the LIFO inventory rule, many US issuers would lose significant tax benefits if they were required to convert to IFRSs. The United States Chamber of Commerce, in a letter dated 20 April 2009 (the deadline for submitting comments), wrote that, in the midst of 'the worst financial crisis in 75 years', the SEC should not be compounding the stresses being felt by companies, auditors, and investors by 'foisting on them a myriad of difficult IFRS transition issues.... Committing to a changeover in the U.S. financial reporting system at this critical juncture risks undermining confidence in our markets when the focus instead should be on restoring it.' The Chamber also opined that 'The framework for and details of the proposed Roadmap are incomplete and need to be reconsidered'.

An AICPA analysis of the comment letters said: 'By far the two most common criticisms of the roadmap were the cost of adoption and the belief that a more measured convergence process was the best option. The current financial crisis was often cited as a deterrent to mandating adoption soon.'[63] Hence, the cacophony of views expressed in the comment letters hardly emboldened the SEC to proceed along the course it had been charting.

---

[62] This analysis of the comment letters performed by Gaylen Hansen, a partner in a CPA firm, was reported in Tom Selling, 'The Comments on the SEC Roadmap Are Clear: Make a U-turn', comment posted 20 July 2009 <http://accountingonion.typepad.com>. A more nuanced analysis of the letters may be found in Tom Tyson, 'The Convergence of IFRS and U.S. GAAP', *The CPA Journal*, 81/6 (June 2011), 26–31. See also Michael Rapoport, 'U.S. Firms Clash over Accounting Rules', *The Wall Street Journal*, 6 July 2011.

[63] 'Where Will the SEC Take the IFRS roadmap? An AICPA Analysis of Comment Letters on the SEC's Proposal', AICPA IFRS Resources, 27 April 2009 <http://www.ifrs.com>.

It could be argued that the reactions of auditors, users, and preparers as outlined above were generally in line with expectations. But a reaction that came as a bolt out of the blue, at least to the IASB, and was the submission by the Financial Accounting Foundation (FAF) and the FASB, signed by John J. (Jack) Brennan and Bob Herz. One year before, the FAF and the FASB, in a letter signed by the then FAF Chairman Robert E. Denham and by Herz, had shown themselves generally in favour of the SEC's concept release on allowing the use of IFRSs on a voluntary basis, and had asserted that a prolonged coexistence of two sets of standards in the United States was undesirable (see Section 8.5). They had therefore argued for a transition of all public companies to an improved version of IFRSs. But now, Brennan and Herz counselled caution. They recommended that the SEC undertake a major study that 'should fully examine and evaluate the strengths, weaknesses, costs, and benefits [of implementing IFRS for US issuers] compared with other possible approaches, such as convergence through continuation of the joint standard-setting efforts of the FASB and the IASB over a longer period as advocated by some investors and other parties'. The FASB and the FAF then raised a host of challenging policy and implementation issues that, they said, the SEC must address in this study. One of the most daunting was: 'The degree of direct and indirect macroeconomic benefits in the near term and over time to the U.S. and to the world economy through U.S. participation in and contribution to a high quality global reporting system.' This would have been a weighty topic for a doctoral dissertation. Thus, the FASB and the FAF not only declined to endorse the aim of the SEC's roadmap proposal, the study they called for effectively obliged the SEC to dispense with the roadmap and go back to 'square one'. David Tweedie was livid with the FASB and FAF for submitting what, to him, was a narrow-minded comment letter on the SEC's roadmap which was 'all America-centric'. He severely reproved Brennan and Herz—likely Brennan more than Herz—in a frosty meeting held in Paul Volcker's offices shortly after he had seen an early draft of the letter.[64]

The FASB and the FAF, on their part, believed that their letter reflected insights gained from ongoing consultation and careful deliberation.[65] They had engaged two independent consultants 'to provide us with objective analyses of the economic and policy considerations that they felt were most salient to a potential U.S. decision to adopt IFRS'. The consultants' reports formed part of their submission. Brennan and Herz cited the following as one of the major findings in the reports: 'Significant political challenges likely would arise in persuading the U.S. Congress to permit the SEC to designate an international body as the standard setter for U.S. companies.'

Jack Brennan, the chairman of Vanguard, had rejoined the FAF board of trustees as chairman in February 2009 after having previously served on the board from 1998 to 2003. Once he became chairman, the attitude towards convergence and especially its implications for the eventual adoption of IFRSs in the United States, as expressed in the chairman's letter which he signed in the

---

[64] Interviews with David Tweedie, 15 October 2009, and Thomas Seidenstein, 7 July 2011.

[65] Robert Herz, *Accounting Changes: Chronicles of Convergence, Crisis, and Complexity in Financial Reporting* (AICPA, 2013), 113. Interview with Robert Herz, 9 June 2013.

FAF's *Annual Reports* for 2008, 2009, and 2010, noticeably cooled from that reflected in the letter for 2007 written by his predecessor, Robert Denham.[66] As noted above, this change in attitude was viewed by David Tweedie as a setback in relations with the FAF.

The FAF–FASB comment letter seems not to have attracted widespread attention, possibly because it was published just when all eyes were on the FASB's attempts to deal at short notice with strong political pressure to modify its guidance on the use of fair value (see Section 13.9).[67]

15.4.3 The Series of Instalments in the SEC Staff's Work Plan, from 2010 Onwards

In 2010, over a year after the publication of the roadmap, the SEC took the next step in the process towards deciding what its policy should be on the use by domestic issuers of IFRSs. In a 'Statement in Support of Convergence and Global Accounting Standards' issued on 24 February, the SEC summarized the feedback in the comment letters:

> The key areas of concern expressed by the commenters include the readiness of IFRS to serve as the set of accounting standards for U.S. issuers, the need for continued convergence of IFRS and U.S. GAAP, and the timeframe set for, and potential costs of, transitioning U.S. GAAP to IFRS.[68]

The Commission said it had:

> directed the staff of the Office of the Chief Accountant, with appropriate consultation with other Divisions and Offices of the Commission, to develop and carry out the Work Plan [which] sets forth specific areas and factors for the staff to consider before potentially transitioning our current financial reporting system for U.S. issuers to a system incorporating IFRS. . . . The Work Plan is designed to provide the Commission the information it needs to evaluate the implications of incorporating IFRS into the U.S. domestic reporting system.[69]

This Statement placed emphasis on convergence ('incorporating IFRS into the U.S. domestic reporting system') as the short-term goal before the Commission was prepared to take the next step.

The initial edition of the Work Plan, formally titled 'Work Plan for the Consideration of Incorporating International Financial Reporting Standards into the Financial Reporting System for U.S. Issuers', was published as an appendix to the Commission's Statement on 24 February 2010. It drew on the comment letters received in response to the roadmap proposal as well as on the Commission's Statement. The Work Plan listed numerous questions on the operation and

---

[66] Letters contained in the Financial Accounting Foundation's *Annual Reports* for 2007 (pages 10–11), 2008 (page 13), 2009 (page 8), and 2010 (page 4).

[67] 'FASB Wants Close Look Before IFRS Switch', *Compliance Reporter*, 20 March 2009; 'Response to SEC Roadmap', *World Accounting Report*, April 2009, 9.

[68] 'Commission Statement in Support of Convergence and Global Accounting Standards', release nos. 33-9109; 34-61587, page 9, footnote omitted.

[69] 'Commission Statement in Support of Convergence', 14.

governance of the IASB and the IASC Foundation, the quality of IFRSs, the capacity of investors to understand IFRSs, the state of the regulatory environment, the potential impact on issuers of incorporating IFRSs into the US financial reporting system, and the readiness of the education and training of accountants and other affected parties, especially within audit firms, to meet the challenge of IFRSs. A further study of these areas and a monitoring of ongoing developments was required, it said, before the SEC could make a decision.

At the open meeting on 24 February, when the Commission's Statement and the staff's Work Plan were unveiled, Chairman Schapiro confirmed that the Commission still planned to follow the timetable in the roadmap with respect to the timing of its decision on IFRSs. She said: 'In 2011, upon conclusion of the fact-gathering and analysis set forth in the work plan—and assuming completion of the convergence projects—the Commission will then be in a position to determine whether to incorporate IFRS into the financial reporting system for U.S. public companies.'[70]

Yet by February 2010 it was already evident that no action had been taken on the proposal in the roadmap to allow selected US companies to begin reporting on the basis of IFRSs in 2009. In the Work Plan, the SEC made it clear that plans for voluntary use were on hold until the SEC decided on the overall approach to incorporating IFRSs into the US financial reporting system.[71] At the open meeting referred to above, Commissioner Kathleen L. Casey, who then chaired IOSCO's Technical Committee, said: 'Notably, although the Commission is not at this time pursuing optional or early adoption of IFRS by U.S. issuers, the Statement clearly signals that optional or early adoption remains viable as a potential element of the transition to the use of IFRS by U.S. issuers.'[72]

Commissioner Elisse B. Walter, who, together with Casey, had voted for the roadmap proposal in August 2008, exuded confidence that the staff would successfully complete the Work Plan in time to enable the Commission to reach the decision point in 2011 to determine whether IFRS reporting by US issuers was in the public interest. Yet, even more emphatically than Chairman Schapiro, Commissioner Walter pointed out that whether and when the SEC would reach the decision point also depended on the IASB and the Financial Accounting Standards Board (FASB): 'Successful completion of the FASB–IASB convergence project and the independence of standard setting for the benefit of investors will remain critical milestones that, in my view, must be achieved before we move forward.'[73]

On 29 October 2010, the SEC published the first progress report on the staff's Work Plan, but the staff was not yet ready to expose any recommendations for

---

[70] 'Speech by SEC Chairman: Statement at SEC Open Meeting—Global Accounting Standards', 24 February 2010.

[71] 'Commission Statement in Support of Convergence and Global Accounting Standards' (February 2010), 23.

[72] 'Speech by SEC Commissioner: Commission Statement in Support of Convergence and Global Accounting Standards, by Commissioner Kathleen L. Casey', 24 February 2010.

[73] 'Speech by SEC Commissioner: Commission Statement in Support of Convergence and Global Accounting Standards, by Commissioner Elisse B. Walter', 24 February 2010.

public comment.[74] The report contained many factual observations on factors that were relevant in developing such recommendations, some favourable to an incorporation of IFRSs into the US reporting system, and some presenting obstacles. It was noted, for instance, that the general absence of industry-specific guidance in IFRSs did cause concern among industry regulators and that, in particular, the absence of a standard on rate-regulated activities 'may create numerous challenges' (page 31). The IASB had issued an exposure draft on the subject in July 2009 but, as it happened, had decided to defer the project in September 2010, just before the SEC issued its progress report.[75] The IASB was not as averse to developing industry standards as was sometimes thought. The insurance contracts standard was intended to result in an industry standard in all but name, and the applicability of some IFRIC interpretations was also largely confined to specific industries.[76]

A notable theme developed in the October 2010 progress report was that only 'a very small minority of the largest jurisdictions' had chosen the 'purest form' of IFRS adoption, that is, making IFRSs applicable once issued by the IASB, without approval by any local body. Most had chosen an incorporation process, not necessarily aimed at adoption of full IFRSs. The report discussed the 'convergence' approach of China and the elaborate 'endorsement' approach of the EU, allowing many bodies a say in the process, with the IAS 39 carve-out and the postponed endorsement of IFRS 9 as demonstrable effects.[77]

The next shoe dropped on 6 December 2010, when Paul A. Beswick, a deputy chief accountant in the Office of the Chief Accountant (OCA) who was the principal draftsman of the roadmap proposal in 2008, said the following in a widely noticed speech:

> In our October update we highlighted that the majority of jurisdictions are following either a convergence or an endorsement approach. In my opinion, if the U.S. were to move to IFRS, somewhere in between could be the right approach. I will call it a 'condorsement' approach. Yes, I admit I just made up a word. And by the way, the patent is pending as we speak.
>
> So how would this approach work? Well, to begin, U.S. GAAP would continue to exist. The IASB and the FASB would finish the major projects in their MOU [Memorandum of Understanding]. The FASB would not begin work on any major new projects in the normal course. Rather, a new set of priorities would be established where the FASB would work to converge existing U.S. GAAP to IFRS over a period of time for standards that are not on the IASB's agenda. This is not meant to be an MOU2 but rather would entail making sure that, on a standard by standard basis, existing IFRS standards are suitable for our capital markets.[78]

---

[74] 'Work Plan for the Consideration of Incorporating International Financial Reporting Standards into the Financial Reporting System for U.S. Issuers: Progress Report' (US SEC, Office of the Chief Accountant/Division of Corporation Finance, 29 October 2010).

[75] ED/2009/8 'Rate-regulated Activities' (IASB, July 2009).

[76] For example, IFRIC 12 *Service Concession Arrangements* and IFRIC 15 *Agreements for the Construction of Real Estate*.

[77] 'Work Plan . . . Progress Report' (October 2010), 9–13.

[78] 'Speech by SEC Staff: Remarks before the 2010 AICPA National Conference on Current SEC and PCAOB Developments, by Paul A. Beswick', 6 December 2010. Beswick, a former partner in Ernst & Young, joined the staff of the OCA in October 2007 and became deputy chief accountant (DCA) for its

Beswick, while not speaking for the staff or the Commission, nonetheless ventured a view that was interpreted as a signal of the staff's thinking.[79] His invented term, 'condorsement', was duly repeated in the next progress report of the Work Plan, issued on 26 May 2011.[80] By this time, the staff was ready to expose for public comment a recommended framework, with a proposal of multiple roles for the FASB. The FASB would undertake a one-way convergence of US GAAP to IFRSs, thus incorporating IFRSs into the US financial reporting system. The FASB would continue to participate, as one of the world's national standard setters, in the standard-setting activities of the IASB. And it would endorse the IASB's modifications to IFRSs for incorporation into US GAAP. In addition, the FASB would be authorized to impose additional disclosures, to prescribe which of two or more alternative accounting treatments permitted by IFRSs on a particular issue should be adopted by US issuers, and to specify interpretive guidance. In this way, the progress report stated, 'a U.S. "flavor" of IFRS could result' (page 10). The report counselled that the FASB's modifications to IFRSs 'should be rare and generally avoidable. The objective would be for U.S. GAAP to remain consistent with IFRSs, and the FASB should find the need to exercise its authority to issue any requirement in conflict with IFRS in only unusual circumstances' (page 10).

The SEC received more than 140 comment letters on the May 2011 progress report.[81] Views were expressed on all sides of the staff's proposed framework. The goal of achieving a single set of high-quality global accounting standards received the greatest support. Most commenters agreed that the FASB should play the convergence and endorsement roles, but there was disagreement about the desired scope of its authority. Some argued that the FASB should not be tightly constrained in these roles, while others expressed a concern that an FASB with a broad mandate to make modifications would lead to troubling deviations between US GAAP and IFRSs, thus diluting worldwide comparability of financial reporting.

In April 2011, the SEC had announced a roundtable for July that would 'discuss benefits or challenges in potentially incorporating International Financial

---

Professional Practice group in September 2008. Then in November 2009 he became DCA over the Accounting group in the OCA and 'will be responsible for resolution of accounting issues, rulemaking projects, and oversight of private sector accounting standard-setting effort'. (See 'Paul Beswick named SEC Deputy Chief Accountant in Charge of Accounting Group', SEC press release 2009-244, dated 13 November 2009.) It was, therefore, something of a surprise that he spoke out on a subject falling under International Affairs, which is the third group within the OCA.

[79] See Jack T. Ciesielski, 'What Keeps the SEC Busy—2011', *The Analyst's Accounting Observer*, 19/14 (14 December 2010), 3–4, and 'Is the IFRS "Condorsement" Coming? Maybe', *The Analyst's Accounting Observer*, 20/8 (20 June 2011, 1–6); Tom Selling, 'IFRS Adoption Is Dead (I Think)', item posted 9 May 2011 <http://accountingonion.typepad.com>; and Floyd Norris, 'Accounting that Comes in Flavors', *The New York Times*, 8 July 2011, B1. For the reaction in April 2011 by FASB Chairman Leslie Seidman, see 'Condorsement: FASB's Potential New Role under IFRS', posted 4 April 2011 <http://www.journalofaccountancy.com>.

[80] 'Work Plan for the Consideration of Incorporating International Financial Reporting Standards into the Financial Reporting System for U.S. Issuers: Exploring a Possible Method of Incorporation', Securities and Exchange Commission staff paper, 26 May 2011.

[81] Accessible at <http://www.sec.gov/comments/4-600/4-600.shtml>.

Reporting Standards (IFRS) into the financial reporting system for U.S. issuers'.[82] There would be panels representing investors, smaller public companies, and regulators. Especially in a weak economy, the SEC was concerned about imposing the cost of transitioning to IFRSs on smaller listed companies that lacked international exposure.

In August 2011, Tom Selling, an avowed opponent of bringing IFRSs into the United States, wrote in his electronic newsletter, *The Accounting Onion*, as follows:

> Except for the Big Four . . . and perhaps a few large companies, the Staff Paper [of 26 May 2011] has gone over like a lead balloon. To start, the handpicked investor panel at July's SEC Roundtable on IFRS provided only tepid encouragement, and the smaller public companies panel could barely be held back from strangling the SEC staff; all they saw in IFRS was a lot of incremental cost and zero incremental benefit.[83]

Nonetheless, opinions remained divided. A survey of senior financial executives held in March and April 2011 indicated that a quarter of respondents supported the immediate adoption of IFRSs for public companies, while half wished to see another five to seven years of convergence before making such a move. The remaining quarter believed that the United States should not adopt IFRSs. Slightly over half of the respondents thought that private entities should be allowed to use the *IFRS for SMEs*.[84]

The ultimate aim of the successive versions of the Work Plan was to provide the Commission with a framework when making its decision about the future of IFRSs in US capital markets. By June 2011, which is the end of the ten-year period encompassed by our history, the Commission's staff was still working assiduously (a) to study how IFRSs were used in practice by a sample of companies, both SEC registrants and others, and (b) to prepare a topic-by-topic comparison of IFRSs and US GAAP.[85] The staff was also analysing the comment letters and the views expressed at the July 2011 roundtable.

Not least because of the SEC's roadmap, the year 2011 had for several years been the focal point of expectations and planning, not just at the IASB, but in many countries that had adopted or were converging with IFRSs. In March, towards the end of his term as IASB chairman, David Tweedie made an

---

[82] 'SEC Announces Roundtable on International Financial Reporting Standards', SEC press release 2011-95, dated 20 April 2011.

[83] Tom Selling, 'Let the "Condorsement" Games Begin', item posted 18 August 2011 <http://accountingonion.typepad.com>.

[84] 'Accounting Issues and IFRS: Selected Results from the CFO Survey Spring 2011' (Grant Thornton, 20 April 2011) <http://www.grantthornton.com>. Previous editions of Grant Thornton's biannual surveys were based on varying questions or were reported using varying classifications of answers. Nonetheless, it would appear from the survey results that support for adoption of IFRSs, either immediately or within a span of several years remained stable or increased somewhat from 2009 to 2011.

[85] The staff issued two papers in the Work Plan series on 16 November 2011 to deal with these projects: 'Work Plan for the Consideration of Incorporating International Financial Reporting Standards into the Financial Reporting System for U.S. Issuers: An Analysis of IFRS in Practice', SEC staff paper, 16 November 2011, and 'Work Plan for the Consideration of Incorporating International Financial Reporting Standards into the Financial Reporting System for U.S. Issuers: A Comparison of U.S. GAAP and IFRS', SEC staff paper, 16 November 2011.

impassioned plea in a speech given in the United States for a clear timetable for the incorporation of IFRSs, as issued by the IASB, into the US financial reporting system:

> Years from now, we will look back on 2011 as a year when the future path of financial reporting was determined.... The SEC's decision will be felt well beyond the borders of the United States.... China, India and Japan have yet to make a formal and full commitment to domestic adoption of IFRSs. Their work towards adopting IFRSs in their countries has been, in part, predicated on the implicit understanding that a truly global accounting standard must include the United States. They are therefore closely watching the SEC's decision.[86]

But the year was allowed to pass without a decision by the SEC. In the minds of many, the silence was as eloquent as any statement could have been. In February 2012, there was still no news other than that the SEC staff had replaced the memorable term, 'condorsement', with the familiar 'endorsement'.[87] Finally, in July 2012, the staff published its final report on the Work Plan, but the Commission was unequivocal about the significance that should be attributed to the report:

> The Commission believes it is important to make clear that publication of the Staff Report at this time does not imply—and should not be construed to imply—that the Commission has made any policy decision as to whether International Financial Reporting Standards should be incorporated into the financial reporting system for U.S. issuers, or how any such incorporation, if it were to occur, should be implemented.[88]

As if the SEC had not been thinking about the issue since its 2007 concept release, the Commission in 2012 could go no further than observe that the question of 'whether transitioning to IFRS is in the best interests of the U.S. securities markets generally and U.S. investors specifically' requires 'additional analysis and consideration'.

15.5 JAPAN PULLS BACK FROM ADOPTING IFRSs

15.5.1 Building Momentum Towards IFRS Adoption

The year 2008 dawned shortly after the US SEC had announced, in November 2007, that it would no longer require foreign private issuers to reconcile their earnings and shareholders' equity to US GAAP equivalents so long as they adopted 'IFRS as published by the IASB'. Another US development of interest

---

[86] 'Sir David Tweedie Addresses the US Chamber of Commerce', speech delivered 10 March 2011 <http://www.ifrs.org>.

[87] See the Editorial and 'No, It's Endorsement After All', *World Accounting Report*, 15/2 (March 2012), 1, 3.

[88] 'Work Plan for the Consideration of Incorporating International Financial Reporting Standards in the Financial Reporting System for U.S. Issuers: Final Staff Report', Office of the Chief Accountant, 13 July 2012.

in 2007 was the SEC's concept release issued in August which explored the possibility that US domestic registrants might one day be allowed to adopt IFRSs. Both of these developments signified the SEC's view that the IASB and IFRSs were following a positive path towards acceptability in the United States. For a country such as Japan which had, since the Second World War, been much influenced by US accounting developments, these were watershed developments.

As discussed in Chapters 4 and 10, the entire dialogue over IFRSs in Japan up to and including the 2007 Tokyo Agreement had been about 'convergence' of Japanese GAAP and IFRSs, with the aim of the international recognition of Japanese GAAP as a set of high-quality accounting standards. The SEC's lifting of the reconciliation requirement for IFRSs with no prospect of a similar move for Japanese GAAP was a cause for concern.

In the course of 2008, the debate in Japan shifted from 'convergence' to 'adoption'. Nippon Keidanren, the highly influential business federation, took the first step towards an adoption mode—although one of our Japanese interviewees has suggested that the Financial Services Agency (FSA) may have encouraged Keidanren to take the initiative. The FSA was at least as attuned to developments in the United States as was Keidanren. For instance, FSA representatives had met in September and November 2007 with the SEC's accounting staff in Washington concerning the concept release and progress towards lifting the reconciliation requirement.[89]

In March 2008, Keidanren sent to Europe a research team headed by Yoshiki Yagi, a former executive vice president of Hitachi Ltd who chaired the business accounting division of Keidanren's committee on economic law. He was already well familiar with the IASB, having served on SAC since 2001. Apart from holding discussions with the IASB, the team met, among others, with officials from the European Commission and members of the European Parliament, with business organizations, and with the accounting standard setters in France and the United Kingdom. The Japanese delegation would have had ample opportunity to learn about the practice of IFRS adoption, both from supporters and critics of the IASB. Undoubtedly, it provided Keidanren with more insight, for instance in the way the EU had separated the regulation of consolidated financial statements from that which governed parent company financial statements in order to enable the adoption of IFRSs.[90] Yet the trip may also, or even primarily, have served to prepare public opinion in Japan for a change of policy on which Keidanren had already decided. This was the case for the Japanese Institute of Certified Public Accountants (JICPA), which had decided that the time for IFRSs had come, and which thereupon sent a similar mission to Europe in July 2008.[91]

An even stronger stimulus to adopt IFRSs was provided on 27 August 2008 when the SEC followed up its concept release of August 2007 by unanimously approving a rule proposal which set out a roadmap leading towards the possible mandatory use by US domestic issuers of 'IFRSs as issued by the IASB'. On 14 October 2008, Keidanren published a major paper, 'Future Directions of

---

[89] See the entries for 24 September 2007 and 15 November 2007 in the list of comment letters received by the SEC on the August 2007 concept release <http://www.sec.gov>.

[90] Interview with Yoshiki Yagi and Shigeo Sakase, 25 January 2011.

[91] Interview with Shozo Yamazaki, 28 January 2011.

Accounting Standards in Japan—The Next Step towards a Single Set of Accounting Standards'. It said:

> Having had the U.S. announcement this year, Japan became the only country among the major capital markets, which has not officially announced the adoption of IFRS. Some of the Japanese companies have already begun the study of IFRS preparing for future adoption. Japan should accelerate the discussion of the future direction of accounting standards and set out a concrete Roadmap as soon as possible, indicating the adoption of IFRS.[92]

This paper marked a turning-point in the replacement of 'convergence' by 'adoption' in the Japanese dialogue over IFRSs. By that time, significant progress had been made by the Accounting Standards Board of Japan (ASBJ) towards converging Japanese GAAP with IFRSs, not least in order to obtain a recognition of equivalence with IFRSs from the European Commission. This phase was now drawing to a close. Already in April 2008, the European Commission's Directorate General for the internal market issued a report which expressed the view that Japanese GAAP was on course towards equivalence with IFRSs. It wrote: 'CESR [Committee of European Securities Regulators] has advised that by June 2008 the Commission should consider Japanese GAAP equivalent unless there is no adequate evidence of the ASBJ achieving to timetable the objectives set out in the Tokyo Agreement.'[93] In December 2008, the ASBJ announced that it had completed the short-term projects of the Tokyo Agreement, that is, the projects directly addressing the concerns expressed earlier by the European Commission.[94] As the ASBJ noted in its press release, the European Commission had already announced two weeks earlier that it had accepted Japanese GAAP as the equivalent of IFRSs, thus enabling Japanese companies listed in European capital markets to continue to use Japanese GAAP in their financial statements.[95] As in the case of US GAAP, the equivalence was granted for an indefinite period of time.

For proponents of convergence rather than adoption, the European Commission's announcement might have been read as a confirmation that 'close is good enough'. But as if in a relay race, the EU's baton had already been taken over by the SEC to maintain or even increase pressure on Japan. One of the senior corporate executives whom we interviewed recalled as follows:

> From around 2005 through to 2008, I would say that one after another, the US authorities started to make public their intent regarding IFRSs and it was an acceleration from our viewpoint. The equivalence assessment by the EU was ongoing at the same time, so it was not one single factor that motivated the Japanese industry, but more than one. I would say not only the awareness was raised by the Japanese

---

[92] 'Future Directions of Accounting Standards in Japan—The Next Step Towards a Single Set of Accounting Standards', executive summary in English, Nippon Keidanren, 14 October 2008 <http://www.keidanren.or.jp>.

[93] 'Report on Convergence between International Financial Reporting Standards (IFRS) and Third Country Generally Accepted Accounting Principles (GAAPs)...' (European Commission, DG Internal Market and Services, 22 April 2008), 6 <http://ec.europa.eu/internal_market/accounting>.

[94] 'ASBJ Completes the Short-term Projects in the Tokyo Agreement', ASBJ press release dated 26 December 2008 <http://www.asb.or.jp>.

[95] Commission decision of 12 December 2008, 2008/961/EC.

companies in general, but almost a sense of crisis asking ourselves: 'are we going to continue on our way in this way, or should we change?'

In the light of the initiatives taken by the SEC in 2007 and 2008, and the number of important countries that had recently announced a commitment to adopt IFRSs, it was felt that Japan might be left behind if it did not begin moving towards adoption, and that it was time for Japan to join the game. A senior official whom we interviewed at Keidanren advised, 'we decided that [Japan] should also jump into the playing-field of the development of the IFRS, so that we should also be involved in rewriting the IFRS, so that it would be more easy to use for the Japanese preparers'.[96]

On 11 June 2009, heeding the encouragement by Keidanren, the FSA issued an opinion paper prepared by its Business Accounting Council (BAC), containing its own proposed roadmap towards the possible future adoption of IFRSs by Japanese companies. Its paper, styled as an 'interim report', was entitled, 'Application of International Financial Reporting Standards (IFRS) in Japan'.[97] It was evidently modelled on the SEC's proposing release issued in November 2008. The FSA recommended that companies meeting certain criteria should be allowed to switch to IFRSs beginning in the financial years ending on or after 31 March 2010. In 2012, the FSA would make a decision on the possible future mandatory use of IFRSs, which, if approved, would begin in either 2015 or 2016.

It may be surmised that the FSA's plan to make a final decision in 2012 was based on the assumption that it could take its cue from the SEC, which was expected to make its own decision on the use of IFRSs by US domestic listed companies in 2011. Yet in one important respect the FSA moved ahead of the SEC. The FSA's proposed roadmap was made final in December 2009 by the issue of revised Cabinet Office Ordinances which allowed some public companies to adopt IFRSs voluntarily in their consolidated financial statements starting from the financial year ended 31 March 2010.[98] As seen in Section 15.4.3, the SEC had originally contemplated the voluntary use of IFRSs by US companies beginning in 2009, but did not actually take a decision to this effect.

Also in December 2009, the FSA commissioner, after receiving advice from the BAC, announced that all IASs, IFRSs, and interpretations issued by the IASB on or before 30 June 2009 were to be 'designated IFRSs', which companies using IFRSs voluntarily would be required to apply when preparing their consolidated statements. In January 2010, the FSA announced that it proposed to designate the standards issued or amended by the IASB between 1 July and 31 December 2009 without any deviations, which meant that Japanese companies were also allowed to apply the IASB's new standard on financial instruments, IFRS 9.[99] Thereafter,

---

[96] Interview with Masakuzo Kubota and Yoshihara Obata, 28 January 2011.

[97] 'Application of International Financial Reporting Standards (IFRS) in Japan', unofficial summary in English by FSA staff, 12 June 2009 <http://www.fsa.go.jp>.

[98] 'Publication of the Revised Cabinet Office Ordinances, etc. for the Voluntary Application of International Financial Reporting Standards in Japan', FSA press release dated 11 December 2009 <http://www.fsa.go.jp>. A summary of the Cabinet Ordinances in English is attached to the press release.

[99] 'Public Consultation on the Designation of the International Financial Reporting Standards for their Voluntary Application in Japan', FSA press release dated 29 January 2010 <http://www.fsa.go.jp>. The FSA's proposal was made final in March.

the FSA continued to designate subsequently issued or amended IASs and IFRSs. The practice of the FSA has been to make these designations two or three times a year in order to avoid time lags between the effective dates of IFRSs and their allowed use in Japan.

For many years, the FSA had allowed the some thirty-five companies whose securities were publicly traded in the United States to use either US GAAP or Japanese GAAP in their filings with the FSA. Apparently all of them used the former. In its final roadmap issued in December 2009, the FSA said that this authority for companies to use US GAAP would terminate for financial years starting in financial years after 31 March 2016. This was another bold step which could seem to prejudge the FSA's final decision on IFRSs in 2012.

In July 2009, following the issue of the FSA's opinion paper containing the roadmap, several private-sector bodies formed the IFRS Council, which brought together all of the parties interested in IFRSs. These bodies were the ASBJ and its Financial Accounting Standards Foundation (FASF), Keidanren, the JICPA, and the Tokyo Stock Exchange.[100] Hiroshi Endo, the secretary general of the FASF, played a leadership role in launching the IFRS Council. Its aim was to address a number of the implementation issues going forward, including education and training and the translation of IFRSs into Japanese, which were raised in the FSA's opinion paper. It was also to convey strong messages of the views of Japanese business to the IASB.[101] The ASBJ, for its part, was now in line with promoting the adoption of IFRSs.[102]

The Tokyo Stock Exchange may well have been concerned that its market would become of lesser international importance if Japan did not go over to IFRSs.[103] In 2009, and again in 2010, the Exchange conducted surveys of its listed companies to determine how ready they were to accomplish the transition to IFRSs, either voluntarily or under the FSA's roadmap for mandatory compliance.[104] The majority of companies that replied to both surveys would thus have become even more sensitized to the need to think about their preparations to move towards IFRSs. Of the 1,416 companies replying to the first survey, 61.8 per cent said they had begun an investigation about the implementation of IFRS, and 3.9 per cent (fifty-five companies) said they were looking into early implementation in 2010 or later. Of the 1,572 companies replying to the second survey, fully 67.4 per cent said they predicted that IFRS implementation would be required by

---

[100] 'Establishment of the IFRS Council, Private Sector Promotion Council to Address Japanese Roadmap towards IFRS Implementation', IFRS Council press release dated 3 July 2009 <http://www.asb.or.jp>.

[101] Interview with Hiroshi Endo, 31 January 2011.

[102] Interview with Ikuo Nishikawa, 24 January 2011.

[103] Interview with Atsushi Saito, 2 February 2011.

[104] 'Kokusai kaikei kijun (IFRS) no tekiyō ni muketa jōjōgaisha ankēto chōsa kekka no gaiyō' [Listed Companies' IFRS Implementation: Summary of Survey Results], (Tokyo Stock Exchange, 30 October 2009) <http://www.tse.or.jp/listing/seibi/b7gje60000005z9h-att/ifrs_enq.pdf>; 'IFRS junbi jōkyō ni kansuru chōsa kekka (gaiyō)' [IFRS Preparation Survey Results (Summary)] (Tokyo Stock Exchange, 15 November 2010) <http://www.tse.or.jp/rules/ifrs/index.html>. For a report in English on the 2010 survey, see David F. Hawkins and Jin Yamamoto, 'Perception and Readiness of Japanese Companies for IFRS Implementation: The Tokyo Stock Exchange Survey', Harvard Business School case 9-112-017, 12 August 2011. The authors thank Rei Morikawa and Kaho Kawamura for translation services.

the year 2015–16, and that they had begun their preparations. Ninety-seven companies, or 6.2 per cent, said they were preparing for optional implementation earlier than the required date. Overall, large market capitalization companies were further along in the implementation phase than smaller market capitalization companies.

15.5.2 Hesitation Sets In

The first company to adopt IFRSs voluntarily under the FSA's new authority was Nihon Dempa Kogyo Co. Ltd (NDK). As discussed in Chapter 4, NDK had been the single Japanese company using IFRSs in its voluntary English annual report since 2002, and thus had been obliged to maintain two sets of accounting records. Prior to 2010, it had filed with the FSA using Japanese GAAP; so NDK's decision to adopt IFRSs in its filing with the FSA in 2010 represented a cost reduction. Yet since then, and until June 2011, only three other companies adopted IFRSs voluntarily: Mitsui Sumitomo Financial Group in 2010, and HOYA Corporation and Sumitomo Corporation, both in 2011. Compared to the expectations raised following the FSA roadmap as reflected in the Tokyo Stock Exchange surveys cited above, this was a very tepid response.

The apparent reason for this small number of voluntary adopters was that uncertainty had set in over whether the FSA would carry out its mandate that all listed companies adopt IFRSs. This uncertainty was fed both by awareness of the faltering progress towards IFRSs in the United States and by a growing chorus of voices raising doubts about the quality of IFRSs and expounding on the challenges to IFRS adoption in Japan.[105]

Divisions arose within Keidanren itself over the move to IFRSs, as between the large multinationals that had driven the shift to a pro-adoption stance in 2008, and the great many smaller listed companies whose reach was domestic. For the large, internationally active companies with many foreign subsidiaries, the use of a single set of accounting standards was an obvious advantage. Sumitomo Corporation, one of the few companies to avail itself of the opportunity to adopt IFRSs voluntarily, was the prime example of a large multinational corporation supporting IFRSs and the work of the IASB. Noriaki Shimazaki, then Sumitomo's chief financial officer, became a trustee of the IASC Foundation (now the IFRS Foundation) in January 2009, with a second term beginning in January 2012. Shimazaki became one of the most active proponents of IFRS adoption in Japan. In July 2011, Takatsugu Ochi joined the IASB Board from his position as assistant general manager of Sumitomo's financial resources management group. Prior to his appointment to the Board, he had been serving on the IFRS Interpretations Committee. As it happens, Tatsumi Yamada, the IASB Board member from

---

[105] The following paragraphs draw on interviews with Noboyuki Hiratsuka, 25 January 2011; Yoshitaka Kato and Akashi Kohno, 3 February 2011; Atsushi Kogasaka, 26 January 2011; Hidenori Mitsui, 1 February 2011; Tetsuo Seki and Hidetake Ishihara, 2 February 2011; Noriaki Shimazaki, 31 January 2011; Yoshiki Yagi and Shigeo Sakase, 25 January 2011; Tatsumi Yamada, 19 May 2011; and Shozo Yamazaki, 28 January 2011.

2001 to 2011, worked for Sumitomo prior to the 1990s.[106] The strong representation of individuals with a Sumitomo connection in the IASB may have been
coincidental, but there could be no doubt about the company's support for IFRSs
in Japan. But many smaller companies saw transition to IFRSs in terms of costs
rather than benefits, and the discussions over the adoption of IFRSs soon became
complicated by suggestions that a large proportion of the thousands of listed
companies should be allowed to continue reporting on the basis of Japanese
GAAP.

One major tangle of issues that lay largely outside the influence of the IASB was
the traditional close relationship between financial reporting, company law, and
taxation in Japan. There was a diversity of views over whether these relationships
could or should be severed upon the adoption of IFRSs, in particular by making a
distinction between accounting standards for consolidated and unconsolidated
financial statements. A strong current of opinion favoured the traditional position
that accounting should be unified, and that it was undesirable to account for the
same item in different ways in different financial statements. The steps taken by
the ASBJ to converge Japanese GAAP with IFRSs had already raised the problem
of what this meant for the calculation of taxable income. A principle of Japanese
tax law was that, for an accounting treatment to be acceptable for tax purposes, it
had to be applied in a company's financial statements. Hence, when the ASBJ
wished to eliminate the LIFO method in order to converge with IFRSs and to
satisfy the European Commission, extensive consultations were required to address the consequences for taxation. In principle, there was a policy to ensure that
convergence with IFRSs would have no tax consequences, but this effect was not
sought by a radical decoupling of tax accounting and financial reporting. Rather,
reliance was placed on consultation between the relevant ministries to ensure that
modifications to accounting standards were, if necessary, offset by corresponding
adjustments to the tax rules. The process was sufficiently complex to inspire
doubts that a transition to IFRSs could ever be completely neutral in terms of
taxation.

The Ministry of Economy, Trade and Industry (METI) took an interest in the
IFRS policy issue from the point of view of furthering the competitive position of
Japanese industry, and it was therefore receptive to concerns over the cost of IFRS
transition and complications arising out of links between the financial reporting
and tax systems. In what may also have included an element of inter-ministerial
rivalry, it took the view that the FSA, and the ASBJ operating under the aegis of
the FSA, were too inclined to view accounting standards from a purely technical
standpoint, without sufficient consideration of the consequences for reporting
companies.

Another challenge to Japanese adoption of IFRSs was that, as in the case of US
GAAP, it would involve a reduction in the amount or detail of implementation
guidance. Over the previous decade, the amount of guidance in Japanese GAAP
had steadily expanded, initially as part of the 'accounting big bang' of the late
1990s, and more recently in response to several company bankruptcies resulting

---

[106] See also 'Sumitomo Veterans Fight for Japan in International Accounting', *Nikkei Report*, 21 July
2010.

from investigations by the FSA's Securities and Exchange Surveillance Commission and several accounting scandals around 2004–6 (Kanebo, Seibu Railway, Livedoor, among others). It became a recurring argument in the debate over IFRSs that detailed guidance and bright-line rules were necessary in the context of increasing litigation against company managers and auditors. Conversely, others would argue that Japanese GAAP itself was uneven and included some areas with very little guidance, or that the courts had shown themselves reticent in questioning managers' or auditors' judgments in cases where accounting standards explicitly called for judgment. But at that point the debate would already have entered the realm of accounting and legal specialists. To the more general observers, it was apparent that the ASBJ had expanded the guidance in Japanese GAAP to the point where it had become more voluminous than IFRSs. With a tradition of following rules, rather than engaging in judgments, one can understand that many in Japan thought that a strengthened and much more active IFRIC, perhaps operating as a full-time body, was a very important condition for ensuring that IFRSs would be appropriate for use in Japan.

An illustration of Japanese preparers' concern about the comparative lack of implementation guidance in IFRSs was the issue they raised in 2010 about the conditions under which IAS 16 *Property, Plant and Equipment* allowed companies to use an accelerated method of depreciation such as declining-balance. This was debated without resolution between companies and auditors in the context of exploring the consequences of a move to IFRSs, as few companies had yet actually adopted IFRSs. They then approached the IASB, and Wayne Upton, the director of international activities, formulated a unique 'education note', dated 19 November 2010, after conferring with the ASBJ and its IFRS Implementation Group as well as with several IASB Board members.[107] The note did little more than reiterate how IAS 16 required the exercise of management judgement in determining various aspects of depreciation, including that a depreciation method should reflect the consumption of future economic benefits.

The episode may serve to illustrate that Japanese auditors were reluctant to abide a management judgement, as required by IAS 16, to support use of a depreciation method other than straight-line. However, it also had another significance. As in Germany, the relationship between accounting and taxation frequently operated in an inverse way, in the sense that the choice of an accounting method for tax purposes was often considered as sufficient justification for its use in the financial statements. As Upton asserted in his note that IAS 16 did not prefer straight-line depreciation over other depreciation methods, it could be used to argue that the IASB sanctioned the continued use of tax-inspired accelerated depreciation in the financial statements as long as the benefit consumption pattern was not obviously linear. The education note was therefore not welcome to those in Japan who wished to sever the link between tax accounting and financial reporting, or who believed that IFRSs should be applied without reference to tax consequences.

---

[107] 'Depreciation and IFRS', Occasional Education Notes, 19 November 2010 <http://www.ifrs.org/Use-around-the-world/Education/Pages/Occasional-Education-Notes.aspx>. Interview with Wayne Upton, 7 July 2011.

David Tweedie tended to favour expedients such as the education note if they could be helpful in responding to Japanese concerns and thus help nudge Japan into opting for IFRSs. Other Board members, as well as some Japanese constituents, were more critical. The IASB has not made public any further education notes on technical issues. But there was one previous note that was not divulged publicly. It discussed whether a special Japanese fund related to retirement benefits met the definition of 'plan assets' in IAS 19 *Employee Benefits*.

Another challenge to Japanese adoption of IFRSs was the perception, especially in the eyes of manufacturing companies, that in IFRSs the focus was too much on measuring changes in the value of assets and liabilities, at the expense of presenting an entity's performance in terms of the realization concept. Japanese preparers favoured the revenue-expense approach over the asset-liability approach, and manufacturing companies, in particular, wanted a 'bottom line' that was an indicator to management of the efforts over which it has control—which measures their achievement. As seen in previous chapters, the IASB's repeated attempts to reform financial statement presentation were followed with misgivings in Japan, and seen as so many attempts to abolish net income. While the main thrust of Keidanren's position paper of October 2008, as noted above, was to propose the adoption of IFRSs in Japan, it also contained a warning to the IASB that some of its projects, in particular on financial statement presentation and post-employment benefits, 'have the potential to cause radical change to the current accounting practice'. The IASB, it was said, should develop standards 'that reflect the voices and the needs of the market'.[108]

The IASB was willing to pay heed to these Japanese concerns, but only up to a point. When, in 2009, the IASB developed what was to become IFRS 9 *Financial Instruments*, the initial plan was that, for financial instruments measured at fair value, all changes in fair value would be recognized in profit or loss. However, the Board then agreed to create a category of investments in equity instruments for which changes in fair value were to be recognized in other comprehensive income (OCI). This was done in particular with a view to gain acceptance for the standard in Japan, where 'strategic investments' in the form of cross-holdings were common, and where the prospect of having to report unrealized gains and losses on such investments was viewed with some anxiety.[109] The Board also agreed, against its initial inclination, that dividends received from these investments would be recognized in net income rather than in OCI. However, it maintained that the fair value changes on the investments would not be recycled to profit or loss which, from the point of view of many Japanese, represented a break with the traditional income concept.

By the same token, a senior executive at a manufacturing company whom we interviewed ventured the following view: 'I believe IASB has been giving too much emphasis on the usefulness for the purpose of investors. I do not deny that investors are essential, but financial activities and economic activities cannot be achieved without corporate management.'[110] The dominant weight given to users

[108] 'Future Directions of Accounting Standards in Japan' (October 2008).

[109] 'Banks Nervous about Fair Value Revamp', *Nikkei Report*, 22 June 2009; 'Japan Wants More Say on Drafting of New Standards', *The Nikkei Weekly*, 8 February 2010.

[110] Interview with Yoshiki Yagi and Shigeo Sakase, 25 January 2011.

by the IASB and in many other major capital market countries was not necessarily found in all quarters in Japan. Moreover, manufacturing companies have had a long tradition of using historical cost, and they would view excessive marking to market or fair value as not reflecting the substance of their corporate activities. Trading companies and financial service companies much more strongly supported the move to IFRSs.

Finally, a source of hesitation for any jurisdiction considering a transition to IFRSs in 2009 or 2010 was that IFRSs were not yet stable. As discussed more fully in Chapter 16, the IASB was still working furiously to complete its ambitious convergence work plan with the FASB. It was an open question whether the outcome of major projects such as insurance contracts, financial instruments, revenue recognition, and leases would be acceptable in Japan. In the Tokyo Agreement, the ASBJ had kept its options open on whether or not to converge its standards on these topics, and there was a perception in Japan that the ASBJ was serious when it said that it was not committed to follow whatever the IASB would decide.

15.5.3 The Prospect of IFRS Adoption Fades

On 21 June 2011, Japan's Minister for Financial Services, Shozaburo Jimi, placed the FSA's roadmap on hold.[111] While the minister did not mention, and thus presumably did not call into question, that a decision on IFRSs would be taken in 2012, he announced that mandatory adoption of IFRSs, if any, would occur after 2015, and that in such a case a preparation period of five to seven years would be provided. Among the cited reasons were the recent developments at the SEC, requests from industry and trade unions for a deferral of a decision on IFRSs, and the 'outbreak of the unprecedented Great East Japan Earthquake and tsunami' of March 2011. The ministerial announcement was interpreted as a sign that the prevailing view among Japanese companies was that Japan should not move out of step with other major countries, where moves to IFRSs were also being delayed or reconsidered.[112]

In his announcement, the minister also revoked the decision to end the use of US GAAP starting in financial years after 31 March 2016. If left intact, this policy would almost certainly have implied the transition of a group of major Japanese companies to IFRSs, as their reversion to Japanese GAAP, which was not accepted for US listing purposes, would have been unlikely. By 2012, the number of US-listed companies using US GAAP in their filings with the FSA stood at thirty-three, as very few had availed themselves of the option to use IFRSs. It is understood that many of these companies were satisfied with their right to report on the basis of US GAAP. Unlike Sumitomo, they had seen no pressing need to switch to IFRSs. The removal of the prospective mandatory requirement to abandon US GAAP, coupled with uncertainty over the future course of IFRSs

---

[111] 'Considerations in the Application of IFRS', statement by Minister for Financial Services Shozaburo Jimi, dated 21 June 2011 <http://www.fsa.go.jp>.

[112] 'Japan Rethinks Intl Accounting Rules as Enthusiasm Recedes', *Nikkei Report*, 21 June 2011.

and the risk of divergence between IFRSs and US GAAP, would then be sufficient reasons to explain why more of these companies had not voluntarily adapted IFRSs in their filings.[113]

The IASB, meanwhile, had not given up hope on Japan. A few weeks before Minister Jimi made his announcement, the IASB and the ASBJ had announced their achievements under the Tokyo Agreement.[114] As seen in Chapter 10, the 2007 Tokyo Agreement envisaged the removal of the remaining differences between IFRSs and Japanese GAAP by June 2011, except for active major IASB projects ongoing when the Tokyo Agreement was signed. In June 2011, the two boards did not go so far as to claim that all differences were eliminated, but the ASBJ could point to a number of completed projects that had brought Japanese GAAP closer to IFRSs. Looking forward, the boards would pursue 'a deepening relationship between the IASB and the ASBJ in preparation for a decision in 2012 on a Japanese adoption of IFRSs'. The semi-annual joint meetings of the ASBJ and the IASB continued. The IFRS Foundation held out the prospect that an Asia-Oceania satellite office might be located in Tokyo. The plans for such an office began to be made in 2009, and other countries, including China and Singapore, competed to host the office, the element of financing being an issue. The choice was made in favour of Tokyo, and the office was opened in October 2012.[115]

15.6 CHINA'S SUBSTANTIAL CONVERGENCE

15.6.1 Application and Development of the Converged Accounting Standards

As discussed in Chapter 10, the Chinese Ministry of Finance ceremoniously unveiled its new set of accounting standards, based on IFRSs, in February 2006 in the presence of David Tweedie.

If these standards had been developed at a great pace in the course of 2005, the speed of their implementation was even more breath-taking: they were mandatorily applicable from 1 January 2007 onwards, giving the approximately 1,570 affected listed companies less than a year to prepare. The 'implementation guidance' and 'explanatory guidance' accompanying the standards only became available over the course of 2006 and in early 2007. The IASB advised the ministry to give companies an additional year, but Vice Minister Wang Jun, in charge of accounting, believed that the ministry had prepared the ground sufficiently to act with decisiveness: 'The development of the Chinese accounting system entered the express lane since 2005. This effort is not built on an adrenaline-driven decision,

---

[113] Interview with Nobuyuki Hiratsuka, 25 January 2011; communication to the authors from Takehiro Okamoto, dated 23 January 2012.

[114] 'IASB and ASBJ Announce their Achievements under the Tokyo Agreement and their Plans for Closer Co-operation', IASB/ASBJ press release dated 10 June 2011 <http://www.asb.or.jp>.

[115] 'IFRS Foundation Opens Regional Office in Asia-Oceania', IFRS Foundation press release, dated 15 November 2012.

but by over two decades of solid efforts of internationalization-oriented accounting standards reform.'[116] As part of the preparations, a massive education campaign was undertaken, targeting the accounting professionals involved in the transition.

The ministry saw its approach vindicated by the results. In its own report on the transition, issued in July 2008, the Ministry of Finance described the implementation of the new standards as 'steady and effective'.[117] The report attracted particular interest because it included aggregate statistics on the impact of the new standards on the accounting numbers reported by companies. The Chinese convergence policy was based on the principle of achieving substantially the same outcomes as IFRSs, even though IFRSs were not adopted in full. One possibility to assess this claim was removed in the course of 2007. China companies with listed 'B' shares (that is, shares listed on Chinese exchanges but traded in foreign currency) had, since the 1990s, been required to report both on the basis of IASs (IFRSs) and Chinese standards. In September 2007, the China Securities Regulatory Commission (CSRC) dropped the requirement to report on the basis of IFRSs, on the ground that IFRSs and Chinese standards were now converged.[118] Yet one source of comparisons between Chinese standards and IFRSs remained. Fifty-three Chinese companies with listed 'A' shares (shares listed in mainland China in Chinese currency) and 'H' shares (listed in Hong Kong) had to report both under Chinese standards and under Hong Kong Financial Reporting Standards (HKFRSs). The latter were, since 2005, virtually identical to IFRSs. For these companies, it was found that total net profits aggregated over all companies were 4.69 per cent higher under HKFRSs, while equity was 2.84 per cent higher. No information was given about the range of variation, but it was said that six out of the fifty-three companies reported identical numbers under both standards. In subsequent years, the ministry wished to see a steady reduction of these 'GAAP differences' as evidence of its commitment to convergence. In the report for 2010, the differences had fallen to 0.33 per cent for net profits and 0.01 per cent for equity, with almost half of the companies reporting no differences at all.[119] One reason for the reduction in the 'GAAP differences' was the gradual disappearance of legacy items resulting from different transition arrangements in IFRSs and Chinese accounting standards. Another reason was the continued modification of the Chinese guidance to bring it closer in line with IFRSs.

A peculiar feature of the Chinese convergence process was that the original thirty-eight standards issued in 2006 were not modified in subsequent years, something to which their status as formal law may have contributed. This meant that changes were made by revising the volume of 'explanatory guidance',

---

[116] Written responses to interview questions, communication from Wang Jun to the authors, dated 29 August 2011. The IASB's advice was mentioned by Tatsumi Yamada (interview, 19 May 2011).

[117] 'Guanyu Woguo Shangshi Gongsi 2007 Nian Zhixing Xin Kuaijizhunze Qingkuangde Fenxi Baogao' [Report on the Analysis of the 2007 Implementation Situation of the New Accounting Standards by Chinese Listed Companies] (Ministry of Finance, 3 July 2008) <http://www.mof.gov.cn>.

[118] 'China Drops IFRS Reporting for Listed Companies', news item posted 13 September 2007 <http://www.iasplus.com>.

[119] 'Woguo Shangshi Gongsi 2010 Nian Zhixing Xin Kuaijizhunze Qingkuangde Fenxi Baogao' [Report on the Analysis of the 2010 Implementation Situation of the New Accounting Standards by Chinese Listed Companies] (Ministry of Finance, 29 September 2011) <http://www.mof.gov.cn>.

revised editions of which were published early in 2009 and 2011. More layers of guidance, albeit not nearly as voluminous as the more than 600 pages of 'explanatory guidance', were added in the form of 'questions and answers' and 'interpretations' published on the Ministry of Finance's website. In this way, a quite complex structure of texts was gradually built up which did not in all respects fully mirror the development of IFRSs, and in which the various components sometimes sat uneasily together.

This approach was sustainable for a number of years, not least because the completion of many of the major projects on the IASB's agenda, in particular in the convergence programme with US GAAP, continued to be delayed (see Chapter 16). Hence, while the IASB made numerous changes to existing standards between 2006 and 2011, it did not issue too many completely new standards. The main exception was the revision of IFRS 3 *Business Combinations*, issued in 2008. As a result, by 2011 the Chinese accounting standard on business combinations still suggested the step-by-step determination of goodwill for business combinations achieved in stages, in line with IFRS 3 (2004), whereas the explanatory guidance had been adjusted to reflect the revision of IFRS 3 in 2008.[120] Similarly, while the Chinese standard on segment reporting continued to be based on IAS 14 *Segment Reporting*, the implementation guidance was modified in line with IFRS 8 *Operating Segments*.[121] When the IASB issued IFRS 9 *Financial Instruments*, China did not integrate it into its body of standards, but because the effective date of IFRS 9 was repeatedly deferred by the IASB, this did not create a difference with IFRSs. It was not until 2014 that the first revisions of the thirty-eight basic standards appeared, and that a few new standards were added, reflecting among others the completion of the IASB's new standard on consolidation and related topics (IFRSs 10 to 12) and the standard on fair value measurement (IFRS 13) in 2011.

In modifying its guidance, the Ministry of Finance consulted regularly with the IASB. These communications were greatly facilitated by the appointment of Zhang Wei-Guo to the IASB Board in 2007. The working relations were formalized in a Memorandum of Understanding signed in July 2008 by Liu Yuting, the director general of the ministry's Accounting Regulatory Department, and Wayne Upton, the IASB's director of international activities, which envisaged several annual meetings at director level and the permanent secondment of a Chinese staff member at the IASB in London. These arrangements were similar to those agreed with the Japanese ASBJ in the Tokyo Agreement, but, unlike the agreement with Japan, no regular meetings at Board level were planned.

While most of the convergence consisted of adjusting the Chinese standards to IFRSs, the Ministry of Finance believed that convergence ought to be a two-way process in which the IASB should be sensitive to the needs and particular circumstances of emerging economies such as China. It therefore attached great importance to two changes made by the IASB at the request of China. As mentioned in Chapter 10, the Ministry of Finance wished to see the re-introduction of an exemption in IAS 24 *Related Party Disclosure* for transactions between

---

[120] See CAS 20.11.2; compare *Kuaijizhunze Jiangjie* 2006 edition, 315, and 2010 edition, 331.
[121] CAS 35; compare *Kuaijizhunze Jiangjie* 2008 edition, Chapter 36, and 2010 edition, Chapter 36.

state-owned, or state-controlled, enterprises. The exemption had been cursorily removed as one of the myriad changes made in the course the IASB's initial improvements project.[122] As it was clearly of great practical significance to China, the IASB issued an exposure draft in 2007 to reinstate the exemption.[123] The Board was not at first willing to provide a blanket exemption, and in the exposure draft it sought to limit the exemption to cases where there were no indicators of influence of one state-controlled entity on another. This made the proposal complex, as many respondents pointed out, and the IASB spent considerable time reconsidering the criteria. Nor did the exposure draft fully resolve the concerns of the Chinese Ministry of Finance, a point which was made clear both in writing and in discussions with the IASB.[124] Following a second exposure draft, proposing a general exemption, IAS 24 was finally revised in 2010 to China's satisfaction.

Another change introduced by the IASB related to the Chinese government's policy of requiring that state-owned enterprises revalue their assets to current values prior to an initial public offering of their shares. While this policy made sense from the point of view of not selling state-owned assets too cheaply, it created a problem in that IFRSs did not allow the incidental revaluation of property, plant, and equipment and of intangible assets. A revaluation implied that the company would permanently measure the assets on the basis of regular revaluations. The problem was not new, and had existed as long as Chinese companies had sought listings in Hong Kong, reporting on the basis of IASs. Yet in 2007 it became visible as a significant source of the 'GAAP differences' in the dual reporting of Chinese companies listed both in China and Hong Kong which the Ministry of Finance sought to eliminate. Aided by the Hong Kong Institute of Certified Public Accountants (HKICPA), the Ministry of Finance campaigned hard for a change in IFRSs, with the result that IFRS 1 *First-time Adoption of International Financial Reporting Standards* was amended in 2010 to allow revalued amounts determined in cases such as this to be carried forward as the 'deemed cost' of the assets, and accounted for on a cost basis.[125]

15.6.2 China Seeks Recognition of Equivalence

From the Chinese point of view, strengthening the domestic regulatory frame-work was an important reason for converging Chinese standards with IFRSs. Yet it was also an element in its policy to support Chinese companies 'going out' into the world. Obtaining recognition of equivalence therefore became an important project of the Ministry of Finance.[126] As the ministry also continued to insist on

[122] AP 10/2001 paper 9A, 14; IASB meeting of 18–20 October 2001, minute X.

[123] Exposure draft 'State-controlled Entities and the Definition of a Related Party' (IASB, February 2007).

[124] IAS 24 exposure draft (2007), CL 13 (Ministry of Finance/China Accounting Standards Committee), filed 24 May 2007 <http://www.ifrs.org>. Liu Yuting, *Zhongguo Qiye Kuaijizhunze: Gaige yu Fazhan* [Chinese Accounting Standards: Reform and Development] (Beijing: Renmin Chubanshe, 2010), 71–2.

[125] *Improvements to IFRSs* (IASB, May 2010), 9–13.

[126] Liu Yuting, 'Chinese Accounting Standards System: Structure, International Convergence and Equivalence', *Accounting Research in China*, 1/1 (2009), 98–112.

the need to take account of China's circumstances in converging with IFRSs, and thus not necessarily to adopt IFRSs in full, deciding on the equivalence of Chinese accounting standards with IFRSs was not a trivial question.

At an early stage, China found support for its approach in Europe. In November 2005, before the new Chinese standards were published, Vice Minister Wang Jun visited Brussels for talks with the staff of the European Commission. In a joint statement issued after the meeting by Wang and Director General Alexander Schaub, both the importance of accounting convergence and its limits were emphasized: 'Convergence does not mean creating identical accounting standards as national and regional economic environments must be taken into account when elaborating and implementing international accounting standards.'[127] In 2007, China was included in the EU's assessment of the equivalence of third-country GAAP with IFRSs, and CESR, as well as the Commission's staff, began to follow developments in China. In March 2008, CESR issued a cautious report in which it noted the ongoing efforts of China, in consultation with the IASB, to converge its standards, but it also noted that China was taking an approach to convergence that was different from that pursued in Japan or the United States, because of adjustments made to IFRSs in order to adapt some standards to local circumstances. According to CESR, which had had to rely on information supplied by the Ministry of Finance and the IASB: 'On the basis of a technical analysis of the standards alone, CESR would . . . have to conclude that Chinese GAAP could on the surface qualify as equivalent to IFRS as it appears largely to be IFRS.' Yet, the evidence of equivalence would have to come from the application of the standards, which had only begun in 2007. CESR also pointed to the importance of a supporting infrastructure of auditing and regulatory oversight.[128] For the European Commission, this was sufficient to accept Chinese standards as equivalent to IFRSs in December 2008. Unlike Japanese GAAP and US GAAP, the equivalence status of Chinese standards was accorded on a temporary basis, awaiting 'further evidence of their proper application'.[129]

China also proposed that its converged standards be recognized as equivalent with HKFRSs, but the HKICPA, Hong Kong's independent accounting standard setter, insisted that this first required a detailed, standard-by-standard comparison on the basis of the completed package of Chinese standards and related implementation guidance. Following such an assessment, a joint declaration was issued in December 2007, concluding that, as of that date, financial statements prepared under Chinese standards 'should achieve substantially the same effect' as when prepared under HKFRSs.[130] Accordingly, steps would be taken with the relevant

---

[127] 'Joint Statement by the Ministry of Finance of China and the Internal Market and Services Directorate General of the European Commission on International Convergence of Accounting Standards and Bilateral Cooperation', Brussels, 24 November 2005 <http://ec.europa/internal_market/accounting>.

[128] 'CESR's Advice on the Equivalence of Chinese, Japanese and US GAAPs' (CESR, March 2008), paragraph 12 and Section IV <http://www.esma.eu>.

[129] 'Commission Decision of 12 December 2008 on the Use by Third Countries' Issuers of Certain Third Country's National Accounting Standards and International Financial Reporting Standards to Prepare their Consolidated Financial Statements', 2008/961/EC, recital 11.

[130] 'Joint Declaration of the China Accounting Standards Committee and the Hong Kong Institute of Certified Public Accountants on the Converged China Accounting Standards for Business Enterprises and Hong Kong Financial Reporting Standards', 6 December 2007 <http://www.hkicpa.org.hk>.

authorities in each of the two jurisdictions with a view to mutual acceptance, for listing purposes, of financial statements prepared and audited on the basis of the standards of each jurisdiction. A proposal to accept, for listings in Hong Kong, financial statements prepared on the basis of Chinese accounting and auditing standards and audited by mainland audit firms, was put forward by the Hong Kong Stock Exchange in 2009. A final decision was made in line with the proposal in December 2010.[131]

The HKICPA's scrutiny of Chinese accounting standards, as well as its continued involvement with both the IASB and the Ministry of Finance, was an important factor in engendering confidence at the IASB that the Chinese standards were a good approximation of IFRSs.[132] By 2010 it would seem that it was generally accepted in Hong Kong that Chinese accounting standards were broadly equivalent to IFRSs, but that the quality of auditing was the vital issue. This was in line with a World Bank report published in October 2009, which noted the 'impressive progress' made in China in putting in place an institutional framework for accounting, auditing, and corporate financial reporting. The report accepted that Chinese standards and IFRSs were 'basically comparable', but pointed to a considerable variation in compliance with auditing standards.[133]

In 2007, it was reported that the Ministry of Finance was also raising the question of mutual recognition of accounting standards with the United States.[134] It is not apparent that the US SEC encouraged the Ministry to pursue this possibility. However, Sino-American ties in the area of accounting were strengthened in 2008, when the Chinese Accounting Standards Committee and the FASB signed a Memorandum of Understanding, expressing a general intention to improve communication and exchange views about each body's efforts to converge with IFRSs.[135] A second Memorandum of Understanding was signed in 2009, in which the two sides endorsed the G20's call for a single, high-quality global accounting standard.[136] China did not relinquish the idea of mutual acceptance, and saw the memoranda as aimed at the equivalence of Chinese and US accounting standards.[137] The FASB, on its part, also appeared interested in developing contacts with China. In 2008, Li Feilong, an executive at the oil company CNOOC (subsequently appointed to the IFRS Interpretations

---

[131] 'Consultation Conclusions on Acceptance of Mainland Accounting and Auditing Standards and Mainland Audit Firms for Mainland Incorporated Companies Listed in Hong Kong', Hong Kong Exchanges and Clearing Limited, December 2010 <http://www.hkex.com.hk>.

[132] Interview with David Tweedie, 29 July 2008.

[133] *Report on the Observance of Standards and Codes (ROSC)—Accounting and Auditing: People's Republic of China* (The World Bank, October 2009), executive summary and paragraphs 65 and 73.

[134] 'Efforts Made to Equal Accounting Standards', Comtex News Network news item dated 17 August 2007, accessed through LexisNexis.

[135] 'The Financial Accounting Standards Board and the China Accounting Standards Committee Sign Memorandum of Understanding', FASB press release dated 28 April 2008 <http://www.fasb.org>.

[136] The 2009 Memorandum of Understanding does not appear on the FASB website, but is reproduced in Liu Yuting, *Zhongguo Qiye Kuaijizhunze*, 252.

[137] Written responses to interview questions, communication from Wang Jun to the authors, dated 29 August 2011. On the significance attributed to the two memorandums of understanding with the FASB, see 'The Experience of China's Accounting Standards Setting and Convergence with IFRSs', PowerPoint presentation by Liu Yuting, European Commission conference on international developments in accounting and auditing, 8 February 2008 <http://www.ec.europa.eu/internal_market/accounting>.

Committee), was appointed to the FASB's advisory body, the Financial Accounting Standards Advisory Council (FASAC), as one of the few members from outside the United States.

As seen in Section 15.4.3, China began to figure in the SEC's thinking as an example of a country that was committed to international convergence but retained its sovereignty over accounting standards. It would seem that the Ministry of Finance would not discourage the view that China and the United States could learn from each other. Director General Liu Yuting observed in 2010 in the context of a conference on developments in US GAAP organized by his ministry: 'For China and the United States, which are large economies, it is very difficult to adopt IFRSs directly and fully, as other countries do.'[138]

China took stock of its situation vis-à-vis IFRSs in a 'Roadmap for Continuing Convergence of Chinese Accounting Standards for Business Enterprises and International Financial Reporting Standards'. A draft version was published in September 2009, perhaps not coincidentally a few months after the publication of the Japanese FSA's draft roadmap in June. The final version of the Chinese roadmap was issued by the finance ministry in April 2010.[139] In contrast to the roadmaps of the SEC and the FSA, the Chinese roadmap did not outline any radical departures, but rather contemplated what needed to be done to consolidate and continue the status quo. The ministry sketched China as fully committed to shoulder its international responsibilities, as outlined by the G20, to achieve a single, high-quality global accounting standard. It pointed to the recognition of Chinese standards by the IASB, in Hong Kong, and by the EU as evidence that convergence had been achieved. Yet it was affirmed that, while other countries might choose a policy of literal adoption of IFRSs, China would maintain a policy of continuing convergence, as determined by 'China's special political, economic, legal, and cultural environment'. As if to underline the point, the central phrase of the 2009 draft roadmap, 'continuing and full convergence', was changed to 'continuing convergence' in the final version. While the ministry sought to cooperate actively with the IASB, it also expected convergence to be 'interactive', as the IASB should be attuned to the needs and circumstances of emerging economies.[140] China seemed to see a role for itself in championing the cause of emerging economies in accounting standards, as witnessed by its willingness to host the IFRS Foundation's Emerging Economies Group, set up in 2011 (see Section 11.7).

15.7 ATTEMPTS IN INDIA TO ADOPT IFRSs

The World Bank observed in its 2004 report on India that, while the Institute of Chartered Accountants of India (ICAI) had been using IFRSs extensively when

---

[138] Liu Yuting, *Zhongguo Qiye Kuaijizhunze*, 85.

[139] 'Zhongguo Qiye Kuaijizhuze yu Guoji Caiwu Baogao Zhunze Chixu Qutong Luxiantu', Ministry of Finance, 1 April 2010 <http://www.kjs.mof.gov.cn>. An English translation of the September 2009 draft roadmap is included as an appendix to the World Bank's October 2009 ROSC on China.

[140] Interview with Yang Min, 7 April 2011. See also Liu Yuting, 'Woguo Kuaijizhunze Quoji Qutong Zou Xiang Zongshen Fazhan Jieduan' [China's International Accounting Standards Convergence Moves to the Stage of In-depth Development], statement explaining April 2010 roadmap, dated 14 April 2010 <http://www.mof.gov.cn>.

developing its accounting standards, there were nonetheless significant differences, especially in regard to the extent of disclosure, between Indian accounting standards and IFRSs.[141] The Bank concluded that 'Immediate steps should be taken to issue IFRS-equivalent national standards that are not yet adopted' (paragraph 73, footnote omitted). One supposes that, in addition to a recommendation from the World Bank, responsible figures in India were also urging a move towards the adoption of IFRSs, as had IASB Chairman David Tweedie. India was too important a country to be left outside the IFRS tent.

It took some years for India to begin organizing an effort, involving ICAI and government, to converge Indian accounting standards to IFRSs. The IASC Foundation trustees, for their part, recognized the importance of India by specifically looking for an Indian candidate to fill one of the additional positions reserved for Asia-Oceania in the first review of the Constitution.[142] In January 2006, T.V. Mohandas Pai, chairman of the board of Infosys BPO Limited, became the first Indian trustee on the IASC Foundation. This appointment, as well as arguments made within Indian business and government circles, may have been precipitating factors. Once again, the European Commission may also have been a force for change. In December 2006, it had made continued acceptance of third-country GAAP in the capital markets of the EU dependent on a public commitment to convergence with IFRSs by the relevant national authority in charge of accounting standards (see Section 9.5). As India had not yet made such a commitment, it would either have to make one in 2007, or see European capital markets close to Indian GAAP. David Tweedie, meeting with several top-level officials during a visit to India early in 2007, did not fail to make a strong case for India to join the growing number of countries adopting IFRSs in full.[143]

Whatever the precise motivation, in July 2007 the ICAI announced its decision to 'fully converge' Indian accounting standards with IFRSs, with a view to adoption of the converged standards by listed companies and other public interest entities beginning in April 2011.[144] Although the ICAI issued a draft roadmap later in 2007, and the April 2011 deadline continued to be cited throughout the following years, it soon appeared that India's course towards IFRSs was not to be a straight line. Although it could be argued that Indian accounting standards were, by 2007, already to a considerable extent converged with IFRSs, the future status of the remaining differences continued to be a matter of extensive debate. Already in 2008, the Ministry of Corporate Affairs, which took the lead in organizing the preparations for IFRSs, made the point that India would 'converge' but not 'adopt', thus keeping open the possibility of a degree of divergence from IFRSs.[145]

Further work on the roadmap was undertaken in meetings with representatives of the following parties: the Ministry of Finance, the Securities and Exchange

---

[141] *Report on the Observance of Standards and Codes (ROSC), Accounting and Auditing: India* (The World Bank, 20 December 2004), paragraphs 41, 57, and 58. The authors are grateful for advice received on this section from Prabhakar Kalavacherla.

[142] IASCF trustees meeting of 14–15 November 2005, agenda paper 3, paragraph 15.

[143] '"Converge Fully with Global Financial Reporting Standards"', *The Hindu* (business line), 14 February 2007.

[144] 'India Announces Convergence with IFRSs for Public Interest Entities from 2011', IASB press release, dated 24 July 2007.

[145] '"Converge, not Adopt"', *The Hindu* (Business Line), 14 August 2008.

Board of India (SEBI), the Reserve Bank of India, the Insurance Regulatory and Development Authority, the Comptroller and Auditor General of India, the Pension Fund Regulatory and Development Authority, the ICAI, and industry representatives and other experts. The Ministry of Corporate Affairs set up this 'core group' in July 2009, and obtained the services of IASC Foundation trustee Mohandas Pai to chair one of its working parties. The 'core group' also included the National Advisory Committee on Accounting Standards (NACAS), an expert body set up by the government in 2001 to recommend to the government its approval of accounting standards proposed by the ICAI. All of the relevant bodies within the government, as well as the ICAI, NACAS, and industry, were included in this broad church, and it did not take long before interested parties, especially from the preparer community, began aggressively lobbying ICAI and NACAS as well as the two ministries and SEBI for carve-outs.

During India's period of preparation, in January 2009 Prabhakar ('PK') Kalavacherla, a KPMG partner based in San Francisco and an Indian citizen, became the first IASB Board member from India.

In January 2010, a little more than a year before the planned transition date, the Ministry of Corporate Affairs established what was still known as a 'roadmap' for convergence with IFRSs. The roadmap foresaw the application of a converged set of accounting standards by the larger listed companies as of April 2011. The transition by mid-sized and smaller listed companies was deferred by two and three years, respectively. In what appeared to be a last-minute decision, all but the largest private companies would continue to use non-converged standards. A separate roadmap for banking and insurance companies was established in March.[146] In January 2010, the Ministry of Corporate Affairs still needed to ensure the enactment of the various legal and regulatory amendments identified in the roadmap.

As if to speed up the movement to IFRSs, SEBI announced a change in listing requirements in April 2010. 'In order to familiarize listed entities with the IFRS requirements', it allowed companies, with immediate effect, to submit consolidated financial statements in accordance with IFRSs.[147] The result was limited; in June 2013, it was reported that some eleven companies, mainly ones with foreign listings, had taken up the option.[148] One assumes that the continuing requirement to file financial statements on the basis of Indian GAAP for company law purposes reduced the attractiveness of the option for most companies.

The loss of momentum towards IFRSs that became manifest in 2011 in several countries also occurred in India. Shortly after the text of a set of thirty-five Indian accounting standards based on IFRSs, but with carve-outs, had been published,

---

[146] Ministry of Corporate Affairs, press release 2/2010, dated 22 January 2010; press release 3/2010, dated 31 March 2010 <http://www.mca.gov.in/Ministry/press>; 'Core Panel for Two Sets of Accounting Standards', *The Financial Express* (India), 24 January 2010.

[147] 'Listing Conditions—Amendments to the Equity Listing Agreement', Securities and Exchange Board of India, circular CIR/CFD/DIL/1/2010 dated 5 April 2010 <http://www.sebi.gov.in>.

[148] See 'IFRS Application around the World: Jurisdictional Profile: India' <http://www.ifrs.org>, consulted June 2013.

the Ministry of Corporate Affairs announced in February 2011 that the date for their implementation would be notified at a later date, 'after various issues including tax-related issues are resolved'.[149] It was reported in the press: 'The government today postponed the convergence with Indian accounting standards with the international standards, thanks to the relentless lobbying by corporates, and unresolved taxation issues.... corporates have been lobbying hard to defer the implementation, arguing that they were not prepared for such a convergence right now.'[150]

A press report in May 2011 said that the IASB was 'none-too-pleased that India has retreated from plans to fully adopt International Financial Reporting Standards this year and is making a push to get the country back on track'.[151] Clearly, at this point in time it was a matter of great interest to the IASB that countries would follow each other in adopting IFRSs in full, and to prevent a negative spiral in which one country's delay or carve-outs would provide justification for another's. In May 2011, IASB Board member Kalavacherla made an attempt to reverse the tide. Speaking in India at an 'IFRS Summit' hosted by the Confederation of Indian Industry, he mentioned progress towards IFRSs in the United States, Japan, and China, suggesting that, before long, there would be few countries left in the world that had not incorporated IFRSs into their reporting systems. If India had to keep its carve-outs, it should at least allow companies the option to use full IFRSs.[152]

In August 2012, the Minister of Corporate Affairs set a new deadline of April 2013 for implementation of the converged standards. Much of the long delay, it was reported, was due to differences between the Ministry of Corporate Affairs (a junior ministry) and the Ministry of Finance (a senior ministry) over tax issues.[153] Moreover, the issue of the carve-outs remained. In Kalavacherla's 2011 speech, cited above, he said he had seen analyses showing more than forty, and in one case more than eighty differences between IFRSs and the proposed Indian accounting standards. The website of the Ministry of Corporate Affairs and the IASB's jurisdictional profile for India itemized a number of the deviations.[154]

With or without carve-outs, the adoption of India's converged standards remained an elusive objective. Pai's term on the IFRS Foundation trustees ended in December 2011. His successor, C. B. Bhave, was a former chairman of SEBI. Kalavacherla retired from the Board in December 2013. No Board member from India was appointed in his place.

---

[149] Ministry of Corporate Affairs press release 7/2011(No. 1/1/2009–IFRS) dated 25 February 2011 <http://www.mca.gov.in>.

[150] 'India Inc Has Its Way, IFRS Put Off', *The Indian Express*, 26 February 2011.

[151] Emily Chasan, 'Accounting Board Stung by India's Retreat from IFRS', item posted 24 May 2011 <http://mobile.blogs.wsj.com>.

[152] Prabhakar Kalavacherla, 'Convergence in India—IASB's Perspective' undated speech [18 May 2011] <http://www.ifrs.org>; 'Call for Unmodified IFRS Option in India', news item posted 26 May 2011 <http://www.iasplus.com>.

[153] '"Will Ensure IFRS Implementation by April 2012"', *The Indian Express*, 9 August 2012.

[154] 'IFRS Application around the World: Jurisdictional Profile: India' <http://www.ifrs.org>, consulted June 2013; untitled document [June 2011] <http://www.mca.gov.in/Ministry/pdf/nacas_30jun2011.pdf> accessed April 2014.

15.8 THE ASIAN-OCEANIAN STANDARD-SETTERS GROUP (AOSSG)

An early form of cooperation among standard setters in Asia had been the three-country meetings held by China, Japan, and South Korea, which had begun in February 2002 (see Section 4.6). At their meeting in Beijing, in October 2008, the three countries agreed to study 'how to enhance communication and exchange with standards setters in other Asian countries and Oceanic countries with an eye to promoting the adoption of, or convergence to IFRSs by more jurisdictions in Asia and Oceania and making constructive inputs to IASB projects'.[155]

At that time, there were already forms of periodic consultation in existence between standard setters in the Asia-Pacific region and the IASB. From 2003 to 2009, a series of annual meetings were held, usually in Kuala Lumpur or Singapore, of the IASB with standard setters from the countries of the Association of Southeast Asian Nations (ASEAN), with standard setters from other countries or jurisdictions, including Australia, Japan, South Korea, and Taiwan also in attendance. David Tweedie and Warren McGregor usually took part in these annual meetings.[156] In addition, the IASB sent representatives to meetings of standard setters from the Indian subcontinent, as well as to the China–Japan–Korea meetings. From the point of view of the IASB, a consolidation of these various meetings into a single group would be welcome, if only from the point of view of simplifying the travel schedule. More importantly, it was hoped that a strengthened regional group could provide the IASB with high-quality input on issues that were said to be problematic in the region, such as the application of the rather sophisticated, fair value-based standard IAS 41 *Agriculture*.[157]

The result was the creation of the Asian-Oceanian Standard-Setters Group (AOSSG) which, following a preparatory meeting in April 2009, held its first meeting in November 2009 in Kuala Lumpur. Subsequent meetings were held in Tokyo (September 2010), Melbourne (November 2011), Kathmandu (November 2012), and Colombo (November 2013). The IASB Board chairman, two or three Board members, and senior staff have always attended the AOSSG's annual meetings. In 2010, the AOSSG began commenting on IASB exposure drafts and discussion papers. It also produced a first report of its own, on financial reporting issues arising out of Islamic finance.

In June 2011, the AOSSG issued a 'vision paper' which described its plans and activities, and pointed to a membership consisting of twenty-five jurisdictions from a region that extended from Saudi Arabia and Dubai in the west to Australia and New Zealand in the east.[158] The aim of the AOSSG is to communicate views from the region on the agenda of, and drafts issued by, the IASB Board and IFRS

---

[155] 'China–Japan–Korea Accounting Standards Setters Meeting 2008 Held in Beijing', ASBJ press release dated 21 October 2008 <http://www.asb.or.jp>.

[156] See for example 'Regional Accounting Standard Setters Meet in Singapore to Provide Feedback to IASB on Implementation of IFRSs', Ministry of Finance (Singapore) press release dated 17 July 2008 <http://app.mof.gov.sg>.

[157] Interview with David Tweedie, 15 October 2009.

[158] 'A Vision Paper of the Asian-Oceanian Standard-Setters Group 2011: A Driving Wind for IFRS from Asia-Oceania' (AOSSG, June 2011) <http://www.aossg.org>.

Interpretations Committee and to provide a support system for countries in the region. During the meeting in Kathmandu, the AOSSG took steps to build Nepal's standard-setting capacity.[159]

15.9 OTHER FORMS OF REGIONAL COOPERATION IN ASIA

Whereas the AOSSG and its precursors brought together standard setters, a broader-based series of meetings was known as the IFRS Regional Policy Forum. The initiative for this series was taken by the Australian Treasury, together with its New Zealand counterpart, who had since 2004 sponsored a Trans-Tasman Accounting Standards Advisory Group on issues relating to the adoption of IFRSs. In 2005, it was decided to host a regional forum on IFRSs that, like the Trans-Tasman group, would bring together not only the accounting standard setters, but also their oversight bodies, policy makers, and professional accountancy bodies. The forum was held in October 2005, in Sydney.[160] Subsequent meetings were held in Tokyo, Beijing, Singapore, and Bali, and they continued after 2011. Participants came from some fifteen to twenty countries in the Asia-Pacific region. IASB Chairman David Tweedie regularly attended, usually accompanied by other Board members and senior staff. The Forum 'was intended to bring together policy makers, regulators and national standards setters from jurisdictions in different stages of their IFRS adoption roadmap to share and learn from one another's experiences in adopting the global standards, both the challenges faced and in taking advantage of opportunities offered'.[161]

The three-country meetings among China, Japan, and South Korea continued after the formation of the AOSSG. In January 2011, they renewed their commitment to work together both in the AOSGG and vis-à-vis the IASB in a memorandum of understanding.[162] Japan also attempted to establish ties with India. IFRS Foundation trustee Noriaki Shimazaki played a leadership role in starting an India–Japan Dialogue in July 2010, by which India and Japan could share each other's experiences in moving towards adoption of IFRSs.[163]

Although Japan's ASBJ has played an active role in the various forms of regional cooperation outlined above, there is a belief in Hong Kong and some Asian countries that Japan is more or less in its own orbit with its own distinctive history and accounting culture. Its issues and problems do not mesh easily with those in much of the rest of Asia. One can find partners in major Hong Kong audit

---

[159] 'The Fourth Annual AOSSG Meeting: Communiqué—November 2012' <http://www.aossg.org>.

[160] See 'International Financial Reporting Standards Regional Policy Forum Australia 2005: Communiqé' <http://www.frc.gov.au>; letter from Jim Murphy to David Tweedie, dated 8 February 2005, IASB archive, file 'Australia'.

[161] 'The 5th International Financial Reporting Standards Regional Policy Forum 2011', Communiqé, Bali Indonesia, 24 May 2011 <http://www.ifrs.org>.

[162] 'Memorandum of Understanding (MoU) of High-level Meeting of Accounting Standards Setters among China, Japan and Republic of Korea (January 25, 2011 Beijing)' <http://www.asb.or.jp>.

[163] 'Inauguration of India-Japan Dialogue', ASBJ press release, dated 28 July 2010 <http://www.asb.or.jp>.

firms whose calling cards draw attention to their coverage of Asia but with the proviso, 'ex-Japan'.

15.10 THE EU HOLDS ON TO IFRSs

The EU's requirement that all its listed companies report on the basis of IFRSs, beginning in 2005, had been of vital importance to the IASB. Although the relations between the IASB and its 'first customer' had often been difficult, the EU's IFRS policy was not fundamentally called into question, at least not by a majority of member states, nor by the European Commission. But by the end of the IASB's first decade, there was no support for an expansion of the role of IFRSs in the EU's policies beyond the consolidated financial statements of listed companies.

The member state options to allow or require the use of IFRSs in the parent company financial statements of listed companies, or in the financial statements of non-listed companies, remained in place. The exercise of these options resulted in a decidedly mixed record of the reach of IFRSs across the EU.[164]

As seen in Section 12.10, suggestions that the *IFRS for SMEs* might play a role in accounting regulation at the level of the EU had fallen flat. An attempt by the European Commission to simplify the accounting requirements for smaller entities, beginning in 2007, evolved into a more ambitious project to modernize the Fourth and Seventh Accounting Directives. The Commission completed its legislative proposals in October 2011, but well before that stage it was evident that there was no support for an EU-wide adoption of the *IFRS for SMEs*. The adoption, or not, of the *IFRS for SMEs* would be a matter for the member states, but the revised directives contained some provisions that prevented a straightforward, unmodified adoption.[165]

Earlier in the decade, the European Commission had suggested that IFRSs might be used as the starting point in a project to harmonize the calculation of taxable profits across the EU (the so-called common consolidated corporate tax base, CCCTB), but the possible role of IFRSs in that project soon became very attenuated.[166]

The European Commission remained the linchpin of the EU's original policy of applying IFRSs to the consolidated financial statements of listed companies. In this capacity, it was interested to see IFRSs succeed both in the EU and elsewhere. At the European Commission, there was a degree of frustration that the IASB did not appreciate just how much work the Commission was doing to assure the

---

[164] 'Implementation of the IAS Regulation (1606/2002) in the EU and EAA' (European Commission, 1 July 2010) <http://ec.europa.eu/internal_market/accounting>.

[165] 'Proposal for a Directive of the European Parliament and of the Council on the Annual Financial Statements, Consolidated Financial Statements and Related Reports of Certain Types of Undertakings', COM(2011) 684 final, 25 October 2011, and 'Financial Reporting Obligations for Limited Liability Companies—Frequently Asked Questions', European Commission, MEMO/11/732, dated 25 October 2011, question 14 <http://ec.europa.eu/internal_market/accounting>.

[166] Lida Jaatinen, 'IAS/IFRS: A Starting Point for the CCCTB?', *Intertax*, 40/4 (2012), 260–9.

success of the IASB's programme, both in piloting the IASB's standards through the shoals of a politicized endorsement process, and in promoting the adoption of IFRSs in jurisdictions in other parts of the world. As discussed in this and other chapters, the Commission's equivalence assessments beginning in 2004 played a significant role in nudging other jurisdictions towards adoption of, or convergence with, IFRSs. But it seems that the IASB, when contemplating its relation with the European Commission, perceived it more as an obtrusive Mr Hyde than as a friendly Dr Jekyll. What registered with the IASB was the Commission's unceasing insistence on the need for European influence on the development of IFRSs. This insistence was real enough. To the Commission's staff, it was self-evident that the IASB should operate under a form of accountability to public authorities in adopting jurisdictions, among which the EU still ranked prominently. Moreover, it was a political necessity for the Commission to be seen as responsive to criticisms of the IASB both within the European Parliament and the member states.

The Commission's elementary but blunt tool for influencing the IASB was the threat of not endorsing a standard, endorsing with carve-outs, or delaying endorsement. That this mechanism could be used in practice had been demonstrated on several occasions, but the normal practice of the Commission's staff was to try to make the endorsement process as efficient as possible. By the end of 2008, a significant backlog of unendorsed pronouncements, in particular IFRIC interpretations, had built up, but this was probably the result of the cumbersome endorsement procedure rather than any deliberate delays. With the increased role asserted by the European Parliament and its insistence on impact assessments (see Section 9.6), the endorsement process could take up to a year even in the absence of political complications.[167] The continually postponed endorsement of IFRS 9, beginning at the end of 2009, was the clearest example of how the EU sought to use the endorsement instrument to maintain pressure on the IASB to re-open discussions on parts of a standard.

The creation of the Monitoring Board provided the Commission with an important new platform for interaction with the IASB and the IFRS Foundation (see Chapter 14). As seen in Section 11.10, the Commission's initiative to provide funding to the IASB was meant to ensure the IASB's independence vis-à-vis private-sector donors, but could give rise to concerns that the IASB would become too dependent on European political decision-making.

Finally, the Commission could seek to enhance Europe's influence by encouraging Europe to speak with one voice, an ideal dating back to the days of the IASC. As seen in the following sections, the Commission confirmed its choice of the European Financial Reporting Advisory Group (EFRAG) as the preferred instrument for conveying the European point of view to the IASB. However, the EU member states continued to differ markedly in their attitudes towards IFRSs, as witnessed by the divergent policies adopted with respect to their national accounting standard setters.

---

[167] EFRAG *Annual Review 2008*, 14; interview with Jeroen Hooijer and Alain Deckers, 19 January 2009.

15.10.1 Another Enhancement of EFRAG

Following an earlier 'enhancement' in 2004 (see Section 9.3), EFRAG's supervisory board agreed in November 2008 on a package of further reforms, with the backing of the European Commission. The reason given was: 'With more and more jurisdictions moving towards IFRS, and some able to mobilise significant resources and expertise, European input to the International Accounting Standards Board (IASB) standard-setting process needs to be strengthened.'[168] One assumes this was a reference to the possibility that the US SEC might act on its roadmap, which would bring the full weight of the SEC and of all other interested parties in the United States to bear on the IASB. The response to this challenge, as approved in 2008, was that EFRAG would be given a larger budget, and thus a larger staff. Its existing proactive work to provide input into the early stages of the IASB's process was to be strengthened, not least by better cooperation with European national standard setters. EFRAG was changed from a private-sector body, paid for and governed by its sponsoring organizations, to a semi-public body. The European Commission signalled its intention to contribute up to 50 per cent of EFRAG's budget, matching private-sector contributions euro for euro up to a maximum of €3 million. This promise was given effect in 2010, a year before the start of the Commission's financial contribution to the IASB, but based on the same legal instrument.

As part of the enhancement, EFRAG's supervisory board was reconstituted to become broadly representative of European stakeholder groups, and was committed to act in the public interest. EFRAG's Technical Expert Group (TEG) continued much as before, on a part-time basis. EFRAG's proactive agenda was henceforth set by a 'planning and resource committee' consisting of the TEG chairman, at least two members of the supervisory board, and the chairmen of national standard setters that had committed to pool part of their resources with EFRAG. The details of this pooling became clearer in 2009, when EFRAG signed memoranda of understanding with the French, Italian, and UK national standard setters, each of which committed to provide staff resources as well as an annual cash grant of €350,000 to EFRAG.

The resulting EFRAG was a complex body, but probably approximated what many in Europe had in mind for the IASB: close links with practice but with safeguards to ensure a reasonable degree of independence, and means for stakeholder groups and national standard setters to participate in setting the agenda.

Because of EFRAG's reconstitution as a semi-public body, the Standards Advice Review Group, which had been founded in 2006 as a check on EFRAG, became superfluous and was disbanded in July 2011 (see Section 9.6.1).

Stig Enevoldsen, chairman of TEG until March 2010, actively sought to turn EFRAG into a stronger European voice, but tempered the pursuit of European influence with reminders of the importance of the ultimate objective of global standards. In Enevoldsen's view, an important element of EFRAG's influence was its draft comment letters. By following the IASB's deliberations closely, EFRAG

---

[168] 'Strengthening the European Contribution to the International Standard-setting Process: Final Report on Enhancement of EFRAG' (EFRAG, December 2008) <http://www.efrag.org>.

attempted to be ready to publish a draft comment letter on its website soon after the publication of an IASB exposure draft or discussion paper. EFRAG believed that its drafts were an important point of reference for many other parties around the world in writing their own comments to the IASB.[169] In addition, Enevoldsen held up Europe as a role model for the adoption of IFRSs, and EFRAG as an example for regional bodies such as the AOSSG, set up in other parts of the world to interact with the IASB.[170] But he also warned Europe to remain committed to the idea of a global standard: 'If we do not strongly support the IASB or should we decide to make more carve-outs, the US and Japan might decide not to adopt a set of accounting standards that are not supported or properly used in Europe.'[171] Under his successor, Françoise Flores, EFRAG expressed itself ever more critically about the pace of the IASB's single-minded pursuit of convergence with US GAAP, but EFRAG remained opposed to suggestions that Europe should distance itself from IFRSs. Looking back on the year 2011, Pedro Solbes, the chairman of EFRAG's supervisory board, noted the 'step backwards', away from a global standard, by the deferral of decisions on IFRSs in the United States and Japan, and the policies of China and India not to adopt IFRSs in full: 'Voices have started . . . to be heard in Europe asking why we should continue endorsing IFRS as published by the IASB when other significant economic areas consider that convergence—and full sovereignty retention—is good enough. EFRAG strongly believes that indeed we should.'[172]

15.10.2 UK GAAP Moves Closer to IFRSs

In 2009, the UK Accounting Standards Board (ASB) issued a consultation entitled 'The Future of UK GAAP'.[173] In the paper, the ASB asserted that its 'overarching strategy is to achieve convergence with IFRS. The widespread adoption and recognition of IFRS around the world make them the most obvious basis for UK GAAP. That view received strong support from our constituents' (paragraph 1.11). In consequence, the ASB proposed to withdraw the extant body of UK GAAP, as applicable to financial statements not prepared voluntarily or manda- torily on the basis of IFRSs, and to replace this with the *IFRS for SMEs*, 'wholesale and not amended' (paragraph 2.22). The smallest entities would for the time being remain subject to the ASB's Financial Reporting Standard for Smaller Entities (FRSSE). The proposal was not implemented in exactly this form. As mentioned in Chapter 12, a new UK reporting standard based on, but not identical to, the *IFRS for SMEs* was introduced in 2013. By that time, the ASB itself had disap- peared in a general restructuring of the Financial Reporting Council (FRC) over- seeing the ASB as well as a number of other bodies. Apart from a desire to simplify the FRC's structure, the implication of moving all of UK GAAP closer to IFRSs was that there was less need for a national standard setter. Instead, the FRC envisaged its responsibilities as 'taking a lead role influencing the development of

---

[169] EFRAG *Annual Review 2008*, 11; interview with Stig Enevoldsen, 3 July 2009.
[170] EFRAG *Annual Review 2009*, 10; interview with Stig Enevoldsen, 3 July 2009.
[171] EFRAG *Annual Review 2008*, 8.   [172] EFRAG *Annual Review 2011*, 12.
[173] 'Policy Proposal: The Future of UK GAAP' (ASB, August 2009) <http://www.frc.org.uk>.

[IFRSs]' and of the IASB's strategy after the ending of the IASB's convergence project with US GAAP in 2011, and playing an active role in EFRAG and 'seeking to ensure continued support in the EU for implementing IFRS as issued by the IASB'.[174]

15.10.3 The French Standard Setter Strikes Out on its Own

France moved in a direction that was completely opposite to that taken in the United Kingdom. In January 2010, the Ministry of Finance decided to fortify its standard setter when dealing with the IASB. It remade the old Conseil National de la Comptabilité (CNC, National Accounting Council) into the Autorité des Normes Comptables (ANC, Accounting Principles Authority) with a remit to expand its outreach and adopt a more proactive approach. It replaced its director, Jean-François Lepetit, with Jérôme Haas, a senior civil servant in the Treasury who had been serving as the French representative on the Accounting Regulatory Committee. Haas quickly came to be seen as more assertive in standard-setting circles than his predecessor.

The tone was set in a wide-ranging strategic plan published in June 2010. Here, the ANC presented itself as a strong believer in the need to adjust accounting standards to their context. This implied, among others things, an assertion that both the body of French national standards and the European approach to accounting as embodied in the directives needed to be preserved and brought up to date. Conversely, an 'uncontrolled' introduction of IFRSs beyond the listed companies targeted in the IAS Regulation was to be prevented. In particular, the *IFRS for SMEs* was rejected as untested, too complex, still too close to the original IFRSs, and as an unnecessary complication: a 'third' standard next to IFRSs and national standards based on the European directives. The suggestion was made that France, or Europe, might modify IFRSs for smaller listed companies by cutting out some of the disclosure requirements. The ANC argued that IFRSs reflected too much of a narrow financial or investor perspective—epitomized by fair value and a disregard for the prudence principle—instead of the broader general-interest perspective underlying the European approach to accounting. The ANC pointed out the reservations or hesitations in IFRS adoption in the United States, Japan, and China, implying either that the EU, at least for the time by far the most important adopter of IFRSs, should gain a greater weight in the governance of the IASB, or that the EU would be justified in going further in adjusting IFRSs to suit its own economic and legal circumstances.[175]

In the following years, the ANC continued to build support for its view of the IASB and of IFRSs. Haas travelled to Japan, for instance, for discussions with METI, which also harboured a degree of scepticism about the suitability of IFRSs

---

[174] 'Proposals to Reform the Financial Reporting Council: A Joint BIS and FRC Consultation' (Department for Business Innovation & Skills/Financial Reporting Council, October 2011), 15 <http://www.frc.org.uk>.

[175] Autorité des Normes Comptables, *Plan Stratégique 2010–2011* (ANC, June 2010), *passim*. See in particular 16, 19, and 24.

for smaller enterprises.[176] To support its mission of asserting a French or, more broadly, a Continental European point of view, the ANC sought to invigorate French accounting research by holding an annual conference and by commissioning research projects. Haas increased his contacts with accounting academics in Europe through the European Accounting Association and in the United States at annual meetings of the American Accounting Association.

The cumulative effects of the ANC's stance on public opinion in France were felt mainly beyond the period covered by this book, but they may be judged by the unprecedented step by Board member Philippe Danjou to rebut the ANC openly. In a speech given in France early in 2013, Danjou refuted 'ten great misconceptions' about IFRSs, such as claims about the preponderance of fair value in IFRSs. In his opening remarks, he pointed out that IFRSs were at that time subject to important criticisms in the press and elsewhere, 'in particular on the part of the president of the ANC'. Yet IFRSs had been adopted by the EU, and were part of the law of the French Republic; hence, 'An issuer wishing to comply with legal requirements cannot therefore fail to be disturbed by a hostile attitude shown, apparently as a matter of principle, by the ANC's leadership'.[177] Haas passed away in May 2014, leaving a question mark over the future direction of the French accounting standard setter.

15.10.4 Standard-Setter Crisis in Germany

In 2010, the Deutsches Rechnungslegungs Standards Committee (DRSC) was confronted with the inability to secure continued funding because it had lost the support of the preparer community. Apart from complaints about free-riding by the relatively small number of companies that were fee-paying members of the DRSC, the main source of the dissatisfaction was a loss of confidence in the DRSC as a useful interlocutor with the IASB. As discussed in Chapter 12, many non-listed, family-owned enterprises in Germany were unhappy with the *IFRS for SMEs*. They believed that not only the IASB but also the DRSC was insufficiently attuned to their views, and that they were inadequately represented in the latter. Among companies that did apply IFRSs, there was a view that the DRSC had failed in forcefully representing German companies' views to the IASB. Dissatisfaction with the DRSC had frequently prompted German companies to approach the IASB directly. This allowed the IASB, it was believed, to pick and choose from among conflicting German positions.[178] It may be noted that a desire for a

---

[176] Interview with Nobuyuki Hiratsuka, 25 January 2011.

[177] Philippe Danjou, 'Une mise au point concernant les International Financial Reporting Standards (Normes IFRS)', 1 February 2013 <http://www.ifrs.org>. For an assessment of the tension between the IASB and the ANC prior to Danjou's speech, see 'IFRS: la planète comptable au bord de la crise des nerfs', *Les Echos*, 14 January 2013, 28.

[178] See '"Wir brauchen diesen Standard nicht": Der Finanzchef und Vertreter von Familienfirmen über Ziele der Rechnungslegung—Harte Kritik am Deutschen Bilanzgremium DRSC', *Börsen-Zeitung*, 3 August 2010, 10; Tim Büthe and Walter Mattli, 'Mehr deutscher Einfluss auf die Bilanzierungsregeln', *Frankfurter Allgemeine*, 30 May 2011, 14; Dieter Fockenbrock, 'Letzte Chance für den Bilanzierungsrat', *Handelsblatt*, 30 May 2011, 28; Ana Gyorkos, 'German Standard Setter Secures Future Funding', posted 1 June 2011 <http://www.theaccountant-online.com>; and 'German Standard Setter Continues to Exist', news item posted 31 May 2011 <http://www.iasplus.com>.

strong, unified German position had its counterpart in long-standing calls for a 'European voice' in accounting standard setting, and one assumes that similar obstacles stood in the way of such an ideal at both the national and the European level. And even if the DRSC had not in effect become an apologist for the IASB, as some seemed to believe, it was true that its president, Liesel Knorr, a former IASC technical director, was sympathetic to the IASB's objectives and had nurtured an excellent working relationship with the IASB.

In June 2010, the DRSC notified the Ministry of Justice that it was terminating its standardization agreement with the ministry, effective 31 December. Since its founding in 1998, the DRSC was funded entirely by the private sector, mainly by companies. But now the standard setter faced imminent collapse.

A year of negotiations followed, which concluded with modifications to the structure and role of the DRSC. Under the new arrangements, equal prominence was given to the DRSC's roles with respect to IFRSs and to accounting under German company law. This reflected the government's earlier policy choice that German GAAP should not simply be converged with or subsumed within IFRSs, but must be maintained as a distinct alternative. The new structure, with a broadened membership, was ratified in July 2011. New funding commitments were obtained, and the DRSC undertook to renew its contract with the Ministry of Justice.

16

The IASB and the FASB Rush to Complete the Convergence Programme

The IASB's agenda was, from 2006 onwards, increasingly dominated by the Memorandum of Understanding (MoU) signed with the US Financial Accounting Standards Board (FASB) in February of that year. In the MoU, the two boards had committed to converge their standards on a number of topics. The decision in 2008 to accelerate this convergence work programme with the objective of completion by June 2011 led the two boards on a path of ever more intense activity. Combined with a simultaneous struggle to address accounting issues arising out of the financial crisis, the set of convergence projects strained the capacity of the two organizations to the utmost. The stakes were high, as the US Securities and Exchange Commission (SEC) had indicated that completion of the MoU was a vital milestone in its planned decision in 2011 on the use of IFRSs by domestic registrants. The IASB believed it should make every effort to complete the major convergence projects by June 2011 in order to increase the likelihood of a favourable decision by the SEC. The frenetic pace also put a strain on the boards' constituents as they attempted to follow what was happening and to provide their input into the process.

This chapter begins with an overview of the great effort made by both boards to complete the MoU projects by June 2011, an objective which they pursued until the last moment, but did not achieve. The remainder of the chapter consists of a more detailed discussion of the major convergence projects, showing how the MoU work programme consisted of an array of very diverse challenges, apart from the main challenge of getting the two boards to reach the same conclusions. In some cases, the boards were successful by a combination of versatility and sheer hard work, but in other cases the challenge proved too much.

It may be useful to note at the beginning of a chapter devoted to the technical aspects of IASB–FASB cooperation that in 2009 the FASB completed its codification project. Since 1973, US generally accepted accounting principles (US GAAP) had evolved into a very complex literature, including not only the sequentially numbered Statements of Financial Accounting Standards issued by the FASB, which finally reached number 168, but also statements of predecessor bodies, interpretations, staff positions, and other materials. In 2004, the FASB initiated a project to rearrange all of this material in digital form, under a new system of numbered topics. The resulting *FASB Accounting Standards Codification* replaced all outstanding sources of US GAAP, except those issued by the SEC, from September 2009 onwards. The FASB did recommend that the IASB adopt the technical platform developed by the FASB and thus move to codified IFRSs as well, but the IASB did not take up the offer.[1]

16.1 TENSION RISES AS 2011 APPROACHES

16.1.1 A Tight Schedule

The 2006 MoU listed eleven major projects that the IASB and the FASB would conduct jointly in order to develop new standards, as well as a number of short-term convergence projects in which one of the boards would consider converging its standards on a unilateral basis with those of the other board (see Tables 12.1 and 12.2 for an overview of the MoU projects). In September 2008, the boards had issued an updated version of the MoU in which completion of most of the major projects 'by 2011' was envisaged. In practice, this soon came to mean 'by June 2011', as that was when the terms of Chairman David Tweedie and the other two remaining members of the original IASB Board would end.

So where did the Board stand early in 2009, two and a half years before the planned completion of the MoU? The updated technical plan put before the Board in January 2009 showed no fewer than twenty-nine active projects.[2] While a large share of these, certainly if weighed by complexity, was within the scope of the MoU, the non-MoU projects, either jointly with the FASB or IASB-only, still claimed a considerable share of the Board's attention. The two significant non-MoU joint projects with the FASB were the conceptual framework project and the project on insurance contracts. A weighty IASB-only project to develop a standard for small and medium-sized entities (SMEs) was about to be completed, but this still left a number of other IASB-only projects, ranging from rate-regulated activities to annual improvements. Among these other projects, the revision of IAS 37, on provisions, was probably the most substantial.

With respect to the core of the convergence agenda, the number of major MoU projects had fallen from eleven to nine, as business combinations had been completed and intangible assets had been parked indefinitely as an inactive research project. Of the remaining nine, only consolidations had reached the stage of an exposure draft by January 2009. As the staff observed, the outbreak of the financial crisis in the second half of 2008 had placed additional strain on the agenda, as projects with direct relevance to the crisis (consolidation and special-purpose entities, financial instruments, and fair value measurement) had to be accelerated. While nobody had ever thought of the plan underlying the September 2008 MoU update as anything but challenging, the staff warned that at least three major projects (leases, revenue recognition, and financial statement presentation) were at risk of not meeting the target completion date.[3]

---

[1] For the FASB's recommendation, see AP 10/2008 (joint meeting) paper 6.

[2] AP 1/2009 paper 8. The number of twenty-nine follows from counting the several phases of the conceptual framework project as a single project, and omitting the single active research project on extractive industries.

[3] AP 1/2009 paper 8, paragraphs 11–17.

While the task ahead was challenging, early in 2009 the boards had the wind in their sails in the sense that the G20 leaders, in their November 2008 Washington summit, had issued a clear call that 'The key global accounting standards bodies should work intensively toward the objective of creating a single high-quality global standard'.[4] The prospect of such a single global standard appeared real enough, as the SEC was, on the basis of its 2008 roadmap, expected to make a decision in 2011 on the use of IFRSs by US domestic registrants, and as opinion in Japan was shifting towards adoption of IFRSs because of the SEC's expected move (see Section 15.5).

16.1.2 Renewed Commitment

The cause of a single global standard did suffer setbacks in 2009: a change of the guard at the SEC raised doubts about its commitment to its roadmap for IFRS adoption. In early 2009, there was anger at the IASB at what appeared to be lukewarm support for the use of IFRSs by US domestic companies by the FASB and the Financial Accounting Foundation (FAF) in their comment letter on the SEC's roadmap (see Section 15.4); and, as discussed in Chapter 13, the IASB and the FASB drifted apart on financial instruments accounting during the first half of 2009 as each board sought to respond in its own way to the political pressures unleashed by the financial crisis.

In September 2009, the Financial Stability Board, in its progress report to the G20, expressed concern over a possible divergence of standards, and urged the IASB and the FASB on by using such terms as 'additional work' and 'renewed effort'.[5] The G20 leaders amplified the message in the communiqué issued at their Pittsburgh summit when they made their first reference to the target year of 2011: 'We call on our international accounting bodies to redouble their efforts to achieve a single set of high quality, global accounting standards within the context of their independent standard setting process, and complete their convergence project by June 2011.'[6] The precise meaning of this statement could be debated, because it did not spell out the relationship between completion of the MoU work plan, achieving convergence between IFRSs and US GAAP, and a single set of global accounting standards. The IASC Foundation trustees, in their progress report submitted to the G20 prior to the summit, had blithely asserted that the objective of the 2008 MoU was 'achieving convergence of IFRSs and US GAAP by 2011'.[7] Looking back, FASB Chairman Robert Herz observed that any such notion was 'not consistent with the facts', as completion of the MoU work plan would leave many differences between IFRSs and US GAAP.[8] There was some discomfort at

---

[4] 'Declaration: Summit on Financial Markets and the World Economy', 15 November 2008 <http://www.treasury.gov>.

[5] 'Improving Financial Regulation: Report of the Financial Stability Board to G20 Leaders', 25 September 2009 <http://www.financialstabilityboard.org>.

[6] 'Leaders' Statement: The Pittsburgh Summit, September 24–25 2009', paragraph 14 <http://www.treasury.gov>.

[7] Letter from Gerrit Zalm to Barack Obama, dated 15 September 2009, Appendix A <http://www.ifrs.org>.

[8] Robert Herz, *Accounting Changes: Chronicles of Convergence, Crisis, and Complexity in Financial Reporting* (AICPA, 2013), 116.

the FASB that its acquiescence in the IASB's public emphasis on the 2011 date now allowed the G20 to attribute a greater significance to that date than the FASB had intended.[9]

David Tweedie and Bob Herz persuaded a joint meeting of their boards in October 2009 not merely to reaffirm their commitment to the MoU, including the June 2011 target date, but also to plan an intensification of efforts. A joint public statement detailing an updated work plan was issued on 5 November.[10] Ever since the Norwalk Agreement of 2002, the practice had been for the boards to meet jointly twice a year, in April and October. The year 2009 had already seen an extra joint meeting in June, but now the boards agreed to meet on a monthly basis, starting in January 2010. Indeed, during the first half of 2010, the IASB Board held ten one-day meetings in addition to the six regular, multiple-day meetings once a month. Of the sixteen meetings, fourteen were in whole or in part joint meetings with the FASB. Although this implied a significant increase in air travel, the two boards also relied ever more on video conferencing, dealing as best as they could with the inconvenience of the five-hour time zone difference between London and Norwalk. Video conferencing had already been used for many years to allow IASB staff on joint projects to participate in FASB meetings, and vice versa. Occasionally, individual board members had sat in on meetings of the other board by video link. But in November 2009 the boards held their first joint meeting using video conferencing.

Inevitably, this redoubling of efforts placed the boards and their staffs under great pressure. They had to produce and digest an unceasing flow of agenda papers, in addition to maintaining the level of outreach activities that both boards by now had taught their constituents to expect. Members of both boards, but also many constituents, eyed the work programme with mounting concern: would the fast pace be detrimental to quality and limit opportunities for consultation? Could the boards handle the workload? Would the constituents be able to cope with an accumulation of exposure drafts on major projects, whose planned exposure periods were ever more compressed into a short period of time as project plans slipped?[11]

Yet the SEC seemed to express its approval of what the boards were trying to do. As discussed more fully in Section 15.4, the SEC issued a 'Statement in Support of Convergence and Global Accounting Standards' in February 2010, in which it cited the call of the G20 for converged standards by June 2011. In addition, the SEC recalled its own roadmap when it said that, apart from other preparatory work by the SEC staff, 'completion of the convergence projects of the FASB and the IASB according to their current work plan, will position the Commission in 2011 to make a determination regarding incorporating IFRS into the financial

---

[9] Interview with Thomas Linsmeier, 11 June 2013.

[10] 'FASB and IASB Reaffirm Commitment to Memorandum of Understanding: A Joint Statement of the FASB and IASB', 5 November 2009 <http://www.ifrs.org>.

[11] For a sample of criticisms and concerns, see Mario Christodoulou, 'Convergence Talks Accused over Over-ambitious Targets', news item posted 22 April 2010 <http://www.accountancyage.com>; Paul B.W. Miller and Paul R. Bahnson, 'To the SEC: Forget the Timetable and Stop the Runaway Train', *Accounting Today*, 15 March 2010, 14–15; 'Leasingbranche schimpft über Bilanzierungsvorschläge; Verband: Qualität der Standards leidet unter Zeitplan', *Börsen-Zeitung*, 28 May 2010, 4.

reporting system for U.S. issuers'.[12] Although it did not with so many words require completion of the MoU by June 2011, the SEC made it clear that completion of the MoU was a necessary condition for taking its decision on the use of IFRSs in the United States.

16.1.3 An FAF Threat Leads to a Modification of the Work Plan

A few months into the intensified work plan, in May 2010, the FAF, overseeing the FASB, stepped in.[13] When David Tweedie and Robert Glauber, vice chairman of the IFRS Foundation, were attending the IFRS Regional Policy Forum held in Singapore on 12–13 May, Glauber received an unexpected message from Jack Brennan, the FAF chairman. Brennan told Glauber that the FAF was about to issue a press release, unilaterally announcing that the timetable for completing the MoU was unrealistic and needed to be revised. The message was confirmed shortly afterwards in a phone call from Bob Herz to David Tweedie. Glauber and Tweedie had to devise a response on the spot. The chairman of the trustees, Gerrit Zalm, could not be reached. Tom Seidenstein and Warren McGregor, each in his own way a right-hand man to Tweedie, were in Hamburg to watch Fulham play in the Europa League final. Tweedie's response to Herz was that to issue the press release meant the end of IASB–FASB convergence, and that there would be no point in holding the next joint meeting of the boards, scheduled for the following Monday, 17 May. Tweedie also sought contact with the SEC to let them know the consequences of this abrupt decision taken by the FAF. The result of the various hurried consultations was that the FAF press release was not issued, and that the two boards did meet as planned. However, it was a fraught meeting.

On the IASB side, several Board members shared the FASB's and the FAF's doubts over the feasibility of completing the MoU in time, and were also concerned that high speed might endanger quality. However, there was annoyance if not downright anger over the FAF's abrupt tactic. A joint meeting of IFRS Foundation and FAF trustees had taken place as recently as the end of March, and both sides had reiterated their support for the intensified work programme announced in November 2009, including achieving convergence by June 2011.[14] There was a suspicion that the FAF's move was more than a difference of view over planning, and signalled that the FAF and the FASB were not as committed as they had been to convergence and to a single global standard.

From the point of view of the FASB and the FAF, however, it seemed only natural that they should pay heed to the views of the US constituents in whose

---

[12] Securities and Exchange Commission, 'Commission Statement in Support of Convergence and Global Accounting Standards', Release Nos. 33-9109; 34- 61578, 24 February 2010, 2 <http://www.sec.gov>.

[13] The reconstruction of events in this section is, with respect to the perspective of the IASB, based on interviews with David Tweedie, 21 December 2010 and 6 January 2013, and with Warren McGregor, 18–19 May 2011. See also the brief reference in the IFRS Foundation trustees meeting of 5–7 July 2010, agenda paper 4C, 1–2. With respect to the FASB's perspective, we draw on interviews with Robert Herz, 9 June 2013 and with Thomas Linsmeier, 11 June 2013, and on Herz, *Accounting Changes*, 118–19.

[14] IFRS Foundation trustees' meeting of 29 March–1 April 2010, minute 6.

interest they were mandated to work and who showed themselves increasingly sceptical of plans to adopt IFRSs in the United States. Moreover, there had always been an unresolved difference of view between the IASB and the FASB regarding the significance of June 2011. Whereas at the IASB the date was frequently referred to as a 'deadline', the FASB deliberately avoided that word and spoke of a 'target'. The FASB felt committed to making an effort to achieve the target—and was given credit by IASB Board members for its commitment—but it believed it should take as much time as necessary for deliberation and consultation to produce standards of the requisite quality. At the FASB, there was a view that setting a deadline, especially a tight deadline, was difficult to reconcile with due process, as it implied that the boards had already made up their minds on the issues that constituents would bring up and how long it would take to deal with them. There was an impression that the IASB was too intent on making progress towards 2011 and too willing to cut corners or accept pragmatic solutions. Tweedie would, of course, never accept that the IASB might be satisfied with low quality.[15] The FASB's impression had its mirror image at the IASB, where some believed that the FASB could do with an infusion of pragmatism and a sense of urgency.

Although impossible to pinpoint with precision, there was a difference between the points of view prevailing in the two boards, which was felt more acutely as June 2011 drew nearer. At the FASB, it was believed that the IASB was not responsive to concerns raised by the FASB, so that the FAF's sudden announcement could be seen as a means to force the IASB to the table to discuss the issue of scheduling.

However it was intended and perceived, the practical effect of the FAF's sudden intervention was that the two boards, when they met in administrative session the next Monday, agreed not to descend into recrimination but to reconsider their planning. Again, as in early 2008 (see Section 12.2.3), a group of four (Herz and Tweedie, each accompanied by another board member) sat down to pare down the agenda to something that had a reasonable chance of completion by June 2011. Some projects were scaled down, and the completion of others would be postponed.

While it looked as if these modifications would ease the tensions that had arisen between the two boards, unfortunate communication ruffled more feathers. A week after the joint board meeting and before the two boards had made any formal announcements, Tweedie mentioned in general terms, in an interview published in the *Journal of Accountancy*, that the boards were reworking their schedules in order to reduce the number of exposure drafts outstanding at any one time.[16] While Tweedie's comment was tucked away at the end of the interview, Herz was quoted more prominently a week later. In a Reuters interview under the heading 'Accounting Rulemakers to Delay Convergence', it was reported that Herz 'does not expect FASB to meet a June 30, 2011 deadline for convergence

---

[15] See, for instance, his statement on June 2011 in 'Report of the Chairman of the IASB', *IASC Foundation Annual Report 2009*, 21.

[16] Matthew G. Lamoreaux, 'IASB Chairman Outlines Approach for Reconciling Financial Instrument Standards', posted 25 May 2010 <http://www.journalofaccountancy.com>.

with international accounting rules'.[17] This somewhat casual announcement of what appeared to be a major change in plans caused surprise, and led the IASB and the FASB to issue a provisional statement the next day, 2 June, in which they explained in general terms that they had agreed to a modified strategy in response to concerns of constituents over their ability to respond to a large number of exposure drafts outstanding simultaneously.[18] Details of the revised work plan were made public three weeks later.[19]

SEC Chairman Mary Schapiro, in a statement also issued on 2 June, made it known that she welcomed the boards' decision to take more time for the sake of quality, and that she was confident 'that we continue to be on schedule for a Commission determination in 2011 about whether to incorporate IFRS into the financial reporting system for U.S. issuers'.[20] European Commissioner Michel Barnier showed himself more critical. He was quoted in the press as saying that he was 'disappointed' by the way the decision had been taken: 'All jurisdictions represented in the Monitoring Board need to work closely together and that's where the important decisions should be discussed and taken.'[21] While it was an open question, to put it mildly, to what extent the IFRS Foundation's Monitoring Board should be involved in decisions concerning the IASB Board's agenda, Barnier was on firmer ground when he sensed a degree of improvisation in the way the boards had taken and communicated their decision.

The revised work plan as announced later in June showed the following picture. In terms of the remaining nine major projects of the original MoU, four (consolidation, fair value measurement, derecognition, and post-retirement benefits) were in an advanced state and expected to be finished in time, although in some cases with scaled-down ambitions for the scope of the project and the degree of convergence to be attained. The completion date of two others (financial statement presentation and the equity/liability distinction) was to be moved beyond June 2011, but still before the end of that year. This left three major projects (financial instruments, revenue recognition, and leases) requiring a determined push. These three, together with insurance contracts—a joint, non-MoU project which the IASB did want to conclude as well by June 2011—formed a group of four projects on which the boards would henceforth concentrate most of their attention.

While the G20 leaders, in their declaration at the Seoul summit of November 2010, updated their reiterated call on the IASB and the FASB to complete their convergence project 'by the end of 2011', in actual fact *June* 2011 retained most of

[17] Emily Chasan, 'Accounting Rulemakers to Delay Convergence', posted 1 June 2010 <http://www.reuters.com>.

[18] 'Joint Statement by the IASB and the FASB on their Convergence Work', dated [2] June 2010, <http://www.ifrs.org>. For a review of the handling of the communications, see the report by Mark Byatt, IFRS Foundation trustees meeting of 5–7 July 2010, agenda paper 9.

[19] 'Progress Report on Commitment to Convergence of Accounting Standards and a Single Set of High Quality Global Accounting Standards', IASB–FASB statement dated 24 June 2010 <http://www.ifrs.org>.

[20] 'Chairman Schapiro Statement on FASB–IASB Decision to Modify Timing of Certain Convergence Projects', SEC press release 2010-96, dated 2 June 2010 <http://www.sec.gov>.

[21] 'Accounting Standards Delay Criticized', *Financial Times*, 4 June 2010, 24.

its significance in the IASB's planning.[22] This prompted Tommaso Padoa-Schioppa, who was about to take over as chairman of the IFRS Foundation, to ask during the July 2010 meeting of the trustees, 'why June 2011 was such a crucial date'. That was indeed a question which many others were asking themselves. Tweedie was minuted as replying 'that the date was crucial because of the various other countries around the world hoping to converge or move towards adoption by 2011, expected changes and retirements on both the IASB and the FASB, the Japanese and US decisions on their respective roadmaps and pressure from the G20 countries too'.[23] Most of these reasons were valid enough, except that there seems to be no reason to believe that the FASB was greatly concerned about turnover in its board. Opinions could differ about the weight to be attached to these reasons, individually or collectively. A reason that Tweedie did not mention may have been as important as the others: many board members and staff acknowledged the usefulness of a clear target, however arbitrary, to counter the inevitable drift that accounting standard-setting processes were prone to, and which the experience of the IASB's first decade had already amply illustrated.

16.1.4 The Target is Missed

In August 2010, there was another surprise announcement from the FAF: that FASB Chairman Bob Herz would retire, some two years before the end of his second term, and that the FASB board would be expanded to its original size of seven members, having been reduced to five from 1 July 2008. Leslie Seidman, a member of the FASB since 2003, was appointed acting chairman with effect from 1 October. Also on 1 October, Russell G. Golden, the FASB's technical director, was appointed to the board, and two further new members joined the board in February 2011.[24] From the IASB's point of view, these were disquieting developments. To reshuffle the FASB board—by adding three new members and selecting a new chairman—just as the FASB and the IASB were attempting to bring major projects to a close could hardly be conducive to fast progress. The required majority within FASB changed from 3–2 to 4–3, so that three board members who might have previously been in the majority could conceivably become the three in the minority. The loss of Herz was keenly felt. There is no question that Herz was a committed internationalist, and that he been the main driver behind the FASB's convergence work with the IASB. Seidman, confirmed as chairman in December 2010, was as experienced in IASB–FASB convergence as might be desired, and both in public statements and in discussions with the IASB she continued to emphasize the FASB's commitment to work with the IASB. If anything, it was noted that she seemed to focus more resolutely on completing the convergence process with dispatch, in a change from Herz's more relaxed

---

[22] 'The G20 Seoul Summit Leaders' Declaration, November 11–12, 2010', paragraph 38 <http://www.treasury.gov>.

[23] IFRS Foundation trustees meeting of 6–7 July 2010, minute 4.

[24] 'Financial Accounting Foundation to Increase the Size of FASB: FASB Chairman Herz to Retire After More Than Eight Successful Years', FAF press release dated 24 August 2010 <http://www.accountingfoundation.org>.

style. At the personal level, relations between the two boards continued to be as good as they had been over the years, despite the strain of the MoU work plan and the ever-present frictions arising out of different views on technical questions and working methods. And yet there was a sense at the IASB that the FASB had become somewhat more cautious about changing its accounting standards for the sake of convergence.

During the second half of 2010, the IASB continued its heavy schedule of regular and extra meetings. If the number of joint meetings with the FASB dropped (to four such meetings in the four months from September to December) compared to the first half of the year, this reflected the fact that the boards had to wait for comments on a number of exposure drafts rather than any deliberate slackening of the pace. Yet, once again, the boards concluded that their work plan was still too ambitious. In November 2010, in the third of their quarterly progress reports on convergence which they had begun publishing that year as part of the intensified drive to complete the MoU, they announced further modifications to the agenda. The IASB decided to concentrate entirely on the four main projects that had already been identified in June: leases, revenue recognition, financial instruments, and insurance. Consideration of almost everything else which had remained on the agenda until then, including the conceptual framework, was deferred until after June 2011.[25] In January 2011, Leslie Seidman announced that completing the converged standards on financial instruments, revenue recognition, and leasing were the FASB's three highest priorities until June 2011. She added, though: 'I want to underscore that we want these standards to provide useful information and to be understandable and implementable at a reasonable cost. Let me assure you, if it takes a little longer to reach that comfort level, we will take that time.'[26]

Until well into 2011, David Tweedie continued to emphasize the importance of completing the remaining projects by June 2011.[27] He probably did so against his better instincts, but knowing that any sign of a weakened resolve would let the steam out of the process and would reduce to naught any chance there might still be of completing at least some of the projects by then. But the Board's Achilles heel was, as before, the charge that high speed would compromise due process, either in the thoroughness of the deliberations or in the opportunities for constituents to be consulted and provide feedback. The European Financial Reporting Advisory Group (EFRAG), for instance, had raised questions about the IASB's planning with increasing urgency during its regular meetings with a delegation from the IASB Board.[28]

---

[25] 'Progress Report on Commitment to Convergence of Accounting Standards and a Single Set of High Quality Global Accounting Standards', IASB–FASB statement dated 29 November 2010, <http://www.ifrs.org> accessed through web.archive.

[26] David M. Katz, 'The Path to Global Standards?', report on FASB webcast of 25 January 2011, posted 28 January 2011 <http://www.cfo.com>.

[27] See e.g. 'Sir David Tweedie Addresses the US Chamber of Commerce', transcript of a speech delivered on 10 March 2011 <http://www.ifrs.org> accessed through web.archive. See also 'Dash for the Finish Line', *World Accounting Report*, April 2011, 2.

[28] 'Summary of Main Messages Expressed by the EFRAG Delegation' relative to meetings of 26 August and 12 November 2010 <http://www.efrag.org>.

As mentioned above, due process concerns had prompted the FAF to intervene in May 2010. About a year later, similar concerns prompted the Monitoring Board to speak out.[29] In the public meeting of the Monitoring Board with the IFRS Foundation trustees on Friday 1 April 2011, Commissioner Barnier observed:

> Convergence should not be at the expense of quality is my main point. It's essential that IASB responds fully to the concerns that have been expressed by stakeholders, including additional field testing of projects where needed. It seems to me and the Commission that a few more months are required to develop high-quality solutions that meet the interests of users.[30]

As usual, David Tweedie was also in attendance, and it is understood that in the closed part of the meeting he was informed in less ambiguous terms by members of the Monitoring Board that completion of the remaining projects by June 2011 was incompatible with doing justice to constituents' concerns. Tweedie took this as an unwarranted intrusion by the Monitoring Board in the IASB Board's technical work. He might also have pointed out that the trustees' Due Process Oversight Committee had kept a close watch on the Board's plans and activities, and had appeared satisfied with what it saw.[31] During the following weekend, Tweedie considered offering his resignation, leading to hurried consultation among the members of the Monitoring Board and with Tweedie. In the end, he did not resign and agreement was reached on an interpretation of statements made during the Monitoring Board meeting that were acceptable to all. But the effect was as if Tweedie had heeded the Monitoring Board's call. Two weeks later, following a joint board meeting, Tweedie and Seidman used the format of a podcast interview with the IASB's director of communications to announce that they would 'extend the timetable for a few additional months' in order 'to ensure that the standards are of the highest quality'. Seidman reiterated that '[June 2011] was always intended to be a target, not a deadline, and we always said that achieving the target was subject to the nature and extent of the feedback that we got on each of the exposure documents'. Tweedie concurred that 'the June date is a target, it actually gave both boards great focus, and we are probably further ahead than we would have been had we not had that focus'.[32] Details were announced shortly afterwards when the IASB and the FASB published their quarterly progress report in which they announced that they had 'extended the timetable for the remaining priority MoU convergence projects and insurance beyond June 2011 to permit further work and consultation with stakeholders'.[33]

---

[29] The significance of the April 2011 Monitoring Board meeting for abandoning the June 2011 deadline is indicated in EFRAG's *Annual Review 2011*, 17.

[30] 'Monitoring Board and IFRS Foundation Trustees Meeting', 1 April 2011 <http://www.iosco.org>.

[31] See minutes of meeting of Board with Due Process Oversight Committee on 13 September 2010, IFRS Foundation trustees meeting of 11–13 October 2010, agenda paper 8A, attachment (i). From the minutes and other agenda papers of the trustees' meetings in October 2010, February 2011, and March 2011, it is not apparent that the Due Process Oversight Committee raised specific concerns. David Sidwell, chairman of the committee, also reported to the Monitoring Board at the 1 April 2011 meeting.

[32] 'Podcast Summary of the Joint IASB/FASB Board Meeting, 12–14 April 2011' <http://www.ifrs.org> accessed through web.archive.

[33] 'Progress Report on IASB–FASB Convergence Work', joint IASB–FASB statement dated 21 April 2011 <http://www.ifrs.org> accessed through web.archive.

The announcement that the work programme would not be completed by June 2011, led many to ask why it had taken the boards so long to see what was increasingly obvious to most observers. Scepticism was expressed about completion of the remaining projects in the short term.[34] The G20, whose communiqués had provided an important justification for the speed with which the boards had been pursuing the MoU work plan, appeared not to be greatly concerned. While the statement issued at the G20 Cannes summit in November 2011 still called on the boards to complete their convergence project, it no longer mentioned a specific date.[35]

To the IASB, it was a matter of great interest how the SEC would respond to a delay in the completion of the MoU, and one assumes this was among the points discussed when, as indicated above, the Monitoring Board, on which the SEC was represented, raised the matter of postponing the completion of the MoU projects. In May 2011, the SEC staff issued a progress report on its 'Work Plan for the Consideration of Incorporating International Financial Reporting Standards into the Financial Reporting System for U.S. Issuers'. In the report, the staff stated their assumption that 'reasonably converged standards' on each of the projects would be issued in 2011, but otherwise placed no emphasis on a timeline for decisions by the SEC.[36]

By June 2011, the boards could claim with some justification that they had made great progress on the MoU work plan. The publication of no fewer than four new standards in May 2011 (IFRS 10, 11, 12, and 13) looked like a fitting finale. But Jim Leisenring recalled how he used to say to David Tweedie with respect to the MoU work plan as it evolved since 2008: 'What you are going to do is shoot an arrow at the wall and paint a bull's eye around where it lands.'[37] Indeed, to say that the boards were 'nearing completion', as they did in their April progress report, was putting much too bright a gloss on it.[38] In terms of the eleven major projects of the original MoU (see Table 12.1), four had been completed with approximately the scope as originally intended (business combinations, consolidation, fair value measurement, and post-employment benefits). Two more were completed in the form of minor amendments that fell far short of the original ambitions for the project (derecognition and financial statement presentation). One had never been taken up (intangible assets), and one was suspended (liabilities and equity distinction). The remaining three projects (revenue recognition, financial instruments, and leases) were still active, together with the non-MoU project on insurance contracts which was typically viewed with the other three as a

---

[34] 'Editorial' and 'Convergence Programme: New Timings', *World Accounting Report*, May 2011, 1, 10; Stephen Bouvier, 'It's a Target, Stupid!', blog posted June 2011 <http://www.ipe.com>; 'Bilanzräte verschieben Angleichung ihrer Regeln; IASB und FASB geben sich "einige Monate" Aufschub', *Börsen-Zeitung*, 16 April 2011, 3.

[35] 'Cannes Summit Final Declaration: "Building our Common Future: Renewed Collective Action for the Benefit of All", 4 November 2011', paragraph 34 <http://www.treasury.gov>.

[36] 'Work Plan for the Consideration of Incorporating International Financial Reporting Standards into the Financial Reporting System for U.S. Issuers: Exploring a Possible Method of Incorporation', SEC staff paper, 26 May 2011 <http://www.sec.gov>.

[37] Interview with Jim Leisenring, 2 August 2010.

[38] 'Progress Report on IASB–FASB Convergence Work', joint IASB–FASB statement dated 21 April 2011 <http://www.ifrs.org> accessed through web.archive.

group. As it turned out, 'further work and consultation with stakeholders' on the remaining active projects would take years, not months. The project on revenue recognition was the first to be completed, in May 2014.[39] Whatever one might think of the June 2011 target, it had provided momentum that was irrevocably lost when the date had passed.

16.2 REVIEW OF TECHNICAL PROJECTS

The next sections discuss the main projects on which the IASB was working from 2009 to mid-2011. As in other chapters covering technical projects, this often requires that the narrative begins in earlier years, in order to supply background. The sections are organized as follows.

Sections 16.3 to 16.5 discuss projects, or groups of projects, completed by the IASB up to June 2011. All were MoU projects, although their origins went back in some cases before 2006: the package of standards relating to consolidation, interests in associates, and joint arrangements; IFRS 13, the standard on fair value measurement; and a revision of IAS 19, the standard on post-employment benefits.

The next four sections (16.6 to 16.9) discuss the four projects on which the IASB was focusing all of its attention from late 2010 onwards, which it failed to complete by June 2011, but on which it kept working actively afterwards: revenue recognition, leases, financial instruments, and insurance contracts.

A final group of three sections (16.10 to 16.12) covers MoU projects that were abandoned, either because work was suspended indefinitely or because the ambitions for the project were drastically reduced: financial statement presentation, the equity/liability distinction, and the income tax project.

16.3 CONSOLIDATION AND JOINT ARRANGEMENTS

The IASC had dealt with the accounting and disclosure aspects of interests in other entities in a trio of standards: IAS 27 on subsidiaries and consolidations, IAS 28 on interests in associates and the equity method, and IAS 31 on joint ventures. In May 2011, the IASB published three new standards to cover the same ground: IFRS 10 *Consolidated Financial Statements*, IFRS 11 *Joint Arrangements*, and IFRS 12 *Disclosure of Interests in Other Entities*. The Board also published a revised version of IAS 27, a rump standard now dealing with separate (i.e. unconsolidated) financial statements only, and a version of IAS 28 which remained substantially unaltered except for the removal of disclosure requirements. The latter were now brought together for all types of interests in a single disclosure standard,

---

[39] See also Paul Pacter, 'What Have IASB and FASB Convergence Efforts Achieved?', *Journal of Accountancy*, 215/2 (February 2013), 50–9.

IFRS 12. All of these changes had been many years in the making, in a process that illustrated the difficulties in pursuing convergence with US GAAP.

Although finally issued as a package, the new standards had originated in two separate projects, one on consolidation and the other on joint ventures, which were brought together at a late stage. The idea for IFRS 12 appeared as late as February 2010, when it occurred to the Board that it might be helpful to combine the separate disclosure requirements planned for subsidiaries and joint ventures in a single document, and to add those for associates as well.[40] There was no separate exposure draft for IFRS 12, because it was developed on the basis of the exposure drafts for IFRS 10 and 11, and the existing guidance in IAS 28.

16.3.1 Consolidation and Special Purpose Entities

The central question in the project that led to IFRS 10 was not how to prepare consolidated financial statements. The mechanics of consolidation have for many years been well understood in accounting practice, and were just cursorily indicated in IAS 27. The real question was how to draw the line between interests in other entities that are consolidated, and those that are not. All accounting standard setters faced the immense creativity of reporting companies and their advisors in setting up special-purpose entities (SPEs) designed to remove assets, liabilities, and their risks from the consolidated balance sheet. This was by no means a new issue when the IASB was created, but it attracted headlines after the fall of Enron in 2001. Enron became notorious for its tangle of hundreds of SPEs which obscured its financial position.[41] The FASB quickly produced a draft interpretation, made final in January 2003 as FIN46 *Consolidation of Variable Interest Entities*, and revised in December 2003 as FIN46R. Meanwhile, David Tweedie had reported to his trustees in June 2002 that Enron had made the question of consolidation and SPEs 'a matter of great concern' which the IASB would shortly discuss with the German, UK, and US standard setters.[42] In July, after consulting SAC, the IASB added the project to its active agenda.[43]

Any sense of urgency inspired by Enron was soon lost as the Board struggled to find the right strategy for the project. The problem was clear enough: IAS 27 defined a subsidiary, and thus decided the question of consolidation or not, by means of the notion of 'control'. In IAS 27 control was defined, without reference to legal form, in terms of power to govern the operating and financial policies of another entity. While this was an excellent example of a principles-based, substance-over-form approach, without further guidance it was too weak to prevent abuse. SIC-12 *Consolidation—Special Purpose Entities*, issued in 1998, had not been sufficient to fill the gap. The Board therefore sought to retain 'control' as the guiding principle, but to define it with such rigour that it could be applied robustly

---

[40] AP 2/2010 paper 6A.

[41] See for instance George J. Benston and Al L. Hartgraves, 'Enron: What Happened and What We Can Learn from It', *Journal of Accounting and Public Policy*, 21 (2002), 105–27.

[42] IASCF trustees meeting of 12 June 2002, agenda paper 2, paragraph 31.

[43] AP 7/2002 paper 3. In the Foundation's *Annual Report 2005*, 10, the project is said to have been added to the agenda in June 2003, but see 'IASB New Work Programme', *IASB Insight*, July 2002, 1.

both to ordinary operating subsidiaries and to SPEs. For several years, up to the 2006 MoU, the Board made steady progress by refining its control model and considering how it stood up in a wide range of situations, from inactive majority shareholders to SPEs on autopilot and fiduciary relationships. If progress seemed slow, Jim Leisenring could provide comfort by pointing out that the topic 'had been on FASB's agenda for twenty-three years'.[44]

The Board continued to change its mind on whether it would first establish the meaning of control in general, in a revision of IAS 27 or a new standard, and then develop a separate standard on SPEs, or to aim for a single comprehensive standard. All the while, it was also keeping an eye on the FASB, which did not see FIN46R as necessarily the last word on the subject. The IASB clearly was interested in a converged outcome, but there was no plan agreed with the FASB on how to achieve that. In April 2004, it had been agreed that this was an area where the boards would work 'concurrently' rather than jointly (see Section 5.7.4). In practice, this meant that the FASB was thinking about consolidation, but not very actively, and each board was taking note of what the other was doing.

US GAAP also relied on the concept of control, but it was well known that this carried a different meaning. For instance, the formal criterion of owning a majority of shares was much more important under US GAAP than in IAS 27.[45] It was all too likely that the FASB would not be willing to adopt the IASB's more judgemental approach. In July 2005, the staff warned the Board that several of its tentative decisions taken so far had, in the recent past, been considered but rejected by the FASB. The way the Board's project was going would lead to divergence with US GAAP. According to the staff: 'The Board will need to be confident that the lead it is taking will survive the convergence process.'[46] What that convergence process meant was not so clear, though. During the meeting, Technical Director Liz Hickey described the project as a 'possible future joint project', and said that the boards had agreed 'that they would meet at some point along the project'.[47]

Although the 2006 MoU did indicate a degree of commitment by the FASB, the nature of the project did not change. For the time being, it remained an IASB-only project, not a joint project, although the expectation was that the FASB 'will participate more actively in the project as it develops'.[48] When the IASB would publish its first due process document, the FASB would consider how to respond. The Board was briefed by FASB staff about FIN46R and its problems in order to increase the chances of a converged solution.[49]

By December 2006, the Board had finally made up its mind that the first due process document would be a discussion paper for an integral replacement of IAS 27 and SIC-12, and the staff began its drafting.[50] Why that took more than a year

---

[44] *IStaR*, July 2005, 5.

[45] For a more extensive discussion, see Carrie Bloomer (editor), *The IASC–U.S. Comparison Project: A Report on the Similarities and Differences between IASC Standards and U.S. GAAP*, second edition (Norwalk, CT: FASB, 1999), Chapter 20.

[46] AP 7/2005 paper 4, paragraph 6. [47] *IStaR*, July 2005, 5. [48] AP 4/2006 paper 2.

[49] See the presentation given by FASB staff member Ed Trott in April 2006, AP 4/2006 paper 2 and appendices.

[50] AP 12/2006 paper 6.

is not evident, apart from the inherent complexity of the topic. However, early in 2008, more than six years after Enron, the Board had not yet published anything when the financial crisis once again made off-balance sheet vehicles a central part of the public's perception of what was wrong with accounting. This time, the problem appeared in the guise of the unconsolidated structured investment vehicles by which banks had passed on many assets to third parties, while retaining a residual risk that, in the crisis, frequently turned out to be substantial.

As discussed in Chapter 13, the Board came under strong pressure to accelerate its projects that were particularly relevant in the financial crisis. To Tweedie, this was not unwelcome, as he was always looking for ways to keep his Board moving along. When the Financial Stability Board made it known that the IASB could skip the discussion paper and move directly to an exposure draft on consolidation and SPEs, this may well have reflected a suggestion made by Tweedie himself. Whatever the motivation, by April 2008, the Board had decided that the first document would be an exposure draft.[51]

The FASB was under even stronger pressure to act on off-balance vehicles. If there had been an opportunity during the previous years to achieve convergence at leisure, the boards had let it slip. In October 2008, when the boards met in what was then still one of their half-yearly joint meetings, the FASB had already issued an exposure draft of amendments to FIN46R, and the IASB was about to publish its own exposure draft. The question was raised whether one of the boards might drop its own project and adopt the approach of the other. The problem was that the two projects were different in scope. Whereas the IASB was working on generally applicable consolidation criteria, FIN46R and the proposed amendments applied just to SPEs (variable interest entities, in the FASB's wording). Their specific language could not easily be translated into consolidation criteria for all other situations (voting interest entities, in the FASB's wording).[52] Bob Herz said that the FASB liked the IASB's approach but could not afford to wait. The only thing to do seemed to be that each board would go ahead in the short term, trying to align the expected outcome of FASB's amendment and the IASB's exposure draft as much as possible, and then see what could be done further.[53] Accordingly, the IASB published its exposure draft in December 2008. The FASB published its standard FAS 167 *Amendments to FASB Interpretation No. 46(R)* in June 2009.

The IASB's exposure draft was generally well received. Although there were many calls for more clarification, the approach of developing a general consolidation standard seemed widely supported.[54] It seemed possible to issue a final standard by the end of 2009. That would be an important achievement in the light of calls by the G20 for a rapid response to the financial crisis, with off-balance vehicles identified as a central issue.[55] However, a swift conclusion would not really give the FASB, which had now turned its mind to consolidation criteria applicable to entities other than SPEs, the time to join in the project. Yet in the

[51] AP 4/2008 paper 8A; interview with David Tweedie, 5 June 2013.
[52] AP 10/2008 (joint meeting) paper 3, paragraph 10–11.
[53] *IStaR*, October 2008, joint meeting supplement, 5–7.
[54] AP 5/2009 paper 4A, paragraphs 5–6.   [55] AP 5/2009 paper 4.

revised MoU, issued in September 2008, the boards had committed themselves to finding a strategy to develop a common standard.

The two boards decided in October 2009 that the IASB would wait for the FASB to catch up. The project then became a truly joint project. In close consultation with the IASB's staff, the FASB would issue an exposure draft in the first half of 2010. Both boards would consider the responses, and then move towards final, converged standards in the second half of 2010.[56] The ambition was fitting for the upbeat mood on completion of the MoU in the boards' November 2009 joint reaffirmation of commitment to complete the MoU, discussed above. With the intensified schedule of joint meetings in the first half of 2010, the two boards set off at a high speed, in a few months reaching the point where the FASB staff was ready to prepare its exposure draft (that is, a proposed codification update). The IASB, for its part, agreed to reconsider the kind of consolidation exception for investment companies that was included in US GAAP but which the Board, so far, had not wished to include in its consolidation standard.

But following the May 2010 confrontation between the IASB and the FAF over the work plan (see Section 16.1.3), these ambitions were scaled down. The boards now concluded that they had already reached 'substantially converged' conclusions on SPEs.[57] The FASB did not issue an exposure draft of a general consolidation standard, and the IASB went ahead to publish IFRS 10 in May 2011. An FASB roundtable held later in 2010 on the IASB's near-final draft apparently did not persuade the FASB that it should continue to aim for a general consolidation standard.[58] In 2012 the IASB delivered on its undertaking to consider a consolidation exception for investment companies. Although this removed a difference between IFRSs and US GAAP, a single standard on consolidation had not been achieved.

16.3.2 From Joint Ventures to Joint Arrangements

The IASC's standards inherited by the IASB included a number of accounting treatments that were known to be objectionable to some of the members of the new Board, partly because of their weak conceptual underpinning, partly because they allowed similar situations to be accounted for differently, or because they represented free choices. The members of the Board who had participated in the G4+1 discussions during the 1990s tended to frown on, for instance, LIFO, pooling of interests accounting, and deferred recognition of actuarial gains and losses. Among the items that were soon in the cross-hairs of the Board was the option in IAS 31 to account for joint ventures by means of proportionate consolidation, as an alternative to the equity method. Proportionate consolidation

---

[56] AP 8/2010 (joint meeting) paper 8; AP 1/2010 (observer version) paper 3. See also 'FASB and IASB Reaffirm Commitment to Memorandum of Understanding: A Joint Statement of the FASB and IASB, November 5, 2009', IASB–FASB press release, 5 November 2009.

[57] 'Progress Report on Commitment to Convergence of Accounting Standards and a Single Set of High Quality Global Accounting Standards', joint IASB–FASB statement dated 24 June 2010, 5.

[58] See AP 12/2010 paper 13A (Appendix) for a summary of comments received during the roundtables.

had been found wanting in a G4+1 discussion paper published in 1999.[59] The idea of quickly removing the option of proportionate consolidation was discussed in 2002, but one thing that held the Board back was that it was not convinced of the merits of the equity method either. It would not do to require companies to change their accounting, only to tell them subsequently that their new method was also deficient.[60] Moreover, there were more general issues with respect to joint venture accounting, in particular the question whether the legal form of the arrangement should determine the accounting, as was true under IAS 31.

The Board deferred a decision by asking the Australian Accounting Standards Board (AASB) to undertake a wide-ranging research project on behalf of the IASB. As the AASB built up a fully-fledged team with standard setters from Hong Kong, Malaysia, and New Zealand, the Board continued to vacillate on whether it should undertake a short-term project to eliminate proportionate consolidation. As convergence with the United States became more important, the fact that proportionate consolidation was not, as a rule, allowed under US GAAP acquired more significance, even though it had no implications for the Form 20-F reconciliation of foreign registrants using IFRSs.[61] The AASB presented a set of papers on definitions and classifications of joint ventures in March 2006. It was thanked for its work, and then sidelined, as the Board had recently decided that it would, after all, do a short-term convergence project on removal of proportionate consolidation in the context of the recently agreed MoU work programme with the FASB.[62]

The result was a September 2007 exposure draft on 'joint arrangements', which modified the definitions of the various types of joint arrangements to make the accounting less dependent on legal form, and to remove the proportionate consolidation option for joint ventures.[63] But while it may have seemed obvious to the Board members that use of proportionate consolidation produced results that were inconsistent with the conceptual framework, many of the IASB's constituents were not convinced. Because the method had its supporters, it had been made the benchmark treatment in IAS 31, with the equity method as the allowed alternative. Outside the United States, proportionate consolidation was not unusual. In Canada, it had become mandatory in 1995, at the expense of the equity method. In countries where proportionate consolidation had been in use prior to IFRSs, the practice tended to persist as companies made their choice under IAS 31.[64] A common thread in the comment letters received by the Board, preponderantly from Europe, was that the Board had not provided sufficient justification for the elimination of proportionate consolidation.[65] EFRAG, for instance, provided a detailed rebuttal of the assertion that proportionate

[59] J. Alex Milburn and Peter D. Chant, *Reporting Interests in Joint Ventures and Similar Arrangements* (IASC, 1999).

[60] *IStaR*, December 2002, 23–4; AP 12/2002 paper 9.

[61] AP 11/2004 paper 9; AP 12/2005 paper 10A.

[62] 'Joint Ventures', *IASB Update*, March 2006, 3.

[63] 'ED 9 Joint Arrangements' (IASB, September 2007).

[64] KPMG International Financial Reporting Group/Isabel von Keitz, *The Application of IFRS: Choices in Practice* (London: KPMG IFRG, 2006); Christopher Nobes, 'IFRS Practices and the Persistence of Accounting System Classification', *Abacus*, 47/3 (2011), 267–83.

[65] AP 4/2008 paper 10A.

consolidation was inconsistent with the framework, pointing out that various aspects of the framework, including the definition of control, were still being discussed. Both EFRAG and the AASB questioned the justification in terms of short-term convergence, as they observed that US GAAP did allow proportionate consolidation for certain joint ventures in the oil and gas industry.[66] However, the most fundamental concern appeared to be that the Board had not come up with a sound set of concepts to distinguish among the various types of joint arrangements. After discussion in the Board, David Tweedie concluded that the IASB had 'not got its message across'.[67]

The Board and staff took their time to reconsider the project and to consult with a selection of companies that had written comment letters, in order to get a better understanding of the different kinds of joint arrangements occurring in practice.[68] By the middle of 2009, the essential decisions had been taken, but publication of the standard was delayed by the slow progress on the consolidation standard. The two projects originally had had independent timetables, but now that they both neared completion it was natural to see them as related projects, because the joint arrangements standard depended on the same concept of control that was being developed for consolidation. As seen above, the publication date of IFRS 10 was allowed to slip from late 2009 to May 2011. Given the pressures on its agenda, one can see why the Board did not want to publish the joint arrangements standard first in order to have to modify it shortly afterwards in response to the final modifications of IFRS 10.

The decision to eliminate proportionate consolidation was but briefly discussed again by the Board, following the exposure draft, as most Board members believed they had heard no new arguments.[69] Yet the IASB did modify its message. Whereas the exposure draft had emphasized the 'flaws' of proportionate consolidation and its inconsistency with the conceptual framework, the basis for conclusions of the final standard acknowledged that variation in practice represented differences of view about the best way to portray the economic substance of arrangements. The emphasis in justifying the elimination of proportionate consolidation shifted to the need to achieve identical accounting treatment for equivalent arrangements.[70]

16.3.3 A Difficult European Endorsement

Perhaps the IASB had been well-advised to issue IFRS 10, 11, and 12 as a package in May 2011. The endorsement of the standards for use in the European Union (EU) was a difficult process, finally completed in December 2012. There were

---

[66] Letter from Stig Enevoldsen to IASB, dated 6 February 2008 (CL112), letter from David Boymal to IASB dated 25 January 2008 (CL106), ED 9 comment letters at <http://www.ifrs.org>.

[67] *IStaR*, April 2008, 34.

[68] See AP 5/2009 paper 8B for a review of outreach on this project.

[69] See *IStaR*, April 2008, 31–4. The Board's decision to follow a staff recommendation of further comparative analysis of the equity method and proportionate consolidation (AP 4/2008 paper 10A, paragraph 50) was apparently taken with a view towards better communication of the Board's arguments.

[70] Compare BC9–12 from the September 2007 exposure draft with BC41–4 of IFRS 11.

various reasons for this, including a delay because EFRAG first decided to wait for effects studies promised by the IASB and then, as these did not appear until September, decided to undertake a field study itself.[71] But more importantly, elements of the standards remained controversial, and in particular in France the removal of proportionate consolidation continued to be resented.[72] Allowing the European Commission to submit the standards for endorsement in a package may have helped to argue that any specific drawbacks were outweighed by the benefits of the whole, including the improved disclosures.

When the package was endorsed, it was with an effective date of 1 January 2014, compared to the effective date of 1 January 2013 set by the IASB. This 'temporary carve-out' had been proposed by EFRAG, arguing that companies needed more time to prepare. EFRAG had called on the IASB to defer the effective date, but to no avail, because the IASB had, as before, referred to the urgency of the G20's call for improved standards.[73] Yet, when it came to urgency, it would seem that all parties had forgotten that the original impetus for IFRS 10 had been given by Enron.

16.4 FAIR VALUE MEASUREMENT: LEAPFROGGING TO CONVERGENCE

In May 2011, the IASB issued IFRS 13 *Fair Value Measurement*, a standard with the aim of bringing together in one place all guidance for the measurement of fair value that was hitherto scattered across a number of standards. The concept of fair value has had a long history in the US literature on financial reporting, and it made a modest debut in the IASC's standards in the early 1980s. During the 1990s, it gradually assumed a more prominent role, so that, both in US GAAP and in the IASC's standards, references to fair value began to proliferate. Guidance on how to measure it was not necessarily consistent across the various standards where it was used. It might seem both natural and not too difficult to bring more order to the standards by concentrating all of the relevant guidance in a single document, without changing the application of fair value. Yet what might appear as a simple streamlining operation was complicated by the difficulty of reconciling the requirements of due process with the wish to achieve convergence.

The FASB placed a project of this nature on its agenda in June 2003, and moved quickly to an exposure draft published in June the next year. The IASB followed this development with interest and wished to do something similar, but had some difficulty in finding the proper approach. At the root of the FASB's project was the notion of a 'fair value hierarchy', already established in US GAAP, which distinguished between three levels of inputs to be used in estimating fair values. In order

---

[71] See EFRAG *Annual Review 2011*, 20. The IASB's effects analysis of IFRS 11 appeared in July 2011, that of IFRS 10 in September.

[72] See summary record of the ARC meeting of 7 February 2012, 1–2 <http://ec.europa.eu/internal_market/accounting>.

[73] See 'Endorse, But Not Yet', *World Accounting Report*, May 2012, 5; 'ARC Delays Application Date', *World Accounting Report*, July 2012, 6.

of decreasing preference, these were: observable market prices for identical items, adjusted market prices for similar items, and estimations using valuation techniques. In popular language, the three levels ranged from 'mark-to-market' to 'mark-to-model'. An attempt to clarify this hierarchy in the context of the FASB's business combinations project was then broadened into a more general fair value measurement project.

The IASB saw fair value in broadly similar terms as the FASB, and was working to insert ideas closely related to the FASB's fair value hierarchy into IAS 39, its financial instruments standard. It recognized the merit of the FASB's plan to draft a general fair value measurement standard, but apparently it did not feel in a position in June 2003 to follow the FASB immediately by adding such a project to its agenda. At the suggestion of the staff, the Board adopted the interim step of including the FASB's draft clarification of the fair value hierarchy in its exposure draft on business combinations, in which fair value measurement played a pivotal role.[74]

As seen in Section 12.4, this procedure was not received with favour by many of those who commented on the IASB's business combinations exposure draft, which was published in June 2005. Fair value was a sensitive topic. The IASB was frequently stereotyped by its critics as being inordinately fond of fair value and bent on extending its use throughout the financial statements. To introduce fair value measurement guidance in the form of a consequential amendment to another standard could easily give rise to suspicion that the Board was somehow circumventing due process. Before the comment period was over, the Board agreed in September 2005 that the time had come to add a separate fair value measurement project to its agenda.

By then the FASB was well underway towards publishing its final standard, and the question naturally arose what could be done to achieve a converged outcome. The IASB staff's recommendation was to issue the FASB's standard, when issued, as an IASB exposure draft. The staff—Wayne Upton, one assumes—recognized that this was an unusual procedure. But, having pointed out that the IASB was short of staff resources, it was argued that guidance was urgently needed, if possible in time for the completion of the business combinations project, and that, in the absence of such guidance, companies reporting under IFRSs would be directed to US GAAP anyway under the GAAP hierarchy of IAS 8. The staff stressed that the Board would thoroughly debate all of the issues, but after, rather than before, the exposure draft was published.[75] In the Board, Geoffrey Whittington expressed his astonishment over the proposal to issue a standard developed by another standard setter as an exposure draft, calling it a 'total rejection of due process'. He and Jan Engström voted against the proposal. Others, however, emphasized the quality of the FASB's work or accepted Chairman Tweedie's assurance that the Board would have its debate before a standard was issued.[76]

---

[74] See AP 6/2003 paper 2B for an IASB briefing on the FASB's project as well as the staff's recommendation.

[75] AP 9/2005 paper 12, paragraphs 29–36. Staff contacts listed on the paper were Wayne Upton and Amanda Quiring, who arrived in 2005 at the IASB as an assistant project manager, coming from the FASB staff.

[76] *IStaR*, September 2005, 32.

Based on the assumption that the project would move forward expeditiously, it was included in the February 2006 MoU as one of the few major projects expected to be completed by the end of 2008. But this expectation was short-lived. The 2006 MoU was followed by mounting concerns in Europe that convergence would mean the importation of US GAAP into IFRSs, and the combination of fair value and reliance on an FASB document did not go down well.[77] What did not help was that, in November 2005, the staff of Canada's Accounting Standards Board (AcSB) had published a discussion paper on measurement bases for financial accounting.[78] The AcSB had undertaken to prepare the paper on behalf of the IASB, in its role as a liaison standard setter. The paper came out clearly in favour of fair value even though it was limited in scope to the relatively uncontroversial question of measurement upon initial recognition. The IASB had neither discussed nor endorsed the discussion paper's contents, but it was circulated with an IASB cover and therefore could easily support the assumption that it was just another step in the IASB's promotion of fair value. The IASB was faced with strong calls to open up a more fundamental debate on measurement, something which David Tweedie promised, as part of the conceptual framework project, when appearing before the European Parliament in January 2006.[79]

By June, it was put to the Board that there were 'due process concerns' with respect to the fair value measurement project. The staff reported that 'some constituents' had said that fair value measurement was 'an emotive issue and the [fair value measurement] project may significantly change how fair value is measured in some circumstances'.[80] The Board was aware that even the limited objective of clarifying the meaning of fair value would lead to changes in the practice of fair value measurement. It had kept an eye on the FASB's project, and it knew that the standard shortly to be issued by the FASB would be a substantial document. FAS 157 *Fair Value Measurement* as published in September 2006 ran to over forty pages of detailed guidance, not counting the basis for conclusions. Inevitably, some of this would not be in line with interpretations of the existing fair value guidance in IFRSs. The Board also knew that the FASB's standard would define fair value as an exit price, the price to be received upon selling an asset or to be paid for transferring a liability. Views might differ on the extent to which this merely made explicit what was already assumed in US GAAP, but in IFRSs fair value was defined as the price for which an asset or liability could be exchanged, without differentiating between exit and entry prices. Several Board members were concerned that changing to an exit-price definition would change the substance of the concept, in particular for items such as long-lived tangible assets for which the difference between entry and exit prices might be large.[81]

---

[77] See for instance 'EFRAG: Fair Value Issues', *World Accounting Report*, February 2006, 6.

[78] 'Discussion Paper: Measurement Bases for Financial Accounting—Measurement on Initial Recognition: Prepared by Staff of the Canadian Accounting Standards Board' (IASB, November 2005).

[79] 'Prepared statement of Sir David Tweedie, Chairman of the International Accounting Standards Board before the Economic and Monetary Affairs Committee of the European Parliament, 31 January 2006' <http://www.iasplus.org>.

[80] AP 6/2006 paper 9B, paragraph 5.

[81] See report of Board discussion in *IStaR*, May 2006, 24–6.

Against this background, the Board agreed to change the project plan. It would still issue the FASB's standard with an invitation to comment written by the IASB, but it would issue it as a discussion paper, not as an exposure draft. It was expected that this would prolong the project by another year, so that the objective as stated in the MoU would not be met. Apparently the FASB raised no objections on this point.

Accordingly, the Board published a discussion paper in November 2006, consisting of the full text of FAS 157 and a lengthy invitation to comment, including a recapitulation of all of the existing fair value measurement guidance in IFRSs. The Canadian AcSB's paper was quietly forgotten, after the Board had discussed it once in a meeting.

Because the comment period on the Board's discussion paper—i.e. FAS 157—was extended, it was almost a year later, in October 2007, when the Board began to discuss the comment letters. By then, the so-called credit crunch, the harbinger of the 2008 financial crisis, was already making itself felt, and the use of market prices in fair value measurement was swiftly becoming highly topical. While this was noted by the Board, it did not rush, but proceeded to debate at considerable length the many issues involved in transforming the FASB's standard into an IFRS. As noted above, the Board had promised itself this debate at the start of the project, but it was also something that respondents to the discussion paper urged on the Board. However, respondents also emphasized the importance of a converged outcome, but not in the sense of simply adopting US GAAP. In the staff's summary, it was said: 'many respondents are concerned that, because SFAS 157 was issued so recently, the FASB might be reluctant to change it, and they wonder whether the boards will be able to reach the objective of convergence if the IASB does not accept the Statement as it currently stands. Furthermore, many respondents interpret the issuance of a discussion paper based on a US standard as an indication that the IASB is adopting US GAAP.'[82] The problem of leapfrogging, where one board worked ahead of the other, was apparent: how to reconcile an open-minded due process with a desire to arrive at the conclusions which the other board had already reached?

There were many issues in trying to incorporate FAS 157 in IFRSs, not least because the scope of application of fair value differed significantly as between IFRSs and US GAAP. There was no US GAAP equivalent, for instance, of the fair value measurements for biological assets and property, plant, and equipment in IAS 41 and IAS 16, respectively. But the Board also debated fundamental conceptual issues such as whether and how an entity's own credit risk should be considered when measuring the fair value of a liability. In the course of 2008, the Board worked its way to an exposure draft that might be characterized as an edited version of FAS 157. Although much of the text was identical, there were numerous differences. Some were simple matters of style, such as the replacement of 'should' by 'shall'. But the IASB also inserted new paragraphs with additional clarification. In addition, the draft contained a number of acknowledged differences, which the Board believed would be improvements over FAS 157.[83] The basis for conclusions

---

[82] AP 10/2007 paper 2C, paragraph 7.
[83] ED/2009/5 'Fair Value Measurement' (IASB, May 2009), invitation to comment, question 12, and BC110.

developed for the IASB's exposure draft was largely a new document, although there were instances of 'plagiarism' from FAS 157.

Meanwhile, the financial crisis led to intensifying calls for the IASB to come up with improved guidance on fair value measurement, quickly. As seen in Chapter 13, the IASB responded by installing an Expert Advisory Panel in May 2008, consisting of over twenty representatives of the financial industry, prudential supervisors, and the large audit firms, which issued a report in October with advice on how to apply the existing fair value requirements for financial instruments in situations of illiquid markets. The panel operated independently from the IASB's fair value measurement project, but its deliberations suggested that parts of that project might be brought forward in the form of improved disclosure requirements.[84] In October 2008, the Board published an exposure draft of amendments to IFRS 7 *Financial Instruments: Disclosures* calling for disclosures organized according to the principles of the fair value hierarchy, which was therefore formally introduced into IFRSs when IFRS 7 was amended accordingly in March 2009.

In May 2009, the Board issued its fair value measurement exposure draft. Most respondents still strongly supported the idea of a general standard on fair value measurement. Yet it was clear that there were still divergent views on the nature and purpose of fair value. The identification of fair value with exit price and the fair value measurement of liabilities continued to raise questions. And whereas in Europe the Board was sometimes given credit for its effort to improve on FAS 157, some respondents from the United States were more sceptical and urged the Board to stay close to the language of the American standard.[85] Perhaps the most important among the key messages identified by the staff was that the IASB and the FASB should work together to develop fully converged guidance.[86] This is therefore what the boards set out to do. It required careful planning to meet the June 2011 target date while still ensuring that both boards could satisfy their due process requirements. They had to agree on a text that the IASB could issue as a final standard while doing justice to the comments it had received, and that the FASB would have to expose, but with the prospect of issuing the same final standard as the IASB. In the leapfrogging pattern in which the standard had been developed, this meant that the FASB now had to consider the changes to its standard (by then known as Topic 820 in the FASB's codification) implied by the IASB exposure draft.

The boards largely succeeded in their objective. In May 2011, the IASB published IFRS 13 *Fair Value Measurement* and the FASB published its accounting

---

[84] AP 9/2009 papers and 2B and 4. See also record of Board discussion in *IStaR*, June 2008, 25, where the idea of an earlier disclosure amendment is brought up without a reference to the Expert Advisory Panel.

[85] See e.g. letter from Guido Ravoet and others (European Banking Federation) to David Tweedie dated 28 September 2009, CL124; letter from Gottlieb A. Keller and Peter Baumgartner (SwissHoldings) to IASB dated 25 September 2009, CL152; letter from Matthew L. Schroeder (Goldman Sachs) to IASB dated 28 September 2009, CL110; letter from Arnold Hanish (Financial Executives International) to IASB dated 23 September 2009, CL26; ED/2009/5 comment letters at <http://www.ifrs.org>.

[86] See AP 10/2009 paper 2A for the staff's summary of comment letters.

standards update.[87] The standards were almost identical, apart from some style differences. They differed on a small number of substantive points and disclosure requirements.[88] In terms of convergence, the project had been a success. Yet some in the IASB saw it as an example where convergence with the FASB had led the Board to introduce far more detail into its standards than it would have done by itself. Paul Pacter observed that IFRS 13 was a very long standard 'just to define two words'.[89]

16.5 EMPLOYEE BENEFITS: AN MoU PROJECT WITHOUT THE FASB

In its early years, the IASB had made a stab at reforming accounting for pensions. The main ideas in both IAS 19 *Employee Benefits* and the corresponding standards in US GAAP could be traced back to the 1980s, and were considered in need of review both by the IASB and the FASB. One of the most notable features of both sets of standards was the delayed recognition of actuarial gains and losses on defined benefit plans by a form of income smoothing known as the 'corridor'. As seen in Chapter 5, the IASB had proposed a requirement of immediate recognition of these gains and losses, but had in 2004 settled for an option to do so in other comprehensive income, as an alternative to the deferred recognition approach.

In 2005, it was the FASB's turn. In June of that year, the SEC published a major study on off-balance sheet arrangements and related topics, in fulfilment of the requirements of the Sarbanes-Oxley Act of 2002. One of the SEC recommendations was that accounting for defined benefit plans should be reconsidered, and the SEC's staff made it known that it would like to see the end of the complex smoothing of actuarial gains and losses.[90] The FASB duly added a project to its agenda in November 2005. This was to be a short-term project, to deal with selected issues. The second stage of a more comprehensive review of pension accounting was to follow, if possible together with the IASB, as the SEC had suggested. The FASB was quick to act, and in March 2006 it published an exposure draft in which it proposed that, at least in the balance sheet, the defined benefit liability would be recognized on a current basis, including actuarial gains and losses. For the time being, gains and losses would continue to be recognized on a deferred basis in the income statement, using the existing approach, with the difference recognized temporarily in other comprehensive income.[91]

---

[87] *Fair Value Measurement (Topic 820)*, accounting standards update no. 2011-04 (FASB, May 2011).

[88] IFRS 13, BC236–8.   [89] Interview with Paul Pacter, 15 February 2012.

[90] 'Report and Recommendations Pursuant to Section 401(c) of the Sarbanes-Oxley Act of 2002 on Arrangements with Off-balance Sheet Implications, Special Purpose Entities and Transparency of Filings by Issuers', Securities and Exchange Commission, June 2005, 107–9 <http://www.sec.gov>.

[91] Proposed Statement of Financial Accounting Standards, 'Employers' Accounting for Defined Benefit Pension and Other Postretirement Plans: Amendment of FASB Statements No. 87, 88, 106 and 132(R)', Financial Accounting Series No. 1025-300 (FASB, 31 March 2006).

Accounting for post-employment benefits (or post-retirement benefits in the FASB's vocabulary) had already been noted as a possible convergence project of the IASB and the FASB in 2004, and was listed as one of the projects of the February 2006 MoU. What this would mean in practice for the IASB, given the FASB's plans and work in progress, still had to be determined. When discussing a project plan in the first half of 2006, the IASB decided to take a pragmatic approach. David Tweedie asked the staff not to propose a comprehensive review of pension accounting, but rather a limited improvements project that could be completed within four years.[92] When asked in a Board meeting where the four-year limit came from, Wayne Upton replied 'that it had something to do with the remaining period of service of most of the people [here]'.[93] Evidently, Tweedie was already contemplating the retirement of the founding Board members, most of whom were still in place in early 2006, but all of whom would be gone by the middle of 2011. The question, then, was which package of issues could be addressed in such a four-year project? One option was to mirror the FASB's short-term project. Hans-Georg Bruns, whose main objective was the lifting of the reconciliation requirement, was perhaps the most outspoken proponent of that approach.[94] Most other Board members, however, preferred to make their own selection of issues. If this meant a degree of divergence with US GAAP in the short term, this could be resolved in an as yet vaguely defined second stage in which the boards would work together. The Board therefore agreed on a project scope with two main elements. The first was reconsideration of deferred recognition, including presentation of gains and losses in profit or loss or other comprehensive income. The second element was a reconsideration of the basic dichotomy of defined benefit plans and defined contribution plans, in the light of the growing popularity, mainly in the United States and the United Kingdom, of so-called cash-balance plans. These arrangements, while close to defined contribution plans, did expose employers to a degree of investment risk and would normally have to be classified as defined benefit plans. The FASB had deferred consideration of these plans to its second stage. In addition, the IASB's project would consider aspects of curtailment and settlement and some disclosure improvements.

Before the IASB was truly underway with its project, the FASB concluded its first phase in September 2006 with FAS 158 *Employers' Accounting for Defined Benefit Pension and Other Postretirement Plans*. This standard was in line with its earlier exposure draft. While for many years the second phase continued to be mentioned in the FASB's technical plan, it was without any indication of when the next step might be taken. The FASB explicitly marked it as 'not active' in October 2009.[95] Similarly, while the topic of post-employment benefits continued to be listed in the September 2008 MoU update and the subsequent MoU progress report, it was without any indication of active FASB involvement. This was a MoU project undertaken by the IASB on its own.

The first step was a discussion paper published in March 2008, a large part of which dealt with cash-balance plans, expanded to a broader category of

---

[92] AP 5/2006 paper 5, paragraph 2.   [93] *IStaR*, May 2006, 13.
[94] *IStaR*, July 2006, 11.   [95] See archive of FASB technical plans <http://www.fasb.org>.

'contribution-based promises'. Following the discussion paper, this topic was soon dropped from the scope of the project, as it turned out that most constituents were critical of the Board's initial thoughts on creating a third category of post-employment benefit plans, believing that this might create more problems than it would solve.[96]

The main focus of the IASB's project therefore became the recognition of gains and losses. Here, the Board had spent almost no time in debate before agreeing unanimously, in November 2006, that actuarial gains and losses should be recognized as they occur. The Board had already reached the same conclusion in July 2002 (see Section 5.7.5). The arguments were well-rehearsed, and the staff had relied heavily on the 2002 Board papers to support the identical point that 'the conceptual arguments for immediate recognition are overwhelming'.[97] The staff concluded that 'a substantial majority' of respondents to the discussion paper agreed with the Board, or at least did not oppose it.[98] The strong opposition from preparers that had required the reluctant introduction of a smoothing mechanism, first by the FASB in the 1980s and then by the IASC in the 1990s, had died down. The known views of the SEC and the direction the FASB was taking may have played a role in forming the climate of opinion. More generally, there appeared to be a sense of the inevitable among respondents, a view that the removal of the smoothing mechanism was an idea whose time had come.[99]

The more intractable question was how to present changes in the net defined benefit liability in terms of performance, and it was evident that the support of many constituents for eliminating deferred recognition was conditional on how the presentation issue would be resolved. In the discussion paper, the Board had merely outlined several options, without taking a position. Responses to the discussion paper showed that constituents were very much divided. Following the discussion paper, the initial staff proposal, with which a majority of the Board agreed, was to present all changes—whether related to service costs, to financing costs, or to remeasurements—in profit or loss.[100] The staff and the Board knew that this would run into strong opposition. Tatsumi Yamada, who would consistently support presentation of all components of defined benefit cost in profit or loss, while knowing that this was very unpopular in Japan, was jokingly asked by David Tweedie after the first vote on this point whether he would apply for asylum, as he could not return to Tokyo. Tweedie himself was not in favour of a complete profit or loss presentation. He believed that fluctuations in value were not the same as pension costs, a view reinforced by the gyrations in the pension assets and liabilities of many companies during the financial crisis as a result of swings in interest rates and asset prices.[101] Towards the end of 2009, the issue was

---

[96] AP 11/2008 paper 6, paragraphs 5(e) and 25–43.

[97] Compare AP 7/2002 paper 4D, paragraphs 10–15, with AP 11/2006 paper, paragraphs 12–17. For Board discussion, see *IStaR*, November 2006, 22–3.

[98] AP 11/2008 paper 6, paragraph 16–17.

[99] Interview with Andrea Pryde, 15 February 2012, and with Anne McGeachin, 8 June 2012. However, some advocacy of the corridor method continued, in particular from countries where it was widely used. See 'IAS 19 Volatility Danger', item posted 1 October 2010 <http://www.ipe.com>.

[100] AP 1/2009 paper 16C.

[101] On Yamada, see *IStaR*, January 2009, 55. On Tweedie's views, see *IStaR*, January 2009, 45, and November 2009, 4–5.

reopened. This time, a majority of the Board agreed with a package proposal, supported by Tweedie, that remeasurements should be presented in other comprehensive income, with other comprehensive income and profit or loss presented in a single statement. A month earlier, the Board had agreed to a short-term project aimed at just such a single performance statement, justified in part by the needs of the pensions project (see Section 16.11).[102] The result was that an exposure draft to amend IAS 19, issued in April 2010, was followed a month later by the exposure draft proposing a single performance statement.[103] In the end, the Board did not proceed with a mandatory single performance statement, but it mustered enough votes to approve an amended version of IAS 19, issued in June 2011.

As amended, IAS 19 required immediate recognition of gains and losses on both plan assets and the defined benefit liability. Remeasurements of both plan assets and the defined benefit liability would be presented in other comprehensive income, never to be recycled. For a project undertaken as part of a convergence programme with the FASB, this created a considerable difference with US GAAP in terms of net income: under US GAAP, there was recycling in a pattern determined by the traditional 'corridor' smoothing device.

With the publication of revised IAS 19, the Board achieved a major step forward that it had long wanted to take. Yet not all Board members agreed that the step was indeed forward. Jan Engström and Tatsumi Yamada dissented. Engström objected to the non-recycling of remeasurements, which he believed contributed to the 'gradual erosion of the concept of profit or loss'. Yamada dissented, among other reasons, because of his view that all items related to defined benefit plans should be presented in profit or loss.[104]

Throughout the project, the IASB attempted to steer clear of changing the measurements in the standard, in order to achieve the more limited objective of improved recognition and presentation. Avoiding measurement was not easy, if only because it proved difficult to distinguish remeasurements of plan assets from the investment income earned on those assets. While reporting companies wished to avoid significant fluctuations in profit or loss by reporting volatility in asset values in other comprehensive income, they also wished to offset interest costs on the defined benefit liability in profit or loss by returns on plan assets. IAS 19 had resolved this issue by introducing an expected rate of return on plan assets, but the Board was unable to find an objective way to determine such an expected rate of return. A way out was devised by Board member Stephen Cooper, who proposed to use the discount rate of the defined benefit liability to calculate a net interest item on the net defined benefit liability (that is, the balance of the liability and the plan assets). The difference with the actual change in value of the plan assets would be labelled as remeasurements and, in IAS 19 as finally amended, taken permanently to other comprehensive income. This provided some objectivity, as the discount rate was tied to the rate of interest on high-quality corporate bonds.

---

[102] AP 10/2009 paper 10, paragraph 2; AP 11/2009 paper 7A. For Tweedie's preference among the options presented in the latter paper, see *IStaR*, November 2009, 4–5.

[103] ED/2010/3 'Defined Benefit Plans: Proposed Amendments to IAS 19' (IASB, April 2010), and ED/2010/5 'Presentation of Items of Other Comprehensive Income' (IASB, May 2010).

[104] IAS 19 *Employee Benefits* (IASB, June 2011), DO3 (Engström) and DO10 (Yamada).

But it led Yamada to observe, as one of the reasons for his dissent, that the Board was replacing one smoothing mechanism by another.[105]

16.6 REVENUE RECOGNITION

It may be recalled that in December 2008 the IASB and the FASB concluded several years of deliberations on the topic of revenue recognition with the publication of a joint discussion paper (see Section 12.6). The discussion paper proposed a new general model for revenue recognition. Under this model, revenue was conceived in terms of satisfaction of the performance obligations implied by a sales contract. As these obligations were satisfied by the transfer of assets, the timing of the recognition of revenue was determined by the passing of control over the asset from one party to another. The amount of the performance obligation, and thus the amount of revenue to be recognized, was determined on the basis of the consideration to be received. If a contract consisted of multiple elements, the total consideration had to be allocated to these elements, with revenue recognition determined separately for each element on the basis of the passing of control. For simple retail transactions, this was just a convoluted way of describing age-old practices traditionally explained in terms of the realization convention.[106] However, the novelty and the audacity of the discussion paper was that it aimed to capture the essence of revenue recognition for all contracts with customers. This was significant in particular for US GAAP, where industry-specific guidance was said to be dispersed over more than a hundred different standards and an SEC Staff Accounting Bulletin.[107] This was not true for IFRSs, although it did have separate and inconsistent standards for revenue recognition in general (IAS 18) and for construction contracts (IAS 11). Tentatively, the boards recognized that the model might not be fully applicable to financial instruments, insurance contracts, and leases, but they were not done yet with considering the application of the general revenue model to these specific contracts.

This was therefore the main issue facing the boards and their constituents over the next few years: the idea of a single model was attractive, and the proposal looked reasonable enough in theory, but was it robust enough to deal with the huge variety of contracts underlying the vital 'top line' accounting number in companies' financial statements? Was it really feasible to aim for a single model?

---

[105] For Cooper's first introduction of the idea of calculating interest on a net basis, see *IStaR*, February 2009, 6. On Cooper, see also Stephen Bouvier, 'Corridor Demolished', *Investment & Pension Europe*, December 2010 (<http://www.ipe.com>).

[106] There is a large literature on revenue recognition and the realization concept. See for example Arthur L. Thomas, *Revenue Recognition* (Ann Arbor, MI: Bureau of Business Research, University of Michigan, 1966). For a more recent discussion against the background of the IASB–FASB project, see James A. Ohlson et al., 'Accounting for Revenues: A Framework for Standard Setters', *Accounting Horizons*, 25/3 (September 2011), 577–92.

[107] Discussion paper 'Preliminary Views on Revenue Recognition in Contracts with Customers' (IASB, December 2008), paragraph 1.3. See the SEC's Staff Accounting Bulletin 101 issued in 1999, later corrected as 104 in 2003, on revenue recognition.

How much specific guidance would it need to work? And, would it result in more relevant information for users of financial statements compared to recognition criteria that were tailor-made for specific industries? These were the terms in which the staffs summarized the essence of the more than 200 comment letters sent to either one or both of the boards in response to their joint discussion paper.[108]

Given the universal relevance of revenue recognition, it is interesting to consider briefly the geographical provenance of the comment letters. As analysed by the IASB's staff, the United States and Canada, taken together, and Europe made up the lion's share with 36 per cent each. Australia and New Zealand followed with a combined total of 9 per cent. With another 6 per cent classified as 'multinational', this meant that very few came from all other regions and jurisdictions.[109] One of the justifications for accelerating the MoU in 2008 was that several countries were moving towards IFRS adoption in 2011, but judging from this geographical distribution of comment letters, this had not yet translated into widespread participation of constituents from these countries in the IASB's processes. For Japan, it might perhaps be assumed that individual constituents of various kinds felt that they were well represented by the five letters from the Life Insurance Association of Japan, the Security Analysts Society of Japan, the Accounting Standards Board of Japan, Nippon Keidanren, and the Japanese Institute of Certified Public Accountants, although this did not preclude one company, Fujitsu, from writing its own letter.[110] South Africa accounted for all of the five letters received from Africa. The Mexican Institute of Public Accountants was the only one to respond from all of Latin America. No letters were received from any company or other organization in India.[111] No letter was received from mainland China, although that country considered itself substantially converged with IFRSs.

Before the comments came in, the boards had already started to discuss topics not fully developed in the discussion paper, and in line with the content of the responses; they spent most of 2009 and the first half of 2010 turning the discussion paper into as robust an exposure draft as possible, without changing the fundamental approach. This meant lengthy debates on topics such as the definition of 'control', the segmentation of contracts, and the identification of separate performance obligations, uncertain consideration, warranties, and rights of return. A topic that had already occupied much board time prior to the issue of the discussion paper was the remeasurement of the performance obligation on onerous contracts, an exception to the general principle that revenue should be based on the consideration (transaction price). This was a delicate subject because it related directly to the ongoing reconsideration of IAS 37, on provisions. As already discussed in Chapter 12, the IASB was fully aware that establishing basic recognition and measurement principles for non-financial liabilities was the key to many of its projects, but this key remained elusive.

---

[108] AP 7/2009 paper 14A, paragraphs 5–17.   [109] AP 7/2009 paper 14A, paragraph 3.

[110] CL52, CL90, CL98, CL99, CL101, and CL20, respectively, as classified at <http://www.fasb.org>. Comment letters for this joint project were published on the FASB's website.

[111] CL5, CL26, and CL37 were apparently from individuals in India.

At a general level, one might therefore say that the publication of a joint exposure draft in June 2010 and the comments it elicited were a repeat performance of the discussion paper. Again, many respondents agreed with the general model but called for more guidance on control and identifying separate performance obligations. Again, many respondents questioned whether the proposals would amount to a significant improvement over existing standards, and whether they might not reduce comparability within industries: it was clear that many respondents worried about the implications for their particular industry.[112]

At this stage, the difference between the FASB's constituents and those of the IASB began to look more pronounced. This was apparent from the distribution of the comment letters, pooled across both boards. The absolute number of comment letters from Europe had remained almost constant, but the number from Canada and the United States (mainly the latter) had increased ten-fold, thus making up almost three-quarters of the approximately 975 comment letters received.[113] Even allowing for a letter-writing campaign by private US construction companies, on which the FASB had added a specific question in its version of the exposure draft, this was a large shift. Moreover, the staff noted that 'the FASB's constituents seemed to be least convinced of the need for change'. They ascribed this to the introduction of the FASB's Codification, which presumably had made the complex industry guidance more easily accessible, and to the fact that the limited guidance in IFRSs left more scope for improvement.[114]

As to the world beyond Europe, the United States, and Canada, one could now see that South Korea (seven letters) began to show an interest in the run-up to mandatory use of IFRSs in that country in 2011. With some twenty letters from Japan, individual companies and private persons slowly began to emerge from behind the organizations that had hitherto provided collective responses. China remained heavily centralized, though, with a single comment letter from the Chinese Accounting Standards Committee. The response from Latin America remained desultory with just three letters, from the Mexican and Brazilian accounting standard setters and the Brazilian association of listed companies, Abrasca.[115]

During the first half of 2011, the boards discussed many modifications to the exposure draft in a tightly planned series of meetings. By then, Tweedie had privately given up hope that financial instruments and insurance contracts could be finished by June, but he believed there was still a good chance for revenue recognition, as well as for leases.[116] The boards did reach agreement on most changes that had to be made to the exposure draft, but the crucial question then became whether these changes should be re-exposed or whether the boards could proceed to issue a final standard. This question was discussed in June, when all of the redeliberations were complete. The boards agreed with the assessment of the

---

[112] AP 12/2010 paper 3A.

[113] AP 12/2010 paper 3A reports 986 comment letters. However, AP 11/2013 paper 7A, paragraph 9, reports 974 letters, corresponding to the comment letter archive at <http://www.fasb.org>.

[114] AP 12/2010 paper 3A, paragraph 15.

[115] CL389 (CASC, China), CL558 (CINIF, Mexico), CL587 (CPC, Brazil), and CL575 (Abrasca) <http://www.fasb.org>.

[116] Interview with David Tweedie, 5 June 2013.

staffs that a re-exposure was not necessary because the changes that were made all resulted from extensive consultations with constituents and did not introduce substantively new elements.[117] The boards were indeed commended for listening carefully to all the feedback received and for making many changes in response.[118] However, this led some constituents to argue that a further round of exposure was in order. Undoubtedly to Tweedie's disappointment, it was decided to re-expose. Reasons given during the meeting of the boards in June included the significance of the revenue number, and to preclude opposition to the standard on the grounds of insufficient due process.[119] A revised exposure draft was issued in November 2011, but then the project entered a protracted phase of reconsideration. After a seemingly endless series of delays, a converged standard was finally published in May of 2014.[120] The long wait did not diminish the achievement. *The Economist* hailed the standard as 'the biggest success yet in a decades-long effort to standardise company accounts worldwide'.[121]

16.7 LEASES

When the IASB was founded, accounting for leases had for more than twenty years been dominated by the approach embodied in FAS 13 *Accounting for Leases* (1976). The logic of FAS 13 had been adopted by the IASC in IAS 17 *Accounting for Leases* (1982). It was based on a symmetrical treatment by lessees and lessors who were to use the same criteria to classify lease contracts as either operating leases or finance leases. Lessors and lessees accounted for finance leases as the equivalent of a sale, and accounted for operating leases as executory contracts. The practical implication of these accounting standards was that many leases did not qualify for capitalization on the balance sheet of lessees and that, as was often asserted, an important activity of the leasing industry was to structure contracts deliberately so as to avoid capitalization. As with many other topics that ended up on the IASB's agenda, accounting for leases had been explored by the G4+1 in the 1990s. Two reports had advocated that the distinction between operating and finance leases was arbitrary and should be abandoned. Instead, a single method of accounting for leases should be developed under which all rights and obligations arising out of lease contracts should be recognized and measured at fair value.[122]

The initial Board was sympathetic to the idea of revisiting lease accounting. Warren McGregor had been the principal author of the first G4+1 discussion paper, and David Tweedie's standing joke that one of his big ambitions was to fly on an airplane that actually appeared on the airline's balance sheet was well

---

[117] AP 6/2011 paper 4C.

[118] Lynne Triplett and Ryan Brady, 'Revenue Recognition: Comment Letters Help to Shape Future Guidance', *Financial Executive*, 27/8 (October 2011), 30–3; 'Revenue Recognition and Leases: Controversial Changes Drive the Discussion', *CPA Journal*, 81/8 (August 2011), 40–3.

[119] See the report of the Board meeting in *IFRS Monitor*, June 2011, 55–7.

[120] IFRS 15 *Revenue from Contracts with Customers* (IASB, May 2014).

[121] 'Truthful Top Lines; Company Accounts', *The Economist*, 31 May 2014, 59–60.

[122] Warren McGregor, 'Accounting for Leases: A New Approach' (IASC, 1999); Hans Nailor and Andrew Lennard, 'Leases: Implementation of a New Approach' (IASC, 2000).

known.[123] Yet the Board did not immediately place the topic on its agenda. Instead, it looked to the UK Accounting Standards Board (ASB) to conduct a research project on the basis of responses to the G4+1 papers, the second of which had been authored by ASB staff. In 2003 and 2004, the Board regularly discussed papers in which the ASB developed the implications of a single model for all lease contracts, with a view towards an exposure draft to be issued in 2007, perhaps preceded by a discussion paper in 2005.[124] From the ASB's point of view, it was a joint ASB–IASB project, and not just a matter of servicing the IASB. So when it proved difficult to reach agreement between the boards on several issues, the project began to falter.[125] There were no signs of activity on the project during 2005, and it would seem that plans for cooperation with the ASB were once again, as in the case of the performance presentation project (see Section 5.5.2), overtaken by the growing importance of convergence with US GAAP.

Just when the IASB and the FASB began to consider the implications of the SEC chief accountant's roadmap published in April 2005 (see Chapter 8), the SEC published its study on off-balance sheet arrangements and related topics, referred to above. The study noted that, under FAS 13, just a fraction of the total value of lease contracts, perhaps not more than 4 to 8 per cent, was actually shown on lessees' balance sheets. It was also noted that the 'all or nothing' nature of lease classification meant that very small differences in the economic substance of contracts could lead to vastly different accounting treatments. In FAS 13 (but not in IAS 17) the lease classification criteria had been elaborated in a number of quantitative tests, for instance that, if the present value of the minimum lease payments were equal to or greater than 90 per cent of the fair value of the leased asset, the lease should be classified as a finance lease (capital lease, in terms of FAS 13). Rules such as these had become notorious as 'bright line rules', encouraging the structuring of contracts to obtain specific accounting results. Following Enron and the other scandals that had led to the Sarbanes-Oxley Act, the removal of such rules from US GAAP had become an important desideratum of the SEC. The SEC recommended that the FASB undertake a project to reconsider lease accounting, preferably together with the IASB.[126] This was something the two boards could not ignore, and the topic of leases was duly inscribed in the work plan of the February 2006 MoU as one which the two boards would consider adding to their agenda.

When leases returned to the Board in March 2006 it was in the form of a proposal for a joint project with the FASB, 'picking up from the work carried out by the ASB'.[127] The ASB made one of its staff members, Simon Peerless, available

---

[123] See for instance Tweedie's comment in *International Accounting Standards: Opportunities, Challenges, and Global Convergence Issues*, Hearing before Subcommittee on Securities and Insurance and Investment of the Committee on Banking, Housing, and Urban Affairs, United States Senate, 24 October 2007 <http://www.gpo.gov>.

[124] See AP 5/2003 paper 13 and comments by Andrew Lennard in November 2003 Board meeting, as reported in *IStaR*, November 2003, 8.

[125] Interview with Andrew Lennard, 13 October 2008.

[126] 'Report and Recommendations Pursuant to Section 401(c) of the Sarbanes-Oxley Act of 2002', 60–5 and 105–7.

[127] AP 3/2006 paper 4A.

to the IASB on a part-time basis to work on the leases project. The ASB thus resigned itself to a servicing role.

The IASB and the FASB allowed themselves a slow start, taking time to convene an eighteen-member joint advisory group.[128] Board discussions began in 2007, and led to swift agreement to explore a single accounting model for all leases.[129] In this 'right-of-use' model, leases were viewed as rights to use an asset, and these rights would be recognized on the balance sheet of lessees. Hence, all leases would be capitalized by lessees, although often for less than the full value of the underlying assets, depending on the duration of the lease.

The leasing industry was known to be a formidable lobbyist, and it was not reticent in making known its view on the project.[130] A position paper by six leasing associations from Europe, North America, and Australia published in April 2007 showed the industry as not simply arguing for the status quo, or against any increased capitalization of leases. The leasing associations were presumably as aware as the boards that it was common for financial analysts to adjust balance sheets for non-capitalized leases on the basis of information from the footnotes.[131] They would also have been aware of the SEC's views. They therefore drew the battle lines accordingly. If there was to be a single leasing model, the boards should carefully consider the scope. It was suggested they should exclude short-term leases involving small sums of money from the definition of a lease. The boards should consider avoiding complex measurement rules for simple leases. And, not least, the impact on profit or loss of leases currently classified as operating leases should not change when these contracts were capitalized.[132]

The boards attempted to work out the single right-of-use model to ensure it could handle the variety of lease contracts encountered in practice. This was not easy, and the boards found it challenging to deal even with relatively common features such as renewal options and variable lease payments. Moreover, the implications of the model for lessors were not as straightforward as for lessees: to what extent, if any, should the leased asset be derecognized from the balance sheet of the lessor? Or should lessors recognize a performance obligation, in line with the ongoing work on revenue recognition?[133] At this point, while plans were being made for more extensive consideration of these issues, the question of

---

[128] 'IASB and FASB Announce Members of International Working Group on Lease Accounting', IASB–FASB press release dated 7 December 2006.

[129] See AP 3/2007 paper 12 B for the staff recommendation to pursue the right-of-use model.

[130] See for instance Stephen A. Zeff, 'Lobbying on Lessee Accounting in 1972–73, and the Role of the SEC', *World Accounting Report*, August/September 2012, 9.

[131] See for example Jonathan Weil, 'How Leases Play a Shadowy Role in Accounting', *The Wall Street Journal*, 22 September 2004 (<http://online.wsj.com>).

[132] 'Issues Raised by the Joint IASB/FASB Leasing Project', discussion paper dated 27 March 2007 by the UK Finance and Leasing Association, Leaseurope, the US Equipment Leasing and Finance Association, the British Vehicle Rental and Leasing Association, the Australian Equipment Lessors Association, and the Canadian Finance & Leasing Association <http://www.leaseurope.org>. The Leaseurope website shows a publication date of 1 April 2007.

[133] The emergence of a need to reconsider lessor accounting is noted in AP 12/2007 paper 11, page 28; the problem is described in AP 4/2008 paper 3, paragraph 48.

accelerating the completion of the MoU came up early in 2008.[134] While no target date for a final standard on leasing had been set, it seemed that a curtailment of the project was necessary for it to be completed in 2011. Based on the recommendations of the 'gang of four' (see Section 12.2.3), the boards agreed that consideration of lessor accounting would be deferred.[135] This was a major simplification, because it was on lessor accounting that the project was breaking new ground, compared to the earlier G4+1 papers. For lessee accounting, it was agreed not to develop a new model from scratch, but to apply the existing model for finance leases to operating leases, with modifications where necessary.

While simplifications such as these could be seen as necessary to achieve the 2011 target, there may also have been a certain impatience on the part of David Tweedie. In a meeting with EFRAG in May 2008, he gave the usual justification for accelerating the MoU in terms of countries moving to IFRSs in 2011 and the SEC's consideration of domestic use of IFRSs, but he was reported to have observed that: [136]

> in undertaking this work [i.e. the MoU work plan] they had had to adopt the FASB style of working, which involved no peeking ahead—they took things issue by issue. That seemed to us to be taking us far too long, and the Board felt that future developments would have to be done more quickly.... He said he thought that projects suffered from scope growth ... and that they could do things more quickly if they cut down the scope. Leasing was a good example. The US leasing industry was worth US$600bn a year, but the liabilities were not being shown in balance sheets. The Board could spend seven years debating details like renewal options in leases, but instead they could say that the main objective was just to get liabilities reported in the balance sheet.

A joint discussion paper on the basis of the simplified approach to the project was published in March 2009.[137] However, just before the discussion paper was issued, the FASB made known its view that there should, after all, be a discussion of lessor accounting in the paper, because it would otherwise be difficult to say something about sub-leases. The IASB would rather have left sub-leases out of the scope of the discussion paper altogether, but agreed with the addition of a high-level paragraph on lessor accounting after it had been reassured by the staff that this would cause only a minor delay in the publication of the discussion paper.[138]

There was no shortage of critical comments on the discussion paper, but the boards drew the conclusion that the respondents thought that, in terms of overall approach, they were on the right track.[139] That may not have been an easy

---

[134] The December 2007 Technical Plan update (AP 12/2007 paper 11) shows continued Board discussions in the first half of 2008, yet the leases project was not discussed, other than for planning purposes, between October 2007 and July 2008.

[135] See AP 4/2008 paper 3, paragraphs 49–53, and AP 6/2008 paper 13A.

[136] 'EFRAG Questions Future Programme', *World Accounting Report*, May 2008, 9.

[137] Discussion paper DP/2009/1 'Leases: Preliminary Views' (IASB, March 2009).

[138] AP 1/2009 paper 13. See also *IStaR*, January 2009, 47.

[139] See AP 9/2009 paper 6A for the staff summary of comment letters. According to survey results collected in the first half of 2010, 82 per cent of US chief financial executives of public companies supported capitalization of leases, 'National CFO Survey Finds Majority Support Reforming Lease Accounting; Don't Agree on Measurement', Grant Thornton press release dated 27 May 2010 <http://www.grantthornton.com> accessed through web.archive.

conclusion to draw, as respondents who claimed to support the boards' approach in general could still advocate changes, in particular to the scope of the proposed standard, that would result in the continued non-capitalization of many operating leases under a different name. Although the number of user respondents (five out of 290) was as usual very small, it may have been a matter of comfort to the boards that they were all in favour of the right-of-use model. The boards therefore continued with refining their approach, both in terms of scope and application, and in terms of the ever vexing question of renewal options.

Nearly all of the respondents who commented on the decision to leave lessor accounting out of the scope of the paper expressed their disapproval. Leaseurope, the main European leasing association, lodged a formal due process complaint with the IASC Foundation trustees: it had objected to the original decision to remove lessor accounting from the scope of the project, but was now even more aggrieved to see lessor accounting brought in at short notice, with the possibility that the boards might move to an exposure draft on lessor accounting without a proper discussion paper on the subject.[140] Leaseurope had correctly noted that, on lessor accounting, the boards had already changed tack, and were bringing lessor accounting back into the scope of the project. During the comment period, staff had already been put to work on developing a complete set of proposals for lessor accounting. The burden was shared in that the FASB staff took the lead on lessor accounting, while the IASB staff worked mainly on lessee accounting.[141] The IASC Foundation trustees apparently accepted Tweedie's assurance that, even without a discussion paper, there would be sufficient industry consultation on lessor accounting.[142]

From November 2009 on, when the IASB and the FASB redoubled their efforts to achieve the targets of the MoU, the boards worked at high speed to develop an exposure draft, which they published in August 2010. While there was a prevailing and not unjustified perception that the IASB, during these years, rarely achieved its own targets, this exposure draft was published in line with the planning envisaged in 2008.[143] As expected, one of the central issues in the exposure draft was accounting for lessors, for which there were two contending approaches. One was to derecognize the leased asset in whole or in part, and to substitute a receivable. The other was to recognize a performance obligation, representing the commitment to allow the lessee to use the asset, again offset by a receivable. The FASB was in favour of the performance obligation approach. So, it appeared, was a majority of the IASB. However, David Tweedie was not present when this point was tentatively settled, and during a subsequent meeting he exercised his chairman's privilege to reopen the issue. This was typically not allowed to the other Board members in the rush to complete the MoU: once they had lost a vote, they were expected to move on with the rest of the Board.[144]

---

[140] Letter from Tanguy van de Werve and Mark Venus to Gerrit Zalm and Antonio Vegezzi, dated 24 March 2009, IASCF trustees meeting of 6–8 July 2009, agenda paper 6C(i).

[141] AP 9/2009 paper 6B; see also *IStaR*, January 2009, 48.

[142] IASCF trustees meeting of 6–8 July 2009, minute 9.

[143] The revised work plan established in June 2008 envisaged an exposure draft in '2010', which was subsequently refined to the first half of 2010, then to June 2010. See AP 10/2008 paper 10A, AP 1/2009 paper 8A, and the work plan dated 12 April 2010 as posted on <http://www.ifrs.org>.

[144] See 'Boards Compare Financial Instruments Notes', *World Accounting Report*, August 2008, 3.

In this case, Tweedie's intervention may have been justified in the sense that, as the boards reconsidered the two approaches, they gained more insight into the drawbacks of each, and found it increasingly difficult to choose. Each method could yield results with which the boards were not comfortable. In the case of long-term leases of land, for example, the performance obligation approach might mean that the land remained on the balance sheet of the lessor, with a receivable and offsetting performance obligation unwinding over, say, 99 or 999 years. The partial derecognition approach implied that, depending on the length of the lease, Tweedie's famous aircraft might appear on no balance sheet at all, as the lessee would recognize a right-of-use asset and the lessor a residual asset.[145] In May and June 2010, as the exposure draft was nearing completion, the boards were still considering this elementary question, with some last-minute drafting being done during meetings. The IASB began to think about a hybrid model. As the derecognition approach allowed the recognition of day-one profits, it appeared appropriate for manufacturer and dealer lessors. The performance obligation approach could then be used in other cases. It proved difficult, however, to define acceptable criteria to determine which model should be applied, and it did not escape the IASB's notice that they risked replacing the troublesome distinction between operating and finance leases by a very similar and equally troublesome distinction. One of the reasons for the FASB's doubts about the derecognition approach was precisely its potential for excessive upfront revenue recognition, yet it finally accepted a hybrid approach. Partly, this may have been for the sake of convergence, and partly in recognition of the fact that an undiluted performance obligation approach was not without problems either.[146]

After the boards toyed with a business-model criterion, an idea that had gained currency with IFRS 9 (see Section 13.12), they finally chose to distinguish the two approaches on the basis of 'exposure to significant risks or benefits associated with the underlying asset'. That was not identical to the criterion for distinguishing operating and finance leases in IAS 17, but it came close enough for the project manager, Rachel Knubley, to observe at one point that 'they could be accused of not changing the standard at all except for requiring performance obligation accounting for operating leases'.[147] The August 2010 exposure draft was agreed with a unanimous vote of the two boards.

The complete arsenal of outreach formats that the IASB and the FASB had at their disposal was now deployed, showing the extent to which accounting standard setting had evolved from the days when due process amounted to little more than sending out an exposure draft and waiting for the comment letters to arrive. From the publication of the leases exposure draft to January 2011, the boards held seven roundtables and fifteen preparer workshops (in London, Melbourne, Norwalk, São Paulo, Seoul, Tokyo, and Toronto), and members and staff of both boards participated in over 200 events such as conferences, industry forums, investor calls, and meetings with individual organizations or groups. They sent

---

[145] The examples were among several provided to the Board in AP 6/2010 paper 3D.

[146] For reports on these meetings, see 'Insurance Dominates Proceedings Again', *World Accounting Report*, July 2010, 4, and 'Struggling to Meet the Deadline', *World Accounting Report*, July 2010, 2. For a round-up of views of both IASB and FASB board members, see *IFRS Monitor*, June 2010, 56–9.

[147] *IFRS Monitor*, June 2010, 30.

out questionnaires to lessors and lessees, webcasts and podcasts were made available, and articles were published in professional journals and online.[148] In addition, the staffs engaged in field testing, and the IASB discussed the proposals with its standing consultative groups of users and preparers and at a World Standard Setters meeting.

During the first months of 2011, the boards worked intensively to re-deliberate the proposals in the light of all of the intelligence received, including 760 comment letters. The idea that there might be merit in having lessees capitalize more of their leases appeared to be widely accepted by now, although the question of whether such a change was worth the cost continued to be raised. As already shown by the earlier comments from the leasing industry, the discussion was shifting towards the scope of the standard and the definition of a lease, i.e. whether some contracts hitherto classified as operating leases might be left out of the standard altogether, and to a new issue: the pattern of expense recognition on capitalized leases. In addition, the old question of renewal options was still not settled.[149]

With respect to lessor accounting, the transparency of the boards' proceedings had made it well known that the hybrid model of the exposure draft had been decided on at the last moment. It was not surprising that 'Many constituents noted that the lessor accounting proposed in the ED is less developed than the lessee accounting model'.[150] But the boards moved ahead. The plan of having at least the ballot on a standard in June, with publication later that year, was maintained until April.[151] But before that time, it became ever clearer that the boards were willing to contemplate significant changes to the exposure draft, making it more likely that there should be another exposure draft, thus pushing the completion of the project into the more distant future.[152] It would once more seem that the IASB had learned to listen. As observed in *World Accounting Report*:[153]

> The accepted wisdom about the IASB's due process has come to be that anyone wanting the Board to change its collective mind on a project needed to intervene after publication of a preliminary views discussion paper. Thereafter the Board would proceed to an exposure draft, and the exposure draft would differ little from the final standard unless people could produce new arguments. However, the major projects that both IASB and FASB are addressing at the moment are proving to be an exception. In revenue recognition and leasing the Boards have shown a willingness to change their approach from what was in the exposure draft.

As seen above, the boards decided in June 2011 to re-expose their proposals on revenue recognition. Because it was believed to be important that the standard on leases would be consistent with the revenue standard, this implied that the leases

---

[148] See AP 10/2010 paper 15 and AP 1/2011 paper 5A for an overview of activities.

[149] See AP 1/2011 paper 5B for the staff's identification of the main issues raised during outreach.

[150] AP 1/2011 paper 8, paragraph 4.

[151] See IASB work plan as of 28 March 2011 <http://www.ifrs.org> accessed through web.archive.

[152] See e.g. 'Vorschlag zur Leasing-Bilanzierung nach IFRS sollte gründlich überarbeitet werden', *Börsen-Zeitung*, 8 April 2011, 4. See also letter from global leasing associations to Fujinuma and Glauber, dated 30 March 2011 <http://www.leaseurope.org>.

[153] 'Significant Changes in View', *World Accounting Report*, February 2011, 2.

project would be delayed as well. It would take until May 2013 for the boards to issue a new exposure draft.

16.8 FINANCIAL INSTRUMENTS

It was shown in Chapter 12 how the IASB and the FASB had set out on a project to develop a new, comprehensive, and converged standard on accounting for financial instruments. In Chapter 13, we discussed how this plan was overturned by the financial crisis and how both boards struggled in 2008 and 2009 with intense pressure to make short-term amendments to their respective standards, and how, during 2009, each charted its own course towards more fundamental reform of financial instruments accounting. The situation early in 2010 was not at all propitious from the point of view of convergence.

It may be recalled that the IASB had adopted a phased approach. In November 2009, it had issued IFRS 9 *Financial Instruments*, a partial standard dealing with the recognition and measurement of financial assets. With this standard, the IASB had nailed its colours to the mast, in that it established that accounting for financial instruments would in the long term remain characterized by a mixed-measurement approach, with some financial instruments measured at fair value, with value changes normally recognized in profit or loss, and others at amortized cost. While IFRS 9 laid out the groundwork for a new financial instruments standard, work on a number of vital, complex, and controversial topics was still in progress, including recognition and measurement of financial liabilities, de-recognition, impairment of financial assets, and hedge accounting.

The FASB, meanwhile, had decided not to approach financial instruments in phases, and in May 2010 it issued a comprehensive exposure draft covering not only recognition and measurement but also impairment and hedge accounting. On recognition and measurement, it now lagged the IASB, which had already issued a completed standard. On impairment, both boards now had exposure drafts outstanding, but based on different principles. And on hedge accounting the FASB had leapfrogged the IASB, which would not issue an exposure draft until December 2010. The FASB's exposure draft was based on a principle adopted by the FASB, in July 2009, that almost all financial instruments should be measured at fair value, with some value changes recognized in profit or loss and others in other comprehensive income.

To bring the two boards together again was a challenge. In their first quarterly MoU progress report published in April 2010, the boards described their goal with respect to financial instruments, not in terms of arriving at a common standard, but in the more limited terms of 'improvements . . . that will foster international comparability'. They acknowledged that circumstances had forced them into different timetables, and they asserted that they would work together by publishing each other's proposals and by discussing together the comment letters and other feedback received. They expressed confidence in their ability to work together and to publish final standards in the first half of 2011, but they added:

'there is no guarantee we will be able to resolve all, or any, of our differences on this project.'[154] A few days later, Mario Draghi, the chairman of the Financial Stability Board (FSB), echoed the sentiment in his cover letter accompanying the FSB's progress report on the global regulatory reform agenda to the G20 finance ministers and central bank governors, meeting in Washington in April 2010: 'there is a very material risk that the two standard setters may end up with large divergences in accounting for financial instruments.'[155]

Divergence of standards did not just worry the regulators. As an illustration of how interconnected the world of accounting standards had become, some cross-listed companies in Japan faced the prospect that their right to use US GAAP for domestic filing purposes would end in 2016 (see Section 15.5). For these companies, the diverging paths of the IASB and the FASB on financial instruments were a reason for considering an early move to IFRSs, in order to avoid a costly double change in accounting.[156]

Until June 2011, the two boards struggled valiantly but ultimately unsuccessfully to move closer together in what was not so much a single project, but rather a flotilla of subprojects. As will be seen in the following review, the task proved Sisyphean in that progress towards convergence on some subtopics went hand in hand with new difficulties in others. By June 2011, the boards had, as yet, little to show for their labours. The FASB had not proceeded to issue a standard on the basis of its May 2010 exposure draft, and would re-expose important elements in 2012 and 2013. The IASB made some further additions to IFRS 9, but the standard was by no means complete. The IASB would propose, in August 2011, to defer the effective date of the entire standard to 1 January 2015. The EU had not yet endorsed IFRS 9, thus preventing adoption even on a voluntary basis. While IFRS 9 could be applied on a voluntary basis in jurisdictions such as Australia, Hong Kong, and Japan, its distant effective date and the fact that it was still incomplete deterred most companies from doing so. Around the world, accounting for financial instruments continued for the time being in the mould established by the FASB and the IASC in the late 1990s.

16.8.1 Mixed Measurement or Fair Value

While the IASB's choice of a mixed-measurement approach for what would become IFRS 9 was generally welcomed, both financial institutions and prudential regulators watched the Board's actions with suspicion for signs that the Board was attempting to change the mix of fair value and amortized cost measurement. The Basel Committee on Banking Supervision had taken a position in August 2009 with a statement on 'guiding principles for the replacement of IAS 39' in which it

---

[154] 'IASB and FASB Commitment to Memorandum of Understanding': Quarterly Progress Report, 31 March 2010' (IASB–FASB, 14 April 2010).

[155] Letter from Mario Draghi to G20 ministers and governors, dated 19 April 2010 <http://www.financialstabilityboard.org>.

[156] Interview with Yoshitaka Kato and Akashi Kohno, 3 February 2011.

asserted that the mixed-measurement approach of the IASB's July 2009 exposure draft 'should not result in an expansion of fair value accounting'.[157]

In that light, it is not surprising that the FASB's exposure draft proposing fair value measurement for all financial instruments met with strong opposition, in particular from the US banking industry. Already in August 2009, the American Bankers Association had questioned whether the efforts of the IASB and the FASB 'are driven by a search for simplicity, transparency, and accuracy, or by an appetite to expand fair value accounting, no matter the implications'.[158] The sudden retirement of Bob Herz as FASB chairman in August 2010, and the announcement that the FASB would be restored from five to its original seven members provoked immediate speculation about the future development of the financial instruments proposals. That two of the five FASB members had opposed the board's full fair value proposals was apparent from the exposure draft, but it was also known that Herz had tipped the balance in the five-member board in favour. Leslie Seidman, appointed as acting chairman, had been in the minority, with Lawrence Smith.[159] Rumours could be heard that the reshuffling of the FASB board was directly related to the controversy, but one did not have to believe them to see that the tide of opinion against the proposals was so strong that the FASB, recomposed or not, would have to reconsider them.[160] Opponents of an expansion of fair value were not just to be found in the banking sector, but also included users of financial statements. Regulators also weighed in. In its November 2010 progress report to the G20, the Financial Stability Board reiterated its earlier view that it was 'particularly supportive of standards that would not expand the use of fair value in relation to the lending activities (involving loans and investments in debt instruments) of financial intermediaries'.[161] Around the turn of the year from 2010 to 2011, it was widely assumed that the FASB would be moving in the direction of the IASB's approach, with a greater emphasis on amortized costs.[162]

Following publication of IFRS 9 in November 2009, the IASB did not reconsider the basic mixed-measurement approach, and waited for the FASB to see the light. Meanwhile, it did have work of its own to do on the recognition and

---

[157] 'Guiding Principles for the Replacement of IAS 39' (Basel Committee on Banking Supervision, [27 August 2009]) <http://www.bis.org>. See also 'Regulatory Perspectives on the Changing Accounting Landscape', speech by FED Governor Elizabeth E. Duke, 14 September 2009 <http://www.federalreserve.gov>.

[158] American Bankers Association, 'The Current Pace and Direction of Accounting Standard Setting', white paper, August 2009 <http://www.aba.com>.

[159] For the view from the banking industry, see Heather Landy, 'Cost-based Accounting Not Dead Yet', *American Banker*, 175/132 (26 August 2010), 1–2. See also Proposed Accounting Standards Update 'Accounting for Financial Instruments and Revisions to the Accounting for Derivative Instruments and Hedging Activities' (FASB, 26 May 2010), BC244–45; 'FASB Releases Proposals on Financial Instruments, Comprehensive Income', FEI financial reporting blog, posted 27 May 2010 <http://www.financialexecutives.org>.

[160] See Scott Taub, 'Accounting's Wild Times of 2010; 2011 Predictions', *Compliance Week*, December 2010, 1 and 38–9.

[161] 'Progress since the Washington Summit in the Implementation of the G20 Recommendations for Strengthening Financial Stability', report of the Financial Stability Board to G20 Leaders, 8 November 2010 <http://www.financialstabilityboard.org>, 17.

[162] See e.g. Taub, 'Accounting's Wild Times of 2010' and Paul Munter, 'Accounting Standard-setting: Convergence Drives More Change', *Financial Executive*, 27/1 (January 2011), 22–5.

measurement of financial liabilities, as these had been left out of the scope of IFRS 9. The July 2009 exposure draft that formed the basis of IFRS 9 had covered financial liabilities and had proposed the same mixed-measurement approach as it did for assets. The practical result would be that most loans and payables, other than those that were part of a trading portfolio, would be recognized at amortized cost. In addition, there was to be a fair value option.

What held up these proposals was the question of whether gains and losses on loans measured at fair value should be reported in profit or loss even when they reflected changes in the reporting entity's credit status. This was not a new issue, and it was one of the reasons underlying the fair value option carve-out imposed by the EU in 2004 (see Chapter 6). At that time, the issue was largely theoretical, like other concerns which prudential regulators might have over fair value. But, as the financial crisis had led to widespread and significant deteriorations in credit standing, it had become conspicuous how banks and other companies were recognizing gains on their own liabilities as their overall financial position deteriorated. The idea was ridiculed by, among others, French President Nicolas Sarkozy who held it up in a speech at the World Economic Forum in Davos as an illustration of the absurd consequences of fair value accounting.[163]

Already in December 2008, the Board had asked Wayne Upton to develop a discussion paper on this question, which was published with an invitation to comment in June 2009.[164] The Board debated the responses to the discussion paper in the second half of 2009, but agreed with the staff in October that it needed more time, and for that reason had left liabilities out of the scope of IFRS 9. In May 2010, the Board published an exposure draft, proposing to leave the existing requirements for classifying liabilities in IAS 39 unchanged, and to add an exception for liabilities at fair value but not held for trading, that is, liabilities measured at fair value under the fair value option. For these liabilities, fair value changes relating to own credit risk would be reported in other comprehensive income.[165] IFRS 9 was modified to this effect by an amendment issued in October 2010.[166]

The IASB used its May 2010 exposure draft to draw attention to the FASB's full fair-value comprehensive exposure draft on financial instruments, which was then expected any moment, apparently calling on its constituents to nudge the FASB towards convergence with the IASB:[167]

> The IASB has received widespread support for a measurement approach that requires reporting entities to classify financial instruments into two measurement categories— amortized cost and fair value (a 'mixed measurement' approach). Therefore, the IASB has asked its constituents to provide feedback to the FASB on the proposals in the FASB's exposure draft. This is particularly important because this is a joint project with an objective of increasing international comparability.

---

[163] 'Speech by M. Nicolas Sarkozy, President of the French Republic, 40th World Economic Forum, Davos—Wednesday, January 27, 2010' <http://www.weforum.org>.

[164] See AP 5/2009 papers 3 and 3A. The discussion paper was published as DP/2009/2 'Own Credit Risk in Liability Measurement' (IASB, June 2009) with an accompanying staff paper.

[165] ED/2010/4 'Fair Value Option for Financial Liabilities' (May 2010).

[166] IFRS 9 *Financial Instruments* (IASB, October 2010).

[167] ED/2010/4, paragraph 17.

16.8.2 Impairment

As seen in Chapter 13, one of the central criticisms of IFRSs and US GAAP inspired by the financial crisis was that both required credit losses on banks' portfolios of loans and debt securities to be recognized on the basis of an incurred-loss model. With the intention of limiting earnings management, this approach strictly limited the use of forward-looking information in recognizing credit losses. This exposed the standards to the criticism that loan loss provisions had been 'too little and too late' when the crisis broke and that, because bank profits had been overstated in the good years preceding the crisis, the standards had a procyclical effect on the economy.[168] In the first half of 2009, loan loss provisioning ranked at the top of the political accounting agenda as reflected in the statements of the G20 and the Financial Stability Forum (reconstituted in April 2009 as the Financial Stability Board).

The IASB and the FASB both addressed the question, but reached different answers. The IASB issued an exposure draft in November 2009 in which it attempted to bring in more forward-looking information on credit losses.[169] It did so by modifying the amortized cost model to include credit losses expected at the inception of the loan in the calculation of the effective interest rate. The effect would be that relatively high contractual interest rates on risky loans would be offset in the income statement by gradually building up an allowance account. This was not a new idea, and it had been considered by the Board in 2002 and 2003 when improving the original IAS 39. At that time, it was abandoned, not least because of the operational problems it imposed on banks' information systems when the principle was to be applied to open portfolios of financial instruments.[170] In 2009, these operational problems were still seen as an important question mark hanging over the approach, and were one of the reasons cited by Jim Leisenring and Bob Garnett for voting against the IASB's exposure draft. It was also one of the common themes running through responses received on the exposure draft.[171] Another weakness of the IASB's approach, at least from the point of view of banking regulators, was that it might not be sufficiently prudent, in that losses already expected at the origination of the loan would be recognized gradually rather than immediately.

The FASB, in its May 2010 exposure draft, took a different approach, requiring a full allowance for expected losses at any time, making amends, as it were, for a history of underestimating loan losses.[172] Yet in one sense the FASB's proposal was more restrictive than the IASB's approach, because the FASB limited the

---

[168] See e.g. Tim Bush, *UK and Irish Banks Capital Losses—Post Mortem* (Local Authority Pension Fund Forum, 2011). See also 'Final Report of the EFC Working Group on Pro-cyclicality to the EFC/ECOFIN', 29 June 2009, ST 11479 2009 INIT <http://www.consilium.europa.eu>.

[169] ED/2009/12 'Financial Instruments: Amortised Cost and Impairment' (November 2009).

[170] See for a more extensive discussion: Kees Camfferman, 'The Emergence of the "Incurred Loss" Model for Credit Losses in IAS 39', working paper, VU University Amsterdam, 2014.

[171] AP 10/2010 paper 13A (comment letter summary).

[172] See Stephen A. Zeff, 'Political Lobbying on Accounting Standards—US, UK and International Experience', in Christopher Nobes and Robert Parker, *Comparative International Accounting*, 12th edition (Harlow, England: Pearson, 2012), 242–3; Stephen A. Zeff, 'The Evolution of U.S. GAAP: The Political Forces behind Professional Standards (Part II)', 23.

information that could be used in estimating losses to historical data and conditions known to exist on the reporting date. The IASB's proposal would require companies to look ahead over the entire life of the loan and include forecasts of future conditions as well. As the IASB staff's understanding of the nuances of loan loss accounting increased, they established that the FASB and the IASB proposals were just two out of at least twelve possible models that could be developed by the permutations of variables such as the length of time over which companies were expected to look ahead and the pattern of loss recognition.[173]

In the final months of 2010, when both the IASB and the FASB had gathered the feedback on their respective exposure drafts, the two boards worked out a common solution, combining features of each board's approach. The more rigorous FASB approach of recognizing expected losses immediately was to be applied to the more problematic part of the loan portfolio commonly referred to as the 'bad book'. For loans in the 'good book', expected losses over the life of the loan were to be recognized over time, but with the safety check that the loan loss allowance should at least cover losses expected to occur within an undefined 'foreseeable future'. The operational difficulties of the IASB's approach were to be resolved by allowing a simple linear allocation of expected losses rather than the more complicated adjustment of the effective interest rate method. A supplementary exposure draft of the common approach was issued in January 2010.[174]

The supplementary exposure draft announced the IASB's intention to issue a standard by June 2011. With this looming deadline, the impairment project was particularly vulnerable to complaints that the IASB was going too fast. It was a complex topic about which the boards themselves were evidently still learning as they went along. The comment period allowed was relatively short, particularly for many companies where it coincided with their year-end reporting. And many people had difficulty keeping track of the big picture on the basis of a joint supplementary exposure draft tacked on to two different underlying exposure drafts on impairment which, in turn, were part of two different and still evolving packages for financial instruments in general.[175]

Concerns such as these may have helped the IASB to accept that the project could not be completed by June 2011. But the Board's inability to improve its impairment standard swiftly did not look good against the background of the sovereign-debt crisis erupting in Europe in 2010. When a default of the Greek government appeared inevitable and the Eurozone seemed to be heading towards a melt-down, impairment of financial assets was again a highly topical subject. The diverse and often belated recognition of losses on Greek debt by European banks drew adverse comments in the second half of 2011, not least by the IASB's new chairman, Hans Hoogervorst.[176] Inconsistent application and enforcement of

---

[173] See AP 10/2010 paper 10A for staff's analysis of the IASB's and FASB's approaches in the context of the range of possible models.

[174] Supplement to ED/2009/12 'Financial Instruments: Impairment' (IASB, January 2011).

[175] See AP 4/2011 paper 4D, paragraphs 15–18, for a summary of due process issues raised in comment letters on the January 2011 exposure draft.

[176] Floyd Norris, 'Many Views on a Greek Bond's Value', posted 8 September 2011 <http://www.nytimes.com>. See also letter from Hans Hoogervorst to Steven Maijoor, dated 4 August 2011 <http://

the existing provisions of IAS 39 were part of the problem, but it was hard to avoid the impression that these problems might have been alleviated with an improved impairment standard in place.

16.8.3 Derecognition

In April 2005, the IASB and the FASB had agreed to ask their staffs to undertake a research project on derecognition of financial instruments. The timing of the research work was said to depend on staff availability.[177] This proved to be a significant constraint. The February 2006 MoU listed derecognition of financial instruments among the eleven major projects, but indicated that it was still at the research stage. It was not until October 2007 that the topic first came before the Board, in a joint meeting with the FASB.[178] At that point, the boards discussed a fifty-page draft research report that was supposed to lead to a discussion paper sometime in 2008.

As with other financial instruments topics, it gained a new urgency shortly afterwards, as the credit crisis highlighted problems of off-balance sheet exposures and securitization. When the Board discussed, in April 2008, the acceleration of the MoU projects, the 'gang of four' mentioned that the Financial Stability Forum had identified derecognition as a topic requiring urgent attention. Moreover, the relevant US standard, FAS 140 *Accounting for Transfers and Servicing of Financial Assets and Extinguishments of Liabilities* (2000), was believed to be 'irretrievably broken', but on this point IAS 39 was not fit to be adopted in the United States either.[179] The Board therefore agreed to skip the discussion paper and aim for an exposure draft to be developed on the basis of the staff research to date as the first due process step. An exposure draft of amendments to IAS 39 was published in March 2009.[180] It was not an easy birth, as five Board members voted against, arguing among other things that the proposal was not consistent with the conceptual framework's definitions of assets and liabilities.

Another complication was that the IASB and the FASB again fell into a pattern of leapfrogging. The FASB moved first by issuing an exposure draft of amendments to FAS 140 in September 2008, at the request of the SEC. This was intended as a short-term measure, and the FASB intended to revise its standard more comprehensively by inviting comments on the IASB's standard, when issued.[181] When the FASB's revised standard came out in June 2009, the IASB, in turn, decided to give it at least two quarters of implementation before proceeding with its own standard, to make sure that the lessons learned in the United States were properly understood.[182]

---

www.ifrs.org> and 'ESMA Report: Review of Greek Government Bonds Accounting Practices in the IFRS Financial Statements for the year ended 31 December 2011', (ESMA, 26 July 2012) <http://www. esma.europa.eu>.

[177] *IASB Insight*, April 2005, 5.

[178] Apart from a discussion in September 2006, in relation to a request for input and advice from IFRIC, see AP 9/2006 paper 13.

[179] AP 4/2008 paper 3, paragraphs 34–7.

[180] ED/2009/3 'Derecognition' (March 2009).   [181] *IASB Insight*, March 2009, 5.

[182] FAS 166 *Accounting for Transfers of Financial Assets* (June 2009); AP 9/2009 paper 16, paragraph 24.

The substance of the derecognition project consisted in the complexities of financial engineering, made notorious in March 2010 by the publication of the examiner's report into the bankruptcy of Lehman Brothers.[183] The report gave instant fame to the so-called 'repo 105', a type of repurchase agreement that had allowed Lehman to push down its reported leverage around reporting dates. The IASB's discussions of derecognition suddenly gained in news value, but the Board had already been considering repurchase agreements in its March 2009 exposure draft and in the discussion of the feedback received.[184] The conclusion towards which the Board initially tended was that, under its proposed derecognition model, many of these transactions would be sales, and thus be accounted for in the way Lehman had done.[185] Many respondents to the exposure draft did not agree, however, and in February 2010, just before the Lehman report made headlines, the Board had already tentatively decided to introduce an exception by which, under certain conditions, such transactions would be accounted for as secured borrowings.[186] Rightly or wrongly, the Lehman affair provided the Board with an opportunity, reminiscent of the post-Enron period, to suggest that IFRSs would have prevented Lehman from accounting as it did, and thus to make the case for convergence.[187]

By April 2010, the IASB had reached the stage where it felt that it had refined its model to the point where it could be re-exposed. However, it would seem that the Board had somehow lost the FASB along the way. When taken through the model in a joint meeting, FASB members expressed considerable reservations, with Technical Director Russell Golden wondering how the boards 'had got so out of synch'.[188] The implication was that more discussion was necessary before the IASB draft might be a good basis for convergence. But it didn't come to that: as indicated above, the IASB and the FASB removed a number of convergence projects from their agendas in May and June 2010, including derecognition. On the basis of the argument that the IASB had heard from its constituents that the existing requirements had held up well enough during the financial crisis, the IASB reduced its project to an improvement of disclosures, which was completed in October 2010.[189] At the same time, the existing derecognition requirements of IAS 39 were transferred unchanged to IFRS 9. The FASB went off by itself to improve its guidance on repurchase agreements.[190]

---

[183] 'Report of Anton R. Valukas, Examiner, in re Lehman Brothers Holdings Inc., et al., Debtors', United States Bankruptcy Court, Southern District of New York, 11 March 2010 <http://jenner.com>.

[184] See e.g. 'Repo Accounting up for Review', news item posted 8 April 2010 <http://www.accountancyage.com>.

[185] ED/2009/3, BC58–BC61.   [186] See AP 3/2010 paper 5A.

[187] Philippe Danjou, quoted in 'Lehman Case Backs Convergence: IASB Official', *Compliance Reporter*, 23 April 2010.

[188] *IFRS Monitor*, April 2010, 40.

[189] *Disclosures—Transfers of Financial Assets: Amendments to IFRS 7* (October 2010). See IFRS 7, BC65B.

[190] See 'FASB Goes it Alone on Accounting for Repurchase Agreements (Repos)' <http://www.iasplus.com>, posted 29 July 2010. See also proposed accounting standards update 'Transfers and Servicing (Topic 860)' (FASB, 3 November 2010).

16.8.4 Hedge Accounting

Hedge accounting was one of the factors that made accounting for financial instruments complex. The 2008 IASB–FASB discussion paper, 'Reducing Complexity in Reporting Financial Instruments', had raised the question whether hedge accounting could just be eliminated, in particular in combination with a wider application of fair value for financial assets and liabilities. Perhaps recognizing that this would be a bridge too far, if only because a general use of fair value would still not obviate the need for cash flow hedge accounting, the discussion paper had also listed possible simplifications that might be made if hedge accounting were to be retained. Unlike fair value measurement per se, or impairment, hedge accounting was not directly tied up with the financial crisis. Rather, there were known complaints about the restrictive, rules-based approach of IAS 39 which frequently made it difficult to capture the effects of a company's risk management in the financial statements. These concerns had already been expressed when the Board tried to make initial improvements to IAS 39 in 2001–04. At that time, the Board had left much of IAS 39 with respect to hedge accounting intact, leading to complaints that the Board was not responsive to legitimate preparer concerns (see Chapter 6).

This time, the Board took a different approach. It spent most of 2010 developing what it believed was a principles-based hedge-accounting model that would produce useful information because of the alignment between hedge accounting and a company's risk management. An exposure draft embodying this approach was published in December 2010.[191] This more preparer-friendly attitude was recognized and welcomed by many of those who commented on the exposure draft or took part in the extensive outreach activities surrounding the draft. It was reported that Board members and staff took part in 145 meetings all over the world, including ten in Africa and thirty-four in Central and South America. According to the staff, 'All participants appreciate the extensive outreach effort from the IASB and are pleased with the open and continued dialogue with the IASB on this topic'.[192] While this was self-reported, it would seem that there was indeed a great deal of difference between this round of discussions on hedge accounting and the complaints about a Board that 'does not listen' in 2001–4.

One reason for the different climate may have been that the IASB had postponed its consideration of portfolio or macro hedging, which had on an earlier occasion led to a European carve-out. The carve-out was still in place, and a resolution of the issue acceptable to both the IASB and those parts of the European banking industry where the carve-out was still used was an apparent condition for the endorsement of IFRS 9 for use in the EU. For the time being, however, the IASB's exposure draft was welcomed, not least by many non-financial companies which had faced significant restrictions when applying hedge accounting to hedges of non-financial items, such as manufacturing companies hedging purchases of commodities or airlines hedging purchases of fuel.

---

[191] ED/2010/13 'Hedge Accounting' (IASB, December 2010).
[192] AP 3/2011 paper 7A, paragraph 6.

For these companies, early application of IFRS 9 began to look like an attractive prospect.

Some, however, thought that the Board was going too far in making hedge accounting more widely available. John Smith, the Board's expert on financial instruments and always alert to the possibilities of abuse, voted against the exposure draft and wrote an alternative view of more than six pages in which he explained at length that many of the provisions of the draft were:

> not operational, lack rigour, and would produce unintended consequences.... Mr Smith also believes that the proposals would inappropriately expand the use of hedge accounting, provide a virtually free choice to change the measurement attributes of assets and liabilities and portions thereof otherwise carried at amortized cost, are incompatible with and would provide a means of circumventing the existing provisions of IFRS 9 and would reduce comparability.[193]

Similarly, the FASB was willing to work with the IASB on a common hedge accounting proposal, but there was a view that the IASB was going too far and too fast, and the FASB was not yet prepared to follow.[194] The IASB therefore developed its proposal alone, and its December 2010 exposure draft contained no references to convergence. The FASB, however, did circulate the IASB's draft as a discussion paper.[195]

16.8.5 Offsetting

In 2010, the IASB and the FASB added one more element to their plans for revising financial instruments accounting. Compared to US GAAP, IFRSs gave less scope to the netting, or offsetting, of financial assets and liabilities. The result was that balance sheets under IFRSs tended to be longer, as they reflected gross rather than net positions. This was often thought of as a less favourable presentation of an entity's financial position. Some of the respondents to the March 2009 exposure draft on derecognition, in particular from the financial industry, drew attention to this issue, even though it was outside the scope of the draft.[196] The Institute of International Finance called for an urgent levelling of the playing field, and the European Banking Federation clarified that this should take the form of moving the requirements under IFRSs closer to US GAAP.[197] Different offsetting rules were a complicating factor in determining internationally comparable solvency ratios used in the supervision of banks and other financial institutions, so the Financial Stability Board also encouraged the IASB and the FASB to take up the issue.

The boards did so in June 2010. In contrast to what the banks might have wished, the IASB and the FASB agreed on a common approach that was closer to

---

[193] ED/2010/13 'Hedge Accounting', AV1.

[194] Interview with Thomas Linsmeier, 11 June 2013.

[195] Discussion paper 'Selected Issues about Hedge Accounting', Financial Accounting Series No. 2011-175 (FASB, 9 February 2011).

[196] AP 1/2010 paper 11 (observer version).

[197] CL42 (Institute of International Finance) and CL44 (European Banking Federation), ED/2009/3 comment letters <http://www.ifrs.org>.

IFRSs than to US GAAP, and thus had as its main consequence that US GAAP would become more restrictive. The coordinated exposure drafts appeared in January 2011.[198] The proposal was not favourably received in the United States, and when it was time to consider the next step, it appeared that the FASB would no longer support the position taken in the exposure draft. The exposure draft had been agreed with three votes to two when the FASB was still a five-member board. After the FASB had been expanded to seven in February 2011, the balance shifted from four votes against to three in favour, as the two newly appointed members were not in favour of proceeding on the basis of the exposure draft.[199] Within the IASB, this was seen as the most conspicuous example of how the reconfiguration of the FASB affected the convergence programme. As there was apparently no appetite in the IASB to move towards US GAAP, there was little left to do but finish the project with common disclosures of gross and net positions, while leaving the existing balance sheet presentations unchanged.[200]

16.9 INSURANCE CONTRACTS

As seen in Chapter 5, the IASB had inherited the challenge of writing a standard on insurance contacts from the IASC, and, after an initial attempt, had bought time by issuing an interim standard, IFRS 4 *Insurance Contracts*, in 2004. IFRS 4 sanctioned existing practices, providing that certain minimum conditions were met. In early 2005, the Board was ready again to take up the main project, then known as phase II. At that stage, it was an IASB-only project, but in 2004 future FASB participation had been pencilled in: with the so-called 'modified joint approach' chosen for this project, it was expected that the FASB would join once the IASB had issued a discussion paper.[201] The IASB issued its discussion paper in May 2007.[202] The FASB followed with an invitation for comment, but it took the FASB until October 2008 to complete its consultations and to decide to add the project to its active agenda. At the IASB, it was believed that allowing the FASB to catch up delayed the project by about a year. Joint discussions began in earnest in January 2009.

After an initial exploration of the issues, the IASB organized its thinking around the insurance liability, and decomposed the steps required to estimate this liability at a given point in time in three so-called 'building-blocks': estimates of the future cash flows from the contracts (including both premiums and claims settlement), the discount rate for calculating the present value of the cash flows, and a margin.[203] This way of structuring the problem continued to be used and was

---

[198] ED/2011/1 'Offsetting Financial Assets and Financial Liabilities' (IASB, January 2011) and proposed accounting standards update 'Balance Sheet (Topic 210): Offsetting', Financial Accounting Series No. 2011-100 (FASB, 28 January 2011).

[199] 'New Regime Looks to Finish Programme', *World Accounting Report*, July 2011, 2.

[200] *Disclosures—Offsetting Financial Assets and Financial Liabilities: Amendments to IFRS 7* (IASB, December 2011).

[201] AP 4/2004 paper 11B, paragraph 11; *IASB Update*, April 2004, 4–5.

[202] Discussion paper 'Preliminary Views on Insurance Contracts' (IASB, May 2007).

[203] The first reference to the building blocks appears to be in AP 2/2006 paper 10G.

generally appreciated, but it did not by itself answer the tough questions: should assumptions underlying cash flow estimates be 'locked in' at the inception of a contract, or should they be updated on every balance sheet date? Should assumptions be market-based or entity-specific? Should the margin be decomposed in elements relating to the bearing of risk, the provision of services, and an unspecified residual? Should the margin on initial recognition be calibrated to exclude day-one gains or losses? In the discussion paper, the Board stayed close to the approach of the IASC's steering committee which had provided the Board with its starting point on insurance accounting in 2001 (see Section 5.5.1). That is, the Board tended towards answers that were based on current, market-based information, with resulting changes in the liability recognized in profit or loss. In line with this thinking, the income statement would show the release of the margin over time and adjustments to the liability, rather than premiums shown as revenue and settlement of claims as expenses.[204]

As a technical project, accounting for insurance contracts was in a class of its own. It was always an area for specialists, requiring a high frequency of educational sessions given both by the IASB's staff and by industry representatives. Among the staff, Peter Clark had over the years unquestionably become the leading expert. Among the Board members, Warren McGregor had always been the most strongly interested, and the Board's expertise was strengthened in 2010 with the appointment of Elke König. 'Insurance contracts' covered a wide range of arrangements, with every conceivable variation in terms of duration, uncertainty, and options granted to either insurer or policy holder. It presented some well-known challenges, such as profit sharing by policyholders, which was not easy to fit into the IASB's conceptual thinking, with its neat, dichotomous distinction between liabilities and equity. Although the IASB normally eschewed industry standards, here it was writing an industry standard in all but name, and the industry in question was well-organized and took an intense interest in the project. When insurance contracts came on the agenda, observer seats at Board meetings tended to fill up with what was sometimes referred to as the 'insurance groupies'.[205]

As in banking, the activities of the IASB, and the IASC before it, were a catalyst for the insurance industry to organize itself at an international level. European insurers, who had been rather divided in their responses to the IASC's discussion paper, organized themselves in a 'CFO Forum' in 2002, in response to the growing importance of accounting standards generally, and the impending transition to IFRSs in Europe in particular. It was noted in 2011 that accounting was the area where contacts among insurance associations in Europe, Japan, and the United States were the most highly developed.[206] There was no question that

---

[204] For an extensive discussion of the IASB's discussion paper and related literature see Joanne Horton, Richard Macve, and George Serafeim, *An Experiment in 'Fair Value Accounting': The State of the Art in Research and Thought Leadership on Accounting for Life Assurance in the UK and Continental Europe* (London: ICAEW/Centre for Business Performance, 2007).

[205] *IStaR*, September 2008, 44.

[206] Interview with Eiichi Tachibana, 27 January 2011. See also the joint response letter to the IASB's 2007 discussion paper by the CFO Forum, the Group of North American Insurance Enterprises (GNAIE), and the four largest Japanese life insurers, dated 30 November 2007 <http://www.cfoforum.nl>.

the insurance industry was intent on seeing its views reflected in the IASB's standard, for instance in moving the liability away from the IASB's initial conception of an exit-price measurement, including adjustments for the insurance company's own credit risk. But even where the insurers and the Board collided, the tone was generally more moderate than during some of the Board's discussions with parts of the banking industry early in the decade. One reason may have been that, in insurance, the existing situation was not sustainable, in the sense that few if any were prepared to defend the huge diversity in national practices, and that multinational insurance groups themselves would be greatly helped by using a common accounting basis for all of their subsidiaries. Insurance contracts was an area where the potential benefits of an international standard seemed obvious. This may have helped the industry take a constructive rather than a defensive stance.

While accounting for insurance contracts was a specialist topic, it could not be discussed in isolation. At the heart of the project was the question of recognition and measurement of the liability arising out of insurance contracts, which was related to the question of recognizing revenue. As seen elsewhere, liabilities and revenues were two basic themes in the IASB's technical work, and inevitably the relations between insurance contracts and the more general concepts were explored in detail. Also, the insurance liability was matched in the balance sheet of insurance companies by investments, which for the most part were financial instruments. The insurance companies, therefore, had a great interest in ensuring that the Board's deliberations on financial instruments were coordinated with the insurance contracts project. It was here, perhaps more so than in the insurance contracts project per se, that the greatest tensions arose between the insurance industry and the IASB.[207] It was noted in the insurance sector—perhaps with a twinge of jealousy—that in IFRS 9 the IASB had provided for the basic business model of commercial banks, in that both deposits and loans granted could be accounted for on a cost basis. As the contours of the insurance standard became more clearly discernible, it was not evident that the combination with IFRS 9 would fit the business model of insurance companies: the more likely outcome seemed to be a mismatch of gains and losses on the investments and the insurance liability.

A final complication was that the accounting by insurance companies was a matter of interest to the prudential regulators of the industry. Although the Board did not see it as its mission to write standards specifically for regulatory purposes, both the regulators and the industry were anxious to see an outcome where IFRS-based financial statements could be used as the basis for supervision with a minimum of adjustments or 'prudential filters'. The most pressing question in this regard was the development of the European 'Solvency II' directive, adopted in 2009 and thus developed in parallel with the IASB's ongoing project.

In the light of the above, there is no mystery that it took the Board as long as it did to make progress on the project. From early 2005 to early 2007, the Board discussed insurance contracts in virtually all of its monthly meetings, in preparation of the May 2007 discussion paper. This was followed by almost a year and a

---

[207] See for instance 'Versicherer attackieren Bilanzkomitee', *Financial Times Deutschland*, 29 June 2009, 15.

half of inactivity, both because of the response period, and because of the time it took for the FASB to join in the project. But then, from January 2009 to July 2010, discussions resumed their intense meeting-by-meeting frequency until the publication of an exposure draft in July 2010.[208] All the time, the planning was to issue a final standard before June 2011, although, as the publication date of the exposure draft slipped, the time available to process the comments and complete the standard was increasingly compressed. When, in December 2010, the Board began discussing the responses to their exposure draft, they had about half a year left for work that was initially planned, under favourable assumptions, to take a year.[209]

If, on a global basis, the added value of an international standard was evident, this was not necessarily true in the United States. Even if US GAAP for insurance contracts was not perfect, it was at least well-established and understood. When the FASB joined the IASB's project in October 2008, the expressed intention was to develop a 'common high-quality standard', with an exposure draft as the next expected stage.[210] However, by the time the IASB issued its exposure draft, it had become clear that the boards were not able to reach the same conclusions on all issues, in particular on whether it was necessary to identify a separate risk margin (as the IASB wanted), or to treat the entire margin as an unspecified composite (as some FASB members preferred). Moreover, the FASB had reconsidered whether a comprehensive revision of US GAAP was in order. It issued the IASB's exposure draft as a discussion paper, in which it explained the points on which FASB members' views differed from the conclusions in the IASB's draft, or on which the FASB had not yet reached a decision. The FASB left all options open for the future, as it asked respondents to consider the advantages and disadvantages of proceeding with the IASB's approach, either in its entirety or with modifications, compared to making targeted improvements to US GAAP.[211] By the middle of 2010, the FASB's technical plan no longer indicated a date for a final standard.[212]

The question as it presented itself to the IASB at the end of 2010 or early 2011 was whether it should push ahead and publish its standard by June 2011, perhaps accompanied by an FASB exposure draft.[213] This might have been feasible, but there were strong arguments against. The insurance industry was not yet convinced that the IASB had found all the right answers, even though it commended the Board for many of the changes made since the discussion paper. There were strong doubts in Japan whether a standard based on the exposure draft would be designated for use in Japan by the Financial Services Agency. The industry, not merely in Japan, argued that there should be more extensive field-testing of the proposals. Moreover, pressure for a converged solution remained strong, not least

---

[208] ED/2010/8 'Insurance Contracts' (IASB, July 2010).

[209] See AP 9/2008 paper 14C, as well as AP 2/2008 paper 2D for the underlying assumptions.

[210] 'Project Update—Insurance Contracts', posted 16 December 2008 <http://www.fasb.org> accessed through web.archive; see also FASB technical plan as of 1 January 2009 <http://www.fasb.org>.

[211] Discussion paper 'Preliminary Views on Insurance Contracts', Financial Accounting Series No. 1870-100 (FASB, 17 September 2010).

[212] See technical plans as of July and October 2010 <http://www.fasb.org>.

[213] The IASB's AP 12/2010 paper 7 (observer version) contained a plan for an IFRS and an FASB exposure draft to be issued in June 2011. However, the FASB's technical plan had, since October 2010, no longer shown a date for an exposure draft.

within the United States.[214] This implied a joint IASB–FASB exposure draft, which could prolong the project by another two years. As this was not an MoU project, neither the IASB nor the FASB was committed to completion by 2011. When the comments were discussed in January 2011, Warren McGregor expressed himself most strongly of all the IASB Board members against postponed completion: more field tests and a common standard were certainly desirable, he said, but the IASB had worked on the issue for ten years, following three years by the IASC. A new standard, even if issued now, would not come into effect until three years later, which meant that, for nine years, an interim standard, IFRS 4, would let 'insurers do whatever they want to do'. According to McGregor, there was general agreement that a new standard was needed, both among users and within the industry itself: 'I know it would be nice to spend more time and do a lot more polishing, but there comes a point in time when you just got to make some decisions and move ahead.'[215] But the rest of the Board had not yet reached this point, and the deliberations of the two boards continued throughout 2011 at a steady pace, with the publication of a final standard receding further and further into the background. After several years of additional work and another exposure draft in 2013, the FASB decided early in 2014 that it would no longer pursue the objective of a common standard. Instead, as it already suggested in its 2010 discussion paper, it would focus on making targeted improvements to US GAAP, merely 'considering' the IASB's work.

With hindsight, the wisdom of undertaking the project jointly with the FASB was questioned, both in the insurance industry and in the Board. Inevitably, time was lost as the FASB had to come up to speed, and in re-opening debates on which the IASB and the insurance industry had already reached a degree of mutual understanding. Moreover, some believed that US GAAP on insurance was highly developed, but also closely tailored to the types of insurance products that were common in the United States. That was not an easy starting position for the two boards to reach agreement on a standard that would also have to cater for insurance markets with very different characteristics.[216]

16.10 LIABILITIES AND EQUITY

It was seen in Chapter 12 that a considerable amount of conceptual thinking of the IASB and the FASB took place outside the project to revise the conceptual framework. A good example was a long-running and ultimately unsuccessful project to clarify the distinction between equity and liabilities. This began life as an FASB research project with roots in the 1990s, which the IASB, beginning in 2004, began to follow with some interest.[217] The FASB saw this as a major project,

---

[214] Compare AP 1/2011 paper 3F (observer version), paragraphs 7–9, and AP 1/2011 paper 3E (observer version), paragraph 12.

[215] Audio recording of IASB–FASB 18 January 2011 discussion, insurance contracts, 1′54″–4′34″ <http://www.ifrs.org>.

[216] Interview with Susanne Kanngieser, Gabi Ebbers, and Martina Baumgärtel, 19 April 2010.

[217] See the project history on <http://www.fasb.org> as of July 2010, accessed through web.archive.

with outcomes that could be 'dramatically different' from current practice under US GAAP and IFRSs, and with ramifications for the conceptual framework and other standards such as share-based payments.[218] It was agreed between the IASB and the FASB that this would be a so-called modified joint project, that is, a project in which one of the two boards would take the lead to develop a discussion paper, following which the two boards would work jointly on an exposure draft and a final standard. The FASB published its preliminary views (the equivalent of the IASB's discussion papers) in November 2007.[219] Before that, the IASB had regularly discussed and commented on FASB agenda papers for this project, but from the sidelines, without direct involvement. In March 2008, the IASB issued a brief discussion paper of its own, as an invitation to comment on the FASB's preliminary views. In its discussion paper, the Board pointed out that, compared to IAS 32 *Financial Instruments: Disclosure and Presentation*, the FASB's proposal meant that 'significantly fewer' financial instruments would be classified as equity.[220] The project was moved to the IASB's active agenda, and in October 2008 the two boards held their first joint discussion of the project on an equal footing.

Well before that time, the essential problem of the project had already become manifest. Both the IASB and the FASB believed that their current standards did not draw the line between financial instruments classified as equity and those classified as liabilities in a satisfactory manner, nor in a way that was robust to deal with 'structuring', the creativity of the financial industry to develop financial instruments that met the accounting criteria for classification as equity but were, in economic substance, liabilities. It turned out that it was not too difficult to develop several alternative high-level principles, or models, for making the split between equity and liabilities, including the separation ('bifurcation') of equity and non-equity components of a single instrument. The FASB's preliminary views listed three models, and EFRAG had developed a fourth model in one of its pro-active discussion papers.[221] In subsequent years, more models would be developed. Some models were easily dismissed: for instance, the IASB was not enthusiastic about EFRAG's approach.[222] But the boards found it very difficult to agree on which of the plausible models provided an appropriate pattern of classification among the gamut of specific financial instruments considered, ranging from convertible debt to the puttable shares the Board had already been considering, with an eye on New Zealand cooperatives and German partnerships (see Section 12.9.3). In other words, the boards were not quite prepared to adopt a principle and accept the consequences, but were searching inductively for a principle that could capture much of existing practice.

[218] AP 4/2004 paper 11, paragraph 9.

[219] Preliminary views 'Financial Instruments with Characteristics of Equity', Financial Accounting Series No. 1550-100 (FASB, November 2007).

[220] Discussion paper 'Financial Instruments with Characteristics of Equity' (IASB, February 2008), paragraph 46.

[221] Pro-active Accounting Activities in Europe (PAAinE) discussion paper 'Distinguishing between Liabilities and Equity' (EFRAG, January 2008) <http://www.efrag.org>.

[222] See the report of Board discussions in *IStaR*, February 2008, 24–5, and July 2008, 50–4.

The discussion was complicated and prolonged by references to parallel projects such as insurance contracts and, as 2009 progressed, the new financial instruments standard that became IFRS 9. In turn, the discussions on equity and liabilities held back the 'elements' section of the conceptual framework project, which was never concluded (see Section 12.7.3).[223] Not surprisingly, the idea that IAS 32 wasn't too bad after all came back from time to time. Nonetheless, the boards persevered to the point that a staff draft of an exposure draft was circulated to a small group of seven selected external reviewers in April 2010.[224]

The response was devastating. The reviewers provided extremely detailed feedback, but the upshot was that the draft did not appear to be based on a clear principle, arrived in many cases at the same classification as under current US GAAP and IFRSs, yet failed to deal with all of the issues currently covered by the two sets of standards and known practice issues arising out of these standards.[225] It would appear that the boards had somehow lost sight of the principle, and focused too much on preserving existing outcomes and providing patches for problems. In addition, it was apparent that the FASB's constituents would be very reluctant to give up their existing detailed implementation guidance. Neither the staff nor the boards wished to proceed with the draft, but the idea was mooted that an improved version of IAS 32, dealing with the most pressing issues in US GAAP, might be a way forward. Tatsumi Yamada was the most resolute in dismissing this idea. In September 2010, he said:[226]

> [The] IASB wanted to retain what they had got [i.e. IAS 32] because there were no clear principles out there. However, US preparers wanted to preserve their detailed guidance. He could not see how they could satisfy both Boards. They could try to but the American preparers would not be happy. Therefore, he thought they should stop the project right here.

A month later, the two boards agreed, with apologies and thanks to the staff.[227]

16.11 FINANCIAL STATEMENT PRESENTATION: NO SINGLE PERFORMANCE STATEMENT (AGAIN)

In October 2008, the IASB and the FASB had published a discussion paper on financial statement presentation, a further step in a long process, stretching back into the 1990s, to reconsider the structure of the financial statements. As discussed in Chapters 5 and 12, the question at the core of the project was: what would happen with the distinction between net income and other comprehensive income? In the mind of several Board members, that distinction had lost much

---

[223] Interview with Tom Linsmeier, 11 June 2013, for relation with conceptual framework project.

[224] AP 7/2010 paper 4 (observer version) mentions the April date. The number seven is found in AP 9/2010 paper 2 (observer version).

[225] AP 9/2010 paper 2 (observer version) and staff presentation as reported in *IFRS Monitor*, July 2010, 43–5.

[226] *IFRS Monitor*, September 2010, 11.   [227] *IFRS Monitor*, October 2010, 61–2.

of its relevance, and thoughts had for many years gone in the direction of a single statement of performance.

This question was somewhat obscured in the complex, 167-page discussion paper, because much of it dealt with the question of how the coherence among the balance sheet, the income statement, and the cash flow statement could be strengthened. The proposed solution was to organize all three statements in operating, investing, financing, equity, discontinued operations, and taxation sections, applying the same classification criteria in each statement. In an elaborate reconciliation schedule, the cash flows in each section would be related, line by line, to the corresponding items in the statement of comprehensive income, showing the effect of accruals and remeasurements. The schedule would also serve, in a way, as a substitute for a cash flow statement based on the indirect method. The direct method was indicated as the preferred method in the standards of both the IASB and the FASB, but was rarely used in practice. The boards believed that many users found information based on the indirect method useful because it provided a crude reconciliation of profit to cash flow. It was therefore a logical conclusion to recommend both a proper cash flow statement (i.e. one based on the direct method) and a reconciliation schedule designed for the purpose.

As the boards had soon discovered, net income had no natural place in an approach based on a classification in sections such as operating, investing, and financing. Because they knew that any suggestion that net income might be abolished would provoke strong reactions from the business community, the discussion paper was limited to proposing a single statement of performance, in which net income (profit or loss) would be shown as a subtotal.

During the comment period, the staffs of the two boards attempted to field-test the proposals, not least to obtain a basis for evaluating the costs and benefits of the proposals. The staffs found some thirty companies willing to recast their financial statements in the new formats, and to provide the reconciling information. What was more difficult was to use this information to seek the views of financial analysts, because of insider trading laws and regulations banning private disclosures, in particular the SEC's Regulation Fair Disclosure in the United States. This also created a problem in presenting the original and recast information to the boards.[228] One assumes that not all parties calling on the IASB to do more field tests were fully aware of practical difficulties such as these.

In general, the staffs believed that there was majority support for the high-level principles in the standard, such as linking the information across the three financial statements and separating the business and financing activities. The problem was that there was much to dislike in the details of the proposals. The direct-method cash flow statement was an obvious stumbling block, but there were also widespread concerns over the resulting complexity of the financial statements and the costly systems requirements to provide all of the information

---

[228] AP 3/2009 (joint meeting) paper 4. See AP 9/2009 paper 9B for the final approach to, and results from, the analyst field test.

called for in the discussion paper, in particular the reconciliation between cash flows and comprehensive income.[229]

The main thrust of the boards' extensive deliberations from September 2009 onwards was to make the proposals less rigid and more practicable, while maintaining the overall approach. In the case of the cash flow statement, for instance, this still meant the application of the direct method but with less required detail in the reconciliation of cash flow to income. By February 2010, the staff was ready to begin drafting. Four of the five FASB members indicated their support, with Seidman still hesitant. On the IASB side, there were as many as five possible dissenters who either did not support part of the proposals, in particular the direct method, or who thought that the boards were pushing ahead with an unpopular project with uncertain or limited benefits, which took time away from other, more important projects on hand.[230] It never came to a vote, however, because the project was put on hold. When the work plan was reconsidered following the FAF's intervention in May 2010 (see Section 16.1.3), it was Tweedie who proposed to defer the completion date of the project, even though an exposure draft was almost ready for publication. The exposure draft was published on the website as a staff draft in July 2010 as the basis for further outreach. In October, the boards decided that the outreach could continue, but that the project needed a pause. It was agreed that they would not begin to reconsider the project until after June 2011.[231]

This was not quite the end of the financial statement presentation project. In a sense, most of the above could be seen as just a distraction from the question that had occupied the Board for so long: what to do with other comprehensive income? As seen above, this question was just touched upon in the discussion paper by the proposal for a single performance statement. As it was, IAS 1 *Presentation of Financial Statements* allowed a choice between such a single statement and a two-statement approach, with a separate income statement and a statement of other comprehensive income, both to be displayed with equal prominence. In the minds of several Board members, the discussion paper's proposal for a single statement was inconsequential, as it amounted to little more than removing the page-break between the two statements. But if it was inconsequential, one could either decide to leave it alone, or adopt it without much further ado. The Board chose the latter course, prompted by the FASB.

US GAAP at the time had the same two options for the presentation of other comprehensive income included in IFRSs, as well as a third: to present items of other comprehensive income in the statement of changes in equity. Because its project on financial instruments envisaged important movements in other comprehensive income, the FASB decided in July 2009 to remove two options and require a single-statement presentation. In October 2009, the IASB agreed with a staff proposal that it should join the FASB and accelerate this aspect of financial

---

[229] See AP 7/2009 paper 17B for a summary of constituent input. For a range of user and preparer views, see also Christine DiFabio, 'Extreme Makeover for Financial Statements', *Financial Executive*, 25/3 (April 2009), 44–7.

[230] See the Board discussion as reported in *IFRS Monitor*, February 2010, 19–20.

[231] 'Staff Draft of Exposure Draft IFRS X Financial Statement Presentation' (IASB, 1 July 2010) <http://www.ifrs.org>.

statement presentation as a separate project. This meant a short-term project focusing on presentation of other comprehensive income. Apart from introducing the single statement, it would remove presentation options with respect to taxation of items of other comprehensive income, and improve presentation of recycling.

Within the IASB, there were serious misgivings. Jan Engström was particularly strong in advising against the plan, arguing that it was 'stupid' to bring up the issue of a single statement again, less than a year after a revised version of IAS 1 had come into force in which the Board, faced with much opposition, had decided to continue the two-statement option (see Section 12.8). Other Board members, including McGregor, Leisenring, Danjou, Yamada, and Chairman Tweedie, commented on the risks of the plan. No matter how strong the Board would protest that it had no intention to abolish net income, the proposal would be interpreted in that light and the Board could easily have a fight on its hands. Moreover, issuing a separate exposure draft on a portion of the financial statement presentation project just months before the planned publication of an exposure draft on the main financial statement presentation project would complicate the process and allow constituents to claim that they needed to see the full picture before making up their minds. Nonetheless, the Board agreed to the short-term project. It did so in the belief that it was, after all, a rather innocuous change that would bring more comparability to the presentation of comprehensive income. Moreover, it would be helpful for some of the Board's other ongoing projects that would entail significant new movements in other comprehensive income, in particular financial instruments and pensions.[232] The IASB and the FASB issued comparable exposure drafts in May 2010, in the case of the IASB with Jan Engström's alternative view.[233]

When the comments were reviewed in October 2010, the IASB's staff reported that most respondents opposed the removal of the two-statement option, mainly for reasons that were already familiar to the Board, and very similar to arguments advanced when the Board had previously considered a single performance statement. The FASB had received equally discouraging reactions.[234] A frequently made point was that the boards should first consider the conceptual basis for classifying items as part of other comprehensive income before changing the presentation. As seen above, the boards decided in October 2010 that they would postpone the main financial statement presentation project until after 2011, including any fundamental reconsideration of other comprehensive income. There was no majority in the IASB for pursuing the single-statement approach, and therefore the Board agreed with a limited amendment to IAS 1, which left the two-statement option intact but introduced minor improvements intended to provide more insight in the recycling, or absence of recycling, of items of other comprehensive income. The amendment was issued in June 2011, accompanied

---

[232] See Board discussions as reported in *IStaR* (*IFRS Monitor*), October 2010, 38–40, and February 2010, 75–7.

[233] ED/2010/5 'Presentation of Items of Other Comprehensive Income' (IASB, May 2010) and proposed accounting standards update 'Comprehensive Income (Topic 220): Statement of Comprehensive Income' (FASB, 26 May 2010).

[234] AP 10/2010 paper 6; see also *IFRS Monitor*, October 2010, 14–15.

by a similar amendment from the FASB.[235] More than a decade of debate on reconfiguring the basic financial statements ended in a whimper.

16.12 INCOME TAX: THE LAST FAILURE OF SHORT-TERM CONVERGENCE

As discussed in Chapter 5, the IASB and the FASB set out, following the 2002 Norwalk Agreement, on a series of short-term convergence projects intended to remove some of the differences between their standards. It was soon realized that this was not as easy as expected. If it was always difficult to converge IFRSs, written for no jurisdiction in particular, with US GAAP, tailor-made for a specific national context, this was especially true for the project on accounting for income tax. Although the project went on for many years, and there were at one time high hopes of a successful conclusion, it led to only a minor amendment of IAS 12 *Income Taxes*. The final amendment was not even intended to bring convergence with US GAAP any closer, but dealt with a problem of several other jurisdictions such as Hong Kong. Looking back, Anne McGeachin, the leading IASB project manager, commented wryly: 'Seven years of my life. I could have been on holiday all that time, the end result would have been much the same.'[236]

Underlying the project was the view that IFRSs and US GAAP already shared the same 'temporary differences' approach to accounting for deferred taxes. This was the result of an earlier convergence effort by the IASC during the 1990s by which it had revised IAS 12 in line with FAS 109 *Accounting for Income Taxes*.[237] Under this approach, a deferred tax asset or liability is recognized for a difference between the carrying amount of an asset or a liability in the balance sheet and the tax base of that item, as well as deferred tax assets for loss carry forwards and unused tax credits. The objective of the short-term convergence project was therefore to remove differences in the application of this shared principle, in particular the different exceptions made in IFRSs and US GAAP. The expectation was that this would be a process of give and take, rather than one board adopting the solutions of the other.[238] The project appeared to move along well at first and was frequently discussed in Board meetings and in joint meetings with the FASB. In the first half of 2005, the plan was still to issue a joint exposure draft later that year.[239] But then the planning began to slip, and each of the Foundation's *Annual Reports* for 2005, 2006, and 2007 envisaged publication of the exposure draft in the next year, until it finally appeared in March 2009.

---

[235] *Presentation of Items of Other Comprehensive Income: Amendments to IAS 1* (IASB, June 2011) and accounting standards update no. 2011–5 *Comprehensive Income (Topic 220): Presentation of Comprehensive Income* (FASB, June 2011).
[236] Interview with Anne McGeachin, 8 June 2012.
[237] See Kees Camfferman and Stephen A. Zeff, *Financial Reporting and Global Capital Markets: A History of the International Accounting Standards Committee, 1973–2000* (Oxford: Oxford University Press, 2007), 357–61.
[238] AP 4/2003 paper 11, paragraphs 2–3.
[239] IASCF trustees meeting of 20–1 June 2005, agenda paper 2B (chairman's report), paragraph 35.

There were several reasons why the project proved to be difficult. One was that US GAAP continued to develop. In 2003, the SEC had drawn the FASB's attention to possible diversity in practice in accounting for uncertain tax positions, both with respect to current and deferred tax. This led the FASB to issue an exposure draft on the subject in 2005, followed by FASB Interpretation No. 48 *Accounting for Uncertainty in Income Taxes* (FIN48) in June 2006. The IASB considered whether and how it should follow this development, which brought the income tax project into the general conceptual territory of obligations and the role of probability in recognition and measurement that the Board was exploring with the revision of IAS 37 (see Section 12.5).

Another reason was the question of whether the concepts from US GAAP, developed with reference to the US tax system, could be transferred to other tax systems. The IASC had considered this question when revising IAS 12, asking itself whether it could be assumed that the notion of 'tax base' had a comparable meaning in each jurisdiction. In the end, it had avoided answering the question, bequeathing it to the IASB. More generally, it appeared that the topic of accounting for income tax was particularly vulnerable to misunderstandings, as people might use the same words but mean different things.[240] And there were other institutional complications. Whereas FAS 109 required that deferred tax assets and liabilities should be calculated using 'enacted' tax rates, IAS 12 required the use of 'enacted or substantially enacted' tax rates. Again, it was open to question whether the FASB's requirement, which might make sense in the US context, was the best possible answer in countries with different legislative procedures and conventions.[241] The FASB might point out that US companies seemed capable enough of applying FAS 109 around the world, but this was not necessarily persuasive to the IASB and its constituents.[242]

Early in 2007, the IASB learned of a system of investment tax credits in Malaysia, and considered whether any guidance should be given. The IASC had left investment tax credits outside the scope of IAS 12, mainly because they were also outside the scope of FAS 109. The IASB Board was reminded, in a little history lesson by Wayne Upton and Jim Leisenring, that this went back to a major accounting standards controversy in the United States during the 1960s, and that, in the 1990s, the FASB had seen no reason to reconsider the topic because there were no investment tax credits available in the United States at the time. It was recognized that this was not very helpful to many of the Board's constituents outside of the United States, and while the Board was conscious that the income tax project had already taken longer than expected, an attempt was made to provide at least some guidance on investment tax credits without entering into an exhaustive consideration of the issue.[243]

---

[240] Interview with Anne McGeachin, 8 June 2012.

[241] This point was already raised in AP 4/2003 paper 11 Appendix B, but came back in subsequent years.

[242] This point was made by Herz in the joint board meeting of October 2009, as reported in *IStaR*, October 2009, 85–6.

[243] AP 1/2007 paper 6; see also *IStaR*, January 2007, 20–3, and IASCF trustees meeting of 2–3 July 2005, paper 2, paragraph 61. For the investment tax credit controversy, see Thomas F. Keller and Stephen A. Zeff (editors), *Financial Accounting Theory II: Issues and Controversies* (New York:

Despite delays caused by such factors as mentioned above, progress was made, and each board agreed to a number of changes to its own standard.[244] While the IASB was working towards a substantially modified version of IAS 12, it began to look as if the FASB might abandon its own exposure draft and move directly to the IASB's standard. The suggestion emerged, early in 2008, in a Board paper on the acceleration of the MoU, where it was noted that 'The FASB may propose adopting the proposed IFRS as a demonstration of the move to a common, global, principles-based standard'.[245] In June, FASB Member George Batavick was reported as saying, with reference to the revision of IAS 12: 'If ultimately convergence is going to be on IFRS, why not just go ahead and adopt their standard lock, stock, and barrel?'[246] This seemed to be confirmed in August, when the FASB made it known that it would 'suspend indefinitely' its deliberations on the income tax project.[247] When the IASB and the FASB issued their revised MoU in September 2008, it was stated that: 'In the second half of 2008, the FASB will review its strategy for short-term convergence projects in light of the possibility that some or all U.S. public companies might be permitted or required to adopt IFRS at some future date. As part of that review, it will solicit input from U.S. constituents by issuing an Invitation to Comment containing the IASB's proposed replacement of IAS 12.'[248] In line with Batavick's comment, this was interpreted at the time as a sign of a change in the FASB's strategy, by which it would adopt IFRSs rather than developing standards that were mainly but not fully converged with IFRSs.[249] If so, it would have been in line with demands from US preparers, who increasingly began to use the argument that the FASB should be cautious in issuing new standards of its own if there was to be a transition to IFRSs.[250] When the IASB's exposure draft was issued in March 2009, the US firm of PricewaterhouseCoopers alerted its clients to its significance on the basis of the expectation that the FASB would follow shortly with an invitation to comment.[251]

However, the FASB's invitation to comment failed to materialize. By the second half of 2009 the expectation that the FASB might adopt the IASB's standard had

McGraw-Hill, 1969), 417–21, and Maurice Moonitz, 'Some Reflections on the Investment Credit Experience', *Journal of Accounting Research*, 4/1 (Spring 1966), 47–61.

[244] See IASB ED/2009/2 'Income Tax', BC 131–32, for a brief summary of changes accepted in principle by each board.

[245] AP 4/2008 paper 3 (observer version), paragraph 64.

[246] 'Taxation and Representation', news item posted 3 July 2008 <http://ww2.cfo.com>.

[247] The announcement was not made in a published document, but in the course of a meeting (communication from FASB library staff to the authors, dated 10 February 2014). It was reported in professional news media, for instance, 'Standard Setter Updates', *US Week in Review* (Ernst & Young), 15 August 2008 <http://www.ey.com>.

[248] 'Completing the February 2006 Memorandum of Understanding: A Progress Report and Timetable for Completion, September 2008', appendix to IASB–FASB press release 'IASB and FASB Publish Update to 2006 Memorandum of Understanding', dated 11 September 2008.

[249] See for instance the comments in Deloitte's *Heads Up* newsletter, 16 September 2008, 1–2 <http://www.iasplus.com>.

[250] For a selection of preparer views, see Tim Reason, 'Who Should Write the Rules' <http://ww2.cfo.com> posted 19 August 2008.

[251] 'Income Tax Accounting under IFRS: A Look Ahead', PricewaterhouseCoopers LLP, 2009 <http://www.pwc.com>. For a similar view, see Ernst & Young's *Hot Topic* newsletter, 10 April 2009 <http://www.ey.com>.

disappeared, and therefore the FASB's decision to suspend its income tax project was now no longer seen as a sign of its support for convergence, but rather as the opposite. When the responses to the exposure draft were put before the two boards in October, at their joint meeting, the IASB's staff noted that there was very limited support for pursuing the project on the basis of the exposure draft. A main reason given was that it would fail to achieve convergence, because the FASB had no specific plans to resume its project.[252] At the same joint meeting, the IASB also seemed to have lost the will to pursue the project. A few months earlier, in the press release accompanying its March 2009 exposure draft, the IASB had confidently maintained that the effect of the proposal would be 'to simplify the accounting and strengthen the principle in the standard'.[253] Now the Board accepted without demurring the verdict of constituents, as summarized by the staff, that it amounted to 'the introduction of complex new rules, without significantly improving the outcome'.[254] There was some discussion that a fundamental revision would be better than an attempt to modify existing standards, but it was clear that both boards had no appetite to undertake such a project before June 2011.[255]

In the published progress reports on the MoU, the project soon disappeared from sight. What was left for the IASB was to make amendments to IAS 12 in order to deal with practical problems in its application. While a number of such possible amendments were considered, including the issue of uncertain tax positions where IFRSs had nothing to match FIN48, the list was soon narrowed down to a single topic: revaluations of investment property measured at fair value. This was not an issue in the United States, because property was measured at cost under US GAAP. It was seen as a problem in jurisdictions that had adopted IFRSs, but that had no capital gains tax, or a different tax rate for capital gains and other income. For these jurisdictions, of which Hong Kong and New Zealand were well-known examples, IAS 12 already contained the principle that the recognition and measurement of a deferred tax liability depended on the expected manner of recovery of the asset. The problem with investment property was that companies could not objectively determine up front whether they would hold on to the property to collect rents, or sell it if a favourable opportunity were to arise. For many years, these jurisdictions had been told that this problem would be dealt with as part of the short-term convergence project. It was now swiftly settled by an amendment to IAS 12 issued in December 2010, which introduced a rebuttable presumption that investment properties would be recovered through sale.[256]

---

[252] AP 10/2009 paper 12 (observer version), paragraphs 9–13.
[253] 'IASB Seeks Comments on a Proposed New Standard on Income Tax Accounting', IASB press release dated 31 March 2009.
[254] AP 10/2009 paper 12 (observer version), paragraph 9.
[255] See record of discussion in *IStaR*, October 2009, 85–6.
[256] *Deferred Tax: Recovery of Underlying Assets, Amendments to IAS 12* (IASB, December 2010).

17

Epilogue

What are the boundaries we have set for this book? The span of 2001 to 2011, an even ten years, was the tenure of the Board's first chairman, Sir David Tweedie, as well as the period that encompassed the terms of service of all of the Board's original members. The Board from April 2001 to June 2011 could justly be called the 'Tweedie Board'. But the IASB did not end with Tweedie's term, and important developments covered in this book continued to work themselves out in the subsequent years. In this epilogue, we recount some of the more important changes and events between 2001 and 2011 from the perspective of mid-2014, when the drafting of this book was completed.

17.1 A CHANGING BOARD IN A CHANGING WORLD

The world in which the 'Tweedie Board' had to find its place changed significantly during its tenure. In international capital markets, the relative position of the United States, which was always a fundamental factor in the move towards global accounting standards, had declined. Conversely, emerging economies gained in strength, turning a country such as Brazil into one of the IASB's key constituents. Around the world, financial reporting changed in character, becoming less a private affair of companies and their auditors, and more embedded in formal structures of enforcement and compliance monitoring. As a result, the world could hardly be said to have made up its mind on what it expected of the IASB in terms of principles-based standards.

During the decade, organizations of all kinds were faced with demands for increased transparency, reinforced by the continually expanding possibilities of online communication. It may be recalled, for instance, that the IASB started out with printed newsletters as one of its main forms of outreach. Apart from these secular trends, the economic and financial crisis in the later part of the decade greatly destabilized all aspects of the IASB's environment.

Until 2002, when the European Union (EU) approved the IAS Regulation, which required some 6,700 listed companies to adopt IFRSs in their consolidated statements by 2005, the Board viewed itself as more of a think-tank, without an actual clientele of listed companies of importance—although this view probably understated the extent to which companies were already affected by the Board's standards, or preparing for their adoption. Thereafter, as many other countries followed the EU's lead, the Board began thinking of itself more as a consequential standard setter. It was certainly viewed as such by many of its constituents, prompting demands that the Board, as a quasi-legislator, should become more accountable. The decision by the US Securities and Exchange Commission (SEC) in November 2007 to lift its reconciliation requirement for foreign issuers using IFRSs was further confirmation of the IASB's world standing. The SEC continued to raise expectations by developing proposals for use of IFRSs by domestic companies, opening the prospect that the IASB might within a few years become the unrivalled global standard setter.

During the first ten years, the trustees mostly kept a low public profile, protecting the Board's independence, overseeing the Board's performance and specifically its compliance with proper due process, selecting Board members and trustees, and raising the funds necessary to support the organization. Responding to criticism that the IASB's organization was not adequate for its growing responsibilities and lacked accountability for acting in the public interest, the IASC Foundation trustees joined in the creation of a Monitoring Board in 2009, consisting of top regulators from the United States and Japan, the European Commission, and the International Organization of Securities Commissions (IOSCO). The Monitoring Board has met regularly with the trustees and shown its responsiveness to public discussions of the IASB's governance and processes, while emphasizing the fundamental importance of the Board's independence.

The composition of the Board changed during the ten-year period, reflecting the trustees' deliberate choices. The initial Board was heavily drawn from standard-setting or other technical backgrounds—'techies', as they might be called. By the end of the 2001–11 period, the Board's composition was a more balanced mix of users, regulators, preparers, and audit firm partners—sixteen members all serving full-time—with only a few members possessing strong technical backgrounds.

Apart from the interim chairman Philip Laskawy, the chairmen of the Foundation trustees during the first ten years were successively a prominent central banker, Paul Volcker, and two distinguished public figures who served as ministers of finance, Tommaso Padoa-Schioppa and Gerrit Zalm. On 1 January 2012, a former securities market regulator, Michael Prada, became the trustee chairman. Likewise, David Tweedie's successor in July 2011 was Hans Hoogervorst, not an accountant but the chairman of the Dutch securities market regulator. He was assisted as vice chairman by Ian Mackintosh, the former chairman of the UK Accounting Standards Board. The two together were expected to lead the IASB's mission.

17.2 THE SEC's RELUCTANCE TO MOVE TOWARDS IFRSs

Towards the end of the IASB's first decade it was already evident that the SEC was reluctant to decide on the possible future use of IFRSs by US domestic issuers, and this posture was confirmed in subsequent years.

The SEC's unanimous decision in August 2008, enthusiastically supported by its staff, to propose a roadmap for domestic registrants' required transition from US generally accepted accounting principles (US GAAP) to IFRSs represented a strong and serious commitment by the agency. This decision was driven by SEC Chairman Christopher Cox, almost as if it were to be one of his legacy projects.

Under his leadership, the SEC was prepared to go all the way. What, in the end, held the SEC back from converting the proposal into a final rule? A major factor was the onset of the economic and financial crisis, notably the collapse of Lehman Brothers on 15 September 2008. From that point forward, all major initiatives at the SEC were put on hold, as the Federal Reserve Board chairman and the Secretary of the Treasury, assisted by Cox at the SEC, engaged in weeks of crisis discussions to re-establish the soundness of the US financial markets. The SEC was itself under a pall, as it was being criticized for not detecting earlier the weakness of major Wall Street banks and also for its failure to unmask the Madoff fraud. A second factor was the approaching end of the George W. Bush administration in January 2009, when, by tradition, the chairman of an agency such as the SEC steps down to allow the incoming president to choose his own chairman. Accordingly, Cox—the SEC's foremost advocate of IFRSs—resigned, as did his chief accountant and the director of the Division of Corporation Finance. A third factor was the rising chorus of criticism of the SEC's proposed roadmap by US preparers and users, contained in the more than two hundred letters of comment received on the rule proposal. Prominent among the critics were small listed companies that had little, if any, international exposure. To them, the cost of transition well exceeded any benefits. In this roiled environment, the incoming chairman, Mary Schapiro, was quick to disavow the roadmap in testimony to the Senate Banking Committee in January 2009. It was not until August that a new chief accountant was appointed, and in 2009 the Commission directed the staff to execute a major 'work plan' that would assist the Commission in evaluating the impact on the US securities market of the 'incorporation' of IFRSs into the financial reporting system for US issuers. This represented a step back from actual adoption.

In July 2012, the SEC's staff completed the three-year, comprehensive work plan: a factual analysis to inform the Commission about whether to move towards incorporating IFRSs into the financial reporting system. But the work plan did not make any actual recommendations to the Commission, and it is not known what the Commission's views on the desirability of this incorporation are, and when the Commission will begin formulating any such views. The revolving door at the SEC has sometimes made consistent policy making difficult to achieve: between 2001 and 2013, there have been six chairmen and five chief accountants (interspersed around acting chief accountants). In March 2013, when Mary Jo White, Schapiro's successor as chairman, had her confirmation hearing, the subject of IFRSs was not even raised. This suggests how much IFRSs have receded in importance in US political circles, and perhaps also in regulatory circles.

The IASB's organization, like the IASC's before it, devoted much of its energy and structured its activities towards the goal of gaining acceptance for IFRSs in the United States; so the stalling of further moves towards IFRS adoption in that country inevitably created a need for the IASB to rebalance itself and find a new footing.

17.3 MIXED SIGNALS FROM OTHER JURISDICTIONS

While the US capital market has descended from the dominant worldwide position it held prior to Enron, it is still the largest capital market in the world, and other countries, such as Japan, China, and India, may themselves be influenced by what the Americans do. The vital question facing the IASB was therefore whether the SEC's procrastination on some kind of official acceptance of IFRSs for domestic issuers would lead to an unravelling of much of the hard work by the Board and the Foundation. Would jurisdictions that had not yet adopted IFRSs also postpone their decisions? Would jurisdictions that had already adopted IFRSs believe they should in some way 'reclaim sovereignty' and become more relaxed about introducing deviations from IFRSs? The evidence on these points so far has been mixed.

Next to the United States, the IASB had set its sights on Japan as a major capital market that might be won for IFRSs. In 2009, Japan had already gone one step further than the United States by allowing the use of IFRSs by domestic listed companies. The allowed use of US GAAP for Japanese companies publicly traded in the United States was to be terminated in 2016, and a decision on mandatory adoption of IFRSs was scheduled for 2012, one year after the SEC's planned decision in 2011. However, as the SEC failed to make a decision by 2011, second thoughts on IFRSs gained the upper hand in Japan. In 2011, the FSA said that the option for some companies to report in Japan under US GAAP would be maintained, instead of being terminated in 2016. And after a prolonged period of indecision, the FSA announced in 2013 that Japan might actually move to a four-standard system in which Japanese GAAP, US GAAP, IFRSs, and a yet-to-be-designed modified version of IFRSs, adapted to Japanese circumstances, would exist side by side.[1] Voluntary use of IFRSs was slow to develop, but by the middle of 2014 twenty-seven companies had begun filing on the basis of IFRSs, with another fifty said to be preparing to do the same.[2]

The lack of progress in the United States towards IFRSs seems to have given China confidence in its policy of maintaining its own national standards, 'converged in substance' with IFRSs. For both China and Japan, the EU's recognition of the equivalence of their national standards with IFRSs—which had played a major role in pushing these and other countries in the direction of IFRSs—probably weakened the incentives for taking the *final* step from convergence to full adoption of IFRSs. The IASB continued to work with India, hoping that the number of deviations from IASB standards could be rolled back.

On the other hand, the year 2012 was one in which several major countries adopted, or completed convergence with, IFRSs. The list included Argentina, Mexico, Russia, and Malaysia (convergence, but with exemptions for certain classes of companies pending the issue of amendments by the IASB).

Quite independently of any decisions by the United States, the IASB continued after 2009 to build up an important clientele with its standard for small and medium-sized entities. In July 2013, the IASB reported that in excess of eighty jurisdictions had adopted the *IFRS for SMEs* or had announced plans to do so, an increase of a half-dozen since July 2011. The predominant use of the *IFRS for SMEs* has been in the developing countries. The IASB has created a veritable

---

[1] 'The Present Policy on the Application of International Financial Reporting Standards (IFRS)', report of the Business Accounting Council, dated 19 June 2013 <http://www.fsa.go.jp>.

[2] 'More Japanese Companies Embracing IFRS', news item posted 5 June 2014 <http://asia.nikkei.com>.

minor industry to develop free training materials, put on free training workshops, produce guidance booklets, translate all of the materials into more than twenty languages, and provide ongoing support for all adopters.

17.4 RECALIBRATING THE ORGANIZATION

In regard to membership on the IASB Board, voices continued to be raised in Europe questioning whether countries such as the United States and Japan, which do not require domestic listed companies to use IFRSs, should remain eligible. Yet, the United States and Japan have been, year after year, the top two country contributors to the IFRS Foundation's budget. The Constitution, as revised in 2009, introduced geographical criteria for Board membership which retained four seats for North America. This quota could hardly have been composed mostly of Canadians and Mexicans. Even so, there never has been a Mexican member, and there has been no Canadian member since 2007. The trustees could draw from a larger number of countries to fill the four seats for Asia-Oceania. In 2012, they appointed a Board member from South Korea. Japan retained its seat following the retirement of Tatsumi Yamada, and, furthermore, the IASB opened its first regional office in Tokyo in November 2012. Nevertheless, questions of membership are likely to surface again, and they will not be easy to resolve in a world of uneven IFRS adoption.

The Monitoring Board, for its part, proposed a broadening of its membership in its report on the review of the IFRS Foundation's governance, issued in February 2012. Full membership would continue to be restricted to capital markets authorities, but the intention was stated to appoint up to four new permanent members, primarily from major emerging markets, in addition to creating two rotating seats. As provisionally stated, eligibility for membership of the Monitoring Board 'will require domestic use of IFRSs in the relevant jurisdiction and financial contribution by the jurisdiction to the setting of IFRSs'.[3] Going by the plain meaning of the words, the requirement of domestic use of IFRSs would preclude the SEC's continued membership, given the growing consensus, from 2011 onwards, that the idea of IFRSs for US listed companies was apparently dead.

In October 2013, the Monitoring Board published a revised version of its Charter, including elaborated membership criteria.[4] Criteria regarding the use of IFRSs were stated as follows:

(Appendix A):
(b) The jurisdiction has made a clear commitment to moving towards application of IFRSs and promoting global acceptance of a single set of high quality international accounting standards as the final goal. This commitment is evidenced by the

---

[3] *Final Report on the Review of the IFRS Foundation's Governance* (IFRS Foundation Monitoring Board, 9 February 2012), 13. The executive summary (page 4) used a slightly different wording: 'domestic use of IFRSs in the jurisdiction's capital market and participation by the jurisdiction in Foundation funding'.

[4] *Charter of the IFRSF Monitoring Board*, attached to 'Monitoring Board Completes Revisions to Its Charter and the Memorandum of Understanding with the IFRS Foundation', Monitoring Board press release dated 31 October 2013 <http://www.iosco.org>.

jurisdiction mandating or permitting application of IFRSs to consolidated financial statements of companies raising capital in its relevant market with the effect of actually exhibiting prominence of IFRS application, or having made a decision on a transition to such a status to take place in a reasonable period of time.

(c) The IFRSs to be applied should be essentially aligned with IFRSs developed by the IASB, with possible exceptions limited to cases where certain standards or parts thereof are not relevant for economic or other conditions or could be contrary to public interest in the jurisdiction. Any flaw in following due process in developing certain standards or parts thereof could also allow for exceptions or temporary suspensions.

The first modification of the Monitoring Board's membership was made in January 2014, when it was announced that the Comissão de Valores Mobiliários of Brazil and the Financial Services Commission of South Korea were selected as new permanent members. Their compliance with the criteria cited above could not have been a matter of doubt. In June 2014, the position of the founding members was reviewed for the first time, and the Monitoring Board saw its way to the conclusion that 'no member was found non-compliant with the membership criteria'.[5] Japan's Financial Services Agency did indeed allow listed companies to opt for IFRSs as issued by the IASB. The European Commission's remaining carve-out and its non-endorsement of IFRS 9 were presumably covered by criterion (c). Yet, the continued membership of the SEC could have been justified only by considering the use of IFRSs by foreign registrants as evidence of 'prominence of IFRS application' in the US capital market.

When the drafting of this book was concluded, the Monitoring Board had not yet decided on the appointments to the two remaining permanent seats, or to the two rotating seats. The requirement that the standards to be applied should be 'essentially aligned' with IFRSs was apparently meant to open the way for China. Yet, criterion (c) as cited above would seem to raise but a low barrier against jurisdictional variations of IFRSs.

17.5 WINDING DOWN THE CONVERGENCE EFFORT WITH THE FASB

Convergence between the IASB and the Financial Accounting Standards Board (FASB), which began in earnest in 2002, became the main driver of the IASB's technical agenda, almost to the point of excluding any other activities. By the end of the first decade, all energies were concentrated on completing, by June 2011, a reduced set of major and controversial convergence projects, on revenue recognition, leases, insurance contracts, and financial instruments. Following June 2011, it soon became clear that the pressure was off. The pace slackened, and completion of the projects was delayed by years rather than months.

The differences in operation as between the IASB and FASB—two very unlike boards in terms of composition, organizational style, and culture—remained

---

[5] 'The Chairman of the Monitoring Board Reports on the Latest Meeting', IFRS Foundation Monitoring Board press release dated 18 June 2014 <http://www.iosco.org>.

difficult to bridge despite many years of experience with convergence. Further, the projects themselves led to intense lobbying by interested parties—the positions pressed by US interests often differing from positions advocated in the 'rest of the world'—which in turn led to redeliberations and re-exposures that raised increasingly unresolvable issues.

Although for a while both boards remained committed to completing the four projects jointly, it soon appeared that the 'special relationship' between the IASB and the FASB would not be continued beyond these four projects. In 2011, the IASB Board began public consultations on its technical agenda, as it was required to do every three years following the second Constitution review completed in 2010. This was a natural moment for stock-taking, not just because of the need to reconsider convergence, but also because it marked the start of the 'Hoogervorst Board'. In its conclusions published in December 2012, the Board emphasized the beginning of 'a new chapter'. It was characterized by relative calm, a priority for fundamental reflection in the form of continued work on the conceptual framework, targeted improvements to assist new adopters of IFRSs, more emphasis on maintenance and implementation, and 'fewer false starts and more disciplined work plans and timetables for our projects'.[6] The contrast with the breakneck speed with which the IASB and the FASB had, before June 2011, rushed to complete their frequently modified convergence agenda could hardly be more pronounced.

The final four projects with the FASB remained the main items on the IASB's agenda, but results were elusive. In May 2014, the boards brought one of the projects to a successful conclusion by publishing a common standard on revenue recognition. However, in February 2014 the FASB announced it was withdrawing from the project on insurance contracts. Just before, it had decided not to follow the IASB on the classification and measurement of financial instruments. This left leases as the last remaining joint project, but with an uncertain future. The question of whether and how the boards would work together in the future to *maintain* the relatively small number of converged standards they had managed to produce remains largely unanswered.

As a result of the consultations on its agenda review, the Board decided to undertake further work on the conceptual framework by itself. The IASB and the FASB had decided to launch a joint conceptual framework in 2004, a project which was not even half finished when it was suspended in 2010. The IASB then announced in 2012 that it would not work with any standard setter in particular on the remainder of the framework, although it said it looked forward to working with all standard setters having experience with conceptual frameworks. At the IASB's request, a senior member of the FASB's staff agreed to work with the IASB's staff to develop a major discussion paper on the conceptual framework, which was published in July 2013.

Because of the almost single-minded focus on completing the four convergence projects, the Board's agenda had, by 2011, become largely vacant of other projects. This by itself might be sufficient to explain why the IASB's output from the middle of 2011 to the middle of 2014, apart from convergence work, was limited to a number of minor amendments. Adding new topics to the agenda had become a

---

[6] *Feedback Statement: Agenda Consultation 2011* (IFRS Foundation, December 2012), 5.

more complex and slower process, not only because of the requirement for more extensive public consultation, but also because the Board had accepted that its standards should be evidence-based. This required the Board to demonstrate more rigorously the need for any new standards or amendments. The Board resuscitated its 'rate regulated activities' project and issued a new standard, IFRS 14 *Regulatory Deferral Accounts*, in January 2014, but this was an interim standard rather than the result of a comprehensive consideration of the topic.

17.6 EXPANSION OF TRUSTEE AND BOARD ROLES

As the trustees embarked on their second decade, they added a more aggressive outreach to their previous focus on overseeing the Board. The report on their strategy review, published in February 2012, said that one of the trustees' missions was to ascertain 'where adoption of IFRSs is incomplete or where there is divergence from the full set of IFRSs as issued by the IASB' (paragraph A3).[7] The first step the trustees took was for the Foundation to develop its own database on the extent of adoption by the jurisdictions, rather than continuing to rely on the estimates published by one or more of the major audit firms. Towards this end, the Foundation has posted more than 130 'jurisdiction profiles' on its website—to establish the facts of jurisdictions' adoption of IFRSs or their progress towards doing so. In their strategy review, the trustees also said that both the IASB and the Foundation will enquire into whether there has been 'consistent application' of IFRSs across the jurisdictions.[8] The IASB, they said, will 'work with a network of securities regulators, audit regulators, standard-setters, regional bodies involved with accounting standard-setting, accounting bodies and other stakeholders to identify where divergence in practice occurs across borders' (paragraph A5). The Board, 'in partnership with relevant authorities, will identify jurisdictions where IFRSs are being modified and, in these circumstances, encourage transparent reporting of such divergences at the jurisdictional level' (paragraph A5). Without question, this plan marked out a proactive stance. Clearly, the strategy review signified a turning-point in the trustees' view of the role of the Foundation and the Board in seeking to achieve genuine worldwide comparability of financial reporting.

17.7 A WORLD OF NATIONAL STANDARD SETTERS

The rapid progress of the adoption of, or convergence with, IFRSs around the world during the IASB's first decade raised questions about the future role of national standard setters. Although some national standard setters lost budget and

---

[7] *IFRSs as the Global Standards: Setting a Strategy for the Foundation's Second Decade* (IFRS Foundation, February 2012).

[8] For an assessment of the state of IFRS adoption on the basis of these jurisdiction profiles, see Paul Pacter, 'Global Accounting Standards—From Vision to Reality', *The CPA Journal*, 84/1 (January 2014), 6, 8–10.

influence as the IASB's star rose, others increased in strength and positioned themselves as national interlocutors with the IASB. One of the really positive effects of the work of the IASB has been the impact it has had on the quality of the people around the world who are coming to grips with the IASB's drafts and making perceptive and valuable comments and suggestions for improvement. Andrew Lennard, the technical director and then the research director of the UK's Accounting Standards Board, who has attended semi-annual meetings of the National Standard-Setters from the beginning, has said: 'we [i.e. the ASB] can no longer assume we are in the vanguard, because other people have got much better. Around the world, the countries that one used to be disdainful of are now producing very good, very well informed people. So we're getting towards a real global community of people, all of whom can do things well.'[9] At the start of the second decade, not least because of the declining prospect of adoption in the United States, the future of national standard setters looked more secure.

The trustees' strategy review specified that 'The IFRS Foundation and the IASB should encourage the maintenance of a network of national accounting standard-setting bodies and regional bodies involved with accounting standard-setting as an integral part of the global standard-setting process' (paragraph C5). Accordingly, on 1 November 2012, the trustees sought public comment on proposals for the creation of an Accounting Standards Advisory Forum (ASAF). ASAF 'will result in a more streamlined and effective dialogue between the IASB and this important group of stakeholders from the standard-setting community'.[10] With some modifications, ASAF was placed in operation and held its first meeting on 8–9 April 2013. The aim was to provide a productive flow of ideas between stakeholders and the IASB, both from national standard setters and regional bodies. The FASB took its place as one of the members of ASAF, reverting to the situation of more than ten years earlier, when it was formally just one of the IASB's liaison standard setters.

Within ASAF, regional bodies were given a prominent place, in line with the IASB's earlier encouragement of regional organizations of standard setters. The South African Financial Reporting Standards Council was appointed as the member for Africa, supported by the Pan African Federation of Accountants. The Asian-Oceanian Standard-Setters Group (AOSSG), represented by the Hong Kong Institute of Certified Public Accountants, was appointed as one of the four representatives of Asia-Oceania. The European Financial Reporting Advisory Group (EFRAG) was one of the European members, and the Group of Latin American Accounting Standard Setters (GLASS), represented by Brazil's Comitê de Pronunciamentos Contábeis, was one of the four delegations from the Americas.[11]

---

[9] Interview with Andrew Lennard, 13 October 2008.

[10] 'IFRS Foundation Publishes Proposals to Create an Accounting Standards Advisory Forum', IFRS Foundation press release dated 1 November 2012.

[11] 'Trustees Announce Membership of ASAF', IFRS Foundation press release dated 19 March 2013. The representation of GLASS by Brazil is not mentioned in the Foundation's press release but is found in 'ASAF Membership Announced', news item posted 19 March 2013 <http://www.iasplus.com>.

17.8 EUROPEAN PARLIAMENT POLITICIZES FUNDING OF THE IFRS FOUNDATION

Concerns that EU funding of the IASB might become politicized resurfaced during 2013, when preparations were made for the renewal of the three-year operating grant. A budget proposal made by the European Commission for a six-year grant (2014–20) provided the occasion for some members of the European Parliament to raise, once again, questions about the IASB's governance as well as over the compatibility of IFRSs with some of the basic principles of the accounting directives, such as the true and fair view requirement. Also in 2013, Commissioner Michel Barnier solicited a report by a senior Belgian politician, Philippe Maystadt, into ways of 'reinforcing' the EU's contribution to development of IFRSs. The report, published in November 2013, deflected attention from the IASB and concentrated instead on strengthening EFRAG. The report, apparently, helped to clear the way towards a political agreement in December to continue the EU's funding of the IASB.

17.9 US FINANCIAL ACCOUNTING FOUNDATION CONTROVERSIALLY CONTRIBUTES UP TO $3 MILLION TO THE IFRS FOUNDATION

On 28 January 2014, the Financial Accounting Foundation (FAF), which oversees the FASB, announced that it 'will make a non-recurring contribution of up to $3 million' to the IFRS Foundation 'to support the completion of international convergence projects'.[12] This decision stirred controversy because, under the Sarbanes-Oxley Act of 2002, the SEC imposes an 'accounting support fee' on issuers to subsidize the work of the FASB, via a transfer to the FAF. As noted in Section 11.10, the FAF contributed $500,000 to the IFRS Foundation in 2011, without publicly saying that it was doing so. Prior to announcing this most recent contribution, the FAF said it had consulted with 'senior officials' of the SEC. A news report which aired the controversy over the FAF's most recent contribution revealed that the SEC may have played a role in stimulating the contribution, and that the contribution had been approved by the SEC Chairman but had not been voted on by the full Commission. US commentators were reported to have questioned the FAF trustees' authority to make a financial contribution to another standard-setting board.[13] Some called on the SEC to

---

[12] 'Financial Accounting Foundation to Provide up to $3 Million to IFRS Foundation to Aid Completion of Joint IASB Projects', FAF news release dated 28 January 2014 <http://www.accountingfoundation.org>.

[13] Steve Burkholder, 'FASB Parent's $3 million Pledge to IASB's Parent Raises Concerns in Rulemaking Circles', Accounting Policy & Practice Report, *Bloomberg BNA*, 12 February 2014 <http://www.bna.com>. See also 'From the [FAF's] President's Desk', February 2014, <http://www.accountingfoundation.org>.

put an unambiguous stop to any speculation about a possible future for IFRSs in the United States which the FAF grant might encourage.[14]

The FAF's motivation behind its decision to make this sizeable financial contribution to the IFRS Foundation came into question in February 2014, when, as was noted above, it was reported that the FASB had decided to withdraw from two of the three remaining convergence projects.[15] It seemed incongruous for the FAF to authorize the financial contribution in January 2014, followed a month later by the FASB's decision to pull out of the convergence projects.

Hence, both in Europe and in the United States, politically inspired criticisms were made of the funding of the IFRS Foundation.

[14] Paul B. W. Miller and Paul R. Bahnson, 'FAF's "Gift" to the IASB: It's Time to Finally Reject IFRS and the IASB for the U.S.', *Accounting Today*, 28/5 (May 2014), 20–1.

[15] 'FASB: Insurance Shock' and 'FASB: Classification Model Abandoned' in *World Accounting Report*, March 2014, 7.

Trustees, Members of the Board, the Advisory Council, and the Interpretations Committee

This appendix lists individuals serving as trustees, members of the Board, the Advisory Council and the Interpretations Committee with first terms starting up to June 2011. Terms expected to end after June 2014 are shown in brackets. Any affiliations or former affiliations shown are as of the date of first appointment. This information is indicative only and may not reflect multiple affiliations or the range of previous experience.

A1.1 Trustees of the International Accounting Standards Committee Foundation (IFRS Foundation from March 2010)

Trustees served three-year terms, renewable once. Some of the initial trustees served four- or five-year terms in order to achieve staggering. The original Constitution prescribed nineteen trustees. This number was increased to twenty-two as a result of the Foundation's first Constitution review effective as of January 2006.

Chairmen	
Paul Volcker	May 2000–December 2005
Tommaso Padoa-Schioppa	January 2006–May 2006
Philip Laskawy	June 2006–December 2007
Gerrit Zalm	January 2008–July 2010
Tommaso Padoa-Schioppa	July 2010–December 2010
Tsuguoki Fujinuma/Robert Glauber	December 2010–December 2011 (acting co-chairmen)

Vice chairmen	
Bertrand Collomb	January 2007–December 2007
Philip Laskawy	January 2008–December 2009
Tsuguoki Fujinuma	April 2010–[December 2014]
Robert Glauber	April 2010–[December 2014]

All trustees by date of first appointment		
Trustee	Terms of office	Main affiliation or former affiliation
Roy Andersen	May 2000–December 2003 January 2004–December 2006	Liberty Group, South Africa
John Biggs	May 2000–December 2004	TIAA-CREF, United States
Sir Andrew Crockett	May 2000–June 2003	Bank for International Settlements (British)
Roberto Teixeira da Costa	May 2000–December 2004 January 2005–December 2007	Comissão de Valores Mobiliários, Brazil
Guido Ferrarini	May 2000–December 2004	Università di Genova, Italy
Yves Fortier	May 2000–December 2003 January 2004–December 2006	Ogilvy Renault, Canada

(*continued*)

All trustees by date of first appointment

Trustee	Terms of office	Main affiliation or former affiliation
Toshikatsu Fukuma	May 2000–June 2002	Mitsui & Co., Japan
Cornelius Herkströter	May 2000–December 2003	Royal Dutch/Shell Group, the
	January 2004–December 2006	Netherlands
Hilmar Kopper	May 2000–December 2002	Deutsche Bank, Germany
Philip Laskawy	May 2000–December 2003	Ernst & Young, United States
	January 2004–December 2006	
	January 2007–December 2009	
Charles Yeh Kwong	May 2000–December 2002	Hong Kong Exchanges and Clearing
Lee	January 2003–December 2005	
Sir Sydney Lipworth	May 2000–December 2002	Financial Reporting Council, United
	January 2003–December 2005	Kingdom
Didier Pineau-	May 2000–December 2003	Schneider Electric, France
Valencienne		
Jens Røder	May 2000–December 2004	PricewaterhouseCoopers, Denmark
	January 2005–March 2006	
David Ruder	May 2000–December 2002	(formerly) Securities and Exchange
	January 2003–December 2005	Commission, United States
Kenneth Spencer	May 2000–March 2004	Australian Accounting Standards Board
William Steere	May 2000–December 2002	Pfizer, United States
Koji Tajika	May 2000–December 2004	Deloitte Touche Tohmatsu, Japan
Paul Volcker	May 2000–December 2002	(formerly) Federal Reserve Board, United
	January 2003–December 2005	States
Toru Hashimoto	September 2002–December 2002	Fuji Bank, Japan
	January 2003–December 2005	
Max Dietrich Kley	January 2003–December 2005	BASF, Germany
	January 2006–December 2008	
Sir Dennis	January 2003–December 2005	JP Morgan & Co., United States (British)
Weatherstone		
Malcolm Knight	June 2003–December 2004	Bank for International Settlements
	January 2005–December 2007	(British)
Bertrand Collomb	January 2004–December 2006	Lafarge, France
	January 2007–December 2009	
Richard Humphry	January 2005–December 2007	Australian Stock Exchange
Oscar Fanjul	February 2005–December 2007	Omega Capital, Spain
	January 2008–December 2010	
Tsuguoki Fujinuma	February 2005–December 2007	Japanese Institute of Certified Public
	January 2008–December 2010	Accountants
	January 2011–[December 2014]	
Antonio Vegezzi	February 2005–December 2007	Capital International, Switzerland
	January 2008–December 2010	
Tommaso Padoa-	January 2006–May 2006	European Central Bank (Italian)
Schioppa	July 2010–December 2010	
Marvin Cheung	January 2006–December 2008	Hong Kong Exchanges and Clearing
	January 2009–December 2011	
Samuel DiPiazza	January 2006–December 2008	PricewaterhouseCoopers, United States
	January 2009–December 2011	
William McDonough	January 2006–March 2008	Merrill Lynch & Co., United States
Sir Bryan Nicholson	January 2006–December 2008	Financial Reporting Council, United
	January 2009–January 2012	Kingdom
Mohandas Pai	January 2006–December 2008	Infosys Technologies, India
	January 2009–December 2011	
David Shedlarz	January 2006–December 2008	Pfizer, United States
Junichi Ujiie	January 2006–December 2008	Nomura Holdings, Japan

Liu Zhongli	January 2006–December 2008	Chinese Institute of Certified Public
	January 2009–December 2011	Accountants
Alicja Kornasiewicz	March 2006–December 2007	CA IB Group, Poland
	January 2008–December 2009	
Jeff van Rooyen	January 2007–December 2009	Uranus Investment Holdings, South
	January 2010–December 2012	Africa
David Sidwell	January 2007–December 2009	Morgan Stanley, United States
	January 2010–December 2012	
Kees Storm	January 2007–December 2007	Aegon, the Netherlands
Paul Tellier	January 2007–December 2009	Bombardier, Canada
	January 2010–December 2012	
Gerrit Zalm	January 2008–July 2010	Minister of Finance, the Netherlands
Robert Glauber	March 2008–December 2008	National Association of Securities Dealers
	January 2009–December 2011	(NASD), United States
	January 2012–[December 2014]	
Jeffrey Lucy	January 2008–December 2010	Financial Reporting Council, Australia
	January 2011–December 2013	
Pedro Malan	March 2008–December 2010	Unibanco, Brazil
	January 2011–December 2013	
Luigi Spaventa	March 2008–December 2009	Commissione Nazionale per le Società e
	January 2010–July 2010	la Borsa, Italy
Clemens Börsig	January 2009–December 2011	Deutsche Bank, Germany
	January 2012–[December 2014]	
Noriaki Shimazaki	January 2009–December 2011	Sumitomo Corporation, Japan
	January 2012–June 2013	
Scott Evans	January 2009–December 2011	TIAA-CREF, United States
	January 2012–[December 2014]	
Yves-Thibault de Silguy	January 2010–December 2012	VINCI, France
Harvey Goldschmid	January 2010–December 2012	(formerly) Securities and Exchange
	January 2013–[December 2015]	Commission, United States
Duck-Koo Chung	January 2011–[December 2016]	Minister of Commerce, Industry, and
		Energy, South Korea
Dick Sluimers	February 2011–[December 2016]	APG Group, the Netherlands
Antonio Zoido	April 2011–[December 2016]	Bolsas y Mercados Españoles

A1.2 Members of the International Accounting Standards Board (IASB)

Under the original Constitution, Board members were appointed for terms of five years, renewable once. Some of the initial Board members were appointed for three- or four-year terms in order to achieve staggering. The original Constitution prescribed fourteen Board members. This number was increased to sixteen as a result of the Foundation's second Constitution review effective as of January 2009. As part of the same review, any second terms of Board members appointed after 2 July 2009 were limited to three years.

Chairman and vice chairman	
Sir David Tweedie (chairman)	January 2001–June 2011
Thomas Jones (vice chairman)	January 2001–June 2009

All Board members by date of first appointment, terms as part-time member marked (p)

Board member	Terms of office	(Former) affiliation
Mary Barth	January 2001–June 2004 (p)	Stanford University, United States
	July 2004–June 2009 (p)	
Hans-Georg Bruns	January 2001–June 2006	DaimlerChrysler, Germany
	July 2006–June 2007	
Anthony Cope	January 2001–June 2004	Financial Accounting Standards Board,
	July 2004–June 2007	United States
Robert Garnett	January 2001–June 2005	Anglo American, South Africa
	July 2005–June 2010	
Gilbert Gélard	January 2001–June 2005	KPMG, France
	July 2005–June 2010	
Robert Herz	January 2001–June 2002 (p)	PricewaterhouseCoopers, United States
Thomas Jones	January 2001–June 2004	Citigroup, United States
	July 2004–June 2009	
James Leisenring	January 2001–June 2005	Financial Accounting Standards Board,
	July 2005–June 2010	United States
Warren McGregor	January 2001–June 2006	Stevenson McGregor, Australia
	July 2006–June 2011	
Patricia O'Malley	January 2001–June 2004	Accounting Standards Board, Canada
	July 2004–June 2007	
Harry Schmid	January 2001–March 2004	Nestlé, Switzerland
Sir David Tweedie	January 2001–June 2006	Accounting Standards Board, United
	July 2006–June 2011	Kingdom
Geoffrey Whittington	January 2001–June 2006	Cambridge University, United
		Kingdom
Tatsumi Yamada	January 2001–June 2006	ChuoAoyama Audit Corporation,
	July 2006–June 2011	Japan
John Smith	September 2002–June 2007 (p)	Deloitte & Touche, United States
	July 2007–June 2012	
Jan Engström	May 2004–June 2009	Volvo Group, Sweden
	July 2009–June 2014	
Philippe Danjou	November 2006–June 2011	Autorité des Marchés Financiers,
	July 2011–[June 2016]	France
Zhang Wei-Guo	July 2007–June 2012	China Securities Regulatory
	July 2012–[June 2017]	Commission
Stephen Cooper	July 2007–December 2008 (p)	UBS Investment Bank, United
	January 2009–June 2012	Kingdom
	July 2012–[June 2017]	
Prabhakar	January 2009–June 2013	KPMG, United States (Indian national)
Kalavacherla		
Amaro Luiz de	July 2009–June 2014	Banco Central do Brasil
Oliveira Gomes	July 2014–[June 2019]	
Patrick Finnegan	July 2009–June 2014	CFA Institute, United States
	July 2014–[June 2019]	
Patricia McConnell	July 2009–June 2014	Bear, Stearns & Co., United States
Elke König	July 2010–December 2011	Hannover Re, Germany
Paul Pacter	July 2010–June 2012	Deloitte, Hong Kong
	July 2012–December 2012	
Darrel Scott	October 2010–[June 2015]	FirstRand Banking Group, South
		Africa

A1.3 Members of the Standing Interpretations Committee and the International Financial Reporting Interpretations Committee (IFRS Interpretations Committee from 1 March 2010)

The Standing Interpretations Committee (SIC) was established by the IASC in 1997. It remained in function until December 2001 when it was reconstituted under the name of International Financial Reporting Interpretations Committee (IFRIC). IFRIC members served renewable terms of three years, although some of the initial members served a first or single term of four years. The number of members was increased from twelve to fourteen in November 2007 (first appointments as of July 2008), and the name was changed to IFRS Interpretations Committee in January 2010. IFRIC and the IFRS Interpretations Committee had a non-voting chairman.

Chairmen	
Paul Cherry (SIC)	January 1997–December 2001
Kevin Stevenson	January 2002–March 2005
Robert Garnett	June 2005–July 2011

Interpretations committee members, other than the chairmen, in order of appointment[1]

Member	Terms of office	Affiliation at first appointment
Yves Bernheim	SIC (1997)–December 2001	Mazars & Guérard, France
Mary Keegan	SIC (1997)–December 2001	Price Waterhouse, United Kingdom
Harry Schmid	SIC (1997)–December 2001	Formerly Nestlé, Switzerland
Wienand Schruff	SIC (1997)–December 2001	KPMG Deutsche Treuhand Gesellschaft, Germany
John Smith	SIC (1997)–December 2001 January 2002–August 2002	Deloitte & Touche, United States
Kevin Stevenson	SIC (1997)–December 2001	Coopers & Lybrand, Australia
Leo van der Tas	SIC (1997)–December 2001 January 2002–June 2003 July 2003–June 2006	Moret Ernst & Young, the Netherlands
Patricia Walters	SIC (1998)–December 2001 January 2002–June 2003 July 2003–June 2006	AIMR, United States
Junichi Akiyama	SIC (1999)–December 2001 January 2002–June 2003 July 2003–February 2005	Tama University, Japan
Domingo Mario Marchese	SIC (1999)–December 2001 January 2002–June 2004 July 2004–June 2007	Marchese, Grandi, Mesón & Asociados, Argentina
Phil Ameen	January 2002–June 2005 July 2005–June 2008	General Electric Company, United States
Christian Chiarasini	January 2002–mid 2002	Arthur Andersen, France
Claudio de Conto	January 2002–June 2005 July 2005–June 2008	Pirelli, Italy
Clement Kwok	January 2002–June 2004	Hongkong and Shanghai Hotels, Hong Kong
Wayne Lonergan	January 2002–June 2004	Lonergan Edwards & Associates, Australia
Mary Tokar	January 2002–June 2004 July 2004–June 2007	KPMG International, United Kingdom

(*continued*)

Interpretations committee members, other than the chairmen, in order of appointment[1]

Member	Terms of office	Affiliation at first appointment
Ian Wright	January 2002–June 2004 July 2004–June 2007	PricewaterhouseCoopers, United Kingdom
Jeannot Blanchet	December 2002–June 2004 July 2004–June 2007	Morgan Stanley, France
Ken Wild	December 2002–June 2003 July 2003–June 2006 July 2006–June 2009	Deloitte Touche Tohmatsu, United Kingdom
Michael Bradbury	November 2004–June 2005 July 2005–June 2008	Unitec, New Zealand
Jean-Louis Lebrun	November 2004–June 2005 July 2005–June 2008 July 2008–June 2011	Mazars, France
Shunichi Toyoda	March 2005–June 2006	NEC Corporation, Japan
Sara York Kenny	July 2006–June 2009 July 2009–June 2012	International Finance Corporation, United States
Takatsugu Ochi	July 2006–June 2009 July 2009–June 2011	Sumitomo Corporation, Japan
Ruth Picker	July 2006–June 2009 July 2009–June 2012	Ernst & Young, Australia
Guido Fladt	July 2007–June 2010 July 2010–June 2013	PricewaterhouseCoopers, Germany
Bernd Hacker	July 2007–June 2010 July 2010–June 2013	Siemens, Germany
Andrew Vials	July 2007–June 2010 July 2010–June 2013	KPMG, United Kingdom
Darrel Scott	July 2007–June 2010	FirstRand Banking, South Africa
Joanna Perry	July 2008–June 2011 July 2011–[June 2014]	Financial Reporting Standards Board, New Zealand
Luca Cencioni	July 2008–June 2011 July 2011–[June 2014]	ENI, Italy
Margaret Smyth	July 2008–June 2011 July 2011–June 2013	United Technologies, United States
Scott Taub	July 2008–June 2011 July 2011–[June 2014]	Financial Reporting Advisors, United States
Jean Paré	July 2008–June 2011 July 2011–June 2014	Bombardier, Canada
Laurence Rivat	July 2009–June 2012 July 2012–[June 2015]	Deloitte, France
Li Feilong	July 2010–June 2013 July 2013–[June 2016]	CNOOC, China

A1.4 Members of the Standards Advisory Council (IFRS Advisory Council from March 2010)

The initial members of the Standards Advisory Council (SAC) were appointed for renewable terms of three years. Nevertheless, the initial members who did not step down for personal reasons continued to serve until September 2005, when the trustees appointed a new membership following the first Constitution review. The members appointed in October 2005 continued to serve until December 2008 when the membership of SAC was again

---

[1] SIC members retiring prior to 2001 are not shown. The nationality of the member is indicated when this differs from the country where the affiliated organization is based.

renewed en bloc. All terms of the 2009 SAC members expired in December 2011. In July 2011 the trustees announced that they wished to invite 'most organizations' to renew their membership, but proposed to use staggered terms for the appointments as of January 2012.

From 2001 to 2008, members of SAC served in principle in a personal capacity even though it is evident that several were appointed because of their affiliation with particular organizations. From 2009 onwards all SAC members (IFRS Advisory Council members) were explicitly appointed as representatives of organizations. For members reappointed in 2009, both the private affiliation at initial appointment (P) and the organization represented since 2009 (R) are shown. Chairmen and vice chairmen, post-2009, were not seen as representatives of a particular organization.

Over time, the IASB has used various geographical breakdowns in lists of SAC members, and since 2009 Advisory Council membership is typically not represented in geographical order. The main structure of the table below is based on the geographical categories used in the 2007 *Annual Report*. Within these main categories, the ordering of names is intended to reflect continuity of countries or organizations represented on the Advisory Council.

Chairmen	
Peter Wilmot	2001–2005 (formally vice chairman, replacing David Tweedie)
Nelson Carvalho	2005–2008
Paul Cherry	2009–2013

Vice chairmen	
Charles Macek	2009–[2014]
Patrice Marteau	2009–2012

All Advisory Council members

Member	Terms of service	Affiliation and/or represented organization
Africa		
Ndung'U Gathinji	2001–2005	Eastern Central and Southern African Federation of Accountants, Kenya
Benoît Antoine Atangana Onana	2005–2012	(P) Institute of Chartered Accountants of Cameroon (R) Fédération Internationale des Experts-Comptables Francophones
Peter Wilmot	2001–2005	Accounting Practices Board, South Africa
Darrel Scott	2005–2007	FirstRand Banking Group, South Africa
Christine Ramon	2007–2008	Sasol Ltd, South Africa
Moses Kgosana	2009–2011	Accounting Practices Board, South Africa
Asia-Oceania		
Peter Day	2001–2005	AMCOR, Australia
Judith Downes	2005–2012	(P) Australia and New Zealand Banking Group (R) Group of 100, Australia
Feng Shuping	2001–2005	China Accounting Standards Committee
Wang Jun	2005–2008	China Accounting Standards Committee
Liu Yuting	2009–2011	Ministry of Finance, China
Marvin Cheung	2001–2005	KPMG, China and Hong Kong, Hong Kong
P.M. Kam	2005–2011	(P) Jardine Matheson, Hong Kong (R) Hong Kong Institute of Certified Public Accountants
Yezdi Malegam	2001–2005	S.B. Billimoria & Co., India
Shailesh V. Haribhakti	2005–2008	Haribhakti & Co., India

(continued)

All Advisory Council members

Member	Terms of service	Affiliation and/or represented organization
Narendra Sarda	2009–2011	Associated Chambers of Commerce of India/ Mumbai Stock Exchange
Eiko Tsujiyama	2001–2008	Musashi University, Japan
Sei-Ichi Kaneko	2009–2013	Securities Analysts Association of Japan
Yoshiki Yagi	2001–2008	Hitachi, Japan
Shozo Yoneya	2009–2011	Nippon Keidanren, Japan
Il-Sup Kim	2001–2002	Korea Accounting Standards Board
Kyung-Ho Kim	2002–2004	Korea Accounting Standards Board
Chungwoo Suh	2004–2005	Korea Accounting Standards Board
Suk-Jun Lee	2005–2008	Samsung Electronics, South Korea
Changhong Kim	2009–2013	Korea Accounting Standards Board
Raja Arshad-Uda	2001–2005	Malaysian Accounting Standards Board
Ian Ball	2001–2005	Victoria University of Wellington, New Zealand
Fang Ai Lian	2003–2005	Ernst & Young, Singapore
Danny Teoh Leong Kay	2005–2008	KPMG, Singapore
Surya Subramanian	2009–2011	Association of Banks in Singapore
Reyaz Mihular	2001–2013	(P) Sri Lankan Accounting Standards Committee (R) South Asian Federation of Accountants (SAFA)
Europe		
Benoit Jaspar	2001–2005	Generali, Belgium
Stig Enevoldsen	2001–2010	(P) Deloitte & Touche, Denmark (European Financial Reporting Advisory Group) (R) European Financial Reporting Advisory Group
Françoise Flores	2010–[2014]	European Financial Reporting Advisory Group
Rita Ilisson	2001–2005	Estonian Accounting Standards Board
Maija Torkko	2001–2005	Nokia, Finland
Philippe Danjou	2001–2006	Commission des Opérations de Bourse, France
Jean Keller	2001–2005	Lafarge, France
Patrice Marteau	2005–2012	PPR, France
Jochen Pape	2001–2008	PricewaterhouseCoopers, Germany
Heinz-Joachim Neubürger	2005–2008	Siemens, Germany
Alberto Giussani	2001–2008	PricewaterhouseCoopers, Italy
Anna di Michele	2005–2008	UBS, Italy
Willem van der Loos	2001–2005	Philips, the Netherlands
Kees Storm	2005–2007	Aegon, the Netherlands
Ingebret Hisdal	2005–2008	Deloitte, Norway
Larissa Gorbatova	2001–2005	Ministry of Finance, Russia
Vladimir Preobrazhenskiy	2005–2008	Siberian Coal Energy Company, Russia
Carmelo de las Morenas	2001–2005	Repsol YPF Group, Spain
José Antonio Álvarez Álvarez	2005–2008	Banco Santander, Spain
Sigvard Heurlin	2001–2005	Öhrlings PricewaterhouseCoopers, Sweden
Hugo Schaub	2005–2007	UBS, Switzerland
Will Widdowson	2007–2012	(P) UBS, Switzerland (R) Institute of International Finance
David Damant	2001–2005	Sword Management, United Kingdom
Douglas Flint	2001–2005	HSBC Holdings, United Kingdom
Sarah Deans	2005–2008	JP Morgan, United Kingdom
David Lindsell	2005–2008	Ernst & Young, United Kingdom
Liz Murrall	2009–2013	Association of British Insurers/Investment Management Association, United Kingdom

Richard Thorpe	2006–2013	(P) Financial Services Authority, United Kingdom (R) Committee of European Securities Regulators (CESR)
Mauro Grande	2005–2011	(P)/(R) European Central Bank
Jacques le Douit	2009–2013	European Insurance and Reinsurance Federation
Christoph Hütten	2009–[2014]	European Issuers/European Round Table of Industrialists
Piero di Salvo	2009	European National Standard Setters (annual rotation, Italy)
Liesel Knorr	2010	European National Standard Setters (annual rotation, Germany)
Jérôme Haas	2011	European National Standard Setters (annual rotation, France)
Latin America		
Nelson Carvalho	2001–2008	Universidade de São Paulo, Brazil
Geraldo Toffanello	2009–2011	Brazilian Association of Listed Companies (Abrasca), Brazil
Héctor Estruga	2001–2008	Arthur Andersen, Argentina
Rafael Gómez Eng	2001–2005	KPMG, Mexico
Héctor Vela Dib	2005–2008	CEMEX, Mexico
Middle East		
Adir Inbar	2001–2008	Professional Board, Institute of Certified Public Accountants in Israel
Rifaat Ahmed Abdel Karim	2001–2008	Accounting & Auditing Organization for Islamic Financial Institutions, Bahrain
North America		
Jeannot Blanchet	2001–2002	Arthur Andersen, Canada
Paul McCrossan	2001–2005	Eckler Partners, Canada
Michael Conway	2001–2005	KPMG, United States
Trevor Harris	2001–2008	Morgan Stanley, United States
Philip Livingston	2001–2003	Financial Executives International, United States
Colleen Sayther	2003–2006	Financial Executives International, United States
Michael Cangemi	2007–2008	Financial Executives International, United States
Jamie Miller	2009–2011	Financial Executives International, United States
Karyn Brooks	2009–2013	Financial Executives International, Canada
Patricia McConnell	2001–2006	Bear, Stearns & Co., United States (CFA Institute)
Robert Morgan	2007	Consultant in corporate finance, Canada (CFA Institute)
Dane Mott	2008–2011	(P) Bear, Stearns & Co., United States (CFA Institute) (R) CFA Institute
Gabrielle Napolitano	2001–2003	Goldman, Sachs & Co., United States
David Shedlarz	2001–2005	Pfizer, United States
Keith Sherin	2001–2005	General Electric Company United States
David Sidwell	2001–2005	JP Morgan Chase & Co., United States
Norman Strauss	2001–2005	Ernst & Young, United States
Gerald Edwards	2001–2005	Federal Reserve Board, United States
Frank Brod	2005–2008	Dow Chemical, United States
Neri Bukspan	2009–2011	Investors' Technical Advisory Committee, United States
Gail Hanson	2009–2011	Council of Institutional Investors, United States
Jeff Mahoney	2011–2013	Council of Institutional Investors, United States
Jerry de St. Paer	2009–2013	Group of North American Insurance Enterprises
Donald Boteler	2009–2011	Investment Company Institute, United States
International organizations, business associations, and audit firms		
Arnold Schilder	2001–2006	De Nederlandsche Bank, the Netherlands (Basel Committee on Banking Supervision)
Sylvie Matherat	2007–2012	(P) Banque de France (Basel Committee on Banking Supervision)

(*continued*)

All Advisory Council members

Member	Terms of service	Affiliation and/or represented organization
		(R) Basel Committee on Banking Supervision
Ian Mackintosh	2001–2003	IFAC Public Sector Committee
Philippe Adhémar	2004–2005	International Public Sector Accounting Standards Board
Ian Ball	2005–2008	International Federation of Accountants (IFAC)
James Sylph	2009–2013	International Federation of Accountants (IFAC)
Arne Petersen	2001–2005	International Monetary Fund
Kenneth Sullivan	2005–2012	(P)/(R) International Monetary Fund
John Carchrae	2001–2008	Ontario Securities Commission, Canada (IOSCO)
Rafael Sánchez de la Peña	2001–2005	Comisión Nacional del Mercado de Valores, Spain (IOSCO)
Christoph Ernst	2005–2010	(P) Bundesministerium der Justiz, Germany (IOSCO)
		(R) IOSCO, developed economies (shared German/ French seat)
Thomas Blöink	2011–[2014]	IOSCO, developed economies (shared German/ French seat)
Sophie Baranger	2009–2011	IOSCO, developed economies (shared German/ French seat)
Patrick Parent	2011–[2014]	IOSCO, developed economies (shared German/ French seat)
Marcos Barbosa Pinto	2009–2010	IOSCO, emerging economies
Alexsandro Broedel Lopes	2010–2012	IOSCO, emerging economies
Fayezul Choudhury	2001–2005	World Bank
Charles McDonough	2005–2011	(P)/(R) World Bank
Simon Bradbury	2011–2012	World Bank
Florence Lustman	2002–2005	Commission de contrôle des assurances, des mutuelles et des institutions de prévoyance, France (International Association of Insurance Supervisors)
Tomoko Amaya	2005–2006	Financial Services Agency, Japan (International Association of Insurance Supervisors)
Henning Göbel	2006–2010	(P) Bundesanstalt für Finanzdienstleistungsaufsicht, Germany (International Association of Insurance Supervisors)
		(R) International Association of Insurance Supervisors
Michel Colinet	2010–2011	International Association of Insurance Supervisors
Tatiana Krylova	2003–2007	United Nations Conference on Trade and Development (UNCTAD)
Yoseph Asmelash	2007–2008	United Nations Conference on Trade and Development (UNCTAD)
Norbert Barth	2009–2013	Corporate Reporting Users' Forum
Francis Ruygt	2009–2013	International Actuarial Association
Hollis Ashbaugh Skaife	2009–2011	International Association for Accounting Education & Research
Gerben Everts	2009–2011	International Corporate Governance Network
Richard Keys	2009–2010	PricewaterhouseCoopers
John Hitchins	2010–[2016]	PricewaterhouseCoopers
Mark Vaessen	2009–2013	KPMG
April Mackenzie	2009–2013	Grant Thornton
Leo van der Tas	2009–2013	Ernst & Young
Joel Osnoss	2009–2013	Deloitte
Andrew Buchanan	2009–2013	BDO International

Standards and Interpretations

A2.1 Standards and Amendments to Standards

The first part of this appendix shows final standards and amendments to standards issued by the IASB between 2001 and June 2011, as well as the amended conceptual framework and the one practice statement. It does not include consequential amendments unless published as separate documents. Publications are grouped by headings as used in the IASB's published work programmes. As work plan classifications varied over time, the grouping and the choice of headings has required a degree of judgment. The year shown in parentheses after each heading is the year in which a project related to this topic was first placed on the agenda.

Improvements (2001)

Improvements to International Accounting Standards (December 2003)
Includes revised versions of:

IAS 1 *Presentation of Financial Statements*
IAS 2 *Inventories*
IAS 8 *Accounting Policies, Changes in Accounting Estimates and Errors*
IAS 10 *Events after the Balance Sheet Date*
IAS 16 *Property, Plant and Equipment*
IAS 17 *Leases*
IAS 21 *The Effects of Changes in Foreign Exchange Rates*
IAS 24 *Related Party Disclosures*
IAS 27 *Consolidated and Separate Financial Statements*
IAS 28 *Investments in Associates*
IAS 31 *Interests in Joint Ventures*
IAS 33 *Earnings per Share*
IAS 40 *Investment Property*

First-time Adoption (2001)

IFRS 1 *First-time Adoption of International Financial Reporting Standards* (June 2003)

Cost of an Investment in a Subsidiary, Jointly Controlled Entity or Associate, amendments to IFRS 1 *First-time Adoption of International Financial Reporting Standards* and IAS 27 *Consolidated and Separate Financial Statements* (May 2008)

IFRS 1 *First-time Adoption of International Financial Reporting Standards* (reformatted version, November 2008)

Additional Exemptions for First-time Adopters, amendments to IFRS 1 *First-time Adoption of International Financial Reporting Standards* (July 2009)

Limited Exemption from Comparative IFRS 7 Disclosures for First-time Adopters, amendments to IFRS 1 *First-time Adoption of International Financial Reporting Standards* (January 2010)

Severe Hyperinflation and Removal of Fixed Dates for First-time Adopters, amendments to IFRS 1 *First-time Adoption of International Financial Reporting Standards* (December 2010)

Share-based Payment (2001)

IFRS 2 *Share-based Payment* (February 2004)

Vesting Conditions and Cancellations, amendments to IFRS 2 *Share-based Payment* (January 2008)

Group Cash-settled Share-based Payment Transactions, amendments to IFRS 2 *Share-based Payment* (June 2009)

Business Combinations (2001)

IFRS 3 *Business Combinations* (March 2004)

IAS 36 *Impairment of Assets* (revised, March 2004)

IAS 38 *Intangible Assets* (revised, March 2004)

IFRS 3 *Business Combinations* (revised, January 2008)

IAS 27 *Consolidated and Separate Financial Statements* (revised, January 2008)

Insurance (2001)

IFRS 4 *Insurance Contracts* (March 2004)

Financial Statement Presentation and Performance Reporting (2001)

IAS 1 *Presentation of Financial Statements* (revised, September 2007)

Presentation of Items of Other Comprehensive Income, amendments to IAS 1 *Presentation of Financial Statements* (June 2011)

Employee Benefits (2001)

Employee Benefits: The Asset Ceiling, amendments to IAS 19 *Employee Benefits* (May 2002)

Actuarial Gains and Losses, Group Plans and Disclosures, amendments to IAS 19 *Employee Benefits* (December 2004)

IAS 19 *Employee Benefits* (revised, June 2011)

Financial Instruments (2001)

IAS 32 *Financial Instruments: Disclosure and Presentation* (revised, December 2003)

IAS 39 *Financial Instruments: Recognition and Measurement* (revised, December 2003)

Fair Value Hedge Accounting for a Portfolio Hedge of Interest Rate Risk, amendments to IAS 39 *Financial Instruments: Recognition and Measurement* (March 2004)

Transition and Initial Recognition of Financial Assets and Financial Liabilities, amendments to IAS 39 *Financial Instruments: Recognition and Measurement* (December 2004)

Cash Flow Hedge Accounting of Forecast Intragroup Transactions, amendments to IAS 39 *Financial Instruments: Recognition and Measurement* (April 2005)

The Fair Value Option, amendments to IAS 39 *Financial Instruments: Recognition and Measurement* (June 2005)

Financial Guarantee Contracts, amendments to IAS 39 *Financial Instruments: Recognition and Measurement* and IFRS 4 *Insurance Contracts* (August 2005)

IFRS 7 *Financial Instruments: Disclosures* (August 2005)

Capital Disclosures, amendments to IAS 1 *Presentation of Financial Statements* (August 2005)

Puttable Financial Instruments and Obligations Arising on Liquidation, amendments to IAS 32 *Financial Instruments: Presentation* and IAS 1 *Financial Statement Presentation* (February 2008)

Eligible Hedged Items, amendments to IAS 39 *Financial Instruments: Recognition and Measurement* (July 2008)

Reclassification of Financial Assets, amendments to IAS 39 *Financial Instruments: Recognition and Measurement* and IFRS 7 *Financial Instruments: Disclosures* (October 2008)

Reclassification of Financial Assets—Effective Date and Transition, amendments to IAS 39 *Financial Instruments: Recognition and Measurement* and IFRS 7 *Financial Instruments: Disclosures* (November 2008)

Embedded Derivatives, amendments to IFRIC 9 *Reassessment of Embedded Derivatives* and IAS 39 *Financial Instruments: Recognition and Measurement* (March 2009)

Improving Disclosures about Financial Instruments, amendments to IFRS 7 *Financial Instruments: Disclosures* (March 2009)

Classification of Rights Issues, amendments to IAS 32 *Financial Instruments: Presentation* (October 2009)

IFRS 9 *Financial Instruments* (November 2009)

Disclosures—Transfers of Financial Assets, amendments to IFRS 7 *Financial Instruments: Disclosures* (October 2010)

IFRS 9 *Financial Instruments* (revised, October 2010)

Assets Held for Disposal (2002)

IFRS 5 *Non-current Assets Held for Sale and Discontinued Operations* (March 2004)

Segment Reporting (2002)

IFRS 8 *Operating Segments* (November 2006)

Consolidation and SPEs (2002)

IFRS 10 *Consolidated Financial Statements* (May 2011)

IFRS 12 *Disclosure of Interests in Other Entities* (May 2011)

IAS 27 *Separate Financial Statements* (revised, May 2011)

IAS 28 *Investments in Associates and Joint Ventures* (revised, May 2011)

Joint Ventures (2002)

IFRS 11 *Joint Arrangements* (May 2011)

Income Taxes (2002)

Deferred Tax: Recovery of Underlying Assets, amendments to IAS 12 *Income Taxes* (December 2010)

Extractive Industries (2003)

IFRS 6 *Exploration for and Evaluation of Mineral Resources* (December 2004)

Amendments to IFRS 1 *First-time Adoption of International Financial Reporting Standards* and IFRS 6 *Exploration for and Evaluation of Mineral Resources* (June 2005)

Small and Medium-sized Entities (2003)
IFRS for SMEs (July 2009)

Conceptual Framework (2004)
The Conceptual Framework for Financial Reporting 2010 (September 2010)

Management Commentary (2004)
IASB Practice Statement *Management Commentary: A Framework for Presentation* (December 2010)

Net Investment in a Foreign Operation (2005)
Net Investment in a Foreign Operation, amendments to IAS 21 *The Effects of Changes in Foreign Exchange Rates* (December 2005)

Borrowing Costs (2005)
IAS 23 *Borrowing Costs* (revised, March 2007)

Fair Value Measurement (2005)
IFRS 13 *Fair Value Measurement* (May 2011)

Annual Improvements (2006)
Improvements to IFRSs (May 2008)
Improvements to IFRSs (April 2009)
Improvements to IFRSs (May 2010)

Related Party Disclosures (2006)
IAS 24 *Related Party Disclosures* (revised, November 2009)

A2.2 Interpretations

The second part of this appendix shows interpretations issued by SIC and IFRIC from 2001 to June 2011, ordered by date of adoption by the Board (SIC interpretations) or issuance (IFRIC interpretations). The list indicates the withdrawal of interpretations and major amendments, but does not indicate consequential amendments made as a result of new or amended standards.

SIC-27 *Evaluating the Substance of Transactions Involving the Legal Form of a Lease* (December 2001)

SIC-28 *Business Combinations—'Date of Exchange' and Fair Value of Equity Instruments* (December 2001) (superseded by IFRS 3, 2003)

SIC-29 *Disclosure—Service Concession Arrangements* (December 2001) (title changed to SIC-29 *Service Concession Arrangements: Disclosures* in November 2006)

SIC-30 *Reporting Currency—Translation from Measurement Currency to Presentation Currency* (December 2001) (superseded by revised IAS 21, 2003)

SIC-31 *Revenue—Barter Transactions Involving Advertising Services* (December 2001)

SIC-32 *Intangible Assets—Website Costs* (March 2002)

SIC-33 *Consolidation and Equity Method—Potential Voting Rights and Allocation of Ownership Interests* (December 2001) (superseded by revised IAS 27 and IAS 28, 2003)

IFRIC 1 *Changes in Existing Decommissioning, Restoration and Similar Liabilities* (May 2004)

IFRIC 2 *Members' Shares in Co-operative Entities and Similar Instruments* (November 2004)

IFRIC 3 *Emission Rights* (November 2004) (withdrawn 2005)

IFRIC 4 *Determining Whether an Arrangement Contains a Lease* (December 2004)

IFRIC 5 *Rights to Interests arising from Decommissioning, Restoration and Environmental Rehabilitation Funds* (November 2004)

IFRIC 6 *Liabilities Arising from Participating in a Specific Market—Waste Electrical and Electronic Equipment* (September 2005)

IFRIC 7 *Applying the Restatement Approach under IAS 29 Financial Reporting in Hyperinflationary Economies* (November 2005)

IFRIC 8 *Scope of IFRS 2* (January 2006) (incorporated in IFRS 2 and withdrawn, 2009)

IFRIC 9 *Reassessment of Embedded Derivatives* (March 2006) (superseded by IFRS 9, 2010)

IFRIC 10 *Interim Financial Reporting and Impairment* (July 2006)

IFRIC 11 *IFRS 2—Group and Treasury Share Transactions* (November 2006) (incorporated in IFRS 2 and withdrawn, 2009)

IFRIC 12 *Service Concession Arrangements* (November 2006)

IFRIC 13 *Customer Loyalty Programmes* (June 2007)

IFRIC 14 *IAS 19—The Limit on a Defined Benefit Asset, Minimum Funding Requirements and their Interaction* (July 2007). Amended by the Board, *Prepayments of a Minimum Funding Requirement*, amendments to IFRIC 14 (November 2009)

IFRIC 15 *Agreements for the Construction of Real Estate* (July 2008)

IFRIC 16 *Hedges in a Net Investment of a Foreign Operation* (July 2008)

IFRIC 17 *Distributions of Non-cash Assets to Owners* (November 2008)

IFRIC 18 *Transfers of Assets from Customers* (January 2009)

IFRIC 19 *Extinguishing Financial Liabilities with Equity Instruments* (November 2009)

IASC–IFRS Foundation
Summary Financial Data 2001–11

£1,000

	2001	2002	2003	2004	2005	2006	2007	2008	2009	2010	2011
Contributions	12,830	11,675	9,680	9,318	9,374	10,382	11,277	12,747	16,584	16,640	20,562
—subscription and publication sales	1,966	2,303	2,957	4,154	4,514	5,058	4,992	6,481	5,654	5,804	5,522
—direct cost of sales	(675)	(1,250)	(1,398)	(2,924)	(2,753)	(2,922)	(2,623)	(3,136)	(3,260)	(3,246)	(3,323)
Net proceeds from publications	1,291	1,053	1,559	1,230	1,761	2,136	2,369	3,345	2,394	2,558	2,199
Interest and other income	260	302	370	506	561	593	656	594	411	329	46
Total	14,381	13,030	11,609	11,054	11,696	13,111	14,302	16,686	19,389	19,527	22,807
Salaries and wages—Board and staff	(5,563)	(7,265)	(7,897)	(8,195)	(8,316)	(9,177)	(9,738)	(10,983)	(13,955)	(15,282)	(16,377)
Board, SAC, IFRIC and committees—meeting costs	(926)	(1,279)	(1,472)	(1,512)	(1,498)	(1,709)	(1,867)	(2,130)	(2,473)	(2,093)	(2,006)
Trustees—fees and meeting costs	(408)	(487)	(493)	(649)	(541)	(634)	(746)	(763)	(865)	(1,175)	(1,041)
Other costs including accommodation, fundraising, and taxation	(1,905)	(1,686)	(1,518)	(1,610)	(1,669)	(2,050)	(2,163)	(2,342)	(2,343)	(2,360)	(2,969)
Exchange and fair value gains and losses	(62)	1,184	1,261	1,275	(248)	148	0	(2,215)	894	(641)	294
Increase (decrease) in net assets	5,517	3,497	1,490	363	(576)	(311)	(212)	(1,747)	647	(2,024)	708

Source: IASC/IFRS Foundation Annual Reports 2001–11.

List of Interviewees

The interviewees' positions given below were those which were the focus of the interview. No attempt is made to indicate whether the interviewee was serving in the position at the time of the interview or whether the service preceded the interview. Nationality is given in parentheses. In this book we have drawn on three interviews from our book on the IASC. These are included in the following list, but with an asterisk.

Kenichi Akiba (Japan)—senior member of technical staff, ASBJ

Kirill Altukhov (Russia)—partner, KPMG, Moscow

Sophie Baranger (France)—chief accountant, Autorité des Marchés Financiers; SAC member

Richard Barker (United Kingdom)—technical staff, IASB

Mary Barth (United States)—IASB Board member

Martina Baumgärtel (Germany)—preparer, Allianz

Jean-Baptiste Bellon (France)—user, Cheuvreux de Virieu/Crédit Agricole

Pervenche Berès (France)—member, European Parliament; chairman, Economic and Monetary Affairs Committee

Axel Berger (Germany)—vice president, Deutsche Prüfstelle für Rechnungslegung (Financial Reporting Enforcement Panel)

Suzanne Bielstein (United States)—senior member of technical staff, FASB

John Biggs (United States)—IASC Foundation trustee

Jeannot Blanchet (Canada)—user, Morgan Stanley; SAC member; IFRIC member

Frits Bolkestein (Netherlands)—EU commissioner

Tijmen Bout (Netherlands)—preparer, ABN AMRO

Paul Boyle (United Kingdom)—chief executive, Financial Reporting Council

Hans-Georg Bruns (Germany)—IASB Board member

Philippe Bui (France)—director of research, Autorité des Normes Comptables

Neri Bukspan (United States)—user, Standard & Poor's; member, IFRS Advisory Council

Hans Buurmans (Netherlands)—preparer, ING Groep

Mark Byatt (United Kingdom)—director of corporate communications, IASB

Winnie Cheung (Hong Kong)—chief executive, Hong Kong Institute of Certified Public Accountants

Paul Chow (Hong Kong)—chief executive, Hong Kong Exchanges and Clearing Ltd

Jack Ciesielski (United States)—user, R.G. Associates, Inc.

Peter Clark (United Kingdom)—director of research, IASB

Bertrand Collomb (France)—preparer, Lafarge; IASC Foundation trustee; chairman, trustees' nominating committee

Allan Cook (United Kingdom)—technical director and board member, Accounting Standards Board; member, Technical Expert Group, EFRAG; IFRIC coordinator

Stephen Cooper (United Kingdom)—user, UBS; IASB Board member

Anthony Cope (United Kingdom/United States)—IASB Board member

Christopher Cox (United States)—SEC chairman

Kimberley Crook (New Zealand)—technical staff, IASB

Philippe Danjou (France)—SAC member; IASB Board member

Anne d'Arcy (Germany)—preparer, Deutsche Bank

Jackson Day (United States)—SEC deputy chief accountant
Alain Deckers (Belgium)—European Commission staff
Samuel DiPiazza (United States)—IASC Foundation trustee
William Donaldson (United States)—SEC chairman
Paul Dudek (United States)—SEC director of international corporate finance
Gabi Ebbers (Germany)—preparer, Allianz
Paul Ebling (United Kingdom)—technical director, EFRAG
Gerald Edwards (United States)—various capacities, Basel Committee on Banking
   Supervision; senior advisor, Financial Stability Board; member, FASB–IASB Financial
   Crisis Advisory Group
Egbert Eeftink (Netherlands)—partner, KPMG, Amsterdam
Hiroshi Endo (Japan)—managing director, FASF
Stig Enevoldsen (Denmark)—member, chairman, Technical Expert Group, EFRAG
Jan Engström (Sweden)—IASB Board member
Julie Erhardt (United States)—SEC deputy chief accountant
Donna Fisher (United States)—senior vice president, American Bankers Association
Colin Fleming (Bermuda/Canada)—technical staff, IASB
Françoise Flores (France)—member, chairman, Technical Expert Group, EFRAG
Tsuguoki Fujinuma (Japan)—IASC Foundation trustee
Hirokazu Fujita (Japan)—preparer, Tokio Marine Group
Wilson Fung (Hong Kong)—preparer, Jardines; president, HKICPA; member, HK
   Financial Reporting Review Panel
Philippe Gaberell (Switzerland)—preparer, Nestlé
D.J. Gannon (United States)—partner, Deloitte, Washington DC
Robert Garnett (South Africa)—IASB Board member; chairman, IFRIC
Gilbert Gélard (France)—IASB Board member
Gérard Gil (France)—preparer, BNP Paribas
Amaro Gomes (Brazil)—IASB Board member
Mauro Grande (Italy)—director, directorate of financial stability and supervision,
   European Central Bank; SAC member
Michael Gullette (United States)—vice president, American Bankers Association
Jérôme Haas (France)—director, Autorité des Normes Comptables
Toshitaka Hagiwara (Japan)—chairman, FASF; chairman, IFRS Council
Sue Harding (United Kingdom)—technical staff, IASB; user
Trevor Harris (United States)—user, Morgan Stanley; SAC member
Johan van Helleman (Netherlands)—chairman, Technical Expert Group, EFRAG
Robert Herdman (United States)—SEC chief accountant
Cornelius Herkströter (Netherlands)—IASC Foundation trustee
Robert Herz (United States)—IASB Board member; chairman, FASB
Sigvard Heurlin (Sweden)—SAC member; technical staff, EFRAG
Conrad Hewitt (United States)—SEC chief accountant
Elizabeth Hickey (New Zealand)—director of education and director of technical activ-
   ities, IASB
Kazuo Hiramatsu (Japan)—member, ASBJ
Nobuyuki Hiratsuka (Japan)—director, Ministry of Economy, Trade and Industry
Martin Hoogendoorn (Netherlands)—partner, Ernst & Young, Rotterdam; chairman,
   Raad voor de Jaarverslaggeving
Hans Hoogervorst (Netherlands)—vice chairman, IOSCO Technical Committee; vice
   chairman, FCAG; chairman, Monitoring Board
Jeroen Hooijer (Netherlands)—technical staff, European Commission
Adam Hurwich (United States)—user, Jupiter Advisors
Yuichi Ikeda (Japan)—deputy commissioner, Financial Services Agency

Mami Indo (Japan)—user, Daiwa

Hidetake Ishihara (Japan)—preparer, Nippon Steel

Jeremy Jennings (United Kingdom)—chairman, European Contact Group of the top six global audit firms

Thomas Jones (United Kingdom/United States)—IASB Board vice chairman

Joyce Joseph (United States)—user, Standard & Poor's

P.M. Kam (Hong Kong)—preparer, Jardines; chief executive, Financial Reporting Council

Sei-ichi Kaneko (Japan)—user, executive vice president of Security Analysts Association of Japan; member, Analyst Representative Group; SAC member

Susanne Kanngieser (Germany)—preparer, Allianz

Atsushi Kato (Japan)—vice chairman, ASBJ

Yoshitaka Kato (Japan)—partner, Ernst & Young ShinNihon

Jan Klaassen (Netherlands)—Dutch representative on the ARC; member, SARG

Liesel Knorr (Germany)—president, DRSC; non-voting member, Technical Expert Group, EFRAG; member, SARG

Markus Koch (Germany)—preparer, DIC Asset AG

Atsushi Kogasaka (Japan)—technical director, ASBJ

Akashi Kohno (Japan)—partner, Ernst & Young ShinNihon

Jan Kool (Netherlands)—preparer, Rabobank

Masakazu Kubota (Japan)—senior managing director, Nippon Keidanren

Toshitake Kurosawa (Japan)—director, Financial Services Agency

Philip Laskawy (United States)—IASC Foundation trustee and chairman of trustees

James Leisenring (United States)—IASB Board member

Andrew Lennard (United Kingdom)—technical director and director of research, ASB

Alden Leung (China/Hong Kong)—partner, Ernst & Young; member, HK Financial Reporting Review Panel

*Arthur Levitt (United States)—SEC chairman

Thomas Linsmeier (United States)—member, FASB

Sir Sydney Lipworth (United Kingdom)—IASC Foundation trustee

Liu Yuting (China)—various capacities, Ministry of Finance; SAC member

David Loweth (United Kingdom)—senior technical staff, UK ASB

Lu Jianqiao (China)—director, Ministry of Finance; technical staff, IASB

Ian Mackintosh (New Zealand/Australia/United Kingdom)—chairman, UK ASB; SAC member; chairman, NSS/IFASS

Erika Marseille (Netherlands)—preparer, Akzo Nobel; technical staff, Stichting Toezicht Effectenverkeer

Patrice Marteau (France)—chairman, ACTEO; SAC vice chairman

Charlie McCreevy (Ireland)—EU commissioner

Anne McGeachin (United Kingdom)—technical staff, IASB

Warren McGregor (Australia)—IASB Board member

Harm van de Meerendonk (Netherlands)—preparer, ING Groep

Geoffrey Mitchell (Australia)—chairman, IASB's Financial Activities Advisory Committee; chairman, SARG

Hidenori Mitsui (Japan)—director, Financial Services Agency

Christian Mouillon (France)—partner, Ernst & Young, Paris

Hans de Munnik (Netherlands)—chairman, Raad voor de Jaarverslaggeving

Sir Bryan Nicholson (United Kingdom)—chairman, FRC; IASC Foundation trustee; chairman, trustees' nominating committee

Donald Nicolaisen (United States)—SEC chief accountant

Claus Møller Nielsen (Denmark)—partner, KPMG, Moscow

Ikuo Nishikawa (Japan)—executive director, JICPA; vice chairman, chairman, ASBJ; chairman, AOSSG

Yoshiharu Obata (Japan)—senior manager, Nippon Keidanren

Takatsugu Ochi (Japan)—IFRIC member

Patricia O'Malley (Canada)—IASB Board member; IFRIC co-ordinator

Yukio Ono (Japan)—partner, Deloitte Touche Tohmatsu, Tokyo

Danita Ostling (United States)—partner, Ernst & Young, New York

Paul Pacter (United States)—director, Deloitte Hong Kong; director, IASB's IFRS for SMEs project; IASB Board member

Jochen Pape (Germany)—member, DRSC; SAC member

Jim Paul (Australia)—technical staff, IASB and AASB

Janet Pegg (United States)—user, UBS

Kim Petrone (United States)—technical staff, FASB

Paul Phenix (Australia)—partner, Baker Tilly, Hong Kong; member, Financial Accounting Standards Committee, HKICPA; with Hong Kong Stock Exchange and Australian Stock Exchange

Russell Picot (United Kingdom)—preparer, HSBC; member, IASB working groups

Andrea Pryde (United Kingdom)—technical staff, IASB

Alexander Radwan (Germany)—member, European Parliament

Philippe Richard (France)—Banque de France; secretary general, IOSCO

René Ricol (France)—president, International Federation of Accountants; advisor to President Nicolas Sarkozy

Jens Røder (Denmark)—president, Fédération des Experts Comptables Européens; IASC Foundation trustee

David Ruder (United States)—IASC Foundation trustee

Paul Rutteman (Netherlands)—secretary general, EFRAG

Atsushi Saito (Japan)—president and chief executive, Tokyo Stock Exchange Group

Shizuki Saito (Japan)—chairman, ASBJ

Shigeo Sakase (Japan)—preparer, Hitachi

Takafumi Sato (Japan)—commissioner, Financial Services Agency

Alexander Schaub (Germany)—director general, European Commission

Arnold Schilder (Netherlands)—member, managing board, De Nederlandsche Bank; chairman, Basel Committee's Task Force on Accounting Issues; SAC member

Harry Schmid (Switzerland)—IASB Board member

Hans Schoen (Netherlands)—member, Technical Expert Group, EFRAG

Sönke Schwartz (Germany)—preparer, Vivacon

Darrel Scott (South Africa)—IASB Board member

Thomas Seidenstein (United States)—chief operating officer, IASC Foundation

Leslie Seidman (United States)—member, chairman, FASB

Tetsuo Seki (Japan)—managing director, Nippon Steel Corporation; vice chairman, Business Accounting Council

Noriaki Shimazaki (Japan)—preparer, Sumitomo Corporation; IASC Foundation trustee; member, Business Accounting Council; member, FASF; member, IFRS Council

David Sidwell (United Kingdom/United States)—IASC Foundation trustee

Saskia Slomp (Netherlands)—technical staff, Fédération des Experts Comptables Européens

John Smith (United States)—IASB Board member

*Kenneth Spencer (Australia)—IASC Foundation trustee; chairman, trustees' nominating committee

Kevin Stevenson (Australia)—director of technical activities, IASB; chairman, IFRIC; chairman, Australian Accounting Standards Board

Eiichi Tachibana (Japan)—preparer, Dai-Ichi Mutual Life Insurance; member, IASB working group

Ethiopis Tafara (United States)—director, Office of International Affairs, SEC

Hiroki Takeuchi (Japan)—with Japanese Bankers Association; member, ASBJ's Standards Advisory Council

Scott Taub (United States)—SEC deputy chief accountant

Stephen Taylor (United Kingdom)—partner, Deloitte, Hong Kong; member, Financial Accounting Standards Committee, HKICPA

Alan Teixeira (New Zealand)—senior technical staff, IASB

Angus Thomson (Australia)—technical director, Australian Accounting Standards Board

Richard Thorpe (United Kingdom)—head of accounting, auditing, capital and groups policy, Financial Services Authority; SAC member

Göran Tidström (Sweden)—chairman, EFRAG Supervisory Board

Mary Tokar (United States)—partner, KPMG, London; member, IFRIC

Kostas Tsatsaronis (Greece)—head of financial institutions, Bank for International Settlements

Eiko Tsujiyama (Japan)—part-time member, ASBJ; SAC member

*Lynn Turner (United States)—SEC chief accountant

Sir David Tweedie (United Kingdom)—IASB Board chairman

Daisuke Unami (Japan)—senior vice president, Sumitomo Mitsui Banking Corporation

Wayne Upton (United States)—IASB director of research and director of international activities

Karel Van Hulle (Belgium)—head, accounting unit, European Commission

Nicolas Véron (France)—senior fellow, Bruegel, Brussels

Paul Volcker (United States)—IASC Foundation trustees chairman

Peter Walton (United Kingdom)—academic and editor, *World Accounting Report*

Jesse Wang (China)—senior staff member, China Securities Regulatory Commission; executive vice president, China Investment Corporation

Wang Jun (China)—vice minister, Ministry of Finance

Andrew Watchman (United Kingdom)—executive director, Grant Thornton, London; accountancy advisor, DTI

David Webb (United Kingdom)—activist user, Hong Kong

Geoffrey Whittington (United Kingdom)—IASB Board member

Kenneth Wild (United Kingdom)—partner, Deloitte, London; member, IFRIC

Wilfried Wilms (Belgium)—senior staff, European Banking Federation, Brussels

Paul Winkelmann—partner, PricewaterhouseCoopers; chairman, Financial Accounting Standards Committee, HKICPA; member, HK Financial Reporting Review Panel

Hermann Wirz (Switzerland)—preparer, Nestlé

David Wright (United Kingdom)—deputy director general, European Commission

Xu Jingchang (China)—academic, Renmin University of China

Yoshiki Yagi (Japan)—senior adviser, Hitachi; SAC member; chairman, subcommittee on accounting, Nippon Keidanren

Tatsumi Yamada (Japan)—IASB Board member

Shozo Yamazaki (Japan)—chairman and president, JICPA; member, IFRS Council

Yang Min (China)—director general, Ministry of Finance

Ye Kangtao (China)—academic, Renmin University of China

Joseph Yuen (China)—partner, Deloitte, Beijing

Gerrit Zalm (Netherlands)—IASC Foundation trustees chairman

Zhang Wei-Guo (China)—chief accountant and director general of international affairs, China Securities Regulatory Commission; IASB Board member

Zhou Zhonghui (China)—chief accountant, China Securities Regulatory Commission

APPENDIX 5

Sources and Referencing

A5.1 IASB Archive—Digital

Most of the source materials originated by the IASC/IFRS Foundation have been consulted in digital format. The series most frequently referred to are:

- Board agenda papers: these were numbered consecutively from 1 upwards for each meeting. Agenda papers are referred to as 'AP 3/2007 paper 6', meaning agenda paper 6 for the Board meeting of March 2007. When, from 2009 onwards, the Board met more than once a month the normal practice was to number agenda papers consecutively through the month. Where necessary, the precise date of the meeting is supplied in the references. Initially, agenda papers were not, or only partially, published, and without further indications the versions cited are taken from the IASB archive. In later years, agenda papers were published on the IASB's website with few if any modifications. When referred to, these published versions are identified as '(observer version)'.

- Board minutes: separate minutes for Board meetings were prepared until December 2004. These are cited as 'IASB Board meeting of 15–17 May 2003, minute 5', indicating numbered paragraph 5 from the minutes of the May 2003 meeting. In subsequent years, marked-up texts of *IASB Update* took the place of Board minutes.

- Trustee agenda papers: these papers, consecutively numbered for each meeting, are referred to similarly as Board papers: 'IASCF trustee meeting of 15–17 May 2003, agenda paper 4A', or 'IFRS Foundation trustees meeting' from July 2010 onwards.

- Trustee minutes: cited in the format of 'IASCF (IFRS Foundation) trustees meeting of 15–17 May 2003, minute 6', similar to Board minutes.

A5.2 IASB Archive—Other

When this research was undertaken, the IASC/IFRS Foundation's paper archive was not indexed. In general, we have indicated the location of documents by including a 'file' name, which is normally the name indicated on the folder or binder in which the documents are contained.

A5.3 References to Websites

In footnote references, a standing assumption is that documents issued by the IASC/IFRS Foundation, including press releases, exposure drafts, and discussion documents, are available on the website <http://www.ifrs.org>, and this web address is normally not provided. In cases where the documents were no longer found to be available on the website in the first half of 2014 a reference is supplied to a secondary source, in most cases either <http://www.iasplus.com> or one of the Foundation's older websites (<http://www.iasb.org.uk>, <http://www.iasb.org>, and <http://www.iascfoundation.org>) accessed through web.archive, a generic reference to both <http://archive.org/web> and <http://web.archive.org>.

Index

ABN AMRO 263, 268, 475–6
Abrasca 498, 575
academics, in IASB organization:
  Board 16, 25, 26, 175–6, 279
  IFRIC 44
  SAC 40, 41
  staff 46, 277, 305
  trustees 19, 20, 21, 55
'accounting ayatollahs' 283, 333
Accounting Regulatory Committee
  (ARC) 59, 63, 173, 215, 253, 262
  on governance of IASB 171
  on financial instruments 145, 151, 158–9,
  410, 412, 437
  on other standards and
  interpretations 221, 396, 398
Accounting Standards Advisory Forum 615
Accounting Standards Board (AcSB, Canada):
  Canadian adoption of IFRSs 211–12,
  231–2, 369
  comment letters 574, 575
  liaison standard setter 33, 90, 566
  projects with/for IASB 126, 140, 361, 366,
  392, 566
Accounting Standards Board (ASB, UK):
  and national standard setters 615
  liaison standard setter 33
  Mackintosh's background in 281, 479
  projects with/for IASB 121–5, 291, 370,
  396, 577–8
  represented on EFRAG-TEG 299
  *Statement of Principles for Financial
  Reporting* 361
  'The Future of UK GAAP' 542–3
  Tweedie's background in 24, 29, 37, 46, 94,
  161, 364, 483, 484
  views on IASB projects 136, 141, 164, 223
Accounting Standards Board of Japan (ASBJ)
  conceptual framework 82, 86, 244–5, 363
  convergence policy 85–6, 206, 212, 213,
  240–1, 243, 244–7, 299, 519
  created 80–1
  IFRS Council 521
  liaison standard setter 33, 34, 83, 91
  regional cooperation 83, 538
  relations with FASB 243, 244, 371
  relations with IASB 300, 338, 371
  Tokyo Agreement 196, 213, 244–7
  views on IASB projects 114, 123–4,
  157, 574
Accounting Standards Review Board (New
  Zealand) 68, 319, 414
ACTEO 318
Adhikari, Ajay 250 n. 71

Aegon 160 n. 107
Africa:
  adoption of IFRSs 502–3
  interest in IASB 26, 574
  Pan African Federation of Accountants
  (PAFA) 503, 615
African Development Bank 175
Alexander, David 151 n. 62
Alfredson, Keith 67 n. 27, 126
Allianz 119
American Accounting Association 189, 544
American Bankers Association 416, 422,
  425, 585
American Institute of Certified Public
  Accountants 189, 197, 323, 509, 510
Amsterdam Stock Exchange 51
Analyst Representative Group 168, 169, 220,
  275, 296, 352
analysts, financial:
  IASC membership 10, 278
  IASB contacts with 108, 168, 296, 371, 600
  views on IFRSs 191, 578
  see also Analyst Representative
  Group; users
Andersen, *see* Arthur Andersen
Andersen, Roy 20, 51
Anwar, Zarinah 489
APB Opinion 25 *Accounting for Stock Issued
  to Employees* 107, 109
Arai, Kiyomitsu 80 n. 85
Arce, Miguel 109 n. 64
Argentina 49, 469–7, 495, 501, 610
Arthur Andersen 51, 52, 308, 309, 314
Asian Development Bank 175
Asian-Oceanian Standard-Setters Group
  (AOSSG) 501, 537–8, 542, 615
asset and liability approach, *see* conceptual
  framework
Association of British Insurers 222
Association for Investment Management and
  Research 120
audit firms, *see* Big Six/Five/Four
auditor's report, assertion of compliance with
  IFRSs 64, 68–9, 254, 255–7, 392, 459
  double opinion 69, 233, 253, 254
Australia:
  IASB funding 310, 313, 329
  IASC membership 8, 9
  IFRS adoption (2002–5) 66–9, 97, 126, 201,
  213, 229, 231
  IFRS adoption, specific standards 154,
  438, 584
  IFRS adoption, deletion of options 67,
  157, 254

Australia: (*cont.*)
  'true and fair' override 104
  regional cooperation 537
Australian Accounting Standards Board
    (AASB) 81, 369
  IFRS adoption 67, 413
  liaison standard setter 91
  projects with/for IASB 90, 126, 136–7, 344,
    396, 562–3
  sector-neutral standards 67, 100
Australian Stock Exchange 391
Autorité des Marchés Financiers
    (France) 251, 254 n. 83, 260, 425, 543–4
Autoriteit Financiële Markten
    (Netherlands) 201

Baldurs, Jón Arnar 305
Ball, Steve 161 n. 110
Banco de España, *see* Bank of Spain
Bangladesh 70
Bank for International Settlements 51
Bank of Spain 255, 420–1
Barker, Richard 46, 122, 375
Barnier, Michel:
  IASB agenda 552, 555
  IASB chairman search 480–1, 483
  IASB funding 327, 486, 616
  IASB governance 486, 488
  Monitoring Board 472, 475, 477, 487
Barroso José M. 411, 412
Barth, Mary E:
  (re)appointed to Board 31, 32, 36, 270
  Board and post-Board role 277, 284, 412
  views and votes on IASB projects 127, 204,
    284, 349 n. 53, 350, 358, 374, 376
Basel Committee on Banking
    Supervision 116, 418
  cooperation with IASB 144, 163, 285,
    425, 584
  fair value option 155, 203–4, 584–5
  IASB governance 72, 173
  Monitoring Board 444, 448, 450, 456,
    474, 492
Basel II accord 161
Batavick, George 358, 605
Batt, Marie-Christine 46
Baumann, Karl H. 19
Bayer 14, 109
BBVA 255
BDO 189, 314, 508
Bebbington, Joseph 68 n. 31
Bébéar, Claude 144, 333
Begy, Chris 161 n. 110
Belgium 158
Benson, Sir Henry 8
Benston, George J. 80 n. 84, 192 n. 68
Berès, Pervenche 166, 173, 215, 222, 471, 472
Beresford, Dennis R. 113 n. 79
Beswick, Paul A. 514–15
Bezold, Andreas 154
Bhave, C. B. 536

Bielstein, Suzanne 133, 335, 342, 357
Big Six/Five/Four audit firms:
  comments on SEC proposing release
    (2008) 508–9
  IASB funding 49, 51, 313, 314, 315,
    322, 325
  IASC/IASB interpretations committees
    44, 288
  IFRS compliance 249, 253, 394, 459
  IFRS implementation 202
  favouring IFRSs 67, 189, 192
  role in various projects 106, 236, 402,
    404, 568
  in SAC 40, 287
Biggs, John H. 20, 21, 34, 48, 49, 51, 54,
    55, 170
Blanchet, Jeannot 41, 286
Bloomberg, Michael 184, 507
BNP Paribas 155, 160 n. 106, 415; *see also*
    Pébereau, Michel
Boeing 107, 510
Bolkestein, Frits 61, 87, 151, 153, 157,
    270, 311
Bolsas y Mercados Españoles 326
Bonham, Mike 132 n. 158
Bonin, Christoph 303
Börsig, Clemens 266, 488
Bosnia and Herzegovina 70
Botswana 331, 502
Bouton, Daniel 144
Bowles, Sharon 326
BP 132
Bradbury, Michael 392 n. 242
Bradford and Bingley 407
Brady, Nicholas F. 151
Brady, Ryan 576 n. 118
Brazil:
  adoption of IAS 39: 145–6
  adoption of IFRSs 495, 497–9
  IASB funding 49, 321, 329
  involvement with IASB 575, 607
  value-added statement requirement 499
Brennan, John J. (Jack) 511–12, 550
Briloff, A.J. 112 n. 76
Broad, Sarah 304
Bromwich, Michael 80 n. 84, 192 n. 68
Brown, Gordon 411
Brown, Joan 303
Brown, Philip 64 n. 19
Brunnermeier, Markus K. 402 n. 1
Bruns, Hans-Georg:
  (re)appointed to Board 30, 32, 33, 34, 37,
    272, 275
  views and votes on IASB projects 131,
    348, 570
Buchanan, Patrina 303
Buffett, Warren 108, 110 n. 66
Bugg, Kathie 303
Bulgaria 328
Bullen, Halsey G. 360, 366
Bundesverband deutscher Banken 145

Bundesverband Öffentlicher Banken
   Deutschlands 203
Bunting, Mark 305
Burkholder, Steve 36 n. 40, 76 n. 69
Buschhueter, Michael 304
Bush, George W. 188, 418, 609
Bush, Tim 226
Business Accounting (Deliberation) Council
   (Japan) 80, 242, 520
business combinations 74, 96; *see also* IFRS 3
   under common control 115, 237
Business Roundtable (US) 308, 311, 510
BUSINESSEUROPE, 293; *see also* UNICE
Butcher, Michael 47
Byatt, Mark 224, 295–6

Camfferman, Kees 420 n. 71, 587 n. 170
Campos, Roel C. 181–2, 185, 187, 191
Canada:
   adoption of IFRSs 211, 229–33, 245, 246
   comment letters 574
   equivalence assessment (EU) 211, 212, 214,
      232, 238
   IASB funding 323, 329
   IASC membership 8, 9, 230, 231
   rate-regulated activities 232
Canadian Institute of Chartered Accountants
   (CICA) 229, 230–1, 232, 323
   Task Force on Standard Setting
      (TFOSS) 230
Canadian Securities Administrators
   (CSA) 230, 233
Canfield, Charles T. 170 n. 19
Capital Markets Advisory Committee, *see*
   Analyst Representative Group
Caribbean nations 495, 501
Carnall, Wayne 196
Carneiro, Juarez Domingues 499
Carsberg, Sir Bryan 16, 26, 46
Carvalho, L. Nelson 285, 497, 498
carve-outs (general) 69, 159–60, 227, 239,
      391, 535, 536, 540, 542, 564; *see also*
      IAS 39
Casey, Kathleen L. 187, 513
Castelli, Michael J. 161 n. 110
CCS 47, 49, 318, 321
Center for Audit Quality (US) 189
Certified General Accountants Association of
   Canada (CGA-Canada) 230–1
CFA Institute 120, 189, 349
CFO Forum 594
Chamber of Commerce (US) 187, 422, 510
Cheetham, Malcolm 113
Chen Shimin 234 n. 16
Chen Yugui 234 n. 15, 235 n. 17
Cherry, Paul G. 44, 193, 231, 232, 286
Cheung, Dora 305
Cheung, Marvin 41, 264, 266, 285
Cheung, Winnie C.W. 65 n. 20
Chile 70, 369, 495, 496, 501
China:

'Beijing Agreement' 237
'Beijing initiative' 297
   comment letters 574, 575
   convergence with IFRSs 70, 233–8, 236,
      527–33, 610
   equivalence (EU) 213, 214
   IASB funding 309, 322, 328, 329
   and IASC 234
   Ministry of Finance's role 234, 235–7, 297,
      328, 529, 530–1
   MoU with IASB 499
   three-country meetings (Japan, South
      Korea) 83, 234, 238, 537
China Securities Regulatory Commission 528
Chinese Accounting Standards
   Committee 83, 532, 575
Chirac, Jacques 151, 418
Choudhury, Fayezul 481
Christensen, Hans B. 248 n. 65
Chung, Duck-Koo 240, 266
Ciesielski, Jack T. 189, 194, 509
Clark, Peter 46, 303, 306, 421, 594
Clive & Stokes International 25
Coca-Cola 110
Colegio de Contadores de Chile 369
Colignon, Fabienne 305
Collins, Daniel W. 107 n. 50
Collomb, Bertrand 55, 225–6, 260, 264, 317,
      318, 373
   Constitution and strategy reviews
      440, 450
   nominating committee chairman 276,
      476, 478
Colombia 500–1
Comisión Nacional de Valores
   (Argentina) 496
Comisión Nacional Bancaria y de Valores
   (Mexico) 499
Comissão de Valores Mobiliários (Brazil) 612
Comitê de Pronunciamentos Contábeis
   (Brazil) 498
comitology 58, 59–60, 215, 227
Commerzbank 160 n. 106
Commission des Opérations de Bourse
   (France) 11, 19, 477
Committee of European Banking
   Supervisors 406
Committee of European Securities Regulators
   (CESR):
   compliance with IFRSs 182–3, 202, 248–9,
      250, 257, 258
   created 59, 64
   IASB funding 311
   equivalence assessments 211, 213, 241–2,
      519, 531
   Monitoring Board candidate 444, 445
   succeeded by ESMA 249
Committee on the Global Financial System
   (CGFS) 425
competition among accounting standards 73,
      85, 192, 193

competitive disadvantage, *see* level
  playing field
compliance with IFRSs:
  affirmation of, by companies 185, 190, 233,
    247–9, 252, 253, 255–7, 258–60
  quality of 188–9, 202, 247–52
  see also auditor's report; IAS 1; *and under*
    the various enforcement agencies
comprehensive income, *see* performance
  reporting; other comprehensive income
conceptual framework:
  ASBJ's 82, 86, 244–5, 363
  asset and liability approach 117, 148,
    351–2, 356, 360, 525
  IASC's 11, 98
  FASB's 120, 366
  joint project IASB–FASB 133, 334–69, 554,
    561, 597–606, 613
  reliability 359, 361–3, 365, 369
  reporting entity 367–8
  representational faithfulness 361, 363
  significance to IASB 98
  status in adopting jurisdictions 63
  stewardship 363–5
'condorsement', *see* Securities and Exchange
  Commission
Conseil National de la Comptabilité
  (France) 33, 45, 106, 144, 299, 365,
  396, 543
Consejo Mexicano para la Investigación y
  Desarrollo de Normas de Información
  Financiera (CINIF) 500, 575
Consejo Técnico de la Contaduría Pública
  (Colombia) 500
consolidation 197, 202, 348; *see also* IFRS 10
convergence (general) 128–9, 132, 293–6,
  303–4, 466; *see also* Financial Accounting
  Standards Board; *and under the various*
  jurisdictions
Cook, Allan 124, 207 n. 24, 288, 304
Cooper, Stephen 282, 284, 296
  (re)appointed to Board 275, 278, 358
  views and votes on IASB projects 352–3,
    355, 572
Cope, Anthony T. 82, 294
  (re)appointed to Board 25 n. 19, 29, 32,
    34–5, 121 n. 107, 270
  views and votes on IASB projects 100, 251
    n. 77, 284, 364, 372, 374
Copeland, James E., Jr. 19
Cortese, Corinne L. 127 n. 136
country-by-country disclosure 221–2, 226,
  227; *see also* IFRS 8
Cox, Christopher:
  competition among accounting
    standards 191, 197
  IOSCO Technical Committee
    chairman 413
  lifting of reconciliation requirement 186,
    187, 190–1, 193
  Monitoring Board 455, 471

SEC's international policy 182
SEC's proposing release (2008) 194, 196,
  197, 608
  succeeded by Schapiro 505, 609
  supports Nicolaisen roadmap 184, 185–7
Crawford, Louise 219 n. 74
Crédit Agricole 160 n. 106, 415
Crockett, Andrew 20, 50, 51, 55, 401, 422
Crooch, Michael J. 76, 335, 365
Crook, Kimberley 46, 108, 303, 305, 360–1
Cutler, Kit 495 n. 3, 496, 498, 501
Czech Republic 70

Da Costa, Roberto Teixeira 20, 21, 25, 51,
  170, 497
Daimler Benz (DaimlerChrysler) 14, 30, 109
Dallara, Charles 405 n. 22
Damant, David 168
Danjou, Philippe:
  (re)appointed to Board 273, 285, 544
  SAC member 41, 285
  views and votes on IASB projects 283, 354,
    355, 432, 602
Dasgupta, Kumar 303
Davies, Howard 19
Day, Jackson M. 77
De Greling, Stefan 309
De la Rosière, Jacques 431
De Silguy, Yves-Thibault 266
Deemed cost 530
DeKauwe, Kathryn 303
Deloitte 234, 251, 386, 502, 509
Delsaux, Pierre 317, 444, 489
Denham, Robert E. 192 n. 70, 418, 511, 512
Denmark 159
Deutsche Bank 14, 414
Deutsche Börse 311
Deutsche Prüfstellung für
  Rechnungslegung 201
Deutsche Telekom 14
Deutsches Aktieninstitut 316
Deutsches Rechnungslegungs Standards
  Committee (DRSC):
  IASB funding 318, 326
  interpretations 254 n. 83
  liaison standard setter 33, 216
  projects with/for IASB 391–2
  restructured 544–5
  represented on EFRAG-TEG 299
  share-based payment 107
  views on IASB projects 365, 558
Dexia 160 n. 106
DiPiazza, Samuel A. 265, 266, 318, 325, 409,
  440, 450, 488
Diplock, Jane 175, 429, 455, 471
Docters van Leeuwen, Arthur 184
Dodd, Christopher C. 189
Dominican Republic 495
Donaldson, William H. 77, 78, 180, 181, 243, 334
Downes, Judith 161 n. 110
Draghi, Mario 174, 584

Du Plessis, Adel 65 n. 24
due process, of the IASB:
  initial 99–102
  criticism and improvements 146–7, 166,
    167–70, 224, 225, 289–93, 464–7
  Due Process Handbook 170, 289, 290, 291,
    292, 293, 345, 409, 466–7
  fast-track procedure 466–7
  feedback statements 224, 290, 350, 437, 465
  field tests 100, 169, 217, 291, 293, 294, 389,
    466, 555, 582, 596, 597, 600
  impact assessments 171, 217, 218, 222, 223,
    225, 226, 291, 292, 475
  post-implementation reviews 225, 290,
    351, 465
  suspension of 292, 409–10, 412, 413

earnings per share 129, 130, 304, 375
Eastman, Hilary 304
Ebling, Paul 206
Ecuador 70, 496
ECOFIN, *see* European Council of Finance
    Ministers
Edwards, Colin 304
Edwards, Gerald 72, 401 n. 3
Edwards, Iain 65 n. 24
Eeftink, Egbert 121 n. 107
Egypt 70
El Salvador 495
Embraer 255
emerging economies:
  IASB's interest in 33, 88, 89, 175, 297, 387,
    455, 462, 529, 533
  interest in IFRSs 69–70, 495; *see also under*
    the various jurisdictions
Emerging Economies Group (EEG) 297, 533
Emerging Issues Task Force (of the FASB) 44,
    45, 131
Endo, Hiroshi 244, 313
Enevoldsen, Stig 190, 205–6, 208, 405,
    541–2
enforcement of IFRSs:
  G20: 419
  in the EU 64, 201, 211, 248–9
  IOSCO 182, 249
  SEC's views 79, 94, 181, 182, 346
Engström, Jan 284, 287, 295
  (re)appointed to Board 270–1
  views and votes on IASB projects 256, 354,
    355, 357, 565, 572, 602
Enron 52, 61, 73, 74, 75, 110, 145, 232, 249,
    308, 310, 558, 564, 577
equity and liabilities project 135, 344, 366,
    552, 556, 597–9; *see also* liabilities
equivalence (with IFRSs), *see* European
    Commission
Erhardt, Julie A. 177, 185, 196, 258, 303,
    335, 449
Ericsson 109
Ernst & Young 132, 251, 359
Estonia 70

European Banking Federation 147, 153, 154,
    158, 272, 381–2, 592
European Central Bank (ECB):
  IAS 39 improvements (2001–5) 141,
    155–7, 158, 167, 168, 203, 204, 218, 404
  Trustee Appointments Advisory
    Group 175
European Commission:
  and IASB (general relations) 87, 200,
    214–15, 237, 487, 539–40
  and IASC 13–14, 15, 19, 165
  and EFRAG 61–3, 91, 208, 216, 291, 540
  compliance with IFRSs 252, 253, 370, 394
  endorsement process, general 53, 59–62,
    63–5, 159, 215–16, 228, 252, 291,
    481, 540
  endorsement process, specific
    standards 69, 147, 151, 156–9, 208, 370,
    410, 412, 415, 436–8, 564
  equivalence assessments 65, 84–6, 181,
    210–14, 232, 241, 244, 519, 523, 531, 534,
    540; *see also under the various*
    jurisdictions
  financial crisis 408–12, 415, 416, 418, 419,
    427, 434, 436–8
  IAS proposal (2000) 18, 19, 57–8, 95, 97,
    105, 248; *see also* IAS Regulation
  IASCF Constitution, governance, and due
    process 165–7, 168, 171, 173–4, 180,
    200, 217–18, 224, 225, 264, 326, 351,
    483, 486
  IASB funding 53, 309, 311, 314, 316–17,
    321, 323–4, 326, 327, 486, 541, 616
  IFRIC observer 44
  lobbied 144–5, 151, 222, 223
  Monitoring Board 327, 444–6, 448, 450,
    455, 471–2, 473, 485, 540, 552, 612
  SAC observer 40
  translation of IFRSs 53–4, 106
  US convergence and IFRS adoption 77,
    180, 181, 334, 337, 343
  views on IASB projects 109, 142, 145, 153,
    156, 163, 209, 385, 390, 396, 416, 418, 434
European Council of Finance Ministers
    (ECOFIN) 204, 217, 225, 317, 408, 409,
    410, 427
European Financial Reporting Advisory
    Group (EFRAG):
  created and 'enhanced' 61–3, 204–6,
    541–3, 616
  endorsement, specific standards 158, 159,
    208–9, 221, 398, 412, 437, 564
  funding 316, 318, 323
  impact assessments 226, 228, 291
  pro-active role 62, 598
  relations with IASB 91–2, 205–6, 215, 287,
    299, 615
  Technical Expert Group (TEG) 63, 92, 158,
    205, 299, 541
  views on IASB projects 208–9, 363, 365,
    396, 405, 542, 554, 562–3, 598

European Financial Reporting Advisory Group (EFRAG): (*cont.*)
  working arrangement with European Commission 216, 394, 540
European Parliament:
  endorsement, general 53, 58–61, 215–17, 227–8, 291, 398
  endorsement, specific standards 145, 219, 222–3, 225, 227, 291, 412
  IASB funding 323–4, 337, 616
  IASB's relations with 224, 225, 227
  views on IASB 145, 166, 173, 217–18, 227, 327, 351, 445, 448, 471, 477, 540
European Round Table of Industrialists 109, 151, 169, 270–1, 297
European Securities and Markets Authority (ESMA) 64, 249
European Union (EU):
  critical views of IASB/IFRSs in 165, 166, 202, 216, 218, 219, 284, 290, 294, 311, 136, 337
  decision to adopt IFRSs 57–65, 95, 105–6, 178, 200, 231
  Directives, company law 9, 10, 14, 57, 59, 63, 104, 158, 390, 391–2, 427, 539, 543, 616
  Directives, Prospectus and Transparency 210–12
  European accounting standard setter 57, 487
  'European voice' 62, 540, 541, 545
  IAS Regulation 59–61, 63, 97, 113, 159, 210, 215, 248, 252, 370, 607
  IASB's 'first customer' 166, 210
  'IFRS as adopted by the EU' 64, 179, 185, 189, 214, 252–4, 260, 382, 445
  transition to IFRSs (2005) 200, 201–2, 229, 398
  see also European Commission, European Parliament
Evans, Scott 266
Expert Advisory Panel 405, 407, 416, 426, 568
External Reporting Board (New Zealand) 414
extractive industries 90; *see also* IFRS 6
Exxon 13

fair presentation override, *see* IAS 1
fair value:
  concerns over 62, 139, 142–4, 156, 157, 166, 203, 218, 356–7, 363, 415, 422
  financial crisis 402, 404–5, 407, 415, 416, 418, 422–3, 426, 431, 568
  fair value option, *see* IAS 39; IFRS 9
  financial instruments, *see* IAS 39; IFRS 9
  IASB's predilection for, real or imagined 29, 98, 117, 120, 139, 144, 283, 356–8, 362, 363, 367, 544
  projects on measurement, *see* FAS 157; IFRS 13
Fanjul, Oscar 55, 264, 326

FAS 2 *Accounting for Research and Development Costs* 344
FAS 13 *Accounting for Leases* 576, 577
FAS 87 *Employers' Accounting for Pensions* 136
FAS 109 *Accounting for Income Taxes* 603, 604
FAS 115 *Accounting for Certain Investments in Debt and Equity Securities* 406, 412
FAS 123 *Accounting for Stock-based Compensation* 107, 109, 110, 130
FAS 130 *Reporting Comprehensive Income* 120, 370, 372, 373
FAS 131 *Disclosure About Segments of an Enterprise and Related Information* 219–20
FAS 133 *Accounting for Derivative Instruments and Hedging Activities* 379
FAS 140 *Accounting for Transfers and Servicing of Financial Assets and Extinguishments of Liabilities* 589
FAS 141 *Business Combinations* 113, 115, 347, 348
FAS 142 *Goodwill and Other Intangible Assets* 113
FAS 144 *Accounting for the Impairment or Disposal of Long-lived Assets* 131–2
FAS 146 *Accounting for Costs Associated with Exit or Disposal Activities* 351
FAS 151 *Inventory Costs* 130
FAS 153 *Exchanges of Nonmonetary Assets* 130
FAS 154 *Accounting Changes and Error Corrections* 130
FAS 157 *Fair Value Measurement* 162, 416, 423, 426, 566, 567–8
FAS 158 *Employers' Accounting for Defined Benefit Pension and Other Postretirement Plans* 570
FAS 167 *Amendments to FASB Interpretation No. 46(R)* 560
Faull, Jonathan 326
Fearnley, Stella 402 n. 4
Federación Argentina de Consejos Profesionales en Ciencias Económicas 496–7
Federal Reserve Board (US) 51, 72, 609
Fédération Bancaire Française 140
Fédération des Experts Comptables Européens (FEE) 22, 205, 253, 272, 385–6, 437
Federation of Swiss Industrial Holding Companies 13, 30, 113
Feng Shuping 90, 234, 235
Ferguson, Robert 174
Ferrarini, Guido A. 20, 25, 51, 55, 88
Fiechter, Peter 415 n. 54
Figgie, Liz 304
FIN46(R) *Consolidation of Variable Interest Entities* 558–60

FIN48 *Accounting for Uncertainty in Income Taxes* 604, 606
Financial Accounting Foundation (FAF) 21, 34, 172, 418
  IASB funding 309, 312, 323, 329, 616–17
  intervenes in convergence 550–1
  on US adoption of IFRSs 192, 511–12
Financial Accounting Standards Board (FASB) 21, 25 n. 19
  and ASBJ 243, 244
  changes in board size 134, 585, 593
  compared with IASB 36, 48, 53, 103, 133–5, 279, 346–7
  convergence with IASB, process and planning 129–31, 131–2, 132–5, 185, 194–6, 206, 219–20, 246, 284, 333, 342, 403, 447, 513, 515, 547–57, 589, 590, 592–3, 612–14
  convergence with IASB, substance of, *see under the individual projects*
  liaison standard setter 27, 33, 71, 91
  MoU with IASB (2006) 185, 195, 241, 246, 333, 336, 338–43, 378, 380, 403, 559, 566, 577, 589
  MoU with IASB (updated 2008) 195, 196, 246, 341–5, 402, 547, 561, 574, 605
  Norwalk Agreement 39, 75–7, 84, 91, 115, 128–9, 132–3, 135, 212, 219, 245, 299, 338, 347, 351, 371
  on US adoption of IFRSs 192, 511–12
  see also Herz, Robert H.
Financial Accounting Standards Foundation (Japan) 80, 82, 244, 521
  IASB funding 313, 319
financial crisis 156, 197, 380, 382, 398, 401–38, 456, 473, 508, 568
  impact on IASB funding 322, 323
  impact on IASB planning 291, 302, 324, 334, 360, 547, 548, 560, 568, 583, 586, 587, 589
  impact on IFRS adoption in United States 510, 609
  see also fair value; IFRS 9
Financial Crisis Advisory Group (FCAG) 417, 428–9
Financial Executives Institute (FEI; also: Financial Executives International) 26, 108, 293
financial instruments, *see under the various standards*; *see also* Joint Working Group
Financial Markets Regulatory Dialogue 180
Financial Reporting Council (Australia) 66, 310, 313, 321
Financial Reporting Council (UK) 34, 183, 317, 365, 558
Financial Reporting Standards Board (New Zealand) 33, 90, 392, 562
Financial Reporting Standards Council (South Africa) 615
Financial Sector Reform and Strengthening Initiative (FIRST) 495

Financial Services Action Plan (EU) 57–9, 64, 210, 248
Financial Services Agency (Japan) 80, 84, 242, 244, 523
  IASB chairman selection 480, 481
  IASB governance 487
  IFRS policy 82, 245–6, 487, 518, 520–2, 526, 533, 596, 610, 612
  Monitoring Board 444–6, 448, 449, 450, 455, 446, 508
Financial Services Authority (UK) 183, 317
Financial Services Commission (South Korea) 612; *see also* Financial Supervisory Commission
financial stability, *see* stability, financial
Financial Stability Board (FSB) 425, 548, 585, 592
Financial Stability Forum (FSF) 174, 401, 403, 407, 421, 448, 450, 587, 589
financial statement presentation, *see* IAS 1
Financial Supervisory Commission (South Korea) 238, 239; *see also* Financial Services Commission
Financial Supervisory Service (South Korea) 239
Finnegan, Patrick 278, 284, 468
Fisher, Craig 69 n. 37
Fisher, Michelle 305
Fitch Ratings 189
Fleming, Colin 46, 47, 122
Flint, Douglas 161
Flores, Françoise 542
Flower, John 29 n. 25
Fong, Candy 304
Fonterra 382
Fortier, L. Yves 20, 51
Fortin, Henri 495 n. 3, 496, 498, 501
Fortis 160 n. 106, 407
France 87, 487
  critical views of IASB and IFRSs 144, 145, 151, 158, 272, 390, 543–44
  IASB funding 309–10, 318, 321, 326
  IASC membership 8, 9
  IFRS for SMEs 543
  local interpretations of IFRSs 254–5
Francis, Gavin 303, 306
Friedhoff, Martin 305
FRS 3 *Reporting Financial Performance* 120
FRS 17 *Retirement Benefits* 136
Fujinuma, Tsuguoki 55, 264, 266, 319, 450
  co-chairman of trustees 263, 477
  strategy review 440, 488
Fujitsu 574
Fukuma, Toshikatsu 20, 48, 51, 55

G4+1: 13, 16, 21, 23, 24, 27, 89, 300
  disbanded 33
  former members in IASB 27, 28, 29, 35, 36, 37, 47, 167, 372, 561
  IASB projects 95, 96, 107, 108, 112, 113, 121, 169, 371, 484, 562, 576, 579

G7: 15, 403, 404
G8: 404, 408
G20: 417–20, 421, 425, 456, 532, 560, 564, 587
  2011 convergence target (IASB/
    FASB) 548–9, 552, 553, 556, 584
GAAP hierarchy, *see* IAS 8
'gang of four' 342, 579, 589
Garnett, Robert P. 29, 32, 35, 147
  (re)appointed to Board 271
  extractive industries 125, 127
  IFRIC chairman 288, 393
  views and votes on IASB projects 153, 203,
    204, 283, 284, 348, 349 n. 53, 350, 374,
    392, 434, 587
Gélard, Gilbert 147
  (re)appointed to Board 29–30, 32, 33, 35,
    37, 271
  views and votes on IASB projects 123, 127,
    149, 203, 220, 348, 358
General Electric Company 13, 110
Germany 87
  IASB funding 318, 326
  IASC membership 8, 9
  IFRS 9: 437–8, 544–5
  IFRS for SMEs 390
  local interpretations of IFRSs 254–5, 384, 394
Ghana 70
Giner, Begoña 109 n. 64
Glauber, Robert 267, 488
  appointed trustee 266
  co-chairman of trustees 263, 477, 550
Glaum, Martin 250 n. 71
Global Preparers Forum 297; *see also*
  preparers
Global Public Policy Committee 402
Golden, Russell G. 553, 590
Goldschmid, Harvey 266, 428
Gomes, Amaro Luiz de Oliveira 278–9,
  468, 499
Gómez Soto, Denise 304
goodwill, *see* business combinations; IFRS 3
Gornik-Tomaszevski, Sylvia 201 n. 1
'grandfathering' 127, 233, 397
Grant Thornton 189, 192, 314, 508
Grayson, Alan 423
Greece 329, 588
Group of Latin American Accounting
  Standard Setters (GLASS) 501, 615
Group of Thirty 422
Guatemala 70

Haas, Jérôme 543–4
Hack, Sandra 304
Hague, Ian 305, 366
Hail, Luzi 248 n. 65
Harless, David W. 250 n. 71
Hashimoto, Toro 55, 170, 312
Haswell, Stephen 67 n. 26
Hazzis, Kristin 46
hedge accounting, *see* IAS 39; IFRS 9; *see also*
  carve-out

Helliar, Christine 219 n. 74
Herdman, Robert K:
  share-based payment 109
  supports convergence 72, 73, 74, 75–6,
    77, 128
Herkströter, Cornelius A.J. 20, 48, 50, 51, 170,
  311, 315, 318
Herz, Robert H:
  appointed to IASB 31, 32, 35, 39
  appointed FASB chairman 39, 74, 110,
    553, 585
  convergence with IASB 75, 76, 125 n. 129,
    131, 177, 193, 195, 335, 367, 428, 511,
    548–9, 550, 551, 560
  pressure from Congress 423
  retires from FASB 553, 585
  supports transition to IFRSs in US 192
Hewitt, Conrad W. 182, 187, 194, 195–6, 342,
  449, 461
Hickey, Elizabeth 68 n. 31, 89, 277, 303, 304,
  306, 393, 559
Hillen, Karl-Heinz 161 n. 110
Hiramatsu, Kazuo 84
Hirata Barros, Ana Cristina 495 n. 3, 496,
  498, 501
Hodgdon, Christopher 250 n. 71
Hoffmann-La Roche 109; *see also* Roche
Hollister, Hudson T. 170 n. 19
Honduras 495
Hong Kong 87, 562
  adoption of IFRSs 65–6, 106, 201, 229, 254,
    369, 390, 394, 414, 438, 584
  equivalence with Chinese accounting
    standards 531–2, 533
  H-share companies 528, 530
  IASB funding 321, 322
  income tax 606
  leases 104
Hong Kong Institute of Certified Public
  Accountants (HKICPA) 65, 369, 414,
  531–2, 615
Hong Kong Stock Exchange 51
Hoogendoorn, Martin 201 n. 1
Hoogervorst, Hans:
  co-chairman of FCAG 428, 429
  Monitoring Board chairman 470–1,
    474, 488
  appointed Board chairman 269, 281,
    479–83, 488, 608
  Board chairman role 588, 613
Hopkins, Patrick E. 189 n. 56
House of Representatives (US) 422
Howieson, Bryan 67 n. 26
HOYA Corporation 522
HSBC 161, 435–6
Hughes, Caron 304
Humphry, Richard G. 55, 69, 264, 319
Hundred Group of Finance Directors
  (UK) 331, 363
Hungary 70, 329
Hypo Real Estate 407

IAS 1 *Presentation of Financial Statements* 67, 121, 162, 164, 389
 compliance with IFRSs 247, 252, 253, 255–7, 258, 259
 fair presentation override 104, 249–51, 436
 names of financial statements 374–5
 single-statement presentation 137, 370, 374, 601, 602
 see also other comprehensive income; performance reporting
IAS 2 *Inventories* 130
IAS 7 *Cash Flow Statements* 67, 68, 375
IAS 8 *Accounting Policies, Changes in Accounting Estimates and Errors* 130, 369
 GAAP hierarchy 119, 126–7, 129, 565
IAS 9 *Accounting for Research and Development Activities* 344
IAS 10 *Events after the Balance Sheet Date* 251
IAS 11 *Construction Contracts* 399, 400, 573
IAS 12 *Income Taxes* 129, 341, 344, 390, 603–6
IAS 14 *Segment Reporting* 219, 529; *see also* IFRS 8
IAS 15 *Information Reflecting the Effects of Changing Prices* 105
IAS 16 *Property, Plant and Equipment* 126, 130, 524, 567
IAS 17 *Leases* 104, 576, 577, 581;
 see also leases
IAS 18 *Revenue* 355, 399, 400, 573; *see also* revenue recognition
IAS 19 *Employee Benefits* 344, 525
 convergence with UK 135–7
 MoU project (IASB/FASB) 552, 556, 561, 569–73
IAS 20 *Accounting for Government Grants and Disclosure of Government Assistance* 129, 207, 209
IAS 22 *Business Combinations* 112, 115, 343, 353; *see also* IFRS 3
IAS 23 *Borrowing Costs* 239
IAS 24 *Related Party Disclosures* 238, 241, 520
IAS 27 *Consolidated and Separate Financial Statements* 557–9; *see also* IFRS 10
IAS 28 *Investments in Associates and Joint Ventures* 557–8
IAS 30 *Disclosures in the Financial Statements of Banks and Similar Financial Institutions* 96, 103, 161; *see also* IFRS 7
IAS 31 *Financial Reporting of Interests in Joint Ventures* 239, 561, 562
IAS 32 *Financial Instruments: Presentation (and Disclosure)* 138, 158, 310
 adopted in Brazil 145–6
 equity/liability distinction 598–9
 EU endorsement 63, 105, 151, 154, 157
 'HSBC amendment' 435–6
 improvements (2001–5) 96, 140, 141, 145, 152

 partially replaced by IFRS 7: 161–3
 puttable financial instruments 382–4, 390
 see also IFRS 7
IAS 35 *Discontinuing Operations* 131–2
IAS 36 *Impairment of Assets* 114
IAS 37 *Provisions, Contingent Liabilities and Contingent Assets* 207, 251, 547
 attempted revision 130, 293, 348, 351–5, 366, 547
 cross-cutting issues 355, 356, 366, 574, 604
IAS 38 *Intangible Assets* 114, 126, 127, 207, 209, 344, 352
 MoU project (IASB/FASB) 547, 556
IAS 39 *Financial Instruments: Recognition and Measurement* 66, 426
 adopted in Brazil 145–6
 demand deposits 118, 148, 150, 152, 159 n. 100
 developed by IASC 12, 138–9
 EU endorsement 105, 150, 151, 157–60, 316, 412
 EU carve-outs 63, 64, 69, 157–60, 170, 179, 185, 190–1, 202–4, 237, 251, 252–4, 259, 260, 381–2, 409, 435, 514, 586, 591, 612
 fair value option 142, 152, 155–7, 158, 160, 202–4, 218, 404, 433
 hedge accounting 123, 139, 142–4, 146–51, 152–4, 155, 157–60, 179, 191, 194, 381, 382, 383
 Implementation Guidance Committee 39, 139, 140, 142, 143, 148
 improvements (2001–4) 96, 140–2, 144–5, 146–60
 'incurred loss model' 415, 420, 421
 mixed-measurement 139, 140, 142, 155, 379, 381
 reclassification amendment 404–15, 417, 416
 replacement of 378–80, 402, 433
 see also IFRS 9
IAS 40 *Investment Property* 104, 117
IAS 41 *Agriculture* 117, 385, 537, 567
IAS Plus website 71, 281, 386
IAS Regulation, *see* European Union
IASB Insight 45, 46, 47, 295
IASB Update 295
Iceland 83
IFRIC 3 *Emission Rights* 206–10, 395
IFRIC 12 *Service Concession Arrangements* 219, 226, 395–9
IFRIC 15 *Agreements for the Construction of Real Estate* 255, 399–400
IFRS 1 *First-time Adoption of International Financial Reporting Standards* 96, 106–7, 530
IFRS 2 *Share-based Payment* 107–11, 141
IFRS 3 *Business Combinations* 389, 379, 529
 project planning 74, 96, 113, 115, 338, 339, 343

IFRS 3 *Business Combinations (cont.)*
  original (phase I) 112–15, 351
  revision (phase II) 115, 133, 226, 290,
    347–51, 352, 547
  cross-cutting issues 130, 131, 353, 565
  reception in China 529
IFRS 4 *Insurance Contracts* 115–20, 127, 344,
  366; *see also* insurance contracts
IFRS 5 *Non-current Assets Held for Sale and*
  Discontinued Operations 131–2
IFRS 6 *Exploration for and Evaluation of*
  Mineral Resources 125–7, 221
IFRS 7 *Financial Instruments: Disclosures* 96,
  160–4, 407, 412, 416, 568
IFRS 8 *Operating Segments* 219–23, 225–7,
  290, 291, 340–1, 529
IFRS 9 *Financial instruments*:
  pre-crisis project with FASB 378–80
  crisis response phase 417, 421–2, 424–8,
    431–5,
  completion of project 547, 552, 554, 556,
    583–93
  classification and measurement 389, 581,
    583, 584–6, 595
  divergence from FASB approach 583–4,
    585, 586, 587–8, 590
  cross-cutting issues 595, 599
  derecognition 589–90
  fair value option 422, 427, 433, 586
  hedge accounting 420, 583, 591–2
  impairment 587–9
  long-term fair value objective 139, 140,
    141, 148, 246, 378–80, 432, 586
  offsetting 592–3
  application in Hong Kong and
    Australia 438
  not endorsed in EU 436–8
  reception in China 529
  reception in Japan 525, 584
  see also IAS 39
IFRS 10 *Consolidated Financial*
  Statements 292, 344, 368, 402, 403–4,
  529, 547, 557–61
  EU endorsement 563–4
  FASB involvement 135, 547, 552, 556
IFRS 11 *Joint Arrangements* 292, 341, 344,
  529, 556, 557–8, 561–3, 563–4
IFRS 12 *Disclosure of Interests in Other*
  Entities 292, 529, 556, 557–8, 563–4
IFRS 13 *Fair Value Measurement* 292, 344,
  350, 367, 379, 404, 423, 426, 529,
  564–9
  'fair value hierarchy' 564–5
  MoU project (IASB/FASB) 547, 552, 556
  see also FAS 157
IFRS 14 *Regulatory Deferral Accounts*
  232–3, 614
IFRS 15 *Revenue from Contracts with*
  Customers 576 n. 120
IFRS Advisory Council, *see* Standards
  Advisory Council

IFRS for SMEs 95, 385–91, 432–3, 516,
  539, 610
  critical views of 219, 316, 384
  IASCF Constitution and 170, 175, 387
  name 388
IFRS Foundation, *see* International
  Accounting Standards Committee
  Foundation
IFRS Interpretations Committee, *see*
  International Financial Reporting
  Interpretations Committee
IFRS Regional Policy Forum 538
Implementation Guidance Committee, *see*
  IAS 39
improvements, annual 255, 305, 393, 547
improvements project (initial) 96, 103–6, 119,
  128, 130, 169
Inbar, Adir 121 n. 107
India 70, 574
  adoption of IFRSs, expected or
    discussed 245, 533–6, 610
  equivalence (EU) 213, 214
  IASB funding 321, 322
  IASC membership 12
ING Groep 109, 160 n. 106, 179, 191
Institute of Chartered Accountants in England
  and Wales (ICAEW) 8, 201–2
Institute of Chartered Accountants of India
  (ICAI) 533, 534
Institute of International Finance 405, 592
insurance contracts project 82, 96, 103,
  115–20, 169, 354, 366, 514, 526, 593–7
  project planning 119–20, 552, 554, 555,
    556, 557, 575
  financial instruments 203, 437
  cross-cutting issues 354, 366, 573, 599
  FASB involvement 135, 341, 344, 547, 593,
    597, 612–13
  see also IFRS 4
Inter-American Development Bank 175, 495
Intergovernmental Working Group of Experts
  on International Standards of
  Accounting and Reporting (ISAR) 385
Internal Revenue Code (US) 22
International Accounting Standards
  (IASs) 10, 13
  adopted by IASB 93, 98
  'IAS-lite' 247, 249
  name changed to IFRSs 59, 94
International Accounting Standards Board
  (IASB):
  agenda decisions 93–7, 218, 334, 336, 345,
    359, 396, 402, 465–6, 493, 554, 577, 598,
    613–14
  Anglo-American body 36, 144, 218, 283–4
  Board member terms 32, 468
  Board size 171, 172, 175, 345, 449,
    453–5, 459
  branch offices 277, 324, 469
  'brand' issue 229, 247–52, 247–60, 459
  dissents 53, 101–2, 284

FASB model 15, 54, 165, 170, 176, 317, 460
geographical composition 26, 36, 170–1,
    172, 175, 449, 453, 459, 611
independent attitude 144, 443, 458, 465,
    467, 490–1
'independent expert model' 26, 35, 165,
    170, 172, 173, 317, 453
industry standards 116, 514, 594
library 135, 303
London location 24, 469
meetings, open or closed 102, 408, 554
meetings, outside London 75, 87
name 17, 32, 295, 468–9
outreach and communication 86–7, 166–7,
    168, 293–6, 537
'roadshows' 294
part-time members 16, 25, 30–1, 38, 171,
    172, 175, 274, 275, 276, 440, 453, 454, 455
remuneration 31–2
staff, size and composition 46–7, 134,
    301–7, 336, 358, 360, 383, 449, 452,
    453–5, 459
staff, functioning of 38, 101, 102, 103, 302,
    336–7, 347
'think tank' mentality 35
three-tier structure 491
voting procedures and threshold 99, 101,
    175, *see also* dissents
working groups and advisory
    committees 102, 161, 168, 296–8
see also due process
International Accounting Standards
    Committee (IASC):
origin and early activities 8–10
restructuring 15–6, 18, 26, 35, 54,
    165, 172
'core' standards 12, 94
funding 13, 47–54, 195
and G4+1: 95
hexagon logo 295
and IOSCO 11–12, 94, 100, 105, 358–9
legacy of projects 94, 99, 103–4
Statement of Intent 11, 12
International Accounting Standards
    Committee Foundation (IFRS
    Foundation):
Board (re)appointments 23–32, 269–81,
    467, 492
Constitution review (first) 89, 163–76,
    179–82, 200, 218, 235, 262, 270, 289,
    463, 491
Constitution review (second) 277, 326,
    442, 449–55, 460–70, 485–8, 613
database of jurisdictional adoptions 614
Delaware corporation 22
Due Process Oversight Committee 224,
    289–90, 293, 470, 491, 555
education initiative 88–9
FASB model 176, 268
funding and fundraising 195, 267, 307–32,
    469, 491, 611, 616

general functioning of trustees 267–9, 465
geographical balance 263–4, 467
name change 295, 468–9
outreach 87–8, 267, 312
oversight of Board 54, 166, 172, 267,
    289–93, 448, 465, 614
strategy review (2007) 269, 286, 440–4,
    446, 447, 457–60, 469
strategy review (2011) 291, 331, 470, 487,
    488–93, 614, 615
trustee appointment process 172, 173, 180,
    262, 264, 444
trustee appointments 54–5, 262–7
views on IASB's projects 377, 580
International Association of Financial
    Executives Institutes 13, 28
International Association of Insurance
    Supervisors 116, 444, 448, 450
International Auditing and Assurance
    Standards Board 448, 459, 464
reference to applicable reporting
    framework 255–7, 259, 260
International Bank for Reconstruction and
    Development 238
International Banking Federation 139
International Coffee Organization 331
International Corporate Governance
    Network 223
International Emissions Trading
    Association 210
International Federation of Accountants 12,
    16, 19, 20, 47, 323, 448
International Financial Reporting
    Interpretations Committee (IFRIC,
    subsequently IFRS Interpretations
    Committee):
activities 43–6, 88, 206, 254, 392–400, 435
agenda decisions 393–5
Due Process Handbook 394
membership 44–5, 287–8
name change 295, 468–9
procedures 206
International Financial Reporting Standards
    (IFRSs):
adoption of, *see under the various
    jurisdictions*
adoption by 'more than a hundred
    countries' 229, 247
'as issued by the IASB' 64, 67, 179, 185,
    190, 198, 214, 233, 253, 445, 518
basis for conclusions 102
bold-faced lettering 100
compared to US GAAP 57, 73, 81, 145,
    409; *see also* 'principles-based' standards
'globally accepted' 463
name 59, 94
'stable platform' of standards 97, 111,
    131, 154
structure of documents 101–2
translations of 61, 105–6, 374–5, 459,
    501–2

International Forum of Accounting Standard-Setters, *see* National Standard-Setters (NSS)

International Monetary Fund (IMF) 70, 175, 238, 444, 457

International Organization of Securities Commissions (IOSCO) 11–12, 201, 249, 386, 472
  compliance with IFRSs 249, 256, 258–60, 459
  'core' standards, *see* International Accounting Standards Committee
  endorsement of IASs 15, 17, 94–5, 103, 105, 190
  financial crisis 413, 418
  Trustee Appointments Advisory Group 175
  and IASC 11–12, 100, 116, 358–9
  improvements project 99, 103–4, 105
  Monitoring Board 445–6, 448, 450, 455, 470, 471, 479, 608
  Multilateral MoU 183
  IFRIC observer 44
  Standing Committee 1 (SC1) 38, 155, 156, 183, 257, 258
  Technical Committee 38, 182, 258, 413, 450, 452, 471, 489

International Public Sector Accounting Standards Board 221, 464

International Valuation Standards Committee (IVSC) 464

interpretations, *see* IFRS Interpretations Committee; International Financial Reporting Interpretations Committee; Standing Interpretations Committee

Investment Management Association (IMA) 221–2

Investors Technical Advisory Committee 197, 509

Ireland 8, 390

Irvine, Helen J. 127 n. 136

Isern, Mariela 304

Israel 213, 499

Italy 10, 87, 158, 254, 318

Ito, Tatsuya 243

Jamaica 70, 495

Japan 79–86, 240–7, 517–27
  IASC membership 8, 9
  IASB funding 49, 81, 308, 312–3, 319, 322, 611
  representation on IASB 26, 81
  equivalence assessment (EU) 211, 212, 213, 240, 241, 244, 246
  IFRS adoption considered and deferred 395, 517–27, 584, 610
  IFRS Council 521
  insurance contracts project 118
  mutual recognition policy 82, 85, 240, 241, 242–3

net income, views on 82, 124, 165, 246, 372, 376, 378, 525
  regional cooperation 537, 538
  three-country meetings (China, South Korea) 83, 234, 238, 537
  use of US GAAP 81, 517, 519, 521, 526–7, 584

Japanese Institute of Certified Public Accountants (JICPA) 34, 83, 244, 245, 518, 521, 574

Jardine Matheson Holdings 65

Jefferson Smurfit 109

Jenkins, Edmund L. 23, 39, 72

Jepson, Peter 161 n. 110

Jermakowicz, Eva K. 201 n. 1

Johnson, L. Todd 120 n. 106, 133, 359–60, 361–2, 366

Johnson, W. Bruce 107 n. 50

Joint International Group (JIG) 371, 372, 373

joint ventures 67, 344; *see also* IFRS 11

Joint Working Group (financial instruments) 117, 139–40, 141, 142, 148, 155, 156, 161, 344, 378, 421

Jones, Thomas E:
  (re)appointed to Board 28, 32, 35, 270
  post-Board role 277
  attends EFRAG meetings 92
  US contacts 87, 312
  vice chairman role 37, 75, 277
  views and votes on technical projects 108, 149, 157, 203, 373, 385, 386, 387

Jordan 12, 70

Jordan, Jane 304

JSE Securities Exchange (South Africa) 65

jurisdictional variations from IFRS (generic) 64, 179, 185, 188, 190, 193, 252–60; *see also under the various jurisdictions*

Kaberuka, Donald 175

Kaidonis, Mary A. 127 n. 136

Kalavacherla, Prabhakar
  appointed to Board 276, 278, 535, 536
  India 536
  views and votes on IASB projects 355, 365, 392

Kanjorski, Paul E. 423

Kapsis, Manuel 305

Kazakhstan 70

KBC 160 n. 106

Keegan, Mary 123, 124

Keidanren, *see* Nippon Keidanren

Keller, Jean 121 n. 107

Kenya 70

Kerviel, Jérôme 250, 251; *see also* Société Générale

Kim, Kwon-Jung 121 n. 107

Kim, Sunhee 305

Kim, Yung Wook 305

Kimmitt, Annette 46, 114, 303

Kley, Max Dietrich 55, 225, 264, 289
  IASB funding 311, 316, 317, 318, 321
Klinz, Wolf 216
Knight, Malcolm D. 55
Knorr, Liesel 216, 545
Knubley, Rachel 304, 581
Kolb, Wolfgang 161 n. 110
König, Elke 279–80, 282–3, 468, 594
Kono, Masamichi 488, 490
Kopper, Hilmar 20, 48, 51, 55
Korea (South) 70, 279, 537, 575
  adoption of IFRSs 83, 238–40, 245,
    246, 254
  equivalence (EU) 213, 214, 238
  IASB funding 240, 321, 329
  IASB member 611
  IASC membership 12, 238
  Monitoring Board 612
  three-country meetings (China, Japan) 83,
    234, 238, 537
  trustee from 264
Korea Accounting Standards Board 83, 91,
    238, 321
Kornasiewicz, Alicja 265, 266, 267, 319
Koster, Paul 257
Kotz, Sabine 58 n. 6
KPMG 436, 509
Kraehnke, Michael 305
Kroeker, James L. 423, 507
Kuroda, Haruhiko 175
Kusi-Yeboah, Christian 304
Kwiatkowska, Ewa 304
Kyrgyzstan 70

Lafarge 109, 260
Lagarde, Christine 423, 428
Lamfalussy, Alexandre 58
'Lamfalussy process' 58, 60, 64
Landry, Sebastien 304
Langfield-Smith, Ian 67 n. 26
Larraín, Guillermo 470, 475
Larson, Robert K. 209 n. 42
Laskawy, Philip A:
  appointed trustee 20
  Constitution review (first) 170
  Constitution review (second) 450, 451
  IASC Foundation chairman 263, 264,
    320, 608
  Monitoring Board 471
  nominating committee 25, 54
  strategy review 440, 441, 445, 446
  term of service 263
Latin America 467, 575
  attitude towards IFRSs 214
  IFRS adoption 494–502
  participation in IASB 26, 455
  see also Group of Latin American
    Accounting Standard Setters
Lay, Kenneth 52
Leaseurope 580
leases:

Hong Kong 65, 104
  MoU project (IASB/FASB) 336, 344, 526,
    548, 552, 554, 556, 573, 575, 576–83,
    612, 613
  see also IAS 17
Lebanon 70
Lee, Charles Yeh Kwong 20, 25, 51, 309
Lee, Christine 46
Lee, Jenny 303
Lee, Kil-Woo 303
Lehman Brothers 197, 401, 407, 412, 416, 479,
    590, 609
Lehne, Klaus-Heiner 216
Leisenring, James J. 87, 167
  (re)appointed to Board 27–8, 32, 33, 35,
    271–2
  convergence with US GAAP 335, 342
  dissents 284
  JWG member 140
  technical significance 37, 147, 280
  role in Board 36, 282, 284
  views and votes on IASB projects 100, 127,
    162, 220, 343, 350, 354, 372, 374, 376,
    387, 392, 556, 559, 587, 602, 604
Lennard, Andrew 615
Lepetit, Jean-François 543
Leng Bing 305
Leuz, Christian 248 n. 65
level playing field:
  business combinations 60, 113
  fair value measurement 416
  in IAS Regulation 113
  impairment 426, 438
  offsetting 592–3
  reclassification 406, 407, 409
  share-based payments 60, 109
Levin, Carl 52, 506
Levitt, Arthur 19, 21, 23, 72, 77, 81, 497
Li Feilong 288, 532
liabilities:
  fundamental concept for several
    projects 352–4, 360, 383, 595
  fair value of 152, 354–5
  own credit risk 155, 435, 567, 586, 595
  see also equity and liabilities project; IAS 37
Lian, Li Li 304, 361
liaison standard setters 38, 107, 128, 463–4
  abolished 176, 206, 298–9
  access to agenda papers 102, 298
  and Board appointments 26, 31
  projects for/with IASB 98, 106, 298,
    391, 396
  relations with IASB 90, 298
Life Insurance Association (Japan) 574
LIFO inventory method 104, 199, 561
Lion, Jessica 299 n. 75
Linsmeier, Thomas 342, 358, 376
Lipworth, Sir Sydney 21, 34, 48, 51, 54, 170,
    309, 311, 317
Litan, Robert E. 80 n. 84, 192 n. 68
Lithuania 70

Liu Yuting 235 n. 18, 235, 529, 533
Liu Zhongli 235, 265, 266, 267
Livingston, Philip B. 108, 111
Lloyd, Sue 303, 306
London Stock Exchange 51
Lu Jianqiao 303
Lucy, Jeffrey 67, 154, 265–6, 326, 488

Macedonia 70
Macek, Charles 287
Mackintosh, Ian:
    appointed Board vice chairman 281, 479,
        481, 482–3, 608
    convenes National Standard-Setters 299
    SAC member 41
Mahoney, Jeff 194, 197
Maijoor, Steven 489
Malan, Pedro 266, 267, 450, 497, 499
Malaysia 70, 297, 489, 604
    convergence with IFRSs 610
    IASC membership 12
    national standard setter 90, 91, 562
management commentary 94, 391–2
Management's Discussion & Analysis, *see*
    management commentary
Manso Ponte, Eduardo 304
Marchese, Domingo Mario 288
Marteau, Patrice 287
Maruyama, Junichi 471
Matsushige, Tadayuki 161 n. 110
Mauritius 70, 502
Maystadt, Philippe 616
McBeth, Kevin 366
McConnell, Patricia 121 n. 7, 284, 296
    appointed to Board 278, 286, 468
    chairs NSS 300
    SAC member 41, 286
McCreevy, Charlie 200, 262
    financial crisis 406, 410, 428, 438
    IASB funding 312, 323
    IASCF Constitution review (first) 174,
        180–1, 312
    lifting of 20-F reconciliation 174, 184, 186,
        190, 200, 212–13, 334, 337, 338
    Monitoring Board 455, 471, 472, 474, 475
McDonough, William J. 265, 266, 267, 318
McGeachin, Anne 46, 603
McGladrey & Pullen 508
McGregor, Warren 47, 83 n. 96, 412
    (re)appointed to Board 29, 32, 33, 35,
        272, 281
    and Australia 67, 69
    fair value 63, 655, 29, 283
    insurance contracts 115, 118, 594
    and Tweedie 37, 277, 537, 550
    views and votes on IASB projects 100, 127,
        137, 283, 343, 357, 358, 372, 376, 576,
        597, 602
McKinnon, Jill 67 n. 26
McKinsey & Company 184
MEDEF 310

Medina, Luis 304
Medvedev, Dmitry 503–4
Memorandum of Understanding (IASB/
    FASB), *see* Financial Accounting
    Standards Board
Merkel, Angela 187
Mexican Institute of Public Accountants 574
Mexico 70
    IASB funding 49, 329
    IASC membership 8, 494–5
    IFRS adoption 495, 499–500, 610
Mikuniya, Katsunori 475
Milburn, Alex 141
Ministry of Corporate Affairs (India)
    535, 536
Ministry of Economy, Trade and Industry
    (Japan) 523
Ministry of Finance (China), *see* China
Misirlioglu, Ismail Ufuk 250 n. 71
Mitchell, Geoffrey 161, 216
Mitsui Sumitomo Financial Group 522
Mogg, John F. 57 n. 4
Moldova 70
Monitoring Board:
    creation of 195, 326, 444–7, 455, 608
    IASB's agenda 493, 552, 555
    meetings 323, 470–2, 473–5
    membership 470–5, 492, 608, 611–12
    oversight role 325, 473–5, 492
    replaces Trustee Appointments Advisory
        Group 174, 443
    strategy and governance reviews 485–93
    three-tier structure 491
Monitoring Group of the International
    Federation of Accountants (IFAC) 448
Monti, Mario 262
Moreno, Louis Alberto 175
Morocco 70
Morrissey, John M. 72
Mueller, Michael 305
Multilateral Investment Fund (MIF) 495
Murphy, Richard 222, 226
Murray, Angus 303

Nasdaq 51
National Association of Pension Funds
    (UK) 222
National standard setters:
    in Europe 540, 541
    in Latin America 501
    IASC and 12–13, 15
    IASB's relations with 56, 169, 305, 458,
        298–301, 614–15
    local interpretations 394
    see also liaison standard setters; National
        Standard-Setters meetings; World
        Standard Setters Conference
National Standard-Setters (NSS)
    meetings 299–300
Naumann, Thomas 147
Nazareth, Annette L. 187

Nelson, Jon 304
Nestlé 13, 30, 109, 297, 372
net income, *see* performance reporting;
  see also Japan
Netherlands, the 8, 33, 90, 318
Neuer Markt (Germany) 14
New York Stock Exchange 14, 30, 51
New Zealand:
  adoption of IFRSs 66, 68–9, 91, 157,
    413, 414
  IASB funding 313, 319, 320, 321
  income tax issue 606
  jurisdictional variation of IFRSs 68, 157,
    254, 499
  puttable financial instruments 382–4, 598
  regional cooperation 537, 538
  sector-neutral standards 462
Nicaragua 70
Nicholson, Sir Bryan:
  (re)appointed trustee 264, 266
  fundraising 317, 321, 324, 331
  nominating committee chairman 267, 476,
    477, 478–83
  trustee role 268, 410, 424, 488
Nicolaisen, Donald T. 77, 182
  Constitution review (first) 173
  FCAG member 429
  roadmap (2005) 78–9, 177–82, 184, 185,
    186, 191, 200, 231, 241, 334–5, 577
  on US adoption of IFRSs 186, 192
Nielsen, Claus 303
Niemeier, Charles D. 507
Nigeria 10, 70, 330, 502, 503
Nihon Dempa Kogyo 84, 522
Nippon Keidanren 34, 293, 574
  IASB funding 51, 310, 312, 319
  IFRS policy 82, 84–5, 242, 244, 245,
    518–19, 521, 522
Nishikawa, Ikuo 80, 245
Nishino, Yuji 6
Nobes, Christopher 202 n. 6, 254 n. 82
Nokia 109, 132
Nordea 160 n. 106
Nordic countries 90, 139, 309
Nordic Federation of Public Accountants 12
Norris, Floyd 250, 251
Norwalk Agreement, *see* Financial Accounting
  Standards Board
Norway 87, 126
not-for-profit entities:
  scope of IASB mandate 441, 462
  sector-neutral standards 67, 100–1,
    369, 462
Novartis 113
Noyer, Christian 427

Océ 109
Ochi, Takatsugi 281, 522
Oki, Masashi 305
O'Malley, Patricia L. 121 n. 107, 349 n. 53
  JWG member 140

(re)appointed to Board 27, 32, 33, 35, 44,
  231, 270
Board role 36
post-Board role 288, 304, 306
views and votes on IASB projects 118,
  152, 284
One World Trust 296
Ontario Securities Commission (Canada) 11,
  44, 183, 391
Organization for Economic Co-operation and
  Development (OECD) 9–10, 386
Organismo Italiano di Contabilità 254 n. 83,
  318, 365
Organization for Eastern Caribbean
  States 496
Orrell, Magnus 46
Osawa, Eiko 304
other comprehensive income:
  conceptual debate 370–1, 375–6, 377, 601
  financial instruments 423, 425, 426, 433,
    525, 583, 586
  name 136, 139, 374
  recycling 120–1, 122, 377, 433, 572
  retirement benefits 569, 570, 572
  see also IAS 1; performance reporting
override (fair presentation), *see* IAS 1
Oversberg, Thomas 206 n. 23
own credit risk, *see* liabilities
Oxley, Michael 108

Pacter, Paul 75, 557 n. 39
  appointed to Board 279–81, 306
  Board member role 282, 284
  and China 235–6
  IAS Plus website 281, 386
  IASC staff 46, 100
  IASB staff 303, 306
  IFRS for SMEs 298, 303, 306, 386, 389–90
  views and votes on IASB projects
    392, 569
Padoa-Schioppa, Tommaso:
  at ECB 168, 204
  chairman of trustees (first term) 200–1,
    263, 267, 294
  chairman of trustees (second term) 266,
    268–9, 467, 475–8, 481, 482, 488,
    553, 608
  Italian finance minister 201, 318, 476
  removal of fair value option carve-out
    204, 263
  FCAG member 429
  Group of Thirty 422
  IASB funding 314–15, 316, 318, 320
Pai, T.V. Mohandas 265, 266, 401, 534,
  535, 536
Palmer, Frank 46
Pan African Federation of Accountants
  (PAFA) 503
Panama 496
Pape, Jochen 447
Paraguay 496

Parkinson, C. Northcote 480 n. 125
Paton, William Andrew 368 n. 137
Paul, Jim 46
Paulson, Henry M., Jr. 184
Pébereau, Michel 144
Peerless, Simon 304, 305, 577
pensions, *see* IAS 19
performance reporting project:
  begun with UK ASB 120–9
  continued with FASB 133, 135, 169, 339
  broadened to financial statement
    presentation 370–8, 547, 552
  limited achievements 599–603
  'abolition' of net income 124, 165, 246, 297,
    525, 600, 602
  critical views of 82, 219, 525
  G4+1 background 96
  matrix approach 122–4, 136
  single performance statement 122, 371–5,
    377–8, 572, 599–603
  see also IAS 1; other comprehensive income
Perry, Joanna 68 n. 31, 69 n. 37
Peru 70, 496
Petrone, Kim 375
Philippines 70, 159
Philips 109
Picker, Ruth 67
Picot, Russell 161 n. 110, 161
Pineau-Valencienne, Didier 21, 50, 51, 55
Pinelli, Vittorio 161 n. 110
Pirelli 109
Pitman, April 304
Pitt, Harvey L. 72, 73, 77, 309
Poland 70
pooling of interests 112, 237, 561; *see also*
  IFRS 3, phase I
Pope, Lara 304
Power, David 219 n. 74
Prada, Michel 19, 260, 263, 429, 477, 478, 608
Preface to IASs/IFRSs 96, 99–100, 170
preparers of financial statements:
  in IASC 12, 13
  IASB Board membership 16, 25, 26, 28, 30,
    36, 175–6, 271, 273, 275, 278, 279, 284, 608
  IASB's contacts with 90, 294, 296, 297, 458
  interpretations committee membership 44,
    287–8
  SAC membership 41, 286
PricewaterhouseCoopers (PwC) 210, 508,
  509, 605
'principles-based' standards:
  examples of attempts to write 162–4, 558,
    591, 605
  IASB education initiative 88
  IASB objective 98–9, 100, 393, 461–2, 608
  US GAAP versus IFRS 57, 61, 73–4, 78,
    346, 360, 441
  views in Japan 81, 523–4
Prodi, Romano 59, 60, 151
Prospectus Directive (EU) 210–11
Pryde, Andrea 303

prudential supervisors, role in setting
    accounting standards 203, 204, 420–1,
    450, 451, 452, 456, 464, 473–4, 475, 486,
    492, 595; *see also* stability, financial
Public Interest Oversight Board (IFAC/
    IAASB) 323, 444, 448, 459, 464
Publish What You Pay 220–1, 222

Quiring, Amanda 304

Rabobank 160 n. 106
Radwan, Alexander 216
  'Radwan report' 218, 223, 225, 226, 448
Ramanna, Karthik 230 n. 1
Ramin, Kurt 47, 55, 88
rate-regulated activities, *see* IFRS 14
Rato y Figaredo, Rodrigo de 174
Raytheon 510
reconciliation requirement (20-F):
  IASC/IASB pursue lifting of 11, 17–18, 30,
    71, 94, 338
  determines convergence priorities 128, 129
  European companies and 14–15, 57, 61,
    212, 249, 337
  IASCF (first) Constitution review 174,
    179–82
  pressure on SEC to lift 77, 78, 253
  roadmap (2005), *see* Nicolaisen, Donald T.
  SEC prepares to lift 77–9, 173, 177–82,
    184–7, 212, 224, 229, 241
  SEC decides to lift 188–91, 225, 506, 608
  see also Securities and Exchange
    Commission
recycling, *see* other comprehensive income
Reed, Jack 189, 403, 506
Rees, Henry 303
Reichenberger, Wolfgang 297, 372
Reither, Cheri L. 120 n. 106
Repsol YPF 109
retirement benefits, *see* IAS 19
revenue recognition:
  start as joint project with FASB 133, 153
  continued under MoU (2006) 339, 344,
    355–8
  not concluded under MoU (2008) 526, 547,
    554, 556, 573–6, 582
  completed in 2014: 557, 576, 613
  cross-cutting issues 116–17, 130, 354, 359,
    366, 578, 595
  IFRIC interpretations 396, 397, 399–400
  see also IAS 18
Revsine, Lawrence 107 n. 50
Ricardino Filho, Álvaro A. 497 n. 11
Richards, Ryan 305
Ricol, René 406, 407
Roche 13; *see also* Hoffmann-La Roche
Røder, Jens 21, 25, 54, 223, 265, 311, 314
Romania 70
Rouse, Robert W. 505 n. 47
Ruane, Barbara 305
Ruder, David S. 177

appointed trustee 21
champions IASB independence 170,
    268, 289
IASB funding 312
FAF trustee 34, 50
member of initial nominating
    committee 23, 25, 26
trustee role 21–2, 41, 50, 54, 268
on US convergence 183–4
'rules-based' standards, *see* 'principles-based'
    standards
Russia 70, 91, 289, 331, 503–5, 610
Ryltsova, Galina 46

Saint-Gobain 109
Saito, Shizuki 80–1, 82, 85, 86, 124, 241,
    243, 244
Saloman, James S. 46
Sanpaolo IMI 160 n. 106
Sarbanes, Paul S. 52, 74
Sarbanes-Oxley Act of 2002:
    consequences for convergence agenda 75,
        336, 569
    'principles-based' standards 74, 78, 577
    funding of standard-setting body 52–3,
        308, 309, 312, 320, 323, 616
Sarkozy, Nicolas 406, 407, 408, 410, 411, 586
Sato, Takafumi 455, 471
Saudi Arabia 83
Schapiro, Mary L:
    IASB funding 327
    Monitoring Board 471, 475, 508
    on SEC roadmap 506–7, 513, 552, 609
    succeeds Cox 505–8, 609
Schaub, Alexander 59 n. 8, 60 n. 9, 166, 173,
    316–17, 396, 531
Schelluch, Peter 65 n. 24
Schmid, Harry K:
    appointed to Board 30, 32, 35, 37, 269
    IASC Board member 372
    SIC member 44
    views and votes on IASB projects
        132, 348
Schmidt, Amy 304
Schmidt, Peter 250 n. 71
Schoen, Hans 161 n. 110
Schumer, Charles 184
Schuster, Brigitte 303
Schusterschitz, Gregor 58 n. 6
Scott, Darrel:
    appointed to Board 279–80, 286
    IFRIC member 288
Securities and Exchange Commission (SEC)
    restructuring of IASC 15–16, 21, 167,
        170, 172
    represented on initial IASC nominating
        committee 19; *see also* Levitt, Arthur
    IASCF Constitution review (first) 172
    IASB funding 53, 312, 321, 323, 327
    IASB governance 180, 487
    Monitoring Board 443, 445, 446

SAC observer 40
    access to IASB agenda papers 91
    insists on IFRSs as published by IASB 179,
        188, 190, 193, 198, 252–3, 258
    on compliance with IFRSs 79, 178, 248
    support for convergence 72–6, 128, 183,
        191, 212, 549–50, 556
    concept release on IASs (2000) 17, 94, 190
    roadmap (2005), *see* Nicolaisen, Donald T;
        reconciliation requirement
    concept release on domestic use of IFRSs
        (2007) 187, 191–4, 225, 342
    proposing release on domestic use of IFRSs
        (2008 roadmap) 198–9, 247
    staff work plan on incorporating IFRSs in
        the US financial reporting system 487,
        512–17, 556, 609
    'condorsement' 514–15, 517
    declines to decide on domestic use of
        IFRSs 505–12, 608–9
    off-balance sheet arrangements 569, 577
    and CESR 182–3, 242–3
    and IOSCO 11, 15, 104, 182, 183
    and Japan 81, 242–3
    and mutual recognition 183
    Advisory Committee on Improvements to
        Financial Reporting 197
    Emergency Economic Stabilization Act of
        2008: 422
Security Analysts Society of Japan 574
Seidenstein, Thomas R. 476, 482, 550
    appointment 47
    Monitoring Board 445, 449, 451, 454
    fundraising 310, 312, 315, 322, 324,
        326, 327
    significance 47, 307
    strategy review 440, 443, 444, 470, 488
Seidman, Leslie F. 197, 350, 358, 553, 554,
    555, 585, 601
Sen, Anik 161 n. 110
Selling, Tom 516
Senate Banking Committee (US) 52, 73, 74,
    181, 309, 505, 609
share-based payment 60, 74–5, 96, 133;
    see also IFRS 2
Shedlarz, David 41, 265
Sheng, Andrew 19
Shimazaki, Noriaki 266, 522, 538
SIC-12 *Consolidation—Special Purpose
    Entities* 558
SIC-29 *Disclosure—Service Concession
    Arrangements* 396
Sidwell, David:
    SAC member 41, 285
    IASCF trustee 265, 266, 285, 324, 488
Sikka, Prem 226
Singapore 70
Singleton, Jeff 304
Singleton, Kevin 303
Slovakia 70, 329
Slovenia 70

Sluimers, Dick 266
small- and medium-sized entities, *see IFRS for SMEs*
Smith, John T. 147, 197, 251 n. 77, 284, 403
  (re)appointed to Board 39, 269, 274, 275
  implementation guidance committee 139
  views and votes on IASB projects 127, 152, 155, 210, 284, 350, 355, 358, 362, 383, 592
Smith, Lawrence 585
So, Shelley 305
Société Générale 155, 160 n. 106, 249–51, 415
Society of Investment Professionals (UK) 349
Solbes, Pedro 542
Solvency II directive 595
Song, Esther 68 n. 31
South Africa 26, 70, 299, 455, 467, 574
  adoption of IFRSs 65–6, 107, 201, 213, 229, 502
  IASB funding 330
  IASC membership 10, 12
  IFRS for SMEs 389, 502
  projects with/for IASB 126
South Korea, *see* Korea
Spain 158, 326, 396, 398, 502
Spanish Association of Toll Motorways and Tunnels (ASETA) 397
Spaventa, Luigi 266, 267
special-purpose entities, *see IFRS* 10
Spencer, John 68 n. 31, 121 n. 107
Spencer, Kenneth:
  appointed trustee 21, 54
  chairman of trustee nominating committee 25, 26, 29, 31, 37, 40–1, 484
  and Tweedie 23
Sri Lanka 12, 70, 91
stability, financial, and accounting standards 143, 145, 151, 425
Staff Accounting Bulletin No. 101 *Revenue Recognition in Financial Statements* 355
Staff Accounting Bulletin No. 104 *Revenue Recognition* 355
Standard & Poor's 189, 510
Standards Advice Review Group (SARG) 216–17, 228, 412
Standards Advisory Council (SAC) (IFRS Advisory Council):
  advice on IASB agenda and projects 43, 95–6, 97, 99, 108, 136, 385, 493
  advice on IASB governance and processes 170, 447
  advice on other issues 255, 474
  functioning and effectiveness 43, 123, 284–7, 469
  IASB funding 319
  membership 39–43, 105, 284–6, 235, 287, 457
  role 40, 99, 171, 286, 465, 466
  name change 295, 468–9
Standing Interpretations Committee (SIC) 43–6, 104, 396

Starbatty, Nikolaus 305
Steere, William C. 21, 48, 51, 55
Steinbrück, Peer 428
Stevenson, Kevin 29, 44–6, 47, 103, 128, 133, 288, 303, 306
Stewart, Michael 305, 307
Storch, Robert F. 161 n. 110
Storey, Reed K. 359 n. 93
Storey, Sylvia 359 n. 93
Storm, Kees 265, 285
Strategy Working Party (IASC) 15–16, 21, 23, 29, 37, 48, 170, 176, 311
Strauss-Kahn, Dominique 175
Street, Donna 250 n. 71
Struweg, Jean 65 n. 24
Suh, Chungwoo 240
Sumitomo Corporation 281, 522–3, 526
Sun Zheng 234 n. 16
Sunder, Shyam 73, 85, 192 n. 68, 402 n. 4
Superintendencia de Valores y Seguros (Chile) 496
Sweden 159, 329
Swieringa, Robert J. 120 n. 106
Swiss Re 132
Switzerland 114, 264, 283, 321, 331

Tafara, Ethiopis 183, 335, 444, 489
Taiwan 10, 537
Tajika, Koji 21, 25, 55
Tajikistan 70
Tanzania 70, 502, 503
Tarca, Ann 64 n. 19
Taub, Scott A. 77, 79, 182
Technical Expert Group (TEG), *see* European Financial Reporting Advisory Group
Teixeira, Alan 304, 306, 392
Teixeira da Costa, Roberto, *see* Da Costa, Roberto Teixeira
Tellier, Paul 265, 266, 267
Thomas, Arthur L. 149 n. 54, 573 n. 106
Thomas, Michael 304
Thompson, Sandra 46, 147, 303
Thorpe, Richard 161 n. 110
TIAA-CREF 51
Tidström, Göran 91–2
Tietmeyer, Hans 262
Tokar, Mary 95
Tokyo Agreement, *see* Accounting Standards Board of Japan
Tokyo Stock Exchange 51, 521
Tondkar, Rasoul H. 250 n. 71
Torikai, Yuichi 303
Toronto Stock Exchange 230
Transatlantic Economic Council 187
translation, *see* International Financial Reporting Standards
Transparency Directive (EU) 210–11
Treasury (Australia) 321, 538
Treasury (UK) 420
Treasury Department (US) 72, 180, 184, 188, 418, 420, 609

Trichet, Jean-Claude 156, 175, 478
Triplett, Lynne 576 n. 118
Trott, Edward 358
Trustee Appointments Advisory
    Group 174–5, 180, 262, 444, 446
trustees, *see* International Accounting
    Standards Foundation
Tucker, Jon 250 n. 71
Tunisia 70, 213
Turner, Lynn 16, 23, 189
Tweedie, Sir David:
    (re)appointed Board chairman 23–4, 32,
        35, 37, 272, 491
    considers resignation 411, 555
    succeeded by Hoogervorst 281, 429,
        478–83, 608
    chairman role 38, 103, 154, 168, 167, 190,
        283, 346, 428, 483–4, 565, 570, 580, 607
    chief executive role 47, 440, 468, 491
    contact with trustees 267, 268, 276–7, 290,
        440, 468, 558
    education initiative 88–9, 286
    outreach 87, 126, 154, 238, 297
    role in Board selection 26–9, 271, 272
    role in staff selection 46, 387
    strategy review 440
    and Asia 537, 538
    and Brazil 499
    and China 235–6, 237, 297
    and EBF 381–2
    and EFRAG 91
    and EU 61, 105, 160, 200, 213, 224, 427, 566
    and India 534
    and IOSCO 95
    and Japan 81, 82, 86, 241, 243, 246,
        378, 525
    and SAC 42–3, 285
    and Seidenstein 47, 307, 440, 457
    and South Korea 238
    and US 73, 75, 195, 214, 312, 335, 336, 337,
        342, 346, 411, 508, 511, 516–17
    on adoption and use of IFRSs 68–9, 71,
        255, 258, 393
    views on IASB organization and
        strategy 56, 94, 103, 167, 196, 276–7,
        281, 283, 292, 341, 356, 378, 383, 424, 453
    and 2011 convergence target 196, 549, 550,
        551, 553, 555, 547, 575–6, 579
    views and votes on IASB projects 109, 121,
        141, 152, 209, 257, 336, 343, 360, 364,
        365, 372, 373, 383, 385, 386, 399, 403,
        406–7, 426, 432, 563, 571, 576, 601, 602

UBS 109, 132
Uganda 331, 502
Ujiie, Junichi 264, 319
Ukraine 70
UNICE 62, 272, 349; *see also*
    BUSINESSEUROPE
Unicredit 160 n. 106
United Kingdom:

EU carve-out 159
IASB funding 268, 315, 317, 318, 328
IASC membership 8, 9
IFRS 8 controversy 221–2, 223, 226
IFRS for SMEs 390, 542
interest in IASB 26, 39
stewardship tradition 364
UK GAAP 125, 542–3
United Nations (UN) 9, 10
United Nations Conference on Trade and
    Development (UNCTAD) 385
United States:
    events leading to Norwalk Agreement 71–9
    from Norwalk agreement to lifting of
        reconciliation requirement 177–91;
        see also reconciliation requirement
    domestic use of IFRSs considered 191–9,
        334, 342, 411, 412, 473, 505–17, 550–1
    equivalence assessment (EU) 84,
        211–3, 241
    IASB funding 22, 48–50, 53, 268, 309, 312,
        313, 319–22, 323–9, 611, 616–17
    IASB outreach in 71–2, 108, 277, 297,
        516–17, 609
    IASC membership 8, 9
    influence on other jurisdictions' IFRS
        policy 214, 224, 247, 494, 518, 522, 541,
        542, 543, 610
    interest in IASB and IFRSs 26, 39, 73–4,
        461, 574, 575
    US GAAP and IFRSs 11, 16, 57, 73–4, 77,
        99, 116, 145, 186, 193, 194, 230–2, 249,
        337, 346, 441, 546, 566; see also Financial
        Accounting Standards Board; principles-
        based standards; *and under the
        individual standards*
    see also reconciliation requirement;
        Securities and Exchange Commission
Universal Postal Union 331
Upton, Wayne S:
    appointment 47, 103, 306
    education note on depreciation 524
    international activities 235–6, 239, 297,
        307, 524, 529
    role in various projects 116, 128, 133, 146,
        147, 210, 342, 357, 421, 565, 570,
        586, 604
Uruguay 495, 501
users (of financial statements) 371
    difficult to attract as Board members
        176, 275
    IASB's contacts with 90, 294, 296, 407, 426,
        458, 475, 526, 582
    in initial Board 26, 29, 36
    in subsequent Board 275, 279, 608
    in IFRIC 288

Van der Veen, Hans 305
Van Helleman, Johan 63
Van Hulle, Karel 57, 60, 61–2
Van Rooyen, Jeff 265, 266, 267

Van Zijl, Tony 68, 151 n. 31, 152
Vatrenjak, Aida 706, 305
Vegezzi, Antonio 55, 264
  Constitution review (first) 450, 451
  due process 268, 289–90
  strategy review 440
Venezuela 213, 496
Venter, Henri 305
Véron, Nicolas 3, 223, 482
Vietnam 70
Villmann, Rebecca 305
Vogel, Sylvia 250 n. 71
Volcker, Paul A. 19, 20, 22, 54, 73, 75, 511
  appointed chair of trustees 19, 20, 200
  chairman role 268, 401, 272, 373, 478
  Constitution review (first) 89, 170, 171,
    172, 173, 180–1
  defends IASB independence 36, 108, 147,
    153, 166, 167, 170
  Group of Thirty 422
  IASB funding 48–51, 52–3, 308–9, 310,
    312, 314, 317, 320
  outreach 71, 87
  role in appointments 23, 25, 40, 47, 262
  Trustee Appointments Advisory Group
    chairman 174, 262, 608
Von Keitz, Isabel 137 n. 172, 562 n. 64

Wagenhofer, Alfred 80 n. 84, 192 n. 68
Wal-Mart 510
Walter, Elisse B. 513
Walton, Peter 36 n. 41, 76 n. 67, 483
Wang Jun 235, 237, 297, 527, 531
Wang Yuetang 234 n. 16
Weatherstone, Sir Dennis 55
Wells, Michael 304
West, Andrew 65 n. 24
Whelan, Noreen 303
White, Gerald I. 193–4
White, John W. 186, 187, 192, 194, 196,
    507, 508
White, Mary Jo 609
Whittington, Geoffrey 38, 46, 122, 148 n. 44
  appointed to Board 29, 32, 33, 35, 269,
    272, 365
  liaison role 90
  views and votes on IASB projects 98 n. 19,
    111, 114, 137, 140, 157, 203, 204, 348,
    361, 362, 364, 565
Wiedmann, Harald 384
Wilks, Jeff 305
Wilmot, Peter 42, 285, 385
Wilson, Allister 61–2
Winn-Dixie 107
Wolfensohn, James D. 19, 71
Wolfowitz, Paul 175
Wong, Carol 305

World Bank 221, 234, 459, 457, 503, 532,
    533–4
  IASB monitoring body membership 444,
    448, 450, 452, 456, 457
  ROSC A&A series 70, 495, 501, 532, 533–4
  SAC membership 285, 457
  Trustee Appointments Advisory
    Group 175, 262
  support for IFRSs 9, 69–70, 385, 390, 481
World Standard Setters Conference 91, 299,
    478, 582
World Trade Organization 234
WorldCom 232
Wright, David 145
Wright, Luci 305

XBRL 55

Yamada, Tatsumi:
  (re)appointed to Board 30, 32, 35, 37, 81,
    272, 522
  JWG member 140
  liaison role Asia 83, 234, 235, 238
  liaison role Japan 33, 34, 83, 284, 300,
  views and votes on IASB projects 114, 152,
    157, 203, 284, 348, 361, 376, 571, 572,
    573, 602
Yagi, Yoshiki 124, 518
Yanou, Rieko 46
Yohn, Teri 189
Yükseltürk, Osman 250 n. 71

Zalm, Gerrit:
  Constitution review (second) 450, 451,
    452, 454, 455
  IASC Foundation chairman,
    appointed 263, 267
  IASC Foundation chairman, role 268, 324,
    418, 449, 450, 471, 473, 474, 485, 550
  IASC Foundation chairman,
    retirement 475–6
  and EU institutions 227, 427
  Dutch finance minister 318, 608
Zaman, Farhad 303
Zambia 213, 502
Zeff, Stephen A. 73 n. 54, 107 n. 50, 108 n. 54,
    109 n. 62, 113 n. 79, 205 n. 21, 248 n. 66,
    254 n. 82, 301 n. 81, 347 n. 42, 359 n. 91,
    364 n. 118, 578 n. 130, 587 n. 172
Zhang Wei-Guo 412
  (re)appointed to Board 274–5, 279
  liaison role China 284, 529
  views and votes on IASB projects 282, 355
Zhang Xiangzhi 304
Zimbabwe 12, 502
Zoelick, Robert B. 175
Zoido, Antonio 266

Printed and bound by CPI Group (UK) Ltd, Croydon, CR0 4YY